MARITIME LAW

MARITIME AND TRANSPORT LAW LIBRARY

MARITIME AND TRANSPORT LAW LIBRARY

MARITIME LAW
FOURTH EDITION

EDITED BY

PROFESSOR YVONNE BAATZ

informa law
from Routledge

Fourth edition published 2018
by Informa Law from Routledge
2 Park Square, Milton Park, Abingdon, Oxon OX14 4RN

And by Informa Law from Routledge
711 Third Avenue, New York, NY 10017

Informa Law from Routledge is an imprint of the Taylor & Francis Group, an informa business

First edition published 2008 by Informa
Third edition published 2014 by Informa Law from Routledge

British Library Cataloguing-in-Publication Data
A catalogue record for this book is available from the British Library

Library of Congress Cataloging-in-Publication Data
A catalog record for this book has been requested

ISBN: 978-1-138-03771-7 (hbk)
ISBN: 978-1-138-10483-9 (pbk)
eISBN: 978-1-315-16290-4 (ebk)

Typeset in Times New Roman
by Apex CoVantage, LLC

MIX
Paper from
responsible sources
FSC   FSC® C013056
www.fsc.org

Printed and bound in Great Britain by
TJ International Ltd, Padstow, Cornwall

OUTLINE CONTENTS

DETAILED TABLE OF CONTENTS

ILLUSTRATIONS

FIGURES

TABLES

PREFACE TO THE FOURTH EDITION

Maritime Law flourishes at the University of Southampton. Its ever popular maritime courses both at LLB and LLM level continue to attract students from all over the world. The courses run by its Institute of Maritime Law, most notably the three-week course in Southampton every summer and the two-week course in Singapore every May, do the same. The Donald O'May Lecture every autumn continues to be given by speakers held in the highest esteem in the shipping community most recently in 2016 by Elizabeth Blackburn QC and in 2015 by Sir Bernard Eder. Conferences are organised on topical issues and the support of the city firms, most recently Reed Smith and Norton Rose Fulbright, is gratefully acknowledged. Our most recent projects have included work on unmanned ships and the possible consequences of Brexit on maritime law. All these activities contribute to create a vibrant research culture not only amongst academics at the University of Southampton, but also with other academics and practitioners across the globe. This fourth edition of *Maritime Law* is a product of that collaboration.

I am grateful to the authors who have once again contributed to this book. Their expertise, hard work and commitment to meet a tight deadline has made this venture possible. We are a slightly smaller team of authors than for the last edition as Richard Pilley did not take part in this edition. We are very fortunate, however, that Richard continues to play a role in the Institute of Maritime Law where his consistently sound advice, businesslike common sense, knowledge of the shipping world, and immense courtesy have been so greatly valued over so many years. Three of our authors are no longer at the University of Southampton but I am very glad that we still work together.

A very big thank you is due to Robert Veal, Senior Research Assistant at the Institute of Maritime Law, for all the work he has done in providing research assistance and ensuring that this book has a coherent style throughout. He has, as always, been a pleasure to work with and I have found his considerable research skills and steady, meticulous hard work wholly admirable.

I am grateful for the support of the Institute of Maritime Law and its Directors, Professor Mikis Tsimplis, whose term as Director expired at the end of January 2017 and our new Director, Professor Andrew Serdy. Further thanks go to our librarian, Sara Le Bas, who once again contributed the bibliography to this edition, and Clare Brady who keeps the whole enterprise running smoothly. We are very fortunate to have our excellent library so generously supported by Gard.

I would also like to thank our publishers, Routledge at Informa, in particular Amy Jones and Caroline Church, for their support and encouragement.

I hope that readers of this book will find the breadth and depth as useful as it is fascinating.

YVONNE BAATZ
Professor of Maritime Law
Member of the Institute of Maritime Law
University of Southampton
March 2017

PREFACE TO THE THIRD EDITION

The third edition of this book is dedicated to Richard Shaw. Richard played an important role in the Institute of Maritime Law at the University of Southampton for many years right up until his death in 2013. He had a great love of things maritime and of teaching. He was extremely effective. If Richard promised to do something it would be done. He contributed to the success of the first two editions of this book, the book entitled *Maritime Law Evolving* brought out to celebrate the thirtieth anniversary of the Institute of Maritime Law, and to our many courses each year. His wise counsel at Governing Board meetings of the Institute of Maritime law will be gravely missed. His sunny personality at events such as our Donald O'May lecture each autumn and dinner on the Isle of Wight every September at the end of our three-week Short Course will be remembered with pleasure.

I am grateful to all the authors who have contributed to this third edition. We have been joined by Özlem Gürses, who has contributed new sections to the chapter on marine insurance. Mikis Tsimplis has updated the sections originally written by Richard Shaw as well as his own major contributions. We are very fortunate to have the support of the Institute of Maritime Law, so ably directed by Filippo Lorenzon for the last four years and now by Mikis Tsimplis. Thanks are due to our two research assistants, Jack Steer and Mateusz Bek, who have helped all the authors with research and have worked tirelessly to ensure the consistency of the book as a whole. Further thanks go to Sara Le Bas, the Institute of Maritime Law's librarian, who has contributed the bibliography and to Clare Brady for her assistance.

We are also grateful to our publishers, Taylor & Francis, and particularly to Faye Mousley for her efficiency and encouragement, Alexia Sutton and Jessica Moody.

Shipping law continues to thrive at the University of Southampton with increasing numbers of University students keen to study maritime subjects both at LLB and LLM level and practitioners enthusiastic to attend courses. May this book inspire any reader to delve further into the joys of maritime law and enjoy the fascinating practical and academic issues that it involves.

YVONNE BAATZ
Professor of Maritime Law
Member of the Institute of Maritime Law
University of Southampton March 2014

PREFACE TO THE SECOND EDITION

This second edition of what was in its first edition *Southampton on Shipping Law* has now metamorphosed into simply *Maritime Law*. The aims of the book remain the same as those stated for the first edition in 2008. However, there is a new chapter on shipbuilding, sale, finance and registration, an expanded chapter on marine insurance and throughout the book has been updated.

My thanks go to Filippo Lorenzon, the Director of the Institute of Maritime Law at the University of Southampton, who has so skilfully steered the course of the Institute for the last 14 months. In mapping out the aims of the Institute he encouraged us to produce this new edition. None of this would have been possible without the commitment of my co-authors who once again have worked to tight deadlines and have as always been a wonderful team. One member of that team who deserves special mention is Ainhoa Campàs Velasco who, as with the first edition of this book, has helped all the authors with their research for this project. We have very much appreciated her meticulous attention to detail and steady resolve to make this book a consistent whole. The members of the Institute of Maritime Law have also been very fortunate to have the help of our research assistants past and present and our wonderful Institute Secretary, Anita Rogers-Ballanger.

We are also grateful to our publishers, Sweet & Maxwell, and particularly to Nicola Thurlow, Anne Brisby, Steven Warriner, Joanna Southwell, Claire Sharp and David Lloyd, for their help in making this book a reality.

Finally may this book encourage those who already have, or who may discover, a love of maritime law.

YVONNE BAATZ
Professor of Maritime Law
Member of the Institute of Maritime Law
University of Southampton
April 2011

PREFACE TO *SOUTHAMPTON ON SHIPPING LAW* (2008)

Shipping law has a long history at the University of Southampton. Optional subjects like Admiralty, Carriage of Goods by Sea, International Trade and Marine Insurance have been offered to undergraduate and graduate students for almost 40 years. The annual three-week Maritime Law Short Course grew out of those optional subjects into a highly regarded course attracting legal practitioners and members of the shipping industries to Southampton for the last 34 years. In 1982, our interests in shipping law led to the creation of the Institute of Maritime Law, which celebrated its twenty-fifth anniversary last year with its Quartercentenary Donald O'May Lecture delivered in the City of London by The Rt Hon. The Master of the Rolls, Sir Anthony Clarke.

The Institute now numbers no fewer than 13 shipping lawyers, comprising full-time members of the School of Law, Visiting Research Fellows and research assistants. The School's LLM, which offers 26 optional subjects across a wide range of interests, now attracts almost 100 graduate students annually from all around the world, a heavy proportion of whom choose to take one or more of the maritime law subjects. Many of our LLM graduates go on to practise maritime law within the legal professions or the shipping industry in the City or abroad. For its part, the Institute of Maritime Law now constitutes the largest concentration of maritime lawyers in any UK university.

With so many maritime lawyers under one roof, combining practical and academic experience, it is not surprising that we have been asked many times why we did not have our own text covering as wide a gamut as possible of the many areas which make up shipping law. *Southampton on Shipping Law* is the result.

Our purpose in this book was to produce a readable but authoritative work introducing the newcomer to the fascination of the subject which has kept us in, and attracted so many students to, Southampton. Maritime law is a subject which combines the intellectual challenge of the basic principles of contract, tort and property with the fundamentals of the shipping and commodity markets. It is also a subject which cuts across traditional boundaries of private and public law. We have been able to put together a team of ten contributors to this volume, covering a wide area of what most people would class under the title "Shipping Law".

Southampton on Shipping Law is targeted explicitly at solicitors and barristers about to start their practice in maritime law; at claims handlers in P&I Clubs and commodity houses; at professionals in the shipping industry who want a broad but reliable introduction to the basic structure of the subject; and last (but not least, because so many of the former groups emerge from this one), at LLM students taking courses in the way English law regulates international shipping and maritime business.

The book went from design to production in a little over a year – a considerable feat, given the collaboration needed for a crew of ten writers all of whom have many other academic and professional commitments. My first thanks as Director of the Institute must therefore rightly go to my co-contributors, all of whom have worked to very tight deadlines. I must also thank Vicky Ophield and Laura Brown of Informa Publishing, both of whom have had an infectious enthusiasm for this project. All of us as contributors owe a special debt of gratitude to Ainhoa Campàs Velasco, an LLM graduate who returned to Southampton after some ten years' legal practice in Spain. Ainhoa has provided invaluable research assistance for each contributor, encouraging us gently but firmly to avoid repetition, hesitation and deviation. My greatest personal word of thanks must, however, go to my colleague Professor Yvonne Baatz, who kindly and generously agreed to manage the project and who did so from start to finish with her customary tact and efficiency.

We all hope now that you, the reader, enjoy this book. We have written it to entice you to want to become a shipping lawyer, if you are completely new to the area; or to confirm your best instincts if you have recently become one. We very much hope that you do enjoy the book – and that it may, perhaps, provide an opportunity for contact with members of the School of Law and of the Institute of Maritime Law, here at Southampton.

The law is stated as at 1 May 2008.

CHARLES DEBATTISTA
Professor of Commercial Law
Director of the Institute of Maritime Law
May 2008
Preface to *Southampton on Shipping Law* (2008)

AUTHORS' BIOGRAPHIES

YVONNE BAATZ
Professor Yvonne Baatz qualified as a solicitor in 1981. She practised with two leading firms of solicitors in the City of London, specialising in shipping litigation. Since 1991 she has been a lecturer in
the School of Law at the University of Southampton and was made a
professor in 2007. She was Director of the Institute of Maritime Law
from 2003 until 2006.

AINHOA CAMPÀS VELASCO
Ainhoa Campàs Velasco (LLB Hons Degree (Spain), LLM (Soton)).
Member of the Bar Association of Madrid, she practised with two
leading Maritime Law firms in Madrid, specialising substantially in
litigation, cargo claims, charterparty disputes and maritime administrative law sanctioning proceedings. She was a part-time lecturer in
the Law School at the University of Southampton from 2009 to 2013,
where she is currently studying for a PhD for which she obtained a
scholarship.

CHARLES DEBATTISTA
Charles Debattista runs a busy and successful practice in dry shipping,
international trade and general commercial disputes from St Philips
Stone Chambers, located in Gray's Inn. Apart from appearing as counsel
and doing advisory work, Charles also regularly sits as an arbitrator on
LMAA, ICC, LCIA and ad hoc disputes, and has in the past arbitrated in
many GAFTA and FOSFA arbitrations. Recent Directory entries include:
"able to immediately home in on what is important and give the matter his
full and undivided attention" (Chambers & Partners, 2016); "a very fluent
advocate with a superb knowledge of the law". (Legal 500, 2016). Charles

has been closely involved with a good number of international instruments used in the law and
practice of international sales, carriage and trade finance: for example, he chaired the ICC's
International Drafting Group for Incoterms 2000, co-chaired the Drafting Group for Incoterms
2010, and is currently the ICC's Special Advisor advising the Drafting Group for Incoterms
2020. In an earlier life, Charles was a Professor of Commercial Law and Director of the Institute
of Maritime Law at the University of Southampton.

ÖZLEM GÜRSES

Dr Özlem Gürses is a Reader in Insurance and Commercial Law at King's College London. She is the author of the books *Marine Insurance Law* (2nd ed, 2016) and *Reinsuring Clauses* (2010). She has updated the fifth edition of *The Insurance of Commercial Risks: Law and Practice* (2016).

JOHANNA HJALMARSSON

Johanna Hjalmarsson (JUR KAND Stockholm 1995, LLM Soton 2004) trained as a lawyer in Sweden and served as a junior judge there before joining the UN in Vienna as a legal adviser. She was also a deputy head of unit for law reform with the Office of the High Representative in Bosnia & Herzegovina. She has been with the Institute of Maritime Law since 2004 and is the editor of Informa periodicals *Shipping & Trade Law* and *Lloyd's Law Reporter* and a founding editor of the web resource AviationLaw.Eu. She has published numerous books and articles on maritime and insurance law.

ANDREA LISTA

Professor Andrea Lista LLD (Italy), LLM (Soton) PhD (Lond) Chair in Commercial Law, School of Law, University of Exeter. Of Counsel, SLIG Law LLP, London. Andrea has vast experience and has published widely in various areas of commercial law (International Trade, Competition Law, International Commercial Arbitration. Internal Market Law and Corporate Law). In the past he has acted as legal adviser to the European Parliament and the European Commission, and he is a very active legal consultant to companies and law firms.

FILIPPO LORENZON

Filippo Lorenzon ((LLD, Italy), LLM Soton, FCIL, Avvocato (Italy) and Solicitor in England and Wales) is Professor of Maritime and Commercial Law in the School of Law at the University of Southampton. He is qualified as an Avvocato in Italy and as a Solicitor in England and Wales and is a Member of the Italian and British Maritime Law Associations, the European Maritime Law Association (EMLO) and the International Bar Association (IBA). He is a consultant with Campbell Johnston Clark in London.

ANDREW SERDY

Andrew Serdy is Professor of Public International Law and Ocean Governance at the University of Southampton, specialising in the international law of the sea, a field in which he worked from 1995 to 2005 for the Australian Government. He is on the Board of Editors of *Ocean Development & International Law* as well as being a Review Editor handling law-based submissions to the *ICES* (International Council for the Exploration of the Sea) *Journal of Marine Science*. In 2017 he began a three-year term as Director of the Institute of Maritime Law.

MICHAEL TSIMPLIS

Michael Tsimplis is a Professor in Law and Ocean Sciences, jointly appointed by the School of Law at the University of Southampton and the National Oceanography Centre. He is a contributing author to the fourth IPCC report and participates in the activities of various national and international scientific bodies.

TABLE OF CASES

UK

AUSTRALIA

CANADA

EUROPEAN UNION

FRANCE

GERMANY

HONG KONG

INDIA

INTERNATIONAL

NEW ZEALAND

SINGAPORE

UNITED STATES

TABLE OF LEGISLATION, CONVENTIONS AND RULES

UNITED KINGDOM

STATUTORY INSTRUMENTS

EU DIRECTIVES AND REGULATIONS

Regulations

Directives

FOREIGN STATUTES

CONVENTIONS, RULES, TREATIES AND OTHER INTERNATIONAL INSTRUMENTS

CHAPTER 1

THE CONFLICT OF LAWS

Yvonne Baatz

1. INTRODUCTION

When an international dispute arises out of a maritime contract or incident such as a collision, it is necessary to consider at the outset which law applies to the dispute, which tribunal has jurisdiction to determine the dispute on its merits, whether there is any time bar and whether the claimant can obtain security for its claim. Many maritime contracts contain express governing law and jurisdiction clauses. This chapter will consider the extent to which the English courts will give effect to party choice, the limits on that choice as a result of the maritime conventions and what the position is where no choice has been made. First the reason why these issues matter will be explored.

In order to advise a party on their rights and obligations in any situation it is necessary to establish which law governs those rights and obligations. Whether a contract is governed by one law rather than another may mean the difference between total success by the claimant or total defeat if, for example, one law does not recognise a cause of action or provides the defendant with a complete defence, whereas the other does recognise a cause of action and there is no defence.[1]

The issue of jurisdiction may be of great tactical significance as there may be more than one court which has jurisdiction to determine the dispute and then the claimant must make sure that it commences proceedings in the jurisdiction which is most advantageous to it. In maritime disputes there are a number of reasons why one jurisdiction may be more favourable to one party than the other. One of the aims of this chapter when dealing with jurisdiction is to highlight the differences that can occur in one jurisdiction rather than another, due to the different maritime conventions which States are parties to. This creates an incentive to forum shop. For example, different limits of liability for a cargo claim may apply in different jurisdictions depending on whether the Hague,[2] Hague-Visby[3] or Hamburg Rules[4] apply.[5] In the future the Rotterdam Rules may come into force,[6] but can be incorporated voluntarily. A second example is that

---

1. See, e.g. *Mauritius Oil Refineries Ltd v Stolt-Nielsen Nederlands BV (The Stolt Sydness)* [1997] 1 Lloyd's Rep 273 discussed at page 64 of this chapter and *Sapporo Breweries Ltd v Lupofresh Ltd* [2013] EWCA 948; [2014] 1 All ER (Comm) 484.

2. The International Convention for the Unification of Certain Rules of Law Relating to Bills of Lading, Brussels, 25 August 1924.

3. The International Convention for the Unification of Certain Rules of Law Relating to Bills of Lading signed at Brussels on 25 August 1924 as amended by the Protocol signed at Brussels on 23 February 1968 and by the Protocol signed at Brussels on 21 December 1979.

4. The UN Convention on the Carriage of Goods by Sea 1978. See *The Ratification of Maritime Conventions* (Informa 2016). See also Chapter 4 pages 127–128 for the differences between these Conventions.

5. See pages 52–53 of this chapter.

6. The Convention on Contracts for the International Carriage of Goods Wholly or Partly by Sea was adopted in 2008 and the signing ceremony was held in Rotterdam in September 2009. As at 9 February 2017 the Rotterdam Rules have only been ratified by three States and will not come into force until they have been ratified by 20 States – art 91.

different tonnage limits may apply depending on which convention on tonnage limitation, if any, applies.[7] In any case, whether maritime or not, one court may award more interest; award more legal costs; have more favourable procedural rules, for example, in relation to disclosure of documents; proceed to judgment faster, and so on. As we shall see the European rules have sought to harmonise the rules as to how the EU Member States determine the law applicable so that whichever EU Member State court has jurisdiction it should apply the same law thus reducing the incentive to forum shop.[8] However, the "mandatory overriding provisions" of the law of the forum will still apply and the rules of evidence and procedure of the forum will still apply,[9] so that the jurisdiction will still be very important.

If one jurisdiction is more advantageous to one party, the other party would probably prefer to litigate in the other available jurisdiction and this may create a race between the parties to commence proceedings in the jurisdiction of their choice first. Such races have resulted, for example, in a diver being hired to dive down and pin court proceedings on a ship which had sunk in the territorial waters of Singapore to ensure the jurisdiction of the Singapore court as the tonnage limits were lower there.[10] If the arbitration award or judgment that a party would obtain in one jurisdiction is significantly different from that which the other party would be liable for elsewhere, it may be very difficult to settle the case until the issue of jurisdiction has been resolved.

It is of critical importance to commence proceedings in the correct jurisdiction against the correct party within any time limit. Many maritime disputes are subject to relatively short time limits. For example, the Hague, Hague-Visby or Hamburg Rules may apply to a bill of lading or may be incorporated voluntarily into a charterparty and they have a one- and two-year time bar respectively.[11] If the bill of lading provides for London arbitration and the Hague-Visby Rules apply mandatorily, the cargo receiver must identify the carrier[12] and commence arbitration proceedings in London within the one-year time limit, otherwise the carrier is discharged from all liability.[13]

A party must also consider how to secure its claim as soon as any such claim arises. There is no purpose in expending time, effort and expense in obtaining a favourable court judgment or arbitration award if there are no assets against which to enforce that judgment or award.

Thus the claimant should try to obtain security for its claim right at the outset of the dispute. In a maritime dispute there may be a right to arrest a ship[14] or an arrest may be threatened in order to obtain alternative security in the form of a P&I Club letter of undertaking[15] or bank guarantee. Alternatively if no security is forthcoming there may be a judicial sale of the ship and the proceeds of sale distributed amongst the creditors.[16] If there can be no arrest, perhaps because the ship has sunk and is an actual total loss, the claimant may be able to find assets such as the proceeds of the hull and machinery insurance or funds in the shipowner's bank account which can be frozen by means of a freezing injunction.[17]

This chapter will consider first which tribunal, either arbitration tribunal or court, has jurisdiction to determine the dispute on its merits and then how the English court determines which

---

7. See pages 26–27, 29–30, and 48–49 of this chapter.
8. See page 54.
9. See pages 63–65 and 72.
10. See *Owners of the Herceg Novi v Owners of the Ming Galaxy (The Herceg Novi and the Ming Galaxy)* [1998] 2 Lloyd's Rep 454 CA, discussed at pages 48–49 of this chapter.
11. Art III rule 6 of the Hague and Hague-Visby Rules and art 20 of the Hamburg Rules.
12. See Chapter 5, pages 197–200.
13. See *The Stolt Sydness* at fn 1 of this chapter.
14. See Chapter 12.
15. See Chapter 11, page 489.
16. See Chapter 12, page 511.
17. See Chapter 12, page 520.

law is applicable to the dispute. The parties may have chosen which tribunal has jurisdiction to determine their disputes. Many maritime contracts provide for arbitration. If there is no agreement to arbitrate, the parties may have agreed on a court to determine their disputes but, if they have not, it will be necessary to consider which court will have jurisdiction to determine the dispute on its merits.

2. ARBITRATION

Arbitration in London is a popular choice of dispute resolution in maritime contracts. Thus, for example, many standard form charterparties,[18] international sale contracts, salvage contracts,[19] P&I Club Rules, and reinsurance contracts provide for London arbitration. Many bills of lading incorporate the arbitration clause in the charterparty under which the bill is issued.[20]

Arbitration is perceived to have advantages over court litigation including speed, limited right of appeal,[21] lower cost, the parties may choose their own arbitrators and procedure,[22] ease of enforcement of the arbitration award in view of the fact that the New York Convention on the Recognition and Enforcement of Foreign Arbitral Awards 1958 (the "New York Convention") has been widely accepted around the world[23] and confidentiality. Some of these perceived advantages may prove to be illusory where there is a hearing as if the tribunal consists of three busy arbitrators it may take longer to get a hearing than it would in the English court and may cost more as the arbitrators have to be paid. However, the last criterion of confidentiality may be very important, for example, to large companies who do not wish to have their trade secrets aired in the public proceedings of the court. Furthermore arbitration awards are confidential and cannot be published except with both parties' consent. If such consent is given they may be published in *Lloyd's Maritime Law Newsletter*. Although they are not binding precedent, they may provide very useful guidance.

(a) Valid arbitration agreement

The United Kingdom is a party to the New York Convention and it gives effect to its international obligations under that convention in the Arbitration Act 1996. The key principle is that if the parties have chosen arbitration that is what they should get. Sections 5 and 6 of the Arbitration Act 1996 set out the formalities that have to be complied with for there to be a valid arbitration agreement. Where a charterparty containing an arbitration clause has been drawn up and signed by both parties it will satisfy those formalities. Often in practice this will not be done.[24] The arbitration agreement may also be evidenced in writing and this would comply with the Act.

Where arbitration proceedings are commenced by one party and the other party does not consider it is bound by an arbitration agreement in the contract, the respondent should object to the jurisdiction of the arbitration tribunal before it contests the merits of the matter.[25] The

---

18. See e.g. NYPE 1946, cl 17; NYPE 1993, cl 45; NYPE 2015 cl 54(b); Gencon 1994, cl 19; Shelltime 4, cl 46.
19. Lloyd's Open Form 2011, cl I.
20. See e.g. the Congenbill 1994, 2007 and 2016.
21. Arbitration Act 1996, ss 69(2), 69(3), 70(2) and 70(3).
22. The London Maritime Arbitrators Association has very experienced maritime arbitrators. They offer varying types of procedure depending on the amount at stake.
23. As at 9 February 2017, some 156 States are party to the New York Convention.
24. See page 6.
25. Arbitration Act 1996, s 31.

arbitration tribunal may rule on its own substantive jurisdiction.[26] In other words the arbitrators may decide, for example, whether there is a valid arbitration clause or, if there is, whether it is wide enough in scope to cover the dispute which has arisen. A party to arbitration proceedings may apply to the court to determine the jurisdiction of the arbitration tribunal in certain circumstances, for example with the permission of the arbitration tribunal.[27] In *Toyota Tsusho Sugar Trading Ltd v Prolat SRL*[28] such permission was granted. There were factual matters to be resolved in determining the jurisdiction dispute and an appeal might well follow a decision on the matter by the arbitration tribunal. The determination of the court was therefore likely to produce substantial savings in costs. The application had been made without delay and the involvement of the court in Naples by Prolat was an additional good reason why the English court should decide the issues.[29]

It will be necessary to determine whether a contract which states that it incorporates the terms of another contract, such as a bill of lading incorporating the terms of the charterparty pursuant to which it is issued or a reinsurance contract which incorporates the terms of the primary insurance contract,[30] validly incorporates the arbitration clause in that contract. The English courts have taken a liberal approach to incorporation of such clauses. Where a bill of lading incorporates the terms of a charterparty it may clearly identify that charterparty, by date or by the parties to it, or both.[31] If the charterparty clearly identified is a time charterparty, it will be incorporated.[32] Sometimes the bill of lading does not identify the charterparty, the terms of which are to be incorporated into the bill of lading, and there may be more than one if there is a string of charterparties. Where there are two or more potentially relevant charters, the courts are very reluctant to hold that the contract is void for uncertainty, as this does not give effect to the obvious intention of the parties that the terms of a charter are to be incorporated. There are "guidelines for ascertaining the intentions of the parties".[33] Although it is a question of construction in each case, the general rule is that the head charter, to which the shipowner is party, is incorporated.[34] However, the position may well be different where the head charterparty is a time charterparty, on the basis of the presumed unlikelihood of the parties wishing to incorporate the terms of a time charter which are different in kind.[35]

26. Arbitration Act 1996, s 30.
27. Arbitration Act 1996, s 32. *HC Trading Malta Ltd v Tradeland Commodities SL* [2016] EWHC 1279 (Comm); [2016] 2 Lloyd's Rep 130. See also s 67 and R. Merkin and L. Flannery, *Arbitration Act 1996*, (5th Ed, Informa Law 2014) 119–123 and 291–303.
28. [2014] EWHC 3649 (Comm); [2015] 1 Lloyd's Rep 344.
29. Ibid., [1] and [2].
30. *Trygg Hansa Insurance Co Ltd v Equitas Ltd* [1998] CLC 979; [1998] 2 Lloyd's Rep 439.
31. See eg. *Navig8Pte Ltd v Al-Riyadh Co for Vegetable Oil Industry (The Lucky Lady)* [2013] EWHC 328 (Comm); [2013] 2 All ER (Comm) 145. It was subsequently held that Navig8 Pte Ltd was entitled to declarations that it was not a party to the bill of lading contracts, had not been a bailee of or in possession of the cargo and therefore was not liable to the cargo receiver – [2013] EWHC 1565 (Comm).
32. *Sotrade Denizcilik Sanayi Ve Ticaret AS v Amadou LO (The Duden)* [2008] EWHC 2762 (Comm); [2009] 1 Lloyd's Rep 145 and *Southport Success SA v Tsingchan Holding Group Co Ltd* [2015] EWHC 1994 (Comm); [2015] 2 Lloyd's Rep 578 [18].
33. *Partenreederei M/S Heidberg v Grosvenor Grain & Feed Co Ltd (The Heidberg)* [1994] 2 Lloyd's Rep 287, 311 (Judge Diamond QC).
34. *Pacific Molasses Co and United Molasses Trading Co v Entre Rios Compania Naviera SA (The San Nicholas)* [1976] 1 Lloyd's Rep 8, 11 (Lord Denning); *The Sevonia Team* [1983] 2 Lloyd's Rep 640, 644 (Lloyd J); and *Navig8Pte Ltd v Al-Riyadh Co for Vegetable Oil Industry (The Lucky Lady)* [2013] EWHC 328 (Comm); [2013] 2 All ER 145.
35. *Kallang Shipping SA v Axa Assurances Senegal and Comptoir Commercial Mandiaye Ndiaye (The Kallang)* [2008] EWHC 2761 (Comm); [2009] 1 Lloyd's Rep 1245; *National Navigation Co v Endesa Generacion SA (The Wadi Sudr)* [2009] EWHC 196 (Comm); [2009] 1 Lloyd's Rep 666 which was appealed ([2009] EWCA Civ 1397; [2010] 2 All ER (Comm) 1243), but not on this point.

The business practice of concluding charterparties by an exchange of emails has been referred to as "entirely commonplace" by Tomlinson LJ in *Golden Ocean Group Ltd v Salgoacar Mining Industries Pvt Ltd*.[36] A formal charterparty signed by both parties is often not produced, particularly for short haul voyage charterparties. This raises issues as to whether an arbitration clause, which must be in writing or evidenced in writing, can be incorporated into a bill of lading from a charterparty which is recorded in a fixture recap, or series of emails, and in either case may in turn make reference to a proforma contract between different parties which contains an arbitration clause. The Court of Appeal has held that a charterparty which has not been drawn up at the time the bill of lading is issued and is recorded in a fixture recap telex,[37] or has never been drawn up and is in a fixture recap which, in turn, refers to a different charterparty between different parties,[38] can be incorporated into a bill of lading.

General words of incorporation in a bill of lading will not successfully incorporate an arbitration clause in a charterparty.[39] The Court of Appeal in *The Channel Ranger*[40] stressed that this is "an exception to the general approach of English law which in principle accepts incorporation of standard terms by the use of general words".[41] The reason usually given for this exception to the general rule is that third parties under negotiable bills of lading need certainty as they may not be familiar with the charterparty terms.[42] This would also be the case with a straight bill of lading where the consignee is not a party to the charterparty. A carrier who is the shipowner may not be aware of the terms of the charterparty where a sub voyage charterparty is incorporated into the bill of lading.[43]

If, however, specific words of incorporation are used (i.e. the arbitration clause is specifically referred to in the words of incorporation in the bill of lading), that will successfully incorporate

---

36. [2012] EWCA Civ 265; [2012] 1 Lloyd's Rep 542. The issue was whether a guarantee of a charterparty satisfied section 4 of the Statute of Frauds and was therefore enforceable where the written reference to the guarantee was in a series of emails resulting in the conclusion of the charterparty. Tomlinson LJ stated at [22]

> The conclusion of commercial contracts, particularly charterparties, by an exchange of emails, once telexes or faxes, in which the terms agreed early on are not repeated verbatim later in the exchanges, is entirely commonplace . . . The Statute must however, if possible, be construed in a manner which accommodates accepted contemporary business practice. The present case is not concerned with prescribing best or prudent practice. It is concerned with ensuring, so far as is possible, that the adoption of usual and accepted practice cannot be used as a vehicle for injustice by permitting parties to break promises which are supported by consideration and upon which reliance has been placed.

The Court of Appeal held that the guarantee was enforceable. For further discussion of this case see page 59.
37. *Welex AG v Rosa Maritime Ltd (The Epsilon Rosa) (No 2)* [2003] EWCA Civ 938; [2003] 2 Lloyd's Rep 509 distinguishing *Partenreederei M/S Heidberg v Grosvenor Grain & Feed Co Ltd (The Heidberg)* [1994] 2 Lloyd's Rep 287.
38. *Caresse Navigation Ltd v Office National de L'Electricite (The Channel Ranger)* [2014] EWCA Civ 1366; [2015] 1 Lloyd's Rep 256.
39. *Thomas v Portsea* [1912] AC 1; *Skips A/S Nordheim v Syrian Petroleum Company (The Varenna)* [1983] 2 Lloyd's Rep 592; *Federal Bulk Carriers Inc v C Itoh and Co Ltd (The Federal Bulker)* [1989] 1 Lloyd's Rep 103 (the bill of lading provided, "all terms . . . as per Charterparty . . . to be considered as fully incorporated herein as if fully written"); and *Navig8Pte Ltd v Al-Riyadh Co for Vegetable Oil Industry (The Lucky Lady)* [2013] EWHC 328 (Comm); [2013] 2 All ER (Comm) 145; *Golden Endurance Shipping SA v RMA Watanya SA (The Golden Endurance)* [2014] EWHC 3917 (Comm); [2015] 1 Lloyd's Rep 266 in relation to the Owendi and Takoradi bills which were in the Congenbill 1978 form.
40. *Caresse Navigation Ltd v Office National de L'Electricite (The Channel Ranger)* [2014] EWCA Civ 1366; [2015] 1 Lloyd's Rep 256 [26].
41. *Caresse Navigation Ltd v Office National de L'Electricite (The Channel Ranger)* [2014] EWCA Civ 1366; [2015] 1 Lloyd's Rep 256 [26] referring to *Sea Trade Maritime Corp v Hellenic Mutual Association (Bermuda) Ltd (The Athena)* [2006] EWHC 2530 (Comm); [2007] 1 All ER (Comm) 183 [65] per Langley J.
42. *Federal Bulk Carriers Inc v C Itoh and Co Ltd (The Federal Bulker)* [1989] 1 Lloyd's Rep 103 and *Caresse Navigation Ltd v Office National de L'Electricite (The Channel Ranger)* [2014] EWCA Civ 1366; [2015] 1 Lloyd's Rep 256 [15]. In relation to a court jurisdiction clause see *Siboti K/S v BP France SA* [2003] EWHC 1278; [2003] 2 Lloyd's Rep 364 [24].
43. See *The Wadi Sudr* discussed at page 11.

that clause into the bill of lading.[44] This will be so even if it is necessary to manipulate the wording of the charterparty clause, because, for example, that clause refers "all disputes arising out of this charterparty" to arbitration. As the parties have made clear their intention by the specific words that the arbitration clause is to be incorporated into the bill, the court will add the words "and under any bill of lading issued hereunder".

If the bill of lading incorporates the law and arbitration clause in the charterparty this will also work to incorporate the "law and litigation" clause, clause 41 of the Shelltime form, which provides for disputes to be subject to the jurisdiction of the English court, with a right to elect for London arbitration.[45] In a recent decision the Court of Appeal has gone further than this and held that an exclusive court jurisdiction clause in the charterparty will also be incorporated by a reference to the "Law and Arbitration" clause in the Congenbill 1994 bill of lading.[46] As under English law a third party consignee or indorsee of the bill of lading will also be bound by the arbitration clause in a bill of lading,[47] this decision does make it difficult for a third party bill of lading holder who has not seen the charterparty, or indeed the carrier who has not seen the voyage sub-charterparty, to know which tribunal has jurisdiction. This will be the case even if the charterparty was not drawn up and signed at the time the bill of lading was issued.[48]

Issues of jurisdiction, governing law, recognition and enforcement in bill of lading disputes are frequently resolved at the stage of provision of security for the claim, often if an arrest of the ship or a sister ship is threatened or effected.[49] Thus, where the carrier provides security by way of a P & I Club letter of undertaking[50] or bank guarantee in consideration of the cargo claimant agreeing not to arrest its ship or releasing its vessel from arrest, the terms of the security should spell out the trigger for payment by the P & I Club or bank. This should dovetail with the bill of lading. So, for example, if the bill of lading contains a London arbitration clause, the trigger for payment should be the production of a final London arbitration award and not, for example, a judgment of the courts of Senegal.[51]

If agreement cannot be reached on the trigger for payment it may be necessary to leave the issue open and for the letter of undertaking to provide for production of an award or judgment of a competent tribunal. Alternatively it may be possible to resolve any uncertainty as to jurisdiction when the terms of the security are negotiated. Thus, where the position was not clear as to which arbitration clause was incorporated into four bills of lading, Males J held in *Viscous Global Investment Ltd v Palladium Navigation Corp (The Quest)*[52] that an arbitration clause in the P & I Club letter of undertaking replaced the arbitration clause incorporated in the four bills

44. *Daval Aciers d'Usinor et de Sacilor v Armare SRL (The Nerano)* [1996] 1 Lloyd's Rep 1; *Owners of Cargo Lately Laden on Board The MV Delos v Delos Shipping Ltd (The Delos)* [2001] 1 Lloyd's Rep 703; *Welex AG v Rosa Maritime Ltd (The Epsilon Rosa) (No 2)* [2003] EWCA Civ 938; [2003] 2 Lloyd's Rep 509; *Essar Shipping Ltd v Bank of China Ltd (The Kishore)* [2015] EWHC 3266 (Comm); [2016] 1 Lloyd's Rep 427; and *Golden Endurance Shipping SA v RMA Watanya SA (The Golden Endurance)* [2014] EWHC 3917 (Comm); [2015] 1 Lloyd's Rep 266 in relation to the Lome bill of lading.
45. *YM Mars Tankers Ltd v Shield Petroleum Co (Nigeria) Ltd (The YM Saturn)* [2012] EWHC 2652.
46. *Caresse Navigation Ltd v Office National de L'Electricite (The Channel Ranger)* [2014] EWCA Civ 1366; [2015] 1 Lloyd's Rep 256.
47. See page 8.
48. *The Epsilon Rosa (No 2)* (fn 44) and *The Channel Ranger* (fn 46).
49. See Chapter 12.
50. See Chapter 11.
51. See *Kallang Shipping SA Panama v Axa Assurances Senegal and Comptoir Commercial Mandiaye Ndiaye (The Kallang)* [2008] EWHC 2761 (Comm); [2009] 1 Lloyd's Rep 124. Even if the cargo claimants have obtained security from the vessel's P & I Club they may still decide to pursue another party as was the case in *Navig8 Pte Ltd v Al-Riyadh Co for Vegetable Oil Industry (The Lucky Lady)* [2013] EWHC 328 (Comm); [2013] 2 All ER (Comm) 145 and see fn 34.
52. [2014] EWHC 2654 (Comm); [2014] 2 Lloyd's Rep 600. See also *The Pia Vesta* [1984] 1 Lloyd's Rep 169.

of lading from one of three possible charterparties: a time charterparty, a trip time charterparty and a voyage charterparty. All three provided for arbitration but the head charter provided for two arbitrators and an umpire and provided for "claims up to US$100,000 to be dealt with in accordance with LMAA Small Claims Procedure". The voyage charter provided for "Arbitration if any to be settled in Singapore by English law". The carriers' P & I Club gave a letter of undertaking which provided that the claims were subject to London arbitration.

Males J dismissed the carriers' argument that the Small Claims Procedure of the LMAA terms in the head charter still applied for those of the claims under US$100,000, with the result that the cargo claimants had followed the wrong procedure for those claims and were time barred. He held that the arbitration clause in the letter of undertaking replaced the arbitration agreements in whichever charterparty was incorporated in its entirety and did not just vary them in limited respects. Although the letter of undertaking was intended to provide security, "it was at least one purpose of this LOU to make provision for the way in which the parties' dispute was to be arbitrated."[53]

A clear provision in the security can therefore vary the arbitration clause in the bill of lading.[54] The P & I Club must have authority to vary the terms of the bill of lading in the letter of undertaking on behalf of its member. The letter of undertaking should also have its own jurisdiction and governing law provisions, as the letter of undertaking is a separate contract from the bill of lading.

Under English law, as a result of the Carriage of Goods by Sea Act 1992, a third party consignee or indorsee of the bill of lading will also be bound by the arbitration clause in a bill of lading if it chooses to sue on the bill of lading. Thus the Court of Appeal held in *The Epsilon Rosa (No 2)*[55] that the consignee of the bill of lading was bound by the arbitration clause incorporated in the bill of lading from the charterparty evidenced by the fixture recap telex. In *The Channel Ranger*[56] the bill of lading holder of a negotiable bill of lading was bound by the jurisdiction clause incorporated from the charterparty evidenced by the fixture recap referring to a pro forma charterparty.

A subrogated cargo insurer would also be bound by the London arbitration clause in the bill of lading.[57] Furthermore, where the carrier has become insolvent the subrogated insurer may be able to bring a direct action against the carrier's liability insurer.[58] Whether the claimant in the direct action will be bound by the arbitration clause in the insurance contract of the carrier's liability will depend on whether the right of direct action, given by statute in most States, is characterised as contractual or is an independent statutory right. If the former, the claimant will be bound by the arbitration clause.[59]

---

53. Ibid., [29].

54. Contrast *ISS Machinery Services Ltd v Aeolian Shipping SA (The Aeolian)* [2001] EWCA Civ 1162; [2001] 2 Lloyd's Rep 641 where it was held that the P & I Club letter of undertaking did not vary the governing law of the underlying contract.

55. *Welex AG v Rosa Maritime Ltd (The Epsilon Rosa) (No 2)* [2003] EWCA Civ 938; [2003] 2 Lloyd's Rep 509.

56. *Caresse Navigation Ltd v Office National de L'Electricite (The Channel Ranger)* [2014] EWCA Civ 1366; [2015] 1 Lloyd's Rep 256.

57. *Schiffahrtsgesellschaft Detlev von Appen GmbH v Voest Alpine Intertrading GmbH (The Jay Bola)* [1997] 2 Lloyd's Rep 279, 285 and 286 (Hobhouse LJ); *Navigation Maritime Bulgare v Rustal Trading Ltd (The Ivan Zagubanski)* [2002] 1 Lloyd's Rep 106 [52] and [54]; *People's Insurance Company of China, Hebei Branch v Vysanthi Shipping Co Ltd (The Joanna V)* [2003] 2 Lloyd's Rep 617; *The Front Comor* [2005] EWHC 454 (Comm); [2005] 2 Lloyd's Rep 257 [32] and [33]; *Kallang Shipping SA v Axa Assurances Senegal (The Kallang)* [2006] EWHC 2825; [2007] 1 Lloyd's Rep 160; *Starlight Shipping Co v Tai Ping Insurance Co Ltd* [2007] EWHC 1893 (Comm); [2008] 1 Lloyd's Rep 230; *Niagara Maritime SA v Tianjin Iron & Steel Group Co Ltd* [2011] EWHC 3035 (Comm).

58. See Chapter 11.

59. *Through Transport Mutual Insurance Association (Eurasia) Ltd v New India Assurance Co Ltd (The Hari Bhum)* [2004] EWCA (Civ) 1598; [2005] 1 Lloyd's Rep 67; *London Steam Ship Owners Mutual v Spain (The Prestige)* [2015] EWCA Civ 333; [2015] 2 Lloyd's Rep 33; and *Shipowners' Mutual Protection and Indemnity Association (Luxembourg) v Containerships Denizcilik Nakliyat ve Ticaret AS (The Yusuf Cepnioglu)* [2016] EWCA Civ 386; [2016] 1 Lloyd's Rep 641 under appeal.

Where a party to an arbitration clause,[60] which provides for arbitration in England or abroad, commences proceedings in the English court, the court is obliged to stay the court proceedings if the other party applies for a stay, unless satisfied that the arbitration agreement is null and void, inoperative or incapable of being performed.[61] Where, however, a ship has been arrested, the court granting the stay has a discretion to order that the property arrested be retained or that alternative security be provided for the satisfaction of any arbitration award.[62] The court may also grant a freezing injunction in support of the arbitration proceedings.[63]

(b) Anti-suit injunction

Where a party to a London arbitration agreement commences or threatens to commence proceedings elsewhere in breach of the arbitration agreement, the other party to the agreement may apply to the English court for an anti-suit injunction to restrain the first party from commencing or pursuing the proceedings elsewhere, provided the proceedings are in a court of a State which is neither an EU Member State nor Lugano Contracting State.[64] The English courts have a discretion to prevent parallel arbitration and court proceedings at the outset by granting an anti-suit injunction to restrain the respondent in the arbitration proceedings from commencing or pursuing foreign court proceedings in breach of the arbitration agreement where it is just and convenient to do so.[65]

The effectiveness of an anti-suit injunction will depend on where the assets are against which any judgment obtained in breach of the injunction is to be enforced. If they are in England, recognition and enforcement of the foreign judgment may be refused on the grounds of public policy.[66] Furthermore, the injunction will be served with a penal notice and if the injunction is ignored the party will be in contempt of court and may be liable to a fine or imprisonment.[67]

The party seeking the anti-suit injunction must not delay in doing so and the proceedings in the other jurisdiction must not be too advanced. The remedy is an equitable one and if either of these requirements is not satisfied the English court has a discretion to refuse the anti-suit injunction.[68]

Where, however, a claimant who is not a party to the arbitration agreement seeks an anti-suit injunction it must show that the conduct of the other party is unconscionable as the proceedings

---

60. Arbitration Act 1996, ss 9–11 apply even if the seat of the arbitration is outside England and Wales or Northern Ireland or no seat has been designated or determined (s 2(2)(a)).

61. Arbitration Act 1996, s 9(4). *Halki Shipping Corp v Sopex Oils Ltd* [1998] 1 Lloyd's Rep 465 and *Exfin Shipping (India) Ltd Mumbai v Tolani Shipping Co Ltd Mumbai* [2006] EWHC 1090 (Comm); [2006] 2 Lloyd's Rep 389.

62. Arbitration Act 1996, s 11.

63. Arbitration Act 1996, s 44 which applies regardless of the location of the seat of the arbitration (s 2), but not if the contract contains a *Scott v Avery* clause which provides that neither party shall bring "any action or other legal proceedings" against the other party in respect of a dispute until the arbitration award has been made – *B v S* [2011] EWHC 691 (Comm).

64. *AES Ust-Kamenogorsk Hydropower Plant LLP v Ust-Kamenogorsk Hydropower Plant JSC* [2013] UKSC 35; [2013] 1 WLR 1889 (Kazakhstan).

65. Senior Courts Act, s 37.

66. *Phillip Alexander Securities & Futures Ltd v Bamberger* [1997] ILPr 73,104. See page 14.

67. In *Compania Sud Americana de Vapores SA v Hin-Pro Logistics International Ltd* [2015] EWCA Civ 401; [2015] 2 Lloyd's Rep 1; [2014] EWHC 3632 (Comm); [2015] 1 Lloyd's Rep 301. See page 45 and 50–51.

68. *Toepfer International GMBH v Molino Boschi SRL* [1996] 1 Lloyd's Rep 510; *Verity Shipping SA v NV Norexa* [2008] EWHC 213 (Comm); [2008] 1 Lloyd's Rep 652; *Essar Shipping Ltd v Bank of China Ltd (The Kishore)* [2015] EWHC 3266 (Comm); [2016] 1 Lloyd's Rep 427; and *ADM Asia-Pacific Trading PTE Ltd v PT Buda Semestra Satria* [2016] EWHC 1427 (Comm). This is also true of anti-enforcement injunctions – *Ecobank Transnational Inc v Tanoh* [2015] EWCA Civ 1309; [2016] 1 Lloyd's Rep 360.

elsewhere are vexatious and oppressive. *Star Reefers Pool Inc v JFC Group Co Ltd*[69] concerned the guarantees of two charterparties which provided for London arbitration. The guarantor was not a party to the charterparty arbitration clause which had not been incorporated into the guarantees. Although the guarantees were governed by English law the Court of Appeal refused to uphold an anti-suit injunction restraining the guarantors from pursuing proceedings in Russia. Similarly in *Starlight Shipping Co v Tai Ping Insurance Co Ltd*[70] the managers of a ship and in *Navig8Pte Ltd v Al-Riyadh Co for Vegetable Oil Industry (The Lucky Lady)*[71] the charterers of a ship, could not obtain an anti-suit injunction to restrain a breach of the arbitration clause in the bill of lading as they were not a party to it.

(i) Anti-suit injunctions and the Jurisdiction Regulation

The effectiveness of arbitration agreements in Europe has been weakened. If a party commences court proceedings in an EU Member State court to which Council Regulation (EC) No 44/2001 on jurisdiction and the recognition and enforcement of judgments in civil and commercial matters (the Jurisdiction Regulation)[72] applies, in breach of a London arbitration agreement, the English court cannot grant an anti-suit injunction to restrain the respondent in the English arbitration from pursuing the court proceedings in the EU Member State as a result of the decision of the European Court of Justice in *Allianz SpA (formerly Riunione Adriatica di Sicurta SpA) v West Tankers Inc (The Front Comor)*.[73] There must be mutual trust between the EU Member States and the court of the EU Member State must be trusted to come to its own correct determination as to whether there is a valid arbitration clause. If there is, all the EU Member States are parties to the New York Convention and therefore each EU Member State would be obliged to stay its court proceedings in favour of arbitration. In *The Front Comor* the European Court of Justice rejected the argument that as arbitration proceedings fall outside the scope of the Jurisdiction Regulation as they are excluded by Article 1(2)(d),[74] the judgment of another EU Member State in relation to the validity of the arbitration agreement was also not within the Jurisdiction Regulation and therefore for the English court to grant an anti-suit injunction was not inconsistent

---

69. [2012] EWCA Civ 14; [2012] 2 All ER (Comm) 225.
70. [2007] EWHC 1893 (Comm); [2008] 1 Lloyd's Rep 230 (China).
71. [2013] EWHC 328 (Comm); [2013] 2 Lloyd's Rep 104.
72. See page 17.
73. *Allianz SpA (formerly Riunione Adriatica Di Sicurta SpA) v West Tankers Inc (The Front Comor)*, C-185/07, EU:C:2009:69 [2009] 1 AC 1138; [2009] 1 Lloyd's Rep 413; applied in *Youell v La Reunion Aerienne* [2009] EWCA Civ 175; [2009] 1 Lloyd's Rep 586. See Y. Baatz and A. Sandiforth, "A Setback for Arbitration" (2009) 9 STL 1. Doubt was thrown on the decision in *The Front Comor* by Advocate General Wathelet in his Opinion in *Gazprom OAO v Lietuvos dujos AB*, C-536/13, EU:C:2015:316 and Advocate General Jaaskinen in his Opinion in *CDC Cartel Damage Claims Hydrogen Peroxide SA*, C-352/13, EU:C:2015:335. In the former, Advocate General Wathelet considered that the Recast Jurisdiction Regulation (see page 17) should be taken into account when interpreting the exclusion of arbitration from the Jurisdiction Regulation – ". . . the main novelty of [the Recast Jurisdiction Regulation], which continues to exclude arbitration from its scope, lies not so much in its actual provisions but rather in Recital 12 in its preamble, *which in reality, somewhat in the manner of a retroactive interpretative law, explains how that exclusion must be and always should have been interpreted*." This raises the question whether it is now permissible to give an anti-suit injunction to restrain a party from pursuing proceedings in an EU Member State or a Lugano Contracting State in breach of an arbitration agreement both where the Jurisdiction Regulation and the Recast Jurisdiction Regulation applies. The Court of Justice of the European Union in *Gazprom* reference in May 2015 upheld its earlier decision in *The Front Comor* and did not comment on the Advocate General's Opinion.
74. *Marc Rich & Co AG v Societa Italiana PA (The Atlantic Emperor)*, C-190/89, EU:C:1991:319 [1992] 1 Lloyd's Rep 342; *The Heidberg* [1994] 2 Lloyd's Rep 287, at pp 298–303; *Toepfer International GmbH v Societe Cargill France* [1998] 1 Lloyd's Rep 379; *Van Uden Maritime BV v Kommanditgesellschaft in Firma Deco-Line*, C-391/95, EU:C:1998:543 [1999] All ER (EC) 258 (ECJ); *Navigation Maritime Bulgare v Rustal Trading Ltd (The Ivan Zagubanski)* [2002] 1 Lloyd's Rep 106; and *Through Transport Mutual Insurance Association (Eurasia) Ltd v New India Assurance Co Ltd (The Hari Bhum)* [2004] EWCA (Civ) 1598; [2005] 1 Lloyd's Rep 67; *A v B* [2006] EWHC 2006 (Comm); [2007] 1 Lloyd's Rep 237.

with the Jurisdiction Regulation. The court held that as the Italian court in that case was seised of a substantive dispute for damages in a tort claim as a result of the *Front Comor* hitting the Italian claimants' jetty in Syracuse, and the Italian court had jurisdiction to decide the substantive claim under Article 5(3) of the Jurisdiction Regulation unless there was a valid arbitration agreement, the issue as to whether there was a valid arbitration clause was a preliminary issue to the substantive claim which fell within the Jurisdiction Regulation. Therefore it was inconsistent with the Regulation for the English court to grant an anti-suit injunction restraining the Italian claimant from pursuing proceedings within the Jurisdiction Regulation in Italy.

The unfortunate result of the decision of the European Court of Justice in *The Front Comor* is that there may be, and indeed were in *The Front Comor*,[75] parallel arbitration proceedings in one EU Member State and court proceedings in a different EU Member State. There is no mechanism in the Jurisdiction Regulation to prevent such parallel proceedings with the consequent duplication of costs and risk of conflicting decisions, both as to whether there is a binding arbitration agreement and on the substance of the dispute. The resulting problems are all too clearly illustrated by *National Navigation Co v Endesa Generacion SA (The Wadi Sudr)*[76] where the Spanish court held that the London arbitration clause was not binding, whereas Gloster J held that it was. The Court of Appeal held that the Spanish judgment, a Regulation judgment, can give rise to an issue estoppel as much in arbitration proceedings excluded from the Regulation as in any other proceedings in an English court.[77] Both Waller and Moore-Bick LJJ went further and indicated *obiter* that arbitrators bound to apply English law would have to consider under ordinary principles of English law whether a judgment gave rise to an issue estoppel.[78]

The position under the Jurisdiction Regulation is unfairly weighted against the party seeking to rely on the arbitration clause, who can never seise the court of the seat of the arbitration first within that Regulation. Even if the claimant obtains an arbitration award first before the judgment of the other EU Member State if the other party is determined to pursue proceedings in its own court for its own advantage,[79] there remains uncertainty as to whether the foreign court judgment can be refused recognition in the English courts, which is discussed below.[80]

(ii) Anti-suit injunctions and the Recast Jurisdiction Regulation

After a review of the Jurisdiction Regulation[81] the European Commission proposed amendments to the Regulation[82] to "enhance the effectiveness of arbitration agreements in Europe,

---

75. For a history of this litigation see *West Tankers Inc v Allianz SpA* [2012] EWHC 854 (Comm); [2012] 2 Lloyd's Rep 103, [4] – [16].

76. [2009] EWCA Civ 1397; [2010] 2 All ER (Comm) 1243; [2009] EWHC 196 (Comm); [2009] 1 Lloyd's Rep 666, [49] noted in Y. Baatz, "A Jurisdiction Race in the Dark" [2010] LMCLQ 364.

77. [2009] EWCA Civ 1397; [2010] 2 All ER (Comm) 1243, [56] and [119].

78. Ibid., [56] and [118]. In *CMA CGM v Hyundai MIPO Dockyard Co Ltd* [2009] 1 Lloyd's Rep 213 Burton J, without deciding the point, had indicated that he was not persuaded that London arbitrators were wrong when they had decided that they were not bound by the Regulation and were therefore bound to recognise a French judgment.

79. In the case of *The Wadi Sudr* because Spanish law imposed absolute liability rather than an obligation to exercise due diligence under English law. In the case of *The Front Comor* the Italian insurers may have preferred the Italian court's interpretation of the exception of navigational error.

80. See page 14.

81. B. Hess, T. Pfeiffer and P. Schlosser, *The Brussels I: Regulation (EC) No 44/2001 The Heidelberg Report on the Application of Regulation Brussels I in 25 Member States* (Study JLS/C4/2005/03) (C.H. Beck, Hart, Nomos, 2008) (the "Heidelberg Report"). On 21 April 2009 the European Commission adopted a Report COM (2009) 174 and a Green Paper COM (2009) 175 inviting consultation by 30 June 2009.

82. COM (2010) 748. See A. Briggs, "The Brussels I*bis* Regulation Appears on the Horizon" [2011] LMCLQ 157 for a discussion of those proposals.

prevent parallel court and arbitration proceedings, and eliminate the incentive for abusive litigation tactics"[83] which lead to Regulation (EU) No 1215/2012 of the European Parliament and of the Council of 12 December 2012 on jurisdiction and the recognition and enforcement of judgments in civil and commercial matters (recast) (the "Recast Jurisdiction Regulation").[84] It was not possible to agree any rule of priority as to who should determine the validity of an arbitration clause, although priority was granted to the court chosen to determine whether a court jurisdiction clause was valid.[85] Therefore, as before, there is no mechanism to prevent parallel arbitration and court proceedings and again this leaves the resolution of the problem to the enforcement stage. There is much controversy as to whether it would be permissible for the English court to grant an anti-suit injunction where the Recast Jurisdiction Regulation applies.[86]

Article 1(2)(d) of the Recast Jurisdiction Regulation simply excludes arbitration from the scope of the Recast Jurisdiction Regulation and Article 73 provides that the Recast Jurisdiction Regulation shall not affect the application of the New York Convention. The second paragraph of Recital 12 states that a ruling by the court of an EU Member State as to whether or not an arbitration agreement is null and void, inoperative or incapable of being performed should not be subject to the rules of recognition and enforcement laid down in the Regulation, regardless of whether the court decided on this as a principal issue or as an incidental question. The decision of *The Front Comor* has, therefore, been reversed to the extent that neither an English court judgment nor the Italian court judgment as to the validity of the arbitration agreement would be a Regulation judgment. The issue of the validity of the arbitration agreement therefore falls outside the Recast Regulation. Nevertheless, it seems likely that the Court of Justice of the European Union would apply some general principle to reject anti-suit injunctions.[87]

An arbitration tribunal may grant an anti-suit injunction to restrain a party from proceeding in breach of an arbitration agreement. This could not be served with a penal notice or carry the sanction of contempt proceedings. In the *Gazprom*[88] litigation the Stockholm Chamber of Commerce made an arbitration award in arbitration proceedings between Gazprom and the Lithuanian Ministry of Energy which granted an anti-suit injunction restraining the Lithuanian Ministry of Energy from pursuing court proceedings in Vilnius, Lithuania. The Court of Justice of the European Union held that the Jurisdiction Regulation did not preclude the courts of Vilnius from recognising and enforcing the arbitrators' award.

---

83. COM (2010) 748 Explanatory Memorandum, [3.1.4].
84. See page 17.
85. Changes were introduced for court jurisdiction clauses which give priority to the court chosen to determine the validity of the jurisdiction clause and require the court first seised but not chosen to stay its proceedings – see Recital 22 and arts 29(1) and 31(2) and (3) of the Recast Jurisdiction Regulation discussed at page 24. This solution is similar to that adopted by Article 6 of the 2005 Hague Convention on Choice of Court Agreements – see pages 16 and 17.
86. See A. Ippolito and M. Adler-Nissen, West Tankers revisited: Has the new Brussels I Regulation brought anti-suit injunctions back into the procedural armoury? [2013] Arbitration 1; J Lavelle, "The rebirth of anti-suit injunctions in support of arbitration," (2015) 15 STL 1; http://hsfnotes.com/arbitration/2012/12/12/the-revised-brussels-regulation-are-we-back-to-where-we-started/ (accessed 9 March 2017); See A Briggs, *Civil Jurisdiction and Judgments* (6th ed, Informa Law 2015) [8.18]; M Illmer in Gen eds A Dickinson and E Lein, *The Brussels 1 Recast* (Oxford University Press 2015) [2.03] – [2.10] on the legislative history of the Recast Regulation and the maintenance of the status quo for the arbitration exception; R Fentiman, *International Commercial Litigation* (2nd ed, Oxford University Press 2015), [16.142] – [16.149]; R Merkin and L Flannery, *Arbitration Act 1996* (5th ed, Informa Law 2014), page 191 fn 137, which takes the view that the Recast Regulation does not change the position.
87. Cf for example its approach in *TNT Express Nederland BV v Axa Versicherung AG*, C-533/08, EU:C:2010:243. See also fn 316.
88. *Gazprom OAO v Lietuvos dujos AB*, C-536/13, EU:C:2015:316.

(c) Damages for breach of the arbitration agreement

No matter whether the other proceedings are in an EU Member State or Lugano Contracting State or elsewhere, a party to an arbitration which has been breached may be able to recover damages for breach of contract[89] or for the tort of procuring a breach of contract.[90] In the latest twist of *The Front Comor* litigation Flaux J held[91] that the arbitration tribunal was not deprived, by reason of European law, of the jurisdiction to award equitable damages for breach of the obligation to arbitrate. The damages claimed were for legal fees and expenses reasonably incurred in connection with the Italian proceedings and for an indemnity against an award made against the shipowners in the Italian proceedings if it were greater than the liability of the shipowners as established in the London arbitration. Commenting on *The Wadi Sudr* Flaux J stated in *The Front Comor*,[92]

"The Regulation simply does not apply to arbitration or arbitral tribunals. The reason why the arbitrators were bound to recognise the Spanish judgment was nothing to do with any principle of European law derived from the Regulation but because of the English common law doctrine of res judicata."

(d) Recognition and enforcement

Where an arbitration award is made in London arbitration it can be enforced under the New York Convention in any other State which is a party to that Convention. There are limited grounds to refuse recognition and enforcement of an arbitration award under the New York Convention.[93]

Where a court judgment has been given by another State which is neither an EU Member State nor a Lugano Contracting State in breach of a London arbitration award, there may be grounds on which that court judgment will be refused recognition and enforcement in England. This will depend on whether the other State giving the judgment is one to which the common law rules on enforcement apply[94] or whether the foreign judgment can be registered under the Administration

---

89. *Kallang Shipping SA Panama v Axa Assurances Senegal and Comptoir Commercial Mandiaye Ndiaye (The Kallang)* [2008] EWHC 2761 (Comm); [2009] 1 Lloyd's Rep 124*; West Tankers Inc v Allianz SpA* [2012] EWHC 854 (Comm); [2012] 2 All E R (Comm) 395; [2012] 2 Lloyd's Rep 103; and *Golden Endurance Shipping SA v RMA Watanya SA (The Golden Endurance)* [2014] EWHC 3917 (Comm); [2015] 1 Lloyd's Rep 266 in relation to the Lome bills of lading which contained a London arbitration clause (Morocco); but see *Essar Shipping Ltd v Bank of China Ltd (The Kishore)* [2015] EWHC 3266 (Comm); [2016] 1 Lloyd's Rep 427 [74] and [75]. For the position in relation to court jurisdiction clauses see pages 49–51.

90. *Kallang Shipping SA Panama v Axa Assurances Senegal and Comptoir Commercial Mandiaye Ndiaye (The Kallang)* [2008] EWHC 2761 (Comm); [2009] 1 Lloyd's Rep 124;. For the position in relation to damages for the tort of inducing a breach of a court jurisdiction agreement see page 51.

91. *West Tankers Inc v Allianz SpA* [2012] EWHC 854 (Comm); [2012] 2 All ER (Comm) 395; [2012] 2 Lloyd's Rep 103. For a history of this litigation see [4] – [16].

92. [67].

93. The State requested to recognise the arbitration award may seek to rely on the ground of public policy to refuse recognition or its national law. Compare the position in the non-European arena in the Australian case of *Dampskibsselskabet Nordern A/S v Beach Building & Civil Group Pty Ltd* [2012] FCA 696; 292 ALR 161 (Federal Court, Australia) where Foster J held that a foreign arbitration clause was of no effect and therefore would not be enforced. The case went to the Full Court of the Federal Court of Australia (*Dampskibsselskabet Nordern A/S v Gladstone Civil Pty Ltd (The Ocean Baron)* [2013] FCAFC 107) where a majority held that the arbitration clause in the charterparty did not fall foul of the Australian legislation and it was not therefore necessary to decide the recognition and enforcement issues. However, the dissenting judge held that it would not be enforced. See N. Gaskell, "Australian Recognition and Enforcement of Foreign Charterparty Arbitration Clauses" [2014] LMCLQ 174 at page 180 and 181 and in particular fn. 42.

94. See A. Briggs, *Civil Jurisdiction and Judgments* (6th edition, Informa Law 2015), [7.46] – [7.84].

of Justice Act 1920 or the Foreign Judgments (Reciprocal Enforcement) Act 1933.[95] Both these Acts are based on the rules at common law. So, for example, if a court in China ignores a London arbitration agreement and proceeds to judgment, the English court, applying its common law rules, may refuse to recognise and enforce the Chinese judgment, provided that the defendant in the Chinese court has not submitted to the jurisdiction of that court.[96] The most relevant grounds for such refusal include the ground that the Chinese court gave judgment in breach of a valid arbitration agreement;[97] the foreign judgment was obtained by fraud; recognition of the foreign judgment would be contrary to English public policy;[98] or the foreign judgment is inconsistent with a prior judgment.[99]

Where the foreign judgment is that of an EU Member State court there is uncertainty as to whether that judgment could be refused recognition in the English courts where the Recast Jurisdiction Regulation or Jurisdiction Regulation applied to the foreign judgment and there are arbitration proceedings in England. Timing will be very important and this could lead to a race to judgment or award, as if the foreign court gave a judgment that the arbitration clause was invalid first, the Court of Appeal has held that arbitrators would be bound by that judgment.[100] If, on the other hand, the arbitrators held that they had jurisdiction and gave their award first, the Court of Appeal in *The Front Comor*[101] once the arbitration award had been made,[102] but before the decision of the Italian court, held that the English court had jurisdiction to grant leave to enforce it[103] and to enter judgment in terms of the award.[104] The key will be whether any arbitration award enforced as a judgment in England can prevent the enforcement of the judgment of another EU Member State on the merits. This may give a defence to recognition of any subsequent judgment of the other EU Member State court under Article 34(3) of the Jurisdiction Regulation.[105] In *The Wadi Sudr* Waller LJ indicated *obiter* that he thought this would be the position,[106] but the point

---

95. Ibid., [7.85] – [7.93].

96. *Spliethoff's Bevrachtingskantoor BV v Bank of China Ltd* [2015] EWHC 999 (Comm); [2015] 2 Lloyd's Rep 123. See also *Golden Endurance Shipping SA v RMA Watanya SA* [2016] EWHC 2110 (Comm); [2017] 1 All ER (Comm) 438 where Phillips J held that shipowners had not submitted to the Moroccan court, and also *Ecobank Transnational Inc v Tanoh* [2015] EWCA Civ 1309; [2016] 1 Lloyd's Rep 360.

97. S 32 of the Civil Jurisdiction and Judgments Act 1982. In *Ust-Kamenogorsk Hydropower Plant JSC v AES Ust-Kamenogorsk Hydropower Plant LLP* [2010] EWHC 772 Comm [38] – [39] and [51], upheld on these points by the Court of Appeal [2011] 2 Lloyd's Rep 233 [149] and [186] (the case went to the Supreme Court but not on this point), it was held that a decision of the Kazakhstan court that a London ICC arbitration agreement was void would not be recognised.

98. For example if the judgment is obtained in breach of an English anti-suit injunction – *Phillip Alexander Securities & Futures Ltd v Bamberger* [1997] ILPr 73,104.

99. *People's Insurance Company of China, Hebei Branch v Vysanthi Shipping Co Ltd (The Joanna V)* [2003] EWHC 1655 (Comm); [2003] 2 Lloyd's Rep 617.

100. *National Navigation Co v Endesa Generacion SA (The Wadi Sudr)* [2009] EWCA Civ 1397; [2010] 2 All ER (Comm) 1243 noted in Y Baatz, "A Jurisdiction Race in the Dark" [2010] LMCLQ 364.

101. *West Tankers Inc v Allianz SpA* [2012] EWCA Civ 27; [2012] 2 All ER (Comm) 113; [2011] EWHC 829 (Comm); [2011] 2 All ER (Comm) 1.

102. The arbitrators held that the shipowners had no liability whatsoever in contract, tort or otherwise to the jetty owners or their subrogated insurers, and if this were wrong, that any liability was limited under the Convention on Limitation of Liability for Maritime Claims 1976.

103. Pursuant to Arbitration Act 1996, s 66(1).

104. Pursuant to Arbitration Act 1996, s 66(2).

105. Recast Jurisdiction Regulation, art 45(1)(c).

106. [2009] EWCA Civ 1397; [2010] 2 All ER (Comm) 1243, [63]. This was also the view, *obiter*, of Judge Diamond QC in *Partenreederei M/S Heidberg v Grosvenor Grain and Feed Co Ltd (The Heidberg)* [1994] 2 Lloyd's Rep 287, 301–302 where he distinguishes between the position when the judgment of the foreign court is given before (the facts of the case he had to decide) and after the English court appoints an arbitrator; and of R. Merkin and L. Flannery, *Arbitration Act 1996* (5th ed, Informa Law 2014), p. 192.

is controversial as it may be argued that Article 34(3) does not include judgments which give effect to arbitration awards and are not therefore Regulation judgments.[107]

It may be unlikely that a State will recognise and enforce an arbitration award made in another EU Member State if the court of the former has already given judgment that there is no valid arbitration agreement or has given a judgment on the merits of the case that conflicts with the award. It will therefore be very important where the assets of the paying party are or that the successful party has security for its claim so that the uncertainty as to the enforcement of the award may be avoided.

Even if the claimant obtains an English arbitration award first before the judgment of the other EU Member State,[108] and that court judgment can be refused recognition in the English courts, this is only of value if the assets against which the judgment is to be enforced are in England. For example, the judgment of a Spanish court may have to be recognised in the courts of other EU Member States, who could not be bound to refuse recognition on the basis of an English judgment on an arbitration award, i.e. a judgment which is not local to them and which falls outside the Regulation.

The Recast Jurisdiction Regulation does not solve the issue as to whether the English court can refuse to recognise and enforce the judgment of an EU Member State if there is already an English judgment on an arbitration award.[109] If the court of an EU Member State decides that there is not a valid arbitration clause and proceeds to a substantive judgment on the merits, Recital 12 further states that that judgment will not be precluded from being recognised or enforced under the Regulation. This should not prejudice the competence of the courts of the EU Member States to decide on the recognition and enforcement of arbitral awards in accordance with the New York Convention which takes precedence over the Recast Jurisdiction Regulation. Therefore a London arbitration award should be able to be enforced in, for example, Italy under the New York Convention.

3. COURT JURISDICTION

If there is no arbitration agreement it will be necessary to determine whether the English court has jurisdiction either because it has been chosen by the parties or on some other ground such as sufficient connection between the subject matter of the dispute and a particular court. Maritime

---

107. See eg. *African Fertilizers and Chemicals NIG Ltd v B D Shipsnavo GmbH & Co Reederei KG* [2011] EWHC 2452 (Comm); [2011] 2 Lloyd's Rep 531 and *London Steam Ship Owners Mutual v Spain (The Prestige)* [2013] EWHC 3188 (Comm); [2014] 1 Lloyd's Rep 309, [187] – [189] where Hamblen J did not feel it necessary to decide the point as there was no inconsistent judgment of the Spanish court at the time leave to enforce the arbitration award was given. The case went to the Court of Appeal – [2015] EWCA Civ 333; [2015] 2 Lloyd's Rep 33. See A. Briggs, *Civil Jurisdiction and Judgments* (6th edition, Informa Law 2015), [8.17]; Dicey, Morris and Collins, *The Conflict of Laws* (15th ed., Sweet and Maxwell 2012), [14–206] – [14–214]; and H. Van Houtte, "Why not include Arbitration in The Brussels Jurisdiction Regulation?" (2005) 21 Arbitration International, 509 at 514 and 520 where it was proposed that a new fifth ground be added to Article 34 to refuse recognition or enforcement of a judgment which is irreconcilable with an arbitral award. The position does not appear to be uniform throughout the EU Member States – see eg. the Heidelberg Report, [127] which states that "the recognition of judgments of other Member States that were given despite an arbitration agreement is widely accepted in case law and legal doctrine" and the Report from the Commission to the European Parliament COM (2009) 174 final dated 21.4.2009 para 3.7. See also J Lavelle and R. Merkin, "The availability of declaratory relief" (2010) Arbitration Monthly 1.

108. *West Tankers Inc v Allianz SpA* [2012] EWCA Civ 27 which approved *African Fertilizers and Chemicals NIG Ltd v BD Shipsnavo GmbH & Co Reederei KG* [2011] EWHC 2452 (Comm) and *Sovarex SA v Romero Alvarez SA* [2011] EWHC 1661 (Comm); [2012] 1 All ER (Comm) 207.

109. Applying Article 45(1)(c) of the Recast Jurisdiction Regulation, the equivalent of Article 34(3) of the Jurisdiction Regulation, if the definition of judgment in that provision includes an English judgment enforcing an arbitration award. See R. Merkin and L Flannery, *Arbitration Act 1996* (5th ed, Informa Law 2014) pp. 286 and 287.

contracts, such as bills of lading, marine insurance policies[110] and international sales contracts often provide for the exclusive jurisdiction of the High Court in London. We shall consider how effective such a clause is; the effectiveness of a foreign jurisdiction clause both where the defendant is domiciled in an EU Member State and where it is not. We shall also consider the position where there is no jurisdiction clause and either the defendant is domiciled in an EU Member State or it is not.

There is no one convention which operates worldwide as to which court shall have jurisdiction in an international dispute. The first issue is whether the 2005 Hague Convention on Choice of Court Agreements ("the Choice of Court Convention");[111] Regulation (EU) No. 1215/2012 of the European Parliament and of the Council of 12 December 2012 on jurisdiction and the recognition and enforcement of judgments in civil and commercial matters (recast) ("the Recast Jurisdiction Regulation");[112] Council Regulation (EC) No. 44/2001 of December 22, 2000 on Jurisdiction and the Recognition and Enforcement of Judgments in Civil and Commercial Matters ("the Jurisdiction Regulation");[113] or the revised 2007 Lugano Convention applies.[114] If none of those Conventions or Regulations are applicable the English court will apply its national law to determine whether it has jurisdiction to determine an international dispute.

(a) The 2005 Hague Convention on Choice of Court Agreements

Subject to some important differences, the Choice of Court Convention does for court jurisdiction agreements what the New York Convention does for arbitration agreements. Party autonomy is at the heart of both conventions and results in three basic principles: if parties to a contract choose court jurisdiction or arbitration that choice should be given effect to; no other court should take jurisdiction; and any court judgment or arbitration award resulting from such choice should be recognised and enforced. Each of these principles is subject to exceptions. Whereas the New York Convention has been very successful as it has been ratified by more than 150 States worldwide, the Choice of Court Convention has a long way to go.[115] It remains to be seen whether it can attract support from other major economic powers such as the US and China. If it does, it is more likely to attract further support. It is not surprising that the Choice of Court Convention has been ratified by the EU as the approach of the Convention shares much in

110. Marine insurance contracts on the MAR forms contain an exclusive English court jurisdiction clause, as do some P&I Club rules.

111. The Convention entered into force on 1 October 2015 in Mexico and the EU and on 1 October 2016 in Singapore.

112. The Regulation applies to all the EU Member States including Denmark according to the agreement between the European Community and the Kingdom of Denmark on jurisdiction and the recognition and enforcement of judgments in civil and commercial matters (OJ L 79/4, 21.3.2013).

113. The Jurisdiction Regulation replaced the latest Accession Convention to the Convention on Jurisdiction and the Enforcement of Judgments in Civil and Commercial Matters 1968 ("the Jurisdiction Convention"). The Jurisdiction Convention and the Jurisdiction Regulation are often referred to as the Brussels Convention or Brussels Regulation and the Recast Jurisdiction Regulation as Brussels I Regulation, but such descriptions are not used here to avoid confusion as many maritime conventions were concluded in Brussels. Although the Jurisdiction Regulation has been described by the European Parliament as "one of the most successful pieces of EU legislation" (2009/2140 (INI) dated 7 September 2010, Recital A), as it promotes certainty and predictability and avoids parallel proceedings, nevertheless it was acknowledged that it needed modernisation. An excellent review of the Regulation was carried out by Heidelberg University – B. Hess, T. Pfeiffer and P. Schlosser, *The Brussels I: Regulation (EC) No 44/2001 The Heidelberg Report on the Application of Regulation Brussels I in 25 Member States* (Study JLS/C4/2005/03) (C.H. Beck, Hart, Nomos 2008) (the "Heidelberg Report").

114. The revised Lugano Convention entered into force in Denmark (January 1, 2010); Norway (January 1, 2010); Switzerland (January 1, 2011); the European Union (January 1, 2010) and Iceland on May 1, 2011. The revised Lugano Convention replaced the EFTA Convention on Jurisdiction and the Enforcement of Judgments in Civil and Commercial Matters 1988 ("the Lugano Convention").

115. See fn 111.

common with that of the provisions on choice of jurisdiction in the Recast Jurisdiction Regulation discussed below. However, the scope of the Choice of Court Convention is much narrower than the Recast Jurisdiction Regulation as its focus is jurisdiction agreements, and it does not provide which court will have jurisdiction in an international dispute where the parties have not made an agreement as to jurisdiction. Thus if, for example, two parties have entered into a ship sale contract and the contract provides for the courts of, for example, Singapore to determine any disputes under the contract, the courts of the United Kingdom, would be obliged to give effect to the jurisdiction agreement and stay their proceedings in favour of Singapore. If, however, the jurisdiction clause is not valid the Choice of Court Convention does not apply.

Furthermore, unlike the Recast Jurisdiction Regulation, the Choice of Court Convention does not apply to the carriage of passengers and goods,[116] marine pollution, limitation of liability for maritime claims, General Average and emergency towage and salvage.[117] It does, however, apply to contracts of insurance and reinsurance that relate to such matters[118] and to other maritime contracts such as ship building contracts, ship sale and purchase contracts, international sale contracts and probably time charterparties, but not voyage charterparties.[119]

If the United Kingdom is no longer an EU Member State in the future it will need to become a party to the Choice of Court Convention as this was ratified by the European Union and not the United Kingdom. It would be important for the United Kingdom to ratify the Convention speedily so that the other EU Member States would continue to be obliged to give effect to an English jurisdiction agreement. The Recast Jurisdiction Regulation would no longer apply to the United Kingdom if it were not an EU Member State and the United Kingdom is not a party to the revised Lugano Convention, which was ratified by the European Union and not the United Kingdom.[120]

(b) The Recast Jurisdiction Regulation and the Jurisdiction Regulation

The Recast Jurisdiction Regulation applies to legal proceedings instituted on or after 10 January 2015.[121] The discussion below will focus on the Recast Jurisdiction Regulation but the equivalent provisions of the Jurisdiction Regulation will be given in the footnotes if they differ from those of the Recast Jurisdiction Regulation. The rules under the Recast Jurisdiction Regulation, Jurisdiction Regulation, the Lugano Conventions and the EC Jurisdiction Convention shall be treated as if they are identical but where the Jurisdiction Regulation differs from the Recast Jurisdiction Regulation, particularly in relation to jurisdiction agreements, this will be discussed separately below in case the reader is still dealing with proceedings commenced before 10 January 2015. Much of the case law referred to is decided on the provisions of the Jurisdiction Regulation or its predecessors, but where the wording of the provisions has not changed it is equally applicable to the Recast Jurisdiction Regulation.

The Recast Jurisdiction Regulation seeks to determine the international jurisdiction of the courts of the EU Member States so that all EU Member States are bound by the same rules and will therefore recognise and enforce each other's judgments speedily. They provide for

---

116. Choice of Court Convention, art 2(2)(f).
117. Choice of Court Convention, art 2(2)(g).
118. Choice of Court Convention, art 17.
119. Compare the position under Rome I discussed at page 67.
120. On the possible consequences of the United Kingdom leaving the EU ("Brexit") see S. Masters and B. McRae, "What does Brexit mean for the Brussels Regime? [2016] Journal of International Arbitration 483; A. Dickinson, "Back to the Future: the UK's exit and the conflict of laws" [2016] JIPL 195; and R. Aikens and A. Dinsmore, "Jurisdiction, Enforcement and the Conflict of Laws in Cross-Border Commercial Disputes: What are the Legal Consequences of Brexit?" [2016] EBLR 903.
121. Art 66.

certain and predictable rules with little discretion.[122] The European Court of Justice stated that the aim of the Jurisdiction Regulation is that the claimant should be able "to identify easily the court in which he may sue and the defendant reasonably to foresee before which court he may be sued".[123] The Recast Jurisdiction Regulation applies to "civil and commercial matters"[124] with some exceptions and those exceptions which are particularly relevant to maritime disputes are where there are proceedings relating to the winding up of insolvent companies[125] or arbitration.[126]

The basic rule is that a defendant domiciled in an EU Member State must be sued in that State.[127] It does not matter where the claimant is domiciled.[128] Thus if a Japanese claimant sues a defendant domiciled in France the Recast Jurisdiction Regulation applies and the defendant must be sued in France, unless an exception applies such as where the parties have agreed on the court of an EU Member State, in which case the fact that they have chosen the court of an EU Member State is a trigger for the application of the Recast Jurisdiction Regulation and the EU Member State chosen shall have jurisdiction under Article 25 of that Regulation, no matter where either party is domiciled.[129] If there is no jurisdiction clause and the Japanese claimant were to sue the French-domiciled defendant in England, the defendant could ask for a stay of the English proceedings.

Furthermore, in *Owusu v Jackson*[130] the European Court of Justice held that Article 2 of the Jurisdiction Regulation, the equivalent of Article 4 of the Recast Jurisdiction Regulation, will apply if the defendant is domiciled in an EU Member State, in that case England, even if the only other court involved is that of a non-EU Member State, in that case Jamaica. The importance of predictability and certainty was stressed. Thus the English court could not decline the jurisdiction conferred on it by Article 2 on the ground that the Jamaican court would be a more appropriate forum for the trial of the action. Whether there are any exceptions to that decision remains unclear under the Jurisdiction Regulation. The English courts have held that there is an exception where the defendant is domiciled in England but there is a foreign jurisdiction clause;[131] or there

---

122. See e.g. *Owusu v Jackson* C -281/02, EU:C:2005:120 [2005] ECR I-1383; [2005] 1 Lloyd's Rep 452 and *Color Drack GmbH v Lexx International Vertriebs GmbH* C-386/05, EU:C:2007:262 [2007] ILPr35, [19], [20], [32] and [33], but the Recast Jurisdiction Regulation, arts 33 and 34 expressly provide for discretion as discussed at pages 28–29 and 30–31.

123. *Hypotecni banka asa.s. v Lindner* C-327/10, EU:C:2011:745 [2011] ECR I-11543, [44].

124. Recast Jurisdiction Regulation, art 1(1).

125. Recast Jurisdiction Regulation, art 1(2)(b). The reason for this exclusion is that Regulation (EU) 2015/848 of the European Parliament and of the Council of 20 May 2015 on Insolvency proceedings (Recast) (Recast Insolvency Regulation) applies to insolvency proceedings opened after 26 June 2017 (art 84(1)) and Regulation (EC) No 1346/2000 applies to insolvency proceedings opened before that date (art 84(2) of the Recast Insolvency Regulation).

126. Recast Jurisdiction Regulation, art 1(2)(d). See fn 74 of this chapter.

127. Recast Jurisdiction Regulation, art 4; Jurisdiction Regulation, art 2.

128. *Societe Group Josi Reinsurance Company SA v Compagnie d'Assurances Universal General Insurance Company*, C-421/98, EU:C:2000:399; [2000] 2 All ER (Comm) 467.

129. Jurisdiction Regulation, art 23 discussed at pages 22–24.

130. C-281/02, EU:C:2005:120 [2005] ECR I-1383; [2005] 1 Lloyd's Rep 452. Noted by E. Peel, "Forum Non Conveniens and European Ideals" [2005] LMCLQ 363 and A. Briggs, "Forum Non Conveniens and Ideal Europeans" [2005] LMCLQ 378; A. Briggs, "The Death of Harrods: Forum Non Conveniens and the European Court" (2005) 121 LQR 535; D. Jackson, "Jurisdiction in Europe: And Forum Non Conveniens" (2005) 5(2) STLI 33 and C. Hare, "Forum Non Conveniens in Europe: Game Over or Time for Reflexion?" [2006] JBL 157.

131. *Winnetka Trading Corporation v Julius Baer International Ltd* [2008] EWHC 3146 (Ch); [2009] 2 All ER (Comm) 735 and *Plaza BV v Law Debenture Trust Corp Plc* [2015] EWHC 43 (Ch). See also *Konkola Copper Mines Plc v Coromin* [2006] EWCA Civ 5; [2006] 1 Lloyd's Rep 410; [2005] EWHC 898; [2005] ILPr 39; *CNA Insurance Company Limited v Office Depot International (UK)* [2005] EWHC 456; 2005 WL 1033527 and *Koshy v DEG-Deutsche Investitions-und Entwicklungsgesellschaft mbH* [2006] EWHC 17. A. Briggs, *Civil Jurisdiction and Judgments* (6th edn, Informa 2015), [2.303] – [2.311].

is exclusive jurisdiction in another non-EU Member State,[132] or there are proceedings already commenced in a non-EU Member State.[133] The Recast Jurisdiction Regulation does provide for a discretion where proceedings have been commenced first in what it calls a third State. Those provisions will be considered below under *lis pendens*[134] and related actions.[135]

If the defendant is domiciled in a State which is neither an EU Member State nor a Lugano Contracting State, Article 6 of the Recast Jurisdiction Regulation[136] provides that English national law[137] will apply to determine the jurisdiction of the English courts subject to arts 18(1),[138] 21(2),[139] 24[140] and 25.[141] The former two provisions concern consumer contracts and employment contracts, respectively, which are not considered here. The latter two provisions concern exclusive jurisdiction and jurisdiction clauses. Jurisdiction clauses are of particular relevance in the present context and are considered below.[142]

Article 63 of the Recast Jurisdiction Regulation[143] provides that a company is domiciled at the place where it has its "statutory seat" or "central administration" or "principal place of business".[144] The date on which the domicile of a defendant has to be established is the date on which the proceedings are issued.[145]

There are a number of exceptions to the basic rule in Article 4 of the Recast Jurisdiction Regulation[146] that the defendant must be sued where it is domiciled,[147] most notably for present purposes where the parties have chosen the court of an EU Member State to have exclusive jurisdiction and the jurisdiction agreement satisfies the formalities of Article 25;[148] the defendant has submitted to the jurisdiction of the court of an EU Member State without contesting its jurisdiction;[149]

132. *Lucasfilm Limited v Ainsworth* [2011] UKSC 39; [2012] 1 AC 208 and *Ferrexpo AG v Gilson Investments Ltd* [2012] EWHC 721 (Comm); [2012] 1 Lloyd's Rep 588.

133. *Plaza BV v Law Debenture Trust Corp Plc* [2015] EWHC 43 (Ch); *Catalyst Investment Group Limited v Max Lewinsohn* [2009] EWHC 1964 (Ch). The issue was referred to the European Court of Justice in *Goshawk Dedicated Ltd v Life Receivables Irl Ltd* [2009] IESC 7; [2009] ILPr 26. However, the case was settled – see *Catalyst Investment Group Limited v Max Lewinsohn* [2009] EWHC 1964 (Ch), [85].

134. See pages 28–29.

135. See pages 30–31.

136. Jurisdiction Regulation, art 4.

137. See pages 42–51 on English national law.

138. This provision relates to consumer contracts. Jurisdiction Regulation, art 16(1) but that provision has been amended in the Recast Jurisdiction Regulation, art 18(1). Art 16(1) is not mentioned in art 4 of the Jurisdiction Regulation.

139. This provision relates to employment contracts. There is no equivalent provision in the Jurisdiction Regulation and therefore no reference to it art 4 of the Jurisdiction Regulation.

140. Jurisdiction Regulation, art 22. *Said Tony Hamed v Jeremy Stevens* [2013] EWCA Civ 911; *Blomqvist v Zavarco Plc* [2015] EWHC 1898 (Ch); [2016] Ch 128 (corporate governance); *Weber v Weber*, C-438/12, EU:C:2014:212; [2015] Ch 140 (immovable property).

141. Jurisdiction Regulation, art 23.

142. See pages 20–25

143. Jurisdiction Regulation, art 60.

144. *The Rewia* [1991] 2 Lloyd's Rep 325 (CA).

145. *Ministry of Defence and Support of the Armed Forces for Iran v Faz Aviation Ltd* [2007] EWHC 1042 (Comm); [2007] ILPr 42.

146. Jurisdiction Regulation, art 2.

147. Such as Recast Jurisdiction Regulation, art 24; Jurisdiction Regulation, art 22 which provides for exclusive jurisdiction.

148. Jurisdiction Regulation, art 23.

149. Recast Jurisdiction Regulation, art 26; Jurisdiction Regulation, art 24. See, e.g. *Elefanten Schuh v Jacqmain*, C – 150/80, EU:C:1981:148 [1981] E.C.R. 1671; *Ceská Podnikatelská Pojiitovna as, Vienna Insurance Group v Michal Bilas* C-111/09, EU:C:2010:290 [2010] ECR I-4545; [2010] 1 Lloyd's Rep IR 734; *Cartier Parfums-Lunettes SAS v Ziegler France SA*, C-1/13, EU:C:2014:109; *Deutsche Bank AG London Branch v Petromena ASA* [2015] EWCA Civ 226; [2015] 2 Lloyd's Rep 15; *Taser International Inc v SC Gate 4 Business SRL*, C- 175/15, EU: C: 2016: 176.

or an international convention conflicts with the Regulation.[150] If none of the exceptions apply, the claimant may have some additional choices under arts 7,[151] 8[152] or 9,[153] which are considered below.[154]

(i) A jurisdiction clause

Party autonomy is recognised as an important principle, although it is limited in relation to insurance (but not marine insurance),[155] consumer and employment contracts, as the insured, the consumer and the employee are given consumer protection.[156]

Autonomy in this context relates to a jurisdiction agreement. It is irrelevant that the parties have chosen the law applicable to the agreement as this does not found jurisdiction under the Recast Jurisdiction Regulation.[157] Therefore if the parties have provided that their contract shall be governed by English law this will not give the English court jurisdiction under the Recast Jurisdiction Regulation.

The important exception of party autonomy is addressed by Article 25 of the Recast Jurisdiction Regulation.[158] Although party choice is of great importance in both the Recast Jurisdiction and Jurisdiction Regulations there are significant differences between the two and Article 23 of the Jurisdiction Regulation will be discussed below.[159]

Article 25 of the Recast Regulation applies where the parties have chosen the courts of an EU Member State no matter where the parties to the jurisdiction agreement are domiciled. Therefore, if the parties were both domiciled in non-EU Member States but have chosen a neutral venue to determine their disputes in an EU Member State, Article 25 will apply. The court chosen has no discretion.[160]

The parties will only have made a choice within Article 25(1) of the Recast Regulation[161] if the jurisdiction agreement satisfies certain formalities. It must be either:

(a) in writing or evidenced in writing, or
(b) in a form which accords with practices which the parties have established between themselves, or
(c) in international trade or commerce, in a form which accords with a usage of which the parties are or ought to have been aware and which in such trade or commerce is widely known to, and regularly observed by, parties to contracts of the type involved in the particular trade or commerce concerned.

---

150. Recast Jurisdiction Regulation, art 71; Jurisdiction Regulation, art 71. See pages 40–42.
151. Jurisdiction Regulation, art 5.
152. Jurisdiction Regulation, art 6.
153. Jurisdiction Regulation, art 7.
154. See pages 31–40.
155. Recast Jurisdiction Regulation, art 15(5), Jurisdiction Regulation, art 13(5). See J Dunt, *Marine Cargo Insurance* (2nd ed, Informa Law 2015) chapter 2.
156. See Recast Jurisdiction Regulation, Recital 14 and Sections 3, 4 and 5 Jurisdiction Regulation, Recital 14 and Sections 3, 4 and 5.
157. Cf. the position at common law under para 3.1(6)(c) of Practice Direction 6B supplementing Part 6 of the Civil Procedure Rules (CPR). See page 43 of this chapter.
158. Jurisdiction Regulation, art 23.
159. See pages 22–24.
160. *IMS SA v Capital Oil and Gas Industries Ltd* [2016] EWHC 1956; [2016] 4 WLR 163.
161. Jurisdiction Regulation, art 23(1).

The standard of proof is that the claimant must establish that they have the better of the arguments on the material presently available. The question is one of relative plausibility and does not impose a balance of probabilities standard.[162]

A written contract which contains a jurisdiction clause and is signed by both parties at the end of the contract would clearly satisfy the requirements of (a). The contract may not be signed[163] and if it is evidenced in writing by a chain of emails that provision will also be satisfied.[164] A contract which incorporates terms by reference will satisfy the requirements if the reference is express and can be checked by a party exercising reasonable care.[165] An exclusive jurisdiction clause contained in the Terms of Use on a website which was highlighted by way of a hyperlink that the website user was required to view and assent to was binding.[166]

Whether there is a jurisdiction clause that satisfies these requirements may be a complex question. Consider the example of a transferable bill of lading. A bill of lading will often be on a standard form usually only signed by one party, very often the master on behalf of the carrier. There may be no signature by or on behalf of the shipper, let alone by the third party holder of the bill of lading to whom it has been delivered and indorsed. The master's signature is usually on the face of the bill of lading but the jurisdiction clause may be one of many printed conditions on the reverse of the bill. Alternatively, in a charterparty bill of lading the jurisdiction clause is frequently incorporated into the contract by reference to the terms of the charterparty.[167]

To address these difficulties paragraph (c) of Article 25(1) was added when the United Kingdom acceded to the Jurisdiction Convention. The reason that the United Kingdom wanted an amendment to the Jurisdiction Convention was to safeguard the jurisdiction of the High Court in London, which is chosen in many international standard form contracts, including bills of lading. The requirement to satisfy the formalities is to ensure that there is real consent on the part of the parties. However, consensus is presumed where there is a commercial usage in the relevant branch of international trade or commerce of which the parties are or ought to have been aware.[168]

---

162. *Bols Distilleries v Superior Yacht Services Limited* [2006] UKPC 45; [2007] 1 WLR 12; [2007] 1 Lloyd's Rep 683; *Joint Stock Company "Aeroflot-Russian Airlines" v Berezovsky* [2013] EWCA Civ 784; *Quinn Building Products Ltd v P&S Civil Works Ltd* [2013] NIQB 142; *Mar-Train Heavy Haulage Ltd v Shipping.DK Chartering A/S* [2014] EWHC 355 (Comm); *Goldman Sachs International v Novo Banco SA* [2016] EWCA Civ 1092 (under appeal); and *IMS SA v Capital Oil and Gas Industries Ltd* [2016] EWHC 1956; [2016] 4 WLR 163, [45] – [52] where Popplewell J did not think that either party had the better of the arguments.

163. *IMS SA v Capital Oil and Gas Industries Ltd* [2016] EWHC 1956; [2016] 4 WLR 163 [46] – [52].

164. See fn 36.

165. *Estasis Salotti di Colzani Aimo e Gianmario Colzani v RUWA Polstereimaschinen GmbH*, C- 24/76, EU:C:1976:177 [1976] ECR 1831; *Credit Suisse Financial Products v Société Generale d'Entreprises* [1997] CLC 168; *7E Communications Ltd v Vertex Antennentechnik GmbH* [2007] EWCA Civ 140; [2007] 1 WLR 2175; [2007] 2 Lloyd's Rep 411; *Coys of Kensington Automobiles Ltd v Tiziana Pugliese* [2011] EWHC 655; [2011] 2 All ER (Comm) 664; *Höszig Kft v Alstom Power Thermal Services* C-222/15, EU; and *Profit Investment Sim SpA v Ossi* C-366/13, EU: C: 2016: 282.

166. *Ryanair Ltd v Billigfluege de GmbH* [2010] IEHC 47; [2010] IL Pr 22 Irish High Court.

167. This will only be successful if the words of incorporation in the bill of lading specifically refer to the court jurisdiction clause in the charterparty: *Siboti K/S v BP France SA* [2003] EWHC 1278; [2003] 2 Lloyd's Rep 364. However, the English courts have held that a specific reference in the bill of lading to an arbitration clause will incorporate a court jurisdiction agreement – see page 7. For incorporation of arbitration clauses see pages 6–7.

168. *Mainschiffahrts-Genossenschaft eG v Les Gravières Rhénanes (MSG)*, C-106/95, EU:C:1997:70 [1997] All ER (EC) 385 and *Trasporti Castelletti Spedizioni Internazionali SpA v Hugo Trumpy SpA* C-159/97, EU:C:1999:142, [1999] ILPr 492.

The European Court of Justice has held[169] that the validity of a jurisdiction clause in a bill of lading must be assessed by reference to the relationship between the original parties to the contract, the shipper and the carrier. Furthermore, if the clause is effective as between those parties,[170] it is also effective between the carrier and a third party bill of lading holder who was not an original party to the bill of lading, provided that the third party holder of the bill of lading succeeded to the shipper's rights and obligations under the applicable national law when it acquired the bill of lading.[171] The question as to which national law is applicable is not one of interpretation of the Convention. It falls within the jurisdiction of the national court which must apply its rules of private international law.[172] Under English law the "lawful holder" of a transferable bill of lading does have transferred to it the rights and obligations under the bill of lading pursuant to sections 2(1) and 3 of the Carriage of Goods by Sea Act 1992.[173]

If the third party bill of lading holder does not succeed to the rights and obligations of the shipper under the applicable national law when it acquired the bill of lading, it must be established whether it agreed to the jurisdiction clause in accordance with the requirements in Article 25(1) of the Recast Jurisdiction Regulation.[174] In *Dresser UK v Falcongate Ltd*[175] the Court of Appeal held that, even where the doctrine of bailment on terms applied, it could not satisfy the requirements of Article 17 of the EC Jurisdiction Convention (now Article 25 of the Recast Jurisdiction Regulation).

One major change made by the Recast Jurisdiction Regulation is that Article 25 of that Regulation, unlike Article 23 of the Jurisdiction Regulation,[176] makes no distinction according to where the parties to a jurisdiction clause choosing the court of an EU Member State are domiciled. Even if neither party is domiciled in an EU Member State, the court of an EU Member State chosen must take jurisdiction, provided that the jurisdiction agreement satisfies the formalities set out in Article 25(1) of the Recast Regulation. As a result it has been necessary to amend the Civil Procedure Rules, which as we shall see below[177] previously required a claimant to obtain the permission of the court to serve a defendant domiciled outside the EU Member States or Lugano Contracting States. This will no longer be the case where such a defendant has agreed to a jurisdiction agreement for the court of an EU Member State which satisfies the formalities of Article 25(1) of the Recast Jurisdiction Regulation. Therefore Rule 6.33(2)(b) of the Civil Procedure Rules provides for situations where permission of the court is not required for service of the claim form out of the United Kingdom and 6.33(2)(b)(v) prescribes a new situation where

---

169. *Tilly Russ v Nova,* C-71/83, EU:C:1984:217 [1984] ECR 2417, [24]; *Castelletti v Trumpy,* C-159/97, EU:C:1999:142, [1999] ECR I-1597, [41] and [42] and *Coreck Maritime GmbH v Handelsveem BV,* C-387/98, EU:C:2000:606 [2000] ECR 1–09337, [27].

170. The court chosen does not have to be determined on the wording of the jurisdiction clause alone. If the clause states the objective factors on the basis of which the parties have agreed to choose the court (e.g. the country of the carrier's principal place of business) sufficiently precisely, the court seised can determine jurisdiction by the particular circumstances of the case: Case-387/98 *Coreck Maritime GmbH v Handelsveem BV* [2000] ECR 1–09337, [15].

171. *Tilly Russ v Nova* C-71/83, EU:C:1984:217 [1984] ECR 2417 [24]; *Castelletti v Trumpy* C-159/97, EU:C:1999:142 [1999] ECR I-1597, [41] and [42] and *Coreck Maritime GmbH v Handelsveem BV,* EU:C:2000:606, [2000] ECR 1–09337, [22] – [25]. See also *Refcomp SpA v Axa Corporate Solutions Assurance SA,* C-543/10, EU:C:2013:62 [2013] ECR [34] – [36] where the European Court of Justice referred to bills of lading but distinguished the position from a jurisdiction clause in a contract between the manufacturer of goods and a buyer which does not bind a sub buyer as there is no contractual link between them (in *Axa Corporate Solutions Assurance SpA v Refcomp SpA* [2014] the French Cour de Cassation held that there was no jurisdiction clause between the manufacturer of goods and the subbuyer) and *Profit Investment Sim SpA v Ossi* C-366/13, EU: C: 2016: 282 [33].

172. *Coreck Maritime GmbH v Handelsveem BV,* C-387/98, EU:C:2000:606 [2000] ECR 1–09337, [30].

173. See Chapter 5, pages 192–195.

174. *Coreck Maritime GmbH v Handelsveem BV,* C-387/98, EU:C:2000:606 [2000] ECR 1–09337, [26].

175. [1992] 1 QB 502.

176. See page 23.

177. See pages 45–48.

"the defendant is a party to an agreement conferring jurisdiction within article 25 of the [Recast Jurisdiction] Regulation."

Article 23 of the Jurisdiction Regulation differs from Article 25 of the Recast Jurisdiction Regulation as it differentiates between the situation first where at least one of the parties to a jurisdiction agreement for an EU Member State is domiciled in an EU Member State and secondly where none of the parties to such an agreement is domiciled in an EU Member State. In the first situation Article 23(1) provides that the court of the EU Member State shall have exclusive jurisdiction. It does not matter whether it is the claimant or the defendant who is domiciled in the EU Member State as both parties are bound by the agreement. Thus if a Japanese seller is sued by a German buyer in proceedings commenced before 10 January 2015 and their sale contract contains an exclusive English jurisdiction agreement, the English court could not refuse jurisdiction in favour of the courts of another Member State, unless that other court was first seised,[178] nor would the courts of another Member State have jurisdiction. The court chosen has no discretion to stay its jurisdiction in favour of a non-EU Member State by analogy with the decision in *Owusu*.[179]

In the second situation where none of the parties is domiciled in an EU Member State, and they have chosen the court of an EU Member State, Article 23(3) of the Jurisdiction Regulation does not provide that the court chosen shall have jurisdiction, but does provide that the courts of other EU Member States shall have no jurisdiction, unless the court chosen has declined jurisdiction. In this situation the court chosen may apply its own national law to determine whether it has jurisdiction and may decline jurisdiction.[180] We shall consider the English common law below and we shall see that the difference is that instead of the certain rule in the first situation, the English court would have a discretion in the second situation. Although the English court will usually exercise its jurisdiction when it is chosen, it may in rare cases decline to do so, where there are multiple proceedings already commenced in another jurisdiction between multiple parties, some of whom are not bound by the English jurisdiction clause.[181]

The Recast Jurisdiction Regulation strengthens the principle of party autonomy by permitting the court chosen to determine the substantive validity of a jurisdiction clause in accordance with the law of the EU Member State chosen in the jurisdiction agreement.[182] It is for the national

---

178. See *Erich Gasser GmbH v MISAT SRL* discussed at fn 185, now reversed by art 31(2) of the Recast Jurisdiction Regulation.

179. See page 18 of this chapter. *Equitas Limited v Allstate Insurance Company* [2008] EWHC 1671 (Comm); [2009] Lloyd's Rep IR 227 and *Skype Technologies SA v Joltid Ltd* [2009] EWHC 2783 (Ch) [2011] ILPr 8. This point does not appear to have been raised in the Court of Appeal in *OT Africa Line Ltd v Magic Sportswear Corp* [2005] EWCA Civ 710; [2005] 2 Lloyd's Rep 170 discussed at pages 46–47 of this chapter. In *OT Africa Line* the claimant was an English company and therefore under art 60 of the Jurisdiction Regulation presumably domiciled in a Member State, namely the United Kingdom. In that case, it appears that no argument was made that the Jurisdiction Regulation applied, nor does it appear that *Owusu* was cited to the court. For earlier doubts about the process by which the Court of Appeal reached its decision see Y. Baatz, "An English Jurisdiction Clause does Battle with Canadian Legislation Similar to the Hamburg Rules" [2006] LMCLQ 143, at p 148 et seq. A. Briggs, *Civil Jurisdiction and Judgments* (6th edn, Informa 2015), [2.304] fn 1672 expresses the view that *OT Africa Line* "is probably not to be relied on at this point." However, the case is discussed below at pages 46–47 of this chapter as, if the court did have a discretion, it is submitted that it exercised it correctly. See also *Horn Linie GmbH & Co v Panamericana Formas E Impresos SA, Ace Seguros SA (The Hornbay)* [2006] EWHC 373 (Comm); [2006] 2 Lloyd's Rep 44. Compare the position where there is a non-exclusive English jurisdiction agreement – in *Deutsche Bank v Highland Crusader Offshore Partners* [2009] EWCA Civ 725; [2009] 2 Lloyd's Rep 617, [105] – [121] the Court of Appeal refused to extend time for US companies to contest English jurisdiction but allowed an appeal against the grant of an anti-suit injunction.

180. Jurisdiction Regulation, art 4 and pages 46–47 of this chapter.

181. See pages 45–46 of this chapter.

182. Recast Jurisdiction Regulation, art 25(1). There is no equivalent provision in the Jurisdiction Regulation.

court to interpret the jurisdiction clause invoked before it in order to determine which disputes fall within its scope.[183]

Another important difference between the Recast Jurisdiction Regulation and the Jurisdiction Regulation is that the *lis pendens* provisions of the former are subject to Article 31(2)[184] which provides that where a court has been chosen in accordance with Article 25, any court of another EU Member State shall stay its proceedings until such time as the court seised on the basis of the agreement declares that it has no jurisdiction under the agreement.[185] Where the court chosen has established that it has jurisdiction, any court of another EU Member State shall decline jurisdiction in favour of that court.[186] Recital 22 clarifies that the designated court "has priority to decide on the validity of the agreement and on the extent to which the agreement applies to the dispute pending before it",[187] even if it is second seised and irrespective of whether the other court has already decided on the stay of proceedings. Where, however, there is a conflict as to whether both courts have been chosen, then the court first seised will determine the validity of the jurisdiction clause.[188]

The court of an EU Member State has no discretion as to whether to exercise jurisdiction on *forum non conveniens*[189] or other grounds where there is a valid jurisdiction clause in its favour.[190] This must be correct both for the reasons given in the discussion on Article 23(1) of the Jurisdiction Regulation[191] and because the Recast Jurisdiction Regulation does now provide for discretion in limited circumstances in Articles 33 and 34,[192] but such discretion does not apply where the jurisdiction of the EU Member State court is based on Article 25.

Where the parties have chosen the court of a third State, ie a State which is not an EU Member State, then the English court has a discretion to stay its proceedings in some circumstances under the new provisions in Articles 33 and 34 of the Recast Regulation where there are proceedings in a third State and an EU Member State, and the EU Member State has jurisdiction based on arts 4, 7, 8 or 9 of the Recast Jurisdiction Regulation. The court of the third State must be seised first and the EU Member State must be satisfied that a stay is necessary for the proper administration of justice.[193] Recital 24 provides that an EU Member State should assess all the circumstances of the case including, amongst other matters, whether the court of the third State has exclusive jurisdiction in the particular case in circumstances where a court of an EU Member State would have exclusive jurisdiction. This would include a jurisdiction clause in favour of the third State. This provision helps to clarify the limits of the decision of the European Court of Justice in *Owusu*[194] and introduces discretion into the Recast Jurisdiction Regulation. For example, if

---

183. *Hoszig Kft v Alstom Power Thermal Services,* C-222/15, EU:C:2016:525.

184. *Perella Weinberg Partners UK LLP v Codere SA* [2016] EWHC 1182 (Comm) (non-exclusive jurisdiction agreement); *Commerzbank Aktiengesellschaft v Liquimar Tankers Management Inc* [2017] EWHC 161 (Comm); [2017] Lloyd's Rep 273 (asymmetric jurisdiction clause). In *Dexia Crediop SpA v Provinicia Brescia* [2016] EWHC 3261 (Comm) it was held that there was not the same cause of action in the Italian and English proceedings but had there been, Article 31(2) would have applied.

185. See Recital 22 and arts 29(1) and 31(2). This solution is similar to that adopted by art 6 of the Choice of Court Convention – see page 16. These provisions reverse the decision in *Erich Gasser GmbH v MISAT SRL,* C – 116/02, EU:C:2003:657 [2003] E.C.R. I – 14693; [2005] QB 1, which applies to the Jurisdiction Regulation. They are a major improvement.

186. Recast Jurisdiction Regulation, art 31(3).

187. See also *CDC Hydrogen Peroxide,* C-352/13, EU: C: 2015: 335.

188. Recast Jurisdiction Regulation, Recital 22 para 2.

189. See page 44.

190. *IMS SA v Capital Oil and Gas Industries Ltd* [2016] EWHC 1956; [2016] 4 WLR 163.

191. See fn 185.

192. There are no equivalent provisions in the Jurisdiction Regulation.

193. For further discussion of the requirement under Articles 33 and 34 see pages 28–29 and 30–31 respectively.

194. Case-281/02, EU:C:2005:120; [2005] QB 801.

proceedings are commenced in England against a defendant domiciled in England and thus the English court has jurisdiction under Article 4 of the Recast Jurisdiction Regulation, if proceedings had previously been commenced in Jamaica, the English court has a discretion to stay its proceedings in favour of Jamaica under Article 33. The discretion can only arise if the third State is first seised and thus even if there is an exclusive choice of jurisdiction clause in favour of the courts of Jamaica this can only be given effect to by the English court if the Jamaican court proceedings were commenced before the English proceedings. This is an unfortunate restriction which does not give sufficient weight to the principle of party autonomy. It does not reflect the position under Article 31(2) of the Recast Jurisdiction Regulation itself which gives priority to the court chosen rather than the court first seised. However, one can argue that the third State is not entitled to priority as there is no reciprocity between the EU Member States and third States, whereas as between the EU Member States there is. If third States want to protect their position where parties have chosen their court they can always ratify the Choice of Court Convention.[195]

One question which arises is whether Articles 33 and 34 of the Recast Jurisdiction Regulation define the limits of any discretion available to the EU Member State seised where a third State is also seised or whether the English court still has a residual discretion at common law, so that, for example, it could still stay its proceedings where, for example, it has jurisdiction over a defendant domiciled in England and is first seised, but the parties have concluded a jurisdiction agreement in favour of a third State, such as South Korea. It seems to this author that no such residual discretion should be available as the discretion in Articles 33 and 34 is intended to be exclusive and provide for the only situation in which there are exceptions to jurisdiction founded on Articles 4, 7, 8 or 9.

(ii) Multiple proceedings

Section 9 of the Recast Jurisdiction Regulation (Articles 29 to 34)[196] contains provisions which seek to prevent multiple proceedings and thus avoid differing judgments being given in more than one jurisdiction. This last situation might lead to non-recognition of a judgment on the ground that it is irreconcilable with a judgment given in proceedings between the same parties in the EU Member State in which recognition is sought.[197]

The classic case of multiple proceedings would be where a seller sues the buyer in England for non-payment of the purchase price and the buyer sues the seller in another EU Member State for a declaration that it is not liable under the contract. In those circumstances Article 29 of the Recast Jurisdiction Regulation[198] provides for a simple, cut and dried rule that has been described as "first come first served". Where the proceedings involve the same cause of action, are between the same parties and are brought in the courts of different EU Member States, any court other than the court first seised shall of its own motion stay its proceedings until such time as the jurisdiction of the court first seised is established. Once the jurisdiction of the court first seised has been established,[199] any court other than the court first seised shall decline jurisdiction in favour of the latter court. The new Article 31(2) of the Recast Jurisdiction Regulation makes an exception where the court chosen by the parties is seised second.[200]

---

195. See page 16.
196. Jurisdiction Regulation, arts 27–30. Section 8 of the EC Jurisdiction and Lugano Conventions, arts 21–23.
197. Recast Jurisdiction Regulation, art 45(1)(c); Jurisdiction Regulation, art 34(3); or EC Jurisdiction Convention, art 27(3).
198. Jurisdiction Regulation, art 27.
199. *Cartier Parfums-Lunettes SAS v Ziegler France SA,* C-1/13, EU:C:2014:109.
200. See page 24.

Even if those requirements are not satisfied, Article 30 of the Recast Jurisdiction Regulation[201] provides that any court other than the court first seised may stay its proceedings where related actions are brought in the courts of different Member States. Actions are "related" where they are so closely connected that it is expedient to hear and determine them together to avoid the risk of irreconcilable judgments resulting from separate proceedings.[202] Article 31 of the Recast Jurisdiction Regulation[203] further provides that where actions come within the exclusive jurisdiction of several courts, any court other than the court first seised shall decline jurisdiction in favour of the court first seised. Under Articles 29 and 31 of the Recast Jurisdiction Regulation[204] a stay is mandatory, whereas under Article 30[205] it is discretionary. Article 32 of the Recast Jurisdiction Regulation[206] provides that a court is seised when proceedings are commenced.[207]

To determine whether the proceedings involve the same cause of action under Article 29 the courts must look to the substance of the matter and not simply to the form.[208] The French version of the same cause of action is "*le même objet et la même cause*". The "*objet*" is "the end the action has in view" and the "*cause*" comprises the facts and the rule of law relied on as the basis of the action. Thus if in one set of proceedings in the Netherlands the carrier seeks a declaration that it has no liability under a bill of lading and in England the cargo interests seek damages from the carrier for breach of the bill of lading contract, the proceedings will involve the same cause of action. This was the decision of the European Court of Justice in *The Maciej Rataj*.[209] The reason that the cargo interests preferred to sue in England rather than the Netherlands, was that, at that time,[210] the Netherlands applied the 1957 International Convention relating to the Limitation of the Liability of Owners of Sea-Going Ships (the "1957 Limitation Convention"). Under that Convention the owners would be entitled to limit their liability to approximately

201. Jurisdiction Regulation, art 28.
202. Recast Jurisdiction Regulation, art 30(3); Jurisdiction Regulation, art 28(3). See, e.g. *The Tatry (sub nom. The Maciej Rataj)* C-406/92, EU:C:1994:400, [1994] ECR I-5439; [1995] 1 Lloyd's Rep 302; *Maersk Olie & Gas A/S v Firma M de Haan en W de Boer* C-39/02, EU:C:2004:615 [2004] ECR I-9657; [2005] 1 Lloyd's Rep 210; *Bank of Tokyo-Mitsubishi Ltd v Baskan Gida Sanayi Ve Pazarlama* [2004] EWHC 945 (Ch), [2004] 2 Lloyd's Rep 395 and *JP Morgan Europe Ltd v Primacom AG* [2005] EWHC 508; [2005] 2 Lloyd's Rep 665.
203. Jurisdiction Regulation, art 29.
204. Jurisdiction Regulation, arts 27 and 29.
205. Jurisdiction Regulation, art 28.
206. Jurisdiction Regulation, art 30.
207. See, e.g. *Tavoulareas v Tsaviliris* [2005] EWHC 2140, [2006] 1 All ER (Comm) 109; *Royal & Sun Alliance v MK Digital FZE* [2005] EWHC 1408 (Comm); [2005] 2 Lloyd's Rep 679; *Arbuthnot Latham & Co Ltd v M3 Marine Ltd* [2013] EWHC 1019; *Lehman Brothers Finance AG v Klaus Tschira Stiftung GmbH* [2014] EWHC 2782 (Ch) (initiation of mandatory conciliation proceedings in Switzerland falls within Article 30(1) of the Lugano Convention) so that the Swiss courts were first seised; and *Maxter Catheters SAS v Medecina Ltd* [2015] EWHC 3076 (Comm).
208. E.g. *Gubisch Maschinenfabrik KG v Giulio Palumbo*, C-144/86, EU:C:1987:528 [1987] ECR 4861; *Sarrio SA v Kuwait Investment Authority* [1997] 4 All ER 929 (HL); [1997] 1 Lloyd's Rep 113 (CA); [1996] 1 Lloyd's Rep 650; *Gantner Electronic GmbH v Basch Exploitatie Maatschappij BV*, C-111/01, EU:C:2003:257, [2003] ECR I-4207; *Maersk Olie & Gas A/S v Firma M de Haan en W de Boer*, C-39/02, EU:C:2004:615 [2005] 1 Lloyd's Rep 210; *Katsouris Bros Ltd v Haitoglou Bros Ltd* [2011] EWHC 111 (QB); *Masri v Consolidated Contractors International Co SAL* [2011] EWHC 1780 (Comm); *FKI Engineering Ltd v Stribog Ltd* [2011] EWCA Civ 622; *Nordea Bank Norge ASA v Unicredit Corporate Banking SpA* [2011] EWHC 30 (Comm) and *Starlight Shipping Co v Allianz Marine & Aviation Versicherungs AG (The Alexandros T)* [2013] UKSC 70; [2014] 1 Lloyd's Rep 223.
209. *The Tatry (sub nom. The Maciej Rataj)*, C-406/92; EU:C:1994:400 [1994] ECR I-5439; [1995] 1 Lloyd's Rep 302. Although the English courts were previously hostile to negative declarations of liability, they appear to have overcome their antipathy to this remedy: see, e.g. *Boss Group Ltd v Boss France SA* [1996] 4 All ER 970; *Maas Logistics (UK) Ltd v CDR Trucking BV* [1999] 2 Lloyd's Rep 179; *Messier-Dowty Ltd v Sabena SA* [2000] 1 Lloyd's Rep 428; *Phillips v Symes* [2001] CLC 1,673 [38]; *Bristow Helicopters Ltd v Sikorsky Aircraft Corporation* [2004] EWHC 401 (Comm); [2004] 2 Lloyd's Rep 150 and *Bhatia Shipping v Alcobex* [2004] EWHC 2323 (Comm); [2005] 2 Lloyd's Rep 336 [24]–[26]. L. Collins, "Negative Declarations and the Brussels Convention" (1992) 108 LQR 545; A. Bell, "The Negative Declaration in Transnational Litigation" (1995) 111 LQR 674.
210. The Netherlands ratified the 1976 LLMC in 1990 and has now ratified the 1996 Protocol – see page 285.

US$1.25 million, whereas under the 1976 Convention on Limitation of Liability for Maritime Claims ("1976 LLMC") which applied in England,[211] the limit of owners' liability would be more than three times as much, at approximately US$4.225 million. This would be of enormous significance in this claim because the total of the cargo owners' claim could amount to approximately US$3.5 million, i.e. almost three times the Dutch limitation figure.

In contrast in *Maersk Olie & Gas A/S v Firma de Haan en W de Boer*[212] the European Court of Justice held that an application by shipowners for limitation of their liability under the 1957 Limitation Convention in the courts of the Netherlands did not involve the same subject matter and cause of action as an action for damages for damage to their oil and gas pipelines in the North Sea brought by Maersk against the shipowner before the Danish courts. The subject matter was clearly not the same, as an action for damages seeks to have the defendant declared liable, whereas an application to limit liability is designed to ensure that, in the event the defendant is found liable, such liability will be limited.[213] The cause of action comprises the facts and the legal rule invoked as the basis for the application. Even if it were assumed that the facts underlying the two sets of proceedings were identical, the legal rule which formed the basis of the application was different. The action for damages was based on the law governing non-contractual liability, whereas the application for the establishment of a limitation fund was based on the 1957 Limitation Convention and the legislation of the Netherlands giving effect to it.[214]

In *Starlight Shipping Co v Allianz Marine & Aviation Versicherungs AG (The Alexandros T)*[215] insurers settled claims which had been brought against them in the English court for the insured value of the *Alexandros T* which had sunk. The claims were settled and paid by the insurers. Tomlin orders were made staying the English proceedings. However, over three years later the insured commenced proceedings in the Greek court claiming damages in tort under the Greek Criminal and Civil Code. They alleged that the insurers had fabricated false evidence and disseminated false information to third parties, to avoid paying under their insurance indemnity contrary to their contractual obligations. Such claims were not recoverable under English law which governed both the insurance policies and the settlement agreements. Those contracts also provided for the exclusive jurisdiction of the English courts. The Supreme Court held that the insurers' claims for a declaration that they were entitled to an indemnity in respect of any liability in Greece and for a declaration that they were entitled to damages for breach of the jurisdiction agreement were not the same cause of action as the claims in Greece as the English claims were based in contract and those in Greece in tort.

Under the provisions on recognition and enforcement of judgments in the Recast Jurisdiction Regulation it is not permissible for the court of an EU Member State requested to recognise a judgment of another EU Member State to review the jurisdiction of the latter court to give that

211. For the current position, see page 285.
212. *Maersk Olie & Gas A/S v Firma M de Haan en W de Boer*, C-39/02, EU:C:2004:615 [2004] ECR I-9657; [2005] 1 Lloyd's Rep 210. See also the decision of Longmore J in *The Happy Fellow* [1997] 1 Lloyd's Rep 130 discussed at pages 29–30 of this chapter (although the case went to the Court of Appeal, the issue on "same cause of action" was left open – [1998] 1 Lloyd's Rep 13). See also *Dresser UK Ltd v Falcongate Ltd* [1991] 2 Lloyd's Rep 557 and *The Volvox Hollandia* [1988] 2 Lloyd's Rep 361.
213. *Maersk Olie & Gas A/S v Firma M de Haan en W de Boer*, C-39/02, EU:C:2004:615, [2004] ECR I-9657; [2005] 1 Lloyd's Rep 210, [35].
214. Ibid., [38].
215. [2013] UKSC 70; [2014] 1 Lloyd's Rep 223. See also *JP Morgan Europe Ltd v Primacom AG* [2005] EWHC 508 (Comm); [2005] 2 Lloyd's Rep 665; *Nomura International Plc v Banca Monte Dei Paschi di Siena SpA* [2013] EWHC 3187 (Comm); [2014] 1 WLR 1584; *Barclays Bank Plc v Ente Nazionale di Previdenza ed Assistenza Dei Medici E degli Odontoiatri* [2016] EWCA Civ 1261; and *Dexia Crediop SpA v Provinicia Brescia* [2016] EWHC 3261 (Comm).

judgment.[216] Thus the recognising court cannot refuse to recognise a judgment on the ground that there was an exclusive jurisdiction agreement in favour of the court of a State other than that of the court which has given the judgment which is to be recognised. In other words by the time the recognition stage has been reached jurisdiction is no longer an issue.

However, the decision of the court of an EU Member State that it does not have jurisdiction because there is a valid jurisdiction agreement in favour of a Lugano Member State court is binding on any other EU Member State court. In *Gothaer Allgemeine Versicherung AG v Samskip GmbH*[217] the Court of Justice of the European Union held that where the Belgian court had dismissed actions on the ground that the bill of lading contained a jurisdiction clause providing that any dispute arising thereunder was to be decided by the Icelandic courts according to Icelandic law the German Court was not only bound by the decision that the Belgian court did not have jurisdiction, but also by the reason for that decision which was that there was a valid Icelandic jurisdiction clause.

Article 29 of the Recast Jurisdiction Regulation[218] also requires the parties in the different sets of proceedings to be identical. In *The Maciej Rataj* the carrier had commenced proceedings in Rotterdam against some, but not all, of the cargo interests. Some of the cargo interests had commenced proceedings in England by arresting a sister ship of the carrying ship. The equivalent provision of Article 29 of the Recast Jurisdiction Regulation applied to those proceedings where the cargo interests were involved in both the Dutch and the English proceedings but not to those where the cargo interests were only involved in either the Dutch or the English proceedings, but not both.

The European Court of Justice looks at the substance of the issue rather than the detail of procedure and also held in *The Maciej Rataj* that *in rem* proceedings in England against the ship were against the shipowner and therefore involved identical parties as proceedings commenced in Rotterdam by the shipowner.[219] Similarly an insured shipowner and its hull underwriter will be treated as the same party where the insurer is exercising its subrogated rights and stands in the shoes of the insured, provided the interests of the insured and the insurer do not conflict.[220]

New provisions have been added to the Recast Jurisdiction Regulation to deal with the situation where there are proceedings in a third State and an EU Member State and the EU Member State has jurisdiction based on Article 4, 7, 8 or 9 of the Recast Jurisdiction Regulation. Article 33(1)[221] stipulates that provided proceedings were pending before the third State when the court of an EU Member State was seised of an action involving the same cause of action and between the same parties as the proceedings in the third State, the court of the EU Member State may stay its proceedings if it is expected that the court of the third State will give a judgment capable of recognition and, where applicable, enforcement in that EU Member State; and the court of the EU Member State is satisfied that a stay is necessary for the proper administration of justice. Recital 24 provides that an EU Member State should assess all the circumstances of the case including connections between the facts of the case and the parties and the third State concerned, the stage to which the proceedings have progressed by the time proceedings are initiated in the

---

216. Recast Jurisdiction Regulation, art 45(3), except as provided in art 45(1)(e) in the case of insurance, consumer contracts or exclusive jurisdiction under art 24; Jurisdiction Regulation, art 35(3), except as provided in art 35(1) in the case of insurance, consumer contracts or exclusive jurisdiction under art 22.
217. C-456/11, EU:C:2012:719.
218. Jurisdiction Regulation, art 27.
219. See Chapter 12.
220. *Drouot Assurances SA v Consolidated Metallurgical Industries,* C-351/96, EU:C:1998:242 [1998] All ER (EC) 483. See also *Kolden Holdings Ltd v Rochette Commerce Ltd* [2008] ILPr 20 (assignor and assignee).
221. See also Recast Jurisdiction Regulation, Recitals 23 and 24. There were no such provisions in the Jurisdiction Regulation, art 27 of which only applies to *lis pendens* in EU Member States.

court of the EU Member State, whether or not the court of the third State can be expected to give a judgment within a reasonable time, and whether the court of the third State has exclusive jurisdiction in the particular case in circumstances where a court of an EU Member State would have exclusive jurisdiction. Article 33(2) provides for the court of the EU Member State to continue the proceedings at any time in certain circumstances and Article 33(3) provides for dismissal of the proceedings.

This provision helps to clarify the limits of the decision of the European Court of Justice in *Owusu*[222] and introduces discretion into the Recast Jurisdiction Regulation. For example, if proceedings are commenced in England against a defendant domiciled in England and thus the English court has jurisdiction under Article 4 of the Recast Jurisdiction Regulation, if proceedings had previously been commenced in Jamaica, the English court has a discretion to stay its proceedings in favour of Jamaica under Article 33. The discretion can only arise if the third State is first seised.[223]

(iii) Related actions

As we have already seen, if Article 29 of the Recast Jurisdiction Regulation[224] does not apply because, for example, the cause of action is not the same or the parties are not identical in both sets of proceedings in different EU Member States, the court second seised may stay its proceedings if the proceedings are related.[225] The European Court of Justice held that the actions were related in *The Maciej Rataj* where some were brought by the cargo interests who had not been sued in Rotterdam but had sued in England, as they involved alleged contamination of the soya bean oil cargo on the same voyage on bills of lading in the same form.

We have already seen that the European Court of Justice has held that liability and tonnage limitation proceedings in different jurisdictions are not the same cause of action within the equivalent provision of Article 29 of the Recast Jurisdiction Regulation, but they may well be related actions. This issue arose in *The Happy Fellow*.[226] The ships *Happy Fellow* and *Darfur* were in collision on the river Seine. The *Darfur* was arrested at Le Havre. Seven claimants, including the owners of the *Happy Fellow*, commenced proceedings in Le Havre against the owners of the *Darfur*, which they were entitled to do both because the collision occurred in France and because the ship had been arrested there. After the collision the time charterers of the *Darfur*, Baco-Liner, agreed an exclusive English law and jurisdiction clause. They commenced proceedings in London claiming damages for breach of the charterparty. The owners of the *Darfur* accepted service of the writ and instituted limitation proceedings in the same court. They purported to constitute a limitation fund. The Court of Appeal held that a limitation action in England and liability proceedings in France were related actions and that Longmore J at first instance had clearly exercised his discretion correctly to stay the English proceedings in favour of the French courts. Longmore J did not, however, consider that liability and limitation proceedings will always be related actions. He said,

it does not seem to me necessarily to follow that any action in which it is alleged that a shipowner is liable must inevitably be related to any action in which a shipowner is seeking to limit his liability. If, for example, it is clear that the Court trying the liability action does not consider itself seised of the issue of

---

222. See page 18.
223. See also page 25 for the position where there is a jurisdiction agreement in favour of the court of the third State.
224. Jurisdiction Regulation, art 27.
225. See page 26 of this chapter.
226. [1998] 1 Lloyd's Rep 13 (CA); [1997] 1 Lloyd's Rep 130 (Longmore J).

limitation and the main issue in the liability action is, for example, whether a duty of care is owed by the defendant to the plaintiff, it might well be that the actions would not be related actions.[227]

However, on the facts of the case he held that the French proceedings and the English limitation proceedings were related for two main reasons. First, at the time of the first instance hearing the owners of the other ship involved, the *Darfur*, had not admitted liability.[228] Thus the issues of the failure of the *Darfur*'s steering gear, the reasons for the failure and the owners' fault and the degree of such fault would be raised in the French proceedings. Very similar issues would arise in the limitation action, which would consider whether the claimant's loss resulted from the personal act or omission of the shipowners "committed recklessly and with knowledge that such loss would result" within Article 4 of the 1976 LLMC. Second, the French court would regard itself as seised of limitation as well as liability.

It is worth noting that the reason that one party wanted the limitation proceedings to be determined in France, rather than in England, was that, although the courts of both countries would apply the 1976 LLMC, it was thought that it would be easier to break the limits in France than in England, as it was believed that the French courts apply a more objective approach to the test for breaking the limits under Article 4, than the subjective approach followed in the English courts. If this perception were correct, this does illustrate how even if two States are parties to the same Convention, there may still be reason to forum shop if those two States interpret that Convention differently.

Where actions are related the court second seised has a discretion as to whether to stay. In his Opinion in *Owens Bank Ltd v Bracco*[229] Advocate General Lenz identified three particular factors as being of importance in determining the exercise of the discretion: first the extent of the relatedness between the actions and the risk of mutually irreconcilable decisions; second the stage reached in each set of proceedings; and third the proximity of the courts to the subject matter of the case. Regard may be had to the court which is in the best position to decide a given question. These factors were applied in *The Alexandros T*.[230] There the Supreme Court held that where the proceedings in the English court and the Greek court were related, if the English court were second seised, the Supreme Court would not exercise its discretion to stay the English proceedings in light of the exclusive English jurisdiction agreement. Thus the English court would give effect to the parties' choice of jurisdiction and limit the effect of the decision in *Gasser*.[231]

The Recast Jurisdiction Regulation has a new provision in Article 34 which gives the court of an EU Member State a discretion to stay its proceedings where they are based on Article 4, 7, 8 or 9 of the Recast Jurisdiction Regulation. If an action is pending before a court of a third State at the time when a court in an EU Member State is seised of an action which is related to the action in the court of the third State, the court of the EU Member State may stay its proceedings if it is expedient to hear and determine the related actions together to avoid the risk of irreconcilable judgments resulting from separate proceedings; it is expected that the court of the third State will give a judgment capable of recognition and, where applicable, of enforcement in that EU Member State; and the court of the EU Member State is satisfied that a stay is necessary for

227. [1998] 1 Lloyd's Rep 130, at pp 135–136.
228. Such an admission had been made by the time the appeal was heard. The Court of Appeal held that this should not be taken into account.
229. C-129/92, EU:C:1994:13 [1994] QB 509, [74]–[79].
230. See fn 215. See also *JP Morgan Europe Ltd v Primacom AG* [2005] EWHC 508 (Comm); [2005] 2 Lloyd's Rep 665; *Nomura International Plc v Banca Monte Dei Paschi di Siena SpA* [2013] EWHC 3187 (Comm); [2014] 1 WLR 1584; *Barclays Bank Plc v Ente Nazionale di Previdenza ed Assistenza Dei Medici E degli Odontoiatri* [2016] EWCA Civ 1261 affirming the exercise of discretion by the judge at first instance – [2016] EWCA Civ 1261; *Commerzbank Aktiengesellschaft v Liquimar Tankers Management Inc* [2017] EWHC 161 (Comm); [2017] 1 Lloyd's Rep 273 [83] – [102].
231. See fn 185.

the proper administration of justice. The same factors as can be taken into account under Article 33(1) apply.[232] Article 34(2) provides for the circumstances in which the court of the EU Member State may continue its proceedings and Article 34(3) when it may dismiss them.

(iv) No jurisdiction clause

Where none of the exceptions to the rule that the defendant must be sued where it is domiciled, such as a jurisdiction clause, apply the claimant may have a choice to sue the defendant where it is domiciled in accordance with Article 4 of the Recast Jurisdiction Regulation,[233] or, if there is sufficient link with another EU Member State, in that State. Section 2 of the Recast Jurisdiction Regulation[234] entitled Special Jurisdiction gives the claimant additional choices where there is a particularly close connection between the subject matter of the dispute and the courts of a particular place. Some of these provisions are particularly relevant to maritime disputes. Thus Article 7 of the Recast Jurisdiction Regulation[235] gives the claimant the option to sue the defendant "in matters relating to a contract, in the courts for the place of performance of the obligation in question",[236] "in matters relating to tort, delict or quasi-delict in the courts for the place where the harmful event occurred or may occur",[237] "as regards a dispute arising out of the operations of a branch, agency or other establishment, in the courts for the place in which the branch, agency or other establishment is situated"[238] or "as regards a dispute concerning the payment or remuneration claimed in respect of the salvage of a cargo or freight, in the court under the authority of which the cargo or freight" has been arrested or could have been so arrested but security has already been provided.[239] Article 8 of the Recast Jurisdiction Regulation[240] provides for multiple defendants, third party proceedings and counterclaims, and Article 9 of the Recast Regulation[241] deals with tonnage limitation.

As the special jurisdiction is a derogation from the basic rule that the defendant must be sued where it is domiciled, the European Court of Justice has held that the articles on special jurisdiction must be interpreted restrictively.[242] The provisions must be given a European interpretation rather than in accordance with national law as the aim is to seek a uniform interpretation throughout the EU Member States so that each State has equal jurisdiction.[243]

(v) Contract claims

Article 7(1) of the Recast Jurisdiction Regulation[244] may be very useful where the place of performance of the obligation in question is in a different EU Member State from the place where

---

232. See pages 28–29.
233. Jurisdiction Regulation, art 2.
234. Jurisdiction Regulation, Section 2.
235. Jurisdiction Regulation, art 5.
236. Recast Jurisdiction Regulation, art 7(1), Jurisdiction Regulation, art 5(1).
237. Recast Jurisdiction Regulation, art 7(2), Jurisdiction Regulation, art 5(3).
238. Recast Jurisdiction Regulation, art 7(5), Jurisdiction Regulation, art 5(5).
239. Recast Jurisdiction Regulation, art 7(7), Jurisdiction Regulation, art 5(7).
240. Jurisdiction Regulation, art 6.
241. Jurisdiction Regulation, art 7.
242. *Kalfelis v Bankhaus Schroder, Munchmeyer, Hengst & Co,* C-189/87, EU:C:1988:459 [1988] ECR 5565; *Andreas Kainz v Pantherwerke AG,* C-45/13, EU:C:2014:7 [2014] ILPr 16; *Universal Music International Holding BV v Schilling* C-12/15, EU:C:2016:449 [25] and cases cited there.
243. See, e.g. *Reunion Europeenne SA v Spliethoff's Bevrachtingskantoor BV,* C-51/97, EU:C:1998:509 [1999] CLC 282; *Deutsche Bank AG London Branch v Petromena ASA* [2013] EWHC 3065 (Comm) upheld on appeal in [2015] EWCA Civ 226; [2015] 2 Lloyd's Rep 15; *Impala Warehousing and Logistics (Shanghai) Co Ltd v Wanxiang Resources (Singapore) Pte Ltd* [2015] EWHC 811 (Comm); [2015] 2 All ER (Comm) 234 [62] – [81].
244. Jurisdiction Regulation, art 5(1).

the defendant is domiciled and the claimant would prefer to sue there. For example, if an English seller sells goods to a French buyer it has a choice to sue in France where the buyer is domiciled or the place where the goods were delivered. If the goods were delivered in England the seller has a choice of England or France.

There must be a contractual relationship between the parties. In *Jakob Handte & Co GmbH v Société Traitements Mécano-Chimiques des Surfaces (TMCS)*[245] the European Court of Justice held that a French sub-buyer could not sue the German manufacturer of goods within Article 5(1) of the then Jurisdiction Convention, equivalent to Article 7(1) of the Recast Jurisdiction Regulation, even though French law transmits to the sub-buyer the intermediate seller's contractual rights against the manufacturer, as there was no contractual link between the sub-buyer and the manufacturer.

In *Réunion Européenne SA v Spliethoff's Bevrachtingskantoor BV*[246] the lead insurer brought proceedings exercising its subrogated rights for damage to pears. The pears were carried from Melbourne to Rotterdam on the *Alblasgracht VOO2* under a bill of lading issued by Refrigerated Container Carriers Pty Ltd (RCC) and on their headed note paper. RCC had its registered office in Sydney. The pears were carried by Spliethoff's Bevrachtingskantoor BV, the actual carrier, who was not mentioned on the bill of lading and whose registered office was in Amsterdam. The pears were discharged in Rotterdam and then carried by road under an international consignment note to Rungis in France, where the insured consignee had its registered office. The cargo insurers sued RCC, the contractual carrier, the actual carrier and the master of the carrying ship, who resided in the Netherlands, in the French courts. The first issue before the European Court of Justice was whether the claim against the actual carrier was based on the contract of transport and whether the claim for that or any other reason fell within the scope of "matters relating to a contract" within the meaning of the equivalent of Article 7(1) of the Recast Jurisdiction Regulation. The European Court of Justice held that it did not. The bill of lading disclosed no contractual relationship freely entered into between the consignee and the actual carrier or the master of the ship.

As the words must be given a European interpretation, this may result in there being a contractual relationship even if under the stricter English law requirements, e.g. on consideration, there would not be.[247]

The English courts have distinguished between the situation where a contract is void, for example, for illegality or *ultra vires* and where the contract is voidable, for example, for misrepresentation or non-disclosure.[248] Thus in *Kleinwort Benson Ltd. v Glasgow City*

---

245. C – 26/91, EU:C:1992:268 [1993] I L Pr 5. See, e.g. *Effer SpA v Kantner,* C-38/81, EU:C:1982:79 [1982] ECR 825 where the European Court held that art 5(1) can apply even where the existence of the contract on which the claim is based is in dispute between the parties; *Boss Group Ltd v Boss France SA* [1996] 4 All ER 970 where the Court of Appeal held that the English court had jurisdiction under art 5(1) where the appellant sought a negative declaration relying on the respondents' allegation that a contract existed; Case 156/07 *Re Place of Performance of an FOB Contract* [2010] I.L.Pr. 17 German Federal Supreme Court; Case C-548/12 *Brogsitter v Fabrication de Montres Normandes* EU:C:2014:148; *Harald Kolassa v Barclays Bank plc,* C-375/13; EU:C:2015:37; *Canyon Offshore Ltd v GDF Suez E&P Nederland BV* [2014] EWHC 3810 (Comm); [2015] ILPr 8 and *Profit Investment Sim SpA v Ossi* C-366/13, EU: C: 2016: 282 [58].

246. C-51/97, EU:C:1998:509, [1999] CLC 282. See A. Briggs, "Claims against Sea Carriers and the Brussels Convention" [1999] LMCLQ 333. See also *Deutsche Bank AG London Branch v Petromena ASA* [2015] EWCA Civ 226; [2015] 2 Lloyd's Rep 15; [2013] EWHC 3065 (Comm); and *Impala Warehousing and Logistics (Shanghai) Co Ltd v Wanxiang Resources (Singapore) Pte Ltd* [2015] EWHC 811 (Comm); [2015] 2 All ER (Comm) 234 [62] – [81].

247. Similar issues could arise under, e.g., Rome I which only applies to contractual obligations and the Unfair Terms in Consumer Contracts Regulations 1999.

248. See Marine Insurance Act 1906, ss 17–20. Sections 18–20 of the Marine Insurance Act 1906 have now been repealed by the Insurance Act 2015 which provides for the duty of fair presentation of the risk discussed in Chapter 11.

Council.[249] a majority of the House of Lords[250] held that the bank's claim for restitution where a contract was void for *ultra vires*, was not a matter relating to a contract within the equivalent of Article 7(1). However, in *Profit Investment Sim SpA v Ossi*[251] the Court of Justice of the European Union held that an action seeking the annulment of a contract and the restitution of sums paid but not due on the basis of that contract constituted "matters relating to a contract". In *Agnew v Lansforsakringsbolagens AB*[252] a majority of the House of Lords held that claims for alleged precontractual non-disclosure and misrepresentation in a reinsurance contract which make the contract voidable, fell within the equivalent of Article 7(1) of the Recast Regulation. It is not clear, however, whether *Agnew* can be distinguished from the decision of the European Court of Justice in *Fonderie Officine Meccaniche Tacconi SpA v Heinrich Wagner Sinto Maschinenfabrik GmbH*.[253] There it was held that the equivalent of Article 7(1) of the Recast Jurisdiction Regulation did not apply where the claim was that the defendant had broken off negotiations for a contract in breach of good faith with the result that no contract was ever concluded. In light of the provisions of Regulation (EC) No 593/2008 on the Law Applicable to Contractual Obligations ("Rome I")[254] and Regulation (EC) No 864/2007 on the Law applicable to non-contractual obligations ("Rome II")[255] discussed below it seems likely that where a claim is made to avoid a contract voidable for misrepresentation or non-disclosure this would now be characterised as non-contractual because it is a breach of a pre contractual obligation and would not fall within Article 7(1) of the Recast Jurisdiction Regulation, but would fall within Article 7(2) of that Regulation.[256]

Where national law gives a right to claim in tort this may still fall within Article 7(1) as a matter relating to contract. In *Marc Brogsitter v Fabrication de Montres Normandes EURL*[257] Mr Brogsitter, a seller of luxury watches, brought a claim in the German courts against a French company and their manager. Mr Brogsitter had entered into a contract with the defendants to develop movements for luxury watches but he alleged that the defendants were in breach of the terms of the contract and claimed damages in tort under German law on unfair competition. The Court of Justice of the European Union held that such claims, made in tort under national law, must none the less be considered as concerning "matters relating to contract" within the equivalent of Article 7(1)(a) of the Recast Jurisdiction Regulation where the conduct complained of may be considered a breach of the terms of the contract, which may be established by taking into account the purpose of the contract.

The parties are free to agree the place of performance but that place must bear some relation to the actual performance of the contract. The parties cannot provide for a place of performance which does not reflect the performance which is actually required by the contract. *Mainschiffahrts-Genossenschaft e.G. v Les Gravières Rhénanes*[258] concerned an oral agreement for the charter of an inland waterway vessel. The European Court of Justice held that where there is no

---

249. [1997] 4 All ER 641 (HL); [1996] 2 All ER 257 (CA); *Barclays Bank v Glasgow City Council* [1994] 4 All ER 865 (Hirst J). See E. Peel, "Jurisdiction over Restitutionary Claims" [1998] LMCLQ 145 and A. Briggs, "Jurisdiction over Restitutionary Claims" [1992] LMCLQ 283.

250. Lord Goff, Lord Clyde and Lord Hutton with Lord Mustill and Lord Nicholls dissenting.

251. C-366/13, EU: C: 2016: 282.

252. [2000] 1 Lloyd's Rep 317 (HL); [1997] 4 All ER 937 (CA); [1996] 4 All ER 978 (Mance J). See H.N. Bennett, "Mapping the Doctrine of Utmost Good Faith in Insurance Contract Law" [1999] LMCLQ 165, at pp 193–196.

253. C-334/00; EU:C:2002:499 [2002] ECR I-7357.

254. See pages 53–67.

255. See pages 70–73. However, see *Kainz v Pantherwerke AG* C-45/13, EU:C:2014:7 [2014] ILPr 16.

256. Jurisdiction Regulation, art 5(3). See Rome I, Recital 10 and art 1(2)(i) (see page 56 of this chapter) and Rome II, Recital 30 and art 12 (see page 70 of this chapter).

257. C-548/12, EU:C:2014:148.

258. C-106/95; EU:C:1997:70 [1997] All ER (EC) 385.

valid jurisdiction clause, an oral agreement that Germany is the place of performance, which was designed not to determine the place where the person liable is actually to perform its obligations (which was France), but solely to establish that the courts for a particular place have jurisdiction, was not valid under the equivalent of Article 7(1) of the Recast Jurisdiction Regulation. The place of performance designated had no real connection with the reality of the contract. Otherwise it would be open to a party to circumvent the formalities required by the equivalent of Article 25 of the Recast Jurisdiction Regulation for a jurisdiction agreement. Thus an oral agreement on the place of performance which is designed solely to establish that the courts for a particular place have jurisdiction is not governed by Article 7(1), but by Article 25, and is valid only if it complies with the formalities of the latter Article.

Article 7(1)(b) of the Recast Jurisdiction Regulation[259] provides that, unless otherwise agreed, in the case of sale of goods[260] and provision of services,[261] the place of performance of the obligation in question shall be where, under the contract, the goods were delivered or should have been delivered or the services were provided or should have been provided. This provision was new in the Jurisdiction Regulation and was intended to provide as the place of performance the place where the obligation which characterises the contract is to be performed.[262] It may be difficult to determine where the place of delivery under a sale contract is.[263] The goods may be delivered in several places in one EU Member State,[264] or the services provided in more than one EU Member State;[265] or the contract may be for both delivery of goods and provision of services in different EU Member States.

Article 7(1)(b) of the Recast Jurisdiction Regulation does not apply where the contract is neither for goods nor services or, if it is, the place of performance is in a non-EU Member State. In that event, the "obligation in question" is the obligation arising under the same contract and forming the basis of the proceedings commenced by the claimant and not the obligation which characterises the contract.[266] Where there are a number of obligations in issue the principal obligation will determine the court's jurisdiction.[267] If several obligations are in dispute but there is no principal obligation, there will only be jurisdiction in State A for the claim in respect of the obligation to be performed in State A and jurisdiction in State B for the obligation to be performed in State B.[268] Although this would lead to the fragmentation of the litigation, the claimant

---

259. Jurisdiction Regulation, art 5(1)(b).

260. *Car Trim v KeySafety Systems Srl,* C-381/08, EU:C:2010:90 [2010] ECR 1–000. See also F. Lorenzon and Y. Baatz, *CIF and FOB Contracts,* (6th ed., Sweet & Maxwell 2017) [15–067] – [15–072]. *Granarolo SpA v Ambrosi Emmi France SA* C-196/15; EU:C:2016:559.

261. *Corman-Collins SA v La Maison du Whisky SA,* C-9/12; EU:C:2013:860 [2014] 2 WLR 494 (distribution agreement) and *Krejci Lager & Umschlagbetriebs GmbH v Olbrich Transport und Logistik GmbH,* C-469/12; EU:C:2013:788 [2014] CEC 654 (warehouse storage of goods).

262. *Color Drack GmbH v Lexx International Vertriebs GmbH,* C-386/05; EU:C:2007:262 [2007] ILPr 35.

263. *Scottish & Newcastle International Limited v Othon Ghalanos Limited* [2008] UKHL 11; [2008] 1 CLC 186; *Car Trim v KeySafety Systems Srl,* C-381/08, EU:C:2010:90 [2010] ECR 1–000; and *Masai Clothing Co APS v Targa di Badash Tzuri Sciaddai EC SAS* [2015] ILPr 22; *Granarolo SpA v Ambrosi Emmi France SA* C-196/15, EU:C:2016:559.

264. *Color Drack GmbH v Lexx International Vertriebs GmbH* C-386/05, EU:C:2007:262 [2007] ILPr 35.

265. *Wood Floor Solutions Andreas Domberger GmbH v Silva Trade SA,* C-19/09, EU:C:2010:137 [2010] 2 Lloyd's Rep 114 and *Peter Rehder v Air Baltic Corporation,* C-204/08; EU:C:2009:439 [2009] ECR I-6073.

266. *Ets A de Bloos SPRL v Société en Commandite par actions Bouyer,* C-14/76; EU:C:1976:134 [1976] ECR 1497; *Shenevai v Kreischer* C-266/85; EU:C:1987:11 [1987] ECR 239; *Atlas Shipping Agency (UK) Ltd v Suisse Atlantique Société D'Armement Maritime SA (The Gulf Grain and El Amaan)* [1995] 2 Lloyd's Rep 188; *Mainschiffahrts – Genossenschaft eG (MSG) v Les Gravières Rhénanes Sarl,* C-106/95, EU:C:1997:70 [1997] All ER (EC) 385; *Domicrest Ltd v Swiss Bank Corp* [1998] 3 All ER 578; *Viskase Ltd v Paul Kiefel GmbH* [1999] Comm 641 (CA); *RPS Prodotti Siderurgici SRL v The Owners of the Sea Maas (The Sea Maas)* [1999] 2 Lloyd's Rep 281.

267. *Union Transport Group plc v Continental Lines SA* [1992] 1 All ER 161; *Source Ltd v TUV Rheinland Holding AG* [1997] 3 WLR 365; and *AIG Group (UK) Ltd v The Ethniki* [2000] 1 Lloyd's Rep 343.

268. *Leathertex Divisione Sintetici SpA,* Case C-420/97, EU:C:1999:483 [1999] CLC 1983.

always has the option to sue for all its claims where the defendant is domiciled under Article 4 of the Recast Jurisdiction Regulation.[269]

The place of performance of the obligation in question is determined as a matter of national law.[270]

(vi) Tort claims

Article 7(2) of the Recast Jurisdiction Regulation[271] provides that "in matters relating to tort, delict or quasi-delict" the courts for the place where the harmful event occurred shall also have jurisdiction. The European Court of Justice has held that the concept of "matters relating to tort, delict or quasi-delict" is an autonomous one. *Kalfelis v Bankhaus Schroder, Munchmeyer, Hengst & Co*[272] involved claims against three defendants, based on contractual liability for breach of the defendants' duty to provide information, tort and unjust enrichment. The court held that in order to ensure uniformity in all the EU Member States the concept covers all actions which seek to establish the liability of a defendant and which are not related to "contract" within the meaning of the equivalent of Article 7(1) of the Recast Jurisdiction Regulation. The English courts have, however, interpreted this as meaning that the liability referred to must be interpreted as connoting liability in tort, delict or quasi-delict and not as a catch-all provision for any liability other than in contract.[273]

In *Kalfelis* the European Court of Justice went on to hold that where a court has jurisdiction under the equivalent of Article 7(2) of the Recast Jurisdiction Regulation over an action in so far as it is based on tort or delict, it does not have jurisdiction over that action in so far as it is not so based. Simply because the court has jurisdiction over a claim in tort it will not also have jurisdiction over a claim between the same parties based on contract. This can lead to fragmentation of claims so that a party can rely on Article 7(2) to bring its claim in tort, for example, in England but as regards any claim in contract it would have to rely on Article 7(1), and if the place of performance of the obligation in question was France, it would have to bring its contract claim there and could not bring it in England. This is clear from *Domicrest Ltd v Swiss Bank Corp*,[274] a case on the Lugano Convention. There Rix J held that Domicrest could sue in England under the equivalent of Article 7(1) of the Recast Jurisdiction Regulation on its contractual claim against the bank for failure to honour a payment order. However, Domicrest also had claims in tort alleging negligent misrepresentation by the bank as to the effect of the payment order and the client's credit. Rix J held that the place where the harmful event occurred was Switzerland and Italy. Therefore Domicrest could not pursue both its contract and tort claims in England. The solution for Domicrest, if it did not wish to pursue different aspects of the same dispute in different courts, would have been to pursue all its claims in Switzerland, where the bank was domiciled.

---

269. Jurisdiction Regulation, art 2.
270. *Tessilli v Dunlop,* C-12/76 [1976] ECR 1473; *Besix,* C-256/00, EU:C:2002:99 [2002] ECR I-1699. *GIE Groupe Concorde v The Master of the vessel Suhadiwarno Panjan* C-440/97, EU:C:1999:456 [1999] CLC 1976.
271. Jurisdiction Regulation, art 5(3).
272. Case 189/97 [1988] ECR 5565.
273. In *Barclays Bank Plc v Glasgow City Council (No 2)* [1997] 4 All ER 641 (HL); [1996] 2 All ER 257 (CA) (see the dissenting judgment of Leggatt LJ); see also *Kleinwort Benson Ltd v Glasgow City Council (No 1)* [1994] 4 All ER 865 (Hirst J). The House of Lords held that the bank's claim for restitution did not fall within the equivalent of Article 7(2) of the Recast Regulation. A claim based on unjust enrichment did not, exceptional circumstances apart, pre-suppose either a harmful event or a threatened wrong. Compare *Profit Investment Sim SpA v Ossi* C-366/13, EU: C: 2016: 282.
274. [1998] 3 All ER 578.

In *Bier v Mines de Potasse d'Alsace*[275] the European Court of Justice held that the "place where the harmful event occurs" has an autonomous meaning and covers both the place where the damage occurs and the place of the event giving rise to that damage. If those places are different the claimant can choose to bring proceedings in either of them.

In *Réunion Européenne SA v Spliethoff's Bevrachtingskantoor BV*[276] the European Court held that the cargo insurers' claims against the actual carrier and the master of a ship did not fall within the equivalent of Article 7(1) of the Recast Jurisdiction Regulation as there was no contractual relationship between the parties. Therefore, following *Kalfelis v Schröder*,[277] the court held that such an action must be a matter relating to tort, delict or quasi-delict within the equivalent of Article 7(2). On the question of "the place where the harmful event occurred", the consignee could bring proceedings against the actual carrier either before the courts of the place where the damage occurred or the courts of the place of the event giving rise to it. The problem for the consignee was that in an international transport operation of this kind, where the goods had been carried by sea to Rotterdam but then on-carried by road to Rungis in France, the consignee might not be able to determine where the event giving rise to the damage occurred. The place where the damage occurred cannot be either the place of final delivery, which can be changed in mid-voyage, or the place where the damage was ascertained. To allow the consignee to bring the actual carrier before the courts for the place of final delivery would in most cases mean attributing jurisdiction to the claimant's domicile and would depend on uncertain factors. Therefore the place where the damage arose in this type of international transport operation could only be the place where the actual maritime carrier was to deliver the goods, as that place meets the requirements of foreseeability and certainty imposed by the Convention.

The courts have given a narrow interpretation to the place where the damage occurs and the European Court of Justice held in *Kronhofer v Maier*[278] that it does not refer to the place where the claimant is domiciled or where "his assets are concentrated" by reason only of the fact that he has suffered financial damage there resulting from the loss of part of his assets which arose and was incurred in another State. For example, in a claim for misrepresentation it is not the place where the misrepresentee had a bank account and made a payment in reliance on the misrepresentation. Thus in *Domicrest Ltd v Swiss Bank Corp*[279] Rix J considered whether Domicrest could sue in England for claims in tort alleging negligent misrepresentation by the bank as to the effect of the payment order and the client's credit. Domicrest argued that the relevant event which gave rise to the damage was the receipt by Domicrest in England of the statements and

---

275. Case 21/76, EU:C:1976:166 [24] and [25]. See also *Katsouris Bros Ltd v Haitoglou Bros Ltd* [2011] EWHC 111(QB) and Case C-45/13 *Andreas Kainz v Pantherwerke AG* [2014] ILPr 16 (where a manufacturer faced a claim of liability for a defective product, the place of the event giving rise to the damage was the place where the product in question was manufactured); *Coty Germany GmbH v First Note Perfumes NV* Case C-360–12, EU:C:2014:1318 [46] (trade mark); and *Pinckney v KDG Mediatech AG* C-170/12, EU:C:2013:635 (copyright); and *Holterman Ferho Exploitatie* Case C-47/14, EU:C:2015:574 [72].

276. Case C-51/97 [1999] CLC 282.

277. See fn 272.

278. Case C-168/02 *Rudolf Kronhofer v Marianne Maier and Others* [2004] ECR I 06009. See also *Dumez France v Hessiche Landesbank (Helaba),* C-220/88 [1990] ILPr 299; *Marinari v Lloyds Bank Plc,* C-364/93 [1996] QB 217; *Dolphin Maritime & Aviation Services Ltd v Sveriges Angfartygs Assurans Forening (The Swedish Club)* [2009] 1 CLC; Case C-228/11 *Melzer v MF Global UK Ltd* [2013] QB 112 (investment losses); *Hi Hotel HCF SARL v Spoering* C-387/12, EU:C:2014:215 [2014] 1 WLR 1912; *Cartel Damage Claims (CDC) Hydrogen Peroxide SA v Akzo Nobel NV* C-352/13 [2015] QB 906 (breaches of EU competition law); *AMT Futures Limited v Marzillier* [2017] UKSC 13; [2017] 2 WLR 853; *Universal Music International Holding BV v Schilling* C-12/15; EU:C:2016:449 [29]–[40] (negligence of lawyers in drafting a share purchase option).

279. [1998] 3 All ER 578. See also *ABCI v Banque Franco Tunisienne* [2003] 2 Lloyd's Rep 146, [41]; *London Helicopters Ltd v Heliportugal LDA-INAC* [2006] EWHC 108 and *Newsat Holdings Ltd v Zani* [2006] 1 Lloyd's Rep 707.

assurances which the bank intended Domicrest to rely upon and which Domicrest did rely upon. As for the damage itself, England was the place where the economic loss was suffered, for it was where Domicrest maintained its bank account, where it received and acted upon the assurances, and where its commercial operations were based. Rix J considered that the place giving rise to the damage in a case of negligent misstatement occurs where the misstatement originates and not the place of receipt and reliance, i.e. in this case Switzerland. The place where the damage itself occurs may be somewhere other than the place of the event giving rise to the damage and is quite likely to be where the misstatement is heard and relied upon. However, on the facts of the case he did not consider that that place was in England but was in Switzerland and in Italy where the goods had been released to the bank's customer in reliance on the bank's assurances that the bank would pay the purchase price.

Domicrest was approved in *Sunderland Marine Mutual Insurance Co Ltd v Wiseman (The Seaward Quest)*[280] which involved a choice of jurisdiction between England and Scotland, and therefore Schedule 4 to the Civil Jurisdiction and Judgments Act 1982 applied.[281] Rule 3(c) of that Schedule is equivalent to Article 7(2). A mutual insurance company pleaded that the three defendants had conspired to sink the *Seaward Quest* deliberately and had fraudulently misrepresented the circumstances of the loss to the insurers who had paid out under the insurance policy. Langley J held that the "harmful event" alleged occurred in Scotland. The conspiracy to scuttle the ship and alleged misrepresentations were made there. The only connection with England was that that was the place where the insurers made the decision to pay the claim and it was assumed that payment was made from there.

In *Anton Durbeck GmbH v Den Norske Bank ASA (The Tropical Reefer)*[282] the claimant cargo interests alleged that a Norwegian bank, the mortgagee of the vessel, *Tropical Reefer*, had wrongfully interfered with the claimants' contracts for the carriage of a cargo of bananas by arresting the ship in Panama. Nigel Teare QC held that the English court did not have jurisdiction to determine the claimants' claim for damages for wrongful interference with the cargo under the equivalent of Article 7(2), as Panama, rather than London, was the place where the event which gave rise to the damage occurred.

In *AMT Futures Limited v Marzillier*[283] a claim was brought by a derivatives broker against German lawyers for the tort of inducing the broker's former clients to breach their contracts which contained an exclusive English court jurisdiction clause by bringing claims in Germany. The event occasioning the damage, the alleged inducement of the former clients by the German lawyers to commence the German legal proceedings occurred in Germany. The broker therefore relied on the alternative basis ie the place where the relevant damage occurred, in support of its argument that the English court had jurisdiction. At first instance[284] it was held that the place where the damage occurred was England, where the alleged tort deprived the claimant of the contractual benefit of the exclusive jurisdiction clause which ought to have been enjoyed in England. The Court of Appeal[285] overruled that decision and held that the place where the damage occurred was Germany. That decision was upheld by the Supreme Court. The direct harm that the claimants suffered from the alleged tort was the expenditure occasioned by the German proceedings and therefore the place where the harmful event

---

280. [2007] EWHC 1460 (Comm); [2007] 2 Lloyd's Rep 308.
281. Which applies *intra* United Kingdom.
282. [2002] EWHC 1173, [2002] All ER (D) 67. The case subsequently went to the Court of Appeal but not on this point – [2003] EWCA Civ 147; [2003] 2 All ER (Comm) 411.
283. [2017] UKSC 13; [2017] 2 WLR 853.
284. [2014] EWHC 1085 (Comm); [2014] 2 Lloyd's Rep 349 [46].
285. [2015] EWCA Civ 143; [2015] QB 699.

occurred was Germany. The result of this decision is that the broker would have to pursue its contractual claims against its former clients in England but its tortious claim against the lawyers of the former clients in Germany ie fragmentation of the litigation. Thus "the ancillary claim in tort ...for inducing the breach of the contracts could not be made in the court which the contract breaker had agreed would have exclusive jurisdiction over the contract."[286] Lord Hodge, delivering the judgment of the Supreme Court, said that "such inconvenience is the price of achieving the legal certainty and foreseeability which are among the principal aims of the Judgments Regulation".[287] It was not necessary to refer the issue as to where the damage occurred to the Court of Justice of the European Union.

A claim for a negative declaration falls within the scope of Article 7(1) or (2) of the Recast Regulation.[288]

(vii) Agency

A person domiciled in an EU Member State may also be sued in another EU Member State "as regards a dispute arising out of the operations of a branch, agency or other establishment, in the courts for the place in which the branch, agency or other establishment is situated" pursuant to Article 7(5) of the Recast Jurisdiction Regulation.[289]

In *Anton Durbeck GmbH v Den Norske Bank ASA (The Tropical Reefer)*[290] the Court of Appeal held that the decision by the London branch of a Norwegian bank to arrest the *Tropical Reefer* in Panama meant that the dispute arose out of the activities of the London branch within the equivalent of Article 7(5) of the Recast Jurisdiction Regulation. The activities which had given rise to the dispute had arisen out of the London banking business conducted by the defendant's London branch. The loan in respect of which the security over the ship had been taken had been negotiated in London, the decision to enforce the security had been taken in London, and the London branch had given instructions to enforce the security and the power of attorney to enable it to be done. Therefore the English court had jurisdiction under the equivalent of Article 7(5) of the Recast Jurisdiction Regulation but the Court of Appeal stayed the proceedings on the grounds of *forum non conveniens*,[291] in favour of Panama.

(viii) Remuneration for salvage of cargo or freight

The claimant may sue for remuneration for salvage of cargo or freight in the court where the cargo or freight has been arrested or could have been arrested and bail or security has been provided under Article 7(7) of the Recast Jurisdiction Regulation.[292]

---

286. [2017] UKSC 13 [6]; [2017] 2 WLR 853.
287. Ibid., [35].
288. *Folien Fischer AG v Ritrama SpA*, C-133/11, EU:C:2012:664 [2013] QB 523.
289. Jurisdiction Regulation, art 5(5).
290. [2003] EWCA Civ 147, [2003] 2 All ER (Comm) 411. See also *Deutsche Bank AG London Branch v Petromena ASA* [2015] EWCA Civ 226; [2015] 2 Lloyd's Rep 15; [2013] EWHC 3065 (Comm) and *AMT Futures Ltd v Marzillier, Dr Meier & Dr Guntner Rechtsanwaltsgesellschaft mbH* [2017] UKSC 13; [2017] 2 WLR 853.
291. This decision precedes the decision of the European Court of Justice in *Owusu v Jackson* C – 281/02, EU:C:2005:120 [2005] ECR I – 1383; [2005] 1 Lloyd's Rep 452 – see page 18. It might be argued that by analogy if the court of an EU Member State has jurisdiction under arts 2,5 or 6 of the Jurisdiction Regulation there is no discretion to stay the proceedings. Whether there would be a discretion to stay in favour of the courts of a third State would now be determined by arts 33 and 34 of the Recast Jurisdiction Regulation – see pages 28–29 and 30–31. There are no such provisions in the Jurisdiction Regulation but the English courts have held that there may be an exception to *Owusu* in some circumstances – see pages 18–19.
292. Jurisdiction Regulation, art 5(7).

(ix) Multiple defendants

Article 8(1) of the Recast Jurisdiction Regulation[293] provides that where there is more than one defendant, the courts for the place where any one of the defendants is domiciled are recognised as having jurisdiction "provided the claims are so closely connected that it is expedient to hear and determine them together to avoid the risk of irreconcilable judgments resulting from separate proceedings". The words in quotes did not appear in Article 6(1) of the EC Jurisdiction and Lugano Conventions but they reflect the decision of the European Court of Justice in *Kalfelis v Schröder*.[294] Thus if, for example, a carrier brings proceedings against different cargo interests, A, B and C, seeking a declaration that it is not liable for cargo damage to cargo shipped on the same voyage under bills of lading in the same terms, and A is domiciled in England, B is domiciled in France and C is domiciled in Spain, the carrier can sue all three cargo interests in either England, France or Spain. The claimant must establish a good arguable case that the defendant is domiciled in England.[295] If there were also a defendant domiciled in Turkey the English courts would apply their national law to determine whether the Turkish defendant could also be sued in England.[296]

Until *Freeport plc v Olle Arnoldsson*[297] it had been debated whether it was possible to apply the equivalent of Article 8(1) of the Recast Regulation in a situation where claims were brought against two or more defendants and one action was based in contract, whereas the other was based in tort. In *Freeport* Mr Arnoldsson sued Freeport plc on an agreement that he would be paid a fee by a company which was to become the owner of a factory shop in Sweden. This company was subsequently incorporated under Swedish law as Freeport AB. Mr Arnoldsson brought proceedings in Sweden against both Freeport plc and Freeport AB. Freeport plc argued that the action against it had a contractual basis, whereas the action against Freeport AB was based in tort, delict or quasi-delict since there was no contractual relationship between Mr Arnoldsson and that company. Freeport plc further argued that as the legal bases of the actions against Freeport plc and Freeport AB were different, Article 8(1) could not apply as it could not be shown that the two actions were connected. The European Court of Justice held that Article 8(1) can apply if the *Kalfelis* test is satisfied, "without there being any need for the actions brought to have identical legal bases".[298]

A valid jurisdiction clause within Article 25 of the Recast Jurisdiction Regulation prevails over the special jurisdiction of Article 8(1) of that Regulation.[299] Therefore if three defendants, A, B and C, are domiciled in England, France and Spain respectively but C has agreed to jurisdiction in Germany, the claimant could sue both A and B in either England or France but must sue C in Germany in accordance with Article 25. The claimant could not sue A, B and C in Germany as only C has agreed to jurisdiction there and none of the defendants is domiciled there, so Article 8(1) does not apply.

---

293. Jurisdiction Regulation, art 6(1).

294. See fn 272. See also e.g. *Roche Nedeland and others* [2006] ECR I-6535; *FKI Engineering Ltd v Dewind Holdings Limited* [2008] EWCA Civ 316; [2008] All ER (D) 417 and Case C-103/05 *Reisch Montage AG v Kiesel Baumachinen Handels GmbH* [2007] ILPr 10.

295. *Canada Trust Co v Stolzenberg & Co KG (No 2)* [2002] 1 AC 1; *Bols Distilleries v Superior Yacht Services Limited* [2006] UKPC 45; [2007] 1 WLR 12; *Benatti v WPP Holdings Italy Srl* [2007] EWCA Civ 263; [2007] ILPr 33, [37] – [44].

296. See pages 42–48.

297. C-98/06; EU:C:2007:595 [2007] WLR (D) 252. See also *Profit Investment Sim SpA v Ossi* C-366/13, EU: C: 2016: 282.

298. Ibid., [46].

299. *Deforche (Société) v Tomacrau (Société)* [2007] ILPr 25 (French Cour De Cassation).

(x) Third party proceedings

Article 8(2) of the Recast Jurisdiction Regulation[300] provides that an action against a third party may be brought in the court seised of the original proceedings. There must be a close connection between the proceedings commenced by the original claimant and the third party proceedings commenced by the original defendant.[301] There was not such a close connection in *Barton v Golden Sun Holidays Ltd*.[302] There the claimants were a group of holidaymakers and the defendant was a tour operator. The tour operator admitted liability when the holidaymakers became ill and settled the case with the amount of costs to be agreed at a later date. The tour operator applied to serve third party proceedings on the hotelier in Cyprus. It was held that the claim brought by the holidaymakers was for causes of action and remedies based solely in English law for the protection of English consumers, whereas the claim against the hotelier had consequences under Cypriot law. Furthermore, as the claim between the claimant and defendant had been settled and was no longer active, there was no realistic prospect that the claim between the claimant and the defendant and the third party would be tried together. Therefore there was no risk of irreconcilable judgments.

Article 8(2) will also cover the situation where the third party brings an action against the defendant in the original proceedings, which is closely linked to those original proceedings and this can be heard in the same court as that determining the claim between the claimant and the defendant. This will be the case provided that the action was not instituted solely with the object of removing that defendant from the jurisdiction of the court which would be competent in the case.[303]

Again where the third party and the defendant have a jurisdiction agreement that satisfies Article 25 of the Recast Regulation, that will prevail over Article 8(2) of that Regulation.[304]

(xi) Limitation

As the Recast Jurisdiction Regulation seeks to minimise the risk of irreconcilable judgments and ensure that liability and limitation proceedings are determined by the same court, Article 9[305] provides that a court of an EU Member State which has jurisdiction in "actions relating to liability from the use or operation of a ship" shall also have jurisdiction over claims for limitation of such liability. So, for example, if the shipowner is domiciled in Greece, the court of that State would have jurisdiction to determine the limitation proceedings where the shipowner is sued for liability for a collision in Greece. Without Article 9 the shipowner would not be able to commence a limitation action in Greece but would have to sue where the other party or parties were domiciled. Article 9 allows the shipowner to bring proceedings to limit where it could be sued.[306]

(xii) Other international conventions

Article 71 of the Recast Jurisdiction Regulation[307] provides that that Regulation shall not affect any conventions to which the EU Member States are parties and which in relation to particular

---

300. Jurisdiction Regulation, art 6(2).
301. *Kongress Agentur Hagen GmbH v Zeehaghe BV*, C -365/88, EU:C:1990:203 [1990] ECR 1–1845.
302. [2007] ILPr 57.
303. *SOVAG Schwarzmeer und Ostsee Versicherungs-Aktiengesellschaft v If Vahinkovakuutusyhtiö Oy* C-521/14, EU:C:2016:41.
304. *Groupement D'Intérêt Economique (GIE) Réunion Européenne v Zurich España,* C-77/04, EU:C:2005:327 [2005] ILPr 456.
305. Jurisdiction Regulation, art 7.
306. See N. Meeson "Jurisdictional Aspects of Limitation of Liability for Maritime Claims" in D.R. Thomas (ed.), *Liability Regimes in Contemporary Maritime Law* (Informa Law 2007), at pp 306–308 and chapter 7.
307. Jurisdiction Regulation, art 71, EC Jurisdiction Convention, art 57 and Lugano Convention, art 57. See Y.Baatz, "Forum selection in Contracts for the Carriage of Goods by Sea: the European Dimension [2011] LMCLQ 208.

matters, govern jurisdiction. The Choice of Court Convention[308] will be important in relation to jurisdiction agreements. A number of conventions may be of great significance in maritime matters such as the International Convention for the Unification of Certain Rules Relating to the Arrest of Seagoing Ships of 1952 (the "Arrest Convention"), the International Convention on the Arrest of Ships 1999 (the "1999 Arrest Convention"),[309] the International Convention for the Unification of Certain Rules Concerning Civil Jurisdiction in Matters of Collision 1952 (the "Collision Convention") and the Hamburg Rules.[310] If the Rotterdam Rules come into force[311] and the EU also opts into chapter 14 of that convention on jurisdiction, that convention will also be relevant.

The Arrest Convention is of particular significance as Article 7 gives the English courts jurisdiction on the merits of the dispute if a ship is arrested in England. Therefore, if it is possible to arrest the ship in respect of which the claim arose or a sister ship when it comes into territorial waters, the English court will have jurisdiction on the merits of the dispute, even though the shipowner is domiciled in another EU Member State. The ship must be arrested[312] for the Arrest Convention to apply.[313] It is not sufficient that an arrest has been threatened and security, for example, by means of a P&I Club letter of undertaking or bank guarantee, has been provided in order to avoid arrest. If the claimant agrees not to arrest it should ask the shipowner to agree to English jurisdiction within Article 25 of the Recast Jurisdiction Regulation or submit to the jurisdiction within Article 26 of that Regulation.[314]

The Arrest Convention may be contrasted with the Collision Convention, Article 1(1) of which provides that a collision action can only be brought before the courts there set out including the court where the ship or a sister ship has been arrested or could have been arrested but bail or other security has been provided.[315]

The Recast Jurisdiction Regulation and the other international convention must be read together where that is possible. Where, however, there is a conflict between the Recast Jurisdiction Regulation and the other convention, the latter will prevail. The European Court of Justice considered whether there was a conflict between the Arrest Convention and the EC Jurisdiction Convention in *The Maciej Rataj*.[316] There a sister ship had been arrested in England so that England had jurisdiction on the merits under the Arrest Convention. However, proceedings had already been brought in relation to the same claim in Rotterdam and the shipowner argued that the English court, as the court second seised, must stay its proceedings because of the multiple proceedings provisions in the EC Jurisdiction Convention. The European Court of Justice held that as the Arrest Convention does not contain any multiple proceedings provisions there was

---

308. See page 16.
309. The 1999 Arrest Convention entered into force on 14 September 2011. The State parties are Albania, Algeria, Benin, Bulgaria, Congo, Ecuador, Estonia, Latvia, Liberia, Spain and Syria as at 23 March 2017.
310. See fn 4 of this chapter.
311. See fn 6 of this chapter.
312. See Chapter 12.
313. *The Deichland* [1989] 2 All ER 1066. The claimant can arrest to found jurisdiction even if the shipowner has acknowledged issue of the writ in *rem* and filed a bail bond (*The Prinsengracht* [1993] 1 Lloyd's Rep 41) or entered a caveat against the arrest of the ship (*The Anna H* [1995] 1 Lloyd's Rep 11).
314. E.g. by acknowledging service of a writ in *rem* and by providing a bail bond – *The Prinsengracht* [1993] 1 Lloyd's Rep 41.
315. Art 1(1)(b). See *The Po* [1991] 2 Lloyd's Rep 206. Cf. 1999 Arrest Convention, art 7, Jurisdiction Regulation, art 5(7) and Recast Regulation, art 7(7).
316. Case C-406/92 [1995] 1 Lloyd's Rep 302. See pages 26–29. See also *Frans Maas Logistics (UK) Ltd v CDR Trucking BV* [1999] 1 Comm 737; *Nurnberger Allgemeine Versicherungs AG v Portbridge Transport International BV*, C-148/03, EU:C:2004:677 [2003] ILPr 44; *TNT Express Nederland BV v Axa Versicherung AG*, C-533/08, EU:C:2010:243 [2010] ECR I-04107; *Nipponkoa Insurance Co (Europe) Ltd v Inter-Zuid Transport BV*, C-452/12, EU:C:2013:858 [2014] 1 All ER (Comm) 288; *Nickel & Goeldner Spedition GmbH v Kintra UAB*, C-157/13 EU:C:2014:2145 [2014] WLR 387. In *British American Tobacco Switzerland SA v Exel Europe Ltd* [2015] UKSC 65; [2016] 1 Lloyd's Rep 463 the Supreme Court held that there was no gap in the CMR Convention in relation to where successive road carriers could be sued and therefore the rules of the Jurisdiction Regulation did not apply.

no conflict and the multiple proceedings provisions of the EC Jurisdiction Convention applied. Therefore the English court, as the court second seised, had to stay its proceedings in favour of the court first seised, Rotterdam, in so far as they were between the same parties.

The English court has held that there is a conflict between Article 17 of the EC Jurisdiction Convention, now Article 25 of the Recast Jurisdiction Regulation (which provides that the court chosen shall have jurisdiction), and the Arrest Convention (which provides that the courts of the country in which the arrest was made shall have jurisdiction).[317] Therefore the Arrest Convention prevailed.[318] However, the English court exercised its discretion at common law to stay its proceedings in favour of the court chosen.[319]

Another example of an international convention prevailing would be where the Hamburg Rules apply to a bill of lading which provides for the exclusive jurisdiction of the courts of an EU Member State. Article 21 of the Hamburg Rules provides that the cargo claimant can choose from a number of different fora including the court chosen and this would prevail over Article 25 of the Recast Jurisdiction Regulation which provides that the court chosen shall have exclusive jurisdiction.

It is doubtful whether the Hague-Visby Rules would fall within Article 71 as it may be argued that they do not govern jurisdiction.[320] Thus the position under the Recast Jurisdiction Regulation would be different from that at common law. In *The Morviken*[321] the House of Lords struck out a jurisdiction clause where the court chosen would have applied the Hague Rules which would have imposed a lower package limit than that under the Hague-Visby Rules which applied mandatorily under English law. If, as in *The Morviken* the English court had jurisdiction as a result of the arrest of a sister ship, the English court would have jurisdiction under the Arrest Convention which would prevail provided it was seised first. It could still apply *The Morviken*. The English court would apply the rules in Rome I to determine the law applicable to the contractual obligations under the bill of lading, unless Rome I did not apply to those obligations because they arose out of the negotiable character of the bill of lading.[322] Where Rome I applies the English court could apply the "overriding mandatory provisions" of the law of the forum which probably include the Hague-Visby Rules.[323] Where Rome I does not apply, the English court would apply its national law including *The Morviken*.

(c) Common law

If the defendant is not domiciled in an EU Member State, pursuant to Article 6 of the Recast Jurisdiction Regulation,[324] the English courts determine their jurisdiction in accordance with

---

317. *The Bergen (No 1)* [1997] 1 Lloyd's Rep 380. Cf. *The Bergen (No 2)* [1997] 2 Lloyd's Rep 710 on *forum non conveniens*.

318. Cf. 1999 The Arrest Convention which has an express provision on jurisdiction clauses, as does Chapter 14 of the Rotterdam Rules.

319. *The Bergen (No 2)* [1997] 2 Lloyd's Rep 710. See pages 44–45 of this chapter on *forum non conveniens*.

320. Cf. J. Cooke, T. Young and A. Taylor, *Voyage Charters* (4th edn, Informa Law 2014), [85.27] expresses the view that the Hague-Visby Rules would probably override art 23 of the Jurisdiction Regulation; R. Aikens, R. Lord and M. Bools, *Bills of Lading* (2nd edn, Informa Law from Routledge 2016) (hereinafter "Aikens") expresses the view that the Hague-Visby Rules are not within the terms of art 71 – see [10.55], fn 85; and G. Treitel and F. Reynolds, *Carver on Bills of Lading* (4th edn, Sweet & Maxwell 2017) ("*Carver*"), [9–077], fn 298, which suggests that "Such a jurisdiction clause would however now normally require to be accepted by virtue of art 25 of the [Recast Jurisdiction Regulation]".

321. [1983] 1 AC 565. See page 63 of this chapter. The decision can only apply if the Hague-Visby Rules apply compulsorily – see *The Komninos S* [1991] 1 Lloyd's Rep 370 and *Trafigura Beheer BV v Mediterranean Shipping Co SA (The MSC Amsterdam)* [2007] EWCA Civ 794; [2008] 1 All ER (Comm) 385 discussed at page 52 of this chapter, and see Chapter 5, pages 200–201.

322. See pages 54–95.

323. Rome I, art 9(2).

324. Jurisdiction Regulation, art 4.

the common law, i.e. the Civil Procedure Rules[325] and case law. This provision is subject to the provisions on exclusive jurisdiction[326] and jurisdiction agreements.[327]

At common law jurisdiction is founded as of right for *in personam* proceedings where a defendant is served with proceedings within the jurisdiction in accordance with Part 6 of the Civil Procedure Rules.

Where the defendant is not within the jurisdiction the claimant requires the permission of the court in order to serve proceedings on the defendant outside the jurisdiction. The application for permission is made by the claimant without notice to the defendant. The claimant must satisfy the court that it has a good arguable case that the claim against the foreign defendant falls within one or more of the grounds in paragraph 3.1 of Practice Direction 6B supplementing Part 6[328] of the Civil Procedure Rules. The claimant must state in its application which ground or grounds it relies on.[329] Those most likely to apply to maritime contractual claims are under paragraph (6) where the claim is made in respect of a contract[330] which (a) was made within the jurisdiction; or (b) was made by or through an agent trading or residing within the jurisdiction; or (c) is governed by English law; or (d) contains a term to the effect that the court shall have jurisdiction to determine any claim in respect of the contract.[331] Alternatively, the claim may be made under paragraph (7) in respect of a breach of contract committed within the jurisdiction or paragraph (8) for a claim for a declaration that no contract exists where, if it was found to exist, it would comply with the conditions set out in paragraph (6).

Although there is some overlap these grounds differ considerably from the grounds of jurisdiction under Articles 25, 7(1) and 7(5) of the Recast Regulation. Article 25 of the Recast Jurisdiction Regulation and paragraph 3.1 of Practice Direction 6B supplementing Part 6 of the Civil Procedure Rules recognise party autonomy. However, there is nothing in the Recast Jurisdiction Regulation which confers jurisdiction on the basis of where the contract is concluded, or the governing law of the contract or where the breach of contract is committed. At common law where, for example, a bill of lading provides for English law

---

325. The Civil Procedure Rules replaced the Rules of the Supreme Court in April 1999. The Civil Procedure Rules will be referred to except where case law is discussed which was decided on the Rules of the Supreme Court.

326. Recast Regulation, art 24, Jurisdiction Regulation, art 22.

327. Recast Regulation, art 25, Jurisdiction Regulation, art 23.

328. Formerly CPR, Part 6, r 20 which replaces Order 11, r 1(i) of the Rules of the Supreme Court.

329. Part 6.37(1)(a) CPR.

330. *Global 5000 Ltd v Wadhawan* [2012] EWCA Civ 13; [2012] 1 Lloyd's Rep 239 noted in A. Dickinson, "Service out of the Jurisdiction in Contract Cases: Straightening out the Deck Chairs" [2012] LMCLQ 181.

331. This latter provision is only relevant where the Jurisdiction Regulation, art 23(3) applies, i.e. the proceedings were commenced before 10 January 2015, and neither party is domiciled in an EU Member State; or the revised Lugano Convention applies and neither party is domiciled in a Lugano Contracting State; or the formalities of art 23(1) have not been satisfied. If the proceedings were commenced after that date the Recast Jurisdiction Regulation applies and where the parties have chosen the courts of an EU Member State, such as the London High court, that court shall have jurisdiction no matter where the parties are domiciled. Even if neither party is domiciled in an EU Member State, the court of an EU Member State chosen must take jurisdiction, provided that the jurisdiction agreement satisfies the formalities set out in art 25(1) of the Recast Jurisdiction Regulation. As a result it has been necessary to amend the Civil Procedure Rules, which previously required a claimant to obtain the permission of the court to serve a defendant domiciled outside the EU Member States. This will no longer be the case where such a defendant has agreed to a jurisdiction agreement for the court of an EU Member State which satisfies the formalities of art 25(1) of the Recast Regulation. Therefore Rule 6.33(2)(b) of the Civil Procedure Rules provides for situations where permission of the court is not required for service of the claim form out of the United Kingdom and 6.33(2)(b)(v) has a new situation where "the defendant is a party to an agreement conferring jurisdiction within art 25 of the [Recast Jurisdiction] Regulation."

the court may grant permission to serve a claim form outside the jurisdiction in Canada, as in *The Spiliada*.[332]

The claimant must show that it is, or has become, a party to the bill of lading contract. For example, if it is the transferee of a bill of lading it must show that it is the holder of the bill and that rights have been transferred to it by virtue of section 2 of the Carriage of Goods by Sea Act 1992[333] or where there is an implied contract on the terms of the bill of lading.[334]

Permission to serve the claim form out of the jurisdiction cannot be granted unless the court is "satisfied that England and Wales is the proper place in which to bring the claim".[335] This issue will be considered next.

(i) Forum non conveniens

In a case where the defendant has been served within the jurisdiction a stay will only be granted on the ground of *forum non conveniens* where the defendant can show that England is not the natural or appropriate forum for the trial and that there is another available forum which is clearly or distinctly more appropriate than England, i.e. the case may be tried more suitably for the interests of all the parties and the ends of justice.[336] Thus in *Caltex Singapore Pte Ltd v BP Shipping Ltd*[337] BP was served as of right in England as it was resident in England, but BP sought a stay of the English proceedings on the ground that Singapore was the natural or appropriate forum. The burden was on BP to show that England was not the appropriate forum. BP admitted liability for the damage caused when their ship, the *British Skill*, collided with Caltex's jetty in Singapore, so that only the issues of quantum and limitation remained. Considering such factors as whether there was any connection with England; the place of the tort (Singapore); where the parties were based (Singapore and England); the applicable law (Singapore); where it would be more convenient to have the trial (Singapore as all the witnesses of fact as to the damage to the Caltex jetty were in Singapore); and existing proceedings elsewhere, Clarke J, as he then was, held as a first stage that Singapore was the natural forum for the determination of the issues in the action. At the second stage he asked whether the plaintiff had established that there was some special circumstance as a result of which justice required that the action be allowed to proceed in England.[338]

Where, however, the defendant is outside the jurisdiction the court will not grant permission unless satisfied that England and Wales is the proper place in which to bring the claim. The burden of proof is on the claimant. In *The Spiliada*[339] shipowners claimed against Canadian shippers, Cansulex, for alleged corrosion and pitting of the holds and tank tops of their ship due

---

332. *Spiliada Maritime Corp v Cansulex Ltd (The Spiliada)* [1987] AC 460 – see page 44 of this chapter; *Navig8Pte Ltd v Al-Riyadh Co for Vegetable Oil Industry (The Lucky Lady)* [2013] EWHC 328 (Comm); [2013] 2 All ER (Comm) 145; and *Golden Endurance Shipping SA v RMA Watanya SA (The Golden Endurance)* [2014] EWHC 3917 (Comm); [2015] 1 Lloyd's Rep 266.
333. See Chapter 5, page 192.
334. *Brandt v Liverpool* [1924] 1 KB 175. See Chapter 5, pages 195–196.
335. CPR, r 6.37(3).
336. *The Spiliada* [1987] AC 460.
337. [1996] 1 Lloyd's Rep 286.
338. This is the correct question but his decision not to stay the English proceedings as the tonnage limit was higher there was subsequently overruled in *The Herceg Novi*, discussed at pages 48–49 of this chapter.
339. [1987] AC 460. See also *Connelly v RTZ Corporation Plc* [1997] CLC 1357; *Lubbe v Cape Plc* [2000] 1 Lloyd's Rep 139; *Carlson v Rio Tinto Plc* [1999] CLC 551; *Cherney v Deripaska* [2009] EWCA Civ 849; [2010] 2 All ER 456; *VTB Capital plc v Nutritek* [2013] UKSC 5; [2013] 2 WLR 398 (torts of deceit and conspiracy to defraud); *Alliance Bank JSC v Aquanta Corp* [2012] EWCA 1588; [2013] 1 All ER (Comm) 819 [83] – [118]; *Navig8 Pte Ltd v Al-Riyadh Co for Vegetable Oil Industry (The Lucky Lady)* [2013] EWHC 328 (Comm); [2013] 2 All ER (Comm) 145. Field J subsequently held that Navig8 was not the carrier under the bill of lading – [2013] EWHC 1565 (Comm).

to a cargo of wet sulphur. The bills of lading provided that the bills were to be construed and governed by English law. Leave was obtained by the shipowners to issue and serve a writ upon Cansulex in Canada on the ground that the contract was governed by English law under Order 11 rule 1 of the Rules of the Supreme Court, which has now been replaced by paragraph 3.1 of Practice Direction 6B supplementing Part 6[340] of the Civil Procedure Rules. Cansulex applied for an order to set aside such leave. A very similar action was at that time proceeding in the Admiralty Court in London in which Cansulex were also defendants. That action concerned a ship called the *Cambridgeshire*. After reviewing the authorities, Lord Goff, in a judgment with which all the other Law Lords agreed, stated that where the defendant is outside the jurisdiction the claimant is seeking to persuade the court to exercise its discretionary power to permit service on the defendant outside the jurisdiction. That jurisdiction may be exorbitant. His Lordship also considered that the court should not be deterred from granting a stay of proceedings, or from exercising its discretion against granting leave under Order 11 simply because the plaintiff would be deprived of a legitimate personal or juridical advantage, provided that substantial justice would be done in the available appropriate forum. The plaintiffs were time barred in Canada. The House of Lords upheld the judge's exercise of discretion that England was the appropriate forum. The factors which he had taken into account included the availability of witnesses, the multiplicity of proceedings and the *Cambridgeshire* factor, i.e. the fact that experienced teams of lawyers and experts were already aware of the issues involved and this would contribute to efficiency, expedition and economy and, in Lord Goff 's view, to promoting the possibility of settlement. Lord Goff indicated that, even if the judge had erred in exercising his discretion, he would only have set aside the proceedings on the condition that Cansulex waive their right to rely on the time bar in British Columbia.

Where the defendant is served with English court proceedings it should acknowledge service pursuant to Part 10 of the Civil Procedure Rules. Where it fails to do so, the court may enter judgment by default. If, on the other hand, the defendant wishes to contest the jurisdiction of the English court it may do so by acknowledging service and contesting jurisdiction in accordance with Part 11 of the Civil Procedure Rules, either on the grounds that the court does not have jurisdiction and/or that it should not exercise jurisdiction.[341]

(ii) Jurisdiction agreement

As seen above,[342] if proceedings are commenced on or after 10 January 2015 and the parties have chosen the court of an EU Member State such as the English court, that court shall have jurisdiction and has no discretion. If, however the proceedings were commenced before 10 January 2015 Article 23 of the Jurisdiction Regulation will apply. Under Articles 4 and 23(3) of the Jurisdiction Regulation the common law rules will apply where neither party to the English jurisdiction clause is domiciled in an EU Member State. Thus if, for example, a shipper domiciled in Hong Kong wishes to rely on an English jurisdiction clause in a bill of lading with a carrier also domiciled in a non-EU Member State, the English court will apply the common law rules under which it has a discretion.[343]

At common law the English court has adopted a robust defence of English jurisdiction clauses in most circumstances. Thus the English court will uphold a jurisdiction clause, unless there are

---

340. Formerly CPR, Part 6, r 20 which replaces Order 11, r 1(i) of the Rules of the Supreme Court.
341. *IMS SA v Capital Oil and Gas Industries Ltd* [2016] EWHC 1956; [2016] 4 WLR 163 [13] – [42].
342. See page 17.
343. *Compania Sud Americana De Vapores SA v Hin-Pro International Logistics Ltd* [2015] EWCA Civ 401; [2015] 2 Lloyd's Rep 1; [2014] EWHC 3632 (Comm); [2015] 1 Lloyd's Rep 301.

strong reasons for staying the proceedings in the forum in which the parties have agreed that they will be litigated.[344] This is the case even though proceedings have already been commenced elsewhere,[345] as the court chosen would be the appropriate forum, unless there are multiple proceedings between multiple parties in the other forum, some of whom have not agreed to English jurisdiction.[346]

Two decisions on bills of lading illustrate this, even in the face of legislation in the other jurisdiction which would make the English jurisdiction clause invalid. In *OT Africa Line Ltd v Magic Sportswear Corp*,[347] O. T. Africa Line Ltd (OTAL), an English company which also had offices in Toronto, carried goods from New York on their vessel *Mathilde Maersk* to Monrovia. OTAL issued a bill of lading in Toronto where the ocean freight was payable. The bill of lading named Magic Sportswear Corporation (Magic), a Delaware corporation with business interests in New York, as the shippers and the intended receivers were Blue Banana, a Liberian corporation. It was alleged that the goods were short delivered and Magic and Blue Banana commenced proceedings in Toronto in August 2003. The instigators of those proceedings were the Canadian cargo insurers exercising their subrogated rights to bring the claims in the name of the insured, as Magic and Blue Banana were dormant.

The bill of lading contained an English law and exclusive English court jurisdiction clause. The basis on which the jurisdiction of the Canadian courts was invoked was section 46(1)(b) and (c) of the Canadian Marine Liability Act 2001. Although Canada does not give the force of law to the Hamburg Rules, this section is a similar jurisdiction provision to Article 21 of the Hamburg Rules, which provides that the cargo claimant has an option to bring proceedings in a number of places including the place designated by the contract of carriage. The Canadian legislation is more favourable to the cargo claimant in that it permits an action to be brought if the defendant has *a* place of business, branch or agency in Canada, rather than *the* principal place of business or the habitual residence of the carrier provided for by the Hamburg Rules. The rationale for section 46 included giving Canadian importers and exporters the right to pursue cargo claims in Canada and an attack on what was perceived to be a monopoly of the British courts over such claims. The Canadian court retained a discretion to refuse jurisdiction on grounds of *forum non conveniens* and the choice of law provision remained effective. The Hamburg Rules are not in force in England and Wales and there are no current plans to change this. The case therefore challenged the principle of the supremacy of party autonomy, long recognised by the English courts.

The Court of Appeal held that the conflict between the provisions of the Canadian legislation and the agreed jurisdiction of England was to be resolved by the rules of private international law of the court in which the question has to be resolved, i.e. the English court. One of those rules is that questions of interpretation and enforcement of contracts are resolved by reference to the proper law of the contract, which was English law.[348] The Court of Appeal concluded that there was no strong reason not to hold the parties to the English jurisdiction clause. Furthermore, the Court of Appeal upheld the anti-suit injunctions to restrain the

---

344. *The Eleftheria* [1970] P 94; *The El Amria* [1981] 2 Lloyd's Rep 119 and *Donohue v Armco Inc* [2001] UKHL 64; [2002] 1 Lloyd's Rep 425.

345. Contrast the approach under the Jurisdiction Regulation and the decision in *Gasser* discusssed at fn 185 which has fortunately been reversed by art 31(2) of the Recast Jurisdiction Regulation.

346. *Bouygues Offshore SA v Caspian Shipping Co* [1998] 2 Lloyd's Rep 461 and *Donohue v Armco Inc* [2001] UKHL 64; [2002] 1 Lloyd's Rep 425. For the converse situation where the English court refuses to enforce a foreign jurisdiction agreement because of multiple proceedings in England see page 47.

347. [2005] EWCA 710; [2005] 2 Lloyd's Rep 170. See page 23 and fn 179.

348. The Court relied on the decision of Thomas J in *Akai Pty Ltd v People's Insurance Co Ltd* [1998] 1 Lloyd's Rep 90.

defendants from pursuing the Canadian proceedings.[349] The Canadian court ultimately stayed the shippers' action in Canada.[350]

Magic Sportswear has been followed in *Horn Linie GmbH & Co v Panamericana Formas E Impresos SA, Ace Seguros S.A. (The Hornbay).*[351] The claimants, a German shipowning company that operated a liner service to South America, loaded a cargo of printing machinery on board the *Hornbay*. The cargo was shipped on board at Hamburg for delivery in Cartagena, Colombia. Due to bad weather it was necessary to land the goods at Le Havre where they were found to be a constructive total loss. The bill of lading provided for English law and the exclusive jurisdiction of the High Court in London. The bill of lading also expressly incorporated the Hague-Visby Rules and a Himalaya Clause.

The second defendants were the cargo insurers, ACE, who had procured proceedings to be issued in Colombia against Maritrans, the claimants' agents in Colombia, seeking judgment for the full value of the cargo. The claim was founded upon the contract of carriage and provisions of the Colombian Code of Commerce which the defendants argued imposed liability on Maritrans as agent of the shipowners. The defendants challenged the jurisdiction of the English court in the proceedings for a negative declaration brought by the claimants contemporaneously with the commencement of the Colombian proceedings. The claimants sought an anti-suit injunction against the defendants in respect of the Colombian proceedings. The commercial significance of the dispute on jurisdiction was that, if it remained in England, the cargo interests would be likely to recover nothing because of the one-year time bar. Morison J held that there was no exceptional reason why the English court would not exercise the jurisdiction conferred on it and granted an anti-suit injunction. He joined ACE as a necessary and proper party to the proceedings pursuant to CPR 6.20(3)(c) and (d), as an injunction against them would be more effective than against the first defendants alone. The claimants were also permitted to join Maritrans as a party and to amend their claim for a negative injunction to plead the time bar point.

The English court will also uphold a foreign jurisdiction clause in favour of the courts of Mexico or Singapore under the Choice of Court Convention.[352] It will also do so for a foreign jurisdiction clause which falls outside the scope of the Choice of Court Convention, such as a choice of Singapore jurisdiction in a bill of lading, or a foreign jurisdiction clause in favour of the courts of any non-EU Member State or non-Lugano Contracting State other than Mexico or Singapore, such as China, unless there is strong cause not to, for example, because there are multiple proceedings already in existence in England.[353] This assumes the jurisdiction agreement is valid. It will not be if the English court would apply the Hague-Visby Rules[354] and the effect of the jurisdiction clause would be to lessen the carrier's liability. Thus in *The Morviken*[355] the House of Lords held that an Amsterdam court jurisdiction clause was null and void and of no effect in accordance with Article III rule 8 of the Hague-Visby Rules, which applied mandatorily in that case. The Amsterdam court would have applied lower limits than the English court. A forum clause would not always be invalid but would depend on the type of claim brought. For example, a claim by the carrier for freight would not be affected by the Hague-Visby Rules. In

349. See pages 49–51 of this chapter.

350. *OT Africa Line Ltd v Magic Sportswear Corp* [2007] 1 Lloyd's Rep 85.

351. [2006] EWHC 373 (Comm); [2006] 2 Lloyd's Rep 44. See also *Aline Tramp SA v Jordan International Insurance Company* [2016] EWHC 1317; [2017] 1 Lloyd's Rep Plus 27.

352. See pages 16–17.

353. See, e.g. *Citi-March Ltd v Neptune Orient Lines Ltd* [1996] 2 All ER 545; [1997] 1 Lloyd's Rep 72 and *The MC Pearl* [1997] 1 Lloyd's Rep 566; *obiter Konkola Copper Mines Plc v Coromin* [2006] EWCA Civ 5; [2006] 1 Lloyd's Rep 410 and *Gaskell*, [20.213] – [20.219].

354. As to when the Hague-Visby Rules apply see pages 63–64 of this chapter and Chapter 5 pages 200–201.

355. [1983] 1 AC 565. See page 63 of this chapter.

The Benarty[356] the Court of Appeal gave a stay on the basis of an exclusive jurisdiction clause in favour of the court of Djakarta unless the carrier elected otherwise, on the ground that the carrier sought the benefit of lower tonnage limitation in Indonesia and not lower package limitation, a situation expressly permitted by Article VIII of the Hague-Visby Rules. In that case the defendants had given an undertaking not to rely on the lower package limits applicable in Indonesia. Lord Ackner gave the practice of giving such an undertaking his approval.[357] In *Baghlaf Al Zafer Factory Co v Pakistan National Shipping Co*[358] the shipowners gave an undertaking that they would not rely on the lower limits applicable in Pakistan where the Hague Rules apply and the limit is £100 sterling per package rather than £100 gold value. Had they not done so, Phillips LJ, with whom the other members of the Court of Appeal agreed, said that any application to stay English proceedings where there was an exclusive Pakistan jurisdiction agreement would have been doomed to failure, as the jurisdiction agreement would have had no effect.[359] Subsequently it transpired that it might not be possible to waive the time bar under Pakistani legislation and therefore the English Court of Appeal lifted the stay.[360]

(iii) Tonnage limitation

As we have already seen, a major cause of forum shopping is where a claimant in a maritime incident prefers one jurisdiction rather than another due to the differences in the tonnage limits applicable.[361] There is not a level playing field internationally in relation to tonnage limits. Some States give effect to the 1996 Protocol to the 1976 LLMC with high limits but which may be difficult to break, whereas other States give effect to the 1957 Limitation Convention with lower limits but which may be easier to break.[362]

The English courts have held that where proceedings have been commenced elsewhere first and then in England and the other forum is the natural or appropriate forum, the English court should stay its proceedings in favour of the natural forum, even though that forum will apply the 1957 Limitation Convention, rather than the 1976 LLMC which would have been applied in England. In *The Herceg Novi and Ming Galaxy*[363] the *Herceg Novi* and the *Ming Galaxy* were involved in a collision in the Straits of Singapore. Two days after the collision the Taiwanese owners of the *Ming Galaxy* commenced proceedings in Singapore. They subsequently sought to limit their liability. The writ *in rem* was served by fixing it to the mast of the *Herceg Novi* where she had sunk inside Singapore waters. Ten days after the collision the Maltese owners of the *Herceg Novi* issued a writ *in rem* against the *Ming Galaxy* which was served on a sister ship, the *Ming South*, two days later at Felixstowe. The claims by the owners of the *Herceg Novi* amounted to US$10,353,000, but they could not recover that in either Singapore, where the 1957 Limitation Convention applied,[364] or England, where the 1976 LLMC applied, as there was no suggestion that the limit could be broken under either Convention. The *Ming Galaxy*'s limit in

356. [1984] 2 Lloyd's Rep 244.
357. Ibid., at p 249.
358. [1998] 2 Lloyd's Rep 229, and see J Edwards, "Exclusive Jurisdiction Clauses and Forum Non Conveniens" [1998] IJOSL 193. See also *Pirelli Cables Ltd v United Thai Shipping Corporation Ltd* [2001] CP Rep 7; [2000] 1 Lloyd's Rep 663 (Langley J).
359. Ibid., at p 238.
360. *Baghlaf Al Zafer Factory Co v Pakistan National Shipping Co (No 2)* [2000] 1 Lloyd's Rep 1.
361. On tonnage limitation see pages 3, 26–27 and 29–30 of this chapter and Chapter 7 pages 284–310.
362. See J. Hare, "Shopping for the Best Admiralty Bargain" Chapter 5 in M. Davies (ed.), *Jurisdiction and Forum Selection in International Maritime Law Essays in Honor of Robert Force* (Kluwer Law International 2005); P. Griggs, R. Williams and J. Farr, *Limitation of Liability for Maritime Claims* (4th edn, LLP 2005); N. Meeson (fn 306).
363. [1998] 2 Lloyd's Rep 454.
364. Singapore now gives effect to the 1976 LLMC but not the 1996 Protocol.

England was US$5,800,000, whereas it was US$2,900,000 in Singapore. In addition, the *Herceg Novi* cargo owners had claims of US$4,000,000. Thus the owners of the *Herceg Novi* had every reason to want the English court to determine limitation. The *Ming Galaxy's* claim did not exceed the limit of the *Herceg Novi* under either convention, but they obviously preferred the issue of limitation to be resolved in Singapore to minimise their liability. They applied for a stay of the English proceedings.

The Court of Appeal gave an unconditional stay of the English action. Sir Christopher Staughton, giving the judgment of the court, said that it was accepted that England was not the natural or appropriate forum. Singapore was clearly and distinctly a more appropriate forum than England. Therefore there ought to be a stay of the English action unless that course would deprive the owners of the *Herceg Novi* of some juridical advantage so as to justify the refusal of a stay. The Court of Appeal did not accept that there was a juridical advantage for three reasons. First, the 1976 LLMC has not received universal acceptance and thus is not "an internationally sanctioned and objective view of where substantial justice is now viewed as lying". Second the IMO is not a legislature and cannot be found to have enacted an international consensus. Lastly it is quite impossible to say that substantial justice is not available in Singapore. The preference for the 1976 LLMC has no greater justification than for the 1957 regime.

Bouygues Offshore SA v Caspian Shipping Co[365] concerned multiple parties, two of whom had agreed English jurisdiction and governing law. The Court of Appeal stayed the English proceedings on liability in favour of South Africa where the court had jurisdiction over all the parties, but refused a stay of the limitation actions in England and in this way gave effect to the English jurisdiction agreement. The difference between the two jurisdictions was acute as the whole of the claim for £50 million might be recovered in South Africa which applied the 1957 Limitation Convention with lower limits but which are easier to break, whereas the limit in England was one-hundredth of the amount of the claim.

In *Seismic Shipping Inc v Total E&P UK PLC (The Western Regent)*[366] the Court of Appeal has held that the 1976 LLMC does not require liability proceedings to have been commenced in England before the shipowner can invoke limitation.

(d) Anti-suit injunctions

The English court has a discretion to grant an anti-suit injunction to restrain a party from commencing or continuing proceedings in a foreign court if it would be just and convenient to do so under section 37 of the Senior Courts Act 1981.[367] It is important to stress that the injunction restrains the defendant to the English court proceedings and not the foreign court.[368] Nevertheless the foreign court may take the view that such an order is an interference with its sovereignty,[369] and the European Court of Justice held in *Turner v Grovit*[370] that an anti-suit injunction should not be granted to restrain a defendant from pursuing proceedings in another EU Member State as there should be mutual trust between all the EU Member States. Furthermore as a result

---

365. [1998] 2 Lloyd's Rep 461.
366. [2005] 2 Lloyd's Rep 359. See Chapter 7, page 308.
367. Formerly the Supreme Court Act 1981 but renamed by the Constitutional Reform Act 2005, Schedule 1, para 1.
368. *Turner v Grovit and Others*, 2004 WL 5400365, House of Lords.
369. The Dusseldorf Court of Appeal held that an English anti-suit injunction could not be served on the ground that it was unconstitutional and interfered with its sovereignty: *Re the Enforcement of an English Anti-Suit Injunction* [1997] ILPr 320.
370. *Turner v Grovit*, C-159/02; EU:C:2004:228 [2004] ECR I-3565; [2005] 1 AC 101.

of the decision in *Erich Gasser*[371] an English court which is second seised where the Jurisdiction Regulation and its predecessors applied would have to stay its proceedings until the court first seised has declined jurisdiction and therefore could not grant an anti-suit injunction to enforce an English jurisdiction agreement if the court first seised is within an EU Member State. In theory an anti-suit injunction should not be necessary where the Recast Jurisdiction Regulation applies as the court chosen does not have to stay its proceedings and the courts of any other EU Member State must stay its proceedings even if it is first seised as a result of Article 31(2).

However, the use of anti-suit injunctions to restrain a defendant from pursuing proceedings in a court of a non-EU Member State is permissible.[372] Different considerations apply where there is no mutual agreement as to jurisdiction between two States.[373] The House of Lords stated in *Donohue v Armco*[374] that the English court will usually exercise its discretion and grant an anti-suit injunction to enforce a jurisdiction agreement unless the party suing in the non-contractual forum can show that there is strong reason for suing in that forum.[375] However, in that case an anti-suit injunction was not granted to enforce an exclusive English jurisdiction clause as there were already proceedings between multiple parties in New York, some of whom were not bound by the English jurisdiction agreement.[376]

Where there is no choice of jurisdiction the court will grant an anti-suit injunction where the ends of justice require it and in general two conditions must be satisfied: the English court must be the natural forum for the resolution of the dispute and the conduct of the defendant must be vexatious, oppressive or unconscionable.[377]

The injunction will be served with a penal notice and if the injunction is ignored the party will be in contempt of court. In *Compania Sud Americana de Vapores SA v Hin-Pro Logistics International Ltd*[378] the English court held that Hin-Pro and their director, Miss Sui Wei, were

---

371. *Erich Gasser GmbH v MISAT SRL*, C-116/02, EU:C:2003:657 [2003] ECR I-14693; [2005] QB 1 applied in *Starlight Shipping Co v Allianz Marine & Aviation Versicherungs AG (The Alexandros T)* [2013] UKSC 70; [2014] 1 Lloyd's Rep 223.

372. See e.g. *Compania Sud Americana de Vapores SA v Hin-Pro Logistics International Ltd* [2015] EWCA Civ 401; [2015] 2 Lloyd's Rep 1; [2014] EWHC 3632 (Comm); [2015] 1 Lloyd's Rep 301; *OT Africa Line Ltd v Magic Sportswear Corp* [2005] EWCA 710; [2005] 2 Lloyd's Rep 170 and *Horn Linie GmbH & Co v Panamericana Formas E Impresos SA, Ace Seguros SA (The Hornbay)* [2006] EWHC 373 (Comm); [2006] 2 Lloyd's Rep 44, all bill of lading cases, the latter two discussed on pages 46–47 of this chapter.

373. See e.g. A. Briggs, "Anti-Suit Injunctions in a Complex World" Chapter 12 in F. Rose (ed.), *Lex Mercatoria, Essays on International Commercial Law in Honour of Francis Reynolds* (LLP 2000).

374. [2001] UKHL 64; [2002] 1 Lloyd's Rep 425.

375. See e.g. [24] (Lord Bingham). See also *Impala Warehousing and Logistics (Shanghai) Co Ltd v Wanxiang Resources (Singapore) Pte Ltd* [2015] EWHC 811 (Comm); [2015] 2 All ER (Comm) 234 [60] and [107] – [143]; *Compania Sud Americana De Vapores SA v Hin-Pro International Logistics Ltd* [2015] EWCA Civ 401; [2014] EWHC 3632 (Comm). Applying the same principles, the Court of Appeal (Guernsey) held that it may also grant an anti-anti-suit injunction – *Carlyle Capital Corp Ltd (In Liquidation) v Conway* [2013] 2 Lloyd's Rep 179 (Court of Appeal (Guernsey)).

376. See also *Bouygues Offshore SA v Caspian Shipping Co* [1998] 2 Lloyd's Rep 461.

377. *Societe Nationale Industrielle Aerienne v Lee Kui Jak* [1987] 1 AC 871; *Star Reefers Pooling Inc v JFC Group Co Ltd* [2012] EWCA Civ 14; [2012] 1 CLC 294; *Navig8Pte Ltd v Al-Riyadh Co for Vegetable Oil Industry (The Lucky Lady)* [2013] EWHC 328 (Comm); [2013] 2 Lloyd's Rep 104; *SwissMarine Group Ltd v OW Supply and Trading AS (In Bankruptcy)* [2005] EWHC 1571 (Comm); [2016] 1 All ER (Comm) 1144; and *Axa Corporate Solutions Assurance SA v Weir Services Australia Pty Ltd* [2016] EWHC 904 (Comm); [2016] Lloyd's Rep IR 578 where there was no jurisdiction clause in a global insurance policy but it was governed by English law. The court declined to grant an anti-suit injunction to restrain the insured from pursuing an indemnity claim in Australia. It considered the issue of Australian proceedings was a legitimate tactical step and did not amount to unconscionable conduct. In *Magellan Spirit ApS v Vitol SA* [2016] EWHC 454 (Comm); [2016] 2 Lloyd's Rep 1 it was held that the charterer did not act as agent for the trader, Vitol SA, as undisclosed principal. Therefore Vitol SA was not bound by the jurisdiction clause in the charterparty. Even if it had been, an anti-suit injunction would not have been granted on the grounds of delay (see fn 68 for cases in which an anti-suit injunction to restrain a breach of an arbitration clause has been refused due to delay).

378. [2015] EWCA Civ 401; [2015] 2 Lloyd's Rep 1; [2014] EWHC 3632 (Comm); [2015] 1 Lloyd's Rep 301.

in contempt of court as they were in breach of an anti-suit injunction restraining them from pursuing proceedings in China in breach of an exclusive English jurisdiction clause. Miss Wei was sentenced to imprisonment for three months and permission was given for writs of sequestration to be issued against Hin-Pro. The effectiveness of such sanctions may depend on whether the director ever comes to England.

(e) Damages for breach of a jurisdiction agreement

Where the common law rules apply, a party to an exclusive jurisdiction agreement which has been breached may be able to recover damages for breach of contract[379] or for the tort of procuring a breach of contract.[380]

The English courts will also grant damages for breach of an English jurisdiction agreement where the other proceedings are in the courts of an EU Member State.[381] Where the other proceedings are in the courts of another EU Member State it has been suggested that to grant damages for breach of an English jurisdiction agreement where the Jurisdiction Regulation applied was an inappropriate means of getting around the ban on anti-suit injunctions which are contrary to the principle of mutual trust.[382] The English court has, however, dismissed that argument in *Barclays Bank plc v Ente Nazionale Di Previdenza Ed Assistenza Dei Medici e Degli Odontoiatri*.[383]

A party may recover indemnity costs where the other party has acted in breach of a jurisdiction clause, an arbitration clause or an anti-suit injunction.[384]

4. GOVERNING LAW

Our purpose in this section is to consider how the governing law of obligations in maritime disputes is determined. Following the harmonisation of the rules as to when a court of an EU Member State had jurisdiction, the rules as to how such a court should determine what law governs a contractual or non-contractual obligation were also harmonised. The starting point is to characterise the obligation as either contractual or non-contractual as this will dictate which set of rules applies. Thus if the obligation is contractual and the contract was as from 17 December 2009,

---

379. *Union Discount Co v Zoller* [2002] 1 WLR 1517; *Donohue v Armco Inc* [2001] UKHL 64; [2002] 1 Lloyd's Rep 425, [36], [48] and [75]; and *Compania Sud Americana de Vapores SA v Hin-Pro Logistics International Ltd* [2015] EWCA Civ 401; [2015] 2 Lloyd's Rep 1; [2014] EWHC 3632 (Comm); [2015] 1 Lloyd's Rep 301.

380. See *Horn Linie GmbH & Co v Panamericana Formas E Impresos SA Ace Seguros SA (The Hornbay)* [2006] EWHC 373 (Comm); [2006] 2 Lloyd's Rep 44, [26] (Morison J).

381. *Starlight Shipping Co v Allianz Marine & Aviation Versicherungs AG (The Alexandros T)* [2014] EWCA Civ 1010 upholding the decision of Burton J at first instance – [2011] EWHC 3381(Comm); [2012] 1 Lloyd's Rep 162. The decision of the Court of Appeal was applied in *Starlight Shipping Company v Allianz Marine and Aviation Versicherungs AG (The Alexandros T) (No 3)* [2014] EWHC 3068 (Comm); [2015] 2 All ER (Comm) 747; *Barclays Bank plc v Ente Nazionale Di Previdenza Ed Assistenza Dei Medici e Degli Odontoiatri* [2015] EWHC 2857; [2015] 2 Lloyd's Rep 527 which was upheld by the Court of Appeal – [2016] EWCA Civ 1261.

382. See eg. A Dickinson, "Once bitten – mutual distrust in European private international law" [2015] LQR 186.

383. [2015] EWHC 2857; [2015] 2 Lloyd's Rep 527. [2016] EWCA Civ 1261.

384. *Kyrgyz Mobil v Fellowes International* [2005] EWHC 1314 (Comm) (London arbitration agreement); *Travelers Casualty and Surety Company of Canada v Sun Life Assurance Company of Canada (UK) Ltd* [2006] EWHC 2885 (Comm); *A v B (No 2)* [2007] EWHC 54 (Comm), [2007] 1 Lloyd's Rep 358 (Swiss arbitration subject to the jurisdiction of the Swiss courts); *National Westminster Bank v Rabobank Nederland RV* [2007] EWHC 1742 (Comm) (breach of jurisdiction clause and anti-suit clause), but not in *C v D* [2007] EWCA Civ 1282; [2008] 1 Lloyd's Rep 239.

Regulation (EC) No 593/2008 on the law applicable to contractual obligations (Rome I)[385] will apply, provided no exception applies. If, however, the contract was concluded before 17 December 2009, the Convention on the Law Applicable to Contractual Obligations of 1980 (the "Rome Convention")[386] will apply, provided no exception applies. Where the contract is for a lengthy period, e.g. a contract was entered into in 1996 but is still continuing, the Rome Convention will apply, unless on or after 17 December 2009 the contract was subject to an agreed variation of such magnitude that it gave rise to the creation of a new legal relationship.[387] Alternatively as the general time limit applicable to a contractual claim under English law is six years from the date of the breach of contract, subject to any shorter time limits expressly agreed or imposed, e.g. by a Convention, the Rome Convention may still apply to any claim brought on a contract concluded before 17 December 2009. Rome I follows the same pattern as the Rome Convention but has some differences. This chapter will therefore focus on the main provisions of Rome I that are relevant to maritime contracts. It may be assumed that the provisions of the Rome Convention are similar unless a difference is highlighted in the footnotes.

Where the obligation in question is non-contractual because, for example, it is a tort claim in relation to a collision, neither Rome I nor the Rome Convention will apply but Regulation (EC) No 864/2007 on the law applicable to non-contractual obligations (Rome II)[388] may. In *Homawoo v GMF Assurance SA & Ors*[389] the European Court of Justice held that Rome II applies to events giving rise to damage occurring after 11 January 2009. The date on which the proceedings seeking compensation for damage were brought or the date on which the applicable law is determined are not relevant to the issue of when Rome II applies. If the events giving rise to damage occurred before 11 January 2009, sections 9 to 15 of the Private International Law (Miscellaneous Provisions Act) 1995[390] may apply. As claims can still be brought in relation to events giving rise to damage before 11 January 2009 as the time bar for tort claims is usually six years from the date the damage occurred, the 1995 Act will be considered very briefly after Rome II.

Recital 7 of Rome I provides that the substantive scope and the provisions of Rome I should be consistent with the Jurisdiction Regulation and Rome II.[391] Both Rome I and Rome II provide

385. Rome I came into force on 17 December 2009 in all EU Member States, except Denmark, and applies to contracts concluded as from 17 December 2009 (art 28 as amended). The United Kingdom opted in to Rome I.

386. Section 2 of the Contracts (Applicable Law) Act 1990 gives the force of law to the Rome Convention, as amended by subsequent accession conventions, with the exception of Articles 7(1) and 10(1)(e). It came into force on 1 April 1991.

387. *Republik Griechenland v Nikiforidis* C-135/15, EU:C:2016:774.

388. See generally A. Dickinson, *The Rome II Regulation: The Law Applicable to Non Contractual Obligations* (Oxford University Press 2008) and Supplement thereto.

389. C-412/10, EU:C:2011:747 [2011] ECR I-11603.

390. Which entered into force on 1 May 1996.

391. There is no such provision in the Rome Convention which preceded the Jurisdiction Regulation and Rome II. Section 3(1) of the Contracts (Applicable Law) Act 1990 provides that any question as to the meaning or effect of any provision of the Conventions set out in the Schedules to the Act shall be referred to the European Court of Justice in accordance with the Brussels Protocol or determined in accordance with the principles laid down by, and any relevant decision of, the European Court. Although the Rome Convention has been in force since April 1, 1991, the First Protocol of December 19, 1988 on the interpretation of the European Communities of the Rome Convention did not come into force until August 1, 2004. Therefore although the European Court of Justice has referred to the Rome Convention when interpreting other conventions and regulations, it did not consider the Rome Convention itself until its judgment in *Intercontainer Interfrigo SC (ICF) v Balkenende Oosthuisen BV, MIC Operations BV*, C-133/08, EU:C:2009:617. In addition the report on the Rome Convention by Professor Mario Giuliano and Professor Paul Lagarde which is reproduced in the Official Journal of the Communities of October 31, 1980 may be considered in ascertaining the meaning or effect of any provision of the Convention. Article 18 of the Convention further provides that in the interpretation of the rules of the Convention regard shall be had to their international character and to the desirability of achieving uniformity in their interpretation and application. In interpreting the Rome Convention the European Court of Justice has had regard to the provisions of Rome I in support of its interpretation – *Heiko Koelsch v Etat du Grand-Duche de Luxembourg*, C-29/10; EU:C:2011:151 [46].

for "provisions which cannot be derogated from by agreement", "overriding mandatory provisions", international conventions, Community law and public policy.

Although it is usual for maritime contracts such as charterparties, bills of lading and marine insurance contracts, to contain an express jurisdiction and governing law clause or for a bill of lading to incorporate the jurisdiction and governing law clause contained in any charterparty pursuant to which the bill of lading has been issued, this is not always the case. Furthermore, even where there is an express clause, as we shall see, the parties' choice may be subject to restrictions. Where there is no choice we need to consider what guidelines are available to determine the governing law.

The governing law chosen is usually, but not always,[392] the law of the place that the parties have chosen to have jurisdiction. Thus where, for example, a bill of lading provides for jurisdiction in the country of the carrier's principal place of business, it will also usually provide for the law of this country to apply. This is simply for the common sense reason that a tribunal is best placed to adjudicate on its own law with which it is familiar, rather than on a foreign law. It is much quicker and cheaper for the High Court in London to apply English law than to hear evidence from foreign lawyers on the law of another country and then determine that law. Proper law and jurisdiction may therefore be inextricably linked. An express choice of jurisdiction may indicate the parties' choice of governing law. However, if the parties have chosen English court jurisdiction and the English courts determine that Italian law applies, they will apply Italian law.

(a) Rome I

(i) The scope of Rome I

Article 1(1) of Rome I provides that it applies "in situations involving a conflict of laws, to contractual obligations in civil and commercial matters".[393] Rome I only applies to contractual obligations.[394] Whether a contractual obligation is involved raises similar issues in other contexts such as whether a claim relates to a contract in Article 7(1) of the Recast Jurisdiction Regulation or the Regulations on Unfair Terms in Consumer Contracts and case law in those contexts may assist here.

Any contract concluded on or after 17 December 2009 which involves "a conflict of laws" will be subject to Rome I, unless it is specifically excluded. Many maritime contracts involve such a conflict. For example, bills of lading do so in a peculiarly acute form. This is because the number of different laws which could be involved may be considerable: the nationality of the carrier, shipper, consignee or indorsee, the flag of the ship, the place of loading and discharge, the governing law of any charterparty under which the bill of lading has been issued and any governing law chosen by the parties may all be different. Reinsurance contracts similarly may also involve many different laws, for example, because of the different nationalities of the reinsurer, reinsured and primary insured, the risks may be situated in many different countries, the governing law of the primary insurance and the choice of law of the reinsurance policy may all be different.

---

392. See e.g. the Bermuda Form for liability insurance which provides for London arbitration and New York law which was considered in *C v D* [2007] EWCA Civ 1282; [2008] 1 Lloyd's Rep 239.

393. Article 1 of the Rome Convention is slightly differently worded and refers to "any situation involving a choice between the laws of different countries".

394. *Base Metal Trading Ltd v Shamurin* [2002] CLC 322. See also *Committeri v Club Mediterranee SA* [2016] EWHC 1510; *Pan Oceanic Chartering Inc v UNIPEC UK Ltd* [2016] EWHC 2774 (Comm).

The application of Rome I is not limited to contracts which have some connection with an EU Member State. In this respect Rome I may be contrasted with the Recast Jurisdiction Regulation, the application of which is generally triggered by the domicile of the defendant in an EU Member State or the choice of the courts of an EU Member State. Rome I will apply to a contractual obligation within its scope which comes before the court of an EU Member State provided it involves a conflict of laws i.e. of any laws and not simply those of EU Member States. Thus, for example, if the English court has to determine whether Japanese or New York law applies to a charterparty it will apply Rome I.

Article 1(2) of Rome I excludes certain obligations from its scope. These include "obligations arising under bills of exchange, cheques and promissory notes and other negotiable instruments to the extent that the obligations under such other negotiable instruments arise out of their negotiable character".[395] The main reason for this exclusion is that many EU Member States, although not the UK, are parties to the Geneva Conventions which deal with these matters. It was not clear under the Rome Convention whether this exclusion included bills of lading but Recital 9 of Rome I clarifies that the exclusion covers obligations under "bills of lading to the extent that the obligations under the bill of lading arise out of its negotiable character". It is clear that Rome I applies to the obligations between the original parties to the contract, the carrier and the shipper as the obligations under the bill of lading between the original parties to the bill of lading do not "arise out of its negotiable character". For example, where the shipper, who is not the charterer, sues the carrier on a bill of lading contract dated 1 October 2010, Rome I applies. Where the shipper is the charterer, the contract of carriage is usually the charterparty,[396] unless the bill of lading supersedes the charterparty which is rare, and Rome I would apply to the charterparty. What still remains unclear is whether the exclusion should be given a wide interpretation[397] and the bill of lading is not covered by Rome I in all cases where the bill comes into the hands of a third party or there should be a narrower interpretation so that only proprietary obligations are excluded.[398] In the case of the wider interpretation, where the bill of lading is negotiable as it is an order bill[399] or a bearer bill, Rome I will not apply as the obligations under it "arise out of their negotiable character". Where, however, the bill of lading is a straight bill of lading as it is made out to a named consignee, the bill of lading is not negotiable although it may well be transferred by the shipper (who may be the seller) to the consignee (who may be the buyer)[400] in exchange for payment where the sale contract or the letter of credit so requires. Moreover, the terms of the straight bill of lading may well require it to be presented to the carrier in order to obtain delivery of

---

395. Rome I art 1(2)(d) and Rome Convention art 1(2)(c).

396. See pages 208–209.

397. See the view of H. Boonk, "Determining jurisdiction and choice of law in contractual disputes coupled with property-related claims" [2011] LMCLQ 227 at 231–232.

398. See the view of Professor Erik Rosaeg that bills of lading are only excluded where the issue is a proprietary one as opposed to a contractual one – see his paper at the Colloquium on Maritime Conflict of Laws held at Southampton, 2010. In the Giuliano Lagarde Report No C 282/11 it is stated that "certain Member States of the Community regard these obligations [arising from bills of exchange, cheques, promissory notes] as non-contractual".

399. In *Parsons Corp v CV Scheepvaartonderneming "Happy Ranger" (The Happy Ranger)* [2002] EWCA Civ 694; [2002] 2 Lloyd's Rep 357 the Court of Appeal held that the bill of lading issued was a document of title within art 1(b) of the Hague-Visby Rules as, although only a named consignee appeared in the consignee box, the printed words on the front of the bill referred to delivery of the goods to the "consignee or to his or their assigns". Read together, this made the bill of lading transferable and not a straight bill of lading.

400. In *Welex AG v Rosa Maritime Ltd (The Epsilon Rosa)* discussed at page 8 Steel J and the Court of Appeal applied the Rome Convention to the contract between the carrier and the consignee. See also *Caresse Navigation Ltd v Office National de L'Electricite (The Channel Ranger)* [2014] EWCA Civ 1366; [2015] 1 Lloyd's Rep 256; [2013] EWHC 3081; [2014] 1 Lloyd's Rep 337.

the cargo.[401] Do the obligations of the carrier to the named consignee under the bill of lading arise out of its negotiable character? It might seem odd if Rome I does not apply to some third parties but does to others.

In *Caresse Navigation Ltd v Office National de L'Electricite (The Channel Ranger)*[402] Males J applied Article 3 of Rome I to a negotiable bill of lading between the original parties to the bill of lading, the carrier and the shipper,[403] and then said that there was "no reason why this common form bill of lading should not be transferred to a consignee who (upon becoming a holder of the bill) would succeed to the rights contained therein, which rights were subject to English law".[404] This is very similar to the two-stage approach applied to jurisdiction clauses in bills of lading by the European Court of Justice in *Castelletti*[405] and *Coreck Maritime*.[406] First it must be determined whether the jurisdiction clause satisfies the formalities as between the original parties and then, if it does, national law applies to determine whether a third party is bound by the clause.

By Article 1(2)(e) of Rome I[407] the rules of Rome I do not apply to arbitration agreements and agreements on the choice of court. The reason for this exclusion is that such agreements are subject to other international conventions such as the New York Convention, and Article 25 of the Recast Jurisdiction Regulation.[408] It is necessary to distinguish the governing law of the underlying contract and the arbitration agreement which is a separable and separate agreement.[409] Although the law of the underlying contract, the arbitration agreement and the law of the place where the arbitration is to be conducted will often be the same, they may not be. A contract may be governed by one law but the arbitration governed by a different law. It would be rare for the law of the arbitration agreement and of the seat of the arbitration to be different. However, in *C v D*[410] an insurance policy provided for London arbitration and was governed by New York law. The parties had further agreed that the seat of the arbitration was London and the law of the arbitration was English law. The US insurer applied to the arbitration tribunal to correct its award alleging that the award was manifestly in disregard of New York law and it threatened to commence proceedings in a US Federal Court. The Court of Appeal upheld the anti-suit injunction granted by Cooke J. By choosing London as the seat of the arbitration, the parties must be taken to have agreed that proceedings on the award should be only those permitted by English law. Proceedings in a US Federal Court would negate the whole framework in which the arbitration took place and was vexatious and oppressive, unconscionable and an abuse of process.[411] As the arbitration provision expressly referred to English law and the Arbitration Act 1996 the parties

---

401. In *JI MacWilliam Co Inc v Mediterranean Shipping Co SA (The Rafaela S)* [2005] UKHL 11; [2005] 1 Lloyd's Rep 347 the House of Lords held that a straight bill of lading is a "similar document of title" and therefore the Hague-Visby Rules apply to it. The bill of lading in that case provided: "IN WITNESS whereof the number of Original Bills of Lading stated above [viz. three] all of this tenor and date, has been signed, one of which being accomplished, the others to stand void. One of the Bills of Lading must be surrendered duly endorsed in exchange for the goods or delivery order". However, Rix LJ in the Court of Appeal, at [145] and Lords Bingham and Steyn in the House of Lords, at [20] and [45] stated *obiter* that a straight bill of lading would be a document of title even if it contained no express provision requiring surrender. See also *Peer Voss v APL Co Pte Ltd* [2002] 2 Lloyd's Rep 707 Singapore Court of Appeal.
402. [2014] EWCA Civ 1366; [2015] 1 Lloyd's Rep 256; [2013] EWHC 3081; [2014] 1 Lloyd's Rep 337.
403. [33].
404. [36].
405. Fn 171.
406. Fn 172.
407. Rome Convention, art 1(2)(d).
408. Jurisdiction Regulation, art 23. See *Höszig Kft v Alstom Power Thermal Services* C-222/15, EU:C:2016:525 [50].
409. Arbitration Act 1996, s 7. See *Fiona Trust & Holding Corporation v Privalov* [2007] UKHL 40; [2008] 1 Lloyd's Rep 254.
410. [2007] EWCA Civ 1282; [2008] 1 Lloyd's Rep 239.
411. Applying *Noble Assurance Co v Gerling-Konzern General Insurance Co* [2007] EWHC 253 (Comm), [2007] 1 CLC 85.

had not only agreed to arbitration itself but also that any challenge to an award would only be made to the courts of the place agreed as the seat of the arbitration.[412] The choice of New York law as the governing law of the insurance policy did not mean that the parties had replaced the framework of the Arbitration Act 1996.[413]

Article 25(1) of the Recast Jurisdiction Regulation provides that the court chosen shall determine the substantive validity of a jurisdiction clause in accordance with the law of the EU Member State chosen in the jurisdiction agreement.[414] Where the English court has to consider the law applicable to determine the validity of a jurisdiction or arbitration agreement it will apply its national law.[415]

Article 1(2)(f) of Rome I[416] excludes matters governed by the law relating to such bodies including the creation, legal capacity, internal organisation or winding up of such bodies and the personal liability of officers and members for the obligations of such bodies.

Article 1(2)(g) of Rome I[417] excludes "the question whether an agent is able to bind a principal, or an organ to bind a company or body corporate, or unincorporate, to a third party".[418] Such an issue may arise in relation to bills of lading, e.g. whether a forwarding agent had actual or ostensible authority to sign a bill of lading on behalf of the carrier.

Article 1(2)(i) of Rome I[419] provides that "obligations arising out of dealings prior to the conclusion of a contract" are outside the scope of Rome I. The reason for this is that such obligations are within the scope of Article 12 of Rome II.[420]

Rome I consolidates the current rules on insurance and reinsurance contracts which are to be found in the Rome Convention[421] and the Insurance Directives in Article 7.[422] It can only be helpful to have all the rules in one instrument. The substance of the law remains the same. Thus under Article 7(2) of Rome I the parties can choose the law applicable to marine insurance,

412. Applying *A v B* [2006] EWHC 2006 (Comm), [2007] 1 Lloyd's Rep 237 and *A v B (No 2)* [2007] EWHC 54 (Comm), [2007] 1 Lloyd's Rep 358.

413. Applying *XL Insurance Ltd v Owens Corning* [2000] 2 Lloyd's Rep 500.

414. There is no equivalent provision in the Jurisdiction Regulation.

415. See *Sul America Cia Nacional De Seguros SA v Enesa Engenharia SA* [2012] EWCA Civ 638; [2012] 1 Lloyd's Rep 671; *Arsanovia Ltd v Cruz City 1 Mauritius Holdings* [2012] EWHC 3702; [2013] 2 All ER 1; *Habas Sinai Ve Tibbi Gazlar Istihsal Endustrisi AS v VSC Steel Company Ltd* [2013] EWHC 4071 (Comm); [2014] 1 Lloyd's Rep 479; *Beijing Jianlong Heavy Industry Group v Golden Ocean Group Ltd* [2013] EWHC 1063 (Comm); and *Mauritius Commercial Bank Ltd v Hestia Holdings Ltd* [2013] EWHC 1328 (Comm); [2013] 2 Lloyd's Rep 121.

416. Rome Convention, art 1(2)(e).

417. Rome Convention, art 1(2)(f).

418. The law applicable to determine whether an agent had actual or ostensible authority to bind Daehan Shipbuilding Company to two guarantees of two charterparties was considered in *Rimpacific Navigation Inc v Daehan Shipbuilding Co (The Jin Man and the Jin Pu)* [2010] 2 Lloyd's Rep 236 (Steel J); [2011] EWHC 2618 (Comm); [2010] 2 Lloyd's Rep 236 (Teare J). See also *Habas Sinai Ve Tibbi Gazlar Istihsal Endustri v VSC Steel Co Ltd* [2013] EWHC 4071; [2014] 1 Lloyd's Rep 479; and *Integral Petroleum SA v SCU-Finanz AG* [2015] EWCA Civ 144; [2015] 1 Lloyd's Rep 545.

419. There is no equivalent provision in the Rome Convention which preceded Rome II. It is a controversial question whether the Rome Convention covered pre-contractual obligations. It seems likely that the Court of Justice of the European Union would conclude that it does not in light of the case law of that court in relation to art 5(1) of the Jurisdiction Regulation – see page 33. Furthermore Rome II treats such obligations as non contractual – see Recital 30 and Article 12 of Rome II.

420. Discussed below at page 70.

421. The Rome Convention does not apply to "contracts of insurance which cover risks situated in the territories of the Member States of the European Economic Community" (article 1(3)). The English court must apply its own law in order to determine whether a risk is situated in these territories. The reason for this exclusion is that such risks are covered by the EC Second Directive on Non-Life Insurance which has its own special rules on governing law which are similar to those in the Rome Convention. Contracts of reinsurance are not covered by art 1(3) (art 1(4)).

422. For discussion of issues such as assignment of insurance, subrogation and direct action against a liability insurer see Y. Baatz, "Recent Developments in Party Choice of the Applicable Law and Jurisdiction in Marine Insurance and Reinsurance Contracts" in D.R. Thomas (gen. ed.), *The Modern Law of Marine Insurance, Volume 3* (Informa Law, 2009) and J Dunt, *Marine Cargo Insurance* (2nd ed, Informa Law, 2015), ch 2.

provided their choice is made expressly or clearly demonstrated by the terms of the contract or the circumstances of the case. If there is no choice, the insurance contract will be governed by the law of the country where the insurer has its habitual residence. Where it is clear from all the circumstances of the case that the contract is manifestly more closely connected with another country, the law of that other country shall apply.

(ii) Freedom of choice

Party autonomy is a fundamental principle of Rome I. Article 3(1)[423] provides that the contract is to be governed by the law chosen by the parties. Rome 1 provides that the parties must make their choice "expressly" or it must be "clearly demonstrated by the terms of the contract or the circumstances of the case". Thus if a charterparty expressly provides that English law is to govern the contract, that choice clearly falls within Article 3(1) and will be the applicable law, unless one of the restrictions dealt with below applies.

Standard form bills of lading are intended to be used by parties of any different nationality. They may therefore seek to retain a degree of flexibility rather than providing for any particular law to govern. Many, but not all, standard bill of lading forms are more advantageous to the carrier than to the consignee as they often provide for the jurisdiction and governing law to be that of the principal place of business of the carrier.[424] Thus the carrier will have the comfort of knowing that any disputes will be determined by the courts in its own country in accordance with the law of that country. Such a clause does demonstrate with reasonable certainty what the choice of law is, provided that the identity of the carrier and its principal place of business can be ascertained.[425]

If the contract contains no express choice of law provision the parties may still have clearly demonstrated their choice. Recital 12 of Rome I[426] states that, "An agreement of the parties to confer exclusive jurisdiction on one or more courts or tribunals of a Member State to determine disputes under the contract should be one of the factors to be taken into account in determining whether a choice of law was clearly demonstrated." This raises the question whether an exclusive jurisdiction agreement for the courts of a non-EU Member State, whether a Lugano Contracting State or not, or an arbitration clause should not be taken into account. It seems very unlikely that the English courts would not take such agreements into account, as where, for example, the parties have chosen a particular forum, such as London arbitration, it has been held that this does demonstrate with reasonable certainty that they wanted the law of that forum to govern the contract under the Rome Convention. In *Egon Oldendorff v Libera Corporation*[427] Clarke J had to consider whether the London arbitration clause in the charterparty on the NYPE form demonstrated with reasonable certainty that the parties had chosen English law within Article 3 of the Rome Convention. He also had to consider a Memorandum of Agreement in the Norwegian Sale Form to be attached to the charterparty which provided for arbitration in a city to be specified by the parties and the contract to be subject to the law of the country agreed as the place of arbitration. A footnote in the standard wording provided that if the line was not filled in, it was understood that arbitration would take place in London in accordance with English law.

---

423. Rome Convention, art 3(1). The wording of this provision differs very slightly as it provides that "The choice must be express or demonstrated with reasonable certainty by the terms of the contract or the circumstances of the case".

424. See e.g. Conlinebill, cl 3.

425. The facts of *The Rewia* [1991] 2 Lloyd's Rep 325 illustrate how difficulties may arise on both these issues.

426. There is no equivalent Recital in the Rome Convention but it is in the Giuliano and Lagarde Report at C-282/12 and 282/17.

427. [1996] 1 Lloyd's Rep 380.

The clause further provided for three arbitrators. Another footnote provided that if the parties did not complete who was to appoint the third arbitrator, the third would be appointed by the London Maritime Arbitrators' Association (LMAA) in London. It was held that there was no reason to disregard the footnotes and that therefore the parties had agreed London arbitration and that the Memorandum of Agreement was to be subject to English law as the country agreed as the place of arbitration.

Clarke J concluded that the parties had demonstrated their choice in the charterparty with reasonable certainty. On all the facts of the case, when set in the context of the terms of the contract as a whole and of the circumstances of the case, the arbitration clause was a strong indication of the parties' intention to choose English law as the applicable law as well as the curial law. Having agreed English arbitration for the determination in London of disputes arising out of a well-known English language form of charterparty which contains standard clauses with well-known meanings in English law, it was to be inferred that the parties intended that law to apply. Having agreed a neutral forum the reasonable inference is that the parties intended the forum to apply a "neutral" law, namely English law and not either German or Japanese law. The parties made a tacit choice of English law as the applicable law of both the charterparty and the Memorandum of Agreement which was not surprising as they undoubtedly chose English law in the case of the Memorandum of Agreement and it was an express term of their Agreement that the Memorandum of Agreement would be attached to the charterparty.

Clarke J accepted that the plaintiff's case would have been even stronger if the charterparty had contained wording similar to the Memorandum of Agreement providing for arbitration in London by LMAA arbitrators or London brokers or by a local association or exchange. The charterparty clause here simply provided that all arbitrators were to be conversant with shipping matters.

In *Martrade Shipping & Transport GmbH v United Enterprises Corporation (The Wisdom)*[428] Popplewell J held that the Late Payment of Commercial Debts (Interest) Act 1998 does not apply to a trip time charterparty of a Panamanian-registered vessel made between the owners, a Marshall Islands Company, and German charterers through Greek shipbrokers. The vessel was not going to trade to England and the hire was payable to a bank account in Greece. The Act imposes a penal rate for two purposes: to protect commercial suppliers whose financial position makes them particularly vulnerable if their debts are paid late and general deterrence of late payment of commercial debts. Section 12 of the Act provides that where parties to a contract with an international dimension have chosen English law to govern the contract, the choice of English law is not of itself sufficient to attract the application of the Act. There must be a significant connection between the contract and England (section 12(1)(a)); or the contract must be one which would be governed by English law apart from the choice of law (section 12(1)(b)). The fact that the contract contained a London arbitration clause which in turn would have meant that the contract was governed by English law[429] was not a relevant connecting factor. Nor was the fact that the contract was in English; adjustment of general average was in London in accordance with English law; the entry of the vessel in a P & I Club with London managers; the NYPE Interclub agreement provides that its governing law is to be that of the charterparty; or the fact that the standard for classification was set by Lloyd's Register and that basic war coverage was to be as defined by Lloyd's of London.

---

428. [2014] EWHC 1884 (Comm); [2014] 2 Lloyd's Rep 198 [27]–[30].
429. See *Egon Oldendorff* fn 427.

In *Gan Insurance Co Ltd v Tai Ping Insurance Co Ltd*[430] the Court of Appeal upheld the decision of Cresswell J that there was an implied choice of English law demonstrated with reasonable certainty by the terms of the contract which contained the clauses commonly used in the London market within Article 3 of the Rome Convention. Although the reinsurance slip stated "as original" it did not incorporate all the terms of the Taiwanese insurance policy including the Taiwanese choice of law clause, but only the provisions which defined the extent of the risk insured.

Where there is a connection between two contracts the fact that there is an express choice of law in one may demonstrate that there is an implied choice of that law in the other connected contract. Thus in *Star Reefers Pool Inc v JFC Group Co Ltd*[431] there were two charterparties between Star Reefers and Kalistad Ltd. JFC Group Co Ltd signed two guarantees of the performance of the charterparties. Teare J held that the circumstances of the case demonstrated that English law had been chosen as the law applicable to the guarantees. The circumstances were the very close connection between the charterers and the guarantor and the express choice of law in the charterparty. The judge rejected the argument that there was no implied law and that the applicable law was Russian which was the law with which the guarantee was most closely connected in that the party who was to effect the performance which is characteristic of the contract of guarantee was the guarantor whose central administration was in Russia under Article 4(2) of the Rome Convention.

A similar decision was reached by the Court of Appeal in *Golden Ocean Group Ltd v Salgaocar Mining Industries PVT Ltd*[432] where again a charterparty was governed by English law and by including a guarantee within the charterparty the parties had demonstrated with reasonable certainty a choice of English law to govern the guarantee under Article 3 of the Rome Convention. The proper law of the claim against the broker for breach of warranty of authority was also English law; the circumstances of the implied contract demonstrated with reasonable certainty a choice that it should be governed by the same law as the proposed principal contract to which it was ancillary. The same result could be achieved by application of Articles 4(1) and/or 4(5) of the Rome Convention.[433]

Some bills of lading specifically incorporate the choice of law clause in the charterparty pursuant to which the bill of lading is issued.[434] Recent case law indicates that general words of incorporation in a bill of lading will be sufficient to incorporate the governing law clause from a charterparty. In *Navig8Pte Ltd v Al-Riyadh Co for Vegetable Oil Industry (The Lucky Lady)*[435] Andrew Smith J held that the general words of incorporation in the bill of lading as follows,

This shipment is carried under and pursuant to the terms of the [subcharter] between [Navig8] as Owners and [the sellers] as charterers, and all conditions liberties and exceptions whatsoever of the said Charter apply to and govern the rights of the party concerned in this shipment gave Navig8 a sufficiently strong

---

430. [1999] CLC 1270.
431. [2010] EWHC 3003 (Comm) [13] – [15]. The case went to the Court of Appeal but this aspect was no longer in issue before that court – [2012] EWCA Civ 14; [2012] 1 Lloyd's Rep 376 [14] and [17]. See also *Emeraldian Wellmix Shipping* [2010] EWHC 1411, [170] and *Global Distressed Alpha Fund 1 Ltd Partnership v PT Bakrie Investindo* [2011] EWHC 256 (Comm).
432. [2012] EWCA 265, [42] – [45] affirming [2011] EWHC 56 (Comm); [2011] 1 WLR 2575 applied in *Alliance Bank JSC v Aquanta Corp* [2012] EWCA Civ 1588; [2013] 1 All ER (Comm) 819 and *Mitsui OSK Lines Ltd v Salgaocar Mining Industries Private Ltd (The Unta)* [2015] EWHC 565 (Comm); [2015] 2 Lloyd's Rep 518 [37].
433. Ibid., [49].
434. E.g. Congenbill 1994, Congenbill 2007, Congenbill 2016, Heavyconbill, HIBL and Orevoybill.
435. [2013] EWHC 328 (Comm); [2013] 2 All ER 145.

argument, on an application for permission to serve proceedings out of the jurisdiction on Jordanian receivers, that the bill of lading was governed by English law.[436]

If there is a dispute as to the validity of a contract or as to the validity of the choice of law clause, e.g. on the grounds that the incorporation is ineffective, Article 3(5) of Rome I[437] provides that the existence and validity of the consent of the parties as to the choice of the applicable law shall be determined in accordance with the provisions of Articles 10, 11 and 13.[438] Article 10(1) of Rome I[439] provides that the existence and validity of a contract, or of any term of a contract, shall be determined by the law which would govern it under Rome I if the contract or term were valid. Nevertheless, under Article 10(2)[440] in order to establish that it did not consent, a party may rely upon the law of the country in which it has its habitual residence to establish that it did not consent if it appears from the circumstances that it would not be reasonable to determine the effect of its conduct in accordance with the law specified in Article 10(1). Mance J considered both rules of Article 8 of the Rome Convention, the equivalent of Article 10 of Rome I in *Egon Oldendorff v Libera Corporation*.[441] There German charterers alleged that they had concluded a charterparty with Japanese owners. The latter argued that the agreement was subject to two conditions which had not been satisfied. One of those conditions was subject to details of a previously concluded fixture which provided for London arbitration. Mance J held that if the arbitration clause was validly incorporated, any contract which was validly made was subject to English law and not Japanese law. Therefore, English law applied to determine whether the subject details had been lifted. Even on the assumption in the Japanese owners' favour that Japanese law would have reached a different conclusion, Mance J held that they could not rely on Article 8(2). He thought that the onus must be on the party who sought to invoke Article 8(2) to negative consent, to bring himself within the provisions of that Article. Whether or not that was right, there were very strong grounds for regarding it as unreasonable to determine the effect of the owners' conduct on either the formation of a valid contract or the agreement on a valid arbitration clause in accordance with Japanese law. The natural implication of the London arbitration clause in the charterparty on which the negotiations were based was that English law governed. It would be contrary to ordinary commercial expectations to ignore that clause when everything suggested that the owners must have considered and accepted the clause and, even if they had not done so, should have done. Furthermore, the arbitration clause was precisely the sort of clause which they might have expected in such an international charterparty (indeed the charterparty form which the owners had originally proposed was amended to provide for London arbitration).

Similarly in *Welex AG v Rosa Maritime Ltd (The Epsilon Rosa)*[442] the Court of Appeal upheld the decision of Steel J that, assuming that English law was applicable under Article 8(1) of

436. See also *Caresse Navigation Ltd v Office National de L'Electricite (The Channel Ranger)* [2013] EWHC 3081, [2014] 1 Lloyd's Rep 337 [34], upheld on appeal – [2014] EWCA Civ 1366; [2015] 1 Lloyd's Rep 256, where Males J held that general words of incorporation were sufficient, applying *The Njegos* [1936] P 90 and *The San Nicholas* [1976] 1 Lloyd's Rep 8, although in that case there were specific words referring to the law and arbitration clause, and *The Dolphina* [2011] SGHC 273, a decision of the Singapore High Court. General words of incorporation cannot incorporate an arbitration clause – see page 8.
437. Rome Convention, art 3(4).
438. Rome Convention arts 8, 9 and 11.
439. Rome Convention, art 8(1).
440. Rome Convention, art 8(2).
441. [1995] 2 Lloyd's Rep 64. See also *Höszig Kft v Alstom Power Thermal Services* C-222/15, EU:C:2016:525.
442. [2003] EWCA Civ 938; [2003] 2 Lloyd's Rep 509; [2002] EWHC 762 (Comm). See also *Raiffeisen Zentralbank Osterreich Aktiengesellschaft v National Bank of Greece SA* [1999] 1 Lloyd's Rep 408, at pp 412 and 413 and *Horn Linie GmbH & Co v Panamericana Formas E Impresos SA, Ace Seguros SA (The Hornbay)* [2006] EWHC 373 (Comm); [2006] 2 Lloyd's Rep 44. On a letter of credit, see *Marconi v PT Pan Indonesia Bank Ltd TBK* [2004] 1 Lloyd's Rep 594.

the Rome Convention and applying that law, the arbitration clause referred to in an executed charterparty was incorporated into the bill of lading. In *Welex AG v Rosa Maritime Ltd (The Epsilon Rosa) (No 2)*[443] the claimant sought to rely on Ukrainian or Swiss law to establish it did not consent to incorporation by virtue of Article 8(2) of the Rome Convention. Steel J held that the burden was on Welex to displace the effect of Article 8(1). The shippers presented the Congenbill to the master for signature; it was not suggested that there was anything unreasonable in holding Welex to the contract of carriage as a whole; an arbitration clause was commonplace in contracts of this kind; in due course Welex succeeded to the shippers' rights and obligations; and there was nothing "eccentric" let alone unjust in the English law to hold that both shipper and consignee were bound by the terms of the dispute resolution clause. The transaction was an entirely conventional one, nothing in the circumstances rendered it unreasonable to determine the effect of Welex's conduct by reference to English law.

More recently in *Toyota Tsusho Sugar Trading Ltd v Prolat SRL*[444] Cooke J held that where the subject matter of the application to the English court was the existence or otherwise of an agreement to arbitrate as Prolat argued that it was not a party to such an agreement, English law as the putative proper law of the sale contract for sugar was the applicable law. Article 10(2) of Rome I did not apply.[445] Cooke J found that Mr Dibranco had both actual and ostensible authority to act on behalf of Prolat and to bind them to the sale contract containing the arbitration agreement.[446]

Article 3(1) of Rome I[447] provides that the parties can choose the law applicable to the whole or a part only of the contract.

Article 3(2) of Rome I provides that the parties may at any time agree to vary the law which previously governed the contract. Thus, for example, where the parties had already agreed that Italian law should govern the contract, they could at any time thereafter agree that the contract should be governed by English law. Similarly, if the contract did not contain any choice of law either express or demonstrated by reasonable certainty, the contract would have an applicable law which would fall to be determined in accordance with Rome I but the parties would be free to agree a new applicable law. There may be a floating proper law which is objectively ascertainable.[448]

(iii) Limits on party choice

Where Rome I applies, there are a number of limitations on the parties' freedom to choose the proper law. Articles 6, 7 and 8 of Rome I[449] have provisions on consumer, some insurance and individual employment contracts respectively but it is assumed for present purposes that these are not relevant. Article 3(3) provides for provisions which cannot be derogated from by agreement;[450] Article 3(4) for provisions of Community law which cannot be derogated from by agreement;[451] Article 9 for overriding mandatory provisions;[452] Article 21 for public policy of the

---

443. [2002] 2 Lloyd's Rep 701.
444. [2014] EWHC 3649 (Comm); [2015] 1 Lloyd's Rep 344.
445. Ibid., [18].
446. Ibid., [43] and [44].
447. Rome Convention, art 3(1). *Centrax Ltd v Citibank NA* [1999] 1 All ER (Comm) 557 (CA).
448. *Bhatia Shipping v Alcobex* [2004] EWHC 2323 (Comm); [2005] 2 Lloyd's Rep 336.
449. Rome Convention, arts 5 (certain consumer contracts), 6 (individual employment contracts) and 1(3) (contracts of insurance which cover risks situated in the territories of the Member States of the European Economic Community were excluded from the scope of the Rome Convention as such insurance contracts were governed by the Insurance Directives which gave protection to some insureds).
450. Art 3(3) of the Rome Convention differs in its wording but not its substance.
451. There is no equivalent provision in the Rome Convention.
452. Art 7 of the Rome Convention differs as discussed below.

forum;[453] Article 23 for conflict of laws rules in provisions of Community law[454] and Article 25 for conflict of law rules in international conventions.[455]

(iv) Provisions which cannot be derogated from by agreement in a domestic contract

Article 3(3) of Rome I deals with the situation where a contract is domestic as all the elements relevant to the situation are connected with country A,[456] save that the parties have provided for the law of country B. In that event provisions of the law of country A "which cannot be derogated from by agreement" cannot be prejudiced by the parties' choice of law. Recital 15 of Rome I states that the rule should apply whether or not the choice of law is accompanied by a choice of jurisdiction. The wording of Article 3(3) of Rome I is slightly different from Article 3(3) of the Rome Convention which refers to "rules of the law of that country which cannot be derogated from by contract, hereinafter called 'mandatory rules'". Recital 15 further provides that no substantial change was intended and the change of wording in the two provisions was to align this provision and Article 14 of Rome II.[457] However, Recital 37 of Rome I provides that the "concept of 'overriding mandatory provisions' should be distinguished from the expression 'provisions which cannot be derogated from by agreement' and should be construed more restrictively".

Article 3(3) will not apply to a contract for the international carriage of goods but could apply to purely coastal trade, e.g. from an English port to another English port on an English registered ship. Were the parties to provide for a foreign law which would apply the Hague Rules and a party brings a claim against the carrier in contract, the English court would be entitled to apply the Hague-Visby Rules as section 1(3) of the Carriage of Goods by Sea Act 1971 extends the application of the Hague-Visby Rules and gives them the force of law in relation to coastal trade where the port of shipment is a port in the United Kingdom, whether or not the carriage is between ports in two different States.

(v) Community law in a domestic contract

Article 3(4) of Rome I[458] provides that where all other elements relevant to the situation at the time of the choice are located in one or more of the EU Member States, the parties' choice of applicable law other than that of an EU Member State shall not prejudice the application of provisions of Community law, where appropriate as implemented in the EU Member State of the forum, which cannot be derogated from by agreement.

---

453. Art16 of the Rome Convention.
454. Art 20 of the Rome Convention differs.
455. Art 21 of the Rome Convention differs as discussed below.
456. For the case law on this requirement in art 3(3) of the Rome Convention see the *dicta* of Longmore J in *Bankers Trust International v RCS Editori SpA* [1996] CLC 899 at pp. 904–905, and, in particular, *obiter* at page 905H where the judge doubted whether all the elements relevant to the situation were connected with Italy. *Ingmar GB Ltd v Eaton Leonard Technologies Inc* [1999] ECC 49 (CA) and *Emeraldian Limited Partnership v Wellmix Shipping Ltd (The Vine)* [2010] EWHC 1411 (Comm), where the elements were not all connected with China as the guarantee covered the obligations under a charterparty which provided for English law and English jurisdiction and the beneficiary of the guarantee was a Liberian company. *Caterpillar Financial Services Corp v SNC Passion* [2004] EWHC 569 (Comm); [2004] 2 Lloyd's Rep 99; *Dexia Crediop SpA v Comune di Prato* [2015] EWHC 1746 not followed in *Banco Santander Totta SA v Companhia de Carris de Ferro de Lisboa SA* [2016] EWCA Civ 1267; [2017] 1 Lloyd's Rep 113.
457. Discussed below at pages 71–72.
458. There is no equivalent provision in the Rome Convention.

(vi) Overriding mandatory provisions

A further exception to the law determined by Rome I based on "considerations of public interest" which only applies in exceptional circumstances[459] is where there are "overriding mandatory provisions".

"Overriding mandatory provisions" are defined in Article 9(1) as provisions the respect for which is regarded as crucial by a country for safeguarding its public interests, such as its political, social or economic organisation, to such an extent that they are applicable to any situation falling within their scope, irrespective of the law otherwise applicable to the contract under this Regulation.

Article 9(2)[460] provides that nothing in Rome I restricts the application of the overriding mandatory provisions of the law of the forum. As Articles 9(2) and (3) are a derogation from the general principle that the parties may choose the law applicable to their contract they must be interpreted strictly.[461] An issue which is particularly relevant to bills of lading is whether, applying the law of the forum, the Hague-Visby Rules apply mandatorily even if they would not apply under the law chosen by the parties. The Hague-Visby Rules are given the force of law by the Carriage of Goods by Sea Act 1971 and apply mandatorily where the provisions of section 1 of the Carriage of Goods by Sea Act 1971 or Article X of the Rules are satisfied. Prior to the coming into force of the Rome Convention, the parties' express or inferred choice of law could be rendered null and void where the Hague-Visby Rules applied mandatorily and the effect of the choice of law would have been to render the carrier's liability less than that which would have been imposed by the Hague-Visby Rules. In *The Morviken*[462] a bill of lading expressly applied "the law of the Netherlands in which the Hague Rules . . . are incorporated". It further provided for the exclusive jurisdiction of the Amsterdam court unless the carrier elected otherwise. The shippers commenced an action *in rem* in England as a sister ship belonging to the carrier was within the jurisdiction of the Admiralty Court. The carriers sought a stay on the grounds of the foreign jurisdiction clause. The carrier preferred to have the case tried in the Netherlands where its liability would be about £250 under the Hague Rules, whereas if the English court applied the Hague-Visby Rules, the limit would be approximately £11,000. The Hague-Visby Rules have the force of law in the United Kingdom and thus are to be treated as if they are part of directly enacted statute law. The rules applied as the bill of lading was both issued in a Contracting State and it covered a contract for carriage from a port in a Contracting State within Article X(a) and (b). The House of Lords held that the choice of law provision purported to lessen the carrier's liability and was therefore null and void and of no effect in accordance with Article III rule 8 of the Rules.

The effect of Article 9(2) of Rome I would be the same as that of the decision in *The Morviken*. The law otherwise applicable to the contract as determined under Articles 3 or 5, could not restrict the application of the Hague-Visby Rules where they apply mandatorily. It is important to stress that Article 9(2) of Rome I would not apply where the Hague-Visby Rules only apply contractually to a contract, as opposed to mandatorily. For example, the Hague-Visby Rules never apply mandatorily to a charterparty, although they are often incorporated voluntarily into standard form charterparties.[463] Although they frequently apply mandatorily to bills of lading, this is not always the case. It should be noted that the fact that English law governs

---

459. Rome I, Recital 37.
460. Rome Convention art 7(2) is similar. See *United Antwerp Maritime Agencies (Unamar) NV v Navigation Maritime Bulgare,* C-184/12, EU:C:2013:663; [2014] 1 Lloyd's Rep 161.
461. Ibid., and *Republik Griechenland v Nikiforidis,* C-135/15, EU:C:2016:774.
462. [1983] 1 AC 565.
463. See Chapter 4, pages 128–132.

the contract, does not necessarily trigger the application of the Hague-Visby Rules. Thus in *Trafigura Beheer BV v Mediterranean Shipping Co SA (The MSC Amsterdam)*,[464] 360 tonnes of copper cathodes were shipped from South Africa to China. The bill of lading was expressly governed by English law and the clause paramount provided,

(a) For all trades, . . . this B/L shall be subject to the 1924 Hague Rules with the express exclusion of Article IX, or, if compulsorily applicable, subject to the 1968 Protocol (Hague-Visby) or any compulsory legislation based on the Hague Rules and/or said Protocols.

South Africa was not a Contracting State to the Hague-Visby Rules although its legislation, the South African Carriage of Goods by Sea Act 1986, does apply the Hague-Visby Rules to any shipment from a South African port. The Court of Appeal held that the Hague Rules, not the Hague-Visby Rules, were applicable. In order to determine whether the Rules are compulsorily applicable one had to look to the proper law of the contract and not the law of the country of shipment or of destination. The law of the forum might also have to be considered. The Court of Appeal held that Aikens J had correctly held that English statute law did not make the Hague-Visby Rules applicable and therefore neither the proper law nor the law of the forum made the Hague-Visby Rules compulsorily applicable and they did not therefore apply to the bill of lading.

In *Sideridraulic Systems SpA v BBC Chartering & Logistic GmbH & Co KG (The BBC Greenland)*[465] the bill of lading contained a clause paramount which provided for the Hague Rules to apply but continued,

In trades where [the Hague-Visby Rules] apply compulsorily, the provisions of the respective legislation shall be considered incorporated in this Bill of Lading. . . . Unless otherwise provided herein, the Carrier shall in no case be responsible for loss of or damage to deck cargo.

There was a London arbitration and English law clause. However, the bill of lading further provided that "In the event that US COGSA applies, then the Carrier may at the Carrier's election, commence suit in a court of proper jurisdiction in the United States in which case this court shall have exclusive jurisdiction." Hamblen J held that the Hague-Visby Rules did not apply compulsorily and therefore there was US jurisdiction.

Where a charterparty incorporates foreign legislation, for example, the US Carriage of Goods by Sea Act 1936, which gives effect to the Hague Rules, the question of construction of the legislation must be determined by the proper law of the contract. Thus in *The Stolt Sydness*[466] it made a difference whether the time bar in the US Carriage of Goods by Sea Act 1936, which was incorporated into the voyage charterparty, was interpreted under English law or United States law. Under the latter "suit" in Article III rule 6, which is reproduced in section 3(6) of the US Act, was confined to litigation and did not extend to arbitration. By contrast under English law "suit" includes arbitration and thus arbitration must be commenced within the one-year time limit.[467] As the charterparty expressly provided for London arbitration and English law, Rix J held that the English law interpretation applied and the claim was time barred as arbitration had not been commenced within the one-year time limit.

464. [2007] EWCA Civ 794; [2008] 1 All ER (Comm) 385; [2007] EWHC 944 (Comm). See also *The Komninos S* [1991] 1 Lloyd's Rep 370. See also the *obiter dicta* of Tuckey LJ with whom Aldous LJ agreed, Rix LJ dissenting, in *Parsons Corporation v CV Scheepvaartonderneming "Happy Ranger" (The Happy Ranger)* [2002] EWCA Civ 694; [2002] 2 Lloyd's Rep 357, [19].
465. [2011] EWHC 3106 (Comm); [2012] 1 Lloyd's Rep 230.
466. *Mauritius Oil Refineries Ltd v Stolt Nielsen Nederland BV (The Stolt Sydness)* [1997] 1 Lloyd's Rep 273.
467. *Owners of Cargo on Board the Merak v The Merak (Owners) (The Merak)* [1964] 2 Lloyd's Rep 527.

Where the Hamburg Rules are incorporated into a bill of lading, or where the proper law is that of a Contracting State to the Hamburg Rules where that law would mandatorily apply the Hamburg Rules, the English courts would apply those Rules provided they impose a greater liability on the carrier than that under the Hague-Visby Rules. The parties are free to increase their liabilities but not to seek to lessen them. The effect of the Hamburg Rules is that they would usually impose a greater liability on the carrier than the Hague-Visby Rules.

The United Kingdom and several other EU Member States[468] did not give the force of law to Article 7(1) of the Rome Convention which dealt with mandatory rules of a third country. There is no possibility of reservation to a Regulation and therefore Article 9(3) of Rome I, which is the equivalent of Article 7(1) of the Rome Convention, applies to all the EU Member States. The forum has a discretion to apply the law of a third country as pursuant to Article 9(3) overriding mandatory provisions of the law of the country where the contract is to be performed or has been performed may be given effect to the extent that they render the performance of the contract unlawful. It is relevant to consider the nature and purpose of those provisions and the consequences of their application or non-application.[469] Article 9(3) has been described as a "welcome development",[470] as it reflects existing case law under English common law.[471]

In *Republik Griechenland v Nikiforidis*[472] the Court of Justice of the European Union held that Article 9(3) must be interpreted as precluding overriding mandatory provisions other than those of the State of the forum or of the State where the obligations arising out of the contract have to be or have been performed from being applied, as legal rules, by the court of the forum, but as not precluding it from taking such other overriding mandatory provisions into account as matters of fact in so far as this is provided for by the national law that is applicable to the contract pursuant to the Regulation. This interpretation is not affected by the principle of sincere co-operation laid down in Article 4(3) of the Treaty on European Union.

(vii) Public policy

Article 21 Rome I[473] provides that the application of the law of any country specified by Rome I may be refused only if such application is manifestly incompatible with the public policy of the forum. "Public policy" will be very restrictively interpreted as it is only to apply in exceptional circumstances.[474]

(viii) International conventions

Article 25 of Rome I deals with the relationship between Rome I and "international conventions to which one or more EU Member States are parties at the time when Rome I is adopted and which lay down conflict-of-law rules relating to contractual obligations". Rome I will not prejudice the application of such a convention, as the EU Member States are obliged to honour their

---

468. Germany, Ireland and Luxembourg (1980 Rome Convention), Portugal (1992 Accession Convention), Latvia and Slovenia (2005 Accession Convention) reserved the right not to apply art 7(1).
469. Cf. *Emeraldian Limited Partnership v Wellmix Shipping Ltd (The Vine)* [2010] EWHC 1411; [2011] 1 Lloyd's Rep 301.
470. See A. Chong, "The Public Policy and Mandatory Rules of Third Countries in International Contracts" [2006] JPIL 27, at p 70.
471. See *Foster v Driscoll* [1929] 1 KB 470 (smuggle alcohol into US during prohibition) and *Reggazzoni v KC Sethia* [1958] AC 301 (sale of jute from India to South Africa in breach of Indian law).
472. C-135/15, EU:C:2016:774.
473. Rome Convention, art 16. See e.g. *Emeraldian Ltd Partnership v Wellmix Shipping Ltd (The Vine)* [2010] EWHC 1411; [2011] 1 Lloyd's Rep 301.
474. See Rome II, Recital 32.

international commitments.[475] The wording of Article 25 of Rome I is more restricted than the equivalent provision, Article 21 of the Rome Convention, in two ways. First, the Rome Convention refers to "international conventions to which a Contracting State is, or becomes, a party". Rome I only permits international conventions to which one or more EU Member States are parties at the time when Rome I is adopted, and not thereafter.[476] Article 26 of Rome I required EU Member States to notify the Commission of the international conventions referred to in Article 25(1) by 17 June 2009 and the Commission to publish the list of those conventions "to make the rules more accessible".[477] The United Kingdom notified that there were no conventions.

Second, Article 25 of Rome I specifically requires the international convention "to lay down conflict-of-law rules relating to contractual obligations". There is no such requirement in Article 21 of the Rome Convention. The Hague-Visby Rules do not provide expressly for any conflict of law rules and, therefore, even though in *The Morviken* it was held that the effect of Article III rule 8 of those Rules is to nullify the express choice of law, this convention does not appear to fall within Article 25 of Rome I.

(ix) Community law

Article 23 provides that Rome I shall not prejudice the application of provisions of Community law[478] which in relation to particular matters, lay down conflict-of-law rules relating to contractual obligations, with the exception of insurance matters.[479]

(x) No choice

Where the parties have not chosen the law applicable to the contract in accordance with Article 3, Rome I provides for a number of rules that apply to specific types of contracts.[480] Thus for example, a contract for the sale of goods[481] shall be governed by the law of the country where the seller has his habitual residence;[482] and a contract for the provision of services by the law of the country where the service provider has his habitual residence.[483] If a contract is not one of those mentioned in Article 4(1) of Rome I, or where the contract is for more than one of the types specified, for example it is a contract for the sale of goods and the provision of services, the contract shall be governed by the law of the country where the party required to effect the characteristic performance of the contract has his habitual residence.[484] Where it is clear from all the circumstances of the case that the contract is manifestly more closely connected with a country other than that indicated in Article 4(1) and (2), the law of that other country shall apply.[485] Where the law applicable cannot be determined pursuant to Article 4(1)

---

475. Rome I, Recital 41.
476. This change is also seen in the amendments made to art 57 of the EC Jurisdiction Convention which has now become art 71 of the EC Jurisdiction Regulation and Recast Jurisdiction Regulation.
477. Rome I, Recital 41.
478. Rome I, Recital 40.
479. Special rules on insurance are set out in art 7 of Rome I.
480. The Rome Convention does not have these specific rules and is discussed below.
481. There are similarities with Article 5(1)(b) of the Jurisdiction Regulation. As in that provision there is no definition of "sale of goods" but the case law on Article 5(1)(b) will be applicable here as the Jurisdiction Regulation and Rome I should be interpreted consistently – Recital 7 of Rome I.
482. Rome I, art 4(1)(a).
483. Rome I, art 4(1)(b).
484. Rome I, art 4(2). See eg. *Taurus Petroleum Ltd v State Oil Marketing Company of the Ministry of Oil, Republic of Iraq* [2015] EWCA Civ 835; [2016] 1 Lloyd's Rep 42 (letter of credit).
485. Rome I, art 4(3).

or (2), the contract shall be governed by the law of the country with which it is most closely connected.[486]

Article 5 provides for special rules for contracts of carriage of goods[487] and carriage of passengers.[488] For contracts of carriage the law shall be that of the country of the habitual residence of the carrier, provided that the place of receipt or the place of delivery or the habitual residence of the consignor is also situated in that country. If those requirements are not met, the law is that of the country where the place of delivery as agreed by the parties is situated. Those rules are subject to an escape in Article 5(3) of Rome I if it is clear from all the circumstances of the case that the contract, in the absence of a choice of law, is manifestly more closely connected with a country other than that indicated, in which case the law of that country shall apply.

The provisions of the Rome Convention where there is no choice are rather different. Article 4(1) of the Rome Convention provides that where there is no choice the contract shall be governed by the law of the country with which it is most closely connected. That Article further provides that a severable part of the contract which has a closer connection with another country may be governed by the law of that other country.

In order to determine which country the contract is most closely connected with, there are a number of presumptions in Article 4(2), (3) and (4), all of which may be disregarded in accordance with Article 4(5), if it appears from the circumstances as a whole that the contract is more closely connected with another country. If the contract is not for the carriage of goods (such as a bill of lading or voyage charterparty)[489] but is, for example, an international sale contract,[490] time[491] or demise charterparty, insurance contract to which the Rome Convention applies, reinsurance contract or letter of credit, the presumption in Article 4(2) applies. That presumption is that the contract is most closely connected with the country where the party who is to effect the performance which is characteristic of the contract has, at the time of the conclusion of the contract, its principal place of business or where the contract provides that performance is to be effected through another place of business, the country in which that other place of business is situated. This involves first working out what the characteristic performance of the contract is. This will be the performance in return for which payment is promised.[492] Thus, for example, the performance characteristic of a contract of sale is delivery of the goods,[493] not payment of the purchase price, and of a contract of insurance is the provision of insurance cover,[494] not payment of the premium. Thus the governing law of a contract of sale would usually be the principal place of business of the seller.[495] Under the Recast Jurisdiction Regulation if the parties have not

---

486. Rome I, art 4(4).
487. Rome I, art 5(1) and Recital 22.
488. Rome I, art 5(2).
489. Rome Convention, art 4(4). See page 68.
490. *Air Transworld Ltd v Bombardier Inc* [2012] EWHC 243 (Comm); [2012] 1 CLC 145 [101]–[106].
491. See *Martrade Shipping & Transport GmbH v United Enterprises Corp* [2014] EWHC 1884 (Comm) on a trip time charterparty.
492. See also *Print Concept GmbH v GEW (EC) Ltd* [2001] EWCA Civ 352, [2002] CLC 352, [2001] ECC 36 (distributorship agreement); See also *Iran Continental Shelf Oil Co v IRI International Corp* [2002] EWCA Civ 1024, [2004] 2 CLC 696. On letters of credit see *Bank of Baroda v Vysya Bank* Limited [1994] 2 Lloyd's Rep 87 (letter of credit between the confirming and the issuing bank); *PT Pan Indonesia Bank Ltd TBK v Marconi Communications International Limited* [2005] EWCA Civ 422 (CA); [2004] 1 Lloyd's Rep 594 (QB) (letter of credit between the beneficiary and the confirming bank). *Tavoulareas v Tsavliris (The Atlas Pride)* [2005] EWHC 2140 (Comm) [49]–[52].
493. *Air Transworld Ltd v Bombardier Inc* [2012] EWHC 243 (Comm); [2012] 1 CLC 145 [101]–[106].
494. *Credit Lyonnais v New Hampshire Insurance Co* [1997] 2 Lloyd's Rep 1 applied in *American Motorists Insurance Co v Cellstar Corporation Welex* [2003] EWCA Civ 206; [2003] Lloyd's Rep IR 295 (CA); [2002] EWHC 421 (Comm), [2002] 2 Lloyd's Rep 216 (QB). Compare art 7(2) second paragraph of Rome I. *Dornoch Limited v The Mauritius Union Assurance Company Ltd* [2006] EWCA Civ 389, [2006] 2 Lloyd's Rep 475 [41]–[43], the characteristic performance of a reinsurance contract was payment in the event of a claim.
495. *Sapporo Breweries Ltd v Lupofresh Ltd v* [2013] EWCA Civ 948; [2014] 1 All ER (Comm) 484.

chosen the jurisdiction under Article 25 the claimant may sue where the defendant is domiciled or where, under the contract, the goods were delivered or should have been delivered. There may be no connection between the place of delivery and the principal place of business of the seller, with the unfortunate result that the court with jurisdiction has to apply the law of a different country. For example, a seller whose principal place of business is in Switzerland, sells a cargo of oil on f.o.b. terms so that the buyer must provide a ship to take delivery of the goods in Singapore for carriage to Rotterdam. Therefore it is very important that the parties choose both jurisdiction and governing law. Article 4(3) relates to immovable property and is not therefore relevant for present purposes.

There is a special presumption in Article 4(4) of the Rome Convention for contracts for the carriage of goods which is slightly different from that in Article 5(1) of Rome I. Unlike Rome I there is no special presumption for contracts for the carriage of passengers. Article 4(4) of the Rome Convention states that single voyage charterparties and other contracts, the main purpose of which is the carriage of goods, shall be treated as contracts for the carriage of goods.[496] In such a contract if the country in which the carrier has its principal place of business, is also the country in which the place of loading or the place of discharge or the principal place of business of the consignor is situated, it shall be presumed that the contract is most closely connected with that country. The time for applying this test is when the contract is concluded as we look to the formation of the contract. Thus if an Italian charterer who is also the carrier issues bills of lading for carriage of goods from Rotterdam to Genoa, the presumption is that Italian law applies, unless it appears from the circumstances as a whole that the contract is more closely connected with another country. However, there will frequently be no presumption as often the principal place of business of the carrier is not the same as the loadport, discharge port or principal place of business of the consignor. It is common for bills of lading to contain express clauses providing for jurisdiction in the courts of and the governing law of the principal place of business of the carrier. If, however, the parties have not made an express choice nor demonstrated it with reasonable certainty by choosing the jurisdiction, one of three other factors must point to the principal place of business of the carrier for the presumption to apply. This presumption has been considered by the European Court of Justice in *Intercontainer Interfrigo SC (ICF) v Balkenende Oosthuizen BV, MIC Operations BV*[497] and *Haeger & Schmidt GmbH v Mutuelles du Mans assurances IARD*.[498]

The presumptions will apply unless it appears from the circumstances as a whole that the contract is more closely connected with another country.[499] Circumstances such as where the performance of all the contractual obligations is to be given and the governing law of an independent but interconnected contract may be relevant.[500] In *Definitely Maybe (Touring) Ltd v*

---

496. In *Martrade Shipping & Transport GmbH v United Enterprises Corporation* [2014] EWHC 1884 (Comm); [2014] 2 Lloyd's Rep 198 [27]–[30] Popplewell J held that a trip time charterparty, like a term time charter, is not an undertaking by the owner to carry goods, but is to make the vessel and her crew available to the charterer as a means for the charterer to transport goods. Therefore the presumption in Article 4(2) applies to a trip time charter.

497. C-133/08, EU:C:2009:617 [2009] ECR I-9687.

498. C-305/13 EU:C:2014:2320 [2015] QB 319.

499. Article 4(5). See Case C-133/08; EU:C:2009:617 *Intercontainer Interfrigo SC (ICF) v Balkenende Oosthuizen BV, MIC Operations BV* [2009] ECR I-9687, applied in *British Arab Commercial Bank Plc v Bank of Communications* [2011] EWHC 281 (Comm); *Martrade Shipping & Transport GmbH v United Enterprises Corp* [2014] EWHC 1884 (Comm); [2014] 2 Lloyd's Rep 198 and *Case* C-305/13; EU:C:2014:2320; *Haeger & Schmidt GmbH v Mutuelles du Mans Assurances IARD* [2015] QB 319.

500. *Bank of Baroda v Vysya Bank Limited* [1994] 2 Lloyd's Rep 87 (letter of credit between the confirming and the issuing bank). See also *HIB Ltd v Guardian Insurance Co Inc* [1997] 1 Lloyd's Rep 412. The decision of the Court of Appeal in *Crédit Lyonnais v New Hampshire Insurance Co* [1997] CLC 909 is relevant to Article 4. Although the court was there considering the Second EC Directive on Non Life Insurance, it recognised that there are many similarities between the Rome Convention and the second directive (p. 913).

Marek Lieberberg Konzertagentur GmbH [501] the characteristic performance of the contract was for Oasis to perform in two concerts in Germany and thus the presumption under Article 4(2) was that as the party to effect the characteristic performance was located in England, English law would be the governing law of the contract. However, the defendant established factors which showed the contract had a closer connection with Germany than with England, as the contract required performance of contractual obligations by both parties in Germany. Therefore the presumption did not apply and German law applied.

In *Gan Insurance Co Ltd v Tai Ping Insurance Co Ltd* [502] the Court of Appeal agreed with Cresswell J at first instance that if there were no choice within Article 3 of the Rome Convention, the reinsurance had its closest connection with English law under Article 4(2) and it did not appear from the circumstances as a whole that the reinsurance contracts were more closely connected with Taiwan under Article 4(5).

(b) The common law

Where neither Rome I nor the Rome Convention applies, for example because the bill of lading was concluded after 17 December 2009 and the issue is one excluded under Article 1(2)(d) of Rome I, the common law rules in relation to conflict of laws apply. The proper law of the contract means the system of law which the parties intended to apply to the contract. The parties may express their intention or where there is no express written choice their intention may be inferred from the terms and nature of the contract. So, for example, where the contract contains a choice of forum clause, but no express choice of law clause, the court will infer that the parties intended the contract to be governed by the law of the forum where disputes are to be tried unless there are strong indications that they did not intend or may not have intended this result. [503] The English court would hold an express choice of law void where the choice would lessen the carrier's liability if the Hague-Visby Rules are mandatorily applicable as in *The Morviken*. [504]

Where the intention of the parties as to the governing law is not expressed and cannot be inferred from the circumstances, the contract is governed by the system of law with which the transaction has its closest and most real connection. [505]

As in common with many other jurisdictions England will not apply a foreign law which is contrary to public policy.

---

501. [2001] 2 All ER (Comm) 1. See also *Iran Continental Shelf Oil Co v IRI International Corp* [2002] EWCA Civ 1024, [2004] 2 CLC 696; [2002] CLC 372 (QB); *Samcrete Egypt Engineers & Contractors SAE v Land Rover Exports Ltd* [2001] EWCA Civ 2019, [2002] CLC 533; *Ennstone Building Products Ltd v Stanger Ltd* [2002] EWCA Civ 916, [2002] 2 All ER (Comm) 479 (CA); applied by *Waldwiese Stiftung v Lewis* [2004] EWHC 2589 (Ch), 2004 WL 2652645 (Ch D); *Kenburn Waste Management Ltd v Bergmann* [2002] EWCA Civ 98, [2002] CLC 644; *Caledonia Subsea Ltd v Micoperi SRL* [2003] SC 70 (Inner House Court of Session) and *Ophthalmic Innovations International (UK) Ltd v Ophthalmic Innovations International Incorporated* [2004] EWHC 2948 (Ch) [2005] ILPr 10.

502. [1999] CLC 1270 per Beldam LJ at p. 1279 and *per* Cresswell J [1998] CLC 1072, 1082. See also *Raiffeisen Zentralbank Osterreich Aktiengesellschaft v National Bank of Greece SA* [1999] 1 Lloyd's Rep 408, 412 and 413 and *Ferguson Shipbuilders v Voith Hydro GmbH and Co KG* [2000] SLT 229, a decision of the Scottish Outer House; *ISS Machinery Services Ltd v Aeolian Shipping SA (The Aeolian)* [2001] 2 Lloyd's Rep 641; *Star Reefers Pool Inc v JFC Group Col Ltd* [2010] EWHC 3003 (Comm) discussed at page 59. See also *Emeraldian Ltd Partnership v Wellmix Shipping Ltd (The Vine)* [2010] EWHC 1411 (Comm) [170].

503. *Compagnie D'Armement Maritime SA v Compagnie Tunisienne de Navigation SA* [1971] AC 572; *The Al Wahab* [1983] 2 Lloyd's Rep 365; *Hellenic Steel Co v Svolamar Shipping Co Ltd (The Komninos S)* [1991] 1 Lloyd's Rep 370.

504. See page 63.

505. *Compagnie D'Armement Maritime SA v Compagnie Tunisienne de Navigation SA* [1971] AC 572; *Trade Indemnity plc v Forsakringsaktiebolaget Njord* [1995] 1 All ER 796. Compare *Baring Brothers & Co Ltd v Cunninghame District Council* [1997] CLC 108, a decision of the Scottish Court of Session concerning a void contract.

(c) Rome II

Recital 7 of Rome II provides that the substantive scope and the provisions of Rome II should be consistent with the Jurisdiction Regulation and the Rome Convention and Rome I.[506] Non-contractual obligation is an autonomous concept and also covers non-contractual obligations arising out of strict liability.[507] If the dispute between the parties involves, for example, a tort committed after Rome II applies[508] the governing law will be determined by the rules set out in Rome II.

Like the Rome Convention and Rome I, Rome II applies to any choice of law situation which comes before the courts of an EU Member State, whether the damage occurs within or outside the European Union, and may result in the court applying the law of a non-EU Member State.

The general rule is that the law applicable to a non-contractual obligation arising out of a tort or delict is the law of the country in which the damage occurs,[509] unless both parties have their habitual residence in the same country at the time when the damage occurs, in which case the law of that country applies.[510] An escape clause provides that the law of another country shall apply where it is clear from all the circumstances of the case that the tort or delict is manifestly more closely connected with that country. There are specific rules for special torts such as product liability,[511] unfair competition,[512] environmental damage,[513] infringement of intellectual property rights[514] and industrial action.[515] There are also special rules where damage is caused by an act which is not a tort or delict, such as unjust enrichment,[516] *negotiorum gestio*[517] and *culpa in contrahendo*.[518]

Where there is a maritime tort and the damage occurs on the high seas Rome II may not apply.[519] For example, if there is a collision which occurs in French territorial waters then the rule that the law of the country in which the damage occurs can be applied, but if the collision occurs on the high seas then the rule cannot be applied because the law of no particular country is triggered. However, in that event the Collision Regulations would apply.[520]

A major change from the rules under the Private International Law (Miscellaneous Provisions Act) 1995 is that the scope of Rome II is wider and the law determined as applicable under Rome II will also govern the assessment of damages.[521] However, the law applicable under Rome II is subject to a number of restrictions, such as "overriding mandatory provisions" which probably includes the Hague-Visby Rules.

---

506. "[T]he instruments dealing with the law applicable to contractual obligations". See also Recital 7 of Rome I which is in similar terms.

507. Rome II, Recital 11.

508. See page 52.

509. Art 4(1). See also *Committeri v Club Mediterranee SA* [2016] EWHC 1510; *Pan Oceanic Chartering Inc v UNIPEC UK Ltd* [2016] EWHC 2774 (Comm).

510. Rome II, art 4(2).

511. Rome II, art 5.

512. Rome II, art 6.

513. Rome II, art 7.

514. Rome II, art 8.

515. Rome II, art 9.

516. Rome II, art 10.

517. Rome II, art 11.

518. Rome II, art 12.

519. M. George, "Choice of Law in Maritime Torts" (2007) 3 J Pr Int L 137, at pp 170–171; A. Dickinson, *The Rome II Regulation: The Law Applicable to Non-Contractual Obligations* (Oxford University Press 2008), [3.311]–[3.314].

520. See Chapter 7, pages 236–237.

521. Rome II, art 15(c).

(i) Freedom of choice

As in Rome I party autonomy is recognised, although conditions are imposed on the choice to protect weaker parties.[522] Thus the parties may choose to submit non-contractual obligations to the law of their choice in two situations: first where an agreement is concluded after the event giving rise to the damage[523] or second where all the parties are pursuing a commercial activity, by an agreement freely negotiated before the event giving rise to the damage occurred.[524] In either case the choice must be express or demonstrated with reasonable certainty. It is important to note that the choice shall not prejudice the rights of third parties. So once again there is some doubt as to whether such a choice of law in a bill of lading would bind the third party bill of lading holder.

Article 18 of Rome II deals with direct action against the liability insurer and provides that the person who has suffered damage may bring its claim against the insurer of the person liable to provide compensation if the law applicable to the non-contractual obligation or the law applicable to the insurance contract so provides.[525] Thus if the owners of a ship which has been involved in a collision have a claim against the other ship which has caused the collision in the tort of negligence, they can bring a direct action against the other ship's liability insurers, usually their hull insurers and P&I Club,[526] if either of two laws permits this: the law applicable to the tort or the law applicable to the insurance contract.

Article 19 of Rome II which deals with subrogation is along similar lines to Article 15 of Rome I as it provides that where an insured has a non-contractual claim against another, for example, the other vessel with which it has been in collision, and the insurer is obliged to indemnify or has indemnified the insured, the law which governs the insurer's duty to indemnify the insured shall determine whether, and the extent to which, the insurer is entitled to exercise against the debtor, the other vessel, the rights which the insured had against the other vessel under the law governing their relationship.

Again like Rome I, the choice made by the parties shall not prejudice exceptions based on public policy and overriding mandatory provisions which will apply in exceptional circumstances.

(ii) Provisions which cannot be derogated from by agreement in a domestic contract

Article 14(2) of Rome II is similar to Article 3(3) of Rome I and the Rome Convention which deal with a domestic situation as all the elements relevant to the situation at the time when the event giving rise to the damage occurs are located in country A, save that the parties have provided for the law of country B. In that event provisions of the law of country A "which cannot be derogated from by agreement" cannot be prejudiced by the parties' choice.[527]

This provision will not apply to a contract for the international carriage of goods but could apply to purely coastal trade, e.g. from an English port to another English port on an English registered ship. Were the parties to provide for a foreign law which would apply the Hague Rules and a party brings a claim against the carrier in tort, the English court would be entitled to apply

---

522. Rome II, Recital 31 and art 14.
523. Rome II, art 14(1)(a).
524. Rome II, art 14(1)(b).
525. Y. Baatz, "Recent Developments in Party Choice of the Applicable Law and Jurisdiction in Marine Insurance and Reinsurance Contracts" in D.R. Thomas (gen. ed.), *The Modern Law of Marine Insurance, Volume 3* (Informa Law, 2009); J. Hjalmarsson, "Direct Claims against Marine Insurers in the English Legal System" (2010) 18 APLR 269; V. Ulfbeck, "Direct Actions Against the Insurer in a Maritime Setting: The European Perspective" [2011] LMCLQ 293.
526. See pages 487–488 of Chapter 11.
527. See page 62.

the Hague-Visby Rules as section 1(3) of the Carriage of Goods by Sea Act 1971 extends the application of the Hague-Visby Rules and gives them the force of law in relation to coastal trade where the port of shipment is a port in the United Kingdom, whether or not the carriage is between ports in two different States. Furthermore Article IV*bis* of the Hague-Visby Rules provides that the defences and limits of liability apply to any action against the carrier whether the action be founded in contract or in tort.

(iii) Community law in a domestic contract

Article 14(3) of Rome II also reflects Article 3(4) of Rome I and provides that where all the elements relevant to the situation at the time when the event giving rise to the damage occurs are located in one or more of the Member States, the parties' choice of a law other than that of a Member State shall not prejudice the application of provisions of Community law, where appropriate as implemented in the Member State of the forum, which cannot be derogated from by agreement.

(iv) Overriding mandatory provisions

As in Rome I there is a further exception to the law determined by Rome II based on "considerations of public interest" which only apply in exceptional circumstances[528] where there are overriding mandatory provisions.

Article 16 provides that nothing in Rome II restricts the application of the law of the forum in a situation where they are mandatory irrespective of the law otherwise applicable to the non-contractual obligation.[529]

(v) Public policy

Article 26 of Rome II is identical to Article 21 of Rome I and provides that the application of the law of any country specified by Rome II may be refused only if such application is manifestly incompatible with the public policy of the forum. "Public policy" will be very restrictively interpreted as it is only to apply in exceptional circumstances. Recital 32 of Rome II gives an example and states that a law which grants "non-compensatory exemplary or punitive damages of an excessive nature" may be regarded as being contrary to the public policy of the forum. Equivalent situations in a non-contractual context could include economic duress.

(vi) Community law

Article 27 provides that Rome II shall not prejudice the application of provisions of Community law[530] which in relation to particular matters, lay down conflict-of-law rules relating to non-contractual obligations.

(vii) International conventions

Article 28 deals with the relationship between Rome II and "international conventions to which one or more EU Member States are parties at the time when [Rome II] is adopted and which lay

---

528. Rome II, Recital 32.
529. This provision is very similar to art 9(2) of Rome I and art 7(2) of the Rome Convention. A definition of "overriding mandatory provisions" is given in Rome I, art 9(1) discussed at page 63.
530. Rome II, Recital 35.

down conflict-of-law rules relating to contractual obligations". Rome II will not prejudice the application of such a convention, as the EU Member States are obliged to honour their international commitments.[531]

The wording of Article 28 reflects that of Article 25 of Rome I.[532] Article 29 of Rome II required EU Member States to notify the European Commission of the international conventions referred to in Article 28(1) by 11 July 2008 and the European Commission to publish the list of those conventions "to make the rules more accessible".[533] The United Kingdom has done so and does not list the Hague-Visby rules.

(d) Sections 9 to 15 of the Private International Law (Miscellaneous Provisions) Act 1995

Part III of the Private International Law (Miscellaneous Provisions) Act 1995 entered into force on 1 May 1996 and determines the law applicable to torts committed before Rome II is applicable.[534] It only deals with tort and delict and does not cover other non-contractual obligations such as restitution including unjust enrichment or equitable obligations.

The 1995 Act abolished the rule at common law of double actionability.[535] That rule had required that in order to be actionable in England, conduct abroad had to be actionable in accordance with the law of the forum and the law of the place where it occurred, subject to a flexible exception based on the most significant relationship.[536] The 1995 Act provided new statutory rules, except in relation to issues arising in any defamation claim which are excluded by section 13. Section 11(1) provides for a general rule that "the applicable law is the law of the country in which the events constituting the tort or delict in question occur". Section 11(2) provides for the position where those events occur in different countries. In the case of a claim for personal injury the law of the country where the individual was when he sustained the injury applies (s 11(2)(a)); for damage to property the law of the country where the property was when it was damaged applies (s 11(2)(b)); and in any other case the law of the country in which the most significant element or elements of those events occurred.[537]

The general rule may be displaced. Pursuant to section 12(1), if on comparing the significance of the factors which connect a tort with the country whose law would apply under the general rule with the significance of any factors connecting the tort with another country, it appears that it would be substantially more appropriate for the law of that other country to determine the issues, or any of those issues, then the law of that other country may apply to determine those issues or that issue. Section 12(2) provides that the factors which may be taken into account in considering all the circumstances include factors relating to the parties, to any of the events which constitute the tort or to any of the circumstances or consequences of those events. The

---

531. Rome II, Recital 36.

532. See pages 65–66 of this chapter.

533. Rome II, Recital 36.

534. Rome II applies to events which occurred after 9 January 2009. See page 52 of this chapter.

535. s 10.

536. *Phillips v Eyre* [1870] LR 6 QB 1; *Boys v Chaplin* [1971] AC 356; *Red Sea Insurance Co Ltd v Bouygues SA* [1995] 1 AC 190.

537. *Roerig v Valiant Trawlers Ltd* [2002] EWCA Civ 21 [2002] 1 WLR 2304; *Morin v Bonhams & Brooks* [2004] EWCA Civ 1802; [2004] 1 Lloyd's Rep 702; *Anton Durbeck GmBH v Den Norske Bank ASA* [2005] EWHC 2497 (Comm); [2006] 1 Lloyd's Rep 93; *Trafigura Beheer BV v Kookmin Bank Co* [2006] EWHC 1450 (Comm); [2006] 2 Lloyd's Rep 455; *VTB Capital plc v Nutritek* [2013] UKSC 5; [2013] 2 AC 337 (torts of deceit and conspiracy to defraud); *Alliance Bank JSC v Aquanta Corp* [2012] EWCA 1588; [2013] 1 All ER (Comm) 819 (alleged conspiracy to defraud Alliance Bank of £1.1 billion); *Sapporo Breweries Ltd v Lupofresh Ltd* [2013] EWCA 948; [2014] 1 All ER (Comm) 484, [43]–[46].

1995 Act does not provide for party choice but a choice of law or jurisdiction provision in a contract could be taken into account in applying the displacement rule in section 12.[538]

A public policy exception is provided for in section 14(3)(i). Matters of evidence and procedure remain governed by the law of the forum – section 14(3)(b). Quantification of damages has been determined to be a matter of procedure and is therefore determined by the law of the forum.[539]

---

538. *Morin v Bonhams & Brooks* [2004] EWCA Civ 1802; [2004] 1 Lloyd's Rep 702; *Trafigura Beheer BV v Kookmin Bank Co* [2006] EWHC 1450 (Comm); [2006] 2 Lloyd's Rep 455 and *Sapporo Breweries Ltd v Lupofresh Ltd* [2013] EWCA 948; [2014] 1 All ER (Comm) 484, [46].

539. *Harding v Wealands* [2006] UKHL 32; [2007] 2 AC 1; A. Scott, "Substance and Procedure and Choice of Law in Torts" [2007] LMCLQ 1.

CHAPTER 2

SHIPBUILDING, SALE, FINANCE AND REGISTRATION

Filippo Lorenzon and Ainhoa Campàs Velasco

1. INTRODUCTION[1]

Maritime law would certainly not have developed as it has in the last 500 years without the desire of mankind to explore the unknown and its keenness for trading with far away nations.

---

1. Sections 1, 2 and 3 have been written by Filippo Lorenzon, and sections 4 and 5 have been written by Ainhoa Campàs Velasco.

75

However, although the lifeblood of commercial shipping is unquestionably international trade,[2] the chattel symbol of the entire maritime community is certainly the *ship*.

Tens of thousands of merchant ships are currently in service worldwide and – although constantly affected by the cycles typical of the shipping economy – this figure appears to be steadily growing in the long term.[3] All going well, ships have a long life cycle which starts with their commissioning from a yard, goes through decades of service under bareboat, time and voyage charters and eventually ends in a scrap yard. For some there is a life after "retirement" and conversion into yachts, floating warehouses, FPSOs or even a floating hotel (in the case of the famous Cunard passenger ship *Queen Elizabeth II*). This appears to be becoming less rare than in the past.

This chapter discusses the four key initial stages of a vessel's life cycle through an analysis of the legal instruments making it possible for her to start trading: shipbuilding and ship sale contracts allow the owner to increase the tonnage of its fleet and generate more business for its holding group or shipping pool; the registration of the ship in the owner's name will then follow in order for her to be assigned a flag, a nationality and – rather importantly – a fiscal regime; and lastly possibly the most essential ingredient for the life of a ship: its financing by lenders.

2. SHIPBUILDING AND ITS CONTRACTUAL FRAMEWORK

Shipbuilding contracts are very complex transactions and the contractual framework under which they are commissioned reflects such complexity. It is very common in shipping contracts, whether in the context of shipbuilding, sale, charterparties or bills of lading for there to be standard form contracts which the parties may amend at will or incorporate in the course of their negotiations. In shipbuilding, there are a good number of standard form contracts widely used as templates on which individual agreements are negotiated, although the contract eventually concluded may depart significantly from the standard form proposed. The popularity of each form depends on a number of factors among which the geographical location of the yard, the habit of the owner and the strength of the trade association concerned appear to be the most influential. The most common forms are: the Shipbuilders' Association of Japan Form (hereinafter "SAJ Form"), the Association of European Shipbuilders and Shiprepairers' Form (hereinafter "AWES Form"), the Norwegian Standard Form of Shipbuilding Contract (hereinafter "Norwegian Form") and the Baltic and International Maritime Council (BIMCO) Standard Newbuilding Contract (hereinafter "NEWBUILDCON") although other forms are available in the market.[4] Unlike in chartering where the use of riders tends to preserve the integrity of the model form, in shipbuilding the practice appears to be to use the standard clauses as a mere sample which is heavily amended with increased risk of internal conflicts and inconsistencies. Interpretation issues may also arise from the fact that the amended standard form makes numerous references to a number of external sources such as classification societies' rules and regulations and the all important technical schedules where the detailed requirements of the newbuild and her designs are necessarily contained.

---

2. See Chapter 3.
3. See Commission of the European Communities, "Seventh Report from the Commission to the Council on the Situation in World Shipbuilding", COM (2003) 232 final.
4. For example, the MARAD Form by the Maritime Administration of the United States Department for Commerce.

A full discussion of the legal issues revolving around the law of shipbuilding contracts is beyond the scope of this work.[5] In the following pages the crucial features of shipbuilding contracts will be dealt with: namely (a) the nature of shipbuilding contracts and the legal framework to which they are subject; (b) the formation of the contract and "subject to details" arrangements; (c) the structure and main terms of the most common standard terms currently used in the market.

(a) The nature of shipbuilding contracts

A shipbuilding contract is one directed towards the regulation of a substantial and complex construction project involving the supply of workmanship and materials. The final product however – the ship – is not excluded from the definition of "goods" contained in the Sale of Goods Act 1979[6] and under English law the traditional view is that shipbuilding contracts are in fact agreements to sell[7] future goods[8] by description.[9] This proposition however should be handled with care as it has been doubted twice by the House of Lords in more recent years.[10] In the last of these cases, *Stocznia Gdanska SA v Latvian Shipping Co*,[11] the shipyard rightly terminated the contract and sued the buyer for payment of the first two instalments of the purchase price due at the time of rescission. The buyers claimed that no property in the ship had ever passed to them under the rescinded contract and therefore the total failure of consideration made the instalments not due. Refusing to depart from the *Hyundai* precedent, Lord Goff asked himself the following question:

Is the contract in question simply a contract for the sale of a ship or is it rather a contract under which the design and construction of the vessel formed part of the yard's contractual duties, as well as the duty to transfer the finished object to the buyers? If it is the latter, the design and construction of the vessel form part of the consideration for which the price is to be paid. [. . .] I am satisfied that the present case falls into the latter category.[12]

It seems, however, that the fact that the ship has to be designed by the builders is not enough, in principle, to disqualify the shipbuilding contract as one for the sale of future goods by description and qualify the contract as a hybrid one;[13] with respect, the better view appears to be that the parties to the contract, in the exercise of their freedom, may include the design and building processes as further preparatory stages for the delivery and the transfer of the property in the ship and should be remunerated as provided for in the contract. These further obligations are

5. For a full analysis of issues concerning shipbuilding contracts concluded on the SAJ form see S. Curtis, *The Law of Shipbuilding Contracts* (4th edn, Informa Publishing 2012). See also M. Clarke, *Shipbuilding contracts* (2nd edn, Sweet & Maxwell 1992); A. Mandaraka-Sheppard, *Modern Maritime Law volume II: Managing Risks and Liabilities* (3rd edn, Informa Publishing 2013), at pp 221–289 (hereinafter "Mandaraka-Sheppard") and C. Hill, *Maritime Law* (6th edn, LLP 2003), at p 75 and ff.
6. s 61.
7. As defined by ss 2(5) and 5(3) of the Sale of Goods Act 1979.
8. Which are defined in s 5(1) as "goods to be manufactured by the seller after the making of the contract of sale [are] called future goods".
9. This has been the traditional view since *Lee v Griffin* [1861] B&S 272; *McDougalle v Aeromarine* [1958] 2 Lloyd's Rep 345.
10. *Hyundai Heavy Industries Co v Papadopoulos* [1980] 2 Lloyd's Rep 1; and *Stocznia Gdanska SA v Latvian Shipping Co* [1998] 1 Lloyd's Rep 609. See also M. Clarke, "In Consideration of Building Ships" [1981] LMCLQ 235.
11. [1998] 1 Lloyd's Rep 609.
12. [1998] 1 Lloyd's Rep 609, [620].
13. As suggested by Mandaraka-Sheppard (fn 5), at p 223.

usually well catered for by the standard forms in use and, it seems, should not affect the categorisation of the contract as one for the sale of future goods by description to which the Sale of Goods Act 1979 applies.[14]

It must be noted that different jurisdictions treat shipbuilding contracts as construction contracts instead with rather important differences in the legal framework surrounding their performance and thus the choice of the law applicable to the deal concerned is crucial. Choice of law clauses in these complex agreements may opt expressly for the law of a given country[15] or be less straightforward and make reference to the law of a place which has a particular connection with the contract at stake.[16]

(b) Formation of the shipbuilding contract

As for any contract, under English law offer, unconditional acceptance and consideration are essential ingredients for there to be a valid and binding shipbuilding contract.[17] However, the complexity of such agreements and the unavoidable influence that third parties such as classification societies, designers and lenders have on their terms often makes the negotiation of shipbuilding agreements lengthy and the interpretation of resulting agreements at times problematic.[18]

In order to prevent a binding agreement being formed *before* all terms of the contract have been agreed upon and approved, it is not uncommon for all drafts and any other written exchange during – and at times after – the negotiations to include a statement that it is "subject to details".[19] The question has arisen as to what this means and what are the legal implications of the use of such *term of art*. English law is very clear on this point and the courts have repeatedly held that the words "sub details" are the shipping law equivalent of the more general contract law expression "subject to contract"[20] and therefore any exchange made "subject to details" is not a binding agreement.[21] While this is perfectly reasonable in cases where the negotiations are at an initial stage, this interpretation becomes more difficult where – for example – the owner walks out of advanced negotiations due to an unexpected fluctuation in the market.

However unfair the outcome may be, English law seems well settled in holding that there is no binding contract at "subject to details" stage and it would always be advisable for both owners and yards to protect themselves from the risk of withdrawal by a *separate* indemnity

---

14. Of the same view see M.G. Bridge (ed.) *Benjamin's Sale of Goods* (9th edn, Sweet & Maxwell 2014), [1–041] and S. Curtis, *The Law of Shipbuilding Contracts* (4th edn, Informa Publishing 2012), at p 2. The classification of a shipbuilding contract as one for the sale of goods is crucial for the application of the Sale of Goods Act 1979. The terms implied by the Act may have significant effects on the working of the contract as the facts in the ship sale case, *Dalmare SpA v Union Maritime Ltd (The Union Power)* [2012] EWHC 3537 (Comm); [2013] 1 Lloyd's Rep 509 and more recently in the shipbuilding context, *Neon Shipping v Foreign Economic and Technical Co-operation* [2016] EWHC 399 Comm; [2016] 2 Lloyd's Rep 158, have demonstrated.

15. See NEWBUILDCON, art 41 and box 23(a) which makes express reference to English Law.

16. See for example art XIII(1) states, "Arbitration in Tokyo by the Japan Shipping Exchange" and art XX(1) "shall be governed by the law of the country where the VESSEL is built". See also Chapter 1 above.

17. Among the many cases see *Brogden v Metropolitan Railway* [1877] 2 App Cas 666; see also H. Beale, *Chitty on Contracts* (32nd edn, Sweet & Maxwell 2015), [2–001] and ff.

18. Mandaraka-Sheppard (fn 5), at p 229.

19. For a full discussion on this topic in the context of charterparty negotiations, see C. Debattista, "Charterparties 'Subject Details': Further Reflections" [1985] LMCLQ 241, and "Charterparties Sub Details" [1988] LMCLQ 439.

20. *Star Steamship Society v Beogradska Plovidba (The Junior K)* [1988] 2 Lloyd's Rep 583; *Welex AG v Rosa Maritime Ltd (The Epsilon Rosa) (No 2)* [2003] 2 Lloyd's Rep 509; *Thoresen & Co v Fathom Marine Co Ltd* [2004] 1 Lloyd's Rep 622. Contra *Hanjin Shipping Co Ltd v Zenith Chartering Corp (The Mercedes Envoy)* [1995] 2 Lloyd's Rep 559, a decision taken in the special circumstances of that case.

21. Cf. the American position as expressed in *The Cluden* [1982] AMC 2321; and *US Titan v Guangzhou Zhen Hua Shipping,* 241 F 3rd 135 (2nd Cir 2001); where a distinction is drawn between the *main terms* of the agreement – sufficient for a binding contract to come into existence – and its *details*.

agreement.[22] It must be noted that in *RTS Flexible Systems Ltd v Molkerei Alois Muller*,[23] a non-shipping case, the Supreme Court held that a "subject to contract" clause had been waived, given that all relevant terms had been agreed between the parties; the Court thus decided that the agreement was – in the circumstances – legally binding. This may be the beginning of a shift towards a more American[24] approach and only time will tell whether subject to details shipping contracts will be affected by the *RTS* case.

(c) The terms of the contract

The most popular standard forms of shipbuilding contract are the SAJ Form, the NEWBUILD-CON and the AWES Form. The purpose of this section is to discuss briefly the general structure of a shipbuilding agreement based on these standard forms, leaving their clause-by-clause analysis to more specialist works.[25]

A preliminary point of great practical importance is that of understanding whether a specific term of the contract is to be regarded as a condition, a warranty or an innominate term as the breach of a term categorised as a condition and that of a warranty give the innocent party very different remedies. This matter is discussed in full elsewhere in this work.[26] It suffices here to say that although guidance can be sought from sections 13 to 15A[27] of the Sale of Goods Act 1979, which imply certain conditions into any contract for the sale of goods, including a shipbuilding contract, the exact wording of individual clauses are much more useful to determine whether a term is a condition, warranty or innominate term.[28] For example, the SAJ Form Article IX(4)(c) displaces entirely any further conditions which would normally be implied by the Sale of Goods Act 1979 or the common law as the clause reads:

(c) The guarantee contained as hereinabove in this Article replaces and excludes any other liability, guarantee, warranty and/or condition imposed or implied by the law, customary, statutory or otherwise, by reason of the construction and sale of the VESSEL by the BUILDER for and to the BUYER.[29]

This is a truly remarkable clause with very far-reaching effects. For this reason and given their complexity and value it is crucial that shipbuilding contracts are drafted extremely carefully and that standard forms are amended with caution and care to avoid inherent contradictions.

The key obligation of the builder/seller under a shipbuilding contract is always that of *delivering* a vessel as *described* in the contract[30] while the owner/buyer must take delivery[31] and pay the contract price.[32] As the terms relating to the description of the goods and payment in international sales are dealt with elsewhere in this work, the following pages will focus on three important features specific to shipbuilding contracts: (i) pre-delivery inspection: trials; (ii) delivery of the "good"; and (iii) warranties under the contract.

---

22. A good example of which can be found in *Radiant Shipping Co Ltd v Sea Containers Ltd* [1995] CLC 976.
23. *RTS Flexible Systems Ltd v Molkerei Alois Muller GmbH & Co KG* [2010] UKSC 14; [2010] 3 All ER 1.
24. See again *The Cluden*.
25. For example, for the SAJ Form see S. Curtis, *The Law of Shipbuilding Contracts* (fn 14).
26. See Chapter 4.
27. For a dispute on the application of s 14(3) of the Act to a shipbuilding contract see, *Neon Shipping v Foreign Economic and Technical Co-operation* [2016] EWHC 399 Comm; [2016] 2 Lloyd's Rep 158.
28. See *The Seaflower* and the discussion on the "Waller Test" at page 103 of Chapter 3, or more extensively see F. Lorenzon, *CIF and FOB Contracts*, (6th edn, Sweet & Maxwell 2017), at [4–009] and ff.
29. See also NEWBUILDCON, art 37(d). In the same vein see AWES, art 12(a).
30. See SAJ Form, art VII.
31. See SAJ Form, art VII(4) and (6), and NEWBUILDCON, art 28.
32. See SAJ Form, arts II and III, and NEWBUILDCON, art 7 and 15.

(i) Pre-delivery inspection: trials

One of the features of shipbuilding contracts is that the owner usually has the right to have its representative on board the ship during her sea trials[33] and – on the basis of the outcome of such trial run – decide whether to accept or reject the newbuild.[34] In case the buyer is inclined to reject the ship, Article VI(4) of the SAJ form requires it to give notice to that effect to the yard specifying in which respect the ship or her equipment does not conform with her contractual description; if the buyer fails to do so it will – under the SAJ Form – be deemed to have accepted the ship.[35]

If the buyer decides to accept the ship or is deemed to have accepted her as complying with the contract description, the seller will be under the duty to deliver the newly built ship as agreed in the contract.

(ii) Delivery of the "good"

As part of the seller's obligation delivery of the ship must be made at the time and place agreed in the contract, including any postponement or alteration allowed therein.[36] The matter of timing of the delivery is particularly important to the buyer for it to be able to keep its chartering commitments (often essential to secure the financing of the whole project) and settle all matters related to the registration of the ship,[37] her insurance and all other financial and other arrangements revolving around the acceptance of a new ship. However, whether the time of delivery is of the essence of the contract or not depends squarely on the terms of the delivery clause.[38] If the contract is silent then it appears that time will not be treated as of the essence of the contract.[39]

As far as the place of delivery is concerned, the ship must be delivered at the place stipulated for in the contract[40] although usually this is the main yard or the last yard where the ship has been fitted. If the contract is silent as to the place of delivery,[41] the delivery is to be that of the seller's place of business.[42]

(iii) Warranties under the contract

There may be two types of warranties in contracts for the sale of goods: express warranties and implied warranties. Express warranties are those set out specifically in the contract itself and will usually state clearly what the warranty covers and – most importantly for both seller and buyer – what it does *not* cover. For example, Article IX(1) of the SAJ Form makes it clear that the express warranty therein contained covers "Any defects in the VESSEL which are due to defective material and/or bad workmanship on the part of the Builder [. . .] discovered within

---

33. E.g. SAJ Form, art VI(1).
34. SAJ Form, art VI(4), and NEWBUILDCON, art 23.
35. SAJ Form, art VI(4)(a).
36. SAJ Form, art VII.
37. See below.
38. SAJ Form, art III(1)(c); see also the various "delay clauses" the effect of which is discussed in *Stocznia Gdynia SA v Gearbulk Holdings Ltd* [2009] EWCA Civ 75; [2009] 1 Lloyd's Rep 461. See also *Sea-Cargo Skips AS v State Bank of India* [2013] EWHC 177 (Comm); [2013] 2 Lloyd's Rep 477.
39. See *Lindvig v Forth* [1921] 7 Ll L Rep 253, at p 255.
40. SAJ, art VI(1).
41. Which is today most unusual.
42. See Sale of Goods Act 1979, s 29(2).

[. . .] twelve months after the date of delivery"[43] provided the buyer gives formal notice of defect to the seller as provided in Article IX(2), failing which no warranty is due.[44]

Express warranties invariably contain exclusions[45] and – in the case of shipbuilding contracts – these are quite far reaching as the warranty therein contained does not cover any other defects whatsoever, any consequential loss, damage or expense, any parts originally provided by the buyer and any parts replaced by the buyer.[46] Moreover:

(b) The BUILDER shall not be responsible for any defects in any part of the VESSEL which may subsequent to delivery of the VESSEL have been replaced or in any way repaired by any other contractor, or for any defects which have been caused or aggravated by omission or improper use and maintenance of the VESSEL on the part of the BUYER, its servants or agents or by ordinary wear and tear or by any other circumstances beyond the control of the BUILDER.[47]

As the wording of this last clause completely relieves the builder from liabilities for defects in case of the buyer's contributory negligence, the issue has arisen of how to establish whether the original defect or the owner's contribution is the *dominant* cause of the failure of the vessel or her part. The matter was decided in *Ackerman v Protim*,[48] a case where the ship's failure was contributed to by defective workmanship and a proven lack of maintenance. The Court of Appeal applied the *contra proferentem* rule and held that the yard would only be excused from liability if its initial breach of contract was less significant than the lack of maintenance in causing the event. Such predominance appears to be a matter of fact. Builders can protect themselves from such liability through the use of a separate "Guarantee risk" insurance policy.[49]

Warranties may also be implied into the contract by the common law – when applicable – depending on the surrounding circumstances. The difficulty here is that implied warranties add some degree of uncertainty into contractual performance and may become real issues when the shipbuilding contract proper and the agreements concluded between the yard and its suppliers are subject to different laws and/or different jurisdictions. To avoid such uncertainties Article IX(4)(c) of the SAJ Form[50] excludes "any other liability, guarantee, warranty and/or condition imposed or implied by the law, customary, statutory or otherwise".[51]

3. THE SALE OF SECOND HAND TONNAGE

If a shipowner or pool manager is looking to increase its fleet on a permanent basis, the purchase of second hand tonnage[52] could represent a quicker and cheaper alternative to a shipbuilding project. The purchase is almost invariably negotiated through sale and purchase brokers (S&P

---

43. SAJ Form, art IX(1). See *China Shipbuilding Corporation v Nippon Yusen Kabukishi Kaisha and Anr (The Setu Maru, The Saikyo and The Suma)* [2000] 1 Lloyd's Rep 367.
44. SAJ Form, art IX(2).
45. See NEWBUILDCON, art 37.
46. SAJ Form, art IX(4)(a). See also *Star Polaris LLC v HHIC PHIL Inc* [2016] EWHC 2941 Comm.
47. SAJ Form, art IX(4)(b).
48. [1988] 2 EGLR 259.
49. For an example of such a clause see *Heesens Yacht Builders BV v Cox Syndicate Management Ltd (The Red Sapphire)* [2006] EWCA (Civ) 384; [2006] 2 Lloyd's Rep 35.
50. See above.
51. SAJ Form, art IX(4)(c).
52. For a detailed account of the topic see I. Goldrein, M. Hannaford and P. Turner, *Ship Sale and Purchase* (6th edn, Informa 2012) (hereinafter "Goldrein"); M. Strong and P. Herring, *Sale of Ships: The Norwegian Saleform* (3rd edn, Sweet & Maxwell 2014) (hereinafter "Strong & Herring"); and C. Debattista and F. Lorenzon, *Sale of Ships under the Singapore Form* (LexisNexis 2012) (hereinafter "Debattista & Lorenzon").

Brokers as they are usually called)[53] and may require the owner to set up a lease agreement and the other securities connected thereto.[54]

From a legal point of view, the sale of second hand ships is a very similar deal to a shipbuilding contract as both agreements are categorised as sales of goods covered by the Sale of Goods Act 1979[55] but the sale and purchase agreement is indeed a much simpler legal transaction. As is the case with most shipping contracts, there are a number of standard forms commonly used for sale and purchase transactions and the individual agreements are usually negotiated by exchanging amended versions of the electronic template and eventually consolidating all changes in a final document subject to approval or details.[56] Once the subjects are lifted the contract becomes binding. Again the popularity of these forms depends on very much the same factors which affect the choice of other standard terms and conditions, but for sale and purchase agreements brokers appear to have considerable influence over which form will eventually be used.

The most common forms currently in the market are the Norwegian Sale Form (hereinafter "NSF "),[57] the Japan Shipping Exchange Form (hereinafter "Nipponsale Form")[58] and the Singapore Shipsale Form (hereinafter "SSF 2011")[59] launched in Singapore in January 2011. In the yachting market the most common standard form in current use is the Mediterranean Yacht Brokers Association Memorandum of Agreement (hereinafter the "MYBA MOA").[60] None of these forms however is perfect for every deal. Quite the contrary: standard form contracts must be considered as a "set menu" of clauses, carefully drafted for the "average deal" and as such not ready for use yet. Every buyer, seller, ship and deal is different and whichever the standard form used by the parties, it must be adapted to the deal at stake.[61] There are of course risks in amending standard form contracts, the most prominent of which is that every time one word is added to or deleted from a clause the entire meaning of that clause – and at times a number of other clauses in the contract – may be affected while earlier decisions interpreting the same clause may be distinguished by virtue of the new wording, hence generating a certain degree of unpredictability and – regretfully – litigation on matters of construction and interpretation.

The issues related to whether there is a concluded sale and purchase agreement at *sub details* stage,[62] the implied conditions under sections 13 to 15A of the Sale of Goods Act 1979, and the issues related to express and implied warranties have already been discussed above when dealing with shipbuilding contracts and need not be repeated here. The only difference which is worth noting is that the contract – once all subjects are lifted – is not one for the sale

53. On which see Goldrein, ibid., at p 21 ff.

54. See below.

55. *Dalmare SpA v Union Maritime Ltd (The Union Power)* [2012] EWHC 3537 (Comm); [2013] 1 Lloyd's Rep 509. See also the extensive discussion in Debattista & Lorenzon (fn 52), [17–01] and ff.

56. See above.

57. The Norwegian Shipbrokers' Association's Memorandum of Agreement for sale and purchase of ships, adopted by the Baltic and International Maritime Council (BIMCO) in 1956, currently in its 2012 revision. A full commentary on the new edition can be found in Goldrein (fn 52).

58. The Nipponsale Memorandum of Agreement of the Documentary Committee of the Japan Shipping Exchange Inc. 1965, currently in its 1999 revision.

59. Memorandum of Agreement Singapore Ship Sale Form SSF 2011, available at www.singforms.com (accessed 9 February 2017). For a full study of this particular form see Debattista & Lorenzon (fn 52). See also C. Debattista and F. Lorenzon, "The New Singapore Sale Form: A Commentary on the New Sale Form", available at www.singforms.com/theforms_ssf_unisouthampton.php (accessed 9 February 2017).

60. Memorandum of Agreement approved by the Mediterranean Yacht Brokers Association, on which see F. Lorenzon and R. Coles, *The Law of Yachts and Yachting* (Informa Law 2012), [10–001] and ff.

61. For a fuller discussion on the use of standard form contracts in the sale of second hand ships see Goldrein (fn 52), [4.5]; see also Strong & Herring (fn 52), [2A-36].

62. Or other subjects as was the case in *Metal Scrap Trade Corp Ltd v Kate Shipping Co Ltd (The Gladys) (No 2)* [1994] 2 Lloyd's Rep 402, where the contract was concluded "sub recon".

of future goods by description but rather one of existing goods and hence the issue of misrepresentation may arise.[63] In this section three features which are peculiar to the sale of second hand tonnage will be discussed: (i) the deposit; (ii) the notice of readiness; and (iii) the matter of encumbrances. These three issues will be briefly dealt with in turn mainly with reference to the latest 2012 version of the NSF and – for its novelty and the interesting solutions adopted – the SSF 2011.

(a) The deposit

Both clause 2 of the NSF and clause 1 of the SSF 2011 deal with the important issue of the deposit.[64] The two clauses are very different in length and level of detail but most of the extra wording in the SSF 2011 is aimed at clarifying the duties of sellers and buyers as far as the deposit is concerned and reflects both current market practice and the stringent anti money-laundering requirements with which banks must now comply.

The buyer's failure to pay the price will entitle the seller to the deposit and any interest earned thereon as a minimum amount of liquidated damages;[65] the action for further damages in the measure determined according to the rules of causation and remoteness of the law chosen by the parties is always available.[66] Furthermore, in the event of failure by the buyer to pay the deposit or to provide the bank-to-bank confirmation[67] the seller has the right to cancel the contract and claim compensation for its losses and expenses. In *The Griffon*,[68] the buyer under an amended NSF 1993 contract failed to pay the deposit altogether and the seller exercised its right to cancel the contract and sued for damages. In what was considered by the market a rather surprising decision Teare J held that the quantum of losses claimable by the sellers under clause 13 of the contract was the full 10 per cent deposit rather than their actual losses and expenses.[69] On the wording of the NSF 1993, and indeed the NSF 2012, the decision seems – with respect – correct and has been subsequently approved by the Court of Appeal. It is however submitted that the outcome of the case would have been different had the contract been concluded on the SSF 2011. Clause 12 of that form excludes expressly any liquidated damages for the buyer's default in the amount of the deposit.[70] On the other hand, in case of the seller's default the deposit and any interest accrued shall be returned.[71]

The deposit is normally paid into a joint escrow account and is usually released to the seller as part of the purchase price.[72]

Among the NSF, the Nipponsale 1999 and the SSF 2011, the latter is the one which clarifies in greater detail the obligations of both parties regarding the payment. The SSF 2011, in fact, imposes on the seller the duty to open the joint escrow account in the nominated bank within a specified time and on the buyer the duty to arrange bank-to-bank confirmation from the remitting bank to the seller's nominated bank, for which the buyer (and any different remitting party) are

---

63. In general see Chitty (fn 17), [6–001] and ff.; for the specific application to MOAs see Strong & Herring (fn 52), [2A-26] and ff.
64. Goldrein (fn 52), [5–14] and ff.; Strong & Herring (fn 52), [5–01] and ff.; Debattista & Lorenzon (fn 52), [1–01] and ff.
65. SSF 2011, cl 12(b), on which Debattista & Lorenzon (fn 52) [12–05] and ff.; 1993, cl 13 on which Strong & Herring (fn 52), [16–05] and ff.; NSF 2012, cl 13 on which Goldrein (fn 52) [5.50] and ff.
66. SSF 2011, cl 12(b); NSF 1993 and 212, cl 13; Nipponsale 1999, cl 14(a), ll 248–251.
67. See below.
68. *Griffon Shipping Ltd v Firodi Shipping Ltd (The Griffon)* [2013] EWCA 1567; [2014] 1 Lloyd's Rep 15.
69. *Griffon Shipping Ltd v Firodi Shipping Ltd (The Griffon)* [2013] EWHC 593 (Comm); [2013] 2 Lloyd's Rep 50.
70. For a detailed discussion on the point see Debattista & Lorenzon (fn 52), [12–08].
71. SSF 2011, cl 13(c).
72. See Goldrein (fn 52), [5. 11. 2] and Strong & Herring (fn 52), [5–07].

known customers of the bank thereby facilitating basic due diligence required by the nominated bank to hold the deposit funds. It must however be noted that in practice the buyers and the sellers at times nominate a firm of solicitors or brokers to act as escrow agents and an escrow agreement is entered into with details of the closing necessary mechanics.

(b) The notice of readiness

When the ship is ready for delivery, the seller will issue a number of notices of expected readiness and – upon arrival at the delivery port – eventually a notice of her being "in every respect physically ready for delivery"[73] ("notice of actual readiness" in the SSF 2011).[74] The sellers must give four consecutive advance written[75] notices of the estimated time and port of delivery[76] and – in the NSF and the SSF 2011 – the ship's route.[77] Another special feature of the SSF 2011 is that as soon as any notice of estimated time and port of delivery is given, the seller is under a positive duty to take reasonable steps not to hinder delivery by the date given in the notice thus preventing deliberate over-trading. However, the consequences of breaching this duty – as those of failure to give any of the notices of expected delivery – are unclear and would appear to be absorbed in the right to cancel the contract for failure to give notice of actual readiness by the cancelling date.[78]

The Notice of Readiness (NOR) is a well-known document to the seller and buyer under both the NSF and the Nipponsale 1999, where it is called Notice of Readiness for Delivery (NORD). Under all forms the NOR or NORD – if validly given – has the function of triggering the buyer's duty to pay the contract price[79] and take delivery of the vessel. Under the NSF the NOR will be validly given if two conditions are fulfilled: (i) the ship is at the place of delivery; and (ii) is physically ready for delivery in accordance with the contract.[80] Under Nipponsale 1999, the NORD is validly given "when the vessel becomes ready for delivery"[81] although presumably she must be "within the Delivery Range".[82] However, none of these two forms makes any reference to any kind of readiness which is not purely physical. This is where the SSF 2011 has broken new ground with the introduction of a substantially different notice: the Notice of Actual Readiness (NOAR).[83] The function of the NOAR under the SSF is exactly the same as the NOR under the NSF or Nipponsale 1999 but the requirements for its validity are radically different. For the NOAR to be valid three conditions must be fulfilled: (i) the ship must have arrived at the Delivery Place agreed in the contract or notified under clause 5(a); (ii) the ship must be physically

---

73. As in cl 3 of the NSF.

74. See Debattista & Lorenzon (fn 52), [5–01] and ff.

75. Under the SSF 2011 any *written* notice must be given by registered letter, telex, fax, e-mail or other modern form of written communication.

76. The same notices (30, 15, 7 and 3 days) are stipulated in the NSF, cl 5(a), the SSF 2011, 5(b), and the Nipponsale 1999, cl 4(b).

77. NSF 1993, cls 5 and 52, NSF 2012, cl 5(b); SSF 2011, cls 5(a) and 69.

78. See below.

79. Under the NSF, cl 3, ll 27–29, together with the requirement that the vessel is "in every respect physically ready for delivery in accordance with the terms and conditions of [the contract]" and *simpliciter* under Nipponsale 1999, cl 2(b) ll 26–29, and the NSF 2012, ll 83–84.

80. NSF 1993, cl 5(a), ll 54–56 ; NSF 2012, cl 5(b), ll 83–84 where the words "in every respect" have been omitted.

81. Nipponsale 1999, cl 7(a).

82. Nipponsale 1999, cl 4(a), cl 50; see Strong & Herring (fn 52), [8–28]; *contra* see Goldrein (fn 52), [5.12.12] who appears to infer that the ship does not need to be at the place of delivery for the NORD to be validly given.

83. SSF 2011, cl 5(b); Debattista & Lorenzon (fn 52), [5–04]–[5–09].

ready for delivery;[84] and (iii) the seller must have ready all of the seller's documents required by clause 8[85] save for the Certificate of Ownership, Class Maintained Certificate, Invoice for Bunkers and Lubricants and the Protocol of Delivery and Acceptance. This last condition may appear a minor alteration from the familiar concept of NOR in a ship sale context but it certainly is not as the lack of any of the numerous documents required under clause 8 (save those expressly excepted) appears to make the NOAR invalidly given[86] and hence unable to trigger the buyer's duty to pay the price and take delivery and – most remarkably – unable to stop the running of time towards the cancelling clause. In fact, if the NOAR is not validly given by the cancelling date, the buyer has the option to cancel the contract.[87]

(c) Encumbrances

All forms insist that the seller warrants that the ship be delivered free of encumbrances[88] but whether this term is a condition, warranty or innominate term is a matter which has caused some debate.[89] Uncertainty is usually unwelcome in commercial contracts, either requiring detailed negotiation or leading to difficult disputes. The odd one out is again the SSF 2011, under which it is very clear that this clause is a condition of the contract,[90] breach of which entitles the buyer to reject the ship and claim damages. Given the draconian consequences for the breach of clause 9 of the SSF 2011, the widened list of encumbrances of which the ship should be delivered free becomes even more important to both the buyer and seller and will probably be one of those parts of the form which will be looked at very carefully during negotiations. Against a NSF list of only five items,[91] the SSF requires the ship to be delivered "free from all encumbrances, charters, mortgages, maritime liens, writs (save where security has been furnished), port State and other administrative detentions, stowaways, trading commitments and any other debts whatsoever".[92] Under the SSF 2011 therefore the ship may be rejected if delivered under arrest[93] or Port State Control detention on virtually any ground, with stowaways on board (supposedly at the time of the NOAR, on delivery or any time in between) and if encumbered by any other trading commitment. As far as the words "any other debts whatsoever" are concerned, it may be worth noting that they have been held by the English Court of Appeal to include debts which, at

---

84. The express reference to cl 4 of the SSF 2011 here means that physical readiness has a very well defined meaning:

> in substantially the same condition as the Vessel was at the time of inspection, with the exception of fair wear and tear, with present Class maintained free from any outstanding Class conditions and/or recommendations, free from damage affecting Vessel's Class, with all Class and trading certificates (both national and international) clean and valid at the time of delivery. All cargo spaces shall be clean and free of any cargo, subject only to immovable residues.

85. For an interesting case where the MOA required tender of a "portworthy certificate", see London Arbitration 14/00 in LMLN 546, at p 3.

86. This amendment reflects market practice which has inserted documentary readiness as a rider to the NSF 1993 form.

87. SSF 2011, cl 13(a).

88. NSF 1993, cl 9, l 100; NSF 2012, cl 9; Nipponsale 1999, cl 13; and NSF 2012 cl 9.

89. See Goldrein (fn 52) [5. 37 .6]; Strong & Herring (fn 52), [12–03]–[12–05].

90. *B S & N Ltd (BVI) v Micado Shipping Ltd (Malta) (The Seaflower) (No 1)* [2001] 1 Lloyd's Rep 341.

91. NSF 1993, cl 9. The five items are: (1) charters, (2) encumbrances, (3) mortgages, (4) maritime liens and (5) any other debts whatsoever. In the 2012 version of the NSF, ll 302–303 also require the vessel to be free from any Port State or other administrative detentions.

92. SSF 2011, cl 9(a); see Debattista & Lorenzon (fn 52), [9–05] and ff.

93. Cf. *Athens Cape Naviera SA v Deutsche Dampfschiffartsgesellshaft "Hansa" Aktiengesellshaft (The Barenbels)* [1985] 1 Lloyd's Rep 528.

the time of delivery, had given rise to actual existing rights affecting the property in or the use of the ship.[94]

The NSF[95] and the Nipponsale 1999[96] impose on the seller the duty to indemnify the buyer against "all consequences of claims made against the Vessel"[97] while the indemnity under the SSF 2011 is due against "all consequences of any *claims against the Buyers* that may arise due to claims against the Vessel". In order to trigger the indemnity under the SSF 2011 therefore the buyer must prove that: (1) it suffered a quantified loss; (2) as the consequence of a claim against it; (3) arisen due to a claim against the ship.[98]

4. SHIP REGISTRATION

From its early days at the Lloyd's Coffee House, claimed to be at the origin of the Register of Shipping in 1760, the organisation, modus operandi and purpose of ship registration in the United Kingdom have evolved dramatically, adapting to the economic and social circumstances of the times. This section of the chapter considers the current legal framework for the registration of ships in the British Register, in order to give the reader a basic picture of its organisation, structure and functions. The criteria established to define who is qualified to own a British ship and which ships are entitled to be entered in Part I of the register will also be outlined. Finally, special attention will be paid to the type of evidence the Register provides.[99]

(a) Key features of a centralised ship registration system

Part II of the Merchant Shipping Act 1995 (hereinafter "MSA 1995")[100] defines the legal framework of the British ship registration system, which is detailed in the Merchant Shipping (Registration of Ships) Regulations 1993, as amended (hereinafter "1993 Regulations").[101] The MSA 1995 continues the innovative centralised Register created under the Merchant Shipping Act 1993 (hereinafter "MSA 1993")[102] and the 1993 Regulations.[103] The Central Register of British Ships is based in Cardiff and consists of both paper and computerised records to fulfil its purpose of a public record.[104] The Register is maintained by the Registrar General of Shipping and

---

94. Ibid. and Goldrein (fn 52), [5. 37. 9] ; Strong & Herring (fn 52), [12–12] and [12–13]; and Debattista & Lorenzon (fn 52), [9–15].

95. NSF 1993, cl 9, ll 209–211; NSF 2012, cl 9, ll 303–305.

96. Nipponsale 1999, cl 13, ll 232–235.

97. Ibid.

98. See Debattista & Lorenzon (fn 52), [9–17] ff.

99. It is not the aim of this section to cover all the aspects of ship registration. For a more comprehensive view see R. Coles and E. Watt, *Ship Registration: Law and Practice* (2nd edn, Informa Law 2009) (hereafter referred to as "Coles and Watt"). See also C. Hill, *Maritime Law* (6th edn, LLP 2003), Chapter 1, G Bowtle,, C Buss and D Osborne, *The Law of Ship Mortgages* (2nd edn, Informa Law 2016) ("Bowtle"), [2.3]–[2.9].

100. 1995 MSA, Chapter 21, "An Act to consolidate the Merchant Shipping Acts 1894 to 1994 and other enactments relating to merchant shipping", as complemented by Schedule 1, on Private Law Provisions for registered ships. The MSA 1995 entered into force on 1 January 1996.

101. SI 1993/3138, in force on 21 March 1994, as amended by the Merchant Shipping (Registration of Ships) (Amendment) Regulations 1994 (SI 1994/541), the Merchant Shipping (Registration of Ships) (Tonnage Amendment) Regulations 1998, SI 1998/1915, the Merchant Shipping (Registration of Ships) (Amendment) Regulations 1998, SI 1998/2976 and the Merchant Shipping (Registration of Ships, and Tonnage) Regulations 1999, SI 1999/3206.

102. MSA 1993, s 1.

103. MSA 1995, Part II, s 8.

104. MSA 1995, s 1, and 1993 Regulations, Part II, regs 2(2) and 2(3).

Seamen[105] whose functions may be discharged fully or partially by the Secretary of State by means of Directions.[106]

Interestingly, since 1761 and until the entry into force of the MSA 1993 and the 1993 Regulations, the UK registration system relied on a completely different organisation made up by local registers kept in each port, and operated by customs officers.[107] Traces of the old system are retained in the new centralised process as ships registered under Part I and Part II of the register[108] are allocated a port of their choice.[109] However, this allocation is nowadays deprived of any legal effect.[110]

The centralised registry system in the UK is complemented by the registers in the relevant British possessions.[111] Such registers are classified into two categories[112] – for ships other than small ships and fishing vessels[113] – and the assignment of each relevant British possession to a category of registry is done by means of Orders in Council.[114] Section 18(3) of the MSA 1995 limits its statutory capacity in favour of the legislation of the relevant British possession, which may provide for further or different accessibility restrictions. The 1993 Regulations[115] provide for the procedures of transfer of registration of ships registered in Part I of the Central Register to the register of a port in a relevant British dependent territory and vice versa.[116]

(b) Basic features

This section will focus on some key aspects of ship registration, in particular (i) the public and private law aspects of ship registration, (ii) the division of the Central Register into four parts corresponding to four different categories of ships and (iii) the voluntary character of registration.

(i) Public and private law aspects of ship registration

The main function and purpose of the ship Central Register is the public record of ships and their particulars, which have implications in their legal status both in the public and the private law spheres. This duality is also reflected in the two bodies of legislation currently in force, and more

---

105. MSA 1995, s 8(2).

106. MSA 1995, s 8(4).

107. The National Archives, Registration of Merchant Ships, http://www.nationalarchives.gov.uk/help-with-your-research/research-guides/merchant-ships/ (accessed 10 January 2017).

108. 1993 Regulations, reg 2.

109. From a list contained in Schedule 2 to the 1993 Regulations. The port allocation is still marked on the stern of the ship, pursuant to Schedule 3 to the 1993 Regulations.

110. 1993 Regulations, Part VI, reg 31. See N. Gaskell and A. Clarke, "Sailing Towards Consolidation" [1994] LMCLQ 146.

111. See the MSA 1995, s 18 and s 315 in Part XIII. British possessions are defined and listed in s 313 in Part XIII of the MSA 1995, as follows "*(a) The Isle of Man, (b) any of the Channel Islands; and (c) any colony*". As to the latter, see the Merchant Shipping (Categorisation of Registries of Relevant British Possessions) (Amended) Order 2008, SI 2008/1243 and the list contained in fn 112.

112. *Category* 1: unlimited tonnage, type and length is defined in Schedule to the 2008 Order as "Registry to which no restriction such as is mentioned in s 18(2)(a) of the Merchant Shipping Act 1995 applies". *Category 2*: limited type and tonnage is defined in Schedule to the 2008 Order as "Registry in which ships may be registered, subject to the restrictions specified in column (3)", i.e. " (i) passenger ships, (ii) pleasure vessels of more than 150 tons and (iii) ships which are not passenger ships or pleasure vessels, but which are of more than 150 tons".

113. MSA 1995, s 18 and reg 3 of the Order in Council 2008.

114. The Order in Council under section 18 presently in force is the Merchant Shipping (Categorisation of Registries of Relevant British Possessions) Order, SI 2003/1248, as amended, according to which Bermuda, the British Virgin Islands, Gibraltar and Isle of Man have been assigned to Category 1, and Anguilla, Falkland Islands, Guernsey, Jersey, Montserrat, St Helena, and Turks and Caicos Islands have been assigned to Category 2.

115. Part IX, regs 71 and 72.

116. See also N. P. Ready, *Ship Registration* (3rd edn, LLP 1998), at pages 61 and 62.

precisely in Part II of the MSA 1995 together with its Schedule 1,[117] and the 1993 Regulations as amended.

The main public law implication of registration relates to the nationality of the ship and hence the duties of the flag State to exercise effective jurisdiction with regards to its ships and control over administrative, technical and social matters.[118] In the field of private law, two fundamental issues will be addressed – the ship's registered title[119] and the registered mortgage.

(ii) The four parts of the Register

In compliance with the MSA 1995, section 8(5), the 1993 Regulations, regulation 2 in Part II, provides for the division of the Central Register of British ships into four separate parts, distinguishing between different categories of ships. These are:

1. Part I, devoted to ships owned by qualified persons[120] excluding fishing vessels and small ships;
2. Part II, devoted to fishing vessels;
3. Part III, devoted to small ships;[121] and
4. Part IV, devoted to bareboat charter ships.[122]

For the sake of completeness it is worth mentioning that Part II for fishing vessels hosts two types of registration, namely, the "simple registration" where the private provisions regarding ownership transfers and registration of mortgages are not made public in the register,[123] and the "full registration", to which provisions of Schedule 1 to the MSA 1995 apply.

Regulation 5 of the 1993 Regulations sets out the principle that a ship may only be registered in one Part of the register.

(iii) The voluntary character of registration

As opposed to the repealed registration system, which established the compulsory registration of British-owned ships, under the current legal framework the registration of British-owned ships is voluntary.[124] Section 2 of the MSA 1894, entitled "Obligation to Register British Ships", provided for the detention of those ships not exempted from registry under the Act, until the master, if so required, produced the ship certificate of register.[125] The compulsory system dates back to the Navigation Acts from 1660 which sought to implement a protectionist policy over the

---

117. Schedule 1 to the MSA 1995 is devoted to Private Law Provisions for registered ships, and Part II of the MSA 1995 and the 1993 Regulations are dedicated to the public law aspects.

118. Art 94 of the United Nations Convention on the Law of the Sea (Montego Bay, 10 December 1982) 1833 UNTS 3. See Chapter 8, pages 331–332 and Chapter 9.

119. See the 1993 Regulations, reg 28 on evidence of title to be submitted to the Registrar to register a ship for the first time.

120. Part III of the 1993 Regulations, regs 7 to 9.

121. Defined in reg 1 of the 1993 Regulations as "*a ship which is less than 24 metres in overall length and is, or is applying to be, registered under Part VI*" of the Regulations.

122. MSA 1995, s 17.

123. 1993 Regulations, regs 3 and 4.

124. MSA 1995, s 9.

125. MSA 1894, s 2(3), www.legislation.gov.uk/ukpga/1894/60/pdfs/ukpga_18940060_en.pdf (accessed 11 January 2017).

shipbuilding industry, according to which British merchants had to carry their goods on board British-built ships.[126]

Presently, the 1993 Regulations establish the entitlement to register a ship in the Central Register coupled with a newly introduced period of validity limited to five years as from the date of registration of the certificate of registry.[127] To avoid the expiry and hence the termination of the registration, an application for renewal needs to be produced in accordance with regulation 42. The entitlement to register a ship allowing it to become a British ship, or to renew its registration, is conditional on the verification that a number of eligibility criteria are met. The requirements to be met in order to own a ship entitled to be registered in Part I of the register are discussed below.

(c) Requirements for registration under Part I of the Register

In accordance with Article 91 of UNCLOS, "Nationality of ships", which provides that "[e]very State shall fix the conditions for the grant of its nationality to ships, for the registration of ships in its territory, and for the right to fly its flag", regulations 7 and 8 in Part III of the 1993 Regulations establish the requirements for eligibility to own a ship to be registered on Part I of the Register and which ships are entitled to be registered therein.[128] The requirements are to be analysed both from a subjective and an objective perspective. These three elements will be dealt with in turn.

(i) Qualified persons to own a British ship: the subjective approach

British citizenship, or nationality, are traditional conditions to be eligible to register a ship in the British Register, with individuals or bodies corporate of EU Member States also eligible.[129]

Bodies corporate need to be either incorporated in an EU Member State with no further requirement as to the location of their principal place of business[130] or incorporated in any relevant British dependent territory with the additional requirement in that case to have the principal place of business in the United Kingdom or in any such possession.[131]

European Economic Interest Groupings (EEIGs), as defined by Council Regulation (EEC) No 2137/85 of 25 July 1985,[132] may also qualify to own ships to be registered in Part I, provided they are registered in the UK.[133] Their registration in the UK enables the EEIGs to acquire legal personality as bodies corporate from the date shown in the certificate of registration.[134]

---

126. The National Archives, Registration of Merchant Ships. See fn 107.

127. 1993 Regulations, reg 39.

128. These provisions do not apply to small ships, fishing vessels and government ships.

129. 1993 Regulations, reg 7(1)(a)–(e). It remains to be seen what the effect of Brexit will be on the eligibility of the latter.

130. Ibid., reg 7(1)(f).

131. Ibid., reg 7(1)(g). As to the meaning and extent of "principal place of business", see *Owners of Cargo Lately Laden on Board the Rewia v Caribbean Liners (Caribtainer) Ltd (The Rewia)* (CA) [1991] 2 Lloyd's Rep 325; [1993] ILPr 507.

132. OJ L 199, 31 July 1985, 1–9. This Regulation was implemented in the UK by means of The European Economic Interest Grouping Regulations 1989 (SI 1989/638); The European Interest Grouping (Amendment) Regulations 2009 (SI 2009/2399) and The European Economic Interest Grouping and European Public Limited-Liability Company (Amendment) Regulations 2014 (SI 2014/2382). As commented above, the impact Brexit will have on the eligibility criteria is still to be seen.

133. 1993 Regulations, reg 7(1)(h).

134. The European Economic Interest Grouping Regulations 1989 (SI 1989/638) reg 3, giving practical effect to the Council Regulation (EEC) No 2137/85.

A person not qualified under regulation 7(1) to own a British ship is nevertheless exempted from complying with any of the above requirements in case of co-ownership of the ship, provided the majority interest in the ship[135] is owned by persons who are so qualified[136] and the ship is registered in Part I of the Register.[137]

(ii) Ships entitled to be registered in Part I of the Register: the objective approach

As a general rule[138] a ship is entitled to be registered and hence become a British ship, if a majority interest in the ship is owned by one or more persons qualified to be owners of British ships pursuant to regulation 7. This general rule is however subject to the Registrar's refusal, in accordance with regulation 36, and to the specific requirements set out in paragraphs 2 and 3 of this regulation, the applicability of which will depend on the characteristics of the person (or persons) forming the majority interest in the ship.

Accordingly, where the person or persons forming the majority interest in the ship are:

- British citizens or other EU Member States nationals established in the UK,[139]
- British Dependent Territories citizens,[140]
- British nationals (overseas) under the Hong Kong (British Nationality) Order 1986,[141]
- bodies corporate incorporated in an EU Member State, or
- European Economic Interest Groupings (EEIGs) pursuant to Article 1 of the Council Regulation (EEC) No 2137/85, registered in the United Kingdom,[142]

the ship will be entitled to be registered only if the owner (or, in case more persons are to be registered as owners, at least one of them) is resident in the United Kingdom.[143] Where none of the above conditions is met, the entitlement to register arises only if a ship's representative is appointed in accordance with Part V of the 1993 Regulations. This would be either an individual resident in the UK or a body corporate incorporated in an EU Member State with a place of business in the UK.[144]

Where the person or persons forming the majority interest in the ship are British overseas citizens[145] or British subjects under the British Nationality Act 1981, the ship's entitlement to register arises provided the person or any of those persons, as the case may be, is resident in the UK. If that requirement is not met, a subsidiary condition is introduced, namely that the Secretary of State issues a declaration of consent for the ship to be registered and in addition that the appointment of a representative person in relation to the ship is made, pursuant to Part V of the 1993 Regulations.[146]

---

135. Where the legal title is to 33 or more shares in the ship pursuant to reg 9. Regulations 2(5)(a) and (b) establish that the property in a ship can be divided into 64 shares, and that not more than 64 persons are entitled to be registered at the same time as owners of any one ship, subject to the exceptions therein contained.
136. 1993 Regulations, reg 7(2)(a) in conjunction with reg 8.
137. Ibid., reg 7(2)(b).
138. Ibid., reg 8.
139. 1993 Regulations, reg 7(1)(a).
140. Ibid., reg 7(1)(b).
141. SI 1986/948, reg 7(1)(e).
142. 1993 Regulations, reg 7(1)(h).
143. According to reg 9(b) "a body corporate shall be treated as resident in the United Kingdom, if, being a body incorporated in a member State, it has a place of business in the United Kingdom".
144. 1993 Regulations, reg 18(2).
145. Ibid., reg 7(1)(c).
146. Ibid., 8(4)(a).

Where the person or persons forming the majority interest in the ship are bodies corporate incorporated in any relevant British possession, the ship's entitlement to register arises if the body corporate has a place of business in the United Kingdom or, in the absence of that requirement, if a representative person is appointed in relation to the ship.[147]

The Regulations finally contemplate the possibility of certain combinations of persons qualified on different grounds pursuant to regulation 7 forming part of the majority interest in the ship, and establish different requirements to entitle the registration of the ship. For example, if the majority interest in a ship is owned by one or more persons qualified under regulation 7(1)(c) or (d) together with one or more persons qualified under regulation 7(1)(a), (b), (e), (f) or (h), the declaration of the Secretary of State consenting to the ship to be registered will no longer be needed when none of the persons is resident in the United Kingdom, provided a representative person is appointed pursuant to Part V of the 1993 Regulations.[148]

(iii) The British connection

The aim of the requirements discussed above is doubtless to ensure the British connection of the ships entered in the Register.[149]

This purpose is contained in regulation 8, according to which the concept of British connection lies chiefly in the ownership of the ship by one or more persons qualified to be owners of British ships by virtue of regulation 7, provided it represents the majority interest in the ship. This concept is also dealt with in section 9(9) of the MSA 1995, where it is merely stated that a ship having a British connection is a ship which complies with the requirements set in subsections 9(1)(a), 9(1)(b) and 9(2)(a) to be registered in the Central Register of British ships, i.e. the ship is "owned, to the prescribed extent, by persons qualified to own British ships"; and other requirements established by the 1993 Regulations are met "to secure that, taken into conjunction with the requisite of ownership, only ships having a British connection are registered".

The British connection is therefore the cornerstone for a ship to be registered in the Register of British Ships entitling the ship to fly the British flag. In this way, the MSA 1995 and the 1993 Regulations are ensuring the existence of what has been named in international law the *genuine link* between the ship and her flag State. However, there remains controversy given the lack of a definition of this concept in the international legal framework.

In particular, the 1982 United Nations Convention on the Law of the Sea (UNCLOS), Article 91,[150] along the lines of its predecessor, the 1958 Convention on the High Seas, Article 5,[151] refers to this term without giving a definition of this concept. A further opportunity to define the concept arose with the 1986 United Nations Convention on Conditions for Registration of Ships (the "Registration Convention"), concluded under the auspices of the United Nations Conference on Trade and Development (UNCTAD), which is not yet in force.[152] The aim of the Registration Convention is quite ambitious: as described in its Article 1, the purpose is to ensure or, as the case may be, strengthen the genuine link between a State and the ship flying its flag. The Registration Convention further tries to provide a uniform legal framework for the States

---

147. Ibid., 8(4)(b).
148. 1993 Regulations, reg 8(5)(a) and (b).
149. See equivalent provisions set for the registration of fishing vessels in Part II (reg 14) and the registration of small ships in Part III of the Register (reg 90).
150. United Nations Convention on the Law of the Sea (Montego Bay, 10 December 1982) 1833 UNTS 3.
151. Convention on the High Seas (Geneva, 29 April 1958) 450 UNTS 11.
152. United Nations Convention on Conditions for the Registration of Ships (Geneva, 7 February 1986) UN doc TD/RS/CONF/23 (13 March 1986) which requires 40 signatories, the combined tonnage of which exceeds 25 per cent of the world tonnage to enter into force. As at 9 January 2017, it has received only 15 ratifications and accessions.

parties to exercise effective jurisdiction and control over the ships flying their flags, with regard to a higher degree of transparency enabling *inter alia* the identification and accountability of shipowners and operators, and with regard to administrative, technical, economic and social matters. Article 7 is dedicated to the levels of participation by nationals in the ownership and/or manning of ships and may be regarded as the key enabling instrument to accomplish the aim of the Convention. However, the Registration Convention leaves to the States parties the discretion to define these levels of participation within general parameters and the minimal requirements set out in Articles 8(1) and (2), 9(1) to (3) and 10.[153]

(d) Evidentiary value of the Register

The purpose of the Register, other than to entitle a ship to become a British ship, is to constitute an official record of, and provide the public access to, all the information relating to the ships therein registered. In this respect, it is relevant to consider what kind of evidence the Register actually provides for both (i) public and (ii) private law purposes, and leaving as a separate and last point for consideration (iii) the statutory treatment of the evidentiary value given by the MSA 1995 to the documents purporting to be copies of the information contained in an entry in the Register.

(i) Public law

The registration of a ship as a British ship was held to be prima facie evidence of her nationality in *R v Adolph Bjornsen*.[154] In this case the nationality of the barque ship *Gustav Adolph* had to be established for jurisdictional purposes over a homicide committed on board while the ship was plying the high seas. The *Gustav Adolph* sailed under the British flag and was registered as a British ship under the Merchant Shipping Act 1854. The Court held that the registration record of the *Gustav Adolph* in conjunction with the fact that the ship was flying the British flag and that the owner was resident in England, constituted prima facie evidence that the ship was a British ship. However, the said evidence was rebutted by the fact that the owner was not a "natural-born British subject" and no proof was produced that the owner was qualified to own a British ship, i.e. had been naturalised or denizen in the manner prescribed in the MSA 1854.[155]

The effect of this prima facie evidence is also relevant to other aspects of public law, which affect the flag State duties over the ship.[156]

(ii) Private law

A number of private law implications derive from the registration of the ship in the British Register and an exhaustive discussion of these would be beyond the scope of this work.[157] The cases below, however, provide good examples of what is the most relevant practical aspect of registration: that of its evidentiary value. Given the different legal aspects arising in each of the

---

153. See Chapter 8, pages 330–331. See also Coles and Watt, at [2.8]–[2.20], and George C. Kasoulides, "The 1986 United Nations Convention on the Conditions for Registration of Vessels and the Question of Open Registry" [1989] *Ocean Development and International Law*, 543–576. See further J-A Witt, *Obligations and Control of Flag States: Developments and Perspectives in International Law and EU Law* (Lit Verlag Münster 2007), 26–34.

154. *Leigh v Cave* 545, [1865] 169 ER 1508.

155. See also MSA 1995, s 1.

156. See Chapter 8, page 331 and Coles and Watt, [1.2]–[1.21].

157. See A.R.M. Fogarty, *Merchant Shipping Legislation* (2nd edn, Informa 2004) (hereafter referred to as "Fogarty") Chapter 1; Coles and Watt, [1.24]–[1.29].

cases cited here, a more detailed account of the relevant facts and the courts' judgments has been considered necessary.

Hibbs v Ross[158] concerned an action for personal injury suffered by the plaintiff while lawfully crossing the deck of the ship *Jarnia*, which was laid up in a public dock for the winter, to reach the quay from another ship lying in the same dock, alongside the *Jarnia*. The claim was brought against the registered owner according to the certificate of registry on the grounds of negligence of the ship-keeper in charge of the *Jarnia*. It was held by the court that the certificate constituted prima facie evidence of ownership. This was in fact only the preliminary point in the legal analysis of whether ownership, once proved, amounted to a presumption that the persons in charge of the ship (in that case, the ship-keeper) were employed by the owner, in order to establish the owner's vicarious liability. The first presumption, i.e. the certificate of registry being prima facie evidence of ownership, was based on the Merchant Shipping Act 1854,[159] the *Jarnia* being a ship registered in 1864, under the said Act. Section 107 provided, *inter alia*, that the Certificate of Registry was prima facie evidence of all the matters therein contained or thereon endorsed, and read as follows:

17 & 18 Vict. c. 104, s. 107: – Every register of or declaration made in pursuance of the second part of this act in respect of any British ship may be proved in any court of justice, or before any person having either by law or by consent of parties authority to receive evidence, either by the production of the original or by an examined copy, or by any copy thereof purporting to be certified under the hand of the registrar or other person having the charge of the original, which certified copies he is hereby required to furnish to any person applying at a reasonable time for the same, upon payment of 1s. for each such certified copy; and every such register or copy of a register, and also *every certificate of registry of any British ship, purporting to be signed by the registrar or other proper officer, shall be received in evidence in any court of justice, or before any person having by law or by consent of parties authority to receive evidence, as primâ facie proof of all the matters contained or recited in such register when the register or such copy is produced, and of all the matters contained in or indorsed on such certificate of registry, and purporting to be authenticated by the signature of a registrar, when such certificate is produced.*[160]

(emphasis added)

Consequently, the Courts would accept contradictory evidence and look beyond the Register evidence into the validity of the underlying transactions performed, in order to confirm and protect the rights of the lawful owner should the need arise.[161]

This need arose in the context of the MSA 1894, in *Dalby v Others claiming to be Owners of Motor Yacht Bineta (The Bineta)*,[162] where an application was made by the purchaser of the yacht *Bineta* to be registered as owner under the MSA 1894. It was held that the plaintiff had acquired good title to the motor yacht *Bineta* even though the seller he had purchased her from was not at the time the registered owner of the yacht. The seller had previously sold the *Bineta* to Garthwaite who then became the registered owner. However, Garthwaite failed to pay the purchase price and consequently the seller retained possession of the yacht, exercising a lien as an unpaid seller. Two years later the seller resold the yacht to the plaintiff, who paid the purchase price and applied to be registered as owner of the vessel under the MSA 1894. This application was refused because the seller did not appear as the registered owner, instead

---

158. (1865–66) LR 1 QB 534.
159. 17 & 18 Vict c 104.
160. Extract quoted from *Hibbs v Ross* [1866] LR 1 QB 534, 536.
161. See also *The Innisfallen* [1865–67] LR 1 A & E 72, in the context of the MSA 1854, s 66, and the MSA Amendment Act 1862, s 3.
162. *Dalby v Others claiming to be Owners of Motor Yacht Bineta (The Bineta)* [1967] 1 WLR 121; [1966] 2 Lloyd's Rep 419.

Garthwaite did. The plaintiff commenced an action for an order that he be declared the lawful owner of the *Bineta* and entitled to be registered as such. The application was successful on the grounds of the seller's right of re-sale under sections 39(1) and 48(3) of the Sale of Goods Act, 1893.[163]

It would be safely pointed out that it is the most common practice for the prospective buyer to be advised to verify that the identity of the seller in the Memorandum of Agreement and the Bill of Sale match the identity of the registered owner before executing the bill of sale. In case of discrepancy, it would be doubtless in the interest of the intended buyer to request from the seller to update the registered information on the legal status of the ship and avoid further costs and, more importantly, risks vis-à-vis a third bona fide purchaser relying on the registered title, as it will be seen hereunder.

As a result of the evidential nature of the Register, it has been stated that the court "has power, by virtue of its inherent jurisdiction" to order the rectification of the Register and in some circumstances the expunction of entries relating to transactions declared void.[164]

The question which immediately arises is what type of protection is afforded, for example, to the bona fide purchaser who relies upon the evidence of title of the seller provided by the Register. An answer was given in cases where fraud had arisen, whereby a bona fide buyer relying on the evidence of title provided by the Register, would acquire good title over the ship for valuable consideration, by execution and registration of the bill of sale. Such a scenario was presented and decided upon in *The Horlock*,[165] in the context of the MSA 1854. The dispute concerned an action of co-ownership in which the plaintiff, G. Wright, had purchased for valuable consideration half of the shares from the seller, T. Worraker, who appeared as the registered owner of the said shares. According to the bill of sale, registered under the MSA 1854, the defendant, J Horlock – at the time sole owner of the *Horlock* – had transferred his shares to T. Worraker who in turn resold them to the plaintiff. The defendant denied that he had ever signed a bill of sale transferring any shares of the *Horlock* and claimed that the bill of sale was fraudulent. The key question arising here was whether the plaintiff, who was assumed to have purchased from the registered owner 32 sixty-fourth shares of the ship for valuable consideration and without notice of fraud, had good and equitable title to those shares. In his decision, Sir Robert Phillimore considered two legal grounds governing the case before him, i.e. section 43 of the MSA 1854, and the Court of Appeal in Chancery decision in *Heath v Crealock*.[166]

Section 43 had a major impact in the legal reasoning in *The Horlock*. Its meaning was considered to be the "material point" in that case, in particular, the passage cited hereunder:

[S]ubject to any rights and powers appearing by the register book to be vested in any other party, the registered owner of any ship or share therein shall have power absolutely to dispose in manner hereinafter mentioned of such ship or share, and to give effectual receipts for any money paid or advanced by way of consideration.[167]

---

163. For a detailed view on yacht registration, see F. Lorenzon and R. Coles, *The Law of Yachts and Yachting* (Informa Law 2012), Chapter 2.

164. *Brond v Broomhall* [1906] 1 KB 57, and *Glatzer v Bradston Ltd (The Ocean Enterprise)* [1997] 1 Lloyd's Rep 449.

165. [1876–77] LR 2 PD 243. Contrast *Glatzer v Bradston Ltd (The Ocean Enterprise)* [1997] 1 Lloyd's Rep 449, where the subsequent buyers did not act in good faith.

166. [1874–75] LR 10 Ch 22, at p 33, a dispute regarding land sale.

167. *The Horlock*, 248.

Sir Robert Phillimore also weighed the predominance of authority in the cases cited before him, particularly, the Court of Appeal in Chancery decision in *Heath v Crealock*, which supported the proposition, in Sir Robert Phillimore's words, that:

[A] purchaser purchasing from an owner of registered property for a valuable consideration without any notice of fraud, and combining therefore a legal and equitable title, is not liable to have such title impeached on the ground of fraud to which he was not a party; such fraud being between the person who at the time of the purchase appeared on the register as owner and another person. I should observe here that the ownership is still registered, according to the bill of sale in question.[168]

Whereas the first ground focuses solely on the registered owner's right to sell, the second one may seem to allow some space for the doctrine of "foi publique" of the Register, with the inherent requirement of lack of notice of fraud by the purchaser, by virtue of which, the purchaser relying upon the registered information would be protected.

Although Sir Robert Phillimore expressly considered the fact that the bill of sale had been registered, the protection afforded to the bona fide purchaser would arguably also apply when valuable consideration has been transferred and the bill of sale has been executed and exchanged, even though the bill has not been later registered.

In the present legal framework, the protection afforded to the bona fide purchaser is to be analysed in accordance with sub-paragraphs 1(1) to 1(3) of Schedule 1 to the MSA 1995, entitled *Private Law Provisions for registered ships*. On the one hand, sub-paragraph 1(1) combined with sub-paragraph 1(3) mirrors, to an important extent, the old section 43 of the MSA 1854, re-enacted as section 56 of the MSA 1894, with the same effect as described in *The Horlock*. On the other hand sub-paragraph 1(2), which finds a predecessor in section 57 of the MSA 1894, aims to protect interests arising under contract or other equitable interests acquired in a ship or share in the same manner as in respect of any other personal property and making them enforceable against a registered owner.[169]

However, there will inevitably be situations where paragraph 1 cannot afford protection to conflicting innocent interests. This could be the situation in a scenario similar to *The Bineta* where, for instance, the buyer had not yet obtained a declaration from the court that he be declared the lawful owner of the ship and entitled to be registered as such and, additionally, the registered owner had in the meantime fraudulently sold the ship to a third purchaser who had relied on the registered title, just as in *The Horlock*.

(iii) Statutory treatment given to the Register documents

The 1995 MSA contains one provision relevant to the evidentiary value of documents issued by the Register, with potential implications both in the public and the private law spheres. This provision is sub-section 10(8), under section 10 "Registration Regulations" in Part II of the MSA 1995. This sub-section is, strangely, the only one not related to the registration Regulations and therefore stands alone in that section.

Sub-section 10(8) provides as follows:

Any document purporting to be a copy of any information contained in an entry in the register and to be certified as a true copy by the registrar shall be evidence (and, in Scotland, sufficient evidence) of the matters stated in the document.

168. Ibid., 249.
169. MSA 1894, fn 125.

A predecessor of this sub-section is to be found in section 107 of the Shipping Act 1854,[170] stating that every register, certified copy, or certificate of registry, as therein described, was prima facie proof of all the matters therein contained or thereon endorsed. However, the present wording has been drafted in a much more succinct fashion, choosing as a general reference the term "any document" to cover *inter alia*, certificates and transcripts, provided it is certified by the Registrar to be a true copy of any information contained in an entry in the Register. It is also to be noted that the qualifying words "prima facie" have been omitted, leaving the key element in this sub-section, i.e. "evidence", bare and subject to interpretation by the English courts.

5. BASIC SHIP FINANCE AND REGISTRATION OF MORTGAGES

The financial effort necessary to build[171] or purchase new tonnage is so great that very few companies wish to tie up their liquid assets in ships without the support of highly specialised lenders providing tailor-made ship finance products under increasingly complex agreements, the details of which are well beyond the scope of this work.[172] However, in order to understand shipping in its entirety it seems necessary to give a brief illustration of the structure of a basic ship finance agreement and to discuss the basic elements of the registration of mortgages. The main purpose of the multi-guarantee structure of security documents (including the loan agreement) and indeed of the possibility of registering ship mortgages is that of providing lenders with as much security as possible for the money lent to the owner for the purpose of acquiring new tonnage or (re)financing existing tonnage. The level of the security provided by the network of guarantees however depends on the market and in the current post-2008 era direct interests in ships themselves are arguably considered to offer far less attractive security than in the past. The market has reacted relatively quickly to the new financial situation and it is now more common than in the past for banks to lend on a project-based finance structure rather than on an old-fashioned asset-based one. This notwithstanding, obtaining finance remains difficult and many banks are still unwilling to return to this particular form of investment.

(a) The basic structure of a ship finance agreement

Ship finance agreements are usually individually negotiated from a standard structure on which terms the lender is prepared to make funds available to the borrower. Negotiations will depend on a variety of factors including the parties involved, the market, the general availability of credit and the direct and indirect guarantees offered by the owner.[173] The result of these negotiations will be contained in the so-called *Term Sheet* drafted by the lender; essentially an offer which details the maximum amount the lender is prepared to loan, the validity period of the offer, the type of asset the borrower is authorised to buy and the specific conditions upon which the amount will be made available. Ship finance therefore differs

---

170. 17 & 18 Vict c 104, see page 93 and fn 159 of this chapter.
171. On the specific issues related to shipbuilding finance see F. Paine, *The Finance of Ship Acquisitions*, (Fairplay Publications 1989) at p 5 ff.; and Stephenson Harwood (ed.), *Shipping Finance* (3rd edn, Stephenson Harwood 2006), (hereinafter "Stephenson Harwood").
172. In general Bowtle (fn 99); J.E. Sloggett, *Shipping Finance* (Fairplay Publications 1984); and again Stephenson Harwood, ibid.
173. See P. Stokes, *Ship Finance, Credit Expansion and the Boom-Bust Cycle* (2nd edn, LLP Professional Publishing 1997).

from general corporate finance as the loan is primarily – although not exclusively – linked to the asset to be purchased, invariably itself a guarantee and the main earner of proceeds assigned to the lender as security for the loan. Once the *Term Sheet* is in place the owner will to a great extent take comfort that financing should be available and will further their plans to acquire new tonnage.

Once the tonnage is identified the actual *Loan Agreement* is drafted containing the main terms of the agreement between the lender and the borrower and all the collateral guarantees the borrower will make available to the lender, as conditions precedent to the draw-down. The most basic *Loan Agreement* will be structured around five main securities:[174]

a   a mortgage over the ship;
b   an assignment of the earnings of the ship;
c   an assignment of the benefit of insurance on the ship;[175]
d   an assignment of the earning account; and
e   a guarantee from the holding company of the subsidiary in which title to the ship is usually registered.[176]

The purpose of these securities is not surprising: the mortgage, and thus the ship herself, is one of the main securities for the loan and the assignment of the insurance will protect the lender should the ship for any reason become a total loss, whether actual or constructive.[177] The guarantee will instead give further security to the lender that usually makes the finance available based on the financial solidity of the group of companies behind the owner/borrower and the earnings expected from the project. Finally, the assignment of the earnings and of the earning account will give the lender greater flexibility in case of the borrower's default or insolvency,[178] as before foreclosure on the ship – said always to be a last resort from a lender's perspective – they will be able to satisfy their credit, at least in part, on the earnings of the ship.

What must be borne in mind however is that each loan facility is different from another and the terms of the loan agreement, the lending structure and the issue of collateral guarantees securing the lender's position vary considerably from case to case. On this latter issue of security, mortgages and the possibility of registering them against the ship's entry play an extremely important role. A brief overview of the registration of ship mortgages is given below.

(b) The registration of mortgages

Earlier in this chapter the basic principles of the registration system were dealt with, focusing on the register of ships. In this last stretch, the key aspects of registering ship mortgages as special entries in the Register will be outlined.[179] The main legal effect of these entries can be readily identified: they afford lenders involved in ship finance transactions invaluable protection in situations of default of the borrower.

---

174. See Stephenson Harwood (fn 173) where seven "principal types of security" are listed. This account is a simplified version.

175. The alternative possibility of lender and owner to be co-assured under the policy is discussed in detail in Bowtle (fn 99), at p 438 and ff., and the cases cited therein.

176. See *Citibank NA v Hobbs, Savill & Co (The Panglobal Friendship)* [1978] 1 Lloyd's Rep 368, at p 371 (Roskill LJ). On the registration of securities see above and Bowtle (fn 99), at Chapter 3.

177. See Chapter 11.

178. See in detail Bowtle (fn 99), at p 475 and ff.

179. For a more detailed view on this subject, see Bowtle (fn 99), Chapter 6. See also Fogarty (fn 159), Chapter 1.

Section 16 of the MSA 1995, Schedule 1 to the MSA 1995, in particular paragraphs 7 to 14, and the 1993 Regulations, Part VII, contain the relevant provisions regarding registration of mortgages over registered ships and the so-called priority notices.

The term mortgage is defined for the purpose of Schedule 1 as the instrument creating "a security for the repayment of a loan or the discharge of any other obligation".[180] The mortgage produced for registration, as well as the transfer and the discharge of registered mortgages needs to be executed in a form approved by the Registrar.[181]

As already seen, the MSA 1995 gives continuity to a centralised register where registration is an entitlement as opposed to an obligation. The question which therefore arises is: why would a mortgagee be keen on having the mortgage entered in this public record? The answer is doubtless protection, as a registered mortgagee is given (i) power of sale and (ii) priority among mortgagees. Both issues will be discussed in turn.

(i) Power of sale

Paragraph 9(1) of Schedule 1 to the MSA 1995 provides the registered mortgagee with a statutory right against the mortgagor and its subsequent buyers to sell the ship or share in respect of which it is registered, *if* the mortgage money or any part of it is due. This right constitutes an exception to the principle that the mortgagor is treated "as not having ceased to be owner of the ship or share".[182] Where prior registered mortgagees exist, the subsequent mortgagee will only exercise the right to sell with the concurrence of every prior mortgagee, as requested in paragraph 9(2), unless the sale takes place under an order of a court of competent jurisdiction.[183]

(ii) Priority among mortgagees

In case of two or more competing registered mortgages, priority between themselves is given to the mortgage, entry of which is recorded earlier in time, favouring the first registered mortgage over any other.[184] However, this rule is not without exception as an intending mortgagee can notify the Registrar of its prospective interest under a proposed mortgage on a registered ship or a share therein. Provided the notification is made on a standard form approved by the Secretary of State, the Registrar will then record the said interest. The effect of this so-called priority notice is that, if the mortgage is subsequently executed and registered, it will take priority over any mortgage registered after the notice was recorded.[185] This benefit is extended even to cases where the ship is not yet registered at the time of notification by the intended mortgagee. In such a case the Registrar shall record the interest under the intended mortgage, and if the ship is later registered, the Registrar shall enter the ship subject to that interest. If however the mortgage has by then been executed pursuant to regulation 57 of the 1993 Regulations and duly produced to the Registrar by the time the ship is registered, the ship shall be registered subject to that

---

180. Schedule 1, para 14 in conjunction with paras 7(1) and 7(2).
181. Pursuant to paras 7(2), 11 and 13 of Schedule 1 to the MSA 1995, together with regs 57, 58 and 60 to 62 of the 1993 Regulations.
182. MSA 1995, Schedule 1, para 10(b).
183. See Fogarty (fn 157), [1.119] – [1.124]. Regarding a sale taking place under a court order, see for a recent example *The m/v Union Gold the m/v Union Silver the m/v Union Emerald the m/v Union Pluto* [2013] EWHC 1696 (Admlty), [2014] 1 Lloyd's Rep 53 on the application by the mortgagee for sale of vessels *pendente lite*, where the court decided to depart from the conventional process of sale involving appraisal, advertisement and invitations to bid, due to exceptional circumstances.
184. *Qui prior est tempore potior est jure.* See para 8 in conjunction with para 7(4) of Schedule 1 to the MSA 1995.
185. 1993 Regulations, reg 59(5).

mortgage.[186] The notification will cease to have effect unless it is renewed or executed within 30 days from notification. The renewal is made by means of a further notice to the Registrar and it is also valid for 30 days.[187] The 1993 Regulations do not establish a limit to the number of renewals.

This chronological hierarchy will consequently affect directly the "power of sale" of the registered mortgagee who coexists with prior registered mortgagees, and, as already commented, the subsequent mortgagee shall not proceed to sell the ship (unless pursuant to a court order) "without the concurrence of every prior mortgagee".[188]

Moreover, the registered mortgagee has priority over any unregistered mortgages, whether or not pre-existing the registration of the mortgage.[189]

Both the MSA 1995[190] and the 1993 Regulations[191] further strengthen the protection of the registered mortgagee by establishing that the ship's cancellation from the register[192] will not affect the entries of any undischarged mortgage on that ship or any share in it.

---

186. Ibid., reg 59(3).
187. Ibid., reg 59(6) and (7).
188. MSA 1995, Schedule 1, para 9(2).
189. See *Black v William* [1895] 1 Ch 408, a case decided under the MSA 1894. See Fogarty (fn 157) at [1.112]. Also, for a view on the ranking of registered mortgages with regards to maritime liens, statutory liens and possessory liens, see further [1.115]–[1.117]. Concerning the latter, see the High Court of New Zealand decision in *Babcock Fitzroy Ltd v The ship m/v Southern Pasifika* [2012] NZHC 1254; [2012] 2 Lloyd's Rep 423. Cf. Chapter 12 pages 513–514.
190. S 16(4).
191. Reg 63.
192. See reg 56 of 1993 Regulations for circumstances giving rise to the termination of a ship's registration.

CHAPTER 3

INTERNATIONAL TRADE AND SHIPPING DOCUMENTS

Filippo Lorenzon

1. INTRODUCTION: SHIPPING AND INTERNATIONAL TRADE

Thousands of commercial vessels sail daily across the oceans, operated by companies incorporated in different jurisdictions, under charterparties and bills of lading imposing duties and liabilities on all parties concerned. These vessels are built by hundreds of shipbuilding facilities and have to comply with a multitude of international, regional and national regulations in order to call safely at a worldwide network of commercial ports. The shipping industry as a whole employs millions of people worldwide and feeds a great number of service providers and public servants. However, the purpose of the world's commercial fleet, the main reason why vessels are built, registered, chartered and insured is not *maritime* at all: vessels sail to carry goods bought in one market to be sold in another. The real purpose of the entire commercial shipping industry and its regulatory and contractual framework is to make *international trade* possible, safe and efficient.

This chapter will give a brief overview of the basic concepts of international commercial sales on shipment terms in order to provide the reader with the commercial background to understand shipping law as a whole better.

2. INTERNATIONAL COMMERCIAL SALES ON SHIPMENT TERMS

International trade law is a specialist area of commercial law dealing with the sale of goods for commercial purposes. Contracts for the international sale of goods may be further divided into three main groups depending on the mode and place of delivery of the consignment sold: *E terms*[1] (or *ex works* contracts), *D terms*[2] (destination/arrival or delivered contracts) and *shipment terms*.[3] Broadly speaking, the delivery of the goods is made at the seller's premises in *EX terms*, at the buyer's premises in *D terms* and generally on board a vessel at the loading port in *shipment terms*. The following pages are dedicated to the identification of the main features of this latter type of commercial sale, where the link between the sale contract and the shipping documents becomes more complex.[4]

(a) The contract and its terms

In current commercial practice, sale contracts are concluded by exchanges of short e-mails, faxes or telexes, *confirmation notes* focusing mainly on the description of the goods to be sold and the main delivery and payment terms. Very often though, these *notes* provide for express incorporation of one of the Incoterms®[5] and/or longer and considerably more detailed standard forms such as the ones provided by trade associations like GAFTA[6] and FOSFA.[7] These forms – when correctly incorporated by reference – constitute a second layer of contractual clauses with an equally binding effect between seller and buyer. It is not uncommon for these forms to incorporate further terms from other standard forms or in-house models, rules and/or procedures which will come to form a third layer of contractual clauses.[8] In this *millefoglie* of contractual clauses, identifying the exact terms agreed upon by the parties may not be straightforward.[9]

The importance of the correct ascertainment of the parties' intentions is, however, paramount since it is essential at the very early stages of any claim to establish – for example – the correct

---

1. EXW in Incoterms® 2010 Rules language, see fn 17 of this chapter. Common in practice are also "*ex store*" and "*ex warehouse*".
2. The current Incoterms® Rules D terms are as follows: DAT (Delivered At Terminal), DAP (Delivered At Place) and DDP (Delivered Duty Paid). The terms DAF (Delivered At Frontier), DES (Delivered Ex Ship), DEQ (Delivered Ex Quay), DDU (Delivered Duty Unpaid) as they appear in Incoterms 2000 have in fact been replaced by the new DAT and DAP above. Incoterms 2000 can still be used if the parties to the contract choose to incorporate them.
3. C.i.f., c.&f. and f.o.b. contracts; in Incoterms® 2010 Rules language the shipment sales for maritime transport are CIF (Cost Insurance and Freight), CFR (Cost and FReight), and f.o.b. (Free On Board); for other means of transport FCA (Free CArrier), CPT (Carriage Paid To) and CIP (Carriage and Insurance Paid to) should be used.
4. See in general F. Lorenzon, *C.i.f. and f.o.b. Contracts* (6th edn, Sweet & Maxwell 2017) (hereinafter "Lorenzon").
5. See below.
6. The Grain and Feed Trade Association.
7. The Federation of Oils, Seeds and Fat Associations Ltd.
8. E.g. FOSFA 54 ll 31–33.
9. See *Tekdata Interconnections Ltd v Amphenol Ltd* [2009] EWCA Civ 1209; [2010] 1 Lloyd's Rep 357; and *Claxton Engineering Services Ltd v TXM Olaj-és Gázkutató KFT* [2010] EWHC 2567 Comm; [2011] 1 Lloyd's Rep 252. See also *Proton Energy Group SA v Orlen Lietuva* [2013] EWHC 2872 (Comm); [2014] 1 Lloyd's Rep 100.

law applicable to the contract and the correct forum where the claim should be brought.[10] Because of the number of contractual layers forming the agreement of the parties, it is not unusual to have clauses in the confirmation note interacting with clauses in one or more of the standard forms or rules incorporated by reference. In these circumstances it becomes crucial to identify correctly the relationship between the various layers of the contract. The basic principle here is that the arbitrator or judge will try to identify the intention of the parties as it appears from the contract.[11] Hence, if the contract contains a clear hierarchy clause making one layer prevail over the others, the clause will be given full effect.[12] Where no hierarchy clause is drawn up, the principle is that where there is clear conflict between two clauses,[13] specially negotiated terms would prevail over standard terms and conditions of sale.[14] The rule is apparently simple but when, as often happens, the confirmation note incorporates general terms and conditions of sale which in turn incorporate standard additional clauses containing ad hoc amendments, the relationship between the various layers of the contract may become less straightforward. Occasionally the courts have refused to uphold the validity of the incorporation of unusual[15] or unreasonable[16] clauses, but – it is submitted – this string of authorities should be read with caution and with reference to the special circumstances of the cases concerned.

It may be worth at this stage discussing the incorporation of the International Chamber of Commerce's (ICC) *Official Rules for the Interpretation of Trade Terms* (more commonly known as the *Incoterms®*[17]) and the effect of their incorporation into the contract. The Incoterms® 2010 Rules (in their latest edition)[18] are a set of standard trade terms compiled by the ICC. They are not, nor are they meant to be, an international convention and are regarded – at any rate under English law – as just another set of standard forms. From this it follows that under English law the mere agreement that a contract is fixed "on c.i.f. terms" is not enough to trigger the application of the Incoterms® and that, once correctly incorporated, they become just another layer of the contract to which the ordinary rules of construction discussed above apply.[19] It is therefore crucial for the parties who intend to make use of the Incoterms® 2010 Rules not only to incorporate expressly the right term[20] of the right vintage,[21] but also to draft a detailed confirmation note to record the special terms agreed between them for the particular transaction at stake.

---

10. See Chapter 1.

11. *Charles Robert Leader and Henrietta Ada Leader v Duffey and Amyatt Edmond Ray* [1888] 13 App Cas 294 (HL).

12. *Pagnan SpA v Tradax Ocean Transportation SA* [1987] 2 Lloyd's Rep 342.

13. English courts, however, will seek to construe every contract as a whole and if a reasonable commercial construction of the whole could reconcile two provisions (whether typed or printed) then such a construction could and should be adopted; *Bayoil SA v Seawind Tankers Corp (The Leonidas)* [2001] 1 Lloyd's Rep 533.

14. *Indian Oil Corporation v Vanol Inc* [1991] 2 Lloyd's Rep 634.

15. *OK Petroleum AB v Vitol Energy SA* [1995] 2 Lloyd's Rep 160.

16. *Ceval Alimentos SA v Agrimpex Trading Co Ltd (The Northern Progress) (No 2)* [1996] 2 Lloyd's Rep 319.

17. International Chamber of Commerce, *Incoterms 2010: ICC Rules for the Use of Domestic and International Trade Terms* (ICC 2009), ICC publication n. 715E; in force from 1 January 2011.

18. At the time of going to press, the process of updating the Rules had just been triggered with a new edition, the Incoterms® 2020 Rules, being planned for publication in 2019.

19. For a case of construction where CIP Incoterms 2000 were incorporated together with a set of rules for the specific trade concerned see *Stora Enso Oyj v Port of Dundee* [2006] CSOH 40; [2006] 1 CLC 453. It must be noted that this approach to the Incoterms is not necessarily followed in some civil law jurisdictions where contracting on c.i.f. basis alone may be deemed to be enough to incorporate the CIF Incoterm in its entirety.

20. In case of carriage by air on CIF terms, for example, it would be advisable to incorporate the CIP Incoterms 2010 rather than the CIF term, specifically designed for maritime transport.

21. Incorporation of CIF Incoterm may in fact not be enough to prefer Incoterms® 2010 Rules over Incoterms 2000 whereas – it is suggested – reference to the "CIF Incoterm in force at the date of the conclusion of the contract" would indeed suffice.

(b) C.i.f. and f.o.b. contracts and carriage arrangements

Once the terms and conditions of the agreement between the parties are located and identified, it becomes necessary to illustrate the key features of commercial sales on shipment terms. First of all it must be made clear that both c.i.f. and f.o.b. sales are *shipment* contracts where the duty of the seller as to the delivery of the cargo is fulfilled by shipping goods on board a vessel (or procuring goods shipped on board a vessel) rather than by handing them over to the buyer at the port of discharge. But whereas the duty to procure the cargo always rests with the seller, the duty to fix a vessel suitable to carry the cargo from the port of loading to the port of discharge does not always follow. Generally speaking, in c.i.f. (or c.&f.) agreements it is the seller who is under the obligation to fix the vessel whereas in bare (or straight) f.o.b. sales such duty falls on the buyer. Particular care, however, should be taken with regard to f.o.b. contracts where – in practice – such default position is often amended by way of contractual variations the most common of which is often referred to as "f.o.b. of the classic type".[22] In its "classic" form the f.o.b. contract provides for the seller to conclude a contract of carriage as an agent for the buyer, at all material stages the original party to the contract of carriage with the carrier; the commodity will be still invoiced by the seller at f.o.b. rate but a commission for the fixture is usually added as a separate item. Another common alternative may be referred to as "f.o.b. with additional carriage services" where the seller fixes the contract of carriage with the carrier in his own name and then transfers its contractual position by endorsing the bill of lading. In this case again the commodity is invoiced at f.o.b. rate and freight and commission are charged separately or specifically itemised. Distinguishing between c.i.f. sales and the various sub-types of f.o.b. terms is crucial both for (i) understanding the apportionment of the risk of market fluctuations between seller and buyer and (ii) for the identification of the terms of the contract of carriage governing the cargo claim in case of loss of or damage to the cargo.[23]

(i) The risk of market fluctuations

Because of the timing of international commercial transactions – where sale contracts (and price) may be agreed upon long before or indeed long after the actual date of shipment – and the high volatility of the freight and insurance markets, selling on c.i.f. terms means retaining the risk of fluctuations of effectively three separate markets (the commodity, the freight and the insurance) whereas opting for an f.o.b. solution leaves fluctuations in the freight and insurance markets for the buyer to bear. This is particularly significant when comparing a sale on "f.o.b. terms with additional carriage services" with a c.&f. contract: both arrangements see the seller providing the fixture and paying for it as agreed with the carrier; however, where the c.&f. contract involves an all-in quote by the seller who carries the risk of any increase (and the benefit of any reduction) in the cost of carriage, the f.o.b. seller would be immune from any such fluctuations: he may well have negotiated and paid for the contract of carriage but the risk and the benefits of variations in the freight market would clearly be for the buyer's account.[24]

(ii) The parties to the contract of carriage

Identifying correctly which of the parties to the sale contract is also a party to the carriage contract allows for the correct identification of the terms on which this contract is concluded, i.e. the

---

22. See Lorenzon (fn 4), [9–001] and ff.
23. See Chapter 5.
24. *Scottish & Newcastle Int Ltd v Othon Ghalanos Ltd* [2008] HKHL 11; [2008] 1 Lloyd's Rep 462, [35].

terms on which the carrier may eventually be sued to recover losses which have arisen in transit.[25] From what we have seen above it follows that in c.i.f. and c.&f. contracts the seller is the original party to the carriage contract – e.g. a voyage charterparty, a contract of affreightment or liner booking – and the terms of its agreement with the carrier will always be found in that original contract.[26] However, as soon as a negotiable bill of lading is transferred by the seller to the buyer in exchange for payment, the buyer acquires rights of suit under the contract evidenced by the bill.[27] In this situation both seller and buyer will have an enforceable contract with the carrier but the terms of such contract will be contained in different documents, the seller's agreement being recorded in the charterparty (or other agreement arrived at between them) and the buyer's in the bill of lading. The situation changes considerably when the sale contract is concluded on f.o.b. terms. In case of bare f.o.b. contracts, where the charterparty is negotiated and fixed by the buyer as charterer, the buyer is and will always be the carrier's original contractor and the terms of the agreement between buyer and carrier will be – at all material times – contained in the charterparty, whether or not a bill of lading is issued and tendered.[28] The situation remains factually unaltered in f.o.b. classic arrangements when the charterparty is concluded by the seller as agent for the buyer. However, if additional carriage services are added to the f.o.b. seller's duty the situation is reversed and the buyer – non-charterer – will only become a party to a contract of carriage through transfer of the bill of lading and on the terms of such bill.[29]

3. THE PASSING OF RISK AND PROPERTY IN THE GOODS

The parties to every sale contract have an interest in the quality and condition of the goods they trade in but – when the sale at stake is an international one – there is a further cause for concern: to reach their buyers the goods sold have to be carried across international, political and geographical boundaries. It may well happen that such goods are shipped in lorries at the producers' plant, transhipped on to barges or lighters, transhipped again on a seagoing vessel to be discharged at destination, several weeks after they have left the seller. While carried, the goods are in the control of a network of carriers, independent contractors working neither as agents of the seller or for the buyer. But what happens if the goods are damaged or lost in transit? Although both the carrier (or its liability insurer) and the cargo insurer will provide compensation for transit losses, within the framework discussed elsewhere in this work,[30] the identity of the party which will have suffered the loss depends on the answer to a rather different question: who bears the risk of loss of or damage to the goods while in transit?

According to the maxim *res perit domino* only the owner of the cargo can suffer an actual loss as a result of its cargo being lost or damaged. And in fact section 20 of the Sale of Goods Act

---

25. See again Chapter 5.

26. *Rodocanachi, Sons & Co v Milburn Brothers* [1887] LR 18 QBD 67.

27. See Carriage of Goods by Sea Act 1992 ("COGSA 1992"), s 2(1)(a) and Chapter 5. See also *Tate & Lyle, Ltd v Hain Steamship Company Ltd* [1936] 2 All ER 597 and *Brandt v Liverpool Brazil & River Plate Steam Navigation Co Ltd* [1924] 1 KB 575. Where a "straight consigned bill of lading" or a seawaybill is issued the buyer acquires rights of suit under that contract at the time of issue by virtue of being identified as the consignee by the document itself and transfer of the document may only be necessary for the purposes of obtaining delivery *if* the contract so provides; see COGSA 1992, s 2(1)(b).

28. *President of India v Metcalfe Shipping Ltd (The Dunelmia)* [1970] 1 QB 289; [1969] 2 Lloyd's Rep 476.

29. COGSA 1992, s 2(1).

30. See Chapters 5 and 12.

1979[31] clearly states that: "Unless otherwise agreed, the goods remain at the seller's risk until the property in them is transferred to the buyer." However, when goods are sold on shipment terms the situation is more elaborate and risk and property are very seldom transferred at the same time.

(a) Risk passes on or as from shipment

Given the key importance of risk in international trade transactions it may happen that the parties expressly clarify the allocation of transit risks in their contracts with ad hoc clauses saying e.g. that "risk . . . shall pass to Buyers at the loading port or terminal as the oil passes the loading vessel's permanent hose connection". In such cases it is clear that risk of transit loss will pass to the buyer at that very precise moment in time. On the other hand, if the parties have not given special consideration to the issue of risk, risk will pass according to the type of contract stipulated by the parties.

In *ex works* contracts the duty of the seller is to place the goods at the disposal of the buyer at the agreed point, if any, at the named place of delivery (e.g. seller's warehouse) not yet loaded on any collecting vehicle,[32] whereas the buyer has the duty to take delivery of them and bears all risks of loss of or damage to the goods from the time they have been so delivered.[33] The main consequence of this is that the risk of transit loss rests with the buyer from the point of collection at seller's premises onwards.[34] At the opposite end of the spectrum, in contracts concluded on *D terms* the seller undertakes to arrange the carriage of the goods to the agreed point, if any, at the named destination in the country of import, whereas the buyer has to take delivery only if the goods it receives at destination are as agreed in the contract. From this it follows that the risk for transit loss of, or damage to, the goods whilst being carried rests squarely with the seller.[35] If the sale is concluded on *shipment terms* either the seller (in c.i.f. and c.&f./CFR sales) or the buyer (in f.o.b. sales) may undertake to make transport arrangements, but delivery of the goods always takes place on board the nominated vessel at the port of shipment.[36] If the obligation of the seller is one to deliver the goods on board a vessel – in other words to *ship* the goods – it must follow that the risk of transit loss of such goods passes from the seller to the buyer from that moment on: i.e. across the ship's rail *on (or as from)*

---

31. Ch 54. The Act covering the sale of goods in the UK. The Sale of Goods Act 1979 (as amended) only applies to contracts for the 'sales of goods' as defined in s 2(1). In case the Act does not apply, a contract which is subject to English law will be subject to the common law only and all the statutory provisions of the Act will be irrelevant. For an important decision in which a sale of bunker oil was held not to be a sale of goods for the purposes of the application of the Sale of Goods Act see *PST Energy 7 Shipping LLC v OW Bunker Malta Ltd (The "Res Cogitans")* [2016] UKSC 23; [2016] 1 Lloyd's Rep 589.

32. Incoterms® 2010 Rules EXW, A4. The risk term is actually A5 which reads: "the seller bears all risks of loss of or damage to the goods until they have been delivered in accordance with A4".

33. Ibid., B4 and B5.

34. Ibid., A5 and B5.

35. E.g. "Ex Ship deliveries: The risk and property in the crude oil delivered under the agreement shall pass to the Buyer as the crude oil passes the Vessel's permanent hose connection at the Discharge Port." See also Incoterms 2000 DES, A5 and B5. In Incoterms® 2010 Rules this term together with the DAF, DEQ and DDU terms has been replaced by the DAT and DAP terms – see fn 2 of this chapter.

36. Incoterms® 2010 Rules CIF, A4, CFR, A4 and f.o.b., A4. It must be noted that under Incoterms® 2010 Rules CIF, CFR and "FOB" A4 the seller may deliver the goods in two ways: (i) by placing them on board the vessel or (ii) by procuring them to be so placed.

shipment irrespective of where the property in the goods lies.[37] If the Incoterms® 2010 Rules are incorporated in the contract the exact moment in time at which risk passes to the buyer is less clear as the new terms have done away with the concept of ship's rail altogether and state that under "CIF", CFR and FOB terms risk passes when "the goods have been delivered in accordance with A4".[38] A4 in turn provides that delivery may take place by (a) placing the goods on board or by (b) procuring the goods to be so placed.[39] The effect of the changes appears twofold: (i) a container dropped on board a vessel during the loading operation would still be at the risk of its seller as it had not been placed on board at the time of the damage or loss;[40] and – perhaps more worryingly – (ii) the seller of goods in a string may not be able to pass the risk on to its buyer retroactively from shipment anymore as risk appears to be transferred on the action of "procuring the goods so delivered" rather than on the physical act of delivery. Whenever the moment of transfer, the fact that the buyer bears such a significant risk is balanced by some degree of control over the goods through the documents which the seller has delivered to it: by holding a bill of lading which gives constructive possession of the goods, the buyer can ask the carrier for the goods and sell them on; by becoming a party to the contract of carriage with the carrier, it acquires title to sue the carrier in case the goods are damaged in transit[41] and finally by being the beneficiary under the contract of insurance, the buyer has recourse against the insurer for transit loss.[42]

The common law rule that risk in goods sold on c.i.f., c.&f. and f.o.b.[43] terms passes on or *as from shipment* also responds to the commercial reality that a seller might have shipped goods before it has reached a binding agreement with a buyer or situations where a trader might have sold goods it has yet to buy. In these cases, if the goods are lost or damaged in transit prior to the conclusion of the contract of sale, it is still the buyer who bears the risk for such loss retroactively[44] and its duty to pay the seller against conforming documents remains unaffected. But what if a buyer of goods in transit, with knowledge that the goods have perished, sells on to another buyer? Does this on-buyer inherit retroactively a risk which has already materialised in a loss? It is suggested that whether the seller's duty is one to *ship goods of the contract description* or one to *procure the same goods shipped as promised*, the obligation of the seller under a sale contract on shipment terms is one to *ship* the goods, never one to deliver them at destination. Hence, in order to understand whether the risk has passed to the buyer, the right questions to be asked should be: (a) did the seller procure goods that – *at the time of shipment* – conformed to the requirements set in the sale contract? (b) Do the documents tendered evidence that goods of the contract description were in fact shipped?

---

37. *Comptoir d'Achat et de Vente du Boerenbond Belge SA v Luis de Ridder Limitada (The Julia)* [1947] 1 All ER 118; Incoterms® 2010 Rules, CIF, CFR and "FOB", A5; the presumption made by s 20(2) of the Sale of Goods Act 1979 (hereinafter "SOGA 1979") that the risk passes together with property, being defeated by the express choice of the parties of contracting on shipment terms. The retroactivity of the passage of risk appears less obvious under Incoterms® 2010 Rules. For the same statement as to the rule on passage of risk see Lorenzon (fn 4), [2–010], approved by the High Court of Singapore in *Profindo Pte Ltd v Abani Trading Pte Ltd (The M/V Athens)* [2013] SGHC 10; [2013] 1 Lloyd's Rep 370, [39].
38. Incoterms® 2010 Rules, A5.
39. Incoterms® 2010 Rules, CIF, CFR and FOB, A4.
40. A similar issue may present itself with liquid cargo where the concept of "placement" is often associated with that of the "settlement" of the product on board the tanker, clearly well after any contamination may have occurred.
41. See COGSA 1992 and Chapter 5.
42. See Chapter 11.
43. On which see specifically *Soufflet Negoce SA v Bunge SA* [2009] EWHC 2454 (Comm); [2010] 1 Lloyd's Rep 718, per Steel J, [16]. Affd [2010] EWCA Civ 1102; [2011] 1 Lloyd's Rep 531.
44. For doubts on the position under Incoterms® 2010 Rules, see above.

Were both questions to be answered in the affirmative the seller has performed its duty and risk lies with the buyer.[45]

(b) The exceptions to the rule

The rule that risk passes on or as from shipment is not without exceptions which – if triggered – would relieve the buyer from bearing all or part of the risk of transit loss or damage. Such exceptions may be divided into two main categories: (i) the *contractual exceptions* arising out of express agreement between the parties and (ii) the *legal exceptions*, where they find their source in statutory provisions or in the common law.[46] They will be dealt with in turn.

(i) Contractual exceptions

In the exercise of their freedom of contract the parties may well decide to allocate the risks associated with the carriage of the goods sold as they see fit. In practice this is usually done with specifically drafted *out turn* clauses commonly related to the quantity,[47] quality or condition[48] of the cargo at the port of discharge. Such clauses usually provide for an adjustment in price in case the commodity reaches destination falling short – in quantity, quality or condition as the case may be – of the contract specifications with the effect of reversing the risk of such losses back on to the seller's shoulders.[49] *Out turn* clauses are interpreted strictly *contra proferentem* by the courts and hence do not cover the total loss of the consignment.[50]

(ii) Legal exceptions

Whether or not the contract contains specific clauses on the reallocation of risks, both the Sale of Goods Act 1979 and the common law provide for a limited number of exceptions to the rule that risk passes on or as from shipment. The legal exceptions are five: (i) where delivery has been delayed through the fault of the seller any loss which might not have occurred but for such fault is for the seller's account;[51] (ii) where the seller acts as bailee or custodian of the goods, losses caused by breach of the duty to take reasonable care of such goods is for the

---

45. *Manbre Saccharine Co v Corn Products Co* [1919] 1 KB 198; *C Groom Ltd v Barber* [1915] 1 KB 316. For the same conclusion see C. Debattista, *Bills of Lading in Export Trade* (3rd edn, Tottel Publishing 2008), (hereinafter "Debattista"), ch 4; and D.M. Sassoon, *C.i.f. and f.o.b. Contracts* (4th edn, Sweet & Maxwell 1995), (hereinafter "Sassoon"), [253]. *Contra*, for cases of total loss in c.i.f. contracts only see *Couturier v Hastie* [1856] 5 HLC 673. See also E. Mckendrick (ed.), *Goode on Commercial law* (5th edn, Penguin 2017), (hereinafter "Goode"), at p 1047; and M. Bridge (ed.), *Benjamin's Sale of Goods* (9th edn, Sweet & Maxwell 2015), (hereinafter "Benjamin"), [19–114].

46. See also Lorenzon (fn 4), [2–018] ff.

47. For example, providing for the *out turn* quantity "to be settled at the market price of the last day of discharge of the last ship to arrive", FOSFA 54, cl 16, l 171.

48. Typically providing for a discount proportionate to the deterioration in the quality or condition of one or more items of the description; e.g. GAFTA 119, cl 5.

49. The seller at this stage has probably lost its title to sue the carrier under s 2(5) of COGSA 1992 and care should be taken to ensure the *out turn* clause provides expressly for an assignment back of the buyer's action against the carrier.

50. *Soon Hua Seng Co Ltd v Glencore Grain* [1996] 1 Lloyd's Rep 398 (QBD), at p 405 (Mance J):

> If the goods covered by the shipping documents and invoice are lost in transit and do not arrive at all, the risk of loss remains on the buyers and no question of any adjustment to the payment due against the commercial invoice can arise.

51. SOGA 1979, s 20(2) and *Gatoil International Inc v Tradox Petroleum Ltd* (*The Rio Sun*) [1985] 1 Lloyd's Rep 350.

seller's account;[52] (iii) where the seller has failed to make a reasonable contract of carriage for the benefit of the buyer, the loss of or damage to the goods is also for the seller to bear;[53] (iv) if the seller has failed to pass on information to enable the buyer to insure goods during their sea transit, again the goods will be at the seller's risk during such sea transit;[54] and finally (v) if the consignment gets damaged or lost in transit because its condition at the time of shipment was such as to make it unlikely to withstand normal sea transit, they will be at seller's rather than at buyer's risk.[55]

(c) Property passes when intended to pass

Although the transfer of risk is certainly a more significant issue to traders, there are circumstances in which it may be important to establish where property in the goods lies, the most obvious being where it is necessary to start a tortious action against the carrier[56] or where either of the parties becomes insolvent. The default position under the Sale of Goods Act 1979 is that property will pass at such time as the parties to the contract intend it to be transferred,[57] such intention to be ascertained having regard to the terms of the contract, the conduct of the parties and the circumstances of the case.[58]

So, where the contract makes it clear that the property in the goods shall only pass on payment of the price or on delivery of the relevant shipping document then the situation is clear. In case the contract is silent about the transfer of property, it will be necessary to refer to section 18 of Sale of Goods Act 1979, which provides a series of rebuttable presumptions, the most relevant for international commercial sales being that where there is a contract for the sale of unascertained or future goods by description, and the goods are unconditionally appropriated to the contract through delivery to a carrier, the property in the goods passes to the buyer at the time of delivery to such carrier.[59]

4. PERFORMANCE OF THE CONTRACT

The Sale of Goods Act 1979 states very clearly that a sale contract is an agreement by which the seller undertakes to deliver the goods in accordance with the terms of the contract of sale.[60] However, in international commercial sales on shipment terms *physical* delivery of the goods is not enough to discharge the seller's duty as to delivery: he has also a *documentary* duty to

---

52. SOGA 1979, s 20(3).
53. Ibid., s 32(2); see also F. Lorenzon, "When is a CIF Seller's Carriage Contract Unreasonable? Section 32(2) of the Sale of Goods Act 1979" (2007) 13 JIML 241.
54. SOGA 1979, s 32(3).
55. *Mash & Murrell v Joseph I Emanuel Ltd* [1961] 2 Lloyd's Rep 326 (CA). See also *Navigas Ltd v Enron Liquid Fuels Ltd* (unreported, 22 May 1998, Colman J) and *KG Bominflot Bunkergesellshaft für Mineraloele mbH & Co v Petroplus Marketing AG (The Mercini Lady)* [2010] EWCA Civ 1145; [2011] 1 Lloyd's Rep 442.
56. *Leigh & Sillivan Ltd v Aliakmon Shipping Co Ltd (The Aliakmon)* [1986] AC 785; [1986] 2 Lloyd's Rep 1 (HL).
57. SOGA 1979, s 17(1).
58. Ibid., s 17(2). For a full and recent account of the rules relating to passage of property under English law see C. Debattista in A. Von Ziegler, C. Debattista, A.B.K. Plegat and J. Windahl (eds), *Transfer of Ownership in International Trade* (2nd edn, Kluwer Law 2011), at p 134 ff.
59. Ibid., s 18, r 5(1). For goods shipped commingled see rr 5(3) and 5(4). See *Lorenzon* (fn 4) [2–040] ff.
60. Ibid., s 27.

tender the documents agreed upon in the contract.[61] The duties to deliver goods and documents are separate and independent from each other[62] and will be dealt with in turn.

(a) The seller's physical duties

On the physical side the seller must (a) ship *contractual goods* (b) *as agreed* in the sale contract. What the expression "*contractual goods*" actually means under English law and how accurately it needs to follow the shipping instructions agreed in the contract will be the subject of the following paragraphs.

(i) Shipping contractual goods . . .

The most obvious obligation imposed on the seller by any sale contract is the duty to ship *exactly* the goods it has promised. However, the extent of precision with which the seller has to perform this basic obligation and the remedies of the buyer for breach of such duty vary according to the *nature* of the contractual term at stake. Under English law, contractual terms relating to the goods are in fact considered either by express choice of the parties, by the relevant market and/or by the law as being so crucial to the trade concerned that their breach gives the buyer the option of rejecting the goods and terminating the contract.

Traditionally contractual clauses have been classified in three different categories: (a) *warranties*, the breach of which entitles the innocent party to a claim in damages;[63] (b) *conditions*, the breach of which gives the innocent party the further option to bring the contract to an abrupt end; and (c) *intermediate* (or *innominate*) terms, whose breach may afford the innocent party the right to terminate provided it can prove that the breach in question went to the root of the contract concerned. Since this classification has very powerful effects on the life itself of the transaction it is crucial for both buyer and seller to be able to identify which terms of their contract are conditions and which are not. The test to be applied here has been authoritatively summarised in *Chitty on Contracts*[64] and approved by Waller LJ in the Court of Appeal in *The Seaflower*[65] as follows:

a term of a contract will be held to be a condition:

 (i) If it is expressly so provided *by statute*;
 (ii) If it has been so categorised as the result of previous judicial decision [. . .];
(iii) If it is so designated in the contract or if the consequences of its breach, that is, the right of the innocent party to treat himself as discharged, are provided for expressly in the contract; or
(iv) If the nature of the contract or the subject-matter or the circumstances of the case lead to the conclusion that the parties must, by necessary implication, have intended that the innocent party would be discharged from further performance of his obligations in the event that the term was not fully and precisely complied with.[66]

If a term in a contract falls within any of the four limbs of this, which we may call the "*Waller Test*", then the parties' rights and liabilities are sharp and clear.

---

61. *Arnhold Karberg & Co v Blythe, Green, Jourdain & Co* [1916] 1 KB 495 (CA).
62. *Kwei Tek Chao & Others v British Traders and Shippers Ltd* [1954] 2 QB 459; [1954] 1 Lloyd's Rep 16.
63. On the matter of damages, see *Bunge SA v Nidera BV* [2015] UKSC 43; [2015] 2 Lloyd's Rep 469.
64. H.G. Beale (ed.), *Chitty on Contracts* (32nd edn, Sweet & Maxwell 2014), (hereinafter "Chitty"), [13-038]–[13-040].
65. *B S & N Ltd (BVI) v Micado Shipping Ltd (Malta) (The Seaflower) (No 1)* [2001] 1 Lloyd's Rep 341.
66. Ibid., [42].

Conditions by contract. Limbs (iii) and (iv) above may be collectively defined as *conditions by contract* on the ground that they find their source in the freedom of the parties to determine the terms of their agreement although it must be said that judges are increasingly reluctant to imply conditions under limb (iv). The bottom line here is that if a particular feature of the goods to be shipped is of crucial importance to the buyer it should be proactive and draft a clause in its contract whereby delivery of goods without such feature would give it the right to reject the consignment.

Conditions by law. On the other hand, clauses falling within limbs (i) and (ii) of the test may be collectively classified as *conditions by law* as they find their source either in statutory provisions or in the common law. Under English law the Sale of Goods Act 1979 implies three types of conditions into all sale contracts.

(1) Terms describing the goods. Section 13 of the Sale of Goods Act 1979 states that where there is a contract for the sale of goods by description, there is an implied condition that the goods will correspond with the description. The key here is that the contract prevails and that if the parties have agreed to allowances and/or price adjustments in their agreements the courts will infer that that particular item of the description was not regarded by the parties as a condition at all. However, where the contract is silent, the court will make its decision on the basis of evidence from the market as to whether the description of the goods in the contract went to the *identity* of the commodity sold.[67]

(2) The goods must be of satisfactory quality. Section 14 of the Sale of Goods Act 1979 further provides that where the seller sells goods in the course of a business, there is an implied term that the goods supplied under the contract are of a satisfactory quality[68] and that this implied term is a condition.[69] In the attempt to clarify what is intended by satisfactory quality, the Act regards as satisfactory the quality of goods meeting "the standard that a reasonable person would regard as satisfactory, taking account of any description of the goods, the price (if relevant) and all the other relevant circumstances".[70] Moreover the quality of the goods is said to include their state, condition, fitness for all the purposes for which goods of the kind in question are commonly supplied, appearance and finish, freedom from minor defects, safety and durability.[71]

(3) The case of goods sold by sample. The third implied condition established by the Sale of Goods Act 1979 relates to the special case of goods sold by sample. A contract of sale is a contract for sale by sample where there is an express or implied term in the contract to that effect.[72] In this case there is an implied condition that the bulk will correspond with the sample in quality[73] and that the goods will be free from any qualitative defect which would not be apparent on reasonable examination of the sample.[74]

Having examined the three conditions implied by the Act, the next question to be addressed is whether any breach – however slight – of these terms entitles the buyer to terminate the contract or whether, together with the term, the law implies also a leeway: the current position is not

---

67. *Tradax Internacional SA v Goldschmidt SA* [1977] 2 Lloyd's Rep 604.

68. SOGA 1979, s 14(2). For a detailed discussion on the scope of the term implied by s 14(2) see *KG Bominflot Bunkergesellshaft für Mineraloele mbH & Co v Petroplus Marketing AG (The Mercini Lady)* [2010] EWCA Civ 1145; [2011] 1 Lloyd's Rep 442.

69. SOGA 1979, s 14(6).

70. Ibid., s 14(2A).

71. Ibid., s 14(2B); on durability in the context of shipment sale as to capability to withstand normal sea transit see again *Mash & Murrell v Emanuel* [1961] 2 Lloyd's Rep 326, fn 55 and the discussion in Lorenzon (fn 4), [2-033]–[2-035].

72. SOGA 1979, s 15(1).

73. Ibid., s 15(2)(a).

74. Ibid., s 15(2)(c).

entirely clear. Section 15A of the Act[75] provides that where the buyer has the right to reject goods by reason of a breach on the part of the seller of a term implied by sections 13, 14 or 15 of the Act but the breach is so slight that it would be unreasonable for the buyer to reject them[76] (the burden of proof is on the seller),[77] the breach may be treated as a breach of warranty.[78] If the discrepancy falls within the known *de minimis* allowance implied by the common law the buyer would not be allowed to reject the goods.[79] It is, however, clear that section 15A is an attempt to broaden considerably the scope of the *de minimis* allowance to avoid so-called technical rejections. On the other hand, this section only applies unless a contrary intention appears in, or is to be implied from, the contract[80] and this is almost invariably the case in commodity sales where allowances and adjustments are commonly catered for or incorporated by reference.

Apart from the Sale of Goods Act 1979 itself, the common law has also made substantial contributions to the categorisation of terms in sale contracts. So terms about the time[81] and place[82] of shipment and the quantity[83] of the goods to be shipped have traditionally been considered as part of the description of the goods and as such held to be conditions now covered by section 13 of the Act. As far as the quantity of the goods is concerned the Sale of Goods Act 1979 (in its amended version) softened the harshness of the buyer's remedy by adding that it may not reject the whole consignment for short or excess delivery if such shortfall or excess is so slight that it would be unreasonable for it to do so.[84] This subsection being subject to any usage of trade, special agreement or course of dealing between the parties[85] – it is submitted – should not ordinarily apply to c.i.f. and f.o.b. sales.

(ii) . . . as agreed in the sale contract

Selecting the goods for shipment represents only one part of the physical duties owed by the seller to its buyer: such goods must also be *delivered as agreed* in the sale contract. This obviously *physical* duty in shipment sales – both on c.i.f. and f.o.b. terms – is performed by loading the goods on board the vessel fixed by the seller or buyer respectively. Section 32(1) of the Sale of Goods Act 1979 in fact provides that where the seller is required to send the goods to the buyer, delivery of the goods to a carrier for the purpose of transmission to the buyer is prima facie deemed to be a delivery of the goods to the buyer.[86] Two issues are crucial here: (i) this is and remains at all material times a *physical* duty to load and stow the cargo in the manner and on the vessel agreed in the sale contract; and (ii) the remedy available to the buyer for breach of such duty will depend entirely on the terms of the sale contract.

As already discussed the duty to make transport arrangements may fall on either the seller or the buyer depending on the terms on which the shipment sale has been concluded. In f.o.b. sales where the contract of carriage is concluded directly by the buyer, the physical duties relating

---

75. Inserted by the Sale and Supply of Goods Act 1994, s 4(1).
76. SOGA 1979, s 15A(1)(a).
77. Ibid., s 15A(3).
78. Ibid., s 15A(1)(b).
79. *Arcos Ltd v E A Ronaasen & Son* [1933] 45 Ll L Rep 33, [1933] AC 470, at p 479 (Lord Atkin): "No doubt there may be microscopic deviations which business men and therefore lawyers will ignore."
80. SOGA 1979, s 15A(2).
81. *Bowes v Shand* [1876–77] LR 2 App Cas 455 (HL).
82. *Petrograde Inc v Stinnes Handel GmbH* [1995] 1 Lloyd's Rep 142.
83. *In Re an Arbitration between Keighley Maxted & Co and Bryan Durant & Co* [1893] 1 QB 405.
84. SOGA 1979, s 30(2A).
85. Ibid., s 30(5).
86. Ibid., s 32(1). In the context of f.o.b. sales, see *Scottish & Newcastle International Ltd v Othon Ghalanos Ltd* [2008] UKHL 11; [2008] 1 Lloyd's Rep 462.

to the choice of the vessel, her route and – often – the details of the loading operations will be agreed upon by the buyer itself at the outset and are unlikely to cause any disputes, at any rate between the parties to the sale contract. On the other hand, where the shipping and carriage arrangements are made by the seller, it ought to comply with the prescriptions contained in the purchase agreement. The seller's duties with regards to the terms of the contract of carriage, at any rate when English law applies to such contract, are to be found in the contract of sale itself (or in the letter of credit) and in section 32(2) of the Sale of Goods Act 1979.

(a) The sale contract. Naturally the buyer is entitled to carriage arrangements it has stipulated for in the contract of sale. So if the sale contract provides for a vessel of a given class or tonnage, imposes restrictions on previous cargos or flag, reefer temperatures or any other specific requirements, the seller shall make the transport arrangement it promised. The fact that the promise is contained in the confirmation note or any of the incorporated standard forms or rules is clearly irrelevant as they are all part of the same agreement.

(b) The letter of credit. A letter of credit is a promise by a bank to pay to the beneficiary – *qua* seller – up to the amount of the credit against presentation of the documents stipulated therein.[87] As the agreed method of payment of the contract price, the credit will invariably contain – expressly or through incorporation of the UCP 600[88] – details relating to the carriage documents to be presented by the seller in order to collect payment. This has two consequences: (i) the bank will honour payment only to a seller who tenders the documents as required by the letter of credit[89] and consequently (ii) shipment will have to be made so as to allow the issue of such documents or certificates. An example may clarify this matter: if shipment on a vessel of a specific class was not required by the sale contract but the letter of credit requires tender of a specific class certificate issued by, for example, an IACS[90] member, the bank will honour the credit only if the seller tenders such a certificate and hence the duty to ship as agreed in the contract of sale can only be performed by shipping on board a vessel classed by a member of the Association.

Section 32(2) of the Sale of Goods Act 1979 provides that any *other* features of the contract of carriage tendered by the seller must be "reasonable having regard to the nature of the goods and the other circumstances of the case" and, if they are not, risk does not pass to the buyer leaving the seller responsible for transit loss.[91] The authorities appear to suggest that the word "reasonable" in this section has a threefold meaning: the seller must provide a contract of carriage (a) on usual terms,[92] (b) giving the buyer "protective rights"[93] against the carrier and (c) which is appropriate[94] to grant sufficient protection to the goods while in transit.[95] At this stage, it may also be interesting to notice the different choice of wording made in the Incoterms® 2010 Rules. The corresponding provisions there – e.g. Article CIF A3(a) – describe the seller's duty as one to tender a contract of carriage on "usual terms". However, the term further prescribes that the carriage of the goods must be made "to the named port of destination [. . .] by the usual route

87. *United City Merchants (Investments) Ltd v Royal Bank of Canada (The American Accord)* [1982] 2 Lloyd's Rep 1; [1983] 1 AC 168.
88. ICC Uniform Customs and Practice for Documentary Credits, 2007 Revision, ICC Publication No 600 (hereinafter "UCP 600").
89. UCP 600, arts 2 and 14(a).
90. The International Association of Classification Societies, see Chapter 9.
91. SOGA 1979, s 32(2).
92. *The Northern Progress (No 2)*, fn 16; and the other authorities cited in F. Lorenzon, "When is a CIF Seller's Carriage Contract Unreasonable? Section 32(2) of the Sale of Goods Act 1979" (2007) 13 JIML 241, at pp 242 et seq.
93. *Elof Hansson v Hamel and Horley* [1922] 2 AC 36, [1922] 10 Lloyd's Rep 507 (HL).
94. *Texas Instruments Ltd and Others v Nason (Europe) Ltd and Others* [1991] 1 Lloyd's Rep 146; *Gatoil International Inc v Tradax Petroleum Ltd (The Rio Sun)* [1985] 1 Lloyd's Rep 350.
95. *Thomas Young and Sons Ltd v Hobson and Partners* [1949] 65 TLR 365.

in a vessel of the type normally used for the transport of the type of goods sold"[96] which clearly indicates that – under the Incoterms® 2010 Rules – the choice has been made to allow the seller to arrange for whatever transport arrangement the market regards as "usual" in the trade concerned, provided it meets the above requirements.

If it is certainly true to say that the seller must make a contract of carriage which conforms to the contract of sale (or the letter of credit) and which is reasonable or usual as the case may be, it is also true to say that this does not imply that the seller guarantees to the buyer any degree of success in an action against the carrier[97] who is certainly entitled to all the protection and exclusions offered to it by the applicable national and international legislation.[98]

(b) The seller's documentary duties

Shipping goods as agreed in the sale contract only fulfils part of the seller's duties under the sale contract; in order to get paid for its goods the seller will also have to tender to the buyer the documents it has promised. The duty to tender documents together with (and at times instead of) goods is deeply embedded in the concept of shipment sales which are also referred to as *documentary* sales on shipment terms. The matter is hardly one of definition, both the physical and documentary tenders being essential parts of the performance of the sale contract.

Which documents will have to be tendered by the seller will clearly depend on the wording of the relevant agreement. Confirmation notes and standard form contracts will invariably list a number of documents to be tendered and will often spell out some of the characteristics these documents will have to have to be acceptable. In general terms, however, it can be said that two documents are essential to every shipment sale: the *commercial invoice* with which the seller quantifies its credit and a clean shipped on board *bill of lading*. If the goods are sold on c.i.f. terms the seller will also need to tender an *insurance policy* covering marine risks and any additional risks agreed in the sale contract.[99] The importance of the documents is crucial to both seller and buyer for different reasons: as far as the seller is concerned, it will only be paid if it can tender the documents promised under the sale contract, physical performance being insufficient to trigger the buyer's duty to pay the price. For the buyer – on the other hand – the documents provide it with evidence of physical performance, possessory rights over the goods and contractual rights against the carrier and the insurer. Where a letter of credit has been agreed as the method of payment for the goods in question, the credit itself will ask for a list of documents to be tendered, each with specific requirements.

Among the many documents which may be required in exchange for payment, the most complex and important is the bill of lading for it performs three crucial functions: (1) it provides evidence of a contract of carriage with the carrier and title to sue such carrier on its terms; (2) it gives constructive possession of the goods and hence the right to control and dispose of them; (3) it functions as a receipt for the goods shipped. Most aspects of the law relating to bills of lading are discussed in the chapter on cargo claims to which full reference is made.[100] The focus there is on the rights and liabilities of the carrier vis-à-vis cargo interests and on how such action can be brought under English law. The following paragraphs, on the other hand, will focus on an

---

96. CIF Incoterms® 2010 Rules, art A3(a).

97. *M Golodetz & Co Inc v Czarnikow-Rionda Co Inc (The Galatia)* [1979] 2 Lloyd's Rep 450, approved by the Court of Appeal at [1980] 1 Lloyd's Rep 453.

98. See Chapter 5 and *Jindal Iron and Steel Co Ltd and Others v Islamic Solidarity Shipping Co Jordan Inc (The Jordan II)* [2004] UKHL 49; [2005] 1 Lloyd's Rep 57.

99. See Chapter 11.

100. See Chapter 5.

entirely different – although connected – issue: what kind of bill of lading is the seller to tender to its buyer in order to be entitled to payment? The answer to this question will depend on the method of payment agreed between the parties: "net cash against shipping documents" or via a letter of credit governed by the UCP 600.

(i) To the buyer under the sale contract in cash against documents transactions

If there is no letter of credit, the seller is bound to tender to the buyer the documents listed in the sale contract.[101] It must be emphasised that very often the confirmation note contains some specific requirements regarding the most obvious or crucial documents to be tendered. However, often several documentary requirements are contained in standard forms incorporated by reference; in such cases the buyer will be entitled to all documents provided for in the note plus every additional document listed in the standard form's documents clause. It is worth noting that when the parties incorporate the Incoterms® 2010 Rules, the requirement becomes one to tender the "usual proof that the goods have been delivered in accordance with A4"[102] if the contract is on f.o.b. terms, or the "usual transport document for the agreed port of destination"[103] in case of CFR or CIF sales. In the latter scenario the transport document tendered must:

- cover the contract goods;
- be dated within the period agreed for shipment;
- enable the buyer to claim the goods from the carrier at the port of destination;
- unless otherwise agreed, enable the buyer to sell the goods in transit by the transfer of the document to a subsequent buyer or by notification to the carrier.[104]

In case the confirmation note refers only to the "usual shipping documents" and no other indication regarding the documents to be tendered may be found elsewhere in the agreement, it will be necessary for the parties (and the arbitrator or judge) to ascertain what "usual" means in the specific circumstances at stake, taking into account their course of dealing, the custom of the particular trade concerned and – where English law applies to the contract – the English common law. At common law, the bill must cover the goods which are the subject matter of the contract,[105] be made out in transferable form,[106] give the buyer a right of action against the carrier[107] and be clean.[108]

Time of presentation. If the sale contract provides for tender by a given time, the documents must be tendered within this time, the provision being regarded as a condition of the contract.[109] If the contract is silent, the seller must tender as soon as possible after shipment.[110]

When the contract stipulates for payment to be made via a letter of credit, all the above will have very limited relevance to ascertain the seller's documentary duties under the sale contract.

---

101. *Bergerco USA v Vegoil Ltd* [1984] 1 Lloyd's Rep 440.
102. Incoterms® 2010 Rules, "FOB", A8.
103. Incoterms® 2010 Rules, CIF and CFR, A8.
104. Ibid.
105. *In Re an Arbitration Keighley, Maxted & Co and Bryan, Durant & Co* (fn 83).
106. *Soproma SpA v Marine and Animal By-Products Corp* [1966] 1 Lloyd's Rep 367. For a full list see Halsbury's Laws of England, Vol. 91, *Sale of Goods and Supply of Services* (5th edn, LexisNexis 2012), [343].
107. *Buckman v Levi* [1813] 3 Camp 414; F. Lorenzon, "When is a CIF Seller's Carriage Contract Unreasonable? Section 32(2) of the Sale of Goods Act 1979" (2007) 13 JIML 241, 246.
108. *The Galatia* (fn 97); see Chapter 5.
109. *Toepfer (Hamburg) v Lenersan-Poortman NV (Rotterdam)* [1980] 1 Lloyd's Rep 143 (CA).
110. *C Sharpe & Co Ltd v Nosawa & Co* [1917] 2 KB 814.

(ii) To the bank under a letter of credit incorporating the UCP 600

In commercial sales of commodities the parties often agree for the buyer to pay via a letter of credit; in such cases the only way for the seller to get to the contract money is through tender of the documents to the bank instructed by its buyer. A letter of credit is – in essence – a series of contracts involving the buyer, one or more banks and the seller,[111] allowing documents and money to change hands in opposite directions, giving the buyer rigorous documentary screening before payment is made on its behalf and giving the seller an additional solvent debtor within its own jurisdiction. The system works as follows: the buyer instructs its bank to open a credit in favour of the seller for the amount of the purchase price. Naturally it must open a credit which conforms to the specifications spelled out in the sale contract. This *issuing* bank will then correspond with a bank within the seller's jurisdiction, which will either *advise* the seller of the opening of the credit in its favour, or *confirm* the credit opened by the issuing bank adding its own direct undertaking to pay the purchase price.[112] At this stage the advising or confirming bank will send the letter of credit to the seller – the beneficiary under the credit – containing a list of documents to be presented in order to obtain release of the money.

Once the letter of credit is received by the seller, the bank's promise becomes irrevocable[113] and the payment mechanism becomes active. This is not to say that the beneficiary itself is bound by it as yet: the letter of credit is a unilateral contract which – as the agreed method of payment – must conform with the requirements set in the sale contract and may well be rejected vis-à-vis the buyer if it does not. So, where the credit was agreed to be confirmed and it is not, or where it requires tender of different documents from the ones agreed in the sale contract, the seller would be entitled to reject it and withhold shipment of the goods.[114] In other words, the buyer is not entitled to amend the seller's documentary duties via the letter of credit after the contract of sale has been concluded. On the other hand, acceptance of a non-conforming credit – both express or through conduct – has been held to amount to a new agreement capable of modifying the contract of sale itself.[115]

Once accepted, the letter of credit becomes the only method of payment available to the seller. Hence, tender of the documents provided for in the letter of credit has a dual effect: on the one hand (i) it constitutes documentary performance under the sale contract and on the other (ii) it triggers the bank's duties under the credit.[116] At this stage the bank will carefully examine the bundle of documents to make sure that it parts with money only where the documents presented comply with the applicant's instructions as they appear in the credit. If they do, the confirming bank will release the funds and pass on the documents to the issuing bank for reimbursement and then eventually to the buyer;[117] if they do not the bank will refuse payment and return the documents.[118] But what criteria will the bank follow to make such a crucial decision?

---

111. *The Bank of Baroda v The Vysya Bank Ltd* [1994] 2 Lloyd's Rep 87, 90.
112. For an example of the different consequences of the bank's position see *Den Danske Bank A/S and Others v Surinam Shipping Ltd* [2014] UKPC 10; [2014] 1 Lloyd's Rep 52.
113. UCP 600, art 2.
114. *Soproma SpA v Marine and Animal By-Products Corp* (fn 106).
115. *Panoutsos v Raymond Hadley Corpn of New York* [1917] 2 KB 473 (CA); *Enrico Furst & Co v W E Fischer Ltd* [1960] 2 Lloyd's Rep 340; *W J Alan & Co Ltd v El Nasr Export & Import Co* [1972] 2 QB 189 (CA); *Ficom SA v Societad Cadex Ltda* [1980] 2 Lloyd's Rep 118; *Glencore Grain Rotterdam v Lebanese Organisation for International Commerce (The Lorico)* [1997] 4 All ER 514; [1997] 2 Lloyd's Rep 386 (CA).
116. UCP 600, arts 8, 14 and 16.
117. UCP 600, art 8. On the consequences of the bank's breach of the duty to return the documents see UCP 600, art 16(f) and *Fortis Bank SA/NV v Indian Overseas Bank* [2011] EWCA Civ 58; [2011] 2 Lloyd's Rep 33.
118. UCP 600, art 16.

(a) The UCP 600. The Uniform Customs and Practice for Documentary Credits are – in essence – standard terms setting out the duties and liabilities of the parties to the letters of credit in which they are incorporated.[119] They are drafted and regularly amended by the International Chamber of Commerce in Paris and they have no international or – as far as English law is concerned – national standing at all. Notwithstanding this, their incorporation in letters of credit is almost universal and their acceptance by bankers and traders alike makes them an essential tool in understanding international commercial sales and supply agreements. In its current edition in force from 1 July 2007, the UCP 600 apply to any documentary credit "where the text of the credit expressly indicates that it is subject to these rules. They are binding on all parties thereto, unless expressly modified or excluded by the credit";[120] in practice they are the universal rule of the game, the instructions the seller has to follow to convert documents into hard cash.

The duties and liabilities of the bank as to the examination and scrutiny of the documents – collectively referred to as *presentation* – are scrupulously defined and limited by the UCP 600 and the decision on whether to accept them or not must be made strictly "on the basis of the documents alone".[121] At common law the decision on whether the presentation is acceptable is made in accordance with the doctrine of *strict compliance* and the bank should pay only if the presentation complies strictly with the terms set out in the letter of credit itself; as Lord Sumner once put it: "There is no room for documents which are almost the same, or which will do just as well."[122] This case was, however, decided by the House of Lords in 1926, in a pre-UCP banking era.

Under the UCP 600 the strict duty imposed by the common law is heavily corrected by a series of carefully drafted clauses, according to which banks must examine the presentation to determine whether or not the documents appear *on their face*[123] to be in accordance with the terms and conditions of the credit, the UCP 600 itself and international standard banking practice.[124] Moreover, in documents other than the commercial invoice the description of the goods, services or performance, may not be stated at all or be in general terms not conflicting with their description in the credit.[125] Furthermore, banks assume "no liability or responsibility for the form, sufficiency, accuracy, genuineness, falsification or legal effect of any documents".[126] These "disclaimers" have two main functions: (i) on the one hand they have the clear intent to protect banks from liabilities which the duty of strict compliance – as it stands at common law – would undoubtedly impose on them; on the other (ii) they allow banks a certain amount of flexibility hence permitting the credit to be a reliable and prompt payment mechanism.

(b) Bills of lading under the UCP 600. A full account of all detailed requirements the UCP set for the acceptability of bills of lading goes beyond the scope of this work.[127] What must be clarified is that the bank, by opening the letter of credit and parting with money against documents, exposes itself to the risks of being unable to be reimbursed by its customer, either because the applicant declines a non-conforming presentation or becomes insolvent. In this case the bank will have an actual – as opposed to vested – interest in getting as much security as it

---

119. UCP 600, art 1. On letters of credit in general see A. Malek and D. Quest, *Jack: Documentary Credits* (4th edn, Tottel Publishing 2009) (hereinafter "Jack's").
120. Ibid.
121. UCP 600, arts 5 and 14 (a).
122. *Equitable Trust Co of New York v Dawson Partners Ltd* [1926] 27 Ll L Rep 49.
123. UCP 600, art 14(a).
124. Ibid., art 2.
125. Ibid., art 14(e).
126. Ibid., art 34.
127. For a full account see Jack's (fn 119) and C. Debattista, "The New UCP 600: Changes to Tender of the Seller's Shipping Documents under Letters of Credit" (2007) 4 JBL 329.

can from the documents and that is where the terms on which shipping documents are issued become extremely important.[128] For these reasons, the UCP 600 list several requirements bills of lading have to comply with in order to be acceptable under the credit. Such requisites may be usefully grouped according to the kind of security the bank (and its customer) may be interested in obtaining from the document in (a) requirements related to the bill as a contract of carriage giving enforceable rights against a contracting carrier, (b) requirements connected to the bill as a document of title to goods and (c) particulars concerning its function as a receipt.

Broadly speaking, (a) as a *contract of carriage* the bill of lading to be acceptable has to:

(i) appear to indicate the name of the carrier;[129]
(ii) indicate that the goods have been actually shipped on board;[130]
(iii) be made out from the port of loading to the port of discharge indicated in the credit;[131] and
(iv) contain the terms of the contract of carriage.[132]

It must be noted, however, that the UCP 600 do not require the bill to be made out in such a way as to give title to sue the carrier under COGSA 1992: detailed indication on how and to whom the bill will have to be made out is left to the applicant and the bank to decide and hence invariably contained in the letter of credit itself rather than the UCP.[133] Once the credit makes such stipulation, the bank will only pay against a bill complying with it. Second, in case something goes wrong with the reimbursement arrangement, the bank has a clear interest in being able to sell the bill of lading on and recover its losses. This may only be achieved if the bill of lading is properly pledged as (b) a negotiable *document of title* giving the bank constructive possession of the goods. Again here the UCP 600 does not contain express requirements on the issue other than for the fact that the bill has to be the sole original or, if issued in a set, it must be tendered as a full set.[134]

Finally, (c) as a *receipt* the bill must

(i) describe the goods in a way which is not inconsistent with the description of the goods in the credit;[135]
(ii) contain data which is not conflicting with data in other parts of the document, any other stipulated document or the credit;[136] and
(iii) bear no clause or notation expressly declaring a defective condition of the goods or their packaging.[137]

---

128. For a full discussion on shipping documents as a form of security for banks involved in letters of credit see C. Debattista, "Banks and the Carriage of Goods by Sea: Secure Transport Documents and the UCP 500" [1994] BJIBFL 329.
129. UCP 600, art 20(a)(i).
130. Ibid., art 20(a)(ii).
131. Ibid., art 20(a)(iii).
132. Ibid., art 20(a)(v) and (vi).
133. See Chapter 5.
134. UCP 600, art 20(a)(iv). Cf. the surprising corresponding requirement under Incoterms® 2010 Rules which make tender of multiple originals under CIF, CFR and CIP contracts necessary "when [the] transport document is issued *in negotiable form* and in several originals", A8. See also *Standard Chartered Bank v Dorchester LNG (2) Ltd (The "Erin Schulte")* [2014] EWCA Civ 1382; [2015] 2 Lloyd's Rep 97.
135. Ibid., art 14(e).
136. Ibid., art 14(d).
137. Ibid., art 27.

(c) *The decision to pay or not to pay.* It has now been seen that the bank is called to decide on the basis of the documents alone whether the presentation has been made in accordance with the requirements expressly set out in the letter of credit, the UCP 600 when incorporated and international standard banking practice. To reach its decision, Article 14(b) of the UCP 600 allows the bank "a maximum of five banking days following the day of presentation".[138] Delay in deciding whether or not to pay may well lead to the bank being estopped from denying that the documents conform to the credit.[139] If the bank decides that one or more of the documents tendered are not in compliance with the terms and conditions of the credit, in order to avoid liability for breach of contract vis-à-vis the applicant it will have to reject the documents.

(d) *Time for presentation.* It is clear that where the letter of credit stipulates a period for tender from the shipment date, the seller must tender the transport document by that date. Article 6(e) of UCP 600 provides that documents must be presented on or before such expiry date. If any of the above dates fall on a non-business day, then the documents must be tendered on the subsequent banking day.[140]

5. REJECTION: THE BUYER'S REMEDY AND THE SELLER'S RIGHT TO CURE

In c.i.f. and f.o.b. contracts, cancellation by rejection may be much more complex than in ordinary sales on delivery terms as the seller actually performs *two* types of delivery, the *documentary* tender and the *physical delivery* of goods. Moreover, whereas the law considers physical delivery the one which takes place at the place and time of shipment, the buyer will have the right to inspect its cargo only several days or weeks later at the port of discharge, at a time when – possibly – it has already taken delivery of the documents, directly or through its bank and parted with its cash. Finally, the costs of rejecting the consignment at the port of discharge are significant and would involve further negotiations (and expenses) aimed at rerouting the vessel to a new buyer or storing the unwanted cargo at the original discharge port awaiting resale.

Furthermore, it will be remembered that the physical duty to ship the consignment on board the vessel and the documentary duty to tender the agreed documentation run neatly separate and independent from each other and have been independently dealt with above. From this follows that serious breaches of each one of them will give the buyer separate and independent rights of termination: a physical breach of condition will entitle the buyer to reject the goods and terminate the sale contract, whereas a breach of the documentary duty to tender contractual documents will entitle the buyer (and the bank) to reject the presentation, withhold payment and terminate the contract in its own right.[141] The further practical difficulty is that documents and goods will rarely reach the buyer at the same time making it even more difficult for it to decide whether or not it actually wishes to terminate: if documents reach the buyer before arrival of the goods, in spotting a documentary defect the buyer may actually wish to withhold its right to reject them awaiting physical inspection of the actual cargo, particularly against a rising market. On the contrary, the buyer may have no option to reject the documentary tender at all as the documents may well be in order whereas the goods – on discharge – may tell a completely different story. Moreover, where banks are involved with the scrutiny of documents, the decision as to whether the presentation complies or not with the terms of the credit will be based exclusively

---

138. Ibid., art 14(b).
139. Ibid., art 14(f).
140. UCP 600, art 29(a).
141. *James Finlay & Co Ltd v Kwik Hoo Tong Handel Maatschappij* [1929] 1 KB 400, [1928] 32 Ll L Rep 245; *Kwei Tek Chao & Others v British Traders and Shippers Ltd* (fn 62).

on the examination of the documents and no regard will be paid to the condition of the goods on shipment.[142] For these reasons the position of buyers and banks with regard to rejection will be dealt with separately.

(a) Rejection of goods and documents by the buyer

The right to reject documents is completely separate and independent from the right to reject goods. The position under English law is quite clear: accepting the documentary tender does not have any implications for the separate and independent right to reject the physical tender on inspection.[143] This principle, however, is not absolute but has two important exceptions: (i) when the contract of sale provides for physical performance to be exclusively evidenced by documents and (ii) when the buyer accepts a documentary tender providing clear evidence of a fatal defect in the *physical delivery*. The two exceptions will be dealt with in turn.

(i) Documents – final evidence of physical performance

The duties to ship the consignment within a certain date or in a given quantity or again to load goods of a specific description are clearly all physical duties the seller has to perform. These duties have all been classified as conditions of the sale contract, breach of which entitles the buyer to reject the goods and declare termination. However, while the seller performs these duties at the time and place of shipment, the buyer will be able to verify physical compliance only much later, at the time and place of discharge. Moreover, in order to reject the cargo rightfully the buyer will have to provide evidence that the goods were non-conforming to the contractual specs at the time and place of shipment, when – at best – it was not there to check. It is hence very common for sale contracts – in particular in commodity trades – to provide for *documentary evidence of physical performance* and to make such evidence *"final" between the parties*: non-rebuttable. So the date of shipment may well be said to be "final as per bill of lading" and the quantity and quality of the goods "final as per certificate issued by independent surveyor", so to provide both parties with conclusive evidence of what has been shipped.[144]

When the parties have agreed upon such terms,[145] breach of the physical duty in question may only be evidenced through the stipulated documents and where the documents indicate correct physical performance the buyer will not be entitled to refuse delivery of a non-conforming cargo: it is *estopped (by convention)*[146] from doing so unless it can prove fraud[147] on the part of the seller or a procedural breach in the collection or examination of the samples.[148]

(ii) Acceptance of documents evidencing a physical repudiatory breach

The other exception to the doctrine of independence of the physical and documentary duties arising under a sale contract is based on the Court of Appeal decision in *Panchaud Frères*.[149] In

---

142. UCP 600, art 5.

143. *Kwei Tek Chao & Others v British Traders and Shippers Ltd* (fn 62).

144. A. Sandiforth, "Certificate Final Clauses in International Trade: Some Recent Developments", in M. Clarke (ed.), *Maritime Law Evolving: 30 Years at Southampton* (Hart Publishing, 2013), 197.

145. This may be a difficult matter of construction requiring careful attention as demonstrated by the facts in *RG Grain Trade LLP v Feed Factors International Ltd* [2011] EWHC 1889 (Comm); [2011] 2 Lloyd's Rep 432.

146. See *Colchester Bc v Smith* [1992] Ch 421, at p 434; and H. Beale (ed.), *Chitty on Contracts* (32nd edn, Sweet & Maxwell, 2014), [4-108]–[4-109].

147. *Gill & Duffus SA v Berger & Co Inc* [1984] AC 382; [1984] 1 Lloyd's Rep 227 (HL).

148. *Soon Hua Seng Co Ltd v Glencore Grain Ltd* (fn 50).

149. *Panchaud Frères SA v Establissements General Grain Co* [1970] 1 Lloyd's Rep 53.

this case the buyers accepted and paid for documents among which there was a bill of lading indicating shipment within the shipment period and a certificate of inspection indicating that samples were collected at the port of loading ashore, *after* the last day allowed for shipment. The bill of lading was clearly antedated and the presentation could have been rejected as a whole, as evidencing shipment outside the permitted time window. However, it was not. On arrival the buyer rejected the goods for breach of the *physical* duty to ship the consignment within the time stipulated in the contract. The buyers then sued the seller to recover the price paid against tender of documents but the claim was unsuccessful: Lord Denning MR held that by accepting documents indicating a defective condition of the goods the buyers are now *estopped (by conduct)* from rejecting the goods on the same grounds.

A last point needs to be made at this stage: what if the goods delivered are only in part compliant with the terms of the contract and the rest is not? Would it be possible for the buyer to take delivery of the good consignment and reject the bad one? The situation is considered by section 35A of the Sale of Goods Act 1979 which – in such cases – allows the buyer an option: reject the non-conforming goods while accepting the rest. The section provides as follows:

> If the buyer has the right to reject the goods [. . .] but accepts some of the goods, including, where there are any goods unaffected by the breach, all such goods, he does not by accepting them lose his right to reject the rest.[150]

(b) Rejection of documents by the bank

The bank's obligation with regard to honouring the credit is determined by the UCP 600 as one to honour[151] a complying presentation or refuse to honour a non-complying one.[152] The bank can hence commit either of two breaches: (a) paying against a non-complying presentation; or (b) refusing to pay against a complying presentation. Should the bank pay against defective documents, it will clearly have no action against the issuing bank or the applicant for reimbursement.[153] Should the bank refuse to pay under conforming documents the beneficiary will have a direct action for breach of the promise contained in the letter of credit.

In order to try and avoid such liabilities banks have two devices: if presented with non-complying documents the confirming bank may in its sole discretion approach the issuing bank and – in turn – the issuing bank approach the applicant for an advanced waiver of the discrepancy.[154] Once permission to pay is granted upstream the bank can safely pay the beneficiary without responsibility. Another way of avoiding liabilities for wrongful payment has been created through the practice of paying "under reserve" against documents known to be defective. However, where the bank is inclined to pay under reserve it has to take great care to clarify its rights and liabilities vis-à-vis the beneficiary in the under reserve arrangement itself so to avoid difficulties when the time to enforce such arrangement comes.[155]

Where the bank intends to reject, however, it is crucial that it follows strictly the prescriptions contained in Article 16(c) of the UCP 600 according to which the bank *must* give a single notice of rejection containing three fundamental elements: (i) a statement that the bank is refusing to

---

150. SOGA 1979, s 35A.
151. UCP 600, art 15(a).
152. Ibid., art 16(a).
153. *Credit Agricole Indosuez v Generale Bank and Seco Steel Trading Inc and Considar Inc (No 2)* [2000] 1 Lloyd's Rep 123.
154. UCP 600, art 16(b).
155. *Banque de l'Indochine et de Suez SA v JH Rayner (Mincing Lane) Ltd* [1983] 1 All ER 1137, [1983] 1 Lloyd's Rep 228; *Co-operative Centrale Raiffeisen-Boerenleenbank BA v Sumitomo Bank (The Royan, The Abukirk, The Bretagne, The Auvergne)* [1988] 2 Lloyd's Rep 250 (CA).

honour the credit, (ii) a list of each discrepancy in respect of which the rejection is grounded and (iii) a declaration indicating what the bank is currently doing with the unsuccessful presentation. The importance of the formalities of such notice are signified by the draconian consequence the bank will have to face in case of failure to act in accordance with the provisions of the article: the bank shall in fact be precluded from claiming that the documents do not constitute a complying presentation and hence will be forced to pay or defend an action for non-payment by the beneficiary.[156]

(c) The seller's right to cure a defective tender

The last question to be addressed is whether – on rejection – the seller has the right to cure *physical* and/or documentary defects. This issue is particularly relevant for if the seller were allowed to cure its defective performance the buyer would still be bound to accept the new conforming performance and pay the contract price.

(i) Curing physical performance

It is quite clear on the authorities and indeed on the wording of the Sale of Goods Act 1979 that if the physical tender was made in breach of condition the remedy available to the buyer is an absolute one: termination of contract.[157] Once the contract is terminated, the seller would be allowed to re-tender only if it can reach a new agreement with the buyer: in substance a new contract.

(ii) Curing documentary tender in cash against documents transactions

It is clear that when the sale contract allows or – more commonly – prohibits the seller to cure a defective tender, the court will give effect to such term. If the contract is silent, however, it is here submitted that – at any rate where the parties did not provide for a time window for the tender of documents – it would not be possible for the seller to tender a complying set of documents after a first non-conforming tender has been rejected. This is argued on the ground that documentary tender *is* performance of the contract and once the document tendered evidences (or is itself) a repudiatory breach, documentary performance is non-contractual and the buyer's remedy remains termination. On the other hand, where the contract provides for a time window for presentation of documents then the seller appears to be entitled to re-tender,[158] the documentary duty becoming a rather different one: to tender conforming documents *within the last available day*. On these terms there can be no breach until the time has elapsed.[159]

(iii) Curing documentary tender in letters of credit transactions

It is clear that where the bank decides to reject the presentation, the seller has the right to re-tender provided it does so within the timeframe allowed by the credit. This is where the notice of rejection the bank must give[160] becomes most relevant as it notifies the beneficiary of the

---

156. UCP 600, art 16(f) and *Fortis Bank SA/NV v Indian Overseas Bank* [2011] EWCA Civ 58; [2011] 2 Lloyd's Rep 33.
157. SOGA 1979, ss 13, 14 and 15; and discussion above.
158. *SIAT di Dal Ferro v Tradax Overseas SA* [1980] 1 Lloyd's Rep 53.
159. See in the same sense Benjamin (fn 45), [19–072] and Debattista (fn 45), [9.18].
160. UCP 600, art 16(c).

grounds on which payment has been refused and hence allows the seller to cure the documents and re-tender what should then be a complying presentation. The promise of the bank under the credit in fact still stands and a new complying presentation will still entitle the beneficiary to full payment provided such new tender is effected within both the expiry date of the credit[161] and the last day for presentation of documents.[162]

161. Ibid., art 16(e).
162. Ibid., art 16(c).

CHAPTER 4

CHARTERPARTIES

Yvonne Baatz

1. INTRODUCTION

A shipowner will wish to ensure that it makes as much profit from its ship as it possibly can. One means of achieving this aim is to charter the ship either on a time charter or on a voyage charter. A demise charterparty is a time charterparty usually for a long term such as ten years and the ship is in the possession of the demise charterer who crews, maintains and insures the ship.[1] Demise

---

1. See e.g. *BW Gas AS v JAS Shipping Ltd* [2010] EWCA Civ 68; [2011] 1 All ER (Comm) 236.

charters are often entered into for tax reasons. They are in a small minority of charters and this chapter will focus on the more usual time and voyage charterparties. In both these cases the ship remains in the possession of the owner who crews, maintains and insures the ship. However, there are very significant differences between time and voyage charterparties, most notably the manner in which the owner is paid. Under a time charterparty the ship is placed at the disposal of the time charterer for a period of time and the time charterer pays hire for every minute that it is so placed, unless the ship is off hire. Under a voyage charterparty the contract is for a voyage and the charterer pays freight and, if the time allowed at either the load or discharge port for the process of loading and discharging the cargo is exceeded, usually demurrage.

This chapter will consider the role of shipbrokers. It will focus on charterparties between commercial parties. Such parties enjoy freedom of contract and can contract on such terms as they have the commercial muscle to obtain. The Hague,[2] Hague-Visby[3] or Hamburg[4] Rules, which impose minimum obligations that cannot be contracted out of, on carriers under bills of lading, do not apply mandatorily to charterparties. However, the parties may voluntarily provide for such conventions to apply to their charterparty. Whether they have done so will be considered so that the terms of the charterparty can be identified before the parties' obligations are discussed.

Standard form charterparties, both time and voyage, almost invariably contain express terms imposing obligations on the owner to make the ship seaworthy, to perform its contractual obligations with reasonable despatch and not to deviate from the contractual voyage. If there were to be no such express terms each of these obligations would be implied. These obligations will be considered together with the impact of any Rules which apply to the charterparty. The remedies that are available to the charterer for breach will be explored. The charterer's obligations in relation to safe ports will be discussed, before considering the circumstances in which a charterparty can be frustrated. Issues specific to time charterparties will then be explored before turning to such issues in relation to voyage charterparties. Time charterparties are considered first as if there are both time and voyage charters in relation to the same ship, the time charter will usually have come into existence first. Finally the issue of liens both over cargo and sub-freights to enforce payment under the charterparty will be considered.

2. SHIPBROKERS

Both the owner and the charterer may each instruct a chartering shipbroker, who will have the best knowledge of the current chartering market. Shipbrokers will often specialise in different types of ships such as oil tankers or general cargo ships. This is both because the owners and charterers of these ships are different and because the standard form contracts which usually form the basis of the negotiations and tailor-made clauses vary according to which type of ship is involved. There are numerous standard form charterparties, both time and voyage, and in each case, for different types of cargo. Thus for a time charterparty for the carriage of general cargo the New York Produce Exchange ("NYPE") form 1946 or 1993[5] is commonly used, whereas for

---

2. The International Convention for the Unification of Certain Rules of Law Relating to Bills of Lading signed at Brussels on 25 August 1924.
3. The International Convention for the Unification of Certain Rules of Law Relating to Bills of Lading signed at Brussels on 25 August 1924 as amended by the Protocol signed at Brussels on 23 February 1968 and by the Protocol signed at Brussels on 21 December 1979.
4. The UN Convention on the Carriage of Goods by Sea 1978.
5. See also the New York Produce Exchange Form 2015.

the carriage of oil a specialist form such as the Shelltime 3 or 4 form may be used. For voyage charterparties the Gencon charterparty 1994 is widely used for general cargo and the Asbatankvoy and Shellvoy forms are used for oil. These particular standard forms will be referred to throughout this chapter to give examples of typical provisions and the problems they may give rise to. Both the NYPE form 1946 and the Asbatankvoy charterparties are now old forms. Although they are both still widely used, they are often extensively amended and numerous additional typed clauses will probably be appended to the standard form. The broker will advise its principal on how to tailor the standard form to the individual transaction.

Once the charterparty has been concluded its terms will usually be recorded in a fixture recap, that is an email or other written form recording the terms of the charterparty and referring to any standard form or pro forma charterparty in relation to another vessel agreed.[6] Sometimes there may be an issue as to whether the amendments recorded in the fixture recap and the standard form contract or pro forma contract incorporated into the fixture can be reconciled. It will be a question of construction[7] as to whether there is an inconsistency between the negotiated terms and the incorporated standard terms or pro forma, in which case the former may prevail, or whether the latter terms qualify the former, in which case they must be read together.[8] A charterparty may be drawn up and signed by both parties but this is often not done and therefore the fixture recap or exchange of emails must be relied on.[9]

It is important to determine whether the broker has contracted as agent for its principal or in its personal capacity as principal.[10] If the broker acts as an agent for its principal, there will be an agency contract between the broker and the party on whose behalf it is acting.[11] That contract will impose obligations on the broker to act, for example, with reasonable skill and care. If the broker fails to comply with those obligations it may be liable to its principal in either contract for breach of the agency contract or in tort for breach of its tortious duty of care. The principal can choose whether to sue in contract or in tort depending on which cause of action is most favourable[12] because, for example, the damages may be assessed differently, the time limit is different in contract and tort[13] and jurisdiction may be different.[14] Where the claim in contract and in tort

---

6. See e.g. *Caresse Navigation Ltd v Office National de L'Electricite (The Channel Ranger)* [2014] EWCA Civ 1366; [2015] 1 Lloyd's Rep 256.

7. The general principles of construction of contract were recently set out by Lord Neuberger delivering the majority judgment (Lord Neuberger delivered a judgment also on behalf of Lord Sumption and Lord Hughes JJSC; Lord Hodge JSC delivered his own judgment in agreement; but Lord Carnwath JSC dissented) of the Supreme Court in *Arnold v Britton* [2015] UKSC 36; [2015] AC 1619 [15], a case concerning the amount of the service charges in a lease. Lord Neuberger also emphasised seven factors at [16]–[23]. The seventh was relevant only to service charge clauses in leases but the first six may be important in the construction of charterparties. See also *Antaios Compania Naviera SA v Salen Rederierna AB* [1985] AC 191; *Investors' Compensation Scheme v West Bromwich Building Society* [1998] 1 WLR 896 followed in *Bank of Credit and Commerce International SA v Ali* [2001] UKHL8; [2002] 1 AC 251; *Rainy Sky SA v Kookmin Bank* [2011] UKSC 50; [2011] 1 WLR 2900; and *Lloyds TSB Foundation for Scotland v Lloyds Banking Group plc* [2013] UKSC 3; [2013] 1 WLR 366, [23], [45] and [54] and *Griffon Shipping LLC v Firodi Shipping Ltd (The Griffon)* [2013] EWHC 593 (Comm) (construction of the Norwegian Sale form discussed at p 83. See also *Wood v Capita Insurance Services Ltd*).

8. See e.g. *Cobelfret Bulk Carriers NV v Swissmarine Services SA (The Lowlands Orchid)* [2009] EWHC 2883 (Comm); [2010] 2 All ER (Comm) 128; [2010] 1 Lloyd's Rep 317 discussed at p 179 considering *Bayoil SA v Seawind Tankers Corporation (The Leonidas)* [2001] 1 Lloyd's Rep 533 and *Ocean Pride Maritime Ltd Partnership v Qingdao Ocean Shipping Co (The Northgate)* [2008] 1 Lloyd's Rep 511.

9. See *Golden Ocean Group Ltd v Salgaocar Mining Industries PVT Ltd* [2012] EWCA 265; [2012] 1 WLR 3674 per Tomlinson LJ [22]. See Chapter 1, page 6.

10. *Polish Steamship Co v AJ Williams (Overseas Sales) Ltd (The Suwalki)* [1989] 1 Lloyd's Rep 511. See also *Fin-Moon Ltd v Baltic Reefer Management Ltd* [2012] EWHC 920 (Comm); [2012] 2 Lloyd's Rep 388.

11. *Pan Ocean Chartering v UNIPEC Ltd* [2016] EWHC 2774 (Comm).

12. *Henderson v Merrett* [1994] 3 All ER 506.

13. Ibid.

14. See Chapter 1, pages 31–38.

is concurrent and both the contractual and tortious duty are coextensive, as they are both to exercise reasonable skill and care, the broker could rely on the defence of contributory negligence.[15]

Provided that the broker has actual or ostensible authority to act on behalf of its principal, when the charterparty is concluded, its principal is bound to the other party to the charterparty.[16] The broker has no obligations under the charterparty as it has acted merely as agent. Were the broker not to have authority to contract on behalf of its principal, it could not bind its principal to the charterparty and would be liable to the other party in tort for breach of warranty of authority.[17] The broker can also incur liability to the other party to the transaction if it makes a misrepresentation in its personal capacity rather than on behalf of its principal, for example, as to the creditworthiness of its principal. This was the situation in *The Arta*,[18] where the charterer's broker indicated to the owner's broker at the commencement of negotiations for a voyage charterparty that the charterer was "okay", meaning that it could meet its financial commitments under the charter. The charterer subsequently failed to pay the freight and the brokers were held liable in tort for breach of their duty of care as they had failed to carry out checks on their new client's creditworthiness. In establishing whether the broker was in breach of its duty of care the court would consider the rules by which the broker was bound, for example, those of the Institute of Chartered Shipbrokers, and the extent to which a broker could rely on information supplied to it by another broker.

The broker is paid commission and the charterparty will usually contain a clause providing who will pay what commission to which broker.[19] The broker is not a party to the charterparty contract. If the party obliged to pay the commission fails to do so, then if that party is the broker's own principal, the broker can sue its own principal in contract under its agency agreement. However, if the other party to the charterparty owes the commission, the broker may be able to overcome the problem of lack of privity if the Contracts (Rights of Third Parties) Act 1999 applies, either because the charterparty expressly provides that the broker may enforce the charterparty[20] or, which is more likely, the term in the charterparty purports to confer a benefit on the broker.[21] In *Nisshin Shipping Co Ltd v Cleaves & Co. Ltd*[22] Colman J held that chartering brokers had the right to enforce commission clauses in charterparties between their principals and the shipowners pursuant to section 1 of the Contracts (Rights of Third Parties Act) 1999 and had the right and the obligation to refer the disputes to arbitration as provided for in the charterparties. Alternatively, the broker can sue both parties to the charterparty as co-defendants to enforce a constructive trust of the commission of which it is beneficiary.[23]

---

15. *Vesta v Butcher* [1988] 2 All ER 43.
16. See *Golden Ocean Group Ltd v Salgaocar Mining Industries PVT Ltd* [2012] EWCA 265; [2012] 1 WLR 3674 affirming [2011] EWHC 56 (Comm); [2011] 1 WLR 2575; whether an agent had actual or ostensible authority to bind Daehan Shipbuilding Company to two guarantees of two charterparties was considered in *Rimpacific Navigation Inc v Daehan Shipbuilding Co (The Jin Man and the Jin Pu)* [2009] EWHC 2941; [2010] 2 Lloyd's Rep 236 (Steel J); [2011] EWHC 2618 (Comm); [2010] 2 Lloyd's Rep 236 (Teare J); *Mitsui OSK Lines Ltd v Salgaocar Mining Industries Private Ltd (The Unta)* [2015] EWHC 565 (Comm); [2015] 2 Lloyd's Rep 518 [37]. See also *Habas Sinai Ve Tibbi Gazlar Istihsal Endustri v VSC Steel Co Ltd* [2013] EWHC 4071; [2014] 1 Lloyd's Rep 479.
17. *Navig8 Inc v South Vigour Shipping Inc* [2015] EWHC 32 (Comm); [2015] 1 Lloyd's Rep 436. Managers were liable for damages for breach of warranty of authority as they did not have authority to bind owners to four charterparties.
18. *Markappa Inc v N W Spratt & Son Ltd (The Arta)* [1985] 1 Lloyd's Rep 534.
19. See e.g. cl 24 of the Baltime form, cls 27 and 28 NYPE 1946, cls 43 and 44 NYPE 1993 and cl 53 of NYPE 2015.
20. s 1(1)(a).
21. s 1(1)(b). The broker must be identified in accordance with s 1 (3).
22. [2004] 1 Lloyd's Rep 38. See also *Starlight Shipping Company v Allianz Marine and Aviation Versicherungs AG (The Alexandros T) (No 3)* [2014] EWHC 3068 (Comm); [2015] 2 All ER (Comm) 747 [83] – [88] in relation to a claim under the Act for damages for breach of a jurisdiction agreement in a settlement agreement.
23. *Les Affreteurs Reunis v Walford* [1919] AC 801.

3. THE HAGUE, HAGUE-VISBY AND HAMBURG RULES

Some time and voyage charterparties provide that the Hague, Hague-Visby or Hamburg Rules apply to the charterparty. The charterparty may contain a clause paramount or set out sections of the rules in the charterparty or provide that any set of Rules that applies to any bill of lading issued under the charterparty shall also apply to any cargo claim under the charterparty.

The development of the Hague, Hague-Visby and Hamburg Rules will be outlined. In the nineteenth century shipowners included wide exclusions of liability in their contracts. This was perceived as unacceptable for bills of lading where the third party consignee or indorsee of the bill of lading, who was not an original party to the bill of lading and had not had an opportunity to negotiate its terms, might find that it had paid for a cargo but had no rights against the shipowner for damage to or loss of that cargo because of those exclusions. Following the lead of the US Harter Act 1893,[24] the international community agreed to the Hague Rules in 1924. Those Rules impose certain minimum obligations on carriers which they cannot contract out of,[25] such as the duty to exercise due diligence to make the ship seaworthy before and at the beginning of the voyage[26] and to care for the cargo.[27] In return the shipowner has certain exemptions or immunities, such as the right to rely on the list of exceptions in Article IV rule 2, provided that it has complied with its seaworthiness obligation, to limit its liability for cargo loss or damage[28] and to be discharged from liability one year after discharge of the goods.[29]

Once the Hague Rules had been in force for some four decades it became apparent that there were some criticisms of the rules, not least that the package limits had become very low. Therefore in 1968 the Visby Protocol was agreed.[30] It is given the force of law in the United Kingdom by the Carriage of Goods by Sea Act 1971. It follows the format of the Hague Rules but made amendments principally to the limits of liability which were in some cases increased,[31] the method of calculation of the limit[32] and the right to break the limit,[33] an extended time limit for indemnity claims,[34] extending the defences and limits of liability to tort claims,[35] and to servants and agents of the carrier.[36]

In 1978 the Hamburg Rules were agreed, which seek to give greater protection to cargo interests. Major differences from the Hague-Visby Rules include a different regime of liability with no exception for negligent navigation,[37] higher limits[38] (but they can be broken[39] and the

---

24. See cl 24 of NYPE 1946.
25. Art III r 8.
26. Art III r 1.
27. Art III r 2.
28. Art IV r 5.
29. Art III r 6.
30. A. Diamond, "The Hague-Visby Rules" [1978] LMCLQ 255.
31. The limits in the Hague-Visby Rules may differ from those in the Hague Rules but are not always higher as is illustrated by *Yemgas FZCO v Superior Pescadores SA Panama (The Superior Pescadores)* [2016] EWCA Civ 101 at [14]; [2014] EWHC 971 (Comm); [2014] 1 Lloyd's Rep 660 at [42] and *Vinnlustodin HF v Sea Tank Shipping AS (The Aqasia)* [2016] EWHC 2514 (Comm); [2016] 2 Lloyd's Rep 510 where it was held that there is no limit under the Hague Rules for bulk liquid cargo, but there would be a limit under the Hague-Visby Rules. See also P. Todd, *Principles of the Carriage of Goods by Sea* (Routledge 2016), section 18.5.
32. Art IV r 5.
33. Art IV r 5(e) and art IV*bis* r 4.
34. Art III r 6*bis*.
35. Art IV*bis* r 1.
36. Art IV*bis* r 2 to 4.
37. Hamburg Rules, art 5.
38. Hamburg Rules, art 6.
39. Hamburg Rules, art 8.

defences and limits of liability of the carrier are extended to claims in tort[40] and to the servant or agent of the carrier[41]), a two-year time bar,[42] and jurisdiction and arbitration provisions.[43]

There is no international harmony on which rules apply compulsorily to bills of lading. Some States still give effect to the Hague Rules (most notably the United States of America by its US Carriage of Goods by Sea Act 1936 ("US COGSA"), but this Act applies the Rules to both inward and outward shipments[44]). Other States give effect to the Hague-Visby Rules (including most EU Member States) and yet other States give effect to the Hamburg Rules. National legislation which gives effect to a set of Rules may provide for some local variation or a combination of more than one set of Rules. In a final bid for international unity by the United Nations Commission on International Trade Law, the Convention on Contracts for the International Carriage of Goods Wholly or Partly by Sea was adopted in 2008 and the signing ceremony held in Rotterdam in September 2009. These Rules are therefore referred to as the Rotterdam Rules.[45] Although they are not yet in force it would be possible to incorporate them into a charterparty. They differ significantly from the Hague-Visby Rules as they have a different regime of liability, higher limits[46] (but they can be broken),[47] a two-year time limit which applies to all claims for breach of obligations under the Convention whether by the carrier or the shipper,[48] and jurisdiction and arbitration provisions,[49] which latter provisions will only apply if a State has specifically opted in to them.[50]

Although the consignee of a non-transferable bill of lading[51] or the third party transferee of a transferable bill of lading deserves protection, there is no reason to restrict the parties' freedom of contract for charterparties. Therefore the Hague, Hague-Visby, Hamburg and Rotterdam Rules do not apply mandatorily to charterparties.[52] However, the parties to the charterparty may wish to ensure that the obligations under both the charterparty and the bill of lading are the same. Some standard form charterparties seek to achieve this by incorporating a clause paramount into the charterparty and providing that it must be incorporated into any bill of lading issued under the charterparty.[53]

---

40. Hamburg Rules, art 7.1.
41. Hamburg Rules, art 7.2.
42. Hamburg Rules, art 20. Art 20 r 5 of the Hamburg Rules also provides for indemnity claims.
43. Hamburg Rules, arts 21 and 22. See Chapter 1, pages 33–34.
44. Contrast the position under the English Carriage of Goods by Sea Act 1924 giving effect to the Hague Rules and the Carriage of Goods by Sea Act 1971 which gives the force of law to the Hague-Visby Rules and apply to outward shipment but not inward shipment.
45. See Y. Baatz, C. Debattista, F. Lorenzon, A. Serdy, H. Staniland and M. Tsimplis, *The Rotterdam Rules: A Practical Annotation* (Informa 2009); D.R. Thomas (ed.), *A New Convention for the Carriage of Goods by Sea: The Rotterdam Rules* (Lawtext Publishing Limited 2009); D.R. Thomas (ed.), *The Carriage of Goods by Sea under the Rotterdam Rules* (Lloyd's List 2010); A. Diamond, "The Rotterdam Rules" [2009] LMCLQ 445; M. Sturley, T. Fujita and G. van der Ziel, *The Rotterdam Rules* (Sweet & Maxwell 2010); and A. von Ziegler, S. Zunarelli and J. Schelin, *The Rotterdam Rules 2008* (Wolters Kluwer 2010).
46. Rotterdam Rules arts 59 and 60.
47. Rotterdam Rules, art 61.
48. Rotterdam Rules, art 62.
49. Rotterdam Rules, Chapters 14 and 15 respectively.
50. Rotterdam Rules, arts 74, 78 and 91.
51. *J I MacWilliam Co Inc v Mediterranean Shipping Co SA (The Rafaela S)* [2005] UKHL 11; [2005] 1 Lloyd's Rep 347.
52. Hague and Hague-Visby Rules, art V; Hamburg Rules, art 2 r 3; Rotterdam Rules, art 6.
53. E.g. cl 24 of NYPE 1946, cl 31(a) of NYPE 1993, and clause 33(a) of NYPE 2015. The NYPE charterparty may also provide that any cargo claims as between the owners and the charterers shall be settled in accordance with the Inter-Club Agreement 1996 (as amended 1 September 2011) or any subsequent modification or replacement thereof – see e.g. clause 27 of NYPE 2015. See *Transgrain Shipping (Singapore) Pte Ltd v Yangtze Navigation (Hong Kong) Co Ltd* [2016] EWHC 3132 (Comm); [2017] 1 Lloyd's Rep 212, under appeal.

Provided a charterparty, either voyage or time, makes clear the parties' intention to incorporate a clause paramount into the charterparty, the English courts will give effect to that intention, even though this may involve some manipulation of the wording of the clause paramount and even though it may mean that part of the Rules referred to in the clause paramount have to be ignored. In *The Saxon Star*[54] the charterparty in its original form was a voyage charterparty which had been amended to cover as many consecutive voyages as the ship could perform within 18 months. It provided that the clause paramount was "to be incorporated in this charterparty". The clause paramount itself provided as follows:

This bill of lading shall have effect subject to the provisions of the Carriage of Goods by Sea Act of the United States, approved Apr. 16, 1936, which shall be deemed to be incorporated herein, and nothing herein contained shall be deemed a surrender by the carrier of any of its rights or immunities or an increase of any of its responsibilities or liabilities under said Act. If any term of this bill of lading be repugnant to said Act to any extent, such term shall be void to that extent, but no further.

The House of Lords held that the charterparty did incorporate US COGSA[55] and that the wording in the clause paramount could be manipulated to read "This charterparty" rather than "This bill of lading" in view of the parties' clear intention to apply the statute to the charterparty as well as the bill of lading,[56] despite the fact that US COGSA itself provides that it does not apply to charterparties.

Applying the decision in *The Saxon Star*, Staughton J held that US COGSA was effectively incorporated into a time charter by the printed clause paramount in clause 24 of the NYPE form in *The Satya Kailash*.[57] Staughton J dismissed the argument that the parties could not have intended to incorporate the duty to exercise due diligence to make the ship seaworthy in US COGSA as they had already provided for an absolute obligation of seaworthiness.

Whereas initially the clause paramount only referred to the Hague Rules or national legislation giving effect to those Rules, clause paramounts in more recently drafted standard form charterparties have become more complicated because the Hague-Visby Rules or the Hamburg Rules or some national legislation giving effect to them may apply mandatorily to the bill of lading.[58] A clause paramount may provide, for example, that the bill of lading is to be subject to the Hague Rules or the Hague-Visby Rules where they are compulsorily applicable.[59]

It will then be necessary to determine which set of Rules applies to the charterparty or to which voyage or voyages under the charterparty. Sometimes it may not matter whether the Hague or the Hague-Visby Rules apply because, for example, in both cases there is a duty to

---

54. *Adamastos Shipping Co v Anglo-Saxon Petroleum Co (The Saxon Star)* [1959] AC 133.
55. This statute gives effect to the Hague Rules with some amendments. See G. Treitel and F. Reynolds, *Carver on Bills of Lading* (4th edn, Sweet & Maxwell 2017) (hereinafter "*Carver*"), [9–089] on the "peculiarities" of this statute and R. Aikens, R. Lord and M. Bools, *Bills of Lading* (2nd edn, Informa 2016) (hereinafter "*Aikens*"), [10.19].
56. This may be contrasted with the incorporation of charterparty clauses into bills of lading where it is not permissible to manipulate the wording of the charterparty clause to make it applicable to the bill of lading – *Miramar Maritime Corporation v Holborn Oil Trading Ltd (The Miramar)* [1984] 2 Lloyd's Rep 129, unless specific words of incorporation are used e.g. *Daval Aciers D'Usinor Et De Sacilor v Armare S S L (The Nerano)* [1996] 1 Lloyd's Rep 1, discussed in Chapter 1, pages 6–7. The difference is due to the fact that bills of lading involve third parties e.g. the named consignee or indorsee of the bill of lading.
57. *Seven Seas Transportation Ltd v Pacifico Union Marina Corporation (The Satya Kailash and Oceanic Amity)* [1982] 2 Lloyd's Rep 465. Although the case went to the Court of Appeal – [1984] 1 Lloyd's Rep 588 – as discussed at page 134 – this point was not appealed. See also *Grimaldi Compagnia Di Navigazione SPA v Sekihyo Lines Ltd (The Seki Rolette)* [1998] 2 Lloyd's Rep 638.
58. See e.g. cl 31(a) of NYPE 1993 and cl 33(a) of NYPE 2015.
59. See e.g. *Trafigura Beheer BV v Mediterranean Shipping Co SA (The MSC Amsterdam)* [2007] EWCA Civ 794; [2007] 2 Lloyd's Rep 622, discussed at page 64.

exercise due diligence to make the ship seaworthy before and at the beginning of the voyage[60] and a list of exceptions in Article IV rule 2.[61] However, in other cases, as we have already seen, there may be significant differences depending on which set of rules applies. It will be a question of construction of both the words of incorporation and the clause paramount itself as to whether the same Rules that apply to each bill of lading issued under the charterparty are to apply to the voyages covered by such bill of lading under the charterparty[62] with the result that, for example, different voyages under a time charterparty are governed by different Rules. An alternative construction would be that the default position under the clause paramount is to apply to all the voyages under the charterparty, with the result that the charterparty and the bill of lading may not be back to back. More sophisticated recent standard form charterparties do not seek to incorporate the clause paramount into the charterparty, but only into any bill of lading issued under that charterparty. There is an express clause stating that the Rules that apply to the bill of lading are also to apply to cargo carrying voyages under the charterparty.[63]

In *Onego Shipping & Chartering BV v JSC Arcadia Shipping (The Socol 3)*[64] Hamblen J considered a time charterparty in the NYPE 1993 form. The charterparty was for one time charter trip from Finland. Deck cargo was lost and the vessel had to take refuge at the port of Halmstad where the deck cargo was discharged and re-stowed. It was common ground that the Hague-Visby Rules were incorporated into the charterparty as Finland was a Contracting State to the Hague-Visby Rules. The first issue in the case was whether, where a charterparty incorporates the Hague-Visby Rules and the charterparty envisages deck cargo will or may be carried but does not state and/or identify what and/or how much deck cargo is being carried ("an on-deck statement"), the Rules apply to the carriage of deck cargo or their application is excluded by virtue of Article I(c) of the Hague-Visby Rules. The charterers contended that the "contract of carriage" referred to in Article I(c) is the charterparty and that since the charterparty does not contain the necessary on deck statement, the exclusion of deck cargo does not apply. The owners contended that the "contract of carriage" refers to the bill(s) of lading issued for the deck cargo, not the charterparty. Hamblen J held that "Contract of carriage" in Article I(c) could only sensibly apply to the bill of lading as it is only the bill of lading which is ever likely to contain an on-deck statement. The practical effect of charterers' construction would be that the carriage of deck cargo would almost invariably be subject to the Hague/Hague-Visby Rules and to render the Article I(c) liberty to contract out of the Rules illusory. It would also mean that the liability for deck cargo under the bill of lading and under the charterparty would differ. In contrast to the position under the bill of lading, owners would not be free to carry deck cargo on their own conditions under the charterparty. The terms of the bill(s) of lading issued under a time charter party will generally be within the control of the charterers as the master is obliged to sign bills "as presented". Therefore the Rules did not apply to the charterparty.[65]

---

60. However, if the owner is in breach of this obligation, the owner can limit its liability – *Parsons Corporation and Others v C V Scheepvaartonderneming "Happy Ranger" and Others (The Happy Ranger)* [2002] 2 Lloyd's Rep 357. The limits differ under the Hague and Hague-Visby Rules (see fn 31) and can be broken under the latter.

61. Thus in *Whistler International v Kawasaki Kisen Kaisha Ltd (The Hill Harmony)* [2001] 1 Lloyd's Rep 147 the charterparty incorporated three clauses paramount but no point arose on their application or on which one was relevant as their effect was to incorporate the exception in art IV r 2(a) – per Lord Hobhouse at p 154.

62. London Arbitration 2/97 LMLN 450; *Onego Shipping & Chartering BV v JSC Arcadia Shipping (The Socol 3)* [2010] EWHC 777 (Comm), [2010] 2 Lloyd's Rep 221; [2010] 1 CLC 601.

63. See e.g. cl 27(c)(ii) of the Shelltime 4 charterparty as amended in December 2003 and T. Coghlin, A. Baker QC, J. Kenny and J. Kimball, *Time Charters* (7th edn, Informa 2014) (hereinafter "*Time Charters*"), [37.142] and [37.143] commenting on cl 27(c)(ii) of Shelltime 4.

64. [2010] EWHC 777 (Comm), [2010] 2 Lloyd's Rep 221.

65. See page 135 for discussion of whether the exclusion clause in the charterparty applied.

Where the charterparty incorporates foreign legislation giving effect to the Hague Rules, such as US COGSA, the construction of the legislation must be determined as a question of the proper law of the contract. In *The Stolt Sydness*[66] that was English law rather than US law.

Sometimes the parties use shorthand and simply provide for "Paramount Clause to be incorporated herein" or "US Clause Paramount" or "Canadian Clause Paramount". In *The Agios Lazaros*[67] the Court of Appeal held that "paramount clause" meant that all the Hague Rules applied. Although this decision was before the Hague-Visby Rules came into force, the words will still mean the Hague Rules unless a party can adduce evidence that shipping men would now understand these words to mean the Hague-Visby Rules,[68] which seems unlikely, as if the Hague-Visby Rules are required, the wording "general clause paramount" is used.[69]

In *Yemgas FZCO v Superior Pescadores SA Panama (The Superior Pescadores)*[70] the issue was whether the limits in the Hague or Hague-Visby Rules applied. In that case the application of the Hague Rules resulted in a higher limit of liability in some cases than the Hague-Visby Rules. The bills of lading were for a shipment of equipment from Antwerp, Belgium to Balhaf in Yemen in early January 2008. As Belgium became a Contracting State of the Hague-Visby Rules in 1978, those Rules applied mandatorily. Some four and a half years after the shipment in October 2012 the Owner's P & I Club gave a letter of undertaking and agreed English law and jurisdiction on behalf of the owner. The question was what Rules applied contractually as if the Hague Rules did, and they provided for higher limits in some situations, the issue was whether there was an agreement for a higher limit pursuant to Article IV rule 5(g) of the Hague-Visby Rules. The clause paramount stated,

2. Paramount Clause The Hague Rules contained in the International Convention for the Unification of certain rules relating to Bills of Lading, dated Brussels the 25th August 1924 as enacted in the country of shipment shall apply to this contract. When no such enactment is in force in the country of shipment, the corresponding legislation of the country of destination shall apply, but in respect of shipments to which no such enactments are compulsorily applicable, the terms of the said Convention shall apply.

The Court of Appeal held that the Hague-Visby limits applied as any case in which a bill of lading was issued in 2008 incorporating the Hague Rules as enacted in the country of shipment and in which the country of shipment had enacted the Hague-Visby Rules should be regarded as a case which was subject to the Hague-Visby Rules, rather than the Hague Rules. Longmore LJ, with whom Tomlinson and McCombe LJJ agreed, commented that the conclusion by the judge that the 1924 Hague Rules applied rather than the 1968 Rules in 2015 in respect of a contract made in 2008 was "odd".[71] He continued,

Most maritime nations have adopted the Hague-Visby Rules; the United Kingdom did so as early as 1971 in the Carriage of Goods by Sea Act of that date; it did not come into force until a certain number of other

---

66. See *Mauritius Oil Refineries Ltd v Stolt Nielsen Nederlands BV (The Stolt Sydness)* [1997] 1 Lloyd's Rep 273, discussed at page 64.
67. *Nea Agrex SA v Baltic Shipping Co Ltd (The Agios Lazaros)* [1976] 2 Lloyd's Rep 47.
68. *Seabridge Shipping AB v A C Orssleff's Eftf's A/S (The Fjellvang)* [1999] 2 Lloyd's Rep 685.
69. See *Lauritzen Reefers v Ocean Reef Transport Ltd SA (The Bukhta Russkaya)* [1997] 2 Lloyd's Rep 744 for the meaning of this wording which is similar in effect to the clause paramount in the Congenbill 1994. On the facts of this case, the Hague Rules applied rather than the Hague-Visby Rules and the charterer's claim for an indemnity for its liability for cargo damage on the voyage in question was therefore time barred.
70. [2016] EWCA Civ 101; [2016] 1 Lloyd's Rep 561; [2014] EWHC 971 (Comm); [2014] 1 Lloyd's Rep 660.
71. [16].

countries had signed up but that happened as long ago as 23rd June 1977. Can it really be the case that a Paramount Clause in a contract made over 30 years later in 2008 is still to be taken as incorporating the 1924 Rules rather than the 1968 Rules?

Where the Rules are incorporated into the charterparty, there may be difficulties of construction as to whether the clause paramount prevails over other clauses in the charterparty.[72] The clause paramount may state that in case of inconsistency the rules are to prevail.[73] Alternatively there may be a provision to the opposite effect.[74]

4. SEAWORTHINESS

If there were no express provision in the charterparty as to seaworthiness, there is an implied obligation of seaworthiness at common law. It is an absolute obligation that the ship will be fit for the purpose intended. However, nowadays one would expect a standard form charterparty to contain express provisions as to seaworthiness, although the word "seaworthiness" may well not be present.[75] For example, the New York Produce Exchange form 1946 expressly provides that on her delivery the ship shall be "ready to receive cargo with clean swept holds and tight, staunch, strong and in every way fitted for the service . . . with full complement of officers, seamen, engineers and firemen for a vessel of her tonnage".[76] Although this provision is clearly confined to the time of delivery in addition there will probably be a description of the ship at the time the charterparty is concluded in the preamble of the charterparty which covers matters such as the ship's class, her capacity and her speed and consumption.[77] Further details may be given in additional typed clauses. There is also a continuing obligation to maintain the ship[78] and a clause paramount which incorporates US COGSA.[79]

Assuming that the Hague or Hague-Visby Rules are incorporated into a charterparty they may have a significant effect on the seaworthiness obligation. If the charterparty provides for an absolute obligation of seaworthiness, the effect will be to reduce the obligation to one to exercise due diligence. This was the effect of the clause paramount in *The Saxon Star*.[80] Although that case concerned a consecutive voyage charterparty the better view is that it applies by analogy to a time charterparty.[81] Article III rule 1 has three parts. First, Article

---

72. See *Marifortuna Naviera v Government of Ceylon (The Mariasmi)* [1970] 1 Lloyd's Rep 247, at p 255; *Nea Agrex SA v Baltic Shipping Co Ltd (The Agios Lazaros)* [1976] 2 Lloyd's Rep 47, per Lord Goff at p 53; *Seven Seas Transportation Ltd v Pacifico Union Marina Corporation (The Satya Kailash and Oceanic Amity)* [1984] 1 Lloyd's Rep 588; *Finagra (UK) Ltd v OT Africa Line Ltd* [1998] 2 Lloyd's Rep 622 and *Dairy Containers Limited v Tasman Orient Line CV (The Tasman Discoverer)* [2004] UKPC 22; [2004] 2 Lloyd's Rep 647; *Trafigura Beheer BV v Navigazione Montanari SpA (The Valle di Cordoba)* [2015] EWCA Civ 91; [2015] 1 Lloyd's Rep 529 (a loss of cargo due to piracy did not fall within a loss in transit clause in a voyage charterparty but, even if it did, the owner could rely on the Hague-Visby exceptions which excluded piracy); Carver, [9–091]; J. Cooke, T. Young and A. Taylor, *Voyage Charters* (4th edn, Informa 2014) (hereinafter "Cooke"), [85.14]–[85.18] and Aikens, [10.33] and n. 38.
73. See e.g. cl 24 of NYPE form 1946.
74. See e.g. *Parsons Corporation and Others v CV Scheepvaartonderneming "Happy Ranger" and Others (The Happy Ranger)* [2002] 2 Lloyd's Rep 357.
75. *Hong Kong Fir Shipping Co Ltd v Kawasaki Kisen Kaisha Ltd* [1962] 2 QB 26; [1961] 2 Lloyd's Rep 478.
76. ll 21–24. See also cl 2 NYPE 1993 and cl 2(b) and (c) of NYPE 2015.
77. ll 3–11.
78. cl 1. See also cl 6 of NYPE 1993 and cl 6 of NYPE 2015.
79. cl 24. See also cl 31(a) of NYPE 1993 and cl 33(a) of NYPE 2015.
80. See fn 54. See also *The Petroleum Oil and Gas Corporation of South Africa (Pty) Ltd v FR8 Singapore Pte Ltd (The Eternity)* [2008] EWHC 2480 (Comm); [2009] 1 Lloyd's Rep 107 considering cl 38.1 of a voyage charterparty on an amended BPVoy 4 form, [3] and [10], [17]–[21].
81. See *Time Charters*, [34.5], discussing the effect of the incorporation of US COGSA into the NYPE 1946 by cl 24.

III rule 1(a) requires the ship to be seaworthy. For example, the ship must not leak and her machinery, such as her engines and steering gear, must be in good working order. Second, Article III rule 1(b) requires the ship to be properly manned, equipped and supplied. Her crew must be sufficient, qualified and trained. The requirements in relation to the number of the crew to be employed on board a particular ship are determined by the ship's flag State. Furthermore the crew must be properly qualified to perform the duties which they are actually employed to perform on the relevant ship. Finally the crew must be properly trained to carry out those duties. The Standards of Training, Certification and Watchkeeping of Seafarers 1995, which is part of the Safety of Life at Sea Convention,[82] require that the crew must be continuously trained to keep abreast of new developments and technology. In *The Star Sea*[83] the ship *Star Sea* was found to be unseaworthy as the master, despite being qualified and very experienced, had not been trained to use the fire-fighting equipment on the ship. When a fire broke out he did not use the carbon dioxide fire fighting system quickly enough, and, when he did give instructions that it should be deployed, he did not order that all the CO_2 be used to flood the hold on fire, as he should have done, but only part of the CO_2, with the result that the fire was not extinguished and the ship became a constructive total loss. The master was held to be incompetent and therefore the ship was unseaworthy.

Third, Article III rule 1(c) requires the ship to be fit and safe to carry her cargo. The test of unseaworthiness is subjective and not objective, i.e. this ship must be fit to encounter the perils of the sea for the contractual voyage and not any other voyage. The perils of a voyage carrying timber on deck across the Atlantic in February are very different from those of a reefer vessel carrying frozen prawns in its refrigerated holds in the Mediterranean in June.

The burden of proving unseaworthiness is on the claimant who must also show that the ship was unseaworthy before and at the beginning of the voyage. If the claimant can establish that, the burden of proof then shifts to the owner to establish that it exercised due diligence to make the ship seaworthy before and at the beginning of the voyage.[84] This is a fairly heavy burden as the duty cannot be delegated.[85] It is not enough for the owner to say that it exercised due diligence in selecting, for example, reputable ship repairers or surveyors. The owner must also establish that those ship repairers or surveyors themselves exercised due diligence. In *The Fjord Wind* the ship was on voyage charter and after leaving her loadport the ship grounded as a result of engine problems. The engines required lengthy repairs and the cargo had to be transshipped. The issue was whether the charterparty had been frustrated or whether the owner was in breach of its seaworthiness obligation. The Court of Appeal had to reconcile an initial seaworthiness clause and the scheme of the Hague Rules. It was held that the owner's obligation as to seaworthiness at each stage was the same, i.e. to exercise due diligence. The owner had failed to exercise due diligence to make the ship seaworthy. Although maintenance work had been carried out on the main engines by two representatives of the engine manufacturers at Durban, the problem for the owner was that it was unable to prove that the representatives had exercised due diligence when making the repairs to the engines and the burden of proof was on the owner to do so.

It is still not clear, however, under a time charter when the obligation to exercise due diligence under the Hague or Hague-Visby Rules bites. The better view is that it applies at the beginning

82. See Chapter 9, page 264.

83. *Manifest Shipping Co Ltd v Uni-Polaris Insurance Co Ltd (The Star Sea)* [1995] 1 Lloyd's Rep 651. Although the case went to the House of Lords the decision of Tuckey J at first instance that the ship was unseaworthy was not appealed. The case concerned s 39(5) of the Marine Insurance Act 1906.

84. Art IV r 1. *The Hellenic Dolphin* [1978] 2 Lloyd's Rep 336.

85. *Riverstone Meat Co v Lancashire Shipping Co (The Muncaster Castle)* [1961] 1 Lloyd's Rep 57; *Eridania SpA v Rudolf A Oetker (The Fjord Wind)* [2000] 2 Lloyd's Rep 191; [1999] 1 Lloyd's Rep 307.

of each voyage under the charterparty.[86] In *Onego Shipping & Chartering BV v JSC Arcadia Shipping (The Socol 3)*[87] Hamblen J stated,

Where there is loading at more than one port under a charterparty, the relevant "voyage" is the voyage for the cargo in question and the duty of due diligence therefore arises at each different load port – see *Cooke on Voyage Charters* at para. 85.106.[88]

This is supported by the continuing obligation to maintain the ship which, although it may appear to be an absolute obligation, is read together with the Rules to become a duty to exercise due diligence.[89] Therefore more modern standard form charterparties expressly provide that the owner shall exercise due diligence to maintain the ship throughout the charter service.[90]

Provided the owner has exercised due diligence to make the ship seaworthy it may rely on the exceptions in Article IV rule 2 of the Hague and Hague-Visby Rules. The exception for "act, neglect, or default of the master, mariner, pilot, or the servants of the carrier in the navigation or the management of the ship" in Article IV rule 2(a), may be of great significance to the owner, not least because the general exception clause in the charterparty may not cover negligent errors of navigation, whereas the Article IV rule 2 exception does. Thus, provided the owner has exercised due diligence in employing a Chief Officer who is properly qualified and trained, if the Chief Officer makes a negligent error of navigation while he is on watch, the owner will not be liable.

The exceptions have been interpreted as applying to the wider range of services which are to be provided under a time charterparty than those which would be provided in relation to the loading, handling, stowage, carriage, custody, care or discharge of the goods under a bill of lading. Thus in *The Satya Kailash*[91] the owner of the *Satya Kailash* chartered the *Oceanic Amity* to lighten the *Satya Kailash*. During the lightening operation damage was caused to the *Satya Kailash* as a result of the negligent navigation of the master of the *Oceanic Amity*. The Court of Appeal held that the owner of the *Oceanic Amity* could rely on the exception of negligent navigation.[92]

In *Trafigura Beheer BV v Navigazione Montanari SpA (The Valle di Cordoba)*[93] the Court of Appeal held that theft of cargo by pirates was excluded by the Hague-Visby Rules and that exception would have been available to the carrier even if an in transit loss clause had applied, which it did not.

---

86. B. Eder, H. Bennett, S. Berry, D. Foxton and C. Smith, *Scrutton on Charterparties* (23rd edn, Sweet & Maxwell 2015) (hereinafter "*Scrutton*"), at pp 360 and 361 and *Time Charters*, [34.5], [34.15] and [34.16], [37.142] and [37.143] on cl 27(c)(ii) of Shelltime 4.

87. [2010] EWHC 777 (Comm); [2010] 2 Lloyd's Rep 221; [2010] 1 CLC 601.

88. Ibid., [38].

89. See *Time Charters*, [34.5], [34.15] and [34.16], discussing the effect of the incorporation of US COGSA into the New York Produce Exchange form 1946 by cl 24 but see the words of caution of Mustill J in *Nitrate Corporation of Chile Ltd v Pansuiza Compania de Navegacion SA (The Hermosa)* [1980] 1 Lloyd's Rep 638, at p 648.

90. See e.g. cl 3 of Shelltime 4. See *Golden Fleece Maritime Inc v ST Shipping & Transport Inc (The Ellie and the Frixos)* [2007] EWHC 1890 (Comm); [2008] 1 Lloyd's Rep 262, affirmed by the Court of Appeal [2008] EWCA Civ 584; [2009] 1 All ER (Comm) 908; [2008] 2 Lloyd's Rep 119.

91. *Seven Seas Transportation Ltd v Pacifico Union Marina Corporation (The Satya Kailash and Oceanic Amity)* [1984] 1 Lloyd's Rep 588 upholding the decision of Staughton J in that case at first instance and *Industrie Chimiche Italia Centrale SpA v Nea Ninemia Shipping Co SA (The Emmanuel C)* [1983] 1 Lloyd's Rep 310 that the mutual exceptions clause, cl 16, of the NYPE form, does not cover negligent errors.

92. See also *Aliakmon Maritime Corporation v Transocean Continental Shipping Ltd and Frank Truman Export Ltd (The Aliakmon Progress)* [1978] 2 Lloyd's Rep 499; *Actis Co Ltd v Sanko Steamship Co Ltd (The Aquacharm)* [1982] 1 Lloyd's Rep 7; *Bayoil SA v Seawind Tankers Corporation (The Leonidas)* [2001] 1 Lloyd's Rep 533 and *Whistler International v Kawasaki Kisen Kaisha Ltd (The Hill Harmony)* [2001] 1 Lloyd's Rep 147 (HL); [1999] 2 Lloyd's Rep 209.

93. [2015] EWCA Civ 91; [2015] 1 Lloyd's Rep 529.

Where the Rules do not apply the parties are free to agree on any exclusions or limitation of liability. Hamblen J determined that the Rules did not apply in *Onego Shipping & Chartering BV v JSC Arcadia Shipping (The Socol 3)*[94] as the cargo was carried on deck and was stated to be so. Thus the next issue was whether the owners could rely on the exclusion clause as follows,

In the event of deck cargo being carried, the Owners are to be and are hereby indemnified by the Charterers for any loss and/or damage and/or liability of whatsoever nature caused to the Vessel as a result of the carriage of deck cargo and which would not have arisen had deck cargo not been loaded.

Hamblen J held that the clause provided the owners with an indemnity in respect of loss and/or damage and/or liability effectively caused by the carriage of deck cargo but not for loss and/or damage and/or liability caused by negligence and/or breach of the obligation of seaworthiness on the part of owners, their servants or agents.

The time bar is also extremely important. The time limit within which claims must be brought under a charterparty is generally six years from the breach of contract, unless the parties have expressly agreed a shorter time limit.[95] However, where the Hague or Hague-Visby Rules apply to the charterparty they contain a one-year time bar in Article III rule 6.[96] Many charterparties contain a provision referring all disputes to arbitration[97] and under English law the arbitration must be commenced within the time limit. The time bar is of even greater import now that section 12 of the Arbitration Act 1996 has narrowed the grounds on which an extension of time can be obtained.[98]

Not all claims under a charterparty will be caught by the time bar in the Rules as there must be a real connection between the loss or damage claimed and the goods being carried, and not just a very tenuous link.[99] Thus, for example, in *The Standard Ardour*[100] Saville J, as he then was, held that the charterer's claim for an indemnity for claims due to delays in the release of bills of lading which the charterer alleged were caused by the failure of the owner to provide a ship properly equipped to measure the quantities loaded, was not time barred. The loss was connected with the shipping documents and not the goods.

---

94. [2010] EWHC 777 (Comm); [2010] 2 Lloyd's Rep 221; [2010] 1 CLC 601 cf. *The Danah* [1993] 1 Lloyd's Rep 351, where Saville J held that "carried on deck at Shipper's risk with responsibility for loss or damage howsoever caused" covered negligence. Similarly in *The Imvros* [1999] 1 Lloyd's Rep 848, Langley J held that "carried on deck at Shippers' risk without responsibility for loss or damage however caused" covered both negligence and unseaworthiness. The decision in *The Imvros* has been criticised (S. Baughen, "Problems with Deck Cargo" [2000] LMCLQ 295) and in *Sunlight Mercantile Pte Ltd v Ever Lucky Shipping Co Ltd* [2003] SGCA 47; [2004] 1 SLR 171 the Singapore Court of Appeal held that such words did not absolve the carrier from liability for unseaworthiness and refused to follow *The Imvros* [1999] 1 Lloyd's Rep 848. See also *Pt Soonlee Metalindo Perkasa v Synergy Shipping Pte Ltd (Freighter Services Pte Ltd, Third Party) (The Limin XIX)* [2007] 4 SLR 51 Judith Prakash J held that the carrying barge was unseaworthy. The words "shipped on deck at shipper's risk" did not exclude the carrier's liability because they did not cover the breach of the fundamental obligation to provide a seaworthy ship.
95. See e.g. *Babanaft International Co SA v Avant Petroleum Inc (The Oltenia)* [1982] 2 Lloyd's Rep 99 (CA); [1982] 1 Lloyd's Rep 448 and page 181.
96. The Hamburg Rules and the Rotterdam Rules provide for a two-year time bar in arts 20 and 62 respectively.
97. E.g. cl 17 of NYPE 1946 and cl 23 of the Baltime form.
98. *Grimaldi Compagnia Di Navigazione SpA v Sekihyo Lines Ltd (The Seki Rolette)* [1998] 2 Lloyd's Rep 638 where Mance J did not grant an extension under s 12 of the Arbitration Act 1996.
99. *Goulandris Brothers Ltd v B Goldman and Sons Ltd* [1957] 2 Lloyd's Rep 207; *Interbulk Ltd v Ponte dei Sospiri Shipping Co (The Standard Ardour)* [1988] 2 Lloyd's Rep 159; *Cargill International SA v CPN Tankers (Bermuda) Ltd (The Ot Sonja)* [1993] 2 Lloyd's Rep 435 (voyage charter – charterers suffering financial loss and expense due to loading delayed due to necessity of cleaning dirty tanks and due to analysis of suspected contamination of cargo); *Noranda Inc v Barton (Time Charter) Ltd (The Marinor)* [1996] 1 Lloyd's Rep 301; *Grimaldi Compagnia Di Navigazione SpA v Sekihyo Lines Ltd (The Seki Rolette)* [1998] 2 Lloyd's Rep 638; *Linea Naviera Paramaconi SA v Abnormal Load Engineering Ltd* [2001] 1 Lloyd's Rep 763 and *Bulk & Metal Transport (UK) LLP v Voc Bulk Ultra Handymax Pool LLC (The Voc Gallant)* [2009] EWHC 288 (Comm); [2009] 1 Lloyd's Rep 418.
100. *Interbulk Ltd v Ponte dei Sospiri Shipping Co (The Standard Ardour)* [1988] 2 Lloyd's Rep 159.

Some standard form charterparties limit the application of the Rules to cargo claims.[101] In *The Stena Pacifica*[102] Evans J concluded that the limited terms of incorporation meant that Article III rule 6 did not apply to claims outside the Hague Rules obligations.

5. REMEDIES FOR OWNER'S BREACH

We shall now consider the remedies that the charterer will have if the ship does not comply with its description or is not seaworthy.

Where the owner has made a representation of fact to the charterer during the negotiations for the charterparty, probably through its broker, which induced the charterer to enter into the charterparty, and the representation is false, the charterer has a right to elect to avoid the charterparty. It must make an election to avoid or affirm the contract once it is aware that it has such a right, or it will be taken to have waived its right and the contract will be affirmed. If the charterer does elect to avoid, it is as if the charterparty had never existed. The charterer is entitled to be put back into the position it was in before the representation was made and it was induced to enter into the contract, as it never would have entered into this contract had it not been misled.

The charterer may also be entitled to damages for misrepresentation. Where the misrepresentation made by the misrepresentor induces the misrepresentee to enter into a contract with the misrepresentor, the Misrepresentation Act 1967 applies. If the owner cannot show that it had reasonable grounds to believe and did believe in the truth of the representation, it will be liable for damages as if the representation were fraudulent under section 2(1). Thus in *Howard Marine & Dredging Co Ltd v Ogden & Sons (Excavations) Ltd*[103] the owner misrepresented the carrying capacity of its two barges. It had relied on incorrect figures given in Lloyd's Register. The Court of Appeal held that it was not reasonable to rely on those figures as the ships' documents giving the true figures were in the owner's possession.

There are two great advantages of section 2(1) of the Misrepresentation Act 1967: the reverse burden of proof on the misrepresentor and the fiction of fraud, which means that the misrepresentee can recover damages as if the misrepresentor were fraudulent, although this is controversial.[104] If the owner could prove that it did have reasonable grounds to believe and did believe in the truth of the representation, the charterer could seek damages in lieu of rescission under section 2(2) of the Misrepresentation Act 1967 but this is in the discretion of the court.

Where the misrepresentee is induced to enter into a contract with a third party rather than the misrepresentor, the Misrepresentation Act 1967 does not apply. This was the case, for example, in *The Arta*[105] referred to above where the charterer's broker made a representation in its personal capacity, rather than as agent on behalf of the charterer and induced the owner to enter into a contract with the charterer, rather than itself. If the charterer can prove that the misrepresentation was made fraudulently, it will be entitled to damages for the tort of deceit for all direct losses, whether foreseeable or not. There is no defence of contributory negligence[106] and the liability

---

101. E.g. cl 27(c)(ii) of the Shelltime 4 form.
102. [1990] 2 Lloyd's Rep 234. See also *Borgship Tankers Inc v Product Transport Corporation Ltd (The Casco)* [2005] EWHC 273 (Comm); [2005] 1 Lloyd's Rep 565.
103. [1978] QB 574.
104. *Royscot Trust Ltd v Rogerson* [1991] 3 All ER 294 applied in *Pankhania v Hackney LBC (Damages)* [2004] EWHC 323 (Ch); [2004] 1 EGLR 135 and *Monde Petroleum SA v Western Zagros Ltd* [2016] EWHC 1472 (Comm); [2016] 2 Lloyd's Rep 229, but see the doubts of the House of Lords in *Smith New Court Securities Ltd v Scrimgeour Vickers Asset Management Limited* [1997] AC 254.
105. *Markappa Inc v N W Spratt & Son Ltd (The Arta)* [1985] 1 Lloyd's Rep 534, discussed at page 126.
106. *Standard Chartered Bank v Pakistan National Shipping Corporation (No 2)* [2003] 1 Lloyd's Rep 227.

cannot be excluded.[107] However, the burden of proof is a heavy one and if it cannot be satisfied the misrepresentor may sue for the tort of negligence.[108] In that case the misrepresentee must establish that the misrepresentor owes it a duty of care. The burden of proving negligence in breaching that duty of care would be on the misrepresentee and it must show that the loss was foreseeable. The owner could rely on the defence of contributory negligence[109] and the liability could be excluded by a carefully drafted contractual term.[110]

Where the failure complained of is a breach of a term of the charterparty the charterer has a number of contractual remedies. In addition the charterparty may give an express remedy such as the right to cancel on the occurrence of a specified event. Standard form charterparties usually give the charterers an express right to cancel if the ship is not delivered ready or in every way fitted for the service by a specific time.[111] This provision is of great importance to the charterer as it may cancel the contract,[112] regardless of fault by the owner and the right is therefore not affected by whether the owner's obligation is absolute or one of due diligence. The only question the charterer has to ask is whether the ship is in the condition contracted for by the time prescribed. If it is not, the charterer may cancel. The charterer does not have to ask why not, unless it also wishes to claim damages, in which case it must show a breach of charterparty.

Where one party has failed to comply with an obligation under the contract, either express or implied, it is in breach of contract. The remedy that the innocent party will have for that breach will depend on the importance of the obligation breached. Provided that the innocent party can show that it has suffered a loss caused by the breach which is not too remote, it will be able to claim damages for breach, unless liability is excluded or limited. However, if the breach is fundamental, the innocent party not only has the right to damages, but also has the right to elect to terminate the contract, thereby discharging the parties from their future obligations under the contract.

Therefore if the charterer accepts delivery of the ship it may never have another chance to terminate the charterparty at common law, even if the ship is defective, unless it can prove a fundamental breach that is either a breach of condition or an innominate term where the consequences of the breach go to the root of the contract; or the owner is in repudiatory breach; or there is another express right to terminate or cancel. It is therefore necessary to be able to determine whether the term breached is a condition or an innominate term.

The parties may expressly provide that a clause in the charterparty is a condition. However, this is neither sufficient nor necessary. Even if the parties have neither expressly stated that an obligation is a condition nor spelled out the consequences of breach, the court may find that the term was of such importance in the contract that it is a condition. In *The Seaflower*[113] a time charterparty for a period of 11 months, maximum 12 months at the charterers' option, contained the following clause 46:

Vessel is presently MOBIL (expiring 27/1/98) CONOCO (expiring 3/2/98) and SHELL (expiring 14/1/98) acceptable. Owners guarantee to obtain within 60 days (sixty) days EXXON approval in addition to present approvals. On delivery date hire rate will be discounted USD 250 . . . for each approval missing. . . . If for any reason, Owners would lose even one of such acceptances they must advise charterers at once and they

107. *HIH Casualty and General Insurance Ltd v Chase Manhattan Bank* [2003] 2 Lloyd's Rep 61.
108. *Hedley Byrne v Heller* [1964] AC 465.
109. See e.g. *Vesta v Butcher* [1988] 2 All ER 43.
110. See e.g. *Howard Marine & Dredging Co Ltd v Ogden & Sons (Excavations) Ltd* [1978] QB 574.
111. E.g. cl 21 of the Baltime 1939 (as revised 2001), cl 14 of NYPE 1946, cl 16 NYPE 1993, cl 3 of NYPE 2015 and cl 5 of Shelltime 4.
112. See further page 139.
113. *BS & N Ltd (BVI) v Micado Shipping Ltd (Malta) (The Seaflower)* [2001] 1 Lloyd's Rep 341.

must reinstate same within 30 (thirty) days from such occurrence failing which Charterers will be at liberty to cancel charterparty. . . . Hire rates will be reinstated once Owner will show written evidence of approvals from Major Oil Companies.

The Court of Appeal unanimously held that the requirement to obtain approval from Exxon within 60 days was a condition, breach of which entitled the charterer to elect to terminate the charterparty. The clause could have been better drafted. One of the charterer's problems was that the clause did not spell out whether the charterer had the right to cancel the charterparty if the Exxon approval was not obtained within 60 days. It only expressly provided for such a right if an acceptance were lost and not reinstated within 30 days. That right clearly applied to the loss of Exxon approval once such approval was obtained. Thus the charterer treated the majors' approval as important and the clause treated a failure to reinstate a lost approval as a breach of condition. The parties should be assumed to have intended to be consistent about the importance of obtaining and maintaining majors' approvals. Thus there should be no inconsistency between the loss of some majors' approvals and that of Exxon or between having the approval at the outset of the charterparty and losing the approval after the commencement of the charter period. It did not matter that the charterparty did not expressly state that the requirement was a condition. As held by the House of Lords in *Bunge Corporation v Tradax Export SA*,[114] a provision for performance of an obligation within a certain time limit in a mercantile contract,[115] particularly if the other party's performance of the contract is dependent on performance of that obligation by a certain time, is presumed to be a condition. The word "guarantee" used in this provision served to emphasise the importance of the provision although it would not on its own justify the conclusion that the provision was a condition.[116]

A term may be an innominate term where the consequences of breach could vary from being very significant to inconsequential. In *The Hong Kong Fir*[117] the Court of Appeal held that the obligation as to seaworthiness is an innominate term and therefore breach of that term would only give rise to a right to elect to terminate if the consequences of the breach are so serious that they deprive the innocent party of substantially the whole of the benefit that it was intended to obtain under the contract – in other words if the breach is fundamental or goes to the root of the contract. This is because of the range of consequences that can result from breach of such a term. At one end of the spectrum the consequences of breach may be very trivial. For example, the radar of the ship may break down. Nevertheless the ship is navigated safely into port without any difficulty. On arrival in port an electrical engineer is requested to fix the radar, which is repaired within a matter of hours and no delay is caused to the ship's operations as cargo operations are

---

114. [1981] 1 WLR 711; [1981] 2 Lloyd's Rep 1. See also *Dolphin Tanker Srl v Westport Petroleum Inc (The Savina Caylyn)* [2010] EWHC 2617 (Comm); [2011] 1 Lloyd's Rep 550. Compare *Transpetrol Maritime Services Ltd v S,7B (Marine Energy) BV (The Rowan)* [2012] EWCA Civ 198; [2012] 1 Lloyd's Rep 564 and *Sea Glory Maritime Co v Al Sagr National Insurance Co (The Nancy)* [2013] EWHC 2116 (Comm); [2014] 1 Lloyd's Rep 14.
115. Whether the time for payment of time charter hire is a condition is discussed at page 164.
116. Per Jonathan Parker LJ, [102].
117. *Hong Kong Fir Shipping Co Ltd v Kawasaki Kisen Kaisha Ltd (The Hong Kong Fir)* [1962] 2 QB 26; [1961] 2 Lloyd's Rep 478 followed in *Star Reefers Pool Inc v JFC Group Co Ltd* [2011] EWHC 2204 (Comm). See also *Sports Connection Pte Ltd v Deuter Sports GMBH* [2009] SGCA 22; [2009] 5 SLR 883, a decision of the Singapore Court of Appeal; *Wuhan Ocean Economic and Technical Cooperation Company Limited v Schiffahrts-Gesellschaft "Hansa Murcia" MBH & Co KG* [2012] EWHC 3104 (Comm); [2013] 1 All ER (Comm) 1277, [32] – [39] where Cooke J held that the obligation of a seller under a shipbuilding contract to extend the Refund Guarantee was an innominate term; *Ampurius Nu Homes Holdings Ltd v Telford Homes (Creekside) Ltd* [2013] EWCA Civ 577; [2013] 4 All ER 377 followed in *Urban I (Blonk Street) Ltd v Ayres* [2013] EWCA Civ 816; [2014] 1 WLR 756. See also *Spar Shipping AS v Grand China Logistics Holding (Group) Co Ltd* [2016] EWCA Civ 982; [2016] 2 Lloyd's Rep 447 discussed at page 164 where the Court of Appeal held that the obligation to pay hire on time was an innominate term.

performed throughout the repairs. At the other end of the spectrum, the ship's steering gear fails in heavy seas and the ship becomes a total loss on the rocks.

The disadvantage of the classification of the term as an innominate one rather than a condition is that, instead of being able to elect to terminate the charterparty immediately on breach, the charterer has to wait to see what the consequences of the breach are. This may be commercially very inconvenient as is illustrated by *The Hong Kong Fir*. There the charterparty was for a term of 24 months. The ship suffered a number of engine breakdowns and it was necessary for repairs to be carried out over a period of five months. The Court of Appeal held that the breach by the owner of the seaworthiness provision did not entitle the charterer to elect to terminate the charterparty as it had not been deprived of substantially the whole benefit it had contracted for: the charterer had lost the use of the ship for five months out of 24.

Commercially the charterer may be in a very difficult position if it does not have the use of the ship for a period of time. This will be exacerbated by the fact that when the ship gets into difficulties it may not initially be clear how long it will take to sort the problem out. For example, if the engines break down and it is necessary to obtain spare parts from the manufacturer and perhaps have the manufacturer's personnel attend the ship to advise on the necessary repairs, it may take some time to estimate how long the repairs will take. This may play havoc with the charterer's planning. The charterer may well have to make decisions such as whether to charter in a substitute ship to perform its contractual commitments to sellers and purchasers and may not know how long to charter such substitute for, so that it will have to enter into voyage charters. Until it becomes clear how long the difficulties will last, or it becomes clear that the difficulties will cause a significant delay, the charterer cannot elect to terminate the charterparty. This is even more frustrating if the market is falling and the charterer would much prefer to charter in a reliable and cheaper substitute ship.

It is for this reason that many of the more sophisticated time charterparties, and particularly those with the oil majors, contain express cancellation clauses entitling the charterer to cancel the charterparty if the owner does not rectify a problem within a specified time[118] and provide for an indemnity.

If a party has a right to elect to terminate the charterparty it must make that election by clearly communicating it, unless its non-performance of the contract clearly demonstrates its election to terminate.[119] It does not matter why the innocent party elects to terminate. It may wish to escape the contract for purely commercial reasons; for example, it could now go out into the market and charter in another ship at a better rate. If the innocent party does make an election to terminate both parties are discharged from future performance of their primary obligations under the contract. The party in fundamental breach has a secondary obligation to pay damages for that breach. The contract itself is not to be disregarded. Indeed, the contract will establish what the liability of the party in fundamental breach is. It will be a question of construction whether clauses of the contract such as exemption clauses, limitation clauses and liquidated damages clauses, are drafted widely enough to apply even to the fundamental breach of contract.[120] If the parties litigate their dispute they will still be bound by any jurisdiction or arbitration clause in the contract.

---

118. E.g. cl 3(iii) of the Shelltime 4 form and additional typed clauses as in *The Seaflower*, discussed at pages 137–138. See also *Dolphin Tanker Srl v Westport Petroleum Inc (The Savina Caylyn)* [2010] EWHC 2617 (Comm); [2011] 1 Lloyd's Rep 550 on the construction of an oil majors' approval and vetting clause in an amended Shelltime 4 charterparty and fn 114.

119. *Vitol v Norelf (The Santa Clara)* [1996] AC 800.

120. *Photo Production v Securicor* [1980] 1 All ER 856.

The election to terminate is irrevocable and once made the innocent party cannot subsequently change its mind. Both parties will be liable for other breaches which occurred prior to the election to terminate.

The innocent party may prefer to elect to affirm the contract, especially if the market has fluctuated so that it would now be more expensive, for example, for the charterer to charter a substitute ship. In that event both parties must continue to perform the charterparty. The party in fundamental breach will be liable for damages for that breach and both parties will be liable for any previous breaches. Once the innocent party has communicated its affirmation it is irrevocable unless the party in breach persists with its non-performance or commits a new fundamental breach, in which case the innocent party can elect to terminate.[121]

Frequently the innocent party will wish to elect to terminate the contract. For example, if a charterer states that it is unable to perform the contract the shipowner may wish to take control of the situation, to elect to terminate the contract and to mitigate its damages by going into the market to find a substitute charterer. This will often be the case if the market is rising and the owner can find a substitute charterer at a better market rate than the charter rate. However, if the market is falling, as it did dramatically in the market crash in the autumn of 2008,[122] the question may arise as to whether the shipowner is obliged to elect to terminate or whether it can affirm the contract and demand payment of the charter hire for the full period of the charterparty.

In many contracts it may not be possible for the innocent party to continue to perform the contract and earn the contract price without the assent or co-operation of the other party. This issue was considered by the House of Lords in *White and Carter (Councils) Ltd v McGregor*.[123] There an advertiser entered into a contract to provide advertising for the owner of a garage for three years. A term of the contract provided that if payment of an instalment was not paid for four weeks, the whole amount due for the three-year contract became immediately due and payable. As the advertiser was able to perform the contract without the co-operation of the garage owner the House of Lords held that it could perform the contract and claim payment for the whole three years. Lord Reid stated,

It might be, but it never has been, the law that a person is only entitled to enforce his contractual rights in a reasonable way, and that a court will not support an attempt to enforce them in an unreasonable way. One reason why that is not the law is, no doubt, because it was thought that it would create too much uncertainty to require the court to decide whether it is reasonable or equitable to allow a party to enforce his full rights under a contract.[124]

Lord Reid, *obiter*, did go on to admit of one possible exception,

It may well be that, if it can be shown that a person has no legitimate interest, financial or otherwise, in performing the contract rather than claiming damages, he ought not to be allowed to saddle the other party with an additional burden with no benefit to himself.[125]

That exception did not apply in that case as it could not be said that the advertisers "should be deprived of their right to claim the contract price merely because the benefit to them, as against claiming damages and re-letting their advertising space, might be small in comparison with the loss to [the garage owner]".[126]

121. *Johnson v Agnew* [1980] AC 369.
122. See the UNCTAD Review of Maritime Transport 2016 Chapter 3 Freight Rates and Maritime Transport Costs.
123. [1962] AC 413.
124. Ibid., p 430. See also Lord Hodson at p 445.
125. Ibid., p 431.
126. Ibid., p 431.

In *Isabella Shipowner SA v Shagang Shipping Co Ltd (The Aquafaith)*[127] Cooke J considered whether owners were entitled to refuse early redelivery of the *Aquafaith* and affirm the time charter or whether they were bound to accept early delivery and merely entitled to sue for damages. The *Aquafaith* was chartered on an amended NYPE form for a duration of 59–61 months and expressly provided that "the vessel will not be redelivered before the minimum period of 59 months". The vessel was redelivered 94 days before the earliest permissible redelivery date. Owners sought an arbitration award declaring that they were entitled to refuse such redelivery and to affirm the charterparty, holding the charterers liable for hire for the balance of the minimum period.

On the first issue as to whether the rule in *White and Carter* applied to a time charter or whether the owners could not complete the contract themselves without the co-operation of the charterers, Cooke J held that a shipowner could perform a time charterparty by keeping the ship at the disposal of the charterer, without the need for the charterer to do anything. He agreed with the view of Kerr J in *The Odenfeld*[128] and of Simon J in *The Dynamic*[129] that the principle in *White and Carter* applied to a time charter. He distinguished a demise charter, where the charterer takes possession of the vessel, provides the crew and typically pays all outgoings on the vessel.[130]

The second issue was whether this was an extreme case where the general rule that the innocent party can elect to affirm or terminate the contract could not apply, because the owners had no legitimate interest in maintaining the charter for the balance of 94 days and claiming hire, as opposed to accepting the repudiatory breach of the charterers as bringing the charter to an end, trading on the spot market in mitigation of loss and claiming damages for the difference. Cooke J held that:

the effect of the authorities is that an innocent party will have no legitimate interest in maintaining the contract if damages are an adequate remedy and his insistence on maintaining the contract can be described as "wholly unreasonable",[131] "extremely unreasonable" or, perhaps, in my words, "perverse".[132]

Damages were not an adequate remedy as the charterers' financial position was uncertain. Termination of the charterparty would deprive the owner of the right to receive hire in advance as opposed to after an arbitration award. Affirmation of the contract would impose the obligation on the charterer to trade the vessel rather than making the innocent party, the owner, mitigate its damages with the risk of subsequent argument as to whether it had done so reasonably.

The *White v Carter* principle will not apply to a case where the commercial purpose of the adventure has been frustrated due to delay as in *MSC Mediterranean Shipping Co SA v Cottonex Anstalt*.[133] There, containers of cotton were shipped to Chittagong but due to a dispute between the shippers and the consignees delivery was not taken and the containers were not redelivered

---

127. [2012] EWHC 1077 (Comm); [2012] 2 All ER (Comm) 461. See also *Barclays Bank plc v Unicredit Bank AG* [2012] EWHC 3655 (Comm) (guarantees) and *Geys v Societe Generale* [2012] UKSC 63; [2013] 2 WLR 50 (employment contract).

128. *Gator Shipping Corp v Trans-Asiatic Oil SA (The Odenfeld)* [1978] 2 Lloyd's Rep 357.

129. *Ocean Marine Navigation Ltd v Koch Carbon Inc (The Dynamic)* [2003] EWHC 1936 (Comm); [2003] 2 Lloyd's Rep 693.

130. Therefore the *obiter dicta* of Orr and Brown LJJ in *Attica Sea Carriers Corporation v Ferrostaal Poseidon Bulk Reederei GmbH (The Puerto Buitrago)* [1976] 1 Lloyd's Rep 250 that the demise charter could not be fulfilled without the co-operation of the charterers did not apply to a time charter.

131. Kerr J in *Gator Shipping Corp v Trans-Asiatic Oil SA (The Odenfeld)* [1978] 2 Lloyd's Rep 357 and Lloyd J in *Clea Shipping Corp v Bulk Oil (The Alaskan Trader)* [1984] 1 All ER 129.

132. [44].

133. [2016] EWCA Civ 789; [2016] 2 Lloyd's Rep 494.

to the carriers. The carriers claimed demurrage for the containers but after several months of delay and when the carrier had offered to sell the containers to the shippers, the Court of Appeal held that the commercial purpose of the adventure had been frustrated so that the containers were lost. Moore-Bick LJ stated:

If it had been open to the carrier to affirm the contract I should have agreed with the judge that it had no legitimate interest in continuing to insist on performance by the shipper of its remaining obligations under the contracts. The accrued demurrage already exceeded by a considerable amount the value of the containers. Replacement containers were readily available at Chittagong and the carrier had no interest in keeping the contract alive other than to earn demurrage pending their return. This is a classic case in which it would have been wholly unreasonable for the carrier to insist on further performance. The only reasonable course for it to take would have been to accept the shipper's failure to redeliver the containers as a repudiation of the contract. However, I do not think that the option of affirming the contracts remained open to the carrier once the adventure had become frustrated, because at that point further performance became impossible, just as it would if the shipper or those for whom it was responsible had caused the containers to be destroyed. With respect to the judge, therefore, I do not think that this is a case in which the White & Carter principle applies. As at 2nd February 2012 the shipper could no longer redeliver the containers and, having brought about that situation by its breach, had become liable in damages for their loss.[134]

A party may be in anticipatory or renunciatory breach of charterparty where it evinces an intention not to perform the contract before the time for performance falls due. In *SK Shipping (S) PTE Ltd v Petroexport Ltd (The Pro Victor)*[135] Flaux J held that the owner was justified in terminating the charterparty after giving the charterer an ultimatum asking for confirmation of performance which went unanswered.

In *Spar Shipping AS v Grand China Logistics Holding (Group) Co Ltd*[136] Gross LJ summarised the position on when a breach of contract would give the innocent party the right to terminate the contract as follows:

Breaches of contract entitling the innocent party to treat the contract as at an end may be classified as follows:

  i) Breach of condition;
 ii) Repudiatory breach, i.e., an actual breach of an innominate term where the consequences are such as to entitle the innocent party to treat the contract as at an end; and
iii) Renunciatory breach, i.e., an anticipatory breach of contract (i.e., in advance of the due date for performance), where the other party makes clear to the innocent party that it is not going to perform the contract at all or is going to commit a breach of a condition or is going to commit a breach of an innominate term and the consequences will be such as to entitle the innocent party to treat the contract as at an end; in each case here, the innocent party has an election to accept the renunciatory breach at once and to terminate the contract, without waiting for the due date of performance: see, Burrows,[137] op. cit., at pp. 116–117.[138]

If the term breached is neither a condition nor an innominate term, it will be a warranty and the only remedy for breach of warranty is damages.

The purpose of damages is to compensate the innocent party for the loss of its contractual bargain and to put the innocent party in the position that it would have been in had the contract been

---

134. [43].
135. [2009] EWHC 2974 (Comm); [2010] 2 Lloyd's Rep 158.
136. [2016] EWCA Civ 982; [2016] 2 Lloyd's Rep 447.
137. A. Burrows, *Commentary in A Restatement Of The English Law Of Contract* (OUP 2016).
138. [2016] EWCA Civ 982; [2016] 2 Lloyd's Rep 447 [21].

performed.[139] It is necessary to ask whether the innocent party would have been able to perform its part of the contract had there been no repudiatory breach, as if it would not have been able to, damages would put the party in a better position than if the charterparty had been performed. That would be a windfall and contrary to the compensatory principle.[140]

In *Omak Maritime Ltd v Mamola Challenger Shipping Co (The Mamola Challenger)*[141] the charterers were in repudiatory breach of a five-year time charterparty. The owners were able to find substitute employment for their ship and earned more than they would have done over the five-year period even had they carried out alterations to the ship required by the contract. They therefore suffered no loss. However, they sought to recover expenditure they had wasted in relation to the alterations. Hamblen J held that they could not recover the wasted expenditure as damages.

The damages must not be too remote. In *Sylvia Shipping Co Ltd v Progress Bulk Carriers Ltd (The Sylvia)*[142] the owners were in breach of their obligation to exercise due diligence and maintenance. As a result the time charterers' sub-charterers cancelled the sub-charterparty. The time charterers were entitled to recover the profits they would have made under the sub-charter.

Off hire is another important remedy for a time charterer.[143] The charterer of the *Hong Kong Fir* did not have to pay hire for the ship during the period that time was lost while repairs to the engines were carried out. Furthermore, some charterparties expressly provide that the charterer is entitled to add off hire periods to the period of the charterparty, as in *The Hong Kong Fir*,[144] so that the charterer does actually have the use of the ship for the time originally contracted for.

6. REASONABLE DESPATCH

There is usually an express term in a charterparty providing that the owner must exercise reasonable despatch, all convenient despatch,[145] utmost despatch[146] or due despatch.[147] Where a contract does not provide for the time within which an obligation must be performed, at common law it will be implied that the obligation must be performed within a reasonable time.[148]

---

139. *Golden Strait Corporation v Nippon Yusen Kubishka Kaisha (The Golden Victory)* [2007] UKHL 12; [2007] 2 Lloyd's Rep 164 discussed at page 157 together with the principles applicable to the early redelivery of the vessel both where there is an available market and where there is not. Clear words would be required for a contractual provision to overcome the compensatory principle where the innocent party would not have suffered any loss – *Novasen SA v Alimenta SA* [2013] EWHC 345 (Comm); [2013] 2 All ER (Comm) 162.

140. *Flame SA v Glory Wealth Shipping Pte Ltd (The Glory Wealth)* [2013] EWHC 3153 (Comm); [2013] 2 Lloyd's Rep 653.

141. [2010] EWHC 2026 (Comm); [2011] 1 Lloyd's Rep 47.

142. [2010] EWHC 542 (Comm); [2010] 2 Lloyd's Rep 81 applied in *Maestro Bulk Ltd v Cosco Bulk Carrier Co Ltd (The Great Creation)* [2014] EWHC 3987 (Comm); [2015] 1 Lloyd's Rep 315. Contrast *The Achilleas* discussed at page 162.

143. See pages 169–171.

144. See also *Petroleo Brasileiro SA v Kriti Akti Shipping Co SA (The Kriti Akti)* [2004] EWCA Civ 116, [2004] 1 Lloyd's Rep 712, discussed at page 155. See also cl 52(c) of NYPE 2015.

145. See e.g. cl 1 of *Asbatankvoy*.

146. See e.g. cl 8 of NYPE 1946.

147. See e.g. cl 8 of NYPE 1993 and cl 8(a) of NYPE 2015.

148. *Wuhan Ocean Economic and Technical Cooperation Company Limited v Schiffahrts-Gesellschaft "Hansa Murcia" MBH & Co KG* [2012] EWHC 3104 (Comm); [2013] 1 All ER (Comm) 1277.

7. DEVIATION

A charterparty may provide for a particular route to be followed or under a time charterparty the time charterer may give express instructions as to the route.[149] If there is a contractually agreed route, the shipowner must follow that route unless an exception applies. If there is no contractually agreed route it is presumed that the contractual route is the direct geographical route, unless the owner can prove that there is a customary route.[150]

Many charterparties contain an express liberty to deviate.[151] Such a clause will be interpreted restrictively against the owner.[152] If the charterparty incorporates the Hague or Hague-Visby Rules, Article IV rule 4 of both sets of Rules provides that the carrier shall not be liable for any loss or damage resulting from any deviation in saving or attempting to save life or property or any reasonable deviation.[153] The Rules do not permit the owner to contract out of the minimum obligations imposed by the Rules,[154] and where there is both a wide express liberty clause and the Rules apply, the question arises whether the liberty clause is an attempt to lessen the owner's obligations and thus void, or defines the scope of the owner's obligations in which case it is valid. The latter interpretation seems likely.[155]

If there is no express liberty clause and the Rules do not apply to the charterparty, the owner can rely on the justifications for deviation at common law. These are narrower than those under the Rules and cover deviation to save human life or to communicate with a ship in distress where there is a risk of loss of life (but not for the sole purpose of saving property);[156] to avoid danger to the ship or her cargo, even if the danger was caused by the vessel being unseaworthy when she went to sea;[157] or where deviation is necessary due to the fault of the charterer.

Unjustified deviation is a fundamental breach of contract and the charterer has the right to elect to terminate or affirm the contract.[158] The breach was treated at common law as of such a serious character as to go to the root of the contract and, if the charterer elected to terminate the contract, the owner could no longer rely on any of its terms, including any exception clauses. This is the doctrine of fundamental breach. That doctrine no longer survives in general contract law as a result of the decision of the House of Lords in *Photo Production v Securicor*.[159] However, in that case Lord Wilberforce left open the question whether maritime contracts are of a special type and therefore whether the doctrine should survive in relation to them.[160] The better

---

149. See e.g. *Whistler International v Kawasaki Kisen Kaisha Ltd (The Hill Harmony)* [2001] 1 Lloyd's Rep 147.

150. *Reardon Smith Line v Black Sea and Baltic General Insurance* [1939] AC 562.

151. See e.g. cl 3 of Gencon 1994.

152. *Glynn v Margetson* [1893] AC 351 and *Stag Line v Foscolo, Mango & Co* [1932] AC 328.

153. See *Stag Line v Foscolo, Mango & Co* [1932] AC 328 and *Lyric Shipping Inc v Intermetals Ltd (The Al Taha)* [1990] 2 Lloyd's Rep 117.

154. Art III r 8 of the Hague and Hague-Visby Rules.

155. *Renton v Palmyra Trading Corp* [1956] 1 QB 462, at p 510, approved in *Jindal Iron & Steel Limited v Islamic Solidarity Shipping Co (The Jordan II)* [2005] 1 Lloyd's Rep 57. See also *Yuzhny Zavod Metall Profil LLC v EEMS Beheerder BV (The Eems Solar)* [2013] 2 Lloyd's Rep 487 – the case was appealed but the Court of Appeal held ([2014] Civ 333) that unless the cargo owner complied with an earlier interim payment order its appeal against the owners in respect of damage caused to its cargo would be struck out. Furthermore it was appropriate to allow the owners to adduce fresh evidence in relation to a point for which the cargo owner had been granted leave to appeal but where the point had been neither pleaded nor argued at trial. *Societe de Distribution de Toutes Merchandises en Cote-D'Ivoire v Continental Lines NV (The Sea Miror)* [2015] EWHC 1747; [2015] 2 Lloyd's Rep 395.

156. *Scaramanga v Stamp* [1880] 5 CPD 295, per Cockburn CJ at p 304.

157. *Kish v Taylor* [1912] AC 604.

158. *Hain Steamship Company Ltd v Tate & Lyle Ltd* [1936] 2 All ER 597.

159. [1980] AC 827.

160. Ibid., at p 845.

view is that it does not.[161] Historically the reason for the draconian response to deviation was that the insurer was discharged from liability if there was a deviation.[162] Nowadays the standard form insurance contracts hold the insured covered if there is a deviation.[163] If the doctrine of fundamental breach no longer survives, it would be a question of construction whether an exemption clause is drafted widely enough to cover the fundamental breach which has occurred.

Where the Hague or Hague-Visby Rules apply to the charterparty, the time bar will probably still apply[164] even if the owner has deviated and the owner can rely on the limits of liability,[165] although it may be possible to break those limits where the Hague-Visby Rules apply.

8. SAFE PORTS

A charterparty either time or voyage will usually provide that the ship may only be ordered to safe ports or places.[166] In some more sophisticated charterparties, the charterer's obligation is limited to one of due diligence to ensure that the ship is only employed between and at safe places.[167] Where there is no such express term there may be an implied obligation.[168]

The classic statement of what constitutes a safe port is that of Sellers LJ in *The Eastern City*,[169]

a port will not be safe unless, in the relevant period of time, the particular ship can reach it, use it and return from it without, in the absence of some abnormal occurrence, being exposed to danger which cannot be avoided by good navigation and seamanship.

Thus a port may be unsafe because the ship cannot safely get to it, for example, because her draft is too great, there is ice, the anchorage is unreliable[170] or there is no adequate system of monitoring the channel.[171] In *Emeraldian Limited Partnership v Wellmix Shipping Ltd (The Vine)*[172] the charterparty provided for "1 or 2 safe berths, 1 safe port Itagui, Brazil, always afloat". It was held that the charterer nominated an unsafe berth, requiring more than ordinary navigation and seamanship to avoid the inherent dangers in the defective berthing dolphins. These were Sumitomo type fenders, the middle and forward one of which had been damaged and needed repair. Masters and pilots were not informed of these dangers.

Simply because there are hazards at a port does not necessarily make that port unsafe as it may be possible to avoid them with good navigation and seamanship. There must be a safe system in the port to warn of hazards and to avoid them. Thus a port is still safe if it is prone to bad weather and it is necessary for the ship to leave the port during such weather, if there is an

161. See e.g. the view of Lloyd LJ in *The Antares* [1987] 1 Lloyd's Rep 424, at p 430. C. Debattista, "Fundamental Breach and Deviation in the Carriage of Goods by Sea" [1989] JBL 22.

162. Marine Insurance Act 1906, ss 45 and 46. H. Bennett, *The Law of Marine Insurance* (2nd edn, Oxford University Press 2006) (hereinafter "*Bennett*"), [18.34]–[18.37].

163. *Bennett*, [18.111]–[18.114]. See page 455.

164. Cf. *The Antares* [1987] 1 Lloyd's Rep 424, at p 479.

165. Cf. *Daewoo Heavy Industries Ltd v Klipriver Shipping Ltd (The Kapitan Petko Voivoda)* [2003] EWCA Civ 451; [2003] 2 Lloyd's Rep 1; *Scrutton*, at pp 435, 447–449 and 452 p 470; A. Diamond, "Hague-Visby Rules" (1978) 2 LMCLQ 225, at pp 246–247.

166. See e.g. cl 5 of NYPE 1993, cl 1(b) and 1(c) of NYPE 2015 and cls 1 and 9 of Asbatankvoy.

167. See e.g. cl 3 of Shelltime 3 and cl 4 of Shelltime 4.

168. There was no implied warranty of safety of the berth in *Mediterranean Salvage & Towage Ltd v Seamar Trading & Commerce Inc (The Reborn)* [2009] EWCA Civ 531; [2009] 1 CLC 909. On implication of terms generally see *Marks & Spencer plc v BNP Paribas Securities Services Trust Co (Jersey) Ltd* [2015] UKSC 72; [2016] AC 742.

169. *Leeds Shipping Co v Societe Francaise Bunge (The Eastern City)* [1958] 2 Lloyd's Rep 127, at p 131 applied in *Gard Marine & Energy Ltd v China National Chartering Co Ltd (The Ocean Victory)* [2017] UKSC 35; [2017] 1 WLR 1793.

170. Ibid.

171. *Independent Petroleum Group v Seacarriers (The Count)* [2006] EWHC 3173; [2007] 1 All ER (Comm) 88.

172. [2010] EWHC 1411 (Comm); [2011] 1 Lloyd's Rep 301.

adequate system for forecasting bad weather, sufficient tugs and pilots, adequate sea room to manoeuvre and an adequate system of making sure that adequate sea room is always available to manoeuvre.[173] A port may also be unsafe for political reasons, for example, as a result of the outbreak of hostilities so that the ship is trapped at her discharge port.[174]

When a time charterer gives voyage instructions its obligation is to nominate a port which is prospectively safe, i.e. the port will be safe at the time that the ship arrives there, uses it and leaves. The port does not need to be safe at the time the order is given, provided it will have become safe for this ship by the time she arrives, for example, because the ice currently at the port will have melted. The charterer is liable for the normal characteristics of the port whether they were known to it or not. However, it does not guarantee the safety of the port, as it will not be liable for abnormal and unexpected events. Thus the charterer was not liable in *The Evia (No 2)*[175] when the ship was trapped in the Shatt al Arab waterway as a result of the outbreak of war between Iran and Iraq. In *The Saga Cob*[176] the vessel was attacked by Eritrean guerrillas in Massawa. The Court of Appeal held that it was impossible to say that such an attack or even the risk of an attack was a normal characteristic of the port. The attack was an abnormal and unexpected event. The charterer's duty in that case was one of due diligence and the Court of Appeal thought that there was a strong argument that the test should be whether a reasonably careful charterer would on the facts known have concluded that the port was prospectively unsafe.[177] What happened after the attack would also be relevant on the question of due diligence.

In *Gard Marine & Energy Ltd v China National Chartering Co Ltd (The Ocean Victory)*[178] the Supreme Court had to consider whether the combination of long waves and severe northerly winds were an abnormal occurrence at the port of Kashima in Japan. Kashima is a large man-made modern port bordering the Pacific Ocean. There were a string of charterparties of the *Ocean Victory* and each of them contained an undertaking to trade the ship between safe ports. The *Ocean Victory*, a Capesize bulk carrier, commenced discharge at Kashima but had to stop on 23 October due to strong winds and heavy rain. There was considerable swell due to the phenomenon known as long waves affecting the ship's berth and high winds. On 24 October the master decided to leave the berth but lost control of the ship while leaving the port due to the strong northerly winds. She was driven on to the breakwater wall and subsequently became a total loss. The owner and the demise charterer claimed that the port of Kashima was unsafe. The charterers denied that the port was unsafe and argued that the conditions on 24 October were an abnormal occurrence. There had never been an incident such as befell the *Ocean Victory* since the construction of the port in 1969. Between 1971 and 2006 some 1,254 VLCCs and some 5,316 Capesize vessels had visited the port. There was limited data relating to long waves. Even when there were long waves they might affect only some ships at a particular quay or none. Strong northerly winds only affected the port less than once a year. The issue was whether Teare J was correct to hold[179] that the combination of two weather conditions on the casualty date (namely the phenomenon of swell from "long waves", which might have forced the vessel to leave the berth, and a very severe northerly gale which meant that the vessel could not safely exit the port) was not to be characterised as an abnormal occurrence, notwithstanding that the coincidence

173. *The Khian Sea* [1979] 545 and *Gard Marine & Energy Ltd v China National Chartering Co Ltd (The Ocean Victory)* [2017] UKSC 35; [2017] 1 WLR 1793.
174. *Kodros Shipping Corp v Empresa Cubana de Fletes (The Evia) (No 2)* [1982] 2 Lloyd's Rep 307.
175. Ibid.
176. *K/S Penta Shipping A/S v Ethiopian Shipping Lines Corporation (The Saga Cob)* [1992] 2 Lloyd's Rep 545.
177. Ibid., at p 551.
178. [2017] UKSC 35; [2017] 1 WLR 1793.
179. [2013] EWHC 2199 (Comm); [2014] 1 Lloyd's Rep 59.

of the two conditions was "rare",[180] because both conditions were physical characteristics or attributes of the port. It was common ground that neither condition on its own rendered the port unsafe. If long waves affected a Capesize when moored at its berth, and its movement could not be controlled by moorings or tugs, the vessel could leave. If northerly gales affected the port, a Capesize did not need to transit the Kashima Fairway: it could safely stay at berth, if it had already entered, or wait outside the port, if it had not.

Longmore LJ, delivering the judgment of the Court of Appeal, overturned the judgment of Teare J as:

> First of all he failed to formulate the critical – and unitary – question which he had to answer: namely, whether the simultaneous coincidence of the two critical features, viz. (a) such severe swell from long waves that it was dangerous for a vessel to remain at her berth at the Raw Materials Quay (because of the risk of damage or mooring break out) and (b) conditions in the Kashima Fairway being so severe because of gale force winds from the northerly/northeasterly quadrant), as to make navigation of the Fairway dangerous or impossible for Capesize vessels, was an abnormal occurrence or a normal characteristic of the port of Kashima? Or put even more simply, was it an abnormal occurrence or a normal characteristic of the port that a vessel might be in danger at her berth at the Raw Materials Quay but unable at the same time safely to leave because of navigation dangers in the Kashima Fairway arising from the combination of long waves and gale force northerly winds which, in fact, occurred.
>
> On the contrary, instead of asking the unitary question directed at establishing the correct characterisation of the critical combination (abnormal occurrence or normal characteristic of the port), the judge merely addressed the respective constituent elements of the combination (swell from long waves making it dangerous for a vessel to remain at the Raw Materials Quay and gale force winds from the northerly/northeasterly quadrant making navigation of the Fairway dangerous or impossible for Capesize vessels) separately. He looked at each component and decided that, viewed on its own, neither could be said to be rare and both were attributes or characteristics of the port. That was the wrong approach; what mattered was not the nature of the individual component dangers that gave rise to the events on 24 October, but the nature of the event (i.e. the critical combination) which gave rise to the vessel (on the judge's findings) effectively being trapped in port.[181]

The judge was wrong to conclude that even if the critical combination was rare, nonetheless it was a characteristic of the port. Even if an event is theoretically foreseeable as possibly occurring at the port it is not sufficient to turn "a rare event in the history of the port" into a normal characteristic of the port. Regard needed to be had to "significant factors such as the actual evidence relating to the past history of the port, the frequency (if any) of the event, the degree of forseeability of the critical combination and the very severe nature of the storm on the casualty date."[182] Longmore continued,

> In deciding whether the critical combination was itself a normal characteristic of the port or an abnormal occurrence, what the judge should have done was to evaluate the evidence relating to the past frequency of such an event occurring and the likelihood of it occurring again. He should have also, in our view, have taken into account what appears to have been the unchallenged evidence of Mr Lynagh referred to above relating to the exceptional nature of the storm that affected Kashima on 24 October 2006 in terms of its rapid development, its duration and its severity. Had he done so, then, on the basis of his own finding that "the concurrent occurrence of those events was rare", and on the basis of the evidence which we have summarised above, there would, in our view, have been only one conclusion which he could have reached – namely that the event which occurred on 24th October 2006 was indeed an abnormal occurrence."[183]

Therefore the charterers were not in breach of the safe port obligation. The Supreme Court upheld the Court of Appeal decision.

---

180. Ibid., [127]–[128].
181. [2015] EWCA Civ 16; [2015] 1 Lloyd's Rep 381 [55] and [56].
182. [58].
183. [63].

The House of Lords also held in *The Evia (No 2)* that if the port which was prospectively safe subsequently becomes unsafe, the charterer has a secondary obligation to order the ship to a new safe port. Where the ship is already at the port no such secondary obligation can arise where it is not possible for the vessel to leave, as was the case in *The Evia (No 2)*. In *The Lucille*,[184] however, the ship could not enter the port due to congestion and the port became prospectively unsafe. The charterer should have ordered the ship to leave and was therefore in breach of its secondary obligation. It is not clear whether the secondary obligation is an absolute one or is based on due diligence or reasonable care or on the actual knowledge of the charterer.

The House of Lords also left open the question as to whether the secondary obligation applies to a voyage charterer. A voyage charterparty may expressly provide that the ship is to proceed to a named port or ports, so that the parties have agreed in advance the contractual ports. *The Livanita*[185] concerned a "time charter trip via St Petersburg". The hull of the vessel was damaged by ice blocks created by ice breakers which assisted her as she left St Petersburg. The charterer contended that there was no relevant express warranty because the risk of the ship encountering ice at St Petersburg was a risk the owner had agreed to bear by agreeing to a charterparty with St Petersburg as a named port in winter. Langley J held that where a charterparty expressly names a loading port and also contains a safe port warranty that warranty applies to the named port. No case was made by the charterer of variation, estoppel or waiver. There was no evidence that either party knew or ought reasonably to have anticipated that the port was unsafe at the time the charter was entered into, or that it was unsafe in a reasonably predictable and expected way. In *The Archimidis*[186] the Court of Appeal held that the express typed provision for "1 safe port Ventspils" constituted a warranty by the charterer of the safety of the port, as opposed to an agreement by both parties that the port was safe.

When a charterer gives voyage instructions under a time charterparty to proceed to an unsafe port the owner is entitled to reject the order as invalid and ask for valid voyage instructions. An analogy may be drawn with the situation where the charterer gives an order to go on an illegitimate last voyage.[187] Thus if the charterer were to insist on invalid voyage instructions, the charterer would be in repudiatory breach of charterparty and the owner would have the right to elect to terminate the charterparty. Where the owner is not aware that the port is unsafe, but it subsequently becomes clear that that is the position, the owner may refuse to enter the port.

The war risks clause in the charterparty may entitle the owner to refuse to proceed to a port in a war zone.[188] This will depend on the construction of the trading limits of the charterparty and the war risks clause in the light of the intended pattern of trading at the time the charterparty was entered into. In *Abu Dhabi National Tanker Co v Product Star Shipping (The Product Star) (No 2)*[189] the Court of Appeal held that the owners were in repudiatory breach of time charter where they had refused to proceed to Ruwais in the United Arab Emirates. When the charterparty was entered into the owners were aware of the charterer's intended trade pattern from Ruwais to Bangladesh during the Iran–Iraq war. The United Arab Emirates was a war risk zone but the charterers had to pay the war risk premiums. The owners had a discretion to decline to enter a "dangerous port". The vessel made four voyages from Ruwais to Bangladesh under the charterparty but then refused an order to load at Ruwais on the ground that it was dangerous.

---

184. *C-Trade of Geneva SA v Uni-Ocean Lines Pte of Singapore (The Lucille)* [1984] 1 Lloyd's Rep 244 (CA).
185. *STX Pan Ocean Co Ltd v Ugland Bulk Transport AS (The Livanita)* [2007] EWHC 1317 (Comm); [2008] 1 Lloyd's Rep 86.
186. *AIC Limited v Marine Pilot Limited (The Archimidis)* [2008] EWCA Civ 175; [2008] 2 All ER (Comm) 545.
187. See pages 161–162 of this chapter and see *The Peonia*, per Lord Bingham at p 107 and *The Gregos*.
188. See e.g.cl 31(e) of NYPE 1993 and the BIMCO War Risks Clause CONWARTIME 2013 in cl 34 of NYPE 2015.
189. *The Product Star (No 2)* [1993] 1 Lloyd's Rep 397.

There had been no attacks on vessels which traded solely to the United Arab Emirates. The owners' discretion had to be exercised honestly and in good faith and not arbitrarily, capriciously or unreasonably. The Court of Appeal upheld the decision of the judge that there was no material on which a reasonable owner could reasonably have considered that the risk of proceeding to Ruwais was a different risk from that which already existed at the date of the charterparty and which had been accepted by the terms of the charterparty. Even if the owners had bona fide considered Ruwais to be dangerous by comparison with the risks at the date of the charterparty, such conclusion would have been unreasonable and capricious.

The Product Star (No 2) was distinguished in *Taokas Navigation SA v Komrowski Bulk Shipping KG (GmbH & Co) (The Paiwan Wisdom).*[190] Teare J held that the owners were entitled to refuse the instruction for the first voyage to proceed to Mombasa, Kenya. The charterparty in the NYPE 1993 form did not exclude Kenya in the vessel's trading limits under the charterparty but the charterparty incorporated the BIMCO War Risks Clause for Time Charters 2004, the 2004 Conwartime clause. This gave the owners the right to refuse to proceed to Kenya due to the risks of Somali piracy despite the fact that the position had not changed between the date of entering into the charterparty and the charterers' order. The owners were not aware at the time the charterparty was entered into that the vessel was likely to be traded to Kenya. It was assumed that the owners had acted bona fide.

Where, however, the owner is aware that the port is unsafe but accepts the order to proceed there, the owner cannot then change its mind although it may still have a right to damages for breach of contract.[191] Where the master ignores obvious danger and proceeds to enter the agreed port, this may constitute a break in the chain of causation so that the owner cannot recover damages from the charterer as the loss resulted from the choice of the owner's servant rather than the charterer's breach.

When the charterer is in breach of its safe port obligation it will be liable in damages for the consequences of its breach such as physical damage to the ship, additional costs incurred at the port, for example if the ship is unable to enter due to her draught being excessive and it is necessary to lighten her. Where the consequence is delay the time charterer would continue to be liable for time charter hire and other expenses incurred such as additional insurance premiums while the delay continued, whereas a voyage charterer would be liable for damages for detention.

9. FRUSTRATION

In *National Carriers Ltd v Panalpina (Northern) Ltd*[192] Lord Simon stated,

Frustration of a contract takes place when there supervenes an event (without fault of either party and for which the contract makes no sufficient provision) which so significantly changes the nature (not merely the expense or onerousness) of the outstanding rights and/or obligations from what the parties could reasonably have contemplated at the time of its execution that it would be unjust to hold them to the literal sense of its stipulations in the new circumstances; in such case the law declares both parties to be discharged from further performance.[193]

---

190. [2012] EWHC 1888 (Comm); [2013] 1 All ER (Comm) 564. See also *Pacific Basin IHX Ltd v Bulkhandling Handymax AS (The Triton Lark)* [2012] EWHC 70 (Comm); [2012] 1 Lloyd's Rep 457 and [2011] EWHC 2862 (Comm); [2012] 1 All ER (Comm) 639 on the meaning of "exposed to War Risks" in cl 2 of CONWARTIME 1993 in so far as it related to acts of piracy.

191. *Motor Oil Hellas Refineries SA v Shipping Corp of India (The Kanchenjunga)* [1990] 1 Lloyd's Rep 391.

192. [1981] AC 675 (HL).

193. Ibid., at p 700.

In the maritime context frustration may occur if the ship is destroyed, requisitioned,[194] seized[195] or trapped due to outbreak of war.[196] Simply because it is more expensive and time consuming[197] to perform the contract will not frustrate it. Thus in *Tsakiroglou & Co Ltd v Noblee Thorl GmbH*[198] a sale contract was not frustrated by the closure of the Suez Canal, even though the freight rate was much higher and it took twice as long to perform the voyage as the ship had to take the route round the Cape of Good Hope. The contract could still be performed. This would not be the case if the ship could not arrive within the contractual delivery date or the cargo would perish on the longer voyage.

Where an event causes delay in performance of contractual obligations it may be possible to say immediately that the prospective delay is so great that the contract is frustrated. In other situations, however, it may be necessary to wait to see whether the delay that has already occurred, and is likely to occur in the future, is so great as to frustrate the contract. The party alleging frustration will seek the earliest frustration date possible and will no doubt argue that it was predictable at an early stage that the delay would be frustrating. It is for the tribunal of fact, properly informed as to the law, to decide the effect of the delay.[199]

It will be necessary to consider the impact of the event on each individual contract. The same event may have a different impact on different contracts depending on what obligations remain to be performed under each contract and whether the contract has provided for the event which has occurred. For example, the outbreak of war between Iran and Iraq on 22 September 1980 frustrated the time charterparty in *The Evia*[200] on 8 October 1980 as, soon after the outbreak of war, it became clear that it would be a long, slow war of attrition and as the ship had completed discharge of her cargo on the day war broke out, the only obligation remaining to be performed by charterers was to redeliver the ship which was not possible. In *The Agathon*,[201] however, the charterparty could still be performed after the outbreak of war, as the ship could still continue to discharge her cargo, albeit slowly. Thus her charterparty was not frustrated until December that year, when discharge was completed.

In *The Sea Angel*[202] Tsavliris, salvors, chartered the *Sea Angel*, a small ship, to transfer the cargo of crude oil from the *Tasman Spirit* which had grounded in the approaches to the port of Karachi, as part of the salvage operation of the *Tasman Spirit*. The time charter of the *Sea Angel* was for 20 days. The *Sea Angel* completed the transfer of the cargo and was due to leave Karachi on 9 September for redelivery at Fujairah three days later. However, the Karachi Port Trust (KPT) refused to grant a No Demand Certificate so that she could not leave. KPT demanded that Tsavliris pay about US$11 million. The ship was detained for 108 days until 26 December. The Court of Appeal upheld the decision of Gross J at first instance that the contract was not frustrated. Tsavliris argued on appeal that the delay which had already taken place by 13 October of about five weeks added to the prospective delay amounted to a total, ongoing, indefinite delay of such unreasonable and inordinate length, especially when compared with the length of the charter and the very short time unexpired, as to frustrate the contract. It was argued that this

194. *Anglo Northern Trading Company Limited v Emlyn Jones & Williams* [1917] 2 KB 78; *Bank Line Limited v Arthur Capel & Co* [1919] AC 435.
195. *Tatem v Gamboa* [1939] 1 KB 132.
196. *Kodros Shipping Corp v Empresa Cubana de Fletes (The Evia) (No 2)* [1982] 2 Lloyd's Rep 307.
197. *Davies Contractors Ltd v Fareham Urban District Council* [1956] AC 696.
198. [1962] AC 93.
199. *Pioneer Shipping Ltd v BTP Tioxide Ltd (The Nema)* [1982] AC 724 (strike).
200. *Kodros Shipping Corp v Empresa Cubana de Fletes (The Evia) (No 2)* [1982] 2 Lloyd's Rep 307.
201. *Kissavos Shipping Co SA v Empresa Cubana de Fletes (The Agathon)* [1982] 2 Lloyd's Rep 211 (CA).
202. *Edwinton Commercial Corporation v Tsavliris Russ (Worldwide Salvage & Towage) Ltd (The Sea Angel)* [2007] EWCA Civ 547; [2007] 2 Lloyd's Rep 517. See also *DGM Commodities Corp v Sea Metropolitan SA (The Andra)* [2012] EWHC 1984 (Comm); [2012] 2 Lloyd's Rep 587.

comparison was the main test to apply. Rix LJ rejected that argument as, although it is an important consideration, it was on the facts "only the starting point".[203] Rix LJ distinguished the cases on requisition, seizure or trapping as there is no possibility in such cases of negotiating or litigating one's way out of such consequences of war. A special factor included the foreseeability of the general risk of the unreasonable detention of a ship participating in salvage services, which was recognised within the salvage industry. The requirement of justice was not an additional test for frustration but was "a relevant factor" and "provides the ultimate rationale of the doctrine". It could be used as "a reality check".[204]

The event may not only have been foreseen by the parties but there may be some express provision in the charterparty.[205] It will be a question of construction whether any provision is sufficient to cover the very serious circumstances which have occurred or whether the supervening event goes beyond the risk assumed under the contract and renders performance radically different[206] from that contracted for.

The supervening event must not be due to the fault of either party. Thus if the event is caused by the fault or breach of either party the contract cannot be frustrated and this is referred to as self-induced frustration. For example, in *The Fjord Wind*[207] the ship ran aground and it was necessary to transship her cargo. The owner argued that the voyage charterparty was frustrated. However, as the grounding was due to the owner's failure to exercise due diligence to make the ship seaworthy there could not be frustration. Furthermore, where it is impossible to perform the contract due to a choice or election made by one of the parties this is self-induced frustration. Thus in *The Super Servant Two*[208] a contract could be performed by one of two ships. The owner allocated one ship to perform another contract and the second ship was lost. The charterparty was not frustrated as it could not be performed due to the owner's choice to use the first ship to perform a contract with a third party rather than using it to perform this contract. The solution would have been for the owner to provide in the contract that it had an option as to which of the ships was to perform the contract. Once such an option was exercised, if the ship chosen is lost the contract could be frustrated, but the owner cannot keep its option open and claim frustration if only one ship is lost.

The consequence of frustration is that the contract is terminated automatically as from the date of frustration, i.e. both parties are discharged from their contractual obligations without either party making any election. At common law any sums that were due by the date of frustration were still due and any sums which had been paid before the date of frustration could not be recovered. Any sums which would have become due after the date of frustration no longer had to be paid. In *Fibrosa v Fairbairn*[209] the House of Lords held that a payment which had been made prior to frustration could be refunded if there was a total failure of consideration.

The Law Reform (Frustrated Contracts) Act 1943,[210] which seeks to apportion losses between the parties, applies to time charters and charterparties by demise, but not to voyage charters and

---

203. Ibid., [118].
204. Ibid., [132].
205. *Ocean Tramp Tankers Corporation v V/O Sovfracht (The Eugenia)* [1963] 2 Lloyd's Rep 381 (CA); *WJ Tatem, Ltd v Gamboa* [1938] 61 Ll L Rep 149; *BTP Tioxide Ltd v Pioneer Shipping Ltd and Armada Marine SpA (The Nema) (No 2)* [1981] 2 Lloyd's Rep 239 (HL); and *Bunge SA v Kyla Shipping Co Ltd (The Kyla)* [2012] EWHC 3522 (Comm); [2013] 1 Lloyd's Rep 565. This latter case went to the Court of Appeal – [2013] EWCA Civ 734; [2013] 3 All ER 1006 – but on the issue of whether the Court of Appeal had jurisdiction to grant permission to appeal from the decision of the judge at first instance, which it held that it did not.
206. Per Lord Radcliffe in *Davies Contractors Ltd v Fareham Urban District Council* [1956] AC 696, at p 729.
207. *Eridania SpA v Rudolf A Oetker (The Fjord Wind)* [2000] 2 Lloyd's Rep 191.
208. [1990] 1 Lloyd's Rep 1 applied in *Melli Bank plc v Holbud Ltd* [2013] EWHC 1506 (Comm).
209. [1943] AC 32.
210. *DVB Bank SE v Shere Shipping Co Ltd* [2013] EWHC 2321 (Ch).

bills of lading. Where a time charterparty is frustrated the hire which has been paid in advance may be repayable under section 1(2) of the Act, although the court has a discretion to allow hire to be retained by the owner where it has expended money in or for the performance of the contract. Section 1(3) provides that where a valuable benefit has been conferred on a party by partial performance of the contract, the court has a discretion to award compensation to the party conferring the benefit. Such compensation cannot exceed the value of the benefit conferred and should take into account the expenses which the party obtaining the benefit has incurred in performing the contract and any circumstances which may have affected the value of the benefit.[211]

10. TIMING AT THE BEGINNING OF THE CHARTERPARTY

Although the ship may already be at the loadport when the charterparty is concluded, this will not usually be the case. The owner will wish to conclude the next fixture in good time before the completion of the current charterparty, so that there is no possibility of the ship being unemployed. The charterer will need to know when the ship will be delivered and ready to load so that it can make arrangements to have the cargo ready at the loadport at that time. The charterer may well have other contractual commitments, such as sale or purchase contracts or a sub-charterparty, to perform and the timing of those contracts and the charterparty must be carefully linked. Thus, for example, the charterer may be the f.o.b. buyer of goods under a contract which provides for shipment within a five-day window. It may also have sold the goods on c.i.f. terms with shipment within the same five-day window. The charterer will wish to have the ship arrive at the appropriate time to enable the ship to load within that window. The charterer will not wish the ship to arrive too early when there is no cargo available if the risk of delay is for the charterer. If this were the case a time charterer would be liable for time charter hire or laytime would commence under a voyage charterparty but the charterer cannot yet use the ship. Furthermore the charterer will not wish the ship to arrive so late that the charterer cannot load within the window as the charterer may then be in breach of its sale and purchase contracts and such breach may be a breach of condition.[212]

The charterer will therefore be protected by a number of clauses in the charterparty. First the charterparty may well record where the ship is at the time that the charterparty is concluded.[213] The charterparty may state "now trading" or "present position". Such a provision will be a condition of the charterparty so that if the ship is elsewhere the charterer would be entitled to elect to terminate the charterparty.[214] In addition the charterparty may state when the ship is "expected ready to load".[215] In *The Mihalis Angelos*[216] the Court of Appeal held that such a provision is also a condition so that if the owner gives a date without any honest belief that the ship will arrive by that date or without any reasonable grounds for it, again the charterer is entitled to elect to terminate the contract. The charterer in that case was entitled to elect to terminate, even though the reason that it gave for terminating the contract was an entirely different one – it sought to rely on a force majeure clause in the contract as it could not provide a cargo.

The "expected ready to load" date is not, however, a guarantee that the ship will definitely arrive by the date given. Provided the date given is both honest and reasonable at the time it was

---

211. *BP Exploration v Hunt* [1982] 1 All ER 925.
212. *Bunge Corporation v Tradax Export SA* [1981] 1 WLR 711; [1981] 2 Lloyd's Rep 1. See page 138.
213. *SK Shipping Co Ltd v BB Energy (Asia) Pte Ltd* [2000] 1 All ER (Comm) 810.
214. *Behn v Burness* [1863] 3 B & S 751.
215. See Box 9 of Gencon.
216. *Maredelanto Compania Naviera SA v Bergbau-Handel GmbH (The Mihalis Angelos)* [1970] 2 Lloyd's Rep 43.

given, the owner will not be in breach of that provision if the ship is then delayed, for example, by an unforeseen tug strike or there is bad weather. Therefore, it is usual for both time and voyage charterparties to provide for a cut-off date so that if the ship has not arrived by that date, the charterer has an express right to cancel.[217] The period of time starting from the earliest date at which hire will commence under a time charter or the earliest time from which laytime can start counting under a voyage charter and the latest time by which the ship can tender a notice of readiness without the risk of being cancelled is often called the laycan.

In *The Niizuru*[218] Mance J held that a clause requiring the owner to narrow the laycan to a 15-day spread 25 days prior to the narrowed laycan was a condition precedent to delivery of the ship under a time charterparty. However, the Court of Appeal held in *Universal Bulk Carriers Ltd v Andre Et Cie*[219] that an obligation on the charterer to narrow the laycan in a voyage charterparty was not always a condition precedent to an obligation to nominate a vessel and was not in that case.

So that the charterer is kept informed of progress it is common for the charterparty to provide that the owner must give notices, for example, 72, 48 and 24 hours before the ship's arrival at the delivery point.[220]

In *Mansel Oil Ltd and another v Troon Storage Tankers SA (The Ailsa Craig)*[221] the Court of Appeal held that the charterers' nomination of a delivery port under a Shell-time 4 charterparty was not a condition precedent to their right to cancel on the cancelling date.

Where a charterer under a voyage charterparty in the BEEPEEVOY3 form gave revised orders for the first load port which it had a liberty to do under clause 24, it lost the right to cancel the charterparty under clause 17 as the estimated time of arrival at the revised load port was after the cancelling date.[222]

The cancellation clause may only give a right to cancel on the cancelling date and not before. In *The Mihalis Angelos*[223] a majority of the Court of Appeal, Lord Denning dissenting, held that the charterer could not exercise its express right to cancel until the cancelling date specified in the clause, even though it was clear some days earlier that the ship would not arrive by the cancelling date. If the charterer purports to cancel before the right to cancel accrues, the charterer will be in repudiatory breach of charterparty, unless it has a right at common law to elect to terminate the charterparty for a breach by the owner. As we have already seen the owner was in breach of the expected ready to load provision in *The Mihalis Angelos* and the charterer was entitled to rely on its right to elect to terminate for that breach. Even if the charterer were in repudiatory breach of charterparty, the owner's damages for that breach would be nominal if the charterer would beyond doubt have exercised its right to cancel when the ship did not arrive by the cancelling date.[224]

A simple cancelling clause may be problematic for the owner as, even if it is clear that the ship will not arrive by the cancelling date, the owner is still obliged to proceed to the loadport with reasonable, due or convenient dispatch, knowing that the charterer may choose to cancel when the ship does not arrive on time. The charterer is not obliged to tell the owner in advance whether it will cancel or not. Therefore the more sophisticated cancellation clauses oblige the charterer to

217. E.g. cl 14 of NYPE 1946, cl 16 of NYPE 1993, cl 3 of NYPE 2015, and cl 5 of Asbatankvoy.
218. *Hyundai Merchant Marine Co Ltd v Karander Maritime Inc (The Niizuru)* [1996] 2 Lloyd's Rep 66.
219. [2001] EWCA Civ 588; [2001] 2 Lloyd's Rep 65 (CA). London Arbitration 5/01 LMLN 557.
220. E.g. cl 2(d) of NYPE 2015.
221. [2009] EWCA Civ 425; [2009] 2 All ER (Comm) 495; [2009] 2 Lloyd's Rep 371.
222. *ST Shipping and Transport Inc v Kriti Filoxenia Shipping Co SA* [2015] EWHC 997; [2015] 2 Lloyd's Rep 609.
223. [1970] 2 Lloyd's Rep 43.
224. *The Mihalis Angelos. Fercometal Sarl v MSC Mediterranean Shipping Co SA (The Simona)* [1988] 2 Lloyd's Rep 199 HL.

advise whether it wishes to cancel if the owner asks prior to the cancellation date, failing which the cancellation date is extended.[225]

The express right to cancel is a very valuable remedy for the charterer. Not only does the ship have to be at the right place by a specified deadline, but she must also be ready. Thus in *The Madeleine*[226] the charterer was entitled to cancel the charterparty in the Baltime form which required the ship to be "in every way fitted for ordinary cargo service" because she did not have a deratisation certificate. However, in *The North Sea*[227] the ship was "in every way fitted for container service" by the cancelling date but did not have the amount of bunkers on board stipulated in the charterparty until two hours after the cancelling time. The Court of Appeal agreed with Mance J that breach of the bunker clause could easily be remedied by a claim for damages and did not attract the more draconian remedy of cancellation, although it could if the ship lacked bunkers to the extent which meant that she was not in every way fitted for her service.

Like an off hire clause,[228] the cancellation clause is a no fault provision. The charterer does not have to ask why the ship is not there by the specified time, or is there, but not ready. All the charterer has to ask is whether the ship is there and ready and, if she is not, the charterer can cancel. However, that is the only remedy the clause gives. If the charterer also wishes to claim damages, then the charterer would have to show that the owner was in breach of charterparty, for example, if the ship had failed to proceed to the loadport with reasonable despatch[229] and cannot rely on the exceptions clause or had broken down en route due to unseaworthiness.

11. TIME CHARTERPARTIES

Under a time charterparty, other than a demise or bareboat charter, the ship remains in the possession of the owner and is not actually delivered to the charterer. Nevertheless the terminology commonly used is that the ship is delivered to the time charterer and redelivered by it at the end of the charter period. What is meant by this is that the ship is placed at the disposal of the charterer, in the sense that the time charterer can give voyage instructions to the owner as to where the ship is to go and what cargoes she is to carry, provided that the instructions are within the limits provided in the contract. In return the time charterer pays hire for the whole time that the ship is placed at its disposal and for the bunkers.

(a) For how long does the time charterer have the use of the ship?

It will be of immense significance to both parties to know how long the charterer has the ship at its disposal. As we have already seen the charterparty will no doubt provide the earliest date on which the charterer will become liable for time charter hire and contain an express cancellation clause entitling the charterer to cancel the charterparty without asking why the ship is late if it is not delivered ready by a specified time.[230]

---

225. See e.g. cl 9 of Gencon 1994.
226. *Cheikh Boutros Selim El-Khoury and Others v Ceylon Shipping Lines Ltd (The Madeleine)* [1967] 2 Lloyd's Rep 224.
227. *Georgian Maritime Corporation PLC v Sealand Industries (Bermuda) Ltd (The North Sea)* [1999] 1 Lloyd's Rep 21.
228. See page 170.
229. *The Baleares* [1993] 1 Lloyd's Rep 215. London Arbitration 13/02 LMLN 594; London Arbitration 12/96 LMLN 445; *The West Islands* LMLN 461; *The North Sea* [1999] 1 Lloyd's Rep 21; Inspection London Arbitration 8/97 LMLN 459.
230. See pages 153–154.

The charterer must redeliver the ship within the contractual period, failing which it will be in breach of charterparty and liable for damages. There is often some leeway as to when the ship must be redelivered as it is difficult for the charterer to predict exactly how long any particular voyage will take. Any number of factors may disrupt the best laid plans, for example, the weather or a strike. Therefore when fixing the length of the charter period the parties will often allow a degree of flexibility. For example, they may provide for a period of about six months; 12 months 15 days more or less in charterer's option; minimum four months maximum six months; "about 50 to maximum 70 days"[231] or for a trip time charter where the period of the charterparty is the length of time it takes to perform a particular trip.[232]

If the express terms of the charterparty do not provide any flexibility the courts will imply a margin of tolerance, unless the charterparty imposes an absolute obligation to redeliver the ship by a certain date.[233] Where the charterparty already provides for an express margin the courts will not extend the period further by adding an implied margin.[234] Thus in London Arbitration 12/02 LMLN 594 the charterparty in the NYPE form provided for a period of 11 to 14 months. The vessel was redelivered five days before the 11 months had expired. The arbitrators held that there was no implied margin allowing the charterer to redeliver before the 11 months had expired.

The parties may provide that the period is "without guarantee". In *The Lendoudis Evangelos II*[235] Longmore J held that where a time charter trip provided "duration about[236] 70/80 days without guarantee" the charterer was only under an obligation to make the estimate of the duration of the trip in good faith and not on a reasonable basis. The trip took over 103 days. The arbitrator found that, as the owner had alleged, the charterer made the estimate negligently, but it was never alleged that the charterer did not have a genuine belief in the estimate and therefore it was not liable.

Sometimes the charterparty gives an express right to the charterer to add any periods of off hire to the charter period.[237] In *The Kriti Akti*[238] the Court of Appeal had to consider how to calculate the final terminal date where the charter was "for a period of 11 (eleven) months, 15 days more or less in Charterers' option" and the charterer had an option to extend the charter period by any period of off hire. It held that a final voyage was legitimate which would finish within 11 months plus any off hire period plus 15 days.

When the charterer will wish to redeliver the ship is often dictated by what the market is doing. Obviously if the market has risen sharply the charterer would be wise to keep the ship until the latest possible date permitted under the charterparty (the "final terminal date"), as the charterparty rate of hire is lower than the rate the charterer would have to pay for another ship. On the other hand, if the market has fallen, the charterer will wish to redeliver the ship as early

---

231. *Torvald Klaveness A/S v Arni Maritime Corporation (The Gregos)* [1995] 1 Lloyd's Rep 1, where the arbitrator held that "maximum 70 days" did not allow for a margin.

232. *SBT Star Bulk and Tankers (Germany) GmbH Co KG v Cosmotrade SA (The Wehr Trave)* [2016] EWHC 583 (Comm); [2016] 2 Lloyd's Rep 170 where Eder J held that it was a question of construction of the terms of the charterparty as to whether the charterers were entitled to order the owners to load another cargo under a trip time charterparty.

233. *Alma Shipping Corp of Monrovia v Mantovani (The Dione)* [1975] 1 Lloyd's Rep 115 (CA).

234. Ibid. *Mareva Navigation Co v Canaria Armadora SA (The Mareva AS)* [1977] 1 Lloyd's Rep 368 and *Arta Shipping Co Ltd v Thai Europe Tapioca Shipping Service Ltd (The Johnny)* [1977] 2 Lloyd's Rep 1 (CA).

235. *Continental Pacific Shipping Ltd v Deemand Shipping Co Ltd (The Lendoudis Evangelos II)* [1997] 1 Lloyd's Rep 404. London Arbitration 5/97 LMLN 458.

236. The arbitrator gave a tolerance of 10 per cent for the word "about", namely eight days.

237. See e.g.clause 52(c) of the NYPE 2015. See page 143.

238. *Petroleo Brasileiro SA v Kriti Akti Shipping Co SA (The Kriti Akti)* [2004] EWCA Civ 116; [2004] 1 Lloyd's Rep 712.

as it is contractually entitled to (the "earliest terminal date"), so that it can charter in another ship at the lower market rate.

The charterparty is likely to have an express obligation on the charterer to give a notice of when and where the ship will be redelivered,[239] in good time before the ship is redelivered to the owner, so that the owner has an opportunity to find employment for the ship at the end of her current charterparty. In *IMT Shipping and Chartering GmbH v Chansung Shipping Company Limited (The Zenovia)*[240] Tomlinson J had to consider whether, after giving a notice of redelivery, the charterer is entitled to change the date of redelivery to a new date which is still within the contractual range of redelivery. Three back to back charters all provided for redelivery "minimum 20 September 2007/maximum 22 November 2007" and each provided,

hire to continue until the day of her redelivery . . . on dropping last outward sea pilot one safe port ADEN/ JAPAN range . . . charterers are to give Owners not less than 30 days followed by 20/15/10/7 days notice of approximate redelivery date and intended port thereafter 5/3/2/1 days definite notice of redelivery date and port.

On 5 October charterers gave "approximate notice of redelivery for the MV Zenovia at DLOSP 1 sp China on about 04 Nov 2007 basis agw [all going well], wp [without prejudice], wog [without guarantee], uce [unforeseen circumstances excepted]". On 15 October they revised the date of redelivery to "abt Nov 20th within the range of redelivery". The owners withdrew the vessel on 2 November. Tomlinson J held that the owners were not entitled to do so. There was no implied term that the charterers would not do anything inconsistent with redelivery on 4 November and no promissory estoppel.

(i) Early redelivery

If the ship is redelivered prior to the earliest terminal date, the charterer is in breach and is liable for damages. The purpose of damages is to compensate the victim of the breach for the loss of its contractual bargain and the shipowner is therefore entitled to be put in the position that it would have been in had the contract been performed.[241]

Where there is an available market the damages are calculated by reference to the difference between the contract rate that would have been earned for the balance of the charter period and the market rate which would have been available to the owners had they entered the market on termination to find a substitute fixture of similar length to the balance of the charter period[242] and for similar routes.[243]

The market price in an available market at the date of termination is deemed by the law to represent reasonable mitigation.[244] In *Star Reefers Pool Inc v JFC Group Co Ltd*[245] there was an available market and the owners did not have to bring into account the fact that since repudiation the vessel had been traded on the spot market at a better rate of hire. Nor would the fact that the

239. In *Maestro Bulk Ltd v Cosco Bulk Carrier Co Ltd (The Great Creation)* [2014] EWHC 3987 (Comm); [2015] 1 Lloyd's Rep 315 damages for breach of the obligation to give a notice of redelivery were considered.

240. [2009] EWHC 739 (Comm); [2009] 2 All ER (Comm) 177.

241. *Golden Strait Corporation v Nippon Yusen Kubishka Kaisha (The Golden Victory)* [2007] UKHL 12; [2007] 2 Lloyd's Rep 164 applied in *Flame SA v Glory Wealth Shipping Pte Ltd (The Glory Wealth)* EWHC 3153 (Comm); [2013] 2 Lloyd's Rep 653.

242. *Koch Marine Inc v d'Amica Societa di Navigazione arl (The Elena D'Amico)* [1980] 1 Lloyd's Rep 85, at p 89.

243. *Zodiac Maritime Agencies Limited v Fortescue Metals Group Limited (The Kildare)* [2010] EWHC 903 (Comm); [2011] 2 Lloyd's Rep 360 discussed below.

244. *Glory Wealth Shipping Pte Ltd v Korea Line Corporation (The Wren)* [2011] EWHC 1819 (Comm); [2012] 1 All ER (Comm) 402; [2011] 2 Lloyd's Rep 370 discussed below and *Star Reefers Pool Inc v JFC Group Co Ltd* [2011] EWHC 2204 (Comm).

245. [2011] EWHC 2204 (Comm), [184] – [189].

owners had subsequently sold the vessels be relevant as the damages had been crystallised "by assessing the rate at which the Claimants could have chartered out the vessels after termination of the charterparties and crediting that against the charter rates which they had lost".[246]

Damages for early redelivery were considered by the House of Lords in *The Golden Victory*.[247] The owner chartered its ship for seven years with one month more or less in charterer's option. In repudiatory breach the charterer redelivered the ship almost four years too early. The charterparty gave the charterer a right to cancel the charterparty if war broke out between any two or more of a number of countries including the United States, the United Kingdom and Iraq. The second Gulf War began some 14 months after the charterer's repudiation and some 32 months before the charterparty would have expired. There was at the time of the repudiation an available market for the charter of ships such as the *Golden Victory*. The arbitrator found that at the time of the acceptance of the repudiation a reasonably well-informed person would have considered war between the United States, the United Kingdom and Iraq "merely a possibility" but not "inevitable or even probable"; and that the charterer would have exercised the right to cancel had the ship remained on charter to it at the outbreak of the second Gulf War. A majority of the House of Lords[248] held that the owner could only recover damages until the outbreak of the war. The principle applicable to time charters was that the innocent party should be placed, so far as damages could achieve it, in the position it would have been in had the contract been performed. If the contract would have terminated early on the occurrence of a particular event, the chance of that event happening had to be taken into account. If it was certain that the event would happen, the damages had to be assessed on that footing. They did not therefore apply the general rule that damages for breach of contract were to be assessed as at the date of breach, as that rule could be subject to another date where that more accurately reflected the overriding compensatory rule.

In *Miranos International Trading Inc v Voc Steel Services BV*[249] Cooke J held that where a time charter trip provided that "The charterers guarantee a minimum 35 days' duration", and the charterer redelivered earlier than 35 days, the arbitrator's decision that the owner was entitled to hire for 35 days without giving credit for any benefit it received from the use of the ship between the actual and charter redelivery dates was wrong. The guarantee of minimum duration cannot amount to a guarantee of remuneration. The breach of the guarantee is the same as a breach of warranty that the charter voyage would be of a certain length and the relief to be granted in respect of such a breach is damages. Where the owner was able to earn the freight under its next fixture one-and-a-half days earlier than it would have done had the ship been delivered on time, the arbitrator must find as to the owner's loss by reference to market rate or to normal and direct loss, if there is no such rate.

In the autumn of 2008 the shipping market collapsed. As a result the issue of damages where a charterer repudiates a time charter has been considered in a number of recent cases where there was no available market, or no available market and then a recovering market.

In *Zodiac Maritime Agencies Limited v Fortescue Metals Group Limited (The Kildare)*[250] Steel J held that a Consecutive Voyage charterparty dated 5 December 2007 for five years to

---

246. *Rimpacific Navigation Inc v Daehan Shipbuilding Co* [2011] EWHC 2618 (Comm), per Teare J at [26]. Compare *Fulton Shipping Inc of Panama v Globalia Business Travel SAU (formerly Travelplan SAU) of Spain (The New Flamenco)* [2015] EWCA Civ 1299; [2016] 1 Lloyd's Rep 383 under appeal where there was no available market and the sale of the ship was taken into account – see pages 160–161.

247. *Golden Strait Corporation v Nippon Yusen Kubishka Kaisha (The Golden Victory)* [2007] UKHL 12; [2007] 2 Lloyd's Rep 164. See also *Dalwood Marine Co v Nordana Line A/S* [2009] EWHC 3394 (Comm); [2010] 2 All ER (Comm) 802 on the measure of damages for repudiation.

248. Lord Scott, Lord Carswell and Lord Brown; Lord Bingham and Lord Walker dissenting.

249. [2005] EWHC 1812 (Comm).

250. [2010] EWHC 903 (Comm); [2011] 2 Lloyd's Rep 360.

carry iron ore from Australia to China had been repudiated by charterers on 9 January 2009 with some four-and-a-half years to run. Expert shipbrokers gave evidence on quantum. Steel J regarded as realistic the charterers' concession that the evidence of the owners' expert that the non-trading period of the vessel during the balance of the charterparty was ten days per annum to allow for heavy weather, dry docking, breakdown and port delays.[251] The parties disputed whether there was an available market at or shortly after the contract was terminated. Steel J held that there was no available market for a four-and-a-half-year consecutive voyage or time charter for broadly the same trading limits (i.e. Western Australia/China). There was no match of supply and demand for charters of this length. It was common ground that an available market later emerged in February 2010 for a three- to three-and-a-half-year charter. The owners argued that where such an available market emerged at a later date, damages for the remaining period should be assessed by reference to the available market. That argument was rejected and Steel J stated:

> It is simply a matter of chance when the vessel completes any spot voyages after the termination date. Indeed they may overrun the emergence of an available market. In short I see no basis for requiring the owner to go back into the term market at the end of every spot voyage or for that matter to disregard short time charters in case the market for longer charters emerges in the meantime.[252]

Where the charterparty is wrongfully terminated by charterers and there is no available market then the court must assess the owners' actual loss by reference to the difference between what the owner would have earned had the charter been performed and the actual position resulting from breach. In *The Kildare* the owners were able to nominate the vessel under a different charter to Guofeng which had been concluded before the *Kildare* charterparty. The judge concluded that it was probable that the *Kildare* would continue to perform under the Guofeng charter until after the expiry date of the *Kildare* charter.[253] The issue was whether the earnings from the Guofeng charter should be taken into account in assessing the owners' loss or whether the relevant earnings would be those available on the market. He found that the cause of the renegotiation of the Guofeng charter was the termination of the *Kildare* charter and therefore it should be taken into account. Finally an allowance of 1.5 per cent was given for accelerated receipt of income reflecting the three-year yield in US Treasury bonds. As stated above an allowance had already been made for downtime. A further discount of 1.5 per cent was made to reflect "more catastrophic contingencies such as total loss, bankruptcy and so on".[254] Applying these findings the owners' damages were likely to be in the region of US$80–85 million.

Although Blair J agreed with the decision in *The Kildare* in *Glory Wealth Shipping Pte Ltd v Korea Line Corporation (The Wren)*,[255] he considered that the reviving market was relevant to mitigation. In that case a charterparty was concluded on 22 February 2008 of a new build for minimum 36 months to maximum 38 months at a daily rate of US$39,800. The vessel was delivered on 21 June 2008 but charterers redelivered her in November 2008 and owners accepted charterers' repudiatory breach as entitling them to terminate the charterparty. At the date of termination there was no available market. Owners claimed damages on a "hybrid basis" by reference first to losses on substitute fixtures in the spot market up to July 2009 and then by reference to market rates for the balance of the charter period from that time, when owners argued

---

251. See also *Star Reefers Pool Inc v JFC Group Co Ltd* [2011] EWHC 2204 (Comm).
252. [66].
253. [69].
254. [73].
255. [2011] EWHC 1819 (Comm); [2012] 1 All ER (Comm) 402.

the market for the equivalent of the unexpired period of the charter had revived. The charterers argued that the market had not revived. The owners did not in fact fix the vessel on a long-term charter at that time but continued to fix her on the spot market. The arbitrators found that there was an available market for a two-year charter at US$15,200 per day, although the market was fragile, and used this rate from July onwards. The charterers argued that "to ask when the market for period charters has revived and then to deem the owners to have entered that market, is almost bound to generate a windfall. Such an approach locks in an artificially low rate, in other words the rate at which the market begins to recover, thereby ensuring maximum damages for the owners."[256]

Owners, however, argued that ignoring the market rate when it revived would postpone the calculation of owners' damages until the end of the repudiated charter period. Blair J agreed with the views of Steel J in *The Kildare* and held that the damages where there was no market at the date of termination and it only later revived, were to be assessed by reference to the actual loss of the owner.[257] The rules as to mitigation would apply and the revival of the market would be relevant to mitigation. The revival of the market might also be a factor in calculating future loss if damages fall to be assessed before the end of the contractual period, even though it does not in itself provide the correct measure of damages.[258]

Usually where a charterparty is wrongfully terminated by charterers the owners' loss is measured by calculating what the owners would have received under the charterparty for the remaining days of that charterparty and deducting what the owners in fact earned during that period. Where the owner has obtained a substitute charterparty the earnings under that charterparty will usually be taken into account up to the date when the original charterparty would have ended had it not been wrongfully terminated. Frequently the substitute charterparty lasts longer than this date and the question then arises whether those earnings should also be taken into account. The general position is that they would not be, unless the owners have obtained a benefit as a result of the longer duration of the substitute voyage.[259] "Otherwise one would be involved in calculations to the end of the ship's working life."[260]

In *Dalwood Marine Co v Nordana Line A/S (The Elbrus)*[261] it was found that a benefit was conferred on the owners by the substitute charterparty and that the latter did have to account for such benefit. On 4 April 2005 the charterers wrongfully terminated the time charterparty of the *Elbrus* while the vessel was at Lobito, Angola. But for that repudiation the vessel would have been employed under the charterparty for some 39 days until redelivery at Houston on 13 May 2005. The owners had already fixed the vessel to Navimed before the charterers' wrongful repudiation at a "good hire rate" of US$18,100 per day (as opposed to US$10,800 per day under her repudiated charter) with a laycan of 1–20 May 2005. She had to be drydocked before she could be delivered to Navimed. Had the charterparty not been repudiated the vessel would have dry-docked in Portugal and would have missed her laycan under the Navimed fixture. There was a possibility that Navimed would not have agreed to an extension of the cancelling date because market rates in the Mediterranean had softened. When the charterers wrongfully terminated the charterparty there was no available market for the *Elbrus* off the West coast of Africa. Therefore the owners drydocked the vessel early thus ensuring that they could meet the

256. [13].
257. [31].
258. [31].
259. *The Concordia C* [1985] 2 Lloyd's Rep 55, at p 58 and *The Noel Bay* [1989] 1 Lloyd's Rep 361.
260. *The Noel Bay* [1989] 1 Lloyd's Rep 361, at p 363 per Staughton LJ.
261. [2009] EWHC 3394 (Comm); [2010] 2 All ER (Comm) 802. See also *Zodiac Maritime Agencies Limited v Fortescue Metals Group Limited (The Kildare)* [2010] EWHC 903 (Comm); [2011] 2 Lloyd's Rep 360.

Navimed laycan. The arbitrators found that the owners acted reasonably and went on to find that the owners did not lose as a result of the early termination but made a gain. They found that the owners would not have been able to deliver the vessel to Navimed, had the charter not been prematurely terminated, until 13 June or 10 July 2005. As a result of the premature termination the owners were able to earn the higher rate under the Navimed charter earlier from 6 May than they would have done had the charterparty been contractually terminated. The arbitrators did not compare the notional and actual earnings of the vessel from 4 April until 13 May 2005, the date when the original charterparty would have ended, but compared the notional and actual earnings of the vessel from 4 April until the date when the vessel would have been delivered to Navimed, either 13 June or 10 July 2005. The owners appealed from that decision. The normal measure of damages for early redelivery under a time charter is the hire which would have been earned under the contract and the hire which was in fact earned during that period from such alternative employment as the owners were able to secure. That prima facie measure reflects at least two matters. First the duty of the owner to mitigate its loss by finding alternative employment for its vessel. Second by assessing the value of the benefit obtained from mitigation by reference to the hire received during the period ending with the date on which the original charterparty would have ended, it recognises the difficulty of assessing that benefit over any longer period which, if there were to be a complete assessment of that benefit, would entail a calculation over the whole of the vessel's working life.[262] Teare J held that the arbitration award should be read as a finding that the owners had secured a benefit from their action to mitigate their loss in addition to the earning of hire from 6 to 13 May 2005, as they were able to earn under the Navimed fixture earlier and they ensured that they did not lose the Navimed fixture. Depending on the nature of the benefit and the approach taken to valuation it may be necessary to take into account earnings after the notional date of redelivery. Whether a particular benefit has been established on the evidence and the assessment of the value of that benefit is a matter for the tribunal to determine as a fact. The arbitration tribunal had found that the benefit was established on the evidence before it and the court had to accept the facts as found by the tribunal.

In *Glory Wealth Shipping Pte Limited v North China Shipping Limited (The North Prince)*[263] sub-charterers wrongfully redelivered a ship early to the time charterers on 16 November 2007 when the charterparty provided for "minimum 27 June 2009". The arbitration tribunal awarded damages representing the difference between the contract rate until 27 June 2009 and the actual earning potential on the market as from 5 January, the date on which the sub-charterers' repudiation had been accepted and 27 June 2009. In fact the time charterers redelivered the vessel to the owners on 5 June 2009 and therefore the sub-charterers on appeal argued that this should be taken into account. Steel J dismissed the appeal.

In *Fulton Shipping Inc of Panama v Globalia Business Travel SAU (formerly Travelplan SAU) of Spain (The New Flamenco)*[264] the owners treated the charterers as in anticipatory breach of contract as they had disputed an agreement extending the charterparty by two years and redelivered the vessel early. The owners accepted the charterers' breach as terminating the charterparty. There was no available chartering market on redelivery. The owners sold the vessel for US$23.7 million. There was a significant difference between the value of the vessel when it was sold and the value it would have had at the end of the charterparty had the charterers performed it. Following the global financial crisis, the value on redelivery would have been US$7 million.

---

262. [32].
263. [2010] EWHC 1692 (Comm); [2011] 1 All ER (Comm) 641.
264. [2015] EWCA Civ 1299; [2016] 1 Lloyd's Rep 383 under appeal. See also *Louis Dreyfus Commodities Suisse SA v MT Maritime Management BV (The MTM Hong Kong)* [2015] EWHC 2505 (Comm); [2016] 1 Lloyd's Rep 197 (voyage charterparty).

The owners claimed damages for loss of profits during the additional two year charterparty. The charterers argued that credit should be given for the difference in value of the sale. The arbitrator agreed but the judge at first instance did not. The Court of Appeal held that the arbitrator was correct.

Another problem is where the vessel may have been better or worse placed for future employment at the end of the substitute voyage rather than at the end of the original charter had it been performed.[265]

(ii) Late redelivery

If the charterer gives instructions to the shipowner for a final voyage which may reasonably be expected to result in redelivery by the final terminal date, this is a legitimate final voyage order and the owner must comply with it. In *The Gregos*[266] the House of Lords held that the legitimacy of the order must be judged not at the time the order is given but at the time for performance. In that case the charterer ordered the ship to proceed from Matanzas to Palua and load a cargo of iron ore for carriage to Italy. At the time the order was given, before the completion of her penultimate voyage, compliance with the order could reasonably have been anticipated to allow redelivery by the final terminal date. However, by the time the *Gregos* completed discharge at Matanzas another ship had grounded in the River Orinoco and was obstructing the navigable channel between Palua and the river mouth. Redelivery would have been two to four days late. The charterer was not entitled to insist on the voyage. This decision can make life difficult for the time charterer. It will wish to fix a cargo in good time before the ship completes her current voyage and not wait until the time for performance of the last voyage with the risk of the ship being unemployed. However, the time charterer takes all the risk of events delaying the anticipated final voyage between the time the last voyage order is given and the time for performance of that order.

If the charterer gives instructions for a voyage which cannot reasonably be expected to be completed by the final terminal date, the owner is entitled to refuse such instructions. The owner cannot at this point elect to terminate the charterparty but must ask for valid voyage instructions. Only if the charterer fails to give valid voyage instructions will it be in repudiatory breach of charterparty and the owner could then elect to terminate or affirm the charterparty. Lord Mustill (with whom three other Law Lords agreed) held in *The Gregos* that the issuing of an invalid order, for example, for an illegitimate last voyage is not an automatic ground of discharge.[267] Lord Mustill saw it as depending "not on the invalid order which was given, but on the valid order which was not".[268] The original order given by the charterer had become ineffectual as at the time for performance it was no longer possible to perform the voyage and redeliver by the final terminal date. The charterer was therefore obliged to replace the original order with one which it was entitled to give. The persistence by the charterer in the order after it had become invalid showed that it did not intend to perform the obligations under the contract. This was an anticipatory breach of contract and the owner was entitled to elect to terminate the contract.

In *The Gregos* it was not necessary to express a firm conclusion as to the nature of the charterer's obligation to redeliver on time. However, Lord Mustill (with whom three other Law Lords agreed) inclined to the view that it was an innominate term and that a short delay in redelivery

265. See Staughton LJ in *The Noel Bay* [1989] 1 Lloyd's Rep 361 at p 363.
266. *The Gregos* [1995] 1 Lloyd's Rep 1. See also B. Davenport and M. White, "Last Voyage Orders: Again (*The Gregos*)" [1994] LMCLQ 154.
267. Ibid., p 9.
268. Ibid., p 9.

would not justify the termination of the contract.[269] In practice if there is a cargo on board at the final terminal date the owner would probably not wish to elect to terminate the charterparty as the owner will still have obligations to deliver the cargo under the bill of lading or in tort or in bailment.[270]

Whether or not the order was legitimate, if the owner performs it and the ship is redelivered after the final terminal date, the charterer is in breach of charterparty, even though the delay was not due to any fault on its part. The owner is entitled to damages for the period between the final terminal date and redelivery (the "period of overlap") at the charterparty rate or the market rate, whichever is the higher.[271] In *Transfield Shipping Inc v Mercator Shipping Inc (The Achilleas)*[272] the House of Lords considered the damages that the owner can recover if the ship is redelivered late. There a vessel was redelivered nine days late. The owner had fixed its next charterparty for about four to six months at a rate of US$39,500 per day. When it realised that the *Achilleas* was going to be redelivered late, it obtained an extension of the cancelling date under its next fixture but, due to the volatile market, at a reduced charter rate of US$31,500 per day, as the market had in the meantime fallen. The owner claimed damages of US$1,364,584.37 representing $8,000 per day for the period of its next fixture less the additional sums earned by reason of the late redelivery. The Court of Appeal held[273] that the owner was entitled to that sum and not simply to the difference between the market rate and the charter rate during the period of overlap. The House of Lords, reversing the judgments of the Court of Appeal and Christopher Clarke J held that the owner was not entitled to that sum but only to the difference between the market rate and the charter rate during the period of overlap.

The parties may insert a clause in the charterparty to seek to overcome the decision in *The Achilleas*, but they must be careful that it is not a penalty and therefore unenforceable. In *Lansat Shipping Co Ltd v Glencore Grain BV (The Paragon)*,[274] it had not been determined whether the final voyage, which took 77 days, was illegitimate or not. The vessel was redelivered 6.166 days late. There was a preliminary issue as to whether the following clause was a penalty:

The Charterers hereby undertake the obligation/responsibility to make thorough investigations and every arrangement in order to ensure that the last voyage of this Charter will in no way exceed the maximum period under this Charter Party. If, however, Charterers fail to comply with this obligation and the last voyage will exceed the maximum period, should the market rise above the Charter Party rate in the meantime, it is hereby agreed that the charter hire will be adjusted to reflect the prevailing market level from the 30th day prior to the maximum period [d]ate until actual redelivery of the vessel to the Owners.

The Court of Appeal upheld the decision of Blair J who held that it was a penalty and therefore unenforceable. The owners are entitled to the normal measure of damages for late delivery,

---

269. Ibid., p 9. Contrast the view of Lord Templeman, at p 3, who held that the time for redelivery is of the essence.

270. See pages 189–190 of Chapter 5.

271. *Hyundai Merchant Marine Co Ltd v Gesuri Chartering Co Ltd (The Peonia)* [1991] 1 Lloyd's Rep 100 (legitimate final voyage).

272. [2008] UKHL 48; [2008] 2 Lloyd's Rep 275. Contrast *Sylvia Shipping Co Limited v Progress Bulk Carriers Limited (The Sylvia)* [2010] EWHC 542 (Comm); [2010] 2 Lloyd's Rep 81 where the owners were in breach of their obligation to exercise due diligence and maintenance. As a result the time charterers' sub-charterers cancelled the sub-charterparty under an express cancellation clause. The time charterers were entitled to recover the profits they would have made under the sub-charter. *The Sylvia* was applied in *Ispat Industries Ltd v Western Bulk Pte Ltd* [2011] EWHC 93 (Comm).

273. [2007] EWCA Civ 901; [2007] 2 Lloyd's Rep 555.

274. [2009] EWCA Civ 855; [2010] 1 All ER (Comm) 459; [2009] 2 Lloyd's Rep 688; EWHC 551 (Comm); [2009] 1 Lloyd's Rep 658. See now on penalty clauses in general *Makdessi v Cavendish Square Holdings BV* [2015] UKSC 67; [2016] AC 1172.

which is the market rate for the period between the last permissible date for redelivery and the date of actual redelivery. The first sentence of the above clause was not a condition.

The parties may include an express clause entitling the charterer to complete any last voyage even if it runs beyond the final terminal date without being liable for damages and only paying hire at the charterparty rate until the actual date of redelivery, unless the delay in completion was due to the charterer's breach of some other term.[275] Thus in *The Peonia*[276] a provision that "Charterers have further option to complete last voyage" was held to give the charterers the right to complete a legitimate last voyage without any liability for damages for the period of overlap. The clause would not have entitled the charterer to order the ship to perform an illegitimate last voyage. By contrast in *The World Symphony*[277] the Court of Appeal held that the crucial addition of the wording at the beginning of clause 18 of the Shelltime 3 form that it was "notwithstanding" the charter period meant that it overrode the charter period and the charterer could give an order for a voyage which would not enable the ship to be redelivered by the final terminal date and pay at the charter rate until she was redelivered.

(b) The charterer's obligation to pay hire

The time charterer agrees to pay hire for every minute that the ship is at the charterer's disposal from her delivery until redelivery. The hire is usually stipulated at a daily rate and payable in advance.[278] It is of great importance to the owner in financing the operation of its ship to receive the hire on time and for the right amount. The shipowner will need to meet outgoings such as any principal and interest due under any loan which it took out to finance the purchase of the ship,[279] insurance premiums and P&I Club calls,[280] maintenance and crew wages. There may be grave consequences for the owner if it cannot meet those outgoings on time. For example, if the owner fails to pay the principal and interest due to its bank on any loan it has taken out to buy the ship, the bank might have the right to sell the ship. In order to encourage the charterer to comply with the obligation to pay hire promptly, the standard form time charterparties give the owner an express right to withdraw the ship, i.e. to terminate the charterparty if the hire is not paid. This section will consider the owner's right of withdrawal; the special typed clauses which are frequently inserted to give the charterer some measure of protection known as anti-technicality clauses; off hire clauses and the charterer's limited right to make deductions from hire.

A time charterparty will typically provide that the charterer must pay the hire "in cash"[281] by the due date. "Cash" includes inter-bank transfers with the correct value date and bankers drafts.[282] Time charter hire will usually be paid by an inter-bank transfer and the money must be in the account of the owner designated in the charterparty value the due date. If the due date

---

275. *Hyundai Merchant Marine Co v Gesuri Chartering Co (The Peonia)* [1991] 1 Lloyd's Rep 100 (CA) and *Marimpex Mineraloel-Handelsgesellschaft GmbH & Co KB v Compagnie de Gestion et d'exploitation Ltd (The Ambor and The Once)* [2001] 1 All ER (Comm) 182. Compare cl 52(a) of NYPE 2015.

276. *Hyundai Merchant Marine Co Ltd v Gesuri Chartering Co Ltd (The Peonia)* [1991] 1 Lloyd's Rep 100 (legitimate final voyage).

277. *The World Symphony and the World Renown* [1992] 2 Lloyd's Rep 115 (CA), applied in *Petroleo Brasileiro SA v Kriti Akti Shipping Co SA (The Kriti Akti)* [2004] EWCA Civ 116; [2004] 1 Lloyd's Rep 712.

278. cls 4 and 5 NYPE 1946, cl 11(a) of NYPE 2015 and cl 6 Baltime 1939.

279. The bank will usually have taken an assignment of the hire as security for the loan. See page 97.

280. The bank will require the owner to have insurance under the loan agreement and will usually take an assignment of the insurance proceeds as security for the loan. See page 97.

281. Cl 5 NYPE 1946 form and cl 6 Baltime 1939.

282. *The Chikuma* [1981] 1 Lloyd's Rep 371.

falls on a weekend or a bank holiday the charterer must make sure that the hire is paid on the last banking day before the due date.[283]

(c) Withdrawal

If the hire is not paid by the due date, or too little hire is paid by that date, most standard form charterparties provide that the owner has the right to withdraw the ship. This means that the charterparty is terminated, i.e. that both parties are released from future performance of their obligations under the charterparty. It is important to include such a clause as at common law the time for payment of hire is not a condition (or not of the essence) of the contract, unless expressly stated to be so. Thus late payment of hire would not entitle the owner to terminate the charterparty and claim damages for the loss of its bargain, unless the late payment constituted a repudiatory breach by the charterer because, for example, the charterer had evinced an intention not to perform and had said that it would not pay or could not pay. In the recent decision of *Spar Shipping AS v Grand China Logistics Holding (Group) Co Ltd*[284] the Court of Appeal upheld the decision of Popplewell J at first instance[285] that as the obligation to pay hire was not a condition but an innominate term, all the withdrawal clause gave the owner was a contractual right to terminate the charterparty but not a right to claim damages for the loss of hire for the balance of the charterparty. This would not matter if the market were going up as the owner would probably not suffer any loss, but could be serious for the owner if the market were falling as it could suffer a significant loss. In *Spar Shipping* the owner of three supramax bulk carriers, *Spar Capella*, *Spar Vega* and *Spar Draco* chartered the ships to Grand China Shipping (Hong Kong) Co Ltd (GCS). The charterparties provided for guarantees by Grand China Logistics Holding (Group) Co Ltd (GCL). The *Spar Draco* was chartered for minimum 35 maximum 37 months in charterer's option with hire of US\$ 16,500 per day payable semi-monthly in advance. She was delivered on 31 May 2010. The *Spar Capella* and *Spar Vega* were new builds and were delivered under the charterparties from a Chinese yard on 6 and 12 January 2011. Those charterparties were for minimum 59 maximum 62 months in charterers' option, with hire of US\$16,750 per day payable semi-monthly in advance. Clause 11 of all three charterparties provided for a withdrawal clause and anti-technicality clause.[286] The Court of Appeal overruled the decision of Flaux J in *Kuwait Rocks Co v AMN Bulkcarriers Inc (The Astra)*[287] on the issue as to whether the obligation to pay hire was a condition. Gross LJ stated:

Pulling the threads together, for both historical and analytical reasons, I was not persuaded that the inclusion of the express withdrawal clause provided a strong or any indication that cl. 11 of the charterparties was a condition. As a matter of contractual construction, the charterparties did not make it clear that cl. 11 was to be categorised as a condition. Considerations of certainty, most important though they are, did not sway me from this conclusion, in particular given the significant certainty achieved by cl. 11 as a contractual termination option, *simpliciter* and the fact that breaches of cl. 11 could range from the trivial to the grave; greater certainty would be achieved by categorising cl. 11 as a condition but at a cost of disproportionate consequences flowing from trivial breaches – in my view, an unsatisfactory balance. I sense that market reaction is generally supportive of the decision of the Judge on Issue I in this case and view it as reassuring. I do not regard as significant the arguments advanced on the basis of a general presumption as to time being of the essence in mercantile contracts or those which relied on the anti-technicality clause.

283. *The Laconia* [1977] 1 Lloyd's Rep 315.
284. [2016] EWCA Civ 982; [2016] 2 Lloyd's Rep 447.
285. [2015] EWHC 718 (Comm); [2015] 2 Lloyd's Rep 407.
286. See page 167 for discussion of the anti-technicality clause.
287. [2013] EWHC 865 (Comm); [2013] 2 All ER (Comm) 689.

For my part, I would reject Spar's arguments on Issue I and I would respectfully hold that *The Astra* was wrongly decided on this Issue.

However, both in *Spar Shipping AS v Grand China Logistics Holding (Group) Co Ltd* and *The Astra* the Court of Appeal and Flaux J respectively held that the charterers were in repudiatory breach of charterparty by failing to pay the time charter hire on time, with the result that the owner could elect to terminate the charterparty and claim damages. Popplewell J at first instance[288] in *Spar Shipping* summarised the facts at the dates of the withdrawal of the ships on 23 and 30 September 2011 as follows:

(1) GCS had regularly failed to pay hire punctually since mid-April 2011, a period of over five months. Almost all payments on all three Vessels were unpaid when they fell due. Some were not paid at all, others only months after they fell due. In those months, only in July were instalments paid on time or within a few days of falling due.
(2) For most of the period the arrears fluctuated between about US$1.5m and US$2.5m, and would have been up to US$1m more but for the exercise by Spar of its lien on sub-hire/sub-freights. If one takes a total of US$2m as a very rough average, this is broadly equivalent to about eight instalments over the three vessels; individually the arrears of hire for the Vessels fluctuated between about one and four instalments.
(3) GCS had made clear that non-payment was due to cash flow difficulties caused by the fall in the market which rendered it unable to meet its hire obligations to all the owners of its chartered fleet. Since June it had repeatedly said that it expected cash injection from its parent which would enable it to make punctual payments and pay off the arrears. Despite such indications it continued to fail to make punctual payments on all three Vessels. It twice promised to pay off half the arrears by 31 August but failed to do so.
(4) By the beginning of September GCS was emphasising its cash flow difficulties, providing no concrete payment proposal, and suggesting that it would merely pass on sub-hires when received, which in a market which had substantially fallen since the date of the charterparties was bound to amount to a significant shortfall on the hire due to Spar. It sought to excuse non payment of a SPAR DRACO instalment by saying that sub-charterers had not paid the sub-hire, suggesting that it would only (part) perform its hire obligations on each vessel if timeously paid the (insufficient) sub hire, an approach aptly described by Spar as hand to mouth.
(5) At no stage did GCS provide any detail of what amounts were expected to be received from its parent, or when; or of how any such receipts would be allocated amongst competing creditor shipowners. It provided no explanation as to why its avowed expectations were unfulfilled, or why it was unable to fulfil its promise to pay off half the arrears by the end of August.
(6) The only response from GCL to the request to fulfil its guarantee obligations was on 23 September 2011, when it indicated that the group was prioritising payment of bank interest over operational payments such as the hire due to Spar, and that 'financial support will come' in October. This gave no explanation of how much financial support would come in October or when in that month. It made no concrete proposal for discharge of the liabilities and belittled the amount outstanding as a "relatively small sum".

The contractual benefit Spar was intended to obtain from the charterparties was that the owner is entitled to the regular, periodical payment of hire as stipulated, in advance of performance, so long as the charterparty continues; hire is payable in advance to provide a fund from which the owner can meet the expenses of rendering the services they have undertaken to provide under the charterparty; the owner is not obliged to perform the services on credit; they do so only against advance payment. A reasonable owner in the position of Spar could have no, certainly no realistic, expectation that GCS would in the future pay hire punctually in advance. The

---

288. [2015] EWHC 718 (Comm); [2015] 2 Lloyd's Rep 407 [210].

prospective non-performance was such as to go to the root of the charterparties. Gross LJ, with whom Hamblen LJ and Sir Terence Etherton MR agreed, stated

> The GCS prospective non-performance would unilaterally convert a contract for *payment in advance* into a transaction for unsecured credit and without any provision for the payment of interest. The importance of the advance payment of hire in time charterparties has already been emphasised and need not be repeated. That any failure to pay a single instalment of hire punctually does not amount to a breach of *condition* (Issue I above) is one thing; an evinced intention not to pay hire punctually in the future is very different (as highlighted by Popplewell J, at [198]) and, in my judgment, goes to the root of the charterparties. Taken to their logical conclusion, Mr Coburn's submissions would mean that charterers could hold owners to the contracts by stating that all payments of hire would be made but late and in arrears – leaving owners obliged to accept this limping performance and attendant uncertainty. In my view, that is not the law, at least in this context. For the avoidance of doubt, whichever test is adopted the answer would be the same; thus I am satisfied that GCS's evinced intention would deprive Spar of "substantially the whole benefit" of the charterparties and, for that matter, that GCS would be seeking to hold Spar to an arrangement "radically different" from that which had been agreed (the test for frustration).[289]

He rejected the arithmetical comparison between the arrears of hire (even comprising a number of instalments of hire) and the total sums payable over the life of the charterparties as demonstrating that Spar would not be deprived of substantially the whole benefit of the charterparties.[290]

The NYPE 2015 form of charterparty expressly provides that if the charterer fails to pay the hire within the period of the anti-technicality notice the owner shall have the right to withdraw the ship and, if they do so, claim damages "for the loss of the remainder of the Charter Party".[291] This provision appears to make the obligation to pay the hire by the expiry of the anti technicality notice a condition.

Late payment by the charterer does not deprive the owner of its right to withdraw,[292] but the owner must then return the hire payment.

There is no right to withdraw temporarily[293] unless the contract so provides. If the contract does not so provide, this may place the owner in difficulties. If the hire falls due but is not paid and the ship is about to load a cargo, the owner would prefer not to load until it has been paid, although the Supreme Court has held that if the owner withdraws and there is cargo on board the charterer will be liable to pay for the time taken and the bunkers used under the express indemnity clause and in bailment.[294] Alternatively if a bill of lading is issued, the owner will be obliged to carry the cargo to the discharge port, whether or not the time charter hire has been paid. Even though the hire has not been paid the owner cannot refuse to load the cargo. It is all or nothing: the owner is entitled to withdraw or it must perform. There is no half way house. Therefore more modern charterparties may expressly allow the owner to withhold performance while awaiting payment of hire.[295]

---

289. [87(i)].
290. [87(iii)].
291. Cl 11(c) of NYPE 2015. See *Spar Shipping AS v Grand China Logistics Holding (Group) Co Ltd* [2016] EWCA Civ 982; [2016] 2 Lloyd's Rep 447, [39(v)].
292. See fn 283.
293. *The Mihalios Xilas* [1978] 2 Lloyd's Rep 186. London Arbitration 10/97 LMLN 460.
294. *ENE 1 Kos Limited v Petroleo Brasileiro SA (The Kos)* [2012] UKSC 17; [2012] 2 WLR 976; [2010] EWCA Civ 772; [2010] 2 Lloyd's Rep 409; [2010] 2 CLC 19; [2009] EWHC 1843; [2010] 1 Lloyd's Rep 87 discussed at pages 168–169.
295. See e.g. ll 153–158 of cl 11 of NYPE 1993 and cl 11(d) of NYPE 2015. See also cl 10(e)(4) of BIMCO Supplytime 89 form which permits the owners to suspend the service temporarily without giving an anti-technicality notice – *Greatship (India) Limited v Oceanografia SA de CV* [2012] EWHC 3468 (Comm); [2013] 1 All ER (Comm) 1244. In that case Gloster J considered that the wording of the revised cl 12(f) of BIMCO Supplytime 2005 form is unclear [40].

The right to withdraw must be exercised promptly. Otherwise the owner will waive its right to withdraw for that payment of hire.[296] Where the owner affirms the charterparty and then withdraws the vessel, the owner will be in repudiatory breach of charterparty, unless the charterers are in continuing repudiatory breach[297] or there is a later failure to pay the hire on time or for the correct amount when a new right to withdraw will arise.

The right to withdraw may in certain circumstances be a draconian remedy. In *The Scaptrade*[298] the charterer argued that there should be equitable relief from forfeiture, as is the case in a lease. The House of Lords distinguished a lease as the charterer, unlike the lessee of land, does not have possession of the ship and held that there is no equitable relief from forfeiture. The position is different under a demise charter where the charterer does have possession of the ship. In *More OG Romsdal Fylkesbatar AS v The demise charterers of the Ship Jotunheim*[299] Cooke J held that the court was in principle entitled to grant relief from forfeiture in the case of a demise charter, but that that was not an appropriate case for doing so.

As the withdrawal clause may operate very harshly against the charterer, especially where the failure to pay hire is not due to any fault on its part, but is due, for example, to a bank error in transmission of the hire as in *The Afovos*,[300] it is usual to include an anti-technicality clause to protect the charterer.[301] Such a clause requires the owner to give notice to the charterer when default has occurred so that the charterer has an opportunity to rectify any error. Unless the charterparty expressly provides a time by which payment must be made on the due date the charterer has the whole of the due date to pay the hire and therefore the owner can only give the anti-technicality notice the following day. If the owner gives the notice as soon as banking hours close on the due date, it will not have given a valid notice and were it then to withdraw the ship, the owner would be in repudiatory breach of charterparty.[302]

An anti-technicality notice must be in the form of a clear and unambiguous ultimatum that unless the hire overdue is paid within the specified period the owner will withdraw the ship.

In *The Li Hai*[303] the anti-technicality notice did not contain such an ultimatum and it was confusing as to what hire was outstanding. Therefore the owner was not entitled to withdraw the ship and was liable to the charterer for the difference between the market rate and the charter rate for the balance of the charter period.

Some anti-technicality clauses are very badly drafted as they only require the owner to give a notice in certain circumstances but it is difficult for the owner to determine whether such circumstances exist and whether a notice should be given.[304] Such a provision was considered

---

296. *More OG Romsdal Fylkesbatar AS v The demise charterers of the Ship Jotunheim* [2005] 1 Lloyd's Rep 181 and *Parbulk II A/S v Heritage Maritime SA (The Mahakam)* [2011] EWHC 2917 (Comm); [2012] 2 All ER (Comm) 418.

297. *White Rosebay Shipping SA v Hong Kong Chain Glory Shipping Limited (The Fortune Plum)* [2013] EWHC 1355 (Comm); [2013] 2 All ER (Comm) 449; *Primera Maritime (Hellas) Ltd v Jiangsu Eastern Heavy Industry Co Ltd* [2013] EWHC 3066 (Comm); [2014] 1 Lloyd's Rep 255.

298. *Scandinavian Trading Tanker Co AB v Flota Petrolera Ecuatoriana (The Scaptrade)* [1983] 2 Lloyd's Rep 253.

299. [2005] 1 Lloyd's Rep 181. Cf. *Celestial Aviation Trading 71 Ltd v Paramount Airways Private Ltd* [2010] EWHC 185 (Comm); [2011] 1 All ER (Comm) 259, an aviation case.

300. *Afovos Shipping Co SA v R Pagnan & Fratelli (The Afovos)* [1983] 1 Lloyd's Rep 335.

301. See e.g. cl 11(b) NYPE 1993, cl 11(b) and cl 9(a) Shelltime 4. However, there is not always such a clause – see e.g. *ENE 1 Kos Limited v Petroleo Brasileiro SA (The Kos)* [2012] UKSC 17; [2012] 2 WLR 976; [2010] EWCA Civ 772; [2010] 2 Lloyd's Rep 409; [2009] EWHC 1843; [2010] 1 Lloyd's Rep 87, [4].

302. *The Afovos* [1983] 1 Lloyd's Rep 335, but see also *Schelde Delta Shipping BV v Astarte Shipping Ltd (The Pamela)* [1995] 2 Lloyd's Rep 249 and London Arbitration 3/01 LMLN 555.

303. *Western Bulk Carriers K/S v Li Hai Maritime Inc (The Li Hai)* [2005] EWHC 735 (Comm); [2005] 2 Lloyd's Rep 389 and *Schelde Delta Shipping BV v Astarte Shipping Ltd (The Pamela)* [1995] 2 Lloyd's Rep 249.

304. Cl 11(b) of the NYPE 2015 form avoids such problems by requiring a notice "Where there is failure to make punctual payment of hire due." Thus a notice must be given whatever the reason for the late payment of the hire.

in *Owneast Shipping Ltd v Qatar Navigation QSC*[305] and was described as "deeply unsatisfactory"[306] by the arbitration tribunal and Christopher Clarke J. Clause 61 of an amended NYPE form of charter provided:

where there is any failure to make "punctual and regular payment" due to errors or omission of Charterers' employees, bankers or Agents or otherwise for any reason where there is absence of intention to fail to make payment as set out, Charterers shall be given by owners 3 banking days notice to rectify the failure and where so rectified the payment shall stand as punctual and regular payment.

Christopher Clarke J upheld the decision of the majority of arbitrators that "intention" could not be extended to include recklessness. Where the majority of arbitrators had concluded that this was a case of severe incompetence but not intentional non-payment, a notice was required. Furthermore the owner relied on the fact that the charterer's intended payment was of hire less an objectively unjustifiable deduction. Christopher Clarke J held that if the failure to make punctual and regular payment arises from any of the specified causes, a notice will be required unless the charterer's intention was to make a payment which involved a calculation of a deduction made in bad faith.[307]

The right to withdraw is an extremely important one for the owner. If the market is rising steeply the owner will be waiting to pounce the moment the charterer makes any small non-payment of hire so that it can withdraw the ship and go out into the market to obtain a new charter at a much higher rate of hire. The sum in dispute in *The Li Hai*[308] was only US$500, but as the market for such a ship had risen about two-and-a-half times the charter rate in ten months, it was extremely tempting for the owner to get out of the charter if it could. This was "commerce, red in tooth and claw".[309] However, the owner will not always wish to exercise its right to withdraw. It may take into account factors such as whether the market is rising or falling, the creditworthiness of the charterer, whether cargo has been loaded,[310] its obligations to third parties under, for example, a bill of lading,[311] whether it has a right to lien the cargo or sub-freights in respect of any sums which have not been paid[312] or whether it can obtain security for sums unpaid, for example, by arrest or freezing injunction.[313]

In *ENE 1 Kos Limited v Petroleo Brasileiro SA (The Kos)*[314] the owner withdrew the ship for non-payment of hire when the ship was loading cargo at Angra dos Reis, Brazil. The cargo was discharged 2.64 days later. The issue was whether following a valid withdrawal of the ship, the charterer was obliged to pay the owner for the use of the ship at the market rate and the bunkers consumed until completion of discharge. The Court of Appeal upheld the decision of Andrew Smith J that the owner was not entitled to recover either under the express employment and indemnity clause; or for damages for failure to pay hire. The owner did not pursue

---

305. [2010] EWHC 1663 (Comm); [2011] 1 Lloyd's Rep 350.
306. Ibid., [10].
307. Ibid., [70].
308. *Western Bulk Carriers K/S v Li Hai Maritime Inc (The Li Hai)* [2005] EWHC 735 (Comm); [2005] 2 Lloyd's Rep 389.
309. Ibid., per Jonathan Hirst QC sitting as Deputy Judge of the High Court, [1].
310. *ENE 1 Kos Limited v Petroleo Brasileiro SA (The Kos)* [2012] UKSC 17; [2012] 2 WLR 976; [2010] EWCA Civ 772; [2010] 2 Lloyd's Rep 409; [2009] EWHC 1843 (Comm); [2010] 1 Lloyd's Rep 87.
311. *Vantage Navigation Corp v Suhail and Saud Bahvan Building Materials (The Alev)* [1989] 1 Lloyd's Rep 138.
312. See pages 182–186.
313. See Chapter 12.
314. [2012] UKSC 17; [2012] 2 WLR 976; [2010] EWCA Civ 772; [2010] 2 Lloyd's Rep 409; [2009] EWHC 1843 (Comm); [2010] 1 Lloyd's Rep 87.

the argument for an implied term which had been rejected at first instance. Furthermore the owner was not entitled to a quantum meruit as they did not perform the contract but insisted on discharge of the goods at the port of loading; nor had the owner acted upon a request by the charterers. However, the Court of Appeal reversed the decision of Andrew Smith J when it held that the owner was not entitled to recover remuneration and expenses incurred in fulfilling its duty as bailees to make the cargo available to the charterer after the charterparty came to an end as there was no element of accident, emergency or necessity. The owner could recover the cost of the bunkers used to discharge the charterer's cargo. The owner was also entitled to recover as costs and not as damages the cost of providing a bank guarantee for US$18 million to release its ship from arrest by the charterer for its claim for wrongful withdrawal. The Supreme Court reversed the decision of the Court of Appeal and held that the owners were entitled to recover under the express employment and indemnity clause, Lord Mance dissenting, and in bailment.

(d) Off hire

Standard forms of time charter provide that hire will cease to be payable on the occurrence of certain events which prevent the full working of the ship either for the time lost[315] to the charterer as a result of such event or during the period that the event continues.[316] Some charterparties provide for a list of specified events which will trigger the off hire clause. Events specified in the off hire clause may include breakdown of the ship's engines, the ship running aground, "detention by average accidents to ship or cargo"[317] (an accident which causes damage), "default and/or deficiency of men"[318] or capture and seizure[319] or "any other cause".[320]

The list may culminate in the wording "or any other cause preventing the full working of the vessel".[321] The words "preventing the full working of the vessel" apply to all the causes and it should first be determined whether the cause does prevent the full working of the vessel. This will be the case, for example, if the ship is arrested[322] or free pratique (medical clearance) is delayed due to suspected typhus on the ship at her previous port,[323] but not where the ship is

---

315. Cl 11 of the Baltime form, cl 15 of NYPE 1946, cl 17 of NYPE 1993, and cl 17 of NYPE 2015. See *The Marika M* [1981] 2 Lloyd's Rep 622; *The Pythia* [1982] 2 Lloyd's Rep 160; *The Ira* [1995] 1 Lloyd's Rep 103; London Arbitration 6/99 LMLN 504; *The Houda* [1994] 2 Lloyd's Rep 541; London Arbitration 11/96 LMLN 442; *Action Navigation Inc v Bottigliere di Navigatione SpA (The Kitsa)* [2005] EWHC 177; [2005] 1 Lloyd's Rep 432, LMLN 660; *Bottiglieri di Navigazione Spa v Cosco Qingdao Ocean Shipping Co (The Bunga Saga Lima)* [2005] EWHC 244; [2005] 2 Lloyd's Rep 1.

316. See e.g. cl 21 Shelltime 4 form and *The Bridgestone Maru No 3* [1985] 2 Lloyd's Rep 62.

317. *The Laconian Confidence* [1997] 1 Lloyd's Rep 139; *Nippon Yusen Kaisha Ltd v Scindia Steam Navigation Co Ltd (The Jalagouri)* [2000] 1 Lloyd's Rep 515; and *Cosco Bulk Carrier Co Ltd v Team-Up Owning Co Ltd (m/v Saldanha)* [2010] EWHC 1340 (Comm); [2011] 1 Lloyd's Rep 187.

318. *Cosco Bulk Carrier Co Ltd v Team-Up Owning Co Ltd (m/v Saldanha)* [2010] EWHC 1340 (Comm); [2011] 1 Lloyd's Rep 187.

319. *Osmium Shipping Corporation v Cargill International SA (The Captain Stefanos)* [2012] EWHC 571 (Comm); [2012] 2 Lloyd's Rep 46.

320. *Cosco Bulk Carrier Co Ltd v Team-Up Owning Co Ltd (m/v Saldanha)* [2010] EWHC 1340 (Comm); [2011] 1 Lloyd's Rep 187.

321. See e.g. cl 15 NYPE 1946.

322. *The Mastro Georgis* [1983] 2 Lloyd's Rep 66. In *NYK Bulkship (Atlantic) NV v Cargill International SA (The Global Santosh)* [2016] UKSC 20; [2016] 1 Lloyd's Rep 629 the ship was off hire where she was arrested by the sub-charterer who for these purposes was not acting as the agent of the charterer.

323. *The Apollo* [1987] 1 Lloyd's Rep 200.

trapped by a boom across the Yangtze river,[324] or her draft is too great for the Panama canal[325] or she is detained by Somali pirates.[326]

"Any other cause" will be construed *ejusdem generis*, that is, it will be limited to the same type as those events which have been specifically identified in the list which has gone before or at least as Rix J, as he then was, said in *The Laconian Confidence*[327] "in some limited way reflecting the general context of the charter and clause". In that case the type of causes were "internal" to the ship as opposed to "external" or "extraneous" and did not therefore include delay caused by an unforeseeable interference by the port authorities regarding disposal of residual sweepings. Where the word "whatsoever" is added after the words "any other cause" there is no limit on the causes, although it must still satisfy any express requirement that it prevents the full working of the vessel.

The off hire clause will not depend on the fault of the shipowner. If the shipowner is actually at fault it may also be in breach of charterparty and the charterer may have remedies such as the right to terminate the charterparty or claim damages in addition to, or in substitution for, the ship being off hire. If the off hire event is caused by a breach of charterparty by the charterer, the ship may still be off hire but the owner will be able to recover damages for the breach including any off hire.

The charterer is obliged to pay hire continuously unless it can show that the wording of the off hire clause applies to the event which has occurred. Where the clause is a net loss of time clause the burden of proof is on the charterer to show not only that the off hire event occurred but also that time has been lost as a result. Once the ship is again in full working order, the ship is no longer off hire even if time is lost thereafter.[328]

The Court of Appeal considered the time lost provision in *Minerva Navigation Inc v Oceana Shipping AG (The Athena)*.[329] The off hire clause provided that, "in the event of loss of time from . . . default of master . . . or by any other cause preventing the full working of the vessel, the payment of hire shall cease for the time thereby lost". The vessel loaded a cargo of wheat at Novorossiysk in Russia for carriage to Syria. The cargo was rejected by the Syrian receivers. The charterers instructed the master to proceed to the roads off Benghazi in Libya. The vessel proceeded to Libya but stopped in international waters about 50 miles from Libya and drifted for 10.9 days. The arbitrators held that had the vessel proceeded directly to Benghazi it would not have berthed any earlier than it did. The Court of Appeal held that there was an immediate loss of time by default of the master so that the vessel was off hire for the 10.9-day period. Since the off hire clause was concerned with the service immediately required of the vessel which was to proceed to the roads at Benghazi, it had to be possible at the conclusion of the off hire event to determine what net time had been lost in consequence of the event. It was thus impermissible to have regard to events occurring after the end of the off hire event.

The charterparty may expressly provide for the situation where the ship has to deviate and state that she will be off hire until she is again in an efficient state to resume her service and in a position not less favourable to the charterer than that at which such loss of time commenced.[330] The ship will come on hire again when she is again in an efficient state and in a position not less

324. *Court Line v Dant & Russell* [1939] 44 Com Cas 345.
325. *The Aquacharm* [1982] 1 Lloyd's Rep 7.
326. *Cosco Bulk Carrier Co Ltd v Team-Up Owning Co Ltd (m/v Saldanha)* [2010] EWHC 1340 (Comm); [2011] 1 Lloyd's Rep 187.
327. [1997] 1 Lloyd's Rep 139.
328. *Vogemann v Zanzibar* [1902] 7 Com Cas 254 (CA); [1901] 6 Com Cas 253 and *The Marika M* [1981] 2 Lloyd's Rep 622.
329. [2013] EWCA Civ 1273; [2014] 1 All ER (Comm) 552.
330. E.g. cl 21(c) Shelltime 4.

favourable even though there is some external cause which will still delay her such as a sunken barge restricting shipping movements in the Mississippi.[331]

In *TS Lines Ltd v Delphis NV (The TS Singapore)*[332] Burton J held that the charterer was entitled to redeliver a ship. There was an express right to do so if the ship was off hire for a period of 20 consecutive days when she was next cargo free. The ship was off hire after hitting a breakwater at Yokohama. Her classification society imposed a condition that she proceed to Hong Kong to discharge her cargo and not to Shanghai, as the charterer had ordered. The owner contended that the ship was on hire when she left Yokohama as the route to Shanghai and to Hong Kong was initially the same and it was only when she diverted from that route for Hong Kong that she went off hire again. Burton J held that the commercial purpose of the charterparty was to comply with the charterer's instructions. The ship was not complying with that commercial purpose when she set off from Yokohama. She was therefore off hire, albeit travelling in the direction of Shanghai, but not intending to go there.

Tailor-made off hire clauses may be included in the charterparty. Thus in *The Doric Pride*[333] a charterparty in the NYPE form contained a special off hire clause as follows:

Should the vessel be captured or seized or detained or arrested by any authority or by any legal process during the currency of this Charter Party, the payment of hire shall be suspended until the time of her release, and any extra expenses incurred by and/or during the above capture or seizure or detention or arrest shall be for Owners account, unless such capture or seizure or detention or arrest is occasioned by any personal act or omission or default of the charterers or their agents or by reason of cargo carried or calling port of trading under this charter.

The ship was detained on her way to call at New Orleans, her loading port, on the orders of the captain of the port, pursuant to the Marine Transportation Safety Act 2002, US legislation designed for security purposes. Under that legislation the ship had been designated as a "High Interest Vessel". She was a first-time caller to the United States and there was a US Coast Guard policy to inspect first-time callers to any US port. Unfortunately, while the ship was at anchor awaiting the coastguard boarding team, there was a serious collision between two other ships which led to the closure of the south-west pass. The available resources of the US Coastguard were engaged in search and rescue operations with the result that the inspection of the ship was delayed. The owner argued that this was a simple case of detention by reason of "calling port of trading under this charter" and fell within the proviso to the clause. The Court of Appeal held that the real problem lay in the ship's status and not in the charterer's trading and the ship was therefore off hire within the main part of the clause.

The charterparty may expressly provide that the charterer has an option to add any period of off hire on to the end of the charter period.[334]

(e) Deductions from hire

It will be of vital importance to the cash flow of the charterer to be able to deduct claims from the hire rather than to have to pay the hire in full and subsequently seek to recover its claims from the owner. The charterer must be careful not to make wrongful deductions as this would

---

331. *Poseidon Schiffahrt GmbH v Nomadic Navigation Co Ltd (The Trade Nomad)* [1998] 1 Lloyd's Rep 57, at p 65; [1999] 1 Lloyd's Rep 723 (CA).
332. [2009] EWHC 933 (Comm); [2010] 1 All ER (Comm) 434; [2009] 2 Lloyd's Rep 54.
333. *Hyundai Merchant Marine Co Ltd v Furness Withy (Australia) Pty (The Doric Pride)* [2006] EWCA l.
334. See e.g. *The Hong Kong Fir* and *Petroleo Brasileiro SA v Kriti Akti Shipping Co SA (The Kriti Akti)* [2004] EWCA Civ 116; [2004] 1 Lloyd's Rep 712. See page 155 of this chapter.

entitle the owner to withdraw the ship. The charterer can make deductions from the hire in two situations: where there is an express right to do so or where there is an equitable right of set off. If there is no such right, the charterer must pursue its claim against the owner and, if it is not paid, bring court or arbitration proceedings. This may take considerable time and meanwhile the charterer should seek security for its claim.

It is usual for the charterer to have an express right to deduct a number of different claims from the hire including advances for the ship's disbursements made by the charterer on behalf of the owner,[335] off hire periods (but not anticipated off hire periods),[336] fuel used while the ship is off hire,[337] the cost of diesel oil consumed for domestic consumption,[338] speed and performance claims[339] and the cost of bunkers on board on redelivery from the last hire payment.

If there is no express provision in the charterparty permitting the charterer to make a deduction from hire for a particular sum, English law recognises limited circumstances in which the time charterer is entitled to deduct from hire by way of equitable set off. This contrasts sharply with the position of the voyage charterer who has no such right to deduct from freight.[340] Where the owner of the ship is in breach of time charter and the effect of such breach is wrongly to deprive the charterer of the use of the ship or to prejudice the charterer in the use of it, the time charterer is entitled to deduct the claim for such breach from hire.[341] Thus the time charterer may deduct a claim for speed and performance from the hire,[342] failure to load a full cargo in breach of charterer's instructions,[343] but not a cargo claim,[344] or claim for misappropriation of the charterer's bunkers,[345] or fee incurred by the charterers because a delivery of bunkers was cancelled.[346]

Whether the deduction is made pursuant to an express clause or by way of equitable set off it must be a reasonable assessment made in good faith.[347] The amount does not have to be agreed by the owner.[348] In *The Nanfri*[349] Lord Denning thought that provided the deduction is bona fide and reasonable and is in respect of a claim for which there is a right to deduct, there is no right to withdraw, even if it subsequently turns out that the sum deducted was too much. Goff LJ differed as in his view the charterer acted "at his peril".[350] The view of Lord Denning has been followed at first instance.[351] The charterer would have to pay the owner the amount over deducted.

335. Line 66 NYPE 1946.
336. *The Lutetian* [1982] 2 Lloyd's Rep 140; *Western Bulk Carriers K/S v Li Hai Maritime Inc (The Li Hai)* [2005] EWHC 735 (Comm), [2005] 2 Lloyd's Rep 389.
337. Cl 20 NYPE 1946.
338. Ibid., *The Sounion* [1987] 1 Lloyd's Rep 230.
339. *The Al Bida* [1987] 1 Lloyd's Rep 124.
340. *Aries v Total Transport* [1977] 1 All ER 398 and *Bank of Boston Connecticut (formerly Colonial Bank) v European Grain & Shipping Ltd (The Dominique)* [1989] 1 Lloyd's Rep 431 (HL).
341. *Federal Commerce and Navigation Ltd v Molena Alpha Inc (The Nanfri, Benfri and Lorfri)* [1978] 2 Lloyd's Rep 132.
342. Ibid. See also London Arbitration 5/08 LMLN 739.
343. *Compania Sud Americana De Vapores v Shipmair BV (The Teno)* [1977] 2 Lloyd's Rep 289.
344. *Federal Commerce & Navigation Co Ltd v Molena Alpha Inc (The Nanfri)* [1978] QB 927 (CA), per Lord Denning at p 976.
345. *Leon Corporation v Atlantic Lines and Navigation Co Inc (The Leon)* [1985] 2 Lloyd's Rep 470.
346. *Western Bulk Carriers K/S v Li Hai Maritime Inc (The Li Hai)* [2005] EWHC 735 (Comm); [2005] 2 Lloyd's Rep 389.
347. *The Nanfri* [1978] QB 927; [1978] 2 Lloyd's Rep 132.
348. Ibid. *SL Sethia Liners Ltd v Naviagro Maritime Corp (The Kostas Melas)* [1981] 1 Lloyd's Rep 18.
349. [1978] QB 927; [1978] 2 Lloyd's Rep 132.
350. [1978] QB 927, at p 981.
351. *The Chrysovalandou Dyo* [1981] 1 Lloyd's Rep 157; *The Kostas Melas* [1981] 1 Lloyd's Rep 18 and *Owneast Shipping Ltd v Qatar Navigation QSC* [2010] EWHC 1663 (Comm); [2011] 1 Lloyd's Rep 350, [46] and [47].

12. VOYAGE CHARTERPARTIES

Under a voyage charterparty the owner pays for the maintenance of the ship, insurance, crew wages and the bunkers. The charterer pays freight to have its goods carried from the loadport to the discharge port. The freight due under a voyage charterparty usually covers the preliminary voyage to the loadport. Sometimes, however, the charterparty will provide for the charterer to pay a ballast bonus for the preliminary voyage. The freight will also cover the voyage from the load port to the discharge port and a limited period to load and to discharge at the loading and discharge ports respectively. That limited period of allowed time is called laytime or laydays. If the charterer exceeds the laytime it is in breach of the charterparty and will be liable to pay damages to compensate the shipowner for that breach. It is usual for the shipowner and the charterer to agree in advance the amount of damages due for such breach. Such liquidated damages are called demurrage. The amount of demurrage agreed will depend on the market rate payable for the ship at the time of fixing the charterparty. The shipowner will not be entitled to terminate the charterparty as a result of the charterer's failure to load or discharge within the laytime, unless the breach is repudiatory (for example, the charterer says that it will not load), or the delay amounts to a frustrating delay,[352] or it is clear that a frustrating delay will occur or there is an express contractual right to terminate.[353]

Some of the most complex problems under voyage charterparties arise as a result of the complicated clauses which the parties may include in an attempt to allocate the risk of delay during the loading and discharging operations between themselves. When it is known at the time the fixture is concluded where the load and discharge ports are it is possible to draft the clauses specifically to deal with any known or anticipated delays which may occur at those ports. Where the ports are not known, for example, because the charterer has the right to nominate a port from a wide range of ports, the shipowner must try to cover itself for all the eventualities that could occur in such ports.

As the freight includes the laytime the charterer pays for the stipulated amount of time allowed for the loading and discharging operations. If that time is not used, it is common for general cargo charters to provide that the owner will pay the charterer despatch. Despatch is often half the rate of demurrage.[354]

(a) Freight

The charterparty will provide what the freight is: it may be a lump sum; or in a tanker charter ascertained by reference to Worldscale; or be calculated by reference to the amount of cargo. In the latter case it is important to know whether the freight rate is to be calculated by reference to the intake quantity,[355] bill of lading quantity or delivered quantity. If the charterer fails to load the amount of cargo agreed it may be liable for deadfreight to compensate the shipowner for the freight that it would have earned had the charterer loaded the agreed amount of cargo.[356]

---

352. *DGM Commodities Corp v Sea Metropolitan SA (The Andra)* [2012] EWHC 1984 (Comm); [2012] 2 Lloyd's Rep 587.
353. See e.g. cl 7 of Gencon 1994.
354. See e.g. *Glencore Grain Ltd v Flacker Shipping Ltd (The Happy Day)* [2002] 2 Lloyd's Rep 487.
355. See cl 2 of Asbatankvoy.
356. *China Offshore Oil (Singapore) International Pte Ltd v Giant Shipping Ltd (The Posidon)* [2001] 1 Lloyd's Rep 697; *Pentonville Shipping Ltd v Transfield Shipping Inc (The Johnny K)* [2006] EWHC 134 (Comm); [2006] 1 Lloyd's Rep 666 and *AIC Limited v Marine Pilot Limited (The Archimidis)* [2008] EWCA Civ 175; [2008] 2 All ER (Comm) 545.

At common law the freight is due on delivery of the cargo. By that time the owner has performed the whole of its obligations under the contract. Therefore it is usual for the charterparty to provide expressly that at least part of the freight is to be paid in advance, so as to have a better balance between the parties. Alternatively the charterparty may provide for freight to be paid "before breaking bulk." This term was considered in *D'Amico Shipping Italia SpA v Endofa DMCC*.[357] The issue was whether the freight became payable once bulk was broken ie when discharge began or when the owner tendered the ship to the charterer and made it available for discharge. Foxton QC sitting as Deputy Judge of the High Court thought that there was "a clear temporal difference between freight being payable before breaking bulk and freight being payable on breaking bulk".[358] An additional clause provided,

If the freight and any other amount due to the owners, including, but not limited to accrued demurrage is not received by the owners before notice of readiness is tendered, the owner may, immediately following such payment refuse to commence discharging the cargo until such time as the payment due is received by the owners.

The judge held:

That clause clearly contemplates that freight will be due, that is to say it will be payable as a debt, not only before discharge has commenced, but even before notice of readiness is served, and it contemplates that an owner can refuse to discharge the cargo until such time as it has received that payment. It seems to me the combined effect of those clauses is clearly that freight was payable at a point when the vessel became an arrived ship and was made available to the charterers for the charterers to procure its discharge and not to postpone the point of payment of freight until discharge began.[359]

A distinction must be drawn between the date on which the freight becomes due and that on which it becomes payable. Once the freight is due the owner will not lose its right to be paid the freight even if the ship is subsequently lost with all her cargo on board.

Unlike the time charterer who can make deductions from hire by way of equitable set off, there is no such right of deduction from freight.[360] There will only be a right to make deductions if the charterparty expressly permits deductions, for example, for the value of cargo remaining on board where the ship carries a crude oil cargo[361] or in transit losses.[362] In *The Dominique* the charterer had to pay the freight which had become due without deduction even though subsequently the ship was arrested by creditors at Colombo and it was unlikely that she would leave Colombo under the same ownership, as the shipowner would not be able to put up security to release the ship from arrest.

(b) When does laytime start?

Subject to the express terms of the charterparty laytime will begin to run when three requirements have been satisfied: first the ship is an "arrived ship" at the load port; second notice of

---

357. [2016] EWHC 2223 (Comm). See also page 184 in relation to exercise of the lien.
358. [11].
359. [12].
360. *Aries Tanker Corp v Total Transport Ltd (The Aries)* [1977] 1 Lloyd's Rep 334; *Bank of Boston Connecticut (formerly Colonial Bank) v European Grain & Shipping Ltd (The Dominique)* [1989] AC 1056.
361. See London Arbitration 3/08 LMLN 734.
362. Such clauses are common in the carriage of oil as there may be unexplained losses during carriage and if they exceed a certain percentage of the cargo, the voyage charterer may have a right to deduct from freight. See *Trafigura Beheer BV v Navigazione Montanari SpA (The Valle di Cordoba)* [2015] EWCA Civ 91; [2015] 1 Lloyd's Rep 529 where the Court of Appeal held that a loss of cargo due to piracy did not fall within a loss in transit clause in a voyage charterparty.

readiness has been given in accordance with the charterparty terms; third the ship is in fact ready. The shipowner will be anxious to get the laytime clock ticking as early as possible for as soon as the laytime expires the shipowner will start earning demurrage. The charterer, however, will seek to ensure that the laytime starts counting as late as possible so that the ship never comes on demurrage. The classic illustration of this is the case of *The Happy Day*, which will be considered below, where not only did the charterer argue that laytime never started, but it also claimed despatch for the laytime never used.

(i) Arrived ship

To determine when the ship is arrived it will be necessary to see where the charterparty stipulates the ship has to proceed to. It may provide for the ship to proceed, for example, to one safe port or one safe berth or sea mooring buoy. If the charterparty provides that the ship is to proceed to a port, the area of that port may be very large and on arrival the ship may be required to anchor while she waits for her berth to become available. The anchorage may be some distance from her berth. However, she will be an arrived ship when she is within the limits of the port[363] and is at the immediate and effective disposal of the charterer so that when a berth becomes available, the ship can proceed straight to it. There is a presumption that the ship is at the disposal of the charterer when she is at the usual waiting place in the port, although that presumption is rebuttable. Thus even if the ship is about 17 miles away from her berth she is an arrived ship if she is at the usual waiting place,[364] provided that she is within the limits of the port.[365] This is harsh on the owner if the usual waiting place is outside the port limits or the ship cannot get into the port due, for example, to congestion. Thus the owner may insist on an express clause entitling it to give notice of readiness "whether in port or not".

Tanker charterparties may provide that notice of readiness can be given "upon arrival at customary anchorage at each port of loading or discharge . . . berth or no berth".[366] London arbitrators have accepted that this provision entitles notice of readiness to be tendered at a customary anchorage which is outside the port.[367]

Although it has been argued that the ship has not arrived until she has anchored at the designated anchorage as her sea voyage has not yet come to an end,[368] an alternative view is that there is nothing in the express wording of Asbatankvoy which requires the ship to have anchored.[369] All she has to have done is arrive at the customary anchorage. Indeed, she may never anchor. It may not be necessary to anchor as the terminal is expecting her and she can proceed straight into berth. It has also been asked whether in such circumstances the ship should proceed via the customary anchorage in order to tender notice of readiness. It is likely that in such circumstances the ship will arrive in the berth and laytime will start counting before the expiry of six hours from giving notice at the customary anchorage.[370]

---

363. *Navalmar UK Ltd v Kalemaden Hammeddeler Sanayi Ve Ticaret AS (The Arundel Castle)* [2017] EWHC 116 (Comm); [2017] Lloyd's Rep Plus 22.

364. *EL Oldendorff & Co GmbH v Tradax Export SA (The Johanna Oldendorff)* [1973] 2 Lloyd's Rep 285.

365. *Federal Commerce & Navigation Co Ltd v Tradax Export SA (The Maratha Envoy)* [1977] 2 Lloyd's Rep 301.

366. E.g. cl 6 of Asbatankvoy.

367. See (2007) 725 LMLN 2, and see *Cooke*, [57.4]. In *Feoso (Singapore)Pte Ltd v Faith Maritime Co Ltd (The Daphne L)* [2003] SGCA 34; [2003] 3 SLR 556 the Singapore Court of Appeal held that where the ship gave notice of readiness when she had reached the recognised waiting place for the port, even though the customary anchorage was some 20 miles from the port, she was an arrived ship.

368. See J Schofield, *Laytime and Demurrage* (7th edn, Informa 2017), [3.312] – [3.322].

369. See (2007) 725 LMLN 2.

370. London Arbitration (2006) 698 LMLN 1.

Where the charterparty provides that the ship is to proceed to a berth, the ship is not arrived until she is in berth. In *Novologistics SARL v Five Ocean Corporation (The Merida)*[371] the charterparty recap provided:

one good and safe chrts' berth terminal 4 stevedores Xingang to one good and safe berth Cadiz and one good and safe berth Bilbao

Clause 2(1)
The vessel to load at one good and safe port/one good and safe charterers' berths Xingang . . .

Clause 2(2)
Shifting from anchorage/warping along the berth at port of load and at ports of discharge to be for owners' account, while all time used to count as laytime.

Gross J held that the charterparty was a berth charterparty and therefore the delay of 20 days between the vessel's arrival at Xingang and berthing was at owners' risk. As this case illustrates a berth charterparty is dangerous from the owner's point of view. The owner usually has no control over the allocation of the berth but takes the risk that there is a delay in getting into berth for whatever reason.[372] The charterer may have some contractual link with the shipper or receiver of the goods and the sale and purchase contract for the goods will usually contain laytime and demurrage clauses so that the seller or buyer can recover demurrage if the shipper or receiver is slow in providing a berth. Therefore even if the charterparty provides that the ship must proceed to a berth, a number of clauses may be used to reallocate the risk of delay in getting into berth back to the charterer.

The first is the berth "reachable on arrival" provision found in clause 9 of the Asbatankvoy charterparty. This was considered by the House of Lords in *The Laura Prima*[373] and it was held that the charterer was in breach of the obligation to designate and procure a berth reachable on arrival where the berth was congested. It has subsequently been held that matters such as lack of tugs and bad weather[374] or lack of pilots and prohibition of night navigation,[375] which were traditionally considered to be the owner's risks, would also mean that the berth was not reachable on arrival so that the charterer was in breach of this obligation.

An alternative is to provide that time is to count "whether in berth or not". This provision was considered by the House of Lords in *The Kyzikos*.[376] It does not provide the owner with as great protection as the berth "reachable on arrival" provision as time will only count if a berth is not available. If a berth is available, but cannot be reached, for example, due to fog, time will not count. Another possibility is to have the provision "time lost waiting for a berth to count as loading . . . time"[377] or a clause tailor-made for delays which are anticipated at a specific port.[378] The parties may agree to split certain delays of getting into berth between themselves.[379]

(ii) Notice of readiness

The charterer requires notice of the arrival of the ship so that it can arrange to load the ship promptly. Indeed the charterparty may provide that the shipowner is also to give notice of the

---

371. [2009] EWHC 3046 (Comm).
372. *The Isabelle* [1984] 1 Lloyd's Rep 366 (CA); [1982] 2 Lloyd's Rep 81 (Robert Goff J).
373. *Nereide SpA di Navigazione v Bulk Oil International (The Laura Prima)* [1982] 1 Lloyd's Rep 1.
374. *Palm Shipping Inc v Kuwait Petroleum Corp (The Sea Queen)* [1988] 1 Lloyd's Rep 500.
375. *K/S Arnt J Moerland v Kuwait Petroleum Corporation (The Fjordaas)* [1988] 1 Lloyd's Rep 336.
376. *Seacrystal Shipping Ltd v Bulk Transport Group Shipping Co (The Kyzikos)* [1989] 1 Lloyd's Rep 1. *Glencore Grain Ltd v Flacker Shipping Ltd (The Happy Day)* [2002] 2 Lloyd's Rep 487. See also London Arbitration (2006) 690 LMLN (2) and *Carboex SA v Louis Dreyfus Commodities Suisse SA* [2012] EWCA Civ 838; [2013] QB 789.
377. Cl 6 Gencon. See *Aldebaran Compania Maritima SA v Aussenhandel AG (The Darrah)* [1977] AC 157.
378. See e.g. *Ellis Shipping Corp v Voest Alpine Intertrading (The Lefthero)* [1992] 2 Lloyd's Rep 109.
379. E.g. the Conoco Weather Clause.

ship's expected time of arrival, e.g. 72, 48 and 24 hours prior to her estimated time of arrival so that the charterer has additional time to ensure that the cargo is ready and a berth is available as soon as the ship arrives. Many standard forms of charterparty provide that laytime will not commence until six hours after notice of readiness has been tendered or received or until the ship has berthed, whichever is the earlier.[380]

An initial question is whether the notice of readiness can be given outside the laycan, i.e. prior to the commencement date or after the cancelling date given in the charterparty. As we have already seen[381] the charterer will not want laytime to start before a specified time, which will usually be the start of the window allocated within the shipper's loading schedule, as it will have no use for the ship. If the ship arrives before that window the owner may invite the charterer to take the ship early and agree that laytime will commence early. The charterer may approach the shipper and if there is some flexibility in the loading schedule, for example, because another ship is late, the shipper may be able to bring forward the loading and the charterer can then agree with the owner to accept notice of readiness early.

The charterparty usually provides that laytime shall not commence before the commencement date, except with the charterer's sanction.[382] If the charterer requests the ship to tender notice of readiness and berth before the earliest layday, then the charterer has sanctioned the earlier commencement of laytime.[383] The charterparty may not provide what is to happen if notice of readiness is given before the commencement date. If the charterer does not want the ship to load early notice of readiness and the six hours after notice of readiness may run before the commencement date,[384] so that laytime would commence at 0001 hours on the first day of the laycan. Other charterparties expressly provide that laytime shall not commence before 0600 hours on the commencement date.[385]

The owner is obliged to proceed "with all convenient despatch" to the loadport even if it is clear that the ship will not arrive by the cancellation date and may be cancelled. The charterer has no right to cancel before the cancelling date even though it may be clear to the charterer for some days beforehand that the ship will not arrive by the cancelling date. If the charterer does not cancel the ship even though the ship is late, the charterer may find that it has to pay for all the time spent waiting for a berth. In *The Nikmary*[386] the Court of Appeal held that the delay resulted from the charterer's failure to have cargo ready for loading.

The charterparty will usually provide for the form in which notice of readiness must be given (for example, in writing, by fax),[387] to whom (for example, to the charterer's load port agents or the loading terminal) and when.[388] Thus it is common in a charterparty for general cargo to find that notice of readiness can only be tendered during working hours and not on a weekend or holiday. By contrast, most oil terminals operate 24 hours seven days a week and notice of readiness can usually be tendered at any time of the day or night. However, in *The Petr Schmidt*[389] the charterparty provided that notice of readiness must be tendered between 0600 and 1700 hours. If a

---

380. See e.g. cl 6 of Asbatankvoy.
381. See page 152 of this chapter.
382. E.g. cl 5 of Asbatankvoy.
383. *Tidebrook Maritime Corporation v Vitol SA (The Front Commander)* [2006] 2 Lloyd's Rep 251 (CA), per Rix LJ, [45].
384. Ibid.
385. cl 13(a) of ExxonMobil VOY2000 and cl 13(1)(a) of Shellvoy 6.
386. *Triton Navigation Ltd v Vitol SA (The Nikmary)* [2003] EWCA Civ 1715; [2004] 1 Lloyd's Rep 55.
387. Where six means of giving notice of readiness were listed in a charterparty but did not include email, notice of readiness given by email was not valid – see *Trafigura Beheer BV v Ravennavi SpA (The Port Russel)* [2013] EWHC 490 (Comm); [2013] 2 Lloyd's Rep 57.
388. See e.g. cl 6 of Asbatankvoy and cl 6(c) Gencon.
389. *Galaxy Energy International Ltd v Novorossiysk Shipping Co (The Petr Schmidt)* [1998] 2 Lloyd's Rep 1 (CA).

notice of readiness was given outside those hours, the notice could not start time counting at the time it was given but, provided it was a truthful notice at the time it was given it was not a nullity. Therefore, when working hours started again time would start counting as long as the notice remained truthful and the ship was still ready. It was not necessary to tender a further notice.

(iii) Readiness

Third, the notice of readiness must contain accurate statements that the ship has arrived and is ready at the time the notice is given. If the statements are inaccurate the notice is a nullity,[390] unless it is accepted by the charterer[391] or its agents[392] or there is a waiver of the requirement for a notice of readiness. The fact that the ship becomes ready or becomes an arrived ship[393] after the notice is given does not give the notice of readiness any subsequent effect. In *The Mexico I*[394] notice of readiness was given when the charterer's cargo was overstowed with the owner's cargo and the ship was therefore not ready to discharge the charterer's cargo until the owner's cargo had first been discharged. No further notice of readiness was given when discharge of the owner's cargo was completed. The Court of Appeal rejected the owner's arguments that the notice of readiness was inchoate and became effective when the ship became ready or when the charterer knew, or ought to have known, that the ship was ready. In that case the charterer conceded that laytime would commence when discharge actually commenced. Mustill LJ indicated that he thought the concession was correctly made.

However, in *The Happy Day*[395] no such concession was made. The ship arrived off Cochin and was unable to enter the port because she missed the tide. Nevertheless the master purported to give a notice of readiness. As the charterparty was a berth charterparty and a berth was available, this was an invalid notice of readiness. The ship entered the port and commenced discharging the following day but discharge was not completed until almost three months later. The shipowner claimed demurrage for the extensive delay. The charterer argued that as no valid notice of readiness had ever been given, laytime never commenced. This despite the fact that the charterer had used the ship for some three months. To add insult to injury, the charterer claimed despatch. This would have been such an unappealing result that the Court of Appeal held that where notice of readiness valid in form had been served on the charterer or receiver prior to the arrival of the ship, the ship thereafter arrived and was or was accepted to be ready to discharge to the knowledge of the charterer, and discharge thereafter commenced to the order of the charterer or receiver without either having given any intimation of rejection or reservation in respect of the notice of readiness previously served, or any indication that further notice of readiness was required before laytime commenced, the charterer could be deemed to have waived reliance on the invalidity of the original notice as from the time of commencement of discharge and laytime would commence as if a valid notice of readiness had been served at that time.

Where the shipowner is in doubt as to whether a notice of readiness is valid, it should tender another notice of readiness when it is clear that the ship is arrived and is ready. There could still

---

390. *Compania de Naviera Nedelka v Tradex International (The Tres Flores)* [1973] 2 Lloyd's Rep 247.
391. *Sofial SA v Ove Skou Rederi (The Helle Skou)* [1976] 2 Lloyd's Rep 205.
392. *Ocean Pride Maritime Ltd Partnership v Qingdao Ocean Shipping Co* [2007] EWHC 2796 (Comm); [2008] 1 Lloyd's Rep 511.
393. *TA Shipping Ltd v Comet Shipping Ltd (The Agamemnon)* [1998] 1 Lloyd's Rep 675.
394. *Transgrain Shipping BV v Global Transporte Oceanico SA (The Mexico 1)* [1990] 1 Lloyd's Rep 507 (CA).
395. *Glencore Grain Ltd v Flacker Shipping Ltd (The Happy Day)* [2002] 2 Lloyd's Rep 487. See also *The Mass Glory* [2002] 2 Lloyd's Rep 244; *Alphapoint Shipping Ltd v Rotem Amfert Negev Ltd (The Agios Dimitrios)* [2005] 1 Lloyd's Rep 23; and *Ocean Pride Maritime Ltd Partnership v Qingdao Ocean Shipping Co (The Northgate)* [2007] EWHC 2796 (Comm); [2008] 1 Lloyd's Rep 511.

be significant delays after giving a valid notice of readiness until the commencement of cargo operations and the shipowner needs to protect its position in respect of such time. If a valid notice of readiness is never given, the owner should clearly plead waiver and request the tribunal at first instance or the arbitrator for clear findings of fact upon which waiver can be based.

The ship must actually be ready[396] when the notice of readiness is given, subject to *de minimis*. Thus she must have clean holds,[397] and be ready to receive cargo, clear customs[398] and receive free pratique (medical clearance). In *AET Inc Limited v Arcadia Petroleum Limited (The Eagle Valencia)*[399] the charterers' argument that the notice of readiness at the second load port, Excravos, was invalidated because the vessel failed to secure free pratique within contractual time limits succeeded on appeal to the Court of Appeal.

The consequence that the notice of readiness will be null if the ship is not ready, even though the master thought she was ready, can be hard on the owner if the ship is not inspected on arrival at the loadport and is kept waiting for a berth. Only when a berth is finally allocated and the ship is inspected is the owner told that the ship is not ready and no time will count at all until she is actually ready, even though it may not take long to make her ready. Therefore, the charterparty may expressly provide that laytime will count even if it is subsequently found that the ship is not ready, except the time making her ready.[400] In *The Linardos*[401] Colman J held that it was necessary to imply a term into such a provision that the notice of readiness must be given in good faith.

(c) The calculation of laytime

The period of laytime may be provided for in the charterparty in a number of different ways, for example, a specified period of time or a formula such as a fixed amount of cargo per day. Thus a tanker voyage charter usually provides for 72 hours of laytime to cover both the loading and discharging operations or alternatively, for 36 hours of laytime at the loadport and 36 hours of laytime at the discharge port. The former would be preferable from the charterer's point of view as if only 30 hours were used at the loadport there would still be 42 hours available at the discharge port, whereas the provision for 36 hours at each port is non-reversible.

Unless provided otherwise, laytime will run continuously from the time the notice of readiness expires. Exceptions must be clear and a general exceptions clause will not usually create an exception from laytime, although it is a question of construction.[402] In a general cargo charterparty it is usual to exclude days which are not worked at the port from the computation of laytime, such as Saturdays and Sundays, or Thursday afternoons and Fridays in Muslim countries, holidays and super holidays.[403] Only "working days" or "weather working days" may count as

---

396. *The Tres Flores* [1973] 2 Lloyd's Rep 247; *The Virginia M* [1989] 1 Lloyd's Rep 603.
397. *Cobelfret NV v Cyclades Shipping Co Ltd (The Linardos)* [1994] 1 Lloyd's Rep 28.
398. *The Antclizo (No 2)* [1992] 1 Lloyd's Rep 558.
399. [2010] EWCA Civ 713; [2011] 1 All ER (Comm) 153; [2010] 2 Lloyd's Rep 257; [2009] EWHC 2337 (Comm); [2010] EWCA Civ 713. Contrast *Feoso (Singapore) Pte Ltd v Faith Maritime Co Ltd (The Daphne L)* [2003] SGCA 34; [2003] 3 SLR 556 where the Singapore Court of Appeal held that the requirement that the vessel declare her arrival to the Chinese authorities within 24 hours of arrival for joint inspection was a mere formality and not a precondition to the tender of notice of readiness. Furthermore, the cargo interests were estopped from arguing that laytime did not commence because joint inspection had not been carried out, as they had instructed the owners not to declare the cargo as crude oil.
400. See *The Linardos* and *United Nations Food and Agriculture Organisation World Food Programme v Caspian Navigation Inc (The Jay Ganesh)* [1994] 2 Lloyd's Rep 358. See also cl 6 of Gencon 1994.
401. [1994] 1 Lloyd's Rep 28.
402. *Cero Navigation Corporation v Jean Lion & Cie (The Solon)* [2000] 1 Lloyd's Rep 292.
403. *Cobelfret Bulk Carriers NV v Swissmarine Services SA (The Lowlands Orchid)* [2009] EWHC 2883 (Comm); [2010] 2 All ER (Comm) 128; [2010] 1 Lloyd's Rep 317.

laytime. In a tanker charterparty there are not likely to be such exceptions to laytime as an oil terminal is likely to operate 24 hours a day seven days a week. However, there will be other express exceptions to laytime such as the time it takes to shift the ship from her anchorage to her berth (in a berth charterparty this will be considered as part of the voyage even though the charterparty has allowed the notice of readiness to be given earlier than on the arrival in berth) or deballasting (as this is a ship operation to make the ship ready to load); or "partial or total interruptions on railway or port" which has been held to cover delays caused by scheduled repairs to defective fenders.[404]

Where the charterparty provides that the charterer must designate a berth reachable on arrival the charterer cannot rely on any exceptions from laytime until it has designated such a berth.[405]

The charterer has paid for the laytime in the freight. Therefore, the charterer is entitled to keep the ship for the whole of the laytime even though it could have loaded in less time.[406] The charterer is entitled to order the master not to berth immediately on arrival at the loadport, so that if the master acts in breach of those orders the owner will be liable for the charterer's loss.[407] However, once loading or discharging has been completed, laytime comes to an end, even if the cargo operations have been concluded within the laytime allowed and there is unexpired laytime. Thus if loading is completed within the laytime allowed but the ship is delayed, for example, due to the charterer's failure to give the master instructions or because cargo documents are delayed, the charterer will be liable for damages for detention.[408]

Some charterparties contain express provisions as to when laytime ends. For example, most tanker charterparties provide that laytime shall run until hoses are disconnected[409] or until cargo documents have been received on board.[410]

(d) The calculation of demurrage

Once the laytime has expired the charterer is in breach and would be liable for damages for detention. However, most standard form voyage charterparties provide for damages at an agreed rate called demurrage. The maxim "once on demurrage always on demurrage" means that time counts for demurrage unless the parties have unambiguously provided otherwise.[411] Thus in the Asbatankvoy charterparty the allowance of six hours after giving of notice of readiness does not apply if the ship is already on demurrage when notice of readiness is given.[412] Exceptions to laytime do not constitute exceptions to demurrage unless they are expressly stated to be exceptions to demurrage as well.[413] A general exceptions clause is unlikely to be specific enough.[414] Furthermore if the wording of the exception is ambiguous it will be construed against the charterer, as

---

404. *Emeraldian Limited Partnership v Wellmix Shipping Ltd (The Vine)* [2010] EWHC 1411 (Comm); [2011] 1 Lloyd's Rep 301. However, in this case the charterer was held liable for demurrage as it had nominated an unsafe berth – see page 145 of this chapter.

405. *Nereide SpA di Navigazione v Bulk Oil International (The Laura Prima)* [1982] 1 Lloyd's Rep 1.

406. *Margaronis Navigation Agency Ltd v Henry W Peabody & Co of London Ltd* [1965] 2 QB 430.

407. *Novorossisk Shipping Co v Neopetro Ltd (The Ulyanovsk)* [1990] 1 Lloyd's Rep 425.

408. *Owners of the Steamship Nolisement v Bunge and Born* [1916] CC 135.

409. E.g. cl 11 Asbatankvoy.

410. Cl 9 Intertankvoy. Cf. cl 13(c) of ExxonMobil VOY2000. See 1993 LMLN 358.

411. See e.g. cl 8 Asbatankvoy.

412. *Nippon Yusen Kaisha v Marocaine de L'Industrie du Raffinage (The Tsukuba Maru)* [1979] 1 Lloyd's Rep 459. Contrast, e.g. cl 7.3.2 of BPVOY 4.

413. *Dias Compania Naviera SA v Louis Dreyfus* [1978] 1 All ER 724. *Nippon Yusen Kaisha v Marocaine de L'Industrie du Raffinage (The Tsukuba Maru)* [1979] 1 Lloyd's Rep 459.

414. *The Lefthero* (fn 378).

the party seeking to rely on it. The burden of proof is on the charterer to show that the terms of the exception apply.

Clear exceptions may include fire, storm, strikes or lockouts; "causes beyond the control of the Merchant" which will cover the breakdown of loading equipment as a result of bad maintenance on the part of the operator, who was an independent contractor of the charterer;[415] or "breakdown of machinery or equipment in or about the plant of the Charterer, supplier, shipper or consignee of the cargo".[416]

Time does not run during the periods where cargo operations have been delayed by the shipowner's fault.[417] This derives from the principle that nobody can benefit from their own wrong. It has been argued that time will run if the shipowner can prove that during that period, no cargo operations would have taken place but *The Stolt Spur*[418] has decided the issue against the owner. Demurrage will, however, continue to accrue where the delay is not due to the fault of either shipowner or charterer, unless an express exception applies.

(e) The distinction between demurrage and damages for detention

It may be important to determine whether a claim is one for demurrage or for damages for detention for a number of reasons. First, the rate of damages is at an agreed rate for demurrage but not for damages for detention, unless the charterparty expressly provides otherwise. Therefore the owner would have to prove its loss. Second, charterparties sometimes require presentation of all documentation relating to a demurrage claim within quite a short time limit, failing which the claim is time barred.[419] If the time bar applies to demurrage claims, but not claims for damages for detention, the latter claim will be subject to the general contractual time bar of six years from the breach of contract. Section 12 of the Arbitration Act 1996 has narrowed the grounds on which an extension of time can be obtained.[420] Third, most charterparties provide for a lien for certain claims. Unless the charterparty expressly provides for a lien for demurrage and damages for detention there will be no lien for either of the claims not expressly referred to.[421]

Demurrage is the agreed amount of damages due to the shipowner if the charterer is in breach of charterparty because the laytime, i.e. the agreed time for loading or discharging the ship, is exceeded. If the charterer is in breach of the charterparty in other respects and delay is caused the charterer will not be liable for demurrage but for damages for detention. Thus, for example, if the charterer delays the ship at the load-port once loading has been completed either because

---

415. *The Mozart* [1985] 1 Lloyd's Rep 239 and *A Meredith Jones & Co Ltd v Vangemar Shipping Co Ltd (The Apostolis) (No 2)* [1999] 2 Lloyd's Rep 292, at pp 300–301.

416. *Portolana Cia Nav v Vitol SA (The Afrapearl)* [2004] 2 Lloyd's Rep 305.

417. *DGM Commodities Corp v Sea Metropolitan SA (The Andra)* [2012] EWHC 1984 (Comm); [2012] 2 Lloyd's Rep 587.

418. *Stolt Tankers Inc v Landmark Chemicals SA (The Stolt Spur)* [2002] 1 Lloyd's Rep 786.

419. *Babanaft International Co SA v Avanti Petroleum Inc (The Oltenia)* [1982] 2 Lloyd's Rep 99 (CA) and [1982] 1 Lloyd's Rep 448 (Bingham J); *Evergos Naftiki Eteria v Cargill Plc (The Voltaz)* [1997] 1 Lloyd's Rep 35 for the construction of a time bar for "any claim"; *Waterfront Shipping Co Ltd v Trafigura AG (The Sabrewing)* [2008] 1 Lloyd's Rep 286; *The Petroleum Oil and Gas Corporation of South Africa (Pty) Ltd v FR8 Singapore Pte Ltd (The Eternity)* [2008] EWHC 2480 (Comm); [2009] 1 Lloyd's Rep 107; *AET Inc Limited v Arcadia Petroleum Limited (The Eagle Valencia)* [2010] EWCA Civ 713; [2010] 2 Lloyd's Rep 257; [2009] EWHC 2337 (Comm); *National Shipping Company of Saudi Arabia v BP Oil Supply Company (The Abqaiq)* [2011] EWCA Civ 1127; [2012] 1 Lloyd's Rep 18; (2010) 160 NLJ 1684; *X v Y* [2011] EWHC 152 (Comm); [2011] 1 Lloyd's Rep 694; and *Kassiopi Maritime Co Ltd v Fal Shipping Co Ltd (The Adventure)* [2015] EWHC 318 (Comm); [2015] 1 Lloyd's Rep 473.

420. *Cathiship SA v Allanasons Ltd (The Catherine Helen)* [1998] 2 Lloyd's Rep 511; London Arbitration 21/98 LMLN 493; and *Bocimar NV v Mira Oil Resources of Tortola (The Obo Venture)* [1999] CLC 819, [1999] 2 Lloyd's Rep 101.

421. See page 182 of this chapter.

it has not paid its agents and therefore the ship is prevented from leaving, or the charterer fails to nominate the discharge port, the charterer is not entitled to use the ship as floating storage space and will be liable for damages for detention. The charter may provide that the demurrage rate applies[422] but if it does not, the owner must prove its loss and adduce evidence (for example, from a chartering broker) as to the market rate for the ship. If the market has risen this will be to the owner's advantage as the owner may well be able to recover more than the demurrage rate. However, if the market has fallen, the owner may recover less than the demurrage rate.

(f) Termination for non-payment

Some voyage charterparties provide for an express right to terminate the charterparty for non-payment of demurrage, such as clause 7 of Gencon 1994. This provision is similar to the right to withdraw under a time charterparty for non-payment of hire. However, the right to terminate under clause 7 of Gencon is restricted to the situation where the ship is at or off the loadport. This no doubt reflects the practical reality that once the ship has loaded and left the loadport the owner may well have an obligation to a third party to carry the cargo to the discharge port under a bill of lading and it will not therefore wish to terminate the charterparty.

13. LIENS

At common law there is a lien for freight payable on delivery, General Average contribution[423] and expenses of preserving goods. Most standard form charterparties, both time and voyage, contain an express contractual right to lien the cargo which is much wider than that at common law. For example, time charters may well provide for a lien on the cargo "for any amounts due under this Charter"[424] and voyage charterparties "for freight, deadfreight, demurrage, claims for damages and for all other amounts due under this Charter Party including costs of recovering same".[425] If, however, the charterparty does not expressly provide for a lien for a claim such as damages for detention, there is no lien for such claim.[426]

(a) On cargo

Most charterparties provide for a lien on "the cargo".[427] The lien on cargo is a possessory lien. The owner has possession of the cargo and the lien, whether at common law or contractual, gives the owner a right to retain possession until it has been paid the sums which the lien covers. If the owner parts with possession it will lose its lien.[428] Usually the owner will wish to discharge the cargo as soon as possible under a voyage charterparty so that the ship can be delivered under its next fixture, rather than just sitting as floating storage at the discharge port. Laytime and demurrage will continue to run during the time that the cargo is retained while the lien is

---

422. See e.g. cl 4(c) of Asbatankvoy.
423. *Metall Market 000 v Vitorio Shipping Co Ltd (The Lehmann Timber)* [2013] EWCA Civ 650; [2013] 2 All ER (Comm) 585 considering the lien for General Average contributions.
424. Cl 18 of NYPE 1946 and cl 23 of NYPE 1993.
425. Cl 8 of Gencon 1994.
426. E.g. cl 21 of Asbatankvoy.
427. E.g. cl 8 Gencon 1994.
428. Cf. the wording of cl 21 of Asbatankvoy which states that the "lien shall continue after delivery of the cargo into the possession of the Charterer, or of the holders of any Bills of Lading covering the same or of any storagemen". It is not clear what the effect of this wording is – see *Cooke*, [79.3].

exercised, provided such exercise is valid. However, if there is already a problem with payment of, for example, demurrage, the owner will not wish further demurrage to accrue while its ship is idle. The owner may therefore decide that the best course of action is to discharge the cargo to its own agents at the discharge port. This is only possible if there are suitable facilities to receive the cargo, such as segregated shore tanks or barges for an oil cargo, or dry, secure warehouse facilities for a general cargo, which is not always the case. The owner can then seek to recover such costs of exercising the lien either if the express terms of the lien clause cover them or as damages from the charterer for failure to pay the sums due.[429]

Where the cargo is owned by the charterer, the owner has the right to lien the cargo under the express terms of the charterparty. Where, however, the cargo is owned by a third party the owner must check that it has the right to lien the cargo vis-à-vis the cargo owner, who cannot be bound by the terms of the charterparty as it is not a party to that contract. The bill of lading may contain a lien clause or, if the bill of lading incorporates the charterparty terms,[430] even general words of incorporation will incorporate the lien clause from the charterparty,[431] as that clause relates to the shipment, carriage and discharge of the goods. Then the owner can lien the cargo, even though the bill of lading holder does not have a personal liability for the sums due. Thus in *The Miramar*[432] owners sought to argue that they could lien against the bill of lading holder for demurrage due under a charterparty as the bill of lading incorporated the charterparty terms, including the lien clause. The demurrage clause in the charterparty provided that the demurrage was payable by the charterers. At first instance Mustill J, as he then was, held that there was no obligation to pay demurrage on the bill of lading holders, but that the owners could recover under a letter of guarantee that had been provided by the bill of lading holders to lift the lien as they were entitled to exercise the lien which was incorporated into the bill of lading. Mustill J's decision that owners could exercise the lien was not appealed but the Court of Appeal and the House of Lords upheld the decision that the wording of the charterparty demurrage provision could not be manipulated to impose the obligation to pay demurrage on the bill of lading holders.[433]

Where the bill of lading does not contain a lien or incorporate the charterparty lien clause there are conflicting decisions. Mocatta J held in *The Agios Giorgis*[434] that although the charterparty provided for a contractual lien on "all cargoes", this could not give the owner the right to lien cargo which did not belong to the charterer and the owner was in breach of the charterparty when it instructed the master to refuse discharge. Donaldson J took a different view in *The Aegnoussiotis*.[435] He held that if the cargo is owned by a third party and not the charterer, the latter is obliged to make sure that there is a contractual lien in favour of the owner. If the charterer does not do this, the owner can still exercise the lien as against the charterer who cannot rely on its own breach of contract. The charterer would remain liable for hire during the period in which the lien had been exercised. The bill of lading holder, however, would have a claim against the owner.

---

429. *Metall Market 000 v Vitorio Shipping Co Ltd (The Lehmann Timber)* [2013] EWCA Civ 650; [2013] 2 All ER (Comm) 585. The owner was entitled to recover storage and other expenses incurred in exercising a lien over cargo following discharge.

430. E.g. the Congenbill.

431. *Miramar Maritime Corporation v Holborn Oil Trading Ltd (The Miramar)* and *Santiren Shipping Ltd v Unimarine SA (The Chrysovalandou Dyo)* [1981] 1 Lloyd's Rep 159.

432. Ibid.

433. [1984] 2 Lloyd's Rep 129. See also *Tradigrain SA v King Diamond Shipping SA (The Spiros C)* [2000] 2 Lloyd's Rep 319.

434. *Steelwood Carriers Inc of Monrovia v Evimeria Compania Naviera SA of Panama (The Agios Giorgis)* [1976] 2 Lloyd's Rep 192.

435. *Aegnoussiotis Shipping Corporation v A/S Kristian Jebsens Rederi (The Aegnoussiotis)* [1977] 1 Lloyd's Rep 268.

The owner is not entitled to protect its lien by refusing to issue bills of lading unless they incorporate the charterparty lien clause and are stamped "freight prepaid". In *The Nanfri*[436] the House of Lords held that the owner would be in repudiatory breach of charterparty if it failed to issue bills of lading in the form chosen by the charterer.

In order to exercise the lien the owner must give a notice stating that it is exercising a lien and stating the sum that must be paid or setting out how that sum can be calculated. A lien can only be exercised for sums which are already due.[437] The owner cannot exercise a lien on the way to the discharge port[438] but can exercise it off the discharge port.[439] The owner must also consult a local lawyer to ascertain whether the local law permits the exercise of the lien; whether, the cargo may be sold if the sums due are not paid[440] and, if so, in accordance with what procedure.[441]

In *D'Amico Shipping Italia SpA v Endofa DMCC*[442] on the ship's arrival at her discharge port neither charterers nor shippers gave any instruction for discharge of the ship, nor was any freight paid. The owner sought the permission of the English court to discharge the cargo and to sell it pursuant to orders dated 11 and 22 September 2015. The cargo of oil was eventually sold for US$3.2 million and the owners sought an order from the court that the sale proceeds would be used to satisfy a default judgment against the shippers for damages for detention, the costs of deviation and in partial satisfaction of the claim for freight. The judge held that the freight was due as a debt before discharge. The doctrine of mitigation does not apply to a debt, whereas it may to a claim for damages. However, *obiter* the judge considered the charterers' argument on mitigation. The charterer argued that it was in repudiatory breach of the charterparty by about June 2015 because of the prolonged failure to discharge the cargo which was sufficiently long to go to the root of the contract or to frustrate the commercial purpose of the venture. The charterer argued that the owner should have accepted that breach at that point and taken steps to discharge the cargo under a lien and sell it. If it had done so, the claim for demurrage or damages for detention would have been much lower, in which case the proceeds of sale would have covered the whole of the freight. The judge dismissed the argument as it was not an argument that the owner should have mitigated the loss claimed i.e. the freight which would have remained the same amount whatever, but that the owner should have mitigated another claim.

(b) On sub-freight

Some charterparties also provide for a lien on "all sub-freights".[443] The nature of this right is very different from the lien on cargo which is founded on the owner's right to retain possession. In *Western Bulk Shipowning III A/S v Carbofer Maritime Trading ApS (The Western Moscow)*[444] Christopher Clarke J preferred the view that the contractual lien creates an equitable assignment by way of charge.[445] The owner's right over the sub-freight is to intercept freight due to the charterer under a sub charterparty or under a bill of lading issued by the charterer, but not hire under

436. [1979]1 Lloyd's Rep 201, at p 211.
437. *The Fort Kipp* [1985] 2 Lloyd's Rep 168.
438. *International Bulk Carriers (Beirut) SARL v Evlogia Shipping Co SA, and Marathon Shipping Co Ltd (The Mihalios Xilas)* [1978] 2 Lloyd's Rep 186.
439. *Santiren Shipping Ltd v Unimarine SA (The Chrysovalandou Dyo)* [1981] 1 Lloyd's Rep 159.
440. See eg. *Castleton Commodities Shipping Co Pte Ltd v Silver Rocks Investments Inc (The Clipper Monarch)* [2015] EWHC 2584 (Comm); [2016] 1 Lloyd's Rep 1
441. Under English law see CPR 25, r 25.1 (m) and the Torts (Interference with Goods) Act 1977, s 12.
442. [2016] EWHC 2223 (Comm).
443. E.g. cl 18 of NYPE 1946 and cl 23 of NYPE 1993 and cl 8 of Gencon 1994, but not cl 21 of Asbatankvoy.
444. [2012] EWHC 1224; [2012] 2 Lloyd's Rep 163.
445. [52]. See also G. Bowtle, "Liens on Sub-freights" [2002] LMCLQ 289.

a sub-time charterparty.[446] In *The Western Moscow* the New York Produce Exchange Form lien clause in clause 18 had been amended to read, (amendments in italics): "That the Owners shall have a lien upon all cargoes, and all sub-freights, *hire and sub-hire* for any amounts due under this Charter, including General Average contributions." Where there is a chain of charters each containing lien clauses, the party at the top of the chain becomes the assignee (in the sense of being the beneficiary of a contract to assign future debts) not only of the sub-hire owed to the head charterer by a sub-charterer, but also of the hire payable under the sub-sub-charter by the sub-sub-charterer. Christopher Clarke J stated,

In using the expression "*all . . . sub-hire*" the draftsman was not simply seeking to make clear that all, as opposed to some, of the sub charter hire was the subject of the lien; but to provide that it was to extend to all sub-hire down the line.[447]

The owner must give a notice to the sub-charterer or bill of lading holder demanding payment of the freight due before the payment is made.[448] If the sub-charterer has already paid the freight before it receives the notice from the owner, the lien is lost. In *The Spiros C*[449] the time charterer failed to pay time charter hire and the owner therefore gave notice of the exercise of a lien on sub-freights to Tradigrain, the sub-charterers of the ship and the shippers under the bills of lading. The owner's bills of lading provided that freight was payable as per charterparty and incorporated "all terms and conditions liberties and exceptions" of the sub-charterparty. Tradigrain had already paid the freight in accordance with the sub-charterparty to the account designated in the sub-charterparty. Tradigrain had made deductions from the freight. The deductions for commission and extra insurance were expressly permitted by a clause in the sub-charter which was in turn incorporated into the bill of lading. However, deductions had also been made in respect of a cash advance to the master and ship's disbursements at the loadport which had been paid by Tradigrain on account of the time charterer for which there was no express right to deduct although the time charterers and the sub-charterers had agreed that such sums could be set off. The Court of Appeal reversed Colman J's decision that it was not open to Tradigrain unilaterally to alter the payment terms of the bill of lading to accommodate collateral arrangements it may have made with the disponent owner for deductions from the sub-charter freight.

If the party receiving the owner's notice is not sure whether the freight should be paid to the owner or to the charterer with whom it has a contract, it can interplead and pay the money into court.[450]

---

446. *Itex Itagrani Export SA v Care Shipping Corp (The Cebu) (No 2)* [1990] 2 Lloyd's Rep 316; *Western Bulk Shipowning III A/S v Carbofer Maritime Trading ApS (The Western Moscow)* [2012] EWHC 1224; [2012] 2 Lloyd's Rep 163 but see now cl 23 of NYPE 1993 which provides for "a lien upon all cargoes and all sub-freights and/or sub-hire for any amounts" and cl 23 of NYPE 2015 which provides for "a lien upon all cargoes, sub-hires and sub-freights (including deadfreight and demurrage) belonging or due to the Charterers or any sub-charterers, for any amounts due under this Charter Party, including general average contributions."

447. [61].

448. *Dry Bulk Handy Holding Inc v Fayette International Holdings Ltd (The Bulk Chile)* [2013] EWCA Civ 184; [2013] 2 Lloyd's Rep 38; *Western Bulk Shipowning III A/S v Carbofer Maritime Trading ApS (The Western Moscow)* [2012] EWHC 1224; [2012] 2 Lloyd's Rep 163 and *Byatt International SA v Canworld Shipping Co Ltd (The Loyalty)* [2013] BCCA 427, a decision of the Court of Appeal for British Columbia, Canada.

449. *Tradigrain SA v King Diamond Shipping SA (The Spiros C)* [2000] 2 Lloyd's Rep 319.

450. Part 35 CPR. For priority of claims see *Samsun Logix Corporation v Oceantrade Corporation, Deval Denizeilik VE Ticaret AS v Oceantrade Corporation, Samsum Logix Corporation* [2007] EWHC 2372 (Comm); [2008] 1 All ER (Comm) 67. See also *Cosco Bulk Carrier Co Ltd v Armada Shipping SA* [2011] EWHC 216 (Ch); [2011] 2 All ER (Comm) 1140 where Briggs J held that the issues in relation to the lien should be determined in London arbitration commenced in accordance with the London arbitration clause in the subcharterparty, and not in the Swiss courts where the time charterer had filed for liquidation.

Voyage charterparties often also contain cesser clauses either as part of the lien clause or separately. The purpose of the cesser clause is to provide that the charterer's liability to pay demurrage ceases but only to the extent that the owner has been able to obtain payment of it by exercising the lien on the cargo.[451] The Court of Appeal has held that the right of lien must be enforceable and effective at the time of discharge for the charterer's liability to cease.[452] The local law may not permit a lien to be enforced or it would be "practically ineffective" if no lien could be exercised ashore and any attempt to exercise it on board would have resulted in the ship being sent to the end of the queue of waiting ships.[453] There are conflicting *obiter dicta* as to whether the charterer or the owner has the burden of proving that the lien was ineffective but the better view is that it lies on the charterer as the cesser clause seeks to exempt or limit the charterer's liability.[454]

---

451. E.g. cl 8 Gencon 1994.
452. *Overseas Transportation Co v Mineralimportexport (The Sinoe)* [1972] 1 Lloyd's Rep 201.
453. *The Tropwave* [1981] 2 Lloyd's Rep 159.
454. See *Cooke*, [17.12] and [17.13].

CHAPTER 5

CARGO CLAIMS AND BILLS OF LADING

Charles Debattista

1. CARGO CLAIMS – THE GENERAL PICTURE

Cargo claims are brought by cargo interests against carriers when the cargo in which they have an interest is not delivered, is delivered short or is delivered damaged. Those cargo interests may be the shippers of the goods; they may be the receivers (or, in the case of non-delivery, the intended receivers) of the goods; they may be charterers or sub-charterers of the vessel on which the cargo was shipped; they may even be banks who have extended a line of credit against the security of the cargo. The carriers sued may be shipowners or charterers. Lurking behind those interests and those carriers, there will typically be insurance entities, cargo insurers or Protection and Indemnity Clubs. The terms on which the cargo interest will claim against the carrier may also vary: in some circumstances, the claim will be brought on the terms of a bill of lading – a document which comes in many shapes and forms; in other circumstances, the claim will properly be brought on the terms of a charterparty. Finally, the law governing the claim will differ according to what the relevant contract of carriage says about the choice of law and other circumstances of the particular case.

The complexities are, it will readily be appreciated, many. The objectives of the parties to the claim, however, are simple: the cargo claimant has suffered a loss which it seeks to recover through an award of damages against the carrier; the carrier, for its part, seeks to deny, exclude or limit liability for that loss. Moreover, whether the ship on which the goods were carried is or is not under charter, and, where it is, whether the claim is brought by a charterer or a non-charterer, the bill of lading will play a central role in the cargo claim.

In this chapter, we shall follow the progress of a cargo claim governed by English law. Despite the complexities referred to above, there are a number of questions which any adviser working on a cargo claim needs to answer. These are:

1. Does the claimant have *title to sue* the defendant?
   This question conceals two quite different but related issues:
   (a) the claimant's title to sue;
   (b) the identity of the responsible carrier.

2. Do the Hague-Visby Rules apply to the cargo claim?

Having established that the right claimant has the right defendant in its sights, the next issue is whether the Hague-Visby Rules (the main international regime governing cargo claims) apply to the claim. The reason this needs to be tackled at this early stage is that the answers to the questions which follow will, at any rate in part, depend on whether the claim is subject to the Hague-Visby Rules.

3. If the right parties are in play, then can the claimant *prove its loss?*

With the stage now set for the cargo claim – with the right parties in the right court and the proper law identified – the claimant needs to prove its loss, the basic reason for the claim. This question focuses on the function of the bill of lading as a receipt: in essence, the claimant is saying that the carrier has failed to discharge what the latter had stated it had shipped in the bill of lading. The evidential force of the bill of lading is consequently of great significance at this stage of the claim.

4. If the claimant has proved its loss, then can it prove that the loss has been caused by a *breach* by the carrier of a duty owed by the carrier to the claimant?

Proof of loss is not enough: to drive home its claim, the claimant needs to prove that that loss has been caused by the carrier's breach of a duty owed to the claimant in law, whether in contract or in bailment or in tort. Behind this question, there lurk two important questions:

(a) Where are the terms of the contract of carriage between the claimant and the carrier: are they in the bill of lading or in a charterparty?
(b) If the terms of the claimant's contract of carriage are in the bill of lading, what are the carrier's duties regarding:
  (i) the ship; and
  (ii) the care of the goods?

5. If the claimant has been able to prove that its loss was caused by the carrier's breach of contract, can the carrier *exclude or limit* its liability?

These questions explain the main headings to this chapter:

- The claimant's title to sue
- The identity of the carrier
- Do the Hague-Visby rules apply?
- Proving the claimant's loss
- Proving the carrier's breach
- Excluding or limiting the carrier's liability

There is a last heading which will be dealt with, at any rate briefly, in this chapter. While not technically part of a cargo claim, a claimant does need to be aware of how its role as claimant in a cargo claim may expose it to liabilities towards the carrier:

- The claimant's potential liability towards the carrier.

2. THE CLAIMANT'S TITLE TO SUE

(a) Who cares about title to sue?

The heading here may give the impression that it is always the claimant who is more interested in establishing its title to sue: without title to sue, the claimant lacks legitimacy – commonly called *locus standi* – against the carrier and the claim is thrown out. It is necessary to point out immediately, however, that the carrier too is concerned about the claimant's title to sue – and not always or only for the obvious reason that demolishing the claimant's *locus standi* is the quickest escape route from the claim for the carrier.

The claimant may have more than one route through which to claim against the carrier. The most obvious is through a contract of carriage, either made or acquired by the claimant. The claimant may, however, have other arrows in its quiver. In certain circumstances, the claimant may bring an action against the carrier in one of two relevant torts recognised by English law, i.e. conversion or negligence. If the carrier fails to deliver goods to which the claimant can prove that it has certain rights, then the carrier is liable to the claimant in conversion. Again, if the carrier short-delivers or damages goods to which the claimant can prove it has certain rights, then the carrier is liable to the claimant in the tort of negligence. Moreover, if the circumstances are such that the carrier is the cargo interest's bailee, holding physical possession of goods to which the cargo interest has a right to possession (commonly called constructive possession) then another possible route – bailment – opens itself up to the cargo interest, outside any contract of carriage that may exist between the parties to the claim. These different routes, tort and bailment, have two things in common. First, they are not special to the law of carriage of goods by sea. They are simply carriage equivalents of more general grounds of liability which arise, for example, when a theatre-goer entrusts his overcoat and umbrella to the theatre cloakroom attendant: the latter must, as a matter of common law, return the same number of items to the same theatre-goer in the same condition in which they were entrusted to the theatre; and failure to do so exposes the theatre to liability in tort or bailment. Second, both routes are alternative to contract in two senses, i.e. (a) that either route may be available even if there *is* no contract of carriage; and (b) that either route may be available *in addition* to the claimant's contractual route of recovery where there *is* a contract of carriage between the claimant and the carrier.

It is in this latter instance that the carrier may, far and away from *denying* the claimant's title to sue in contract, become – somewhat perversely – the party interested in *establishing* it. Where a carrier is threatened by a claim outside the contract of carriage – either because there appears to be *no* contract of carriage or because there is one, but the requirements for recovery in tort or bailment *also* are satisfied – then the carrier is actually assisted if it can establish the cargo interest's *locus standi* in contract. This is not because the carrier can dictate which weapon the cargo interest uses: in English law, choice of weapon is very much up to the claimant. The point is that, while the claimant can choose whether to go in contract, tort or bailment (and claimants typically go in all three, on a belt-and-braces basis), the carrier too can, for its part, choose its shield: whichever sword the claimant chooses to wield, a carrier proving a contract with the claimant can use that contract – in its defence. And here lies the rub: liability, even if grounded in tort or bailment, is limited not only by the *general* rules of causation, remoteness and time-limitation applicable by law, but *also* by the *special* terms of any contract existing between the parties. And, in the nature of things, the terms of that contract, particularly in the liner trade where there are many cargo interests shipping their goods on to one vessel, is a contract the terms of which will have been dictated by (and therefore more likely favour) the carrier.

Thus, for example, a cargo claimant may wish to bring its claim against the carrier in tort or bailment two years after discharge of the goods: the general law would allow such a claim in tort or bailment. However, if the parties are bound by a contract of carriage governed by the Hague-Visby Rules, then the carrier can have the claim thrown out on the basis that the claim is barred by the lapse of one year from delivery under Article III rule 6 of those Rules. Alternatively, a cargo claimant may wish to recover its entire loss, "at large" and without any limitations of *quantum*, other than the general rules of causation and remoteness: a carrier, however, who can establish a contract between it and the claimant, a contract again covered by the Hague-Visby Rules, can limit its exposure through the so-called "package and unit limitation" provided for in Article IV, rule 5 of the same Rules.

For these reasons, both parties to a cargo claim care about the cargo interest's title to sue: the claimant, because it provides the claimant's legitimacy in the claim; the carrier, either because it destroys that legitimacy and throws out the claim, or because it allows the carrier to use a friendly contract shield against a hostile *non*-contractual sword.

(b) Where there is no doubt about title to sue

Given the serious interests at stake in establishing or denying the claimant's title to sue in contract, it is not surprising that this first topic is frequently hotly disputed between parties to a claim. It is important, however, to state that there are two instances where there is no mileage at all in disputing the claimant's *locus standi*.

Charterers. The first is where the cargo claimant is a charterer or a sub-charterer of a chartered ship. There is no doubt here that the claimant has title to sue the party from whom it has chartered the ship, which may be the shipowner or another charterer, under the terms of the charterparty concluded between the claimant and the respondent carrier. The charterer may be the shipper of the goods (in which case it will, if the goods are the subject of a sale contract, be, for example, a c.i.f. seller) or it may be the receiver of the goods (in which case, again if the goods are the subject of a sale contract, the receiver-charterer will likely be an f.o.b. buyer). In either event, the point is that if the claimant is a charterer, its *locus standi* is unassailable: once a charterer, as it were, always a charterer.

Shippers. The second case where there is no problem with the claimant's *locus standi*, at any rate until the moment when the bill of lading issued by the carrier is transferred by the shipper to the receiver, is where the claim is brought by the shipper who has concluded the contract of carriage. This is true whether the goods are carried on a chartered ship (the situation we have just examined) or not. Thus where, for example, S (Shipper) books space with C (Carrier) for the carriage of ten containers on C's ship, then it is that contract between S and C which provides S with *locus standi* to bring a cargo claim against C: for S to establish its title to sue, it need satisfy no further condition, for example the issue or presentation of a bill of lading. If such a bill of lading *is* issued and transferred, then the shipper will, as we shall see later in this chapter, lose its title to sue. It is not quite here once a shipper *always* a shipper: it is true to say, however, that a shipper of goods derives its title to sue the carrier from its role as a shipper, not from the issue or presentation of a bill of lading; it is equally true to say, however, as we shall see, that letting go of any bill of lading issued will extinguish that shipper's *locus standi*.

Charterers, then, are always safe, as far as concerns title to sue; and shippers are too, at any rate until they transfer the bill of lading. In which circumstances, therefore, might there be a question mark over the cargo interest's title to sue the carrier in contract – and over the carrier's ability to defend itself through the terms of the same contract?

(c) Where problems with title to sue arise

(i) The privity problem

The problem of the cargo claimant's title to sue the carrier has been closely associated with English law and other systems in the common law tradition because of the common law's strictures regarding privity of contract. If only those who are parties to a contract can sue on it, then a cargo interest who had not actually itself concluded the contract of carriage cannot sue the carrier on it despite the fact that the loss caused by the carrier's breach of contract was actually incurred by the third party rather than by the cargo interest who concluded the contract with the carrier.

Thus, if S (Shipper) makes a contract of carriage with C (Carrier) for the carriage of goods which S sells to B (Buyer), and if B pays S the purchase price of the goods against tender of a bill of lading by S to B, whether under a c.i.f. sale or under an f.o.b. sale providing that S is to make the carriage arrangements, and if C damages the goods in transit, then the doctrine of privity of contract causes B serious difficulties. B is technically a third party to S's contract with C; the doctrine of privity thus bars him from suing C; S, however, has no interest in suing C, despite having been the initial cargo interest privy to the contract of carriage, because of the simple reason that B has paid S in full and S will have suffered no loss. B, however, the receiver of damaged goods for which B has paid the full price of sound goods under the sale contract when the bill of lading was tendered, is a third party to the carriage contract and is therefore left out in

191

the cold. The consequence is that the person with title to sue, S in this example, suffers no loss; but the person who *has* suffered a loss, here B, has no title to sue.

English law sought to resolve this problem in the context of cargo claims very early on, in the shape of the Bills of Lading Act 1855, now repealed. Indeed, in 1999, English law sought to resolve the *general* problem of privity of contract across the area of contract law through the Contracts (Rights of Third Parties) Act 1999, an Act which, however, was explicitly denied impact in the context of the carriage of goods by sea.[1] The particular Act now seeking to resolve the difficulties caused by the doctrine of privity of contract in the *special* context of cargo claims is the Carriage of Goods by Sea Act 1992.

(ii) The Carriage of Goods by Sea Act 1992

The effect of section 2 of the 1992 Act is to provide the following three types of cargo interest with rights of suit against the carrier: (a) lawful holders of transferable bills of lading; (b) parties for the time being named as consignees on sea waybills and straight bills; and (c) parties to whom the carrier undertakes to deliver the goods under a ship's delivery order.

Each of the terms used in that brief summary of the effect of the Carriage of Goods by Sea Act 1992 – in particular each of the three shipping documents captured by the Act – is carefully defined in the Act. These definitions are important because, where a particular document falls outside them, it becomes necessary to examine whether there is any other basis for title to sue under the common law.

(a) Lawful holders of bills of lading. The first type of cargo interest with title to sue the carrier is the lawful holder of a "bill of lading", a phrase which, for the purposes of this Act, is assumed in section 1(2) to include only transferable bills of lading, that is to say, bills of lading which are either made out to bearer, or simply to order, or to the shipper's or to a named consignee's order. Moreover, for the claimant to have rights of suit under the Act, it must be a "lawful holder" of the bill of lading, a term defined in section 5(2) of the Act as a person with possession of the bill *and*, unless the bill is made out to bearer, either (a) named as consignee on the bill, or (b) to whom the bill is endorsed either in full or in blank. It is clear that the way the bill of lading is "made out" or endorsed is crucial to the transfer of rights of suit under the Act, at any rate where the bill is not a "bearer" bill.

(b) Bearer bills. Where the bill simply names the "bearer" as the consignee, it is the mere holding of the bill – without any need of endorsement by any cargo interest – which endows the holder with rights of suit against the carrier. That holder may be any one of a number of persons, e.g. a buyer of the goods, a bank extending a line of credit to the buyer or indeed a person who simply comes across the bill. This flexibility provides at once the greatest strength and the greatest weakness of bearer bills. On the one hand, bearer bills facilitate the transfer of rights of suit down a string of buyers or through a chain of banks through simple physical transfer of the bills with no requirement of endorsement in one form or another. On the other hand, bearer bills carry with them the risk that they may end up in the wrong pair of hands, those of a holder who simply comes across the bill and presents it under the Act: although the Act does, at section 2(1), somewhat piously, require the holder to be a "lawful" holder, it is difficult to see how a carrier can in practice be expected to assess such a holder's good faith when the bill is presented for delivery of the goods. It is presumably for this reason that bearer bills are far less commonly used in practice than bills of lading made out to the order of a named person, normally the buyer.

---

1. See Contracts (Rights of Third Parties) Act 1999, s 6(5)(a).

(c) Shipper's order bills. Before we come to bills made out to the order of the buyer, however, we need to look at bills of lading made out to the order of the shipper itself. The consignee box in such bills may be completed in one of the following ways: "To Order", "To Shipper's Order" or "(To the Shipper's name) or Order". In these cases, the carrier has agreed to carry the goods and to deliver them to any person to whom the shipper orders the carrier to deliver the goods. The question is: how does the carrier ascertain the shipper's order regarding any particular cargo? Bills made out "to order" are issued in order to dispense with repeated undertakings by the carrier to deliver: their issue constitutes what is called an a priori attornment, i.e. acknowledgement by the carrier, and it can hardly be concluded that where a bill of lading is made out simply "to order", the intention of S and C is that C needs to "attorn to" (i.e. acknowledge) every transfer of the bill. The more likely conclusion to draw from the completion of a bill of lading to Shipper's Order in any of the three ways described here is that the shipper's instructions to deliver the goods to a particular person can safely be inferred by the carrier from the fact that that person holds the bill and physically presents it for delivery of the goods at the agreed discharge port. Looked at from this perspective, there seems to be little difference between bills of lading made out to the order of the shipper and bearer bills. With both types of bill, the holder of the bill of lading has rights of suit under the 1992 Act, with no endorsements required for those rights of suit to travel down a string to the eventual receiver.[2] The strengths – and the weaknesses – of bearer bills are consequently shared with bills of lading made out to the order of the shipper.

(d) Bills of lading made out to the order of a named consignee who is not the shipper. This brings us to somewhat safer – but rather less flexible – transferable bills made out to the order of a named person, normally (but not always) the buyer of the goods. The paradigm example would be where S ships goods on C's ship and has the bill of lading made out to the order of B, the buyer of the goods. Here, if B physically presents the bill of lading at the discharge port, he is the lawful holder of the bill of lading and has rights of suit against the carrier under section 2(1) of the 1992 Act. If, however, B sells the goods on to B1 while the goods are still in transit to the discharge port agreed between S and C, then *B1* is the lawful holder of the bill of lading for the purposes of the Act and consequently has rights of suit against the carrier if two conditions are satisfied: (a) if B endorses the bill to B1, typically on the reverse side of the bill, either in full (by signing it and explicitly naming B1) or in blank (by simply signing the bill), and (b) physically transfers the bill of lading to B1 so that B1 can present the bill of lading at the discharge port. Although the person named as consignee will typically be the buyer of the goods, this is by no means always the case. Where banks extend a line of credit to the applicant under a letter of credit, typically the buyer of the goods, it may well be a condition of the letter of credit that bills of lading be made out to the order of the bank: the bank would here be securing itself against the buyer's default with the letter of credit by ensuring that it, the bank, has direct rights over the goods as against the carrier.[3] This situation has a direct impact on how the bill of lading needs to be endorsed and on who becomes the holder of the bill of lading for the purposes of the 1992 Act – and when.

Before we leave transferable bills of lading, we should say that once S, the shipper, transfers the bill of lading to B, its buyer, S loses its rights of suit against C, the carrier. Where there are several sellers and buyers down a string, each seller transferring a bearer bill or endorsing a

---

2. It would appear, however, that where a bill of lading made out simply "to order" *is* endorsed, then the holder of such a bill is only a "lawful holder" for the purposes of COGSA 1992 if the endorsement is "valid", which it will not be if the endorsement is tainted by fraud: see *The Dolphina* [2011] SGHC 273; [2012] 1 Lloyd's Rep 304.

3. The bank would similarly be secured as a lawful holder of a bill of lading if the bill of lading was endorsed to it: see *Standard Chartered Bank v Dorchester LNG (2) Ltd* (*The Erin Schulte*) [2014] EWCA Civ 1382; [2015] 1 Lloyd's Rep 97.

bill of lading made out to a named consignee's order down a string also loses its own rights of suit against the carrier. In most situations, this tallies precisely with all the parties' commercial expectations: once a seller transfers a bill of lading to a buyer, it no longer expects to be interested in the performance of the contract of carriage by the carrier – and consequently loses interest in, and the rights under, the contract of carriage. It should be remembered, however, that, as we saw earlier, a charterer never loses its title to sue its contractual carrier. Consequently, if S, the original shipper, or any of the sellers down a string, happens to be a charterer, then they retain title to sue under the charterparty even after transferring the bill of lading to their buyer.

(e) Sea waybills and straight bills of lading. Bearer bills, bills made out to the order of the shipper and bills of lading made out to the order of a named consignee all share one feature: by issuing the bill of lading in any of these three forms, the carrier has agreed to deliver the goods to a person who is not necessarily identified on the bill at the time the bill is issued. Even in the third case, where the bill is made out to the name of an identified consignee, typically the buyer, the carrier has agreed to deliver the goods to the named buyer *or* to an endorsee from that buyer – and such endorsees are not identified in the bill at that time.

There may be circumstances, however, where the identity of the *only* party to whom the shipper wants the goods delivered is known when the bill of lading is issued. Thus, for example, where one company in a group ships mechanical equipment to another company overseas in the same group, then it is not typically envisaged that the equipment will be sold in transit. In this case, C, the carrier, happily agrees with S, the shipper, that it will deliver the equipment to B – and only to B. That agreement can be recorded on a shipping document called – and calling itself – a sea waybill. B here has rights of suit against C, in terms of the 1992 Act, solely through it being named as consignee. The way in which the named consignee here acquires rights of suit against the carrier is different from the way in which a lawful holder of a bearer or order bill acquires such rights in two important ways. First, there is no need for any endorsement of the sea waybill by S to B: S and C have agreed that the equipment be delivered to B – and that, as it were, is the end of the line and there is no need for C to have any further evidence (through endorsement) of S's desire that the equipment be delivered to B. For much the same reason, B does not need to be a lawful *holder* of the sea waybill for B to acquire rights of suit: B's identity was known to S and to C at the time the sea waybill was issued. Consequently, the only credentials C needs to see before handing the goods over to B, and exposing itself to rights of suit under the contract of carriage contained in the sea waybill, is proof that B is who it says it is, i.e. B. While with a bearer or order bill – a bill intended to be and capable of being transferred down a string – the best credentials the carrier can look for in order to ensure that the goods are delivered and rights of suit are transferred to the right person is the physical holding of the bill of lading, the same cannot be said of a sea waybill which clearly on its face envisages delivery of the goods to one person and to one person only, the singularly named consignee.

We have assumed so far in this part of the chapter that the carrier has issued a document calling itself a sea waybill. What has been said in respect of sea waybills is also, however, true of documents calling themselves bills of lading but not made out to bearer or to anyone's order. Such bills of lading are commonly called straight or non-transferable bills of lading. These are used – or at least they are best used – where it is not envisaged that the goods shipped will be sold in transit. Just as with sea waybills, B's exclusive identity is known to C at the time C issues the bill to S and rights of suit in B exist because of its named role as B and because B can prove its identity as B at the discharge port, not because of any endorsement and physical transfer of the bill of lading by S.

It is clear that the main advantage of sea waybills and straight bills is that rights of suit against C can travel from S to B without physical transfer of the bill of lading: the relationship between

B and C is not consequently held up by any delay in the physical transfer of the sea waybill or the straight bill of lading by S to B. There are, however, three possible consequences of the use of such documents which need to be weighed up against this advantage. First, because B's rights of suit against C depend exclusively on it being named as consignee on the document, those rights of suit vanish as soon as B stops being named as consignee – and S can, so far as concerns its contract of carriage with C, name another person as consignee at any time until the goods are discharged: B's rights of suit against C are consequently precarious in that S can deprive B of such rights through the simple expedient of giving alternative delivery instructions to C. B may, of course, have rights of action against S under the sale contract in such circumstances, but such rights may provide recourse which is both too little, too late, and possibly in a foreign jurisdiction. Second – and this may be of concern to C – whereas C is free of liability towards S where S transfers a bearer or order bill to B, the same is not true where C issues a sea waybill or a straight bill. Section 2(1) of the 1992 Act makes it clear that S's rights of suit against C co-exist with the rights of suit which B has against C arising out of B's role as named consignee. Third, while it is clear that an order bill of lading is, in stipulated circumstances which we shall examine later on in this chapter, governed by the Hague-Visby Rules, the circumstances in which those Rules apply to a sea waybill and a straight bill of lading are somewhat more complex: we shall return to this later in this chapter.

(f) Ship's delivery orders. Apart from lawful holders of bills of lading and consignees named on sea waybills and straight bills of lading, the third type of cargo interest to whom the Carriage of Goods by Sea Act 1992 transfers rights of suit against the carrier is any person to whom the carrier acknowledges (or "attorns") a right to delivery under a ship's delivery order. Such documents are used where a cargo shipped in bulk needs to be split. So, for example, where S ships 10,000 metric tonnes of rice covered by one bill of lading and then sells 5,000 metric tonnes to each of B and B1, S now needs two shipping documents to tender under its sale contracts to B and Bl. Rather than asking C, the carrier, to re-issue two bills of lading each for 5,000 metric tonnes, S asks C to issue two ship's delivery orders, in which C undertakes to each of B and B1, both explicitly named on their respective documents, that C will deliver 5,000 metric tonnes of rice. Here, by virtue of section 2(1)(c) of the 1992 Act, B and B1 each has rights of suit against C.

As with sea waybills and straight bills of lading, B and B1 have rights of suit because they are named, normally as "consignees", on the ship's delivery orders. The delivery orders consequently do not need to be endorsed to B or B1 for either party to acquire rights of suit; neither do they need physically to be held or presented by B or B1, who simply need to satisfy C, the carrier, that they are the party identified on the ship's delivery order as consignee. Again as with sea waybills and straight bills of lading, S, the shipper, does not lose its own initial rights of suit against the carrier if S transfers the ship's delivery order to either or both of B and Bl.

(d) Where problems with title to sue are not solved by the 1992 Act

(i) The Brandt v Liverpool *contract*

The 1992 Act was passed in order to resolve title to sue issues in as many different situations as were considered to be common at the time of the passing of the Act. This did not mean, however, that other situations might not arise, falling outside the Act, where either a cargo interest or a carrier might seek to establish or deny title to sue. Thus, for example, a cargo interest may be named as consignee not on a *ship's* delivery order, but on what is sometimes called a trader's or mere delivery order, a warrant issued not by C (the carrier) but by S (the shipper) undertaking to B (the buyer) that C (the carrier) will deliver, say, 5,000 metric tonnes of rice. Here, there is no direct undertaking by C towards B; the document is not, therefore, covered by section 1(4) of the 1992 Act and section 2(1) of the same Act does not give B rights of suit. Again, if "B's bank or order" rather than B itself is named as consignee on a bill of lading, and B's bank hands the bill of lading to B but fails to endorse it, B, though in possession of the bill, is not its lawful holder within the terms of section 5(2) of the Act, being neither a consignee nor an endorsee of the bill. In these and other circumstances, B is left out in the cold by the Act, bereft of title to sue C, the carrier, at any rate in contract. Moreover, if B could seek recovery on a cause of action outside contract, then C could not plead the terms of a contract of carriage in its defence. Thus if B could prove that he owned the particular goods damaged at the time the damage was caused, B's cause of action in the tort of negligence would not be subject to any of the contractual defences which would have been available to the carrier had B had contractual title to sue.

The problem in either of the above two cases is technical and legal: privity rears its head again and a factual situation lying ever so slightly outside the precise terms of the 1992 Act leaves cargo and ship unconnected by contract. However, carriers and cargo interests at discharge ports frequently raise their sights above such technicalities and proceed as if there was no problem. Despite the fact that a particular document falls outside the precise strictures of the 1992 Act, the carrier may deliver the goods to a cargo interest which will, for its part, tender the document in its possession to the carrier and pay the carrier any outstanding shipping charges. The courts have for many years recognised in this factual exchange of goods for documents and charges an implied contract of carriage, a contract of carriage sometimes called a *Brandt v Liverpool* contract, after the case which most famously recognised such a contract.[4] The 1992 Act was designed to make recourse to such implications by the common law unnecessary: the Act did not, however, exclude such an implication where a situation arises which falls outside the Act and consequently where the Act fails to work, legal advisers will seek facts which support the implication of a contract at common law.

(ii) The party with title to sue claiming for the benefit of another

The *Brandt v Liverpool* solution to a privity problem had its limitations: the cases where the device worked all involved the surrender of some form of shipping document and the payment of some form of shipping charge by the receiver to the carrier, and the handing over of some goods by the carrier to the receiver. Where one of these factors was absent, the exchange of consideration between the parties to a contract was missing and no amount of judicial ingenuity could solve the privity problem. Section 2(4) of the 1992 Act hands the cargo interest a lifeline: where a bill of lading, a sea waybill or straight bill of lading or a ship's delivery order has been issued but B, a buyer, does not acquire rights against C (a carrier) through section 2(1) of the Act, but such rights of suit reside in another person, say S (the shipper), then S can bring an action against C for the benefit of B. The idea here is to allow the party *with* his own title to sue[5] a right to bring an action against C with any damages recovered from C to be held by S for the benefit of B. It is important to note two limitations to the effect of this subsection. First, for the section to apply, one of the three documents to which the Act applies – a bill of lading, a sea waybill or a ship's delivery order – must still be issued: the section does not apply where no such document is issued. Second, B's position against C here clearly depends on S's co-operation: if that co-op-eration is not forthcoming, as it may not be, say, where the damage to the goods has provoked

4. *Brandt v Liverpool Brazil & River Plate Steam Navigation Co Ltd* [1924] 1 KB 575; [1923] All ER Rep 656 (CA).
5. It is clear that the claimant must be able to establish that he has title to sue in his own right: see *Pace Shipping Ltd v Churchgate Nigeria Ltd (The Pace (No 2))* [2010] EWHC 2828 (Comm); [2011] 1 Lloyd's Rep 537, [28].

not only a dispute between the receiver and the carrier under the alleged contract of carriage but also one between the buyer and the seller under the sale contract, then B is not assisted by the subsection, which simply states that S is entitled to sue for the benefit of B, not that S is obliged so to do.

(iii) The f.o.b. seller and title to sue

So far we have focused on the buyer's title to sue the carrier, a question which arises every time a seller who has made the contract of carriage with the carrier then seeks to transfer its rights against the carrier to a buyer, typically where the sale contract is concluded on c.i.f. terms or on f.o.b. terms where the parties to the sale contract agree that the seller is to make the initial contract arrangements. As we have seen when we looked at the role of shipping documents in international trade contracts in Chapter 3, however, there are other types of f.o.b. contracts of sale. The parties to the sale contract may agree that the seller, S, will make the carriage arrangements with C (the carrier), not as principal but as agent for B (the buyer). In this situation, either cargo interest's title to sue the carrier is clear, B having *locus standi* under the carriage contract as principal and S as agent.

More difficult is the situation where the seller and the buyer agree that the buyer will make the carriage arrangements. Here, there is clearly no problem with establishing the buyer's *locus standi*: the buyer has made the carriage contract and is and will remain (at any rate until it transfers those rights on to an onbuyer through transfer of the bill of lading) an initial cargo party to the contract of carriage. The difficulty lies with the seller. Circumstances may arise where the seller, S, suffers a loss through the carrier's breach of the contract of carriage which C (the carrier) makes with B (the buyer). Thus, for example, where C simply fails to ship goods in space booked by B, S suffers a loss in that, as we have seen in Chapter 3, it will have failed to ship goods free on board the vessel by a date stipulated in the sale contract. Were S to be found liable to B in damages, could S recover such a loss from C under a contract of carriage? The doctrine of privity again threatens S's *locus standi*: if the contract of carriage was concluded by B, then S has no right to sue C on that contract, to which it, S, was not a party. In *Pyrene v Scindia*[6] however, Devlin J came remarkably close to recognising a contract for the benefit of a third party: S had title to sue either because, in a situation broadly analogous to that here described, S was a third party clearly envisaged by C and B when making their contract of carriage as being a party intended to be benefited by that contract; or because it was possible to imply, at any rate where goods were damaged during shipment, a contract of the type recognised in *Brandt v Liverpool*.

3. THE IDENTITY OF THE CARRIER

It may appear strange, outside a shipping law context, that the identity of the carrier should be a problem at all: surely if a claimant's claim is in contract, then the appropriate defendant is simply the claimant's contractual counterparty. The difficulty here, however, is that it is sometimes difficult to identify precisely who that contractual counterparty is. Part of the problem lies in the way ships are used, the way they are chartered and sub-chartered down several layers of charterparties. Another part of the problem – and a part of the solution – lies in the way bills of lading are signed and by whom.

---

6. *Pyrene Co Ltd v Scindia Steam Navigation Co Ltd* [1954] 2 QB 402; [1954] 1 Lloyd's Rep 321.

The problem typically arises in the following manner. S ships its goods on a ship chartered by O, the shipowner, to C; the same ship is sub-chartered by C to C1, which itself sub-sub-charters it to C2; S then transfers the bill of lading to B. If the goods are damaged in transit, B needs to know against which defendant to bring its claim: O, the shipowner or one of the three charterers, C, Cl or C2. Life may become more complex where, for example, S is itself a charterer of the ship and where S itself may therefore join the identity parade facing B as a potential defendant. The problem of the identity of the carrier may also arise in a totally different set of circumstances where there is no charterparty at all: imagine S ships its goods on to O's vessel from which the goods are then transhipped on to O1's vessel: again here, B faces two possible defendants, O and O1: which is B to sue? Which *can* it sue?

(a) Is this a problem?

In a sense, of course, it may seem strange to present this as a problem: surely having more than one possible defendant is a bonus, not a problem. Moreover, the decision is and should be a commercial, tactical one, rather than a purely legal one. The claimant would be well advised to claim against the defendant with the deepest pocket, with assets in the friendliest, most accessible and most litigation efficient jurisdiction. While all of these factors no doubt play a part in every claimant's choice of defendant, it is still important to get the choice right in terms of law. Getting it wrong – pursuing a defendant who then successfully points elsewhere – not only involves unnecessary cost, but also runs the risk of allowing a time bar to lapse vis-à-vis the proper defendant. The claimant's objective is to establish that the defendant against whom it *wishes* to claim (for all the tactical reasons indicated earlier on) is the defendant against whom it *can*, as a matter of law, bring a claim.

Who then *is* the proper defendant? Who is the contractual carrier? The answer depends in large part on the bill of lading covering the goods. There is one situation, however, where the bill of lading will not indicate the identity of the carrier and we need to deal with that situation first.

(b) Where the claimant is a charterer

Where the claimant in a cargo claim is a charterer, then its carrier is the party from whom it chartered the ship. Thus, where S, a shipper who has sub-chartered from C, ships goods on a vessel chartered to C by O, the shipowner, S's defendant is C not O. C and S have contracted for the carriage of goods on the chartered ship; the charterparty is the only contract to which they are both party; and C is consequently S's defendant in a cargo claim. The bill of lading will, as we shall see when we come to proving the claimant's loss, play a part in that claim, but it will not establish who S's defendant is: it will simply help establish S's loss.

(c) Where the claimant is not a charterer

Where the claimant is not a charterer, then the identity of its carrier will depend on the logo or banner heading of the bill of lading covering the goods and on the manner in which the bill of lading is signed. The latter factor has been particularly significant in providing relatively quick answers to most "identity of the carrier" questions since 1994, when the UCP 500, the Uniform Customs and Practice for Documentary Credits, came into force. Those Rules have now, as we have seen in Chapter 3, been superseded by the UCP 600, but for present purposes, there is no relevant difference between the two versions of the Rules. For a bill of lading to be accepted by a bank under a letter of credit, Article 20 of the UCP 600 requires it to "indicate the name of the carrier" and to be signed in one of a number of ways detailing the name of the signatory and the capacity in which it signs the bill.

It is not surprising that a set of banking rules requires such detail: the bill of lading frequently acts as security for the bank against non-payment by the buyer as applicant under a letter of credit and, in such circumstances, the bank has an interest in identifying clearly who physically has the goods represented by the bill of lading. A presumably unintended, but nonetheless welcome, consequence of these banking rules is that it is now relatively easy to identify the carrier for the purpose of identifying the carrier in a cargo claim. The link between the UCP 500 and the significance in particular of the signature at the foot of a bill of lading was explicitly recognised by the House of Lords in *The Starsin*,[7] where the evidence of identity provided by the signature on a bill of lading was held to prevail over an express "identity of the carrier" clause appearing on the reverse of a bill of lading: in effect, what was good enough for a document checker in a bank should be good enough for a cargo claimant when it comes to identifying the contractual carrier responsible for the safe carriage of goods.

The main identifier, then, in discovering whom the claimant can pursue in a cargo claim is the signature at the foot of the bill of lading, assisted by the banner logo at the top of the bill of lading. Consequently, in our example above, where B faced four possible defendants, O (the owner), C (the head-charterer), C1 and C2 (two sub-charterers), B's legal advisers would need to look at the bill of lading, focusing first on the signature at the toe and then at the logo (if there is one) at the top. Given the rigours required by the banking rules, it is now extremely likely that this fairly mechanical scrutiny will answer the carriage question as to the identity of the carrier.

To this, three caveats need to be added. First, if the head-charter between O and C is a demise or bareboat charterparty (as to which see Chapter 4), then O falls out of B's range: one of the effects of such a charterparty is that C acts as disponent owner of the ship and O is out of everyone's sight other than C's. Second, it must be recalled that this entire question is a matter of contract and that it is therefore subject to any clear contra-indication: thus, for example, it is conceivable that a clear and obvious clause on the front of the bill may upset the presumptions raised at the top and toe of the bill of lading. Third, and by the same token, in the rare situation where the logo and the signature fail clearly to identify the carrier, the courts have developed a number of presumptions on which to fall back, the most important of which is that a master is deemed to have signed on behalf of the shipowner rather than a charterer.

(d) Claiming against the "actual" carrier

So far, we have looked at the problem of the identity of the carrier in the context of chartered ships. The problem may, however, also arise where S, a shipper, contracts with O, a shipowner, for the carriage of goods which are then transhipped onto O1's vessel: who can B sue, O, the contractual carrier, or O1, the so-called "actual" carrier?

It is clear that B can sue O, with whom B has a contract. What, however, if O is not worth suing: can B claim against O1, with whom it has no contract? The answer to this question is quite obvious and unremarkable: B can claim against O1 if B can establish a tort committed by O1 or a breach by O1 of O1's duties as B's bailee. Broadly speaking, if B can prove that O1 failed in its duty of care towards B at a time when B owned or was entitled to the possession of the goods, then B has title to sue O1 in tort or bailment.

The real problem is not with B's sword, but with O1's shield. If B could sue O1 in tort or bailment, would O1 be able to use in its defence the terms of the bill of lading issued by O to

---

7. *Homburg Houtimport BV v Agrosin Private Ltd (The Starsin)* [2003] UKHL 12; [2003] 1 Lloyd's Rep 571.

B or of any bill of lading issued by O1 to O? If the answer to this question was "No", the result would be that, even where they *could* sue O, claimants would choose to sue O1 at large and in a claim uncluttered by the contractual defences which would affect an action against O. This consequence is avoided by the decision in *The K H Enterprise,*[8] which held that where O's contract with S allowed O to tranship the goods on any terms, O1 could, if sued by S or B, plead in its defence the terms of a bill of lading issued by O1 to O, i.e. the terms of the bill of lading under which the goods were transhipped by the actual carrier.

4. DO THE HAGUE-VISBY RULES APPLY?

As we proceed through the cargo claim, we shall see that a number of matters depend on whether or not the Hague-Visby Rules[9] apply: we have already alluded to some such matters, like the one-year time bar and the package/unit limitations under the Rules. These Rules, brought into force in the UK by the Carriage of Goods by Sea Act 1971, represent a patchwork quilt of compromises between the interests of cargo claimants and those of carriers. Thus, for example, while time bars and the cap on recoverable damages obviously favour the carrier, the bar on bill of lading clauses which seek to exclude or limit the carrier's liability other than as provided in the Rules (contained in Article III rule 8) is obviously important to cargo interests. It follows that it is difficult to predict before a dispute arises and the claim starts playing itself out which of the two parties to a cargo claim will be arguing for the application of the Rules: this will really depend on which party needs which article in the Rules to drive home the claim or to extinguish or limit it.

We saw in Chapter 1 that the general rules whereby English courts decide which law applies to a particular dispute are now to be found in Regulation (EC) No 593/2008 on the law applicable to contractual obligations ("Rome I") and the Law Applicable to Contractual Obligations (England and Wales and Northern Ireland) Regulations 2009, which came into force on 17 December 2009.[10] We saw there that an express choice of law determines the law applicable to a contractual dispute and one might have thought that, given that most bills of lading contain choice of law clauses, the matter would be relatively uncontroversial: the Hague-Visby Rules would apply only where the parties had expressly incorporated them or, failing that, where the contract of carriage had a close connection with the UK, a Hague-Visby State.

Ever since the House of Lords decision in *The Morviken,*[11] however, a decision made before the 1990 Act but which has, perhaps rather surprisingly, stood since then, the English position regarding the law applicable in particular to cargo claims has been rather special. In summary, rather than following the usual conflicts path of first finding out which national law applies (through the conflicts rules contained in the Contracts (Applicable Law) Act 1990) and then, if English law applies, finding out which *part* of English law applies to the particular dispute (e.g. the Carriage of Goods by Sea Act 1971), the courts will use the 1971 Act itself to decide whether

---

8. *Owners of cargo lately laden on board the KH Enterprise v Owners of the Pioneer Container (The KH Enterprise)* [1994] 2 AC 324; [1994] 1 Lloyd's Rep 593.

9. For a brief history of the Hague-Visby Rules, see Chapter 4, pages 127–128. On 23 September 2009, the United Nations Convention on Contracts for the International Carriage of Goods Wholly or Partly by Sea (the "Rotterdam Rules") was opened for signature. As of 2 March 2017, while the Convention has been signed by 25 States, it had only been ratified by Congo, Spain and Togo. A total of 20 ratifications, acceptances, approvals or accessions are required for the Convention to come into force.

10. SI 2009/3064. The Regulations disapply the Contracts (Applicable Law) Act 1990 regarding contracts concluded as from 17 December 2009. The Rome Convention and the Contracts (Applicable Law) Act 1990 apply to contracts concluded before that date. See more generally Chapter 1, page 53 et seq.

11. *Owners of cargo on board the Morviken v Owners of the Hollandia (The Morviken)* [1983] 1 AC 565; [1983] 1 Lloyd's Rep 1.

the English Carriage regime applies to the cargo claim. In other words, the conflict rules used for cargo claims are contained in the Carriage of Goods by Sea Act 1971 rather than in Rome I. The effect is that if any one of a number of triggers in the 1971 Act is triggered, then the Hague-Visby Rules will apply, even without an express choice of law clause saying so, and indeed (as was the case in *The Morviken* itself), in the teeth of an express choice of law clause choosing some other regime.

The 1971 Act contains four such triggers. The Rules will apply to any bill of lading if (a) the bill of lading is issued in a Hague-Visby contracting State,[12] or if (b) the carriage starts from such a State, or if (c) the bill of lading incorporates the legislation of a State giving effect to the Rules or if (d) the bill of lading expressly incorporates the Rules through what is commonly called a clause paramount. Triggers (a), (b) and (c) only apply to bills of lading covering the carriage of goods between ports in different States and do not apply to the carriage of live animals or to goods carried on deck and stated on the bill so to be carried. Trigger (d), however, applies, by virtue of sections 1(6)(a) and 1(7) of the 1971 Act whether or not the carriage is international and even to live animals and goods carried on deck and stated so to be carried.[13] The effect of using these triggers as conflict rules for cargo claims is that cargo claims in England will almost certainly attract the application of the Hague-Visby Rules as enacted in the Carriage of Goods by Sea Act 1971 even where there is precious little connection between the contract and this country and even if (as was the case in *The Morviken*) the parties choose another law in the bill of lading.[14]

It will be noted that for the Rules to apply, the starting point is that a bill of lading is required. However, three caveats need to be added to this default position. First, it was held in *Pyrene v Scindia*[15] that, where an f.o.b. seller claimed against a carrier in respect of goods damaged by the carrier during shipment, the carrier could plead the terms of the Rules despite the fact that no bill of lading had actually been issued. Second, by virtue of section 1(6)(b) of the 1971 Act, the Rules can, in large part, be made to apply to a non-negotiable receipt through a clause incorporating the Rules into such a document: this would cover a sea waybill containing a so-called "clause paramount". Third, it is now clear since *The Rafaela S*[16] that the Rules apply to straight bills of lading, i.e. bills of lading made out to a named consignee but not to its order.

In the rest of this chapter, we will follow the progress of a cargo claim on the assumption that it is governed by the Hague-Visby Rules.

5. PROVING THE CLAIMANT'S LOSS

Having established its own *locus standi* as claimant and having identified the carrier as a proper defendant, the claimant, whether it be S, the shipper, or B, the buyer of the goods, now needs to

---

12. It is not enough for the bill of lading to be issued in, or for the goods to be shipped from, a State which has enacted into its domestic law, but has not signed, the Hague-Visby Rules. See *Trafigura Beheer BV and Another v Mediterranean Shipping Company SA (The MSC Amsterdam)* [2007] EWCA Civ 794; [2007] 2 Lloyd's Rep 622 (CA).

13. See *Sideridraulic Systems SpA v BBC Chartering & Logistics GmbH & Co KG (The BBC Greenland)* [2011] EWHC 3106 (Comm); [2012] 1 Lloyd's Rep 230, [22].

14. In effect, the Hague-Visby Rules would be treated as overriding mandatory provisions for the purposes of art 9 of Rome I.

15. *Pyrene Co Ltd v Scindia Steam Navigation Co Ltd*, see fn 6. Moreover, the Rules would apply even in respect of that part of the packing operation of a container carried out on land: see *Volcafe Ltd v Compania Sud Americana de Vapores SA (t/a CSAV)* [2015] EWHC 516 (Comm); [2015] 1 Lloyd's Rep 639 [9] and [10], overturned but not on this ground at [2016] EWCA Civ 1103; [2017] 1 Lloyd's Rep 32.

16. *J I Macwilliam Co Inc v Mediterranean Shipping Co SA (The Rafaela S)* [2005] UKHL 11; [2005] 1 Lloyd's Rep 347.

prove its loss. In effect, this means that it is up to the claimant to establish that the carrier has failed to deliver what the shipper shipped. This involves a comparison between two photographs or snapshots of the goods: the goods as they were shipped and the goods as they were discharged.

(a) Notice of loss at discharge

To start with the second of the snapshots, the snapshot at discharge, it is of course important for the cargo interest to preserve, as it were, the evidence. Article III rule 6 of the Hague-Visby Rules provides an incentive: notice of loss or damage must, failing joint inspection when the cargo interest receives the goods, be given in writing to the carrier at the discharge port before or when the cargo interest takes the goods into its custody or, where such loss or damage is not apparent, within three days. If the cargo interest fails to give such notice, in effect presenting a snapshot of damaged goods on discharge, the carrier is prima facie assumed to have delivered the cargo as described in the bill of lading. Such an assumption would not necessarily destroy the cargo claim, but it does seriously wrong-foot the claimant who would now have to upset the presumption by proving one of two negatives, i.e. either that the goods were *not* delivered in the condition or quantity described in the bill of lading or that the goods were not damaged ashore after discharge. Clearly an Article III rule 6 notice, the receiver's "discharge snapshot", is of considerable evidential importance in getting a cargo claim off the ground.

(b) Where the shipper claims: a prima facie presumption

It is, however, the difference between that photograph, taken at discharge, and the photograph taken on loading in the bill of lading which provides real substance to the cargo claim because it is that difference, that discrepancy, which constitutes the claimant's evidence of loss. It is clear that the carrier must, on the shipper's demand, provide the shipper with a snapshot after receiving the goods into its charge, showing among other things, the quantity of the goods as furnished in writing by the shipper (whether by way of the number of packages or pieces or by weight, as appropriate), the apparent order and condition of the goods, and the leading marks necessary for the identification of the goods as furnished in writing by the shipper.[17] It will be noticed that the shipper plays an important role in the taking of this photograph. Thus, the quantity of the goods and the leading marks originate with the shipper: this is hardly surprising, as the shipper is at least as likely as the carrier to have this information.

Once the bill of lading is issued and signed by the carrier, however, the photograph becomes the carrier's: by signing the bill, by autographing the snapshot, the carrier states that the goods identified by the indicated loading marks have been loaded (hence "bill of loading") in the quantity and apparent condition stated in the bill. That statement raises a prima facie presumption against the carrier that the goods *were* so loaded, a presumption which the carrier can, if the cargo claim is brought by the shipper, rebut through evidence contradicting the statements on the bill as to loading marks, quantity and apparent condition.

Given that the information as to leading marks and quantity originates with the shipper and given that both the shipper and the carrier are both physically present at the loading port, it makes sense for the presumption raised against the carrier in a claim by the shipper to be relatively weak, i.e. rebuttable by contrary evidence intended to show that the carrier loaded goods in the quantity and apparent condition in which they were discharged, not the quantity and

---

17. Art III r 3 of the Hague-Visby Rules.

apparent condition stated on the bill of lading. The evidential playing field as between the carrier and the shipper is sensibly level, or at any rate only slightly tilted in the carrier's favour.

(c) Where a third party claims: conclusive evidence

A third party to whom the bill of lading has been transferred, however, needs stronger protection. B, the buyer of goods to whom the bill of lading has been endorsed and transferred, was not the party with whom information about the goods originated; neither was B at the shipment port, nor does B have easy access to evidence as to what was shipped at that port. To allow C, the carrier, to upset the prima facie presumption raised against C by the bill of lading in a claim brought by B would be unfairly to skew the balance in C's favour. This is why Article III rule 4 of the Hague-Visby Rules bars proof contradicting the statements as to quantity, apparent condition and leading marks contained in the bill of lading when the bill has been transferred to a third party acting in good faith, here B, the buyer of the goods: the bar raises an estoppel against the carrier, making the bill of lading conclusive evidence of what it says about the goods. The result is that if B can show that the goods were discharged in a smaller quantity or in a worse apparent condition than that in which they were stated in the bill of lading to have been shipped, it will have proved its loss and the cargo claim is well on its way to success. Given the fact, however, that some of the information to which the carrier is bound – leading marks and quantity – originates with S, the shipper, the Rules provide C with an indemnity against S for all loss, damages and expenses resulting from any inaccuracies in any such particulars.[18]

Before we leave the apparently strong presumption which the Hague-Visby Rules raise in Article III rule 4 in favour of third party transferees of bills of lading against the carrier, it is important to point out that the Article does not apply where the goods are covered not by a transferable bill of lading (a bearer bill or a bill of lading made out to order) but by a sea waybill. Section 1(6)(b) of the Carriage of Goods by Sea Act 1971 makes it clear that where goods carried by sea are covered by a non-negotiable receipt marked as such (in modern practice, a sea waybill), statements on the document regarding leading marks, quantity and apparent condition are not conclusive. Three points need to be made. The first is that where a sea waybill is issued, it will not necessarily be – and it does not need to be – transferred to the person named as consignee. We have already seen that the consignee acquires its rights of suit against the carrier through being named as consignee not through transfer of the document. Second, although the document does not need to be transferred to the consignee, it may be – and where this happens, it may come as a surprise to the consignee that the carrier is not bound by the statements on the sea waybill regarding the goods, particularly given that the sea waybill envisaged in section 1(6)(b) is one which expressly provides that the Rules are to govern the contract as if the sea waybill were a bill of lading. Third, it is not clear whether the transferee of a straight bill of lading – as opposed to a sea waybill – is similarly deprived of the advantages of Article III rule 3 of the Hague Rules. In *The Rafaela S*,[19] the House of Lords held that the Rules applied to such bills of lading on the basis either that a straight bill of lading was nonetheless a bill of lading or that it was a "similar document of title" within the definition of "contract of carriage" in Article I(b) of the Rules. The specific issue in the dispute was whether the carrier could limit its liability rather than whether the bill of lading provided conclusive evidence in the hands of the consignee. It would seem to follow from the decision that the Rules apply to straight bills, however; that a straight bill *does*

---

18. Art III r 5 of the Hague-Visby Rules.
19. See fn 16.

provide the consignee with conclusive evidence of what it says about the goods, although, as we have seen, a sea waybill, curiously, does not.

(d) Why the estoppel is weaker than it seems

The stage seems set for an evidential victory for B, with C having a residual indemnity against S: this would, however, be too simplistic a summary of the position. The effect of Article III rule 4 of the Hague-Visby Rules is to bind C to what is stated about quantity, apparent condition and leading marks in the bill of lading and if the bill of lading states nothing much in this regard, then there is little to which to bind C. Now no carrier is likely to issue a bill of lading saying nothing about the quantity and apparent condition of the goods shipped, for much the same reason that it is unwise to issue a blank cheque in general commercial life: blanks can be filled in later with information which would not assist C. Carriers do, however, so qualify their statements as to make them of little use to B: like all estoppels, the estoppel raised by Article III rule 4 of the Hague-Visby Rules is only as strong as the statements on which it is based and if those statements are weak, then so is the estoppel. Statements as to apparent condition are weakened by so-called "clausing"; those as to quantity, by "weight and quantity unknown" clauses.

(e) Clausing bills

Bills of lading typically state in pre-printed wording that the goods have been shipped in apparent good order and condition. The statement says nothing, of course, about the commercial value or specifications of the goods – it is limited to the *apparent* condition of the goods. This is all that a carrier can reasonably be held to, the carrier not being a trader in the particular goods or commodities being shipped.

The shipment of goods in apparently good condition is, of course, what both C, the carrier, and S, the shipper – and most definitely B, the buyer – hope will happen. C, however, is also wary of being bound to such a statement if it is not true, of being held hostage to a photograph showing goods to have been shipped in good condition when they were not: such a "clean" photograph would give B, the buyer, an unfair advantage in a cargo claim, unfair because the goods were simply not, on this hypothesis, ever shipped in apparently good condition. If the goods are shipped in less than good order and condition, the carrier will therefore want to "clause" the bill qualifying the statement that the goods were shipped in apparent good order and condition, adding words such as "torn bags noted" or "evidence of rust on shipment".[20]

This type of clausing has an unwelcome impact on a c.i.f. seller, who is under an implied duty to tender a clean bill of lading:[21] the clausing of a bill by C in effect puts S in breach of its duties under the sale contract and will also prejudice its chances of payment under any letter of credit. In order to avoid this, S will attempt to persuade C to issue a clean bill where a claused one is warranted, normally by offering to hold C harmless against any consequences of issuing a

---

20. Carriers will frequently seek to engineer the same result when shipping particular types of goods, e.g. timber or steel, by redefining the "condition" which is "apparent[ly] good" to exclude, say, warping or rust: these clauses are known as "Retla" clauses after the American case, *Tokio Marine & Fire Insurance Co Ltd v Retla Steamship Co* [1970] 2 Lloyd's Rep 91, giving effect to such clauses. The protection provided by such clauses under English law is now suspect after the decision in *Breffka & Hehnke GmbH & Co KG v Navire Shipping Co Ltd (The Saga Explorer)* [2012] EWHC 3124 (Comm); [2013] 1 Lloyd's Rep 401, at any rate when there is clear evidence of fraud in the issuing of an apparently clean bill of lading.

21. *M Golodetz & Co Inc v Czarnikow-Rionda Co Inc (The Galatia)* [1980] 1 Lloyd's Rep 453 (CA).

clean bill. Two issues arise: first, is S actually *entitled* to a clean bill of lading; and, second, can C safely issue a clean bill in these circumstances against a letter holding it harmless against the consequences of so doing?

As for the first issue, it is clear that a shipper is *not* entitled to a clean bill where the goods are shipped in less than *good* order and condition. All that Article III rule 3 of the Hague-Visby Rules gives the shipper is the right to demand on shipment of the goods a bill of lading stating the apparent order and condition of the goods, not one stating the apparent good order and condition of the goods. It is for the shipper to ask for, but for the carrier to issue, a clean bill of lading – and if the carrier does so issue, then, of course, as we have seen, the carrier is held to that photograph in a cargo claim brought by any transferees of the bill of lading. This is why carriers who *do* issue clean bills in such circumstances will normally do so only against a letter of indemnity ("LOI") in which the shipper holds them harmless against the consequences of so doing – and this brings us to the second issue: how secure are these LOIs?

There are two problems here. First, the LOI is only, of course, as good as its issuer and a carrier would need to feel sure, before issuing a clean bill in these circumstances, that the issuer is both solvent and easily accessible: this is why carriers frequently ask for an LOI backed by a bank guarantee. Second, however, there is some doubt as to whether such an LOI is actually enforceable under English law: in a majority decision, the Court of Appeal held in *Brown Jenkinson & Co Ltd v Percy Dalton (London) Ltd*,[22] that such an indemnity is unenforceable where its purpose is to make a fraudulent representation as to the apparent condition of the goods – which, it would appear, would be the case by definition in the circumstances here envisaged. It is for these reasons that disputes quite regularly arise between shippers and carriers as to whether goods shipped are or are not in apparent good order and condition – and as to whether carriers are or are not entitled to clause bills of lading; see, for example, the disputes which arose in *The David Agmashenebeli*[23] and *The Sea Success*.[24]

(f) "Weight and quantity unknown" clauses

If there are problems with bills clausing the statement as to the apparent order and condition of goods shipped, there are many more problems with statements on bills regarding the quantity of goods shipped. Bills are not always claused: they are only claused when carriers observe obvious problems with the goods on shipment. The shipper's figures as to quantities are, however, always qualified as a matter of course by carriers, in pre-printed wording varying in ingenuity: "weight and quantity unknown", "shipper's figures, for information only", "said to contain", "said to be", "STC", "STB", etc. Two issues arise: first, what is the effect of such qualifications; second, is the carrier entitled so to qualify the figures given to it by the shipper?

As for the first issue, it is clear that the effect of such qualifications is to deprive the bill of lading of any evidential force regarding the quantity of goods shipped in a cargo claim brought either by a shipper or by a third party transferee of the bill of lading. A statement can only raise a presumption of its truth, whether prima facie or conclusive, if a statement is made; a statement as to quantity involves stating that goods have been shipped in such-and-such a quantity; a

---

22. *Brown Jenkinson & Co Ltd v Percy Dalton (London) Ltd* [1957] 2 QB 621; [1957] 2 Lloyd's Rep 1.

23. Owners of cargo lately laden on board the *David Agmashenebeli v Owners of the David Agmashenebeli (The David Agmashenebeli)* [2002] EWHC 104 (Admlty); [2003] 1 Lloyd's Rep 92.

24. *Sea Success Maritime Inc v African Maritime Carriers Ltd (The Sea Success)* [2005] EWHC 1542 (Comm); [2005] 2 Lloyd's Rep 692.

statement stating that goods *may* have been shipped in such a quantity, but then again may *not* have, is no statement at all and consequently no presumption arises.

As for the second issue, four things are clear. First, the carrier is entitled so to qualify the statements as to quantity where, in the words of Article III rule 3, "he has reasonable ground for suspecting not accurately to represent the goods actually received, or which he has had no reasonable means of checking". Second, however, this is the extent of the leeway allowed to the carrier. It is equally clear from the article that "on demand of the shipper", the carrier "shall" issue a bill of lading giving the quantity of the goods shipped. Consequently, the shipper does have the right, when faced with a bill of lading qualifying out of existence the statement on it as the quantity of goods shipped, to demand that the offending part of the qualification be deleted. Thus, for example, where the bill of lading states that 20,000 mts of a commodity have been shipped, "weight and quantity unknown", the shipper is entitled to ask for the deletion of the qualification, leaving the statement ready to acquire conclusive evidence in the hands of the transferee. Third, and again, however, the shipper is highly unlikely to exercise its rights of demand under Article III rule 3: the reality is that a shipper in receipt of a bill of lading is far likelier to tender it for payment to the buyer than to complain to the carrier about the precise effect of the qualifications as to the quantity of goods shipped: the shipper's objective is to get paid as quickly as possible rather than to return the bill of lading to the carrier for deletion of the qualification. Fourth, where the qualification is not deleted (as is, for the reason just stated, most likely) the qualification cannot, it is suggested, be struck down by Article III rule 8, the article which bars clauses, covenants or agreements which relieve or lessen the carrier's liability under the Rules: a qualification of a statement of fact is not a clause covenant or agreement and therefore falls outside the effect of Article III rule 8.

The net result is that where a cargo claim for short delivery is brought by a transferee of a bill of lading, the transferee has no clear photograph of the quantity of goods shipped and will consequently need to prove not only the quantity in which the goods were discharged (which the transferee can easily do so long as notice of loss is given on discharge) but also the quantity in which the goods were shipped. The estoppel raised by the Rules is consequently of little use to the transferee – and the buyer of commodities where quantity discrepancies are common may need to protect itself against such losses through means other than the contract of carriage, as we have seen in Chapter 3.

6. PROVING THE CARRIER'S BREACH

Proving that the goods discharged were not the goods stated to have been shipped, comparing the difference between the discharge and the loading snapshots, is necessary but not sufficient for the success of the cargo claim. For the claimant to succeed, it needs to prove that its loss was the direct result of a breach by the carrier of any one of three possible sources of obligation, i.e. contract, tort or bailment. We have already seen the requirements for success in tort or bailment, namely a link between the claimant and the particular goods damaged at the time of damage. It is with proof of breach of contract that this part of the chapter is concerned – and this issue revolves around two central questions:

(a) Where are the terms of the contract of carriage between the claimant and the carrier: are they in the bill of lading or in a charterparty?
(b) If the terms of the claimant's contract of carriage are in the bill of lading, what are the carrier's duties breach of which might give success to the cargo claimant?

(a) Where are the terms of the contract of carriage?

If the cargo claimant needs to prove that its loss has been caused by a breach by the carrier of a particular term of a particular contract, it becomes crucial for the claimant to identify the contract on which the claim is being brought. It is easy to draw the conclusion from the fact that the claimant holds a bill of lading, whether as shipper or as transferee, that the terms of its contract with the carrier are contained in the bill of lading and that the claimant's task is to declare the carrier in breach of a term contained in the bill of lading. This conclusion is, however, too simplistic. In identifying the claimant's contract of carriage, there are four possible sources:

(i) The contract itself

It may seem tautological to say that the contract of carriage on which the claim is based is in the contract of carriage: there is, however, a fundamental truth hidden in this circularity. Where a cargo claim is brought by a non-charterer shipper of goods who has actually concluded the contract of carriage with the carrier, then the terms of the contract of carriage are contained in the agreement which they have concluded. The contract pre-exists – and is not exclusively contained in – any bill of lading which may later be issued. The bill of lading is issued after the goods are shipped, performing its role as a snapshot of shipment. Shipment occurs, however, in performance of a contract which already exists – and some of whose terms will already therefore have been agreed, e.g. freight and time of shipment. Those terms will be contained in a variety of exchanges and possibly documents, e.g. telephone or email exchanges and published schedules or booking notes. Other terms will be left to the bill of lading, which will, when it is issued, provide good evidence of the parties' agreement. It is not, however, the only or even the prevailing source of evidence, in the sense that if parties have agreed terms which do not tally with a particular term of the bill of lading, then it is the specially agreed term which prevails over the bill of lading term, not because one is special and the other general, but because the contract exists before the issue of the bill of lading. Thus if, for example, the parties agree that shipment will be direct without calls at intermediate ports, that agreement will prevail over a term in the bill of lading giving the carrier a liberty to call at intermediate ports. The basic point is that the shipper's contract is in the contract evidenced by, but not contained in, the bill of lading.[25]

Who is the shipper here? Two situations are quite simple. First, we are envisaging here a shipper who is not also a charterer: we shall see presently that a shipper who is a charterer contracts with the carrier on charterparty terms, despite the fact that the charterer also holds a bill of lading. Second, the shipper will typically be either a shipper shipping goods for its own account, without selling the goods on, or a c.i.f. seller making the contract of carriage and actually shipping the goods it is selling to a buyer. In either case, the terms of the shipper's contract of carriage are in its contract of carriage with the carrier.

The third situation is a little more complex. We have already looked at the case *Pyrene v Scindia*,[26] where an f.o.b. seller claimed against a carrier in respect of goods damaged by the carrier during shipment: the carrier successfully pleaded the terms of the Rules despite the fact that no bill of lading had actually been issued. We have seen in Chapter 3 that in f.o.b. sales, the party who will typically (but not always) make the contract of carriage is the buyer – this type of f.o.b.

---

25. On the other hand, anything which the carrier seeks to insert into the agreement *after* the issue of the bill of lading is clearly post-contractual and therefore not binding: see *Glencore International AG v MSC Mediterranean Shipping Co SA* [2015] EWHC 1989 (Comm); [2015] 2 Lloyd's Rep 508 (under appeal), where a carrier's attempt to make discharge tantamount to due delivery in a document issued after the bill of lading was hopelessly late and therefore ineffective to protect the carrier from an action for misdelivery. Affirmed, but with no comment on this point, at [2017] EWCA Civ 365.

26. See fn 6.

contract is normally called a straight f.o.b. contract and the sale contract in *Pyrene v Scindia* was on such terms. Now, on the assumption that the buyer is not a charterer, the straight f.o.b. buyer's contract of carriage is contained in its agreement with the carrier: the buyer is here the contractual shipper making its contract of carriage with the carrier, with the bill of lading providing evidence of, but not containing, the terms of that contract. What if, however, a claim is brought against the carrier not by the buyer, the carrier's contractual shipper, but by the seller, who will most likely be the *actual* shipper of the goods? We have already seen that Devlin J recognised the actual shipper's title to sue the carrier; we also saw that the carrier could, in defence to such a claim, plead the terms of a bill of lading which was never issued. This must mean that, as between a straight f.o.b. seller and a carrier, the terms of the contract of carriage are contained in, not just evidenced by, the bill of lading which would have been issued had goods been shipped.

(ii) The bill of lading

This brings us to more typical situations where the contract terms are contained in the bill of lading. Again leaving to one side situations where the goods are carried on a chartered ship, the buyer of goods from a c.i.f. seller, or from an f.o.b. seller where the seller has agreed to conclude and to transfer a contract of carriage to the buyer, obtains, as we saw at the start of this chapter, rights of suit against the carrier through the Carriage of Goods by Sea Act 1992 – and those rights of suit are in a real sense *contained in*, rather than simply evidenced by, the bill of lading. Consequently, any terms of the contract of carriage specially agreed between the seller/shipper and the carrier do not travel to the buyer. To return to the example used earlier, if a shipper agrees with the carrier that there will be no intermediate calls, that term prevails over a bill of lading term permitting such calls; once the bill of lading is transferred, however, and a claim is brought against the carrier by the transferee, then the bill of lading permitting intermediate calls prevails.

(iii) A charterparty

So far, we have not considered situations where the goods are carried on a chartered ship. The issue here is whether either party to a cargo claim, the claimant or the carrier, can plead terms contained in the charterparty or in the bill of lading issued when the goods were shipped. It is impossible to predict which party to a claim will want which document to dictate the terms of the contract on which the claim is brought. The reality is that the parties are not after a *document*: they are after a particular term in a particular document which happens to suit the way the claim has progressed. Thus, for example, a carrier will want a particularly short time bar in a charterparty to prevail over the longer one-year time bar affecting the bill of lading through the Hague-Visby Rules. For its part, the claimant may be after a London arbitration clause in the bill of lading in preference to a possibly less attractive jurisdiction clause contained in the charterparty.

The problem – which document, which contract – arises because the same transaction frequently spawns both a charterparty (clearly a contract of carriage) and a bill of lading (the reverse page of which looks uncannily like a contract). If the resulting but only apparent confusion is to be cleared up, it is helpful to make two crucial points. First, a charterparty is – and can only be – a contract of carriage: it can never perform any other functions; it does not provide a snapshot of the goods on shipment, and neither can it be passed down a string of buyers, transferring rights of suit as it goes. Second, although a bill of lading can, in certain circumstances, contain the terms of a contract of carriage, this is not the only function it performs – and it is not a function it *always* performs. We have already seen that in the contractual shipper's hands, the bill of lading evidences but does not contain the contract of carriage. And whether or not it does contain the terms of the contract, the bill of lading will always perform its original snapshot or receipt function and may, where the requirements of the Carriage of Goods by Sea Act 1992 are satisfied, transfer rights of suit to a succession of buyers of the goods it covers. In sum, a charterparty does one thing; a bill of lading can do different things at different times.

Given this fundamental difference between the two documents, it ceases to surprise that a charterer may hold at one and the same time two documents, a charterparty and a bill of lading, both of which look as though they contain a contract of carriage. The truth is that, in a charterer's hands, only one of those documents contains the terms of its contract of carriage with the carrier: the charterparty. The reason the charterer also holds a bill of lading is that the charterer needs a receipt for the goods shipped, whether for its own reassurance or because it needs to tender such a snapshot under a sale contract with its buyer; a second reason the charterer needs the bill is because it may need the means whereby to transfer to its buyer rights of suit against the carrier. Were such transfer not to happen, however, and were the claim to be brought by the charterer against the carrier, the contract terms covering that claim would be contained in the charterparty not in the bill of lading, and this despite the fact that the bill of lading would still, in that same cargo claim brought by the charterer against the carrier, perform its useful function as a receipt. In essence, the practical consequence is that a c.i.f. seller/charterer and an f.o.b. buyer/charterer bring their cargo claim against the carrier on the terms of the charterparty; a c.i.f. buyer/receiver, however, and (as we have seen) a straight f.o.b. seller, bring their cargo claim against the carrier on the terms of the bill of lading.

(iv) A bill of lading incorporating charterparty terms

There is one additional complication to the issue of whether a cargo claim is brought on bill of lading or charterparty terms: what if the appropriate document is, on the basis of the principles summarised above, the bill of lading, but that bill of lading contains a clause incorporating one, some or all terms from a charterparty? In this situation, is the cargo claim subject to bill of lading or to charterparty terms?

It is common for bills of lading to incorporate terms from a charterparty, largely but not exclusively, in the commodity trades. Where commodities are shipped requiring the full capacity of a single ship, the c.i.f. seller or f.o.b. buyer will typically charter the ship and the bill of lading issued will typically be a so-called short-form bill of lading, marked "for use with charterparties" and incorporating all terms from a charterparty. These bills of lading are commonly called "charterparty bills of lading". Incorporation of charterparty terms into bills of lading is not unknown, however, in the liner trade, where a full-form bill of lading is issued, not intended exclusively for use with a charterparty, but incorporating but one term, e.g. freight or arbitration "as per charterparty".

In either case, where the claim is brought by the charterer, the incorporation of charterparty terms causes no problem: as we have seen, a claim brought against the carrier by the charterer will be on charterparty terms in any event. It is when the bill of lading is transferred to a non-charterer that a problem of known unknowns arises: the bill of lading tells the transferee that charterparty terms are incorporated, but those terms are unknown to the transferee, who was not a party to – and played no part in negotiating – the charterparty. It may seem harsh on the transferee to bind it into charterparty terms in the conclusion of which it played no part and to sight of which at any rate in the absence of express stipulations, it has no right under the sale contract.

It is with these considerations of fairness – in essence considerations of privity of contract and notice – that the courts in England have developed a number of tests intended to protect third party transferees from the untoward effect of unseen contractual terms. First, where the words of incorporation in the charterparty are general in ambit, only those terms which are germane to the carriage of goods are susceptible of incorporation into the bill of lading: thus, for example, while stowage,[27] time bar and limitation clauses would travel into the bill of lading from the charterparty, a bunkering clause or a safe port warranty would not. Second, where more specific terms of incorporation are used in the bill of lading, only those charterparty terms which come strictly within the ambit of the terms of incorporation and which can, with a limited degree of verbal manipulation, be intelligibly applied within the bill of lading, are susceptible of incorporation. Thus, for example, if the bill of lading incorporates "freight" or "destination" as per charterparty, then it is only freight and destination clauses which can travel from the charterparty into the bill of lading, sensibly substituting, for example, the word "shipper" for "charterer". Third, and perhaps most importantly, even if a charterparty term travels successfully from a charterparty into a bill of lading, incorporation does *not* work if an inconsistency results from such incorporation within the bill of lading. Thus, for example, if a bill of lading incorporates a charterparty London arbitration clause, but contains, say, its own Paris arbitration clause, then the charterparty arbitration clause is not incorporated into the bill of lading. This is a particularly obvious form of inconsistency. A less obvious but possibly more important, form of inconsistency may arise through the Carriage of Goods by Sea Act 1971. We have already seen that Article III rule 8 of the Hague-Visby Rules strikes down bill of lading clauses which relieve or lessen the carrier's liability under the Rules. Where a charterparty term successfully negotiates its way through the tests just described, it becomes, for the purposes of the cargo claim to which it now becomes relevant, a bill of lading clause. If the bill of lading is subject to the Hague-Visby Rules, the result is that if the incorporated charterparty clause falls foul of Article III rule 8 (as it would do, for example, if it provided for a nine-month time bar) then the charterparty time bar is in effect not incorporated into the bill of lading.

(b) Breach of which term in the contract of carriage?

Given the complexity involved in identifying the terms of the contract of carriage on which the cargo claim is based, it is obvious that it is impossible to generalise on which particular term the claimant will use to ground its claim: it is in the nature of a cargo claim that a claimant will collect the facts which can plausibly be argued to have caused the loss, and then attempt to characterise those facts as the reverse of a particular term in the claimant's contract of carriage with the carrier.

Having said that, however, where a claim is brought on the terms of a contract of carriage contained in or evidenced by a bill of lading governed by the Hague-Visby Rules, it is clear that the claimant will need to establish facts which put the carrier in breach of one of two types of obligation, those going to the ship, set out in Article III rule 1, and those going to the custody of the goods, set out in Article III rule 2. Moreover, there are tactical advantages for the claimant in pursuing the first route rather than the second.

Article III rule 1 of the Hague-Visby Rules requires the carrier, before and at the beginning of the voyage, to exercise due diligence to make the ship seaworthy, in a broader sense than simply the seagoing viability of the ship: the carrier needs also to ensure that the ship is properly manned and equipped and that its holds are fit to receive the cargo. Not only is the carrier barred by Article III rule 8 from inserting terms in its bill of lading lessening its duties in this regard, but the decision of the House of Lords in *The Muncaster Castle*[28] prevents the carrier

---

27. See, most recently, *Yuzhny Zavod Metal Profil LLC v Eems Beheerder BV* [2013] 2 Lloyd's Rep 487 [94].
28. *Riverstone Meat Co Pty Ltd v Lancashire Shipping Co Ltd (The Muncaster Castle)* [1961] AC 807; [1961] 1 Lloyd's Rep 57. See Chapter 4, page 127.

from escaping from this liability on the simple ground that that due diligence was exercised in selecting a competent independent contractor to make the ship seaworthy. Finally, once the fact of unseaworthiness is established by the claimant, the burden of proof shifts very sharply on to the carrier to prove that it exercised due diligence to make the ship seaworthy.

Article III rule 2 requires the carrier properly and carefully to load, handle, stow, carry keep, care for and discharge the goods carried, "[s]ubject to the provisions of Article IV". The reference in Article III rule 2 to Article IV provides the claimant with the tactical advantage of Article III rule 1 over Article III rule 2. Article IV rule 2 contains a long litany of exceptions to the carrier's liability, e.g. acts of God, perils of the sea, strikes, etc. Where the claimant can only prove facts which would put the carrier in breach of Article III rule 2, the carrier could seek to exclude its liability by proving facts which come within one or more of the exceptions to liability described in Article IV rule 2. Where, on the other hand, the claimant can prove facts which put the carrier in breach of its broad seaworthiness duties under Article III rule 1, those exclusions are not available to the carrier, given that Article III rule 1 does not start (as Article III rule 2 does) with the words "[s]ubject to the provisions of Article IV".

Thus, for example, if containers go overboard during a storm, a peril of the sea for which liability is excluded by Article IV rule 2(c), and the lashing equipment on board is found to have been defective, the carrier's position will depend on what the claimant can prove. If the claimant can establish that the lashing equipment was defective at the beginning of the voyage, this would put the carrier in breach of Article III rule 1 unless the carrier can prove that it exercised due diligence: the ship would be unseaworthy under that article, which is not subject to Article IV and the carrier cannot, consequently, exclude its liability because of the peril of the sea. Alternatively, if the claimant can prove only that the lashings had become defective during the voyage, although this too would be a breach of contract, it is one from which the carrier can escape through the peril of the sea exception in Article IV rule 2. The net result is that it generally pays the claimant to base its claim on unseaworthiness under Article III rule 1 rather than a simple breach of care of the goods under Article III rule 2.

There is, since the House of Lords decision in *The Jordan II*,[29] an additional tactical advantage for the claimant in Article III rule 1 over Article III rule 2. While it is clear that Article III rule 8 bars the carrier from excluding or lessening its duties or liabilities to provide a seaworthy ship under Article III rule 1, it is now clear that it is open to the carrier to craft a term in the bill of lading which allocates the duty of stowage to the cargo interest rather than to the carrier. Such a clause was considered by the House of Lords to be one defining the parties' obligations rather than one relieving or lessening an obligation imposed by the Rules and therefore beyond the reach of Article III rule 8.

7. EXCLUDING OR LIMITING THE CARRIER'S LIABILITY

We have reached the end of the cargo claim. With the right claimant establishing, in a claim against the right defendant, that its proven loss was caused by a breach by the carrier of a term in their contract of carriage or of an obligation owed by the carrier to the claimant in tort or bailment, the claimant will succeed. The carrier will, of course, have fought the claimant all the way: contesting the claimant's title to sue; claiming that it is not the claimant's contractual carrier;

---

29. *Jindal Iron & Steel Co Ltd and Others v Islamic Solidarity Shipping Co Jordan Inc (The Jordan II)* [2004] UKHL 49; [2005] 1 Lloyd's Rep 57, recently followed in *Yuzhny Zavod Metall Profil LLC v EEMS Beheerder BV (The Eems Solar)* [2013] 2 Lloyd's Rep 487.

disputing evidence of loss; denying a breach of any duty owed towards the claimant. If none of these counter-attacks works, however, there are a few remaining routes out of liability or, at any rate, out of as much recovery as the claimant would like. The carrier could extinguish the claim, either by arguing that the claim has been time barred or by pleading one of the exceptions to liability allowed by the Hague-Visby Rules. If neither of those escape routes is available, the carrier could limit its liability through the so-called package and unit limitation imposed by the Rules, a privilege of which the claimant could deprive the carrier through one of two means, i.e. either deviation or by proving that the damage was caused intentionally by the carrier.

Before we deal with these escape routes from and limitations to liability, it would be useful to make one methodological point. Viewed from one perspective, it makes sense to deal with these matters at the end of this chapter on cargo claims: escape routes and limitations should logically come after having established liability. From a more practical perspective, however, it frequently makes sense to examine the facts going to the time bar, exceptions and limitation as soon as the dispute hits the desk. The matters previously discussed in this chapter going to title to sue, proof of loss and liability are obviously crucial: whether the bottom line looks attractive, however, whether anything much at all can be recovered if liability is established, makes it easier to decide whether it is worth pursuing the claim vigorously – or settling it.

(a) The one-year time bar

The normal limitation period for civil liability in English law is six years: cargo claims under the Hague-Visby Rules, however, must be brought within one year of the delivery of the goods or of the date on which the goods should have been delivered. For the reason stated in the immediately preceding paragraph, it is crucial to ensure, at a very early stage of the claim, whether the time bar has lapsed and, if it has, to see whether agreement can be reached with the carrier to extend or waive the time bar.

(b) Exceptions to liability

We have already referred to Article IV rule 2 of the Hague-Visby Rules as the Article containing a long litany of exceptions to the carrier's liability. Some of these exceptions are quite typical of any contracts of carriage, whether covered by a bill of lading or by a charterparty and whether or not governed by the Hague-Visby Rules: acts of God, acts of war, strikes or lockouts etc. Others, however, are quite particular to the Rules and are part of the patchwork compromise between the interests of cargo and carrier arrived at in the Hague-Visby Rules. Thus, for example, it may come as a surprise to a cargo claimant that an act, neglect or default in the navigation or management of the ship has pride of place as the very first exception to the carrier's liability. Moreover, while in most contracts, a list of exclusions of liability is normally closed, the list in Article IV rule 2 ends with an open-ended exclusion: any other cause arising without the actual fault or privity of the carrier, the burden of proving the absence of fault or privity falling on the carrier.

(c) Quantification and limitation of loss

Assuming that neither the time bar nor Article IV rule 2 provides the carrier with an escape route from liability, the claimant's next task is to quantify its loss. If the parties have agreed that loss, in what is commonly called an *ad valorem* box in the bill of lading, then the issue of *quantum* is resolved, at any rate prima facie. In effect, the claimant's loss has been liquidated in advance and the cargo claimant is tied to that declared value as the sum of its loss. In order to guard against inflated valuations, however, the presumption raised by the *ad valorem* declaration is not conclusive against the carrier, who can, therefore, prove that the goods shipped were worth less than the valuation. Moreover, if the carrier can prove that the shipper *knowingly* mis-stated the value of the goods, then the carrier is simply not liable at all, according to Article IV rule 5(h). On the other hand, if the value of the claimant's loss has not been agreed beforehand, or if the valuation has been set aside by the carrier, then there are two stages to be gone through under the Hague-Visby Rules, the first being the usual process of quantification of damages for breach of contract and the second being the limitation of those damages.

First, the basic objective here, as with any award in damages, is to place the claimant, through damages, in the position in which it would have been had the contract been performed, i.e. had the goods arrived in a sound condition. In the context of a contract of carriage, this translates into the following formula: the claimant is entitled to the difference between the market value of the goods had they arrived in sound condition and their value in the condition in which they actually arrived. The formula is used in Article IV rule 5(b) of the Hague-Visby Rules.

Second, once that sum is arrived at, the damages need to be limited by the so-called "package/ unit limitation" contained in Article IV rule 5(a)(c) and (d). The basic principle is that liability is limited to the higher of the following two quantities, either 666.67 special drawing rights of the International Monetary Fund per package or unit or two special drawing rights per kilogramme of gross weight of the goods lost or damaged. It is important to point out that Article IV rule 5(a) does not provide two formulae, one for goods in units or packages and the other for commodities shipped in bulk. The single formula has two alternatives, both of which need to be worked out whatever the cargo – and the applicable limit is the higher of the two. Once the formula has been worked through and the higher of the two alternatives provides the limit of liability, any clause in the bill of lading which seeks to limit the carrier's liability any further would, of course, be struck down by Article III rule 8 of the Hague-Visby Rules, at which we have already looked earlier in this chapter. It is, however, open to the parties to agree a *higher* limit and it has recently been held that the parties could do that by incorporating the limitation formula in the Hague Rules if, but only if, that formula were, on particular facts, to yield a higher limit than that yielded by the formula in the Hague-Visby Rules – and this even where the Hague-Visby Rules had mandatory force.[30]

Moreover, where goods are consolidated in a container, pallet or such like and the bill of lading quantifies the goods as, say, "one container said to contain 10,000 pairs of shoes", then the multiplier for the purpose of the package/unit limitation in Article IV rule 5(a) is 10,000 rather than one. The effect of "said to contain" clauses has already been covered: the evidential force of the bill of lading is emasculated in the sense that no binding photograph exists as to what was shipped. If a cargo claim has reached the stage of quantification, however, this must mean that the claimant has overcome the resulting evidential difficulties by actually proving what was shipped, through tally sheets, alternative exchanges between the parties, oral evidence etc.: the carrier will, as it were, have failed in its attempt to qualify the statement as to quantity on the bill of lading. Having failed in that attempt, the carrier does not get a second bite at the cherry: the claimant having proved that 10,000 pairs of shoes were in fact shipped, the carrier cannot now use one as the enumerator for limitation purposes.[31] To allow the carrier to do so would be to allow the carrier in effect to nullify the evidential gain already made by the claimant.

---

30. See *Yemgas FZCO v Superior Pescadores SA* [2014] EWHC 971 (Comm); [2014] 1 Lloyd's Rep 660, The case went to the Court of Appeal [2016] EWCA Civ 101; [2016] 1 Lloyd's Rep.561 where it was held that the Hague-Visby Rules applied. See page 131 of Chapter 4.

31. See art IV r 5(c) of the Hague-Visby Rules and, under the Hague Rules, *Owners of Cargo Lately Laden on Board the River Gurara v Nigerian National Shipping Line Ltd (The River Gurara)* [1998] QB 610; [1998] 1 Lloyd's Rep 225 (CA).

Finally on limitation, it is important to emphasise that the limitation amounts here described relate to claims brought on bills of lading for the carriage of goods by sea. Other conventions provide different levels of limitation for the carriage of goods by other means[32] and, where carriage is multimodal, bills of lading will frequently contain clauses limiting damages according to whether the location of the loss is or is not known.

(d) Breaking limitation

Limitation of liability is, of course, not something the claimant gladly accepts: it does mean that he may well be left with an uncovered exposure to loss which may or may not be covered by a cargo insurance policy on the goods. The claimant's instinct, at this late stage of the cargo claim is to break or "bust" limitation and there are two recognised means of doing so. The first is the less controversial but also, in English law, the less frequently used. Article IV rule 5(e) states that liability cannot be limited where the damage to the goods results from an act or omission of the carrier done with intent to cause damage or recklessly and with knowledge that damage would probably result. The critical point here is proof of *intent*, a difficult and, in the context of civil liability, an unusual thing for English lawyers to concern themselves with in quantifying damages: and this may be why the article has been somewhat under-utilised in our litigation.

A far more traditional method of breaking limitation is to prove that the carrier has deviated from the contract voyage. The meaning of deviation has already been covered in the context of charterparties in Chapter 4. All Article IV rule 4 of the Hague-Visby Rules adds to the sum of knowledge on deviation is that deviation is permissible not only for the saving of life or property but also for any reasonable cause. The relevance of deviation to the breaking of limitation lies, however, outside the Rules. The position traditionally held in English law is that a carrier who steps outside the contract of carriage and that it consequently cannot plead any of the contractual defences to which it would normally be entitled. This is commonly known as the "deviation rule". Its effect is draconian, leaving the carrier open to liability at large, unrestricted by the package/unit limitation or indeed any of the other defences under the Hague-Visby Rules, like the time bar, whether or not the claim was based on or the loss caused by the deviation. It has been argued, but so far not successfully in litigation, that the deviation rule is a carriage equivalent of the so-called "doctrine of fundamental breach" in general contract law, a doctrine given burial by the House of Lords in *Photo Production Ltd v Securicor Transport Ltd*.[33] Despite these discussions, largely restricted to the legal journals, it is still wise for a cargo claimant faced by unwelcome limitation, to argue that limitation is unavailable where the carrier has deviated from the contract voyage.

8. THE CLAIMANT'S POTENTIAL LIABILITY TOWARDS THE CARRIER

It may seem strange to end a chapter on cargo claims against the carrier with a brief consideration of claims by the carrier against cargo interests. The carrier may be owed freight; the carrier

---

32. Cf. arts 22–25 of the Convention for the Unification of Certain Rules for International Carriage by Air, Montreal, 28 May 1999; art 23 of Convention on the Contract for International Carriage of Goods by Road (CMR Convention), Geneva, 19 May 1956; arts 30(2) and 31 of the Convention concerning International Carriage by Rail (COTIF), Berne, 9 May 1980.

33. *Photo Production Ltd v Securicor Transport Ltd* [1980] AC 827; [1980] 1 Lloyd's Rep 545. See also C. Mills, "The Future of Deviation" (1983) 4 LMCLQ 587; C. Debattista, "Fundamental Breach and Deviation" [1989] JBL 22; F. Reynolds, "The Butterworth Lectures 1990–91" (Butterworths 1991), reviewed by Johan Steyn in [1993] LMCLQ, at pp 272–273; M. Dockray, "Deviation: A Doctrine All at Sea" [2000] LMCLQ 76.

may wish to recover for, say, warehousing charges where the receiver fails to collect; or for damage to the ship caused by the cargo, whether prohibited, dangerous[34] or neither. Now there are two types of cargo interest that are never beyond the reach of a carrier for these types of losses. First, a charterer from the carrier will always be open to attack by the carrier: that charterparty survives any transfer of a bill of lading by or to the charterer. Second, even where there is no charterparty, a carrier never loses its rights of suit against the original shipper with whom the carrier first contracted, again despite the fact that the shipper may have transferred the bill of lading to a third party. The problem arises when a carrier wishes to pursue a claim not against either of these two parties, a charterer or a shipper, but against a lawful holder of a bill of lading, a person named as consignee on a sea waybill or a person to whom a carrier acknowledges a right of delivery under a ship's delivery order. Does the fact that these cargo interests have rights of suit against the carrier mean that the carrier can pursue them under the relevant document? If the answer to this question was yes, difficulties would be caused to banks: a bank named in any of these capacities on any one of the three documents mentioned above would be a likely and attractive defendant for carriers and the result would be that bills of lading and associated shipping documents would become unattractive security documents for banks extending a line of credit to buyers through letters of credit. Section 3 of the Carriage of Goods by Sea Act 1992 consequently makes it clear that for a carrier to have rights of action against a lawful holder of a bill of lading, a consignee named as such on a sea waybill and a party to whom the carrier acknowledges a right of delivery on a ship's delivery order, that person must do one of the following: it must either take or demand delivery of any of the goods to which the document relates or make a claim under the contract of carriage to which the document relates. This means that for the cargo interest to expose itself to liability towards the carrier, the cargo interest needs first to activate liability by exercising its own rights under the 1992 Act. An unintended consequence follows from this: a cargo interest can simply avoid any liabilities towards the carrier under the carriage contract through the simple expedient of failing to receive goods in which it has, for some reason or other, lost interest under the sale contract.

---

34. For a definition of what goods are "dangerous" for the purposes of the Hague-Visby Rules, see *Bunge SA v ADM do Brasil Ltda & Ors. (The Darya Radhe)* [2009] EWHC 845 (Comm); [2009] 2 Lloyd's Rep 175.

CHAPTER 6

CARRIAGE OF PASSENGERS

Michael Tsimplis

1. INTRODUCTION[1]

Claims arising as a result of accidents to passengers on ships have provided a fertile field for maritime lawyers since the loss of the *Titanic* in 1912.[2] An important distinction must however be drawn between *international* and *domestic* carriage of passengers. Domestic carriage is not a matter for international negotiations and is exclusively regulated by national regimes. International carriage does require international regulation because more than one legal system related to the carriage can be identified and conflicts between them may make it particularly difficult for claimants to recover any damage suffered. The principal subject of this chapter is the international legal regime. However, the UK national regime will also be discussed.

The carriage of passengers by sea internationally involves two types of services. First, there are ships which provide public transport to and from islands and between States. Some services in terms of food and entertainment may be provided but the service is primarily one for transport. Second, there are the cruise ships in which passengers live for some periods

---

1. See M. Tsimplis, "Liability in Respect of Passenger Claims and its Limitation" (2009) 15 JIML 123; P. Todd, *Carriage of Passengers by Sea: Athens Conventions and UK Implementation* (CreateSpace Independent Publishing Platform 2013).
2. White Star Line sought to limit its liability in the United States to the value of the life boats which were recovered and brought to New York with the survivors on board the *Carpathia* [1912] 209 Fed Rep 501, *New York Times* 26 May 1912. More recent accidents have also involved significant casualties. The *MS al-Salam Boccaccio 98* (2006) where more than 100 people died, the *Costa Concordia* (2012) and the *Sea Diamond* (2007) groundings, where 33 and two people drowned as well as *the Sewol* (2014) ferry accident, where around 380 people drowned.

of time.[3] These ships provide many more services and are much more expensive. They may provide sightseeing at various ports and include several embarkations and disembarkations for each passenger.[4]

The navigational hazards for both types of services are similar and it makes sense that they are dealt with in a uniform way. However, the hazards that relate to the "living in" part of the transport are very different and pose significantly higher risks for cruise ships than ordinary passenger ships.[5]

Passengers' rights and obligations vis-à-vis the carrier are of a contractual nature with the contract evidenced by the issuance of the ticket. Contractual terms would then apply, but these terms are usually written by the carrier, and the passenger has little or no capability to negotiate. In the past, this has enabled carriers to reduce their liability to passengers significantly, or even exclude it entirely by inserting exemption or limitation clauses at will.[6] The law nationally[7] and internationally has gradually developed extra protection for passengers who are at a disadvantage due to their lack of negotiating power.

2. THE LEGAL FRAMEWORK

Carriage of passengers between different States has however been governed[8] for many years by the 1974 Athens Convention, which entered into force in 1987.[9] The Convention was amended by the 2002 Athens Protocol (the "2002 Athens Convention") and this came into force on 23 April 2014.[10] The 2002 Athens Convention as amended has the force of law in the UK.[11] Thus, its application is automatic and does not depend on contractual incorporation into the contract of carriage with the passenger.[12] The 2002 Athens Convention applies to international carriage[13]

---

3. Of course, it will apply to all kinds of passengers covered by the wording. See *Collins v Lawrence* [2016] 1 Lloyd's Rep Plus, 81, for a claim by a passenger of a fishing boat.

4. One could argue for a third type of carriage of passengers, that provided for pilgrim ships involving large numbers of unberthed passengers. This is regional to the Indian Ocean and is regulated by two international agreements, the Special Trade Passenger Ships Agreement, 1971 and the supplementary Protocol on Space Requirements for Special Trade Passenger Ships, 1973. These, in essence, permit departure from the SOLAS Convention requirements for such ships.

5. For example, in 2010, more than 400 out of the 2,600 passengers of the *Celebrity Mercury* were stricken ill by what was apparently a norovirus outbreak.

6. *Adler v Dickson (No 1)* [1954] 2 Lloyd's Rep 267 (CA); *The Eagle* [1977] 2 Lloyd's Rep 70; *The Mikhail Lermontov* [1991] 2 Lloyd's Rep 155.

7. In England, the Unfair Contract Terms Act 1977 deals with contractual terms excluding or restricting liability for death or personal injury (s 2(1)) or property damage (s 2(2)). Permission to restrict and exclude liability to passengers by sea was granted under section 28 of the Act which has now been removed by the Consumer Rights Act 2015. Therefore, it appears that where a contract for the carriage of passenger contains exclusion clauses these will be scrutinised under the Act.

8. The Carriage of Passengers Convention 1961 and the Passenger Luggage Convention 1967 were agreed before the 1974 Athens Convention, but were not successful. The Carriage of Passengers Convention 1961 came into force on 4 June 1965 and was ratified by 11 states. The Passenger Luggage Convention 1967 was only ratified by Cuba and Algeria but never entered into force, as five ratifications were needed.

9. It has now been ratified or acceded to by 36 States (as at 8 February 2017).

10. As at 8 February 2017, 27 Contracting States.

11. MSA 1995, ss 183, 184.

12. See *The Lion* [1990] 2 Lloyd's Rep 144, where it was held that the omission by the carrier to give notice of some of the Articles of the 1974 Athens Convention, as required by S 1125/1980, although an offence, did not deprive the carrier of his right to limit liability. The right of the Secretary of State to issue such a requirement and establish fines is provided for by MSA 1995, Sch 6, Pt II para 11.

13. Under art 1.9, international carriage is where the port of destination or an intermediate port of call is located in a different State from the port of departure.

where the flag State of the ship is a State party to the Convention[14] or the port of departure or destination is in a State party.[15] The UK[16] has extended its application to carriage of passengers by sea between UK ports including the Isle of Man and the Channel Islands.[17] The 2002 Athens Convention also applies where the contract of carriage was made in a State which is a contracting party.[18] This arrangement would have been enough to make the 2002 Athens Convention applicable in the UK. However, the statutory background is more complicated. The EU has inserted the 2002 Athens Convention, as amended by some additional IMO guidelines, in Regulation (EC) No 392/2009 of the European Parliament and of the Council of 23 April 2009 on the liability of carriers of passengers by sea in the event of accidents (we will refer to this as the Athens Regulation). The Athens Regulation entered into force on 31 December 2012. The Regulation applies to international voyages as defined under the 2002 Athens Convention and the ship is registered in a Member State or the contract of carriage has been made in a Member State or the contractual place of departure or destination is in a Member State.[19] In addition, it applies to certain domestic voyages.[20] Therefore, there is an overlap between Schedule 6 of the 1995 MSA and the Athens Regulation both with respect to the international character of the Convention and in relation to its application to domestic voyages. The substantive provisions are almost identical but the Athens Regulation has some additional features, which may matter to claimants, as will be shown later. The Merchant Shipping (Carriage of Passengers by Sea) Regulations 2012 (SI 2012/3152) amended the 1995 MSA by adding a new subsection to section 183, which provides that Schedule 6 would no longer apply to cases where the Athens Regulation applies.

Thus, the Athens Regulation applies to all voyages involving ships flagged and contracts made in the EU and voyages involving a contractual departure or destination port in the EU. What is left out of the Athens Regulation are voyages involving one or more Contracting States to the 2002 Athens Convention which are not Member States on board a ship which is not a Member State ship and on a contract made outside the EU. Such claims will be covered by

---

14. 2002 Athens Convention, art 2.1(a).

15. 2002 Athens Convention, art 2.1(c). Notably, in multimodal travel, where there is a compulsorily applicable international liability regime, this will prevail over the Athens Convention (art 2.2). See also MSA 1995, Sch 6, Pt II, which states that such Conventions will be treated as applicable to sea carriage if the contract of carriage so states.

16. It is worth noting that commercial carriage by the State or public authorities is subject to the Convention (art 21), provided there is a contract of carriage within the meaning of the Athens Convention.

17. The Carriage of Passengers and their Luggage by Sea (Domestic Carriage) Order 1987/670, Sch 1 para 1.

18. 2002 Athens Convention, art 2.1(b).

19. Athens Regulation, art 2.

20. Art 2. Under EU law, passenger ships larger than 24 m in length are classified in accordance with art 4 of the Council Directive 98/18/EC. The Athens Regulation applies to 'Class A' and 'Class B" ships flying the flag of a Member State, where the carriage contract is made in a Member State or the point of departure or destination is in a Member State. The classification of passenger ships is not done by reference to the size of the ship or the number of passengers. Instead, a system based on the distance from the shore, a place of refuge and a place where the passengers can be landed as well as the dominant wave direction and significant wave height conditions are used. 'Class A" passenger ships are essentially those that venture more than 20 miles from the coast. For those ships, the application of the Athens Regulation is compulsory for domestic voyages since 31 December 2016 as until that time Member States could have deferred its application (art11(1)). For "Class B" passenger ships the Athens Regulation applies unless the Member State chooses to delay the application until at the latest 31 December 2018 (art11(2)). "Class B" passenger ships are those domestic voyages in the course of which it is at no time more than 20 miles from the line of the coast, where shipwrecked persons can land provided that they are not "Class C" or "Class D" ships. This, in essence, means that they go through areas where the significant wave height does not exceed 2.5 m for more than 10 per cent of the time in a year. Section 4 of the Merchant Shipping (Carriage of Passengers by Sea) Regulations 2012 has used the right to defer the application of the Regulation for both "Class A" and "Class B" ships on domestic voyages. Thus, presently "Class B" ships are excluded from the ambit of the Athens Regulation. A further option is provided to Member States to extend the application to all domestic seagoing carriage of passengers (art 2). An earlier option to include inland waterways was abandoned.

Schedule 6 of the 1995 MSA. Similarly, for domestic voyages, the Athens Regulation currently applies to Class A passenger ships on domestic voyages. Class B passenger ships on domestic voyages will be covered from 1 January 2019 while the other two classes of ships are under the domestic implementation of Schedule 6 of the 1995 MSA.

The international legal instrument, the 2002 Athens Convention, will be the focal point in the following discussion. However, the modifications made by the Athens Regulation will also be discussed while comments on the 1974 Athens Convention will be found in the footnotes.

The 2002 Athens Convention applies[21] to international carriage onboard ships registered or flying the flag of a Contracting State. In addition, it covers international carriage where either the port of departure or discharge is in a Contracting State. International carriage requires that the port of departure and the port of destination or an intermediate port are in a different State.[22]

This means that it is always applicable to British ships. For example, if a ship registered in the UK takes a passenger for a voyage between two non-Contracting States to the 2002 Athens Convention, then the carriage of that passenger will still be covered by the 2002 Athens Convention. However, if a ship of a non-Contracting State performs a journey not involving any Contracting State, the contract is not made in the UK and the case is decided in England, the 2002 Athens Convention[23] will be inapplicable despite having the force of law because the contract of carriage does not fulfil the requirements for its application. Similar examples can be made for the Athens Regulation; however the requirement there is that either the contractual ports, the flag or the place where the contract is made are in EU Member States.

The 2002 Athens Convention covers liability to passengers of seagoing ships[24] – defined as persons carried on the ship under a contract of carriage or those accompanying, with the consent of the carrier[25] – and liability for passengers' vehicles or luggage. The 2002 Athens Convention covers liability to persons carried on the ship under a contract of carriage and their vehicles or luggage.[26]

The 2002 Athens Convention arrangements are protected by Article 18 of the Convention. This article renders null and void any contractual clauses which exclude liability or provide lower limits of liability or affect the reverse burden of proof or restrict the jurisdictional options.[27]

The 2002 Athens Convention is designed to be the sole framework by which a passenger can claim against the carrier or the contractual carrier.[28]

---

21. 2002 Athens Convention, art 2.

22. 2002 Athens Convention, art 1.9.

23. And the Athens Regulation "also".

24. In *The Sea Eagle* [2011] EWHC 1438 (Admlty), [2012] 2 Lloyd's Rep 37, the Admiralty Registrar held that for a craft or structure to fall within the Athens Convention ambit, it has to be: (a) a ship or vessel; and (b) seagoing. In that case, the craft was an RIB and as it was designed to go offshore, it was considered to be a ship used in navigation despite the lack of a cabin. The judge considered that in order to decide whether the ship was seagoing or not, the actual use to which the vessel was being put in the context of the claim being brought against her had to be considered. The important issue was not whether a ship could go to sea, but whether she did go to sea. The question was whether the type of trips on which the *Sea Eagle* was engaged could be classified as seagoing. The answer depended upon what was regarded as being sea and what was not. Because, the trip taken by the RIB involved operating in waters that were to be regarded as "sea" it was "seagoing" for the purpose the Athens Convention.

25. The carrier is the contractual carrier whether he performs the carriage or not (art 1(a)).

26. Persons accompanying cargo, or any live animals carried on board under a contract of carriage of goods by sea, are also included in the scope of the Convention, provided they are on board with the consent of the carrier – although cargo and animals are excluded from the regime.

27. For example, by prescribing the only place of business for the carrier.

28. 2002 Athens Convention, art 14.

(a) Basis of liability

(i) Liability for loss of life and personal injury[29]

The contracting carrier[30] is the person liable under the 2002 Athens Convention.[31] The liability regime covers passengers[32] from the point of embarkation until disembarkation.[33] In a recent, rather specific case[34] a passenger of a fishing ship was disembarking from the boat onto a platform at the top of a set of freestanding steps which led down on to the shingle beach. A large plywood board had been put on the shingle at the foot of the steps. The passenger slipped on the board, which was wet, and sustained injury. When sued for negligence under the Occupiers' Liability Act 1957, the defendant claimed the action fell under the two-year time bar of the 1974 Athens Convention.[35] The claimant argued that he had disembarked at the time he stepped onto the board and therefore the accident happened outside the period of application of the 1974 Athens Convention and the time bar did not apply to his claim. The judge considered that disembarkation occurred when the passenger was safely off a gangway and when stepping over the side of the ship when both his feet were on the dock and he had his balance. He found the board was part of the disembarkation equipment. Thus, the accident happened during disembarkation and the action was time-barred.

The 2002 Athens Convention distinguishes between "shipping incidents" and other incidents.[36] Shipwrecks, capsizes, collisions, stranding, explosions, fires and, more controversially, "defects in the ship",[37] are all "shipping incidents".[38] The distinction separates the risks arising from the particularities of carriage by sea from those relating to the use of the ship as living premises. Strict liability for loss of life and personal injury arising from such shipping incidents is limited to 250,000 SDR per passenger.[39] Losses in excess of this limit are recoverable except where the carrier proves that the damage was not caused by its fault or the fault of its servants.[40]

---

29. This is one of the major changes to the 1974 Athens Convention. Article 3 of the 1974 Athens Convention starts by reciting the common law position that the carrier is liable for damages caused by the death or injury of a passenger caused by the fault or neglect of its servants or agents acting within the scope of their employment. In essence the general arrangement is based on negligence by the carrier (contractual and performing) and their servants. This can be a very difficult arrangement for a claimant who needs to discharge the burden of proving fault as most of the information would be in the hands of the carrier. In order to address this problem art 3(3) provides that such fault or neglect is presumed if the death or injury arose from or in connection with shipwreck, collision, stranding, explosion, fire or defect in the ship, i.e. the burden of proof is reversed. However, the burden of proving that the incident causing the loss or damage occurred in the course of the carriage still lies with the claimant. The 2002 Athens Convention has effectively altered the basis of liability, which is now strict.
30. 2002 Athens Convention, art1(1)(a).
31. Ibid., art 3(1).
32. Under art 1(1) passengers are not only those carried under a contract of carriage but also those who, with the carrier's consent, accompany live animals or a vehicle.
33. The definition is broad and includes the transport from the shore to the ship onboard smaller boats unless these are paid in the ticket price or the vessels are provided by the carrier (art 1(8)(a)). It expressly excludes periods "in a marine terminal or station or on a quay or in or on any other port installation".
34. See *Collins v Lawrence* [2016] 1 Lloyd's Rep Plus 81.
35. The decision is equally applicable to the 2002 Athens Convention.
36. It is questionable whether a "man overboard" incident can be properly considered a shipping incident. In *Davis v Stena Line Ltd* [2005] EWHC 420 (QB); [2005] 2 Lloyd's Rep 13 a passenger fell overboard. This was conceded by both parties to be during the carriage and thus dealt with under the 1974 Athens Convention. Negligence was established on the facts of the case in several aspects, including the actions of the master after the man fell overboard and there was an attempt to rescue him, which probably lead to his drowning.
37. 2002 Athens Convention, art 3(5)(c).
38. 2002 Athens Convention, art 3(5)(a).
39. 2002 Athens Convention, art 3(1).
40. 2002 Athens Convention, art3 (1) and see art 3(5)(b) defining the fault of the carrier as including the fault or neglect of the servants of the carrier.

Liability for death or personal injury, which did not occur in a shipping incident, is fault based only, with the burden of proving the fault falling on the claimant passenger.[41] The "fault of the carrier" includes, in shipping as well as in other incidents, the negligence of the carrier's servants and agents acting within the scope of their employment. Fault-based liability for loss of life or personal injury is set, under the Convention, at 400,000 SDR per passenger.[42] It is, however, permissible for Contracting States to provide in their national law for liability to be higher, or unlimited.[43]

The introduction of strict liability for the carrier is accompanied by the introduction of two express exceptions. Under the first exception, the carrier can be exonerated entirely for shipping incidents if it can show that the loss of life or personal injury was caused by acts of war, hostilities, civil war, insurrection or from a natural phenomenon of an exceptional, inevitable and irresistible character.[44] The second exception permits the carrier to escape liability if the incident was caused solely by intentional acts or omissions of a third party.[45] This exception would cover terrorist attacks and piracy, both serious concerns for the passengers, the industry and the insurers. The wording differs significantly between the two exceptions: the first requires that the damage "resulted from..." the second that the damage "was wholly caused..." by the relevant exempted factor. Shipowners and P&I Clubs have been concerned by the wording of the second exception, which would arguably not be available even with the slightest causative mistake by the carrier or its servants.[46] The IMO in 2006[47] developed a reservation and some guidelines to the 2002 Athens Convention, which it recommended Contracting States make at the time they ratified the Convention. The reservation does two things. First, it obliges the Contracting State to limit the carrier's liability to either 250,000 SDR per passenger or 340 million SDR overall, whichever is lower, per incident in relation to a list of causes. This means that when more than 1,360 passengers have lost their lives or are injured by a cause on the list of specified causes, the carrier may pay less than the 250,000 SDR that corresponds to the compulsory insurance amount. The list of specified causes which permit lower compensation are actually wider than that which the aforementioned exemption provides for and covers all insurance risks.[48] Second, the IMO guidelines permit the insurer to reduce its exposure to a number of risks by introducing

---

41. 2002 Athens Convention, art 3.2. In *Dawkins v Carnival Plc (t/a P&O Cruises)* [2011] EWCA Civ 1237; [2012] 1 Lloyd's Rep 1 a passenger slipped on water spilled on the restaurant floor of *The Oriana* and suffered injury. The Court of Appeal held that the existence of water on the restaurant floor created prima facie evidence of liability for negligence by the carrier. The carrier could avoid liability if it could show that the spill was there for a very short time (which was a reasonable time). The burden of proving how long the water spill was there was on the carrier. At first instance, the High Court held that it sufficed for the carrier to show that there was an appropriate inspection system in place that was followed. In *Nolan and others v Tui Uk Ltd* [2013] EWHC 3099 (QB); [2016] 1 Lloyd's Rep 211 the claimants failed because the outbreak of gastroenteritis was caused by norovirus rather than failure of hygiene measures. An attempt to link this with a similar outbreak in the previous voyage failed as the judge considered that it could not be a defect of the ship. Also, it was held that a failure to warn was not something that happened on board and therefore a claim based on it failed as a matter of law.

42. 2002 Athens Convention, art (7). This is another major change from the 1974 Athens Convention which had a limit of 46,666 SDR per passenger.

43. Art 6.

44. 2002 Athens Convention, art 3(1)(a).

45. 2002 Athens Convention, art 3(1)(b).

46. These provisions, combined with the higher limits, caused considerable concern in the world of marine liability insurance, particularly in the International Group of P&I Clubs. The steadily increasing size of passenger ships has raised the spectre of a major accident on a ship carrying more than 3,500 passengers and 1,500 crew. Presently there are several ships able to carry more than 6,000 passengers. At the Diplomatic Conference in 2002, a leading underwriter stated that insurance to meet the Protocol's requirements, particularly with unlimited reinstatements after a casualty, was simply not available on the market.

47. Ref. A1/P/5.01, Circular letter No.2758, 20 November 2006.

48. In particular it covers war, civil war, revolution, rebellion, insurrection, or civil strife arising therefrom, or any hostile act by or against a belligerent power; capture, seizure, arrest, restraint or detainment, and the consequences thereof or any attempt thereat; derelict mines, torpedoes, bombs or other derelict weapons of war; act of any terrorist or any person acting maliciously or from a political motive and any action taken to prevent or counter any such risk; confiscation and expropriation.

a number of Institute clauses[49] into the contract of insurance and entitles the Contracting State to exempt the insurer from such liability. Therefore, where a terrorist attack takes place there would be no liability for the carrier or, in case the carrier is at fault, this would be limited to 250,000 SDR per passenger or 340 million SDR overall and, depending on the type of attack, the carrier may be liable, but without insurance cover for such an event.[50]

(ii) Liability for damage or loss of luggage and vehicles[51]

The carrier's liability covers any article or vehicle carried under the ticket but excludes things carried under a charterparty, a bill of lading or other shipping document "primarily concerned"[52] with the carriage of goods as well as live animals. The items carried are categorised as either cabin luggage or other than cabin luggage. Cabin luggage is luggage which the passenger has in his cabin and remains in the possession of the passenger. The liability of the carrier concerning cabin luggage covers the same period as the liability for the passenger, i.e. embarkation to disembarkation. However, for cabin luggage which has been given temporarily to the carrier, for example to be taken up the stairs of the ship, the period on the quay or in the terminal is also included, provided that it had not been redelivered.[53] Items left in the passenger's car are also considered as cabin luggage under the Convention. However, the carrier's period of liability is not the same as that for cabin luggage[54] but the same as that of other luggage, including the vehicle, which starts at the time such luggage is taken over by the carrier, whether on board or on shore and until it redelivers it.[55]

The carrier's liability for loss of or damage to cabin luggage is fault based.[56] For shipping incidents, the carrier's fault is presumed. For other incidents the claimant must prove fault.[57] For other luggage, the liability is fault-based with a presumption of carrier's fault.[58]

Liability for loss or damage of valuables and money is excluded altogether, unless these effects were handed to the carrier for safekeeping.[59] The application of the exclusion of liability for valuables depends on whether the carrier has facilities on board and does not reject a request for the depositing of valuables in its care. Thus, unless the shipowner gives the passengers the option to hand over to it their valuables for safe keeping it would be unable to rely on the exclusion of liability in respect of these valuables, at least in respect of passengers who intended to deposit their valuables.[60]

---

49. See s 1(9) of the IMO Reservations, and Guidelines s 2(2).
50. Notably not all Contracting States have made the reservation when signing up to the Convention. This can create complications through not being able to obtain appropriate insurance and therefore having ships liable to detention. See IMO LEG 101/8/3, 12 March 2014.
51. The 1974 Athens Convention had the same legal test for liability to luggage but with lower limits of liability.
52. 2002 Athens Convention, art 1(5).
53. 2002 Athens Convention, art 1(6).
54. 2002 Athens Convention, art 1(6).
55. 2002 Athens Convention, art 1(8)(c). Whether and when a vehicle driven and parked in the ship's garage is taken over by the carrier is not clear. It could be the time the driver starts following directions by crew members, or it could be at the time the garage is locked, as happens on some voyages, or it could be argued that it never happens while the keys are held by the passenger.
56. Fault includes fault of its servants.
57. 2002 Athens Convention, art 3(3).
58. 2002 Athens Convention, art 3(4).
59. 2002 Athens Convention, art 5.
60. See *Lee and Another v Airtours Holidays Ltd and Another* [2004] 1 Lloyd's Rep 683, where there was a safe in each cabin of the ship. The passengers requested to put their valuables in the ship's safe, but were told that the cabin's safe would be sufficient. The ship was lost and the passengers claimed for the loss of their valuables. Although the case was not decided under the 1974 Athens Convention, the Central London County Court held that had the 1974 Athens Convention been applicable, art 5 would not have protected the carrier as there was no opportunity given to passengers to deposit their valuables with the carrier for safekeeping.

Where the contracting carrier is not the performing carrier,[61] the 2002 Athens Convention imposes joint and several liability on both carriers for the part of the carriage performed by the performing carrier.[62] Thus the contracting carrier is liable for his actions for the whole of the carriage and, in addition, is liable for the actions of the performing carrier and of the performing carrier's servants or agents,[63] with the burden of proof arrangements as described earlier. Any right of recourse between the carriers is expressly preserved.[64] The defence of contributory negligence, in accordance with national law, is also preserved.[65]

Servants and agents of the carrier and the contractual carrier are covered by the limits of liability and the other defences available to the carrier, provided they prove they were acting within the scope of their employment.[66]

(b) Limits of liability

The original limits of liability under Article 7 of the 1974 Athens Convention for loss of life and personal injury were too low.[67] The 1990 Protocol has not achieved any ratifications.[68] The UK has, however, unilaterally increased the limit per passenger for UK carriers to 300,000 SDR, following the *Herald of Free Enterprise* casualty. The limits of liability are shown in Table 6.1.[69]

Article 13 of the 2002 Athens Convention provides for loss of the right to limit liability in the event of intentional harm or recklessness in terms similar to Article 4 of the 1976 Limitation Convention.[70] Thus, it is extremely difficult for limitation of liability to be affected except where the carrier acts intentionally or recklessly and with knowledge of the particular loss, i.e. the death or the personal injury of the passengers or the loss or damage to the luggage. For this test the act or omission cannot be one of the carrier's servants but must be one of the carrier itself. Limitation of liability rights under other conventions are preserved which creates a potential overlap with the limitation of liability conventions.[71]

(c) Time bar

A two-year time limit on claims is imposed. This starts at disembarkation or the time that disembarkation should have taken place in cases of death or injury during the journey and loss or damage to

61. 2002 Athens Convention, art 1(1)(b).
62. 2002 Athens Convention, art 4(4).
63. 2002 Athens Convention, art 4.
64. 2002 Athens Convention, art 4(5).
65. 2002 Athens Convention, art 6.
66. 2002 Athens Convention, art 11.
67. Equivalent of 1 SDR on 16 June 2017 is £1.080760. For latest equivalent rates see www.imf.org/external/np/fin/rates/rms_five.cfm (accessed 16 June 2017).
68. This figure has been adopted by the Scandinavian countries.
69. Where a State is not a member of the International Monetary Fund and by its own law cannot have the SDR, 15 gold francs 2002 Athens Convention, art 9. The gold franc is defined as 65.5 grams of gold of millesimal fineness 900. Determining the appropriate value of gold is not trivial. See, for example, *SS Pharmaceutical Co Ltd v Qantas Airways Ltd* [1989] 1 Lloyd's Rep 319 where the market price of gold was accepted, although this would clearly create fluctuating limits of liability. By contrast, the US Supreme Court in *Franklin Mint Corporation and others v Trans World Airlines Inc* [1984] 1 Lloyd's Rep 220 adopted the latest official price of gold as the appropriate one.
70. See Chapter 7, page 286. The test in the 1974 Athens Convention is:

> The carrier shall not be entitled to the benefit of the limits of liability prescribed in Articles 7 and 8 and paragraph 1 of Article 10, if it is proved that the damage resulted from an act or omission of the carrier done with the intent to cause such damage, or recklessly and with knowledge that such damage would probably result.

71. 1974 Athens Convention, art 19.

Table 6.1 Limits of liability under the 1974 Athens Convention and its Protocols
Values expressed in SDRs

Loss or Damage	1974 Athens Convention	1990 Protocol[1]	UK Carriers[2]	2002 Athens Convention[3]
Life, personal injury/ passenger	46,666	175,000	300,000	250,000 strict 400,000 (or higher) if fault
Cabin luggage/ passenger	833	1,800	833	2,250
Luggage in the custody of the carrier/passenger	1,200 (1,187)[4]	2,700 (2,565)[4]	1,200 (1,187)[4]	3,375 (3,226)[4]
Vehicle and luggage within	3,333 (3,216)[4]	10,000 (9,700)[4]	3,333 (3,216)[4]	12,700 (12,370)[4]

Notes
1. The 1990 Protocol never came into force.
2. Carriage of Passengers and their Luggage by Sea (United Kingdom Carriers) Order 1998 (SI 1998/2917), which came into force on 1 January 1999.
3. Except where the IMO Reservation and Guidelines are relevant, where there is a cap of 340,000 SDR per incident and a maximum of 250,000 SDR per passenger if the cap is not exceeded.
4. Numbers in brackets are those applicable after the optional deduction.

luggage.[72] The only exception to the two-year time bar is where personal injury occurs during the journey but death occurs after disembarkation. In such a case, the time bar is two years from the day of death but not later than three years from disembarkation. Extension of and interruption to the limitation period is governed by the rules of the court hearing the case, but the overall period cannot be extended more than three years from disembarkation. The time bar also applies to arbitration.[73]

The powers to extend the time bar period are very limited. The Limitation Act 1980 is the relevant legislation in England and section 39 does not exclude the 1974 Athens Convention from the operation of Part II of that Act. However, this was of no assistance to the claimant passenger in *Higham v Stena Sealink Ltd*,[74] who relied on Article 16(3) of the 1974 Athens Convention in order to achieve a time extension in her action. The Court of Appeal considered that section 33 of the Limitation Act 1980, which permits the discretionary extension of time in cases of personal injury or death, was not applicable in relation to Article 16(3) of the 1974 Athens Convention. This is because section 33 refers expressly to time bars set by section 11 of the Limitation Act 1980. The Court of Appeal did not decide the more general question of whether there are any sections of Part II of the Limitation Act 1980 which might assist a claimant under the 1974 Athens Convention in obtaining an extension to the two-year time bar. However, Hirst LJ, who delivered the judgment, noted that although sections 28 to 32 of the Limitation Act 1980 appear to be relevant, they all make specific reference to time bars established by the Limitation Act 1980 itself and this may disqualify them.[75] Thus, it is doubtful whether any of the Limitation Act 1980 provisions may be relied upon to extend the limitation period under the 2002 Athens Convention.

72. 1974 Athens Convention, art 16(2).
73. MSA 1995, Schedule 6 Part II, para 7.
74. *Higham v Stena Sealink Ltd* [1996] 2 Lloyd's Rep 26 (CA). s 39 of the Limitation Act 1980 states that:

This Act shall not apply to any action or arbitration for which a period of limitation is prescribed by or under any other enactment (whether passed before or after the passing of this Act) or to any action or arbitration to which the Crown is a party and for which, if it were between subjects, a period of limitation would be prescribed by or under any such other enactment.

75. *Higham v Stena Sealink Ltd* [1996] 2 Lloyd's Rep 26, 30.

The time bar in the 2002 Athens Convention is one that bars the remedy but not the cause of action.[76] In *South West Strategic Health Authority v Bay Island Voyages*,[77] a claimant injured on a trip in a RIB inflatable missed the two-year time bar to sue the carrier. She sued, instead, her employer, who in turn, sued the carrier for contribution under the Civil Liability (Contribution) Act 1978. The Court of Appeal in reversing the High Court decision held that the time bar did not protect against a claim for contribution as this was not a claim by the passenger under the 2002 Athens Convention. The Court further held that the 2002 Athens Convention was not a complete code governing all liability of sea carriers to whomsoever it might be owed.

(d) Jurisdictional arrangements

The 2002 Athens Convention permits the claimant to select where to pursue the claim from a range of competent jurisdictions. These are:

- the place of residence or principal place of business of the defendant;[78]
- the contractual place of departure or destination;[79]
- the claimant's place of domicile or permanent residency;[80] or
- the place where the contract was made[81] if the defendant has a place of business there and is subject to the jurisdiction of that State.

The parties to the contract of the carriage may agree, after the incident, to a different jurisdiction, as permitted in Article 17(1).[82] The various options for jurisdiction create a risk of multiple proceedings in more than one court. The application of these provisions may lead to different *fora* for a claim against the carrier and the performing carrier.

Final enforceable judgments from a competent court are to be enforced by all courts of Contracting States except where obtained by fraud or where the defendant was not given reasonable notice and a fair opportunity to submit a defence.[83] The wording suggests that two tests should be applicable: lack of reasonable notice and deprivation of a fair opportunity to present the case. It is unclear whether the second condition should flow from the first for this exception to apply, or whether their co-existence without a direct link is sufficient.

The Athens Regulation does not include the jurisdictional provisions of Articles 17 and 17*bis* of the 2002 Athens Convention because jurisdictional issues are within the exclusive competence of the European Union and not that of the Member States. Thus, these issues were said to "form part of the Community legal order when the Community accedes to the Athens Convention".[84] Article 17 and 17*bis* will fall to be implemented through the Recast Jurisdiction Regulation.[85] In terms of the position that will then be applied by the Recast Jurisdiction Regulation, Article 17*bis*(3) of the 2002 Athens Convention permits the application of the Recast Jurisdiction Regulation between Member States for the recognition and enforcement of judgments provided

---

76. *South West Strategic Health Authority v Bay Island Voyages* [2015] EWCA Civ 708; [2015] 2 Lloyd's Rep 652.
77. [2015] EWCA Civ 708; [2015] 2 Lloyd's Rep 652. See also P. Todd, "Athens Convention Time Bar: South West Strategic Health Authority v Bay Island Voyages", [2015] LMCLQ, 477–482.
78. 2002 Athens Convention, art 17(1)(a).
79. 2002 Athens Convention, art 17(1)(b).
80. 2002 Athens Convention, art 17(1)(c).
81. 2002 Athens Convention, art 17(1)(d).
82. 2002 Athens Convention, art 17(2).
83. 2002 Athens Convention art 17bis. This arrangement did not exist under the 1974 Athens Convention.
84. Regulation (EC) No 392/2009, Recital, para. 11.
85. Regulation (EU) No 1215/2012 of the European Parliament and of the Council of 12 December 2012 on jurisdiction and the recognition and enforcement of judgments in civil and commercial matters (recast).

that judgments of courts with jurisdiction under the 2002 Athens Convention are recognised, at least to the extent provided for in that Convention. For jurisdiction allocation, the provisions of the 2002 Athens Convention are therefore to prevail over the more general, existing provisions of the Recast Jurisdiction Regulation.[86]

(e) Compulsory insurance

The 2002 Athens Convention requires compulsory liability insurance accompanied by a right of direct action against the liability insurer.[87] The performing carrier of a ship licensed to carry more than 12 passengers is obliged[88] to carry insurance up to the limits of strict liability multiplied by the number of passengers the vessel is allowed to carry – that is, 250,000 SDR per passenger.[89] Direct action against the insurer can be brought under Article 10. However, the liability of the insurer is limited to 250,000 SDR even if the carrier has lost his right to limit liability. It follows that, even where unlimited liability is prescribed by a State under Article 7.2, the insurer's liability will still be limited to 250,000 SDR per passenger.[90] The insurer can avoid liability relying on the same exceptions as the carrier[91] and, in addition, in cases where the incident has been caused by the wilful misconduct of the carrier. However, the insurer will not be able to rely on the contract of insurance in order to avoid paying a claimant passenger.

The insurer can use any defences available to the carrier, for example the exceptions for act of war or hostility and the like,[92] natural phenomena of an irresistible nature[93] as well as contributory negligence and rights of recovery against third parties.[94] Moreover, the insurer can escape liability if the damage was caused by the wilful misconduct of the insured.[95] However, the insurer will have to make payment up[96] to the limits of liability in all other situations, except for war risks, even where it could have avoided the insurance contract in a claim by the performing carrier.[97] The limit operates per passenger. Thus, if a passenger suffers damage of more than 250,000 SDR in a ship licensed to carry, say, 400 passengers, the insurer will only pay up to 250,000 SDR, even though the total insurance cover would be 100,000,000 SDR. The above-mentioned jurisdictions are also available for a direct action against the insurer.

3. THE ATHENS REGULATION

The 2002 Athens Convention is an Appendix to the Athens Regulation[98] while the main part of the Regulation determines the scope of the 2002 Athens Convention in various respects. The

---

86. For a discussion on potential conflicts, see H. Ringbom, "EU Regulation 44/2001 and its Implications for the International Maritime Liability Conventions", (2014) 35(1) JMLC 1–33.

87. This is a significant improvement over the 1974 Athens Convention.

88. 2002 Athens Convention, art 4*bis* (1).

89. 2002 Athens Convention, art 4*bis*. However, the requirement for compulsory insurance applies only to vessels that carry more than 12 passengers. Detailed provisions for issuing the insurance certificates by the coastal State are also provided in the same Article. Discussion of them is outside the scope of this chapter.

90. Or, for war risks 340 million SDR under the IMO reservation and Guidelines.

91. This has been modified by the IMO Guidelines, which permit the insurers to reduce their exposure by inserting specific Institute Clauses.

92. 2002 Athens Convention, art 3.1(a).

93. 2002 Athens Convention, art 3.1(b).

94. 2002 Athens Convention, art 3.7.

95. 2002 Athens Convention, art 4*bis* 10.

96. The insurer retains the right to join both the contractual and the performing carrier to the proceedings: art 4*bis* 10.

97. 2002 Athens Convention, art 4*bis* 10. For example, where there is a breach of the seaworthiness obligation.

98. The Regulation was published on 28 May 2009.

IMO reservation and most[99] of the guidelines are also included as part of the Regulation (Annex II), with binding character equal to the authentic text of the 2002 Athens Convention. The major changes introduced by the Athens Regulation are the following:

- The Athens Regulation does not depend on the status of the 2002 Athens Convention. It became applicable on 31 December 2012,[100] before the 2002 Athens Convention came into force.
- The IMO Guidelines are included in Annex II and are binding.[101]
- The application of the 2002 Athens Convention is gradually extended to national carriage of passengers.[102]
- Sufficient[103] advance payments will have to be paid out within 15 days from the time the person entitled to damages is identified. Such payments will not be considered an admission of liability. The advance payment provisions apply to carriers flying the flag of, or registered in, a Member State or for damages occurring within a Member State's territory.
- Each carrier is obliged to give out information regarding the rights of passengers under the Athens Regulation, including their rights to compensation, the limits applicable and the possibility of direct action against the insurer.[104]
- Loss or damage to mobility and other specific equipment belonging to a passenger with reduced mobility will be governed by Article 3.3 of the 2002 Athens Convention. The carrier's fault will be presumed if the loss is caused by shipwreck, capsizing, collision or the stranding of the ship, explosion or fire in the ship, or any defect in the ship. Compensation will correspond to the replacement value of the equipment or, where relevant, the cost of the repairs.

The Athens Regulation expressly provides in Article 5.1 that it does not modify the rights or duties of the carrier or the performing carrier under national legislation implementing the 1996 LLMC. Thus, the Regulation seeks to ensure that where Member States are using the limits under Article 7.1 of the 1996 LLMC which concern loss of life or personal injury of passengers these are not overridden by the supremacy of the Regulation over national law. Article 5.1 goes on to provide that where there is no such national legislation then only Article 3 of the Regulation implementing the liability provisions of the 2002 Athens Convention is applicable.[105]

4. INTERACTION BETWEEN THE 1974 ATHENS CONVENTION AND THE 1976 AND 1996 CONVENTIONS ON LIMITATION OF LIABILITY FOR MARITIME CLAIMS

Because Article 19 of the 2002 Athens Convention does not affect the shipowner's right of limitation, it follows that the proper interpretation is that the 1976 LLMC limits as amended co-exist

---

99. Guidelines 4 and 5 are not included.
100. Athens Regulation, art 12.
101. Athens Regulation, art 3.2.
102. Athens Regulation, art 2. See earlier discussion.
103. Athens Regulation, art 6. Sufficient to cover immediate economic needs, not less than EUR 21,000 in case of death.
104. Athens Regulation, art 7. No penalty for non-provision of information is imposed within the proposed Regulation.
105. Athens Regulation, art 5.1.

with the limits of the 2002 Athens Convention. Therefore, the lower limits will arguably apply and this may cause problems.[106]

The problem was more acute under the 1976 LLMC which included, under Article 7, in addition to a limit of 46,666 SDR multiplied by the number of passengers the ship was authorised to carry, an overall cap of 25,000,000 SDR. The 1996 Protocol LLMC has reduced the problem by increasing the limits to 175,000 SDR multiplied by the number of passengers the ship is authorised to carry. Under the 1996 LLMC, the limit is still global, that is, the same amount is available even if one passenger is killed or injured, whereas, of course, the 2002 Athens Convention imposes the limits per passenger.

Furthermore, the 1996 LLMC also permits the increase of the limits above those prescribed under Article 7 through the national law of each State party.[107] Thus, unlimited liability under the 1996 LLMC for loss of life and personal injury to a passenger is now possible.[108]

The UK government has utilised Article 15(3)*bis* of the 1996 LLMC and dis-applied Article 7 in relation to sea going ships.[109] This arrangement permits the higher limits of liability under the 2002 Athens Convention to operate.

For damage to luggage or "other than luggage", the limits under Article 6.1(b) of the 1996 LLMC apply, as well as the limits per passenger under Article 8 of the 2002 Athens Convention. Thus, passengers will be able to recover, for such claims, up to the limits prescribed under the 2002 Athens Convention unless the 1996 LLMC limits are exceeded, in which case recovery for damage to the possessions of the passengers will be further reduced.

Not every State may follow the UK arrangements for passenger limits. Thus, States which are party to the 2002 Athens Convention and are also party to the 1996 LLMC will have the following choices over loss of life and personal injury:

(i) Limit liability for passengers both under the 1996 LLMC and the 2002 Athens Convention. This would imply a limit of liability of 400,000 SDR per passenger[110] under Article 7.1 of the 2002 Athens Convention, capped by an overall limit of 175,000 SDR, multiplied by the number of passengers the ship is authorised to carry, according to the ship's certificate,. This solution may reduce liability below the 250,000 SDR strict liability limits under Article 3.1 of the 2002 Athens Convention to 175,000 SDR per passenger.

(ii) A State could provide for unlimited liability for loss of life or personal injury under the 1996 LLMC under Article 15(3)*bis*. In such a case the limits of the 2002 Athens Convention will apply alone.

(iii) A State could provide unlimited liability under the 2002 Athens Convention and permit limitation of liability under Article 7.1 of the 1996 LLMC.

(iv) A State can remove the limits of liability from both conventions and permit unlimited liability for passenger claims in respect of death or personal injury.

In the UK, until the Merchant Shipping Act 1995 applied the limitation provisions of the 1976 LLMC to vessels which are not seagoing, the provisions of the 1974 Athens Convention and 1976 LLMC did not apply to them. Thus the claims of the passengers on the Thames Cruise

---

106. Among other problems, this doubles the difficulty of updating the limits of liability for passenger claims as they are contained in two Conventions.

107. 1996 LLMC, art 6, inserting art 15(3)*bis*.

108. See N. Gaskell, "New Limits for Passengers and Others in the United Kingdom" (1998) 2 LMCLQ 312–314, which observes that this is the contemporary trend for loss of life and personal property.

109. MSA 1995, Schedule 7 Pt II para 6.

110. Except for war risks as explained where 250,000 SDR per passenger or 340,000 SDR overall whichever is lower will apply.

Boat *Marchioness*, which sank following collision with the dredger *Bowbelle* in 1989,[111] were not subject to any limitation regime. The position has now been changed and the UK implementation[112] establishes a per-head limit of 175,000 SDR.

5. THE COMMERCIAL REALITY

The high media profile of shipping accidents involving passenger ships coupled with the insurance cover provided by the carrier's Protection and Indemnity ("P&I") insurance and the practice of seeking settlement outside courts have led to very few reported cases of death and injury claims being pursued through the courts. The principal value of the limitation provisions in the 2002 Athens and 1996 LLMC Conventions supported by the almost unbreakable tests for removing such rights means that realistic settlements are encouraged since there is not much point litigating for excess recovery.

English courts typically award for personal injury, medical expenses; pain and suffering (past, present and future); loss of amenity and lost earnings (past, present and future). For loss of life, the personal representatives of the deceased will claim for medical, funeral and testamentary expenses, including expenses in connection with a coroner's inquest; the deceased's pain and suffering prior to death; damages for bereavement under the Fatal Accidents Acts 1976 (currently £12,000) to specified dependants; dependency claims by those (e.g. spouse, children or aged parents) whom the deceased was supporting prior to death. Forum shopping is of course common because other courts, such as those of the US, provide better chances for recovery of higher damages. However, US jurisdiction must first be established.

6. THE EU PACKAGE TRAVEL DIRECTIVE

Passengers who are killed, injured or whose belongings are lost or damaged suffer more losses than the 2002 Athens Convention covers. In particular, they lose the money they have paid for the ticket as well as the enjoyment they expected to have. The EU Directive[113] provides the basis for additional recovery. This was introduced in 1990, and is enacted in various forms in the laws of all EU Member States. It applies to all travel which is part of a pre-arranged set of services sold or offered for sale at an inclusive price covering a period of more than 24 hours or including an overnight stay and which combines at least two of the following: transport, accommodation, any other tourist services not related to transport or accommodation which account for a significant proportion of the package price.[114]

---

111. With the loss of 51 lives. The legal proceedings arising out of this accident were all settled out of court.

112. MSA 1995, Schedule 7, Part II, para 6.

113. Directive 90/314/EEC incorporated into English Law by the Package Travel, Package Holidays and Package Tours Regulations 1992, SI 1992/3288. This was amended by Directive (EU) 2015/2302 of the European Parliament and of the Council of 25 November 2015 on package travel and linked travel arrangements, amending Regulation (EC) No 2006/2004 and Directive 2011/83/EU of the European Parliament and of the Council and repealing Council Directive 90/314/EEC. This will apply from 1 July 2018.

114. Articles 4 and 5 of the Directive provide protection to consumers in relation to descriptive matter and the contents of brochures. Article 6 sets out circumstances in which particulars in a brochure are to be binding on an operator. Articles 7 and 8 impose on the operator the obligation to provide certain appropriate information in a timely way. Article 9 sets out certain minimum requirements as to the contents and form of the relevant contract, including the provision that "all the terms of the contract are set out in writing or such other form as is comprehensible and accessible to the consumer". Article 10 to 14 provide the consumer with protection in relation to the transfer of bookings, price revision, significant alteration of essential terms and significant proportion of services not provided.

Article 15 provides:

Liability of other party to the contract for proper performance of obligations under contract

(1) The other party to the contract is liable to the consumer for the proper performance of the obligations under the contract, irrespective of whether such obligations are to be performed by that other party or by suppliers of services.
(2) The other party to the contract is liable to the consumer for any damage caused to him by the failure to perform the contract or the improper performance of the contract . . .
(3) In the case of damage arising from the non-performance or improper performance of the services involved in the package, the contract may provide for compensation to be limited in accordance with the international conventions which govern such services.
(4) In the case of damage other than personal injury resulting from the non-performance or improper performance of the services involved in the package, the contract may include a term limiting the amount of compensation which will be paid to the consumer, provided that the limitation is not unreasonable.

The interaction between this Directive and the 1974 Athens Convention has been the subject of two legal decisions in the UK County Court which are difficult to reconcile with each other and with the Convention. In the first case, *Lee and Another v Airtours Holidays Ltd and Another*,[115] decided in April 2002, Judge Hallgarten QC held that the provisions of the Directive were part of UK domestic law and should be applied unless the provisions of the Convention were specifically referred to in the contract, which they were not on the facts of that case (where a booking was made by internet).

However, in *Norfolk v My Travel Group Plc*[116] Judge Overend in the Plymouth County Court held that the 1974 Athens Convention was given the force of law in the UK by section 183 Merchant Shipping Act 1995, and that it therefore applied even where there was no express reference to it in the contract. He also held that the two-year time bar in the Convention did not conflict with the terms of the Directive.

Judge Overend did not refer to the decision in *Lee v Airtours* in the course of his judgment, or indeed to the cases cited by Judge Hallgarten, although that case had been decided one year earlier. He did however rely heavily on the comments of Lord Hope in the House of Lords case of *Sidhu v British Airways Plc*,[117] which concerned the interaction of the Warsaw Convention and common law claims by passengers in an aircraft, and which was not cited in *Lee v Airtours*.

There is an apparent conflict between the terms of the Directive and the express terms of Articles 11 and 14 of the 1974 Athens Convention, which demonstrate that it is intended that the code contained in the Convention applicable to claims against a carrier should also apply to claims against the servants or agents of the carrier, and, more important, that no claims by passengers should be brought otherwise than in accordance with the Convention. Judge Overend relied on these provisions in *Norfolk v My Travel*[118]. It is strongly arguable that the provisions of the EU Directive, to the extent that they conflict with the Convention, amount to a breach by the EU Member States of their treaty obligations to the other States parties to the 1974 Athens Convention. However, the introduction of the Athens Regulation partly resolves the conflict because as part of the legal order of the EU, the Athens Regulation cannot be overridden by the national implementation of the Directive.

115. [2004] 1 Lloyd's Rep 683.
116. [2004] 1 Lloyd's Rep 106.
117. [1997] AC 430 (HL); [1997] 2 Lloyd's Rep 76.
118. [2004] 1 Lloyd's Rep 106.

7. THE EUROPEAN REGULATION ON PASSENGERS' RIGHTS[119]

This Regulation is intended to strengthen passengers' rights as well as rights of disabled passengers to compensation from the carrier, and to provide for express rights to compensation for delay or cancellation of the service. Passengers whose journey is delayed by more than 90 minutes are entitled to refreshments, re-routing or reimbursement, and if necessary to accommodation for a maximum of three nights up to a cost of EUR 80 per night. Compensation for delayed arrival of up to a half of the ticket price may be payable in the event of delayed arrival at destination, but the right to accommodation does not apply if the delay or cancellation is caused by bad weather. Likewise no compensation for late arrival is due if weather conditions or extraordinary circumstances hindered the performance of the service. Special provisions require facilities and assistance to be provided to passengers with disabilities.

---

119. Regulation (EU) No 1177/2010 of the European Parliament and of the Council of 24 November 2010 concerning the rights of passengers when travelling by sea and inland waterway and amending Regulation (EC) No 2006/2004 A useful summary of this complex legislation is in the short article by J Chuah, "New Rights for Ship Passengers" (2010) 16 JIML 317.

CHAPTER 7

THE LIABILITIES OF THE VESSEL

Michael Tsimplis

1. INTRODUCTION[1]

This chapter deals with liabilities arising from the vessel's operation. These are usually called "wet" topics, to contrast with what are called the "dry" aspects of maritime law which usually refer to cargo and charterparty claims. In this book contracts for the carriage of passengers

---

1. Johanna Hjalmarsson has updated section 4 on General Average. Michael Tsimplis has authored the rest of the chapter.

and cargo as well as charterparty claims are dealt with in separate chapters.[2] Marine pollution which includes an expanding body of rules and international conventions is also described separately.[3]

The aspects of liability we consider in this chapter are those arising from collisions, salvage, General Average, towage, wreck removal, damage occurring when the vessel is under the command of a pilot, the privilege granted to shipowners and others to limit their liability in respect of some types of claim and liabilities in ports and harbours. The final section of this chapter discusses technology and shipping law.

2. COLLISIONS

(a) Introduction

Collisions and groundings are the most common accidents at sea.[4] Liability for damage arising from a collision is, in general, based on tort law and in particular on negligence. In English law negligence is defined as the breach of a recognised duty of care owed to a person who may reasonably be foreseen to suffer loss as a direct result of that breach.[5] However, liability in the absence of negligence is frequently established statutorily for damage to port installations,[6] oil pollution damage,[7] wreck removal costs[8] and loss of life and personal injury of passengers.[9] However, in all cases, the strict liability regimes permit the person liable to claim, under an indemnity claim, all or part of the payments it has made to third parties from the person whose negligence has led to the damage.

(b) Liability for collision damage

There is, in general, a duty of care imposed on every ship against all other users of the seas.[10] Most collision claims are based on the negligent breach of this duty[11] or negligent breach of a statutory duty, although claims in nuisance and trespass have also been made.[12] While collisions occur at sea the cause of a collision can, in some cases, be traced back to negligent acts or omissions that took place well before the collision occurred and sometimes not at sea but in the office of the shipowning or managing company. For example, decisions made by the shipowning company not to undertake the appropriate maintenance of the ship or an engine or, perhaps by failing to ensure that the master and the crew are properly qualified have often been found to contribute

---

2. In Chapters 6, 5 and 4 respectively.

3. See Chapter 10.

4. An excellent practitioner's textbook on collision litigation is S. Gault and S. Hazlewood (Gen Eds), *Marsden and Gault on Collisions at Sea* (14th edn, Sweet & Maxwell 2016). See also A Mandaraka-Sheppard, *Modern Maritime Law: Volumes 1 (Jurisdiction and Risks)* and *2 (Management Risks and Liabilities)* (3rd edn, Informa 2013).

5. *Donoghue v Stevenson* [1932] AC 562.

6. See section 9 of this Chapter on Ports and Harbours.

7. See Chapter 10.

8. See section 6 of this Chapter.

9. See Chapter 6.

10. *Mobil Oil Hong Kong and Dow Chemical (Hong Kong) v Hong Kong United Dockyards (The Hua Lien)* [1991] 1 Lloyd's Rep 309, 328–32.

11. Note that a collision by itself is not proof of negligence (see, for example, *The Cythera* [1965] 2 Lloyd's Rep 454, Supreme Court (New South Wales)). Note also that a duty of care may be imposed in relation to damage caused by young offenders who escaped from a detention centre due to negligence of the public servants overseeing their detention (*Home Office v Dorset Ship Company Ltd* [1970] AC 1004).

12. *Esso Petroleum Co Ltd v Southport Corporation* [1956] AC 218; *Crown River Cruises Ltd v Kimbolton Fireworks Ltd* [1996] 2 Lloyd's Rep 533.

to collisions. Thus in approaching collision liability a distinction between negligence in the navigation of the ship and negligence in the management of the ship must be drawn. The former refers to faults by the master, pilot or crew while the latter is concerned with faults caused either by the crew and the master or the company in ensuring the ship is safe to sail and is operated in a safe way. Where for example the crew is overworked and this leads, through human error, to a collision then the causation of the collision can be considered to be the lack of an appropriate watch system enabling crew members to rest properly. In both negligence in the management of the ship and negligence in navigation vicarious liability will attach to the employer, who could be the registered shipowner or a bareboat charterer. However, negligence in the management of the ship brings the causative act closer to the corporate shipowning entity and, as will be seen, this can affect the shipowner's right to limit liability.[13] In order to avoid liability one has to discharge the duty of care by behaving in accordance with the expected standard. Conversely, liability will be established where the claimant shows that the damage suffered was caused by the conduct of the defendant falling below the required standard. In terms of navigational standards, "good seamanship", which can be taken to mean the ordinary skill, care and nerve of each seaman according to his rank, is required.[14] The duty is very wide and includes observance of local[15] as well as international navigation rules.[16] Negligence in the mooring of the ship may also create liability for subsequent damage.[17] In addition it entails the collection of any relevant information for the place where the ship may sail. Thus, where a port is under dredging operations and the ship sails unaware of them and as a result a collision occurs, the ship is likely to be liable.[18] In relation to negligence in management a similar standard which can perhaps be termed "good shipownership" needs to be observed. There are various conventions and regulations relating to the standards that the crew members should observe. The 1978 International Convention on Standards of Training, Certification and Watchkeeping of Seafarers[19] prescribes the standards for crew training, certification and the working duties onboard the ship. In addition, the 1994 International Safety Management Code[20] provides for the establishment of a safety management system in the shipping company and the ship. Particular codes for ships implementing the international conventions to specific class of vessels in ways which are appropriate also exist and are developed by ship registers under powers granted by the relevant conventions. Negligence in observing these duties and any other statutory duties imposed on the owners, managers or operators of a ship could result in liability for the collision damage. In addition, all actions in breach of statutory or other duties to maintain, keep up, provide for the ship and her equipment, documentation, charts etc may result in liability for the collision.[21] Thus negligence in management can refer to any of the statutory provisions providing for the safety of the ship and its equipment including the manning and the training requirements, the operational procedures onboard the ship, including the ability of the crew to communicate with each other and read the

---

13. See section 8 of this chapter on Limitation of Liability.

14. *The Thomas Powell and the Cuba* (1866) 14 LT 603.

15. *The Fairplay XIV* (1939) 63 Ll L Rep 210.

16. There is case law in support of the view that in some instances compliance with navigation rules made by local bodies that do not have statutory authority is part of the duty of good seamanship (*The Humbergate* [1952] 1 Lloyd's Rep 168; *The Whitby Abbey* [1962] 1 Lloyd's Rep 110 and *The Grampian Coast* [1958] 1 Lloyd's Rep 208).

17. *Voaden v Champion (The Baltic Surveyor and The Timbuktu)* [2002] EWCA Civ 89; [2002] 1 Lloyd's Rep 623. A case where the negligent mooring led to damage to another ship and to the mooring pontoon.

18. *Plumb v Rae* (1935) 51 Ll L Rep 252.

19. This convention was adopted by International Maritime Organisation (IMO) on 7 July 1978. See Chapter 9.

20. This code was adopted by the IMO as Assembly Resolution A.741(18), in November 1993. See Chapter 9.

21. Thus, where the owner undertakes to maintain the ship itself it will still be liable if it is negligent. See for example *The Alastor* [1981] 1 Lloyd's Rep 581.

ship's manuals, the required maintenance and inspections and every other decision or act that a reasonable shipowner would take in order to make the ship's navigation safe.[22]

The claimant must prove that the damage suffered was caused by the negligence of the defendant. In certain cases, the principle of *res ipsa loquitur* applies where the facts of the tort speak for themselves in establishing, at least, prima facie evidence of negligence. Accordingly, where a ship underway strikes a moored vessel in good visibility during the day, an inference of negligence against the moving ship is likely to be made.[23] Where the claimant fails to show that the damage was caused by the fault of the defendant then the claim fails. It follows that if two ships collide but it is unclear whose fault caused the damage then each party bears their own loss.[24]

While in the general case discharging the duty of good seamanship will involve following the applicable national or international navigational rules, there are cases where departure from the manoeuvres required by the Collision Regulations may be needed in order to comply with the duty of good seamanship.[25] The Collision Regulations provide specific guidance on how ships should navigate in situations where they approach other ships, the lights and shapes they should display and their actions in situations of reduced visibility etc. Rule 1 permits the operation of rules of navigation imposed by port authorities or coastal States in appropriate areas.

The standard of good seamanship requires the persons navigating the vessel not to be negligent. However, in situations where a ship:

a) is put in a collision situation by the actions of another vessel, and
b) they are under time pressure to react

liability may not be imposed even if the act is inconsistent with the good seamanship standard. For this exception from liability, named "agony of the moment",[26] to be applicable, the collision danger must be sudden and great. In addition, the ship relying on the agony of the moment defence should not have contributed to the creation of the dangerous situation.

(c) The Collision Regulations

These provide part of the standard of good seamanship. However, failure to comply with them does not necessarily lead to the imposition of civil liability. Firstly, if the action is dictated by the standard of good seamanship it is not against the Collision Regulations and it is not a negligent act.[27] Secondly, causation also needs to be established.[28]

A major obligation is that all vessels should maintain a proper look out by sight and hearing.[29] Vessels should always proceed with safe speed.[30] The Collision Regulations do not specify what a safe speed is but do say that the purpose of this is to be able to avoid collision by turning or

---

22. See e.g. SOLAS, in particular Chapters V (Navigation) and IX (Management for the Safe Operation of Ships).
23. See, for example, *The Merchant Prince* [1892] P 179.
24. *Owners of the SS Olympic v Blunt (The Olympic and the HMS Hawke)* [1913] P 214.
25. See Collision Regulations Rule 2(a).
26. *The Bywell Castle* (1878–79) LR 4 PD 219. But see *Rickman v Railway Executive* (1949/50) 83 Ll L Rep 409, for an explanation that, even where the original negligence and collision is due to the action by the party injured, it is really a question of whether the negligent act that caused the damage is linked with the original negligence.
27. Rule 2.
28. Any negligence which is found by the court to be non-causative will be left out of the reckoning. See: *Owners of the Global Mariner v Owners of the Atlantic Crusader (The Global Mariner and Atlantic Crusader)* [2005] 1 Lloyd's Rep 699.
29. Rule 5. What this means in terms of personnel and instruments depends on the weather conditions and the general situation.
30. Rule 6.

stopping in time, taking into account the prevailing conditions.[31] The Collision Regulations also provide for Traffic Separation Schemes[32] where the traffic is channelled into one-way (notional) lanes in order to increase the safety of navigation.

The Collision Regulations then deal with the situation where ships are in sight of each other. There are different rules applying to instances where a sailing vessel meets a mechanically propelled vessel or a fishing vessel etc. For mechanically propelled vessels in sight of each other the following rules apply. The general principle is that ships "drive on the right". Thus when two ships are approaching each other, they must pass port to port, keeping to the starboard side of mid channel[33] when in a channel, and must alter course to starboard when approaching end-on.[34] In a crossing situation the ship which has the other on her starboard side must give way.[35]

The Collision Regulations include rules applicable to restricted visibility.[36] The steering and sailing rules[37] apply *only* to vessels *in sight* of one another, and not to vessels navigating by reference to one another by radar in fog. The Collision Regulations also contain detailed rules concerning lights and shapes to be displayed by vessels[38] and sound signals to be given by them.[39]

(d) Causation

The breach of the duties in navigation or in the ship's management is not sufficient to establish liability. It must be shown that the negligent act has been causative wholly or partly of the damage. Thus where the defendant can show that the damage was not caused by its negligence but by a new intervening cause then the "chain of causation" is broken and liability is not imposed on the defendant. For example, where a ship is taking in water following a collision to which she had not contributed by negligence but the master unreasonably refuses salvage assistance and tries to take the ship into port but the ship sinks before reaching the port, then the loss of the ship is due to the master's decision and not due to the collision and any negligence of the other party involved. In such a case, the owner of the sunken ship can only recover nominal damage for the collision damage suffered.[40] The same consequence will follow a collision involving a ship where the ship's master, although not responsible for the collision, becomes responsible for the ship's loss through his negligent response to the collision damage.

Another defence available to a defendant is that of "inevitable accident". The defence, to be available, requires the exclusion of any negligence by the party claiming it. This will necessarily

---

31. The outcome of the enquiry to the loss of the *Titanic* includes the following passage concerning the decision of the master not to reduce the speed:

> He made a mistake, a very grievous mistake, but one in which, in face of the practice and of past experience, negligence cannot be said to have had any part; and in the absence of negligence it is, in my opinion, impossible to fix Captain Smith with blame. It is, however, to be hoped that the last has been heard of the practice and that for the future it will be abandoned for what we now know to be more prudent and wiser measures. What was a mistake in the case of the "Titanic" would without doubt be negligence in any similar case in the future.
>
> www.titanicinquiry.org/BOTInq/BOTReport/botRepAction.php (accessed 27 March 2017).

It is submitted that past practice can not avoid the conclusion of negligence any more.
32. Rule 10.
33. Rule 9.
34. Rule 14.
35. Rule 15.
36. Rule 19.
37. Rules 11–18.
38. Rules 20–30.
39. Rules 34 and 35.
40. *Owners of Mitera Marigo v Owners of Fritz Thyssen (The Fritz Thyssen)* [1967] 1 All ER 628.

involve an investigation as to whether any earlier acts were negligent and contributed to the creation of the inevitable accident situation, in which case the defence will not operate.[41]

(e) Time bars

The time bar for actions against the shipowner or that of a claim by a shipowner against another shipowner in a collision case is two years.[42] The time bar applies to loss of life, personal injury and damage to others and property claims. The courts are granted discretion to extend the limitation period as thought fit.[43] The above time bar only applies to collisions between ships. Consequently, collisions between a ship and a jetty or buoy or harbour installation are not covered by the Merchant Shipping Act 1995 time bar; instead, the Limitation Act 1980 would apply. Under section 2 of the Limitation Act 1980 a general limit of six years is introduced for damages arising from a tort. This is further restricted to three years for loss of life or personal injury under section 11. The three years commence under section 11(4) from the date on which the cause of action accrued; or the date of knowledge (if later) of the person injured. Subrogation to insurers of the right of an insured will occur on payment of the insurance.[44]

(f) Who can claim in respect of collision damage?

The registered owners and the demise-charterers of a ship are in general entitled to sue for collision damage suffered by their ship. Other charterers of the ship are not able to sue for collision damage suffered by the ship,[45] although they can sue if they own property on the ship which has been damaged in the collision. Mortgagees who do not have possession of the ship cannot sue for damage done to the ship. Crew members and passengers can sue for personal injury and for damage to their property in tort against another vessel and under contract against the vessel on which they work or are passengers. Where a person is killed his estate may sue[46] for damages caused to the deceased, and his personal representatives or dependants can sue for loss and damages they have suffered.[47]

(g) Apportionment of liability[48]

The liability for loss of life and personal injury following a collision between two ships is joint and several.[49] Thus a claimant can recover from either ship in full. The party that has paid the claimant can recover a contribution from the other party which corresponds to the other party's liability for the damage caused.[50] In respect of property loss or damage caused by the negligence of two or more ships (including a ship and a ship or two ships), the liability

---

41. *The Merchant Prince* [1892] P 179; *The Kite* [1933] P 154; (1933) 46 Ll L Rep 83.
42. MSA 1995, s 190.
43. MSA 1995, s 190(5). For the approach taken to extension of the limitation provision of s 190 MSA 1995 see *CDE SA v Sure Wind Marine Ltd (The Odyssee)* [2015] EWHC 720 (Admlty); [2015] 2 Lloyd's Rep 268. See also *Owners of the Stolt Kestrel v Owners of the Niyazi S* [2015] EWCA Civ 1035; [2016] 1 Lloyd's Rep 125 and *Former Owners of the Melissa K (now named Jasmine I) v Former Owners of the Tomsk (subsequently named Pure Energy and now named Thayer)* [2015] EWHC 3445 (Admlty); [2016] 1 Lloyd's Rep 503.
44. Marine Insurance Act 1906, s 79. See Chapter 11.
45. *Candlewood Navigation Corp v Mitsui Osk Lines (The Mineral Transporter and The Ibaraki Maru)* [1986] AC 1.
46. The Law Reform (Miscellaneous Provisions) Act 1934, s 1(1).
47. The Fatal Accidents Act 1976.
48. The UK has by way of s 187 and s 188 of the 1995 MSA enacted the 1910 Brussels Collision Convention.
49. MSA 1995, s 188.
50. MSA 1995, s 189.

is in proportion to the fault. Thus a claimant can recover from each vessel in accordance with the causative potency of the damage and the blameworthiness of the act. However, when a ship is not at fault but it is damaged following a collision with two or more other ships the above provisions do not apply. In such a case the English law position is that there is a right of recovery from any of the tortfeasors.[51] Where no party is negligent but nevertheless a collision took place each party has to suffer its own losses. It must be noted that the provisions of the 1995 MSA do not cover situations between a ship and a dock or a mooring buoy or a jetty etc. In such a case, apportionment of liability falls under the 1945 Law Reform (Contributory Negligence) Act.[52]

(h) Investigation of a collision

There are several practicalities that need to be resolved following a collision claim. First, there is difficulty in relation to the appropriate jurisdiction. Under the 1952 Collision (Civil Jurisdiction) Convention a claimant has a choice of jurisdiction. It can sue the defendant in the court where the defendant has his habitual residence or a place of business or, where the ship or a sister ship has been arrested or could have been arrested and bail or security has been provided or, if the collision took place within the limits of a port or in the inland waters of a State in the courts of that Contracting State.[53] The parties can agree, of course, on another forum including arbitration.[54] A second consideration is the provision of security. This can be achieved by arresting the ship or a sister ship. In many cases the mutual provision of security in the form of a P&I Club letter of undertaking is negotiated together with the choice of forum.[55]

It is also practically important that all the relevant information is collected and that the court establishes the facts of the case as soon as possible. This is done in various ways. The damage is quantified by surveyors and experts who provide assessments on the details of the collision including the speed at the time of collision, the angle of the blow and the actions of all parties involved before the collision. Because a ship's ability to slow down and turn are limited and depend on various factors, the negligence in navigation that caused the collision may go back 30 minutes or even more in some cases. Thus a detailed scenario of what happened from the moment the ships came in sight of each other needs to be developed. In preparation for the dispute resolution each party assembles all the ship's documents including log books, charts and any data from the automatic data logging devices installed on the ship. Their solicitors interview the officers and crew members on watch on the bridge and in the engine room, and any other member of the crew who witnessed anything relevant, and prepare a written statement of each witness's evidence. Such statements cannot be disclosed to the other parties to the litigation without the agreement of the party on whose behalf they were made, as they are privileged.[56] In practice, most such statements are disclosed in English collision proceedings and treated as evidence of the facts described, except where the witness is called to give oral evidence.

---

51. *Owners of the Steamship Devonshire v Owners of the Barge Leslie* [1912] AC 634; *The Cairnbahn* [1914] P 25.
52. See *Fitzgerald v Lane* [1989] AC 328 for the difference in the effects of contributory action.
53. 1952 Collision (Civil Jurisdiction) Convention, art 1. The UK is a party and has enacted the Convention as a restriction in the action *in personam* under ss 21and 22 of the Senior Courts Act 1981. See Chapter 12.
54. Ibid., art 2.
55. The form of such a guarantee is negotiable, but in English practice all collision security is now given on the terms of the standard forms published by the City of London Admiralty Solicitors Group available, free of charge, from www. admiraltysolicitorsgroup.com (accessed 18 February 2017).
56. For a recent case on waiving privilege in witness statements see *Commodities Research Unit International (Holdings) Ltd v King and Wood Mallesons LLP* [2016] EWHC 63 (QB).

Evidence from external sources, for example, a recording of the radar showing movements of the ships concerned made by an official body such as Dover Coastguard[57] or other Vessel Traffic Surveillance (VTS) service[58] can also be used. Occasionally, independent evidence may be obtained from the officer on watch on another ship in the vicinity of the collision, who may have observed the movements of the two ships on radar.

The Civil Procedure Rules require the submission of a "Collision Statement of Case", formerly known as the Preliminary Act.[59] This contains a series of questions related to the circumstances of the collision, which each party is required to answer and submit to the Court without knowing the answers given by the other party. Answers to the questions are considered to be admissions of fact by the party filing it, and that party cannot advance a case which is inconsistent with their "Collision Statement of Case" without the permission of the judge. The evaluation of the navigational behaviour in collision cases is entrusted to the Elder Brethren of Trinity House, who are retired ships' masters who sit with the Admiralty Judge as Nautical Assessors. It is therefore not normally necessary for the parties to call expert evidence on these matters.[60]

It is the usual practice in collision cases in England for the question of liability (the division of blame) for the collision to be decided separately from the quantum of damages. The sums recoverable in most collision cases are negotiated and settled directly between the solicitors for the parties, but in the event of failure to agree, the disputed item(s) will be decided by the Admiralty Registrar.[61]

3. SALVAGE

(a) Introduction

The sea can be a dangerous place for a ship. Historically the responsibility and the capability of coastal States to assist has been very small or even non-existent in areas beyond their jurisdiction and it was primarily restricted to saving lives without much interest in preserving the ship or its cargo. There is still no general duty to save property at sea although due to the risk of pollution, States' interest has increased. Thus, historically, assistance was most likely to come from other passing ships, or from ships prepared to leave the safety of the port and risk severe weather conditions in order to assist stricken vessels.[62]

In order to facilitate and encourage this practice public policy has been developed encouraging assistance to endangered vessels. This public policy consisted of three elements. It was recognised: (a) that such assistance entitles the salvors of property to a salvage reward, (b) that the right to a salvage reward arises at the time of rendering assistance and it does not depend on the existence of a contract and (c) that this right is protected by a maritime claim of the highest priority, the salvage lien, enforceable by a right to arrest the salved property through an action *in rem*.[63]

---

57. Dover Coastguard monitors and records all traffic passing though the Dover Strait from Langton Battery on the cliffs above Dover.

58. Such services are to be found in many major ports such as London and Southampton.

59. Civil Procedure Rules 61.4(6) and PD 61.4(5).

60. For the way in which the advice of Nautical Assessors is used by the judge see *Owners of the Bow Spring v Owners of the Manzanillo II (The Bow Spring and the Manzanillo II)* [2004] EWCA Civ 1007; [2005] 1 Lloyd's Rep 1.

61. See CPR, PD 61 – Admiralty Claims, [13].

62. The public policy to encourage and reward assistance to endangered property is ancient. For more information, see H.S. Khalilieh, *Admiralty and Maritime Laws in the Mediterranean Sea (c.800–1050): the Kitab Akriyat al-Sufun vis-a-vis the Nomos Rhodion Nautikos* (Brill 2006), at 205.

63. See Chapter 12. Freezing injunctions are also available under general law. See, for example, *Ministry of Trade of Iraq v Tsavliris Salvage (International) Ltd (The Altair)* [2008] EWHC 612 (Comm); [2008] 2 Lloyd's Rep 90.

The liability to pay the reward is incurred by the owners of the salved property in proportion to the relative values of their property. Therefore, the liability will not only attach to the ship-owner but also to the cargo owners whose cargo was saved from danger, to charterers when the bunkers owned by them are salvaged as well as any owner of other property on board a ship.

Problems may arise between the salvor and the shipowner. Clearly the recognition of a right to a salvage reward does not by itself resolve the manner in which the operation should be performed, the respective obligations of the salvor and the salved property, the place and the time when the ship and any property are to be redelivered to their owner or the provision of financial security to the salvor who quite apart from concerns about payment from the shipowner for the services provided, is also concerned that cargo as well as other owners of property may resist the payment of any salvage reward.

These difficulties could partly be resolved by concluding a contract. However, negotiating the salvage reward within such a contract cannot be made, in a situation of danger, at arm's length. For these reasons specialised salvage contracts providing solutions to the practical difficulties and setting out clearly the obligations of the parties, while leaving aside the determination of the salvage reward, have been developed. The most influential of them, the Lloyd's Open Form (LOF), leaves open the extent of the reward to an arbitrator appointed by Lloyd's, thus avoiding negotiations and delays in helping the ship in distress. The LOF contract is associated with the "No Cure – No Pay" principle which reflects the general position in salvage that only where property is salved is there an entitlement to a salvage reward.

During the last 40 years, marine pollution from shipping incidents has made the availability of salvage operations crucial not only for the preservation of property at sea but also for the protection of the marine environment. However, it soon became clear that under the traditional salvage arrangement which required property to be salved in order for the salvor to be able to get a reward, there was no incentive for salvors to assist stricken tankers which were likely to sink and spill all of their cargo as no reward would then be available. This was so, under the older salvage regime, despite the fact that the salvor could have made a significant effort to prevent marine pollution, thus benefiting the owners and users of coastal resources and reducing the exposure of the shipowner to liability.

The salvage industry first modified the 1980 LOF contract to permit the recovery of the salvor's expenses if the salvage reward under the "No Cure – No Pay" principle was insufficient where the salvage operation concerned oil tankers. In addition, the Comité Maritime International (CMI), with the encouragement of the International Maritime Organisation (IMO), salvors and the International Group of P&I Clubs started the process of reviewing pre-existing salvage law[64] and eventually developed the Montreal Draft Convention which provided for the foundations of the International Salvage Convention 1989 (hereinafter the "Salvage Convention").[65]

The Salvage Convention significantly modified the reward scheme for salvage. It is presently consolidated in Schedule 11 to the Merchant Shipping Act 1995.[66] The Salvage Convention is the salvage law for England. Only where the Salvage Convention is unclear or silent there may be some freedom to obtain guidance from the pre-existing law of salvage. However, because international conventions are exactly that, i.e. international, it is suggested that only where the pre-existing English law can be said to reflect international law, can such argument

---

64. The Convention for the Unification of Certain Rules of Law Respecting Assistance and Salvage at Sea 1910 – the Brussels Salvage Convention 1910. Some articles of this convention were enacted into English law by the Maritime Conventions Act 1911, ss 6–8, but the Convention was never formally incorporated into English law. See R. Shaw, "The 1989 Salvage Convention and English Law" (1996) 2 LMCLQ 202.

65. Originally developed by the CMI. See R. Shaw (fn 64).

66. Originally enacted through the Merchant Shipping (Salvage and Pollution) Act 1994.

be persuasive.[67] It is at least comforting to observe that the Salvage Convention is to an extent consistent with the pre-existing English salvage law, thus facilitating its interpretation. However, in cases of conflict the Salvage Convention overrides any pre-existing law of salvage.

(b) The Salvage Convention

The Salvage Convention applies in all cases where salvage matters are brought before an English court or an arbitration panel seated in England.[68] Thus it applies irrespective of the flag of the ships[69] involved or the area of the sea in which the salvage operation was undertaken. The UK has reduced the geographical scope of application of the Salvage Convention by excluding salvage operations that take place in UK inland waters[70] where all vessels involved are vessels of inland navigation, and excluding salvage in inland waters where no ships are involved.[71] The definition of inland waters provided within the same section excludes waters "within the ebb and flow" of the spring tide and any docks connected with such waters. When a vessel is one of inland navigation is unclear. The wording may have various meanings, for example it may mean a vessel designed solely for inland navigation, one that is only employed in inland navigation or one which was employed in inland navigation at the time of the incident necessitating salvage assistance.[72]

Ships, craft and other structures capable of navigation as well as other property not permanently and intentionally attached to the shore can be the objects of salvage.[73] Freight at risk is also subject to salvage.[74] Pipelines and jetties are excluded from the operation of the salvage regime because they are permanently and intentionally attached to the shore. By contrast, cargo adrift or sunken can be the subject of salvage.[75]

Drilling platforms whether floating, fixed or mobile are expressly excluded[76] from the application of the Salvage Convention when they are on location and engaged in their specific operation of drilling. However, when under way these structures are subject to salvage.[77]

---

67. See the Vienna Convention on the Law of Treaties 1969, art 31(1) of which requires that: "A treaty shall be interpreted in good faith in accordance with the ordinary meaning to be given to the terms of the treaty in their context and in the light of its object and purpose." While supplementary means of interpretation, such as the working documents of the treaty, are allowed under art 32 in special circumstances, reference to any national law or pre-existing convention is arguably not permitted.

68. Salvage Convention, art 2.

69. Warships and State-owned vessels are generally excluded from the Salvage Convention unless a government has provided otherwise. See Salvage Convention, art 4.

70. For the position before the Salvage Convention, see *The Goring* [1988] 1 AC 631.

71. The UK entered a reservation under art 30 of the Convention which was then enacted in English law by the MSA 1995, Schedule 11, Part II, para 2. Notably this covers only UK waters and therefore if a salvage case concerning ships in the internal waters of another State comes before the English courts then the Salvage Convention will apply.

72. This latter suggestion is supported by the decision in *The Sea Eagle* [2011] EWHC 1438 (Admlty); [2012] 2 Lloyd's Rep 37 where the Admiralty Registrar, in the context of the 1974 Athens Convention held that the term "seagoing ship" was concerned not with whether a ship could go to sea, but whether she did go to sea.

73. Salvage Convention, art 1.

74. Freight is the amount payable to the owner under a voyage charterparty. The time it becomes payable depends on the particular charterparty. However, in the absence of a contractual arrangement as well as various charterparty forms payment is due on delivery of the cargo. Thus if the cargo is lost and never delivered freight payable on delivery will not be due and will be lost for the owner. When the salvor saves the cargo it confers on the owner the benefit of freight becoming due. Thus freight which according to the contract depends on the delivery of the cargo to be paid is freight at risk, and contributes to the salvage award. If freight is payable earlier, for example on shipment, then freight is not at risk and is not taken into account for the salvage award.

75. For the earlier narrower position under English law, see *Wells and Another (Paupers) Appellant v The Owners of the Gas Float Whitton No 2 Respondents (The Gas Float Whitton No 2)* [1896] P 42 (CA), [1897] AC 337 (HL).

76. Salvage Convention, art 3.

77. *Owners of the Maridive VII, Maridive XIII, Maridive 85 and Maridive 94 v Owners and Demise Charterers of the Key Singapore* [2005] 1 Lloyd's Rep 91.

For an operation to fall under the definition of salvage the relevant property must be in "danger".[78] The Salvage Convention does not define the term "danger". Under pre-existing English law the requirement was one of "real danger", reasonably apprehended, and this appears to be accepted as the correct interpretation under the Salvage Convention too,[79] in spite of the argument that the term should be given an international interpretation. The danger does not need to be present at the time of the sustained damage, provided that it is reasonably expected that it will arise before self-help can remedy the situation. Thus, a ship immobilised by engine failure is generally in danger, even if the weather is calm or it is anchored, if there is no possibility for effective repairs to be done.[80] A vessel breaking one mooring line and swinging around its mooring point may also be in danger if there is a risk of collision with a buoy,[81] or if it is unable to turn around in a strong current.[82] Whether the vessel is in danger or not is to be decided objectively by the judge or arbitrator. The master's opinion is not conclusive in this respect,[83] even if he is the person who will request or accept an offer for salvage assistance.

The salvor is under a duty to perform the salvage operation with due care and in doing so to minimise environmental damage and to seek assistance from other salvors if necessary. If the salvor fails to fulfil these duties it may receive a reduced reward or no reward at all.[84] Under English law the salvor is also liable for damages caused to the property salvaged if negligent.[85] The owners of the property in danger are under an obligation to co-operate fully with the salvor, to prevent or minimise environmental damage and to accept redelivery at a place of safety.[86] It is unclear what the consequences are if the owners of the property or the master do not fulfil these obligations. If, for example, the owner fails to provide information of the cargo's nature to the salvor, and as a result the vessel and the cargo are lost, would then the salvor be entitled to a salvage reward or some compensation? Similar questions can be posed in respect of the environmental duties of the salvor and the owner or master. If there is no property salved then it is clear that no salvage reward could be due. Thus the only available remedies to the salvor would arguably be either breach of the salvage contract, if there is one, or breach of the duties under Article 8 of the Salvage Convention. However, the Salvage Convention does not specify such remedies.[87] In a similar example what would the sanctions be if the salvage is successfully performed but no party pays any attention to environmental protection,[88] for example, by unnecessarily discharging oil at sea in order to refloat a grounded vessel? Within the Salvage Convention there does not appear to be any penalty for the owners of the property. For the salvor, one could argue that a reduction in the reward may be a penalty in view of the criteria for awarding monetary satisfaction which will be discussed below.

The obligation of the owners of property to accept redelivery, when the property is at a place of safety, is also problematic. The Salvage Convention does not define what a place of safety

---

78. Salvage Convention, art l(a).
79. *Owners of the Hamtun v Owners of the St John (The Hamtun and the St John)* [1999] 1 Lloyd's Rep 883.
80. *Owners of Cargo Lately Laden on Board the Troilus v Owners, masters and Crew of the Glenogle (The Troilus and the Glenogle)* [1951] 1 Lloyd's Rep 467; *Tsavliris Salvage (International) Ltd v Guangdong Shantou Overseas Chinese Materials Marketing Co (The Pa Mar)* [1999] 1 Lloyd's Rep 338.
81. *The Hamtun and the St John* (fn 78).
82. *Owners and/or Demise Charterers of the Tug Sea Tractor v Owners of the Tramp (The Tramp)* [2007] EWHC 31 (Admlty); [2007] 2 Lloyd's Rep 363.
83. *The Hamtun and the St John* (fn 78), 889 (Mr Peter Gross QC).
84. Salvage Convention, art 18.
85. See *Owners of the Maridive VII, Maridive XIII, Maridive 85 and Maridive 94 v Owners and Demise Charterers of the Key Singapore* (fn 76).
86. Salvage Convention art 8(2).
87. See R. Shaw (fn 64), at pp 225–226 for a discussion on the subject.
88. An obligation imposed by art 8 on both salvors and property owners.

is. Under pre-existing English law an interpretation requiring that the place of safety not only needed to be physically safe but also to have appropriate facilities to put the vessel back into service appeared to be the correct one.[89] However, it is strongly arguable that the natural meaning of the term, on which its interpretation should be based, only requires the place of safety to be physically safe.[90] One may also argue that once the vessel has been brought into physical safety, cheaper methods for its transportation to a place of repair, for example towage, could and should, if available, be employed.[91]

When a salvage operation has a useful result then, under Article 12, a right to a reward arises. The Salvage Convention does not define what a useful result is. The term *useful* may imply an improvement of the condition/value or quantity of the property salved and not simply that some property has been salved. If, for example, the salvors save some property but as a matter of fact the same property would have been saved without their assistance then arguably no useful result has been achieved and no salvage reward should be given.[92] An alternative interpretation may be that the salvage of any property in itself is a useful result, subject to the reservation that where the salvor has not exercised due care or has not been efficient the salvor may face a reduced reward under the relevant criteria of Article 13, or a reduction in or full deprivation of the reward under Article 18. It is submitted that because it would have been easy to state that "where property is salved a right to a reward arises", the more complex wording of Article 12 suggests that the word "useful" implies more than the mere salvage of property.[93]

Saving people at sea alone does not by itself create a right to a salvage reward. This is partly a result of Article 16 of the Salvage Convention which provides that salved people are not under an obligation to pay salvage but, at the same time, preserves any provisions of national law. English law does not recognise a right to a reward for saving life alone.[94] However, where property is salved and therefore there is a salvage reward, the Salvage Convention provides that the salvor of life is "entitled to a fair share of the payment awarded to"[95] the property salvor. In addition, for salvage of life within UK waters or anywhere in the world if the salvor of life is acting from a UK-flagged vessel the Secretary of State can award an appropriate amount in respect of salvage operations.[96]

(c) The salvage reward

Two ways of calculating the salvor's remuneration are provided under the Salvage Convention. Where there is a useful result the "No Cure – No Pay" principle is applied on the basis of various performance-related criteria under Article 13 and a salvage reward will be due. The criteria employed include: the value of the salved property; the skills of the salvors in minimising

---

89. *Owners of Cargo Lately Laden on Board the Troilus v Owners, masters and Crew of the Glenogle (The Troilus and the Glenogle)* [1951] 1 Lloyd's Rep 467 (fn 81).

90. See also Salvage Convention, art 21(3), where the requirements for security are linked to a right of detention at the "port or place where the property first arrives".

91. This is clearly a matter of interest for all property owners, in particular for cargo interests.

92. Under English law salvors are liable for damage caused by their negligence. See *Bureau Wijsmuller NV v Owners of the Tojo Maru (The Tojo Maru) (No 2)* [1972] AC 242 (HL) concerning a salvage contract. However, the salvor's liability is limited under the general limitation provisions of Schedule 7 to the Merchant Shipping Act 1995 enacting the 1976 Limitation Convention as amended by the 1996 Protocol.

93. See R. Shaw (fn 64) for the view that "useful result" is the same as the requirement of "success" under English law before the introduction of the Salvage Convention.

94. *The Renpor* [1883] LR 8PD 115. The Salvage Convention does impose (art 10) an obligation on masters (only) of ships to render assistance when life is endangered and on the Contracting States to legislate for this (see MSA 1995, Schedule 11, Pt II, para 3). See also MSA 1995, ss 92 and 93.

95. Salvage Convention, art 16.

96. MSA 1995, Schedule 11, Part II, art 5.

environmental damage; the nature and extent of danger, the measure of success and the general skills of the salvors as evidenced in the response time; the risks undertaken; the availability of vessels; the promptness and length of the salvage service. The various criteria listed under Article 13 are not in a hierarchical order and can only be considered as indicators for the adjudicators of the salvage reward. Thus it cannot be said which of these criteria is the most determinative of the amount of the reward. As a result judges and arbitrators have significant discretion in determining the amount awarded.[97] What is certain is that if there is no valuable property salved there will be no reward.[98] It is arguable that the point in time at which the reward is earned is the redelivery of the property to the owners, or, if the owners are avoiding redelivery, the time at which the redelivery should have been accepted.[99]

The salvage reward is payable by the owners of the property salved and in proportion to the value of the salved property.[100] For example, if the ship's salved value is £8,000,000, the salved cargo's value is £90,000,000, the bunkers cost £1,000,000 and the freight at risk another £1,000,000, then, a salvage reward of £100,000 under Article 13 will be payable as follows: the owner of the ship will pay £8,000, the cargo owner £90,000, the owner of the bunkers £1,000 and the party benefiting from the unpaid freight for the salved cargo another £1,000.

The amount awarded is at the discretion of the arbitrators and can be controversial. It has been held that the salvage award must take into account the value of the salved property but cannot be out of proportion to the services rendered.[101] This would probably imply that for the same services a higher reward will be awarded to the salvor of a more expensive ship and cargo. The second part restricts, to an extent, the possibility of providing very high salvage awards without taking into account the type of the actual services rendered. It is submitted that such guidelines cannot alter the principles of Article 13 but they are permissible if they assist with the interpretation of the 1989 Salvage Convention. Situations where the ship is immobilised, there is no immediate danger and the master accepts salvage assistance also pose problems. In such cases towage assistance, if available, would probably have been sufficient so the argument has been made that the money payable under towage should be taken into account when the salvage award is decided. English courts have confirmed that while it is permissible to take into account commercial rates for the services obtained the significance varies with the facts of each situation.[102] Overall, the reward criteria are vague and give to the arbitrators significant discretion, thus making salvage awards primarily an internal matter for the shipping and the salvage industry. While the Salvage Convention was developed for the protection of the salvage industry and the encouragement of salvors the downturn of the economy is not a factor that should lead to a higher award.[103]

A special remuneration is also available to salvors in certain circumstances and is called "special compensation". This is provided for under Article 14. The special compensation is the

97. Note also that many of the criteria are solely applicable to professional salvors. Since vessels passing by cannot possibly satisfy some criteria it can be argued that for the same salvage a professional salvor is likely to be rewarded more under the Convention than a non-professional salvor.

98. See Salvage Convention, art 13(3).

99. Arguably, it is at that time that the "useful" result can be assessed, although difficulties may arise if the property is brought to a place of safety but it is lost between that time and redelivery to the owners.

100. See Salvage Convention, art 13(2).

101. *Compagnie Generale Transatlantique v Owners of the FT Barry and the Auburn (The Amerique)* [1874–75] LR 6 PC 468; confirmed in *Ocean Crown (Owners) & Ors v Five Oceans Salvage Consultants Ltd (The Ocean Crown)* [2009] EWHC 3040 (Admlty); [2009] 2 CLC 878.

102. *The Owners of the Vessel "Voutakos", Her Bunkers, Stores and Cargo v Tsavliris Salvage (International) Ltd* [2008] EWHC 1581 (Comm); [2008] 2 Lloyd's Rep 516.

103. *Ocean Crown (Owners) & Ors v Five Oceans Salvage Consultants Ltd (The Ocean Crown)* [2009] EWHC 3040 (Admlty); [2009] 2 CLC 878.

most significant modification introduced by the 1989 Salvage Convention in the law of salvage and provides incentives for the salvors to get involved in incidents where pollution is threatened, even if there is a risk that very little or no property will eventually be salved.

Before describing the method of calculation of the special compensation it is worth explaining when it becomes payable. The Salvage Convention defines "damage to the environment" as "substantial physical damage to human health or to marine life or resources in coastal or inland waters or areas adjacent thereto, caused by pollution, contamination, fire, explosion or similar major incidents".[104] This definition is restrictive in many ways. First, damage to the environment is only covered in coastal or inland waters and adjacent areas. Therefore, it is arguable that any damage occurring away from coastal areas, presumably within the Exclusive Economic Zone (EEZ) but certainly on the high seas, does not come under this definition[105] with the consequence that the relevant incentives are not available to salvors in circumstances where the oil spill or other type of pollution occurs far from the coast. The second restrictive characteristic of the definition is that it requires "substantial" physical damage, a term which is not clear. Presumably, the "substantial" nature of the damage will depend not only on the extent of the damage but also on the importance and rarity of the marine life and resources affected. With respect to human health, it is submitted that effects on even one person, if serious, would be "substantial". The third way in which the definition is restrictive is the required link with major incidents, indicating that where physical damage to the environment is substantial but the incident is not a major one the environmental damage will probably not be covered by the definition.

Where the salvor has participated in a salvage operation in which there was a threat of environmental damage then there is an entitlement to special compensation. Two situations are provided for. The first occurs where the salvor has been unsuccessful in its attempts to prevent or minimise damage to the environment. In such a case the special compensation will be equivalent to the salvor's expenses.[106] The second situation is where the salvor has been successful in preventing or minimising damage to the environment. In such a case the salvor can recover its expenses plus an increase by anything up to 100 per cent.[107] The extent of the increase is to be decided on the basis of the same reward criteria that apply for the salvage reward under Article 13.

The special compensation is only payable to the extent that it exceeds the ordinary Article 13 reward. Only the shipowner is liable for the payment of the special compensation. This is arguably a fair arrangement as it is usually the shipowner who restricts its pollution liability exposure by the actions of the salvor.

While the whole idea of special compensation appears sound and workable, its practical application has led, under English law, to two significant problems. The first problem is the way in which the salvor's expenses are to be calculated. The Salvage Convention itself under Article 14(3) specifies a way of calculating these expenses. First, actual payments made reasonably by the salvor, for example for hiring equipment, fall under the "out of pocket" expenses and are to be included in the expenses on the basis of which the special compensation is to be calculated.[108] However, Article 14(3) also requires the inclusion in the salvor's

104. Salvage Convention, art l(d).

105. An alternative reading would be to restrict the definition of coastal areas and areas adjacent thereto only in respect of resources thus permitting all damage to human health and marine life to be covered by the definition.

106. Salvage Convention, art 14(1).

107. Note that the text of the Convention under art 14(2) is badly drafted and does not make sense. The wording of art 14(2) can probably be taken to mean that the special compensation should in general be up to 130 per cent of the salvor's expenses and only in exceptional cases should it be increased to 200 per cent.

108. Salvage Convention, art 14(3). See also *Semco Salvage & Marine Pte Ltd v Lancer Navigation Co Ltd (The Nagasaki Spirit)* [1997] 1 Lloyd's Rep 323.

expenses of "a fair rate for equipment and personnel actually and reasonably used in the salvage operation". While it is clear that the intention of the Salvage Convention was to provide reasonable compensation for the use of the salvor's equipment, the question whether "fair rate" should reflect market prices or be decided on some other commercial basis has caused practical problems. The issue was resolved by the House of Lords in *The Nagasaki Spirit*[109] where it was decided that the term "fair rate" referred to expenditure and did not include an element of profit. Determining a "fair rate" in such a way might necessitate the involvement of accountants, an unnecessary and impractical exercise in a market where decision making on whether to get involved in a pollution-threatening incident must be encouraged by providing certainty of an appropriate reward.

The second unclear point regarding Article 14 is whether special compensation is payable only during the period in which a threat of environmental damage is present and ceases to be payable as soon as the environmental damage is averted or whether, once it becomes payable, it is to be calculated until the redelivery of the property to its owners. The House of Lords in *The Nagasaki Spirit* held that, if Article 14 applies, the calculation of the special compensation continues until the redelivery of the property to its owners.[110] This is of course a concern for the shipowners who exercise little control over the salvage operation and who may have to pay more if the salvage operation is prolonged.

The special compensation can be reduced if the salvors act negligently or in breach of their environmental duties under the Salvage Convention.[111]

(d) Who can claim a salvage reward?

Public policy supports salvage and as a result when assistance is rendered at sea a salvage reward is likely. However, certain categories of claimants are not entitled to claim salvage, largely for public policy reasons. For instance, it is reasonable to exclude from the right to claim salvage persons who may deliberately create danger in order to gain a salvage reward. Thus, in general, the master and the crew of the salved vessel, as well as pilots and tugs under contracts of towage, will not be able to claim while performing the services contracted for. The Salvage Convention requires that for a salvage reward to become payable to contractors "the services rendered exceed what can be reasonably considered as due performance of a contract entered into before the danger arose".[112] However, when the services provided do exceed the contractual arrangement, e.g. when the vessel is abandoned by order of the master, then the crew members may act as salvors.[113] Similarly, if during the performance of a towage contract the situation becomes dangerous, towage may turn into salvage. For example, where the tow line parts and the weather conditions put the tow in danger, the service may turn into a salvage operation which in practice means that the towage contract is displaced and the salvage obligations and reward come into play.[114]

Two other categories of person who may find difficulty in claiming salvage are salvors employed by governmental or public services and the governmental or public services

109. See fn 107.
110. Ibid.
111. Salvage Convention, art 14(5).
112. Salvage Convention, art 17.
113. See *The San Demetrio* [1941] 69 Ll L Rep 5 and *The Warrior* [1862] Lush 476. See also *The Albionic* [1942] 72 Ll L Rep 91.
114. *The Texaco Southampton* [1983] 1 Lloyd's Rep 94 (New South Wales Court of Appeal), *Owners of the Maridive VII, Maridive XIII, Maridive 85 and Maridive 94 v Owners and Demise Charterers of the Key Singapore* [2005] 1 Lloyd's Rep 91; *The Hamtun and the St John* [1999] 1 Lloyd's Rep 883. Note, though, that while this is tempting for the tugs, it may be difficult to prove.

themselves, for example the Navy or the Coastguard. In respect of salvors employed by governmental authorities or performing salvage under the control of such authorities Article 5.2 of the 1989 Salvage Convention expressly entitles them to claim for salvage, while in respect of the governmental and public services themselves the issue is subject to the national law of the State in which the public service is situated.[115]

The general encouragement of salvage requires that a shipowner should be allowed to provide salvage assistance to another of its ships.[116] This is consistent with the pre-existing law of salvage[117] under which in the appropriate circumstances a salvage reward may be due to the shipowner or indeed the cargo owner.[118]

(e) Financial security

The right to the salvage reward is supported by a maritime lien of the highest priority[119] and by a possessory lien. However, particularly in respect of the special compensation, salvors need to know as early as possible that payment for their services will be forthcoming and that the shipowner will be capable of paying. Accordingly, the provision of financial security at an early stage is important for the salvors.

The Salvage Convention leaves unaffected maritime liens existing under national law as well as liens under other international conventions. The only restriction imposed is that where security is provided the maritime lien cannot be exercised.[120] However, the amount of the required security is not specified but needs to be "satisfactory" by reference not only to the reward itself but to interest and costs.[121] The duty to provide financial security is put upon the owners of the property. Nonetheless, the shipowner, apart from the obligation to provide financial security for the part of the reward for which it is responsible, is also under a duty to exercise best endeavours to ensure that the cargo interests will also provide security in respect of their part of the reward.[122]

To enhance the probabilities of recovery for the salvor the Salvage Convention provides that the ship or other property salved should not be moved from the port prior to the provision of security.[123] However, the wording employed does not create robust obligations because it is not accompanied by sanctions where, for example, the cargo is removed from the ship and the port. Moreover, it is unclear how the person permitting the unauthorised release of the property can become liable to the salvors. Similarly, the general requirement about the provision of satisfactory security does not spell out what the salvor's options are where such security is not provided. The arrangement under Article 14 is supported by a non-binding Code of Practice between the International Group of P&I Clubs and the International Salvage Union (ISU) regarding the provision of security.[124]

---

115. MSA 1995, s 230(2), entitles the Crown to claim salvage.
116. Salvage Convention, art 12(3).
117. See, e.g. *Owners of Cargo Lately Laden on Board the Troilus v Owners, masters and Crew of the Glenogle (The Troilus and the Glenogle)* [1951] 1 Lloyd's Rep 467.
118. *The Sava Star* [1995] 2 Lloyd's Rep 13.
119. *The Bold Buccleugh* [1851] 7 Moo PC 267; *Owners of the Carbonnade v Owners of the Ruta (The Ruta)* [2000] 1 Lloyd's Rep 359. It is doubtful whether the salvage maritime lien covers special compensation. The maritime lien exists independently of the 1989 Salvage Convention. Thus its scope depends on its characteristics under pre-existing English law.
120. Salvage Convention, art 20.
121. Salvage Convention, art 21.
122. Salvage Convention, art 21(2).
123. Salvage Convention, art 21(3).
124. The Funding Agreement 1989. See R. Shaw (fn 63), at p 228, for a discussion on the issues of obtaining security under the Convention.

(f) Apportionment of the salvage reward

Where more than one salvor is involved in the salvage operation, the question of how the salvage reward should be distributed becomes important. Article 15 of the Salvage Convention requires that any salvage reward or special compensation is to be divided between the salvors in accordance with the criteria set out in Article 13. In addition, the distribution of the salvage reward between salvor's crew is subject to the law of the flag of the salvor's ship. Where salvage is not performed from a ship, the law of the contract between the salvor and its employees will decide how the reward should be split. Of course if there are sub-contracts between the head salvor and other contributors, it is usual that both the law and jurisdiction, and probably the substantive part of the payment, has been agreed.[125]

A different problem arises where the ship performing the salvage is under a demise or time charter. The question whether and to what extent the salvage reward will be split between owners, demise charterers and other charterers will depend on the relevant charterparty.[126]

(g) Time bar and limitation of liability

The time bar for any action relating to payment under the Salvage Convention is two years from the time the salvage operation has been terminated.[127] The period can be extended by the defendant in an action under the 1989 Salvage Convention.[128] Indemnity claims are subject to the time bar for such actions under the national law of the State party. In England this is six years.[129]

Limitation of liability issues are not dealt with under the Salvage Convention but under the 1996 Limitation of Liability for Maritime Claims Convention (1996 LLMC).[130] It is sufficient to clarify two points here. First, that under English law the salvage reward and the special compensation are not subject to limitation of liability.[131] Second, that under the 1996 LLMC, the salvors' liability for damage caused to the property is limited to that of a shipowner of a vessel of 1,500 tons.[132]

(h) Salvage contracts under the Salvage Convention

The right to a salvage reward arises independently of whether there is a contract or not. However, salvage contracts when appropriately drafted can significantly clarify the duties of the parties during the salvage operation. Provisions for the place of redelivery as well as the conditions under which salvage can be terminated including agreement on the forum and the law of the contract can avoid further disputes and expenses. The Salvage Convention permits exclusion of many of its provisions by contract. The default position under the Salvage Convention is that it

125. The International Salvage Union provides standard forms of sub-contracts which can be found at www.marine-salvage.com/documents/ (accessed 15 March 2017).
126. See, for example, Barecon 1989, cl 17, where the benefit and repairs are for the demise charterer, and Baltime, cl 19, where the net profits are to be equally split between owner and charterer.
127. Salvage Convention, art 23.
128. Salvage Convention, art 23(2).
129. Limitation Act 1980, s 5.
130. Convention on Limitation of Liability for Maritime Claims (London, 19 November 1976) (1976 LLMC) and the Protocol of 1996 amending the Convention on Limitation of Liability for Maritime Claims of 19 November 1976 (London, 2 May 1996) (1996 LLMC); see MSA 1995, ss 185–186. See also section 8 on limitation of liability below. Unless specified otherwise, reference to "1996 LLMC" should be treated as a reference to both the 1976 LLMC as amended by the 1996 Protocol and the unamended 1976 LLMC.
131. 1996 LLMC, art 3.
132. Which is presently two million SDR for loss of life and personal injury, and one million SDR for property damage. See section 8 on limitation of liability below.

only applies to the extent that salvage contracts do not provide otherwise.[133] Therefore, salvage contracts can substantially alter most of the conditions under the Convention including the payment options and the time bar. However, the rights granted to courts to review salvage contracts under Article 7 as well as the environmental obligations put on the salvor and the salved property, under Article 8, cannot be contracted out of.

Liability for a salvage reward can be a significant financial burden for the shipowner and the cargo owner. The cargo owner in particular may end up paying for freight, which was agreed to take the cargo to destination and, in addition for salvage. The latter may or may not be recoverable from the carrier depending on the terms of the contract of carriage. It is therefore not surprising that where the master has signed a salvage contract the cargo interests have sought to avoid liability for salvage by claiming that the salvage contract is not binding on the cargo owners because it has not been agreed with them. Of course, where a situation of danger exists, and assistance is successfully provided, the right to claim part of the salvage reward from the cargo owners arises independently of the salvage contract.

Under the Salvage Convention binding authority to sign salvage contracts is granted to the master of the vessel.[134] This authority is binding both on the shipowner and the cargo owner.[135] The shipowner also has authority to bind the cargo to a salvage contract. The wording of Article 6(2) provides binding authority only for the conclusion of contracts concerning salvage operations which must involve a ship or property in danger.[136] As a result where danger is not present, salvage operations, as defined under the Salvage Convention, cannot take place and the master and the shipowner arguably have no authority to bind the cargo interests to a salvage contract.

The extent of the master's authority under Article 6(2) has not yet been interpreted by the courts. However, it appears that after a reasonable contract of salvage is concluded, further modifications agreed between the shipowner and the salvor will not necessarily be binding on the cargo owners.[137] Similarly, it can be argued that where the master breaches the contract of salvage, for example, by unreasonably replacing the salvor, then the cargo owners would probably not be considered in breach of the original salvage contract[138] or bound by the new contract, leaving the shipowner to pay for the contractual breaches.

(i) Dismissal of salvors

Situations may arise where a more competent or cheaper salvor becomes available and then the master or the shipowner may wish to replace the original salvor. The Salvage Convention does not give such rights to either the master or shipowner. It does, nevertheless impose an obligation on the operating salvors to accept the assistance and collaboration of other salvors when reasonably requested by the master. If it is later shown that such intervention was unnecessary then

133. Salvage Convention, art 6(1),
134. Salvage Convention, art 6(2).
135. This is an important modification of the pre-existing English law under which the master of the ship did not in general have authority to bind the cargo interests to a salvage contract, except where a situation creating an "agency of necessity" was created. The creation of the agency of necessity occurs when there is a situation of danger making salvage necessary, coupled with difficulties in communicating with the owners of the cargo such that obtaining their instructions is reasonably impractical. In addition, the actions of the master must be bona fide for the interests of cargo and also reasonable in entering the contract. See *Industrie Chimiche Italia Centrale v Alexander G Tsavliris & Sons Maritime Co (The Choko Star)* [1995] 2 Lloyd's Rep 608.
136. As defined under art l(a).
137. *Tsavliris Salvage (International) Ltd v Guangdong Shantou Overseas Chinese Materials Marketing Co (The Pa Mar)* [1999] 1 Lloyd's Rep 338.
138. Unless, probably, where they have consented to the breach committed by the master.

the reward of the original salvor "would not be prejudiced",[139] probably meaning that the ship-owner would have to remunerate the first salvor fully and also pay salvage to the second salvor according to the relevant criteria under Article 13. However, if the salvor is dismissed it is not clear what the consequences are under the Salvage Convention. Under pre-existing salvage law it was arguable that there was compensation for loss of opportunity and a reward for the period during which the salvor contributed to salvage.[140] However, this depended on the final success of the salvage operation.

By contrast, where a salvage contract has been signed, a dismissal of the salvor is a breach of contract for which the salvor is entitled to claim damages, sounding in the amount of salvage that would have been received had it completed the salvage operation, minus any expenses and costs that would have been incurred by the salvor.[141] This decision is a consequence of the law of contract and it should remain unaffected by the Salvage Convention.[142]

(j) The Lloyd's Open Form – "No Cure – No Pay"

One of the most extensively used salvage contract forms is the Lloyd's Open Form (LOF). The LOF has been repeatedly adjusted to accommodate the needs of contemporary salvage in antic-ipation of developments of national or international law which always took much longer. Thus, the LOF 1980 included the first departure from the "No Cure – No Pay" principle by entitling the salvor of a stricken tanker who had failed to recover an ordinary salvage reward to recover its costs plus a 15 per cent uplift on top of those costs but only to the extent that the expenses together with increment were greater than the ordinary "No Cure – No Pay" award. The 1990 version of the LOF incorporated the Salvage Convention six years before it came into force. The LOF 2000 introduced the first attempt to overcome the difficulties of the Salvage Convention by providing the option to incorporate the special compensation P&I Club's (SCOPIC) Clause.

In brief, the most recent LOF 2011 contract consists of a short form which incorporates a number of standard sets of clauses, namely, the Lloyd's Standard and Arbitration Clauses (LSSA), the Lloyd's procedural rules and, when the option is exercised, the SCOPIC Clause. Signing the LOF constitutes an express choice of arbitration as the means of resolving disputes related to the award.[143]

The main provisions of the LOF 2011 contract are set out in the short form which provides for identification of the parties to the contract and the property to be salved, place and date of the agreement, the agreed place of safety and an agreed currency for the arbitration award. Most importantly, the LOF 2011 provides the parties with an option to have the SCOPIC clause incor-porated. This option radically changes the effects of the contract. The LOF 2011 added two new clauses to the LOF 2000 which do not affect its substantial arrangements.

Whether the SCOPIC Clause 2 is incorporated or not, a contract subject to English law and Lloyd's Arbitration comes into existence when the LOF 2011 is signed. The basic obligation under the LOF 2011 is the salvage of the named property and the redelivery to the agreed place of safety (Clause A). If the salvors bring the ship and/or the property to the agreed place of safety then, provided that the property does not need salvage assistance and the port or government

---

139. Salvage Convention, art 8(1)(d).
140. *The Unique Mariner (No 2)* [1979] 1 Lloyd's Rep 37.
141. Ibid.
142. Such a claim was held in *The Tesaba* [1982] 1 Lloyd's Rep 397 not to be "in the nature of salvage"; but see the Merchant Shipping (Salvage and Pollution) Act 1994, Schedule 2, [6], amending s 20 of the Senior Courts Act 1981 and extending the Admiralty Jurisdiction of the High Court to such claims.
143. See Clause I. The website www.lloyds.com/the-market/tools-and-resources/lloyds-agency-department (accessed 15 March 2017) has information on such arbitrations and on a new form of fixed cost arbitration.

regulations do not require the presence of salvors any further, the salvors have fulfilled their part of the deal (Clause H).

While performing the contract the salvors should use best endeavours to prevent or minimise damage to the environment (Clause B). Note that the term "best endeavours" has been argued to be more burdensome than the obligation under Article 8 of the Convention to "exercise due care".[144] Other views are also arguable and "best endeavours" can be taken to mean a subjective measure of care that depends on the particular salvor while "due care" could reflect the standard of professional care and skill required of professional salvors.[145]

Interestingly, where an LOF 2011 is agreed it applies retrospectively to all previous services rendered.[146] Express obligations are imposed on the owners of the property in danger to allow reasonable use of the machinery onboard the ship and also to provide all necessary information to the salvors and help in obtaining permission for entry into the designated place of safety.

The LOF 2011 provides that the master has authority to act as agent of the property interests (Clause K). Clearly, this is a contractual undertaking from the shipowner, it is actionable against the shipowner alone and cannot replace the Salvage Convention's authority of the master under Article 6.2.[147]

The LOF 2011 also provides for an obligation on the shipowner to inform the cargo owners of the salvage agreement and for the latter to provide security if the salvage is successful.[148]

Where the SCOPIC Clause is not incorporated, the two types of remuneration under the Salvage Convention, namely the reward under Article 13 and the special compensation under Article 14, are available to the salvor.[149]

However, where the SCOPIC 2014[150] Clause is incorporated, Article 14 is excluded as a potential remuneration.[151] Thus the salvor can only rely on an Article 13 reward from the moment the contract is signed until the salvor decides to invoke, in writing, the SCOPIC Clause. From the time the SCOPIC Clause is invoked, it provides an alternative to Article 13 as a way of calculating the salvage reward. However, any services provided before the SCOPIC Clause was invoked remain subject to the salvage reward under Article 13 of the Convention. It is important to note that the SCOPIC reward does not depend on the existence of any threat of damage to the environment, nor is it restricted to a particular jurisdictional or physical area of the seas.[152] Thus it is a more general and readily available compensation for the salvors in all cases in which they may become worried about the possibility of a satisfactory Article 13 reward. The remuneration

144. N. Gaskell, *Merchant Shipping Act 1995, Current Law Statutes Annotated*, at pp 21–390.

145. Consistent with the judgments in *The Tojo Maru* [1972] AC 242.

146. This naturally raises the query whether or not the consequences of a breach of the LOF before it is agreed are also retrospectively actionable.

147. There is, of course, the question whether the master's authority can be removed by contract because the Salvage Convention does not exclude the possibility that art 6 of the Salvage Convention may itself be excluded by contract. Even if this were the case, it is suggested that only a salvage contract can have this effect and exclusions of such authority in other contracts, for example time charterparties, cannot exclude such authority to bind the cargo against a salvor, although they may constitute grounds for damages to be paid under the time charterparty. In such a case as well as in the case that the above interpretation is wrong, and the authority of the master to sign salvage contracts can be removed by other than salvage contracts, the existence of agency of necessity discussed at fn 134 above will become relevant again.

148. Important Note 1 giving notice of cl 4 of the LSSA Clauses.

149. See cl D.

150. Apart from increasing the tariff rates, SCOPIC 2014 also incorporates art 18 of the Salvage Convention into the contract.

151. See SCOPIC, s 1.

152. This is beneficial to salvors both in terms of avoiding the difficulties of art 14 but also by ensuring that the SCOPIC remuneration is equally high regardless of the economic condition of the area of the world in which salvage is undertaken.

under SCOPIC is based on set tariffs[153] contained in a separate appendix (Appendix A) to the clause. There is a standard bonus of 25 per cent on top of the tariffs.[154] Thus, the calculation of the SCOPIC reward is simple and easy to make. The standard of conduct required under the SCOPIC Clause is, as under the LOF, to use best endeavours (Clause 10) for salving the property and in doing so to prevent or minimise damage to the environment.[155]

The SCOPIC reward is only payable by shipowners and only to the extent it exceeds the Article 13 reward under the Salvage Convention. However, there is a discount to the Article 13 reward if the salvor has unnecessarily invoked the SCOPIC clause in a situation where the Article 13 reward would have been larger. In such a case the Article 13 reward is reduced by 25 per cent of the difference between the salvage reward and the SCOPIC remuneration (Clause 7). For this reduction the SCOPIC remuneration is calculated from the beginning of the salvage operation irrespective of the day on which the clause was actually invoked. This retrospective extension maximises the SCOPIC remuneration and minimises the difference from a calculated Article 13 award thus making the penalty's application more unlikely.[156]

Apart from the difference in the salvor's remuneration, the invocation of SCOPIC has several other consequences. First, the owners are obliged to put up a bank guarantee or P&I Club security for US$3,000,000 within two working days.[157] This initial security can be adjusted later as needed or by the arbitrator if there is a dispute. If security is not provided the salvor can withdraw from SCOPIC and revert to the LOF, including Article 14.[158]

Second, a Special Casualty Representative (SCR) is appointed. The SCR is a salvage specialist acting as an independent adviser to the shipowner, assessing the efficiency and the reasonableness of the salvage operation undertaken under the SCOPIC agreement and providing the shipowner with daily estimates of the SCOPIC remuneration. The SCR is to be selected from a list of specialists.[159] Appendix B to SCOPIC sets out the rules of conduct for the SCR. Two other Special Representatives, one for the hull and one for the cargo interests can be appointed under the SCOPIC clause. They are required to be technical men and not practising lawyers. Their role is set out in Appendix C. The aim of having the SCR and the Special Representatives is to provide transparency of the salvage operation, thus removing fears that salvors would unnecessarily prolong salvage in order to achieve higher SCOPIC remuneration. However, the control of the salvage operation remains with the salvage master.

Third, the SCOPIC Clause provides the salvor with the right to terminate the SCOPIC Clause and the LOF contract where the SCOPIC remuneration plus the value of the property that can be salved are lower than the costs of the services provided.[160] The shipowner can also terminate the contract at any time by giving five days' notice and paying for five days' (or as long as needed for demobilisation) worth of salvage remuneration. But the rights to termination only exist if the salvor is not restricted from abandoning the salvage services by the government or the port authorities concerned.[161]

---

153. The rates are agreed by the International Salvage Union and the International Group of P&I Clubs and endorsed by property underwriters and owners.

154. SCOPIC, cl 5. Where the salvor has higher salvage rates than those set out in the SCOPIC tariffs it will receive either the actual costs plus 10 per cent, bonus or the tariff rate plus the 25 per cent bonus, whichever is higher.

155. SCOPIC, cl 10.

156. Arguably it would have been easier in such a case just to replace art 13 reward with that chosen by the salvor, i.e. the SCOPIC remuneration.

157. SCOPIC, cl 3.

158. SCOPIC, cl 4.

159. See www.lloyds.com/the-market/tools-and-resources/lloyds-agency-department/salvage-arbitration-branch/contact-us/special-casualty-representatives (accessed 15 March 2017).

160. SCOPIC, cl 9.

161. Ibid.

The SCOPIC clause is supported by two non-binding Codes of Practice, one applying to the International Group of P&I Clubs and the ISU regarding the provision of SCOPIC security, and the other applying to the International Group of P&I Clubs and the London Property Underwriters and the ISU regarding the contribution to the payment of fees of the SCR by the P&I Clubs and the property insurers.

The SCOPIC Clause has so far been considered successful, resolving most of the problems arising from the Salvage Convention. It is a further example of a successful and well-designed intervention by the salvage industry to avoid the difficulties posed by the Salvage Convention and to satisfy the needs of the market.

(k) The control of the salvage operation by the coastal State

The Salvage Convention preserves any rights available under international law to the coastal State to take measures for coastal protection and pollution prevention and to intervene and give direction in relation to salvage operations.[162] Such rights may arise under UNCLOS,[163] the Intervention Convention 1969,[164] under regional or international conventions, or customary international law.

Therefore, the coastal State is under no obligation to permit the salvors to enter a place where salvage can be more efficient, but on the contrary can order them to move the stricken vessel away from the coast.[165] The freedom of the coastal State is not restricted by the obligation imposed under Article 11 of the Salvage Convention to take into account, when deciding on the provision of a place of refuge, of the need for co-operation between salvors, other interests and the coastal State.

In the UK the Secretary of State appoints the Secretary of State's Representative, "SOSREP", with powers to oversee, control and intervene in salvage operations within UK waters involving vessels or fixed platforms where there is significant risk of pollution. The powers of the SOSREP are set out in the MSA 1995, Schedule 3A, as amended by the Marine Safety Act 2003.

The European Union Directive 2002/59/EC[166] requires each EU Member State to establish a national authority for the purpose of collecting information regarding ship movements and incidents and to which application for entries into ports of refuge should be submitted. Each EU Member State must, under Article 20 of the Directive, designate appropriate places of refuge.

The UK position is more flexible. The MCA 's Duty Operations Director and Counter Pollution and Salvage (CPS) is the first point of contact. The CPS branch in consultation, as far as practicable with environmental groups will assess the situation, conduct risk assessment for potential places of refuge, and submit the information to the SOSREP who takes the decision.[167]

---

162. Salvage Convention, art 9.
163. See Chapter 8, page 308.
164. International Convention Relating to Intervention on the High Seas in Cases of Oil Pollution Casualties (Brussels, 29 November 1969). The Convention was amended by the 1973 Protocol relating to Intervention on the High Seas in Cases of Marine Pollution by Substances other than Oil. The Protocol has been amended in 1996 and 2002 to update the list of substances attached to it.
165. *The Castor* and *The Prestige* are recent examples. In *The Prestige* case it appears that the decision of the Spanish Government to order the vessel away from the coast was disastrous in enhancing the spatial extent of the pollution caused. See www.tsavliris.com/news_details.php?record=1 (accessed 15 March 2017) for the facts on *The Castor*. See also www.iopcfunds.org/fileadmin/IOPC_Upload/Downloads/English/incidents2012_e.pdf (accessed 15 March 2017) on *The Prestige*.
166. Directive 2002/59/EC of the European Parliament and of the Council of 27 June 2002 establishing a Community vessel traffic monitoring and information system and repealing Council Directive 93/75/EEC. See also the relevant IMO Resolution A 949 (23). The Directive has been amended twice by Directives 2011/15 and 2009/17.
167. The National Contingency Plan, https://www.gov.uk/government/publications/national-contingency-planncp (accessed 15 June 2017).

(l) A review of the Salvage Convention?

Salvors have been actively pursuing[168] the adoption of a new environmental award, through a revision of the Salvage Convention, which will recognise the contribution of salvors to environmental protection. It was originally suggested by the ISU that such an award should be paid through a fund created by governments of coastal States. Alternatively, cargo insurers suggested it could be paid directly by the shipowners. The International Chamber of Shipping[169] has voiced a significant concern about the usefulness and the basis of this initiative. Following these disagreements this initiative was focused on an effort to modify the Salvage Convention and the ISU suggested changes with respect to: the definition of environmental damage under Article 1(d); the right of Public Authorities to claim salvage award under Article 5; the Places of Refuge under Article 11; the liability for salvage for container ships through changes under Articles 13 and 21; a new environmental salvage award through modification under Article 14; and changing the responsibility for life salvage claims to property interests rather than the salvor under Article 16. Changes to Article 27 were also suggested. The Comité Maritime International held a Conference on the topic and only the broadening of the environmental damage definition found support by all parties.[170]

Thus a general revision of the Salvage Convention is unlikely as coastal States will not be prepared to undertake to pay salvors for what is presently met by the shipowners and their insurers and the salvage industry has not made a strong case that the present arrangements are insufficient.

The availability of salvage remuneration gives rise to a competition issue as cheaper towage services do not become available to shipowners due to all potential providers refusing to offer assistance on all but salvage terms, even where the ship is simply immobilised but there is not imminent danger. The dominance of the LOF salvage contract referring to Lloyd's arbitration poses additional problems as the same services, even on salvage terms, could have been obtained cheaper if the salvage contract was referred to another State's courts or a different arbitration panel. Practices by which salvage services commence and later a contract is presented for signature by the salvors may also prove problematic, as it is arguable that the owners of the property have to agree to such a contract under duress.

4. GENERAL AVERAGE

(a) What is General Average?

> There is a general average act when, and only when, any extraordinary sacrifice or expenditure is intentionally and reasonably made or incurred for the common safety for the purpose of preserving from peril the property involved in the common maritime adventure.
>
> (York–Antwerp Rules, Rule A.1)

General Average ("GA") is the sharing of the financial consequences of an unexpected casualty between the commercial parties which have a financial interest in seeing the "adventure" completed.

---

168. See e.g. the ISU newsletter, Salvage World, 2010 (December), at p 3.
169. Circular ICS/14/1.
170. See Comité Maritime International Beijing Conference 2012. Report of the Review of the Salvage Convention, available at www.comitemaritime.org/Uploads/Work%20In%20Progress/Salvage%20Convention/Beijing%20 Conf.%20Report%20of%20the%20Review%20of%20the%20Salvage%20Convention.pdf (accessed 15 March 2017).

The expenses which fall within this definition are borne by those parties in proportion to the value of their respective interests at the time when and place where the adventure ends.

The concept is of very ancient origin, and references can be traced to the *Lex Rhodia de Iactu* probably in the fourth century BC.[171] It has, however, been the subject of development over time and still applies to modern seaborne trade. Insurance policies on hull, cargo and freight all provide that the insurers will pay the contribution in GA due from the assured,[172] and GA is therefore closely related to marine insurance.[173]

General Average now forms part of the maritime law of every State with maritime jurisdiction. It arises by operation of law, independently of contract or statute.

It is one of the type of obligations usually classified as "quasi contract", but a reference to GA and the York–Antwerp Rules is also expressly incorporated into most contracts of carriage.[174]

(b) Typical examples of General Average sacrifices or expenditure

Various laws, national and international, for the protection of the marine environment mean that the classic example of a General Average sacrifice, namely the jettison of cargo to lighten a ship in danger of foundering, takes place extremely rarely today. However, the injection of compressed air into the cargo tanks of a grounded tanker, as part of a salvage operation to refloat her, may cause increased cargo leakage through the damaged bottom, and this will be treated as a General Average loss, since the benefits of saving the ship and cargo will be mutual.[175]

More common now are claims based on hull and engine damage caused by efforts to refloat a grounded ship, and the cost of tugs engaged to assist refloating. These expenses must be distinguished from the cost of repairing damage caused by the grounding itself, which is treated as particular average and covered by the ship's hull insurance. Other examples of GA expenses are hull and cargo damage, typically water damage, caused by fire fighting operations, discharge and reloading of the cargo at a port of refuge, and expenses incurred at that port. Expenses incurred, either by the ship or cargo owners, to forward the cargo to its destination onboard another ship where the damage to the original carrying ship renders the continuation of her voyage physically or financially impracticable, will not usually be treated as GA, in the absence of an express agreement between the parties.[176]

(c) Piracy[177]

In recent years there has been a growth of pirate attacks, particularly in the waters off Somalia and Nigeria, and the payment of substantial sums has been made by way of ransom to secure the release of ship, cargo and crew. Ransom payments reasonably made in all the circumstances are probably admissible as GA expenditure.[178] In *Mitsui & Co Ltd and others v*

171. "What is given for everyone should be contributed to by everyone". *Justinian Digest Book* 14 title 2.
172. Institute Time Clauses Hulls 1/10/83, cl 11; ITC (H) 1/11/95, cl 10; International Hull Clauses 1/11/03, cl 8; Institute Cargo Clauses A, B and C (2009), cl 2.
173. Marine Insurance Act 1906, s 66.
174. See, e.g. Congenbill 2007, cl 4 – New Jason Clause, and ASBATANKVOY, cl 20(b)(iii).
175. A modern example of this took place during the salvage of the *Sea Empress* off Milford Haven in 1996, and was recognised as legitimate in Lord Donaldson's Report (1999 Cm 4193).
176. Subject to r G(3) of the York–Antwerp Rules 1994 and 2004.
177. See also Chapters 4, 10 and 11 for Charterparties, Public International Law Aspects of Shipping Regulations and Marine Insurance on Piracy.
178. *Masefield AG v Amlin Corporate Member Ltd* [2010] EWHC 280; [2010] 1 Lloyd's Rep 509, upheld by the Court of Appeal [2011] EWCA Civ 24; [2011] 1 Lloyd's Rep 630 and see *The Longchamp* where the parties agreed that the ransom payment was covered.

Beteiligungsgesellschaft LPG Tankerflotte mbH & Co KG and another (The Longchamp),[179] the parties agreed that the ransom payment itself was covered, but disagreed on whether it was permissible to include in the final assessment the shipowner's expenses incurred while negotiating down the ransom from US$6 million to US$1.85million. During the period of negotiation, some 50 days, the shipowner continued to incur expenses for crew wages, "high-risk area bonus" payments to the crew, food supplies and bunkers consumed. The shipowner sought to include these expenses in the adjustment as substituted expenses under Rule F, which in the 1974 version of the York–Antwerp Rules permitted substitution of any "extra expense incurred in place of another expense which would have been allowable as general average".[180] The average adjuster and judge at first instance permitted their inclusion, but the Court of Appeal held that once the ransom demand was made, there was only one course of action available to the shipowner, namely negotiation. That being the case, the expenses incurred during negotiations could not be regarded as 'extra' expenses. Such expenses were instead to be regarded as operating costs incurred as a result of delay, which could not be substituted for the higher initial ransom demand.

(d) The York–Antwerp rules

The principle of GA was adopted in the medieval maritime codes,[181] but its application varied widely from port to port. Following a series of conferences promoted by marine insurers between 1865 and 1890, a set of Rules codifying the generally accepted practices of average adjusters was adopted in 1890 as the York–Antwerp Rules ("YAR"). These have been updated in 1924, 1950, 1974, 1990, 1994, 2004, and 2016.

The YAR have no statutory or legislative force, but are generally incorporated into contracts of carriage, so are contractually binding on the parties. The contract of carriage may also provide:

* where the adjustment shall be drawn up;
* the currency to be used for the adjustment; and
* the security which may be required.

The modern YAR are divided into lettered rules A to G, and numbered rules 1 to 23. The lettered rules are statements of general principle, while the numbered rules are specific applications of those principles. The Rule of Interpretation set out at the top of the Rules provides that the numbered rules prevail over the lettered rules, and that the YAR shall prevail over any contrary law or practice. From the 2004 Rules onwards, the Rule of Interpretation was supplemented by a Rule Paramount, which imposes a requirement of reasonableness. This was in response to the decision in *The Alpha*.[182] In that case, the damage caused to the engines of a stranded ship was held to be General Average damage, although the master's actions in this respect were considered unreasonable.

Revision of the YAR is now in the hands of the Comité Maritime International (CMI), which most recently adopted new Rules at its conference in May 2016. While the 2004 Rules had failed to find acceptance among the shipowning community, the 2016 Rules have been endorsed by the Baltic and International Maritime Council (BIMCO) and should find wide acceptance.

179. [2016] EWCA Civ 708; [2016] 2 Lloyd's Rep 375.
180. Rule F, York–Antwerp Rules 1974. The 2016 Rules use the word "additional" instead of "extra".
181. See, for instance, *Consolado del Mare* (1494), Laws of Oleron (thirteenth century), *Ordonnance de la Marine* (1681).
182. See *Corfu Navigation Co v Mobil Shipping Co (The Alpha) (No 2)* [1991] 2 Lloyd's Rep 515.

(e) General Average on an unseaworthy ship

It is of the essence of GA that it operates independently of the cause of the GA act. Rule D of the YAR 2016 provides:

Rights to contribution in general average shall not be affected, though the event which gave rise to the sacrifice or expenditure may have been due to the fault of one of the parties to the common maritime adventure, but this shall not prejudice any remedies or defences which may be open against or to that party in respect of such fault.[183]

If therefore the casualty giving rise to the need for extraordinary sacrifice or expenditure was the result of the ship having been unseaworthy at the commencement of the relevant voyage, this will probably be a breach of the relevant contract of carriage. However, the need for extraordinary measures is not diminished, and the underlying philosophy of GA is that such measures should be undertaken promptly, and the liability aspects dealt with afterwards; hence Rule D.

Nevertheless, in *Goulandris Bros Ltd v Goldman & Sons Ltd*[184] it was held that where the GA act was brought about by the shipowner's actionable fault (e.g. failure to exercise due diligence to make the ship seaworthy before and at the commencement of the voyage),[185] the shipowner's claim against the cargo interest for contribution in GA failed. In those circumstances, cargo's contribution would usually be reimbursed by the P&I Club in which the ship was entered, provided that there was no breach of the terms of the club cover.[186]

Any attempt by a carrier to include provisions in its contracts of carriage which purport to permit it to recover General Average contributions notwithstanding its actionable fault will usually be neutralised by the repugnancy provisions in Article III rule 8 of the Hague and Hague-Visby Rules.

(f) How General Average works

Following a marine casualty a "Declaration of General Average" may be made by the master of the ship, although this is not necessary in most legal systems – GA operates as a matter of law. It is, however, customary for the master to put a statement to this effect in the ship's log.

The Average adjuster is usually appointed by the shipowner. He is an independent professional – in some countries he is treated as a judge or arbitrator. He will usually, though not necessarily, be a member of the Association of Average Adjusters, an international body based in London. He will co-ordinate the collection of documents and information and prepare the average adjustment. If a cargo interest is not happy with the appointed adjuster, it may appoint a co-adjuster to supervise the process at his expense.

The adjuster will distribute a valuation form to all parties together with a GA Bond and GA Guarantee which must be completed and returned, usually by the cargo receivers and their insurers.

- The valuation form sets out the value of each cargo interest and the amount of any deductions claimed in respect of damage found at destination.

---

183. The 2016 Rules inserted the words 'common maritime' before adventure. The rule is otherwise unchanged from the 1994/2004 Rules.
184. [1957] 2 Lloyd's Rep 207.
185. Hague and Hague-Visby Rules, art III, r 1.
186. For example, failure to comply with the ISM Code – see Chapter 9, page 341.

- The GA Bond identifies the cargo receiver who undertakes to pay the proportion of GA due from the cargo in question.
- The GA Guarantee is signed by the cargo insurer creating a direct liability to pay the contribution due from the cargo in question.

Collecting these documents is the most time-consuming part of Average adjusting. The terms of YAR Rule E(3) are important. They allow the adjuster to estimate the allowance or contributory value if the party in question fails to supply the necessary information.

Where there are difficult questions of apportionment, e.g. between damage caused by grounding (Particular Average) and damage caused by efforts to refloat (General Average), the adjuster will often appoint a consultant surveyor to advise him. The cost of the consultant's advice will be included in the adjustment. Likewise, a professional ship valuer will usually be engaged to fix the sound market value of the ship, from which the cost of repairing any damage (actual or estimated) will be deducted in order to arrive at the ship's contributory value.

On completion the Average adjuster will publish his adjustment, often a large volume, with details of all General Average sacrifices and allowances which he has admitted (and those which he has not), the contributory values of ship and cargo interests, and the apportionment between those interests. An extract will be sent to each contributing interest setting out the amount due from or to them. The adjuster will also usually act as the clearing house for the payments.

(g) Developments in the York–Antwerp Rules

Changes in the YAR reflect and react to developments in the law. Thus the YAR were amended in 1990 following the adoption by the 1989 Diplomatic Conference of the Salvage Convention including provisions for the assessment of special compensation for measures preventing pollution. An amended version of Rule VI was adopted which makes clear that special compensation payments will not be treated as GA.[187]

The decision in *The Alpha*[188] has already been mentioned – in addition to the requirement of reasonableness, amendments were also made to exclude any expense or sacrifice in connection with pollution save for the exceptional circumstances specified in Rule XI(d).

After the 1994 CMI Conference underwriting interests began a concerted campaign to circumscribe the extent of admissible GA expenditure. An International sub-Committee of the CMI prepared a detailed report[189] with recommendations which was presented to the CMI Conference at Vancouver. The York–Antwerp Rules 2004 were adopted which: (i) excluded salvage from GA (Rule VI); (ii) limited admissible Port of Refuge expenses to those of putting into a port of refuge excluding crew's wages; (iii) clarified the position relating to temporary repairs in the light of *The Bijela* decision;[190] (iv) abolished the allowance of commission; and (v) adopted a variable rate of interest fixed annually.

These changes were not well received by shipowners, and references to the 1994 YAR were retained in charterparties and bills of lading published by BIMCO. A renewed attempt resulted in the 2016 Rules, which reinstated some of the expenses at Ports of Refuge done away with by

---

187. As requested by the Special Resolution annexed to the Salvage Convention. See Rule VI(d) in the 2016 York–Antwerp Rules.
188. See *Corfu Navigation Co v Mobil Shipping Co (The Alpha) (No 2)* [1991] 2 Lloyd's Rep 515.
189. See http://comitemaritime.org/Uploads/Yearbooks/YBK_2003.pdf (accessed 15 March 2017).
190. See *Marida Ltd v Oswal Steel (The Bijela)* [1994] 2 Lloyd's Rep 1.

the 2004 Rules as permissible GA expenses. Salvage expenses, which under the 2004 Rules had been stated to "lie where they fall" are allowed in GA under the 2016 Rules; albeit with significant limitations. As a result of these and other changes, the 2016 Rules are perceived as striking a better balance between the interests of those involved in the maritime adventure and have been endorsed by BIMCO.

(h) The future of General Average

Many writers have suggested that General Average is archaic and should be abolished. However, it forms part of maritime codes and laws throughout so many States that it would require a special international convention (which would have to be ratified worldwide) to achieve this. There is no prospect of such a convention.

Meanwhile, we shall no doubt see a contest between the insurers (led by their association, the International Association of Marine Insurance (IUMI)), who seek to reduce the importance of General Average, and the shipping interests such as BIMCO who will seek to retain it.

5. TOWAGE

(a) Introduction

Towage has been defined as "the employment of one vessel to expedite the voyage of another when nothing more is required than the accelerating of her progress".[191] However, tugs are employed for many more tasks than this definition would imply. Tugs still accompany or speed up the voyage of larger vessels especially at their entry to, manoeuvring within and departure from ports where restrictions in the movement and heavy traffic can pose risks. However, tugs are also used for towing dead ships or unmanned barges between places and they also supply services and assistance to the offshore industry. Thus, modern towage entails many more varieties of service and as a result the original definition appears now to be restrictive and can only be considered as a starting point for the discussion of towage.

Tugs can also be employed for salvage assistance, pollution prevention or clean-up operations. However, such services are not usually in the nature of towage but are remunerated under the legal regime of salvage or under clean-up arrangements with the coastal State.

Towage law involves two different aspects which must not be confused. The first concerns the contractual relationship between the tug and the tow. This is a matter for the towage contract and any implied terms or statutory interventions relevant to this contract.

The second aspect concerns tug and tow liability to third parties in collision or pollution cases. The legal basis for this and the liability vis-à-vis the third party are governed by the law of torts and any statutory regimes concerning pollution. The fact that the tug and the tow are physically connected or commanded by the same person can create problems when one tries to identify to which vessel liability attaches. The third party is not affected by the towage contract between the tug and the tow; thus even where the contract puts liability solely on one party this is not effective vis-à-vis the third party which can recover in tort from whichever party has been negligent. However, because the limits of liability for the tug are many times smaller than those for the tow it is to the advantage of the third party to attempt to attach negligence and consequential liability to the tow thus increasing the amount of recovery available to them.

---

191. *The Princess Alice* [1849] 3 W Rob 138, at p 139.

(b) The contract of towage

Various standard forms of towage contracts are available. However, the arrangements under these forms are not restrictive and parties can agree on any terms they wish subject to restrictions imposed by statute, for example by the Unfair Contract Terms Act 1977.[192] Nonetheless, the commercial reality is quite different. Port services in many cases are monopolised by tugowners working as a group offering exactly the same contractual terms. In addition, standard forms are convenient because they are supposedly better thought out and tested in practice than new arrangements, the parties are used to them and it would be impractical to negotiate a different contract every time a ship enters or leaves a port.

While in general a written contract is available, it is instructive to start by considering the position where the terms of the contract are not expressed by the parties. In the absence of a written contract the courts would imply certain terms and conditions.[193] The contract of towage is one for the provision of services and the Supply of Goods and Services Act 1982 (SGSA 1982) would apply to such contracts. The SGSA 1982 implies an obligation to perform the service with reasonable care and skill (section 13) and within a reasonable time (section 14). However, these implied terms can be excluded under section 16(1) by express contractual agreement, or by a course of dealing or a usage binding between the tug and the tow. They are also very similar if not identical to the requirements under earlier case law stipulating for the use of "best endeavours"[194] or the exercise of "proper skill and diligence".[195] These obligations have been detailed to involve a tug appropriately fitted and manned, acting with reasonable and proper skill, and an obligation to stay with the tow if the towing line breaks and use at least the appropriate skill or possibly best endeavours to reconnect with it.[196]

Several examples of application of these obligations exist in case law. In a case where the tug, fearing a collision, let the towing line go and as a result the tow collided with another ship the tug was held to be under an obligation to reconnect and continue the towage.[197] In another case where the towline broke, the tug was in breach of contract because it did not stand by the tow but sailed away in order to get a new tow line.[198] The obligation to stand by the tow is of course concerned with the safety of the tow. Thus, it is probably not surprising that where a vessel was towed from the anchorage to a berth but could not berth, towage was not finished until the vessel was taken back to the anchorage.[199] In short, towage can only be abandoned if it becomes impossible to perform.[200]

Obligations are not only imposed on the tug but on the tow as well. Thus, the tow is also under an obligation to be fit for towage and appropriately manned. In addition, the persons on board the tow must demonstrate proper skill and diligence in respect of the tow's actions during towage.[201] Accordingly, where the tow collides and sinks the tug because of negligence in its navigation, the tow is liable for breach of the towage contract.

---

192. However, this act is more relevant where towage is provided as a service to small boat or yacht owners who can be considered as consumers.

193. *The Minnehaha* [1861] Lush 335; [1861] 15 Moo PC 133 and *The Julia* [1861] Lush 224.

194. *The Minnehaha* [1861] Lush 335.

195. *The Julia* [1861] Lush 224.

196. See fn 193 and *The Marechal Suchet* [1911] P 1, but see also the discussion in S. Rainey, *The Law of Tug and Tow and Offshore Contracts* (3rd edn, Informa Publishing 2011).

197. *The Golden Light* [1861] Lush 355.

198. *The Refrigerant* [1925] P 130.

199. *The Aboukir* [1905] 21 TLR 200.

200. *The Minnehaha* [1861] Lush 335.

201. *The Julia* [1861] Lush 224.

The law is unclear as to whether the standard of the duty imposed in respect of the fitness of the tug is an absolute one, akin to the obligation of a common carrier to provide a seaworthy vessel or one of due care to provide a tug fitted to the service.[202] It appears that the stronger view under the English system is the latter, while other legal systems favour the former.[203] There is an exception if the contract of towage is for a specified tug in which case there is no implied warranty as to the fitness of the tug.[204]

The implied duties, or indeed the contractual obligations, come into play when towage starts. Where there is a contract it is the contract itself which would probably stipulate the time the various obligations must be performed. In the absence of express contractual stipulation towing starts at the time the towing line is passed and ends when the towing line is slipped.[205]

All contractual and pre-contractual remedies available under English law are applicable to a contract of towage. Thus the contract can be frustrated,[206] and remedies for misrepresentation under the Misrepresentation Act 1967 are available.[207] Issues related to the parties to the contract and the authority of the tug's and tow's masters to bind their principals are also dealt with on the basis of general contract law. Thus the master usually has an express or implied actual authority to bind his principal to a reasonable contract of towage. It is also arguable that where the vessel is in danger (and therefore the master has authority under Article 6.2 of the Salvage Convention to bind the owners of the property onboard the ship as well as the shipowner) this authority would argu-ably cover the situation where the agreement is made on towage terms rather than on a standard contract of salvage. The identity of the contractual parties to the towage contract is important not only in respect of the exercise of contractual rights but also with regard to security proceedings, in particular actions *in rem*.[208] To that extent it is important to ascertain whether the contract of towage is binding on the shipowner, the demise charterer or the time or voyage charterer.

(c) Standard forms of towage

Special forms of contract have been developed reflecting the needs of, mainly, the towage indus-try. This is particularly true of harbour towage where monopoly conditions operate. Exclusions of liability and indemnities are routinely introduced in towage contracts. Under English law such exclusion and indemnity terms are valid if clearly drafted.[209] Moreover, the Unfair Contract Terms Act (UCTA) 1977, which regulates the use of exemption clauses, excludes from its appli-cation towage and salvage contracts,[210] except where such contracts relate to owners of small yachts who are seen as consumers.

The inclusion of wide exclusion and indemnity clauses has led to attempts by shipowners to avoid their consequences by disputing that they are operative in respect of a particular incident

---

202. See the cases above and *The West Cock* [1911] P 208, and the discussion in S. Rainey (fn 196).
203. See the discussion in S. Rainey (fn 196).
204. *Fraser & White Ltd v Vernon* [1951] 2 Lloyd's Rep 175.
205. *The Clan Colquhoun* [1936] 54 Ll L Rep 221.
206. For example, if the tow is lost without fault of the tug or the tow, or the tow and the tug belong to flag States which come into conflict.
207. For instance, where the power of the tug does not correspond to that stated in the negotiations, for an example see the litigation of *Ultisol Transport Contractors Ltd v Bouygues Offshore SA and Comite d'Etudes et des Services des Assureurs Maritimes et Tansports de France (Tigr, Ultisol v Bouyges)* [1996] 2 Lloyd's Rep 140 and *Bouygues Offshore SA v Caspian Shipping Co (No 3)* [1997] 2 Lloyd's Rep 493, involving several issues. See also *Ease Faith Limited v Leonis Marine Management Limited, Cloudfree Ship Management Limited* [2006] EWHC 232 (Comm); [2006] 1 Lloyd's Rep 673 (under TOWCON), where a claim of a tow in "light ballast" failed.
208. See Chapter 12.
209. *The President Van Buren* [1924] 19 Ll L Rep 185. This position is not universally adopted, and in the US such clauses are nullified as being against public policy – see *Bisso v Inland Waterways* [1955] AMC 899.
210. UCTA 1977, Schedule 1, para 2(a).

because towage has either not started or has already finished. This depends on the construction of the contract and will be discussed in detail when the most common contracts are outlined. In other situations the shipowners try to identify a lack of agency or authority of the party signing for the tugowners or themselves. An example would be where a port authority, or terminal operator, or time charterer, makes the towage contract on behalf of independent tug companies.[211]

The parties to these forms are usually termed the "Tugowner" and the "Hirer".

The second term is an indication that it is not necessarily the owner of the tow who is a party to the contract but probably a charterer, demise charterer or some other entity. The question then would be whether the person signing the contract has the authority of the owner of the tow to sign the towage contract. If it does not have the authority then the owner of the tow is not bound by the contract and, in addition, security measures against the tow may not be available to it.

In order to remedy this situation most standard forms include a "warranty of authority" clause[212] under which the "Hirer" warrants that it has authority to sign on behalf of the owner of the tow and that they are both bound by the contract jointly and severally. While such a term can be the basis for a recourse action against the Hirer, where the authority to bind the tow owner does not exist, it cannot on its own bind the owner of the tow to the towage contract.[213]

Below we will use the terms "tug" and "tow" to refer to the parties to the contract. However, this should not be misunderstood as an assumption that the Hirer is always the tow owner, or that there is always an implication of liability *in rem* against the tow.

(i) UK Standard Towing Conditions 1986

The UK Standard Conditions for Towage and Other Services (UKSTC) goes back to 1933 with several subsequent modifications. In addition to towage the UKSTC 1986 also cover "other services". Thus they can be incorporated where ancillary services to oil rigs and the offshore industry are provided. The reference to the UK does not preclude their application to other parts of the world as these are in essence contractual terms.[214] From the variety of forms available worldwide the UKSTC are probably the most favourable to tugowners. The UKSTC include English law and exclusive English jurisdiction except in Scotland where local courts have jurisdiction.[215]

The UKSTC can be incorporated into the towage contract where there is an express incorporation, for example on fixture communication, or where the conduct of past dealing between the parties indicates an intention to be bound by the standard conditions[216] or because they habitually apply to such contracts and this fact is known and expected.[217]

---

211. See *Owners of the Borvigilant v Owners of the Romina G (The Borvigilant and Romina G)* [2003] EWCA Civ 935; [2003] 2 Lloyd's Rep 520, where such an attempt failed. The Contracts (Rights of Third Parties) Act 1999 may now assist tug companies.

212. UKSTC, cl 2; TOWHIRE, cl 22; TOWCON, cl 22.

213. *Lukoil-Kaliningradmorneft Plc v Tata Ltd and Global Marine Inc* [1999] 1 Lloyd's Rep 365; [1999] 2 Lloyd's Rep 129.

214. Subject to the law applicable in that State. See, for example, *PNSL Berhard v Dalrymple Marine Services Pty Ltd; PNSL Berhard v The Owners of the Ship Koumala (The Koumala)* [2007] QSC 101 where the exclusions in the 1974 version of the UKSTC were found to violate the Australian Trade Practices Act 1974 which imposed an implied warranty to provide services with due care and skill (s 74) and which could not be excluded by contract (s 68).

215. UKSTC 1986, cl 9.

216. *The Tasmania* [1888] LR 13 PD 110.

217. For support of this argument see *British Crane Hire Corp Ltd v Ipswich Plant Hire Ltd* [1975] 1 QB 303. See also *Owners of the Wallumba v Australian Coastal Shipping Commission (The Wallumba)* [1964] 2 Lloyd's Rep 387; [1965] 1 Lloyd's Rep 121, an Australian case in which a tug was requested by the central tug control officer of the Port of Melbourne where a pooling arrangement exists between tugowners. The court found that the nomination of the tug gave rise to a contract between the vessel which was to be assisted and the tug providing assistance which was subject to the UKSTC applicable there.

The terms provide for two different types of services: towing and other services. Towing is defined as "any operation in connection with the holding, pushing, pulling, moving, escorting or guiding of or standing by the Hirer's vessel",[218] and the contract applies "whilst towing" which covers the period from when the tug is in position to receive orders or to pick up ropes or when the towing line has passed whichever occurred first until the final orders have been performed or the lines have slipped (whichever is later) *and* the tug or any other assisting vessel is safely clear of the tow.[219]

This definition includes in the towage service any period of interruption but it is not free from difficulty. Consider the situation where the tug arrives early on site and the vessel has not yet finished loading or discharging the cargo. If the tug runs into the prospective tow and damages itself and the tow, could it then be protected by the UKSTC?[220] In *The Apollon*[221] Brandon J reviewing the authorities considered that three conditions must be fulfilled for the tug to be "in a position to receive orders direct from the Hirer's vessel . . . to pick up lines . . . etc". These are, first, that the situation is such that those on board can reasonably expect the tow to give the tug orders or to pick up ropes or lines; second, that the tug is ready to respond to such orders; and, third, that the tug can receive these orders directly, that is, the tug is within hailing distance.[222] One may query whether the requirement that the tug should be at a hailing distance is necessary as in practice orders can and are given in many cases through VHF. However, the orders must be "direct", arguably indicating very close proximity rather than the desired way of communication.[223]

Where more than one tug is involved in the towage it is reasonable to suggest that the UKSTC will start applying separately at the time each tug satisfies *The Apollon* conditions.[224] However, the wording of the contractual arrangement will be significant in this sense and may provide otherwise.

The protection of the tug under the UKSTC 1986 is based on the following contractual arrangements. First, under clause 3, all employees of the tugowner are deemed to be servants of the tow for the duration of the service. This arrangement provides a defence to any claim by the tow against the tug for negligence of the tugowner's employees. In addition, it can provide a cause of action against the tow where the negligence of the tug's crew has caused the damage to the tug. It is important to note again that this contractual arrangement is only binding between the parties to the contract and does not affect third party liability. In other words, vis-à-vis a third party, the tugowner's employees remain the source of vicarious liability for the tugowner.

218. UKSTC 1986, cl 1(b)(i).
219. UKSTC 1986, cl 1(b)(iv). But it does not include an accidental parting of the towing line – see *The Wallumba* [1964] 2 Lloyd's Rep 387; [1965] 1 Lloyd's Rep 121.
220. *The Uranienborg* [1935] 53 Ll L Rep 165; [1936] P 21; see also *The Glenaffaric* [1948–49] 81 Ll L Rep; [1949] 1 All ER 245 where *The Uranienborg* was distinguished.
221. *British Transport Docks Board v "Apollon"* [1971] 1 Lloyd's Rep 476. In this case the tug struck a moored dock gate and sustained propeller damage.
222. In *PSNL Berhard v Dalrymple Marine Services Pty Ltd (The Koumala)* (fn 209), an Australian case, the pilot ordered the two tugs to make fast at the starboard side of the vessel. The tugs crossed ahead of the vessel and turned starboard but one of them lost steering power and collided with the tow. Helman J considered that the tug was not yet in the position to receive orders and thus the UKSTC were not applicable.
223. Without the "hailing distance" requirement the period of the application of the towage contract would expand but arguably not too much. The first and the second conditions of *The Apollon* test require a situation where both tug and tow are ready and a situation in which it is reasonable for the tow to give an order. Thus, a situation of proximity would have been implied bound by a criterion of whether it is reasonable or not to give an order rather than whether the tug is at a hailing distance.
224. In *The Apollon* (fn 221) two tugs were involved. The first had made fast, the second damaged a dock gate before making fast. The argument that the towage terms applied from the moment the first tug started towing was not put forward.

Second, under clause 4, the liability of the tugowner is expressly exempted. This exemption covers any liability for damage caused either by the tug or the tow and it is effected by use of very wide terms. In addition clause 4 expressly imposes an obligation on the tow owner to indemnify the tugowner for any damages sustained or paid out to third parties. The indemnity provision in clause 4(b) is wide enough to cover even the loss of the tug caused by the negligence of the tugowner or the tug's crew or even cases where the tug is unseaworthy.[225] An additional, comparably more modest exemption, is also introduced under clause 8 excluding any liability of the tug in respect of losses suffered by the tow and caused by war, riots, civil commotions, acts of terrorism or sabotage, strikes, lockouts, disputes, stoppages or labour disturbances, etc.

There are only a few instances in which the liability of the tug is not exempted or is not to be indemnified[226] by the tow. The first situation arises where the tugowner itself or the chief management of the tug or the person in the tug company to which the particular duty has been delegated has failed to exercise reasonable care to provide a seaworthy tug. However, any damage arising from the negligence or faults or omissions of any other employees of the tugowner, even if they cause the tug to become unseaworthy and suffer the relevant damage, is to be indemnified by the tow.[227] The second instance in which the tow does not have to pay concerns situations where the tug has temporarily interrupted the provision of towage or other services and has moved away from the tow, for example to take bunkers or replace a tow line. The third instance arises where loss of life or personal injury is caused by the tug's negligence. The liability of the tug is in such cases not excluded.

The UKSTC also provide for the right of the tugowner to substitute tugs or arrange tugs[228] for the tow on behalf of the tow as agent (clause 5), claim salvage in appropriate circumstances (clause 6) and limit liability (clause 6).

(ii) TOWHIRE 2008

Alternatives to the UKSTC have been produced by BIMCO in order to satisfy the needs arising from long haul towage where the UKSTC conditions are financially very risky for the tow (the "Hirer"). The TOWHIRE[229] and TOWCON[230] forms resemble in many aspects time and voyage charterparties and attempt to provide a more balanced solution to the need for standardised contractual forms.

TOWHIRE is a daily hire towage contract. The first three pages of the form identify the details of the contractual arrangement and the parties to the agreement.

Clause 17 of TOWHIRE 2008 imposes an obligation of due diligence on the tugowner to provide a seaworthy ship at the place of delivery of the tug. A similar obligation of tow-worthiness is placed on the tow owner under clause 16. In addition the tow owner has to provide a certificate issued by appropriate marine surveyors stating that the vessel is tow-worthy. However, even after such a certificate has been provided the tugowner can still refuse to start the towage if it is not satisfied that the tow is indeed tow-worthy.

---

225. See *M'Bundis v Waratah Towage* [1992] LMLN 343. Note *The Romina G* (fn 206) on a slightly different version of the form.

226. Note that the issue of who are parties to the contract may be relevant when it comes to looking at indemnities: see *Targe Towing Ltd and Another v Marine Blast Ltd* [2004] EWCA Civ 346; [2004] 1 Lloyd's Rep 721.

227. UKSTC, cl 4(c)(i).

228. Note that the Contracts (Rights of Third Parties) Act 1999 would apply directly to a towage contract as their application is not presumably affected by s 6(5).

229. TOWHIRE 2008 International Ocean Towage Agreement (Daily Hire) can be found at www.marine-salvage.com/documents/TOWHIRE%202008.pdf (accessed 15 March 2017).

230. TOWCON International Ocean Towage Agreement (lump sum) can be found at www.marine-salvage.com/documents/TOWCON%202008.pdf (accessed 15 March 2017).

Allocation of liabilities under TOWHIRE is on a "knock for knock" basis (clause 23). Under this arrangement some liabilities are allocated to the tug or the tow in relation to which they arose irrespective of whether liability would normally attach to the owner of the tug or the tow respectively. There are three parts of clause 23, each working in a slightly different way. Clause 23(a)(i) provides that the tugowner will indemnify the tow owner for liability arising from loss of life or personal injury of the tug's employees or happenings on board the tug. Clause 23(b)(i) similarly provides indemnification to the tugowner for loss of life or personal injury of the tow's employees or people onboard the tow. Clause 23(b)(ii) provides that the tugowner will pay, without having a right of recourse against the tow owner, for loss or damage to the tug or property on board the tug and consequential loss; loss or damage to any other property caused by contact with the tug and consequential loss; wreck removal; and pollution liability for the tug. This is coupled with an obligation imposed on the tugowner to indemnify the tow owner for any such liability imposed on the tow owner by a court or an arbitration award. The reverse arrangement applies for the tow (clause 23(b)). Notably the division of damages under clause 23(b) is stated to be applicable whether or not the damages are "due to breach of contract, negligence or any other fault on the part" of the party to whom liability to pay attaches. Such a statement is not present in the arrangement under clause 23(a).[231] Note that clause 23(c) further restricts the general rights of recovery of the parties against each other.[232]

Difficulty arises when the division of financial liability under the knock-for-knock agreement is considered together with the respective obligations of the tug and the tow to provide, respectively, a seaworthy and tow-worthy ship (clauses 16 and 17). The question of which clause prevails would then arise. If the duty of seaworthiness or tow-worthiness is considered as the primary obligation that needs to be fulfilled, this would then mean that when this obligation is breached the knock-for-knock arrangement can be avoided. The alternative interpretation is that the knock-for-knock agreement applies in spite of the breach of the seaworthiness or tow-worthiness obligation. In *Smit v Mobius*[233] the tow was not entitled to introduce arguments concerning the seaworthiness of the tug in respect of liability arising from a collision between the tow and another vessel because the "knock-for-knock" agreement was a workable allocation of risk and responsibility. Consequently, under a knock-for-knock agreement the significance of the obligation of seaworthiness and tow-worthiness is restricted in respect of the liabilities specified in the knock-for-knock agreement under clause 23.

However, clause 23 does not resolve all liability issues. Only where the particular claims referred to are included in the wording of the clause does the clause operate. For example, where the tug is unseaworthy and there are losses not covered by clause 23, for example by increased bunker consumption, then such operational damage is recoverable provided that it is brought about by a breach of the contract of towage.

---

231. See S. Rainey (fn 196) for an argument that this difference implies that cl 23(1) as well as cl 23(3) do not cover situations where the relevant damages are caused by negligence, because exclusion clauses which can be taken to exclude contractual liability will not normally be considered to extend to cover negligence. The discussion in S. Rainey (fn 196) concerns cl 18 of the 1985 version of TOWHIRE.

232. Note that the exclusion itself contains exclusions in respect of cls 15, 16, 17, 20 and 21. The earlier version of this clause was the issue in the decision in *The Herdentor*, unreported, 19 January 1996, and *Ease Faith Limited v Leonis Marine Management Limited, Cloudfree Ship Management Limited* (under TOWCON) (fn 207). An opposing view is supported by S. Rainey (fn 196). In the second case the delay in the delivery day of the tug led to increased pilotage expenses as well as docking expense and reduced price for the tow which was sold for scrap. All these damages were recoverable by the tow and were not excluded by the knock-for-knock agreement.

233. *Smit International (Deutschland) GmbIJ v Josef Mobius Bau-Gesellsehaft (GmbH & Co)* [2001] 2 All ER (Comm) 265.

Where the "Hirer" under the TOWHIRE or TOWCON agreement is not the owner of the tow but a charterer then the owner of the tow becomes a third party under clause 23. Thus, where the tow has been lost and this third party (the owner) sues and recovers from the tugowner in negligence, then the tugowner can obtain an indemnity from the "Hirer", the charterer in this case.[234]

TOWHIRE provides for the creation of a lien on the tow for any unpaid amounts under the contract. However, this will be enforceable only where the tow owner is bound by the towage contract.[235] The exercise of the lien is always dependent on the power to enforce it at the port of destination as it is the law of the place where the assets are located that will determine the issues related to the ownership and possession of property. Consequently, even if the contract is under English law, the local court may consider the exercise of the lien as against public policy or unenforceable, especially where the tow is owned by the port State. In practice this may lead to the tug avoiding going into port or even staying outside territorial waters while exercising its lien.[236] Such delays, if reasonable, do not deprive the tug of the payment of hire, but if unreasonable and there is a date of delivery of the tow, it may result in the payment of damages to the hirer.[237] The contract provides for a reference to arbitration and the parties have a choice to select the place of arbitration[238] (clause 31) and a one-year time bar (clause 29).

(iii) TOWCON 2008

This contract is used for towage where payment by lump sum has been agreed. However, the form has flexibility in that it permits part payment to be made at particular times, for example, at the time when the contract is agreed, when lines are passed and when the towage is finished. It thus determines when the instalment is earned and when and how payment is to be effected. The major differences with TOWHIRE concern the payment provisions under clause 2, and the place of departure which is more complicated than that of TOWHIRE. As with TOWHIRE, obligations of due diligence to provide a seaworthy tug and a tow-worthy tow are imposed (clauses 18 and 19) as well as the knock-for-knock agreement under clause 25. A duty of reasonable despatch[239] is implied in the contract if no provision about time is contained in it.[240] A tug operating only one of the two engines in order to minimise bunker consumption is in breach of this obligation. The reasoning includes an argument that the towing power of the vessel is included in the consideration of the lump sum payable, because more powerful tugs cost more; thus in general it is not an option for the tugowner to use only part of the power it has agreed to provide.

Reference to arbitration with a choice between English, New York or other place is provided (clause 33)[241] together with a one-year time bar[242] (clause 31) and a warranty of authority exactly the same as that under TOWHIRE.

Because under TOWCON the risk of delay is on the tug, clause 27 provides for "Delay Payment" if the delay is due to unsuitability of the tow for towage. The amount is agreed in advance

---

234. See *Targe Towing Ltd and Another v Marine Blast Ltd* (fn 226).

235. See *Lukoil-Kalingradnorneft plc v Tata Ltd (No 2)* [1999] 2 Lloyd's Rep 129 for the proposition that under the TOWCON contract in certain circumstances a lien based on bailment can be exercised.

236. In *Ease Faith Ltd v Leonis Marine Management, Cloudfree Ship Management Limited* (fn 207), 145, this was accepted as consistent with the contract by the parties.

237. Ibid.

238. TOWHIRE 1985 includes an exclusive English jurisdiction clause under cl 25.

239. The contract may provide for "utmost despatch" which is taken to mean the maximum sustainable speed. See *Ease Faith Ltd v Leonis Marine Management Ltd* (fn 207).

240. *Ease Faith Ltd v Leonis Marine Management Ltd* (fn 207).

241. TOWCON 1985 includes an exclusive English jurisdiction clause under cl 25.

242. *Rowan Companies 1nc & Ors v Lambert Eggink Offshore Transport Consultants VOF & Ors* [1998] CLC 1574.

in Box 30 of the form. What would render the tow unsuitable for towage is a question that is not necessarily answered in exactly the same way as under a time or voyage charterparty.

In *A Turtle Offshore SA v Superior Trading Inc*[243] a drilling rig towed by the *Mighty Deliverer* from Brazil to Singapore via Cape Town ended up on the shores of Tristan da Cunha. The claim was put forward by the rig owners in respect of liability arising for the loss of the rig and the wreck removal costs while the counterclaim put forward by the tug owners concerned entitlement to the outstanding 95 per cent of freight described in the contract to be "due and payable on arrival of tug and tow at the place of destination" and "deemed earned whether the tug or rig was lost or not lost". The *A Turtle* was intentionally released by the *Mighty Deliverer* because the latter was running out of fuel. After its release the rig drifted away from the tug for several weeks before running aground. Without releasing the rig both tug and tow would have been at risk of being lost. By releasing the rig the *Mighty Deliverer* managed to refuel successfully from a sister-tug that arrived on location two weeks after the rig was released. Both tugs searched for the released rig for about six days but without success.

The contract of towage was on the TOWCON 1985 form. Under this contract the tug owners agreed to use their "best endeavours to perform their towage" subject to terms and conditions, in accordance with clause 13, they were under an obligation to exercise due diligence "to tender the Tug at the place of departure in a seaworthy condition and in all respects ready to perform the towage". A similar obligation of tow-worthiness was placed on the tow owner under clause 12. In addition, the tow owner had to provide a certificate issued by appropriate marine surveyors stating that the vessel was tow-worthy. The rig owners did not agree on the towage terms until their retained surveyors issued a "fitness to tow" certificate regarding the *Mighty Deliverer* after surveying the tug and the plans related to the towage of the rig. A first question was whether the owners of the *Mighty Deliverer* were in breach of their obligation to provide a seaworthy tug under clause 13. Teare J considered that a prudent tug owner would have planned to cross the south Atlantic without refuelling. Thus the question was whether the managers of the *Mighty Deliverer* had assessed the amount of bunkers required in a reasonable manner. The answer to this question in turn depended on the predicted speed that would be achieved by the flotilla, taking weather and current into account. The owners of the *Mighty Deliverer* failed to persuade Teare J that their belief that the calculation of consumption on the assumption that the flotilla would progress with three to four knots on average was a reasonable one. Amongst the various reasons Teare J considered that the bollard pull of the tug was lower than that required to achieve the suggested speed of three to four knots. Had the calculation in this respect been made, the problem would have been identified. As a result, the owners of the *Mighty Deliverer* were in breach of their clause 13 obligation.[244]

Complaints were also filed in respect of the performance of the voyage. Thus it was argued that after the towage started the duty to exercise best endeavours meant that the flotilla should either turn back or should have made bunkering arrangements. Teare J considered that on the facts of the case the discharge of the duty of best endeavours demanded that the tug should have returned to South America for refuelling. Even if continuing the journey and arranging for refuelling, as was in fact done, was consistent with the duty of best endeavours, such action would not excuse the breach of the seaworthiness obligation under clause 13.

Teare J did not find that the timing of the disconnection of the rig was a breach of the contractual obligation of best endeavours and rejected an argument that disconnection should have

---

243. [2008] EWHC 3034 (Admlty); [2009] 1 Lloyd's Rep 177.
244. Tugowners further argued that the fact that the TOWCON was signed by the rig owners only after the issuance of the "fitness to tow" certificate by the rig owners' surveyors meant that rig owners had accepted the *Mighty Deliverer* as seaworthy and that they were therefore estopped from arguing otherwise. This argument was rejected.

taken place earlier so that the *Mighty Deliverer* would have had enough bunkers to stand by the rig as it was drifting.[245] In addition, several other assertions by the claimants regarding omissions were rejected by the court.

However, Teare J held that the knock-for-knock arrangement protected the owners of the *Mighty Deliverer* in spite of the breach of the seaworthiness obligation under clause 13 because these were risks expressly accepted to be borne by the owners of the rig. Teare J then responded to a submission that clause 18 would not protect tug owners where, for example, they abandon their tow in order to pursue a more lucrative operation. He considered that clause 18 would not operate to protect tugowners in such circumstances, although the wording would probably cover such a situation. The proper construction requires interpreting clause 18 subject to the 1985 TOWCON contract performance. Thus, clause 18 protects the parties when they perform their duties under the contract although their performance falls short of the required standard, but not where they do not perform in a way consistent with the main objective of the contract. In other words, clause 18 cannot be given a meaning that makes the contract a mere declaration of intent and clearer words would be needed for such an effect. Applying this test to the facts of the case, Teare J found that the two omissions identified, i.e. the deficient bunkering calculations and the breach of the duty of best endeavours by not turning back to South America for refuelling, were efforts to fulfil the contract and therefore clause 18 did protect the owners of the *Mighty Deliverer*. Notably, the court held that the decision to stop the search for the rig after the refuelling of the *Mighty Deliverer* was a breach of the contract which, had it been proven to be causative, would have removed the protection of clause 18 from the tug owners.[246]

The freight arrangement was held to make the 5 per cent of the freight payable irrespective of the loss of the tug or the tow while the 95 per cent was only payable on arrival of the flotilla at the contractual destination, a precondition that was not fulfilled.

The decision in *The A Turtle* under the TOWCON contract confirms the view in *Smit v Mobius* under the 1985 TOWHIRE contract in respect of the coupling of the seaworthiness obligations for tug and tow with the knock-for-knock agreement.[247]

(d) Salvage and towage law

Towage services in admiralty are almost always based on contract.[248] Remuneration for towing a vessel in the absence of a contract is only earned if it is considered as part of a salvage operation.[249] However, the distinction between salvage and towage services is not always easily defined. The two regimes differ significantly as towage is purely contractual and although it is protected by a statutory action *in rem* entitling the parties to a towage contract to arrest each

---

245. Towage can be abandoned if it becomes impossible to perform. Otherwise there is a duty to stand by the tow and attempt to reconnect. See *The Minnehaha* [1861] Lush 335.

246. Finally, although the issue did not arise because of the effects of cl 18 the court indicated that the tugowners would be entitled to limitation of liability under art 4 of the Convention on Limitation of Liability for Maritime Claims 1976.

247. Note that the equivalent cl 25 in the 2008 version of the contract states "whether or not the same is due to any breach of contract, negligence or any other fault on the part of". Thus it can be argued that the application of the knock-for-knock agreement is extended to cover even those breaches that were considered as escaping the clause in the *A Turtle Offshore SA v Superior Trading Inc* (fn 243).

248. The action of towing another vessel which is in difficulty without remuneration is not uncommon, especially in respect of small yachts or between sister ships. In such cases there is no contract but the courts will impose an obligation on both tug and tow to exercise reasonable care in respect of their contribution to the service. For the application of the principle, see, for example, the Canadian case *Maurice Federation v Stewart (The West Bay III)* [1969] 1 Lloyd's Rep 158.

249. As defined under art 1(1) of the Salvage Convention. See section on salvage for details.

other's ship, such claim is of lower priority than a claim for salvage which is supported by a maritime lien.[250] In addition, the right to a salvage reward arises independently of contract,[251] and is payable by the owners of the property in proportion to the relative value of their property.[252] The final remuneration, when no contract of salvage has been signed, or when the salvage contract is in a form similar to the Lloyd's Open Form, depends on several criteria[253] and it is by no means fixed as payment under a towage contract.

For the right to salvage reward to arise, the ship must be in danger. This does not exclude the possibility that a ship in danger may enter into a towage contract, provided that a willing tug is found. This is in practice the preferred, and usually cheaper, option for both shipowners and cargo owners and is feasible in situations where there is no imminent danger to the vessel, for example where the engines have broken down but the vessel is away from the coast and the weather conditions are fair. The acceptance of a contract of towage arguably excludes the possibility for the tugowner to claim salvage unless the situation significantly changes.[254]

The restriction arises from Article 17 of the Salvage Convention which states that a salvage reward is only payable where "the services rendered exceed what can be reasonably considered as due performance of a contract entered into before the danger arose". It must be presumed that a ship under towage, even if disabled, is not in danger and that a situation of danger in respect of the tow should arise. There is agreement between commentators[255] that Article 17 does not change the pre-existing salvage situation. Cases prior to the Salvage Convention suggest that one must look at the contractual towage arrangement to see whether the rendered services exceed those agreed. For example, operational difficulties, including interruptions of the towage service, which are normal and expected, or the parting of the tow line or the deterioration of weather by itself, would not take the tug outside the towage service into salvage.[256]

The test pre-dating the Salvage Convention is one based on the development of new circumstances which create a dangerous situation for the tow and which cannot reasonably be considered as covered by the existing towage contract.[257]

In a recent case a number of tugs were engaged in towing an oil rig between two locations. The hawser of one of the tugs parted under deteriorating weather conditions. The arbitrator held that on the facts a situation of danger arose when the hawser parted and that the services from then on amounted to salvage even if the situation of danger was brought about partly by the negligence of the tugs.[258] The appeal to the High Court did not concern the dispute regarding Article 17 but merely the consequences of the salvor's negligence under Article 18.[259]

Where a towage service changes into salvage the fate of the towage contract must be considered. The view expressed in case law pre-dating the Salvage Convention is that the towage contract is "suspended" until the time when "the special and unexpected danger is over, and

250. See Chapter 12.
251. Salvage Convention, art 12.
252. Salvage Convention, art 13.
253. Ibid.
254. Clause 6 of the UKSTC and other services expressly preserve the rights of the tugowner and the crew to claim salvage. Contrast with TOWHIRE, cl 15, and TOWCON, cl 15, where the tug should make all reasonable efforts to reconnect with the tow where the towing line parts without claiming salvage. In addition the tugowner and its servants are expressly authorised to seek salvage assistance where needed.
255. See F. Rose, *Kennedy and Rose on the Law of Salvage* (8th edn, Sweet & Maxwell 2013); J Reeder QC, *Brice on Maritime Law of Salvage* (5th edn, Sweet & Maxwell 2012) and S. Rainey (fn 196).
256. *The Minnehaha* (fn 193).
257. See S. Rainey (fn 196).
258. A reduction of the salvage reward under art 18 of the Salvage Convention was the consequence for the negligent salvor.
259. *The Owners, masters and Crews of the Tugs Maridive VII, Maridive XIII, Maridive 85 and Maridive 94 v Owners and Demise Charterers of the Oil Rig Key Singapore her Equipment, Stores and Bunkers* (fn 77).

then the salvage service would end, and the towage service would be resumed".[260] An alternative interpretation is that salvage starts when the towage contract becomes impossible to perform at which point in time the towage contract is abandoned.[261] Where an express agreement for salvage is put in place between the same parties this latter position should plainly be the correct one. Where there is no such express salvage agreement difficulties may arise but it is submitted that the latter position should also be adopted. The salvage operation would need to be performed in accordance with the Salvage Convention imposing specific requirements on the parties, binding the cargo and potentially providing for an Article 14 award which, according to *The Nagasaki Spirit*, is payable until redelivery if it exceeds the award under Article 13. In addition, redelivery at a place of safety is required. This does not of course prohibit the parties from accepting redelivery under salvage at sea, even if redelivery is from the tug, as a salvor, to the same tug under the towage contract, and proceed directly to the destination of the contract of towage. The law before the Salvage Convention appears to impose this solution on the parties.[262] One must be aware that complications are bound to arise where the towage contract and the salvage contract are subject to the law of different countries and disputes as to the period of suspension arise.

The right to the salvage reward under the Salvage Convention requires a "useful result" and is not subject to redelivery at a place of safety, which is only mentioned under the obligation of the property owners (Article 8.2) to accept redelivery in such a place. To this extent and regarding the criteria for fixing the salvage reward under Article 13 there is no difficulty in accepting that, unless the owners refuse redelivery at sea, the English law solution that the towage contract is suspended during the performance of the salvage services is not in conflict with the Salvage Convention and is thus still applicable.

However, where special compensation under Article 14 is also to be earned there appears to be a problem in respect of the House of Lords' decision in *The Nagasaki Spirit*,[263] where it was held that the application of Article 14 continues until the salvage operation is completed. To impose on the salvors an obligation to abandon their right of remuneration under Article 14 because of a pre-existing towage contract which has been "suspended" is in our view not justifiable when the purpose of the Salvage Convention is taken into account[264] and, in any case, cannot be confirmed without the courts considering the situation. In order for the "suspended contract" solution to remain valid one must assume that the "suspended" contract imposes on the tug an obligation to redeliver from the salvage operations and return back to the towage contract as soon as practicable which is far from obvious. Thus the fate of the towage contract when special compensation is payable is in our view unclear and we consider the common law position as problematic and in need of revision. It is submitted that the towage contract ends at the point where a situation of salvage arises and that the towage contract can be reinstated by agreement by both parties but subject to rights and obligations created by the Salvage Convention. By contrast, it is clear that where salvage operations have started, whether under a salvage contract or not, the services cannot turn from salvage services to become towage services without an express agreement between the property owners and the salvors.

---

260. *The Minnehaha* (fn 193); *The Leon Blum* [1915] P 90; [1915] P 290.
261. This is neater, easier to apply and describe as part of the contract law solution. However, it has significant drawbacks in relation to the exact point in time at which a new towage contract is reintroduced.
262. *The Leon Blum* [1915] P 290.
263. *Semco Salvage & Marine Pte Ltd v Lancer Navigation Co Ltd (The Nagasaki Spirit)* [1997] 1 Lloyd's Rep 323.
264. One should also take into account that the Salvage Convention imposes additional obligations on the parties in respect of environmental protection which cannot be excluded by contract. The resurrection of the pre-existing towage contract under the common law position cannot arguably remove such obligations.

(e) Towage and carriage of goods by sea

Where unmanned barges or ships are towed, or where a riding crew is put onboard the tow by the tug, then the tug has physical possession of the tow and can be considered to be a bailee of the tow.[265] This legal relationship, which is relevant to towage only where the tug has the physical possession of the tow, imposes on the tugowner the strict liability of a bailee. This is a much heavier duty than the reasonable care and skill implied at common law or imposed statutorily by the Supply of Goods and Services Act 1982 in a contract of towage.

The existence of such a relationship of bailment will also be important for the tow owner who is not a party to the towage contract but can be considered as bound by bailment on terms or sub-bailment.[266]

(f) Collisions during the towage operation

Liability for collision damage between the tug and tow would almost always be governed by their contractual arrangements.

Collision or pollution liability will be based on tort[267] or on special pollution liability regimes.[268] The contractual or other relationship between the tug and the tow will not affect the relationship of either of them with a third party but could provide for indemnification of one party by the other.

However, there are issues which complicate the relationship between the tug and the tow vis-à-vis third parties. First, there is the issue of limited liability. Because the tug is usually a much smaller vessel than the tow, it also has much lower limits of liability. Thus, a third party claimant would be in a better position if it can establish the liability of the tow or if possible the liability of both the tow and the tug.[269]

The second related issue concerns the commanding of the towing operation. English case law has in the past used the misleading expression the "tug is the servant of the tow"[270] and this was considered to be the position as a matter of law. It has now been clarified that this position is wrong and the issue of command and liability is a matter of fact, not a matter of law.[271] Perhaps the best way to explain the position is by considering three proposals. First, that the tug is an independent entity. Second, that liability of the tug or the tow vis-à-vis a third party will arise when any of them acts or fails to act in accordance with the required "good seamanship" standard.[272] Third, that in addition to the liability of the party that acted negligently, whether this was the tug or the tow, liability may also attach to the other party[273] (tow or tug respectively) if that party was in command of the towage operation and acted negligently in this capacity.[274] Of course causation of damage flowing from the negligent command or actions must be proved in all cases for rights of compensation to arise. Limitation of liability would then depend on

---

265. *Lukoil-Kalingradmorneft Plc v Tata Ltd (No 2)* [1999]1 Lloyd's Rep 365. See also *Targe Towing Ltd and Another v Marine Blast Ltd* (fn 226), where the issue was partly discussed.
266. *Owners of Cargo lately Laden on Board the KH Enterprise v Owners of the Pioneer Container (The Pioneer Container, The KH Enterprise)* [1994]1 Lloyd's Rep 593; [1994] 2 AC 324 (PC).
267. See the section on Collisions.
268. See Chapter 10.
269. See *The Bramley Moore* [1963] 2 Lloyd's Rep 429.
270. *Owners of the SS Devonshire v Owners of the Barge Leslie and Others (The Devonshire)* [1912] AC 634.
271. Ibid.
272. See the section on Collisions.
273. For examples, see *Owners of the Steam Barge Trishna v Owners of the Motor Tug Panther (The Panther)* [1957] 1 Lloyd's Rep 57; *San Jose v Socrates and Champion (The Socrates and the Champion)* [1923] 15 Ll L Rep 196.
274. *The Niobe* [1888] LR 13 PD 55; [1888] 59 LT 257; [1891] AC 401.

the entitlement of each liable party in this respect.[275] Where the third party's vessel is innocent then the liability of the tug and the tow will be joint and several. Where the third party's vessel navigates negligently and contributes to the collision, liability for property damage will be apportioned between the wrongdoers[276] while in respect of loss of life and personal injury it will be joint and several.[277]

6. WRECK REMOVAL

(a) Introduction

Wrecks can be viewed in different ways, Some wrecks can be seen as cultural heritage, time capsules, providing information on the past of human civilization. Others are war graves to be protected from interference as a moral principle for respect. Others are dangerous, carrying pollutants which range from chemical weapons to fuel. Others are dangerous to navigation and to other users of the sea. Some have more than one of these characteristics. When a new wreck happens nowadays an environmental risk is almost always present. But if the wreck is left for several decades it gradually becomes part of the heritage and becomes subject to preservation laws. Thus there are competing norms in operation when discussing the management of a wreck. One tension exists between the tendency to protect cultural heritage and exploitation of it by treasure hunters. The second is between war graves and cultural heritage on the one hand and environmental risks on the other. The third tension exists between the environmental and navigational risks posed by wrecks and the exclusive rights the flag State has over such wrecks. This last tension is easily resolved for wrecks in territorial waters.

The maritime law of many States contains provisions empowering governments, usually coastguard, port or lighthouse authorities, to remove wrecks which amount to an obstruction or danger to navigation. In England the relevant provisions are sections 252 to 254 of the Merchant Shipping Act 1995, which not only empower the relevant agency to remove the wreck, but also to recover the cost of doing so from the owner.[278]

The relevant statutory provisions[279] usually give the governmental agency the power to sell the ship or any material recovered from her to defray the costs of the removal operation, and to recover any unrecovered balance from the shipowner.

However, although the statutory definitions rarely state so explicitly,[280] a wreck is, by its nature, a thing of no commercial value.[281] Were it to have such a value, the salvage industry would no doubt undertake its removal and sale in return for a suitable salvage reward. However, a valueless wreck will not yield proceeds of sale equal to the costs involved in its removal, and since most ships are owned by a one-ship company, the prospects of a coastal State recovering by legal proceedings expenses which it has incurred in removing a wreck are very poor.

What happens then when the owner of a wrecked ship (or its insurer) takes no action to remove it? If the wreck is under the jurisdiction of a coastal State in its internal waters or territorial sea,

---

275. *The Bramley Moore* (fn 269).

276. MSA 1995, s 187. This applies also where the wrongdoer is not physically in contact with any other vessel. See *The Cairnbahn* [1914] P 25.

277. MSA 1995, s 188.

278. Similar powers are conferred by s 56 of the Harbour Docks and Piers Clauses Act 1847.

279. See, for instance, MSA 1995, s 252(2)(c) and (d).

280. See, e.g. MSA 1995, s 255(1).

281. A wreck might however have a non-commercial value arising from archaeological or historical significance. See S. Dromgoole and C. Forrest, "The Nairobi Wreck Removal Convention 2007 and Hazardous Historic Shipwrecks" [2011] LMCLQ 92.

that State is likely to invoke its domestic law to issue a Wreck Removal Order, and eventually to undertake the removal itself[282] in order to maintain the safety of those using the waters in which the wreck lies. It will then, as previously mentioned, seek to recover the costs from the shipowner, but if they have no other assets that may prove very difficult. Recovering directly from the P&I Club in which the ship is entered will generally be defeated by the "pay to be paid" rule in the club cover.[283] However, no such rights exist under customary international law outside the territorial sea in respects of ships flying the flag of foreign States. Nevertheless, navigation and pollution threats may occur outside the territorial waters of a coastal State. The need of coastal States to intervene in cases of imminent environmental damage led to the development of the 1969 Intervention Convention.[284] The development of the 1982 United Nations Convention on the Law of the Sea provided some further possibilities of intervention to the coastal State in cases where there was a threat of environmental pollution in the EEZ but these were more of the form of duties imposed on the coastal or other States, and were not supported by rights of recourse against the owner of a ship endangering the environment. Therefore under international law a coastal State arguably has no right to remove a wreck which is a navigational hazard in its EEZ and the cost of wreck removal is unlikely to be recoverable from the shipowner. The situation has radically changed as a result of the 2007 Nairobi Convention which entered into force on 14 April 2015.

(b) The 2007 Nairobi Convention

The 2007 Nairobi Convention has three main actors, namely the Coastal (Affected) State, the registered owner and its insurer. The UK government has passed the Wreck Removal Convention Act 2011 which inserts the 2007 Convention into the 1995 MSA as Schedule 11 ZA, and provides for its implementation by introducing Part 9A of the 1995 MSA. The Wreck Removal Convention Act 2011 (Commencement) Order 2015 SI 2015/133 (c.7) triggers the commencement of the substantive provisions on 14 April 2015. The UK implementation does not remove the rights of lighthouse, port or conservatory authorities. However, it provides the Secretary of State with the power to direct them to act or not to act in relation to wrecks within their areas.[285]

(i) Scope of application

The 2007 Nairobi Convention applies[286] to wrecks within the EEZ of a Contracting State or an equivalent zone of up to 200 miles from the coast.[287] An option is provided for States to extend

282. Or, more probably, to employ a professional salvage contractor to do so.
283. This will be discussed in Chapter 11 – see *Firma C-Trade SA v Newcastle Protection & Indemnity Association (The Fanti)* and *Socony Mobil Oil Inc and Others v West of England Shipowners Mutual Insurance Association (London) Ltd (No 2)(The Padre Island)* [1991] 2 AC 1; [1990] 2 Lloyd's Rep 191.
284. 1969 Intervention Convention and the Protocol relating to Intervention on the High Seas in cases of Pollution by substances other than Oil, 1973. Note though that a right to intervene or direct is not, on its own, the solution to the problem. Establishing appropriate decision-making procedures and separating the technical and environmental protection matters from political consequences and media pressure is also of paramount importance as the *Prestige* incident and the relevant ill-considered decisions of the Spanish Government have demonstrated.
285. MSA 255C s 3 regarding marking locating the wreck and MSA 255F s 2 regarding the removal of the wreck. Both section inserted by the WRC Act 2011.
286. 2007 Nairobi Convention, art 3(1).
287. 2007 Nairobi Convention, art 1(1). The established zone should be in accordance with international law. The Exclusive Economic Zone Order 2013 (SI 2013/3161) delimits the UK EEZ as from 31 March 2014.

its application, in a restricted way as we will see, to territorial waters.[288] The UK has informed the IMO that the UK coastal areas will also be part of its implementation and has nationally defined the Wreck Removal Convention Area as including its EEZ and the United Kingdom waters.[289]

A very wide definition of ships is adopted in Article 1(2) including any seagoing vessel and extends to hydrofoils, air-cushion vehicles, submersibles, floating craft and floating platforms not in location and drilling.

The 2007 Nairobi Convention applies to wrecks "following upon a maritime casualty"[290] within the area chosen[291] by the Contracting State. The word "wreck" is defined as including not only sunken or stranded (seagoing) ships[292] but any of the parts of the ship[293] or any object which has been on the stranded ship.[294] In addition, objects lost at sea from a ship which is not itself stranded are also covered.[295] Article 1(4)(d) extends the definition of wreck to ships "reasonably expected to sink or strand" where no effective salvage is underway.[296]

"Removal" in the 2007 Nairobi Convention is defined as "any form of prevention, mitigation or elimination of the hazard created by a wreck".[297] Thus wreck removal means the removal of the navigational or environmental hazard, rather than the complete physical removal of the wreck from the sea bed.

(ii) Rights of the coastal State

The coastal State which has the wreck in it area is defined, under Article 1(10), as the Affected State which is the main beneficiary of the 2007 Nairobi Convention. The Affected State acquires a general right to take measures in relation to the removal of wrecks which pose a "hazard".[298] In turn, a wreck becomes a hazard when it poses a danger or an impediment to navigation,[299] or when it is reasonable to expect that "major harmful consequences" to the marine and coastal environment or damage to the coastline and related interests would follow.[300]

The Affected State's rights of intervention are not unlimited under the 2007 Nairobi Convention. First, because it only acquires such rights when the wreck becomes a hazard; and secondly,

---

288. 2007 Nairobi Convention, art 3(2), following notification to the IMO Secretary General (see art 1(12) and 1(13)).

289. The Merchant Shipping (United Kingdom Wreck Convention Area) Order 2015, SI 2015/172.

290. The definition of maritime incident is very general and apart from collisions, strandings and other navigational incidents, it also includes all other occurrences whether onboard or external which result in material damage or imminent threat of damage to ship or cargo. Thus an explosion onboard the ship or the disintegration of a rusty plate on the ship would arguably both be considered as maritime casualties.

291. Thus Convention Area can be either the EEZ or equivalent zone, and where the coastal State has opted to include its territory then the term includes such areas art 3(3).

292. 2007 Nairobi Convention, art 1(4).

293. 2007 Nairobi Convention, art 1(4).

294. 2007 Nairobi Convention, art 1(4). This definition covers derelict, flotsam and jetsam (materials jettisoned from the ship) from a stranded ship.

295. 2007 Nairobi Convention 2007, art 1(4). This would cover flotsam but arguably would not cover *jetsam* from a ship which is not stranded.

296. Art 1(4). This arguably permits the coastal State to treat a ship under salvage as falling under the Nairobi Convention 2007 and take appropriate measures in spite of any rights the salvors may have.

297. 2007 Nairobi Convention, art 1(7).

298. Art 2(1).

299. Art 1(5)(a).

300. 2007 Nairobi Convention, art 1(5)(b) and art 1(6). Apart from the requirement that there must be a reasonable expectation of a "major harmful consequence", the wording is very wide in terms of the interests which must be at risk. Marine, coastal, port and estuarine, as well as fishery activities used as living resources, tourist attractions and other economic interests concerned, the health of population and the well-being of living marine resources and wildlife in general are all included.

any measures must be proportional to the hazard and are only taken if they are reasonably necessary in order to remove the hazard posed by the wreck.[301]

When the Affected State becomes aware of a wreck, it becomes subject to a number of obligations. The first obligation, which arises irrespective of whether the wreck is a hazard or not, is immediately to warn mariners and other States concerned about the nature and the existence of the wreck.[302] If the Affected State assesses the wreck to be a hazard,[303] then additional obligations to establish the precise location of the wreck[304] and to mark the wreck appropriately,[305] as well as to inform the flag State and the registered owner, are imposed.[306] In addition, the Affected State should consult with the flag State and other concerned States in respect of the wreck. Note that such consultation should take place irrespective of whether the flag State is also a Contracting State to the 2007 Nairobi Convention or not.[307]

(iii) Rights and obligations of the registered shipowner

Article 9(2) of the 2007 Nairobi Convention imposes an obligation on the registered owner to remove the wreck which is considered a hazard by the Affected State.[308] As explained earlier this is an obligation to remove the hazard, not necessarily the wreck. Evidence of insurance is at that stage required.[309] These obligations appear to be subject to the obligation of the Affected State to inform the registered owner and the flag State. Only upon the receipt of the information that a wreck is considered to be a hazard does the obligation attach to the registered owner. At this stage the registered owner is granted the option to contract for the removal of the wreck subject to conditions imposed by the Affected State, before the wreck removal operations start, in respect (only) of the safety and marine environmental protection.[310] Thus, the Affected State, in general, ought not to prescribe the type of the contractual agreement or the remuneration or even the law of the contract for the wreck removal, or the jurisdiction arrangements under the contract, but could prescribe the depth to which the wreck should be removed and also prohibit

---

301. Art 2(2). In addition art 2(4) makes it clear that no rights over the high seas can be claimed on the basis of the application of the Convention. Note that art 2(4) is not relevant in respect of the application with the territorial sea, thus is excluded in such a case (see art 4(4)).

302. Art 7(1). Under art 5, Contracting States have a general obligation to impose in their laws a requirement that the master or operator, whether this is the registered owner, the demise charterer or the manager of the ship (art 1(9)), report immediately when their ship has been involved in a maritime casualty resulting in a wreck. Within this obligation the general information regarding the wreck, that is, location, type and size, condition and nature of damage, cargo and pollutants on board should all be reported to the Affected State. The way art 5 is worded indicates that if a ship registered in a Contracting State collides with a ship not registered in a Contracting State, and the second ship becomes a wreck, the master of the first ship should make the report in respect of the wreck.

303. Art 7(2). In assessing whether the wreck is a hazard, fifteen criteria set out under art 6 are to be taken into account. These are related to the configuration and the physical environment of the area and the wreck, the traffic as well as the sensitivity of the local environment. The fifteenth criterion relates to "any other circumstances that might necessitate the removal of the wreck". Thus apart from the stated criteria, the coastal State can take into account any other criterion it considers relevant to a particular wreck.

304. Art 7(2) requiring all practicable steps to be undertaken for this purpose.

305. Art 8. Markings should use, where possible the international system of buoyage and should be published in charts and other relevant publications used by mariners.

306. 2007 Nairobi Convention, art 9(1).

307. Where the Affected State has extended the application of the Convention to its territorial sea, for wrecks in this area there is no obligation to notify the registered owner and the flag State if the wreck is in the territorial sea before taking subsequent measures, as these have been excluded under art 4(4).

308. 2007 Nairobi Convention, art 9(2).

309. 2007 Nairobi Convention, art 9(3). Note that under the UK implementation, evidence of insurance is needed for all ships whether flying the flag of a Contracting State or not. See MSA 1995, s 255J.

310. 2007 Nairobi Convention, art 9(4).

methods for cargo removal or the removal of the ship's superstructure if these pose environmental threats or safety concerns.

The Affected State must decide on a reasonable deadline for the wreck removal which must be made known in writing to the registered owner making clear that if there is a failure to remove the wreck by the deadline, or if the hazard becomes particularly severe, the Affected State intends to intervene, in the first case after the deadline has passed and in the second case immediately.[311] Provided that notification to the registered owner and the flag State has been given the Affected State can proceed immediately to wreck removal actions when the hazard posed by the wreck is immediate.[312] This is one of the more controversial positions of the 2007 Nairobi Convention because it is applicable to all wrecks whether registered in Contracting States or not. The Affected State can also intervene where the wreck removal operation underway under the registered owner's authority is not done safely, or the protection of the marine environment is not taken into account; but the right of intervention in such a case is only limited to resolving these particular concerns.[313] Where the registered owner cannot be contacted, the Affected State may remove the wreck.[314]

The registered owner is liable for the costs of locating, marking and removing the wreck.[315] The liability is strict, that is, there is no requirement of proving fault of the registered owner. However, the owner's liability is exempted when the maritime incident that caused the wreck was wholly caused by an intentional act of a third party, that is sabotage or terrorism, or was due to war, hostilities or civil war or due to a natural phenomenon of "exceptional, inevitable and irresistible character" or due to fault of any Government or authority whether in a Contracting State or not in respect of navigational lights and aids.[316] In such cases the costs of wreck removal will fall on the Contracting State. The registered owner's rights of recourse against other parties are expressly preserved.[317]

The 2007 Nairobi Convention does not prescribe limits of liability for the registered owner. However, it leaves any existing rights of the registered owner under national or international limitation of liability regimes unaffected.[318] Thus, the available funds for compensation for wreck removal costs would depend on what limitation of liability regime is nationally available. In the UK wreck raising costs are presently excluded from limitation of liability.[319]

(iv) Compulsory insurance[320]

Compulsory insurance for ships of 300 gross tons and above registered in a Contracting State is imposed under Article 12(1). The applicable insurance should be to the respective national limits of liability but in no case higher than those specified under the 1976 LLMC (in the UK, the 1996 LLMC) in respect of the property damage part of the limitation fund as specified under

311. 2007 Nairobi Convention, art 9(6).
312. 2007 Nairobi Convention, art 9(8).
313. 2007 Nairobi Convention, art 9(5).
314. 2007 Nairobi Convention, art 9(7).
315. 2007 Nairobi Convention, art 10(2).
316. Art 10(1).
317. 2007 Nairobi Convention, art 10(4).
318. Art 10(2).
319. See MSA 1995, Schedule 7, Part II para 3(1).
320. See MSA 1995, s 255J for insurance requirements under the UK implementation, s 255K for the consequences of the failure to insure, s 255L for the powers to detain a ship that does not comply with s 255J, s 255M for the production of the insurance certificate and s 255N, 255O, 255P and 255Q for the issuance of the insurance certificate; its cancellation, third parties rights against the insurer and electronic certificates respectively.

Article 6(1)(b).[321] An insurance certificate must be carried on board[322] and direct action against the insurer is also provided. The insurer's liability[323] is always limited to the prescribed insurance limit, even if the shipowner is not entitled to limit liability under the applicable national regime.[324]

The insurance certificate is a prerequisite to trading in the Contracting States. Thus, ships flying the flag of Contracting States will not be permitted to trade without a valid insurance certificate.[325] In addition, only ships covered by wreck removal insurance would be permitted to use the ports or the offshore facilities of a Contracting State, irrespective of whether these are registered in Contracting States or not.[326] As a consequence a system for certification in relation to ships of a non-Contracting State which wish to trade in Contracting States is provided for.

Ships registered in non-Contracting States and not using the facilities of a Contracting coastal State are not subject to the requirements of carrying an insurance certificate. However, if they become wrecks they will become subject to the 2007 Nairobi Convention as this applies to all wrecks in the EEZ of a Contracting State, irrespective of the vessel's flag.[327]

The strongest argument for extending the application of the 2007 Nairobi Convention to the territorial waters of an Affected State is that some financial security for removal costs would be available, if a port of refuge is granted to the ship. Otherwise, as soon as the ship passes into territorial waters, the wreck removal insurance would not apply unless similar provisions are imposed under national law.

(v) Time bar

Actions for recovery against the registered owner and the insurer are time barred, three years from the date the hazard is determined.[328] In addition, an absolute time bar of six years from the time the casualty that led to the wreck happened is imposed.

(c) Wreck-raising contracts

There are standard form industry contracts namely the "Wreckstage 2010"[329] lump sum stage payment contract; the "Wreckhire 2010"[330] daily rate contract, and the "Wreckfixed 2010"[331] fixed price contract. These include knock-for-knock agreements similar to those which appear in TOWCON and TOWHIRE.

---

321. 2007 Nairobi Convention, art 12(1).
322. 2007 Nairobi Convention, art 12(2)-(9).
323. The insurer is entitled to all exemptions available to the registered owner and, in addition, is exempted when the wreck occurred due to wilful misconduct of the owner, art 12(10).
324. 2007 Nairobi Convention, art 12(10). This covers both the situation where the applicable regime does not provide for limited liability in respect of wreck removal costs, for example the present position under the 1995 MSA, or where limited liability is in general provided but the shipowner has lost its right to limit liability under the applicable regime.
325. 2007 Nairobi Convention, art 12(11).
326. 2007 Nairobi Convention, art 12(12). Such ships are not on innocent passage and therefore there is authority to impose such restrictions.
327. Whether there is a right to impose such liability in the EEZs was extensively disputed.
328. Art 13. In the UK implementation this is three years from the moment a wreck removal notice is given or six years from the incident. MSA 1995, s 255H.
329. Formerly Wreckstage 99.
330. Formerly Wreckhire 99.
331. Formerly Wreckfixed 99.

(d) Historic wrecks[332]

The increasing sophistication of diving equipment and remotely operated submersibles has placed virtually all sunken vessels within the reach of researchers and treasure hunters. This has raised some difficult questions of law. Under English law title to wreck remains in the owner of the ship at the time of her sinking and she remains under the jurisdiction of her flag State if she lies outside territorial waters. This has led to the enactment of statutes to prevent unrestricted "salvage" of historic wrecks where their preservation is considered necessary, in particular the Protection of Wrecks Act 1973 which enables the Secretary of State to designate such wrecks as protected wrecks if they are of historical, archaeological or artistic value. Military wrecks are protected by the Protection of Military Remains Act 1986, which applies to military wrecks outside the UK, but the protection is limited since the sanctions in that Act can only apply to British persons and those operating from British ships.

While these statutes create a legal regime of regulation, it is very difficult in practice to enforce such provisions due to the isolated location of most of the wrecks concerned.

Another problem is that by designating a wreck under the Protection of Wrecks Act 1973, the exact location of the wreck becomes a matter of public record, thus depriving the wreck of the secrecy which is in many cases its best protection.

Section 24 of the Merchant Shipping and Maritime Security Act 1997 contains provisions enabling the Secretary of State to implement international agreements relating to the protection of wrecks. In 2003 an order was made under that section with respect to the RMS *Titanic*,[333] which gives effect to an agreement between the governments of Britain, Canada, France and the USA.

Article 303 of UNCLOS 1982 places a duty on States to protect archaeological and historic objects found at sea and to co-operate for that purpose. Article 303(3) expressly preserves the rights of identifiable owners, the law of salvage and other rules of admiralty, and cultural exchange agreements. Article 149 provides that articles and objects found in the high seas shall be preserved or disposed of for the benefit of mankind as a whole.

The 2001 UNESCO Convention on the Protection of the Underwater Cultural Heritage[334] intends to provide an internationally agreed basis for preserving underwater cultural heritage, including wrecks, in all oceanic areas and expressly provides that these shall not be subject to the law of salvage. The 1989 Salvage Convention permits States a reservation which does not apply its provisions for maritime cultural heritage.[335] Thus the UNESCO Convention can, in principle, co-exist with salvage law. However, the wording refers to reservations made at the time of signing up to the Salvage Convention and does not provide for later reservations in this respect. There is ongoing debate as to whether the UK should become a party to the 2001 Underwater Cultural Heritage Convention.[336] The UK abstained from the vote adopting the Convention in 2001 and has not ratified due to concerns primarily about the influence the 2001 UNESCO Convention

---

332. For a detailed treatment of this interesting subject, see N. Gaskell and S. Dromgoole, "Interests in Wreck", in E. McKendrick and N. Palmer (eds) *Interests in Goods* (2nd edn, LLP 1998). See also N. Gaskell, *Merchant Shipping and Maritime Security Act 1997, Current Law Statutes.*

333. The Protection of Wrecks (RMS Titanic) Order 2003, SI 2003/2496.

334. For the full text of the Convention, see http://portal.unesco.org/en/ev.php-URL_ID=13520&URL_ DO=DO_ TOPIC&URL_SECTION=201.html (accessed 18 February 2017). This convention entered into force on 2 January 2009. It has 55 ratifications as at 18 February 2017.

335. Art 30(1)(d).

336. See UNESCO Convention on the Protection of Underwater Cultural Heritage: Next steps for the UK Government. UK National Commission for UNESCO, 2015.Policy Brief 17 available at: www.unesco.org.uk/wp-content/uploads/2015/05/UKNC-Policy-Brief-17_Underwater-Cultural-Heritage_March-2015_REVISED.pdf (accessed 19 February 2017).

may have on wrecks subject to sovereign immunity and the creeping jurisdiction by coastal States which could be considered to be facilitated by ambiguous wording. The UK has a management system for underwater cultural heritage under which the designation of a site as a monument triggers licensing requirements.[337] These, in turn, are developed by adopting the Rules, which are an Annex to the 2001 UNESCO Convention. Thus the management of UK declared sites is already consistent with the Convention. However, the Convention requires Contracting States to protect underwater cultural heritage generally which, it is feared, will require extensive restrictions and licensing with associated enforcement problems. The fact that the UK licensing system is already in line with the Convention's requirements means that the UK legal framework is compatible with the 2001 UNESCO Convention and the UK could sign up to the Convention without radical changes in its laws. It can also be argued that signing up to the Convention will facilitate the appropriate treatment of UK wrecks which exist in the jurisdictional areas of other States and which at the moment are a matter of bilateral negotiations as not all States consider such wrecks as being subjected to sovereign immunity or owned indefinitely by the flag State. It may be an appropriate act for the UK to ratify the 2001 UNESCO Convention if it wishes to continue to lead the way in underwater exploration and preservation of underwater maritime culture.

Note also that underwater cultural heritage can be protected from the effects of shipping activities under the notion of Particularly Sensitive Sea Areas declared by the IMO after application of interested States.[338]

7. PILOTAGE

(a) Introduction

A pilot is defined to be "any person not belonging to a ship who has the conduct thereof".[339] Pilots are usually master mariners with experience and knowledge of particular sea passages or approaches to harbours. They act as advisers under the ship's master's supervision to enhance the safety of navigation in difficult areas. They also act as a "principal source of skilled marine advice to the harbour authority".[340]

Pilotage can be compulsory or voluntary[341] and can also be distinguished between coastal and deep sea. Deep sea pilots are licensed by Trinity House[342] and coastal pilots by competent harbour authorities. Deep sea pilotage is not compulsory although it may become so in marine protected areas.[343] Compulsory pilotage is much more common in coastal areas and the approaches to harbours where collisions and accidents are more likely to happen. The most important legal issue in respect of pilotage is arguably who has to pay for damages caused by the pilot's negligence when the pilot is employed under compulsory and non-compulsory pilotage respectively. This will be discussed after explaining the statutory liability for the appointment, training and management of pilots.

---

337. This is managed by the Marine Management Organisation for England.

338. See IMO resolution A.982(24) Revised guidelines for the identification and designation of Particularly Sensitive Sea Areas (PSSAs). These can also be designated as Special Areas under the MARPOL Annexes.

339. Pilotage Act 1987, s 31(1).

340. Department for Transport, *Review of the Pilotage Act 1987 – Summary*, [16].

341. Government ships are not subject to pilotage directions.

342. Trinity House is also the Lighthouse Authority for England, Wales, the Channel Islands and Gibraltar. Pilotage Act 1987, s 23 gives power to the Secretary of State to authorise bodies to issue deep sea pilotage certificates.

343. For the difficulties under international law of the sea, see for example S. Bateman and M. White, "Compulsory Pilotage in the Torres Strait: Overcoming Unacceptable Risks to a Sensitive Marine Environment" (2009) 40(2) *Ocean Development and International Law* 184.

(b) Statutory provisions

The law related to pilotage has been radically revised under the Pilotage Act 1987[344] which trans-ferred responsibility from pilotage authorities to certain harbour authorities.[345] Such authorities have the power and the obligation under the Pilotage Act 1987, to decide whether and what type of pilotage services are needed in their area for each type of ship and whether pilotage should be compulsory.[346] In addition, such harbour authorities are authorised to provide the pilotage ser-vices,[347] to set the qualifications of pilots,[348] to authorise pilots[349] and to disqualify incompetent pilots.[350] Compulsory pilotage is determined by the issuance of pilotage directions by the har-bour authorities, empowered under the Pilotage Act 1987.[351] The competent harbour authority may charge for the pilotage services provided.[352]

If a ship is navigated in an area of compulsory pilotage without a pilot or without a master or first mate holding an exemption certificate, then the ship's master is guilty of an offence and liable on summary conviction.[353]

A review of the Pilotage Act 1987 undertaken by the Department of Transport has led to the development of the Port Maritime Safety Code.[354] While the review and the code identified significant improvements that need to be made in respect of the training and licensing of pilots and advocated the use of port passage plans, it did not suggest any changes in the liability regime applicable under the Pilotage Act 1987, except perhaps in clarifying that the performance required by the competent harbour authorities in order to discharge their statutory obligations under the act must be consistent with the Port Maritime Safety Code.

(c) Liability for the faults of ships under pilotage

Where a ship which is under the command of a pilot causes damage the question can be raised as to who would be responsible for the damage. The pilot himself, the owner, as well as the authorising harbour authority have to be considered.

---

344. Partly amended under the Marine Navigation Act 2013.

345. Only harbour authorities of ports within pilotage districts as described under the Pilotage Act 1983 and which already have responsibility for the safety of navigation are authorised as competent harbour authorities. A total of 127 harbour authorities presently have pilotage functions, although over 20 appear not to exercise them. Around 800 pilots are employed, many as part timers, with about 70 per cent of them involved with the ten larger port authorities. See Department for Transport, *Review of the Pilotage Act 1987 – Summary*.

346. See *Oceangas (Gibraltar) Ltd v Port of London Authority (The Cavendish)* [1993] 2 Lloyd's Rep 292 for the rejection of an argument that s 2 imposes a positive liability on the competent authority on which the claimant shipowner can rely for a claim for damages caused by pilot's negligence.

347. Pilotage Act 1987, s 2. In deciding so the harbour authority should take into account the risks of the carriage of hazardous and dangerous goods.

348. Pilotage Act 1987, s 3.

349. The power of the harbour authority to appoint new pilots is subject to the approval of existing authorised pilots. See Pilotage Act 1987, s 4.

350. Pilotage Act 1987, s 3. Disqualification occurs when there is incompetence or misconduct in the capacity of a pilot or when qualifications have expired. Licences can also be revoked when the number of pilots exceeds the set limits or where it is appropriate to do so. See s 3(5). See also *Cooper v Forth Ports Plc* [2009] CSOH 160.

351. Pilotage Act 1987, s 7. If compulsory pilotage concerns areas outside a harbour, the harbour authority should apply for a harbour revision order under s 14 of the Harbours Act 1964 to extend the limits of the harbour (see Pilotage Act 1987, s 7(3)). Exemption certificates may be issued when appropriate (see Pilotage Act 1987, s 8) and ships less than 20 metres long and fishing boats less than 47.5 metres long are exempted (see Pilotage Act 1987, s 7(1)(3)).

352. Pilotage Act 1987, s 9. Claims for pilotage fees are supported by an action *in rem* under the Senior Courts Act 1981, s 20(2), which can lead to the arrest of the ship.

353. Pilotage Act 1987, ss 15(2) and 15(3).The offence is heavier where a pilot has offered services and the master rejected such an offer. See also Pilotage Act 1987, s 17.

354. www.gov.uk/government/uploads/system/uploads/attachment_data/file/564723/port-marine-safety-code.pdf (accessed 19 February 2017).

(i) Liability of the pilot

Pilots are liable for acts or omissions which cause "loss, destruction or serious damage" or "personal injury or death"[355] only where they act deliberately or under the influence of drugs or drink, or their act or omission amounts to a breach or neglect of duty.[356] In such circumstances fines and prison sentences may be imposed upon pilots. The criminal liability provisions under section 21 are not restricted to authorised pilots.[357]

The Pilotage Act 1987 limits the civil liability of an authorised pilot.[358] The liability cannot exceed £1,000 and the pilotage fee.[359] The latter can be up to a few thousand pounds for larger vessels and which varies between ports. The limits of liability available to the pilot are arguably absolute, because there is no provision under which the pilot may lose the right to limit his liability. In addition, claims by third parties against the pilot would be limited under the 1996 LLMC.[360]

There is no limitation for unauthorised pilots under the Pilotage Act 1987. Presumably unauthorised pilots would be considered as crew and will be protected against third party claims by the 1996 LLMC.

(ii) Liability of the harbour authority

The harbour authority is not liable just because it has licensed a pilot whose acts or omissions have caused damage.[361] Fault by the competent harbour authority itself must be demonstrated. Arguably the fault of the competent harbour authority may be based most probably on a breach of its statutory duties.

Pilots usually have a contractual arrangement, normally a contract of employment with the harbour authority.[362] The question then arises whether the negligence of the pilot imposes vicarious liability on the employing harbour authority, or on the shipowner or on both.[363]

In respect of non-compulsory pilotage vicarious liability cannot arise for the harbour authority simply because it does not exercise any statutory power. The owner can employ any adviser he wishes to assist with the ship's navigation. Only where the shipowner requests an appropriately qualified pilot and later it is revealed that the pilot's licence was granted or remained in force in breach of a duty of the licensing authority, liability could potentially arise but not as vicarious liability in respect of the pilot's actions or omissions.

The situation may be different when the ship suffers or causes damage while under the command of a compulsory pilot. There is an argument then to be made that vicarious liability for

355. Pilotage Act 1987, s 21(1).
356. Ibid.
357. Pilotage Act 1987, s 21(2).
358. The limitation of liability applies even where the ship is outside the area of compulsory pilotage provided that she is navigating to or from the usual place where pilots are picked up (Pilotage Act 1987, s 22(2)).
359. Pilotage Act 1987, s 21(2).
360. 1995 MSA, Schedule 7, art 1(4) states: "If any claims set out in Article 2 are made against any person for whose act, neglect or default the shipowner or salvor is responsible, such person shall be entitled to avail himself of the limitation of liability provided for in this Convention." This would cover pilots as, under English law, shipowners are responsible for their acts. In this case, art 4 of the LLMC provides the test for breaking limitation.
361. Pilotage Act 1987, s 22(8).
362. This is not precluded by the fact that the harbour authority discharges statutory duties by employing pilots. See *Transport and General Workers Union v Associated British Ports Limited* [2001] EWCA Civ 2032.
363. The possibility of joint liability arose only recently: *Viasystems (Tyneside) Ltd v Thermal Transfer (Northern) Ltd and Others* [2005] EWCA Civ 1151; [2006] QB 510. No pilotage claim has been decided after this case was considered. However, it is submitted that the interpretation of s 16 of the Pilotage Act 1987 is probably conclusive in restricting any liability to the shipowner alone, especially as there is no particular policy reason to impose liability on the harbour authority too.

damage to third parties may not attach to the shipowner but to the authority imposing the pilot on the shipowner. Moreover, in such a case it may also be argued that any damage to the property of the licensing authority caused by the pilot's negligence should not be recoverable and additionally the shipowner may be able to recover against the harbour authority.

All the above arguments have been rejected either by court decisions or statutorily.

Up to the coming into force of the Pilotage Act 1913, case law supported the proposition that in respect of compulsory pilotage the shipowner's liability was excluded.[364] However, the introduction of section 15(1) of the Pilotage Act 1913 reversed the position.[365] The relevant section states:

Notwithstanding anything in any public or local Act, the owner or master of a vessel navigating under circumstances in which pilotage is compulsory shall be answerable for any loss or damage caused by the vessel or by any fault of the navigation of the vessel in the same manner as he would if pilotage were not compulsory.

Thus in *The Esso Bernicia*[366] the House of Lords held that no vicarious liability attaches to the general employer of a pilot for two reasons. First, because the pilot navigates the ship as a principal, not as a servant of his general employer. Second, because of the application of section 15(1) of the Pilotage Act 1913.

The relevant provision presently is section 16 of the Pilotage Act 1987 which states:

The fact that a ship is being navigated in an area and in circumstances in which pilotage is compulsory for it shall not affect any liability of the owner or master of the ship for any loss or damage caused by the ship or by the manner in which it is navigated.

Taken within the historical context of section 15(1) of the Pilotage Act 1913, section 16 of the Pilotage Act 1987 has been held to impose liability for the negligence of a compulsory pilot on shipowners in respect of claims by third parties and make the pilot the servant of the shipowner in all respects, even where this concerns the damage suffered by the shipowner.[367]

Thus it appears clear that whether the pilotage is compulsory or not there is no vicarious liability[368] attaching to the competent harbour authority for actions of the pilot either in respect of claims by third parties or in respect of claims made by the shipowner.

The liability of the competent harbour authority is anyway limited under the Pilotage Act 1987 in respect of loss of or damage to the ship under pilotage and any property on it, loss of or damage to any other ship or property onboard such ship as well as to any other property or rights.[369] The applicable limits of liability are calculated by multiplying the number of authorised pilots employed by the harbour authority by £1,000. However, the harbour authority loses the right to limit liability if it is proven that the loss or damage was caused by a personal act or omission of the harbour authority which was intentional or reckless and with knowledge that the damage would probably have resulted.[370] The provisions that apply to a competent harbour authority also apply to any agent authorised to undertake pilotage services.[371]

---

364. *The Maria* [1869] 1 W Rob 95.
365. *Workington Harbour and Dock Board v Towerfield (Owners) (The Towerfield)* [1951] AC 112.
366. *Esso Petroleum Co Ltd v Hall Russell & Co Ltd (The Esso Bernicia)* [1989] 1 Lloyd's Rep 8.
367. *The Cavendish* (fn 246).
368. An argument based on a contractual agreement between the shipowner and the harbour authority on implied terms was also rejected in *The Cavendish* (fn 346), where it was held to be no more than an arrangement to facilitate the shipowner to discharge his statutory obligation for compulsory pilotage, no contract existed.
369. Pilotage Act 1987, s 22(3).
370. See Pilotage Act 1987, s 22(3), where the test to be satisfied is that under art 4 of the 1996 LLMC. For the meaning of the test, see Pilotage Act 1987, s 7.
371. Pilotage Act 1987, s 22(4).

There is no right to limit liability for loss of life or personal injury under the Pilotage Act 1987. Consequently, for such claims the liability of the harbour authority or any authorised agent is unlimited.

Provisions for the payment into court of the limitation amount and powers granted to the court to distribute these funds appropriately and stay pending proceedings are provided under section 22(6) of the Pilotage Act 1987.

From the wording of the Pilotage Act 1987 the provisions applicable to competent harbour authorities, the exclusions of liability and the relevant limitation of liability do not extend to any body authorised under section 23 in respect of deep sea pilotage. Thus it appears that the liability of such bodies would be unlimited

(iii) Shipowner's vicarious liability

As explained, section 16 of the Pilotage Act 1987[372] provides that the liability of the owner and the master of the ship is not affected in any way for "any loss or damage caused by the ship or by the manner in which it is navigated".[373] As discussed earlier, this provision has been deemed to impose liability on the shipowner in respect of the acts or omissions of the pilot during compulsory pilotage and to assimilate it to the long-standing position in respect of non-compulsory pilotage that the pilot's actions make the shipowner vicariously liable.[374]

The establishment of limitation rights for pilots and competent harbour authorities does not affect the right of the shipowner or others to limit liability.[375]

8. LIMITATION OF LIABILITY

(a) Introduction

Shipowners and certain others connected with the operation of a ship enjoy the privilege of limiting their liability.[376] Because liability is limited and known the shipowner can deposit with an appropriate court the full amount it may be liable for and thus be free of further liability or legal actions and security measures against its property, such as ship arrest in respect of these claims. The shipowner can therefore avoid multiple litigation and security demands in various jurisdictions and continue trading, leaving the claimants and the court managing the limitation fund to arrange for the distribution of the claims.

Limitation of liability was originally developed to reduce the personal exposure of the shipowner and protect its property in cases where the ship's master and crew were negligent or acted intentionally.[377] Such cases risked financial ruin for the shipowners and were catered for

372. Under common law the liability of the shipowner was excluded when the ship was under compulsory pilotage. See *The Maria* (fn 364).

373. Pilotage Act 1987, s 16.

374. *The Cavendish* (fn 346).

375. Pilotage Act 1987, s 21(7).

376. Arguments for and against limitation of liability can be found in Lord Mustill, "Ships are Different – Or are They?"[1993] LMCLQ 490 and D. Steel QC, "Ships are Different: The Case for Limitation of Liability" [1995] LMCLQ 77.

377. This explanation links vicarious liability with the right to limit and naturally leads to the conclusion that where liability of the shipowner is personal then limitation of liability should not be available. See, for example, D.C. Greenman, "Limitation of Liability Unlimited" (2001) 32(2) *Journal of Maritime Law and Commerce* 279. This arrangement is reflected in the 1851 US Limitation Act and was reflected in the wording of the older international limitation conventions, including the 1957 Limitation Convention, and was changed only in the 1976 LLMC. See also *JD Irving Ltd v Siemens Canada Ltd and Others (The "SPM 125")* 2016 FC 287, a Canadian decision on contractors who are not entitled to limit liability.

by express rights to avoid liability where the ship and freight were abandoned to creditors. This practice was developed in several continental countries, but was not introduced in England until 1733.[378] Limitation of liability has expanded in time to cover more persons and also to protect these persons better by making it almost an undisputable right.

Presently, shipowners (and certain others) are entitled to limit their liability in two different contexts. The original right to limit liability has led to the development of global limitation regimes for which the only purpose is the establishment of the right to limit without altering the applicable substantive liability rules. By contrast, special liability regimes for, *inter alia*, oil pollution and carriage of goods or passengers also provide for an entitlement to limited liability but this is coupled with liability rules which modify the ordinary legal position. In that context limitation of liability is arguably more justifiable as it forms part of the package deal rather than a separate entitlement. In this section we will deal with global limitation regimes.

Three international conventions provide shipowners (and certain others) with an almost global ability to limit. These conventions[379] are the 1924 Limitation Convention, the International Convention relating to the Limitation of Liability of Owners of Sea-Going Ships (Brussels 1957) (1957 Limitation Convention) and the Convention on Limitation of Liability for Maritime Claims (London 1976) (1976 LLMC), together with the Protocol of 1996 amending the Convention on Limitation of Liability for Maritime Claims of 19 November 1976 (1996 LLMC). The 1976 LLMC and its 1996 Protocol are in force in the UK.[380] We will refer to the amended 1976 LLMC as the 1996 LLMC. An amendment to the 1996 Protocol was agreed on 19 April 2012 and came into force on 8 June 2015. The UK enacted the new limits which are, since 30 November 2016, in force in the UK.[381]

These conventions apply whether the claims are classified as occurring in tort, delict, contract or on some other basis.[382] However, not every claim against a shipowner is subject to limitation of liability under these conventions.

Shipowners also in practice limit their liability by forming "one ship" companies; however, this method is part of general corporate law and is not in any way unique to the shipping industry.

(b) Who is entitled to limit liability?

Article 1 of the 1996 LLMC prescribes that "shipowners", salvors, persons for whose acts the shipowner or the salvor are responsible and the insurers of particular liabilities have the right to limit their liability. The registered owner, the charterer, the manager and the operator of a seagoing ship are deemed to be within the Convention's definition of a shipowner[383] and thus entitled to limit their liability. The liability of these persons for actions against the ship (*in rem*) is also subject to limitation.[384]

---

378. The triggering event was, according to K. McGuffie (ed.), *Marsden on the Law of Collisions at Sea* (11th edn, Stevens & Sons Ltd 1961), [175] the case of *Boucher v Lawson* [1734] Cas Temp Hardw 85 in which personal liability of the shipowner was established for the value of a cargo of bullion stolen by the ship's master. This led to legislation establishing rights of limited liability for such incidents which were gradually in time expanded.

379. Parties entitled to limit liability differs between the various conventions.

380. MSA 1995, ss 185–186.

381. The MSA 1995 (Amendment) Order 2016, SI 2016/1061 amends the limits of liability in Schedule 7 of the 1995 MSA and enacts the 2012 LLMC protocol into English law.

382. That is how the somehow misleading term "global limitation" has come into existence. Limitation under these regimes is "global" in the sense that the liability of the shipowner does not have to arise from a specific liability head. However, the term "global" also gives the impression that this right is always available against all shipowners' liability which, as we will see later, is not true.

383. 1996 LLMC, art 1(2).

384. 1996 LLMC, art 1(5).

Demise charterers also enjoy the right to limit liability.[385] The term "charterer" has been decided[386] to include a time charterer and voyage as well as slot charterers.[387] Both decisions were in the context of the Senior Courts Act 1981. However, the same position appears to have been adopted in respect of the 1996 LLMC.[388] Thus demise charterers, voyage and time charterers as well as slot charters can limit liability.[389]

The ship's managers and operators are also entitled to limit their liability. The ordinary meaning of the words would certainly include the managing owners but it is uncertain whether managers and operators of a part of the shipping activity, for example, recruitment, would be covered. The management contract should be valid and not frustrated or repudiated in order for the right of limitation to be available. Where the management of the ship is taken over by a bank or other creditor under a mortgage agreement there could also be difficulties as the mortgagee in possession is not the owner of the ship,[390] but may be considered as the operator of the ship.[391] An alternative route is to suggest that the mortgage agreement provides the consent of the owner for the mortgagee to act as the manager, entitling it to limit liability.

Persons for whose act, neglect or default the shipowner or the salvor are responsible are also entitled to limited liability. The purpose of this provision is to avoid circumvention of the right to limit by claimants suing the individual wrongdoer rather than the shipowner.[392] The extension of the right to limit to persons for whom the shipowner is responsible clearly covers the master and the crew members when they act within the scope of their employment. However, anyone who can show that s/he is linked with the shipowner in a way that makes the shipowner responsible would also be entitled to limit liability. Pilots may be subject to this provision because under English law their negligence makes the owner liable.[393] However, in England pilots may also limit their liability under section 22 of the Pilotage Act 1987 to a much lower limit.[394] Independent contractors as well as others involved in the shipping business are arguably not included in the definition. Thus, ship's agents, stevedores and classification societies[395] are probably not entitled to limit their liability.

Salvors are also expressly entitled to limit their liability.[396] When salvors operate from a ship they are considered to be shipowners and therefore are entitled to limit their liability. However, when they do not operate from a ship they will not fall under the definition of a shipowner.[397]

---

385. *The Hopper No 66* [1908] AC 126 (HL).
386. *The Span Terza* [1982] 1 Lloyd's Rep 225.
387. *MSC Mediterranean Shipping Co SA v Polish Ocean Lines (The Tychy)* [1999] 2 Lloyd's Rep 11.
388. This much can be deduced from *The Aegean Sea*, a voyage charterparty case, and the *CMA CGM SA v Classica Shipping Co Ltd (The CMA Djakarta)* [2003] 2 Lloyd's Rep 50, where the right of the voyage and time charterers to limited liability was challenged by the shipowners only to the extent that it applied to indemnity claims by the shipowners and not in general. In the latter case, Longmore LJ stated that the concession, that a charterer when sued by a cargo-owner is entitled to limit, is "obviously correct" – see *CMA CGM SA v Classica Shipping Co Ltd (The CMA Djakarta)* [2004] 1 Lloyd's Rep 460, [16].
389. *Metvale Ltd v Monsanto International Sarl (The MSC Napoli)* [2009] 1 Lloyd's Rep 246.
390. *Collins v Lamport* [1864] 4 De G J & Sim 500; 46 ER 1012.
391. A statement to this effect is included in G. Bowtle and K. McGuiness, *The Law of Ship Mortgages* (Informa Law 2001), at 189.
392. This was successful in *Adler v Dickson and Another (The Himalaya)* [1954] 2 Lloyd's Rep 267.
393. See *Esso Petroleum Co Ltd v Hall Russell & Co Ltd (The Esso Bernicia)* [1989] 1 Lloyd's Rep 8. In addition authorised pilots are entitled to limit liability under s 16 of the Pilotage Act 1987.
394. £1,000.
395. Under English law classification societies do not owe a duty of care and do not become liable to third parties for financial losses. See *Marc Rich & Co AG and Others v Bishop Rock Marine Co Ltd and Nippon Kaiji Kyokai (The Nicholas H)* [1995] 2 Lloyd's Rep 299. However, where loss of life occurs there could be liability put on them – see *Perrett v Collins and Others* [1998] 2 Lloyd's Rep 255.
396. 1996 LLMC, art 1(1).
397. *The Tojo Maru* [1971] 1 Lloyd's Rep 341 (HL).

Accordingly, the express statement in Article 1(1) ensures that salvors are always entitled to limit their liability. The definition of a salvor is wide and probably includes any person involved in wreck removal.[398]

Liability insurers of shipowners in respect of claims subject to limitation are also given the right to limit liability under the 1976 LLMC[399] "to the same extent" as the insured.[400]

Persons that do not fall within the Article 1 definitions would not be able to limit liability under the 1996 LLMC.[401] Other entities, in particular port authorities as well as owners of docks and canals, can limit liability on the basis of section 191 of the MSA 1995. The right to limit arises on the basis of the relevant section of the MSA 1995 and is therefore independent from the 1996 LLMC.[402]

(c) Can owners limit liability against each other?

Persons entitled to limit liability under the 1976 LLMC may of course bring claims against each other. Their contractual relationship will determine the legal basis of such claims.[403] If, for example, there is a cargo claim against the charterer, the charterer would be entitled to limit its liability against the cargo owner. However, if the charterer pays the claim in full and then tries to recover from the shipowner, the shipowner would be entitled to limit its liability against the charterer in exactly the same way as if the claim was directly from the cargo owner against the shipowner. This is consistent with the historical development of the limitation of liability as a protectionist measure for the benefit of the owner and the extension of the shipowners' privilege to other persons. However, when the cargo claim is brought against the shipowner who pays up and then tries to recover from the charterer, in such a case is the charterer also entitled to invoke limitation of liability against the shipowner? Such a result would be a significant expansion of the scope of limitation beyond the protection of the shipowner, who may consequently face limited recovery for damages incurred in the shipping business.

The historical development of limitation of liability suggests that a charterer would only be entitled to limit its liability where it acts "in the shoes" of the shipowner. To this effect were the first instance decisions in *The Aegean Sea*[404] and in *The CMA Djakarta*.[405]

However, the first instance decision in *The CMA Djakarta* was unanimously reversed by the Court of Appeal.[406] The Court of Appeal noted that the construction of any international convention should be made without any English law preconceptions and that it must not be controlled

---

398. 1996 LLMC, art 2(l)(d), (1)(e) and (1)(t).

399. This was another innovation of the 1976 LLMC.

400. 1996 LLMC, art 1(6). This has been seen as problematic in respect of the interpretation of s 1 of the Third Parties (Right Against Insurers) Act 1930 in *Firma C-Trade SA Respondents v Newcastle Protection and Indemnity Association (The Fanti)* [1990] 3 WLR 78; [1990] 2 Lloyd's Rep 191. Section 1 in essence permits direct recovery by claimants from the insurers in cases where the assured has been wound up. However, the House of Lords in *The Fanti* considered this right to be subject to the express terms of the contract of insurance. In that case there was a requirement that the claimant was to be paid by the insured for the insured to obtain a right of collecting the insurance from its P&I Club. See Chapter 11, page 487.

401. Persons who are not residents or do not have a principal place of business in a party State and would otherwise have been entitled to limit liability can be excluded by a party State under art 15(1). The UK has not provided for any such exclusion.

402. However, the determination of the limits of liability for these entities is based on the tonnage of the largest UK ship that has visited these facilities and they are calculated by reference to arts 6 and 7 of the 1996 LLMC. Similarly, the constitution of a limitation fund is also prescribed on the basis of arts 11 and 12 of the 1996 LLMC.

403. The same applies for all claims subject to limitation of liability.

404. *Aegean Sea Traders Corp v Repsol Petroleo and Another (The Aegean Sea)* [1998] 2 Lloyd's Rep 39.

405. *CMA CGM SA v Classica Shipping Co Ltd (The CMA Djakarta)* [2003] EWHC 641 (Comm); [2003] 2 Lloyd's Rep 50.

406. [2004] EWCA Civ 114; [2004] 1 Lloyd's Rep 460.

by domestic principles of construction.[407] They also noted that the ordinary meaning of the word "charterer" includes a charterer, whether it acts as a charterer or in any other capacity. As a result, charterers as well as managers and operators enjoy the same rights as shipowners, thus making the effect of the 1996 LLMC much wider than shipowners would have expected.

(d) Which ships are subject to limitation of liability?

The 1996 LLMC applies to the owner of a seagoing ship.[408] However, the UK government extended the application of the right to limit to owners of non-seagoing ships,[409] thus removing the need for determining the distinction between seagoing and non-seagoing ships and granting the same right of limited liability to shipowners of non-seagoing ships.

The reference to a ship "includes references to any structure (whether completed or in course of completion) launched and intended for use in navigation as a ship or part of a ship".[410] Under English case law this is usually decided as a matter of fact on a case-by-case basis taking into account the use of the particular structure in question in navigation and also the policy reasons or the practicalities that may suggest that a structure should or should not be described as a ship. The term "used in navigation" is arguably not satisfied by "controlled travel over water" but "ordered progression over the water from one place to another".[411] Thus jet skis do not satisfy the "use in navigation" criterion,[412] while a jack-up oil rig was considered under a different statute[413] to fulfil the navigation criteria[414] even if its primary purpose was not navigation.

Special rights are granted under the 1996 LLMC to each party State in respect of the limitation arrangements for vessels smaller than 300 tons.[415] In the UK the MSA 1995, Schedule 7, Part II, Para 5, sets out the limits of liability for ships smaller than 300 tons. Government ships are also subject to the 1996 LLMC.[416]

The 1976 LLMC expressly excludes aircushion vehicles and floating platforms for the exploration and exploitation of natural resources.[417] However, as the MSA 1995 does not include the

---

407. Ibid. One can of course counter-argue that the development of limitation of liability and the creation of the 1976 LLMC (and its predecessors) can and should be considered in the light of the preconceptions of English law that are common with the other parties to the 1976 LLMC as they must have been part of the basis of the agreement in forming the Convention.

408. 1976 LLMC, art 2.

409. MSA 1995, Schedule 7, Part II, para 2. This was based on an express right under the 1976 LLMC, art 15(2), to legislate for vessels of inland navigation. The extension of the right of a shipowner to limit liability irrespective of whether its vessel is seagoing or not goes back to 1894 (see s 503).

410. MSA 1995, Schedule 7, Part II, para 12. Notably, the inclusion of the term "under construction" would extend the right to limit to shipowners of vessels not yet completed but launched. However, it is unclear when, at the end of the life of the vessel, such right is lost. For example, would under any circumstances a claim by injured workers involved in the dismantling of the ship give a right to limitation to the owner, probably the shipyard? Arguably, while the vessel is still in the water the right would exist. It is also arguable that even if she is out of the water and retains the characteristics of a ship (able to float and capable of use in navigation) the right still exists and is only lost when the structure no longer falls within the definition of a ship.

411. *R v Goodwin (Mark)* [2005] EWCA Crim 3184; [2006] 1 Lloyd's Rep 432, citing with approval *Steedman v Scofield and Another* [1992] 2 Lloyd's Rep 163, and considering *The Von Rocks* [1998] 2 Lloyd's Rep 198, *Perks v Clark* [2001] EWCA Civ 1228; [2001] 2 Lloyd's Rep 431; and *Curtis v Wild* [1991] 4 All ER 172 which contain *dicta* favouring a wider interpretation of the term "navigation". Thus, it was held in that case that "the words 'used in navigation' excluded from the definition of 'ship or vessel' craft that were simply used for having fun on the water without the object of going anywhere, into which category jet skis plainly fell".

412. *R v Goodwin (Mark)* (fn 411); *Steedman v Scofield and Another* (fn 411). Arguably, this is so for most small recreational vessels not capable of navigating long distances.

413. Merchant Shipping Act 1894.

414. *Clark (Inspector of Taxes) v Perks* [2001] EWCA Civ 1228; [2001] 2 Lloyd's Rep 431.

415. 1976 LLMC, art 15(2).

416. MSA 1995, s 192.

417. 1976 LLMC, art 15(5).

particular article, it follows that the exclusion is not operative in England. The question whether such structures can be considered as ships remains and may restrict the application of the Convention to such structures. In relation to hovercraft specific legislation, making part of the 1996 LLMC applicable to them, has been enacted.[418]

Ships engaged in drilling, whether specifically constructed for this purpose or adapted, while engaged in drilling may be excluded from the 1996 LLMC if national legislation provides for higher limits of liability or when the particular State is a party to a specialised convention applicable to such ships.[419] These provisions are not enacted in the MSA 1995 and therefore such craft, provided that they fulfil the definition of a ship, are also subject to the application of the 1996 LLMC.

(e) Claims subject to limitation of liability

Claims under Article 2 and not excluded by Article 3 of the 1976 LLMC are subject to limitation. These are subject to limitation, whether the liability arises in contract, tort or by statute[420] and whether they are enforced by personal action against the owner or other person or against the ship.[421] Provided that the claims are within the words of Article 2(1), they will be subject to limitation of liability even if brought by way of recourse or for indemnity under a contract.[422]

Loss of life, personal injury, loss of or damage to property claims, as well as consequential losses, are all subject to limitation provided that they occur either on board or in direct connection with the operation[423] of the ship or a salvage operation. While damage on board is rather well defined, the extent of the term "direct connection with the operation of the ship" is not as easy to determine. The term expresses the "necessary linkage" between the loss suffered and "the ship in respect of which a claim is made".[424] However, it is unclear which damage and when is in direct connection with the ship's operation.

In *The Caspian Basin*, Rix J considered whether a claim for loss of a tow arising in part out of misrepresentation as to the tug's bollard pull and brake horsepower (BHP) was a claim "occurring . . . in direct connection with the operation of the ship" within Article 2(1)(a) of the 1976 LLMC. His decision was based on the fact that the loss claimed was that of the tow which he held to be in direct connection with the operation of the ship.

In *The Breydon Merchant*[425] Sheen J held that a claim by the charterer for salvage contribution is subject to Article 2(1)(a) even if not accompanied by physical damage to the cargo. The point was conceded in *The Darfur*.[426]

In *The Aegean Sea*[427] destruction of the bunkers, pollution damage and clean-up costs arising from the grounding of a vessel on rocks because of the breach of a safe port warranty under an ASBATANKVOY charterparty were also "in direct connection with the operation of the ship".

---

418. Hovercraft (Civil Liability) Order 1986, amended by the Hovercraft (Convention on Limitation of Liability for Maritime Claims (Amendment)) Order 1998.

419. 1976 LLMC, art 15(4).

420. *The Breydon Merchant* [1992] 1 Lloyd's Rep 373.

421. 1976 LLMC, art 1(5).

422. Ibid., art 2(2).

423. The term "operation of the ship" was considered in *The Aegean Sea* [1998] 2 Lloyd's Rep 39 to include everything that goes to the operation of the ship.

424. See the judgment of Rix J in *Caspian Basin Specialised Emergency Salvage Administration and Another v Bouygues Offshore SA and Others (The Caspian Basin)* [1997] 2 Lloyd's Rep 507, at p 522, upheld by the Court of Appeal [1998] 2 Lloyd's Rep 461, at p 472.

425. *The Breydon Merchant* (fn 420).

426. *Blue Nile Shipping Company Ltd and Another v Iguana Shipping and Finance Inc and Others (The Darfur)* [2004] EWHC 1506 (Admlty); [2004] 2 Lloyd's Rep 469.

427. [1998] 2 Lloyd's Rep 39.

In *The CMA Djakarta* cargo claims arising from the shipment of undeclared dangerous goods under a charterparty were also considered to be "in direct connection with the operation of the ship" and thus subject to limitation.[428]

Both in *The Aegean Sea*[429] and *The CMA Djakarta*,[430] which involved indemnity claims by the shipowners against the charterers, all five judges considered the wording of Article 2(1) (a) as incapable of including in the limitation right damage suffered by the ship by reference to which the limits of liability are calculated.[431] Therefore such claims, usually brought by the owner against the charterer, are not subject to limitation of liability. These decisions also exclude claims related to losses consequential to the loss of the ship, in particular salvage expenses and General Average incurred by the shipowners[432] and a claim for freight not earned.[433] The decision in the CMA Djakarta was confirmed by the Supreme Court in *The Ocean Victory, [2017] UKSC 35, May 10, 2017.*

In *The Darfur*,[434] following the collision of the *Darfur* with the *Happy Fellow*, claims by the charterer of the *Darfur* against the shipowner in respect of the *Darfur* being off hire, increased insurance costs to cover the deviation after the collision, discharge and transhipment costs for the cargo, loss of use of the relevant containers for the period between the casualty and transhipment, hiring, bunkering and insuring alternative tonnage, loss of business and loss of profit were all considered to be claims consequential to the loss of the vessel and thus not subject to limitation.

In *Qenos Pty Ltd v Ship "APL Sydney"*[435] the Federal Court of Australia had to consider whether the reference to consequential loss under Article 2(1)(a) of the 1976 LLMC was restricted to consequential losses incurred by a party that had suffered loss of life, personal injury or property damage. The case concerned the disruption of the provision of ethane by pipeline to two companies involved in the production of derivatives of ethane, neither of which were the owners of the pipeline. The *APL Sydney* had drifted and dragged its anchor into the pipeline, causing an interruption in its use. The owners of the *APL Sydney* had applied to limit their liability. The claimants claimed for their economic losses. The key point at stake was that the claimants had not suffered any loss of life, personal injury or property damage resulting from the incident. The Federal Court of Australia took the view that the meaning of consequential loss in Article 2(1)(a) of the 1976 LLMC is not restricted to losses suffered by claimants who had already suffered loss of life, personal injury or property damage. This approach has merit. Given that the limitation right is granted for the purpose of protecting the shipowners from the consequences of the ship's activities, it is inconsistent to restrict the notion of consequential damage to damage consequent on the claimant's own physical damage or loss of life or personal injury. It is more consistent to interpret the section as covering damage consequential to the incident in which the ship is involved in more general terms. Notably, the issue would not have arisen in this form under English law because recovery for this type of loss, i.e. economic, is not permissible as a

428. *CMA CGM SA v Classica Shipping Co Ltd (The CMA Djakarta)* [2004] EWCA Civ 114; [2004] 1 Lloyd's Rep 460, reversing the first instance decision.
429. [1998] 2 Lloyd's Rep 39.
430. *CMA CGM SA v Classica Shipping Co Ltd (The CMA Djakarta)* (fn 428), in agreement on this point with the first instance decision: [2003] EWHC 641 (Comm); [2003] 2 Lloyd's Rep 50.
431. Probably a stronger argument is the consequence the opposite decision would have had on other claimants of the limitation fund.
432. *CMA CGM SA v Classica Shipping Co Ltd (The CMA Djakarta)* (fn 428).
433. If freight is earned it is due in full.
434. *Blue Nile Shipping Company Ltd and Another v Iguana Shipping and Finance Inc and Others (The Darfur)* [2004] 2 Lloyd's Rep. 469.
435. *Qenos Pty Ltd v Ship "APL Sydney"* [2009] FCA 1090.

matter of English law,[436] whereas the Australian courts have permitted the recovery of at least some types of economic losses.[437]

The 1996 LLMC under Article 7 covers loss of life and personal injury as well as consequential damage. However, in the UK the application of this is excluded pursuant to the right to regulate otherwise contained in the new Article 15(3*bis*) of the 1996 LLMC.[438] As a result, in UK law the 1996 LLMC does not cover passengers of seagoing vessels.

Under Article 2(1)(b) claims in respect of loss resulting from delay in the carriage by sea of cargo, passengers or their luggage are also subject to limitation of liability. Because there is no definition of luggage, the word arguably encompasses in its ordinary meaning all types of luggage including valuables. The 1974 Athens Convention expressly provides that vehicles are luggage for its purpose.[439] It is at least doubtful that the ordinary meaning of luggage includes vehicles. However, the 1974 Athens Convention definition may be used as an indication of the internationally acceptable meaning of the term.

Under Article 2(1)(c) claims in respect of other loss resulting from infringement of rights other than contractual rights, occurring in direct connection with the operation of the ship or salvage operations are also subject to limitation of liability. While Article 2(1)(a) is concerned with losses and damage linked with property damage or loss of life, Article 2(1)(c) covers claims from parties that may have suffered losses not linked to property damage. In *The Aegean Sea*[440] loss of use and loss of profit by users of the sea and the coasts, in particular owners of fishing boats and yachts, fish and shellfish farm owners, local shop owners, local municipalities, local governments and the coastal State, were held to fall in this category. The category is very broad and taking into account that Article 2 is not restricted in general by the legal nature of the claim the only evident exclusion is that of contractual rights as expressed in the provision itself. Therefore, any actionable rights available through national or international law to users of the coastal environment or any relevant infrastructure are probably included in this section and thus subject to limitation. Recovery of freight not earned and lost following damage to the ship has been held not to fall within this category of claims as it is based on a contractual right.[441] In *Qenos Pty Ltd v Ship "APL Sydney"*[442] the Federal Court of Australia held that pure economic loss arising from the physical damage of a pipeline to users of the product carried by the pipeline was covered by Article 2(1)(c) of the 1976 LLMC. In doing so the court considered that the term "rights" in this context "includes a legally enforceable claim which results from the act or omission of another person".[443] In *The Tiruna*[444] the Australian court held that the term covers wreck removal expenses.

Under Article 2(1)(d) claims in respect of the raising, removal, destruction or the rendering harmless of a ship which is sunk, wrecked, stranded or abandoned, including anything that is or has been on board such ship are also subject to limitation of liability. Claims for wreck raising, removal, etc., differ from other property and consequential claims in the sense that the party

---

436. See *Candlewood Navigation Corp v Mitsui Osk Lines (The Mineral Transporter and The Ibaraki Maru)* [1986] AC 1 (PC); *Leigh & Sillivan Ltd v Aliakmon Shipping Co Ltd (The Aliakmon)* [1986] AC 785 and a restatement of the law by Steel J in *Colour Quest Ltd v Total Downstream UK Plc* [2009] EWHC 540 (Comm); [2009] 2 Lloyd's Rep 1.

437. *Caltex Oil (Australia) Pty v The Dredge Willemstad* [1976] 136 CLR 529 (High Court of Australia).

438. This was inserted by the Merchant Shipping (Convention on Limitation of Liability for Maritime Claims) (Amendment) Order 1998 which enacts the 1996 Protocol.

439. 1974 Athens Convention, art 1(5).

440. [1998] 2 Lloyd's Rep 39.

441. Ibid.

442. *Qenos Pty Ltd v Ship "APL Sydney"* [2009] FCA 1090 (Federal Court of Australia).

443. Ibid., [35].

444. *The Tiruna* [1987] 2 Lloyd's Rep 666 (Court of Appeal of Australia).

claiming could be under a duty to keep the waterways clear of objects[445] and therefore public funding will probably have to meet the costs that exceed limitation. To avoid this consequence[446] the UK has made a reservation in respect of this provision[447] and all claims in respect of wreck raising removal, etc., are not subject to limitation of liability.[448]

Article 2(1)(e) provides that claims in respect of removal, destruction or rendering harmless of the cargo of a ship are subject to limitation of liability. This section concerns cargo-related operations in general irrespective of whether the ship is distressed or sunk. It could, for example, cover a claim by cargo owners for the jettison or confiscation of cargo partly infested which makes discharge of the whole cargo, whether infested or not, illegal.[449] It would also cover the destruction or raising of a container with toxic substances lost to the sea. Thus, in the UK, because of the reservation made with respect to Article 2(1)(d), the costs for raising or destroying a ship are not subject to limitation of liability. By contrast, the raising of the cargo would probably be subject to limitation, as it also falls under Article 2(1)(e).[450]

Article 2(1)(f) provides for claims of a person other than the person liable in respect of measures taken in order to avert or minimise loss for which the person liable may limit his liability in accordance with the 1996 LLMC. It further provides for losses caused by such measures to be subject to limitation of liability. These claims are, in essence, assistance services and clean-up costs undertaken by persons who cannot be considered as salvors. This provision avoids the situation by which a claim would be limited but the claim for prevention of the loss would be unlimited. In *The Breydon Merchant*[451] a claim by cargo owners against the shipowner for salvage liability caused by unseaworthiness was considered to be within this article as it was a claim for measures taken to prevent or minimise the loss to cargo for which the shipowner would have been able to limit liability. While in general all claims described above are subject to limitation whether as direct or as indemnity actions, claims under Article 2(1)(d), (e) and (f) are expressly not limited when they relate to remuneration under a contract with the shipowner.[452]

Therefore, contractors undertaking cargo or ship raising otherwise than in salvage or acting for the minimisation of loss under a contract do not face a defence of limitation when demanding payment. However, it appears that it is only in respect of remuneration that such claims are unlimited. Thus, a claim by a person contracted to raise a lost container who suffers damage will probably be subject to limited liability.

---

445. In England the MSA 1995, s 252, describes the powers of the harbour authorities.

446. See *Richard Abel & Sons Ltd v Manchester Ship Canal (The Stonedale No 1)* [1955] 2 Lloyd's Rep 9; [1956] AC 1 for the earlier position.

447. MSA 1995, Schedule 7, Part II, art 3(1), stating:

> Paragraph 1(d) of Article 2 shall not apply unless provision has been made by an order of the Secretary of State for the setting up and management of a fund to be used for the making to harbour or conservancy authorities of payments needed to compensate them for the reduction, in consequence of the said paragraph l(d), of amounts recoverable by them in claims of the kind there mentioned, and to be maintained by contributions from such authorities raised and collected by them in respect of vessels in like manner as other sums so raised by them.

No action has been taken by the Secretary of State, thus the reservation is generally applicable.

448. The Wreck Removal Convention expressly preserves under art 10(2) the right of the registered owner to limit its liability under any applicable international or national regime such as the 1976 LLMC. However, it is not yet clear whether the UK will ratify the Wreck Removal Convention which is not yet in force and whether as a result of this the domestic law regarding limitation of liability for wreck removal would be changed.

449. See, e.g. the facts of *Effort Shipping Co Ltd v Linden Management SA (The Giannis NK)* [1998] AC 605; [1998] 1 Lloyd's Rep 337.

450. One could suggest that art 2(1)(d) refers to cargo of stranded vessels while art 2(1)(e) refers to cargo of vessels not wrecked or sunk, etc. However, the general wording of art 2(1)(e) would arguably be an obstacle to such interpretation.

451. [1992] 1 Lloyd's Rep. 373.

452. 1976 LLMC, art 2(2).

(f) Claims excluded from limitation

Any claim which does not fall within the wording of Article 2 is not subject to limitation of liability. In addition, for general policy reasons some claims under Article 2 are expressly exempted from limitation of liability. These exemptions can be found in Article 3. In particular, claims for salvage including special compensation under Article 14 of the Salvage Convention are not subject to limitation. Otherwise salvors may become reluctant to undertake salvage. However, the exemption only covers direct[453] claims from salvors and not indemnity claims for salvage expenses under the contract of carriage.[454] Moreover, even claims by salvors must be in the nature of salvage and not otherwise in order to be unlimited.[455] Claims for General Average are also not subject to limitation of liability.[456]

Claims for oil pollution damage covered by the 1992 CLC[457] are also excluded[458] as the 1992 CLC and the 1992 FUND[459] conventions contain their independent special liability regimes which include limits of liability. Damages arising from nuclear damage which are subject to national or international legislation are also excluded under Article 3(c). The 1960 Paris Convention[460] and the 1963 Brussels Convention[461] as well as the 1997 Protocol to Amend the Vienna Convention on Civil Liability for Nuclear Damage[462] and the Joint Protocol Relating to the Application of the Vienna Convention and the Paris Convention[463] compose the international liability framework which channels liability exclusively towards the operator of a nuclear installation, making it strictly liable and providing for limitation of its liability. These conventions are applicable to nuclear installations and do not cover liability in respect of nuclear powered ships.[464] Article 3(d) expressly states the liability of the shipowner of a nuclear ship cannot be limited under the 1976 LLMC. Notably salvors assisting nuclear ships in distress will be able to limit liability as usual, as the exception only covers shipowners.

The final category of claims is described in Article 2(e) which concerns the servants of the owner and salvors. Their claims are not universally excluded from limitation, but it is left to the law governing their contract to decide whether these will be allowed in full or limited to any amount which is higher than that under Article 6 of the 1996 LLMC. The provision requires that the servant's duties "are connected with the ship", which would certainly include the master and crew members. Servants whose duties are only temporarily connected with the ship may also be covered by this provision if they are physically located at the time of the damage on board

---

453. Salvage may be contractual or may arise independently as a right under the Salvage Convention which is presently enacted as Schedule 11 to the MSA 1995.

454. See *The Breydon Merchant* [1992] 1 Lloyd's Rep. 373.

455. In *The Tesaba* [1982] 1 Lloyd's Rep 397 salvors attempted to arrest a ship because the shipowners permitted the discharge of the cargo before security was provided by cargo interests, in contravention of an agreement with the salvors. However, it was held that for the purpose of an action *in rem* such a claim was not in the nature of salvage.

456. 1976 LLMC, art 3(1).

457. International Convention on Civil Liability for Oil Pollution Damage 1992. See further Chapter 10 page 374.

458. In the UK the exclusion can be found in MSA 1995, Schedule 7, Part II, para 4(2).

459. International Convention on the Establishment of an International Fund for Compensation for Oil Pollution Damage. See further Chapter 10 page 386.

460. Convention on Third Party Liability in the Field of Nuclear Energy of 29 July 1960, Additional Protocol of 28 January 1964, Protocol of 16 November 1982.

461. Convention of 31 January 1963 Supplementary to the Paris Convention of 29 July 1960, Protocol of 28 January 1964 and Protocol of 16 November 1982.

462. In force but not signed by the UK.

463. In force and ratified by the UK.

464. See Convention on Third Party Liability in the Field of Nuclear Energy of 29 July 1960, as amended by the Additional Protocol of 28 January 1964 and by the Protocol of 16 November 1982, art 1(a)(ii). The 1965 Nuclear Act excludes such ships under art 1(1)(a) which restricts the operation of the act to "any nuclear reactor (other than such reactor comprised in a means of transport, whether by land, water or air)".

or in close proximity to the ship. Section 185(4) of the MSA 1995 excludes from limitation of liability personal injury and death as well as property loss claims made by a person employed under a contract of service governed by the law of any part of the UK. The application of the particular section of the MSA 1995 depends on whether the established relationship between such parties and the shipowner is a contract of service. In *The Maragetha Maria*[465] the Court of Appeal considered that a claim by the estate of drowned fishermen who were working on the vessel under a share profits arrangement meant that losses as well as profits were to be shared. In addition, the deceased paid tax and national insurance on the basis that they were self-employed. These indicated that the deceased were not under a contract of service and their claims were not covered by the exemption under Article 3(3), thus they were subject to the shipowner's right to limited liability.

The claims exempted under Article 3 cover direct claims against a shipowner. These ought to be paid in full to the claimant. However, if after payment the shipowner seeks an indemnity from another shipowner, for example a charterer, the indemnity claim is not generally a claim covered by Article 3, and the second shipowner does have the right to limit liability.

(g) When is the privilege to limited liability lost?[466]

Under Article 4 the shipowner loses the right to limited liability if the damages are caused by "his personal act or omission, committed with the intent to cause such loss, or recklessly and with knowledge that such loss would probably result". This test requires (a) personal act or omission of the shipowner, and (b) culpability which is intentional or almost as bad as intentional.

The personal acts of the shipowner when the shipowner is a company are not always easy to identify and a case-by-case approach is adopted by the courts. The answer depends on the structure of each company[467] and the way responsibilities are allocated within each company.[468] Historically, the case law approached the question in a hierarchical way either starting from the top of the company, the owner or the governing board, and coming down or vice versa. More recent case law recognises that certain actions by the company may be delegated to lower ranking officers who do not in general have decision-making authority in respect of the running of the company. This avoids the difficulty that arises if solely the hierarchical approach is used, namely that the delegation of duties to lower ranking officers would exclude the possibility of attributing the faults of these officers to the company itself and consequently ensure an unbreakable right

---

465. *Todd and Others v Adams and Chope (t/a Tralewney fishing Co) (The Maragetha Maria)* [2002] EWCA Civ 509; [2002] 2 Lloyd's Rep 293.

466. Note that it is possible for the shipowner to contract out of or waive the right to limit liability although it will require very clear words to do so, which in turn may depend on the contractual background. See the Privy Council decision in *Bahamas Oil Refining Company International Ltd v Owners of the Cape Bari Tankschiffahrts Gmbh & Co Kg (Bahamas) (The "Cape Bari")* [2016] UKPC 20; [2016] 2 Lloyd's Rep 469, confirming this possibility first identified in *Clarke v Dunraven (The Satanita)* [1897] AC 59 (CA).

467. See Mustill LJ's judgment in the Court of Appeal decision in *Societe Anonyme des Minerais v Grant Trading Inc (The Ert Stefanie)* [1989] 1 Lloyd's Rep 349.

468. In *Lennard's Carrying Co Ltd Appellants v Asiatic Petroleum Company, Limited Respondents* [1915] AC 705 Viscount Haldane LC, who delivered the leading judgment, stated:

> My Lords, a corporation is an abstraction. It has no mind of its own any more than it has a body of its own; its active and directing will must consequently be sought in the person of somebody who for some purposes may be called an agent, but who is really the directing mind and will of the corporation, the very ego and centre of the personality of the corporation. That person may be under the direction of the shareholders in general meeting; that person may be the board of directors itself, or it may be, and in some companies it is so, that that person has an authority co-ordinate with the board of directors given to him under the articles of association, and is appointed by the general meeting of the company, and can only be removed by the general meeting of the company.

to limit liability. There is significant case law in shipping demonstrating the factual approach adopted by the English courts.

Acts of a member of the board of directors would normally implicate the acts of the company. There could however be circumstances under which such a person may not be representing the company.[469] In the same line, even where there is one person who has the ultimate control of a company, this does not necessarily mean that only this person's acts would count as acts of the company.[470]

The Privy Council decision in *Meridian Global Funds Management Asia Ltd v Securities Commission*[471] confirmed the general position that the primary rules of attribution found in the company's constitution and implied by company law together with the secondary rules of attribution, that is the rules of agency, vicarious liability, etc., determine the natural persons whose acts are to be attributed to the company. However, the Privy Council does not end the story there but explains that, in exceptional cases, even where the particular person cannot be properly described as the "directing mind and will of the company" it may be necessary to devise special rules of attribution where the acts of a duly authorised agent or servant of the company will represent the company. Such exceptional cases are distinguishable by reference to the substantive legal provisions imposing obligations on the company. Thus arguments that acts or omissions by a person statutorily required to act for the company in particular respects, such as the Designated Person under the ISM code[472] or the "Company Security Officer" under the ISPS code,[473] may render her/him the relevant person. However, it is submitted that only in cases where there is a breach of the ISM or the ISPS Code in respect of the company's obligations, to the extent that the right of limitation is challenged and that this obligation was to be discharged by the nominated person himself, there could be a possibility that *Meridian Global Funds Management Asia Ltd v Securities Commission*[474] could be relied upon to establish that the acts of the relevant person were acts of the company. In such cases it can be argued that the legislation has identified the "alter ego" of the company.

---

469. Mustill LJ in *The Ert Stefanie* [1989] 1 Lloyd's Rep 349 said: "It seems to me at least theoretically possible for a situation to exist where a particular director had been formally excluded from participation in the company's business and where, if nevertheless he did trespass upon that territory, his acts in so doing would not be attributed to the company."
470. Ibid.
471. [1995] 2 AC 500.
472. ISM Code, s 4. Designated person(s) (emphasis added):

> To ensure the safe operation of each ship and to provide a link between the Company and those on board every Company, as appropriate, should designate a person or persons ashore *having direct* access *to the highest level of management*. The responsibility and authority of the designated person or persons should include monitoring the safety and pollution-prevention aspects of the operation of each ship and ensuring that adequate resources and shore-based support are applied, as required.

It is difficult to say whether the conduct of the designated person can cause the shipowner to lose its right to limit liability. This will depend on the role of the designated person within the shipowning company, as explained in *Meridian Global v Securities Commissioner* (fn 539). A professional ship manager would normally be the employer of the "designated person" under the ship's safety management system. Where the conduct of the designated person satisfies art 4, then his employer, the ship manager, could arguably lose its right to limited liability. However, when the registered shipowner remains ignorant of the problem, despite having acted reasonably in appointing a competent ship manager, it would arguably be unfair to deprive the owner (and its P&I Club) of limitation of liability.
473. Where the "Company Security Officer" is described as:

> the person designated by the company for ensuring that a ship security assessment is carried out; that a ship security plan is developed and submitted for approval, and thereafter implemented and maintained and for liaison with port facility security officers and the ship security officer.

See SOLAS/CONF.5/3A4N, NEX1, Part A, s 2.7. See also Chapter 9.
474. [1995] 2 AC 500.

In the absence of these exceptional circumstances there is still a need to search for the "directing will and mind of the company",[475] which involves a hierarchical approach to the company. Thus, acts of the master or a marine superintendent cannot be considered as personal acts of the company.[476] The acts of the chief navigator and his staff in a large State-owned shipping company are not the acts of the company,[477] while the acts of his superior, the director of technical and investment affairs, would, in that particular case, have represented the company.

Fault may also be found in the way the constitution of the company attributes duties. However, such fault would arguably be relevant only where the company directors are in fact aware of the fault and they do not perform the necessary duties.[478]

From a practical point of view, the above would mean that, provided that appropriate procedures are established by the company's constitution, faults by officers operating or supervising the operation of the vessel would not normally be considered as faults of the company.

The entrusting of the running of the vessel by the registered owner to a management company does not exclude the possibility that there is fault or privity by the registered owners.[479] This position would arguably be also applicable to operating companies.

Where the time or voyage or slot charterer or the salvor tries to limit under a regime that gives them such right[480] the same rules as in respect of the registered owner will also apply.

Having discussed the conditions under which the personal act or omission of the shipowner is established we now need to discuss the type of conduct that needs to be proved in order to deprive the shipowner of its right to limit liability under the 1976 LLMC. If intention can be shown, for example where the vessel is scuttled, the test will be satisfied. However, difficulties arise in the interpretation of the term "recklessly and with knowledge that such damage would probably result".

In interpreting a provision very similar to Article 4 of 1976 LLMC, i.e. Article 25 of the Warsaw Convention 1929, the Court of Appeal in *Goldman v Thai Airways International Ltd*[481] held that the phrase means a person's act which indicates a decision to run the risk or a mental attitude of indifference to the risk's existence.[482]

This creates the need to understand the risk involved in order to decide whether a particular act or omission is indeed reckless.[483]

Moreover, it is also necessary to show that the wrongdoer had knowledge that damage would probably result. The term "with knowledge" was held to refer to the actual knowledge held by the wrongdoer in respect of the damage that would probably result and not to knowledge that the wrongdoer ought to have had.[484] The Court of Appeal in *Nugent and Killick v Michael Goss*

---

475. *Lennard's Carrying Co Ltd Appellants v Asiatic Petroleum Co, Limited Respondents* [1915] AC 705.

476. *Arthur Guinness, Son & Co (Dublin) Ltd v Owners of the Motor Vessel Freshfield (The Lady Gwendolen)* [1965] 1 Lloyd's Rep 335 and *The Garden City (No 1)* [1982] 2 Lloyd's Rep 382.

477. *The Garden City (No 1)* [1982] 2 Lloyd's Rep 382.

478. See, for example, *The Garden City (No 1)* [1982] 2 Lloyd's Rep 382.

479. *Charlotte v Theory and Others (The Charlotte)* [1921] 9 Ll L Rep 341, *The Lady Gwendolen* [1965] 1 Lloyd's Rep 335, *The Marion* [1982] 2 Lloyd's Rep 52, at p 54 and *The Ert Stefanie* [1989] 1 Lloyd's Rep 349, where Mustill LJ said:

> While the doctrines of corporate personality call for a ritual nod in the direction of the owners, nobody in practice pays any attention to these one-ship companies registered under flags of convenience; and the law takes the same view when questions of limitation are in issue.

480. The 1996 LLMC does provide for such right.

481. [1983] 1 WLR 1186. Note, however, that the word "such" does not appear before "loss" in the Warsaw Convention 1929.

482. *Goldman v Thai Airways International Ltd* [1983] 1 WLR 1186, at pp 1193–1194.

483. Ibid.

484. An attempt by the claimants in *Gunter and Others v Beaton and Others* [1993] 2 Lloyd's Rep 369, to qualify the knowledge as the knowledge that such damage would occur "if the risk materializes" was expressly rejected by the Court of Appeal.

Aviation Ltd and Others[485] held that anything less than "actual conscious knowledge" cannot satisfy Article 25.[486] Thus, "turning a blind eye" knowledge is in essence excluded from the ambit of the required knowledge.[487]

The word "probably" has been distinguished from the word "possibly" and was taken to mean "something likely to happen".[488] With "rather less confidence"[489] the Court held in the same case that the word "damage" refers to damage of the same kind as that which had occurred.

The case law on Article 25 of the amended Warsaw Convention can be considered at least as containing persuasive arguments in relation to the interpretation of Article 4 of the 1976 LLMC, although in principle each convention is independent and has to be interpreted in accordance with its scope.[490] The close similarity of the words and the similar function within each convention of these articles supports a common interpretation in spite of the modification of the term "loss" to "such loss" in the 1996 LLMC. Arguably, the word adds clarification to the need for knowledge of the particular loss that occurred. However, the test may be even narrower than suggested above and may not only refer to the kind of damage but to the damage actually suffered.

Two possible interpretations have been outlined in respect of the collision between two vessels (A and B). The Court of Appeal stated that in such a situation the required test under Article 4 could have two interpretations: either that the cargo-/shipowners of ship A must prove that the owner of ship B intended that it should collide with ship A, or acted recklessly with the knowledge that it was likely to do so or that the claimant merely has to prove that the owner of ship B intended that his ship should collide with another ship, or acted recklessly with the knowledge that it was likely to do so.[491]

The Court of Appeal did not decide this point which therefore remains open.

The burden of proving that Article 4 is fulfilled is on the claimant,[492] since the shipowner has no interest in proving the fulfilment of conditions under Article 4.

The generally accepted strictness of the test, which only slightly lowers the requirement from one of an intentional act, has led to the statement that as long as collisions are concerned Article 4 cannot, in general, be satisfied. Consequently, the liability of the shipowner will be limited in all but the most exceptional cases[493] and the court will issue a declaration to this effect, i.e. a limitation decree would be directly available to the shipowner.[494]

---

485. [2000] 2 Lloyd's Rep 222.

486. For two reasons, first that anything less would cause uncertainty and second because the intention of the Convention was taken to be that art 25 would be applicable in very rare circumstances.

487. However, the third judge, Pill LJ, considered that the wrongdoer cannot limit his liability just because he made a conscious decision to put the knowledge out of his mind, and he was prepared to infer the general knowledge that an experienced pilot would have. See *Nugent and Killick v Michael Goss Aviation Ltd and Others* [2000] 2 Lloyd's Rep 222.

488. *Goldman v Thai Airways International Ltd* [1983] 1 WLR 1186, at p 1196.

489. Ibid.

490. Art 31 of the 1969 Vienna Convention on the Law of Treaties states that: "A treaty shall be interpreted in good faith in accordance with the ordinary meaning to be given to the terms of the treaty in their context and in the light of its object and purpose." The object and purpose of the liability regime established under the 1929 Warsaw Convention for air carriage is clearly not the same as that of the 1976 LLMC thus, at least in theory, some differences could exist.

491. *Schiffahrtsgesellschaft MS Merkur Sky GmbH & Co KG v MS Leerort Nth Schiffarts Gmbh & Co KG (The Leerort)* [2001] 2 Lloyd's Rep 291.

492. See *The Bowbelle* [1990] 1 Lloyd's Rep 532 and *MSC Mediterranean Shipping Co SA v Delumar BVBA (The MSC Rosa M)* [2000] 2 Lloyd's Rep 399; *The Leerort* [2001] 2 Lloyd's Rep 291; *Margolle and Another v Delta Maritime Co Ltd and Others (The Saint Jacques II and Gudermes)* [2002] EWHC 2452 (Admlty); [2003] 1 Lloyd's Rep 203. See also the decision of the Court of Appeal in *Goldman v Thai Airways International Ltd* [1983] 1 WLR 1186 on the Warsaw Convention which provides for a similar test.

493. *The Leerort* [2001] 2 Lloyd's Rep 291.

494. See Chapter 12, page 514.

In one exceptional case, the limitation decree was not granted. The facts of the case[495] can be summarised as follows: a fishing vessel which routinely[496] navigated the Channel on the wrong side of the traffic separation scheme, under the command of her owner who was also the master, collided with an oncoming vessel. The owner/master admitted that the navigation was reckless but claimed that the element of knowledge was missing because the real test was one that required knowledge of the particular loss that occurred, which in this case was collision damage caused to the specific vessel[497] and that, as at the time of the collision he was in his cabin sleeping, he did not have such knowledge. The question was whether the limitation decree would be issued without a hearing as suggested for the routine collision cases in *The Leerort*. However, the judge declined to grant the limitation decree as he considered this to be a case where there was a reasonable prospect that Article 4 could be fulfilled. The case was settled before reaching the court. Thus the case provides only an example of what type of conduct may be considered as possibly risking the loss of the right to limit liability and confirms the discretion of the courts to issue a limitation decree, but arguably not much more.

In a Canadian case considering the right to limit liability the Canadian Supreme Court, reversing the lower court decision held that the defendant fisherman was entitled to limit liability despite the fact that the damage was caused by an intentional act.[498] The master and owner of the fishing vessel got his fishing gear caught in a cable belonging to a communication company and, thinking that it was abandoned, brought it on board and cut it with an electric saw. This happened twice. As the fisherman was also the owner of the fishing boat his actions were the company's actions. The Canadian Appeal Court held that as a result of cutting the cable he was deprived of the right to limit liability. Notably, the conduct was also considered wilful misconduct, enabling the insurers to avoid the contract of insurance. The decision with respect to the right to limit liability was reversed by the Supreme Court of Canada on the basis that the fisherman did not intend to cause the specific loss. Thus, the Supreme Court read the test for limitation as one that is not satisfied by any intentional act or omission but only by an intentional act or omission which is undertaken with knowledge that such damage would probably result. The Supreme Court confirmed the decision of the Appeal Court with respect to the insurance contract. This means that the standard of wilful misconduct is easier to fulfil than that satisfying Article 4 of the LLMC.

Under English law, the right to limit liability was removed in *The Atlantik Confidence*[499] where the cargo claimant successfully proved that the test under Article 4 of the 1976 LLMC as amended was satisfied. The court decided that the appropriate approach is the same as that followed when determining "whether a hull underwriter had proved on the balance of probabilities that a vessel was scuttled" with a standard of proof which "would fall not far short of the rigorous criminal standard". This statement is not necessarily contradictory with that made in *The Realice* because in *The Atlantik Confidence* the possession of the required knowledge, under Article 4, of the resulting damage was not challenged. The case does, however, have a number of interesting points. First, the involvement of the shipowner in the scuttling was inferred by a number of contributing factors and unexplainable navigational and other reactions. It was found that the occurrence of the fire that

---

495. *Margolle and Another v Delta Maritime Co Ltd And Others (The Saint Jacques II and Gudermes)* [2002] EWHC 2452 (Admlty).

496. The judge considered that prior to the accident repetition of the same reckless navigation, i.e. contravening r 10 of the Collision Regulations, without the occurrence of a collision, did not indicate that such action did not carry with it the probability of damage.

497. An arguable option, as suggested in *The Leerort* [2001] 2 Lloyd's Rep 291.

498. *Telus Communications v Peracomo Inc and Réal Vallée* [2011] FC 494, 27 April 2011 and *Peracomo Inc. v. Société Telus Communications Co*, 2014 SCC 29.

499. *Kairos Shipping Ltd and Another v Enka & Co Llc and Others (The "Atlantik Confidence")* [2016] EWHC 2412 (Admlty), [2016] 2 Lloyd's Rep 525.

started in the storeroom of the engine room, the flooding of the engine room and the flooding of two ballast double bottom tanks, individually, were improbable to have happened unless caused by a deliberate act. Furthermore, the combination of these three improbable events, which led to the sinking of the ship, took place after the ship was instructed to change route to deeper waters and were followed by a number of actions by the master and the chief engineer which, while on their own were not determinative, when considered in context, suggested a scuttling effort. There were successive visits to the ship after it was abandoned by the chief engineer and superintendents who failed to take photographs or collect evidence, a failure properly to inform salvors and other omissions all indicating a scuttling plan. The link with the shipowner was based on the absence of any allegation that the master and the chief engineer acted for their own reasons, a number of navigational and other actions taken and the use of the insurance money for paying off debts of other companies in the same group. The shipowner was the one to benefit from the scuttling. A point of interest was the decision that the scuttling effort was by itself incompetent. The flooded engine room and ballast tanks were not sufficient to sink the ship. There was probably an intention to flood other parts of the ship but the valves did not operate properly. In the end the ship sank because of the flooding of hold No. 5 through corrosion in a ballast water pipeline which permitted water to go in. Thus in this case there was deliberate act or omission with knowledge of the probable damage but the act was by itself inadequate to cause the intentional damage. The court held that this did not alter the conclusion. The test under Article 4 requires that the loss "resulted from" an act or omission. This term refers to causation but not directly. It is significantly different from what it would have been if the term "caused by" had been used. It arguably includes the case where the act or omission is the initial cause but additional contributing factors finally lead to the loss. If this is correct, as the judgment suggests it is, then the test would be satisfied even where the damage is caused by another subsequent event provided that the operation of the other reason was facilitated by the intentional or reckless act or omission by the shipowner so that in the absence of the wrongful action, the other cause would not have been effective. Such an example would be an instruction to the master to enter a war zone or a hurricane which then leads to the loss of the ship. The interpretation of Article 4 in *The Atlantik Confidence* indicates that it is the intention and the recklessness of the shipowner (with knowledge) that lead to the loss of right to limit and not the actual causation of the loss by such actions.

More difficult would be cases where the ship is, for example hit in a war zone, and while having a risk of being lost, the shipowner decides to scuttle it. It would be more difficult then to argue that the loss of the ship resulted from the shipowner's action, unless of course the ship could have certainly been salved but for the scuttling effort.

(h) The limits of liability

The 1996 LLMC, which is presently in force in the UK,[500] calculates the applicable limits on the basis of the tonnage of the ship[501] as defined under the International Convention on Tonnage Measurement of Ships 1969.[502] Only in relation to limitation of liability in respect of loss of life and personal injury to passengers a different system based on the number of passengers is used. The limits of liability are shown in Table 7.1. To determine the limits of liability one has to distinguish between loss of life and personal injury claims on the one hand and property damage

---

500. The Merchant Shipping Act 1995 (Amendment) Order 2016, SI 2016/1061 amends the limits of liability in Schedule 7 of the 1995 MSA and enacts the 2012 LLMC protocol into English law. The amendment came into force on 30 November 2016.

501. Arguably, with the exception of liability against passengers where a separate limit per passenger is provided.

502. SI 1997/1510, as amended by SI 1998/1916, SI 1999/3206 and SI 2005/2114, applies in the UK.

Table 7.1 Limits of liability under the 1996 LLMC as amended by the 2012 Protocol

Tonnage grt	Limitation Fund Property Damage		Limitation Fund Loss of Life/Person	
	Million SDR	SDR/Per Ton	Million SDR	SDR/Ton
<2000	1.51	–	3.02	–
2001–30,000	1.51	604	3.02	1,208
30,001–70,000	1.51	453	3	906
>70,000	1.51	302	3	604

claims on the other. In the case of property damage the limits of liability provide for a smaller fund than where there is also loss of life or personal injury, in which case the fund is three times as large. In general the loss of life/personal injury claimants are entitled to two-thirds of such a fund and any excess of such claims rank equally with property damage in respect of the residual third of the fund

(i) Limits of liability for property damage

Where there is only property damage, determining the amount of money available to the property claimants is straightforward. Note that in fact the claimants for property damage will have the full amounts described in Table 7.1 only where the loss of life/personal injury claims are fully satisfied by their exclusive part of the limitation fund.

As an example let us consider a ship of 50,000 tons under the 1996 LLMC. The tonnage of the ship spans three ranges, the first of 2,000 tons, the second of 2,001–30,000 tons and also 20,000 in the third range of 30,001–70,000. Therefore, the first 2,000 tons correspond to 1,510,000 SDR,[503] the next 28,000 tons, up to the 30,000 limit, correspond to 28,000 tons × 604 SDR/ton which equals 16,912,000 SDR.

The 20,000 tons in excess of 30,000 correspond to 20,000 tons × 453 SDR/ton which equals 9,060,000 SDR. Thus, the limit of liability for this ship is the sum of 1,510,000 + 16,912,000 + 9,060,000 = 27,482,000 SDR.

There is no right to obtain funds from the loss of life and personal injury part of the limitation fund for property damage. Therefore where the limits of liability for property damage are exceeded the payment will be in proportion to the confirmed claims.

(ii) Limits of liability for loss of life or personal injury

For non-passenger claims, the loss of life and personal injury part of the fund is by definition twice that of the property fund (see Table 7.1). Furthermore, loss of life and personal injury claimants are entitled to be paid from the property part of the limitation fund. As a result, where there are no claims for property damage but only claims for loss of life or personal injury, the limits of liability are three times those available for damage to property.[504]

---

503. The unit of account for the 1996 and the 1976 LLMC is the Special Drawing Right, a unit defined by the International Monetary Fund – see 1996 LLMC, art 8. The daily value of this unit is routinely quoted in financial newspapers or can be retrieved through the IMF's internet website. As of 16 June 2017, 1 SDR is the equivalent of £1.074 and $1.386. See www.imf.org/external/np/fin/data/param_rms_mth.aspx (accessed 16 June 2017).

504. See Table 7.1 (page 300).

When there are both loss of life and personal injury claims on the one hand and damage to property claims on the other hand then the loss of life and personal injury claims are paid by the earmarked part of the fund, (two-thirds of the total limitation amount) and the other one-third is left to satisfy the property claimants and any unsatisfied balance of claims for loss of life or personal injury not met by the dedicated personal injury fund in proportion to the amounts claimed.

The way this happens is as follows: Article 6(1)(a) provides for the limits of liability for loss of life or personal injury. Article 6(1)(b) provides for the limits of liability for damage to property. Article 6(2) provides for the participation of any unsatisfied loss of life and personal injury claims in the property damage part of the limitation fund.

As an example let us consider again a ship of 50,000 tons under the 1996 LLMC. The limitation fund when only property damage is caused has already been calculated above as being 27,482,000 SDR.

In respect of loss of life or personal injury claims, the limits of liability would be 3,020,000 for the first 2,000 tons, $28,000 \times 1,208 = 33,824,000$ SDR for the following 28,000 tons and $20,000 \times 906 = 18,120,000$ SDR for the other 20,000 tons. Thus, the limitation fund for loss of life and personal injury is then 54,964,000 SDR and the total limitation fund is 82,446,000.

The significance of Article 6(2) can be demonstrated if the property damage is considered to be 27,482,000 SDR and the loss of life/personal injury claims 82,446,000 SDR, respectively. In such a case the personal claims will be paid first to cover 54,964,000 SDR. We would then have 27,482,000 SDR of personal claims unpaid as well as an equal amount of property damages. These would rank equally and will both be paid in proportion from the property-related limitation fund.

Thus, 13,741,000 SDR will be paid out to the property claimants and 68,705,000 SDR to the claims for personal injuries or death.

Accordingly, the existence of claimants for loss of life/personal injury which exceed the relevant part of the limitation fund can significantly reduce the recovery by property damage claimants.

For passenger claims, a separate limit for loss of life and personal injury of passengers against the carrying ship is established by Article 7 of the 1996 LLMC. The limits imposed are 175,000 SDR per passenger times the number of passengers the ship is authorised to carry. However, Article 15.3*bis* of the 1976 LLMC permits the fixing by each State of limits higher than those imposed by the new Article 7 and by implication also permits the removal of limits of liability for loss of life and personal injury of passengers.[505] It is worth noting that the beneficiaries of the inclusion of the passenger fund in the 1996 LLMC are not only the passengers themselves who have an earmarked fund but all other claimants who, in cases of passenger loss of life or personal injury, do not have to share the fund under Article 6 with passengers. The UK has restricted the application of Article 7 of the 1996 LLMC, thus it is only the limits of the 2002 Athens Convention, as enforced through the Athens Regulation,[506] that limits the shipowner's liability for such types of damage.

Article 15(2) of the 1976 LLMC gives the right for a State party to provide limits of liability for vessels less than 300 tons.[507] In the UK, for such vessels the limits have been specified to be 1,000,000 SDR for loss of life and personal injury and 500,000 SDR for property damage on its

---

505. Each Contracting State using art 15.3*bis* must inform the Secretary-General of the IMO in respect of these higher limits or the absence thereof.

506. See Chapter 6.

507. There is an obligation imposed on each State party to inform the depositary about the limits of liability for smaller vessels.

own.[508] Thus loss of life and personal injury claimants can have access to up to 1,500,000 SDR where there are no property claimants.

(i) Multiplicity of defendants and counterclaims

The limits of liability apply to all claims arising from a "distinct occasion".[509] Whether a series of accidents belong to the same occasion or distinct occasions is of paramount importance because two separate incidents would require two limitation funds. Under English law, the question of whether two accidents are separate appears to depend on whether the accidents are linked in such a way that the second can be shown to be the natural consequence of the first.[510] Where counterclaims exist, Article 5 provides that the limits of liability apply to the balance of the claim and the counterclaim.[511] For example, where two ships collide and they are both to blame, their claims must be set off against each other and then the net balance would be subject to limitation of liability of the party that has to pay the net balance.

The issue of when two incidents are separate so as to merit two limitation funds has been addressed under English law in *The Schwan*,[512] a case involving the collision of a ship with two other ships successively. The Court of Appeal held that the two incidents were separate and therefore two limitation funds should be established. The test was considered to be whether both collisions were the result of the "same act of want of seamanship".[513] Accordingly, where there is a lapse of time between successive accidents during which appropriate action could have prevented the later accident, there are two separate incidents.[514]

The issue has been reassessed by Rares J in *Strong Wise Ltd v Esso Australia Resources Pty Ltd*,[515] a decision of the Federal Court of Australia. In that case the container ship *APL Sydney* was brought to the anchorage at Port Phillip Bay Melbourne by the pilot. The pilot left the ship before the anchoring procedure was completed so when the vessel started drifting the port authority refused the master's request to take the anchor up and retry anchoring and instructed the master to wait for a pilot to arrive. As a result, the anchor fouled a gas pipeline which was buried three metres below the seabed. The master stopped the engine until the pilot arrived. After the pilot returned to the ship and under his instructions the ship moved, dragging the anchor, and as a result ruptured the pipeline. The shipowner went to court in order to establish a limitation fund while the owners of the pipeline asked the court to declare that there were four separate incidents and that four funds should be established.

The four incidents were alleged to be: (i) the navigational errors leading to the initial fouling of the pipeline by the anchor; (ii) the order that the ship's engine go astern (allegedly this caused

---

508. Merchant Shipping (Convention on Limitation of Liability for Maritime Claims) Amendment Order 1998 (SI 1998/1258). Before the coming into force of this amendment (13 May 2004) the previous established limits were 250,000 SDR and 83,333 SDR, respectively.

509. 1996 LLMC, art 9.

510. See, for example, *The Lucullite (Owners) v The R Mackay (Owners)* [1929] SC 401 and *The Harlow* [1922] 10 Ll L Rep 488.

511. 1976 LLMC, art 5.

512. *The Schwan* [1892] P 419.

513. Ibid., 439.

514. See also *The Creadon* [1886] 5 Asp MLC 585, 54 LT 880 and *The Rajah* [1872] LR 3 A & E 539. In both cases a second collision was considered to be inevitable after the first one and one limitation fund was established. See also *The Lucullite* [1929] SC 401. For the US position, see *Exxon Shipping Company v Cailletau* 869 F 2d 843; [1989] AMC 1422. See also *Ballast Trailing NY v Decca Survey Australia Ltd* (NSWCA, unreported, 29 September 1981), a New South Wales Court of Appeal decision, mentioned in *Strong Wise Ltd v Esso Australia Resources Pty Ltd* [2010] FCA 240, where a dredger had hit the same pipelines in each of nine passages over them. The court held that these were nine distinct occasions.

515. *Strong Wise Ltd v Esso Australia Resources Pty Ltd* [2010] FCA 240 (Federal Court of Australia).

the pipeline to be pulled further out of its trench for an appreciable distance and bent more); (iii) the order that the engine go ahead (allegedly causing the pipeline to rupture and gas to escape); and (iv) the further order that the engine go astern (allegedly causing the pipeline to be dragged further out of its trench and severing a section of the pipe).

Rares J took account of the common law treatment of the subject but noted that the interpretation of the "distinct occasion" must be considered by taking into account the objective of the 1996 LLMC to protect the shipowner from financial ruin. The judge stated that:

whether one occasion is distinct from another will depend upon whether the causes of the claims that arise from each act, neglect or default are sufficiently discrete that, as a matter of commonsense, they can be said to be distinct from one another.[516]

Further, he said:

The Convention focuses attention on an act, neglect or default that constitutes the occasion from which claims arise. In such a case, it is often the last avoidable error that, not having been averted, will be seen as the commonsense cause of the casualty. Then the proceeding errors are not the relevant act, neglect or default because they do not, as a matter of commonsense, necessarily lead to what followed.[517]

As a result, Rares J found on the facts that there were two separate incidents, one relating to the fouling of the pipeline by the ship's anchor and the second relating to the manoeuvring of the ship about half an hour later that led to the rupturing of the pipeline, and consequently the establishment of two limitation funds was required. There is nothing to prevent different claims being submitted to each of the funds. Rares J suggested that the additional damage done to the pipeline during the second incident, the extra repair time required and additional consequential losses and the loss of gas that escaped, were to be subject to the second fund while all the other damage was to be recovered under the limitation fund corresponding to the first incident.[518]

It is worth noting that where separate incidents occur, the test for breaking limitation of liability should apply separately to each incident. Thus, if on the above facts it had been shown that the shipowner itself had instructed the negligent manoeuvring of the *APL Sydney* after the pipeline was fouled but before it was ruptured, then, depending on whether the action could be considered as reckless and depending on the knowledge available to the shipowner, the right to limit liability could have been removed for claims against the second fund without affecting the limits of liability applicable to the damage arising from the first incident.

It is also worth noting that such separation of incidents would arguably lead to separate rights for the arrest of the ship and the establishment of a limitation fund for one incident would not necessarily cover an arrest based on another incident. This would naturally pose some difficult practical questions both regarding arrest as well as over obtaining a limitation decree where the claimants consider that many separate incidents have taken place. In *Strong Wise Ltd v Esso Australia Resources Pty Ltd* the claimants wished to establish four separate incidents and the shipowner wished to limit to one limitation fund. It was only after a very detailed examination of the facts of the case that Rares J reached the decision on how many limitation funds should be established. In addition, there was only one claimant in this case and the entire dispute was under one jurisdiction. Where there is more than one claimant and the actions are dispersed in various jurisdictions it could defeat the 1996 LLMC's objectives if each claimant could, by pointing at

516. Ibid., [80].
517. Ibid., [83].
518. Ibid., [363].

different negligent acts and arguing that more than one incident has taken place, force the shipowner to establish several limitation funds and thus put it to considerable expense. Moreover, if a claimant can avoid the consequences of the establishment of a limitation fund[519] by arguing that a particular claim arose from a separate incident, significant pressure will be imposed on the shipowner who would not, a priori, know how many limitation decrees it should apply for.

It is submitted that as the ship was not disengaged from the pipeline and safely anchored before the second incident occurred, it is arguable that there was one incident in this particular case.

(j) Constitution of the limitation fund and priority of claims

Where legal proceedings[520] have been initiated in a State party in respect of claims subject to limitation any person entitled to limit and alleged in these proceedings to be liable is entitled to constitute a limitation fund with one of the courts in which proceedings are pending.[521] A fund constituted by one of the persons entitled to limit is considered to be constituted by all persons entitled to limit liability.[522] The provision restricts the establishment of the limitation fund (and therefore the protection available under Article 13) only to courts in States parties to the Convention. Thus, where a limitation fund is established under a different limitation regime such limitation fund would not be sufficient for the purpose of the 1996 LLMC. The same applies for a limitation fund established in a State party to the 1976 LLMC in respect of limitation proceedings and/or arrest of a ship in a 1996 LLMC State party.

Where there are no legal proceedings in any Contracting State there are strong arguments supporting the assertion that a shipowner may choose in which Contracting State it will constitute the limitation fund and when.[523] This is supported by noting that the purpose of the limitation fund is to provide security up to the limit prescribed and to free the vessel and the shipowner from further inconvenience. Waiting for the initiation of legal proceedings before facilitating this process through the establishment of a limitation fund arguably defeats one of the advantages of limitation of liability. However, such an argument is not sufficient and one should look for support in the text of the 1996 LLMC. Article 11 establishes that where there are legal proceedings the limitation fund may[524] be constituted in one of these courts. This is consistent with the purposive interpretation suggested above because the objective of providing security and releasing the vessel is served better when the limitation fund is established where a claim has been submitted than elsewhere. However, until such an action is established there is no reason to restrict the shipowner's options.

It can also be argued that "legal proceedings" under Article 11 cover not only liability claims against the shipowner but also limitation proceedings and negative declaratory relief proceedings initiated by the shipowner. Thus, provided that negative declaratory relief is sought by the shipowner in a court of a Contracting State that has jurisdiction on the merits, it then becomes automatically entitled to constitute a limitation fund in that State in accordance with Article 11.

---

519. Namely, the release of the arrested vessel and protection for the shipowner from re-arrest or security measures.

520. Legal proceedings include arbitration proceedings – see *ICL Shipping Ltd, Steamship Mutual Underwriting Association (Bermuda) Ltd v Chin Tai Steel Enterprise Co Ltd and Others (The ICL Vikraman)* [2003] EWHC 2320 (Comm); [2004] 1 Lloyd's Rep 21, following *Afromar Inc v Greek Atlantic Cod Fishing Co (The Penelope II)* [1980] 2 Lloyd's Rep 17.

521. 1996 LLMC, art 11(1).

522. 1996 LLMC, art 11(3).

523. It is arguable that liability proceedings in a non-Contracting State will not be considered as covered by art 11 and the options of the shipowner will be the same as when no liability proceedings have been constituted.

524. The wording of art 11 is permissive and does not state that the shipowner *must* constitute a limitation fund in one of these courts.

It is worth mentioning that Article 11(1) does not question the validity of such proceedings or whether such court has jurisdiction on the merits in respect of claims subject to limitation of liability but only requires the existence of such legal proceedings.

In conclusion, we submit that arguably the most efficient interpretation of the 1996 LLMC would recognise a right to establish a limitation fund in any Contracting State until proceedings against the shipowner have started. Even if proceedings against the owner have commenced in another jurisdiction the shipowner has the option to start limitation proceedings and establish the limitation fund in any Contracting State. However, such choice may be impractical where for example the ship is arrested, in which case a limitation fund would be most efficient at the place of arrest, as will become evident later.

The fund should be for the amounts determined by Articles 6 and 7, increased by interest from the day of the incident to the day of the constitution of the fund. The way the interest is calculated is not prescribed in the 1996 LLMC but is determined by the national rules.[525] Thus, where there are proceedings in several jurisdictions the shipowner can find some variation in the amounts paid out.

The 1996 LLMC makes it clear that the fund should include interest on the appropriate amount calculated under Articles 6 and 7 for the period between the incident and the establishment of the limitation fund.[526] Thus, payment of the limitation amount without the accrued interest would not be an appropriate fund in accordance with the 1996 LLMC and the shipowners would not be entitled to the protection of Article 13.

Depending on the type of the account in which the limitation amount is held, the interest gained may be compound or simple.[527] The question is to be answered by national law. English courts can only grant simple interest, thus any additional interest is for the shipowner's benefit.[528]

The unit of account for the 1996 and the 1976 LLMC is the Special Drawing Right.[529] The value of the fund is determined at the date the limitation fund is established or payment is made or security is deposited.[530] The exchange rates for the currency of countries which are Member States of the International Monetary Fund (IMF) are determined through the IMF.[531] If a State is not a party to the IMF then that State will have to determine[532] the exchange rate for the SDR and its national currency.[533] The fund can be constituted either by payment into court of the monies required or "by producing a guarantee acceptable under the legislation of the State party where the fund is constituted and considered to be adequate by the court or other competent authority".[534] This wording ensures that where the sum of money corresponding to the limitation fund is paid into court, then the limitation fund is properly constituted but the provision of any other form of financial security or guarantee is possible only where the national court approves it.[535]

---

525. In England, the MSA 1995, Schedule 7, Part II, para 8(1), states that the Secretary of State may prescribe the rate applied. This is done through appropriate statutory instruments – see para 8(2).

526. The position differs under the 1924 and 1957 Limitation Conventions.

527. This means that the interest itself accumulates interest which is added to the capital invested.

528. *Polish Steamship Co v Atlantic Maritime Co (The Garden City (No 2))* [1984] 2 Lloyd's Rep 37.

529. See fn 503.

530. 1996 LLMC, art 8.

531. Accessible through the internet at the IMF website, see www.imf.org (accessed 15 March 2017).

532. Where a State is not a member of the IMF and its national law does not permit the determination of exchange rates the 1996 LLMC permits that such a State can declare the limits of liability of art 8(2) which use as monetary unit 65.5 milligrams of gold of millesimal fineness 900 (art 8(3)).The way of converting such units to national currency is left to the law of the State concerned (art 8.3).

533. 1996 LLMC, art 8(1).

534. Ibid., art 11(2).

535. In *Kairos Shipping Ltd And Another v Enka & Co Llc And Others (The Atlantik Confidence)* [2013] EWHC 1904 (Comm); [2013] 2 Lloyd's Rep 535 Simon J held that under English law only payment into court suffices. The Court of Appeal, [2014] EWCA Civ 217; [2014] 1 Lloyd's Rep 586 reversed the decision holding that the proper interpretation of the 1996 LLMC expressly permits the use of a guarantee and the position under earlier English Law is not relevant.

(k) Which claims are paid out of the limitation fund?

Claims subject to limitation of liability[536] are paid out of the fund. Where the shipowner or its insurer or any third party settles or pays out a claim which would otherwise have been subject to limitation of liability the rights of the claimant are subrogated to shipowner or its insurer or to that third party[537] who is then entitled to claim against the limitation fund. This means that the shipowner or its insurer cannot always recover the full payment they have made prior to the distribution of the fund but only that part of the claim that would have been paid to the claimant had it retained its claim to the fund.

Provision is also made under the 1996 LLMC for situations where a settlement has not yet been reached at the time the fund is distributed. In situations where the person limiting liability or any other person can show that "he may be compelled to pay, at a later date"[538] such a settlement for which had he paid before the distribution of the limitation fund, he would be entitled to claim against the fund having been subrogated to the claimant's rights. The court has discretion to order that a part of the limitation fund should be retained for the payment of the respective proportion of this claim.

Although the 1996 LLMC does not clarify the point, it is strongly arguable that litigation costs are not to be paid out of the limitation fund because otherwise the shipowner would be encouraged to embark upon long litigation knowing that it will not have to pay any additional costs.

The fund is distributed proportionally to the "established claims". The law applicable to the constitution and the distribution of the fund is the law of the State in which the fund is constituted.[539] Apart from the larger amounts available and the priority given in the payment of the loss of life and personal injury claims under Article 6, no other priority is provided for. Thus, any priority of claims *in rem* does not affect the distribution of the limitation fund and it does not matter whether the claims are based on maritime liens or other statutory rights *in rem*. This is further clarified in the MSA 1995, where it is stated that "no lien or other right in respect of any ship or property" shall affect the distribution of the fund.[540]

(l) Consequences of the constitution of the limitation fund

The constitution of a limitation fund which fulfils Article 11 requirements brings immediate protection to the shipowner in respect of any claim made against the fund. Therefore, all other rights against either the person that has established the fund or on behalf of whom the fund is established, i.e. all the "shipowners", salvors and their insurers, are barred.[541] The wording is very general and refers to "any rights", thus it is arguable that security proceedings as well as relief by injunction are also barred.

Where the claimant has succeeded in obtaining security through arrest of the ship or attachment of other property or security in any other form before the establishment of the fund, the establishment of the fund may affect the release of the ship or the security depending on the Contracting State in which the limitation fund is established. Accordingly, where the fund

---

536. That is claims under art 2 not excluded under art 3 of the 1996 LLMC.
537. 1996 LLMC, art 12(2).
538. Ibid., art 12(4).
539. Ibid., art 14.
540. MSA 1995, Schedule 7, Part II, para 9. Because, loss of life and personal injury have a larger fund available and the claims under art 3 are not subject to limitation of liability, there is an indirect priority which partly reflects the *in rem* priority because salvage and crew claims are not subject to limitation. Thus, collision claimants are the primary losers of this arrangement.
541. Ibid., para 13(1).

is constituted at the first port of call after an incident,[542] or at the place of disembarkation in respect of passengers,[543] or the port of discharge in respect of cargo,[544] or the port where the ship is arrested,[545] then the ship or other property or security should be released. While it is not expressly stated it appears reasonable to assume that the obligation to release any arrested ship or security applies equally to all courts in States which are party to the 1996 LLMC. Both the release of the property and the bar against other actions are subject to the condition that the fund is accessible to the claimant.[546] This means that if, for example, a vessel collides with another vessel at a foreign port and the shipowner establishes a limitation fund at that foreign port, the English courts would have to release any vessel arrested in England in respect of that collision. If the collision takes place outside a port, and the limitation fund is not established at the first port of call either because it is established elsewhere or because the ship is lost due to the collision, the English court has discretion to deal with the release of the ship/security.[547]

The discretion of the court refers to security, ship arrest and attachment of property that has happened before the establishment of the fund. Such rights are barred under Article 13(1) after the establishment of a suitable fund. This provides strong imperatives for the shipowner to establish a limitation fund if it wishes to avoid further arrest or freezing measures for security.

The court is authorised to order not only the release of the vessel or the return of bail but also the security provided under contractual terms between the parties,[548] provided that it is subject to that court's jurisdiction.

Where a claim against the limitation fund is made then the claimant is not permitted to enforce its claim against any of the assets of the defendant.[549] This would probably apply whether or not the claim is finally considered to be under the 1996 LLMC. However, if the claim is not under the 1996 LLMC there could be a problem of the action becoming time barred, in particular where specific claims are subject to exclusive jurisdictions and have to be submitted to courts in countries other than that where the limitation fund is established. Because the wording of Article 13 does not restrict the initiation of proceedings on the merits, but only proceedings against assets arguably providing some sort of pre-trial security, it is wise to start proceedings at the appropriate *forum* within time, irrespective of the position on limitation of liability.

Whether Article 13 restricts in any way the right of a claimant to obtain a freezing injunction[550] or any similar restraining order from an English court is questionable.

Freezing injunctions are only viewed as orders against the defendant and not as creating rights against the property.[551] Therefore, it is unlikely that Article 13 restricts by itself the right to apply

---

542. Ibid., art 13(2)(a), or at the port where the incident happened if it did happen within a port. Presumably, the word "port" denotes the administrative characteristics of the port area rather than the physical location within the breakwaters and docks.

543. 1996 LLMC, art 13(2)(b).

544. Ibid., art 13(2)(e).

545. Ibid., art 13(2)(d).

546. Ibid., art 13(3): "only if the claimant may bring a claim against the limitation fund before the Court administering that fund and the fund is actually available and freely transferable in respect of that claim".

547. See *Owners of the Zenatia v Owners of the Putbus (The Putbus)* [1969]1 Lloyd's Rep 253, deciding the point in respect of the 1957 Limitation Convention.

548. See *The Wladyslaw Lokietek* [1978] 2 Lloyd's Rep 520, under s 5 of the Merchant Shipping (Liability of Shipowners and Others) Act 1958. See also *ICL Vickraman* [2003] EWHC 2320 (Comm); [2004] 1 Lloyd's Rep 21, where the same issue was not challenged.

549. See 1996 LLMC, art 13. See also P. Griggs, R. Williams and J. Farr, *Limitation of Liability for Maritime Claims* (4th edn, Informa Law 2005), at 69.

550. See Chapter 12.

551. Freezing injunctions are not pre-trial attachments and they do not give rise to a lien. See *The Cretan Harmony* [1978] 1 Lloyd's Rep 425. See also Chapter 12 page 520.

for a freezing injunction or prejudices the outcome of the application. However, in order to obtain a freezing injunction, the claimant has to show that there is a risk of removal of assets of the defendant.[552] Where the defendant has already established a limitation fund and the claimant has claimed against the fund it would be virtually impossible to demonstrate that the risk of dissipation of assets exists, so it is unlikely that such an order would be granted.

(m) Limitation of liability without the constitution of the fund

The constitution of a limitation fund is particularly useful where there are several claimants. In such a case the establishment of a fund acts as the provision of security for all claims collectively, thus permitting the release of the ship from detention[553] and an assessment of the prospects of recovery for the various claimants. However, where there is only one claimant the constitution of the limitation fund may not be necessary. In such a situation limitation of liability can be used as a defence.[554] Even more, where liability is admitted it is more efficient to order the direct payment of the limitation amount to the sole claimant without the intermediate steps of constituting and administering a fund.

The 1996 LLMC provides as the default position that limitation of liability may be invoked without the constitution of a limitation fund.[555] However, it also provides that the Contracting State may in its national law restrict this position by providing that a person is entitled to limit liability only where an appropriate limitation fund has been constituted.[556] The procedure is left to be decided by the Contracting State.[557]

The UK has not made use of this option;[558] thus under English law, limitation of liability does not depend on the constitution of a limitation fund.[559] English case law strongly supports the assertion that Article 10 provides a free-standing ground for limitation of liability without the establishment of a limitation fund even where no proceedings have yet started, or are not going to be started, in front of an English court.[560] This interpretation considers the issue of jurisdiction in respect of limitation of liability as completely separate from the issue of jurisdiction on the merits of the dispute and permits the shipowner entitled to limit liability under English law to pre-empt the limitation issue by applying for a limitation decree in England.[561]

552. *The Genie* [1979] 2 Lloyd's Rep 184; *Ketchum International Plc v Group Public Relations* [1997] 1 WLR 4. The contact details and the financial standing of the defendant is relevant as well as the type of assets; see, for example, *The Genie* [1979] 2 Lloyd's Rep 184; *Ninemia Maritime Corp v Trave Schiffahrtsgesellsschaft mbH (The Niedersachsen)* [1984] 1 All ER 398. See Chapter 12, page 521.
553. See Chapter 12.
554. Ibid.
555. 1996 LLMC, art 10(1).
556. Ibid., art 10(1).
557. Ibid., art 10(2).
558. MSA 1995, Schedule 7, Part I, para 10(1) only contains the first sentence of the corresponding article of the Convention and states: "Limitation of liability may be invoked notwithstanding that a limitation fund as mentioned in Article 11 has not been constituted."
559. For a discussion of the procedure and case law, see Chapter 12.
560. See *Seismic Shipping Inc and Another v Total E&P UK plc (The Western Regent)* [2005] EWCA Civ 985; [2005] 2 Lloyd's Rep 359 and [2005] EWHC 460 (Admlty); [2005] 2 Lloyd's Rep 54. See also *The Denise*, unreported, 3 December 2004. There is a contradictory *obiter dictum* in *ICL Vickraman* [2003] EWHC 2320 (Comm), which both the High Court and the Court of Appeal in *The Western Regent* have rejected after noting that the working documents of the Convention are in essence neutral on the subject and that the wording of art 10 does not permit such restriction to be applied. However, the English courts retain discretion to order the constitution of a limitation fund under CPR 61.11 13(a)(ii).
561. Note that in the case of *The Western Regent* the defendant demise charterer was registered in England and therefore the English court had personal jurisdiction. Permission to serve out of the jurisdiction is required in other cases which will be discussed in Chapter 12.

(n) Jurisdictional issues

Limitation proceedings should be distinguished from any proceedings on the merits of claims which are subject to limitation of liability.[562] The two jurisdictional issues arising from the limitation proceedings will be now discussed. These are: (a) the relevance of limitation of liability proceedings in determining the jurisdiction on the merits of a claim; and (b) the problem of conflicting limitation of liability provisions in parallel proceedings.

It is beyond the scope of this book to discuss in detail these two very important questions. Thus, only the position under English law will be described.[563]

The English courts consider that a shipowner can start limitation proceedings in respect of any incident as of right even where no claim against it has yet been launched in England.[564] The nature of limitation is not seen as qualifying the substantive right of the claimant.[565] Two consequences follow. First, in a case of *forum non conveniens* the fact that the foreign court applies other limitation of liability arrangements is not a contributing factor to grant a stay of the English proceedings.[566] However, for claims subject to Regulation (EU) No 1215/2012 of the European Parliament and of the Council of 12 December 2012 on jurisdiction and the recognition and enforcement of judgments in civil and commercial matters (recast)[567] (the "Recast Jurisdiction Regulation") where another EU court was first seised on the merits of the dispute, the English court may exercise the discretion granted through Article 30 and stay its own proceedings.[568] However, such a stay must surely be subject to an assessment of the speed at which the other court is expected to progress. If the foreign court is expected to delay resolution of the dispute, it would arguably be best to determine the limitation of liability issue separately by granting the limitation decree and probably making orders for the establishment of the limitation fund, thus liberating the shipowner from protracted litigation in respect of the limitation of liability. Second, where an English limitation decree is issued its effectiveness would, according to the English courts, be left to the courts of non-EU Member States which have jurisdiction on the merits and will not be supported by an anti-suit injunction. For the courts of EU Member States a limitation decree is directly enforceable.[569]

In respect of limitation decrees issued abroad, the position would be as follows: where a limitation decree has been granted in an EU Member State this must be recognised and enforced by an English court subject to Article 45 of the Recast Regulation;[570] where a foreign limitation decree from a non-EU Member State is issued, then its recognition will arguably depend on whether such a decree is from a 1996 LLMC country. Difficulties may arise where a shipowner has lost the right to limit liability in a State applying the 1957 Limitation Convention[571] and then attempts to limit liability in England. Provided that the decision fulfils the common law rules for

---

562. See Chapter 1, page 48.

563. For a detailed analysis, see M.N. Tsimplis, "Law and Jurisdiction for English Limitation of Liability Proceedings" (2010) 16(4) JIML 289.

564. See *The Western Regent* [2005] EWCA Civ 985; [2005] 2 Lloyd's Rep 359.

565. "The effect of the Convention . . . is not to qualify the substantive right of the claimant against the shipowner, but to limit the extent to which that right can be enforced against the limitation fund". See *Caltex Singapore Pte Ltd v BP Shipping Ltd* [1996] 1 Lloyd's Rep 286, 294; approved in *The Western Regent* (fn 553).

566. *The Herceg Novi* [1998] 2 Lloyd's Rep 454. See Chapter 1, page 40.

567. OJ L 351/1, 20 December 2012.

568. *Blue Nile Shipping Co Ltd v Iguana Shipping & Finance Inc (The Happy Fellow)* [1998] 1 Lloyd's Rep 13.

569. *Maersk Olie & Gas A/S v Firma M de Haan en W de Boer* C-39/02 [2004] ECR I-9657.

570. Ibid. This would be the case even if the limitation decision is contradictory to the UK Limitation system.

571. A shipowner may prefer the 1957 Limitation Convention in view of the lower applicable limits.

the recognition of judgments, the shipowner will probably be estopped from retrying the case because the action will be considered as unconscionable.[572]

9. PORTS AND HARBOURS

(a) Introduction

The safety of navigation in British waters, formerly the entire responsibility of Trinity House (in England and Wales), the Commissioners of Northern Lighthouses (in Scotland) and the Commissioners of Irish Lights (in Northern Ireland), has, since the Ports Act 1991, been divided between them and the relevant Statutory Harbour Authorities.[573] The maintenance of lights, lighthouses and buoys has now been taken over by the latter in the waters subject to their jurisdiction, while the former, now collectively referred to as General Lighthouse Authorities, are responsible for the waters not within the jurisdiction of harbour authorities.

Another important function delegated to Harbour Authorities is the administration of the Pilotage service in the port. The pilots are not considered as employees of the port authority, which is not liable for their negligence.[574]

The *Sea Empress* case is the most significant recent decision in this context. A tanker laden with 130,000 tons of crude oil ran aground on 15 February 1996 while entering the Port of Milford Haven with a duly licensed pilot on board. It was admitted that the pilot, but not the port authority, was negligent. The vessel was eventually salved successfully but only after some 70,000 tons of crude oil had been released into the sea. The Milford Haven Port Authority ("MHPA") was prosecuted under an obscure provision of the Water Resources Act 1991. They pleaded guilty to the offence, which was one of strict liability, and were fined £4,000,000 at first instance, reduced on appeal to £750,000. Although the case was a criminal prosecution, it did involve detailed consideration of the role of a statutory port authority and its relationship with the pilotage service in its waters. In the course of his judgment Steel J said:

The significance of these matters is all the greater in the context of a scheme of compulsory pilotage. Shipowners and masters must engage a pilot. They have to take the training, experience and expertise of the pilot provided at face value. While the master remains nominally in command, it has to be recognized that the pilot had the "con" and a master can only intervene when a situation of danger has clearly arisen. The port authority imposes a charge for pilotage but in the same breath has the added advantage of the pilot being treated for purposes of civil liability as an employee of the shipowner. All this calls for the highest possible standards on the part of the port authority.

The MHPA was a public trust set up as statutory body under the Milford Haven Conservancy Act 1958. It was thus typical of the port authorities round the coast of the UK, most of which

---

572. *Henderson v Henderson* [1843] 3 Hare 100. Civil Jurisdiction and Judgments Act 1982, s 34 states:

No proceedings may be brought by a person in England and Wales or Northern Ireland on a cause of action in respect of which a judgment has been given in his favour in proceedings between the same parties, or their privies, in a court in another part of the United Kingdom or in a court of an overseas country, unless that judgment is not enforceable or entitled to recognition in England and Wales or, as the case may be, in Northern Ireland.

This would arguably not apply if a foreign decision removing the right to limit liability from a shipowner has been issued simply because such a judgment cannot be considered as being in his favour. However, if the limitation of liability issue has not been claimed in the foreign or English liability proceedings, there is authority under earlier limitation law that limitation of liability can be raised after the judgment on the merits. See *Baltic Shipping Co v Owners of Cargo on the Mekhanik Evgrafov (The Mekhanik Evgrafov and The Ivan Derbenev)* [1988] 1 Lloyd's Rep 330.

573. MSA 1995, ss 193–223.

574. See the dicta of Steel J in *Environment Agency v Milford Haven Port Authority (The Sea Empress)* [1999] 1 Lloyd's Rep 673. The appeal is reported at [2000] JPL 943. Ibid. at page 679.

have their own enabling legislation derived from similar nineteenth century statutes incorporating the terms of the Harbour Docks and Piers Clauses Act 1847.

(b) Port safety management

The principles applicable to matters of safety in port operations are now set out in the Port Marine Safety Code and the associated Guide to Good Practice on Port Marine Operations both published in 2016,[575] following an extensive review of the laws relating to port authorities and pilotage. This code is not written in mandatory terms, but represents a clear statement of best practice in all aspects of port operation, and is likely to be accepted by courts as the yardstick by which port authorities will be judged if civil claims are brought against them.

(c) Limitation of liability

The subject of limitation of liability of the owners of ships is dealt with elsewhere in this chapter,[576] but in the context of the liabilities of port authorities it should be noted that English law contains an exceptional provision, now in section 191 of the Merchant Shipping Act 1995. This entitles a port authority to limit its liability to the amount of the limitation fund of the largest UK ship which is in the port at the time of the damage giving rise to the claim, or has been within the preceding five years. The provision, which does not derive from any international convention,[577] but which would apply to a claim by a foreign claimant as much as a British port authority, is rarely invoked. It would have been applicable to civil claims against the MHPA arising out of the *Sea Empress* case.

(d) Claims by port authorities

One of the last vestiges of the nineteenth century statute applicable to port authorities is to be found in section 74 of the Harbours Docks and Piers Clauses Act 1847. It creates strict liability on the owner of any vessel causing damage to the harbour dock or pier. That liability is independent of any negligence on the part of the shipowner, but does not prevent him from limiting his liability under the MSA 1995.

(e) Port state control

One of the most important results of the Merchant Shipping and Maritime Security Act 1997, following the publication of the Donaldson Report[578] in the light of the *Braer* casualty in 1992, was to define the powers of detention by harbour authorities of unsafe ships under the regime of Port State Control established, in the case of the UK, by the Paris Memorandum.[579] This was a result of the growing concerns of coastal States at the failure of flag States to enforce their own rules regarding ship safety. The coastal States have now given their port authorities very

---

575. Full details are available from the website of the Department for Transport at www.gov.uk/government/uploads/system/uploads/attachment_data/file/564723/port-marine-safety-code.pdf and www.gov.uk/government/uploads/system/uploads/attachment_data/file/590160/guide-good-practice-marine-code.pdf (accessed 15 March 2017).

576. Section 8 of this chapter.

577. It was first enacted in the Merchant Shipping (Liability of Shipowners and others) Act 1900. A similar provision applies to claims against pilots under the Pilotage Act 1987, s 22.

578. *Safer Ships, Cleaner Seas: Report of Lord Donaldson's Inquiry into the Prevention of Pollution from Merchant Shipping* (HMSO 1994, Cm 2560).

579. See Chapter 9. See also www.parismou.org/ (accessed 15 March 2017). For a full review of this subject, see N. Gaskell, *Merchant Shipping Act 1995, Current Law Statutes Annotated*.

extensive powers of inspection and detention of ships which do not comply with the internationally recognised standards. The results of the inspections are posted, on an open access basis, on the www.equasis.org website.

(f) Places of refuge[580]

The question of the right of the master of a ship in distress to seek shelter in a place of refuge has become topical as a consequence of two well-publicised incidents involving the ships *Castor* and *Prestige*.[581] Both were tankers and both suffered structural failure in heavy weather off the coast of Spain, the *Castor* in the Mediterranean and the *Prestige* in the Atlantic. In both cases permission to enter a Spanish port was refused. The *Castor* was eventually salved successfully after a long and difficult operation, but the *Prestige* broke in two and sank, causing very extensive pollution of the coasts of Spain, Portugal and France.

International law has long recognised the duty of a coastal State to allow entry of a ship in distress.[582] This right, which was largely based on humanitarian considerations for the safety of the crew, has however been eroded by increasing concerns for the protection of the coastal State's marine environment, and by the availability of helicopters to rescue the crews of ships in distress.

The IMO has adopted Guidelines on Places of Refuge which set out criteria for the objective assessment of the condition of a ship in distress but which do not create binding obligations to coastal States.[583]

The European Union has taken a more active stance[584] in pressing Member States to adopt clear rules, based on the IMO Guidelines, for the admission of ships to places of refuge, and the designation of such places on the coasts of such States.[585]

10. TECHNOLOGY AND SHIPPING LAW

Technological development has historically challenged contemporary shipping laws. The development of mechanically propelled ships required the development of special navigational rules when such ships encountered sailing ships which have less manoeuvrability. Hovercrafts, jet-skis, inflatables, offshore platforms and mobile offshore drilling units, submarines and

580. The best collection of papers on this subject is in the 2003 CMI Year Book at www.comitemaritime.org/Uploads/Yearbooks/YBK_2003.pdf and in the 2004 Year Book at www.comitemaritime.org/Uploads/Yearbooks/YBK_2004.pdf (accessed 15 March 2017).

581. The facts of these cases are set out in R. Shaw, "Places of Refuge: International Law in the Making", CMI Year Book 2003, at pp 332–333 accessible at the web address cited above.

582. *Kate A Hoff v The United Mexican States (The Rebecca)* [1929] 4 RAAA 444. The material section of the award is cited in E.D. Brown, *The International Law of the Sea* (Dartmouth Publishing Co 1994), at p 39.

583. Adopted by IMO Resolution A949(23) and the IMO Guidelines on the control of ships in an emergency, adopted as IMO Circular MSC.1/Circ.1251. The nub of these guidelines states in paragraph 1.7:"granting access to a place of refuge could involve a political decision which can only be taken on a case by case basis with due consideration given to the balance between the advantage for the affected ship and the environment resulting from bringing the ship into a place of refuge and the risk to the environment resulting from that ship being near to the coast."Again at paragraph 3.12: "When permission to access a place of refuge is requested, there is no obligation for the coastal State to grant it, but the coastal State should weigh all the factors and risks in a balanced manner and give shelter whenever reasonably possible."

584. See Directive 2002/59/EC of the European Parliament and of the Council of 27 June 2002 establishing a Community vessel traffic monitoring and information system and repealing Council Directive 93/75/EEC, arts 20 and 21.

585. The CMI has maintained an active working group on places of refuge and a draft instrument has been prepared, which would give greater legal force to the principles set out in the IMO Guidelines, and which would create a presumption of a right of access to a place of refuge for a ship in distress. That presumption would be rebuttable on proof by the coastal State that the risk of environmental damage caused by admitting a ship to its harbours outweighs the risks of leaving the ship at the mercy of wind and waves in the open sea. See http://comitemaritime.org/Places-of-Refuge/0,2733,13332,00.html (accessed 15 March 2017).

submersibles all present two challenging questions, one legal, and one of policy. The legal question is whether, on the basis of existing laws, they fall within one or more of the legal arrangements discussed above in this chapter as well as in other parts of this book. Are their owners entitled to the shipowner's limitation rights and the specific maritime time bars? Should they be subject to the same criminal and civil liabilities as ordinary ships? Practically the legal question is answered by courts on a case-by-case basis. The second question is whether, as a matter of policy, such craft ought to be covered by one or another instrument of shipping law. Such discussion is rather difficult especially where the established rights and obligations have been in existence for so long that the original policy considerations underpinning them are no longer directly relevant.[586]

Recent technological developments promise to revolutionise shipping by enabling "unmanned" ships, that is, ships which will be either remotely controlled or which will be able to navigate on their own, guided by a computer program.[587] Craft with such characteristics are already in use for marine exploration and naval operations but plans are afoot for test applications of this technology in passenger ferries and container ships within the next few years. Of course automation has been happening for decades leading to the reduction of crew on board but the possibility of wholly unmanned ships challenges the existing legal framework in various ways. Important questions include whether such craft are to be covered by shipping legislation, who is the master and how would the master's duties and the criminal and administrative liability imposed on a master be discharged. There could be a need to amend the Collision Regulations if the available technology cannot provide collision avoidance where conventionally navigated ships meet unmanned ships. However, if such craft are not covered by the shipping legislation then a new legal framework should be developed if they are going to be used. This is probably a more difficult proposition because their use in international trade would require international consensus. To the extent this is already available for ships, based on the extensive work undertaken within the IMO framework, what would the benefit be for a separate legal regime, rather than an appropriately modified one? The technology may be developed so that ships move autonomously with a caretaker crew ready to intervene if the systems fail. Does it make sense to differentiate, for regulatory purposes, craft performing the same functions on the basis of whether it is on autopilot with a master at the bridge or a controller in a shore-based facility?

Commercial and safety considerations will, in the end, decide whether unmanned ships will replace manned ships in the future. Their commercial advantages in terms of scientific research and for supporting naval operations and offshore work are already proven but this is not yet the case for large commercial ships. However, it is not obvious whether salvage operations would be easy for such craft and whether the risk of minor incidents turning into major catastrophes will be larger. The view of the author is that the major safety risk is in the mix of manned with unmanned ships rather than in any inherent risk in autonomy. Management of the voyage so that collision risks are minimised by sharing information about voyage planning and the development of sea traffic management systems can be the basis of increasing safety in the future. This may be considered as restricting the freedoms of navigation. However, the arguments about safety and efficiency that such systems can deliver would force shipping law to adopt them in one form or another.[588]

---

586. One such example is limitation of liability which was developed for the purpose of protecting shipowners and encouraging national investment in shipping and trade but which is extended to recreational ships.

587. For a detailed discussion see R. Veal and M. Tsimplis "The integration of unmanned ships into the *lex maritima*" [2017] LMCLQ 303. See also A. Serdy, M. Tsimplis, R. Veal et al., *Liability for Operation in Unmanned Maritime Vehicles with Differing Levels of Autonomy*, (European Defence Agency, Brussels 2016). To obtain a copy, please contact Mr Paul O'Brien of the EDA at paul.obrien@eda.europa.eu.

588. See, for example, the Sea Traffic Management Validation project: http://stmvalidation.eu/

CHAPTER 8

PUBLIC INTERNATIONAL LAW ASPECTS OF SHIPPING REGULATION

Andrew Serdy

1. INTRODUCTION – THE PLACE OF INTERNATIONAL LAW IN THE SHIPPING WORLD AND ITS SOURCES

In the regulatory framework for shipping, no less than for most other fields of human endeavour, it is not possible to escape the influence of public international law.[1] This is the system of law that governs relations between States[2] and other actors whose personality is recognised on the international plane, most relevantly for present purposes international organisations established by States.[3]

Every State is a single legal person in international law, even if it is federal in character like Australia, Brazil, Canada, Germany, India, Malaysia, Mexico, Nigeria, Switzerland or the United

---

1. A fine and still up-to-date general introduction to public international law is V. Lowe, *International Law* (Oxford University Press 2007). For an even briefer introduction from a law of the sea perspective, see Chapter 1 of R.R. Churchill and A.V. Lowe, *The Law of the Sea* (3rd edn, Manchester University Press 1999) (hereinafter "Churchill & Lowe"), at pp 1–13 and 22–25.

2. "State" is the term preferred in international law parlance to "country" or "nation"; "country" has a much looser meaning, e.g. Hong Kong may for most purposes be thought of as a country, but formally it is a Special Administrative Region of the People's Republic of China, the State ultimately responsible for its international relations, whereas "nation", though part of an older name by which public international law was once known (the law of nations) too easily risks confusion with the people(s) inhabiting a given State.

3. Non-governmental organisations are thus excluded.

States (US), or, like the United Kingdom (UK), has devolved substantial governmental powers to regional authorities in parts of its territory. International organisations are established by treaties between States, which usually provide that the organisation is to have independent legal personality. The oldest international organisations such as the Universal Postal Union appeared in the late nineteenth century, but it is since the Second World War that the growth in their number has been most rapid. Examples include the United Nations (UN) and its specialised agencies like the International Maritime Organization (IMO) discussed below,[4] as well as regional organisations such as the European Union (EU) or the North Atlantic Treaty Organization (NATO).[5]

Natural and legal persons, i.e. human beings and companies or other entities that the law of a given country endows with personality, were until quite recently not subjects of international law, and their role in it today remains fragmentary.[6] While treaties might be entered into by States for their benefit, they did not confer rights on those persons under international law – rather, they conferred rights on their States of nationality to insist that all other States party to the treaty comply with its provisions. Although some modern treaties confer rights directly on individuals (usually in the field of human rights) and companies (usually in the field of investment protection), it does not automatically follow – unless, that is, the treaty specifically provides a mechanism for it – that they will have some means of enforcing these rights on the international law plane. For example, if a company's rights are violated by a foreign State, it must rely on its own State of nationality (normally the State under whose laws it was incorporated) to espouse a diplomatic claim on its behalf against the delinquent State.

Thus, while today it is accepted that private shipping interests as natural or more frequently legal persons, even though not subjects of international law under the traditional view, can have certain rights and obligations under international law, these are far more limited in extent than those of States. An illustration of this is the 2008 decision of the European Court of Justice (ECJ) in the *Intertanko* case[7] declining to rule on whether Directive 2005/35/EC of the European Parliament and Council on Ship-Source Pollution, which requires EU Member States to ensure that within their legal systems pollution caused by "serious negligence" attracts criminal sanctions, was contrary to the United Nations Convention on the Law of the Sea (UNCLOS).[8] This was on the basis that UNCLOS as a treaty created rights and obligations only for States, not for the applicants, who were a coalition of shipping industry associations.[9] Another way of putting this is to say that, at least in the UK and other States whose legal system is based on the common law,[10] international law works on private companies and individuals by way of interposition: if, for example, the master of a ship is charged with an offence as a consequence of a collision, the offence tried before the UK court will be described not as a contravention of the COLREG

---

4. See section 4 below.

5. International organisations are not always as large or well known as these. Those with specialised functions such as managing world supply and demand of a commodity, e.g. the International Coffee Organization, or regulating international fisheries, such as the North-East Atlantic Fisheries Commission, had a staff small enough in the cases of these examples to be able to share between them, until the mid-2010s, a modest office building in central London.

6. Underscoring its exceptional nature, the most prominent direct application of public international law to natural persons in recent years has been by way of prosecutions of individuals accused of war crimes, crimes against humanity and genocide before the International Criminal Court and the tribunals established by UN Security Council resolutions after the Yugoslavia and Rwanda conflicts.

7. *R (Intertanko and Ors) v Secretary of State for Transport,* C-308/06, EU:C:2008:312, [2008] ECR I-4057.

8. United Nations Convention on the Law of the Sea (Montego Bay, 10 December 1982); 1833 United Nations Treaty Series (hereinafter "UNTS") 3.

9. See fn 7, at [64] – [66].

10. The situation may be different in other States such as Germany whose constitutions provide for international law to be directly effective in creating rights and obligations for natural and legal persons (see art 25 of the *Grundgesetz für die Bundesrepublik Deutschland* (23 May 1949; BGBl. I S. 1), as most recently amended on 23 December 2014 (BGBl. I S. 2438) – but even in this case, the result is brought about by a rule of the State in question, not anything inherent in international law itself.

Convention,[11] but rather of the provision of the Merchant Shipping (Distress Signals and Prevention of Collisions) Regulations 1996[12] under the Merchant Shipping Act 1995 which enacts these rules into UK law. The UK, by virtue of being party to that convention, has to legislate domestically in order to be able to implement and comply with its obligations.

One of the crucial differences between the international legal system and its national counterparts is that there is no international legislature which can enact laws binding on all States. The two main sources of international law affecting shipping (and everything else) are custom, also known as customary international law, and treaties.[13]

(a) Customary international law

This refers to the body of international law rules having their source in the settled practice of States. Not all practices which States customarily observe, however, are required by international law – the reason for them may be no more than courtesy, or the relevant State's own self-interest. To be a rule of customary international law, the practice of States must meet two requirements:

- constant and uniform usage practised by States (State practice for short); and
- recognition by them that this practice is the result of a rule of law or legal obligation (this psychological element is called *opinio iuris sive necessitatis*, usually abbreviated simply to *opinio iuris*).[14]

Some rules of custom have evolved over centuries of practice, such as those regulating diplomatic immunity. It is, however, possible for a permissive rule (i.e. a State may do X) to be established by the practice of just a few States over a short period if other States acquiesce in it, as occurred at the beginning of the space age when States began to send satellites into orbit passing over other States' territories. Until then a State's sovereignty had been thought to extend infinitely upwards from the earth above its territory, but henceforth it was confined to airspace only, beyond which a new set of rules operated in outer space. On the other hand, a mandatory rule (i.e. a State must [not] do Y) requires the widespread practice of States acknowledging its existence, especially by those States particularly affected – though it need not be completely uniform (since States do after all sometimes breach international law).

---

11. Convention on the International Regulations for Preventing Collisions at Sea (London, 20 October 1972); 1050 UNTS 16.

12. SI 1996/75, reg 4(1).

13. From time to time suggestions are made that modern developments have produced additional avenues for creating international law, the most frequently mentioned being acts of international organisations and so-called non-binding "soft law", but these always, when they produce results recognisable as law, do so directly or indirectly by way of one or other of custom and treaties. Some international organisations are authorised by the treaties that establish them to adopt resolutions automatically binding on all members, for example certain decisions of the UN Security Council under art 25 of the UN Charter. Resolutions of international organisations can also be evidence of rules of customary international law if supported by most States with few or none voting against them. This is so especially where the resolution itself asserts the existence of a particular rule of international law, e.g. the UN General Assembly's Declaration on Principles of International Law Concerning Friendly Relations and Co-operation Among States (UN General Assembly Resolution 2625/XXV of 24 October 1970). Similarly, the prescriptions in soft-law instruments, typically phrased in the form "States should . . ." rather than "States shall . . ." to avoid being binding as treaties, may subsequently harden into custom.

14. State practice and expressions of *opinio juris* by governments can take many forms, e.g. national legislation, parliamentary or other policy statements, press releases, official publications, diplomatic correspondence and protests, statements in international organisations, arguments before international courts and tribunals, comments on draft international treaties or decisions by States' domestic courts. See D. Harris and S. Sivakumaran, *Cases and Materials on International Law* (8th edn, Sweet & Maxwell 2015), at p 19 and sources there cited.

One of the uncertainties about rules of customary international law is that it is often difficult to know whether, and if so when, they have been modified by the subsequent practice of States. A new customary rule often begins life by way of an apparent breach of the old one that goes largely unchallenged. Thus, the various claims made by States from the 1960s onwards to extend their fisheries and pollution jurisdiction beyond the territorial sea were, on their face, contrary to the customary rule codified in the 1958 Convention on the High Seas, that "[t]he high seas being open to all nations, no State may validly purport to subject any part of them to its sovereignty".[15] Since not all States accepted the validity of such claims, there ensued a period of chaos in the law of the sea, putting an end to which was one of the aims of the Third United Nations Conference on the Law of the Sea. The proceedings at this conference confirmed that such jurisdictional claims were valid at customary international law, even before UNCLOS, the product of the conference, entered into force on 16 November 1994.

(b) Treaties

UNCLOS, the central instrument of the modern law of the sea, is a treaty.[16] Treaties come under a variety of formal titles (apart from "treaty" itself, "convention" as in UNCLOS, "protocol", "covenant", "agreement", "exchange of letters" are often encountered), but their essence is that they are agreements between States or international organisations intended by their parties to be binding in international law. They are a versatile instrument. Bilateral treaties (those concluded between two States) serve some of the same functions as contracts under national law, particularly where they are for a specific purpose. By contrast, multilateral treaties – those laying down general rules of conduct for all States parties – are to a lesser degree comparable to legislation in national law, for instance the many shipping-related conventions negotiated under the aegis of the IMO.[17] The most important distinction from legislation, however, is that a treaty is only ever binding on those States which are parties to it.[18]

The last sentence does, however, require a qualification, for treaties can themselves be a source of customary international law. If many States are parties to a multilateral treaty containing a certain rule, and there is no practice of other States inconsistent with that rule, then the treaty may be evidence of a rule of custom. Thus over time treaties exert what Mendelson has called a "gravitational pull" on the pre-existing custom, so that even non-parties become bound – not by the treaty as such, but by some or all of the substantive rules within it.[19] Some multilateral treaties are expressed to codify existing rules of international law in a given field, the 1958 Convention on the High Seas being a prominent example.[20]

15. Convention on the High Seas (Geneva, 29 April 1958); 450 UNTS 11, art 2.

16. Most treaties are registered with the UN Secretariat under art 102 of the UN Charter and are then published, with some time lag, in the UNTS, whose online version is available at https://treaties.un.org/Pages/Content.aspx?path=DB/UNTS/pageIntro_en.xml (accessed 30 January 2017).

17. An incomplete list of these is given at page 331 of this chapter.

18. This rule, sometimes called the *pacta tertiis* principle after the Latin maxim *Pacta tertiis nec nocent nec prosunt* (treaties neither harm nor favour third parties) is found in art 34 of the Vienna Convention on the Law of Treaties (Vienna, 23 May 1969; 1155 UNTS 331), and, like most of that convention, represents a codification of the pre-existing customary law regarding treaties.

19. M.H. Mendelson, "Fragmentation of the Law of the Sea" (1988) 12 *Marine Policy* 192, at p 199. Some technical or procedural treaty provisions, such as those relating to the settlement of disputes arising under the treaty, can never enter the realm of custom. The general rule as expressed by the International Court of Justice in the *North Sea Continental Shelf case (Federal Republic of Germany/Denmark; Federal Republic of Germany/Netherlands)*, ICJ Reports 1969, 3 at pp 41–42 ([72]) is that only those provisions can do so which are "of fundamentally norm-creating character", thus capable of forming the basis of a general rule of law.

20. See fn 15; see both paragraphs of the preamble.

As between parties to a treaty, its provisions prevail over rules of customary international law (though occasionally, as seen above, new rules of custom may displace older treaty rules). Thus, by entering into treaties, States modify their mutual rights and obligations under custom. Because of the relative certainty and ease of reference they offer as a source of law by comparison with custom, treaties have become the major vehicle for international co-operation. Developed States are commonly party to thousands of treaties affecting all areas of governmental activity; for the UK the number is over 13,000.[21]

(c) Judicial decisions and academic writings

As there is no doctrine of precedent in international law,[22] decisions of international courts and tribunals are binding only on the parties to the actual dispute. (Nor does international law impose judicial settlement and arbitration *a priori* as methods of settling disputes – the basic obligation is no more than that it be done peacefully.)[23] Even so, they are influential as a subsidiary means for determination of rules of international law, especially judgments of the International Court of Justice (ICJ) and, specifically for shipping and other uses of the ocean, of the International Tribunal for the Law of the Sea (ITLOS).[24]

Academic writings can also be evidence of a rule of international law, if the writer is eminent, and the study is based on a comprehensive and impartial examination of State practice. Also significant in this regard, and frequently cited by the ICJ in its judgments, are reports of the International Law Commission (ILC), a body of eminent international lawyers established by the UN General Assembly in 1947 to promote the codification and progressive development of international law.[25]

21. A. Aust, *Handbook of International Law* (2nd edn, Cambridge University Press 2010), at p 106.

22. This is the effect of the provision in art 59 of the ICJ Statute, annexed to the UN Charter, that "The decision of the Court has no binding force except between the parties and in respect of that particular case." Art 296(2) of UNCLOS is a parallel provision for disputes under that convention.

23. UN Charter, art 2(3). Judicial settlement and arbitration are merely two of a non-exhaustive list of means offered by art 33(1) of the Charter. The jurisdiction of international courts and tribunals is therefore ultimately always based on the consent of the disputing parties – there is no way of compelling a non-consenting State to appear. So-called "compulsory" jurisdiction, for example the elaborate compulsory dispute settlement mechanism contained in UNCLOS (see fn 8, Part XV, arts 279–299), can only be based on a treaty into which there is no compulsion to enter, so that the obligation to submit to a particular body's jurisdiction is itself always ultimately voluntarily undertaken. (This is a different issue from the non-appearance by respondent States not accepting the jurisdiction of a court or tribunal in a particular case despite having consented to it via such a treaty. Since by art 36(6) of the ICJ Statute, mirrored by art 288(4) of UNCLOS, the decision as to whether the body concerned has jurisdiction is one for the body itself to take, which normally treats the non-appearance as a preliminary objection to its jurisdiction, absent respondents take the risk that their objection will be dismissed, and the case can proceed without them if they persist with their election not to defend themselves. This occurred in the *Arctic Sunrise* and *South China Sea* arbitrations, PCA Cases 2014–02, In the Matter of the Arctic Sunrise Arbitration before an Arbitral Tribunal Constituted under Annex VII to the 1982 United Nations Convention on the Law of the Sea between the Kingdom of the Netherlands and the Russian Federation, Award on the Merits, 14 August 2015, https://pcacases.com/web/sendAttach/1438 and 2013–19, In the Matter of the South China Sea Arbitration before an Arbitral Tribunal Constituted under Annex VII to the 1982 United Nations Convention on the Law of the Sea between the Republic of the Philippines and the People's Republic of China, Award, 12 July 2016, www.pcacases.com/pcadocs/PH-CN%20-%2020160712%20-%20Award.pdf respectively (both accessed on 31 December 2016). A further risk to the non-appearing respondent is that the court or tribunal may inadvertently overlook an argument favourable to it despite its duty to satisfy itself that any finding it makes for the applicant is well founded in fact and law; for a possible example of this in the *Arctic Sunrise* case see below, at page 336.)

24. The ICJ at The Hague is a permanent judicial body for the settlement of disputes between States. All members of the UN are automatically parties to its Statute. By arts 3(1) and 9 of its Statute, the Court has 15 judges representative of the "main forms of civilization" and principal legal systems of the world. Other permanent bodies besides the ICJ exist for settling international disputes, for example UNCLOS is also the vehicle by which ITLOS was established. The Statute of ITLOS forms Annex VI to UNCLOS.

25. See art 13(1) of the UN Charter, which gave this role to the General Assembly itself, and General Assembly Resolution 174/II of 21 November 1947, by which the ILC was created and to which its Statute is annexed.

2. MARITIME ZONES RELEVANT TO SHIPPING

In this work, concentrating as it does on navigation, it is not necessary to consider the full panoply of maritime zones known to the contemporary law of the sea, as most of the modern ones were created in order to deal with problems of the exploitation of oceanic resources. The following introduction is based on the two "traditional" zones only, expanded where appropriate to take into account developments in the twentieth century.

(a) The two traditional maritime zones

The traditional zones are (i) a narrow belt of water running along the coast, known as the territorial sea, beyond which are (ii) the high seas. The territorial sea is in places supplemented by internal waters (under the full sovereignty of the coastal State, and treated as equivalent to land) lying landward of the baselines from which the breadth of the territorial sea is measured. The territorial sea is also under the coastal State's sovereignty, but subject to the right of innocent passage for foreign ships, a concept considered further below. The high seas were defined negatively as an area beyond the territorial sea, in which no claim to sovereignty or jurisdiction by any State was permitted.[26] Freedom of navigation thus prevailed on the high seas, as well as certain other well-recognised freedoms such as fishing. This is not to say that States could act as they pleased on the high seas, for that would have been anarchy; rather, States had to exercise their freedoms with reasonable regard for the like exercise of freedoms by other States.[27]

Through the advent of the exclusive economic zone (EEZ) the high seas are now much reduced in area, and the seabed is subject to changed rules, but the outlines of the regime affecting the surface and water column – which is all we are interested in for shipping purposes – are largely left unaltered by UNCLOS. Instead of the four freedoms in the 1958 Convention (navigation, fishing, laying of submarine cables and pipelines, overflight) there are now six: the new ones are the freedom to construct artificial islands and other installations permitted under international law, subject to Part VI, and freedom of scientific research, subject to Parts VI and XIII. (This does not mean that the high seas are becoming freer, for neither the 1958 nor the UNCLOS list is exhaustive, and their elements are better thought of as instances of a single undifferentiated freedom of the high seas, which over the years has become subject to more qualifications, as is apparent in the UNCLOS list itself.) The EEZ, as explained below, can by virtue of Article 58 also be treated as equivalent to the high seas for most navigational purposes.

In the pre-UNCLOS era the major controversies were over the maximum permissible breadth of the territorial sea and the use of straight baselines, from which that breadth is measured, to enclose areas of ocean as internal waters. The major maritime powers of the day – the UK, US, Germany, Japan, France – maintained that the territorial sea was 3 nm (nautical miles),[28] but even then there were widely tolerated regional departures from this practice, such as 4 nm in Scandinavia and 6 nm in parts of the Mediterranean. The twentieth century saw the making of claims by increasingly numerous States to a territorial sea of 12 nm, mainly because of security and fisheries concerns, and in the 1940s and 1950s a number of mostly Latin American States made claims to a territorial sea of 200 nm. Reaching agreement on the maximum breadth was

---

26. See fn 15. That provision is now reproduced in art 89 of UNCLOS (fn 8).

27. The "reasonable regard" standard was codified in art 2(2) of the High Seas Convention (fn 15), but replaced by the slightly more rigorous "due regard" in UNCLOS (fn 8), art 87(2).

28. A nautical mile equals exactly 1,852 metres and is a close approximation to one minute of latitude anywhere on the Earth's surface and one minute of longitude at the equator. See International Hydrographic Organization (IHO), *Hydrographic Dictionary, Part I, Vol. I.* (5th edn, IHO 1994), at p 116.

one of the aims of the 1930 League of Nations Conference on the Codification of International Law, but this effort ended in failure. Attempts to reach a compromise of a six-mile territorial sea plus a further six miles of exclusive coastal State fishery jurisdiction came close to success at the First (1958) and Second (1960) UN Conferences on the Law of the Sea, but agreement remained elusive. All that the ILC could conclude in the commentary to its draft articles prepared for the 1958 conference was that the limit was certainly no more than 12 nm, but might be less.[29]

UNCLOS Article 3 has now settled the maximum breadth of the territorial sea at 12 nm. The rules on straight baselines and bay-closing lines (Articles 7 to 10), however, though admittedly putting some discipline on the drawing of baselines as a way of expanding the area under a coastal State's sovereignty, still leave quite some leeway for their manipulation to this end. Only the US through its Freedom of Navigation programme dating from the 1970s systematically challenges baselines it believes to have been improperly drawn, by a combination of diplomatic protest and directing the US Navy to exercise its navigational rights in the area concerned without seeking prior permission from the relevant coastal State. By contrast, other States tend to protest at only those baselines that directly affect the extent of their own maritime zones, i.e. those of their near neighbours, and take interest in the baselines of more distant States only if they impinge on some specific navigational interest.[30]

Why was the breadth of the territorial sea so controversial? The long insistence by maritime States on 3 nm was fuelled by the fear that certain narrow straits essential for military and commercial communication would lose the high seas corridor through their middle if a broader territorial sea were to become the norm. Innocent passage was not an acceptable substitute because it could be suspended by the coastal State.[31] Ultimately they accepted 12 nm as the maximum only on condition of a new regime of transit passage through straits used for international navigation that forms Part III (Articles 34–45) of UNCLOS.[32] This regime incorporates wider navigational rights (subject to the requirement that the transit be "continuous and expeditious") into a new concept of non-suspendable transit passage in those straits, which the littoral State may not hamper, superimposed on the territorial sea status of the strait.[33]

(b) New maritime zones in the modern law of the sea

Several more zones now exist, but some of them are of limited relevance to shipping:

1. Archipelagic waters, added by Part IV (Articles 46–54) of UNCLOS. This concept recognises the special interest of States such as Indonesia and the Philippines, whose

29. *Report of the International Law Commission covering the work of its eighth session, 23 April–4 July 1956* (UN doc A/3159), reprinted in *Yearbook of the International Law Commission 1956*, Vol II (United Nations 1957) 253, at p 265.

30. See J.R.V. Prescott, "Straight Baselines: Theory and Practice", in E.D. Brown and R.R. Churchill (eds), *The UN Convention on the Law of the Sea: Impact and Implementation* (Law of the Sea Institute 1987), 288 for a pessimistic account of this state of affairs, concluding that inaction by other States has amounted to their acquiescence in the capture of large areas of ocean without any basis in UNCLOS. Seafarers would certainly be well advised to proceed on the presumption that baselines are valid or have become validated in this way, absent an assurance from the flag State of the ship that it has protested against the baseline in timely fashion – and even this is no guarantee against an incident occurring that will result in at best delay and at worst the ship's prolonged detention.

31. Convention on the Territorial Sea and Contiguous Zone (Geneva, 29 April 1958), 516 UNTS 205, art 16(3); see now UNCLOS, art 25(3).

32. In the late 1960s the US circulated to other States a list of 116 straits between 6 nm and 24 nm wide at their narrowest point, which would thus become completely overlapped by territorial sea. The list was incomplete, as, according to A.R. Thomas and J.C. Duncan (eds), *Annotated Supplement to the Commander's Handbook on the Law of Naval Operations* (US Naval War College 1999), at pp 207–208 (Table A2–5), there are in fact 153 such straits. Many of these are of little or no navigational importance, but several are crucial for international commerce: the Straits of Dover, Gibraltar, Malacca, Singapore, Bab-el-Mandab at the southern end of the Red Sea and Hormuz at the mouth of the Persian Gulf.

33. UNCLOS (fn 8), art 38(1) and (2).

territory consists of many islands, in the waters within the archipelago previously regarded as high seas. They wished to be permitted to draw baselines around the archipelago, but this would have transformed the waters within into internal waters. The compromise solution is for archipelagic States (defined in Article 46) to have such baselines,[34] but within them the waters – known as archipelagic waters – have a status more akin to the territorial sea, including the rules on innocent passage,[35] while the routes hitherto used for transit through the archipelago now have a special regime of archipelagic sea lanes passage (Article 53) modelled on the transit passage regime for straits of Part III.[36]

2. The contiguous zone. From the early twentieth century many States made claims to jurisdiction over certain matters falling short of full territorial sea rights in a zone adjacent to and seaward of the territorial sea. Article 24 of the 1958 Convention on the Territorial Sea and Contiguous Zone permitted any State claiming a territorial sea of less than 12 nm to exercise out to 12 nm jurisdiction to prevent and punish infringements of its customs, fiscal, immigration and sanitary (that is, animal and plant quarantine) laws in its territorial sea or land territory, including implicitly any water between the two.[37] Article 33 of UNCLOS retains the 1958 regime but extends the outer limit of the contiguous zone to 24 nm from the baselines.

3. The exclusive economic zone. This is another of the compromises in UNCLOS, added by Part V (Articles 55–75). Up to a maximum of 200 nm from the baselines from which the breadth of the territorial sea is measured,[38] the coastal State may claim sovereign rights over the exploration, exploitation, conservation and management of the living and non-living resources, jurisdiction over artificial islands, protection of the marine environment (including against pollution) and certain other matters.[39] In this zone the coastal State in exercising its rights and duties must have "due regard to the rights and duties of other States" (Article 56(2)), which by Article 58(1) include the freedoms of navigation and overflight as well as laying cables and pipelines and "other internationally lawful uses of the sea related to these freedoms, such as those associated with the operation of ships". Article 58(2) imports into the EEZ the high seas rules (other than on resources) "in so far as they are not incompatible with this Part". The net result is that for almost all navigational purposes, although the EEZ is no longer part of the high seas,[40] it can still be treated as though it were. This explains the frequency of reference in navigational circles to "international waters", a term unknown to the law of the sea, but useful nonetheless, as it refers to the area seaward of the territorial sea, i.e. an amalgam of the EEZ and the high seas.

4. The continental shelf. Dating from the mid-twentieth century,[41] this zone, in which the coastal State has sovereign rights over mineral resources and sedentary living species

34. The UK as well as other island States such as Japan and New Zealand, though they meet the definition of archipelagic States in art 46 of UNCLOS, are not permitted to draw archipelagic baselines because they do not satisfy one of the conditions in art 47 for doing so: that between 10 and 50 per cent of the area enclosed by baselines be land. In other words, they have too much land relative to the water between their islands.

35. See also below the *Duzgit Integrity* arbitration, text at fnn 74–78.

36. For the role of the IMO in approving the axis lines defining these sealanes, see pages 346–347.

37. Note that this is enforcement rather than legislative jurisdiction, so making this a buffer zone in which the laws themselves do not apply, in the sense that acts within the contiguous zone as opposed to the territorial sea cannot themselves attract criminal sanctions.

38. Thus if the State has a 12 nm territorial sea, the maximum breadth of its EEZ is 188 nm, not 200 nm.

39. See UNCLOS (fn 8), art 56(1).

40. Ibid., art 55.

41. See the Treaty between His Britannic Majesty and the President of Venezuela relating to the Submarine Areas of the Gulf of Paria (Caracas, 26 February 1942), 205 League of Nations Treaty Series (hereinafter "LNTS") 122, and the Truman Proclamation (Proclamation No 2667, *Concerning the Policy of the United States with respect to the Natural Resources of the Subsoil and Sea Bed of the Continental Shelf*, (1945) 10 *Federal Register* 12303).

(those which at the harvestable stage of their life cycle are unable to move except in constant physical contact with the seabed or subsoil), introduced for the first time a vertical separation into the law of the sea, as the waters above retained their high seas status, as confirmed by the 1958 Continental Shelf Convention.[42] The seaward extent of the continental shelf was originally based on the 200-metre isobath or beyond to the maximum exploitable water depth, but this provoked concern that the progress of technology would eventually result in the whole ocean becoming exploitable and thus, inequitably, falling under the jurisdiction of the nearest coastal State. In UNCLOS Article 76 the outer limit has therefore been changed to a complicated formula approximating the geologically inexact boundary between continental crust and oceanic crust[43] but, reflecting the introduction meanwhile of the EEZ, if this formula leads to a continental shelf extending less than 200 nm from the baselines, the coastal State is entitled in any event to a flat 200 nm.[44]

5. The seabed beyond national jurisdiction (i.e. beyond the continental shelf). An internationalised deep seabed mining regime exists here under Pt XI of UNCLOS (arts 133 to 191), administered by the International Seabed Authority.[45]

The main remaining task for States as regards the spatial division of the ocean is to delimit their overlapping entitlements to maritime zones and establish the outer limit of the continental shelf where it extends beyond 200 nm, both matters being beyond the scope of this chapter.

3. COASTAL AND FLAG STATE RIGHTS OVER SHIPPING IN THE MAIN MARITIME ZONES

The main tension in the shipping world is between coastal or port States on the one hand and flag States on the other, particularly as regards pollution. The measures favoured by coastal States to minimise the risk of pollution to their coastlines may well have adverse economic consequences for shipping. Let us now examine the principal zones in turn.

---

42. Convention on the Continental Shelf (Geneva, 29 April 1958), 499 UNTS 311, art 3. See now UNCLOS, art 78 (fn 8).

43. Despite this zone in fact thereby coming to encompass the entire continental margin (shelf, slope and rise) rather than just the shelf, it is still known by its old name.

44. Notwithstanding the general irrelevance of this zone to shipping – after all, it can be expected that shipping interests would actively seek to avoid coming into contact with the seabed – it is curious that the rules in the Nairobi International Convention on the Removal of Wrecks (Nairobi, 18 May 2007; IMO doc LEG/CONF.16/19 (23 May 2007)) that apply to the EEZ have not been extended to the continental shelf, inasmuch as wrecks settle on the seabed rather than remaining suspended in the water column. The reason may be that water shallow enough for wrecks to be hazardous to navigation rarely extends far beyond the 12 nm limit of the territorial sea, so that coverage solely of the EEZ (which includes the seabed) is adequate.

45. Contrary to the expectations held while UNCLOS was under negotiation, deep seabed mining looks set to remain uneconomic for some time, whereas genetic resources, from which valuable chemical compounds usable in pharmaceuticals may be extracted, have a ready market. This generated controversy over whether non-mineral resources are, as arts 133(a), 136 and 137 of UNCLOS together imply, excluded from the regime and thus still subject to the high seas rules. The question may be tackled in the negotiations for an international legally binding instrument under UNCLOS on the conservation and sustainable use of marine biological diversity of areas beyond national jurisdiction set in train by UN General Assembly Resolution 69/292 (UN doc A/RES/69/292 (6 July 2015)) but not scheduled to commence until 2018 at the earliest. A Preparatory Committee has been established to make substantive recommendations to the General Assembly by the end of 2017 on the elements of a draft text of such an instrument.

(a) Internal waters (including ports)

A State's ports are part of its internal waters, since Article 11 of UNCLOS provides that "[f]or the purposes of delimiting the territorial sea, the outermost permanent harbour works which form an integral part of the harbour system are regarded as forming part of the coast". The clear position is that foreign ships have no general right to enter internal waters,[46] although there may still be a customary exception for ships in distress, preserved by the preambular paragraph of UNCLOS "affirming that matters not regulated by this Convention continue to be governed by the rules and principles of general international law".[47] This gives the port (coastal) State the upper hand, since if it can withhold permission to enter, then *a fortiori* it can grant such permission on whatever conditions it chooses. This, however, is only the default position in the law of the sea. A right of ships flagged to State A to enter the ports of State B may be contained in a treaty between those States. Such provisions were typically included in the many bilateral "friendship, commerce and navigation" treaties common in the late nineteenth and early twentieth centuries, and some multilateral treaties also accord a right to parties for their ships to enter each other's ports, such as the 1923 Statute on the International Regime of Maritime Ports,[48] of which Article 2 requires *inter alia* that each party must allow all other parties' ships into its ports on the same terms as its own ships. Note also that in the General Agreement on Tariffs and Trade,[49] by which all members of the World Trade Organization (WTO) are bound, Article V(2) on freedom of transit may prevent closure of ports to a ship wanting to unload goods destined for a third State. A claim of breach of this provision was brought by the European Community (as it then was) against Chile in the WTO in 2000, but proceedings were soon suspended and in 2010 ultimately discontinued.[50] A like claim was made by Denmark (for the Faroe Islands) against the EU in 2013, but settled the following year.[51]

A ship voluntarily in port subjects itself to the jurisdiction of the port State. Because its presence is only temporary, often there will be practical reasons for the port State to refrain from exercising this jurisdiction, but it retains the right to do so.[52]

---

46. A.V. Lowe, "The Right of Entry into Maritime Ports in International Law" (1977) 14 *San Diego Law Review* 597, at p 621; L. de La Fayette, "Access to Ports in International Law" (1996) 11 *International Journal of Marine and Coastal Law* 1, at p 12.

47. Others such as E.J. Molenaar, "Port State Jurisdiction: Towards Comprehensive, Mandatory and Global Coverage" (2007) 38 *Ocean Development & International Law* 225 at 227–228 argue that the practice of many States in recent decades shows that they no longer believe this is warranted in the modern age, when the underlying goal of the exception, to save human lives, can often be more safely achieved by evacuating the crew and any passengers but leaving the ship to its fate. While avoidance of danger to the coastal population and environment is also advanced as a justification for denying stricken ships entry to port, this can sometimes prove counterproductive, as the outcome of the *Prestige* incident (see below, page 326) shows.

48. Part of the 1923 Convention and Statute on the International Régime of Maritime Ports (Geneva, 9 December 1923), 58 LNTS 285.

49. Since 1995 GATT has been maintained in force among Members of the World Trade Organization pursuant to the Agreement Establishing the World Trade Organization (Marrakesh, 15 April 1994), 1867 UNTS 3, arts II(2) and II(4).

50. See WTO docs WT/DS193/3 (6 April 2001), "Chile – Measures Affecting the Transit and Importation of Swordfish: Arrangement between the European Communities and Chile" and WT/DS193/4 (3 June 2010), "Chile – Measures Affecting the Transit and Importation of Swordfish: Joint Communication from the European Union and Chile".

51. WTO docs WT/DS469/2 (10 January 2014), "European Union – Measures on Atlanto-Scandian Herring: Request for the Establishment of a Panel by Denmark in Respect of the Faroe Islands" and WT/DS469/3 (25 August 2014), "European Union – Measures on Atlanto-Scandian Herring: Joint Communication from Denmark in respect of the Faroe Islands and the European Union".

52. Harris & Sivakumaran (fn 14), at p 363 indicate that this position is taken by States having a common law heritage, while those with civil law systems are often said to treat the non-exercise of jurisdiction as *opinio iuris* for the proposition, contrary to what is maintained here, that no such jurisdiction in fact exists. The old French authorities usually cited in support of that proposition, however, in fact take a position identical to that of the common law, with which modern French practice is consonant: P. Bonassies, "Faut-il abroger l'avis du Conseil d'État du 28 octobre 1806?", in V. Coussirat-Coustère, Y. Daudet, P.-M. Dupuy, P.M. Eisemann and M. Voelckel (eds), *La mer et son droit: Mélanges offerts à Laurent Lucchini et Jean-Pierre Quéneudec* (Pedone 2003), 101 at pp 102–103.

(b) The territorial sea

The principal qualification of a coastal State's sovereignty over the territorial sea is that foreign ships have a right of innocent passage.[53] UNCLOS Article 18 defines this as "continuous and expeditious" navigation through the territorial sea to or from the internal waters or a port of a coastal State, or a traverse without entering its internal waters. Stopping and anchoring are not allowed, except as incidental to ordinary navigation or necessary due to *force majeure*, distress or in order to render assistance to persons, ships or aircraft in danger or distress. The definition excludes cabotage, the term for coastal shipping between two ports of the same State, leaving States free to reserve this for their own nationals or ships. A notorious example is the Jones Act in the US, which requires not only that goods transported by water between US ports be carried in US-flagged ships, but also that these must be constructed in the US, owned by US citizens and crewed by citizens or permanent residents of the US.[54]

In the territorial sea the main duties of the coastal State are not to hamper innocent passage and to publicise any danger to navigation of which it knows.[55] It may not levy any toll for passage,[56] but may temporarily suspend innocent passage for weapons exercises or other essential security reasons on due advance publicity.[57]

UNCLOS Article 19 elaborates to a much greater degree than the equivalent 1958 Convention[58] the activities which render passage no longer innocent if the ship engages in them. These comprise the threat or use of force against the coastal State's sovereignty or territorial integrity,[59] exercise or practice of weapons of any kind,[60] collection of information prejudicial to the security of the coastal State,[61] any act of propaganda aimed at the coastal State's defence or security,[62] the launching or taking on board of any aircraft or military device,[63] the loading or unloading of any commodity, currency or person contrary to the coastal State's laws,[64] any act of wilful and serious pollution,[65] fishing activity,[66] research or survey activities,[67] interference with communications,[68] or any other activity not directly related to passage.[69] The coastal State may prevent passage which is not innocent.[70]

The only other significant qualification is that coastal States may not prescribe their own conditions for the construction, design, manning and equipment of ships in the territorial sea, but can instead only enact and enforce the regulations contained in "generally accepted international

---

53. UNCLOS, art 17 (fn 8).
54. Merchant Marine Act of 1920 (PL 66–261), s 27, recodified in 2006 as 46 USC ss 8103, 12103, 12112, 12131 and 55102.
55. UNCLOS, arts 24(1) and 24(2) (fn 8) respectively.
56. Ibid., art 26(1).
57. Ibid., art 25(3). Mexico is the only State that regularly notifies such closures to the UN, though two instances of Guatemala and Syria doing so in 2008 and 2012 respectively are also recorded; see www.un.org/depts/los/convention_agreements/innocent_passages_suspension.htm (accessed 17 January 2017).
58. See fn 31.
59. UNCLOS, art 19(2)(a) (fn 8).
60. Ibid., art 19(2)(b).
61. Ibid., art 19(2)(c).
62. Ibid., art 19(2)(d).
63. Ibid., art 19(2)(e) and 19(2)(f).
64. Ibid., art 19(2)(g).
65. Ibid., art 19(2)(h).
66. Ibid., art 19(2)(i).
67. Ibid., art 19(2)(j).
68. Ibid., art 19(2)(k).
69. Ibid., art 19(2)(l). Although the aim of this list is sometimes said to have been to enhance legal certainty by enumerating exhaustively what makes passage non-innocent, this last catch-all provision has the effect of undermining that aim.
70. Ibid., art 25(1).

rules or standards".[71] It will readily be seen that this is necessary if the right of innocent passage is to be at all meaningful, since otherwise ships could be subject to several different and potentially contradictory design rules in the course of a single voyage, with the result that compliance with one such rule may make compliance with another impossible.

A chance to elaborate on innocent passage was declined by the ECJ in 2008 when it declined to entertain a challenge to Directive 2005/35/EC of the European Parliament and Council on Ship-Source Pollution, mandating criminal sanctions for pollution caused by "serious negligence", as contrary to UNCLOS.[72] Such a possibility arises since by Article 19(2)(h) only an act of "serious *and* wilful" pollution would deprive passage of its innocence, hence pollution caused by serious negligence, by definition not wilful, cannot have this effect. The applicants had also argued that the mere presence of these laws on EU Member States' statute books, whether or not they were enforced, would have the effect of hampering innocent passage contrary to UNCLOS Article 24(1) (though note that this provision speaks of the "application" of coastal State regulations).[73] The issue has thus not been definitively disposed of, but may resurface through challenges to the implementing laws of one or more EU Member States by a non-EU flag State. Had there been proceedings by the Commission against any EU Member States failing to implement the Directive (which was opposed by several of them), these could conceivably have defended their position by arguing that, under the EU hierarchy of norms, the Directive yields to any treaty obligation of the EU with which it is inconsistent.

Although the events occurred in archipelagic waters rather than in the territorial sea, the *Duzgit Integrity Arbitration*[74] is mentioned here because the basic regime of archipelagic waters – sovereignty of the coastal State subject to innocent passage for foreign-flagged ships – parallels that of the territorial sea. The dispute arose in 2013 out of the attempt by the *Duzgit Integrity*, flagged to Malta, which had been bunkering other ships, to transfer its remaining supplies to another ship operated by the same enterprise that had come to relieve it. As a result of linguistic and other misunderstandings, although the master of the *Duzgit Integrity* repeatedly indicated his willingness to move outside São Tomé's territorial sea in order to make the transfer, it was in São Tomé's archipelagic waters that the attempt occurred, without the prior authorisation required for this under São Tomé law. Subsequently São Tomé detained the ship and its master; a local court ordered the master's imprisonment and imposed a €5,000,000 fine jointly against the master, owner and charterer of the ship as well as ordering the confiscation of the vessel and its cargo; other administrative fines exceeded €1,000,000. An arbitral tribunal constituted under Annex VII to UNCLOS upheld Malta's claim that the measures taken by São Tomé violated Article 49(3) of UNCLOS, which relates to the exercise of a State's sovereignty over its archipelagic waters.[75] Malta also claimed that São Tomé had breached various provisions of Part XII of

---

71. Ibid., art 21(2).

72. See fn 8 and accompanying text.

73. Note also the opinion of Advocate-General Kokott in this case, available at http://curia.europa.eu/juris/recherche.jsf [102] – [138], that, because the impugned instrument as a directive did not govern shipping of its own force but needed to be transposed into the national law of the EU Member States, it would be for the EU Member States to ensure that the transposed laws remained in conformity with UNCLOS. The rather surprising suggestion is made in this context that, in order to bring this about, "serious negligence" might need to be equated with recklessness outside the territorial sea (as well as in the territorial sea part of straits used for international navigation, which are subject to the right of transit passage – see p 320) but could be given a broader interpretation within it.

74. PCA Case N°2014–07, In the Matter of the Duzgit Integrity Arbitration before an Arbitral Tribunal Constituted under Annex VII of the 1982 United Nations Convention on the Law of the Sea between the Republic of Malta and the Democratic Republic of São Tomé and Príncipe, Award, 5 September 2016, https://pcacases.com/web/sendAttach/1915 (accessed 31 December 2016).

75. Ibid., [219] – [236].

UNCLOS relating to protection of the marine environment.[76] The tribunal held that enforcement measures taken by a coastal State against unlawful activity within its archipelagic waters must be reasonable, which means respecting the general principles of necessity and proportionality.[77] It found unanimously that the initial measures taken by São Tomé – detaining the ship, requesting the master to come ashore to explain the circumstances, and imposing an administrative fine – were well within its law-enforcement jurisdiction, but found by majority that the other penalties imposed by São Tomé taken together – the prolonged detention of ship and master, the monetary sanctions and the confiscation of the entire cargo – could not be regarded as proportionate to either the offence or São Tomé's interest in ensuring respect for its sovereignty and exceeded what was permissible under Article 49.[78] For this Malta was entitled to compensation in a quantum to be determined in a succeeding phase of the arbitration. Malta's claims relating to the marine environment under Part XII of UNCLOS were dismissed, the tribunal not being persuaded on the evidence before it that São Tomé had exposed the marine environment to an unreasonable risk.

(c) The EEZ: "creeping jurisdiction", bunkering, law enforcement

Maritime States keep a keen eye out for what they term "creeping jurisdiction", that is, jurisdictional claims by coastal States in the EEZ beyond what the Part V regime allows them, such as the closure of the EEZ to a single-hulled oil tanker in 2003 by Spain for fear of a repetition of the disastrous pollution consequences of the sinking of the *Prestige* in 2002.[79] Fears of the EEZ hardening in this way into a 200 nm territorial sea are often overplayed, as many coastal States themselves rely on the freedom of navigation, and creeping jurisdiction tends to be used as a pretext to oppose new rules placing additional regulatory powers into coastal States' hands even where there are good reasons to do so. Yet such fears are not entirely fanciful, as this is in fact how the modern doctrine of the territorial sea itself, which grew out of claims to jurisdiction over specific subjects, originally came about.[80]

Similarly, one of the string of cases on bunkering in recent years[81] shows that, while bunkering in itself may be thought of as belonging more to the freedom of navigation preserved by Article 58(2) of UNCLOS, it yields to the specific powers of the coastal States as regards marine living resources. In the first such case, *The M/V Saiga (No 2)*, ITLOS held that the coastal State Guinea had no right to apply its customs legislation prohibiting importation of gas oil into the customs radius (*rayon des douanes*) of Guinea extending to 250 nautical miles from the coast and thus including Guinea's EEZ, where the incident of which the flag State complained took place. ITLOS concluded that Article 58(3) of UNCLOS made it competent to determine the

---

76. Ibid., [278] – [293].

77. Ibid., [254].

78. Ibid., [254] – [262].

79. C. de la Rue and C.B. Anderson, *Shipping and the Environment* (2nd edn, Informa 2009), at pp 1064–1065. These authors defend ibid., at p 901, the actions of Portugal and Spain in relation to the *Prestige* itself, also apparently contrary to UNCLOS, art 58, as an exception permitted by art 221, essentially replicating the International Convention Relating to Intervention on the High Seas in the case of Oil Pollution Casualties (Brussels, 29 November 1969), 970 UNTS 211; see further Chapter 10.

80. J Crawford, *Brownlie's Principles of Public International Law* (8th edn, OUP 2012), at pp 256–257.

81. Bunkering, though in different maritime zones, was also the cause of action taken against ships in both *The Norstar* (fn 90), where all the trouble that followed could have been avoided if the Italian authorities had realised earlier that they had no jurisdiction over foreign ships engaging in bunkering on the high seas, and indirectly in the *Duzgit Integrity* (fn 74), where it can be inferred from the case report that the legally risky course of action taken by the master may have been motivated by the mistaken belief that, because the ship-to-ship transfer of bunkers did not involve an ordinary commercial sale, no such risk existed.

compatibility of Guinea's laws and regulations with UNCLOS. Beyond the contiguous zone overlapping with the innermost 12 miles of the EEZ, the only other part of the EEZ in which the coastal State could apply its customs laws was to artificial islands, installations and structures under Article 60(2), thus Guinea's actions in pursuing and detailing the *Saiga*, prosecuting and convicting its master, confiscating the cargo and seizing the ship were contrary to UNCLOS. It rejected Guinea's argument that the principle of "public interest" could serve as a basis for its laws, observing that this would curtail the rights of other States in the EEZ, contrary to Articles 56 and 58. It similarly rejected a plea of necessity under general international law: however essential Guinea's interest in protecting its tax revenue from the sale of bunkers to fishing vessels, it could not be said that the only means of safeguarding that interest was to apply its customs laws to the whole of its EEZ. While both parties made submissions on the broader question of the rights of coastal and other States in connection with offshore bunkering, ITLOS was able to reach its decision on whether Guinea's actions were consistent with the applicable provisions of UNCLOS without needing to address that issue and thus forbore from making any findings on it.[82]

In *The Virginia G*,[83] however, decided in 2014, ITLOS accepted that bunkering of fishing vessels falls under coastal State fisheries jurisdiction, confirming that coastal States are entitled to prohibit bunkering of such vessels and even confiscate ships engaging in it unlawfully, but only to the extent necessary to ensure compliance with coastal State regulations pursuant to Article 73(1), so the coastal State was ordered to reverse the confiscation in this case. This potentially opens the way to making significant inroads into the residual freedom of navigation preserved by Article 58, which the flag State here unsuccessfully argued should have been the dominant principle.

The *Arctic Sunrise* arbitration[84] concerned a claim before an Annex VII tribunal brought by the Netherlands as the flag State arising out of the pursuit and detention by the Russian authorities of a Greenpeace ship, from which activists protesting against exploration for oil in Arctic waters had unlawfully established themselves aboard a drilling rig in the Barents Sea in Russia's EEZ. Addressing the lawfulness of the measures taken by Russia against the eponymous ship and the 30 persons on board, the tribunal stated that, while protest at sea is an internationally lawful use of the sea related to the freedom of navigation, the right to protest does not override relevant coastal State rights. This led it to consider the possible legal bases for Russia's boarding, seizure and detention of the *Arctic Sunrise*. Of those related to the protection of the coastal State's rights and interests in the EEZ, the tribunal accepted that Russia had a right as a coastal State to enforce its laws regarding non-living resources in its EEZ, but found no specific Russian laws on the subject that the *Arctic Sunrise* might have contravened. Most plausibly, the tribunal noted that a coastal State may act to prevent interference with its sovereign rights for the exploration and exploitation of those resources, but held that none of the actions of the *Arctic Sunrise* up to the time it was boarded constituted such an interference.[85] It also considered whether the measures taken by Russia could have been based on the enforcement jurisdiction of the coastal State with respect to protection of the marine environment, but found no support in the relevant provisions of Part XII of UNCLOS for the particular measures taken.[86] The tribunal did not exclude that the coastal State might be justified in taking some kind of preventive action in its EEZ against a ship when there was reason to believe that it was involved in a terrorist attack on

82. *M/V Saiga (No 2) (Saint Vincent and the Grenadines v Guinea)*, ITLOS Reports 1999, 10, at [138]
83. *M/V "Virginia G" (Panama/Guinea-Bissau), Judgment*, ITLOS Reports 2014, 4.
84. See fn 223.
85. Ibid., [324] – [333].
86. Ibid., [297].

an installation or structure of the coastal State, but considered that there was no reasonable basis for Russia to suspect that the *Arctic Sunrise* was engaged in terrorism.[87]

(d) The high seas: nationality of ships, Flag State duties, piracy

Nationality of ships. This is the most fundamental regulatory matter pertaining to the high seas. The basic rule is set out in Article 92 of UNCLOS, identical (but for a cross-reference) to Article 6 of the 1958 High Seas Convention:

Article 92
Status of ships

1. Ships shall sail under the flag of one State only and, save in exceptional cases expressly provided for in international treaties or in this Convention, shall be subject to its exclusive jurisdiction on the high seas. A ship may not change its flag during a voyage or while in a port of call, save in the case of a real transfer of ownership or change of registry.
2. A ship which sails under the flags of two or more States, using them according to convenience, may not claim any of the nationalities in question with respect to any other State, and may be assimilated to a ship without nationality.

There are two frequently encountered misconceptions as to the effect of this rule. The first is that high seas freedoms and exclusivity of flag State jurisdiction are absolute, so that States cannot enforce their laws even in their own ports where this would prevent a foreign ship from returning to the high seas, as occurred when the New Zealand Court of Appeal in *Sellers v Maritime Safety Inspector*[88] quashed a conviction for leaving port without the prescribed safety equipment. ITLOS by necessary implication rejected such reasoning in *The Louisa*, a case brought by the flag State of a ship detained in port pending investigation of offences relating to unauthorised removal of underwater cultural heritage objects, alleging *inter alia* an interference with the freedom of navigation guaranteed to its ship by UNCLOS Article 87. In dismissing this claim for want of jurisdiction *ratione materiae*, ITLOS took the view that the facts did not even engage Article 87.[89]

It is not certain whether this robust attitude will survive the decision on the merits, expected in 2018, in *The Norstar*. In late 2016 ITLOS dismissed a preliminary objection by Italy to the Article 87 claim of the flag State, Panama, arising out of the detention of the *Norstar* prompted by the Italian authorities' mistaken belief that it had committed tax fraud by bunkering another ship on the high seas, a charge dismissed by an Italian court which found that the high seas location meant that the conduct in question did not constitute an offence.[90] The decision to reject the preliminary objection means that ITLOS accepted that there was a plausible claim, distinguishing this case from *The Louisa* on the basis that the acts alleged to constitute an offence warranting the ship's detention, pleaded to have interfered with the flag State's freedom of navigation, occurred on the high seas, even though the detention itself occurred during its next port call. Whatever the outcome of this case, because there are several exceptions to exclusivity considered below, primacy rather than exclusivity for the flag State gives a truer picture of the actual

---

87. Ibid., [314] – [323].
88. [1999] 2 NZLR 44.
89. *The M/V Louisa (Saint Vincent and the Grenadines v Kingdom of Spain)*, Merits, *Judgment of 28 May 2013*, ITLOS Reports 2013, 4 at pp 36–37, [109].
90. *The M/V Norstar (Panama v Italy)*, Preliminary Objections, *Judgment*, ITLOS Reports 2016, to be published, www.itlos.org/fileadmin/itlos/documents/cases/case_no.25/Preliminary_Objections/Judgment/C25_Judgment_04.11.16_orig.pdf (accessed 31 December 2016).

position. Flag State jurisdiction should instead be seen as a way of preventing a legal vacuum on the high seas, given that no State has the competence to regulate activities there on a spatial basis. In *The Saiga (No 2)*, ITLOS held that UNCLOS

considers a ship as a unit, as regards the obligations of the flag State with respect to the ship and the right of a flag State to seek reparation for loss or damage caused to the ship by acts of other States and to institute proceedings under article 292 of the Convention. Thus the ship, every thing on it, and every person involved or interested in its operations are treated as an entity linked to the flag State. The nationalities of these persons are not relevant.[91]

Seen in this light, allocating primacy of jurisdiction to the flag State, irrespective of the States of nationality of the owners and the various other interests connected with the ship – crew, cargo, insurers – ensures that the ship presents a single legal "face" to the outside world.

Second, the provision that ships must "sail under the flag of one State only" does not mean that ships can have only a single nationality at any given time.[92] The possibility of multiple nationalities is an unavoidable consequence of UNCLOS Article 91:

Article 91
Nationality of ships

1. Every State shall fix the conditions for the grant of its nationality to ships, for the registration of ships in its territory, and for the right to fly its flag. Ships have the nationality of the State whose flag they are entitled to fly. There must exist a genuine link between the State and the ship.
2. Every State shall issue to ships to which it has granted the right to fly its flag documents to that effect.

Since States are free to grant their nationality or the right to fly their flag on whatever basis they choose, provided there is a genuine link between ship and State, it follows that inevitably States will do so on different bases and that there will thus be instances in which a ship satisfies distinct nationality criteria of two or more States simultaneously.[93] While from a policy perspective there is much to be said for the practice of many States that refuse to register a ship without proof that the previous flag State has deleted it from its own registry, there is no legal requirement underpinning this.[94]

Another matter on which Article 91 – indeed the whole of UNCLOS – is silent is the definition of "ship". While several of the IMO Conventions listed below have their own varying definitions, these do not extend beyond the narrow confines of each of these treaties.[95] The consequence of this is that it is left to each State to decide for itself what physical and other characteristics qualify a vessel to be accepted onto its register as a ship, and once registered this would probably oblige other States to treat it as a ship even if it would not qualify as such under their own laws. Should another State have reason to dispute whether the vessel is a ship (though only

---

91. *The Saiga (No 2)*, fn 82, at p 48, [106], reaffirmed in *The Arctic Sunrise*, fn 23, at pp 39–40, [170]–[172]. As to art 292, see section 5 below.

92. *Contra* the otherwise highly recommended D. Anderson, "Freedoms of the High Seas in the Modern Law of the Sea", in D. Freestone, R. Barnes and D. Ong (eds), *The Law of the Sea: Progress and Prospects* (Oxford University Press 2006), 327 at p 333 ("dual nationality is permissible in the case of individuals but not ships").

93. The only way of avoiding this consequence would be if the granting of nationality to a ship by one State automatically extinguished any other nationality, but this would reduce the art 91 right to near-worthlessness, and is contradicted by the widespread practice in the context of bareboat chartering of a ship temporarily taking a second flag and thus a second nationality that eclipses its first (which revives automatically at the end of the charter period, indicating that it has not been extinguished). See Chapter 4, pages 117–118 and 146 on bareboat charters.

94. See also Chapter 2, pages 86–92 on registration.

95. See e.g. Chapter 10, page 388 and 416.

one incident of this kind has come to light, and it is a military one),[96] the compulsory dispute settlement provisions of UNCLOS may offer a way out of the impasse. This may become more of an issue in the coming years with the likely advent of unmanned vessels.

The "genuine link" wording is taken from Article 5 of the High Seas Convention,[97] which in turn was inspired by the ICJ decision in the *Nottebohm Case*,[98] where the facts concerned an individual with, at least on one view, multiple nationalities. Just as such an individual can only present one passport when entering a State, and thereafter that State can insist on treating him or her as a national of the issuing State and no other, a ship must elect one of its nationalities under which to undertake any given voyage; the penalty for using more than one flag is that it cannot claim any of the relevant nationalities and may be treated as though it were stateless.[99]

Another factor leading to the "genuine link" requirement losing much of its significance is the 1960 Advisory Opinion[100] sought from the ICJ by the Intergovernmental Maritime Consultative Organisation (as it then was) on the meaning of the "largest shipowning nations" in Article 28(a) of its 1948 Convention,[101] which the Court interpreted to mean those with the largest registered tonnage. These would be easily ascertainable, whereas attempting to establish the legal or beneficial ownership of ships, which often cannot be done directly but must instead be traced through a series of holding companies whose share registers are not readily available, would be a much more difficult exercise. This has favoured the growth of flags of convenience or open registers, maintained by States which require little or no prior link and often lack the personnel and administrative infrastructure necessary in order to enforce labour and safety standards on board the ships. Precisely for this reason, however, they are popular among shipowners anxious to minimise their costs, and it is generally these interests which shape the positions taken by their States of nationality at the IMO. This is no doubt also the reason why the 1986 United Nations Convention on Conditions for the Registration of Ships[102] fails to specify what constitutes a genuine link,[103] yet even so has received only 15 of the 40 ratifications and accessions accounting for 25 per cent of world shipping tonnage it needs to enter into force,[104] and is now widely regarded as unlikely ever to do so. Note also that this Convention lays down the rule that a ship can only be on one State's register at a time.[105] This would not have been necessary had that been the position anyway under Article 5 of the 1958 High Seas Convention and its successor in UNCLOS, Article 91.

---

96. See the US Department of Defense statement at www.defense.gov/News/Article/Article/1032823/chinese-seize-us-navy-underwater-drone-in-south-china-sea (accessed 15 February 2017).

97. See fn 15.

98. *Nottebohm Case (Liechtenstein v Guatemala), Second Phase*, ICJ Reports 1955, 4 at p 23 ("genuine connection").

99. Churchill & Lowe (fn 1) point out at p 214 that, even where there is thus no flag State to complain of action taken against the ship on the high seas by any other State, the persons on board, and the owners of its cargo still have legitimate interests that their States of nationality, which would normally have been eclipsed by the flag State, are able to protect. This passage should not, however, be read as implying that some other State, e.g. the State of nationality of the owner of the (deemed) stateless ship, then steps into the shoes of the flag State.

100. *Constitution of the Maritime Safety Committee of the Inter-Governmental Maritime Consultative Organization*, ICJ Reports 1960, 150.

101. Convention on the Intergovernmental Maritime Consultative Organization (Geneva, 6 March 1948), 289 UNTS 3.

102. Geneva, 7 February 1986; UN doc TD/RS/CONF/23 (13 March 1986).

103. By art 7, a flag State need only either require in its laws and regulations for the ownership of ships flying its flag such level of participation by itself or its nationals as is sufficient to permit it to exercise effectively its jurisdiction and control over those ships (see arts 8(1) and 8(2)), or require a "satisfactory part" of the officers and crew of ships flying its flag to be nationals or persons domiciled or lawfully in permanent residence in that State (art 9(1)), or both.

104. Art 19(1); the tonnage is to be calculated in accordance with the figures given in Annex III. For the status of ratifications and accessions to the Convention, see https://treaties.un.org/Pages/ViewDetails.aspx?src=IND&mtdsg_no=X-II-7&chapter=12&clang=_en (accessed 18 January 2017).

105. See fn 102, art 4(4), which provides also for certain exceptions.

Flag State duties. An opportunity to restore teeth to the genuine link requirement of Article 91 was not taken by ITLOS in *The Saiga (No 2)*, where it concluded that its purpose was "to secure more effective implementation of the duties of the flag State, and not to establish criteria by reference to which the validity of the registration of ships in a flag State may be challenged by other States".[106] That is, the existence of a genuine link is not a condition precedent to registration, but an obligation that arises as a consequence of it, since without it the flag State would not be in a position to perform the significant duties that it has pursuant to Article 94 of UNCLOS in respect of its ships:

Article 94
Duties of the flag State

1. Every State shall effectively exercise its jurisdiction and control in administrative, technical and social matters over ships flying its flag.
2. In particular every State shall:
    (a) maintain a register of ships containing the names and particulars of ships flying its flag, except those which are excluded from generally accepted international regulations on account of their small size; and
    (b) assume jurisdiction under its internal law over each ship flying its flag and its master, officers and crew in respect of administrative, technical and social matters concerning the ship.
3. Every State shall take such measures for ships flying its flag as are necessary to ensure safety at sea with regard, inter alia, to:
    (a) the construction, equipment and seaworthiness of ships;
    (b) the manning of ships, labour conditions and the training of crews, taking into account the applicable international instruments;
    (c) the use of signals, the maintenance of communications and the prevention of collisions.
4. Such measures shall include those necessary to ensure:
    (a) that each ship, before registration and thereafter at appropriate intervals, is surveyed by a qualified surveyor of ships, and has on board such charts, nautical publications and navigational equipment and instruments as are appropriate for the safe navigation of the ship;
    (b) that each ship is in the charge of a master and officers who possess appropriate qualifications, in particular in seamanship, navigation, communications and marine engineering, and that the crew is appropriate in qualification and numbers for the type, size, machinery and equipment of the ship;
    (c) that the master, officers and, to the extent appropriate, the crew are fully conversant with and required to observe the applicable international regulations concerning the safety of life at sea, the prevention of collisions, the prevention, reduction and control of marine pollution, and the maintenance of communications by radio.
5. In taking the measures called for in paragraphs 3 and 4 each State is required to conform to generally accepted international regulations, procedures and practices and to take any steps which may be necessary to secure their observance.
6. A State which has clear grounds to believe that proper jurisdiction and control with respect to a ship have not been exercised may report the facts to the flag State. Upon receiving such a report, the flag State shall investigate the matter and, if appropriate, take any action necessary to remedy the situation.
7. Each State shall cause an inquiry to be held by or before a suitably qualified person or persons into every marine casualty or incident of navigation on the high seas involving a ship flying its flag and causing loss of life or serious injury to nationals of another State or serious damage to ships or installations of another State or to the marine environment. The flag State and the other State shall co-operate in the conduct of any inquiry held by that other State into any such marine casualty or incident of navigation.

Note the numerous cross-references to international regulations and standards, which are provided by IMO conventions among those listed below, and the requirement for periodic surveys

---

106. *The Saiga (No 2)* (fn 82), at p 42 ([83]).

in subparagraph 4(a), a task that many States delegate to private-sector classification societies.[107] The fact that the performance of the duty is thus delegated to a private body does not absolve the State from the obligation to ensure that it is properly discharged. In *The Erika*,[108] the defendant classification society unsuccessfully claimed sovereign immunity from the French court's jurisdiction, derivative of that of the flag State.

Piracy. There was an upsurge of piracy off Somalia from 2007 which has in recent years largely abated, though the Gulf of Guinea has at the same time emerged as a new area of concern. The relevant international law is for the most part straightforward and well settled. Importantly, despite occasional calls for action implying the contrary, States already have under international law all the legal authority they need to combat piracy by capturing and prosecuting its perpetrators, as set out in Article 105 of UNCLOS below. What frequently stops them from doing so tends instead to be how their own domestic legal systems implement, either generally or in individual cases, the duty in Article 100 of UNCLOS to repress piracy: "All States shall co-operate to the fullest possible extent in the repression of piracy on the high seas or in any other place outside the jurisdiction of any State." This duty, along with the other provisions of UNCLOS quoted or paraphrased below, is accepted as customary international law applying to all States whether or not they are party to UNCLOS, in as much as it reproduces the equivalent articles of the 1958 Convention on the High Seas. Yet Article 100 falls short of imposing an actual duty to do anything in particular in exercise of their Article 105 powers. In economic terms this has allowed States to be free-riders on each other's contributions to securing the oceans against piracy, making such contributions less likely and thus leading to an inefficient global underprovision of efforts in this regard. There is no realistic prospect of amending Article 100 to cure this defect, however, as many States, including most developed ones, are opposed in principle to reopening the text of any part of UNCLOS.

Article 101 of UNCLOS defines piracy as consisting of any of the following acts:

(a) any illegal acts of violence or detention, or any act of depredation, committed for private ends by the crew or the passengers of a private ship or a private aircraft, and directed:
   (i) on the high seas, against another ship or aircraft, or against persons or property on board such ship or aircraft;
   (ii) against a ship, aircraft, persons or property in a place outside the jurisdiction of any State;
(b) any act of voluntary participation in the operation of a ship or of an aircraft with knowledge of facts making it a pirate ship or aircraft;
(c) any act of inciting or of intentionally facilitating an act described in subparagraph (a) or (b).

There are three main limitations under this definition. First is its geographic scope: it is sometimes asserted that piracy can occur only on the high seas, but in the shipping context this needs a twofold qualification: (a) there is no such restriction affecting the acts of incitement or intentional facilitation of piratical acts, which can accordingly take place anywhere, including on land;[109] (b) most importantly, under Article 58 of UNCLOS States' EEZs are taken as still being part of the high seas for this purpose, so that in effect all waters outside the territorial sea of any State are covered. Moreover, similar acts committed within a territorial sea fall under the sovereignty and jurisdiction of the coastal State (although, in the case of Somalia only, a succession of

---

107. See Chapter 9.
108. Cour de cassation, arrêt n 3439 du 25 septembre 2012 (10–82.938) de la Chambre criminelle, Bull crim 198.
109. See *United States v Ali* (2013) 718 F 3d 929, in which the Court of Appeals for the District of Columbia Circuit declined to dismiss a charge of aiding and abetting piracy merely because the acts took place elsewhere than on the high seas, though it did dismiss a charge of conspiracy to commit piracy for the same reason.

UN Security Council Resolutions has established a system for States co-operating with Somalia to operate in its territorial sea).[110]

Second, because of the need for two ships (or aircraft) to be involved, hijacking of ships (or aircraft) by stowaways or persons posing as passengers is not piracy. The same applies if the second craft is not a ship or aircraft, as was the case in the *Arctic Sunrise* arbitration,[111] where Russia initially laid charges of piracy against the Greenpeace protesters but later downgraded these to hooliganism; the arbitral tribunal reasoned that, since the oil rig to which two of them gained access was not a ship, the Russian measures could not be considered as an exercise of the right of visit against ships suspected of piracy. Last, there is debate over whether the specification of "private ends" means that acts of politically motivated violence otherwise fitting the definition cannot be piracy, or simply reflects the rule that government vessels cannot commit piracy.[112]

Article 105 provides as follows:

On the high seas, or in any other place outside the jurisdiction of any State, every State may seize a pirate ship or aircraft, or a ship or aircraft taken by piracy and under the control of pirates, and arrest the persons and seize the property on board. The courts of the State which carried out the seizure may decide upon the penalties to be imposed, and may also determine the action to be taken with regard to the ships, aircraft or property, subject to the rights of third parties acting in good faith.

This has led to suggestions that suspected pirates seized by a State may be tried only by that State and cannot subsequently be transferred to another State (such as Kenya or the Seychelles under agreements reached with States patrolling waters affected by Somalia-based pirates) for trial and, if convicted, imprisonment. Note, however, that while Article 105 assumes that the capturing State will be also be the prosecuting State, it does not actually require this, and does not disturb the customary international law rule that all States have what is known as "universal jurisdiction" to try alleged pirates subsequently found in their territory, without the need for any other links with the piracy offence[113] – though again there is no duty to accept suspects for trial. States willing to use Article 105 that are party to the IMO's 1988 Convention for the Suppression of Unlawful Acts against the Safety of Maritime Navigation,[114] which appears to be drafted broadly enough to cover the acts of violence and hostage-taking often associated with piracy, may in addition rely on the mechanism in Article 8 of the latter Convention for delivering suspects to the authorities in a foreign port.

Note that by Article 107 seizures on account of piracy "may be carried out only by warships or military aircraft, or other ships or aircraft clearly marked and identifiable as being on government service and authorized to that effect". When naval forces engage with pirate vessels, they may fire in self-defence or defence of others on any pirates who pose a clear threat to human life. On the other hand, Article 106 makes a State seizing a ship or aircraft on suspicion of piracy without adequate grounds liable to the flag State for any loss or damage caused by the seizure, somewhat undercutting the exception in Article 110 discussed below to exclusivity of the flag

---

110. The first was Resolution 1816, UN doc S/RES/1816 (2 June 2008) and the most recent at the time of writing is Resolution 2246, UN doc S/RES/2246 (18 November 2015).

111. See fn 23 and the facts of the incident detailed at page 327.

112. Other than those whose crew has mutinied and taken control of the vessel: UNCLOS, art 102.

113. The universal jurisdiction principle was already recognised as a rule of customary international law in the Advisory Opinion of the Privy Council in *In re Piracy Iure Gentium* [1934] AC 586, which arose out of an attempted pirate attack off China and where the issue was whether, since the attempt was unsuccessful, the perpetrators could properly have been tried as pirates (it was held that they could, though the quashing of their conviction by a lower appellate court on the opposite reasoning was not reversed).

114. Rome, 10 March 1988, 1678 UNTS 221.

State's jurisdiction over law enforcement on the high seas, by which all States' warships may board and inspect vessels suspected of piracy.

In the light of the foregoing, a number of factors may contribute to the continuing reluctance of most States to prosecute pirates they capture, as opposed to disarming and releasing them instead with enough food and fuel to make landfall. One is evidential difficulties: physical evidence such as boarding ladders and weapons will often have been dumped into the sea, and the victims who would be called as witnesses at trial are typically seafarers not easy to release from their duties, yet if they make only written statements and are not presented for cross-examination by the defence, their evidence will, depending on the legal system, be discounted or possibly not admitted into court at all. Another is that many States do not have an offence of piracy on their statute books and, even if they do, their navies may – despite their clear international law powers – lack the domestic authority to arrest criminals if that is reserved to the police. Finally, logistics may be an issue; a warship taking captured pirates into port for prosecution is diverted from its principal task of protecting shipping in the vulnerable sea lanes, increasing the risks to other vessels.

In the United Kingdom, Articles 100 to 107 of UNCLOS are expressly recognised as customary international law by section 26(1) of the Merchant Shipping and Maritime Security Act 1997. This ensures that, even though the offence of piracy is committed outside the normal territorial jurisdiction of the UK courts, they will have jurisdiction to try a person accused of the offence, wherever captured, and if the person is convicted, to impose sanctions.

In response to the revival of large-scale piracy, the IMO in 2009 led the formation of the Contact Group on Piracy off the Coast of Somalia, subsequently endorsed by the UN Security Council. One of its fruits was a paper[115] presented to the November 2010 meeting of the IMO Legal Committee, concentrating on the possible courses of action in the legal field. This includes assistance to coastal States to adopt legislation which will empower their courts to prosecute and imprison pirates. The IMO has succeeded in persuading States in the region of Somalia to subscribe to the Djibouti Code of Conduct.[116]

The most significant development since then has been a debate on whether merchant ships should carry armed personnel. It was generally accepted previously that live firing on board a ship was likely to cause more problems than it solved, particularly if the ship in question was a tanker laden with volatile cargo, but the majority view has now changed.[117] The dangers are illustrated by the *Enrica Lexie* incident of 2012, in which Italian naval personnel posted on board a merchant ship for its protection shot and killed two Indian fishermen whom they mistakenly believed to be pirates. The charges of murder filed by Indian prosecutors against the two Italians who fired the fatal shots have been stayed pending resolution of a dispute between Italy and India as to whether, since the incident occurred outside India's territorial sea, Article 97(1) of UNCLOS ("In the event of a collision or any other incident of navigation concerning a ship on the high seas, involving the penal or disciplinary responsibility of the master or of any other person in the service of the ship, no penal or disciplinary proceedings may be instituted against such person except before the judicial or administrative authorities either of the flag State or of

---

115. IMO doc LEG 97/9/1 (30 September 2010), "Piracy: Review of National Legislation". The title is misleading.

116. The Djibouti Code of Conduct concerning the Repression of Piracy and Armed Robbery against Ships in the Western Indian Ocean and Gulf of Aden was adopted in 2009 and is annexed to IMO doc C 102/14 (3 April 2009), Protection of Vital Shipping Lanes: Sub-regional meeting to conclude agreements on maritime security, piracy and armed robbery against ships for States from the Western Indian Ocean, Gulf of Aden and Red Sea areas, Note by the Secretary-General. It has now been adopted by 20 of the 21 eligible States in the region, but is not of treaty status.

117. See IMO doc MSC.1/Circ.1405/Rev.2 (25 May 2012), Revised Interim Guidance to Shipowners, Ship Operators and Shipmasters on the Use of Privately Contracted Armed Security Personnel on Board Ships in the High Risk Area, the latest iteration of a document first issued in 2011.

the State of which such person is a national") operates to give Italy exclusive jurisdiction to try them. If not, then under the general international law rules on criminal jurisdiction India as well as Italy may do so.[118]

(e) Exceptions to exclusivity of flag State jurisdiction on the high seas

Article 110 of UNCLOS, little changed from Article 22 of the 1958 High Seas Convention, sets out a number of bases on which a warship of one State has a right of "visit" (boarding and inspection) over a ship flagged to another State.

Article 110
Right of visit

1. Except where acts of interference derive from powers conferred by treaty, a warship which encounters on the high seas a foreign ship, other than a ship entitled to complete immunity in accordance with articles 95 and 96, is not justified in boarding it unless there is reasonable ground for suspecting that:
    (a) the ship is engaged in piracy;
    (b) the ship is engaged in the slave trade;
    (c) the ship is engaged in unauthorized broadcasting and the flag State of the warship has jurisdiction under article 109;
    (d) the ship is without nationality; or
    (e) though flying a foreign flag or refusing to show its flag, the ship is, in reality, of the same nationality as the warship.
2. In the cases provided for in paragraph 1, the warship may proceed to verify the ship's right to fly its flag. To this end, it may send a boat under the command of an officer to the suspected ship. If suspicion remains after the documents have been checked, it may proceed to a further examination on board the ship, which must be carried out with all possible consideration.
3. If the suspicions prove to be unfounded, and provided that the ship boarded has not committed any act justifying them, it shall be compensated for any loss or damage that may have been sustained.
4. These provisions apply *mutatis mutandis* to military aircraft.
5. These provisions also apply to any other duly authorized ships or aircraft clearly marked and identifiable as being on government service.

As is seen from the foregoing, the bases fall into two classes: (i) where there is reasonable ground for suspecting the ship is engaged in a specified unlawful activity (piracy,[119] slave trading or unauthorised broadcasting); (ii) the ship is either stateless or actually of the same nationality as the warship, despite either failing to fly or refusing to show its flag. If the suspicions prove unfounded, however, and the ship boarded did nothing to justify them, it must be compensated for any loss or damage sustained.

There is no readily available information on the frequency of such boardings or on the level of compliance with the obligation to pay compensation. No disputes between States arising out of them have become publicly known through litigation, although it is possible that disputes of this kind may have occurred but been settled by diplomatic means. The US Coast Guard maintains a

---

118. See *"Enrica Lexie" Incident (Italy v India), Provisional Measures, Order of 24 August 2015*, ITLOS Reports 2015, 182. The ship itself was briefly detained but subsequently released pursuant to the order of the Supreme Court of India in *MT Enrica Lexie & Anor v Doramma & Ors* (2012) 6 SCC 760, Civil Appeal No 4167/2012. Art 97 of UNCLOS provides in para 3 that, after an incident to which para 1 applies, "No arrest or detention of the ship, even as a measure of investigation, shall be ordered by any authorities other than those of the flag State." This was applied by the tribunal in the *Arctic Sunrise* arbitration, in relation to the allegations by the Russian authorities that the ship had engaged in dangerous manoeuvring in contravention of international rules and standards, finding that it did not permit States other than the flag State to board a vessel in the EEZ or commence judicial proceedings as Russia had done: fn 23, at pp 74–76, [298] – [305].
119. See pages 332–334.

fund for this purpose, but makes disbursements from it only for physical loss and damage, and denies compensation to ships for economic loss such as may, for example, be sustained through delays in arrival in port due to the boarding and inspection.[120]

A second exception is "hot pursuit" of a fleeing ship from one of the coastal State's maritime zones where it is suspected of having committed a relevant offence. That is, pursuits arising out of fisheries offences and others falling under the jurisdiction of the coastal State in the EEZ may be commenced from that zone; those arising out of offences against customs, fiscal, immigration and sanitary laws may be commenced in the contiguous zone (though the offences must have taken place within or landward of the territorial sea);[121] pursuit for any other offences must be commenced in the territorial sea. The conditions for valid commencement and maintenance of such a pursuit are to be found in Article 111 of UNCLOS, also little changed from Article 23 of the High Seas Convention, and were considered and applied in the *Arctic Sunrise* arbitration.[122] There an arbitral tribunal formed under Annex VII to UNCLOS found that one of the conditions, that the pursuit must be continuously maintained, had not been satisfied, since it took place in two distinct phases separated by an intervening period in which the pursuing Russian ship, though never losing visual contact with the *Arctic Sunrise*, had acted in a way inconsistent with an intention to maintain an active pursuit. While there is no cause to disagree with these factual findings, the applicability at all of Article 111 may be doubted: the pursuit began and ended in the Russian EEZ without ever reaching the high seas. The tribunal questionably treated the safety zone around the rig, mentioned in paragraph 2 of Article 111 as well as Article 60, as a separate maritime zone from which the pursuit into the surrounding EEZ for possibly relevant offences[123] needed to comply with the rules on hot pursuit. While it is possible to read the ambiguous words "including safety zones around continental shelf installations" in Article 111(2) this way, it implies that the safety zone is not part of the EEZ, and nothing in Article 60 supports this. Article 111(8) provides that "Where a ship has been stopped or arrested outside the territorial sea in circumstances which do not justify the exercise of the right of hot pursuit, it shall be compensated for any loss or damage that may have been thereby sustained." A final phase of the *Arctic Sunrise* arbitration is underway at the time of writing to determine the quantum of compensation due.

Note also that the opening words of UNCLOS Article 110(1) above preserve the right of visit where a separate treaty basis for it exists. The US under the Proliferation Security Initiative has concluded a number of treaties with prominent flag States such as Panama and Liberia by which such visits may occur.[124] The most prominent example of such a treaty provision is Article 21 of the 1995 UN Fish Stocks Agreement,[125] which has the effect of advance consent by its parties to boarding and inspection of their fishing vessels by any State that is a member of a regional

---

120. See the edited transcript of a question-and-answer session at the University of Virginia Center for Ocean Law and Policy's 31st Annual Conference, in M.H. Nordquist, R. Wolfrum, J Norton Moore and R. Long (eds), *Legal Challenges in Maritime Security* (Martinus Nijhoff Publishers 2008), at pp 98–99.

121. UNCLOS, art 111.

122. See fn 23 and text following fn 87.

123. Such as hooliganism, with which the activists on board were charged, based on the entry of some of them into the safety zone around the rig where navigation was prohibited, and terrorism, of which they were accused without any charges ultimately being laid,

124. The State Department website formerly listed 11 flag States (Antigua and Barbuda, Bahamas, Belize, Croatia, Cyprus, Liberia, Malta, the Marshall Islands, Mongolia, Panama and Saint Vincent and the Grenadines) with which the US has such agreements: www.state.gov/t/isn/c27733.htm (accessed 19 January 2017). Nine of these (all but the first and last) can still be seen at https://www.state.gov/t/isn/trty/ (accessed 17 May 2017).

125. Agreement for the Implementation of the Provisions of the United Nations Convention on the Law of the Sea of 10 December 1982 Relating to the Conservation and Management of Straddling Fish Stocks and Highly Migratory Fish Stocks (New York, 4 December 1995), 2167 UNTS 3.

fisheries management organisation or arrangement, whether or not the flag State is itself a member.

Also in force since 2010 is the IMO's 2005 Protocol[126] amending its 1988 Convention for the Suppression of Unlawful Acts against the Safety of Navigation[127] to cover carriage of weapons of mass destruction at sea. This inserts new Article 8*bis* on co-operation and procedures where a State Party desires to board a ship flying the flag of another party on reasonable suspicion that the ship or a person on board is, has been or is about to be involved in committing any of the offences in the revised Article 3[128] and new Articles 3*bis*,[129] 3*ter*[130] and 3*quater*.[131] Article 3*bis* prohibits a person from using against or on a ship or discharging from a ship any explosive, radioactive material or biological, chemical or nuclear weapon, using a ship in a manner that causes death or serious injury, transporting any explosive or radioactive material knowing that it is intended to cause death or serious injury, or committing any of a number of ancillary offences with intent to intimidate a population or to compel a government or international organisation to do or refrain from doing any act.

The flag State's authorisation and co-operation are required before a boarding may take place. The Protocol offers two ways for a State Party to give this authorisation in advance, by making either of the following notifications to the IMO Secretary-General in his capacity as depositary of the 1988 Convention, who then circulates them to the other parties (though, as far as is known, no such notifications have actually been made). One is a general authorisation to board and search a ship flying its flag, its cargo and persons on board, and to question those persons to determine whether a relevant offence in Article 3 as revised or any of Articles 3*bis*, 3*ter* or 3*quater* has been, is being or is about to be committed.[132] The second way is that the flag State's permission must still be sought through the usual channels, but is deemed to have been given if no response to the request to confirm nationality is received from the flag State within four hours of the request being made.[133] No use of force is allowed, unless either it becomes necessary to ensure the safety of the inspecting officials and other persons on board, or the officials are obstructed in the execution of authorised actions; it must then not exceed the minimum degree of force which is necessary and reasonable in the circumstances.[134]

4. THE IMO AND ITS CONVENTIONS

(a) Role of the IMO

The IMO is one of the 17 specialised agencies of the UN,[135] and is the only one whose headquarters are in the UK. Because both the UN and the IMO are created by treaties (the UN Charter

---

126. IMO doc LEG/CONF.15/21 (1 November 2005), Protocol of 2005 to the Convention for the Suppression of Unlawful Acts against the Safety of Maritime Navigation (London, 14 October 2005). By the end of 2016 40 States had ratified or acceded to the Protocol: see www.imo.org/en/About/Conventions/StatusOfConventions/Documents/Status%20of%20Treaties.pdf (accessed 30 January 2017).

127. See fn 114. This is the IMO's anti-terrorism convention.

128. Amended by art 4(1) – (4) of the 2005 Protocol.

129. Inserted by art 4(5) of the 2005 Protocol.

130. Inserted by art 4(6) of the 2005 Protocol.

131. Inserted by art 4(7) of the 2005 Protocol.

132. New art 8*bis*(5)(e) of the 1988 Convention.

133. New art 8*bis*(5)(d) of the 1988 Convention. This procedure may prove most useful to the inspecting State when it is night in the flag State or on weekends and public holidays when the decision makers are not at their desks.

134. New art 8*bis*(9) of the 1988 Convention.

135. Some of the best known of the others are UNESCO, the World Health Organization, the Food and Agriculture Organization and the International Labour Organization. Another that is relevant to shipping is the World Meteorological Organization.

and the Convention on the International Maritime Organization[136] respectively), and there is no hierarchy among treaties, the IMO, like the other specialised agencies, is not formally subordinated to the UN, but rather has been "brought into relationship" with the UN by an agreement with it under Articles 57 and 63 of the UN Charter, and reports each year to the UN's Economic and Social Council on its activities.

As at 31 December 2016 the IMO had 172 Member States and three Associate Members.[137] Because the 1948 Convention is only open to States,[138] the EU is not among them, but has expressed the view that the Convention should be amended to allow it to accede.[139] Not all of its Member States, however, are enthusiastic about such a proposal.[140] Of the various conventions negotiated at the IMO, only the 2002 Protocol to the 1974 Athens Convention relating to the Carriage of Passengers and their Luggage by Sea[141] allows international organisations to become party, which the EU did in 2011.[142]

Under its Convention, the IMO is responsible for both shipping and, since a 1977 amendment,[143] its effect on the marine environment. Its purposes and functions are enumerated in Articles 1 and 2 (originally 3) respectively, namely:

Article 1

The purposes of the Organization are:

(a) To provide machinery for co-operation among Governments in the field of governmental regulation and practices relating to technical matters of all kinds affecting shipping engaged in international trade; to encourage and facilitate the general adoption of the highest practicable standards in matters concerning the maritime safety, efficiency of navigation and prevention and control of marine pollution from ships; and to deal with administrative and legal matters related to the purposes set out in this Article;

(b) To encourage the removal of discriminatory action and unnecessary restrictions by Governments affecting shipping engaged in international trade so as to promote the availability of shipping services to the commerce of the world without discrimination; assistance and encouragement given by a Government for the development of its national shipping and for purposes of security does not

136. See fn 101. As this cross-reference suggests, the IMO was originally known as IMCO. The change of name to IMO was included in one of the several subsequent amendments to this convention, namely those adopted in 1975 (by Resolution A.358(IX)) (1276 UNTS 468), which entered into force in 1982.

137. See www.imo.org/About/Membership/Pages/Default.aspx (accessed 19 January 2017).

138. Arts 4 and 76. Article numbers here and henceforth are cited as those of the text of the Convention as it stands after entry into force of the last outstanding amendments in 2008 (see fn 145), except where otherwise indicated.

139. See the 2001 White Paper *European Transport Policy for 2010: Time to Decide*, COM(2001) 370 final, at p 98; and the 2006 Green Paper *Towards a Future Maritime Policy for the Union: A European Vision for the Oceans and Seas*, COM(2006) 275 final, at p 5; also N. Liu and F. Maes, "Legal Constraints to the European Union's Accession to the International Maritime Organization" (2012) 43 JMLC 279.

140. The UK's opposition was expressed in the Department for Transport's response to the 2006 Green Paper, http://tna.europarchive.org/20081106105415/www.dft.gov.uk/pgr/shippingports/shipping/govresponseeumaritimegreen (accessed 20 January 2017):

> [T]he UK believes that the current arrangements for co-ordination and Community involvement are working and that an attempt to seek a wider Community role is likely to be counterproductive as it carries the risk that non-EU IMO actors will perceive the EU bloc as a threat to IMO's tradition of honest, open technical debate.

Perhaps bowing to this sentiment, in the 2007 "Blue Paper" *An Integrated Maritime Policy for the European Union* COM (2007) 575 final, the only mention (at p 13) is an anodyne one to "promot[ing] co-ordination of European interests in key international fora".

141. IMO doc LEG/CONF.13/20 (19 November 2002), in force since April 2014 according to the IMO's Status of Conventions webpage (fn 126).

142. See IMO doc PAL.4/Circ.5 (19 December 2011), Protocol of 2002 to the Athens Convention relating to the Carriage of Passengers and their Luggage by Sea, 1974: Accession by the European Union. See Chapter 6.

143. The amendments were adopted by Assembly Resolution A.400(X) of 17 November 1977, which entered into force in 1984: see 1380 UNTS 268, in particular the new text of art 64 as compared with the original art 45 of 1948.

in itself constitute discrimination, provided that such assistance and encouragement is not based on measures designed to restrict the freedom of shipping of all flags to take part in international trade;

(c) To provide for the consideration by the Organization of matters concerning unfair restrictive practices by shipping concerns in accordance with Part II;

(d) To provide for the consideration by the Organization of any matters concerning shipping and the effect of shipping on the marine environment that may be referred to it by any organ or specialized agency of the United Nations;

(e) To provide for the exchange of information among Governments on matters under consideration by the Organization.

Article 2

In order to achieve the purposes set out in Part I [i.e. Article 1] the Organization shall:

(a) Subject to the provisions of Article 3, consider and make recommendations upon matters arising under Article 1 (a), (b) and (c) that may be remitted to it by Members, by any organ or specialized agency of the United Nations or by any other intergovernmental organization or upon matters referred to it under Article 1 (d);

(b) Provide for the drafting of conventions, agreements, or other suitable instruments, and recommend these to Governments and to intergovernmental organizations, and convene such conferences as may be necessary;

(c) Provide machinery for consultation among Members and the exchange of information among Governments;

(d) Perform functions arising in connexion with paragraphs (a), (b) and (c) of this Article, in particular those assigned to it by or under international instruments relating to maritime matters and the effect of shipping on the marine environment;

(e) Facilitate as necessary, and in accordance with Part X, technical co-operation within the scope of the Organization.

The purposes of countering discrimination and restrictive practices in shipping were controversial, which is one of the main reasons for the Convention taking a decade to enter into force. Initially, therefore, the focus of the IMO's activity was on safety of navigation, but more recently it has also engaged in related matters such as prevention of pollution. In both capacities the IMO is given a variety of roles in many provisions of UNCLOS, where, with one exception, it is mentioned not by name but as the "competent international organisation".

(b) Structure of the IMO

By Article 12 of the 1948 Convention, the IMO consisted at first of an Assembly, a Council, a Maritime Safety Committee, such subsidiary organs as it "may at any time consider necessary" and a Secretariat. The 1975 amendments that included the name change also entrenched the Legal and Marine Environment Protection Committees in the structure, as did the 1977 amendments for the Technical Co-operation Committee[144] and the 1991 amendments for the Facilitation Committee.[145] The IMO is currently (2017) in its first prolonged period of constitutional stability, as since 2008 there have been neither any outstanding amendments adopted but awaiting entry into force, nor plans to draft new ones.

144. See fns 136 and 143 respectively.
145. The amendments were adopted by Assembly Resolution A.724(17) of 7 November 1991 and entered into force in 2008: see www.imo.org/blast/blastDataHelper.asp?data_id=22582&filename=A724(17).pdf (accessed 20 January 2017); see the latest text in art 11 as substituted by the latter.

The Assembly consists of all the Member States[146] and meets in regular session every two years, with provision for extraordinary sessions to be convened on 60 days' notice.[147] Among its functions are to elect the Members to be represented on the Council,[148] to determine the budget and financial arrangements of the IMO and approve its accounts[149] and to recommend to Members for adoption regulations and guidelines (or amendments to these) concerning maritime safety, the prevention and control of marine pollution from ships and other matters concerning the effect of shipping on the marine environment which have been referred to it.[150]

The Council consists of 40 Members, comprising: (a) ten States with the largest interest in providing international shipping services; (b) ten other States with the largest interest in international seaborne trade; (c) 20 further States having special interests in maritime transport and navigation elected so as to ensure the representation of all major geographic areas of the world.[151] It meets on a month's notice as often as necessary on the summons of its Chairman or on request by not less than four of its members; in recent years there has been a pattern of meeting twice yearly.[152] It receives the recommendations and reports of the various committees and transmits them to the Assembly together with its own comments and recommendations.[153]

The Council, with the approval of the Assembly, also appoints the Secretary-General.[154] It reports to the Assembly at each regular session on the IMO's work since the previous regular session,[155] and submits to the Assembly budget estimates and financial statements together with its comments and recommendations.[156] Between sessions of the Assembly, the Council performs all the functions of the IMO other than making recommendations for the adoption of regulations.[157]

The Maritime Safety Committee now consists of all IMO Members,[158] as do all other IMO Committees.[159] It meets once a year and at other times upon request of any five of its members.[160] The Committee's main duty is to consider matters concerned with aids to navigation, construction and equipment of vessels, manning from a safety standpoint, rules for the prevention of collisions, handling of dangerous cargoes, maritime safety procedures and requirements, hydrographic information, log-books and navigational records, marine casualty investigation, salvage and rescue, and any other matters directly affecting maritime safety.[161] It submits to the Council

---

146. IMO Convention (fn 101), art 12.
147. Ibid., art 13.
148. Ibid., art 15(d).
149. Ibid., arts 15(g) and 15(h).
150. Ibid., art 15(j).
151. Ibid., arts 16 and 17, as amended by Assembly Resolution A.735(18) adopted on 4 November 1993, which entered into force in 2002: see 2199 UNTS 122. The original art 17 of 1948 had a Council of 16 and it has undergone three expansions to reach its present size and composition. By art 18 of the original 1948 Convention, the Council itself determined which Members had the largest or a substantial interest in providing international shipping services, and the Members with the largest interest in international seaborne trade, but this was removed with the first of the expansions and the Convention is now silent on the matter; presumably by default the calculation is left to the Secretariat to perform.
152. Ibid., art 19(c).
153. Ibid., art 21(b).
154. Ibid., art 22.
155. Ibid., art 23.
156. Ibid., art 24.
157. Ibid., art 26.
158. Ibid., art 27; art 28(a) of the original 1948 Convention provided for only 14 Members, elected by the Assembly, of which no fewer than eight had to be the "largest shipowning nations"; it was this phrase that fell to be interpreted in the ICJ advisory opinion of 1960 (fn 100).
159. See e.g. ibid., arts 32 (Marine Environment Protection Committee) and 37 (Legal Committee).
160. Ibid., art 30.
161. Ibid., art 28(a). Note that the International Hydrographic Organization based in Monaco is the international organisation mandated to deal with matters of hydrography (though it is not *stricto sensu* a UN specialised agency).

proposals for new safety regulations or amendments to existing ones, as well as recommendations and guidelines,[162] and reports to the Council on its work since the previous session of the latter.[163]

The Marine Environment Protection Committee, first established by the Assembly in 1973 as a subsidiary body of the Assembly,[164] was made permanent by the 1975 amendments to the IMO Convention.[165] Its remit is to consider any matter concerned with prevention and control of pollution from ships, in particular the adoption and amendment of relevant conventions and other regulations and measures for their enforcement.[166] Meeting at least once a year,[167] it submits to the Council proposals for regulations on prevention and control of marine pollution from ships or amendments to existing ones, as well as recommendations and guidelines,[168] and reports to the Council on its work since the previous session of the latter.[169]

Reporting to both the Maritime Safety Committee and the Marine Environment Protection Committee are seven subcommittees that are open to all Member States.[170] These are reorganised periodically, most recently in 2013 to reduce their number from nine.[171]

The Legal Committee traces its history to 1967 when it was established as a subsidiary body of the Council to deal with legal issues arising from the sinking of the *Torrey Canyon*.[172] Meeting twice a year, usually in April and October (though it is only required to do so annually),[173] it now oversees all the IMO's legal work, including the negotiation of IMO conventions, which are submitted in draft to the Council,[174] and reports to the Council on its work since the previous session of the latter.[175] The detailed drafting of conventions is largely delegated to correspondence groups working intersessionally, usually under the supervision of an appointed "lead delegation". Occasionally instruments are adopted without reference to the Legal Committee, such as the Ballast Water Convention.[176]

There are also two committees of lesser importance: the Technical Co-operation Committee is concerned with the implementation of technical co-operation projects in which the IMO participates and any other matters related to its activities in this field. It was first established

162. Ibid., art 29(a) and (b).

163. Ibid., art 29(c). Under the original art 30 of the 1948 Convention, the Committee reported to the Assembly rather than the Council.

164. See Resolution A.297(VIII).

165. See fn 136.

166. Ibid., art 38(a) and (b).

167. Ibid., art 40. In more recent practice, as can be seen from the number of meetings held since its inception (70 by January 2017), it often meets twice a year.

168. Ibid., art 39(a) and (b).

169. Ibid., art 39(c).

170. These are the Subcommittees on (i) Human Element, Training and Watchkeeping; (ii) Implementation of IMO Instruments; (iii) Navigation, Communications and Search and Rescue; (iv) Pollution Prevention and Response; (v) Ship Design and Construction; (vi) Ship Systems and Equipment; (vii) Carriage of Cargoes and Containers.

171. See www.imo.org/MediaCentre/PressBriefings/Pages/26-restructuring.aspx#.Uwj1sIV8CSo (accessed 20 January 2017).

172. See R.P. Balkin, "The Establishment and Work of the IMO Legal Committee", in M.H. Nordquist and J. Norton Moore (eds) *Current Maritime Issues and the International Maritime Organization* (Martinus Nijhoff 1999), 291 at pp 293–297.

173. IMO Convention (fn 101), art 36.

174. Ibid., arts 33(a) and 34(a). For a fascinating view of the Committee's *modus operandi*, see also N.J.J. Gaskell, "Decision Making and the Legal Committee of the IMO" (2003) 18 *International Journal of Marine and Coastal Law* 155. The Maritime Safety Committee and the Marine Environment Protection Committee are also asked for their views on amendments to the public law regulatory conventions: ibid., at p 166.

175. IMO Convention (fn 101), art 34(b).

176. International Convention for the Control and Management of Ships' Ballast Water and Sediments (London, 13 February 2004); IMO doc BWM/CONF/36 (16 February 2004).

in 1969 as a subsidiary body of the Council,[177] but since 1984 has had a permanent existence by virtue of an amendment to the 1948 Convention.[178] The Facilitation Committee was created in 1972[179] as a focal point for the IMO's work in eliminating unnecessary formalities and bureaucracy in international shipping. It too was a subsidiary body of the Council until the entry into force in 2008 of the IMO Convention amendment that elevated it to the same status as the other Committees.

The IMO's Secretariat with its headquarters in London[180] consists of the Secretary-General and some 300 staff who service the meetings of the various organs and committees[181] as well as the diplomatic conferences at which IMO convention texts are finalised for adoption. The Secretary-General serves as the depositary of these conventions.

(c) IMO Conventions as multilateral treaties

Although the law of treaties applies equally to bilateral and multilateral treaties, the latter are a relatively new phenomenon.[182] The dynamics of multilateral negotiations with many States taking part means that in the drafting of the treaties clarity often has to be sacrificed.[183] The IMO is somewhat unusual among international organisations in that it first works through its own Legal Committee to develop and draft its conventions, and then convenes diplomatic conferences at which the draft texts will be refined and ultimately adopted.

The IMO has the reputation of being among the least politicised of the UN specialised agencies and political considerations rarely interfere with the negotiation of conventions in the Legal Committee or have a disproportionate impact on their largely technical content. (The continuing impasse at the time of writing on how shipping should play its part in combatting climate change in terms of to which State greenhouse gas emissions from the operation of ships should be attributed[184] is, and it must be hoped will remain, an exception.) Once the Legal Committee has developed a text as far as it can, it reports to that effect to the Council, which then calls a diplomatic conference, at which the final remaining points of disagreement – usually the more political ones such as the precise figures for liability limits – are resolved and the treaty is formally adopted.[185] Although the Rules of Procedure at international conferences may provide for the resulting treaty to be adopted by a vote,[186] in multilateral negotiations it is generally preferable to adopt texts by consensus where

177. By Council Resolution C.49 (ES.IV) of 13 March 1969.

178. See now arts 42–46 of the IMO Convention, inserted by the 1977 amendments (fn 143).

179. By Council Resolution C.54 (XXVIII) of 24 May 1972.

180. IMO Convention (fn 101), art 63(a).

181. Ibid., art 52.

182. The idea of one instrument reflecting the will of a large number of States began only with the Vienna Congress of 1815. This was the origin of the Final Act (see fn 187) and was the first time a single instrument had been signed by multiple parties. In fact the Final Act was the only document that all parties at the Congress signed, uniting the range of traditional bilateral treaties under it into a coherent whole.

183. As to how this affects the IMO, see Gaskell (fn 174), particularly at pp 181–182 and 207–211.

184. See section 12 in Chapter 10.

185. Negotiations tend to involve a combination of formal and informal mechanisms. Often the informal side is more productive, with many decisions being made through "corridor chat" outside the main meeting hall, where more genuine debate is possible than in the series of usually prepared statements that tends to characterise the formal proceedings: see Gaskell (fn 174), at pp 188–189. Nonetheless, it is what happens in the main forum that counts in terms of the final text of a treaty – the informal substantive discussions are merged with the official process, creating the instrument to be formally adopted.

186. Art 9(2) of the Vienna Convention on the Law of Treaties (fn 18) provides that, for treaties negotiated at international conferences, adoption of the text requires a two-thirds majority of States present and voting, unless by the same majority they decide to adopt a different procedure. The Rules of Procedure at IMO diplomatic conferences seldom if ever depart from this default rule.

possible, usually defined as the absence of a formal objection, since that maximises the chances of States going on to become party to the treaty, albeit at the cost of dilution of many of its provisions to forestall objections.

(d) Becoming party to IMO Conventions – "final clauses"

A special set of provisions in multilateral treaties known as final clauses governs such mechanical matters as the requirements for entry into force.[187] Under customary international law, as codified in the Vienna Convention on the Law of Treaties, there are two basic modes for expressing consent to be bound, one involving a single step and the other two steps. The two-step procedure is more common for multilateral treaties and is used in the IMO. It consists of signature, followed by ratification.[188] The second step, ratification, is the one by which the State establishes on the international plane its consent to be bound vis-à-vis all other ratifying States. Usually some time elapses between signature and ratification, to permit States to decide whether they wish to or can enact internal laws so as to put the treaty into operation domestically, or consult their legislature where the internal constitutional arrangements require this. This is done in the UK by tabling in Parliament all treaties signed subject to ratification under section 20 of the Constitutional Reform and Governance Act 2010, replicating and replacing the long-standing Ponsonby Rule which was no more than a conventional practice and was not required by law.

Treaties are typically left open for signature for a year or two, though the period can be shorter. By Article 18 of the Vienna Convention, which is considered to be a codification of the pre-existing customary rule, the effect of signature subject to ratification is that the State is obliged to refrain from acts which would defeat the object and purpose of the treaty, unless it makes clear that it will not ratify it. This obligation continues after ratification if the treaty is not yet in force, until entry into force actually occurs or it lapses because entry into force is "unduly delayed". Signature not subject to ratification, sometimes known as definitive signature, is the one-step process, but this is more common for bilateral treaties.[189]

After the treaty closes for signature, the process reverts to a single step, in this case called accession: this allows States to become party to the treaty even if they did not take part in its original negotiation.

In multilateral treaties a certain number of ratifications or accessions is required before a treaty comes into force for any party. IMO final clauses often say these must in addition account for a given proportion of world shipping tonnage.[190] Alternatively, entry into force may also be on a particular date as stipulated in the treaty.

---

187. These should not be confused with the Final Act of the conference, to which the text of a multilateral treaty negotiated at the conference is normally annexed. The Final Act is a record of the proceedings of the conference and includes, besides the text of the treaty, such matters as the way in which the conference's work was organised, a list of the States represented, the delegates' names and any resolutions adopted by the conference. Nowadays the Final Act also plays a formal role of authenticating the text: art 10(b) of the Vienna Convention on the Law of Treaties (fn 18). By signing the Final Act of a conference, a State is not expressing any view on the treaty and its signature neither binds the State nor commits it eventually to become party to the treaty.

188. Ibid., art 14. The heading is "Consent to be bound by a treaty expressed by ratification, acceptance or approval", but as para 2 of this article makes clear, the terms acceptance and approval are functionally equivalent to ratification, which will be the sole term used from this point.

189. Note that, since signature can either (in the one-step process) be sufficient to bind a State or (in the two-step process) not, to describe a State as a "signatory" of a treaty without further explanation is ambiguous as to whether it is bound by the treaty or merely obliged not to defeat its object and purpose, so that a more precise term will always be preferable.

190. In addition, the EU is not counted towards the number of parties for the purposes of this requirement under art 19(3) of the 2002 Protocol to the Athens Convention (fn 141).

Box 8.1 Selected IMO Conventions in force
- Convention on Facilitation of International Maritime Traffic[191]
- International Convention on Load Lines[192]
- International Convention on Tonnage Measurement of Ships[193]
- International Convention Relating to Intervention on the High Seas in the case of Oil Pollution Casualties[194]
- International Convention on Civil Liability for Oil Pollution Damage[195]
- Special Trade Passenger Ships Agreement[196]
- Convention relating to Civil Liability in the Field of Maritime Carriage of Nuclear Materials[197]
- International Convention on the Establishment of an International Fund for Compensation for Oil Pollution Damage[198]
- International Convention for Safe Containers[199]
- Convention on the International Regulations for Preventing Collisions at Sea[200] (COLREG)
- International Convention for the Prevention of Pollution from Ships[201] (MARPOL)
- International Convention for the Safety of Life at Sea[202] (SOLAS)
- Convention relating to the Carriage of Passengers and their Luggage by Sea[203]
- Convention on the International Maritime Satellite Organization[204]
- Convention on Limitation of Liability for Maritime Claims[205]
- International Convention on Standards of Training, Certification and Watchkeeping for Seafarers[206]
- International Convention on Maritime Search and Rescue[207]
- Convention for the Suppression of Unlawful Acts Against the Safety of Maritime Navigation[208]
- International Convention on Salvage[209]
- International Convention on Oil Pollution Preparedness, Response and Co-operation[210]
- International Convention on Maritime Liens and Mortgages[211]
- Convention on the Arrest of Ships[212]
- International Convention on Civil Liability for Bunker Oil Pollution Damage[213]
- International Convention on the Control of Harmful Anti-fouling Systems on Ships[214]
- Nairobi International Convention on the Removal of Wrecks[215]

191. 591 UNTS 265. The purpose of this Convention is to simplify governmental formalities and documentary requirements.

192. 640 UNTS 133.

193. 1291 UNTS 3. See further section on Limitation of Liability in Chapter 7.

194. See fn 79. See further Chapter 10.

195. 973 UNTS 3. See further Chapter 10.

196. 910 UNTS 61.

197. 974 UNTS 255. See further Chapter 10.

198. 1110 UNTS 57. See further Chapter 10.

199. 1064 UNTS 3.

200. See fn 11. This Convention makes the IMO responsible for traffic separation schemes (a role reserved in UNCLOS arts 22(3)(a) and 41(4) and 41(5) for the unnamed "competent international organization" regarding the territorial sea and in particular in straits used for international navigation). Independently of the Convention, the IMO has a parallel role for archipelagic sea lanes and any traffic separation schemes within them under UNCLOS art 53(9). See further section on Collisions in Chapter 7.

201. 1340 UNTS 61. Of this convention's six annexes (on oil, bulk noxious liquids, harmful packaged substances, sewage, garbage, air pollution) only the first two are compulsory, but when it appeared that the inability of many States to comply with Annex II was delaying its entry into force, an amendment negotiated in 1978 changed this so that compliance with it became optional for the first three years. For this reason the Convention is often referred to as MARPOL 73/78. This enabled the Convention to enter into force in 1983. All the other annexes are also now in force. See further Chapter 10.

202. 1184 UNTS 3. This is a frequently amended Convention, e.g. in 1983 to incorporate the previously non-binding Code for the Construction and Equipment of Ships carrying Dangerous Chemicals in Bulk. See further Chapter 9.

203. 1463 UNTS 19. See further Chapter 6.

204. 1143 UNTS 105.

205. 1456 UNTS 221. See further section on Limitation of Liability in Chapter 7.

206. 1361 UNTS 2. See further Chapter 9 on this Convention as amended in 1995 (STCW95); further major amendments were adopted in 2010 and entered into force on 1 January 2012, with a five-year transitional period; these are contained in IMO doc STCW/CONF.2/33 (1 July 2010).

207. 1405 UNTS 97.

208. See fn 114.

209. 1953 UNTS 165. This convention replaces the traditional "no cure no pay" rule with a system of reward to the salvor for preventing a major pollution incident, even if the ship itself is not saved. See further section on Salvage in Chapter 7.

210. 1891 UNTS 51. See further Chapter 10.

211. 2276 UNTS 39. The aim of this Convention is to promote uniformity in private law, but few of its 18 parties are common law jurisdictions. See further Chapter 12.

212. 2797 UNTS 3, though with only 11 parties as at 31 December 2016. See further Chapters 1 and 12.

213. IMO doc LEG/CONF.12/19 (27 March 2001). See further Chapter 10.

214. IMO doc AFS/CONF/26 (18 October 2001). See further Chapter 10.

215. See fn 44. See further section on Wreck Removal in Chapter 7.

The IMO conventions adopted by this process, most of which have been amended or supplemented by protocols (some of them many times) not separately listed, are enumerated in Box 8.1. In addition, the IMO serves as the secretariat to the 1972 Convention on the Prevention of Marine Pollution by Dumping of Wastes and Other Matter[216] and its 1996 Protocol.[217]

The texts of these conventions are available from the IMO, which also as the depositary maintains status lists indicating which States are party to which conventions. Since, under Article 102(1) of the Charter of the United Nations, treaties are supposed to be registered with the Secretariat and published by it, they also appear, once they have entered into force, in the United Nations Treaty Series, which can be accessed online free of charge.[218]

There are relatively few IMO conventions still not in force: the 1996 International Convention on Liability and Compensation for Damage in Connection with the Carriage of Hazardous and Noxious Substances,[219] the 2004 International Convention for the Control and Management of Ships' Ballast Water and Sediments[220] and the 2009 Hong Kong International Convention for the Safe and Environmentally Sound Recycling of Ships.[221]

Relevant conventions negotiated elsewhere than in the IMO include the 1974 Convention on a Code of Conduct for Liner Conferences,[222] the 1978 United Nations Convention on the Carriage of Goods by Sea[223] and the 1986 United Nations Convention on the Conditions for Registration of Ships,[224] all negotiated in the UN Conference on Trade and Development (UNCTAD), while the 2008 UN Convention on Contracts for the International Carriage of Goods Wholly or Partly by Sea[225] was the work of the UN Commission on International Trade Law (UNCITRAL). The 1993 International Convention on Maritime Liens and Mortgages[226]

---

216. London, Mexico City, Moscow and Washington, 29 December 1972; 1046 UNTS 120. See further Chapter 10.

217. The text of the Protocol as amended in 2006 is available at www.imo.org/blast/blastData.asp?doc_id=13203&-filename=PROTOCOL%20Amended%202006.doc (accessed 1 February 2017).

218. See fn 16. Regrettably, however, the UNTS is running some years in arrears and its website is not especially user-friendly. Another way of circumventing the IMO charge is to find the treaty on the treaties website of one of the parties, an especially easy-to-use one being that maintained by the Australian Legal Information Institute at www.austlii.edu.au/au/other/dfat/ (accessed 28 January 2017). (NB: if Australia has signed but not yet ratified the Convention, it will be found under Australian Treaties Not in Force rather than in the Australian Treaty Series.)

219. IMO doc LEG/CONF.10/8/2 (9 May 1996). By art 46(1), it requires 12 States including four each with 2,000,000 units of gross tonnage to consent to be bound by it in order to enter into force. As at 31 March 2017, 14 had done so according to the IMO's Status of Conventions webpage (fn 126), so it is the second condition that remains unfulfilled. A 2010 Protocol (IMO doc LEG/CONF.17/10 (4 May 2010)) amended the Convention to replace certain provisions that had been discouraging many States from expressing that consent, but is itself not yet in force: ibid. See further Chapter 10.

220. See fn 176. By art 18(1), it requires 30 States representing 35 per cent of gross registered tonnage to consent to be bound by it in order to enter into force. The first condition was met in 2011 but the second not until 8 September 2016 according to the IMO's Status of Conventions webpage (fn 126), which will bring the Convention into force a year from the latter date. See further Chapter 10.

221. IMO doc SR/CONF/45 (19 May 2009). By art 18(1), in order to enter into force it requires 15 States representing 40 per cent of gross registered tonnage, and whose combined maximum annual ship recycling volume during the preceding ten years constituted at least 3 per cent of their combined merchant shipping tonnage, to consent to be bound by it. As at 31 March 2017 only five had yet done so according to the IMO's Status of Conventions webpage (fn 126). See further section on Recycling in Chapter 10.

222. Geneva, 6 April 1974; 1334 UNTS 15.

223. Hamburg, 31 March 1978; 1695 UNTS 3. See further Chapter 4.

224. See fn 102, not in force.

225. New York, 11 December 2008. The text is annexed to UN General Assembly Resolution 63/122 (UN doc A/RES/63/122 (2 February 2009)). By art 18(1), it requires 20 States to consent to be bound by it in order to enter into force. As at 31 March 2017 only three had done so according to the UN treaties website (fn 16). See further Chapter 4.

226. See fn 211.

and the 1999 Convention on the Arrest of Ships[227] were negotiated under the joint auspices of IMO and UNCTAD.

Amending treaties is often a problem for international law because it is normally more difficult to gain governments' attention and legislative time for amendments than for the original treaty negotiations, with the result that they typically take a very long time to enter into force, and even then bind only the parties to them,[228] while as between a State party to the amendment and a State only party to the original treaty, it is the latter that remains in force. The IMO has, however, pioneered a "tacit acceptance" procedure for technical amendments, which allows these to come into force after a specified period for all parties other than those that specifically object to them. This is why it has been possible to amend some of the IMO Conventions, notably those on safety of life at sea and the collision regulations, many times. Substantive amendments are still subject to the Vienna Convention rules, however, the 2002 Protocol to the 1974 Athens Convention relating to the Carriage of Passengers and their Luggage by Sea[229] and the 2010 Protocol to the 1996 International Convention on Liability and Compensation for Damage in Connection with the Carriage of Hazardous and Noxious Substances[230] being examples.

(e) IMO as the "competent international organization" in UNCLOS

Being in some respects a framework convention, UNCLOS in many of its provisions does not itself set out binding rules but instead incorporates by reference those made by what it refers to as the "competent international organization(s)" in various fields, which it never names. In the field of navigation and pollution from ships, IMO is universally regarded as the body meant by this phrase.[231] In the territorial sea in general, the coastal State is free to prescribe sea lanes and traffic separation schemes as it sees fit, and need only take into account the IMO's recommendations.[232] In waters where the interests of unimpeded navigation have required special regimes, by contrast – that is, straits used for international navigation and archipelagic sea lanes – the coastal or archipelagic State must refer its proposals to the IMO for adoption, which in turn may adopt only such sea lanes and traffic separation schemes as are agreed with that State.[233] The Assembly in 1997 delegated the Maritime Safety Committee to act on the IMO's behalf in these matters.[234] Traffic separation schemes, of which there are many, are notified to the shipping community by means of Circulars in the COLREG.2 series available on the IMO website.[235] The only instance to date of archipelagic sea lanes is the partial designation by Indonesia.[236] The Philippines was also understood to have been working for some years on bringing a designation to the IMO, but

---

227. See fn 212.

228. See Vienna Convention on the Law of Treaties (fn 18), art 40(4).

229. See fn 141.

230. See fn 219.

231. See the papers by R. Wolfrum, S. Rosenne and A. Blanco-Bazán all entitled "IMO Interface with the Law of the Sea Convention" in M.H. Nordquist and J Norton Moore (eds), *Current Maritime Issues and the International Maritime Organization* (Martinus Nijhoff 1999), at pp 223, 251 and 269 respectively, especially that of Rosenne at p 254.

232. UNCLOS (fn 8), art 22(3)(a).

233. Ibid., arts 41(4) (straits) and 53(9) (archipelagic sea lanes).

234. Assembly Resolution A.858(20) (undated), para 1. Independently of UNCLOS, the IMO has power to adopt such schemes: see r 1(d) of the International Regulations for Preventing Collisions at Sea 1972 annexed to the COLREG Convention (fn 11).

235. See https://docs.imo.org/Category.aspx?cid=126 (accessed on 30 January 2017, requires registration as public user).

236. IMO doc SN/Circ.200 (26 May 1998) annexing Maritime Safety Committee Resolution MSC.72(69) (adopted on 19 May 1998), Adoption, Designation and Substitution of Archipelagic Sea Lanes, para 1.

subsequent indications suggest that it has had second thoughts about the utility of doing so.[237] The effect of archipelagic sea lanes remaining undesignated is that the right of archipelagic sea lanes passage may continue to be exercised through all routes "normally used for international navigation".[238]

The "generally accepted international regulations" emanating from IMO's work are given indirect legal force by UNCLOS where mentioned in the context of rules to be complied with, including, it would seem, by non-parties to the relevant IMO conventions.[239] Thus the rules on safety of navigation are incorporated by reference on such matters as traffic separation schemes in straits and archipelagic sea lanes,[240] as well as the rules on the construction, design, equipment and manning of ships and the prevention of collisions at sea.[241] Of the numerous provisions of this type in Part XII on protection of the marine environment, Article 211 on pollution from ships is particularly significant – the essence of the scheme established by this article is that the coastal State may make and enforce pollution regulations in its EEZ in order to implement the rules formulated through the IMO, but may not ordinarily have more stringent ones.[242] For any defined area within its EEZ where the coastal State nevertheless has reasonable grounds for believing that these rules are inadequate for the special circumstances of that area, and that special mandatory measures (other than design, construction, manning and equipment standards) for preventing pollution are necessary because of oceanographic or ecological conditions, the coastal State may submit scientific and technical information to the IMO, which within 12 months of the receipt of the communication must determine whether the conditions do in fact warrant such measures. If so, the coastal State may adopt the special regulations proposed, though they become binding on foreign ships no earlier than 15 months from the original communication.[243] The IMO has grouped this provision procedurally with similar ones in other instruments within its process for establishing what it calls Particularly Sensitive Sea Areas, not necessarily confined to EEZs, in which special rules apply (each set of rules being unique to each such area).[244] The IMO's website lists several such areas including the Great Barrier Reef off Australia, the Florida Keys, Western European Waters, the Canary Islands, the Galapagos Archipelago and the Baltic Sea.[245]

237. See the chapter by a senior Philippines official, A.A. Encomienda, "Archipelagic Sea Lanes Passage and the Philippines Situation", in M.H Nordquist, T.T.B. Koh and J Norton Moore (eds), *Freedom of Seas, Passage Rights and the 1982 Law of the Sea Convention* (Martinus Nijhoff 2009), 393 at p 405, where seeking designation of the archipelago as a Particularly Sensitive Sea Area (see fn 244 and accompanying text) is canvassed as a potentially more acceptable alternative.

238. UNCLOS (fn 8), art 53(12).

239. Blanco-Bazán (fn 231), cautions at pp 281–282 against taking this too far – the failure by non-parties to ensure compliance by their ships with the more technical provisions of these IMO conventions does not automatically place them in breach of UNCLOS.

240. UNCLOS (fn 8), arts 41(3) (straits) and 53(8) (archipelagic sea lanes).

241. Ibid., art 21(2) and 21(4) respectively. An example of the former is the requirement for new oil tankers to be fitted with double hulls separated by a space of at least 2 metres (on tankers of 5,000 dwt or above) or of at least 0.76 metres (tankers below 5,000 dwt), contained in reg 13F of Annex I to MARPOL 73/78 (fn 201), inserted by Resolution MEPC.52(32) adopted in 1992 and in force since 1993, reproduced at 1733 UNTS 385. A very long list of such requirements, though only up to November 1998, is in IMO doc MSC/Circ.815 (13 November 1998). The latter may be taken as a reference to the COLREG Convention (fn 11).

242. See in particular paras 1 and 5 of art 211. In the territorial sea the coastal State is given more latitude: by para 4, echoing art 24(1), its rules on prevention of pollution from ships must merely "not hamper innocent passage of foreign vessels".

243. UNCLOS (fn 8), art 211(6).

244. See IMO doc A 24/Res.982 (6 February 2006). "[Assembly] Resolution A.982(24) Adopted on 1 December 2005 (Agenda item 11), Revised Guidelines for the Identification and Designation of Particularly Sensitive Sea Areas".

245. See www.imo.org/en/OurWork/Environment/PSSAs/Pages/Default.aspx (accessed 28 January 2017).

Finally, the single mention of the IMO by name in UNCLOS occurs in Annex VIII, making it responsible for drawing up and maintaining a list of experts in the field of navigation including pollution from vessels by dumping, who are available to serve on special ad hoc arbitral panels that States parties may constitute to decide disputes in this field if they so elect.[246] To date, however, Annex VIII has never been invoked.

5. THE UNCLOS ARTICLE 292 PROMPT RELEASE PROCEDURES

Under Article 220 of UNCLOS, a coastal State may detain and prosecute a foreign ship voluntarily present in one of its ports for violating pollution laws in its territorial sea or EEZ, or may inspect ships in the territorial sea for such violation there and, where the evidence so warrants, institute legal proceedings against the ship, which may include its detention.[247] Detention may also occur in the case of "clear objective evidence" that a ship has in the EEZ "committed a violation . . . resulting in a discharge causing major damage or threat of major damage to the coastline or related interests of the coastal State, or to any resources of its territorial sea or exclusive economic zone".[248] This is subject to Article 226(1)(b), which requires that, if the investigation indicates a violation of international environmental rules, "release shall be made promptly subject to reasonable procedures such as bonding or other appropriate financial security".[249]

This in turn is subject to Article 292, whose paragraph 1 provides that, if the detaining State is alleged not to have complied with any provision in UNCLOS for the prompt release of a ship and its crew,[250] the question may be submitted to any court or tribunal agreed on by the parties or, failing such agreement within ten days from the detention, to ITLOS. Paragraph 2 adds that the application may be made only by or on behalf of the flag State, in other words the flag State need not take part in the proceedings, but must give its consent to them if they are to be admissible. By paragraph 3, the court or tribunal must deal without delay with the application for release – but only with the question of release, without prejudice to the merits of the case before any domestic forum against the ship, its owner or its crew.

There have been several such prompt release cases taken to ITLOS under this procedure, which made up the bulk of its judicial activity in its first decade, though the last such case was

---

246. UNCLOS (fn 8), art 287(1)(d) and Annex VIII, art 2(2).
247. Ibid., art 220(1) and 220(2).
248. Ibid., art 220(6).
249. See also ibid., art 226(1)(c), by which the release of an unseaworthy ship presenting an unreasonable threat of damage to the marine environment may be refused or made conditional on proceeding to the nearest appropriate repair yard. In that event, the flag State must be promptly notified.
250. The only provisions relevant are those cited above and art 73 on the enforcement of resources laws in the EEZ. For reasons that are unclear, shipping interests have not used this procedure, and all the cases on it have been in respect either of fishing vessels or of ships servicing fishing vessels. The most recent flag State applications for prompt release of a ship, in *The M/V Louisa (Saint Vincent and the Grenadines v Kingdom of Spain), Provisional Measures*, ITLOS Reports 2008–2010, 58, *The ARA Libertad (Argentina v Ghana), Provisional Measures*, ITLOS Reports 2012, 332 and *The Arctic Sunrise (Kingdom of the Netherlands v Russian Federation), Provisional Measures*, ITLOS Reports 2013, 230, were sought as provisional measures under art 290 of UNCLOS rather than art 292, as the ships were detained for reasons other than suspicion of pollution or fisheries offences. The first of these applications was rejected but the other two succeeded. The judgments, orders and written and oral pleadings in this and all other ITLOS cases are available on its website, www.itlos.org/en/cases/list-of-cases/ (accessed 28 January 2017).

in 2007.[251] Although they all concern fishing vessels,[252] the principles enunciated apply equally to detentions arising from pollution incidents. In *The Camouco*, ITLOS set out the criteria by which the reasonableness of any bond such as that required under Article 226(1)(b) would be judged:

[F]actors . . . relevant in an assessment of the reasonableness of bonds or other financial security . . . include the gravity of the alleged offences, the penalties imposed or imposable under the laws of the detaining State, the value of the detained vessel and of the cargo seized, the amount of the bond imposed by the detaining State and its form.[253]

In the next case, *The Monte Confurco*, the majority judgment noted that under UNCLOS Article 292, ITLOS "is not an appellate forum against a decision of the national court", but added that "nevertheless . . . the Tribunal is not precluded from examining the facts and circumstances of the case to the extent necessary for a proper appreciation of the reasonableness of the bond".[254] In doing so, it criticised the French court of first instance's assumption that half the catch seized by the French authorities was taken illegally in the EEZ, stating that the information before it "does not give an adequate basis to assume" this. The majority thus found that the bond fixed by the French court (FF56.4 million) was not reasonable, and substituted a total of FF18 million.

It is submitted, however, that this reasoning is questionable, and the dissenting opinions were more persuasive. Judge Anderson, who dissented on all substantive points, took the view that the assumption that the seized fish had been caught in French waters was not unreasonable.[255] Judge Jesus thought that ITLOS had intervened in the merits contrary to Article 292(3).[256] Judge Mensah, though not dissenting, agreed that the majority had "come perilously close" to trespassing upon the merits, and criticised the direct approach taken by ITLOS in assessing the facts, forming a view on the merits different from that of the French court and so finding its bond unreasonable, overlooking the possibility that the bond the latter had imposed could be "reasonable" within the meaning of Article 73 of UNCLOS without necessarily being the exact amount that ITLOS itself would have imposed:

The Tribunal is, of course, entitled to disagree with the actual figure chosen by the court of first instance. This is because there is no single correct figure in the circumstances of the case . . . [This] does not mean that the basis of computation adopted by the court of first instance is "inconsistent" with the facts.[257]

---

251. For a survey of the prompt release cases up to 2004 by the first President of ITLOS, see T.A. Mensah, "The Tribunal and the Prompt Release of Vessels" (2007) 22 *International Journal of Marine and Coastal Law* 425.

252. Albeit at one remove in the first, *The M/V Saiga (No 1) (Saint Vincent and the Grenadines v Guinea)*, ITLOS Reports 1997, 16, where the offence which led to the detention was the supply of bunkers to a fishing vessel in the EEZ, which ITLOS elected to treat as a fisheries offence attracting art 292 rather than as a customs offence for which art 292 would not have been available.

253. *Camouco (Panama v France)*, ITLOS Reports 2000, 10 at p 31 ([67]). For a useful case note see B.H. Oxman and V.P. Bantz (2000) 94 *American Journal of International Law* 713.

254. *The Monte Confurco (Seychelles v France)*, ITLOS Reports 2000, 86 at p 109 ([74]). For criticism of this judgment see A. Serdy and M. Bliss, "Prompt Release of Fishing Vessels: State Practice in the Light of the Cases before the International Tribunal for the Law of the Sea" in A.G. Oude Elferink and D.R. Rothwell (eds), *Oceans Management in the 21st Century: Institutional Frameworks and Responses* (Martinus Nijhoff 2004), 273 at pp 280–290.

255. *The Monte Confurco (Seychelles v France), Dissenting Opinion of Judge Anderson*, ITLOS Reports 2000, 127 at pp 128–131.

256. *The Monte Confurco (Seychelles v France), Dissenting Opinion of Judge Jesus*, ITLOS Reports 2000, 139 at pp 142–143 ([24] – [30]).

257. *The Monte Confurco (Seychelles v France), Declaration of Judge Mensah*, ITLOS Reports 2000, 118 at pp 118–119.

Although the outcome in *The Monte Confurco* might appear to suggest that, in effect if not in name, belying the passage quoted above, an appeal to ITLOS is indeed possible from a decision of a domestic court as to bond, a salutary lesson to litigants tempted to try that is given by the 2001 case of *The Grand Prince*. The facts here were that Belize, notified by France of its vessel's arrest for illegal fishing, cancelled its registration and sent a diplomatic Note to France to that effect. Later, however, the Belizean registry stated in a letter to France's Honorary Consul in Belize that:

while we were in the process of cancelling ex-officio the vessel's status, the owners requested an opportunity to defend themselves of the accusations by submitting an appeal to [ITLOS]. Under this context and Belize being a [party to UNCLOS] we considered fair to allow the affected party to file its petition. . . . Depending on the result of this court proceeding we will decide whether or not to enforce our decision to delete the vessel from our records.[258]

Treating the earlier Note as conclusive, a narrow majority found the ship as at the date on which the application was made did not in fact have Belizean nationality, so that ITLOS lacked jurisdiction to hear it.[259] Nine judges dissented jointly, arguing that the official documents issued by Belize subsequent to the Note indicated that the deregistration was not definitive, and had been suspended.[260]

Overall, however, the subsequent prompt release decisions indicate that ITLOS and Article 292 are still a very worthwhile avenue for shipowners to pursue should the occasion arise. In *The Volga*, ITLOS by majority found unreasonable the bond set by Australia for release of a Russian-flagged fishing vessel because it included an amount of A\$1 million as a bond securing compliance with a condition of release, being the installation and operation of a satellite-based vessel monitoring system (VMS) to allow for tracking of the *Volga*. This was based on its interpretation of Article 73 of UNCLOS as not allowing for the imposition of non-financial conditions for releasing a ship, such as the VMS bond and disclosure of its beneficial ownership which the Australian authorities had also demanded.[261] Nonetheless, in this case for the first time ITLOS was prepared to set a bond equal to the full value of the ship,[262] disregarding an argument on behalf of the shipowner that its own case law dictated a going rate for bonds of about 25 per cent of the ship's value.

Although forfeiture of the ship involved is more commonly a penalty for fisheries than for pollution offences, ITLOS has shown itself prepared to go behind the wording of the coastal State's forfeiture law. In *The Juno Trader*[263] ITLOS treated the ostensibly definitive forfeiture of a ship under the law of Guinea-Bissau as reversible as long as proceedings of some kind to overturn it were still on foot. On the other hand, in *The Tomimaru*,[264] the flag State (Japan) and owner delayed too long before invoking Article 292, by when the last possible window of remedial opportunity in the Russian courts had closed, and the application was as a consequence declared without object. This stands to reason, as a ship is released to its owner or a nominated

---

258. *The Grand Prince (Belize v France)*, ITLOS Reports 2001, 17 at p 40 ([74]).

259. Ibid., at p 44 ([93] and [95]). See also the case note by B.H. Oxman and V.P. Bantz, "The 'Grand Prince' (Belize v. France)" (2002) 96 *American Journal of International Law* 219.

260. *The Grand Prince (Belize v France)*, *Dissenting Opinion of Judges Caminos, Marotta Rangel, Yankov, Yamamoto, Akl, Vukas, Marsit, Eiriksson and Jesus*, ITLOS Reports 2001, 66.

261. *The Volga (Russian Federation v Australia)*, ITLOS Reports 2002, 10 at pp 34–36 ([75] – [80]) and 37 ([88]).

262. Ibid., at p 34 ([73]).

263. *The Juno Trader (St Vincent and the Grenadines v Guinea-Bissau)*, ITLOS Reports 2004, 17. See further V.P. Bantz, "Views from Hamburg: The Juno Trader or How to make Sense of the Coastal State's Rights in Light of its Duty of Prompt Release" (2005) 24 *University of Queensland Law Journal* 415.

264. *The Tomimaru (Japan v Russian Federation)* ITLOS Reports 2005–2007, 68.

representative, and if the owner is by then the respondent, any application by the former owner becomes futile.

Since detention of the ship rather than of the crew is the necessary condition for its invocation, the Article 292 procedure was not available to assist the master of the *Prestige*, controversially detained by the Spanish authorities after her sinking in 2002.[265] Even so, this seems insufficient to account for the forbearance of shipping interests from using this procedure. Since the prompt release procedure has lived up to its name and the reputation of ITLOS as an international court capable of applying and developing the public international law of the sea is now well established, the imbalance may begin to be redressed in the coming years.

---

265. See page 312.

CHAPTER 9

SAFETY AND COMPLIANCE

Filippo Lorenzon

1. INTRODUCTION

This chapter is dedicated to some of the most relevant international conventions concerning the safety of life at sea and the security of ships, crews, cargo and ports. The Conventions discussed are very diverse but have a common *leitmotif*: they all focus on the human and technical element of shipping, aiming at preventing human error, enhancing the working and living conditions of seafarers and – in the broadest sense – preserving life at sea.

Another element these conventions have in common is that they all provide detailed regulations with which shipowners and operators are required to comply. Such compliance is achieved by a system of certification and control largely performed by classification societies on behalf of the flag State administration (or Flag State Control) and enforced by the port State (or Port State Control) according to very specific rules set by the International Maritime Organization (IMO). A system of mutual recognition of certification and – within the EU – the important intervention of the European Maritime Safety Agency (EMSA) further enhances compliance with the Conventions.

It is to follow this *leitmotif* that the following analysis will start from the instruments that are obviously connected to *safety*, the 1974 SOLAS Convention and the ISM Code. The focus will then shift to the issue of *safety through security* and the ISPS Code, *safety through manning* where the STCW95 and the Maritime Labour Convention 2006 bring their contributions. Finally *safety compliance* will be looked at and the role of the European Union, EMSA and classification societies in both flag and port State control.

The picture which emerges is one of a sea swimming with codes, rules and regulations where – some may say – the purpose of safety is out of sight, swallowed by waves of bureaucracy and lost among piles of certificates. It seems indeed that the purpose of enhancing safety through compliance could be better achieved if the rules to be followed were unified in a single international instrument easily enforceable around the globe. We are certainly not there yet but the perseverance of the IMO, the International Labour Organization (ILO), the Comité Maritime International and EMSA have contributed significantly to make shipping much safer than it was just a few decades ago. The system is not perfect but work is in progress.

2. THE INTERNATIONAL CONVENTION FOR THE SAFETY OF LIFE AT SEA

The purpose of the SOLAS Convention[1] is to promote safety of life at sea by establishing rules which govern the safe construction of ships,[2] the safety equipment with which ships are required to be fitted and the standards to which they should be operated in order to avoid accidents.[3] It is the role of the IMO regularly to review the Convention and to draft any necessary amendments,[4] but the responsibility for enforcement of the provisions of the Convention lies with the

---

1. International Convention for the Safety of Life at Sea, adopted on 1 November 1974 and entered into force on 25 May 1980 with the Protocol of 1988 as amended (hereinafter "SOLAS"). A full list of amendments and ratifications is available at www.imo.org/About/Conventions/StatusOfConventions/Pages/Default.aspx (accessed 14 February 2017).
2. SOLAS, Chapter II.
3. See also SOLAS, Chapter III.
4. According to the procedure set up in art VIII.

flag State.[5] The flag State must ensure that the ships which trade under its flag are surveyed when they are first registered, in order to establish compliance with SOLAS.[6] Thereafter ships are periodically surveyed at stipulated intervals by the flag State, which also issues certificates prescribed by the Convention. The flag States are permitted to delegate these responsibilities to a recognised body such as a classification society (or Recognised Organizations within the EU).[7] Port States, operating under administrative agreements such as the Paris Memorandum of Understanding on Port State Control – the Paris MoU[8] – have authority to inspect those ships which they have ground to believe not to be in compliance with SOLAS and if necessary detain them.[9]

There have been several versions of the SOLAS Convention, the first was adopted in 1914 following the loss of the RMS *Titanic*, the second in 1929, the third in 1948 and the fourth in 1960. In 1974 the current convention was adopted which includes the new amendment procedure of tacit acceptance. Its inclusion is due to the fact that the formal procedures within the IMO can be lengthy and time consuming, and the need for necessary amendments to be quickly brought into force. Tacit acceptance provides for an amendment to enter into force on a specified date, unless objections are received beforehand from an agreed number of Member States. The procedure has, since 1974, been utilised by the IMO on a number of occasions, notably with the introduction of the International Safety Management (ISM) Code, the International Ship and Port Security (ISPS) Code and more recently the requirement that containers have a verified gross mass (VGM), in force from 1 July 2016.

It must be noted that for EU Member States, Directive 2008/106/EC requires that crew members, who must be certified in accordance with Regulation III/10.4 of the SOLAS Convention, are trained and certificated in accordance with the Directive.[10]

3. THE INTERNATIONAL SAFETY MANAGEMENT CODE

The main objectives of the International Safety Management (ISM) Code[11] "are to ensure safety at sea, prevention of human injury or loss of life, and avoidance of damage to the environment in particular to the marine environment and to property".[12] The ISM Code was adopted by the IMO in 1993 and in 1994 it was inserted into the SOLAS Convention as Chapter IX. On 1 July 1998, the code became mandatory for passenger ships, high speed ships, tankers and bulk carriers

---

5. SOLAS, art I.

6. See SOLAS, art I. For the EU see also Directives 2009/21/EC of the European Parliament and of the Council of 23 April 2009 on compliance with the flag State requirements and 2009/15/EC of the European Parliament and of the Council of 23 April 2009 on common rules and standards for ship inspection and survey organisations and for the relevant activities of maritime administrations, and Regulation (EC) No 391/2009 of the European Parliament and of the Council of 23 April 2009 on common rules and standards for ship inspection and survey organisations (as amended). See p 364 et seq.

7. See below and SOLAS, Chapter I, reg 6.

8. The Paris MoU is an administrative agreement adopted in January 1982. Initially signed by 14 European countries at a Ministerial Conference held in Paris, it entered into operation on 1 July 1982. It now counts 27 Maritime Administrations. See www.parismou.org/about-us/organisation (accessed 1 March 2017).

9. Paris MoU, s 3.

10. Directive 2008/106/EC of the European Parliament and of the Council of 19 November 2008 on the minimum level of training of seafarers, OJ L 323, 3 December 2008, at pp 33–61, art 3.2.

11. The International Management Code for the Safe Operation of Ships and for Pollution Prevention, 2014 consolidated edition, as amended by resolutions MSC.104(73), MSC.179(79), MSC.195(80), MSC.273(85), which entered into force on 1 July 2002, on 1 July 2006, on 1 January 2009, and on 1 July 2010, respectively, and resolution MSC.353(92), which entered into force on 1 January 2015.

12. ISM Code, art 1.2.1.

of more than 500 gross tonnes. Later, from 1 July 2002, it became mandatory for all other types of ship, excluding warships, auxiliaries or other government operated ships, used for non-commercial purposes.[13]

The Code provided for earlier implementation by Member States where it was deemed appropriate. On 9 December 1995, the Council of the European Union adopted the ISM Code and declared that from 1 July 1996 it would become mandatory for operators of Ro-Ro passenger ferries operating to or from any port within the European Community.[14] Even before the code became mandatory, it was held by the courts that ISM represented a set of internationally recognised principles embodying best practice in ship management.[15]

The wording of the ISM Code is admirably brief and clear setting out principles for ship operators – owners or managers – requiring them to:

- adopt a Safety Management System;[16]
- appoint a designated person with responsibility to monitor the implementation of the Safety Management System;[17]
- ensure that adequate resources and support are available;[18]
- establish procedures for all operations and maintenance tasks;[19]
- ensure good safety practices afloat and ashore;
- improve communication between ship and shore;[20]
- establish emergency procedures;[21] and
- put in place a system of verification, review and evaluation (internal audits).[22]

It should be noted that while the shipboard aspects of the Code are important, equal emphasis is placed upon the role and responsibilities of the operator.

While a full and detailed discussion on the ISM Code is beyond the scope of this chapter, three of its key aspects require further analysis because of their importance and practical relevance. These are (a) certification issues, (b) the creation of the designated person and (c) the impact of the Code in litigation. These three issues will be dealt with in turn.

(a) Certification, verification and control

The flag States – referred to as "Administrations" in the Code – are required to institute systems of certification, verification and control,[23] which may be carried out either by the flag States themselves or delegated to a Recognised Organisation, such as a classification society.[24] Those operators who

---

13. For the United Kingdom, this was done through the Merchant Shipping (International Safety Management (ISM) Code) Regulations 1998, SI 1998/1561, since repealed by the Merchant Shipping (International Safety Management (ISM) Code) Regulations, SI 2014/1512, reg 3. On the ISM Code and Regulations see P. Anderson, *ISM Code: A Practical Guide to the Legal and Insurance Implications* (3rd edn, Informa Law 2005).

14. Council Regulation (EC) No 3051/95 of 8 December 1995 on the safety management of roll-on/rolloff passenger ferries (ro-ro ferries), OJ L 320, 30 December 1995, at pp 14–24.

15. See *Papera Traders Co Ltd and Others v Hyundai Merchant Marine Co Ltd and Another (The Eurasian Dream) (No 1)* [2002] 1 Lloyd's Rep 719, [143] and [144].

16. As defined in ISM Code, art 1.1.4.

17. ISM Code, art 4.

18. Ibid., art 6.

19. Ibid., arts 6–10.

20. *Inter alia* through the Designated Person, see ISM Code, art 4, s 1.4.

21. ISM Code, art 8.

22. Ibid., art 12.

23. Ibid., art 15.

24. See in detail below.

comply with the Code receive a Document of Compliance (DOC) drawn up according to a standard model appended to the Code. The DOC[25] is valid for five years,[26] subject to annual verification.[27] Similarly, each ship, after audit, is issued with a Safety Management Certificate (SMC) valid for five years, subject to one intermediate audit.[28] Ships are required to carry on board the original SMC and a copy of the DOC as well as a copy of the documents used to describe and implement the safety management system, collectively referred to as the Safety Management Manual.[29]

(b) The designated person

Article 4 of the ISM Code creates the role of the "designated person" for the purpose of "ensur[ing] the safe operation of each ship and [of] provid[ing] a link between the Company and those on board". The designated person should be suitably qualified, properly experienced and fully conversant with the company's Safety Management System; it must also have the independence and authority to report all non-conformities to the "highest levels of management".[30] According to the International Chamber of Shipping "Guidelines on the application of the ISM Code",[31] the role of the designated person is one of line management responsibility; for this reason it will hardly be a member of the senior management of the company, but must have access to it and must also be provided with adequate financial, human and material resources to carry out its tasks. The responsibility and authority of the designated person should include, but not necessarily be limited to, monitoring the safety and pollution prevention aspects of each ship operated by the company, and ensuring that adequate resources and shore-based support are applied, as required.[32]

(c) The impact of the ISM Code on litigation

The ISM Code has an important impact on day-to-day legal practice as compliance with its procedures is now often used as evidence in litigation. In fact, many of the certificates and documents required under the ISM Code will be standard items for disclosure including all records of communications with the designated person, and between the designated person and the highest level of management in the company.

The Woolf Report on Access to Justice[33] emphasises that the disclosure of documents must not impose an unfair burden on the court or the parties, but must be confined to the issues as pleaded. The judges are encouraged to take an active role in case management and ensure that the disclosure of documents is controlled. Furthermore the International Chamber of Shipping (ICS) "Guidelines on the application of the ISM code"[34] refer to records of maintenance and inspection and to documentation control, but makes clear that the purpose of the ISM Code is not proliferation of paperwork, adding to the workload of ship board personnel. However, the Code does require the production of more documentation and will affect – at least in part – the cost of disclosure. Brevity and conciseness are certainly valued even in the realm of management

---

25. ISM Code, art 13.
26. Ibid., art 13.2.
27. Ibid., art 13.4.
28. Ibid., art 13.8.
29. Ibid., art 11.3.
30. Ibid., art 4.
31. ICS & ISF, *Guidelines on the Application of the IMO International Safety Management (ISM) Code* (4th edn, 2010).
32. ISM Code, art 4.
33. Access to Justice Final Report by The Right Honourable the Lord Woolf, Master of the Rolls, July 1996.
34. See fn 31.

control systems. However, brevity should not stand in the way of completeness and striking a fair balance should be the aim of any twenty-first century operator. This should control, at least in part, extra discovery costs.

The outcome of the discovery may be of particular importance in three litigation or mediation scenarios, (i) when unseaworthiness is at stake in a cargo claim, or (ii) insurance claim, and (iii) for limitation of liability purposes. These three aspects will be dealt with in turn.

(i) Cargo claims and unseaworthiness

When the Hague or Hague-Visby Rules apply to a claim for loss of or damage to cargo carried under a bill of lading, Article III rule 1 requires the carrier to exercise due diligence to make the ship seaworthy before and at the beginning of the voyage.[35] The Hamburg Rules impose a higher level of obligation upon the carrier.[36] Where the Hague or Hague-Visby Rules apply, carriers will be unable to benefit from the exclusion from liability for negligence in the navigation or management of the ship or the other exceptions contained in Article IV rule 2, if at any time the damage to the cargo is due to the unseaworthiness of the carrying vessel, unless they are able to prove the exercise of due diligence to make the ship seaworthy before and at the beginning of the contract voyage. This duty is non-delegable.[37] It is immediately apparent to see the link between due diligence as to seaworthiness and an effective system of ship and safety management.

The ISM Code represents the internationally recognised standard of good ship and safety management and failure to comply with its principles, as opposed to the simple failure to produce a valid certificate, could be argued to render the vessel unseaworthy on the basis that "there is something about it [. . .] which renders it legally or practically impossible for the vessel to go at sea or to load or unload its cargo",[38] or at least negatively affect the position of the operator *qua* carrier's ability to provide evidence of having exercised due diligence at the relevant time.[39] A well-documented Safety Management System would be of considerable help in establishing the exercise of due diligence and, as such, should be considered an important tool for defending claims based on unseaworthiness.

(ii) ISM and insurance cover

ISM Compliance may be relevant for the purpose of section 39(5) of the Marine Insurance Act 1906[40] to exclude liability of the insurer if the ship is sent to sea in an unseaworthy condition with the privity of the assured. It is, however, common for policies of insurance to contain specific ISM-related warranties.

The words "Vessel classed and class maintained. Vessel ISM Compliant" were included in an amended hull and machinery policy concluded on ITC – Hulls 95 terms for the M/V *Nancy*, a bulk carrier, which became a constructive total loss after a serious fire on board while in the port

---

35. The International Convention for the Unification of Certain Rules of Law Relating to Bills of Lading signed at Brussels on 25 August 1924 as amended by the Protocol signed at Brussels on 23 February 1968 and by the Protocol signed at Brussels on 21 December 1979. See also Chapter 5.

36. The UN Convention on the Carriage of Goods by Sea 1978, art 5.

37. *Riverstone Meat Co Pty Ltd v Lancashire Shipping Co Ltd (The Muncaster Castle)* [1961] 1 Lloyd's Rep 57. See also Chapter 5.

38. *Athenian Tankers Management SA v Pyrena Shipping (The Arianna)* [1987] 2 Lloyd's Rep 376, at p 389 (Webster J); for the corresponding issue under the ISPS code see B. Soyer and R. Williams, "Potential Legal Implications of the International Ship and Port Facility Security (ISPS) Code on Maritime Law" (2005) 2 LMCLQ 515 (hereinafter "Soyer & Williams").

39. See *The Eurasian Dream* (fn 15).

40. Marine Insurance Act 1906.

of Nokhodka, in Russia. The insured perils under the policy included fire but the insurers denied liability on a number of grounds including misrepresentation, non-disclosure and – most relevantly for present purposes – breach of the express ISM warranty. In the circumstances, the Safety Management System of the company managing the vessel was found to suffer from six areas of major non-conformity with the ISM Code. The claimants argued that the vessel possessed documentation certifying compliance with the Code. Blair J held that the insurers were liable for the sums claimed as the words "Vessels ISM Compliant" required only documentary compliance and that there was a distinction between compliance with the warranty and compliance with the Code.

The decision is based on a number of practical considerations and supported by a number of authorities on the matter of class compliance[41] and seems, with respect, in line with current insurance practice. The decision however is not in the spirit of the Code which is very much aimed at substantive compliance for the purposes of increasing the actual safety of the ship, her crew and cargo rather than mere paper compliance.[42]

(iii) Limitation of liability

Under the 1957 Limitation Convention, which is no longer in force in England, the right to limit liability is granted to the shipowner "unless the occurrence giving rise to the claim resulted from the actual fault or privity of the owner".[43] The requirement under the ISM Code to appoint a designated person with access to the highest levels of management, with express duties to monitor the safety and pollution prevention aspects of the operation of each ship, makes it harder for the owner of a ship trying to rely on the limitation procedure afforded by the 1957 Convention to prove the absence of fault or privity if the problems which give rise to the casualty were already known to the designated person and duly raised at the "highest level of management".[44]

Under the 1976 Limitation Convention it is more difficult to lose the right to limit. Article 4 of the Convention reads:

A person shall not be entitled to limit his liability if it is proved that the loss resulted from his personal act or omission, committed with intent to cause such loss or recklessly and with the knowledge that such loss would probably result.[45]

The ISM clearly defines the term "company" as including the owner of the ship and any organisation including a professional ship manager or bareboat charterer who has assumed responsibility for the operation of the ship (the "operator").[46] The question arises whether the "act or omission" of such a manager would be imputed as "personal" to the person entitled to limit in the context of the 1976 Limitation Convention. The ship manager may well be the employer of the designated person and if that person is found to be at fault, with the true owner ignorant of the problem, it may be considered unfair to deprive him of the right to limit. The wording of the Convention does not assist, although the insertion of the word "personal" may suggest a Rule of Attribution[47] pointing to the owner himself or to the person in a corporate ownership most closely corresponding to the individual shipowner.

---

41. *French v Newgass* (1878) 3 CPD 163, *Marina Offshore Pte Ltd v China Insurance Co (Singapore) Pte Ltd* [2006] SGCA 28; [2007] 1 Lloyd's Rep 66, *Transpetrol Maritime Services Ltd v SJB (Marine Energy) BV (The Rowan)* [2012] EWCA Civ 198; [2012] 1 Lloyd's Rep 564.
42. See also Chapter 11.
43. 1957 Limitation Convention, art 1.1. See in general Chapter 7.
44. ISM Code, art 4.
45. See Chapter 7.
46. ISM Code, art 1.1.2.
47. See *Meridian Global Funds Management v Securities Commission* [1995] 2 AC 500, 507.

The benefit of limitation under the Hague-Visby Rules can also be lost by the carrier or the ship if the claimant can prove that the damage resulted from an act or omission of the carrier done with intent to cause damage, or recklessly and with knowledge that damage would probably result.[48] The notable absence of the word "personal" would appear to make compliance with the ISM Code even more important when the issue of limitation is brought within the four corners of the Hague-Visby system.[49]

The ISM Code requires management arrangements to be more transparent than had formerly been the case and the Code subjects these arrangements to increased scrutiny, meaning that owners' rights to limitation are likely to be challenged more frequently.[50]

(d) Conclusion

It must be stressed that the objectives of the ISM Code are the "safety at sea and the prevention of marine pollution". The Code is drafted in a simple and easily legible manner and is based upon basic general principles and clear objectives. It recognises that no two shipping companies, shipowners or operators are the same and that ships operate under varying conditions. Legal decisions involving the ISM Code have been refreshingly few: brief reference to the ISM Code was made in *The Eurasian Dream (No 1)*,[51] although the code was not in force for that ship at the material time.

The question arises as to whether the ISM Code has succeeded in its aim of reducing the number of marine accidents. Some underwriters claim that it has had a positive impact, although it is not clear precisely how this is substantiated. Many of those ship operators who willingly embraced the Code claim to have benefited in terms of efficiency, economy and safety; others may have regarded the document of compliance as just another trading certificate and may not have adopted the spirit of the Code so wholeheartedly. Seafarers not infrequently complain of the extra burden of paperwork involved and it seems likely that, contrary to the spirit of the Code, many Safety Management Systems are over lengthy and over complicated. On the other hand, some ship operators have progressed further and have adopted standards of the International Organization for Standardization, particularly those in the ISO-9000 family of standards, which relate to Quality Management systems, or ISO-14000 relating to Environmental Management.[52] Independent tanker owners are encouraged by the oil majors in addition to compliance with ISM, to undergo "Tanker Management Self Assessment" (TMSA) and to establish risk assessment procedures when planning shipboard operations.[53]

4. THE INTERNATIONAL SHIP AND PORT FACILITY SECURITY CODE

Since the events of 11 September 2001, terrorism has attracted the attention of governments and intergovernmental organisations as being a major threat to the safety of life and property, including ships and port facilities. In December 2002, the IMO adopted amendments to the SOLAS

---

48. Hague-Visby Rules, art IV r 5(e).
49. See Chapter 5 and above, p 357.
50. See Chapters 7 and 10.
51. [2002] EWHC 118 (Comm); [2002] 1 Lloyd's Rep 719.
52. The standards can be found at www.iso.org/iso/home.html (accessed 1 March 2017).
53. Further information on the ISM Code can be obtained from the ICS/ISF booklet *Guidelines on the Application of the IMO International Safety Management (ISM) Code* (fn 31).

Convention[54] requiring some physical modifications to ships for the purpose of enhancing security[55] and a number of important requirements which governments with port facilities have to comply with in order to ensure adequate port security.[56] These amendments are implemented by way of a further instrument known as the International Ship and Port Facility (ISPS) Code.[57]

The ISPS Code consists of two parts: Part A (mandatory) and Part B (advisory).[58] It covers passenger ships, all types of cargo ships, including high-speed craft, of 500 gt and over, and mobile offshore drilling units.[59] It applies also to port facilities which handle ships engaged on international voyages but does not apply to warships or other government-operated ships used for non-commercial purposes.[60] There are provisions for contracting governments to reach agreement with others to provide alternative security arrangements on ships making short international voyages.[61]

In parallel, the United States of America has enacted the Maritime Transportation Security Act 2002[62] which imposes additional requirements on passenger ships and ships over 500 gt calling at US ports and which makes ISPS (Part B) mandatory for US flag ships. This Act came into force at the same time as ISPS on 1 July 2004.

(a) An overview of the ISPS Code

The main aim of the ISPS Code is to establish an international framework involving co-operation between contracting governments, government agencies, local administrations, shipping and port industries, in order to detect security threats and take preventive measures against security incidents affecting ships or port facilities used in international trade.[63] This is achieved through setting a number of requisites for ship operators and port facilities contained in the 19 articles of Part A of the Code.

Each ship operator must obtain an International Ship Security Certificate (ISSC) for each ship which must be retained on board the ship at all times.[64] A company security officer must be appointed[65] who is required to carry out a security assessment on each ship and thereafter with the approval of the flag State, formulate a ship security plan.[66] This plan must be available on the ship and will provide for the appointment of a ship security officer,[67] who may be the ship's master and should provide for the appropriate training and exercises.[68] Other duties of the com-

---

54. Contained in Chapters V and XI-2 of the Convention.
55. SOLAS, Chapter XI-2, reg 4 and ISPS Code, Part A. Among the most important physical modifications: all ships must be fitted with an automatic identification system (SOLAS, Chapter V, reg 19.2.4), display the ship's identification number externally and internally (SOLAS, Chapter XI, reg 3) and instal a ship security alert system (SOLAS, Chapter XI, reg 6).
56. SOLAS, Chapter XI-2, regs 10–12 and ISPS Code, Part A.
57. Since the adoption of Regulation (EC) No 725/2004, integrating the ISPS Code into Community law, the Community has enjoyed exclusive competence to assume international obligations in the area covered by that Code. See *Commission of the European Communities v Hellenic Republic* (Case C-45/07) [2009] 1 Lloyd's Rep 425.
58. SOLAS, Chapter XI-2, regs 1.1.12 and 2.1.
59. SOLAS, Chapter XI-2, reg 1.2. For its applicability to superyachts see F. Lorenzon, R. Coles, *The Law of Yachts and Yachting*, (Informa 2012), Ch. 11.
60. SOLAS, Chapter XI-2, reg 2.1.3.
61. SOLAS, Chapter XI-2, reg 2.1.2.
62. Maritime Transportation Security Act of 2002 (MTSA), Pub L No 107–295, ii codified at 46 USC §§70102, 70103, 25 November 2002.
63. ISPS Code, Part A, s 1.2.
64. Ibid., s 19.
65. Ibid., s 11.
66. Ibid., s 9.
67. Ibid., s 12.
68. Ibid., s 13.

pany security officer include assessing likely port security threats and maintaining awareness of terrorist activities. The master always has the ultimate responsibility for the safety of the ship. The ship security assessment identifies any existing security measures and any operations where security may be an issue.[69] The plan will vary according to the ship and any potential threats must be approved by the flag State, as must any later amendments.[70] Security plans are not normally subject to inspection by port State Control unless the inspectors have "clear grounds" to believe that the ship is not in compliance with the Code.[71] Security levels are defined within the Code[72] and controlled by the flag State. These are:

1. Security Level One: *normal* – the level at which ships and ports will usually operate, with controlled access to the ship, controlled embarkation of all persons and their effects. Restricted areas, including deck areas and areas surrounding the ship must be monitored and the handling of cargo and stores must be supervised.[73]
2. Security Level Two: *heightened* – in this case, additional security measures apply as specified in the Security Plan.[74]
3. Security Level Three: *exceptional* – the level applying while there is a probable or imminent risk, when further specific measures must be adopted.[75]

If the security level of a port State is higher than that set by the flag State, then the higher level must be adopted before entering port and both parties must be advised.[76]

In addition to the ship security plan and the ISPS certificate, the ship must be provided with, a "Continuous Synopsis Record" issued by the flag State. Also on board should be any additional information relating to joining crew, parties to charterparties and those deciding the employment of the ship as well as any security information regarding previous port calls. Records must also be kept of training exercises, any security threats, changes in security level, internal audits, reviews of the ship security plan, amendments to the plan, testing of security equipment and the ship security alert system.[77]

The Continuous Synopsis Record, which must be in English, Spanish or French,[78] provides an onboard history of the ship dating from 1 July 2004, including:

- the name of the flag State;
- the date of the ship's registry;
- ship's ID number;
- name of ship;
- port of registry;
- name and address of registered owner;
- name and address, if applicable, of registered bareboat charterer;
- name and address of the ISM operator;
- classification society;
- the name of the issuing authority of the ISM certificates and the name of the auditor;

69. Ibid., s 8.
70. Ibid., s 9.
71. Ibid., s 9.8.1.
72. Ibid., s 2.1.
73. For operations at this security level see ISPS Code, Part A, ss 7.2 for board and 14.2 for shore.
74. For operations at this security level see ISPS Code, Part A, ss 7.3 for board and 14.3 for shore.
75. For operations at this security level see ISPS Code, Part A, ss 7.4 for board and 14.4 for shore.
76. ISPS Code, Part A, ss 7 and 14.
77. SOLAS, Chapter XI-1, reg 5.
78. A translation in the official language or languages of the Administration may be provided but is not necessary, see SOLAS, Chapter XI-1, reg 5.5.1.

- the name of the authority which issued the ISSC and details of the verification process; and
- any change of flag.

(b) The legal and commercial implications of the ISPS Code

All the above imposes important obligations on all stakeholders and, in particular, (i) shipowners and ships operators, (ii) contracting governments, (iii) ports, with (iv) significant commercial and insurance implications for the shipping world. These obligations and implications are the subject of the reflections contained in the following paragraphs.

(i) Ships entering port

At the earliest opportunity the ship must contact the port facility security officer at the next port of call. Non-compliance with either the SOLAS regulations or Part A of the ISPS Code or with the requirements of the port State, must be notified before attempting entry into port.[79] The ship is likely to undergo routine port State inspection but this will not normally include the ship security plan. If officers authorised by the port State have "clear grounds" for believing that the ship does not comply with SOLAS or the ISPS Code, they must inform the ship and the flag State.[80] They may require the ship to undergo further inspection or they may deny entry into port. The ship must be kept fully informed and the master may decide not to enter that port.

Contracting governments may require advance information, including the continuous synopsis record, the ship's position, the estimate time of arrival (ETA), details of passenger and crew lists, cargo manifest and any other information required under SOLAS. Further information may be required such as the details of the ISSC, the security level currently in operation and the security level in the previous ten ports of call, including details of any extra security measures taken in the previous ten ports, records of security measures taken in any port in the territory of a non-contracting government and any "Declarations of Security" entered into within port facilities. Also required may be any records of ship to ship activity with ships from a non-contracting government or with ships not required to comply with ISPS. Any information about persons rescued at sea must be reported. Sometimes a "Declaration of Security" may be agreed between ship and port on the security measures to be adopted during the ship's call.[81] It might, for example, be required when the ship and port are operating at different levels of security.

Chapter XI of SOLAS describes control measures which apply to ships as from 1 July 2004 including those ships which fly the flag of a State which has not ratified the 1988 SOLAS protocol. Vessels below the Convention tonnage must comply with whatever local measures the State may see fit to enforce.

(ii) Contracting governments

Contracting governments have responsibility for security levels on ships[82] and in port facilities,[83] testing ship security plans,[84] declarations of security,[85] security threats and the provision of the

---

79. ISPS Code, Part A, s 7.6.
80. ISPS Code, Part A, s 9.8.1.
81. SOLAS, Chapter XI-2, reg 1.1.15 and ISPS Code, Part A, s 5.
82. ISPS Code, Part A, s 7.
83. Ibid., s 14.
84. Ibid., s 9.
85. Ibid., s 5.

continuous synopsis record.[86] The flag State is also responsible for setting manning levels on all ships within its registry,[87] always bearing in mind that any additional workload imposed by the Code may require increased manning levels. Contracting governments also have responsibility for approving ship security plans, verifying the compliance of ships, issuing security certificates to ships under its flag and overseeing the obligations of port facilities.[88] All information regarding security must be communicated by contracting governments to both the IMO and to registered companies and ships.

(iii) Ports and port facilities

SOLAS Chapter XI-2 and Part A of the ISPS Code set out the requirements for port facilities which are similar requirements to those for ships.[89] Contracting governments must supervise port security assessments and the development of port security plans as well as setting security levels.[90] Each port facility is required to appoint a security officer, similar to that required of companies and ships.[91]

(iv) Commercial and insurance implications of ISPS

A breach of the ISPS Code on the part of the operator – owner, carrier or assured as the case may be – carries similar consequences to those illustrated above in relation to breaches of the ISM Code.[92] When fixing charters, the rights and duties of each party and the apportionment of costs must be taken into account. BIMCO has published ISPS Clauses for both time and voyage charters, which offer a sound framework for the sharing of specific costs and duties.[93] For example the time charter clause states that owners, as from 1 July 2004 and for the duration of the charter, must comply with the ISPS Code. Owners must furnish charterers with evidence of compliance and are accountable for any failure to comply. Some of the owners' obligations can be met only with the co-operation of the charterer and of course the charterers will be liable for any damage due to their failure to co-operate with the owner. The clauses are comprehensive and allocate expressly responsibilities for delays, costs and expenses imposed by a port authority under the Code for charterers' account; while the costs of preparing and complying with the Ship Security Plan are for owners' account.

The trading history of the ship, covering the last ten voyages, is deliberately not covered in the clause. A wise charterer, before fixing a ship, will ascertain the ship's recent trading history and in case it emerges that the ship has visited a non-ISPS compliant port, take a commercial decision as to whether to proceed with the charter and to accept the risk of possible delays. United States authorities, for example, are known to maintain records of facilities which are considered to be insecure. Provided that the owners have always complied with the Code, then the risk rests with the charterers for the contracted voyage. It is important to include one of the BIMCO clauses, or a rider dealing otherwise with ISPS compliance matters, in each charter party.

---

86. SOLAS, Chapter XI-1, reg 5.
87. SOLAS Chapter V, reg 14.
88. ISPS Code, Part A, s 5.
89. Ibid., ss 14–18.
90. Ibid., s 14.
91. Ibid., s 17.
92. For an in-depth analysis of such implications see Soyer & Williams (fn 38).
93. Both clauses are available at www.bimco.org.

P&I Clubs within the International Group[94] have made it a condition of cover that ships must have and maintain on board a valid certificate confirming compliance with the ISPS Code. Failure to do so will result in any claims being paid only at the discretion of the Club's board of directors.

(c) Conclusions

Doubts have been expressed about the practicality of ensuring security on ships and in port facilities, particularly in the face of determined terrorist attacks. Security has not in the past, been a priority for seafarers and many need extensive encouragement and training to gain awareness of potential security risks. Other concerns include the failure of many ports to comply effectively with the Code and the possible later consequences for ships calling at such ports. Port operators who are non-compliant may face claims from ship operators who suffer losses as a result of such non-compliance. There has been criticism of some governments, who fail to ensure that ports within their jurisdiction are ISPS compliant. Questions have been raised about the consistency of ISPS enforcement and about the practice of appointing the master as security officer, with some countries discouraging or even opposing it. It has also been suggested that while ships may comply with the requirements for automated identification systems, shore-side monitoring stations may not be adequate. Proponents of the Code will doubtless contend that, if properly implemented, it should reduce the opportunities for terrorists and others to attack ships or use them in any way to promote terrorist activities and that a strong commitment to the Code by all will yield unexpected safety benefits.[95]

5. THE INTERNATIONAL CONVENTION ON STANDARDS OF TRAINING, CERTIFICATION AND WATCHKEEPING AS AMENDED IN 1995 (STCW95)

The aim of the STCW95 is to ensure seafarers worldwide are trained to consistent standards and that seafarers' certificates of competency are issued to similar acceptable and consistent standards. The training and certification of seafarers has always been the responsibility of flag administrations and before 1978 when the first STCW Convention was drafted, most of the recognised or traditional maritime administrations had in place their own established procedures in order to satisfy these requirements, always to the highest standards. The emergence and growth of non-traditional flag States often not equipped to implement such procedures and sometimes without a robust maritime administration, led to the introduction by the IMO of the International Convention on Standards of Training, Certification and Watchkeeping (STCW) 1978, which came into force in 1984.

However, in the 1990s it became clear that the original convention required further strengthening and clarification if it was to fulfil the perceived needs of the changing maritime world. A detailed analysis of maritime accidents shows the significance of the human element in most casualties and the need to raise awareness among the shipping community of the urge to improve training and competency among seafarers, and to impose stricter and more accurately defined regulations.

---

94. See Chapter 11.
95. More information on the ISPS Code can be obtained from the ICS/ISF booklet *Guidelines on the Application of the IMO International Safety Management (ISM) Code* (fn 31).

The revised convention, which was published in 1995 (STCW95), and which came fully into force in February 2002, aims to ensure precisely defined uniform standards of training, certification and competency; better procedures to guarantee that STCW Convention is implemented and enforced worldwide; and the flexibility to meet the demands of the industry in the twenty-first century.

Both the ISM Code and the STCW Convention relate to the human element being closely related and complementary to each other. ISM Code states that: "The company must ensure that each ship is manned with qualified, certificated and medically fit seafarers in accordance with national and international requirements."[96] It is the STCW Convention, which defines these international requirements and it may be said that it is in some respects an amplification of the ISM Code. Any failure by a shipowner to comply with the requirements of the STCW Convention could be construed as a breach of the ISM Code and such a failure, if sufficiently serious in nature, could be interpreted as a major ISM non-conformity.

Unlike the ISM Code, the STCW Convention is lengthy. It may be divided broadly into two parts, one relevant to flag administrations – representing the bulk of the Convention – and the other relevant to shipping companies and operators. Some of the provisions of the STCW Convention, applying to shipowners, came into force in February 1997. Other provisions have been in force since August 1998, whilst the remainder did not apply until February 2002. For EU Member States, Directive 2008/106/EC requires that seafarers are trained, as a minimum, in accordance with the requirements of the STCW Convention.[97] The latest amendments to the Convention are known as the 2010 Manila Amendments and entered into force on 1 January 2012.

In the following paragraphs a brief account of the duties and liabilities of both (a) flag administrations and (b) ship operators will be given, followed by (c) a discussion of the legal consequences of non-compliance.

(a) Flag administrations

The STCW95 Convention lays down new responsibilities for flag administrations. These responsibilities relate in the main, to the establishment of suitable training centres, uniform standards of training and competency, and measures to ensure uniform, worldwide implementation.[98] Flag States are likely to issue their own certificates of competency to seafarers of their own nationality. Where foreign seafarers are concerned, their country of nationality will either issue their own certificates or issue individual endorsements to any certificates issued by other States.[99] The ultimate responsibilities of the administration cannot be delegated and there is no provision in the Convention for flag States to delegate their responsibilities to other parties, such as classification societies. Flag States are required to have in place an infrastructure, which provides for legislation, documentation procedures, compliance administration and record keeping.[100]

Governments issuing STCW certificates were required by August 1998, to submit to the IMO documentary evidence of compliance with the standards of the Convention.[101] This was in order to facilitate the compilation of the "white list" of countries who are deemed to be properly

---

96. ISM Code, art 6.2.

97. Directive 2008/106/EC of the European Parliament and of the Council of 19 November 2008 on the minimum level of training of seafarers, art 3.1.

98. STCW95 Convention, reg I/6.

99. Ibid., reg I/10.

100. Ibid., art IV.

101. Ibid., reg I/7.

implementing the STCW95.[102] The information required included details of legal and administrative measures in place to ensure compliance, of all training courses and assessment regimes and verification procedures.[103]

Since the Convention came fully into force in 2002, governments are required to demonstrate that all training, assessments of competence, certification, endorsement and revalidation activities carried out whether by themselves or by non-governmental agencies are monitored through a quality standards system.[104] Even those States which may have elected to proceed by not issuing their own certificates but by endorsing and recognising the certificates and training provided by other States, still need to establish infrastructures not dissimilar to those of the issuing States.[105]

Another important feature of the STCW Convention is the provision for the involvement of port State control whereby port State control inspectors are authorised to verify the qualifications and competence of seafarers. Following an accident, inspectors will also be empowered to assess the abilities of seafarers, subject to certain provisions.[106]

(b) Responsibilities of shipowners

It may be helpful to look at the obligations imposed on shipowners always bearing in mind the significant link between the ISM Code and STCW95 referred to earlier.

(i) Certification

The seafarers employed on board must hold the certificates stipulated in the Safe Manning Certificate unless they have valid dispensations.[107] Owners must ensure that officers serving on their ships hold valid certificates of competency for the responsibility which they hold.[108] Ratings also must, when watch-keeping, hold the appropriate certificate.[109] From 2012, the STCW contains new requirements relating to training and certification in modern technology such as electronic charts and information systems (ECDIS), as well as new requirements for marine environment awareness training and training in leadership and teamwork, and – given the current global relevance of piracy – new requirements for security training, as well as provisions to ensure that seafarers are properly trained to cope if their ship comes under attack by pirates. Officers' certificates must be revalidated every five years.[110] Every five years all seafarers must undergo a medical examination recognised by the authority issuing the certificate.[111] All such certificates must be endorsed in English to certify that they meet STCW standards.[112] Officers and ratings employed on certain types of ships, for example, tankers, must hold the relevant special endorsements certifying that they are properly trained in that specific trade.[113] The original certificates

---

102. The latest list compiled by the Maritime Safety Committee can be found at www.imo.org (accessed 27 February 2017).
103. STCW95 Convention, art IV.
104. Ibid., reg I/8.
105. Ibid., reg I/8.
106. Ibid., reg I/4.
107. Ibid., reg I/10.
108. Ibid., regs II/1, II/2 and II/3.
109. Ibid., reg II/4.
110. Ibid., reg I/11.
111. Ibid., reg I/11.
112. Ibid., reg I/2.
113. Ibid., regs II/1, II/2 and II/3.

must be available for scrutiny on board, photocopies will not be accepted.[114] All possible precautions must be taken in order to ensure that the certificates are valid.[115]

(ii) Crew co-ordination

Seafarers employed on board must be able to demonstrate that they are able to co-ordinate their actions in an emergency and communicate in a common language.[116] Drills and exercises simulating various situations must be carried out and recorded.[117]

(iii) Minimum rest periods

All watchkeeping personnel must be provided with at least the prescribed rest periods.[118] Watch schedules must be posted where they are readily accessible. Part B of the code suggests that records of working hours should be accurately maintained in order to demonstrate compliance.[119]

(iv) Safety training

All personnel involved with safety or pollution prevention duties must receive basic training in personal survival techniques, fire prevention and fire-fighting as well as elementary first aid and emergency procedures, pollution prevention and occupational safety.[120] Personnel must be able to demonstrate that they are competent in these procedures. All other personnel – including riding crews and catering staff – must undergo elementary training in safety matters, including attending shore-side training courses.[121] Full records of any such training must be maintained.

(v) Ship-specific familiarisation

The company must provide the master with written instructions on the familiarisation of newly recruited personnel with equipment and operating procedures, ensuring that sufficient time is allocated to this procedure.[122] A member of the crew must be appointed for the purpose of ensuring that newly embarked seafarers receive all relevant information in a language that they can understand.[123] A full record of such familiarisation procedure should be made, be properly maintained[124] and be available.[125]

(vi) Record-keeping and documentation

The shipowner or operator must maintain readily accessible records of:

- seafarers' experience (i.e. service record before and during the current employment);
- training received before and during employment;

---

114. Ibid., reg I/2.
115. Ibid., reg I/9.
116. Ibid., reg I/14.
117. STCW95, s A-I/12.
118. STCW95 Convention, reg VIII/2; see also the Maritime Labour Convention 2006, below.
119. STCW95 Convention, s B-VIII/1, as revised by the 2010 Manila Amendments.
120. STCW95 Convention, reg VI/1; STCW95 Code, s A-VI/1.
121. STCW95 Code, s A-VI/1.
122. Ibid., s A-I/14.
123. Ibid., s A-I/14.
124. STCW95 Convention, reg I/14.
125. Ibid.

- medical fitness; and
- competence.[126]

Companies must be able to demonstrate compliance with proper record-keeping and documentation ready for inspection.[127] Many of these responsibilities are derived from the ISM Code[128] but the STCW Convention requires a much greater level of detail.

(vii) Responsibility for STCW compliance

If a shipowner decides to delegate the responsibility for personnel matters and STCW compliance to a third party, the contractual arrangements between the owner and the third party must clearly indicate who assumes responsibility for STCW compliance.[129]

(c) Non-compliance and the legal consequences

When dealing with the ISM Code, reference has been made to the consequences of any failure on the part of a shipowner to comply with its provisions. That section referred to unseaworthiness and the likely consequences with respect to cargo claims, prejudice of insurance cover and limitation of liability. Any unseaworthiness arising from a breach of the STCW Convention is likely to have similar consequences, as non-compliance with the STCW Convention might be construed as non-conformity with the ISM Code.[130]

6. THE MARITIME LABOUR CONVENTION 2006

The Maritime Labour Convention (MLC) 2006,[131] was the result of a long process of review and research by the International Labour Organization (ILO) over a period exceeding five years. The ILO was founded in 1919 soon after the end of the First World War, in order to promote the interests of workers worldwide. It is a United Nations agency which brings together representatives of governments, employers and workers in order to draft international conventions and supervise labour standards worldwide.[132] In the maritime field, the ILO has produced a number of international conventions concerned with the working conditions of seamen. The new convention is intended to consolidate and supersede a large number of these conventions in the attempt to simplify and harmonise this complex area of maritime law; in the words of its preamble, it seeks "to create a single, coherent instrument embodying as far as possible all up-to-date standards of existing international maritime labour conventions and recommendations, as well as the fundamental principles to be found in other international conventions".[133]

---

126. Ibid., reg 1/14.
127. Ibid., reg I/14.
128. See above.
129. STCW95 Convention, reg I/1.
130. Further information about STCW can be obtained from the ICS/ISF booklet, *The STCW Convention Guidelines on the Application of the IMO International Safety Management (ISM) Code* (4th edn, 2010).
131. See J. Lavelle (ed.), *The Maritime Labour Convention 2006: International Labour Law Redefined* (Informa Law 2013), (hereinafter "Lavelle").
132. For more information, see ILO website www.ilo.org/ (accessed 1 March 2017).
133. The full text of the Maritime Labour Convention is to be found at www.ilo.org/ (accessed 27 February 2017).

At the outset, it must be pointed out that the MLC came into force on 20 August 2013.[134] As at 27 February 2017, 81 countries have ratified the Convention.[135] The EU is actively encouraging all of its 28 Member States to ratify the Convention and has adopted a Directive[136] which, by incorporating a social agreement reproducing almost verbatim titles I to IV of the MLC, forces all EU Member States to adopt national legislation reproducing in part the MLC. The Directive came into force on the date of entry into force of the MLC[137] and national legislation should be in place 12 months thereafter.[138] This dual implementation appears highly undesirable, particularly from the perspective of EU Member States which have ratified or will ratify the MLC itself as it creates a system whereby the same subject matter is regulated by two different legal instruments: the MLC and the national legislation transposing Directive 2009/13. This could be partly avoided if ratification of the MLC by an EU Member State was accepted as Implementation of Directive 2009/13, but from informal discussions with the European Commission during the research leading to this chapter this does not appear to be the case. The UK started the implementation process early on with the European Communities (Definition of Treaties) (Maritime Labour Convention) Order 2009.[139] The process has resulted in a number of statutory instruments so far and it is still likely that more will come in the near future. The list of the statutory instruments which have entered into force so far includes: the Merchant Shipping (Maritime Labour Convention) (Medical Certifications) Regulations 2010,[140] the Merchant Shipping (Maritime Labour Convention) (Survey and Certification) Regulations 2013,[141] the Merchant Shipping (Maritime Labour Convention) (Hours of Work) (Amendment) Regulations 2014 which came into force on 17 March 2014,[142] the Merchant Shipping (Maritime Labour Convention) (Minimum Requirements for Seafarers) Regulations 2014,[143] the Merchant Shipping (Maritime Labour Convention) (Consequential and Minor Amendments) Regulations 2014,[144] the Merchant Shipping (Maritime Labour Convention) (Recruitment and Placement) Regulations 2014,[145] the Merchant Shipping (Maritime Labour Convention) (Health and Safety) (Amendment) Regulations 2014.[146]

(a) Fundamental rights and principles

The following pages are meant as a simple overview of the structure and content of the MLC and the most relevant differences between the Convention itself and its European counterpart. From the outset it must be stressed again that the MLC is an instrument of consolidation rather than innovation and hence a good number of the provisions of the Convention are already in force either through other ILO conventions or – in Europe – through an increasing number of EU instruments.

---

134. MLC, art VIII.
135. The full list of ratifications can be found at www.ilo.org/dyn/normlex/en/f?p=1000:11300:0::NO:11300:P11300_INSTRUMENT_ID:312331 (accessed 1 March 2017).
136. Council Directive 2009/13/EC of 16 February 2009 implementing the Agreement concluded by the European Community Shipowners' Association (ECSA) and the European Transport Workers' Federation (ETF) on the Maritime Labour Convention, 2006, and amending Directive 1999/63/EC, OJ L 124/30, 20 May 2009.
137. Directive 2009/13/EC, art 7.
138. Ibid., art 5.
139. SI 2009/1757.
140. SI 2010/737.
141. SI 2013/1785.
142. SI 2014/308; reg 2 contains a long series of detailed amendments to the Merchant Shipping Act 1995 to achieve compliance with the MLC.
143. SI 2014/1613.
144. SI 2014/1614.
145. SI 2014/1615.
146. SI 2014/1616.

The structure of the Convention is rather complex as it provides for three different kinds of provisions: Articles, Regulations and the so-called Code. The Articles and Regulations set out the core rights and principles and the basic obligations of States ratifying the Convention, while the Code contains the details for the implementation of the Regulations. It comprises Part A (mandatory Standards) and Part B (non-mandatory Guidelines). The Regulations and the Code are organised into general areas under five Titles as follows:

1. minimum requirements for seafarers to work on a ship;
2. conditions of employment;
3. accommodation, recreational facilities, food and catering;
4. health protection, medical care, welfare and social security protection; and
5. compliance and enforcement.

Each of the five Titles contains provisions relating to a particular right or principle, duly enforced in Title 5. Every Title comprises a number of Regulations, followed by the standards which together form the Code.

(i) Minimum requirements to work on a ship

This Title sets out the minimum requirements that crew members have to meet to be allowed to work on a ship. Under the Convention no person below the minimum age of 16 shall be employed or engaged to work on a ship,[147] and in certain circumstances, a higher minimum age may apply.[148] No seafarer under 18 years of age shall work at night.[149] Every seafarer must be certified as medically fit to perform his duties[150] and properly trained or certified as competent or otherwise qualified to perform its duties.[151] Furthermore, seafarers shall not be permitted to work on a ship unless they have successfully completed training for personal safety on board a ship.[152] Training and certification in accordance with the mandatory instruments adopted by the IMO are considered as meeting the above requirements.[153] The efficiency, adequacy and accountability of the process of recruitment and placement of seafarers are also ensured by the Code.[154]

(ii) Conditions of employment

Title Two of the MLC is dedicated to the conditions under which seafarers have to work and covers a number of important issues. Under the Convention, the terms and conditions of a seafarer's employment shall be set out in a clear written legally enforceable agreement.[155] The seafarer should be given an opportunity to review and seek advice on the terms and conditions

---

147. MLC, reg 1.1; Directive 2009/13/EC, Title 1, reg 1.1(1).

148. MLC, reg 1.1.3; Directive 2009/13/EC, Title 1, reg 1.1(2). The minimum age in the EU is regulated by Council Directive 1999/63/EC of 21 June 1999 concerning the European Agreement on the organisation of working time of seafarers.

149. MLC, Standard A1.1(2).

150. MLC, reg 1.2. Within the EU, Clause 13.1 of the Annex to Directive 1999/63/EC states that "all seafarers shall possess a certificate attesting to their fitness for the work for which they are to be employed at sea".

151. MLC, reg 1.3.1; Directive 2009/13/EC, Title 1, reg 1.3(1).

152. MLC, reg 1.3.2; Directive 2009/13/EC, Title 1, reg 1.3(2).

153. MLC, reg 1.3.3; Directive 2009/13/EC, Title 1, reg 1.3(3). See also Directive 2008/106/EC of the European Parliament and of the Council of 19 November 2008 on the minimum level of training of seafarers; and above.

154. MLC, reg 1.4.

155. MLC, reg 2.1.1; Directive 2009/13/EC, Title 2, reg 2.1(1).

of the agreement and freely accept them before signing.[156] All seafarers shall be paid regularly and in full as agreed in their contract,[157] have firm rules on the maximum hours of work or minimum hours of rest[158] and paid annual leave[159] and shore leave[160] under appropriate conditions. An important provision in this Title is that for repatriation according to which seafarers have a right to be repatriated at no cost to themselves, and that each State party shall require ships to provide financial security to ensure that seafarers are duly repatriated.[161] Seafarers are also entitled to adequate compensation in the case of injury, loss or unemployment arising from the ship's loss or foundering.[162] The shipowner is to pay each seafarer on board an indemnity against unemployment resulting from such loss or foundering.[163]

(iii) Accommodation, recreational facilities, food and catering

This Title deals with the living conditions of seafarers and contains a number of very specific requirements that will – when implemented – force ship designers, builders and fitters to make significant changes in new building projects.[164] To comply with the MLC ships shall provide and maintain decent accommodation and recreational facilities on board[165] in full compliance with the Code.[166] Ships shall carry on board and serve food and drinking water of appropriate quality, nutritional value and quantity that adequately cover the requirements of the ship and take into account the differing cultural and religious backgrounds[167] against minimum standards to be set by national legislation.[168]

(iv) Health protection, medical care and welfare and social security protection

This Title of the MLC focuses on social welfare and requires that seafarers are covered by adequate measures for the protection of their health and that they have access to prompt and adequate medical care.[169] State parties to the Convention must provide seafarers with a right to material assistance and support from the shipowner with respect to the financial consequences of sickness, injury or death occurring during their employment.[170] Moreover shipowners are responsible for health protection and medical care of all seafarers under their employment in

---

156. MLC, reg 2.1.2; Directive 2009/13/EC, Title 2, reg 2.1(2).

157. MLC, reg 2.2.

158. MLC, reg 2.3; Directive 2009/13/EC, Title 2, reg 2.3. In the EU, seafarers' hours of work and rest are regulated by Council Directive 1999/63/EC of 21 June 1999 concerning the Agreement on the organisation of working time of seafarers concluded by the European Community Shipowners' Association (ECSA) and the Federation of Transport Workers' Unions in the European Union (FST) – Annex: European Agreement on the organisation of working time of seafarers, OJ L 167, 2 July 1999.

159. MLC, reg 2.4; Directive 2009/13/EC, Title 2, reg 2.4(1). See again Directive 1999/63/EC.

160. MLC, reg 2.4.2; Directive 2009/13/EC, Title 2, reg 2.4(2).

161. MLC, reg 2.5 and Standard A2.5; Directive 2009/13/EC, Title 2, reg 2.5.

162. MLC, reg 2.6; Directive 2009/13/EC, Title 2, reg 2.6.

163. MLC, Standard A2.6; Directive 2009/13/EC, Title 2, Standard A2.6(1).

164. See Chapter 2.

165. MLC, reg 3.1; notably the text of the MLC is very different from that of the Annex to Directive 2009/13/EC.

166. MLC, Standard A3.1.

167. MLC, reg 3.2; Directive 2009/13/EC, Title 3, reg 3.2(1).

168. MLC, reg 3.2; Directive 2009/13/EC, Title 3, Standard A3.2(2).

169. MLC, reg 4.1; Directive 2009/13/EC, Title 4, reg 4.1(1). For the EU see also Directive 1992/29/EEC of the Council of 31 March 1992 on the minimum safety and health for improved medical treatment on board vessels, as amended by Directive 2007/30/EC of the European Parliament and of the Council of 20 June 2007, which sets out detailed requirements in relation to medical care on board vessels.

170. MLC, reg 4.2; Directive 2009/13/EC, Title 4, reg 4.2.

accordance with certain minimum standards.[171] They shall be liable to pay wages in full or in part where the sickness or injury results in incapacity to work,[172] and shall take measures for safeguarding property left on board by sick, injured or deceased seafarers.[173] The Convention also requires its State parties to ensure that seafarers are provided with occupational health protection and live, work and train on board in a safe and hygienic environment.[174] National guidelines should be developed[175] and regularly reviewed.[176] Last, the Convention requests State parties to ensure that the social security protection in place ashore is extended to seafarers, in conformity with the principles set out in the Code.[177]

(v) Compliance and enforcement

Compliance and enforcement are ensured by both the flag State and port State control, through their own maritime authorities or by taking advantage of the expertise of recognised organisations.[178] Each State party shall establish an effective system for the inspection and certification of maritime labour conditions, ensuring that the working and living conditions for seafarers on ships that fly its flag meet, and continue to meet, the standards set.[179] The certificates issued will be of two types: (i) the Maritime Labour Certificate (MLCert), issued by the flag State, which needs to be kept on board as evidence that the working and living conditions of the seafarers on board have been inspected and found to meet the standards required at national law level; and (ii) the Declaration of Maritime Labour Compliance (DMLC) also issued by the flag State, to be kept on board, stating such national requirements and setting out the measures adopted by the shipowner to ensure compliance with the requirements on the ship.[180] Inspection and enforcement are left to the port State in compliance with its national law or – within the EU – with Directive 2009/16/EC.[181] The Merchant Shipping (Maritime Labour Convention) (Survey and Certification) Regulations 2013[182] contain detailed rules on the issue and validity of both the certificate and the declaration and provide a clear framework for the inspection of non-UK ships by UK authorities.[183]

7. THE EUROPEAN MARITIME SAFETY AGENCY

It has been seen in the present chapter that compliance with international regulatory requirements is evidenced by certificates such as the ISM Document of Compliance (DOC) and the ISM Safety Management certificate (SMC) as well as other certificates confirming compliance with SOLAS, ISPS and the MLC. It has also been seen that the responsibility for issuing these certificates, and indeed to control correct implementation of the international conventions concerned,

---

171. Ibid.
172. Ibid.
173. Ibid.
174. MLC, reg 4.3; Directive 2009/13/EC, Title 4, reg 4.3(1).
175. MLC, reg 4.3; Directive 2009/13/EC, Title 4, reg 4.3(2).
176. MLC, reg 4.3; Directive 2009/13/EC, Title 4, Standard A4.3(3).
177. MLC, reg 4.5. This is not reproduced in the Annex to the Directive.
178. MLC, reg 5.1.
179. MLC, reg 5.1.
180. MLC, reg 5.1.3.
181. Directive 2009/16/EC of the European Parliament and the Council of 23 April 2009 on port State control, OJ L 131, 28 May 2009, at pp 57–100.
182. SI 2013/1785.
183. SI 2013/1785, reg 9.

lies squarely with the flag State administrations on the one hand and on port State control on the other.[184] The European flag States have a clear interest in co-ordinating their national processes and in exchanging relevant information about vessels in their fleets and/or calling at their ports and for many years now the EU has been increasingly active in facilitating such exchanges. However, the sinking of the tanker *Erika* in December 1999 with 30,000 tonnes of heavy fuel just off the coast of Brittany further accelerated this process and led in 2002 to the creation of a new European body: the European Maritime Safety Agency (EMSA).

EMSA, now based in Lisbon, was established in the aftermath of the *Erika* disaster as a "specialist branch" of the European Commission[185] for the purpose of ensuring a high, uniform and effective level of maritime safety; maritime security; prevention of, and response to, pollution caused by ships; as well as response to marine pollution caused by oil and gas installations.[186] Generally speaking the main function of the agency is to provide the EU Member States and the Commission, with the technical and scientific assistance needed to help them apply Community legislation in the field of maritime safety, prevention of pollution from ships[187] and pollution response,[188] to monitor its implementation and to evaluate the effectiveness of the measures in place.[189]

To fulfil its role, Regulation 1406/2002 (as amended)[190] gives EMSA several tasks which are divided into "core tasks" and "ancillary tasks". EMSA's *core tasks* may be summarised as follows:

(a) *Assisting the Commission*. EMSA's main function is that of a specialist technical aid to the Commission; as such it shall provide assistance in the preparatory work for updating and developing EU legislation in the fields of maritime safety and maritime security, the prevention of pollution and response to pollution caused by ships and oil and gas installations, in line with the development of international legislation in that field.[191] Once legislation has been adopted, EMSA shall assist the Commission in its effective implementation by monitoring the overall functioning of the Community port State control regime,[192] performing specific tasks on maritime safety, ship pollution prevention and ship pollution response, and performing the inspection tasks assigned to it pursuant to the Port Facility Security Regulation.[193] EMSA also provides technical and scientific

184. See also Directive 2009/16/EC of the European Parliament and of the Council of 23 April 2009 on port State control OJ L 131, 28 May 2009, at pp 57–100; and Directive 2009/21/EC of the European Parliament and of the Council of 23 April 2009 on compliance with flag State requirements OJ L 131, 28 May 2009, at pp 132–135.

185. Regulation (EC) 1406/2002 of European Parliament and Council of 27 June 2002, Establishing a European Maritime Safety Agency, OJ L 208, 5 August 2002, at pp 1–9, as amended by Regulation (EC) 1644/2003, OJ L 245, 29 September 2003, at pp 10–12; Regulation (EC) 724/2004, OJ L 129, 29 April 2004, at pp 1–5; Regulation (EC) 1891/2006 OJ L 394, 30 December 2006, at pp 14–16; and Regulation (EC) 100/2013 OJ L 39, 9 February 2013, at pp 30–40.

186. See art 1.1 as amended.

187. Both accidental and deliberate according to art 1.3 of the Regulation, added by art 1.1(b) of Regulation (EC) 724/2004.

188. Regulation (EC) No 2038/2006 of the European Parliament and of the Council of 18 December 2006 on multiannual funding for the action of the European Maritime Safety Agency in the field of response to pollution caused by ships and amending Regulation (EC) No 1406/2002, OJ L 394, 30 December 2006, at pp 1–4. EMSA will only provide operational assistance upon request of the State affected, Regulation 1406/2002, art 1.2.

189. Regulation (EC) 1406/2002, as amended, art 2(b).

190. The Regulation has been amended four times now, particularly in the aftermath of the *Prestige* disaster in 2002. A full consolidated version of the Directive is available at www.emsa.europa.eu (accessed 1 March 2017).

191. Regulation (EC) 1406/2002, as amended, art 2.2(a).

192. EMSA is expected to provide the Commission with the technical assistance necessary to take part in the work of the technical bodies of the Paris Memorandum of Understanding on Port State Control; Regulation (EC) 1406/2002, art 2.2(b).

193. Regulation (EC) 725/2004 of the European Parliament and of the Council of 31 March 2004 on Enhancing Ship and Port Facility Security, OJ L 129, 29 April 2004, at pp 6–91, art 9(4).

support for participation at meetings in international fora such as the IMO and the IOPC Fund.

(b) *Working with the EU Member States*. The second cluster of functions of EMSA is that of co-operation with the EU Member States to organise training activities in fields which are the responsibility of the port State and flag State, develop technical solutions and technical assistance for the implementation of EU legislation, provide information to support the monitoring of Recognised Organisations[194] and support pollution response actions in case of accidental or deliberate pollution caused by ships.[195]

(c) *Facilitating co-operation between EU Member States and the Commission*. The agency's third – but equally important – cluster of functions is that of a facilitator for the co-operation between the EU Member States and the Commission on several but quite specific matters, all listed in Article 2.4 of the consolidated version of the Regulation. Most interestingly the development and operation of the EU vessel traffic monitoring and information system[196] and establishing the fundamental principles governing the investigation of accidents in the maritime transport sector.[197] EMSA is also called to provide the EU Member States with objective, reliable and comparable information and data on maritime safety, maritime security and pollution from ships and offshore installations with the aim of enabling them to take the necessary steps to improve their actions in these fields and to evaluate the effectiveness of existing measures. EMSA will also assist the EU Member States in their activities to improve the identification and pursuit of ships making unlawful discharges.[198] The list of tasks attributed to EMSA has grown dramatically since the 2013 amendment and the trend seems to be that of increasing its influence particularly in matters involving safety, security and monitoring.

EMSA has been given a further series of tasks which are referred to as "ancillary" and listed in Article 2a of the Regulation. The list is unsurprisingly long and detailed and has been added by Regulation 100/2013 to ensure EMSA creates "substantiated added value" and avoids "duplication of efforts" always without infringing upon port States', EU Member States' and coastal States' rights and obligations.

As far as its internal organisation is concerned, EMSA's main administrative bodies are its Administrative Board[199] and the Executive Director.[200]

The Administrative Board is formed by one representative of each EU Member State, four representatives of the Commission and four professionals from the relevant sectors also nominated by the Commission.[201] Professional members have no voting rights.[202] All members of the

---

194. See p 38.

195. Regulation (EC) 1406/2002, art 2.2. This may also be done through workshops and/or inspections. For an example of such functions see Directive 2009/16/EC, whereas (10).

196. The system – known as the SafeSeaNet project – has been introduced by Directive 2002/59/EC, OJ L 208, 5 August 2002, at pp 10–27:

> with a view to enhancing the safety and efficiency of maritime traffic, improving the response of authorities to incidents, accidents or potentially dangerous situations at sea, including search and rescue operations, and contributing to a better prevention and detection of pollution by ships.

See Directive 2002/59/EC, art 1.

197. Regulation (EC) 1406/2002, art 2.4.

198. Regulation (EC) 1406/2002, art 2.4(f).

199. Regulation (EC) 1406/2002, arts 10, 11 and 12.

200. Regulation (EC) 1406/2002, art 15.

201. Regulation (EC) 1406/2002, art 11.1.

202. Ibid.

Administrative Board will be in office for five years; the term of office may be renewed.[203] The Board is chaired by a Chairperson elected from among its members for a three-year term.[204] The main functions of the Board are the election of the Executive Director, to report on EMSA's activities to the European Parliament, the Council, the Commission, the Court of Auditors and the EU Member States and to adopt EMSA's work programme and its budget.[205]

The Executive Director is – in all relevant respects – the "manager" of EMSA and its full independence is expressly guaranteed by Article 15 of the Regulation.[206] The Director is appointed and dismissed by the Administrative Board: "on grounds of merit and documented administrative and managerial competence, as well as documented experience in the fields referred to in Article 1".[207] The Director stays in office for five years, renewable for another four-year term,[208] but can be dismissed by a four-fifths majority of the Administrative Board.[209] Among the most relevant duties of the Director are the preparation of EMSA's work programme,[210] the estimates of revenue and expenses[211] and – in general – the overall functioning of EMSA.[212]

In conclusion, EMSA evolved as a result of recent major shipping disasters in European waters, such as the sinking of the ferry *Estonia* and the tankers *Erika* and *Prestige*, to become very active and effective in supporting the preparation and implementation of the ever-increasing European intervention in the field of maritime safety and pollution prevention.

8. COMPLIANCE AND THE ROLE OF CLASSIFICATION SOCIETIES

Throughout this chapter the focus has been on the safety standards and requirements which owners and operators have to follow in the matters of safety and security. A number of compliance certificates have been mentioned and reference to the Maritime Administration of the flag State as the body responsible for such certifications has been made several times. The complexity of the legal framework involved and the technical background required to perform a thorough assessment however are such that in practice the duties of the flag State to verify, certify and control its fleet for compliance with international standards are not always carried out directly by the Administration, but often delegated to specialist private bodies known as classification societies.

In the following paragraphs, (a) the role of classification societies in shipping and (b) their liabilities in performing their statutory certification duties will be addressed.

(a) Classification societies and their role

Classification societies are independent private bodies engaged in the study, development and surveillance of the technical side of ship structural safety and as such they have achieved a pivotal role within the shipping world. Generally speaking the work of classification societies is based on service contracts with shipowners and shipbuilders alike.[213] However, the impor-

---

203. Regulation (EC) 1406/2002, art 11.3.
204. Regulation (EC) 1406/2002, art 12.
205. The detailed powers of the Board may be found in Article 10 of the Regulation.
206. "Without prejudice – in the words of the norm – to the respective competencies of the Commission and the Administrative Board", art 15.1.
207. Regulation (EC) 1406/2002, art 16.1.
208. Regulation (EC) 1406/2002, art 16.2.
209. Regulation (EC) 1406/2002, art 16.1.
210. Regulation (EC) 1406/2002, art 15.2(a).
211. Regulation (EC) 1406/2002, art 15.2(f).
212. Regulation (EC) 1406/2002, art 15.2(c).
213. See Chapter 2.

tance of class certificates extends well beyond the interests of owners and builders since class documents are relied upon not only by flag States and port State control, but also by charterers and traders keen to see their products shipped on board staunch vessels[214] and insurers who need to know the condition of the ships they insure in order to calculate the relevant risks and set the premium.[215] Buyers of vessels may also need the classification certificates to ensure the future employability of the vessel and it does not stop there: other users of the sea, seafarers and coastal interests such as beach resorts and fishing reserves rely on class certificates almost as a form of guarantee for the safety of the world's fleet.

To better understand the work performed by classification societies and the different liabilities which may arise in respect thereof it is necessary to divide it into two categories, (i) *statutory* work and (ii) *non-statutory* work.

(i) *Statutory surveys* are performed by classification societies as representatives of the administration under formal authorisation granted by flag States. In performing these surveys classification societies discharge obligations imposed on the flag State by international or national law. These functions comprise the assessment of the flag fleet in order to determine the compliance of registered vessels with the applicable requirements of the international conventions and codes,[216] EU Directives[217] and national legislation and the issue of statutory certificates.

(ii) *Non-statutory surveys* include any other contractual work carried out by classification societies which does not involve the performance of statutory surveys or the issue of statutory certificates.

The distinction is extremely important and often misunderstood: for the purposes of this chapter – i.e. safety and security compliance – only *statutory* work is relevant as the responsibility for the certificates issued is imposed by international conventions on the flag States and then delegated to the society. In fact, in order to perform statutory work classification societies have to become "Recognised Organisations" ("ROs") and go through a special procedure now standardised within the European Union through Regulation (EC) 391/2009.[218] Recognition will only be granted to organisations meeting specific "minimum criteria"[219] and may be withdrawn in case of serious failure in safety and pollution prevention performance.[220]

(b) ROs' liabilities in the performance of statutory duties

Once duly recognised, an RO may be contracted by the flag State to perform its certification duties. Such delegation referred to as "authorisation" is dealt with by Directive 2009/15/EC,[221] which in its latest recast attempts to create some degree of uniformity across Europe on the

214. See Chapter 4.
215. This was, in origin, the *raison d'être* for the development of classification societies.
216. Some of which, such as the ISM Code, SOLAS etc., were discussed above.
217. Such as Directive 2009/13/EC also discussed above.
218. Regulation (EC) 391/2009 of the European Parliament and of the Council of 23 April 2009 on common rules and standards for ship inspection and survey organisations, OJ L 131, 28 May 2009, at pp 11–23.
219. Ibid., Annex I.
220. Regulation (EC) 391/2009, art 7.
221. Directive 2009/15/EC of the European Parliament and of the Council of 23 April 2009, on common rules and standards for ship inspection and survey organisations and for the relevant activities of maritime administrations (hereinafter "Directive 2009/15/EC"), OJ L 131, 28 May 2009, at pp 47–56; as amended by Directive 2014/111/EU of 17 December 2014 amending Directive 2009/15/EC with regard to the adoption by the International Maritime Organization (IMO) of certain Codes and related amendments to certain conventions and protocols, OJ L 366, 20 December 2014, at p. 83.

specific issue of liability between the authorising States and the classification societies in respect of damages arising from faults of the classification societies in performing statutory surveys.[222] Unsurprisingly, within the scope of their various tasks and duties, classification societies may make mistakes that can cause damage either to the shipowner or to third parties.[223] The extent of their liability in such events would vary depending on the type of survey that has been performed.

While performing non-statutory tasks – where the parties' duties and liabilities are regulated by agreement – the contract itself will usually include clauses to the effect of excluding or limiting the liability of the surveyor and the classification society. However, where the organisation is carrying out statutory work, its negligence may lead to third party claims against the State or the relevant Maritime Authority. In such cases the liability of the State or authority will depend on general principles of the national law concerned, whereas the recourse action against the organisation will depend entirely on the actual wording of the agreement in place between the society and the relevant administration.

When acting on behalf of national administrations the vast majority of ROs in Europe have a contractual arrangement in place, generally called "Model Agreement". Such agreements do contain a schedule with a full list of all functions which are *delegated* to the organisations by the administration concerned. Generally speaking the agreements impose a duty of care on the classification societies and a liability towards the Administration for breach of such duty, on the basis either of Directive 2009/15/EC or of IMO MSC Circular 710 and MEPC Circular 307. Of course, for a national authority to claim against a classification society under the relevant agreement there must be a breach of the agreement and there must be damage suffered as a consequence thereof. Damages may be suffered by the authorising State if the classification society has been negligent and the State was sued and found liable to pay damages for such breach of statutory duty. This is where Directive 2009/15/EC had a major impact on the European liability regime of classification societies.

In its original text, the Directive imposed on the EU Member States the obligation to put in place a quality monitoring system[224] for selecting classification societies to whom they were allowed to delegate,[225] in full or in part, performance of statutory surveys. Only organisations which met the criteria to obtain recognition as set out in the Annex of the Directive could be authorised to carry out statutory work.[226] The third amendment to this instrument[227] and its 2009 recast require all EU Member States to insert in their agreements with such ROs the following clause concerning liability:

(i) if liability arising out of any incident is finally and definitely imposed on the administration by a court of law or as part of the settlement of a dispute through arbitration procedures, together with a requirement to compensate the injured parties for loss or damage to property or personal injury or death, which is proved in that court of law

---

222. The attempt however can only be partly successful as demonstrated in a study by the Institute of Maritime Law of the University of Southampton; see Commission of the European Communities, "Commission Working Document on the Control of Recognised Organisations by the Commission and on the Impact of the Civil Liability Regime in Accordance with Directive 94/57/EC", COM (2006) 588 final, 11 October 2006.

223. As charterers or cargo owners, as happened in *Marc Rich & Co AG v Bishop Rock Marine Co Ltd (The Nicholas H)* [1996] AC 211; [1995] Lloyd's Rep 299 (HL).

224. Directive 94/57/EC, art 11(1) of the original text.

225. Art 3(2).

226. Art 4(1) of the original text.

227. Directive 2001/105/EC of the European Parliament and of the Council of 19 December 2001 amending Council Directive 94/57/EC on common rules and standards for ship inspection and survey organisations and for the relevant activities of maritime administrations, OJ L 19, 22 January 2002, at pp 9–16.

to have been caused by a wilful act or omission or gross negligence of the recognised organisation, its bodies, employees, agents or others who act on behalf of the recognised organisation, the administration shall be entitled to financial compensation from the recognised organisation to the extent that the said loss, damage, injury or death is, as decided by that court, caused by the recognised organisation;

(ii) if liability arising out of any incident is finally and definitely imposed on the administration by a court of law or as part of the settlement of a dispute through arbitration procedures, together with a requirement to compensate the injured parties for personal injury or death, which is proved in that court of law to have been caused by any negligent or reckless act or omission of the recognised organisation, its employees, agents or others who act on behalf of the recognised organisation, the administration shall be entitled to financial compensation from the recognised organisation to the extent that the said personal injury or death is, as decided by that court, caused by the recognised organisation; the Member States may limit the maximum amount payable by the recognised organisation, which must, however, be at least equal to EUR 4 million;

(iii) if liability arising out of any incident is finally and definitely imposed on the administration by a court of law or as part of the settlement of a dispute through arbitration procedures, together with a requirement to compensate the injured parties for loss or damage to property, which is proved in that court of law to have been caused by any negligent or reckless act or omission of the recognised organisation, its employees, agents or others who act on behalf of the recognised organisation, the administration shall be entitled to financial compensation from the recognised organisation, to the extent that the said loss or damage is, as decided by that court, caused by the recognised organisation; the Member States may limit the maximum amount payable by the recognised organisation, which must, however, be at least equal to EUR 2 million.[228]

The addition of this clause to the agreements between classification societies and the States may have very serious financial implications, indeed exposing classification societies to unlimited financial exposure for negligent acts or omissions. However – it is submitted – the clause cannot be triggered unless two conditions are satisfied: (a) the liability of the Maritime Administration is positively established through (b) the negligence of the class surveyor. If this is true, this situation can only arise in respect of *statutory surveys* where the surveyor is performing inspections by express authorisation of the maritime administration. On the other hand, where a non-statutory survey is performed, the liability of the Administration cannot arise and the classification society will be liable in contract and tort according to the ordinary rules of the law applicable to the relevant claim.

After the decision of the Tribunal de Grande Instance de Paris in the *Erika* case[229] it is now clear that – at least under French law – classification societies may be liable to pay huge compensation for pollution damage caused or contributed to by their own negligence. On the other hand they may be able to limit or exclude their liability under specific conventions[230] or national law, as it is clearly the case in England where claims in tort against classification societies have

---

228. Art 5.2(b).

229. Tribunal de Grande Instance de Paris, 11ème Chambre – 4ème section, 16 January 2008, unreported, affirmed by the Paris Court of Appeal on 30 March 2010, Jugement du 16 Janvier 2008, Tribunal de Grande Instance de Paris, 11ème Chambre – 4ème section, No 9934895010.

230. *Reino de Espana v American Bureau of Shipping et al.*, sub nom. *The Prestige*, US District Court, Southern District of New York, 3 August 2010.

been effectively restricted, mainly on policy considerations.[231] But the *Erika* decision appears to be taken on the, with respect, dubious basis that the class surveyors were negligent in performing *non-statutory* rather than *statutory* surveys. As such, the liability regimes classification societies may fall in are far from being uniform and the distance between the various regimes – even within the European region – are such as to encourage shopping for a convenient forum. The domicile of a company is established in the country where it has its statutory seat, central administration or principal place of business.[232] Thus jurisdiction can be seized on the basis of the registered office of a classification society under Article 63(1) of the Recast Jurisdiction Regulation (EU) 2015/2012.[233] And this without taking into account special conflict provisions contained in specialist conventions.[234]

On the other hand, in the case of statutory surveys, where uniform legislation is put in place by Directive 2009/15/EC, uniform results are equally difficult to achieve since the liability provision in Article 5(2)(b) may only be triggered if the Maritime Administration's liability is established which, in turn, will depend on the court seized and its internal constitutional, administrative and procedural laws.[235]

---

231. *Marc Rich & Co. AG v Bishop Rock Marine Co. Ltd (The Nicholas H)* [1996] AC 211; [1995] Lloyd's Rep 299 (HL). This is not the case in Italy where Lloyd's Register has been found liable in tort for damages caused to the charterer of a vessel detained due to SOLAS and MARPOL deficiencies not discovered by the Lloyd's Register inspector who issued the relevant certificates; Tribunale di Genova, 18 February 2010, *Argos Shipping Agency S.r.l. v Lloyd's Register of Shipping (The Redwood)*, unreported in English.

232. Previously Council Regulation (EC) 44/2001, art 60(1); now Regulation (EU) No 1215/2012 of the European Parliament and of the Council of 12 December 2012 on jurisdiction and the recognition and enforcement of judgments in civil and commercial matters (recast) OJ 20 December 2012, L 351/1, 20 December 2012, at pp 1–32, art 63, applicable from 10 January 2015.

233. Ibid.

234. *The Prestige* (fn 230).

235. See F. Lorenzon and M. Tsimplis, "Classification Societies and Directive 94/57/EC: Time for Rethinking the Unlimited Liability Issue?" (2006) 6(7) STL 1.

CHAPTER 10

MARINE POLLUTION FROM SHIPPING ACTIVITIES

Michael Tsimplis

1. INTRODUCTION

Up to the early 1970s marine pollution from ships was in essence unregulated. In the name of business efficiency ships regularly cleaned their tanks en route and discharged their residues at sea together with all rubbish overboard. This attitude was not assisted by the fact that the jurisdiction of coastal States extended only to territorial waters of, in general, three nautical miles from the coast. Pollution damage recovery for contaminated property was based on national law, in England in tort, and was not always easy to achieve.[1] Today there is an extensive legislative framework attempting to prevent or mitigate pollution[2] at sea and reduce the degradation of the marine environment. The jurisdiction of the coastal States in respect of the protection of the marine environment has significantly expanded and technology, in particular, satellite observations, provide better opportunities for identifying malpractice resulting in marine pollution.

It was the image of big tankers[3] leaking large quantities of oil, polluting extensive areas and destroying wildlife that raised public awareness about the threats to the environment posed by large-scale transportation of oil by sea. Triggered by these high profile incidents the law started developing into a very distinct and separate field involving regulatory obligations coupled with penal and civil liability.[4] The shipping industry played a leading role in the development of the new law, and in several instances overtook the international legal negotiations by adopting innovative private schemes. This positive attitude ensured that the solutions adopted were

---

1. *Esso Petroleum Co Ltd v Southport Corp* [1956] AC 218; [1955] 2 Lloyd's Rep 655.
2. It should not be assumed that shipping is the major source of oceanic pollution. Land-based activities are far more damaging not only in terms of volume of pollutants but also because most of the oceanic life is concentrated in the coastal zone. However, as these are within the jurisdiction and the politics of each coastal State only "soft" international law under regional international instruments has been developed.
3. A detailed review of the history, the well known incidents and the political and financial conflicts involved is beyond the scope of this work. The interested reader is advised to read Colin de la Rue and Charles B. Anderson, *Shipping and the Environment* (2nd edn, LLP 2009) where a good summary of the history is provided.
4. It cannot be seriously argued that the shipping industry and the coastal authorities could not predict that serious pollution incidents were likely to happen. However, before major pollution incidents started happening there was not much public interest in developing pollution prevention and compensation regimes. In addition the shipping industry's lobbying of various governments was probably strong enough to delay these developments.

acceptable both to the industry and to States and reduced the consequences of multiple litigation and security measures when an incident occurred. Most of the drafting work in creating the legal framework has been achieved within the negotiating environment of the International Maritime Organization. However, the resulting legal instruments are the minimum common standards achievable on an international basis and do not cover the needs of all States.

Ships are, in general, regulated by the laws of the flag State but they become subject to the laws applicable to the jurisdictional zones of the States they transit and those they trade to. It is the coastal State rather than the flag State which has the pressing interest to protect its coastal environment and at the same time facilitate trade. Before 1982 the rights of the coastal State were restricted to internal and territorial waters. The development of the 1982 United Nations Convention on the Law of the Sea (UNCLOS) has improved the governance of pollution incident situations in three respects.[5] First, it extended the jurisdiction of the coastal State's rights and obligations to 200 nautical miles from the coast by accepting the exclusive economic zone (EEZ);[6] second, it imposed general duties on coastal States to protect the marine environment;[7] and third, it weakened the right of innocent passage by providing that this is to be exercised subject to the protection of the marine environment.[8]

An important increase of the rights of the coastal State that comes under threat of pollution from a shipping incident has been provided under the Intervention Convention 1969 and its protocols.[9] Under Article 1 of the Intervention Convention 1969 the coastal State is entitled to take measures on the high seas which it thinks necessary in order to avoid grave and imminent pollution threats arising from shipping incidents. In the UK the government's intervention powers can be found in the Merchant Shipping Act 1995.[10]

In addition to UNCLOS other framework conventions have introduced State obligations which concern the environment in general and have an impact on shipping activities too. Examples are the Convention on Biological Diversity,[11] the Basel Convention on Hazardous Wastes 1992[12] and the United Nations Framework Convention on Climate Change 1992, the Kyoto Protocol[13] and currently the 2015 Paris Agreement.[14] These conventions lay down general principles and objectives which are not necessarily directly applicable to or enforceable against ships but which affect ships though the implementation of their general principles.

---

5. We only refer to the three more important effects here. It should be stressed that UNCLOS has several other provisions affecting the marine environment, but these are dealt with in Chapter 8.

6. Part V of UNCLOS.

7. Part XII of UNCLOS.

8. Art 21 of UNCLOS. However, legislation regarding the construction of ships has to be based on international agreement rather than national standards art 21(2).

9. International Convention Relating to Intervention on the High Seas in Cases of Oil Pollution Casualties, 1969, came into force 6 May 1975. The original convention covered only some types of oil but its 1973 Protocol extended to other substances. The list of substances has further been revised in 1991, 1996 and 2002 with successive protocols modifying the list of substances to which the Convention applies.

10. Schedule 3A was introduced under Schedule 1 of the Marine Safety Act 2003.

11. Signed at the Rio Earth Summit in 1992 by 150 government leaders, and dedicated to promoting sustainable development. Entered into force on 29 December 1993. It presently has 196 parties (on 22 February 2017). The Convention establishes the role of biological diversity for people, food security, medicines, fresh air and water, shelter, and a clean and healthy environment. The Convention covers all biological diversity including the marine environment.

12. Basel Convention on the Control of Transboundary Movements of Hazardous Wastes and their Disposal. Adopted on 22 March 1989, entered into force on 5 May 1992. It has 185 parties (22 February 2017).

13. UN Framework Convention on Climate Change 1992. The Convention entered into force on 21 March 1994. The Kyoto Protocol was adopted in Kyoto, Japan, on 11 December 1997 and entered into force on 16 February 2005. There are 197 parties to the Convention and 192 Parties to the Kyoto Protocol (on 22 February 2017).

14. The 2015 Paris Agreement on the Implementation of the United Nations Framework Convention Climate Change was agreed on 12 December 2015 and entered into force on 4 November 2016. It currently has 129 Contracting States (as at 11 February 2017).

Overall, international policy regarding the protection of the marine environment has been unfocused and in some respects inconsistent. Part-solutions to pressing problems have been developed, but the legal framework is, as will become evident, a labyrinth starting with good intentions and ending in incomplete parts or sometimes dead ends. Despite the haphazard development of the legal framework, the most regulated part of the industry that concerned oil tankers has dramatically increased its environmental record. Despite the significant increase in oil trade, marine pollution from oil spills from accidents involving tankers has been significantly reduced, both in the number but also in the total amount of oil spilled during such accidents.[15] There are still however significant polluting events and tackling the largest of those, which are the cause of around three quarters[16] of the oil spilt, is a significant challenge.

However, the development of environmental law in relation to shipping has by no means stopped. Environmental pressures increase with time and widen in scope. Atmospheric pollution and greenhouse gas emissions from ships are now important problems that need to be resolved together with the transportation of alien species by ships, the effects noise has on mammals and the collisions between ships and particular marine species. Due to its international character the shipping industry requires uniformity of environmental measures and regulations for ships to the greatest extent possible as otherwise it may become subjected to unilateral legal provisions and demands by each coastal State. At the same time the needs of the coastal States differ with developed States more concerned for their environment and developing States focused on economic development. Environmentally safe shipping requires prevention of shipping incidents and operational pollution alike. This is achieved by developing five equally important tools. First, by improving the construction and maintenance standards for ships so that the carriage of pollutants is more resilient to the dangers of the sea and to human fault. Second, by improving training standards for crew members so that the risk of human fault is reduced and awareness of the significance of marine pollution develops. Third, by establishing management systems for ships, ports and shipping companies which ensure early identification and minimisation of risks taken, or, in the case of an accident, confirmation of the causes of the pollution accident and appropriate attribution of responsibility. Fourth, by establishing liability regimes which ensure that pollution victims will be compensated and that the polluting industry, in other words shipowners, cargo owners, insurers and importers, will strive to avoid pollution because of the imposed liability. The final tool in the legal framework is the imposition of criminal liability and fines for pollution incidents.

2. SHIP STANDARDS IN CONSTRUCTION, OPERATION AND MANNING

Standards for the ship's safety are contained in the International Convention for the Safety of Life at Sea 1974 (SOLAS),[17] the cornerstone of a technical and managerial framework ensuring the safety of ships which in turn also impacts on marine pollution.[18] Flag and port State control are utilised as methods of implementation and enforcement. The International Safety Management Code contained in Chapter IX and the International Ship and Port Facilities Security Code (ISPS Code) contained under Chapter XI-2 of SOLAS indicate the breadth of issues covered.

15. See Oil Tanker Spill Statistics 2017, The International Tanker Owners Pollution Federation Limited, www.itopf. com/fileadmin/data/Photos/Publications/Oil_Spill_Stats_2016_low.pdf (accessed 11 February 2017).
16. Ibid.
17. Which entered into force on 25 May 1980.
18. See Chapter 9.

Standards for the operation of ships and the reduction of accidental and operational pollution are dealt with under the International Convention for the Prevention of Pollution from Ships 1973, as modified by the Protocol of 1978 relating thereto (MARPOL 73/78).[19] MARPOL 73/78 has been extended and modified by several successive protocols. It contains regulations for prevention of oil pollution (Annex I), prevention of pollution by hazardous and noxious substances in bulk (Annex II) and harmful substances in packaged form (Annex III), sewage and garbage pollution from ships (Annex IV and V), as well as air pollution from ships (Annex VI).[20] Only the first two annexes are compulsory for Contracting States.[21]

Contracting States undertake to develop criminal liability and disciplinary procedures for violations of MARPOL and SOLAS. Parts of MARPOL 73/78 are also implemented in European Law by the EU Ship Source Pollution Directive.[22] The Directive uses the same definition of illegal, operational or accidental discharges as MARPOL 73/78.[23] However, the Directive provides for criminal sanctions when caused intentionally, recklessly or by "serious negligence"[24] which is in contrast to the similar test under MARPOL 73/78 which refers to "the owner or the master" acting "either with intent to cause damage or recklessly and with knowledge that damage would probably result".[25] The lower threshold applies[26] to discharges in the territorial sea.[27] In addition criminal liability under the Directive is not restricted to the owner and the master of the ship but extends to "any other person involved" which would include many other entities, for example charterers, classification societies and operators not presently covered under MARPOL 73/78. The Directive applies[28] not just to territorial waters but also EEZs and the high seas.[29] A distinction between minor and other cases of pollution is created by the Directive. The Directive imposes criminal liability even for minor cases of pollution when committed with intent,

19. MARPOL 1978 which also includes the 1973 MARPOL entered into force on 2 October 1983 (along with Annexes I and II).

20. The air pollution regulations relate to sulphur oxide and nitrogen oxide emissions from ship exhausts and prohibit deliberate emissions of ozone depleting substances. Special emission areas are designated and lower emissions than the global cap of 4.5 per cent on the sulphur content of fuel oil are established for such areas (1.5 per cent). Greenhouse gases from shipping which are probably between 1.5 and 3.0 per cent of the global emissions are not regulated under any international or national instrument yet and are excluded under art 2.2 of the Kyoto Protocol 1997 from the general counting of greenhouse gas emissions. Annex VI provides that the IMO should seek to regulate such emissions. But see s 25 of the UK Draft Climate Change Bill where power is granted to the Secretary of State to count such emissions in this respect.

21. The UK is a signatory to all annexes. General authority to issue orders in this respect is granted under s 128 of the MSA 1995. Note also that the International Convention for the Control and Management of Ships Ballast Water and Sediments was adopted by consensus at a Diplomatic Conference at IMO in London on 13 February 2004. The latest Annex VI is the lowest in ratification with 62 countries covering approximately 85 per cent of the world tonnage. Thus the non-obligatory character of the annexes has not prevented extensive ratification. However, the major concern is the enforcement of the various measures. The Ballast Water Convention will enter into force on 8 September 2017. For an analysis see: M. Tsimplis, "Alien species stay home: The International Convention for the Control and Management of Ships' Ballast Water" (2004) 19, (4), International Journal of Coastal and Marine Law, 411–482.

22. Directive 2005/35/EC. See also Directive 2009/123/EC of the European Parliament and of the Council of 21 October 2009 amending Directive 2005/35/EC on ship-source pollution and on the introduction of penalties for infringements.

23. The Directive does not apply to pollution from warships and in cases where the ship or human life is in danger.

24. Art 4 EU Ship Source Pollution Directive 2005/35/EC amended by Directive 2009/123/EC, art 4.

25. Annex I Regulation 11(b) of MARPOL 73/78.

26. Arguably "gross negligence" includes breach of pollution or other shipping regulations thus it broadens the scope of criminal liability significantly.

27. Art 5 of the original Directive has been amended by Directive 2009/123/EC to ensure consistency with MARPOL 73/78.

28. The Directive has been transposed into English law by Statutory Instrument 2009 No 1210, as the Merchant Shipping (Implementation of Ship-Source Pollution Directive) Regulations 2009 which came into force on 1 July 2009. The relevant provisions have been inserted in the Merchant Shipping (Prevention of Oil Pollution) Regulations 1996 (SI 1996/2154). Note that the UK implementation protects persons connected with a ship's business and this is defined under Regulation 11C(d) to owner, master, seafarer, cargo owners and the classification society.

29. Directive 2005/35/EC, art 3.

recklessly or with serious negligence in the territorial waters or internal waters of a Member State.[30] Otherwise minor cases which do not individually and, if repeated, collectively affect "the quality of water"[31] are not infringements under the Directive.[32]

3. LIABILITY FOR OIL POLLUTION FROM SHIPS

(a) Civil liability for oil pollution

Civil liability for oil pollution is covered by various international conventions. Tankers are treated differently from other ships because they have a higher potential of causing extensive pollution. For tankers compensation for pollution damage is provided by the shipowner up to a limit and in addition by a specially formed intergovernmental legal entity called the International Oil Pollution Compensation Fund (IOPC Fund) funded from money collected from oil importers.

The 1969 Civil Liability Convention (1969 CLC)[33] establishes strict but limited liability for the shipowner, coupled with compulsory insurance and direct action against the insurer. The 1969 CLC has been updated by a 1976 Protocol and, in many States including the UK, by the 1992 Protocol which forms the 1992 Civil Liability Convention (1992 CLC).[34] The 1969/1992 CLC are each supplemented by the International Convention on the Establishment of an International Fund for Compensation for Oil Pollution Damage (IOPC Fund) 1971[35]/1992 respectively. The 1971 Fund Convention ceased to be in force on 24 May 2002 and the Fund was wound up with effect from 31 December 2014. Thus only the 1992 IOPC Fund is presently active. The role of the IOPC Fund is twofold. First, it provides additional compensation to victims of oil pollution in cases where compensation cannot be received under the CLC because the shipowner's liability is exempted or where the shipowner and its insurer are financially unable to provide for compensation. In addition it provides compensation to marine pollution victims to limits of liability higher than those available against the shipowner. The CLC/IOPC Fund system has been very successful as shown by the wide ratification of the 1992 CLC by 136 States and the 1992 IOPC Fund, by 114 States.[36] A Protocol to the 1992 IOPC Fund was agreed on 27 May 2003 for the creation of a voluntary third tier of liability for oil pollution. This third tier came into force

30. Directive 2009/123/EC, art 4.1.
31. Note that the Directive does not specify this term. There are several EU instruments which affect the water quality in general. It is not clear whether the intention is that criminal liability will only be established if the quality of water is affected under one of these instruments or whether the term is to be interpreted in a more general way.
32. Directive 2009/123/EC, art 5.
33. International Convention on Civil Liability for Oil Pollution Damage, Brussels, 29 November 1969 which came into force on 19 June 1975. The Protocol to the International Convention on Civil Liability for Oil Pollution Damage, London, 19 November 1976, which came into force on 8 April 1971, has been used as an interim solution to increase the low limits of liability agreed within the 1969 CLC. As at 11 February 2017, there were 34 States party to this Convention. The US has its own system of compensation for oil pollution damage which contains a tonnage rather than a value limit system, in contrast to the US approach to issues of global limitation.
34. International Liability Convention on Civil Liability for Oil Pollution Damage, London, 2 December 1992, which is created by the modification of the 1969 CLC in a 1992 Protocol to the 1969 CLC: see art 11(2) of the 1992 Protocol and also art 12(5). There was a not too dissimilar 1984 Protocol to the 1969 CLC also, which, despite being ratified by various major trading nations (e.g. France, Germany and Australia), was ratified by insufficient countries for it to be in force anywhere and its provisions have largely been included in the 1992 CLC. The 1992 Protocol came into force on 30 May 1996. On 11 February 2017 the 1992 Protocol had 136 Contracting States.
35. International Convention on the Establishment of an International Fund for Compensation for Oil Pollution Damage (FUND), adopted 18 December 1971, entered into force 16 October 1978. Convention on the Establishment of an International Fund for Compensation for Oil Pollution Damage, 27 November 1992. While the 1971 Fund Convention is not in force any more, it continued to exist because of outstanding claims until 31 December 2014.
36. See the status of International Maritime Organization Conventions at www.imo.org/ (accessed 11 February 2017).

in 2005, currently has 31 Contracting States[37] is available only in those States which are party to it and is supported by importers of those States. It was produced following recognition that, in spite of successive increases in the limits of liability for oil pollution, the "maximum compensation afforded by IOPCF 1992 might be insufficient to meet compensation needs in certain circumstances in some Contracting States to that Convention".[38] The *rationale* for the Supplementary Fund is that it provides higher levels of compensation in States which choose to become parties, while enabling States which do not wish to burden their oil importers with the higher levels of contribution involved to remain outside. Oil spill damage from bunkers and lubrication oils from ships not employed for the carriage of oil are covered by the 2001 Bunker Oil Pollution Convention (2001 BOPC)[39] which establishes strict but limited liability for the shipowner and other persons associated with the running of the ship coupled with compulsory insurance and direct action against insurers. However, unlike the CLC/IOPC Fund/Supplementary Fund system, the 2001 BOPC does not provide for a separate "stand-alone" limitation fund but preserves existing rights to limit liability whether under national or international law.[40]

In the UK, the Merchant Shipping Act 1995 rewrites the 1992 CLC (in Chapter III)[41] and the Fund Convention (in Chapter IV) into English law.[42] The 2003 Supplementary Fund has been enacted in the UK through the Merchant Shipping (Oil Pollution Compensation Limits) Order 2003.[43] The 2001 BOPC is implemented through the Merchant Shipping (Oil Pollution) (Bunkers Convention) Regulations 2006.

(b) The Civil Liability Convention 1992

The 1992 CLC and Fund Conventions apply to oil pollution damage caused in the territory, including the territorial sea, of a Contracting State,[44] and to damage caused within 200 miles from the coast.[45] It also covers the costs of preventive measures "wherever taken".[46]

---

37. As at 11 February 2017.

38. IMO LEG/CONF.14/20 the Preamble to the Supplementary Fund. The development of the 2003 Supplementary Fund to the IOPC Fund was initiated as a response to a European Union White Paper on Environmental Liability (Brussels, 9 February 2000, COM (2000) 66), a Communication from the Commission to the European Parliament and the Council on the Safety of the Seaborne Oil Trade (COM (2000), 142 final) which found the liability regime for oil pollution to be unsatisfactory in two respects. First, the limits were considered to be too low and second, the right of the shipowner to limit liability was considered to be almost unbreakable. The Communication suggested (1) an EU-wide solution which would involve establishing a third-tier Fund, supported by the industry, with an overall ceiling of one billion euros, (2) strict liability for the person who causes pollution (i.e. not only for the sea carriers) and (3) sanctions for gross negligence imposed on the negligent party and payable to the State where the pollution occurs. The 2003 Supplementary Fund was created to avoid unilateral measures by the EU. As concluded, the European Directive 2004/35/CE of 21 April 2004 excludes from its application all major maritime conventions included in its Annex IV.

39. Adopted on 23 March 2001 in London. Closed to signature on 30 September 2002. It came into force on 21 November 2008. 83 parties, as at 11 February 2017.

40. 2001 BOPC, art 6. In other words, while the CLC produced new money from the shipowners to pay out for pollution damage the 2001 BOPC does not do so but relies on the general limitation of liability fund.

41. ss 152–172 as amended by the Merchant Shipping (Oil Pollution) (Bunkers Convention) Regulations 2006, SI 2006/1244. These Regulations came into force on 21 November 2008.

42. ss 173–181.

43. By replacing the limits of liability for the Fund under s 157 of the MSA 1995.

44. However, there is no requirement that the damage should be only in one Contracting State. See also *Landcatch Ltd v International Oil Pollution Compensation Fund* [1999] 2 Lloyd's Rep 316, 328.

45. That is either an EEZ of a Contracting State, established in accordance with international law, or, if the State has not established such a zone, an area beyond and adjacent to the territorial sea of that State extending no more than 200 nautical miles from the baselines from which the breadth of its territorial sea is measured – 1969 CLC, art II. MSA 1995 ss 152–170 refer to damage and measures in the territory of the UK (s 153(1)) and to damage and measures in the territory of another CLC State. In turn the UK territory consists of the territorial sea and the British Fishery limits set out under the Fishery Limits Act 1976 and the territorial waters and the EEZs (or 200 mile zones) of other CLC States (s 170(4)).

46. 1992 CLC, art II(b). Which must be taken for the purpose of preventing damage to a Contracting State.

Thus it does not matter where the incident that caused the pollution has taken place but rather where the pollution damage occurred. Even where the incident has taken place within the waters of a non-Contracting State or on the high seas, if a Contracting State has suffered oil pollution damage in its EEZ or territorial waters, the 1992 CLC will apply and will cover preventive measures wherever undertaken including those in the jurisdictional zones of the non-Contracting coastal State or the high seas provided that they were preventing pollution damage to a Contracting State. Note also that the application of the 1992 CLC does not depend on whether the polluting ship is registered in a Contracting State or not.

The 1992 CLC/Fund defines oil as any persistent hydrocarbon mineral oil such as crude oil, fuel oil, heavy diesel oil and lubricating oil, whether carried on board a ship as cargo or in the bunkers of a ship.[47] However, the 1992 CLC wording does not define precisely which types of oil are persistent and thus included within the scope of the Convention.[48]

The difficulty of defining the scope of the 1992 CLC is resolved partly by the express reference to some types of oil within the oil definition[49] and partly by the development of a definition of non-persistent oils by the IOPC Fund.[50] Under this definition non-persistent oil is that which at the time of shipment, consists of hydrocarbon fractions, (a) at least 50 per cent of which, by volume, distils at a temperature of 340°C and (b) at least 95 per cent of which, by volume, distils at a temperature of 370°C when tested by the ASTM Method D86/78 or any subsequent revision thereof.[51]

All oils that do not fall within the non-persistent oil definition are persistent oils and thus subject to the CLC/Fund system. This working definition is more accurate than that included in the 1992 CLC.[52] The IOPC Fund will determine compensation on the basis of this definition. However, the working definition[53] cannot be considered binding on any national court because it does not legally carry the weight of a definition within the meaning of the Convention. As a result, it is open to claimants to challenge the persistent character of specific oil, presumably on evidence of its actual persistence despite the IOPC Fund definition.

The establishment of liability for pollution damage only for persistent oils arises from their evident impact on wildlife, beaches and ecosystems. When the 1969 CLC was developed it was, and still is, assumed that non-persistent oils will dissipate rapidly through evaporation into the atmosphere thus not causing significant damage or cleanup costs.[54] However, it would be wrong to assume that there is no pollution impact from incidents involving non-persistent oils.[55]

47. Art I(5).

48. s 170(1) of the MSA 1995 specifies "oil" as persistent hydrocarbon mineral oil. This excludes the examples given in the 1992 CLC definition. However, it does not appear to produce a different result as the term is the same and must be interpreted by reference to the 1992 CLC. The Merchant Shipping (Oil Pollution) (Bunkers Convention) Regulations 2006 amend the term to read as: "oil" except in the term "bunker oil" means persistent hydrocarbon mineral oil. No practical change is made by this modification.

49. 1992 CLC, art I(5).

50. See, for example, Caryn Anderson, "The International Tanker Owners Pollution Federation Limited (ITOPF) Persistent vs Non-Persistent Oils: What You Need to Know", article in: "Beacon" (Skuld Newsletter) July 2001, available at www.itopf.com/fileadmin/data/Documents/Papers/persistent.pdf where damage to paint coatings in marinas and harbours and to marine organisms are suggested as potential damage arising from non-persistent oils. Atmospheric pollution can also be an issue although it has not at the moment been considered as a consequence that should create civil liability.

51. Ibid.

52. However, it presents difficulties as it cannot be applied to non-mineral oils because they cannot tolerate the distillation process. These have to be distinguished on the basis of their mineral character. Caryn Anderson (fn 50).

53. Liquefied natural gas (LNG) and liquefied petroleum gas (LPG) as well as other gas products, gasolines, kerosenes and light distillates are non-persistent oils and are therefore not covered by the CLC/Fund framework.

54. In this context the distinction is not necessary as any claim for damage arising from non-persistent oil would have been difficult to prove.

55. Caryn Anderson (fn 50).

(c) What types of vessel are covered?

The 1992 CLC covers ships defined[56] as "any sea-going vessel and any seaborne craft of any type whatsoever". There is no definition of "seagoing",[57] "vessel", "seaborne" or "craft" in the Convention. The 1992 CLC does not apply to warships and other government ships used for non-commercial activities.[58]

The 1992 CLC further restricts its application to ships "constructed or adapted for the carriage of oil in bulk as cargo",[59] thus giving emphasis to the requirements of approval of ships as physically suitable for the carriage of oil.[60] The 1992 CLC applies always to ships which are only capable of carrying oil in bulk. In addition the 1992 CLC extends[61] the scope of coverage to oil spillage from Oil/Bulk/Ore ships (OBOs) which arguably fulfil the requirement to be constructed for the carriage of oil provided that these vessels are laden with oil or that they are on their first voyage after the carriage of oil and they have oil residues from the previous voyage on board.[62]

Oil pollution damage arising from barges without steering and propulsion, or floating storage units (FSU) as well as floating production, storage and offloading units (FPSO) also raises the question of applicability of the 1992 CLC.[63] While for barges with no propulsion or steering it is, under English law, well established that these are to be treated as ships, such an answer is not obvious for the other types of craft and is to be decided on a case-by-case basis.

The application of the 1992 CLC will also turn upon whether the structure under discussion is "carrying oil in bulk as cargo".[64] The notion of carriage usually involves transportation rather than containment thus making it strongly arguable that where the intention is storage rather than carriage the 1992 CLC would be inapplicable. While this interpretation is literally consistent with the wording of Article I(1) it would practically mean that pollution damages from such structures used for storage would require further legislation to achieve the same coverage as under the CLC.[65]

---

56. The enactment of the 1992 CLC into English law employs the same definition, s 170 MSA 1995.

57. See *Michael v Musgrove (t/a YNYS Ribs)* [2011] EWHC 1438 (Admlty); [2012] 2 Lloyd's Rep 37 where the Admiralty Registrar held that the important issue was not whether a ship could go to sea, but whether she did go to sea in the context of the claim. This case was within the Athens Convention. While it is possible to apply it in the 1992 CLC context it is difficult to see, in case of an accident while transporting oil in inland water, that the courts will accept that, despite the fact that the ship is continuously insured and not only when it is on seagoing voyages, pollution damage would not be recoverable for claimants.

58. 1992 CLC, art XI.

59. There is no definition of what "in bulk" may mean but the whole term arguably focuses on the words "as cargo". Thus, any quantity of oil carried under a contract of carriage of goods should trigger the application. By contrast, where oil is not part of the cargo but, for example, is contained in tanker trucks which are then carried on a ship (whether capable of carrying oil or not) the 1969 and the 1992 CLC will arguably not be applicable, irrespective of the amount of oil transported.

60. The corresponding restrictions in the definition of ship can be found in s 153(3) of the MSA 1995.

61. 1992 CLC, art I.I, see also s 153(3) and (4) of the MSA 1995.

62. Oil residues may be pumpable or non-pumpable oil mixtures caused by contamination of the oil by seawater or chemicals or simply by reduction in the oil temperature.

63. In the UK as part of the licence approval procedures operators of offshore oil and gas installations and pipelines must become members of the voluntary scheme Offshore Pollution Liability Association Limited (OPOL) or provide alternative liability coverage of the same value. Strict liability under the Agreement is limited to $120 million per incident and $240 million aggregate is imposed. Clean-up costs claimed by public authorities and "pollution damage" (cl 15 of OPOL agreement) means only direct loss or damage by direct contamination from a discharge of oil. Claimants are clearly not precluded from seeking compensation in courts. FPSOs and FSUs used in the production process as well as when temporarily removed from their normal station are covered by this agreement.

64. As required under art I(1) of the 1992 CLC.

65. The oil contained in such craft is not included in the tonnage of imported oil on the basis of which contributions to the IOPC Fund are levied. In 2006 the Greek Supreme Court held that the *Slops*, a former tanker from which the propeller and main machinery had been removed, was a "ship" for the purpose of the 1992 Fund Convention, although the Executive Committee of the Fund had decided that it was not. See IOPC Fund document 92FUND/EXC.34/7 at http://documentservices.iopcfunds.org/meeting-documents/download/docs/2867/lang/en/ (accessed 22 February 2017).

The IOPC Fund has extensively discussed the possibility of expanding its coverage after the Greek Supreme Court held that the *Slops*,[66] a decommissioned tanker used for storage of oil, was covered by the definition of ship.[67] In April 2016, the IOPC Fund Assembly accepted[68] a "Guidance Document for Member States". The Guidance Document "should not be seen as an authoritative interpretation of the relevant international Conventions"[69] but, nevertheless, it includes an illustrative list of craft falling within the definition of the ship and a list of craft falling outside the definition of the ship. Member States have agreed to rely on these lists as starting points and, for craft not clearly falling in either category, the concept of "maritime transport chain" has been agreed to be used as the interpretive tool in a case-by-case approach.[70] The maritime transport chain starts after the loading of oil and ends with final discharge. It includes ship-to-ship transport and temporary storage, provided the storage facility has navigational capability.[71] Notably, all structures that fall under the definition of ship in Article I(1) would be subject to the 1992 CLC irrespective of their size. However, compulsory insurance is only required for vessels larger than 2,000 grt.[72] For vessels smaller than 2,000 grt no compulsory insurance and no direct action against the insurer is available but the same type of liability is imposed as with larger vessels.

(d) Who is liable?

The 1992 CLC imposes strict liability on the owner of the ship causing pollution damage.[73] Strict liability in this context means the claimant needs only to prove that the pollution damage suffered was caused by a type of oil covered by the Convention which came from a ship covered by the Convention. There is no need to prove fault of the shipowner. The shipowner can avoid liability only under some limited exceptions. Strict liability does not prevent the shipowner from claiming against the party responsible for the pollution damage, nor does it remove the defence of contributory negligence by any victim of pollution damage. In essence it provides an obligation to pay out the claims by third party claimants thus channelling the claims, making the payment of compensation easier and quicker, reducing the litigation and minimising or excluding the possibility of security measures against the shipowner's property.

The owner is defined as the registered owner[74] or, in the absence of registration, the persons(s)[75] owning the ship.[76] Ownership at the time of the incident is relevant.[77] Where the incident consists of several occurrences then the material time for determining the owner is the time where the first of the occurrences took place (Article III(1)).

---

66. See fn 65.
67. See IOPC/MAY14/8/1 for an update of the unresolved debate which has been going on for a significant period of time.
68. IOPC/APR16/4/1. The Guidance document appears as Annex II.
69. Ibid., Annex II, Preface.
70. Ibid., s 2.1.
71. Ibid., s 5.3. A list of examples is also provided for the maritime transport chain in an Annex.
72. 1992 CLC, Art VII(1).
73. Art III(1). Section 153 of the MSA 1995 makes reference to the "owner" defined as the "registered owner" under s 170(1). The amendment by the Merchant Shipping (Oil Pollution) Bunkers Convention) Regulations 2006, SI 2006/1244, replaces the word "owner" with the term "registered owner" and also amends s 170(1) to point to the new section 153A(7) which states "In this Chapter (except in section 170(1) 'owner' except when used in the term 'registered owner', means the registered owner, bareboat charterer, manager and operator of the ship".
74. This is made express by the Merchant Shipping (Oil Pollution) Bunkers Convention) Regulations 2006, SI 2006/1244 amending s 170(1) of the MSA 1995.
75. 1992 CLC, art I.2. Individuals, partnerships, public and private bodies, corporate or not, including States, are covered by the term person.
76. Art I. Where the vessel is State owned but operated by a company, that company is the owner under art I.3.
77. See s 170(2) of the MSA 1995.

If the oil has escaped or been discharged from two or more ships and pollution damage has resulted, their owners are jointly and severally liable for all damage which is not reasonably separable.[78] Thus in such a case there is no need for the claimant to prove which ship caused the damage.

(e) When liability may arise

The 1992 CLC imposes an exclusive system of strict liability[79] for pollution damage caused by oil which has escaped or been discharged from a ship as a result of an incident.[80] Distinguishing between incidents is important as the limits of liability apply per incident.[81]

"Incident" is defined as any occurrence, or series of occurrences with the same origin, which cause(s) pollution damage. Occurrences which create a grave and imminent threat of causing pollution damage are also covered by the term "incident".[82] Thus preventive measures taken before an incident happens are covered by the 1992 CLC.

"Pollution damage" is defined as loss or damage outside the oil carrying ship caused by contamination resulting from the escape or discharge of oil from the ship, wherever this escape or discharge may occur. It includes the costs of preventive measures and further loss or damage caused by preventive measures.[83] These measures are defined as reasonable measures taken by any person after the incident occurred to prevent or minimise pollution damage.[84]

Under the 1992 CLC, the definition of "pollution damage" also includes the stipulation that compensation for impairment of the environment, other than for loss of profit from such impairment, shall be limited to costs of reasonable measures of reinstatement actually undertaken or to be undertaken.[85]

The wording of the pollution damage definition and in particular the "loss of profit" arising from the impairment of the environment creates rights for recovery of economic losses which are otherwise not recoverable under English law.

The IOPC Fund practice[86] is that loss of earnings caused by oil pollution suffered by persons whose property has not been polluted (pure economic loss)[87] may be covered.[88] In particular the manual suggests as permissible claims: loss of earnings by fishermen whose nets were not contaminated but who may be prevented from fishing because of the pollution of the area they normally fish; loss of income by hotel owners located close to a contaminated public beach; even costs of marketing campaigns to prevent or reduce economic losses by counteracting the negative publicity arising from a major pollution incident. The discrepancy between the common law

---

78. Art IV and s 153(5) of the MSA 1995 for the UK enactment.

79. In *Landcatch Ltd v International Oil Pollution Compensation Fund*, see fn 44, the liability was described as "in compensation as distinct from liability in damages at common law".

80. Arts I.8, III.1 and 4. The shipowners can of course pursue third parties for some or all of their resulting losses: art III.5.

81. See the *Strong Wise Ltd v Esso Australia Resources Pty Ltd (The "APL Sydney")* [2010] FCA 240, Federal Court of Australia, Rares J, 18 March 2010 for a discussion of the term in the context of the 1996 LLMC.

82. Art I.8.

83. 1969/1992 CLC, art I.6 and 7. See s 153 of the MSA 1995 for the damages for which liability is imposed and s 170 (1) for the statement that "damage" includes "loss".

84. Art I.7.

85. Art I.6 and s 153(3) of the MSA 1995 for the English enactment.

86. IOPC Fund Claims Manual 2016. www.iopcfunds.org/uploads/tx_iopcpublications/IOPC_Funds_Claims_Manual_ENGLISH_WEB.pdf (accessed 11 February 2017).

87. Note that in Australia where recovery for pure economic loss has been permitted in some cases it was held in *The APL Sydney* [2009] FCA 1090 that such losses are subject to limitation.

88. Note that expanding the scope of claims within a limited fund implies that other claimants who had suffered physical damage and consequential loss will in some cases recover less so that pure economic loss claimants can recover.

position and the IOPC Fund practice has led to litigation[89] in order to clarify the extent to which the common law rule of non-recovery has been modified by the introduction of the CLC/Fund legal framework into English Law.

In *Landcatch Ltd v International Oil Pollution Compensation Fund*,[90] smolt providers to the salmon farming industry in the Shetland Islands claimed against the shipowners, their insurers and the IOPC Fund for economic loss arising from the grounding of the *Braer*. The loss was caused by the pollution of the area and subsequent restrictive orders of the Secretary of State. The restrictive orders defined an exclusion area where pollution may have affected the food chain thus making fish dangerous to human health. As a result the demand for smolt was reduced, and prices fell. Lord Cullen delivered the leading judgment of the Scottish Inner House Court of Session rejecting the claims as being for indirect and relational economic losses. The judgment also rejected the suggestion that the IOPC Fund criteria and decisions are an aid to the construction of the legislation[91] and the suggestion that these claims are distinguishable from claims for damages for economic loss at common law.[92] In particular, the claimants suggested that it was unnecessary to constrain economic loss claims, contrary to the normal approach under common law, because there was no risk of exposing the shipowner or the Fund to an unlimited number of claims as their liability was limited under the Conventions. However, the court rejected the suggestion that the particular section replaced the common law liability with its restrictions on recovery for economic loss.[93] The decision in *Landcatch Ltd* was followed by the rejection by courts of several related claims.[94]

The English Court of Appeal, in rejecting a claim for secondary/relational economic loss[95] arising from the pollution caused by the grounding of the *Sea Empress*,[96] endorsed the *Landcatch* decision and, without deciding the precise scope of the recovery, accepted that "damage consisting of economic loss may well be recoverable under the statute by persons such as fishermen accustomed to fish in waters which become contaminated".[97] Thus the requirement for direct links of the economic loss on the one hand and the claimant's activity on the other hand with the polluted area appears to be the primary restriction in the type of claims recoverable.[98]

(f) Exclusion of liability

No liability for pollution damage will attach to the owner under the 1992 CLC if it proves that the damage resulted from an act of war, hostilities, civil war, insurrection or a natural phenomenon

89. *Landcatch Ltd v International Oil Pollution Compensation Fund* (fn 44); *Smith v Braer Corp* [1999] GWD 21–1023; *P&O Scottish Ferries Ltd v Braer Corp* [1999] 2 Lloyd's Rep 535; *Skerries Salmon Ltd v Braer Corp* [1999] SLT 1196; *Alegrete Shipping Co Inc v International Oil Pollution Compensation Fund 1971 (The Sea Empress)* [2003] EWCA Civ 65; [2003] 1 Lloyd's Rep 327.
90. See fn 44.
91. [2003] 1 Lloyd's Rep 327 at p 320.
92. Ibid., at p 328.
93. The counter-argument is, of course, that if all economic loss is to be compensated then claimants suffering physical damage will have to accept lower compensation.
94. See *Smith v Braer Corp* (fn 89), where the claims of the owner of a slaughter house within the restriction area were concerned; *P&O Scottish Ferries Ltd v Braer Corp* (fn 89), concerning claims for loss of revenue in relation to ferrying activities to and from the Shetland Islands due to the bad publicity following the incident; *Skerries Salmon Ltd v Braer Corp* (fn 89) where a fish farm outside the restriction area claimed for loss of earnings due to adverse publicity.
95. *The Sea Empress* (fn 89). The claim was under the 1995 Merchant Shipping Act. It concerned loss of earnings by a company involved in fish processing and sought to be distinguished from the *Landcatch Ltd* case on the basis that the company relied on provision of fish from the area in which a fishing ban was imposed.
96. The oil tanker *Sea Empress* grounded in the entrance to Milford Haven on 15 February 1996. A total of 72,500 tons of oil was spilled and extensive pollution to more than 200 km of the coastline was caused.
97. *The Sea Empress* (fn 89), at p 336, col 1.
98. In *The Sea Empress* (fn 89), at p 336 this was expressed as "the interest and losses of such fishermen could be very closely related to the physical waters and the physical contamination that occurred".

of an exceptional, inevitable and irresistible character; or was wholly caused by a third party's act or omission done with intent to cause damage.[99] Furthermore no liability attaches where the oil pollution damage was wholly caused by the negligence or other wrongful act of any government or other authority responsible for the maintenance of lights or other navigational aids in the exercise of that function.[100] The exceptions cover situations where the shipowner is not negligent. In fact, if the shipowner is negligent and this contributes to the damage, the exceptions will not apply. This is clear in relation to the second and third exceptions where the requirement for their application is that the damage was "wholly caused" by the relevant exception. It is submitted, nevertheless, that even if the different term "resulted from" is used in relation to the first exception in case there is negligence by the shipowner, the exception will not protect the shipowner either. If the shipowner sails the ship negligently into an area of war, then the pollution damage would arguably not be considered to arise from the act of war but from the shipowner's negligence.[101] However, the shipowner is not exempted from liability simply because it has not been negligent. For example, where pollution damage is caused by a collision between a tanker and another ship and liability for the collision damage is that of the other ship, the shipowner of the tanker will still have to compensate the victims for the pollution damage under the 1992 CLC but could of course sue the other shipowner for recovery.

Contributory negligence is also available as a defence reducing the liability of the registered owner.[102]

The 1992 CLC provides for a direct right of action by third party claimants against the insurer or other person providing financial security for the owner's liability for pollution damage.[103] This ensures that recovery may be available even if the owner is not financially capable of paying.

Insurers will not be liable if the shipowner's liability is excluded by the above-mentioned provisions.[104] The insurer can also avoid liability if it can show that the pollution damage resulted from the wilful misconduct of the owner.[95] However, the insurer is not entitled to[105] rely on any other contractual defence which it might have been entitled to take in proceedings brought by the owner against it,[106] for example for a breach of warranty or for the breach of the duty of fair presentation of the risk under the Insurance Act 2015.[107]

Rights of compensation under the Civil Liability Convention are extinguished unless an action is brought within three years from the date on which the damage occurred.[108] In no case may an action be brought after six years from the date of the incident which caused the damage.[109] The dual time bar covers situations[110] where the pollution does not arise immediately but is for

99. Art III.2(a).
100. Art III.2 and s 155 of the MSA 1995.
101. This interpretation is supported by the way the similar exception in the Hague-Visby Rules art IV r.2 has been interpreted by the English Courts. See, generally, R Aikens, R Lord and M Bools, *Bills of Lading* (2nd edn, Informa Law 2015) [10.218] – [10.286].
102. Art III.3 and s 169 of the MSA 1995.
103. Art VII.8. Government ships used commercially are able to escape this provision and not maintain insurance or other financial security: art VII.12 and s 167(2) of the MSA 1995.
104. 1992 CLC art VII.8 and s 165(2) of the MSA 1995.
105. Art III.3 and s 165(2) of the MSA 1995.
106. Ibid. One of the reasons for the extensive provisions covering insurers in the 1969 and 1992 CLC is that insurance is compulsory for the owners of ships registered in a Contracting State carrying more than 2,000 tons of oil in bulk as cargo: art VII.1.
107. In addition the UK enactment expressly excludes the compulsory insurance contract from the provisions of the Third Parties (Rights against Insurers) Act 2010 – see s 165(5) of the MSA 1995. See Chapter 11.
108. 1992 CLC art VIII and s 162 of the MSA 1995.
109. Ibid. Where this incident consists of a series of occurrences, the six-year period runs from the date of the first occurrence.
110. See Lord Gill's statement in *Gray and Another v The Braer Corporation and Others and International Oil Pollution Compensation Fund* [1999] 2 Lloyd's Rep 541, 544.

some reason delayed, for example, where a fully laden tanker sinks without much oil leaking but subsequently the oil is released following the deterioration of the wreck.[111]

The 1992 CLC prohibits in general[112] any claim for pollution damage as defined under the Civil Liability Conventions or otherwise against crewmembers and other servants or agents of the owner, the pilot (or any other person who, without being a member of the crew,[113] performs services for the ship), any charterer,[114] any manager or operator of the ship, any person performing salvage operations with the consent of the owner or on the instructions of a competent public authority, and any person taking preventive measures to avoid oil pollution damage.[115] Servants or agents of the charterer, manager, operator, salvor or other person taking oil pollution prevention measures are also protected. Thus for any pollution damage claim the shipowner or its insurer are the only persons a claimant may sue under the 1992 CLC.

Persons not protected under the 1992 CLC, for example shipbuilders and arguably Classification Societies, can be sued directly thus potentially becoming exposed to unlimited, fault-based, liability. In the first instance decision of *The Erika*[116] the Paris Criminal Court considered the list of the persons protected as restricted. As a consequence it held that the Italian classification society RINA, together with the technical manager of the ship and also Total SA, which had vetted the vessel which was then chartered by one of its subsidiaries, were not protected under the 1992 CLC and were liable for damages for the pollution caused on the basis of negligent practices. RINA was fined on the basis of French national law and its conviction was upheld by the Court of Appeal. The Court of Cassation found that in principle a classification society can rely on the CLC channelling provisions but in this case RINA would not have been successful because the damage arose from its recklessness.[117]

(g) Limitation of liability

Under the 1992 CLC scheme limitation of liability can be argued as protection provided to the shipowner in exchange for the imposition of strict liability. Thus, limitation of liability under the 1992 CLC may be invoked only in circumstances in which liability is imposed under the 1992 CLC[118] and only for damages covered by the 1992 CLC.

Owners of ships covered by the Convention[119] and their insurers are entitled to limit their liability for oil pollution damage.[120] The liability of the insurer is always limited[121] and the insurer

111. The Nairobi Wreck Removal Convention 2007, provides the basis for the removal of wrecks which threaten the marine environment. The wreck removal expenses under this convention are payable by the shipowner or covered by the compulsory insurance the shipowner has to carry. However, the 1992 CLC provisions will continue providing compensation for pollution damage.

112. Art III.4 "except in so far as the damage resulted from their personal act or omission, committed with the intent to cause such damage, or recklessly and with knowledge that such damage would probably result". For the meaning of these terms.

113. Art III.3 and s 156 of the MSA 1995.

114. "[H]owsoever described" (art III.4(c)) includes demise, time and voyage as well as slot charterers.

115. 1992 CLC, art III.4 but see s 156 of the MSA 1995.

116. See the report on the case submitted by France to the IOPC Fund 92FUND/EXC.40/4/1, 19 February 2008 and a summary provided by the Fund's French lawyer at 92FUND/EXC.40/4.

117. Arrêt n° 3439 du 25 Septembre 2012 (10–82.938) – Cour de cassation – Chambre criminelle – ECLI:FR:C-CASS:2012:CR03439. In the *Prestige* case, the French Courts have held that ABS had sovereign immunity in a claim brought by the State of France.

118. Art V.1: the liability is stated to be "under this Convention".

119. Arts V.11 and VII.8, provided that the type of damage suffered and the jurisdictional zone in which they have occurred is covered by the relevant convention.

120. See s 157(1) of the MSA 1995 for the right of the (registered) shipowner to limit liability and s 165(3) for the insurer's right to do so.

121. Art VII.8.

can always constitute a limitation fund[122] even if the owner is itself unable to limit liability.[123] The insurer is also entitled to use any defences which the owner would be entitled to use and to require the owner to be joined in the proceedings.[124] Liability may be limited for any one occurrence or series of occurrences with the same origin which causes pollution damage.[125]

The types of vessel subject to limitation are the same as those for which liability may arise under the Conventions. Thus there is no size-related restriction on the imposition of strict and limited liability. However, only ships of 2,000 grt or larger are obliged to have oil pollution damage insurance.[126]

The limits of liability are based on the tonnage of the ships and are as set out in Table 10.1. The 1976 Protocol to the 1969 CLC increased these limits for States party thereto.[127] The 1992 CLC further increased the applicable limitation of liability limits and contains provisions for the amendment of limits without the need for a new convention.[128]

The enacted limits can be found at section 157 of the MSA 1995 as last updated by the Merchant Shipping (Oil Pollution Compensation Limits) Order 2003[129] giving effect to the 2000 Amendment agreed by the IMO.[130]

(h) When does the shipowner lose the right to limit liability?

Only acts or omissions of the owner may remove the owner's right to limit liability under the 1992 CLC. Where, as is the usual case, the shipowner personally is not directly involved in the running of the ship, a search for the "alter ego" of the shipowner in respect of the particular act or omission needs to be undertaken.[131] This must be resolved on a case-by-case basis depending

Table 10.1 Limits of liability for the owner of a ship under the CLCs and their protocols

	Minimum liability for ships of 5,000 grt or less	Liability per ton in addition to minimum liability per ton	Maximum liability
1969 CLC	No special provision	2,000 gold francs	210 million gold francs
1976 CLC Protocol	No special provision	133 SDR	14 million SDR
1992 CLC Protocol	3 million SDR	420 SDR	59.7 million SDR
2000 Amendment	4.51 million SDR	631 SDR	89.77 million SDR

122. Art V.11 and s 165(4) for the situation where both the shipowner and the insurer apply to limit their liability.
123. Arts V.11, VII.8 and see s 165(3) of the MSA 1995.
124. Art VII.8. The insurer cannot however plead the bankruptcy or winding-up of the owner: art VII.8 although they can claim their own bankruptcy or winding-up.
125. Arts I.8., V.1.
126. 1992 CLC, art VII.1 and s 163(1) of the MSA 1995.
127. Protocol to the International Convention on Civil Liability for Oil Pollution Damage, London, 19 November 1976. There was also a 1984 Protocol to the 1969 CLC, which was ratified by insufficient countries for it to be in force anywhere. Its provisions have largely been included in the 1992 CLC.
128. 1992 CLC, art 15, the so-called "tacit amendment procedure".
129. SI 2003/2559.
130. IMO Legal Committee Resolution Leg. 1/82. The amendment was effected by power given to the Secretary of State under s 157(2) MSA 1995 to give effect to alterations of the limits of liability.
131. However, in the first instance decision in *The Erika* the shareholder of the owning company was held liable for the pollution damage as not covered by the protection of the 1992 CLC. See the report on the case submitted by France to the IOPC Fund 92FUND/EXC.40/4/1, 19 February 2008. Such a solution is arguably unacceptable under English law where the shareholders are not considered liable for the liability of the company (see for example *The Evpo Agnic* [1988] 1 WLR 1090; [1988] 2 Lloyd's Rep 411).

on the structure of each company[132] and the way responsibilities are distributed within each company either by the company's constitution or by statutory responsibility or by fact.[133]

The conduct required for the shipowner's act is intention to cause damage, or, recklessness coupled with knowledge that such damage would probably result.[134] Thus where the shipowner or his "alter ego" is reckless, but does not have actual knowledge of the particular kind of loss that occurred, the right to limit liability is preserved.[135] The burden of proving the shipowner's conduct is on the claimant.[136]

The condition under which the shipowner may lose its right to limit liability under the 1992 CLC is very similar to the test applied under the 1996 LLMC where a full discussion is provided.

The wording of the 1992 CLC (Article V.2) is as follows:

The owner shall not be entitled to limit his liability under this Convention if it is proved that the pollution damage resulted from his personal act or omission, committed with the intent to cause such damage, or recklessly and with knowledge that such damage would probably result.

This has been rewritten under section 157(3) of the MSA 1995 stating.[137]

Subsection (1) above shall not apply in a case where it is proved that the discharge or escape, or (as the case may be) the relevant threat of contamination, resulted from anything done or omitted to be done by the owner either with intent to cause any such damage or cost as is mentioned in section 153 or recklessly and in the knowledge that any such damage or cost would probably result.

Three issues need to be discussed in respect of the different wording used. First, whether under section 157(3) the point of reference is the discharge or escape or the relevant threat of contamination, rather than the pollution damage as under Article V(2). It is submitted that this is unlikely to make a difference in practice because the words under section 157(3) refocus the test to intentional or reckless (with knowledge) act to cause *such damage*. The second issue is the change of the term of the 1992 CLC "such damage" to the term "any such damage". Whether this resolves the difficulty under the 1976/1996 LLMC by specifying that the required knowledge refers to knowledge of the general kind of damage rather than the specific one[138] is not clear. The third aspect is that under section 157(3) "anything done or not done by the owner" has replaced his "personal act or omission" under the 1992 CLC. There are several decisions discussing the latter term which exists in the global limitation conventions.[139] However, the removal of the word "personal" may be taken to indicate an intention to break away from the relatively well understood but strict test and develop a new one where the act or omission making the shipowner lose its right to limit does not have to be attributed to the "alter ego" of the shipowner but also to lower ranking persons in the shipowning company. It is submitted that

---

132. See Lord Mustill's judgment in the Court of Appeal decision *Societe Anonyme des Minerais v Grant Trading Inc (The "Ert Stefanie")* [1989] 1 Lloyd's Rep 349. Also the judgment of the Privy Council in *Meridian Global Funds Management Asia Ltd v Securities Commission* [1995] 3 All ER 918 at pp 922–927.

133. See *Lennard's Carrying Company, Limited v Asiatic Petroleum Company Limited* [1915] AC 705 (HL).

134. 1992 CLC, art V.

135. See Chapter 7 p 294 for a discussion on whether knowledge of the type of loss caused is enough for the owner to lose the right to limit or whether knowledge of the exact loss that was suffered is required.

136. Art V.2. It is implicit in the wording.

137. The same modification has also been introduced in the similar test applying to the protection from liability of other persons under s 156(1)(ii).

138. In a collision case, whether negligent navigation would lead to collision with some ship rather than collision with the specific ship see *Schiffahrtsgesellschaft MS "Merkur Sky" MBH & Co KG v MS Leerort Nth Schiffahrts GMBH & Co KG (The Leerort)* [2001] 2 Lloyd's Rep 291.

139. See Chapter 7, p 294.

as the intention of the enactment was to give effect to the 1992 CLC section 157(3) should be interpreted in a way consistent with the 1992 CLC.[140]

(i) The Shipowner's Limitation Fund

Under the 1992 CLC the right to limit liability is available to the shipowner and its insurer[141] only after they have constituted a limitation fund which satisfies the following conditions:[142]

- if an action is brought before one or more competent courts or authorities then the limitation fund must be constituted at one of the competent courts or authority;
- if no action is brought before a competent court the limitation fund can be established at any of the competent courts;[143]
- the fund must be for the full limitation sum;
- the fund must be cash or bank guarantee – alternatives are available only where the competent court accepts other type of guarantees.

After the establishment of a limitation fund which satisfies the 1992 CLC conditions and which is accessible to the claimant,[144] and, provided that the right to limit liability has not been lost, no other assets of the owner, apart from the limitation fund, can be targeted by claimants and the release of any ship or property and relevant security must be ordered.[145]

If the right to limit liability has been lost, presumably, additional security to the extent of the claim including costs and interest would be required for the release of the ship, however this would not be an issue for the 1992 CLC but one for the Admiralty rules of the relevant court. Where the right to limit has not been lost the limitation fund represents the only asset available for the claimants.[146] The limitation fund is to be distributed to all entitled claimants pro rata.[147] However, parts of the fund may be set aside for satisfaction of future claims if the owner or any other person can show that they will be compelled to pay such sums.[148] However, if the limitation fund is exhausted any new claims are likely to remain unsatisfied as the shipowner has paid out its obligations in full, under the 1992 CLC, by establishing a limitation fund. Under English law, section 158 of the MSA 1995 provides for the relevant English procedure and the release of the vessel where an appropriate fund is constituted.[149]

The establishment of a limited fund as the only asset of the owner against which rights can be exercised creates conflicts amongst the claimants of an incident. For every new claim introduced against the fund can potentially restrict the amount recoverable by the other claimants. Thus

---

140. Numerous other international conventions that have the same test, e.g. the Athens Convention relating to the Carriage of Passengers and their Luggage by Sea, 1974 and its 2002 Protocol (art 13), and the International Convention on Liability and Compensation for Damage in Connection with the Carriage of Hazardous and Noxious Substances by Sea, 1996 (art 9.2).

141. 1969 CLC, art V.11. The insurer has the right to establish a limitation fund even where the shipowner's right to limit liability is challenged or lost. However, the 1992 CLC amendment to this article clarifies that the establishment of the limitation fund by the insurer does not prejudice a claimant's rights against the owner where the owner has lost the right to limit liability.

142. 1992 CLC, art V.

143. For the meaning of a competent court see below.

144. 1992 CLC, art VI.2.

145. 1992 CLC, art VI 1.b.

146. Unless they can sue other persons not covered or protected by the CLC under other regimes of liability.

147. 1992 CLC, art V.4.

148. 1992 CLC, art V.7.

149. MSA 1995, s 159. Notably, s 159 will also apply in respect of limitation funds and foreign courts which are parties to the 1992 CLC (s 161).

every claimant within the fund can and in practice will, if they have grounds, resist the addition of a new claim.[150]

(j) Jurisdictional issues

The coastal States which suffer oil pollution damage either in the territorial waters or in the EEZs[151] or where preventive measures have taken place, have jurisdiction over claims under the 1992 CLC. These States are termed competent jurisdictions. After the limitation fund is constituted the courts of the State where the fund is constituted has exclusive jurisdiction in respect of the management and distribution of the limitation fund.[152]

Under the 1992 CLC the owner can establish a limitation fund in any of the competent jurisdictions before any claim has been brought. Thus, the jurisdictional initiative, under the 1992 CLC can be with the shipowner who may wish to invoke one of several competent jurisdictions by establishing a limitation fund there.

The UK enactment[153] restricts the jurisdiction of the UK courts both *in personam* and *in rem* in relation to discharges that do not cause, or threaten pollution damage and no preventive measures are taken in UK territory. This restriction applies in respect of actions against the shipowner and also in actions against any of the other persons protected under section 156(1)(ii).[154]

Final judgments of a competent court must be recognised by all Contracting States.[155]

(k) The role of the 1992 IOPC Fund

The creation of the 1971[156] and the 1992 IOPC Fund Conventions crystallised the undertaking of the oil industry and, in particular, oil importers to contribute to the compensation of oil pollution damage. The management and organisation of their contribution is effected by the creation of an intergovernmental organisation: the IOPC Fund.

The 1992 IOPC Fund covers situations in which the owner's liability is excluded under Article III.2 of the 1992 CLC. Thus the Fund will pay out[157] where the pollution damage was caused by a natural phenomenon of an exceptional, inevitable and irresistible character, or was wholly caused by an act or omission done with intent to cause damage by a third party. In addition the IOPC Fund will pay where the damage was wholly caused by the negligence or other wrongful act of any Government or other authority responsible for the maintenance of lights or other navigational aids.[158] Thus in the situations mentioned above, although the shipowner will not be liable, an equal amount of compensation will be provided by the IOPC Fund.

---

150. See for example the Scottish Outer House decision in *Anderson Ors v International Oil Pollution Compensation Fund* [2001] Scottish Court of Session 34 (14 February 2001) where the right is accepted on the basis of *van Eijck & Zoon v Somerville* [1906] 8 F 22 (HL).

151. 1992 CLC, art IX.1. The reference to the art II defining zones which are the EEZ or equivalent jurisdictional zones, was made by the 1992 Protocol. Under the 1969 CLC art IX.1 the competent jurisdiction (is) for the actions for compensation for damages or preventive measures in the territorial waters or on land of a Contracting State, will be in the courts of such Contracting State.

152. 1992 CLC, art IX.3.

153. MSA 1995, s 166.

154. Unless the actions of such persons have the consequence that they lose the protection under the test in s 156(1)(ii).

155. 1969 and 1992 CLC, art X, unless obtained by fraud or without reasonable notice to the defendant and a fair opportunity to defend. See also s 166(4) of the MSA 1995.

156. The 1971 IOPC Fund ceased to be in force on 24 May 2002.

157. The liability of the Fund in UK is prescribed under s 175 of the MSA 1995.

158. s 175(1)(a)(iii) of the MSA 1995.

The IOPC Fund also covers oil pollution liability in cases where, and to the extent that, the shipowner and its insurer are financially incapable of providing the required compensation under the 1992 CLC Convention[159] or where the damages exceed the owners' liability.[160]

In situations where there is oil pollution damage but the vessel that caused the oil spill has not been identified the claimant can still be compensated by the IOPC Fund if it can prove that the oil that caused the damage came from at least one ship.[161] Thus the Fund is liable for compensation from "mystery" oil spills where the ship that caused the damage is not identified.[162]

However, the IOPC Fund will not be liable where the damage arises from acts of war, hostilities, civil war, insurrection or from a governmental ship used in a governmental mission or where the claimant cannot prove that damage resulted from a ship.[163] In such cases neither the shipowner nor the IOPC Fund have any liability under the 1992 CLC and thus the claimants will have to try and recover against other parties.

The shipowner's expenses for preventive measures falling under the definition of the 1992 CLC Article I.6 rank equally with the pollution damage or clean-up claims by other parties. Thus to the extent the shipowner's limit is exceeded these are recoverable from the IOPC Fund[164] in the same way and in the same proportion as other claims.[165]

(l) Time bar

Claims against the IOPC Fund must be brought before a competent court within three years of the incident that caused the pollution.[166] However, situations may arise where it is not evident immediately after the incident that the shipowner is either exempted from liability under Article III.2. of the 1992 CLC, is unable to pay,[167] or simply that damages will exceed the shipowner's limits of liability. To avoid unnecessary claims against the IOPC Fund the Fund Convention enables the claimant to avoid the three-year time bar by just providing a notification to the IOPC Fund in a way that will enable the Fund to intervene in the legal proceedings if it decides to do so.[168]

However, such notification will be sufficient to avoid the three-year time bar only and unless the claimant brings a lawsuit within six years from the time the damage occurred the action will be time barred nevertheless.[169] Although the use of the notification to avoid the three-year time bar is clearly stated in Article 6 this mechanism is somewhat surprising. For example, assume that the IOPC Fund decides to intervene in an action against the shipowner. Such intervention

---

159. 1992 Fund Convention, art 4.1(b) and s 175(1)(b) of the MSA 1995.
160. 1992 Fund Convention, art 4.1(c) and s 175(1)(c) of the MSA 1995.
161. For methods employed in identifying the pollution source see: S. Stout, G.Douglas, A. Uhler, K. McCarthy and S. Emsbo-Mattingly, "Identifying the Source of Mystery Waterborne Oil Spills: A Case for Quantitative Chemical Fingerprinting" (2005) 17(1) *Environmental Claims Journal* 71.
162. However, because of the existence of alternative sources of pollution, for example tank washing, it may be difficult to establish liability under the Fund without identifying an occurrence that causes pollution damage, that is, the "incident" under the CLC, a definition preserved in the Fund Convention art I.1.
163. 1992 Fund Convention, art III.2.a and s 175(7) of the MSA 1995.
164. 1992 Fund Convention, art 4.1.
165. 1992 CLC, art V.8 and s 175(6) of the MSA 1995.
166. 1971/1992 Fund Convention, art 6.1. MSA 1995, s 178(1) stated originally that the limit when a note to the Fund is given is "not later than three years after the claim against the Fund arose". This has been modified under the Merchant Shipping (Pollution) Act 2006 to "not later than three years after the damage arose". This makes the provision consistent with the wording of the Fund Convention.
167. Under s 175(5) the owner and the insurer are considered unable to meet their obligations if all reasonable steps to obtain legal remedies have been taken but were not sufficient to make them pay.
168. 1971/1992 Fund Convention, art 7.6.
169. 1971/1992 Fund Convention, art 6.1.

would not by itself initiate claims against the IOPC Fund. Why in such a case a new action needs to be started within six years is not clear.[170]

Provided action has started within the appropriate limits and the damage is covered by the 1992 IOPC Fund Convention, the claimant will be entitled to recover compensation for pollution damage in addition to the amount received under the 1992 CLC. The limits of liability payable under the 1992 Fund and the 1992 CLC are available as an overall total amount against which recovery is possible. In other words, the limits of liability established by the Fund include the owners' limits of liability under the 1992 CLC, meaning that whether the shipowner pays its part or whether it does not pay anything, the overall available compensation will be the same. Thus in cases where the shipowner pays its part the IOPC Fund will "top-up" the amount, while in other cases the whole compensation will be paid by the IOPC Fund. The limits of liability under the various versions of the Fund Convention and Protocols can be seen in Table 10.2.

The limits of liability for the IOPC Fund can be found in section 176 and appear in Part I of Schedule 5 to the MSA 1995 which has been updated by the Merchant Shipping (Oil Pollution Compensation Limits) Order 2003[171] giving effect to the 2000 Amendment agreed by the IMO.[172]

The 1992 IOPC Fund is supported financially by every oil importer who has imported within a year 150,000 tons or more of contributing oil[173] into a Contracting State.[174] Only direct imports by sea or imports by land from a non-Contracting State to which they were carried by sea count.[175] In addition, breaking up the importer into smaller companies[176] so that their import drops below the 150,000 tons limit cannot be used to evade liability because the obligation is preserved under Article 10.2 of the 1992 IOPC Fund Convention where the import is made by associated persons, defined, as "any subsidiary or commonly controlled entity".[177]

(m) Jurisdiction for actions under the 1992 IOPC Fund Convention

Jurisdiction under the 1992 IOPC Fund Convention is more complicated than the distribution of jurisdiction under the 1992 CLC. This is because States having competent jurisdiction under the 1992 CLC may or may not be party to the 1992 IOPC Fund Convention. Thus, two situations are provided for. First, where an action has started before a competent jurisdiction under the 1992 CLC;

---

170. See N. Gaskell, *Merchant Shipping Act 1995, Current Law Statutes Annotated Vol 2* (Sweet and Maxwell 1995), at pp 21–204 for discussion of incidents where the claimant considered that notification had been given but the IOPC Fund took the view that the Convention's time bar should operate.

171. SI 2003/2559.

172. IMO LEG. 2/82. The amendment was effected by power given to the Secretary of State under s 176(5) of the MSA 1995 to give effect to alterations of the limits of liability.

173. Contributing oil is defined under art 1.3 of the 1992 IOPC Fund Convention to include crude oil and fuel oil which are further defined as follows: "crude oil" as any liquid hydrocarbon mixture occurring naturally in the earth whether or not treated for transportation. It also includes crude oils from which certain distillate fractions have been removed (sometimes referred to as "topped crudes") or to which certain distillate fractions have been added (sometimes referred to as "spiked" or "reconstituted" crudes). "fuel oil" means heavy distillates or residues from crude oil or blends of such materials intended for use as a fuel for the production of heat or power of a quality equivalent to the "American Society for Testing and Materials' Specification for Number Four Fuel Oil (Designation D 396–69)", or heavier. See s 173(10) of the MSA 1995 for the UK enactment.

174. s 173 of the MSA 1995 provides for contributions to the Fund and also empowers the Secretary of State to collect the necessary information in order to identify the contributing parties (s 174); s 174 also provides for penalties in case of non-compliance or provision of false information in respect of a request for information under this section.

175. 1992 IOPC Fund Convention, art 10.1.

176. According to the Final Regulatory Impact Assessment on the Supplementary Fund Protocol (Department of Trade, UK) in 2003, 13 companies in the UK have exceeded the limit. The range of contribution varies between years as contributions are made after incidents involving the Fund occur. In some years no contributions were requested while in others contributions up to £0.08 per ton of oil imported were made.

177. Art 10.32(b). The question whether a person comes within this definition is to be determined by the national law of the Contracting State. See s 173 of the MSA 1995.

Table 10.2 Limits of liability for oil pollution damage under the Fund conventions

Convention/Protocol	Limits of liability (million)	Monetary unit
1971 Fund	450–900[1]	Gold francs
1976 Fund Protocol	60	SDR
1992 Fund Protocol – not in force	135[2]	SDR
2000 Fund Amendment (tacit acceptance)	203[3]	SDR
2003 Supplementary Fund	750	SDR

Notes

The 1971 Fund and its 1976 Protocol are no longer in force and are included here for the purposes of comparison. Only the 1992 Fund limits, its Protocol of 2000 and the supplementary Fund are currently applicable.

1. The original limit was 450 million which was gradually increased to 900 million in accordance with the 1971 Fund, arte 4.6.

2. The limit is to be raised to 200 million SDR when three States contributing to the Fund receive more than 600 million tons of oil per annum (1992 Fund Convention, art 4.4(c)).

3. The limit is to be raised to 300.7 million SDR when three States contributing to the Fund receive more than 600 million tons of oil per annum.

if this State is also a party to the 1992 Fund Convention, then the same court has jurisdiction against the 1992 IOPC Fund.

However, where the action has started in a competent jurisdiction, under the 1992 CLC, which is not a party to the 1992 Fund Convention, then the IOPC Fund may be sued either at its place of business (England) or in any of the other competent jurisdictions which are parties to the 1992 IOPC Fund Convention.[178]

There are no provisions in either of the CLCs for multiple proceedings, thus the conflict of laws provisions for each Contracting State would apply in such cases.

Final judgments of a competent court must be recognised by all Contracting States,[179] however the IOPC Fund is not bound by judgments in proceedings in which it has not participated.[180]

Subrogation of rights of claimants who have been paid out by the IOPC Fund is also provided for.[181] This subrogation covers third party claims against the shipowner and its insurer. In addition it covers subrogation of rights against third parties, for example where the shipowner pays for pollution mitigation and prevention expenses which it can then recover against another ship following a collision. Thus presently, if the IOPC Fund fully settles the pollution damage claim with a victim, the IOPC Fund is then entitled under section 179(1) by subrogation to recover the shipowner's part of liability.

Where public authorities pay compensation to victims of pollution damage then the public authorities acquire any rights the victims have against the IOPC Fund.[182]

(n) Challenges to the 1992 CLC and the 1992 IOPC Fund system

There are some indications that the established system is under pressure. Indeed, the *Prestige* incident appears to be testing the entire arrangement. There is ongoing litigation in several States 15 years after the incident and payments have only partly been made hitherto.[183] Thus, the objec-

178. 1992 Fund Convention, art 7.3. The IOPC Fund also has rights to intervene (art 7(4)).

179. 1992 CLC, art X, unless obtained by fraud or without reasonable notice to the defendant and a fair opportunity to defend. See s 177 of the MSA 1995 for the UK Enactment.

180. 1992 Fund Convention, art 7.5.

181. 1992 Fund Convention, art 9; s 179(1) MSA 1995.

182. s 179(2) MSA 1995. The Fund as a legal person or the Fund's Director can sue and be sued (s 180 MSA 1995).

183. IOPC/APR16/3/2.

tive of quick settlement of claims and avoidance of court proceedings in this case have not been achieved. Probably the most controversial decision is that of the Spanish Supreme Court of January 2016. The Supreme Court reversed the decision on the facts of a lower Court and found the master criminally liable for damages to the environment with civil liability. Recalling that the master is, in general, immune from proceedings unless acting intentionally or recklessly and with knowledge of the relevant damage, this was arguably a breach of the channelling of liability. It further held the shipowner to have subsidiary civil liability without a right to limit its liability. Perhaps even more controversially, the P&I Club was held to be directly liable to the limit of the insurance policy of US$1,000 million, instead of the 1992 CLC limits despite the express protection afforded to the liability insurer under the 1992 CLC. In addition, the Supreme Court also recognised the possibility of moral damage claims and other heads of claims, which arguably do not fall within the pollution damage definition of the Convention, at least as this was agreed during the negotiations. Some of the claims made by Spain are based on economic models, a practice discouraged by the IOPC Fund.[184] The decision provides an example in which the national court had reached a decision through a national interpretation of the 1992 CLC utilising the liability regime and the supporting financial security mechanisms but ignoring the compromises on which the Convention was based and the counterbalancing limitation of liability arrangements and the extent of damages recoverable under this international convention. The *quantum* in the Spanish proceedings remains to be decided in further proceedings. Because the 1992 CLC and the IOPCF provide for enforcement of final decisions in all Contracting States, the consequence is that there ought to be little discretion in delaying the enforcement of such decisions after the final judgment of the court that has jurisdiction. In addition, such decisions could be directly enforceable in England against the P&I Club. If enforced and the P&I Club becomes directly liable to the limit of insurance cover,this would require alterations in the way the insurance cover is provided in order to reduce the exposure of the insurer. The P&I Club in question, to protect itself against enforcement, argues that there were two distinct categories of claims pursued against it by Spain and France in their respective courts. The first category includes those claims under the CLC for which it accepted liability. However, for the other claims it successfully argued that these are claims under the insurance contract which are expressly agreed to be determined by English arbitration and which are subject to the pay-to-be paid rule. On this basis they applied for a non-liability arbitration award which they then successfully enforced in the High Court.[185] It remains to be seen whether the decision will provide a successful defence in relation to the Spanish court decisions in respect of liability in excess of the 1992 CLC limits and for claims not considered by the IOPC Fund as falling under the regime. In any case, the master of the *Prestige* has appealed his conviction.

In another pollution case[186] where the tanker *Plate Princess* polluted lake Maracaibo in 1997 the claimants attempted to enforce the Venzuelan judgment of around £51 million in the UK against the IOPC Fund. At the time of the incident the 1992 Fund was not applicable to Venezuela which was still under the 1971 IOPC Fund. The successful defence, was that the judgment was against the 1971 IOPC Fund, which is a different legal person from the 1992 IOPC Fund.[187] In this way the international organization set up to pay compensation avoided a judgment against

---

184. IOPC/APR16/3/2.

185. *The London Steam Ship Owners Mutual Insurance Association Ltd v The Kingdom of Spain and Another (the "Prestige") (No 2)* [2013] EWHC 3188 (Comm); [2014] 1 Lloyd's Rep 309. See the Court of Appeal decision [2016] EWCA Civ 386; [2016] 1 Lloyd's Rep 641.

186. *Sindicato Unico de Pescadores del Municipio Miranda del Estado Zulia v International Oil Pollution Compensation Fund* [2015] EWHC 2476 (QB); [2016] 1 Lloyd's Rep 332.

187. Ibid., [62] – [63].

it by a national court of one of the Contracting States. A third case was the successful effort of another P&I Club to freeze assets of the 1971 IOPC Fund which at the time was in the process of being wound up, for a contribution owed to shipowners after a Venezuelan court judgment in respect of pollution arising from the grounding of the *Nissos Amorgos*.[188] Claims in the Venezuelan courts, considered by the IOPC Fund as time-barred, were successful and the shipowner's P&I Club tried to obtain security for the contribution by the IOPC Fund to claims exceeding its liability. The IOPC Fund contested the claim on the basis of the Headquarters Agreement of 27 July 1979, which afforded to the 1971 IOPC Fund various privileges and immunities. This was, in turn, enacted in the International Oil Pollution Compensation Fund (Privileges and Immunities) Order 1979 (SI 1979/912). The court found that the protection provided to the IOPC Fund under the Headquarters Agreement was not enacted properly in the relevant statutory instrument and, as a result, the IOPC Fund could be subjected to a freezing order for the claims brought in England.[189]

This series of cases, as well as, the outstanding cases for the *Prestige* as well as other incidents demonstrate that the protection of the balance agreed under the 1992 CLC and the 1992 IOPC Fund, can be significantly undermined by national courts. It appears that the preservation of the current system is reliant on the application of English law.

(o) The 2003 Supplementary Fund

The 2003 Supplementary Fund was created following major oil incidents at the Spanish and French coast which made clear that the limits of liability under the two-tier system of the 1992 CLC and Fund were inadequate, especially for coastal areas where the clean-up costs were expensive. Following very strong political pressure from the EU, the IMO quickly developed a third tier of compensation which is available but not compulsory for all parties to the 1992 CLC and IOPC Fund Conventions. In this way States who may consider that the 1992 IOPC Fund limits are adequate to cover their needs in case of an accident can preserve the expenses imposed on their oil importers without burdening them with the additional costs to support the 2003 Supplementary Fund, while other States may opt to include the 2003 Supplementary Fund as a third tier of compensation for oil pollution victims.

The 2003 Supplementary Fund increases the compensation available to victims of oil pollution damage to a total of 750 million SDR.[190] This third tier of compensation is available only to those Contracting States of the 1992 IOPC Fund which are also Contracting States to the 2003 Supplementary Fund. Any importer of 150,000 tons of oil or more, in any given year, to any Contracting State will have to contribute to the Supplementary Fund. In the UK the Merchant Shipping (Oil Pollution) (Supplementary Fund Protocol) Order 2006 incorporates[191] the 2003 Supplementary Fund in the MSA 1995.[192]

188. *Assuranceforeningen Gard Gjensidig v The International Oil Pollution Compensation Fund* [2014] EWHC 1394 (Comm); [2014] 2 Lloyd's Rep 219.

189. In a decision contained in IOPC/OCT16/11/1 the 1992 Fund Assembly approved an Agreement on standard terms relating to interim payments. This gave an option to shipowners to choose, where there were interim payments, to make the payments on behalf of the shipowner or the shipowner and the Fund. This, it is hoped, will avoid complications similar to those that arose in the *Nisos Amorgos* case.

190. Adopted on 16 May 2003, entered into force 3 March 2005. Enacted in England, by the Merchant Shipping (Supplementary Fund Protocol) Order 2006. The Supplementary Fund Protocol entered into force in the UK on 8 September 2006.

191. According to the Final Regulatory Impact Assessment on the Supplementary Fund Protocol (Department of Trade, UK) the worst case scenario will burden the oil importers to the UK by £82.7 million or £1.44 per ton.

192. SI 2006/1265 introducing changes in sections 172–178 and adding Schedule 5ZA to the MSA 1995. The Admiralty jurisdiction of the High Court is also modified (s 20(5a)) to include claims related to the Supplementary Fund.

(p) STOPIA 2006 and TOPIA 2006

The creation of the 2003 Supplementary Fund may have resolved the demands of the EU for higher compensation to pollution victims but has disturbed the agreed balance between shipowners and the oil industry. The reason is that the funds for the 2003 Supplementary Fund are solely provided by the oil importers. The issue has been resolved by two private voluntary agreements:[193] the Tanker Oil Pollution Indemnification Agreement (TOPIA) 2006 and the Small Tanker Oil Pollution Indemnification Agreement (STOPIA) 2006.[194]

TOPIA 2006 applies in pollution accidents in countries which are members of the 2003 Supplementary Fund. Under this contract the shipowners agree to pay 50 per cent of the money paid out by the Supplementary Fund to which rights are given under Clause XL of this agreement.

STOPIA 2006 covers pollution damage to all States party to 1992 CLC, arising from tankers smaller than 29,548 grt, insured by a Club and reinsured under the Pooling arrangement of the International Group of the P&I Clubs. The owners of such ships are undertaking, in effect, to voluntarily raise their limit of liability to 20,000,000 SDR. Rights are given to the 1992 Fund under Clause XL. In the case of excessive damage by small tankers in a Supplementary Fund State, both TOPIA 2006 and STOPIA 2006 are relevant.[195]

These arrangements do not affect the rights of claimants for pollution damage and only concern the arrangement between shipowning and cargo interests on who contributes how much in the compensation.

4. THE 2001 BUNKER POLLUTION CONVENTION[196]

The CLC/IOPC Fund framework applies only to pollution damage from bunker oil and cargo for tankers. Thus pollution damage for bunker oil from other ships was not subject to any international convention until the entry into force of the 2001 Bunker Oil Pollution Convention (2001 BOPC).[197]

The 2001 BOPC establishes strict liability for the registered owner, bareboat charterer, manager and operator of the ship[198] in respect of oil pollution damage from bunker oil. It also establishes compulsory insurance[199] for the registered owner and direct action of third party claimants

---

193. See 92FUND/A.ES.10/131 SUPPFUND/A/ES.2/February 2006. Both agreements are applicable to ships entered in one of the P&I Clubs which are members of the International Group and reinsured through the pooling arrangements of the International Group (see p 458 of Chapter 11). Ships insured by an International Group Club but not covered by the pooling arrangement may agree with the Club concerned to be covered. Both agreements are subject to English law and jurisdiction and have two time bars one at four years after the pollution damage occurred and an absolute one after seven years.

194. 92FUND/A.ES.10/131 SUPPFUND/A/ES.2/February 2006 states that most of the global tonnage is subject to these arrangements. In addition it appears that as the premium paid by the P&I Clubs is the same irrespective of whether the shipowner volunteers to be party to these agreements or not, there is, in effect, no benefit in opting out.

195. The STOPIA 2016 and TOPIA 2016 have been modified to provide for the situation where sanctions prohibit them from paying under the schemes. See IOPC/OCT16/4/3/2/Rev.1.

196. See also: M.N. Tsimplis, "The Bunker Pollution Convention 2001: Completing and Harmonising the Liability Regime for Oil Pollution from Ships?" [2005] LMCLQ 83–100; N. Gaskell and C. Forrest, "Marine Pollution Damage in Australia: Implementing the Bunker Oil Convention 2001 and the Supplementary Fund Protocol 2003" (2008) 27 UQLJ 103–165.

197. The 2001 BOPC came into force on 21 November 2008. Before that date the Merchant Shipping Act 1995, s 154 provided strict liability for bunker oil pollution damage under English law. The Convention was enacted through the Merchant Shipping (Oil Pollution) (Bunkers Convention) Regulations 2006, SI 2006/1244, which modifies Chapter 3 of Part 6 of the Merchant Shipping Act 1995, implementing Council Decision 2002/762/EC which authorises Member States to sign, ratify or accede to the 2001 BOPC (OJ L 256, 25 September 2002, at p 7).

198. 2001 BOPC, art 1.3 and MSA 1995, s 153A (7).

199. 2001 BOPC, art 7 and MSA 1995, s 163A(2).

against the insurer.[200] The Convention does not affect any right of limitation of liability established in national legislation or by international conventions, although it does give a clear suggestion to parties that the 1996 Protocol to the 1976 Convention on Limitation of Liability for Maritime Claims (LLMC 1996) provides the best background for its application.[201] While the Convention applies to all ships, compulsory insurance applies only to the registered owner of ships larger than 1,000 grt.[202] The amount for which this insurance is required corresponds to the limits of liability available to the shipowner under applicable national law but may not exceed the 1976 LLMC limits, as amended.

(a) The scope and definitions of the Convention

The 2001 BOPC has been developed for the purpose of filling in the gap left open by the CLC/IOPC Fund 1992 scheme regarding pollution from bunkers. There is no overlap between the 1992 CLC and the 2001 BOPC because the latter does not apply to pollution damage as defined by 1992 CLC[203] whether or not compensation can be retrieved under the 1992 CLC.[204] The avoidance of overlap with the 1992 CLC under English law is achieved by having two sections for liability in the MSA 1995, section 153 which governs the 1992 CLC and section 153A introduced by the Merchant Shipping (Oil Pollution) (Bunkers Convention) Regulations 2006. Section 153A excludes liability for bunkers from a ship to which section 153 applies. Thus, section 153A creates liability for the owner of any ship for pollution damage from bunker oil for all situations the 1992 CLC does not cover.

The 2001 BOPC covers only hydrocarbon mineral oils used or intended to be used for the operation or propulsion of the ship as fuel or lubrication as well as the residues from the use of such oil. These are defined as "bunker oil".[205] Thus, the distinction between cargo and bunkers is based on the demonstration of intention of use. The presence of such oil in the consumption tanks or the pipelines would probably provide such evidence but where the oil is stored in other tanks this may not be as easy to demonstrate.[206]

The 2001 BOPC covers liability arising from incidents[207] which either cause pollution damage or create a "grave and imminent threat to cause pollution damage".[208] In turn, "pollution dam-

---

200. 2001 BOPC, art 7.10 and MSA 1995, s 165(1A).

201. MSA 1995, s 168 deems any liability to damages arising from bunker oil pollution damage as defined to be damage to property under paragraph 1(a) of art 2 of the 1976/1996 LLMC.

202. 2001 BOCP, art 7 and MSA 1995, s 163A(2); s 163A(7) creates a right to detention if a ship leaves a port without a valid insurance certificate.

203. CLC 1992, art 1.1 defines pollution damage as:

> (a) loss or damage caused outside the ship by contamination resulting from escape or discharge of oil from the ship, wherever such escape may occur, provided that compensation for impairment of the environment other than loss of profit from such impairment shall be limited to costs of reasonable measures of reinstatement actually taken or to be undertaken; (b) the cost of preventive measures and further loss of damage caused by preventive measures.

This wording is very similar to that of 2001 BOPC but the difference in the two conventions arises from (a) the definition of ship which under 1992 CLC art 1.1 covers only ships actually constructed for the carriage of oil and actually carrying oil and (b) from the difference in the terms of "oil" in CLC 1992, art 1.5 and "bunker oil" under 2001 BOPC, art 1.5.

204. 2001 BOPC, art 4.1.

205. 2001 BOPC, art 1.5.

206. See s 170(1) of the MSA 1995 as amended by the Merchant Shipping (Oil Pollution) (Bunkers Convention) Regulations 2006, Statutory Instrument 2006 No 1244 for the equivalent definition in the UK enactment.

207. Defined as an event or series of events having the same origin (2001 BOPC, art 1.8). This definition is identical to CLC 1969 art 1.8. It is unclear whether the definition of incident covers the bunkering process (LEG 74/4/1).

208. 2001 BOPC, art 1.8. See s 153A(1) and (2) of the MSA 1995 as amended by the Merchant Shipping (Oil Pollution) (Bunkers Convention) Regulations 2006, SI 2006/1244 for the UK enactment.

age" is defined as any loss or damage caused outside the ship[209] by spilled bunker oil[210] and the costs of preventive measures and any further damage caused by the preventive measures. Thus damage by explosion or fire is not covered although the damage arising from the bunker oil spill that followed the explosion or the fire is covered. Similarly, claims related to general damage to the environment which are unquantifiable are probably not covered although the exclusion of such claims is subject to the interpretation of the 2001 BOPC by national courts as the experience of the CLC and IOPC Fund Conventions has indicated.[211]

Any seagoing vessel and seaborne craft of any type whatsoever are covered by the 2001 BOPC definition of ship.[212] The term seagoing vessel is also used in other conventions[213] but it is not free of uncertainty.[214]

The 2001 BOPC application is consistent with that of the 1992 CLC.[215] That is, it applies only to pollution damage on the territory, the territorial sea or the EEZ or an equivalent zone[216] of a Contracting State.[217] In addition, the 2001 BOPC applies to preventive measures wherever these are taken.[218] It suffices that the pollution damage has been suffered within these jurisdictional zones.

(b) Liability for bunker oil pollution

The shipowner is strictly liable for pollution damage from bunker oil spilled.[219] The definition of shipowner includes the registered owner, the bareboat charterer, the manager and the operator of a ship.[220] Thus it is much wider than the equivalent definition under 1992 CLC, which imposes liability only on the registered owner. Moreover there is no requirement that the shipowner should actually be using the ship at the time of the incident. Thus the 2001 BOPC makes more than one person liable but only one, the registered shipowner, has to carry compulsory

209. 2001 BOPC, art 1.9(a).
210. With the limitation that in relation to the impairment of the environment only loss of profit and reasonable reinstatement measures (undertaken or to be undertaken) are covered (2001 BOPC, art 1.9). The definition of pollution damage in 2001 BOPC, art 1.9 is identical to CLC 1969, art 6.
211. Italian courts, for example, have repeatedly allowed claims for environmental damage (Colin de La Rue and Charles B. Anderson, *Shipping and the Environment* (2nd edn, LLP 2009), at pp 484–485). Notably it appears that the wording of art III.4 of the 1992 CLC, although intended to exclude any such possibility of claims in fact does not clearly do so. M.N. Tsimplis (fn 196).
212. 2001 BOPC, art 1.1. See also CLC 1992, art 1.1. "Ship means any seagoing vessel and seaborne craft, of any type whatsoever". The definition was considered unclear by the International Association of Drilling Contractors in relation to mobile offshore drilling units (MODU) in two respects: (a) whether for a vessel to be covered by 2001 BOPC it must be both a seagoing vessel and seaborne craft (MODUs are probably not as they are floating during part of their operation); and (b) the meaning of the term seagoing (LEG 79/6/2). See s 170(1) of the MSA 1995 for the UK definition.
213. For example, in art 1.3 of the 1974 Athens Convention relating to the Carriage of Passengers and their Luggage by Sea.
214. See for example the comments of N. Gaskell, *Merchant Shipping Act 1995, Current Law Statutes* (fn 171) cl 21 at pp 21–360 and 21–431 and the discussion in Chapter 6 and the decision in *Michael v Musgrove* (t/a YNYS Ribs) [2011] EWHC 1438 (Admlty); [2012] 2 Lloyd's Rep 37.
215. Compare 2001 BOPC, art 2 to CLC 1992, art 2 and 2001 BOPC, art 1.9(a) to CLC 1992, art 1.6(a).
216. Art 2(a)(ii).
217. s 153A refers to damage and measures in the territory of the UK (s 153A(1)) and, if liability arises under the section, for liability for damage and measures in the territory of other 2001 BOPC States. In turn the UK territory is defined to consist of the territorial sea and the British fishery limits set out under the Fishery Limits Act 1976 and the territorial waters and the EEZs (or 200 mile zones) of other CLC States (s 170(4)).
218. Art 2(b) but for the purpose of prevention of damage from bunker pollution in the territorial waters of a coastal State party to 2001 BOPC.
219. 2001 BOPC, art 3.1.
220. 2001 BOPC, art 1.3. This definition can be found in the UK enactment in s 153(7) of the MSA 1995, introduced by the Merchant Shipping (Oil Pollution) (Bunkers Convention) Regulations 2006.

insurance. There is no requirement of fault for the liability to arise but the shipowner can nevertheless avoid liability if it can prove that the damage was caused by an act of war,[221] an unpredictable natural phenomenon,[222] an act of sabotage[223] or (wholly) caused by defective navigational aids due to the fault of the responsible authority. Contributory negligence or sabotage by the victim of pollution damage may also exonerate the shipowner partly or fully.[224] If only one vessel is involved but more than one person under the definition of shipowner is liable, the liability is joint and several.[225] This means that State authorities can recover from the financially stronger or more accessible shipowner. The 2001 BOPC is the only way to claim against the shipowner.[226] In the UK enactment this is also reflected in section 156(2A) of the MSA 1995 which precludes any recovery other than under the particular section irrespective of whether liability arises or not.

The channelling of claims within the 2001 BOPC is restricted to the shipowner only.[227] The UK enactment modifies the 2001 BOPC and excludes from liability any servant or agent of the owner and any person engaged in any capacity on board or performing any service for the ship; salvors, their servants and agents and any person involved in pollution prevention or mitigation activities and their servants or agents.[228] Thus these persons are protected[229] under the MSA 1995 whether they become liable for oil or bunker pollution from tankers or non-tankers. This is arguably an improvement on the 2001 BOPC and, strictly speaking, is not against the implementation of the 2001 BOPC as the Convention is silent on the liability of these parties.

Where bunker oil from more than one ship causes pollution damage there could be a problem in determining which of the two or more shipowners will be liable under the 2001 BOPC if the damage caused is not separable. To resolve this problem the Convention provides for the owners of both (or all if there are more than two) vessels concerned to be jointly and severally liable but only for the non-separable part of damage.[230]

The 2001 BOPC liability does not apply to government vessels used for non-commercial purposes[231] unless the Contracting State so prescribes.[232] All commercial ships whether private or State-owned are subject to liability and jurisdiction as determined by 2001 BOPC.[233]

---

221. 2001 BOPC, art 3.3(a) "act of war, hostilities, civil war, insurrection". These words are not defined in the Convention.

222. 2001 BOPC, art 3.3(a) "the damage resulted from . . . a natural phenomenon of an exceptional, inevitable and irresistible character". Since there is no requirement for the natural phenomenon to be unforeseeable it is presumably correct to argue that the availability of weather forecasts and warnings would not deprive the shipowner of the benefit of this section, unless there is negligence that caused the damage.

223. 2001 BOPC, art 3.3(b). See also s 155 as amended for the exceptions in the UK enactment.

224. 2001 BOPC, art 3.4.

225. 2001 BOPC, art 3.2. As pointed out by the US submission to the IMO (LEG 77/4/3) joint and several liability essentially means that State authorities can ignore litigation between the parties and recover from the financially healthiest shipowner.

226. 2001 BOPC, art 3.5.

227. By contrast with the equivalent more protective restriction under the 1992 CLC which protects numerous other parties: see art III.4 of the 1992 CLC.

228. MSA 1995, s 156 (2B) introduced by the Merchant Shipping (Oil Pollution) (Bunkers Convention) Regulations 2006.

229. Unless the damage has resulted by their "personal act or omission, committed with intent to cause damage, or recklessly and with knowledge that such damage would probably result", see MSA 1995, s 156(2) (ii).

230. The test is whether the damage is "reasonably" separable (art 5) under the 2001 BOPC. See s 153A(6) of the MSA 1995 as amended.

231. 2001 BOPC, art 4.2. See s 167 of the MSA 1995 as amended by the Merchant Shipping (Oil Pollution) (Bunkers Convention) Regulations 2006.

232. 2001 BOPC, art 4.3: in which case the Secretary-General of IMO shall be notified of the terms and conditions under which this will happen.

233. 2001 BOPC, art 4.4. The Contracting States undertake to waive any rights as sovereign States in respect of these vessels. See s 167 (3) of the MSA 1995 as amended for the relevant provision in the UK enactment.

(c) Time bar

A six-year absolute time bar from the time of the incident and a three-year bar from the time of the damage are prescribed.[234] The UK enactment contains both time bars in section 162 of the MSA 1995.[235] The dual time bar reflects the possibility of oil pollution damage arising later than the shipping incident, for example by leakage of bunker oil from a wreck and the need to provide some leeway for this possibility.

(d) Limitation of liability

The 2001 BOPC does not set new limits of liability.[236] Nor does it affect the right of the ship-owner or the insurer to limit liability "under any applicable national or international regime".[237] The 1976 LLMC, as amended, is expressly given as such an example.[238]

Thus, pollution damage by bunker oil, if covered by the 1992 CLC and IOPC Fund 1992 Conventions, is subject to the limits of those conventions. However, if bunker oil pollution damage is not covered by the 1992 CLC, it falls under the 2001 BOPC and would be subject to any limitation of liability applicable in each State party, including by way of the relevant global limitation regime.

Potentially, bunker pollution damage claims may not be subject to limitation of liability at all under a national regime. With respect to the 1996 LLMC Article 2.1(a) would arguably cover property damage and consequential loss linked to the property damage. However, it is unlikely that pure economic loss suffered by, for example, fishermen and hoteliers will be subject to Article 2.1(a) of the 1996 LLMC when they are not linked to property damage. Similarly questions related to clean-up and consequential damages in marine areas may be an issue. Article 2.1(b) referring to damage for "infringement of rights" can be argued as covering pollution clean-up costs as well as economic loss claims.[239] Article 2.1(c) of the 1996 LLMC applies where the ship is sunk, wrecked, stranded or abandoned and cover amongst other things, "rendering harmless" anything that is or was onboard the ship, which arguably would include cleaning up or neutral-ising bunkers. However, this section does not cover consequential losses. Thus where following the clean-up operation there are losses, for example, by restrictions in fishing or by tourists choosing to stay away because of the chemicals used in the clean-up operation, such losses will not be covered by this section and are likely to remain unlimited.

Therefore, even where there is a national limitation of liability regime it is not certain that all pollution damage claims would be subject to limitation under the corresponding regime simply because that regime, on its wording, may not be able to cover the claims. In such a case these claims will be unlimited.[240]

In the UK's case, the applicable global regime is the 1996 LLMC. Section 168 of the MSA 1995 expressly deems liability for damage caused by bunker oil that arises under section 153A to constitute "property damage" within the meaning of the 1996 LLMC. This arguably resolves

---

234. 2001 BOPC, art 8. As under the 1992 CLC.
235. As amended by the Merchant Shipping (Oil Pollution) (Bunkers Convention) Regulations 2006.
236. This was a much-debated issue. See M.N. Tsimplis (fn 196) for the various options discussed during the nego-tiation stages.
237. 2001 BOPC, art 6.
238. 2001 BOPC, art 6. A resolution to include in the 2001 BOPC preamble words encouraging countries to adopt the 1992 CLC and IOPC Fund 1992 Convention and denounce all previous conventions was also agreed (see LEG/CONF.12/14 and LEG/CONF.12/18, also LEG 82/3/2).
239. See N. Gaskell and C. Forrest (fn 196).
240. N. Gaskell and C. Forrest (fn 196) suggest that this is remedied to an extent by the multiplicity of defendants who, if financially healthy, can be made to contribute to recovery of the unlimited liability for such claims.

most of the problems that are inherent to the linkage between the 2001 BOPC and the 1996 LLMC. As the 2001 BOPC does not cover death and personal injury claims,[241] the available limits are those relevant to property damage, at most one-third of the total limitation fund.[242]

(e) When does the owner lose the right to limit liability?

The 2001 BOPC does not include a test for breaking limitation because it does not include independent rights of limitation of liability but relies on nationally applicable regimes. The application of such differing limitation regimes in conjunction with the 2001 BOPC affects not only the applicable limits of liability but also the test applied for breaking limitation. Thus the test applicable under the 1996 LLMC will be relevant in the UK case.[243] Because the protection of the shipowner's employees and crew members as well as salvors and others is prescribed under section 156(2A) the test under which they lose the right to limit their liability is not consistent with that applied under the 1996 LLMC.[244] Thus there is a possibility that, for the same type of conduct, the shipowner will be able to limit liability under the 1996 LLMC while the crew members will lose their protection under section 156(2A). However, because the 2001 BOPC only provides protection for the owner there is no conflict between the 2001 BOPC and the MSA 1995 at this point.

(f) Direct action against the insurer

A claimant under the 2001 BOPC can directly sue[245] the insurer[246] whether or not the shipowner is solvent or is in breach of its insurance contract and therefore cannot recover under it.[247] Nevertheless the insurer is entitled to limit liability even if the shipowner is not.[248] The insurer can invoke all the defences the shipowner would have invoked in an action against the shipowner. In addition the insurer may avoid liability if the pollution was a result of wilful misconduct by the shipowner.[249] Defences that could have been invoked under the insurance contract, for example breach of the duty of fair presentation of the risk such as non disclosure or misrepresentation etc., would not allow the insurer to avoid liability against third parties under the 2001 BOPC.[250] The insurer is explicitly given the right to join the shipowner in the proceedings under the 2001 BOPC.[251]

(g) Jurisdiction and enforcement of judgments

The jurisdictional arrangements mirror those of the 1992 CLC. Thus, courts of Contracting States which have suffered damage in their territory, territorial seas or their EEZ[252] have juris-

---

241. 2001 BOPC, art 1.9.
242. 1996 LLMC, art 6.1 provides limits of liability for (a) personal injury or death (art 6.1(a)) and (b) other damage (art 6.1(b)). The limits of liability for personal injury or death are twice the limits of liability for other damage. Nevertheless, these limits are not completely independent. Although the limits of liability for personal injury or death are not available when only other damage takes place, the limits of liability for other damage are available for satisfaction of personal injury or death claims and rank equally with those claims (1996 LLMC, art 6.2).
243. MSA 1995, Schedule 7, Part I, para 4.
244. See Chapter 11 on Marine Insurance.
245. Art 7.10.
246. Or the person providing financial security (art 7.10).
247. See s 165(1A) of the MSA 1995 as amended by the Merchant Shipping (Oil Pollution) (Bunkers Convention) Regulations 2006.
248. Art 7.10 and s 165(4B) of the MSA 1995 as amended.
249. Art 7.10 and s 165(4A) of the MSA 1995 as amended.
250. Art 7.10. In such cases the insurer (or provider of guarantee) will have a claim under the insurance contract against the shipowner which may be worthless if the shipowner has gone into liquidation.
251. Art 7.10.
252. Or the equivalent 200-mile zone under art 2(a)(ii).

diction[253] to hear any claim against the shipowner and the insurer or provider of security.[254] The Convention does not specify a period of notice of a commenced action to the defendant but only requires that this should be reasonable.[255] Thus the national law periods for service of the claim forms should apply.[256] The UK enactment implements the above by restricting the jurisdiction of the UK courts to hear actions *in rem* or *in personam* unless bunker pollution damage has occurred in UK territory or prevention measures have been undertaken in UK territory.[257]

Final judgments from a State that has jurisdiction under Article 9 should be recognised[258] and are enforceable[259] in all Contracting States whichever limitation regime applies in the State where enforcement is sought.[260] Thus a judgment obtained in a State which gives effect both to the 2001 BOPC and the 1996 Protocol of 1976 LLMC would arguably be enforceable in a State which is also a party to the 2001 BOPC even if the limitation regime applicable is the 1957 LLMC or if no limitation applies there.[261] Only if the judgment was obtained by fraud or the defendant was not given a fair opportunity or reasonable notice to defend may the judgment not be recognised. No other reason, whether related to public policy or otherwise, would allow a Contracting State to fail to recognise a foreign judgment.

Notably there is no mechanism for resolving jurisdictional conflicts under the 2001 BOPC although multiple jurisdictions may be invoked when neighbouring Contracting States all suffer pollution damage from the same incident. National conflict of laws rules will then resolve the case.

5. LIABILITY UNDER SECTION 154 OF THE 1995 MERCHANT SHIPPING ACT

Section 154 applies generally to all ships whether seagoing or not[262] and all persistent mineral hydrocarbon oil whether carried as cargo or as bunker oil. However, it excludes from its application all liability arising under sections 153 and 153A. As a result it covers liability for damages for oil pollution from tankers or non-tankers which are non-seagoing vessels and imposes liability arrangements similar to the CLC to vessels not covered by the CLC.

Liability under this section is channeled only to the registered owner of the ship.[263] The liability of servants, agents, charterers, manager, operators, salvors and persons performing services on board the ship or taking pollution prevention measures outside the ship as well as the servants or agents of the last three categories of persons are excluded,[264] unless the damage has been caused by an action or omission which is either intentional or reckless and with knowledge that

---

253. The Contracting States are under an obligation to ensure that their courts have such jurisdiction (art 9.3).

254. Art 9.

255. Art 9.2.

256. Where pollution damage gives the right to arrest the ship, a direct conflict between the 2001 BOPC and the 1952 Arrest Convention exists as the latter convention gives jurisdiction at the place of arrest if the national law provides so (art 7.1). The ordinary rules for conflict of laws should then apply. The same conflict exists with the 1999 Arrest Convention.

257. s 166 of the MSA 1995 as amended.

258. Art 10.1.

259. When all required formalities are complied with. These formalities should not allow re-opening of the merits of the case (art 10.2).

260. s 166(4) of the MSA 1995 as amended.

261. See also the submission to the IMO of the International Chamber of Shipping (LEG/CONF.12/10).

262. MSA 1995, s 154(5).

263. s 154(1) as modified by the Merchant Shipping (Oil Pollution) (Bunkers Convention) Regulations 2006, SI 2006/1244.

264. MSA 1995, s 156 (2).

any such damage or cost would probably result.[265] There is no restriction on the size of the ships which are subject to this liability, thus all small ships are covered. The liability is limited under the 1996 LLMC as enacted in the UK by Schedule 7, Part II of the MSA 1995.[266] There are no provisions for compulsory insurance in respect of this section.[267]

6. SPILLED OIL AS WASTE

EC Directive 75/442 provides strict liability for the clean-up of wastes. The European Court of Justice in *Commune de Mesquer v Total France SA, Total International Ltd*[268] held that spilled oil mixed with sand and sediment falls under the definition of waste under Article 1(a) of EC Directive 75/442 on waste,[269] as amended by Decision 96/350,[270] if the spilled oil can no longer be exploited or marketed without prior processing. The European Court of Justice held that this liability attaches to the holder of the waste as well as the seller or the previous holders such as a charterer if it can be shown that such persons "contributed to the risk that the pollution caused by the shipwreck would occur, in particular if [they] failed to take measures to prevent such an incident, such as measures concerning the choice of ship". Thus charterers as well as shippers may find themselves liable for such costs. These parties are not covered by the limitation of liability provisions of the 1969 or 1992 CLC.

The ECJ held that where the operation of the 1992 CLC and the 1992 IOPC Fund is insufficient to cover liability for these damages either because no such liability is covered or because the limitation of liability available under these international instruments restricts the recovery of damages then the EU Member States must provide laws for the liability to be covered by the producer of the product from which the waste that is spread actually came. However, the producer's liability would be fault based and not strict.[271]

The approach adopted by the ECJ indicates that any relevant EC directives are likely to be interpreted in a way that considers international conventions on oil pollution as, where possible, fulfilling Member States' duties under those directives. However, they also indicate that the application of an international convention does not necessarily comprise the complete implementation of such a directive. Thus there is the possibility of looking at third parties where they are at fault to recover damages in excess of, or not covered under, the international conventions. Consequently, the channelling of liability provisions of the international oil pollution conventions will only work to protect the various parties from liability under each of the Conventions and not from liability imposed under European law where it arises more generally. Such liability for the shippers, charterers or previous owners may, depending on the circumstances, be unlimited.

---

265. MSA 1995, s 156(1)(ii).
266. MSA 1995, s 168 expressly considers pollution damage under s 154 to be covered by art 2(1)(a) of the 1996 LLMC.
267. However, Directive 2009/20/EC of the European Parliament and of the Council of 23 April 2009 on the insurance of shipowners for maritime claims (OJ L 131 28 May 2009), enacted in the UK by the Merchant Shipping (Compulsory Insurance of Shipowners for Maritime Claims) Regulations 2012, SI 2012/2267, provides for compulsory insurance up to the limits of the 1976 LLMC, as amended. However, these apply only to sea going vessels larger than 300 grt.
268. *Commune de Mesquer v Total France SA, Total International Ltd*, C-188/07, EU:C:2008:359, [2008] 3 CMLR 16.
269. Council Directive of 15 July 1975 on waste, 75/442/EEC (OJ L 194, 25 July 1975). Note that this Directive as amended has been codified in Directive 2006/12/EC of the European Parliament and of the Council of 5 April 2006 on waste (OJ L 114, 27 April 2006).
270. Commission Decision 96/350/EC of 24 May 1996 adapting Annexes IIA and IIB to Council Directive 75/442/EEC on waste, (OJ L 135, 6 June 1996).
271. Ibid.

7. POLLUTION DAMAGE UNDER THE EC DIRECTIVE 2004/35 AND OTHER EU PROVISIONS

Liability for environmental damage including clean up is imposed by the 2004/35 European Directive[272] on "environmental liability with regard to the prevention and remedying of environmental damage"[273] (ELD), which came into force on 30 April 2004. The ELD imposes strict and unlimited liability on the operator of a facility (which includes shipowners)[274] for environmental damage, but does not cover loss of (human) life or damage to property. The claims are brought by public administrators,[275] not by injured parties, with the damages paid being for the remedy of the environment rather than compensation for losses by private parties.

The ELD imposes liability for preventive measures when a threat of environmental damage occurs[276] and remedial actions when environmental damage occurs.[277]

The ELD covers three types of damage:[278] damage to land, damage to water and damage to protected species and natural habitats. Each type of damage is treated differently in terms of the liability imposed, the area covered and the standards for reparative action.

Operators who professionally conduct the potentially hazardous activities specified in Annex III are strictly liable for damage to land, damage to water and damage to protected species and habitats. The liability of operators of other activities under the ELD is fault based and is restricted to damage to protected species and habitats.[279] Annex III includes all transport of dangerous or polluting goods and the performing carrier is subject to strict liability. Thus the ELD applies, in general, to ships.

Land damage is defined as contamination of land that creates a significant risk of affecting human health. Its remediation requires, as a minimum, clean up and the removal of the threat to human health.[280]

Water damage covers "damage that significantly adversely affects the ecological, chemical and/or quantitative status and/or ecological potential, as defined in the Water Framework Directive 2000/60". The original version of the ELD referred to the marine areas one mile from the coast. Following the Deep Water Horizon incident, the scope was extended in order to bring offshore platforms within the ambit of the ELD. This was achieved by amending its Article 2(1) (b)[281] to include "marine waters" as defined in Article 3(1)(a) of the Marine Strategy Framework

---

272. The Directive has been transposed to English law through SI 2009/153, The Environmental Damage (Prevention and Remediation) Regulations 2009, which came into force on 1 March 2009. This has been replaced by The Environmental Damage (Prevention and Remediation) (England) Regulations 2015, SI 2015/810.

273. Directive 2004/35/EC of the European Parliament and of the Council of 21 April 2004 on environmental liability with regard to the prevention and remedying of environmental damage (OJ L 143, 30 April 2004).

274. The operator is defined under art 2.6 as

any natural or legal, private or public person who operates or controls the occupational activity or, where this is provided for in national legislation, to whom decisive economic power over the technical functioning of such an activity has been delegated, including the holder of a permit or authorisation for such an activity or the person registering or notifying such an activity.

Shipowners may fall with the definition. In addition, owners of jetties and oil storage facilities and refineries are also subject to this definition.

275. The competent authorities are under an obligation to act to remedy environmental damage whether this damage is caused by a private or public entity.

276. ELD, art 5.

277. ELD, art 6.

278. ELD, art 2(1).

279. ELD, art 3(1).

280. ELD, Annex II (2).

281. Art 38(1)(b)(ii) of Directive 2013/30/EU on safety of offshore oil and gas operations. The language of the amendment is general and not limited to the subject of offshore oil and gas operation safety.

Directive.[282] Thus, "water damage" includes all the jurisdictional areas of each Member State.[283] Although the change was introduced to cover offshore facilities the extension is more general and will apply to ship-source pollution too.

Damage to protected species and natural habitats covers the land, the sea bed of the continental shelf and all other parts of the environment, the water column, in the renewable energy zone of each Member State.[284] The species and areas protected are those identified in the relevant EU Directives[285] plus any nationally declared protected areas and species.[286] The remedial action required for water damage aims for the "restoration of the environment to its baseline condition by way of primary, complementary and compensatory remediation".[287] The ELD permits each EU Member State to impose more stringent measures. This naturally leads to variations in the national legislation.

The ELD currently excludes from its application[288] damage arising from incidents covered by some of the major conventions concerned with liability for marine pollution arising from carriage of goods by sea, namely the 1992 CLC,[289] the IOPC Fund 1992 Convention,[290] the 2001 BOPC,[291] the 2010 HNS Convention,[292] as well as the 1971 Nuclear Material Convention,[293] and their future amendments. Thus, the potential scope of the ELD in the marine environment is significantly reduced. However, the exclusion applies only to the extent that the relevant international convention is in force in the Member State concerned.[294] Thus, the ELD directly presented EU governments with a dilemma: either to ratify the existing international conventions or to remain within the liability framework of the ELD. The 2010 HNS Convention is not currently in force. Therefore the ELD will be relevant for any incident involving a cargo of hazardous and

282. Directive 2008/56/EC.

283. The Marine Strategy Framework Directive defines "marine waters" as "waters, the seabed and subsoil on the seaward side of the baseline from which the extent of territorial waters is measured extending to the outmost reach of the area where a Member State has and/or exercises jurisdictional rights", typically the seaward edge of the exclusive economic zone. This has been enacted by s 2(1) of The Environmental Damage (Prevention and Remediation) (England) Regulations 2015, SI 2015/810 and applies to water damage in marine waters occurring after 19 July, 2015.

284. Ibid. The Continental Shelf is defined as the area designated under s 1(7) of the Continental Shelf Act, 1964 and the renewable energy zone as the waters over the seabed designated under s 84(4) of the Energy Act 2004. Some Member States extended the ELD's application during the implementation process with respect to biodiversity to the exclusive economic zone or EEZ. The ELD Implementation Study Final Report (BIO Intelligence Service (2013)), "Implementation Challenges and Obstacles of the Environmental Liability Directive, Final Report", prepared for European Commission – DG Environment in collaboration with Stevens & Bolton LLP found that "Some Member States such as Denmark, Germany, Spain, and the UK, which have a maritime border, provide that the ELD regime applies to biodiversity in the exclusive economic zone. Other Member States are silent on the issue."

285. The Birds Directive 79/409 and the Habitats Directive 92/43.

286. An exception to this is the concept of "coastal waters" which is defined in art 2(7) as surface water on the landward side of a line, every point of which is at a distance of one nautical mile on the seaward side from the nearest point of the baseline from which the breadth of territorial waters is measured, extending where appropriate up to the outer limit of transitional waters.

287. ELD, Annex II(1).

288. ELD, art 4.2 and Annex IV(a) – (d).

289. ELD, Annex IV(a).

290. ELD, Annex IV(b).

291. ELD, Annex IV(c).

292. ELD, Annex IV(c). This convention is not in force. See p 402.

293. ELD, Annex V(e).

294. The Environmental Damage (Prevention and Remediation) (England) Regulations 2015, SI 2015/810 under art 8 have the UK exclusions which includes "any activity carried out in the course of commercial sea fishing if all legislation relating to that fishing was complied with."

noxious substances if damage as defined under the ELD is caused. The ELD will also be relevant to damage arising from non-persistent oils.

Rights of global limitation of liability under the 1976 LLMC and its future amendments[295] are expressly preserved.[296] This, in effect, reduces further the significance of the ELD for shipowners because, even if strict liability is imposed under the ELD for a particular incident, the effect would be merely to force the relevant claimant(s) to share a part of the property damage related limitation fund with any other claimants. No increased liability for the shipowner will result provided, of course, that such damage is subject to limitation. The exclusion of the maritime legal regimes was reviewed together with the whole framework in 2016 and the report identified, with respect to the oil pollution regimes, differences in the remediation standards[297] which the Commission will try to reduce by working with the IOPC Fund in "developing common understanding of concepts".[298] However, the report did not identify evidence of insufficient compensation for environmental damage. Consequently, no changes in the legal text is expected.

The ELD requires transposition into the laws of EU Member States. This has created a patchwork of legislation with significant and important differences in the practical application. Furthermore only a few cases based on the ELD have been reported.[299]

In the UK the transposition of the ELD can be found in the Environmental Damage (Prevention and Remediation) Regulations 2015, SI 2015/810. These include exceptions for the 1992 CLC/IOPCF and 2001 BOPC.[300] However, a ship subject to strict liability under section 154 of the MSA 1995 will be covered by the 2015 Regulations. There is presently no exclusion for incidents that would be covered by the 2010 HNS Convention so the 2015 Regulations apply to such damage. Clean-up and remediation are requirements under the 2015 Regulations.

Where the 2015 Regulations apply to a ship carrying polluting goods it imposes specific obligations to prevent environmental damage. Thus where there is an imminent threat of damage there is a duty for the operator to take all practical steps and notify the relevant authority.[301] In addition the relevant authority is obliged to act on notification by any interested party.[302]

Under the 2015 Regulations a person authorised by the Secretary of State can at any time embark and inspect a ship or maritime installation in UK territorial waters or a UK ship or

---

295. Which includes the 1996 LLMC.

296. ELD, art 4.3 and s (7)(2) of the UK 2015 Regulations.

297. Report from the Commission to the Council and the European Parliament under Article 18(2) of Directive 2004/35/EC on environmental liability with regard to the prevention and remedying of environmental damage 14.4.2016 COM(2016) 204 final.

298. Ibid., s 4.1. Notably the report also admits the lack of data for evaluating the impact of ELD.

299. BIO Intelligence Service (2013), fn 284.

300. s 8(d). It also rather surprisingly excludes liability from fishing activities if all legislation relating to fishing was complied with.

301. Reg 13 of the 2015 Regulations. The enforcing authority depends on the activity and the damage. For waters beyond the 12 nautical miles as well as for damage to species in the EEZ and the continental shelf the Secretary of State.

English Nature is the relevant authority for land, the Environment Agency for water damage not in the sea and for authorised offshore activities in the continental shelf and the limits of the renewable energy zone or the Secretary of State. Failure to comply is an offence.

302. An interested party is defined as a party affected or likely to be affected by environmental damage or someone who has a sufficient interest (s 29). The 2015 Regulations do not specify either of these categories. Explanatory guidelines issued by DEFRA include as examples in the first category, birdwatchers, ramblers, recreational fishermen, residents, those whose health may be at risk from contaminants, those responsible for children or elderly persons whose health may be at risk. In the second category charities registered with the Charity Commission whose objects include environmental protection are included.

offshore installation in the renewable energy zone with powers to stop and embark for enforcement purposes. Arguably, this power is not exercisable with regard to vessels on innocent passage.

8. LIABILITY FOR POLLUTION FROM HAZARDOUS AND NOXIOUS SUBSTANCES

(a) Introduction

Liability for damage arising from the carriage of hazardous and/or noxious cargo is presently, under English law, based in tort. Limitation of such liability is currently covered by the 1996 LLMC for those claims covered by the wording of Article 2. Pure economic losses arising from the escape of HNS cargo is currently non-recoverable. The 1996 International Convention on Liability and Compensation for Damage in Connection with the Carriage of Hazardous and Noxious Substances by Sea (the 1996 HNS Convention)[303] was designed for the purpose of establishing strict liability and providing compensation in respect of such damage.

However, the 1996 HNS Convention faced significant practical difficulties related to the HNS Fund and failed to come into force. Following extensive discussions within the IOPC Fund, the 2010 HNS Protocol was adopted in May 2010.[304] The 2010 HNS Protocol attempts to resolve the most pressing problems with the 1996 HNS Convention but it remains to be seen whether the amendments will persuade States to bring the revised 2010 HNS Convention, into force.[305] The amended 2010 HNS Convention will be discussed here.

The 1996 HNS Convention was modelled in many aspects on the 1992 CLC/IOPC Fund system. Thus, a two-tier system, expressing the joint responsibility of the shipowner (first tier) and the importers/traders (second tier) was devised. However, instead of having two independent conventions the HNS opted for one convention dealing with both tiers. The choice to bundle together the liability of the shipowner with that of the importer was made in spite of the very important practical difference between the oil trade and the trade in hazardous and noxious substances. The financial capability of the IOPC Fund is based on contributions by importers of fuel oil and crude oil with perhaps about 500 traders contributing globally. By contrast, around 6,000 types of cargo are covered by the 1996 HNS Convention with perhaps 500,000 traders involved.[306] Thus, significant issues regarding implementation have arisen in respect of the reporting requirements for imports and the development of methods for collecting the relevant contributions. In addition, during the negotiations leading to the 1996 HNS Convention, conflicts arose between sectors of HNS traders. In particular the importers of comparatively safer cargoes were unwilling to

303. Adopted 3 May 1996. Not yet in force. The United Kingdom signed the 1996 HNS Convention on 16 October 1996. The Merchant Shipping and Maritime Security Act 1997 contains the necessary enabling legislation. This inserts Schedule 5A to the MSA 1995 by the 1997 Maritime Security Act which also provided for a power to the Queen to bring Schedule 5 into force by Order in Council which, in turn has first to be approved by the House of Parliament as a Draft Order.

304. IMO LEG-CONF.17/DC/1, 29 April 2010. Protocol of 2010 to amend the International Convention on Liability and Compensation for Damage in Connection with the Carriage of Hazardous and Noxious Substances by Sea, 1996. It consists of 29 Articles, which significantly amend the Convention in various ways. Art 2 of the 2010 Protocol requires the parties to the Protocol to give effect to the 1996 HNS Convention as amended by the Protocol. The 1996 HNS Convention, together with the 2010 Protocol, form the 2010 HNS Convention.

305. The European Parliament has given its consent to the ratification and accession to the HNS 2010 by EU member states. (European Parliament legislative resolution of 5 April 2017 on the draft Council decision on the ratification and accession by Member States, in the interest of the European Union, to the Protocol of 2010 to the International Convention on Liability and Compensation for Damage in Connection with the Carriage of Hazardous and Noxious Substances by Sea, with regard to the aspects related to judicial cooperation in civil matters (14112/2015 – C8-0409/2015 – 2015/0136(NLE))). Norway has been the irst state to ratify the HNS 2010 on April 21, 2017.

306. See the documents in LEG\CONF \1O\6(a).

contribute to a general HNS Fund as they feared that they would end up subsidising some accident-prone and relatively unsafe parts of the market. These problems, which had been identified from the start,[307] continued to impede its wide ratification and entry into force.

All of the identified problems relate to the organisation of the HNS Fund. The first tier of liability, that is the shipowner's liability and its limitation are not problematic. However, coming into force will either happen for both parts or for neither.

(b) Scope of application

The 2010 HNS Convention covers hazardous and noxious substances carried as cargo and in some cases as residue from previous cargoes. The substances covered by the 2010 HNS Convention are identified by reference to various lists of international codes designed to ensure maritime safety and prevention of pollution.[308] Thus it covers cargoes of oils,[309] noxious liquids,[310] dangerous liquid substances,[311] liquefied gases,[312] liquid substances with flashpoint less than 60°C[313] and solid bulk materials possessing chemical hazards[314] as well as residues from previous carriage in bulk.[315] In addition it covers the transport of packaged dangerous, hazardous and harmful cargoes covered by the International Maritime Dangerous Goods Code.[316]

307. Three problems were identified and dealt with by the 2010 HNS. First, the issue of accounting for imported packaged dangerous goods for the purpose of having them contribute to the HNS Fund. This has been resolved by excluding packaged goods from contributing. To keep the balance between the carrier and the traders the limits of liability for the shipowner who carries packaged goods have been increased. The second issue was that the contribution to the LNG account was to be made by the last person that held title to the goods before discharge. This was very difficult to ascertain and has been modified so that the receiver is the person to pay the contribution. The third issue was the lack of information on imports of HNS by States who had ratified the 1996 HNS Convention. Without such reports the various accounts would not be able to function. This is dealt with under the 2010 HNS in the following ways. Firstly, the liability on the State Party to compensate the HNS Fund where the HNS Fund has suffered losses because of a breach of the reporting obligations in art 21.2 is reaffirmed. Second, the HNS Fund is to refrain from paying damages in respect of a State Party which has failed to pay contributions during the years leading up to an incident when those contributions are still due. When such a State Party is notified of its failure to fulfil its obligations and does not remedy the situation within a year, compensation is to be denied permanently. However, this non-payment option is only available for pollution and property damage and does not apply to loss of life or personal injury losses.

308. It is therefore very different from the 1992 CLC which includes generally persistent oils without specifying exactly which oils are included. Thus the 2010 HNS Convention definition is more precise and, in the case where a particular substance needs to be included, this can be achieved by amending the relevant list.

309. Art 1.5(a)(i): as defined under Annex I, Appendix I of MARPOL 73/78. This includes persistent and non-persistent oils: for example, crude oil, fuel oil, jet oil, gasoline (petrol), etc.

310. Art 1.5(a)(ii): as defined under Annex II, Appendix II of MARPOL 73/78. This includes amongst others tetra-ethyl lead, coal tar, styrene monomer, chloroform, sulphuric acid, coconut oil, sodium hydroxide solution, fish oil etc.

311. 2010 HNS Convention, art 1.5(a)(iii):

dangerous liquid substances carried in bulk listed in chapter 17 of the International Code for the Construction and Equipment of Ships Carrying Dangerous Chemicals in Bulk, 1983, as amended, and the dangerous products for which the preliminary suitable conditions for the carriage have been prescribed by the Administration and port administrations involved in accordance with paragraph 1.1.3 of the Code such as sodium chlorate solution.

312. 2010 HNS Convention, art 1.5(a)(v) when:

listed in chapter 19 of the International Code for the Construction and Equipment of Ships Carrying Liquefied Gases in Bulk, 1983, as amended, and the products for which preliminary suitable conditions for the carriage have been prescribed by the Administration and port administrations involved in accordance with paragraph 1.1.6 of the Code such as LPG, LNG ammonia, chlorine etc.

313. 2010 HNS Convention, art 1.5(a)(vi) for example acetone and ethyl alcohol.

314. 2010 HNS Convention, art 1.5(a)(vii) covered by appendix B of the Code of Safe Practice for Solid Bulk Cargoes, as amended, to the extent that these substances are also subject to the provisions of the International Maritime Dangerous Goods Code when carried in packaged form: for example, potassium nitrate, sulphur.

315. 2010 HNS Convention, art 1.5(b).

316. 2010 HNS Convention, art 1.5(a)(iv), for example cyanides, pesticides and ammunition.

A notable omission from the list of hazardous cargoes is coal which has been found under certain circumstances to become dangerous.[317] Certain radioactive materials are also excluded.[318]

It is worth noting that in general the cargo covered is referred to as being in bulk. Only in relation to dangerous hazardous and harmful cargoes covered by the International Maritime Dangerous Goods Code is the reference to packaged goods.[319]

(c) Which ships are subject to the 2010 HNS Convention?

A "ship" is defined as "any seagoing vessel and seaborne craft, of any type whatsoever".[320] The definition is very wide and not restricted to any particular construction of ship. Whilst the term "seagoing" can be uncertain there appears to be no other restriction in this respect. Mobile off-shore units are clearly within the definition of ship under the 2010 HNS Convention. However, if they are used for storage rather than transportation they would arguably be excluded from its scope.

State ships, not used in commercial tasks and war ships are also excluded from the scope of the 2010 HNS Convention.[321]

Small vessels less than 200 grt employed in coastal trade of a Contracting State or employed exclusively in trade between neighbouring States can be excluded from the application of the 2010 HNS Convention, after such declaration by the Contracting State(s),[322] provided that such vessels only carry HNS cargoes in packaged form and only while they remain in the coastal trade. Exclusion of such vessels means that no compensation is payable under the 2010 HNS Convention[323] from the shipowner or the HNS Fund. Consequently the national law and global limitation regime will apply to damages arising from the excluded ships and carriage.

(d) Damage covered

The 2010 HNS Convention covers damage by contamination caused by any of the hazardous and noxious substances carried. Thus, physical damage by contamination to property out-side the ship, financial loss arising from damage to the environment,[324] costs for reasonable measures for the reinstatement of the environment[325] and the costs of and damage caused by preventive measures.[326] This damage is in essence the same as the damage covered by the 1969/1992 CLC.[327]

---

317. See LEG/CONF. 10/6(a)/16 by Korea arguing that coal is a relatively safe cargo and warning that inclusion of coal in the Convention, with the required contributions to the established Fund would make the 2010 HNS Convention less attractive to several States.

318. 2010 HNS Convention, art 4.3(b). C. de la Rue and C.B. Anderson, *Shipping and the Environment*, (2nd edn, LLP 2009), attribute this exclusion to the absence of P&I cover for such damage, the lack of uniformity of liability regimes in respect of carriage of nuclear material and the financial exposure that would be imposed on the HNS Fund following a major nuclear accident.

319. 2010 HNS Convention, art 1.5(a)(iv): for example, cyanides, pesticides and ammunition.

320. 2010 HNS Convention, art 1.1.

321. 2010 HNS Convention, art 4.4. A Contracting State may opt to have the 2010 HNS applicable to their State vessels (art 4.5).

322. Both Contracting States must agree and make a declaration in the case of trade between these States. Arts 5.3 and 5.4.

323. 2010 HNS Convention, arts 5.5 and 5.6.

324. 2010 HNS Convention, art 1.6(c).

325. 2010 HNS Convention, art 1.6(c).

326. 2010 HNS Convention, art 1.6(d).

327. 1992 CLC, art 1.6.

However, the 2010 HNS Convention also covers two additional heads of damage. First it covers loss of life and personal injury on board as well as outside the ship[328] only excluding such loss when there is a contract of carriage of passengers.[329] Second, it covers property damage outside the ship. Thus its scope is much wider than that of the 1992 CLC.[330]

The inclusion of persistent oils within the scope of the 2010 HNS Convention overlaps with the 1992 CLC/Fund regimes. To avoid the conflict, oil pollution damage covered by the 1992 CLC is excluded from the scope of the 2010 HNS Convention whether compensation is available under the 1992 CLC or not.[331] While the 1992 CLC only covers damage by contamination[332] from persistent oils from tankers there is significant scope for the application of the 2010 HNS Convention in three respects. First, in respect to loss of life and personal injury, second, in respect to property damage outside the ship[333] arising from persistent and non-persistent oils and finally in respect to damage by contamination[334] outside the ship caused by non-persistent oils. This in effect means that in an incident arising from a ship subject to the CLC separate funds and different limits of liability will be available for loss of life and property damage, in addition to pollution damage. The former would be subject to the 2010 HNS regime whereas the latter will be subject to the 1992 CLC regime.

Where the damage is caused by substances covered by the 2010 HNS Convention and by other substances unless the damage is separable it will be wholly covered by the 2010 HNS Convention.[335] Thus if there is an explosion onboard a vessel carrying hazardous and non-hazardous materials then, unless it can be proved that the damage or part of it was caused by the non-hazardous materials, the 2010 HNS Convention will be applicable.

(e) Where does the 2010 HNS Convention apply?

The application of the 2010 HNS Convention depends on the type of damage suffered, the jurisdictional zone in which this damage was suffered and the flag of the ship.

In respect of pollution damage the HNS 2010 applies in the EEZ[336] the territory and the territorial sea of the Contracting State. In respect of preventive measures these expenses are recoverable wherever they occur subject to the requirement that the preventive measures are taken in respect of pollution damage, actual or threatened,[337] in the territorial waters or the EEZ of a Contracting State. Loss of life and personal injury as well as physical damage outside the ship are covered in the territory or territorial sea of a Contracting State. In addition, these are also covered anywhere outside the territory of the Contracting State provided they were caused by HNS cargo onboard a ship registered in a Contracting State.

---

328. 2010 HNS Convention, art 1.6(a).
329. 2010 HNS Convention, art 4.1.
330. Warships naval auxiliaries and other State ships are in general excluded. See art 4.
331. 2010 HNS Convention, art 4.3.
332. Also including the costs of preventive measures and further loss or damage caused by preventive measures.
333. For example, from an explosion or fire.
334. Including the costs of preventive measures and further loss or damage caused by preventive measures.
335. Art 1.6. There is an exception in respect of damage covered by the CLC and radioactive materials (art 4.3), however this is also applicable if the extent of damage caused by the materials covered by the CLC or radioactive materials can be determined. Thus, where a tanker explodes and there is oil leakage the damage from the explosion will certainly be covered by the 2010 HNS Convention while the oil spill damage would arguably be covered by the CLC.
336. In the UK, the Exclusive Economic Zone Order 2013, SI 2013/3161 of 2013 establishes the EEZ.
337. Note that art 1(8) defines "incident" as "any occurrence or series of occurrences having the same origin, which causes damage or creates a grave and imminent threat of causing damage". Thus threatened pollution that does not materialise is covered provided that such threat is "grave and imminent".

(f) Who is liable?

The registered[338] owner of a ship[339] carrying hazardous or noxious substances which causes damage is, under the 2010 HNS Convention, strictly liable for such damage.[340] The requirement that the damage must be caused "in connection with the carriage"[341] of hazardous and noxious substances "by sea" imposes restrictions on the claims that fall under the 2010 HNS Convention.

"Carriage by sea" is defined as the period which starts when the hazardous and noxious cargo during loading enters any part of the ship's equipment until the time during discharge it stops being present in any part of the ship's equipment.[342] If there is no equipment involved the time of crossing the ship's rail is the boundary of application of the Convention.[343] This definition imposes liability on the shipowner irrespective of who is responsible under the contract of carriage for loading or stowing the hazardous or noxious cargo. However, the shipowner's rights of recovery against third parties are expressly preserved.[344]

The 2010 HNS Convention does not cover the period before loading or after the discharge of the hazardous and noxious substances even where the cargoes are in the possession of the owner. Thus the application of the 2010 HNS Convention depends on whether the damage occurred before or after the cargo crossed the ship's rail or the ship's loading line. It is unclear whether temporary discharge or transhipment would stop the application of the 2010 HNS Convention or whether the term discharge in Article 1.9 refers solely to discharge for the purpose of delivery of the cargo. It is submitted that the latter is the better view.[345]

The literal interpretation of Article 1.9 suggests that the 2010 HNS Convention will not apply if the hazardous substances are not on board at the time of the incident. Thus even where there is partial discharge, for lightering, and the damage arises because of the partially discharged cargo, the 2010 HNS Convention would not be applicable in respect of the carrying vessel but will be applicable in respect of the lightering vessel.

(g) Type of liability imposed

Under the 2010 HNS Convention strict liability is imposed on the registered shipowner[346] and its insurer[347] and joint and several liability is imposed when two or more ships carrying hazardous and noxious substances are involved unless the damage is separable.[348] Some exceptions are available to the owner, who can escape liability if the damage is caused by "an act of war, hostilities, civil war, insurrection or a natural phenomenon of exceptional, inevitable and

---

338. 2010 HNS Convention, art 1.3. If there is no registration then persons owning the vessel qualify as owners. For State-owned ships registered by a company, the company is the owner. A person includes individuals as well as legal persons at corporate levels as well as States (for the exact wording see art 1.2).

339. 2010 HNS Convention, art 1.1.

340. 2010 HNS Convention, art 7.1.

341. 2010 HNS Convention, art 7.1.

342. 2010 HNS Convention, art 1.9.

343. 2010 HNS Convention, art 1.9.

344. 2010 HNS Convention, art 7.6.

345. The "maritime chain transport" approach, discussed within the IOPC Fund in relation to the definition of ship under the 1992 Fund Convention may be helpful in this respect.

346. 2010 HNS Convention, art 7.1.

347. 2010 HNS Convention, art 12.8. Compulsory insurance is required for all ships covered by the 2010 HNS Convention (art 12.1). Contracting States may exclude ships less than 200 grt, which carry hazardous and noxious substances only in packaged form and which are involved in coastal trade within the same State or between neighbouring States. In such a case no contribution to the HNS Fund is required for such cargo. However, the HNS Fund will not pay for damage caused by excluded ships and suffered in the territorial waters or the EEZ of these countries or in respect of preventive damages (art 5). Such exclusion will also apply to the requirement of compulsory insurance in respect of such ships.

348. 2010 HNS Convention, art 8.1.

irresistible nature".[349] The owner also avoids liability where the damage was wholly caused by an act of a third party with intention to cause damage,[350] or was wholly caused by negligent acts by a government or authority in respect of maintenance of navigational aids.[351] The owner also escapes liability where it was not informed by the shipper of the dangerous and noxious nature of the cargo and that lack of information caused, at least partly, the damage or led to a failure to obtain the compulsory insurance provided for under Article 9 of the 2010 HNS Convention.[352] The owner may also avoid liability, partly or fully, where it can prove that intentional acts or omissions by the victim of the incident, with the intent to cause damage, contributed to that person's damage.[353] The shipowner can be sued for HNS damage exclusively under the 2010 HNS Convention. No claims under other legal basis are permitted.[354] Protection against claims is provided for the owner's servants or agents, pilots, charterers of all types, the manager and operator of the ship, salvors and others involved in preventive measures and the servants and agents of those entities.[355]

(h) Insurance issues

Compulsory insurance for the owner[356] and direct action against the insurer[357] is provided for by the 2010 HNS Convention. The insurer is entitled to limit its liability[358] and can use the same defences as the owner has available under the 2010 HNS Convention.[359] In addition it is exempted from liability where it can show that it was the owner's wilful misconduct that caused the damage.[360] However, the insurer cannot rely on any other contractual defences which might have enabled it to avoid paying the insured as against a third party initiating a direct action. All ships carrying HNS cargoes are subject to the compulsory insurance provisions. The only possible exceptions are in relation to small vessels which have been declared as excluded under Article 5.1 by a Contracting State and in relation to State ships involved in non-commercial service.

(i) Limitation of liability

(i) The applicable limits

The liability of the owner and its insurer is limited.[361] The limits, which are applicable per incident,[362] are shown in Table 10.3. The limits are set on the basis of the tonnage of the vessel rather

---

349. 2010 HNS Convention, art 7.2(a).
350. 2010 HNS Convention, art 7.2(b).
351. 2010 HNS Convention, art 7.2(c).
352. 2010 HNS Convention, art 7.2(d).
353. 2010 HNS Convention, art 7.3.
354. 2010 HNS Convention, art 7.4.
355. 2010 HNS Convention, art 7.5. However, the protection is removed if "the damage resulted from 'the personal act or omission, of the protected person' . . . committed with the intent to cause such damage, or recklessly and with knowledge that such damage would probably result".
356. Art 12.1. An insurance certificate is required (art 12.2) and has to be carried on board (art 12.4) otherwise the vessel will not be permitted to trade (art 12.10).
357. 2010 HNS Convention, art 12.8.
358. 2010 HNS Convention, art 12.8.
359. Art 12.8. The owners' exemptions are set out in arts 7.2, 7.3 and 7.4 of the 2010 HNS Convention. However, the insurer cannot rely on bankruptcy or winding up of the owner.
360. 2010 HNS Convention, art 12.8.
361. 2010 HNS Convention, art 9.
362. See fn 347. The restriction to "grave and imminent threat of causing damage" do not apply where damage has occurred even where the extent of the damage is small.

Table 10.3 Limits of liability under the 2010 HNS

Tonnage (T) grt[1]	Shipowner's imitation (bulk HNS) SDR[2]	Shipowner's limitation[3] (packaged HNS)[4] SDR		HNS FUND Limitation (inclusive of shipowner's limits)[5] SDR
Less than 2,000	10,000,000	11,500,000		250,000,000
2,001–50,000	$1,500 \times (T\text{-}2000) + 10,000,000$	$1,725 \times (T\text{-}2000)$	$+ 10,000,000$	250,000,000
50,001 to 100,000	$360 \times (T\text{-}50,000) + 82,000,000$	$414 \times T\text{-}50,000)$	$+ 82,000,000$	250,000,000
100,001 and over	100,000,000	115,000,000		250,000,000

Notes
1. Article 9.10 of the 2010 HNS Convention states that the ship's gross tonnage as calculated on the basis of Annex 1 of the International Convention on Tonnage Measurement 1969 is to be used.
2. The term unit of account is used in the relevant article (Article 9) of the 2010 HNS Convention. This is set by default to be the Special Drawing Right (SDR) under Article 9.9(a) and this is the formula followed in the UK. However, for Contracting States of the 2010 HNS Convention which are not members of the International Monetary Fund special provisions under Article 9.9(b) and (c) are made, permitting the use of 15 gold francs as the unit of account.
3. These limits are introduced by Article 7 of the 2010 HNS Convention (Protocol of 2010 to the International Convention on Liability and Compensation for Damage in Connection with the Carriage of Hazardous and Noxious Substances by Sea 1996, LEG/ CONF.17/10, 4 May 2010).
4. Where both packaged and HNS goods have caused damage or where their damage is not separable these higher limits apply.
5. For the HNS Fund, see Section 2.

than the amount of hazardous and noxious substances actually carried. The limits of liability are higher per ton for small ships. Where two or more ships carrying hazardous and noxious substances are involved in an incident the limits of liability are applicable to each vessel independently[363] although the liability may be joint and several.[364]

(ii) Loss of the right to limit liability

The owner loses its right to limit liability if it is proved by the claimant that the damage resulted from the owner's "personal act or omission . . . committed with the intent to cause such damage, or recklessly and with knowledge that such damage would probably result".[365] Thus the test is very similar to that employed by the 1996 LLMC as well as all the other recent maritime conventions agreed from 1976 onwards.[366] It is worth noting once again that the test is satisfied only when the owner's conduct is intentional in causing damage or where it just falls short of it since it requires recklessness coupled with knowledge of the particular damage that occurred. As a result it will need very special circumstances under English law for the right to limit liability under the 2010 HNS Convention to be challenged,

The liability of the insurer is always limited even where the owner has lost the right to limit liability.[367]

363. 2010 HNS Convention, art 8.2.
364. 2010 HNS Convention, art 8.1.
365. 2010 HNS Convention, art 9.2.
366. Information regarding the problems and the application of this test can be found in Chapter 7 pp 286–291.
367. 2010 HNS Convention, art 8.8.

(iii) Establishment and distribution of the limitation fund

The provisions of the 2010 HNS Convention relating to the establishment of a limitation fund are very similar to those applicable to the 1992 CLC. For the owner to benefit from limited liability a limitation fund should be established[368] for the amount corresponding to the size of its vessel under Article 9.1,[369] in any of the competent courts or authorities[370] before which an action has been started.

Where an action has not started the owner can establish the fund in any of the competent courts. Cash or a bank guarantee would be sufficient ways of establishing the fund while other types of guarantee can also be used if they are acceptable under the law of the court in which the limitation fund is established. It is worth noting that the national court does not have any discretion in either setting the amount of security or denying that sufficient security is furnished if cash or a bank guarantee is provided. Moreover, the court has no jurisdiction to decide on a case-by-case basis whether a guarantee for the amount specified under the 2010 HNS Convention is acceptable if the national law generally permits such type of guarantee.

When the limitation fund is established by the owner,[371] and provided that the owner is entitled to limit liability and the fund is accessible to any claimant,[372] the ship if arrested or detained in relation to claims subject to the 2010 HNS Convention must be released and any security provided by the owner in respect of such arrest should be returned.[373] Moreover no other assets of the owner should be accessible to claimants.[374] Thus, the practical consequence of establishing the limitation fund is that the owner is able to continue trading as it has in essence discharged its liability in the form of the limitation fund, leaving the claimants and the courts to sort out compensation. The insurer can establish a limitation fund in exactly the same way as the owner.[375]

A particularity of the HNS limitation fund is that loss of life and personal injury claims are paid first up to two-thirds of the fund.[376] The residual one-third is distributed pro rata between any unpaid loss of life and personal injury claims and all other property, environmental damage and preventive measure claims.

(j) Time bars

A three-year time bar is applicable for claims against the owner or the insurer.[377] In respect of claims against the owner, the starting date for the running of the limitation period is the moment the claimant knows or should reasonably have known of the damage *and* the identity of the owner.[378]

---

368. 2010 HNS Convention, art 9.3.
369. See also Table 10.2.
370. 2010 HNS Convention, art 9.2. The competent courts under the Convention are those defined in art 38.
371. Establishment of a fund by the insurer would not be sufficient.
372. 2010 HNS Convention, art 10.2.
373. 2010 HNS Convention, art 10.1(b).
374. 2010 HNS Convention, art 10.1(a).
375. The rights of claimants against the owner are not affected by the constitution of such fund by the insurer, when the owner is not entitled to limitation of liability.
376. 2010 HNS Convention, art 11.
377. 2010 HNS Convention, art 37.1.
378. 2010 HNS Convention, art 37.1.

An additional time bar of ten years from the date of the incident[379] is also provided for claims against the HNS Fund to cover cases where the starting date of the time bar period is delayed and is not caught by Article 37.1 or 37.2 because, for example, the damage is identified late or the identity of the owner is not revealed.[380]

(k) Jurisdictional issues

Two issues must be distinguished: first, jurisdiction on the merits in respect of actions under the 2010 HNS Convention, and, second, jurisdiction in respect of the management and the distribution of the shipowner's limitation fund. The jurisdiction on the merits of the courts is closely linked with the jurisdictional zone where the damage was suffered. Two situations need to be distinguished here depending on whether the damage was suffered within the territorial waters or the EEZ of one or more Contracting States or elsewhere. Where damage covered by the 2010 HNS Convention is suffered in the territorial waters or the EEZ or equivalent 200 miles zone of one or more Contracting States then only[381] these States have jurisdiction to hear the claims. However, in situations where liability under the 2010 HNS Convention is established but no damage has been suffered in the territorial sea of the EEZ (or equivalent zone) of any Contracting State Article 38.2 provides for alternative jurisdiction in either the courts of the State where the ship is registered,[382] or where the owner has its habitual residence or a principal place of business, provided that these are in a Contracting State or the State party where the required limitation fund is established.[383] Such situations could arise where there is an accident and loss of life, personal injury and damage to property outside the ship arise in the waters or in the port of a non-Contracting State. Of course, the State where the damage occurred will have jurisdiction but claimants may wish to proceed in a Contracting State where strict liability will be available. The shipowner can establish the limitation fund in any competent court in which an action is brought or if an action has not been brought (yet) it can establish the fund in any of the competent courts. However, the courts of the State party where the limitation fund is established retain exclusive jurisdiction in relation to the distribution of the fund[384] irrespective of whether it also has jurisdiction on the merits in respect of all claims or no claim at all.

Under Article 40 of the 2010 HNS Convention, judgments by a competent court[385] which are final, that is, not subject to any formal appeal or review, are to be recognised by all State parties to the 2010 HNS Convention[386] and must be directly enforceable as soon as the formalities for recognition[387] at each State party are fulfilled.[388] Only where the judgment was obtained by fraud or the defendant was not given reasonable notice and a fair chance to defend the claim may such a judgment not be recognised by other State parties.[389]

---

379. Where there is a series of occurrences, the date of the last occurrence is the starting point for the ten-year period (art 37.4).
380. 2010 HNS Convention, art 37.3.
381. 2010 HNS Convention, art 38.1.
382. 2010 HNS Convention, art 38.2(a). If unregistered then the flag State.
383. 2010 HNS Convention, art 38.2.
384. 2010 HNS Convention, art 38.5.
385. Under 2010 HNS Convention, art 38.
386. 2010 HNS Convention, art 40.1.
387. It is expressly prohibited to reopen the merits of the case within the context of the required formalities (art 40.2).
388. 2010 HNS Convention, art 40.2.
389. 2010 HNS Convention, art 40.1.

(l) The 2010 HNS fund

The 2010 HNS Convention provides for the establishment[390] of a Fund (HNS Fund) which will provide compensation in cases covered by the Convention and where:

- either the damages exceed the owner's limit of liability;[391] or
- the owner and its insurer are financially incapable of covering their part of liability;[392] or
- the owner is exempted from liability under the 2010 HNS.[393]

The HNS Fund is only exempted from liability where the damage was caused by war, hostilities, insurrections etc., or where the damage was caused by ships excluded from the application of the 2010 HNS Convention.[394] In addition, the HNS Fund will not pay where the claimant cannot demonstrate that the damage involved one or more ships.[395] Therefore if the damage is caused by a drum of chemicals which was floating but could not be linked with a ship then the liability of the HNS Fund is exempted. In all other cases the claimants will be compensated to the same extent even if the shipowner or its insurer are unable to cover the first tier of liability. Partial exoneration of the HNS Fund, to the same extent as that of the owner,[396] is also possible where the damage was caused by the claimant's negligence or intentional act.[397]

The HNS Fund provides compensation up to 250 million SDR[398] inclusive of any compensation provided by the owner under the 2010 HNS Convention. Owner's expenses and sacrifices for pollution minimisation and prevention during an incident can be claimed against the HNS Fund.[399] Personal injury claims are paid out first up to two-thirds of the total amount of the HNS Fund (166.667 million SDR).[400] The remaining personal claims together with any other property or loss claims are paid out in proportion up to the limit of liability. When making payments the HNS Fund acquires by subrogation any rights any claimant may have against the owner.[401]

The 2010 HNS Convention provides for the creation of a general account divided into sectors[402] and, in addition, when adequate contributions are available for the sectors, the development of an oil account,[403] an LNG account[404] and LPG account.[405] The reason for the various separate accounts appears to be the unwillingness of the various sectors to cross-subsidise damages. Thus, relatively safe sectors like the LNG lobbied and achieved the creation of separate

---

390. 2010 HNS Convention, art 13.
391. 2010 HNS Convention, art 14.1(c).
392. 2010 HNS Convention, art 14.1(b).
393. 2010 HNS Convention, art 14.1(a).
394. 2010 HNS Convention, art 14.3(a). However, the 2010 HNS Fund has the burden of proving the exemption.
395. 2010 HNS Convention, art 14.3(b).
396. 2010 HNS Convention, art 7.3.
397. 2010 HNS Convention, art 14.4. The burden of proving the negligence or the intentional acts is on the HNS Fund.
398. 2010 HNS Convention, art 14.5.
399. 2010 HNS Convention, art 14.2. However, interest accrued on the owner's fund is not used in calculating the limits of liability for the HNS Fund (art 14.5(c)).
400. 2010 HNS Convention, art 14.6.
401. 2010 HNS Convention, art 41. The rights of recourse acquired include those against the shippers of dangerous goods (art 41.2)).
402. 2010 HNS Convention, art 16.1.
403. 2010 HNS Convention, art 16.2(a) with oil as defined in art 1.5(a)(1).
404. 2010 HNS Convention, art 16.2(b), liquefied natural gases of light hydrocarbons with methane as the main constituent.
405. 2010 HNS Convention, art 16.2(c), liquefied petroleum gases of light hydrocarbons with propane and butane as the main components.

accounts. However, for the system to work each account needs to be viable, that is, there should be enough contributors for the account to be capable of compensating accidents arising from contributing cargo. One major difficulty with the 1996 HNS Convention was the lack of reporting to the IMO by the few States that have ratified it. A second problem has been the difficulty in accounting for the imports of packaged dangerous goods. The 2010 HNS Convention has removed the obligation to report packaged dangerous goods and has imposed measures to ensure reporting in relation to other cargoes.

Separate accounts are triggered depending on different criteria. Article 19.3 sets minimum limits of 350 million tonnes, 20 million tonnes and 15 million tonnes of contributing cargo respectively for the oil, LNG and LPG accounts. Until these amounts of contributing cargo are achieved only the general account will operate. In addition if, after the separate accounts have started operating, the contributing cargo drops below the relevant threshold, or more than 10 per cent of the most recent levy remains unpaid six months after it is due, the Assembly can suspend the account and turn the contributions to the general account.[406]

Contributions to the oil account are due by two categories of oil receivers.[407] First, oil receivers of more than 150,000 tonnes of oil which contribute to the 1992 Fund will also contribute to the oil account of the HNS Fund. Second, any other oils[408] in excess of 20,000 tonnes for the year.

Contributions to the LPG account are due from any receiver of 20,000 tonnes or more of LPG.[409]

Contributions to the LNG account are due from any person holding title to an LNG cargo discharged in a port or terminal of a Contracting State.[410] Note that two differences exist between the LNG account and the other accounts. First, there is under Article 19.3, a minimum amount of contributing cargo that needs to be reached in order for the separate LNG account to become active. After the LNG account becomes active every LNG importer should pay contributions without having to pass any minimum cargo per year threshold. Second, the liability for contributions in respect of the LNG account is on the person holding title rather than the receiver, a difficult assessment which may be due to the law applicable to the sale contract. This is in fact one of the obstacles in moving towards the ratification of the 1996 HNS Convention and has been amended by the 2010 Protocol.

Receivers of 20,000 tonnes or more of solid bulk materials or other substances per year excluding substances not included in the separate accounts, contribute to the general account.

(m) Time bars

As with actions against the owner or its insurer a three-year time bar is applicable in respect of claims against the HNS Fund.[411] The starting point for the calculation of the three-year period is the time at which the claimant "knew or ought to have known of the damage".[412] The time bar is

---

406. 2010 HNS Convention, art 19. The relevant contributions to the general account by the different sectors is based on a point system described in Annex 2 of the 2010 HNS. This consists of the proportion of accidents per year from the particular sector and also includes a "memory" or "history" taking into account the safety behaviour of the sector over the past ten years. During the first ten years of the 1996 HNS artificial weights for this history have been agreed.
407. 2010 HNS Convention, art 19.1(a).
408. Listed in Appendix I of Annex I to the International Convention for the Prevention of Pollution from Ships 1973, as modified by the 1978 Protocol and as further amended.
409. 1996 HNS Convention, art 19.1(c).
410. 1996 HNS Convention, art 19.1(b).
411. 2010 HNS Convention, art 37.2.
412. 2010 HNS Convention, art 37.2.

defeated either by the initiation of a claim against the HNS Fund or, more simply, by serving a notification to the HNS Fund of proceedings that have started against the owner.[413] The formalities to which the notification applies depend on the court that has jurisdiction to hear the claim.

The additional time bar of ten years from the date of the incident[414] applicable to claims against the owner and its insurer is also applicable to claims against the HNS Fund.

(n) Jurisdictional issues

The jurisdiction on the merits for legal actions against the HNS Fund is closely linked with the jurisdiction on the merits against the owner and its insurer. Thus claims against the HNS Fund are only permitted where a court of a Contracting State is a competent court for an action against the shipowner.[415] Where the shipowner's liability is exempted or the ship that caused the damage is not identified there are no actions against the shipowner and thus no competent courts. In such case the competent courts for actions against the HNS Fund are identifiable as those which would have jurisdiction had the owner been liable.[416] There is no choice of jurisdiction in respect of actions against the HNS Fund if there is already an action pending against the shipowner before a competent court. In such a case the same court has exclusive jurisdiction for claims against the HNS Fund for the same damage.[417] Where there is no action pending against the owner in any competent court then the courts that have jurisdiction in respect of a claim against the owner or its insurer also have jurisdiction to hear claims against the HNS Fund.[418]

Judgments in proceedings against the owner or its insurer are binding against the HNS Fund only where the HNS Fund has been notified about the claims brought in such a manner that it permits the HNS Fund to intervene in the proceedings.[419] Such notification must be in the formalities required by the court that is hearing the claim.

Judgments of competent courts against the HNS Fund are also recognised and enforceable as soon as they are not subject to review and become enforceable by the issuing State party.[420] However, this is subject to any rights of the HNS Fund to pay pro rata in accordance with Article 14.6 when the claims exceed the HNS Fund limits of liability and where there are claims for loss of life and personal injury.[421]

9. POLLUTION FROM RADIOACTIVE SUBSTANCES

The 1960 Paris Convention and the 1963 Brussels Convention as well as the 1997 Protocol to Amend the Vienna Convention on Civil Liability for Nuclear Damage and the Joint Protocol Relating to the Application of the Vienna Convention and the Paris Convention compose the international liability framework which channels liability exclusively to the operator of a nuclear installation on the basis of strict liability. They also provide for limitation of liability for the operator. The International Convention relating to Civil Liability in the Field of Maritime

---

413. 2010 HNS Convention, art 37.2 and art 39.7.
414. Where there is a series of occurrences the date of the last occurrence is the starting point for the ten-year period (art 37.4).
415. 2010 HNS, art 39.1.
416. 2010 HNS, art 39.1 and 39.2.
417. 2010 HNS, art 38.4.
418. 2010 HNS, art 39.1.
419. 2010 HNS, art 39.5.
420. 2010 HNS, art 40.3.
421. 2010 HNS, art 40.3.

Carriage of Nuclear Material (NUCLEAR), 1971 also relates to the issue of liability of sea carriers of nuclear materials. Where these international instruments or other national instruments are applicable there is no limitation of liability for the shipowner of a ship carrying nuclear substances by virtue of the exclusion under Article 3(c) of the 1976 LLMC. However, this would only be relevant where the operator of a nuclear site is also the shipowner, charterer, manager or operator of the ship as otherwise by virtue of the aforementioned conventions there is no liability on the legal persons owning or running the ship.

In the UK this framework as provided by the 1960 Paris Convention and the 1963 Brussels Convention is enacted in the Nuclear Installations Act 1965. The enactment of the 1976/1996 LLMC in the UK clarifies that the claims under this section are those under sections 7–11 of the Nuclear Installations Act 1965. The Nuclear Installations Act 1965 does not impose liability for foreign operators or other relevant persons carrying excepted matter, defined as nuclear matter that consists of isotopes for medical, industrial or commercial purposes; or uranium either in natural form or with less than 0.72 per cent concentration of U235; or indeed any other matter which is excepted as a matter of foreign law applicable to a foreign operator. The abovementioned conventions related to the carriage of radioactive materials are applicable to nuclear installations and do not cover liability in respect of nuclear-powered ships. The liability of the shipowner of a nuclear ship is excluded from limitation under Article 3(d) of the 1996 LLMC.

10. LIABILITY ARISING FROM CARRIAGE OF HAZARDOUS WASTES[422]

Dumping of substances at sea is generally prohibited under the Convention on the Prevention of Marine Pollution by Dumping of Wastes and Other Matter, 1972 (London Convention 1972) as amended by its 1996 Protocol. In this section we will be concerned with the influence of the international legal framework for hazardous wastes on shipping. This influence is important in two respects. First, in relation to the liability of the owner of a ship carrying hazardous wastes and, second, and perhaps more surprising, in relation to scrapping of ships.

The export of hazardous wastes is regulated by the 1989 Basel Convention on the Control of the Transboundary Movements of Hazardous Wastes and Their Disposal (the Basel Convention).[423] In the UK any export of hazardous wastes to a non-OECD[424] country is completely banned, by virtue of the EU adoption of the 1995 amendment to the Basel Convention.[425] The Basel Convention applies to hazardous wastes[426] which are subject to transboundary movement[427] (hereinafter "transport"). Such wastes are hazardous if they fall within the rather involved

---

422. See also, M.N. Tsimplis, "Liability and Compensation in International Transport of Hazardous Wastes by Sea: The 1999 Protocol to the Basel Convention" (2001) 16(2) *International Journal of Coastal and Marine Law* 295.
423. The Convention entered into force on 5 May 1992. The UK ratified the Basel Convention in February 1994.
424. Organisation for Economic Co-operation and Development.
425. Ban Amendment to the Basel Convention on the Control of Transboundary Movements of Hazardous Wastes and their Disposal, Geneva, 22 September 1995. The Ban Amendment must be ratified by three-fourths of the Parties who accepted it in order to enter into force. At the moment the Protocol is not in force.
426. Art 2.1 of the Basel Convention defines "wastes" as "substances or objects which are disposed of or are intended to be disposed of or are required to be disposed of by the provisions of national law".
427. Art 2.3 of the Basel Convention defines "transboundary movement" as

any movement of hazardous wastes or other wastes from an area under the national jurisdiction of one State to or through an area under the national jurisdiction of another State or to or through an area not under the national jurisdiction of any State, provided at least two States are involved in the movement.

convention definition[428] or if they are deemed hazardous under the domestic legislation of a party to the Convention that is involved in the transport of the waste. Radioactive wastes and wastes which are derived from the normal operations of a ship[429] are excluded from the Basel Convention, provided they are subject to an international regulatory system.[430] The Basel Convention applies to all international carriage of hazardous wastes whether by land, air or sea but not to national carriage. Parties to the Basel Convention are under a general obligation to minimise the generation of hazardous wastes[431] and to ensure that there are adequate disposal facilities within the generating State.[432] Five natural or legal persons[433] that could be involved in the transport of hazardous wastes are identified: the producer of the wastes is termed the "Generator";[434] the "Exporter"[435] is any person under the jurisdiction of the State of export[436] who arranges for the export of hazardous wastes; the "Importer"[437] is any person under the jurisdiction of the State of import[438] who arranges for the import of hazardous wastes; the "Carrier" is the performing carrier;[439] and finally, the "Disposer" is any person who receives and disposes of cargo deemed hazardous waste.[440] Another role, taken either by the "Generator" or the "Exporter" under the Basel Convention is that of the notifier, the person responsible to inform and seek permission from the relevant authority for the export of the hazardous wastes.[441] States party to the Basel Convention can only transport hazardous wastes to other States party to the Convention, whilst transport from and to non-party States is precluded.[442] Transports are authorised and monitored[443] through the dual requirements of the "movement document"[444] and the "notification document".[445] Compulsory insurance is also provided for under the Convention.[446] The State of export, at the end of the transport, has to be informed by the Disposer of the receipt and of the disposal of the

---

428. Under art 1.1(a) of the Basel Convention hazardous wastes are those listed in Annex I of the Convention, unless they are devoid of the characteristics that are contained in Annex III.

429. Ibid., art 1.4.

430. Basel Convention, art 1.3.

431. Ibid., art 4.2(a), "taking into account social, technological and economic aspects".

432. Ibid., art 4.2(b).

433. Ibid., art 2.14.

434. Ibid., art 2.18.

435. Ibid., art 2.15.

436. Art 2.10 of the Basel Convention defines a "State of export" as one "from which a transboundary movement of hazardous wastes or other wastes is planned to be initiated or is initiated".

437. Basel Convention, art 2.16.

438. Art 2.11 of the Basel Convention defines a "State of import" as one to which a transboundary movement of hazardous wastes or other wastes is planned or takes place for the purpose of disposal therein or for the purpose of loading prior to disposal in an area not under the national jurisdiction of any State.

439. Basel Convention, art 2.17.

440. Ibid., art 2.19. By virtue of art 2.4, disposal is defined in Annex IV of the Convention and includes conventional disposal (e.g. incineration, landfill, release into the sea or lakes, permanent storage, included in categories D1 – D12) and reuse/recycling of components of the waste (categories R1 – R11). Both categories include the accumulation/modification of the wastes before disposal (category D13 – D15 for conventional disposal and R1 – R12 for reuse of the material).

441. Basel Convention, arts 4 and 6.

442. Basel Convention, art 4.5.

443. Because seeking permission and providing notice to transit States when carrying hazardous wastes by sea is arguably a restriction on the right of innocent and transit passage, the UK, on signing the Basel Convention, made the following declaration: ". . . the provisions of the Convention do not affect in any way the exercise of navigational rights and freedoms as provided for in international law. Accordingly, nothing in this Convention requires notice to or consent of any state for the passage of hazardous wastes on a vessel under the flag of a party, exercising rights of passage through the territorial sea or freedom of navigation in an exclusive economic zone under international law."

444. A requirement by virtue of art 4.7(c) of the Basel Convention. The information that is required under the document is set out in Annex V, Part B of the Convention.

445. A requirement by virtue of art 6.1 of the Basel Convention. The information that is required under the document is set out in Annex V, Part A of the Convention.

446. Ibid., art 6.11 states that "any transboundary movement of hazardous wastes or other wastes shall be covered by insurance, bond or other guarantee as may be required by the State of import or any State of transit which is a Party".

wastes.[447] Notification of all States through which the hazardous goods are to be transported is required.[448]

Failure to comply with the procedures of the Basel Convention renders the transport "illegal traffic"[449] and this is deemed a criminal offence.[450] This term includes cases where documentation was obtained fraudulently or by misrepresentation[451] or, notwithstanding the absence of fraud or misrepresentation, where the transport fails to comply with the documentation.[452] The transport of wastes for dumping in breach of the Basel Convention is also classed as illegal traffic.[453] If the Generator or Exporter is the person liable for the illegal traffic, then the State of export is under an obligation to dispose of the wastes rendered illegal traffic.[454] Likewise for the State of import if the Importer or Disposer is the person liable.[455]

In December 1999, the fifth Conference of the Parties to the Basel Convention agreed on a Liability Protocol which will enter into force 90 days after 20 States have ratified it.[456] The 1999 Basel Liability Protocol deals with liability and compensation arising from hazardous wastes in transboundary transport, whether this transport is in compliance with the provisions of the Basel Convention or considered as illegal traffic. The Basel Liability Protocol ensures that there should be compensation available for damage caused during the transport of hazardous wastes by providing both for strict liability[457] of one of the designated persons[458] and, in addition, provides for fault-based[459] liability. The strict liability fails to attach where the damage is caused by extreme political events or natural disasters;[460] or where the damage is a result of compliance with State regulations,[461] or sabotage.[462] No strict or fault-based liability attaches to a person if it controls and/or possesses hazardous wastes solely for the purpose of preventing pollution.[463] Persons who are strictly liable are not excluded from fault-based liability. However, if their liability is not fault based, then limits of liability can be introduced under national law. Minimum amounts for such limits are prescribed under Annex B of the Liability Protocol.[464] A carrier will,

447. Ibid., art 6.9.
448. Note that in relation to transport by sea the requirement of notification by the coastal State may be considered as an intervention to the right of innocent passage. The UK made a declaration upon signing, which was confirmed upon ratification, that the provisions of the Convention do not affect in any way the exercise of navigational rights and freedoms as provided for in international law.
449. Failure to comply with procedures for notification or consent is covered in art 9.1(a) and 9.1(b) of the Basel Convention, respectively.
450. Ibid., art 4.3.
451. Ibid., art 9.1(c).
452. Ibid., art 9.1(d).
453. Ibid., art 9.1(e), which states: "That results in deliberate disposal (e.g. dumping) of hazardous wastes or other wastes in contravention of this Convention and of general principles of international law."
454. Ibid., art 9.2. The State of export must either take the waste back or arrange for its disposal elsewhere, in accordance with the Convention provisions.
455. Ibid., art 9.3.
456. As of 12 February 2017, 11 States have accepted the Liability Protocol. The UK signed the Liability Protocol in 2000 but has not ratified it yet.
457. Basel Protocol, art 4.
458. I.e. the Exporter, the Importer and the Disposer.
459. Basel Protocol, art 5.
460. I.e. resulting from an act of "armed conflict, hostilities, civil war, insurrection" (Basel Protocol, art 4.5.a) or resulting from natural phenomena of "exceptional, inevitable unforeseeable and irresistible character" (Basel Protocol, art 4.5.b). The strict liability attaches, presumably, even if the causes described in art 4.5. are foreseeable.
461. This holds only if the compulsory measures are of the State in which the damage occurred (Basel Protocol, art 4.5.c).
462. "[W]rongful intentional conduct of a third party" (Basel Protocol, art 4.5.d).
463. Basel Protocol, art 6.2. Provided that the measures this person takes are reasonable and lawful.
464. These increase with the size of the cargo. Thus every participant in the transport is liable for damage arising from its own faults and in addition, the responsible person (i.e. the exporter or the importer or the disposer) is also strictly liable for all the damage. The minimum limit of (maximum) liability that can be imposed for cargoes larger than 10,000 tonnes is 30,000,000 SDR.

in general, face unlimited, fault-based, liability under the Liability Protocol. If it is also one of the designated persons then its liability will be strict but probably limited. The Liability Protocol arguably permits[465] the application of other liability regimes. Thus, for example, where the carrier is also liable for damage under the 2010 HNS then the 2010 HNS Convention will prevail, thus limiting the carrier's liability.

11. SCRAPPING OF SHIPS[466]

(a) Introduction

Ship-breaking, an integral part of the shipping industry, is a profitable activity concentrated in developing States and considered as an area in need of regulation. India, Bangladesh, Pakistan, China and Turkey are some of the most important ship-breaking countries. The existence of ship-breaking operations is essential for the livelihoods of thousands of families from the most deprived parts of these countries.[467] However, this comes at a price. Accidents,[468] damage to workers' long-term health as well as longterm contamination of the environment are the normal consequences of such industry.[469] However, notwithstanding the physical risks the industry poses to workers, it remains attractive to them because the pay is much higher than in other sectors. Employers can afford higher daily rates because of the profit margins they have.[470] In addition the shipowner gets much more money from the final sale of the ship and thus has a financial incentive to recycle the ship rather than abandon it or scuttle it.

When a ship is sent off for scrapping it may be considered as a hazardous waste within the meaning of the Basel Convention. The majority of ships that are at the end of their lives contain hazardous chemical constituents within their structural make-up, if not in their cargo residues.[471] State-owned ships and war ships are not excluded from the scope of the 1989 Basel Convention. Thus the procedure applicable for all hazardous wastes and the restrictions in exports are also applicable to ships destined for recycling. The Basel Convention also prohibits the exportation of hazardous wastes if a State of export believes that the wastes will not be managed in an environmentally sound manner.[472] There is a reciprocal obligation upon the State of import as well.[473] Environmentally sound management is defined as meaning: "taking all practicable steps to ensure that hazardous wastes or other wastes are managed in a manner which will protect human health and

---

465. Art 11, but the wording is ambiguous.

466. See also D. Wall and M.N. Tsimplis, "Selling Ships for Scrap" (2003) 1 LMCLQ 254; M.N. Tsimplis, "The Hong Kong Convention on the Recycling of Ships" [2010] LMCLQ 305; M.N. Tsimplis, "Recycling of EU ships: From Prohibition to Regulation?" [2014] LMCLQ 415.

467. See for example the report by Prasanna Srinivasan "The Basel Convention of 1989: A Developing Country's Perspective" available from www.libertyindia.org/pdfs/basel_convention_srinivasan.pdf (accessed 22 February 2017).

468. Ibid., at p 19. Srinivasan's study suggests a range between a death of a worker per day to official estimates of 50 deaths of workers per year.

469. Ibid.

470. These are determined by the demand for steel and the values of ore and finished steel as well as the oversupply of ships.

471. A ship can certainly be classed as an "object" under art 2(1) of the Basel Convention, and the further definition of "disposal" encompasses those operations which lead to recovery/recycling. Bearing in mind that scrapping of vessels is generally undertaken to recover material, e.g. scrap steel for steel mills and also fuel oils and machinery components, ships destined for ship-breaking will typically contain several of the materials listed in Annex I as hazardous wastes. In addition to this there are a host of other specific wastes contained in ships destined for shipbreaking, which are listed in Annex VIII of the Basel Convention. Under the above arguments ships are considered as falling under the Basel Convention's scope. However, the literal reading of the Convention indicates that ships were not considered when the Convention was agreed and they fall uneasily within the scope of the Basel Convention (M.N. Tsimplis (fn 421)).

472. Ibid., art 4(2)(e).

473. Ibid., art 4(2)(g).

the environment against the adverse effects which may result from such wastes."[474] It is well documented that ship-breaking operations in non-OECD countries, such as India, Pakistan and Bangladesh, do not always constitute environmentally sound management as defined in the Convention. Consequently, trans-boundary movement of ships destined for ship-breaking are prohibited under the Convention since it does not constitute environmentally sound management, as well as falling within other prohibition measures which were outlined above. As a result, transport of such ships is illegal traffic, thus rendering the persons involved liable to criminal sanctions.[475]

This results in a major problem not only for commercial ships but also for older war ships which are then sold to governments of developing States for further use. It is questionable whether the 1989 Basel Convention permits such transactions because if it does indeed permit them, then sham sales of ships or other wastes would also be able to circumvent the Convention's restrictions. In addition the 1995 Basel Convention Ban Amendment completely prohibits exports of hazardous wastes for final disposal and recycling from OECD countries to non-OECD countries. Although not yet in force, the European Union has implemented its provisions in the form of a Regulation in 1993.[476]

(b) The Ship Recycling Convention

The Conference of the Parties to the Basel Convention has passed the problem of avoidance of the 1989 Basel Convention in shipping to the IMO. The Hong Kong International Convention for the Safe and Environmentally Sound Recycling of Ships, 2009 (SRC),[477] developed in the IMO, attempts to provide a solution to several of the problems raised. It does so, not only by adopting general principles of law but also by devising a system of control and standards through both the ship construction and the ship recycling industry.

The SRC accepts that ship recycling is the best option for decommissioned ships. This is certainly correct as the alternative options of scuttling or abandonment of ships means the uncontrollable release of hazardous materials in the environment with unknown risks involved. The general obligations imposed on the Contracting States are: an obligation to implement the SRC fully and completely,[478] to co-operate with other Contracting States for the purpose of effective implementation[479] and to encourage the continued development of technologies and practices for environmentally safe recycling of ships.[480] The SRC does not restrict Contracting States from taking more stringent measures in order to prevent, reduce or minimise adverse effects to human health and the environment. Other obligations imposed on SRC Contracting States relate to the exchange of information with other Contracting States[481] and technical assistance to Contracting States that require it.[482]

---

474. Ibid., art 2(8).
475. Basel Convention 1989, arts 4.3 and 4.4.
476. Council Reg. 259/93/EEC on the Supervision and Control of Shipments of Waste within, into and out of the European Community (OJ 1993 L30/1). This has been transposed into English law by the Trans-frontier Shipment of Waste Regulations 1994.
477. SR/CONF/45, 19 May 2009. The SRC was agreed on 15 May 2009. It is not yet in force.
478. SRC, art 1(1). This includes the implementation of the Annex which under art 1(5) is stated to be an integral part of the SRC.
479. SRC, art 1(3).
480. SRC, art 1(4).
481. Art 12 which obliges the information to be sent to the IMO which in turn is obliged to disseminate information on ship recycling facilities, Competent Authorities in each State, recognised organisations and surveyors in each Contracting State, names of ships to which a Ready for Recycling certificate has been granted, names of ships recycled each year, list of violations of the SRC and actions taken against recycling facilities.
482. Art 13. No provision for funds to be spent on such assistance is included.

(c) To which structures does the SRC apply?

Ships larger than 500 grt[483] entitled to fly the flag of Contracting States[484] are subject to the provisions of the SCR. In addition Ship Recycling Facilities[485] operating in Contracting States are also subject to the application of the SRC.[486] The term "ship" includes vessels of any type whatsoever which are or have been operating in the marine environment even where they have been stripped of equipment or are under towage.[487] Thus the only restriction is the requirement for these to operate in the marine environment. Vessels operating only within waters under the sovereignty and jurisdiction of the flag State are excluded from the application of the SRC.[488] This is relevant for areas of the marine environment, probably the territorial sea of the Contracting State, as fresh water bodies will be excluded by virtue of the definition of ship under Article 2(7). A very important exclusion concerns military ships and any governmental ship of a Contracting State employed in non-commercial service.[489]

(d) The regulations for safe and environmentally sound recycling of ships

The text of the SRC is supplemented by the annex containing the regulations for the environmentally safe recycling of ships which is an integral part of the SRC.[490] The annex applies to the design, construction, survey and certification of ships larger than 500 grt.[491] The implementation of the annex is to be done in conjunction with the relevant International Labour Organization standards, and the 1989 Basel Convention. The regulations provide for the design, operation and maintenance of ships. Hazardous materials listed in Appendix 1[492] are prohibited to be introduced in new or old ships. Each SRC Contracting State must ensure that ships operating under its authority and ports, ship yards or other facilities in its jurisdiction involved in the building, repair, maintenance and operation of ships would also comply with the prohibition or restricted use permitted under the SRC.

(e) Regulation of hazardous materials used for the construction of ships

The recycling of ships is regulated under the SRC through the International Inventory of Hazardous Materials Certificate (IHM), a key certificate for the operation of the SRC. The IHM is issued

---

483. Gross tonnage is defined under art 2(8) as that calculated under the International Convention on Tonnage Measurement of Ships, 1969 and its successors.

484. Or operating under the Contracting State's authority, art 3(1).

485. The definition of a ship recycling facility is very broad. Any defined area or site, yard or facility used for the recycling of ships falls under this definition, art 2(11).

486. SRC, art 3(1.2).

487. SRC, art 2(7). Expressly included are submersibles, floating craft, floating platforms, self-elevating platforms, floating storage units, floating production storage and offloading units.

488. SRC, art 3(3). The term used is "operating throughout their life". Whether the "life" of a ship stops and starts again when a ship is significantly modified is unclear. For example, where a ship is transformed into a storage facility after a number of years of service and it is then used as such for an equally long period of time would the exception be applicable? Or where a ship is converted into a passenger ship and then is operated within the jurisdiction of a State would it also be excluded from the operation of the SRC? It is suggested that relatively simple conversions of the ship that was subject to the SRC should not enable the converted structures to avoid the SRC regime simply by being used for a period of time within the jurisdiction of a Contracting State. However, where major changes are effected and the new structure is clearly different from the pre-existing ship the exception would arguably be applicable. For example where a part of a ship is used in the construction of a new ship with additional new material. However, depending on the interpretation adopted a potential loophole appears to be present under this article.

489. Art 3(2).

490. Art 1(5).

491. Reg 2.

492. Reg 4. Asbestos, ozone depleting substances (with some exceptions applying until 1 January 2020), polychlorinated biphenyls, antifouling components and systems prohibited under the 2001 Harmful Antifouling Systems on Ships are included in Appendix I.

by the flag State[493] or a recognised organisation or surveyor.[494] The IHM must be on board every ship to which the SRC applies prior to recycling. New ships[495] must have an IHM on board from the time of their construction. Through its role as a record of change of hazardous materials on board the ship the IHM should be the basis for ensuring compliance with regulation 4, that is, to indicate either that no hazardous materials have been used in repairs, maintenance or operation of the ship[496] after the coming into force of the SRC, or if they have been used that this use was in agreement with the restrictions provided under the SRC and the IMO provisions.[497]

When a ship is destined to be recycled, two further parts of the IHM must be completed. The first part lists operationally generated wastes and the second part lists the stores. Both parts should be completed and authorised by the flag State or a recognised organisation.[498]

Existing ships are under an obligation to comply with the requirement to have onboard an inventory of hazardous materials at the latest five years after the entry of the SRC into force[499] or before recycling if this is less than five years from the entry into force of the SRC.[500] However, the IHM for an existing ship, defined as being a ship other than a new ship,[501] is to be produced before recycling as an initial and final survey.[502] Ships registered in non-Contracting States cannot be issued with an IHM certificate.[503] The SRC requires that with respect to ships flying the flag of States that are not Contracting States to the Convention the Contracting States should ensure that "no more favourable treatment is given to such ships".[504] How this will be achieved is not clear and guidelines will be developed.[505]

Rights of inspection are provided to other SRC Contracting States in respect of ships subject to the SRC. The purpose of the inspection is to ensure compliance with the requirements of the SRC. In the general case the rights of inspection are restricted to verifying that there is onboard an International Certificate on Inventory of Hazardous Materials or an International Ready for Recycling Certificate.[506] If there is such a certificate onboard then this must be accepted.[507] A detailed inspection can be carried out by the port authorities but only where there is no appropriate certificate onboard, or where there are substantial discrepancies between the certificate

493. The form is provided under Appendix 3 of the SRC. Contracting States should recognise each other's certificate as equally valid, reg 11.2. The flag State may request that another Contracting State surveys the ship and issues or authorises the issuance of the IHM or endorse it in case of ship repairs or modifications (reg 12(1)). The issued certificate must be transmitted to the flag State and shall contain a statement of its equivalence to certificates issued by the flag States (regs 12(2) and 12(3)).

494. Reg 11(12). Under reg 13, the IHM should be in the official language of the flag State issuing the certificate and translated, if not already in one of these languages, into either English, French or Spanish. An option to avoid the translation in respect of ships not moving to other States is also provided.

495. A new ship is defined under reg 1.4 as one for which the building contract is placed on or after the entry into force of the SRC; or, where there is no shipbuilding contract, a ship with a keel laid six months after the entry into force of the Convention or the delivery is 30 months after the entry into force of the SRC. It is suggested that where more than one of these is satisfied then the ship is a new ship.

496. This is achieved through additional general or partial surveys made under the shipowner's request after major repairs or replacement of parts of the ship or its equipment and results in ensuring compliance with the SRC and amendment of Part I of the IHM; reg 10.3.

497. For existing ships the plan describing the visual or sampling checks used in determining the hazardous materials should be prepared.

498. This is achieved through a final survey, reg 10.4.1.

499. The five-year period applies only if it is not practicable to have the IHM inventory onboard earlier.

500. Reg 5.2.

501. Reg 10.3.

502. Reg 11.

503. Reg 12.4.

504. Art 3(4).

505. See MEPC 59/3/4.

506. This certificate is provided by the flag State, when the formalities of the SRC are complied with in order to enable the ship to be recycled.

507. Art 8.

and the condition of the ship or equipment or there are no procedures for the maintenance of the IHM.[508] The inspection should follow the IMO guidelines.

(f) Authorised ship recycling facilities

Under the SRC, recycling is permitted only at authorised,[509] ship recycling facilities[510] which, in addition, are authorised to perform all the necessary recycling actions the ship recycling plan provides for.[511]

The SRC avoids the solution adopted by the 1989 Basel Convention, where it is up to the exporting State to decide whether environmentally sound recycling can be achieved at the State of import. It also clearly contradicts and is incompatible with the 1995 Basel Amendment (Ban), through which no hazardous wastes are to be exported to developing countries. By contrast it attempts to ensure that, in all countries, including developing countries, the lucrative ship-breaking sector can become part of the sustainable development by adopting measures for workers' safety and for minimisation of the environmental degradation. The costs of the changes in these practices and associated increased costs will probably be met in most cases by a reduction in the money earned by the shipowner through recycling. Contracting States must ensure appropriate authorisation and compliance with the SRC of any recycling facilities operating under their jurisdiction and sanctions for breach of the SRC obligations,[512] severe enough to discourage violations from occurring,[513] should be introduced by all Contracting States' national laws.[514]

(g) Entry into force

Article 17 of the SRC requires three criteria to be met in order for the SRC to come into force. First, it requires at least 15 Contracting States.[515] This should have been relatively easy to achieve, given the support provided by the European Parliament,[516] but have not yet been achieved eight years after the Convention. Second, it requires that the Contracting States represent at least 40 per cent of the gross tonnage of the global merchant shipping. This requirement cannot be met presently by the EU and other developed States.[517] However, this criterion was required to ensure that a significant percentage of the world's fleet will comply with the requirements set out in the SRC. The third criterion is that it requires that the maximum annual ship recycling volume of all

---

508. If there is evidence that a ship has violated, is violating or will violate the SRC arrangements a Contracting State that has evidence can request that the ship is investigated at the port or offshore terminals of another Contracting State. The inspection reports are then sent to the requesting party, the flag State and the IMO (art 9(1)).

509. The final survey provides for compliance with the IHM, that the Ship Recycling Plan reflects appropriately the IHM information as well as the requirement for safe-for-entry and safe-for-hot work requirements and that the Ship Recycling facilities hold a valid authorisation under the SRC (reg 10.4).

510. Ship Recycling facility is, under art 2.11, a defined area, site, yard or facility, used for the recycling of ships. Thus, any area where intentionally activities of ship recycling take place is subject to this definition provided that it is somehow defined as such, probably under the requirements of national law.

511. Reg 8(1.2).

512. Art 10.

513. Art 10(3).

514. When a violation is confirmed the Contracting State is obliged under art 10(1.2) to initiate proceedings against the recycling facility and also inform the IMO of the breach and actions taken and, failing to act within a year after receiving information from another Contracting State, explain why no action has been taken.

515. In accordance with the art 16 requirements for ratification, accession, etc. On 11 February 2017 five countries, representing around 20% of the global grt, had ratified the Convention.

516. See MEPC 59/3/6. This includes the European parliament resolution of 26 March 2009 on an EU strategy for better ship dismantling (para E).

517. More than half of the global tonnage is registered in open registries of which only two, Malta and Cyprus, are EU countries.

the Contracting States during the past ten years is at least 3 per cent of the gross tonnage of these States.[518] It is unclear whether the time period referred to concerns the ten years before the time of the signing of the SRC or before the time the last Contracting State has signed. The issue is resolved by a resolution prescribing the methodology for determining the maximum annual ship recycling volume.[519] The reason a reference to the recycling volume of the Contracting States is included[520] is the need to ensure that when the SRC comes into force the Contracting States have the capacity between themselves to recycle at least 3 per cent of their fleet, otherwise there is a risk of having several ships destined for recycling and not enough facilities within the SRC to recycle them.

The SRC has been considered a success by the IMO and, apparently, by the ILO.[521]

The SRC is clearly inconsistent with the 1995 Basel Amendment Protocol (Ban) because under the latter recycling of ships in a developing State is completely forbidden, irrespective of whether the facility involved is capable of providing environmentally sound recycling. It can further be argued that insistence on the application of the 1995 Basel Amendment Protocol Ban is a breach of the SRC. In particular it can be argued that the SRC Contracting States have undertaken to recycle ships in an appropriate way and for this purpose they have agreed the use of services of appropriate standards. Thus prohibition of export to developing States under the 1995 Basel Amendment Protocol would be directly in conflict with the SRC arrangements.

In conclusion, the documentary framework for the environmentally safe dismantling of ships has been agreed through the SRC. Whether this will lead to substantial improvement of the risks posed by the ship recycling industry especially in the developing States is as yet unclear as many of the important technical aspects have not yet been agreed or have been avoided. However, the achievement of establishing a documentary control system both for ships and ship recycling facilities cannot be underestimated and is certainly, partly at least, a fulfilment of the 1989 Basel Convention.

(h) Equivalent level of control

For Contracting States of the 1989 Basel Convention it is important to identify the extent the SRC fulfils their obligations under the 1989 Basel Convention because additional measures would need to be adopted if the SRC is not sufficient to fulfil the relevant 1989 Basel Convention obligations. Discrepancies between the two legal instruments would mean parallel obligations and duplication of actions. The 1989 Basel Convention itself permits additional agreements on the subject-matter provided that these do not derogate from the 1989 Basel Convention and that they are not less environmentally sound, in particular with respect to the interests[522] of develop-

518. See SR/CONF.41.

519. MEPC 59/3/9 by which the IMO Secretary has to extract the recycled tonnage per year for each of the Contracting States by reference to the table of ship breaking in each year's Lloyd's Register – *Fairplay* – annual publication World Casualty Statistics and determine "the maximum annual ship recycling volume" by selecting the highest value occurring in the previous ten-year period for each Contracting State.

520. See SR/CONF/41. An express suggestion to require the participation of five recycling States ensuring an agreed number of recycled tonnage (see SR/CONF/37) was not followed. This would have even made it more controversial as it would then be a matter of a few developing States whether the SCR would come into force.

521. ILO welcomes new regulations on ship breaking as crisis boosts the industry, see http://www.ilo.org/global/about-the-ilo/newsroom/features/WCMS_106542/lang--en/index.htm (accessed 22 February 2017), where, despite the title, there is no express endorsement of the arrangement in the interview.

522. It can be argued that the reference to the "interests" is not as narrow as including solely environmental interests but includes the interests of the developing States as part expressed within the notion of sustainable development.

ing States.[523] Thus some form of equivalence or certification of the SRC for the purpose of the Basel Convention obligations has to be developed.

It was hoped that ships covered by the SRC could be excluded from the ambit of the Basel Convention. However, when the SRC was discussed in the tenth Conference of the Parties to the Basel Convention (COP) there were differing views as to whether the SRC provides a level of control and enforcement equivalent to that of the Basel Convention.[524] The tenth COP of the Basel Convention encouraged Contracting States to ratify the SRC and enable its early entry into force while "acknowledging that the Basel Convention should continue to assist countries to apply the Basel Convention as it related to ships". In other words the parties to the Basel Convention envisage that ship recycling will be subject to both conventions, in reality not resolving the difficulties of implementation of the Basel Convention to ships but expecting that its implementation will be assisted by the SRC.

(i) The European Ship Recycling Regulation

The EU has taken the view that the SRC provides the same level of control as the Basel Convention.[525] Consistently with this assessment the EU has adopted a new regulation[526] (this will be called here the EU-SRR) which uses the SRC as its basis but significantly modifies the SRC system with respect to the requirements for ship recycling facilities by imposing stricter requirements than the SRC standards. Ships registered in EU Member States (these will be called EU-ships) covered under the EU-SRR are excluded from the legal framework of the Basel Convention as implemented in the EU. The EU-SRR has legal and policy implications and significant commercial and policy ramifications. The EU-SRR will come into force at the earliest on 31 December 2015 and at the latest by 31 December 2018[527] with some of its sections related to older ships and foreign ships coming into force at other times. The most important points are outlined below.

The EU-SRR provides for additional prohibited materials in the IHM. It requires not only EU ships but also foreign ships to carry an IHM certificate after 31 December 2020. It establishes a European list of Ship Recycling Facilities which will consist of such facilities authorised by EU Member States but also those in non-EU Member States. The latter should comply with the EU

---

523. Art 11 of the 1989 Basel Convention states:

> Notwithstanding the provisions of art 4 paragraph 5, Parties may enter into bilateral, multilateral, or regional agreements or arrangements regarding transboundary movement of hazardous wastes or other wastes with Parties or non-Parties provided that such agreements or arrangements do not derogate from the environmentally sound management of hazardous wastes and other wastes as required by this Convention. These agreements or arrangements shall stipulate provisions which are not less environmentally sound than those provided for by this Convention in particular taking into account the interests of developing countries.

524. UNEP/CHW.11/16.
525. The EU's submission to the tenth COP of the Basel Convention states that the SRC provides "a level of control and enforcement at least equivalent to that one provided by the Basel Convention", UNEP/CHW.10/INF/18 at p 39. The US also submitted a preliminary assessment finding an equivalent level of control and enforcement (ibid., at p 71). Japan also submitted a preliminary analysis. Several NGOs submitted analyses suggesting that there is no equivalent level of control and enforcement.
526. Regulation (EU) No 1257/2013 of the European Parliament and of the Council of 20 November 2013 on ship recycling and amending Regulation (EC) No 1013/2006 and Directive 2009/16/EC, OJ L 330 56, 10 December 2013.
527. The Regulation will apply 6 months after the date when the EU Ship Recycling List will exceed 2.5 million LDT. As at February 12 2017 there were 18 solely European recycling facilities on the list which covered anything between 20 per cent and 40 per cent of the threshold. The difference in the estimate arises because both actual and theoretical capacities can be reported. It is reasonable to assume that the end of 2018 is more likely as a date for the application of the Regulation.

standards and should be authorised and inspected by the European Commission. The EU-SRR modifies the requirements for Ship Recycling Facilities so that beaching is not consistent with its application.

12. SHIPPING AND CLIMATE CHANGE

Apart from the impact on the marine environment, shipping affects the atmospheric environment through engine emissions of harmful gases and particles. MARPOL Annex VI provides the framework for reducing emissions of sulphur oxides, adopting even more stringent limits in special areas and planning for the reduction of nitrogen oxide emissions from marine engines by demanding minimum standards for ships constructed on or after 1 January 2016 and operating in emission control areas.[528]

Ship emissions also contribute to greenhouse gas emissions and under the 1992 United Nations Framework Convention on Climate Change (UNFCCC) all states are under an obligation to stabilise greenhouse gas concentrations in the atmosphere at a level that "would prevent dangerous anthropogenic interference with the climate system".[529] The Convention confirms the principle of "common but differentiated responsibility and respected capabilities".[530] The legal instrument that quantifies the amounts of reductions of greenhouse emissions for the period 2008–2012 is the 1997 Kyoto Protocol.[531] New voluntary commitments for Annex I Parties to the Kyoto Protocol were agreed under the Doha Amendment to the Kyoto Protocol.[532]

An overall obligation is imposed on Annex I countries, in essence developed countries, to reduce their emissions by their respective amount so as their total emissions are reduced by 5 per cent in the period 2008–2012 in relation to emissions in 1990. In addition Annex I States[533] are obliged under Article 2(2) "to pursue limitation or reduction of emissions of greenhouse gases . . . from . . . marine bunker fuels, working through the International Maritime Organization". The work of the IMO has historically been in developing legal instruments applicable to all ships irrespective of whether they are registered in developed or developing States. Thus an IMO-based instrument can be argued as going against the common but differentiated responsibility principle and not fulfil Article 2(2) of the Kyoto Protocol which requires developed States to pursue limitation or reduction options. This has for the time being put a brake on these negotiations as the IMO was seen by many developing States as an inappropriate forum to discuss the issue.[534]

Developed States counter-argue that there is competency in the IMO both under its constitution and UNCLOS to deal with pollution from ships. There is little doubt that this view is correct. However, it is also correct that the reference in the Kyoto Protocol expressly puts the obligation on developed States. It appears that for the moment the developing States do not wish

---

528. Ship's bunkers are notoriously dirty. In the European Pollution Control area the permitted sulphur content is 100 times higher than that for cars and in non-control emission areas they have currently 3,500 times higher concentrations which will fall after 2020 to 500 times higher concentrations (Prevention of Air Pollution from Shipping – Implementation of Directive 2012/33/EU – Impact assessment – Annex B, DEFRA). Air pollution is not visible like oil pollution and it is very difficult to attribute atmospheric pollution problems in ports where traffic, industries and households as well as ships each contribute to create major problems.
529. UNFCCC, art 2.
530. UNFCCC, art 3(1).
531. The Kyoto Protocol to the UNFCCC, agreed at the third session of the Conference of the Parties (COP 3) in Kyoto, Japan, on 11 December 1997, entered into force on 16 February 2005.
532. Agreed on 8 December 2012, at Doha, Qatar.
533. Kyoto Protocol, art 3(1).
534. See MEPC 60/22, 12 April 2010.

to lose a negotiating point by conceding to an IMO led agreement without an overall conclusion for greenhouse gas (GHG) emissions under the UNFCCC. However, their argument is merely technical as most ships even when registered in developing States are in fact owned by entities based in the developed world. Applying emission reductions to ships flagged to developed States would in essence push shipowners to reflag their ships to developing States, but the benefits of inaction are not enjoyed by the developing States. Options for unilateral measures by developed States in the form of conditions for entry to their ports are being discussed.

In response to calls for reduction of GHG from shipping, the IMO has adopted the Energy Efficiency Design Index (EEDI) for new ships[535] and the Ship Energy Efficiency Management Plan (SEEMP) for all ships. This happened 20 years after the 1992 UNFCC has been agreed – the equivalent of one generation of ships. The EEDI concerns the gradual development of an engineering index which will, in the future, depending on further negotiations, lead to improvements in energy efficiency from ships and possibly reduction of emissions.[536] The SEEMP is mandatory for ships over 400 grt from 1 January 2013.[537]

Overall the EEDI/SEEMP system will deal with GHG emissions for the next generation of ships which will become fully efficient in 20–25 years and which will reduce the emissions in relation to what would have been emitted without these arrangements. However, the inefficiency of these measures is demonstrated by the fact that the total emissions from ships will increase by more than 40 per cent from its present situation. In the meantime, the focus of the organisation will naturally be on the technical implementation of the EEDI while GHG emission from shipping will grow.

The 2015 Paris Agreement came into force in November 2016 and marks a significant change in the attitude to GHG emissions control. While the Kyoto Protocol was based on specific undertakings for target reductions, the Paris agreement is based on National Determined Contributions with an overall target to keep global atmospheric temperature increase below 2 degrees C and closer to 1.5 degrees C. The 2015 Paris Agreement does not provide for any obligations for shipping.[538] It is unlikely that the current situation can be tolerated for long as ships' engines are, both in respect of atmospheric pollution and GHG emissions, much worse than engines used in other transport sectors.[539] The European Parliament's Environment committee has recently proposed amendments to legislation to include the CO_2 emissions from shipping in the EU Emission Trade System[540] from 2023 in " the absence of a comparable system operating under the IMO" in 2021.

---

535. For an outline of the EEDI, see A. Chrysostomou and E.E Vogslid, "Climate Change: A Challenge for IMO Too" in R. Asariotis and H. Benamara (eds), *Maritime Transport and the Climate Change Challenge* (Earthscan/Routledge 2012), pp 75–111. According to this report (and the IMO GHG study of 2009) ships have emitted 870 million tonnes of CO_2. The projections for all SRES scenarios except the A1FI are bound by emissions of around 1,500 million tonnes of CO_2 annually by 2030 (figure 6.9 of Chrysostomou and Vogslid, 2012) The EEDI is projected under the same paper to reduce the emissions by up to 240 million tonnes of CO_2 annually by 2030. This means that the emissions from shipping in 2030 will be around 1,260 million tonnes of CO_2 annually, that is an increase of emissions from shipping by 44 per cent on the 2009 IMO study estimate. Taking into account that the normal way of estimating reduction/increase of emissions globally is by reference to 1990 one can argue that by 2030 the emissions from ships would be even higher.

536. The EEDI will apply to new ships only thus in essence gradually improving the emissions from the sector as older ships are taken out of use. This exception of old ships coupled with exemptions granted to developing States until 2019 will reduce the effects of the EEDI.

537. See IMO Guidelines (Resolution MEPC.213(63)).

538. The IMO Secretary-General called on global leaders at the Conference of the parties not to intervene and not to insist that the IMO sets a clear and ambitious sector target for shipping. The Ministry of Foreign Affairs of the Marshall Islands called the view a danger to the planet see http://worldmaritimenews.com/archives/173535/marshall-islands-se-kimizus-view-on-co2-emissions-danger-to-the-planet/ (accessible as at 22 February 2017).

539. The counter argument relies on the fact that when emissions are counted per cargo weight, shipping is relatively more efficient. However, the issue is one of absolute reduction of GHG not solely an issue of efficiency and no sector can stay immune.

540. Committee on the Environment, Public Health and Food Safety, 2015/0148(COD), 14/12/2016.

It is unclear whether such plans will prompt the IMO to act. The first International Panel for Climate Change Report was in 1990 and since then every IPCC report confirms the hazardous effects CO_2 emissions have for the global climate. The UNFCC came into force in 1992 but the IMO moved on the topic twenty years later and, as explained above, it is nowhere near stabilising shipping emissions, which are projected to increase dramatically. If shipping is left unregulated all other sectors will have to undertake the emission reductions necessary to meet the 2015 Paris Agreement's targets. This would be contrary to common sense and to the "polluter pays" principle in both its economic and legal context.

CHAPTER 11

MARINE INSURANCE

Özlem Gürses and Johanna Hjalmarsson

1. INTRODUCTION[1]

Much of modern marine insurance owes its current appearance to a gradual introduction of new features over the years, and to case law that has addressed specific issues such as the introduction of steamships, the First and Second World Wars, the container revolution and Somali piracy. The law continues to develop, which makes marine insurance a challenging and stimulating field to study and work in. This chapter deals in turn with the law surrounding marine insurance and with three main forms of marine insurance: hull and machinery insurance, cargo insurance and P&I insurance.

---

1. Sections 1 and 5 were written by Özlem Gürses, sections 2, 3 and 4 by Johanna Hjalmarsson.

The London Market is one of the largest insurance and reinsurance markets insuring and reinsuring risks not only in England but in several continents. Moreover, there are a number of Protection and Indemnity Clubs whose headquarters are in London and who insure shipowners' liabilities to third parties such as oil pollution, loss of or damage to cargo, and liability to passengers and members of crew. In the following paragraphs we will analyse the insurance procedure in London and the law applicable to marine insurance contracts which are governed by English law.

The previous edition of this book referred to the Draft Bill which aimed to reform some of the main principles of English insurance law. The Bill referred to was enacted in February 2015 as the Insurance Act 2015 (IA 2015) and came into force on 12 August 2016. The new law will apply to the policies that are taken out after the IA 2015 came into force. The insurances that were dated before 12 August 2016 will be subject to the law before the law reform. Thus, there will still be some time to come before the IA 2015 will be disputed and the law before the IA 2015 will still be relevant due to the law reform being recent. In this chapter, therefore, both the law before and after the IA 2015 will be referred to.

(a) Formation of insurance contracts

(i) Terminology

Whilst reading the cases that are involved in insurance contracts taken out in the London market it is important to understand the terminology to be able to illustrate the formation procedure. In London an insurance may be placed either in the company market or at Lloyd's. Lloyd's is not an insurance company but it is a market where brokers may place risks by negotiating the risk with several different underwriters. The company market is the market where the insurers are placed outside the Lloyd's building market. In the Lloyd's building there are also representatives of the company market underwriters. With regard to the principles applicable to formation of insurance, no distinction is to be drawn between insurances at Lloyd's and those placed by means of slips in the company market.[2]

Lloyd's has two distinct parts: the market, which is made up of many independent businesses, and the Corporation of Lloyd's, which is there – broadly speaking – to oversee that market.[3] Both work closely to maintain high standards of performance across the market.

Members of Lloyd's organise into *syndicates* who accept insurance business only through a professional (corporate) *managing agent*, who employs professional underwriting and other staff for that reason. A syndicate, that has no legal personality and is not a partnership, is merely the administrative arrangement through which its members underwrite insurance risk.

The Lloyd's Market may place business – especially overseas – under a *binding authority* given to an *overseas broker (coverholder)*. Under the binding authority agreement (contract of delegation) the managing agent delegates its authority, to enter into a contract of insurance to be underwritten by the members of a syndicate managed by it, to the coverholder in accordance with the terms of the agreement. They also set out the coverholder's other responsibilities, such as handling premiums or agreeing claims.

By a *lineslip* underwriter (A) authorises another underwriter (B) to accept risk on A's behalf.

A lineslip is a contract between the underwriters setting out the terms on which one underwriter (B) can accept a risk on behalf of others (A). For instance, in *Involnert Management Inc v*

---

2. See Kerr LJ *General Reinsurance Corp v Forsakringsaktiebolaget Fennia Patria* [1983] Q 856; [1983] 2 Lloyd's Rep 287, at 290.
3. www.lloyds.com/lloyds/about-us/what-is-lloyds.

Aprilgrange Ltd[4] two lineslips were led by Travelers Syndicate 5000, one was for yachts with a value below €10m; the other was for "mega yachts" with a value in excess of €10m up to €50m. Such a facility assists the broker in placing insurance as it avoids the demands of having to broker each risk individually to each insurer.[5]

(ii) Open market placement

A legally binding agreement is formed by an offer and a matching acceptance, and consideration is required to enforce a contractual promise. In the insurance context, the assured provides consideration by paying the premium in return for the policy coverage. The procedure followed in the London Market is called "Open Market Placement". The broker takes round a "slip"[6] to various underwriters at Lloyd's or in the London Company market. The underwriter who is willing to insure the risk "scratches", i.e. initials, the slip and puts his stamp on it as a form of acceptance of the broker's offer. The London Market is a subscription market, meaning that the insurers normally participate in insuring the entire risk by covering given percentages of the risk, to the extent each of them is willing to insure. Thus, the underwriters who accept the broker's offer write "lines" by way of participation towards the 100 per cent cover which the broker and his client seek from the market.

In the London Market, insurance contracts used to be formed by scratching a one-page document, a slip, containing very little information about the terms of the contract. The policy then used to be issued sometimes much later than the contract was formed by a slip (or there never was an issued policy). Such procedure used to be called "deal now detail later". It was abandoned in 2007 and now the document that is used by the brokers is the "Market Reform Contract" (the "MRC"),[7] which provides a standard form of submissions. One of the objectives of introducing the MRC is to have a clear structure whereby brokers present contracts in a consistent manner, which in turn adds clarity to the broker/underwriter discussion and thus enhances the efficiency of the placing process.[8] A further objective is to ensure that the content aligns with the needs of contract certainty.[9]

In a number of cases where the policy was issued much later than the contract had been formed by virtue of a slip, discrepancies between the wording of the slip and the policy arose. While such issues had not been conclusively determined[10] and the latest view was in favour of resolving the dispute according to the rules applicable to interpretation of contracts,[11] the market introduced the MRC. The MRC now contains all the details that otherwise a policy would contain, thus the likelihood of such discrepancies is minimised, as the market's current position is "deal and detail now".

A contract may be formed before the policy is issued, however, section 22 of the Marine Insurance Act 1906 (MIA 1906) provides that "a contract of marine insurance is inadmissible in evidence unless it is embodied in a marine policy in accordance with this Act." The MRC slip contains the detailed terms that a policy would include. Therefore, the contract formed by a MRC will also be embodied by a policy.

---

4. [2015] EWHC 2225 (Comm); [2015] 2 Lloyd's Rep 289 [5].
5. *Involnert Management Inc v Aprilgrange Ltd* [2015] EWHC 2225 (Comm); [2015] 2 Lloyd's Rep 289 [5].
6. After the Market Reform Contract procedure was put in place the document is called the MRC slip.
7. See www.londonmarketgroup.co.uk/mrc (accessed 5 January 2017).
8. See www.londonmarketgroup.co.uk/mrc (accessed 5 January 2017).
9. See www.londonmarketgroup.co.uk/mrc (accessed 5 January 2017).
10. *New Hampshire Insurance v MGN* [1996] CLC 1692 (Potter J); *Youell v Bland Welch & Co (No. 1)* [1992] 2 Lloyd's Rep 127.
11. *HIH Casualty & General Insurance Ltd v New Hampshire Insurance Co* [2001] 1 Lloyd's Rep 378.

As stated above, given that in Lloyd's much of business works by subscription the broker will need to engage with the underwriters in the market until 100 per cent subscription is reached.[12] The question may then arise as to the status of scratches of the underwriters before the 100 per cent subscription is obtained. If a loss occurs before the 100 per cent subscription is obtained, those who had already agreed to insure the risk might want to argue that they can rescind the contract given that there was not a binding agreement before the 100 per cent subscription was reached. In *General Reinsurance Corp v Forsakringsaktiebolaget Fennia Patria*[13] the Court of Appeal held that the presentation of a slip by the broker constitutes an offer, and the writing of each line constitutes an acceptance of this offer by the underwriter *pro tanto*.[14] Thus, once the underwriter scratches the MRC, he cannot rescind the contract in between him signing the contract and the broker obtaining 100 per cent subscription. Equally, the assured cannot insist on the insurer cancelling the endorsement, which is more insurer friendly, before the 100 per cent subscription for the endorsement is obtained.

A binding agreement is formed when the underwriter scratches a MRC slip unless he makes it clear that he does not intend to be bound by his scratch. The courts have decided that scratching by pencil,[15] underlining the signature[16] or adding "TBE"[17] next to the signature is not an indication by the underwriter as to withholding his commitment to the risk. The courts emphasised that to qualify the scratching further words were needed on the slip to indicate the intention not to be bound by the contract yet. On the three occasions mentioned above, the courts found that the examples were purely administrative and they might have had some meaning internally but they did not mean anything to the assured or any other third parties. For instance, scratching by pencil was found as being nothing more than a reflection of the fact that another document would, for purely administrative reasons, have to be drawn up and signed. Underlining the initials with two little lines was found to have been the underwriter's private note for himself or for his partner; it might have had some internal significance for the insurer or his partner but it had no significance whatsoever so far as the other underwriters were concerned. Thus, the underwriter's signature confirming "it is agreed" was unqualified. "TBE", standing for "to be entered", in itself connoted only that the underwriter did not have his records readily available to mark up his entry.

(iii) Leading underwriter

It is likely that a particular underwriter might have a reputation in the market as an expert in the kind of cover required and his lead is likely to be followed by other insurers in the market. Therefore, it might be businesslike for the broker to approach the leading underwriter first and obtain his initial on the slip which might then persuade the following underwriters that it is an acceptable risk to insure. For instance, in *Aneco Reinsurance Underwriting Ltd (In Liquidation) v Johnson & Higgins Ltd*[18] the leading underwriter, K, was referred to as "a prominent figure in

---

12. If the broker achieves more than 100 per cent subscription every line will require to be written down proportionately to some extent, in order to produce a total cover of no more than 100 per cent. This procedure is called signing down and there is now an express provision about signing down on the MRC.

13. [1983] QB; QB 856; [1983] 2 Lloyd's Rep 287.

14. See also *Eagle Star v Spratt* [1971] 2 Lloyd's Rep 116, at p 127 (Lord Denning) and *American Airlines Inc v Hope* [1974] 2 Lloyd's Rep 301.

15. *Bonner v Cox* [2004] EWHC 2963 (Comm); [2005] Lloyd's Rep IR 569. The point did not arise on appeal [2006] 2 Lloyd's Rep 152.

16. *Eagle Star Insurance Co Ltd v Spratt* [1971] 2 Lloyd's Rep 116.

17. *ERC Frankona Reinsurance v American National Insurance Co* [2005] EWHC 1381 (Comm); [2006] Lloyd's Rep IR 157.

18. [2001] UKHL 51; [2002] 1 Lloyd's Rep 157, [165].

the XL market." The leading underwriter may, but is not required to, take a larger share than the following underwriters.[19]

The assured will have separate insurance agreements with the leading underwriter and each of the followers.[20] When a leading underwriter is involved in the subscription to the risk the insurance contract may contain a leading underwriter clause which may clarify the leading underwriter's authority to modify the terms of the insurance contract or to settle the claims by the assured. Consequently, if the leading underwriter is authorised to agree on changes to the contractual terms on behalf of the following market, his consent would be sufficient to bind the following underwriters should the brokers seek any modifications. In this respect, the obvious commercial purpose of the leading underwriter clause may be described as "simplifying administration and claims settlement".[21] In *Roadworks (1952) Ltd v Charman*[22] Judge Kershaw QC explained:

[i]n the London insurance market a risk is often underwritten by several insurers – Lloyd's syndicates, several companies or a combination of both. It is in the interests of both underwriters and brokers that time should not be spent in obtaining the express agreement of every underwriter to every change, even such as a change in the spelling of the name of the insured. Hence, the leading underwriter system has evolved.[23]

The leading underwriter's authority to make changes to the insurance contract had been disputed in the past which then led to the discussions as to the leading underwriter's legal status. It was debated whether he is the agent[24] of the following underwriters or if he is not the agent but his actions are simply the "trigger" by which the following market becomes bound.[25] While a conclusive view had not been expressed on the matter,[26] the market began using the MRC which refers to the General Underwriters Agreement (the "GUA").[27] The GUA contains detailed sections as to the changes which require the leading underwriter's agreement only, or all the following underwriters' consent, as the case may be. Therefore, if there is a dispute on an amendment to the agreement which was agreed only by the leading underwriter, the parties would be referred to the GUA to determine whether the leading underwriter's consent to the amendment is binding on the following underwriters. However, this does not mean that the discussion as to the legal status of a leading underwriter has disappeared. Recently interpretation of the "follow the leader" clause in terms of the settlement agreement reached by the leader and the assured came twice before Teare J.. In *Buana Samudra Pratama v Maritime Mutual Insurance Association (NZ) Ltd*[28] the judge held that the clause covers the quantification of the loss as well as the leader's acceptance that there is no policy defence available, for instance in terms of breach of warranty. In a more recent case, *San Evans Maritime Inc v Aigaion Insurance Co SA*,[29] the "follow clause" was in the following terms: "Agreed to follow . . . Syndicate in claims excluding ex-gratia payments". Teare J held that by agreeing to this clause the following underwriter

19. *Roar Marine Ltd v Bimeh Iran Insurance Co (The Daylam)* [1998] 1 Lloyd's Rep 423, at p 426.
20. *International Lottery Management v Dumas* [2002] Lloyd's Rep IR 237, at [71].
21. *Roar Marine Ltd v Bimeh Iran Insurance Co (The Daylam)* [1998] 1 Lloyd's Rep 423, at p 430; see also *PT Buana Samudra Pratama v Maritime Mutual Insurance Association (NZ) Ltd* [2011] EWHC 2413 (Comm); [2011] 2 Lloyd's Rep 655.
22. [1994] 2 Lloyd's Rep 99.
23. Ibid., at p 104.
24. *Roadworks (1952) Ltd v Charman* [1994] 2 Lloyd's Rep 99.
25. *Mander v Commercial Union Assurance Co Plc* [1998] Lloyd's Rep IR 93.
26. *Unum Life Insurance Co of America v Israel Phoenix Assurance Co Ltd* [2001] EWCA Civ 129;1 [2002] Lloyd's Rep IR 374; *American International Marine Agency of New York Inc v Dandridge* [2005] EWHC 829 (Comm); [2005] Lloyd's Rep IR 643.
27. See www.londonmarketgroup.co.uk/gua (accessed 10 February 2017 update).
28. [2011] EWHC 2413 (Comm); [2011] 2 Lloyd's Rep 655.
29. [2014] EWHC 163 (Comm); [2014] 2 Lloyd's Rep 265

simply agreed to follow the leader in claims and therefore in settlements. The follow clause was an agreement between the following insurer and the assured that the former will follow the settlement of claims by the leader. Teare J stated that the purpose of the follow clause was to simplify the process of claims settlement and that this construction was consistent with that purpose. The judge referred to the discussion whether the leader is an agent of the following market and held that here the operation of the follow clause did not depend on the agency relationship between the leader and the following underwriters. Teare J did not express a concluded view on whether the leading underwriter owed a duty of care to the following underwriters.

General Reinsurance Corp v Forsakringsaktiebolaget Fennia Patria[30] is a case illustrating the formation of insurance contracts, the status of the underwriters' scratching and the independent contracts formed between the assured and each of the underwriters subscribed to the risk. In that case, a reinsurance policy was taken out and after the contract was concluded the reinsured decided to amend it. There were 25 underwriters who followed the leader in this subscription. The leader signed the endorsement which contained the amendment that the reinsured wished to make. Subsequently, the reinsured noticed that without the amendment the reinsurers' exposure would be much larger for a very substantial loss which had just occurred. The reinsured thus insisted that the leader cancel the endorsement. The problem then went before the court and the issue was whether the reinsured could rescind the endorsement unilaterally. The court decided in favour of the leader that every underwriter's scratching creates a binding agreement at the time of the scratching *pro tanto*. Therefore, in *Fennia Patria* the leading underwriter was bound by the amended reinsurance contract, whereas the followers who had not signed the amendment were bound by the original form of the agreement.

(b) Brokers

(i) Dual agency

It is a requirement for the assured to appoint a broker in order to be able to obtain a policy in the London market. Lloyd's brokers bring business into the market on behalf of clients – policyholders, and shop around to see which syndicates can cover their specific risk and on what terms. A broker who does not have direct access to the Lloyd's market, particularly overseas producing brokers, will have to appoint a Lloyd's broker to place the risk. A broker is entitled to a commission in return for taking out the insurance policy for the assured. The commission is deducted from the premium.

In the majority of cases, an insurance broker acts for the person seeking insurance and not for the insurer.[31] However, there are some cases where brokers may act as a dual agent – both for the assured and the insurer. In *Woolcott v Excess Insurance Co Ltd (No 2)*[32] the brokers acted for the assured but were also authorised by the insurers to bind insurance for their account, and initial documents of insurance and endorsements on their behalf. In *Drake Insurance Plc (In Provisional Liquidation) v Provident Insurance Plc*[33] the broker, as well as acting for the assured,

---

30. [1983] QB 856; [1983] 2 Lloyd's Rep 287.
31. In *HIH Casualty & General Insurance Ltd v JLT Risk Solutions Ltd* [2007] EWCA Civ 710; [2007] Lloyd's Rep IR 717 the role of a broker is described as "notoriously anomalous for its inherent scope for engendering conflict of interest in the otherwise relatively tidy legal world of agency, in that the broker is paid by the underwriters and may well act for both parties".
32. [1979] 2 Lloyd's Rep 210.
33. [2003] EWCA Civ 1834; [2004] 1 Lloyd's Rep 268, at p 283.

had authority to rate each proposal and to determine the premium on the basis of the insurer's underwriting criteria.

(ii) Duties

The relationship between the assured and the broker is contractual. In contract the broker is under an implied duty to exercise reasonable skill and care in performing his contractual obligations.[34] The broker also owes a parallel duty of care in tort.[35] The broker's duties apply at the placement of the risk as well as during the currency of the policy and in making the claim against the insurer. Thus, if the broker takes out a policy under which it will never be possible to make a claim against the insurer due to the size of the deductible in the policy compared to the average size of a potential claim by the assured,[36] or if the broker neglects to warn the assured about risk protection measures which were requested by the insurer, the broker will be liable for the loss that the assured suffers as a result.[37] In *Tudor Jones v Crowley Colosso Ltd*[38] the broker breached his duty of care to the assured when the policy coverage obtained was for a shorter period of time than the assured required. Another example in which the broker was in breach of his pre-contractual duties is *Sharp v Sphere Drake Insurance (The Moonacre)*,[39] where the subject matter insured was a yacht on which the crew employed by the assured lived during the time that the yacht was laid up at Majorca in winter. The proposal form contained a question about the yacht being used as a houseboat and the policy contained a clause excluding coverage for any period for which the vessel is used as a houseboat – unless notice be given to and an additional premium agreed by Underwriters. Having regard to the ordinary and natural meaning of the houseboat question in the proposal form and taking into account the expert evidence, Deputy Judge Mr Colman QC held that it was the professional duty of the broker dealing with a client's proposal for yacht insurance to advise his client that the underwriters had to be told if anyone, including a permanent crew, was to use the vessel as living accommodation during the period of lay-up. It should be noted there was a time when the courts were inclined to impose a duty on the assured to make sure that what the broker drafted and the insurer accepted accorded with the assured's instruction to the brokers.[40] However, the modern approach is that a broker is under a duty to exercise reasonable skill and care in the performance of the functions which he has undertaken and the assured has a right to rely on the broker's professionalism.[41]

A broker's pre-contractual duties to his clients include to inform the client of the duty of fair presentation of the risk. In *Jones v Environcom Ltd*[42] the broker's duties in this respect were listed as

- to advise his client of the duty to disclose all material circumstances;
- to explain the consequences of failing to do so;

---

34. *Youell v Bland Welch (No 2)* [1990] 2 Lloyd's Rep 431; *Dunlop Haywards (DHL) Ltd v Barbon Insurance Group Ltd* [2009] EWHC 2900 (Comm); [2010] Lloyd's Rep IR 149, at pp 168–170.

35. *Dunlop Haywards (DHL) Ltd v Barbon Insurance Group Ltd* [2009] EWHC 2900 (Comm); [2010] Lloyd's Rep IR 149, at p 176.

36. In *Standard Life Assurance Ltd v Oak Dedicated Ltd* [2008] EWHC 222 (Comm); [2008] Lloyd's Rep IR 55 while the average size of each claim was about £10,000, the policy had a £25 million deductible per claim.

37. *Ground Gilbey Ltd v Jardine Lloyd Thompson UK Ltd* [2012] Lloyd's Rep IR 12.

38. [1996] 2 Lloyd's Rep 619.

39. [1992] 2 Lloyd's Rep 501.

40. *Waterkeyn, The v Eagle Star & British Dominions Insurance Co Ltd* [1920] 5 Ll L Rep 42.

41. *Dunlop Haywards (DHL) Ltd v Barbon Insurance Group Ltd* [2009] EWHC 2900 (Comm); [2010] Lloyd's Rep IR 149.

42. [2011] EWCA Civ 1152; [2012] Lloyd's Rep IR 277.

- to indicate the sort of matters which ought to be disclosed as being material (or at least arguably material);
- to take reasonable care to elicit matters which ought to be disclosed but which the client might not think it necessary to mention.

In *Involnert Management Inc v Aprilgrange Ltd*,[43] the broker was held to be in breach of the abovementioned duties. The subject matter insured was a yacht which the assured purchased in 2007 for €13 million. A professional valuation in 2009 confirmed that the yacht's value was about €7 million and in 2011 she was advertised for sale at an asking price of €8 million. Between 2007 and 2011 she was insured year by year without giving too much consideration to the variation of her value after she was purchased. These facts were not disclosed to the insurers who successfully avoided the policy after the yacht was severely damaged as a result of a fire. Leggatt J applied *Jones v Environcom Ltd* and held that the brokers were in breach of the duty in failing to warn the managers of the duty of disclosure, but that duty did not extend to asking the managers whether there had been a recent valuation of the yacht or whether, and, if so, at what price, the yacht was to be marketed for sale. It was also held that the brokers' duty was not limited to advising the client in general terms of the duty to disclose material facts, but extended to eliciting from the client matters which ought to be disclosed. Leggatt J held that the brokers in *Involnert* ought to have asked the managers about the market value of the yacht in order to address the question in the proposal form about the "hull market value", but could not be criticised for not eliciting information as to the professional valuation and the planned marketing of the vessel when there was no reason to suspect those possibilities.

(iii) Producing and placing brokers

As stated above, a producing broker may enter into a sub-agency agreement with a placing broker who will place the risk with the insurer. In such a case there is no contractual relationship between the assured and the placing broker, therefore, in principle, the placing broker does not owe contractual or tortious duties to the assured.[44] The placing broker's contractual claims are to be brought against the producing broker who then may turn to the assured if he has a contractual claim against him. The contractual and parallel duties in tort apply between the producing and placing brokers as well as between the assured and the producing brokers.[45] If the producing and placing brokers were both in breach of their duties, the assured's claim in principle will be against the producing broker who then may seek contribution from the placing broker reflecting the placing broker's negligence.[46] It was held in *Involnert Management Inc v Aprilgrange Ltd*[47] that any liability of the producing broker for the negligent acts or omissions of the placing broker could not be a vicarious liability, as it was a basic principle that a person is not vicariously liable for the negligence or other wrongful act or omission of an independent contractor. Leggatt J explained that the basis of such liability is that the producing broker is under duties of a "non-delegable" kind, and liability is co-extensive with what has been contractually agreed. In this case, however, where the producing broker agrees, rather than to arrange insurance for its client, but gets another broker to do so, the duty of the producing broker, both in contract and in

---

43. [2015] EWHC 2225 (Comm); [2015] 2 Lloyd's Rep 289.
44. *Pangood Ltd v Barclay Brown Co Ltd* [1999] Lloyd's Rep IR 405.
45. See *Dunlop Haywards (DHL) Ltd v Barbon Insurance Group Ltd* [2010] Lloyd's Rep IR 149.
46. Ibid. See also *Tudor Jones v Crawley* [1996] 2 Lloyd's Rep 619.
47. [2015] EWHC 2225 (Comm); [2015] 2 Lloyd's Rep 289.

tort, would be limited to taking care to choose a competent sub-broker and giving appropriate instructions to the sub-broker.

The assured does not have a contractual relationship with the placing broker. If assumption of responsibility by the placing broker is proved by the assured, the assured then may sue the placing broker in tort.[48] In *BP Plc v AON Ltd (No 2)*[49] it was held that the direct communication between the assured and the placing broker, on the facts, established the assumption of responsibility. An assumption of responsibility was alleged but rejected in *Involnert Management Inc v Aprilgrange Ltd*[50] in which the assured's knowledge of a sub-broker's involvement in the placement of the risk was no more than the fact that the sub-broker's name was printed on the quote slip, proposal form and cover note for the insurance. There was no evidence that the assured was relying on the expertise of the placing broker, the assured had no contact at all with the placing broker and dealt exclusively with the producing broker.

(c) The premium

The assured pays the premium in exchange for the coverage provided by the policy. In marine insurance a broker is personally liable to pay the premium as a result of the custom[51] which was codified by section 53 of the MIA 1906. Accordingly, it is presumed that the broker already paid the premium to the insurer, that the insurer lent it to the broker and that it is now the broker's personal liability to repay the premium to the insurer. It was suggested that a broker is personally liable because he is deemed to be a principal, receiving the premium for the assured, and not merely an agent, and that a fiction is established that the broker had actually paid the premium but then borrowed the money from the underwriter so as to make himself personally liable to repay it.[52] As a result, the insurer is not able to sue the assured for non-payment of the premium, the responsible party for such a non-payment is the broker and the action has to be brought against him.[53] However, if the premium is to be returned,[54] the insurer is obliged to return the premium to the assured.[55] It is a general rule in these circumstances that "unless otherwise agreed" the broker has a cause of action in its own right against the assured[56] (or reinsured in the context of reinsurance)[57] in respect of unpaid premiums.

Section 53(1) sets out the rules about the payment of premium with the preceding words "unless otherwise agreed"; therefore it is possible to oust[58] the custom which was codified by the section. The custom basically addresses two matters: (1) the broker, not the assured, is personally liable to pay the premium to the insurer (or the reinsurer as the case may be); and (2) the insurer had received the premium which was now lent to the broker, requiring him to repay it to the insurer. The obligation of the broker under the usage is to pay the premium when it falls due under the policy.

---

48. *BP Plc v AON* [2006] Lloyd's Rep IR 577.
49. [2006] EWHC 424 (Comm); [2006] Lloyd's Rep IR 577.
50. [2015] EWHC 2225 (Comm); [2015] 2 Lloyd's Rep 289.
51. *Universo Insurance Co of Milan v Merchants Marine Insurance Co Ltd* [1897] 2 QB 93.
52. See *Power v Butcher* [1829] 10 B & C 329; see also J. Gilman QC, R. Merkin, C. Blanchard QC and M. Templeman (eds), *Arnould's Law of Marine Insurance and Average* (18th edn, Sweet & Maxwell 2013), [6–06]; R. Merkin, "The Duties of Marine Insurance Brokers", in R. Thomas (ed.), *The Modern Law of Marine Insurance: Volume 1* (Informa Law 1996), at p 283.
53. *Universo Insurance Co of Milan v Merchants Marine Insurance Co Ltd* [1897] 2 QB 93.
54. For instance for a non-fraudulent breach of the duty of good faith. MIA 1906, s 84(1).
55. MIA 1906, s 53(1).
56. *JA Chapman & Co Ltd (In Liquidation) v Kadirga Denizcilik ve Ticaret AS* [1998] Lloyd's Rep IR 377.
57. *Heath Lambert Ltd v Sociedad de Corretaje de Seguros* [2004] EWCA Civ 792; [2004] Lloyd's Rep IR 905.
58. See the discussion in *Universo Insurance Co of Milan v Merchants Marine Insurance Co Ltd* [1897] 2 QB 93.

Thus, if the premium had already been paid, it would always be controversial to argue a non-payment of premium. The problem is illustrated by the fact that insurers may include a premium payment warranty in the insurance contract and in such case the question will arise as to the function of the warranty in the policy and whether such a warranty ousts the custom. For instance, in *JA Chapman & Co Ltd (In Liquidation) v Kadirga Denizcilik ve Ticaret AS*[59] the policy contained the following warranty: "Warranted each instalment of premium paid to underwriters within 60 days of due dates." The question in this case was whether the broker was entitled to claim the premium from the assured. The assured shipowners argued that because of the warranty the custom was ousted so that they were liable for the premium to the insurers, not to the broker. A further argument in *Chapman* was that the premium payment warranty clearly contemplated that the underwriter was able to assert that the premium had not been paid to him and that if the underwriter did not receive the actual payment on time there would be a breach of warranty. Such a provision, however, as the argument went, would be wholly inconsistent with the general custom and practice as recognised in section 53(1) of the MIA 1906 which is founded on the hypothesis that as between broker and underwriter premiums are considered as paid. The Court of Appeal was not satisfied that the custom was ousted. It accepted that the presence of the premium payment warranty plainly supported the argument that it was inconsistent with the operation of the general rule and was thus an indication of an agreement ousting it. Nevertheless, the Court of Appeal read the policy as a whole and found that the broker's cancellation clause clearly suggested that the ordinary rule was to apply.

On the other hand, a differently worded premium payment warranty was held to have ousted the custom in *Heath Lambert Ltd v Sociedad de Corretaje de Seguros*,[60] where the relevant clause was in the following terms: "Warranted premium payable on cash basis to London Underwriters within 90 days of attachment." The Court Appeal held that the provision that premium was payable on a cash basis displaces the fiction that the broker was deemed to have paid the premium when due. The court held that the premium due date depends upon the true construction of the relevant premium payment clause. The effect of section 53(1) of MIA 1906, unless otherwise agreed, is that that obligation is the obligation of the broker, not the assured. It followed that the broker, Heath Lambert, could not be in breach of its obligation to pay the premium until the 90 days expired. The combined effect of the clause and section 53 of the MIA 1906 was that premium was payable in cash by the broker to the underwriters within 90 days of attachment and that the assured was liable to the broker on the same basis and that there was no room for a fiction that the broker paid the underwriters in cash when he did not. In *Chapman* the warranty was that each instalment of premium would be "paid to underwriters within 60 days of due dates" and the due dates were separately set out. In *Heath Lambert* the trial judge held, and the Court of Appeal approved that judgment, that a warranty as to when premium will in fact be paid is different from a warranty as to when premium is payable. Thus, a warranty as to when premium will be paid suggests that the premium is payable earlier, whereas a warranty as to when it is payable indicates when the obligation to pay arises. Conclusively, no premium is due immediately but is payable within 90 days of inception and in cash failing which there will be a breach of warranty. The Court of Appeal was satisfied that the policy was to work this way in the light of section 53(1) of the MIA 1906. Heath Lambert owed a duty to the underwriters to pay the premium in cash within 90 days of the attachment of the risk. Failure to pay would put the assured in breach of warranty.

---

59. [1998] Lloyd's Rep IR 377.
60. [2004] EWCA Civ 792; [2004] Lloyd's Rep IR 905.

In the absence of an express term[61] in the policy, premium is payable when the contract is made.[62] The parties may agree that it will be paid in instalments. In such a case the premium is indivisible,[63] therefore the whole premium is earned in full at the inception of the risk; the risk and the premium are apportionable or divisible between successive periods throughout the term. If the contract is terminated after it came into force, the assured is still obliged to pay the entire premium unless the policy expressly provides otherwise. The standard clauses used in marine insurance generally provide terms in respect of refund of premium, for example in case of cancellation of the policy.[64]

The brokers normally insert into the policy a broker's cancellation clause to protect them against non-payment of premium by the assured. The clause entitles the broker to cancel the contract in case the assured fails to pay the premium.[65] Even if the contract does not provide a cancellation clause, the broker has, as against the assured, a lien upon the policy for both the amount of the premium and his charges in respect of effecting the policy.[66]

(d) The duty of fair presentation of the risk

The IA 2015 came into force in August 2016, reforming the rules on the pre-contractual information duty. This duty, before the IA 2015, was referred to as the duty of utmost good faith. The IA 2015 redefined the pre-contractual information duty as the duty of fair presentation of the risk. Under section 17[67] of the MIA 1906 insurance contracts are contracts of utmost good faith. The duty of utmost good faith and the duty of fair presentation of the risk are thus separated. The duty of fair presentation of the risk applies only at the pre-contractual stage,[68] whereas the duty of utmost good faith is a broader duty and applies pre and post-contractually.

The pre-contractual information duty in consumer insurance was reformed by the Consumer Insurance (Disclosure and Representations) Act 2012. The 2012 Act falls outside the scope of this chapter given that marine insurance is in most cases not consumer insurance. The IA 2015 reformed the duty in the context of business insurance. The IA 2015 repealed sections 18, 19 and 20 of the MIA 1906 but the new provisions introduced by the IA 2015 retained the two limbs of the duty: (1) the duty of disclosure and (2) the duty not to misrepresent material facts.

---

61. See cl 35 of the International Hull Clauses 1 November 2003 for such an express clause setting out some detail regarding the time for payment of the premium and the consequences of non-payment.

62. *Heath Lambert Ltd v Sociedad de Corretaje de Seguros* [2004] EWCA Civ 792; [2004] Lloyd's Rep IR 905, [24].

63. *JA Chapman & Co Ltd (In Liquidation) v Kadirga Denizcilik ve Ticaret AS* [1998] Lloyd's Rep IR 377.

64. See e.g. Institute Time Clauses Hulls, 1 November 1995, cl 23; International Hull Clauses, 1 November 2003, cl 25.

65. See *JA Chapman & Co Ltd (In Liquidation) v Kadirga Denizcilik ve Ticaret AS* [1998] Lloyd's Rep IR 377 in which the broker's cancellation clause was in the following terms:

> It is hereby agreed between the underwriters and the assured that in the event of the assured or their agents on whose instructions this insurance may have been effected, failing to pay [Chapman] the premium or any instalment thereof on the due date, this policy may be forthwith cancelled by [Chapman] giving to the underwriters notice in writing, and the underwriters will thereupon return to the brokers through whom this policy as effected pro rata premium from the date of notice or from such later date as cancellation may be required in the said notice.

66. MIA 1906, s 53(2).

67. The IA 2015 retained the following words in section 17 of the MIA 1906 "A contract of marine insurance is a contract based upon the utmost good faith" but it repealed the following words from section 17 of the MIA 1906 ". . . , and, if the utmost good faith be not observed by either party, the contract may be avoided by the other party."

68. IA 2015, s 3(1).

(i) Disclosure

The assured is required to volunteer every material circumstance which the assured knows or ought to know. What the IA 2015 added to this rule is describing the form of satisfactory disclosure by the assured and the definition of "assured's knowledge" in this respect.Under the IA 2015 the assured satisfies the duty of disclosure if the circumstance is reasonably clear and accessible to a prudent insurer.[69] This provision is to prevent data dumping. The assured is required to indicate which of the documents in the data submitted are especially relevant to the risk insured. With regards to the assured's knowledge section 4 of the IA 2015 separates where the assured is an individual and where the assured is not an individual. In the former the assured knows (1) what is known to the individual and (2) what is known to the persons who are responsible for the assured's insurance (section 4(2)). Where the assured is not an individual (e.g. a company) the assured knows what is known by persons who are either (1) part of the assured's senior management, or (2) responsible for the assured's insurance (section 4(3)). The person "responsible for the assured's insurance" is defined by section 4(8)(b): "an individual is responsible for the insured's insurance if the individual participates on behalf of the insured in the process of procuring the insured's insurance (whether the individual does so as the insured's employee or agent, as an employee of the insured's agent or in any other capacity)". This definition is expected to catch, for example, the assured's risk manager if it has one, and any employee who assists in the collection of data or negotiates the terms of the insurance. It may also include an individual acting as the assured's broker.[3]

Unlike section 19 of the MIA 1906, the IA 2015 does not include a separate duty on the agent to disclose information to the insurer. The agent's knowledge or other information held by the agent may be caught under section 4(2) and (3) as stated above.

IA 2015 section 4(6) states that an assured ought to know what should reasonably have been revealed by a reasonable search of information available to the assured (whether the search is conducted by making enquiries or by any other means). Additionally, section 4(7) defines "information" in this context as information held within the assured's organisation or by any other person (such as the assured's agent or a person for whom cover is provided by the contract of insurance). Thus, it appears that relevant information subject to the reasonable search may be held by persons other than the assured itself. The reasonable search may extend beyond the assured itself to other persons, where such a search would be reasonable in the circumstances and where information is available to the assured.

Further, under section 6 of the IA 2015, what an individual knows includes not only what it actually knows but also "blind eye" knowledge. In other words knowledge includes cases where someone has deliberately failed to make an enquiry in case it results in the confirmation of a suspicion.[70]

(ii) Deemed full disclosure

Section 3(4) of the IA 2015 provides that the assured satisfies the duty of disclosure either by (a) disclosure of every material circumstance which the insured knows or ought to know, or (b) failing that, disclosure which gives the insurer sufficient information to put a prudent insurer on notice that it needs to make further enquiries for the purpose of revealing those material circumstances.

Section 3(4)(b) means that if the assured provides some limited information to the insurer which then should have put the insurer on inquiry as to the existence of some

69. IA 2015, s, s 3(3)(b).
70. Explanatory note to the Insurance Bill 2014, para 70. www.publications.parliament.uk/pa/bills/cbill/2014-2015/0155/en/15155en.pdf (accessed on 10 February 2017).

further facts which the assured has not disclosed, this should be deemed a full disclosure because the insurer could have investigated the facts further but chose not to do so. This may be described as the insurer having waived the full disclosure after the assured has disclosed sufficient information to put the insurer on inquiry by not asking for further information. It is yet to be tested by the courts how section 3(4)(b) will apply. Whether or not the information provided was "sufficient" within the meaning of this section will be a matter of an analysis of facts in each case. The test is a reasonably careful insurer rather than the actual insurer. Under the MIA 1906 the courts rejected the arguments to the effect that the assured provided sufficient information to put a prudent insurer on inquiry.[71]

(iii) Facts that need not be disclosed

Section 18(3) of the MIA 1906 contained a list of the facts that need not be disclosed. Accordingly, (1) if a fact diminishes the risk, e.g. a yacht being kept in a marina where there are strict security precautions for the residents;[72] (2) if the fact is known to the insurer;[73] (3) if a particular issue is drafted as a warranty;[74] (4) if the insurer waives the disclosure. Such waiver may be express[75] or implied. Implied waiver may be discussed in a case in which the assured disclosed some facts but there still exist further facts which have not been disclosed and which could have been discovered if the insurer had asked the obvious question. The courts have been reluctant to impose such a duty on the insurer and the emphasis was generally on the assured's duty which was to make a presentation of the risk. Nevertheless, if it is established that the insurer had not asked the obvious question and therefore chose not to discover further facts about the risk, then he is not to be entitled to argue non-disclosure of such facts.[76] This type of waiver may be analysed under section 3(4)(b) of the IA 2015 as discussed above.

With one modification, the IA 2015 retained the above list. Under section 3(5) of the IA 2015, in the absence of enquiry, the assured does not need to disclose a fact if:

(a) it diminishes the risk,
(b) the insurer knows it,
(c) the insurer ought to know it,
(d) the insurer is presumed to know it, or
(e) it is something as to which the insurer waives information.

The IA 2015 did not include the exception which used to appear under section 18(3)(d) of the MIA 1906 that "Any circumstance which it is superfluous to disclose by reason of any express or implied warranty." Section 18(3)(d) disappeared as the IA 2015 also abolished creating warranties by virtue of the basis of the contract clauses which used to render statements made by the assured in the proposal form warranties.

---

71. *Marc Rich & Co AG v Portman* [1997] 1 Lloyd's Rep 225

72. *Decorum Investments Ltd v Atkin (The Elena G)* [2001] 2 Lloyd's Rep 378.

73. See *Garnat Trading & Shipping (Singapore) Pte Ltd v Baominh Insurance Corp* [2010] EWHC 2578 (Comm); [2011] 1 Lloyd's Rep 589, approved by the Court of Appeal [2011] EWCA Civ 540; [2011] 2 Lloyd's Rep 492 in which Christopher Clarke J noted that a reasonable underwriter, in the business of insuring the ocean towage of a floating dock, is presumed to have had the knowledge that a towage plan would contain some general limitations upon the circumstances in which such a vessel could be towed across the ocean.

74. *Garnat Trading & Shipping (Singapore) Pte Ltd v Baominh Insurance Corp* (fn 67).

75. *HIH Casualty & General Insurance Ltd v Chase Manhattan Bank* [2003] UKHL 6; [2003] 2 Lloyd's Rep 61.

76. See *Garnat Trading & Shipping (Singapore) Pte Ltd v Baominh Insurance Corp* (fn 67); *WISE Underwriting Agency Ltd v Grupo Nacional Provincial SA* [2004] EWCA Civ 962; [2004] Lloyd's Rep IR 764, [65] – [66] (Rix LJ); *Marc Rich & Co AG v Portman* [1996] 1 Lloyd's Rep 430, at p 445 (Longmore J) regarding port characteristics.

The insurer's knowledge within the meaning of section 3(5)(b)(c) and (d) is described under section 6 of the IA 2015.

(iv) Misrepresentation

The duty is not to misrepresent material facts. Materiality will be analysed below. The rule under the MIA 1906 was that if the assured's representation was a statement of fact, that it had to be true (section 20(4)). If it was not true the assured was in breach of the duty. On the other hand if the representation was a statement of an expectation or belief the assured may defend the false statement by proving that he had reasonable grounds to believe that what he stated was the truth (section 20(5)). In *Sealion Shipping Ltd v Valiant Insurance Co,*[77] it was held that the statement that there had been an "excellent hull record" was a statement of the brokers' opinion under section 20(5) of the MIA 1906 and it was made in good faith. On the other hand in *Eagle Star Insurance Co Ltd v Games Video Co (GVC) SA (The Game Boy)*[78] the assured overvalued the vessel. The actual value was about US$150,000; the assured declared her value as US$1.8 million. The judge rejected the assured's argument that the assured had reasonable grounds to believe that the vessel was worth $1.8 million. The difference between the actual and declared value was too great to persuade the judge that a reasonable assured would have believed that $1.8 million represented the true value of the vessel. The IA 2015 repealed section 20 of the MIA 1906 but recodified the duty by sections under Part 2 of the Act. Since the duty of fair presentation of the risk is pre-contractual, the assured, who made a misstatement of fact, can correct the statement before the contract is concluded.[79] The correction has to be fairly made to the insurer, such that the corrected picture is fairly presented to the insurer, and comes to his knowledge[80] Moreover, a material representation is substantially correct if a prudent insurer would not consider the difference between what is represented and what is actually correct to be material.[81]

(v) Materiality

The assured is to disclose the information regarding the facts which "would influence the judgment of a prudent insurer in fixing the premium, or determining whether he will take the risk".[82]

The House of Lords in *Pan Atlantic Insurance Co Ltd v Pine Top Insurance Co Ltd*[83] authoritatively decided that the test of materiality, interpreting the words "would influence the judgment", is the mere influence test, namely every fact which a prudent insurer would want to know in assessing the risk is material and requires disclosure. This is a broad test given that to prove materiality it is not required to establish that the insurers' judgment would have been adversely affected upon disclosure of the fact in question. A mere proof that the prudent insurer would be interested to know – irrespective of the decisive influence of the disclosure – satisfies the test. The test of materiality is an objective test given that the actual insurer's view on the matter is to be disregarded and the insurer has to prove materiality by bringing an expert from the relevant

---

77. [2012] EWHC 50 (Comm); [2012] 1 Lloyd's Rep 252. This issue was not disputed on appeal [2012] EWCA Civ 1625; [2013] Lloyd's Rep IR 122.
78. [2004] EWHC 15 (Comm); [2004] 1 Lloyd's Rep 238.
79. IA 2015, s 7(6).
80. *Western Trading Ltd v Great Lakes Reinsurance (UK) Plc* [2015] EWHC 103 (QB); [2015] Lloyd's Rep IR 561 this issue was not disputed on appeal [2016] EWCA Civ 1003; [2016] Lloyd's Rep IR 643.
81. IA 2015, s 7(5).
82. MIA 1906, s 18(2).
83. [1995] 1 AC 501; [1994] 2 Lloyd's Rep 427.

market who would testify that the fact in question is material, or the judge may decide on materiality as a matter of common sense.[84]

The materiality test applies in the same way in the case of a non-disclosure and a misrepresentation of a fact. The test was retained by the IA 2015 with no change in the principles applicable to it.[85]

(vi) Material facts

Whilst the MIA 1906 did not provide any examples of material facts, the IA 2015 does provide a non-exhaustive list.[86] Accordingly, the following facts may be material:

(a) special or unusual facts relating to the risk,
(b) any particular concerns which led the assured to seek insurance cover for the risk,
(c) anything which those concerned with the class of insurance and field of activity in question would generally understand as being something that should be dealt with in a fair presentation of risks of the type in question.

The common law also has established material facts which will still be applicable under the IA 2015. Material facts are analysed under two difference categories: (1) Physical hazard and (2) Moral hazard.

Physical hazard includes the port characteristics,[87] for instance whether it is a congested port in an insurance of the charterer's liability for demurrage or the location of the vessel insured; or if it is a pleasure yacht, where the yacht is moored while she is not sailing.[88] Compared to the physical hazard, moral hazard is a more complicated issue and is more controversial than the topic of physical hazard. Moral hazard can include anything which might indicate whether the assured is a desirable person to do business with or not. The courts established that criminal convictions,[89] civil and criminal charges against the assured,[90] the assured's previous loss experience (if substantial),[91] general dishonesty of the assured (attempt to defraud a third party)[92] and previous breaches of the duty[93] are material facts. Overvaluation, unless it is so excessive that it indicates fraud, is not material.[94] There have been contradicting statements as to the materiality of non-payment of premium in previous policies but the latest view is that it goes to the credit

---

84. *Brit UW Ltd v F&B Trenchless Solutions Ltd* [2015] EWHC 2237 (Comm); [2016] Lloyd's Rep IR 69, [139]; *Synergy Health (UK) Ltd v CGU Insurance Plc (t/a Norwich Union)* [2010] EWHC 2583 (Comm); [2011] Lloyd's Rep IR 500.

85. IA 2015, s 7(3).

86. IA 2015, s 7(4).

87. *Marc Rich & Co AG v Portman* [1996] 1 Lloyd's Rep 430, approved by the Court of Appeal [1997] 1 Lloyd's Rep 225.

88. *Decorum Investments Ltd v Atkin (The Elena G)* [2001] 2 Lloyd's Rep 378.

89. *Inversiones Manria SA v Sphere Drake Insurance Co, Malvern Insurance Co and Niagara Fire Insurance Co (The Dora)* [1989] 1 Lloyd's Rep 69.

90. *North Star Shipping Ltd v Sphere Drake Insurance Plc* [2006] EWCA Civ 378; [2006] 2 Lloyd's Rep 183.

91. *Marc Rich & Co AG v Portman* [1996] 1 Lloyd's Rep 430. However, if the losses that the assured claimed in the past fall below the deductible of the (current) contract which the insurer purports to avoid, the previous losses are not material. *Sealion Shipping Ltd v Valiant Insurance Co* [2012] EWHC 50 (Comm); [2012] 1 Lloyd's Rep 252.

92. *Insurance Corp of the Channel Islands v Royal Hotel Ltd* [1998] Lloyd's Rep IR 151.

93. *Joseph Fielding Properties (Blackpool) Ltd v Aviva Insurance Ltd* [2010] EWHC 2192 (QB); [2011] Lloyd's Rep IR 238.

94. *North Star Shipping Ltd v Sphere Drake Insurance Plc* [2006] EWCA Civ 378; [2006] 2 Lloyd's Rep 183; *Eagle Star Insurance Co Ltd v Games Video Co (GVC) SA (The Game Boy)* [2004] EWHC 15 (Comm); [2004] 1 Lloyd's Rep 238.

risk rather than the assured's characteristics or the risk itself, and therefore it is not material.[95] However, combined with the assured's poor financial condition non-payment of premium might be material.[96]

(vii) Inducement

The House of Lords in *Pan Atlantic* also implied in the MIA 1906 the test of inducement, so that an underwriter who seeks a remedy for breach of the duty of fair presentation of the risk is required to prove two matters: (1) the fact which was not disclosed/or which was misrepresented was material under the mere influence test; and (2) the underwriter was induced to enter into the contract by such non-disclosure.

Inducement is the causal link between non-disclosure/misrepresentation and the making of the contract of insurance,[97] thus proving that the insurer's mind was so affected by a material non-disclosure/misrepresentation that the policy was thereby obtained. Inducement is a subjective test which concerns the insurer's actual mind, so that if the insurer attempts to prove inducement by bringing evidence from an underwriter other than the actual underwriter who wrote the risk, it is unlikely that it will satisfy the burden of proof.[98]

By the IA 2015 inducement has become a statutory requirement for the insurer to seek a remedy for breach of the duty of fair presentation of the risk.[99] The position is the same under the MIA 1906 (which was repealed by the IA 2015) and under the IA 2015 that only proof of materiality is not sufficient for the insurer to seek remedy for breach of the duty but the insurer also needs to establish inducement. However, a major law reform introduced by the IA 2015 is that different types of remedy apply in different circumstances that prove inducement. The remedy for breach of the duty of fair presentation of the risk will be analysed below.

As held in *Involnert Management Inc v Aprilgrange Ltd (The Galatea)*[100] the question to be asked that will prove inducement differs in the case of non-disclosure and misrepresentation. For non-disclosure it is "what the insurer would have done if the true position had been disclosed to him prior to the conclusion of the contract".[101] In *The Galatea* Leggatt J stated that in misrepresentation the answers are different to the questions of (1) what would the insurer have done if there had been no misrepresentation (2) what would the insurer have done if the assured had told the truth. The facts of *The Galatea* were stated above.[102] The difference between the asking price (€8 million) and the insured value (€13 million) of the insured yacht was a material fact to be disclosed to the insurer. When the proposal form was filled in the broker asked the assured's manager about the value of the yacht and the manager said it was purchased for €13million. The broker inserted this value without questioning the currency of this information. Leggatt J stated that the critical counterfactual question to ask is in principle whether the representee would still

---

95. *North Star Shipping Ltd v Sphere Drake Insurance Plc* [2006] EWCA Civ 378; [2006] 2 Lloyd's Rep 183, [50] (Waller LJ); *O'Kane v Jones (The Martin P)* [2003] EWHC 3470 (Comm); [2004] 1 Lloyd's Rep 389.

96. *North Star Shipping Ltd v Sphere Drake Insurance Plc* [2005] EWHC 665 (Comm); [2005] 2 Lloyd's Rep 76, [235] – [236] (Colman J). But see Waller LJ's inconclusive statement in the Court of Appeal where his Lordship stated that non-payment of premium is either material itself or not and since it goes to the credit risk it is probably not material [2006] EWCA Civ 378; [2006] 2 Lloyd's Rep 183, [50].

97. *Pan Atlantic Insurance Co Ltd v Pine Top Insurance Co Ltd* [1995] 1 A.C. 501; [1994] 2 Lloyd's Rep 427, at p 447 (Lord Mustill).

98. *Lewis v Norwich Union Healthcare Ltd* [2010] Lloyd's Rep IR 198.

99. IA 2015, s 8(1).

100. [2015] EWHC 2225 (Comm); [2015] 2 Lloyd's Rep 289.

101. *Synergy Health (UK) Ltd v CGU Insurance Plc (t/a ??Norwich Union)* [2010] EWHC 2583 (Comm); [2011] Lloyd's Rep IR 500.

102. See above 'Brokers' (b)(ii) 'Duties' on page 446.

have contracted (on the same terms) "if the representation had not been made" but not "what the insurer would have done if he had been told the truth".[103] The reason for this separation is that in the case of misrepresentation, it was what was actually said to the insurer – rather than what was not said – which was the foundation of the claim. The distinction was not merely theoretical. In *The Galatea* the judge decided that if the insurer had been told the actual value of the yacht, they would not have insured the yacht for €13 million, however, if the misrepresentation had not been made, e.g. if the value in the proposal form was left blank, it would not have made a difference for the insurers, as they regularly insured yachts without being provided with that information.[104]

(viii) Presumption of inducement

As mentioned above the burden of proof of both materiality and inducement is on the insurer. A question may arise as to whether proof of materiality creates a presumption to the effect that the insurer was induced to enter into the contract so that the burden of proof shifts to the assured who should prove that the insurer was not induced to enter into the insurance. The answer is that there is no general principle of presumption of inducement;[105] thus upon proof of materiality it is still the insurer's burden to prove inducement. However, there are a small number of cases in which the court accepted the presumption upon the facts. The presumption of inducement is not a rule of law but an exception which may be proved as a matter of fact.[106] For instance, in *St Paul Fire & Marine Insurance Co (UK) Ltd v McDonnell Dowell Constructors Ltd*[107] three of the four underwriters who subscribed to insure the risk brought evidence establishing inducement but the fourth underwriter could not submit any evidence. Evans LJ was persuaded that if the true facts had been disclosed, the four of them would have either refused the risk or accepted it on different terms.

As referred to above[108] where a contract is signed by the leading underwriter and the followers, the assured enters into independent contracts with each of the underwriters.[109] A question may arise in terms of whether a misrepresentation or non-disclosure to the leading underwriter could " travel" so as to avail following subscribers to the same slip? The following underwriters' subscription is upon the basis that the leading underwriter had been given a full and fair presentation so that he was in a position to make a proper evaluation of the risk.[110] If the leading underwriter was given a materially incomplete and misleading presentation which induced his acceptance, each of the followers would be entitled to claim the unfair presentation of the risk.[111] In *International Management Group (UK) Ltd v Simmonds*[112] whilst each of the following underwriters who gave evidence told the judge that he had made his own underwriting decision, it was plain to the judge that they placed considerable reliance upon the leading underwriters' assessment of this risk.

---

103. *Involnert Management Inc v Aprilgrange Ltd* [2015] EWHC 2225 (Comm); [2015] 2 Lloyd's Rep 289 [212], [214], and [215].
104. *Involnert Management Inc v Aprilgrange Ltd* [2015] EWHC 2225 (Comm); [2015] 2 Lloyd's Rep 289 [222].
105. *AXA Versicherung AG v ARAB Insurance Group (BSC)* [2015] EWHC 1939 (Comm); [2016] Lloyd's Rep IR 1 [62]; *Brit UW Ltd v F&B Trenchless Solutions Ltd* [2015] EWHC 2237 (Comm); [2016] Lloyd's Rep IR 69, [114].
106. *AXA Versicherung AG v ARAB Insurance Group (BSC)* [2015] EWHC 1939 (Comm); [2016] Lloyd's Rep IR 1 [119].
107. [1996] 1 All ER 96; [1995] 2 Lloyd's Rep 116.
108. See above " leading underwriter".
109. *International Lottery Management v Dumas* [2002] Lloyd's Rep IR 237 [71].
110. Which was proved upon the facts in *International Lottery Management v Dumas* [2002] Lloyd's Rep IR 237. *Aneco Reinsurance Underwriting Ltd v Johnson & Higgins Ltd* [1998] 1 Lloyd's Rep 565.
111. *International Management Group (UK) Ltd v Simmonds* [2003] EWHC 177 (Comm); [2004] Lloyd's Rep IR 247, [150].
112. [2003] EWHC 177 (Comm); [2004] Lloyd's Rep IR 247.

(ix) Remedy for breach of the duty of fair presentation of the risk

The remedy for breach of the pre-contractual information duty was "avoidance" of the contract only.[113] Avoidance means treating the contract as if it never existed, so that the remedy aims to put the parties in the position which they would have been in had there been no contract between them.

A major reform on this matter was introduced by the IA 2015. Under the new regime the insurer may seek remedy for breach of the duty of fair presentation of the risk only if inducement is proved.[114] Inducement was discussed above. A breach for which the insurer has a remedy against the assured is described as a "qualifying breach".[115] The IA 2015 provides different types of remedies where the breach is either (a) deliberate or reckless or (b) neither deliberate nor reckless. A breach is deliberate or reckless if the assured knew that he was in breach of the duty of fair presentation or did not care whether or not he was in breach of that duty.[116] The burden of proof that a qualifying breach was deliberate or reckless lies on the insurer.[117]

The remedies are set out in Schedule 1 of the IA 2015. The insurer may avoid the contract if the qualifying breach was either deliberate or reckless. In this case the insurer need not return any of the premiums paid. If the breach was neither deliberate nor reckless, the insurer's remedy will depend on what the insurer would have done in the absence of the breach. The insurer may avoid the contract if he establishes that he would not have entered into the contract on any terms. In this case the insurer must return the premium paid. Alternatively it may be proved that in the absence of the breach the insurer would still have entered into the contract but on different terms. This would establish inducement but would not give the right to avoid. Alternative remedies are available for the insurer so that if, for instance, the insurer would have entered into the contract by including an exclusion clause in it, the contract is treated as if the exclusion is part of the contract. If the claim falls into the exclusion clause the insurer may claim a contractual remedy and may deny liability for that reason. If the different terms that would have been included in the contract in the absence of the breach is about the premium and if the insurer would have charged a higher premium, upon discovery of the breach, if the risk occurred, the insurer may deduct from the insurance indemnity. Such a deduction will be proportionate, the formulation of which is provided by Schedule 1 as:

$$X = \frac{\text{Premium actually charged}}{\text{Higher Premium}} \times 100$$

For instance, if the insurer charged £1,000 premium but actually would have charged £1,250, the policy indemnification would be reduced by 20 per cent and the insurer would pay 80 per cent of the insured loss.

(x) Waiver of breach

The party who is entitled to avoid the contract will need to elect between two inconsistent choices: to avoid the contract or to affirm it. If the insurer elects to affirm the contract, the contract continues and the insurer will have to indemnify the assured despite the breach. To elect

113. MIA 1906, ss 17, 18(1) and 20(1) (before they were repealed – for s 17 before it was partly repealed).
114. IA 2015, s 8(1).
115. IA 2015, s 8(3).
116. IA 2015, s 8(5).
117. IA 2015, s 8(6).

to affirm the contract, the insurer is required to know about the circumstances which entitle the insurer to avoid the contract, and he should communicate his election to the assured. He must have actual, not merely constructive, knowledge of the facts giving rise to the right to avoid.[118] The law recognised such an election even though the party making such an election was unaware that this would be the legal entrenchment of what he did.[119] An objective assessment of the impact of the relevant conduct on a reasonable person in the position of the other party to the contract can determine whether the contract was affirmed or not.[120] If the insurer's words or conduct may be interpreted by the reasonable person as an election, the insurer will lose his right to avoid the contract. In *WISE Underwriting Agency Ltd v Grupo Nacional Provincial SA*[121] as soon as the reinsurers found out about the loss and the breach of the duty of good faith, they attempted to cancel the policy by relying on a contractual clause, and later when they were asked to reconsider the notice of cancellation they refused to. When the reinsurers purported to avoid the contract to defend the claim in an action brought by the assured the majority of the Court of Appeal decided that they waived the breach by affirming the contract, having relied on a contractual provision. All the reinsurers were required to do was to ignore the contract and treat it as if it never existed.

An insurer is required to communicate his intention to avoid the contract. If the insurer does not do so once it knows of the right to elect to avoid, depending on the period of time between knowledge of the breach and actual attempt to avoid, he may be taken to have waived the breach and to have affirmed the contract. In *Argo Systems FZE v Liberty Insurance Pte Ltd*[122] it was held that having not returned the premium for almost seven years after having found out about the breach and purporting to avoid the contract seven years later was found as a powerful indication of waiving the assured's breach of the duty of good faith.

(xi) The post-contractual duty of good faith

The duty of fair presentation of the risk is pre-contractual; it comes to an end once the contract is concluded.[123] However, the duty to act in good faith continues throughout the contractual relationship between the parties.[124] The courts have been careful not to extend the pre-contractual obligations in respect of the duty of good faith to the post-contractual stage.[125] For example, the argument that the assured is required to disclose at the post-contractual stage the facts which might lead the insurer to cancel the contract pursuant to a cancellation clause was rejected.[126] Nonetheless, the existence of the continuing duty is unanimously accepted by the courts. Instances where the post-contractual duty might be highlighted include the insured's obligation not to prejudice the insurer's subrogation rights[127] and the insurer's duty to act in good faith

---

118. *Persimmon Homes Ltd v Great Lakes Reinsurance (UK) Plc* [2010] EWHC 1705 (Comm); [2011] Lloyd's Rep IR 101, [111]; *Insurance Corp of the Channel Islands v Royal Hotel Ltd* [1998] Lloyd's Rep IR 151, at p 161 (Mance J).
119. *Kammins Ballrooms Co Ltd v Zenith Investments (Torquay) Ltd (No 1)* [1971] AC 850, at p 883 (Lord Diplock).
120. *Insurance Corp of the Channel Islands v Royal Hotel Ltd* [1998] Lloyd's Rep IR 151, at p 163 (Mance J).
121. [2004] EWCA Civ 962; [2004] Lloyd's Rep IR 764.
122. [2011] EWCA Civ 1615; [2011] Lloyd's Rep IR 427, [40]. The case went to the Court of Appeal ([2012] Lloyd's Rep IR 67) but Liberty did not appeal the judge's conclusion on affirmation.
123. IA 2015, s 3(1).
124. MIA 1906, s 17; *K/S Merc-Scandia XXXXII v Lloyd's Underwriters (The Mercandian Continent)* [2001] EWCA Civ 1275; [2001] 2 Lloyd's Rep 563, [21]. *Manifest Shipping Co Ltd v Uni-Polaris Insurance Co Ltd (The Star Sea)* [2001] UKHL 1; [2001] 1 Lloyd's Rep 389.
125. *The Star Sea* (fn 78), [48] and [95] (Lord Hobhouse and Lord Scott, respectively).
126. *New Hampshire Insurance Co Ltd v MGN Ltd* [1997] LRLR 24.
127. *Horwood v Land of Leather Ltd* [2010] EWHC 546; [2010] Lloyd's Rep IR 453.

where the assured is obliged to hand over the dispute of a claim by a third party against the assured.[128]

The reason for the courts being cautious about the use of the words "good faith" at the post-contractual stage was the single remedy of avoidance for breach of the duty of utmost good faith which used to encompass all the pre- and post- contractual information duties imposed on the insurer and assured. Avoidance may not be adequate due to the fact that it would require as a restitutionary remedy the return of all valid payments made under the policy prior to the exercise of the right. Such an effect would render avoidance a one-sided remedy which protects the insurer and may punish the assured disproportionately.[129] Assume that the assured was held to be in breach of a post-contractual duty of good faith, the insurer would have been entitled to avoid the contract and the payments made before the post-contractual breach would have been returned to the insurer. Equally, if the insurer was in breach, the only available remedy for the assured would have been avoidance of the contract, which the assured would not have desired if the insured risk had occurred.[130] The courts, nevertheless, used the good faith argument at the post-contractual stage to prevent the insurer from seeking the remedy where it would be a breach of the duty of good faith to do so[131] or the assured would lose a claim which is tainted by the breach.[132]

The IA 2015 repealed sections 18 and 20 of the MIA 1906 which provided that the remedy for pre-contractual non-disclosure or misrepresentation was avoidance of the contract only. Moreover, it repealed the words ". . . and, if the utmost good faith be not observed by either party, the contract may be avoided by the other party" from section 17 of the MIA 1906 which now reads "A contract of marine insurance is a contract based upon the utmost good faith." As referred to above, the pre-contractual information duty, that used to be named as the duty of utmost good faith and analysed under sections 18–20 of the MIA 1906, is now renamed as the duty of fair presentation of the risk under IA 2015. As a result, the duty of "utmost good faith" and the "duty of fair presentation of the risk" were separated by the IA 2015. This means that the above mentioned examples in which the duty of good faith applied to provide a fair and just outcome may now be more openly applicable as a principle of the duty of utmost good faith without the worry that the only remedy would be avoidance of the contract. A contract of insurance is a contract based upon utmost good faith which requires the parties to act openly, fairly and in a businesslike manner. Breach of the duty will result in different outcomes depending on the facts and nature of each case. It may prevent the insurer from seeking a remedy which would be acting in bad faith or the assured losing a claim under the insurance contract which will not necessarily be avoided by the insurer.

(e) Marine insurance warranties

Insurance contract terms may be classified as warranties and conditions. Insurance warranties used to create draconian consequences in case they were breached by the assured. The remedy for breach of an insurance warranty was reformed by the IA 2015. This will be analysed below.

---

128. *K/S Merc-Scandia XXXXII v Lloyd's Underwriters (The Mercandian Continent)* [2001] EWCA Civ 1275; [2001] Lloyd's Rep IR 802.
129. *The Star Sea* (fn 78), [51] and [57] (Lord Hobhouse).
130. See *Banque Financiere de la Cite SA (formerly Banque Keyser Ullmann SA) v Westgate Insurance Co (formerly Hodge General & Mercantile Co Ltd)* [1991] 2 AC 249; [1990] 2 Lloyd's Rep 377.
131. See *Drake Insurance Plc v Provident Insurance Plc* [2003] EWCA Civ 1834; [2004] 1 Lloyd's Rep 268, [87] (Rix LJ).
132. *Horwood v Land of Leather Ltd* [2010] EWHC 546 (Comm); [2010] Lloyd's Rep IR 453.

(i) Creation of a warranty

Marine insurance warranties may be implied or express. For instance, in a voyage policy there is an implied warranty that at the commencement of the voyage the ship shall be seaworthy for the purpose of the particular adventure insured.[133]

Determining whether an express clause is a warranty is a matter of construction. Express warranties may be created by the use of the word "warranty" or "it is warranted". For a recent example, see *Amlin Corporate Member Ltd v Oriental Assurance Corp*[134] where the clause stated:

it is expressly warranted that the carrying vessel shall not sail or put out of Sheltered Port when there is a typhoon or storm warning at that port nor when her destination or intended route may be within the possible path of the typhoon or storm announced at the port of sailing, port of destination or any intervening point.

However, the absence of the word warranty is not conclusive in determination of the nature of the clause. In *HIH Casualty & General Insurance Ltd v New Hampshire Insurance Co*,[135] Rix LJ stated that a term which was not expressly described as a "warranty", might still be regarded as such if (1) the term goes to the root of the transaction, (2) the term bears materially on the risk and (3) damages would not be an adequate remedy for breach.

On the other hand, despite the use of the word warranty, the particular term may not be construed as a warranty or it may be construed narrowly. The general rules applicable to contractual construction apply to interpretation of insurance contracts. Accordingly, insurance contracts will be construed objectively and the court will try to ascertain what a reasonable person having all the background knowledge, which would reasonably have been available to the parties, would have understood the parties to have meant by the language of the contract.[136] The factual matrix and surrounding circumstances are taken into account in such a construction but previous negotiations are excluded.

Before the IA 2015 the law permitted the creation of a warranty by virtue of basis of the contract clauses. The statements made by the assured in the proposal form could be converted into warranties by a statement in the insurance contract to the effect that the assured's statements in the proposal form are the basis of the contract.[137] Basis of the contract clauses were first abolished in consumer insurance by the Consumer Insurance (Disclosure and Representations) Act 2012.[138] The IA 2015 abolished the clause in non-consumer insurance under section 9 of the Act. As will be mentioned below, contracting out of IA 2015 section 9 is not permitted under any circumstances.

Under the MIA 1906 marine warranties had been subject to interpretation by the courts and three examples are particularly worth mentioning due to the similarities of the wording of the warranties and the contrast in the outcome of the judgments. "Warranted professional skippers and crew in charge at all times" was the wording of the warranty in *Brownsville Holdings Ltd v Adamjee Insurance Co Ltd (The Milasan)*.[139] The assured, who did not employ a professional skipper to look after or "be in charge" of the vessel "all the time" during the period from 1 May 1995 to 1 July 1995, was held to have breached the warranty. In *GE Frankona*

---

133. MIA 1906, s 39(1).
134. [2014] EWCA Civ 1135; [2014] 2 Lloyd's Rep 561.
135. [2001] EWCA Civ 735; [2001] Lloyd's Rep IR 596.
136. *Arnold v Britton* [2015] UKSC 36; [2015] A.C. 1619; *Rainy Sky SA v Kookmin Bank* [2011] UKSC 50; [2012] 1 Lloyd's Rep 34; *Chartbrook Ltd v Persimmon Homes Ltd* [2009] 1 AC 1101; *Investors Compensation Scheme Ltd v West Bromwich Building Society (No. 1)* [1998] 1 WLR 896.
137. *Dawsons Ltd v Bonnin* [1922] 2 AC 413.
138. s 6(2).
139. [2000] 2 All ER (Comm) 803; [2000] 2 Lloyd's Rep 458.

Reinsurance Ltd v CMM Trust No 1400 (The Newfoundland Explorer)[140] the assured warranted "vessel fully crewed at all times". The court decided that the assured was in breach of the warranty when the Master left the vessel to go home which was a 30-minute drive away and there was no one else on board. The court stated that the warranty did not apply to some situations such as when the crew needed to leave the vessel for duties to be completed ashore or when there was an emergency on board. The interpretation of a similar warranty was different in *Pratt v Aigaion Insurance Co SA*[141] in which a fishing vessel was insured and the crew left the vessel after fishing to have dinner in a pub. The vessel then became a total loss upon a fire on board. The contract provided "Warranted Owner and/or Owner's experienced skipper on board and in charge at all times and one experienced crew member". The court interpreted the warranty *contra proferentem* as it was found to be ambiguous. The court also held that stipulating for an "experienced skipper" must have meant that the warranty was to be complied with when the vessel sailed, not when she was moored after fishing.

The abovementioned interpretations are also relevant to determine whether a warranty is a present or a continuing warranty. Whilst a present warranty requires compliance at a particular specified time, for instance only at the outset of the contract, a continuing warranty requires a continuing compliance – as the word speaks for itself.[142] The IA 2015 did not change the rules on creation of warranties – except for the basis of the contract clauses mentioned above. Warranties also have to be strictly complied with. This was the case before the law reform and the IA 2015 retained the position. Breach of a warranty, therefore, will entitle an insurer to seek a remedy although the breach did not cause the loss suffered by the assured.

(ii) Remedy

The position before the IA 2015, in other words under the MIA 1906 and the common law, was as follows: Breach of warranty terminated the risk automatically.[143] The risk terminated but the assured's obligation to pay the premium survived.[144] Upon breach the insurer was discharged from liability automatically.[145] To be discharged from liability the insurer was not required to prove the chain of causation between the breach and the loss. All the insurer had to prove was that the assured breached a warranty.

Section 10(1) of the IA 2015 abolished any rule of law that breach of a warranty (express or implied) in a contract of insurance results in the discharge of the insurer's liability under the contract. Instead, the IA 2015 introduced a new remedy under which "an insurer has no liability under a contract of insurance in respect of any loss occurring, or attributable to something happening, after a warranty (express or implied) in the contract has been breached but before the breach has been remedied."[146]

Whilst a breach of an insurance warranty could not be remedied under section 34(2) of the MIA 1906 and the common law,[147] the IA 2015 repealed those rules and it is now possible to reinstate the insurance cover by remedying the breach. If an assured breaches an insurance warranty, the cover is suspended from the time of the breach until the breach is remedied by the

---

140. [2006] EWHC 429 (Admlty); [2006] Lloyd's Rep IR 704.
141. [2008] EWCA Civ 1314; [2009] Lloyd's Rep IR 149.
142. For instance see *The Milasan* above.
143. MIA 1906, s 33.
144. *JA Chapman & Co Ltd (In Liquidation) v Kadirga Denizcilik ve Ticaret AS* [1998] Lloyd's Rep IR 377.
145. *Bank of Nova Scotia v Hellenic Mutual War Risk Association (Bermuda) Ltd (The Good Luck)* [1992] 1 AC 233; [1991] 2 Lloyd's Rep 191.
146. IA 2015, s 10(2).
147. *Quebec Marine Insurance Company v Commercial Bank of Canada* [1869–71] LR 3 PC 234.

assured. It should be remembered that this applies only if the breach can be remedied. If a loss occurs during the suspension of the cover the insurer is not liable for the loss. If the loss occurs after the assured remedies the breach but the loss is attributable to something happening during the time that the warranty was breached, the insurer is not liable for that loss either. However, it may be the case that an insured risk occurs after the breach is remedied in which case the insurer will not be able to argue breach of warranty as a defence to the assured's claim.

(iii) Waiver

It is yet to be tested by the English courts how an assured can prove that the insurer waived the breach of a warranty which now suspends the insurance cover until the breach is remedied. The IA 2015 does not expressly state whether the remedy set out under section 10 arises automatically. If it is the case, the waiver will be proved by promissory estoppel. The automatic discharge from liability, before the IA 2015, could be waived only by promissory estoppel. The reason was that the automatic effect of the breach did not leave any room for any election/or affirmation as such. The author is of the view that the same principles of waiver by promissory estoppel will apply under the IA 2015 too because the Act does not expressly state that the insurer may elect to be or not to be liable upon breach of a warranty. As mentioned above, section 10(2) of the IA 2015 uses the words "an insurer has no liability...". To prove promissory estoppel three elements[148] have to be established: (1) that the insurer unequivocally represented that it will not rely on the breach, (2) that the assured relied on the insurer's representation and (3) that it is not inequitable for the insurer to go back from his representation.. In a recent case, *Argo Systems FZE v Liberty Insurance Pte Ltd*,[149] the assured argued waiver of breach of warranty for the reason that in the action brought by the assured in the USA seven years before the action in England and which was dismissed for lack of jurisdiction, the insurer relied on a breach of a weather warranty as a defence and did not mention a breach of a hold harmless warranty. Seven years later when the assured sued the insurer in England the insurer included breach of the hold harmless warranty in its defence. The court rejected the waiver of breach of the hold harmless warranty argument for the reason that there was no unequivocal representation by the insurer who described his defence in a letter to the assured seven years before the English action with a reservation in the following terms: "without prejudice to all the remaining terms and conditions of the policy, along with any other defenses which may be discovered after further investigation". This letter was clearly an example of an equivocal representation by the insurer.

(f) Insurance conditions

Insurance conditions are varied; they may be in the form of a mere condition or a condition precedent. Mere conditions[150] are seen as equivalent to innominate terms in general contract law. The remedy for breach of a mere condition entitles the insurer to terminate the contract if its breach creates serious consequences. If the consequences of the breach are trivial the insurer may only claim damages. Breach of a condition precedent creates more draconian effects.[151] A condition precedent may be (1) a condition precedent to contract, or (2) a condition precedent to attachment of the risk, or (3) a condition precedent to insurer's liability. As may be inferred from their

---

148. *Central London Property Trust Ltd v High Trees House Ltd* [1947] KB 130.
149. [2011] EWCA Civ 1572; [2012] Lloyd's Rep IR 67.
150. *Friends Provident Life & Pensions Ltd v Sirius International Insurance Corp* [2005] EWCA Civ 601; [2005] 2 Lloyd's Rep 517.
151. *Kosmar Villa Holidays Plc v Trustees of Syndicate 1243* [2008] EWCA Civ 147; [2008] Lloyd's Rep IR 489.

names, there is no contract if (1) is not complied with. There is a contract but the risk does not attach if (2) is breached. There is a contract, the risk has attached but the insurer's liability for a loss that is covered by the insurance contract depends on the compliance with the condition precedent in (3). If a condition precedent to insurer's liability is not complied with the insurer is automatically discharged from liability that is tainted by the breach. The breach does not affect the validity of the policy; therefore, the assured may comply with the condition precedent in the future and may be able to make a claim when a risk occurs again.

The IA 2015 has introduced a section which is new to English law that the insurer's ability to rely on breach of a warranty or a condition/condition precedent will be subject to section 11 of the IA 2015. It is important to analyse in detail under what circumstances section 11 applies. Section 11 is important because, once the requirements listed under this section are satisfied, although the assured may be in breach of a contractual term, warranty or condition, the assured may still be successful in its claim against the insurer. In other words, if the term in question falls within one of the three categories listed under section 11(1) and if the assured satisfies section 11(3), the remedies stated above for breach of an insurance condition or a warranty do not apply but the insurer will be liable for the loss despite the assured's breach of the term.

(i) Section 11 of the Insurance Act 2015 – terms that are not relevant to the actual loss

The first point to bear in mind in application of section 11 is that it does not apply to terms that define the risk as a whole. The IA 2015 does not further define the phrase "terms that define the risk as a whole". It is yet to be tested by the Courts what type of terms describe the risk as a whole. If a term is not of this category but it is inserted in the policy as a risk mitigation clause; in other words, if compliance with it would tend to reduce the risk of one or more of the following –

    (a) loss of a particular kind,
    (b) loss at a particular location, or
    (c) loss at a particular time

section 11 might apply.

Once it is determined that the clause that has not been complied with by the assured falls within one of the three categories listed above, the next question will be whether breach of the term increased the risk of the loss which actually occurred in the circumstances in which it occurred.[152] The burden of proof of this is on the assured and if the assured satisfies the burden the insurer may not deny or limit liability for the breach of the term that is not relevant to the actual loss. For instance, in the case of a breach of a fire alarm warranty,[153] the assured is recommended to try to prove that the term was not relevant to the actual loss which occurred, for instance, as a result of a burglary. It is clearly arguable that the risk of theft could not have been increased by the breach of the fire alarm warranty. Section 10 of the IA 2015 may apply together with section 11 of the Act.[154] Therefore, whilst under section 10 of the IA 2015 the insurance cover is suspended upon breach of a warranty, the insurer's ability to deny liability for that reason will yet depend on section 11. The same analysis applies if the fire alarm and burglar alarm terms are drafted as a condition or condition precedent. Section 11 of the IA 2015 attempts to change the rule on the interpretation of insurance contract terms from purely depending on the

---

152. IA 2015, s 11(2)(3).
153. Assuming that that warranty in the contract does not define the risk as a whole.
154. IA 2015, s 11(4)

term's form to its substance. However, it is important to separate conditions which aim to mitigate the risk from those which apply only after the risk occurs. The latter are more procedural and impose obligations on the assured such as prompt notification of a loss or co-operation with the insurer in dealing with a claim by a third party against the assured. This type of condition or condition precedent are outside the scope of section 11. Section 11 applies only to the risk mitigation clauses which do not define the risk as a whole.

(g) Contracting out of the Insurance Act 2015

The IA 2015 does not permit contracting out of its provisions in consumer insurance. The rules on the duty of fair presentation of the risk as set out in the IA 2015 apply only to non-consumer insurance. However, sections 10 and 11 referred to above with regard to the interpretation of insurance contract terms apply both in consumer and business insurance. It is not possible to contract out of those sections to the detriment of the assured in consumer insurance.[155]

With one exception it is permitted to contract out of the IA 2015 in non-consumer insurance. That exception is that it is not possible to contract out of section 9 of the Act which abolished basis of the contract clauses in business insurance.[156]

Section 16(2) concerns the situations in which an insurer can "contract out" by using a term of the non-consumer insurance contract to put the assured in a worse position than it would be in under the default rules contained in the IA 2015. A contractual term to this effect is referred to as a "disadvantageous term".[157] Parties can include a disadvantageous term in their insurance contract if the insurer has complied with the "transparency requirements".[158] Accordingly, the insurer is required to take sufficient steps to draw the term to the assured's attention so that the assured is given a reasonable opportunity to know that the disadvantageous term exists before it enters into the contract.[159] The term must also be clear and unambiguous as to its effect.[160] This is intended to require the consequences of the disadvantageous term to be set out explicitly, not merely that the language is clear and unambiguous.

(h) Subrogation

(i) Definition and requirements

The insurer, upon payment under the insurance contract, steps into the assured's shoes in respect of the assured's right against a third party for the loss suffered. The requirements of subrogation are: (1) the assured should have a claim against the third party; (2) the subrogation action has to be brought in the name of the person insured;[161] (3) the insurer subrogates only for the amount paid to the assured but no more than that;[162] (4) the insurer cannot be subrogated into a right of action until he has paid the sum insured and made good the loss.[163] The proposition that "an express provision in the contract providing the insurer with a right to subrogate the assured's

155. IA 2015, s 15(1).
156. IA 2015, s 16(1)
157. IA 2015, s 17(1).
158. IA 2015, s 16(2).
159. IA 2015, s 17(2).
160. IA 2015, s 17(3).
161. The insurer's action brought in its own name was rejected in *London Assurance Company v Sainsbury* [1783] 3 Doug KB 244. See also *Simpson v Thomson* [1877] 3 App Cas 279; *Yates v Whyte* [1838] 4 Bingham New Cases 272.
162. *Yorkshire Insurance Co Ltd v Nisbet Shipping Co Ltd* [1961] 1 Lloyd's Rep 479.
163. *Castellain v Preston* [1883] 11 QBD 380, at p 389.

action 'before or after any payment under this policy' overrides the ordinary presumption that subrogation can only arise once payment has been made by the insurer claiming subrogation" was rejected by Burton J in *Rathbone Brothers Plc v Novae Corporate Underwriting*.[164]

The justification for subrogation can be explained by the premise that a recovery upon a contract of insurance does not alter the position between the assured and the third party. The latter caused the loss of the former by his wrongdoing; thus a recovery from the insurer is no bar to a claim for damages against the wrongdoer.[165] On the other hand, a marine insurance contract is a contract of indemnity under which the assured is not entitled to be indemnified for more than the loss that he has suffered.[166] Thus, the insurer steps into the assured's shoes with regard to the claim by the third party and if there is a recovery from the wrongdoer the insurer is entitled to it. The assured might sue the third party for the benefit of the insurer or the insurer might claim against the third party in the name of the assured. If the assured recovers from a third party – despite the fact of having been indemnified by the insurer already – it receives the damages in trust for the insurer[167] who is then entitled to receive it up to the amount it paid the assured. If the assured is not fully indemnified and if there is still some loss that has to be covered, whatever is obtained from the third party is used to indemnify the assured fully first, and any remaining amount will be paid to the insurer.

(ii) Subrogation against a co-assured

One of the controversial issues about subrogation is action against a co-assured when the insurance contract is composite in nature and one of the co-assureds has caused the other's loss. The matter has mostly been disputed in relation to construction contracts in which a number of sub-contractors are involved and such contracts require the contractors or the employer – as the case may be – to take out a composite insurance policy insuring both employer and contractor and sometimes sub-contractors. If the contractor's negligence causes damage to the work which belongs to the employer and which is insured under the policy, the insurer will indemnify the employer. The insurer then may want to bring a subrogation action against the contractor who might then argue that he is also insured under the policy and it would be unreasonable if the insurer is permitted to bring a subrogation action against him. The issue has been discussed in numerous cases. In *The Yasin*[168] Lloyd LJ was of the view that the reason for the insurer being prevented from bringing a subrogation action against the co-assured was not a fundamental principle to this effect but was based on ordinary rules about circuity, i.e. when the insurer indemnifies co-assured A and then brings a subrogation action against co-assured B who caused the loss, the insurer will need to indemnify B under the policy for his liability to A. Later, in *Petrofina (UK) Ltd v Magnaload Ltd*,[169] Lloyd LJ reiterated that the reason for precluding the insurer from a subrogation action against a co-assured is circuity. But in recent cases the circuity argument seems to have fallen out of favour for the reason that the contract of insurance insures the property, not B's liability to A. In *Co-operative Retail Services Ltd v Taylor Young Partnership Ltd*[170] – although the House of Lords did not need to decide the point – Lord Hope[171]

164. [2013] EWHC 3457 (Comm); [2014] Lloyd's Rep I.R. 203.
165. *Mason v Sainsbury* (1782) 3 Doug. K.B. 61; *Yates v Whyte* [1838] 4 Bingham New Cases 272.
166. *Castellain v Preston* [1883] 11 QBD 380, at p 386 (Brett LJ). Towards the end of his judgment, at p 392, Brett LJ added that the rule is subject to the exception of awarding sue and labour expenses under certain circumstances.
167. *Blaauwpot v Da Costa* [1758] 1 Eden 130.
168. [1979] 2 Lloyd's Rep 45, at p 55.
169. [1984] QB 127; [1983] 2 Lloyd's Rep 91.
170. [2002] UKHL 17; [2002] Lloyd's Rep IR 555.
171. Ibid., p 571.

expressed his agreement with Mr Recorder Jackson QC in *Hopewell Project Management Ltd v Ewbank Preece Ltd*[172] that it would be nonsensical if the parties who were co-insured under a policy could make claims against one another in respect of the loss insured. Like Mr Recorder Jackson QC, Lord Hope was in favour of the argument that it is to be implied into the underlying contract that the parties will not make claims against each other with regard to the loss insured as they could not possibly have intended that they could sue each other for the same loss which was co-insured. Lord Bingham stated in the *Taylor Young* case that it would be an absurdity to permit an insurer to bring a subrogation claim against a co-assured who can then claim indemnity from the insurer in relation to the loss which the insurer subrogated into. Lord Bingham said: "The rationale of this rule may be a matter of some controversy . . . but the rule itself is not in doubt."[173]

In *Tyco Fire & Integrated Solutions (UK) Ltd (formerly Wormald Ansul (UK) Ltd) v Rolls Royce Motor Cars Ltd (formerly Hireus Ltd)*[174] Rix LJ confirmed that the circuity argument was not favoured and, as held in *Taylor Young*, the issue depends on the true construction of the underlying contract between the parties – in most cases the construction contract which sets out the rights and liabilities of the parties in relation to the work being carried out.[175] The outcome of the *Tyco* decision is that: (1) there is no implied term to the effect that only the existence of composite insurance prevents the insurer from bringing a subrogation action against another co-assured who caused the loss; (2) if the insurance policy contains an express waiver of subrogation clause, that has to be given effect so that the insurer cannot bring a subrogation action against the assured because of the express waiver; (3) in the absence of express waiver of subrogation rights, the issue as to whether or not one co-assured can claim against another co-assured, which would then form the basis for the insurer's subrogation rights against the co-assured responsible for the loss, depends on the construction of the underlying contract between the parties. If the outcome of the true construction of the terms of such contract excludes liability between the parties (who are also co-assureds under the insurance contract) there is no possibility for a claim between the parties which would then give no subrogation right to the insurer. If, however, the contract does not exclude liability but provides that – despite the composite insurance contract – the co-assureds are still liable to each other under the underlying contract, a co-assured can claim from another co-assured which would then give a subrogation right to the insurer.

The Court of Appeal in *Gard Marine & Energy Ltd v China National Chartering Co Ltd (The Ocean Victory)*[176] however disagreed with *Tyco*.[177] In *Gard Marine* the vessel was first demise chartered and there were a number of time charterparties following that. The vessel was lost and the insurer, upon indemnifying the owner for the loss, brought a subrogation action against the time charterers alleging that the vessel was lost due to the nomination of an unsafe port. The time charterers argued that because the demise charterer was a co-assured the owner had no claim against the demise charterer who then can turn to the time charterers. The issue therefore focused on whether the requirement for taking out an insurance policy for the benefit of both the owner and the demise charterer exempted the demise charterer from a contractual liability under the demise charterparty. The demise charter provided a safe port warranty. At first instance Teare J[178] said that this is an express clause imposing liability on the demise charterer; if it is argued that

---

172. [1998] 1 Lloyd's Rep 448, at p 458.
173. See fn 111, [7].
174. [2008] EWCA Civ 286; [2008] Lloyd's Rep IR 617.
175. Ibid., [76] – [77].
176. [2015] EWCA Civ 16; [2015] 1 Lloyd's Rep 381.
177. See also *Rathbone Brothers Plc v Novae Corporate Underwriting* [2014] EWCA Civ 1464; [2015] Lloyd's Rep IR 95
178. [2013] EWHC 2199 (Comm); [2014] 1 Lloyd's Rep 59.

such an express liability is excluded, there should be an express term to this effect. The insurance provision, according to Teare J, was not sufficient to imply an exemption of liability for breach of a safe port warranty. The Court of Appeal disagreed and held *obiter*[179] that there was no liability to pass on from the demise charterers for the reason that the demise charterparty provided for joint insurance, the premium for which was paid by the demise charterer. Thus, the insurance provision overrode the fact that the liability of the demise charterer was not expressly excluded. The Supreme Court, by a majority, upheld the Court of Appeal's view.[180]

(iii) Assignment and abandonment

Other issues to be noted about subrogation is that subrogation is different from assignment for the reason that an assignee of a policy can sue in its own name while subrogation has to be brought in the assured's name. Subrogation is again different from abandonment[181] given that the latter has effect only in cases of total loss, whereas subrogation can be exercised for partial as well as total loss. Another separation between the two doctrines is that, as stated above, upon subrogation the insurer steps into the assured's shoes only up to the amount that the insurer paid the assured; this is a right independent of the ownership of the subject matter insured. In abandonment, however, the insurer becomes the owner of the subject matter insured which was lost.[182]

(iv) The duty not to prejudice insurer's subrogation rights

The assured is under a duty not to prejudice the insurer's subrogation rights. For instance, if the assured waives any subrogation rights in an agreement with a third party, determination of the remedy depends on the timing of such waiver. If the waiver agreement was reached before the insurance contract is concluded, such a waiver will be a material fact which should be disclosed to the insurer, breach of which will entitle the insurer to avoid the contract. If the assured reached a waiver agreement that prejudiced the insurer's rights against a third party after the insured risk has occurred, that will be a breach of an implied term of the contract[183] for which the insurer can claim damages from the assured. As a result the assured is unlikely to be indemnified under the insurance contract for the relevant loss and if the breach is so serious that it goes to the root of the contract the insurer may elect to terminate the contract. Such a breach will also be a breach of the duty of good faith at the post-contractual stage.[184]

(i) Sue and labour expenses

(i) The existence of the duty to mitigate in insurance

Sue and labour expenses are expenses that an assured may recover from the insurer where they have been incurred to prevent or minimise an insured loss. Whether the assured can claim such expenses and the amount of recovery available will depend on the terms of the insurance contract.

179. The view is *obiter* because the port was held to be safe.
180. [2017] UKSC 35.
181. See p 26.
182. MIA 1906, s 79(1). *Simpson & Co v Thomson* [1877] 3 App Cas 279, at p 292 (Lord Blackburn).
183. *Horwood v Land of Leather Ltd* [2010] EWHC 546 (Comm); [2010] Lloyd's Rep IR 453.
184. Ibid.

Section 78(1) of the MIA 1906 provides that where an insurance contract contains a sue and labour clause, the assured may recover from the insurer any expenses properly incurred pursuant to the clause. Under section 78(1) such a recovery will be in addition to the insured amount; in other words, it will be a supplementary payment. However, the parties may agree otherwise by the insurance contract and the maximum limit provided for the insured risks may also include any payment for the sue and labour expenses.[185] The sue and labour expenses are paid as a supplementary cover under the IHC 2003 Clause 9.5. The maximum limit that the insurer pays for the sue and labour expenses is equal to the insured amount.

In marine insurance the policies commonly include a clause giving the assured the right to claim sue and labour expenses from the insurer. For instance, 2009 Institute Cargo Clauses (A,B,C) Clause 16 is titled: "MINIMISING LOSSES Duty of Assured" and it provides:

It is the duty of the Assured and their employees and agents in respect of loss recoverable hereunder

16.1 to take such measures as may be reasonable for the purpose of averting or minimising such loss, and

16.2 to ensure that all rights against carriers, bailees or other third parties are properly preserved and exercised and the Insurers will, in addition to any loss recoverable hereunder, reimburse the Assured for any charges properly and reasonably incurred in pursuance of these duties.

In the absence of an express clause which provides that the assured is entitled to claim the sue and labour or mitigation expenses from the insurer, the English courts have not implied a term in the insurance contract to this effect in non-marine insurance.[186] Flaux J[187] recently held

. . . as a matter of English law, in non-marine liability insurance, there is no concept of "sue and labour", so that, if the insured acts to defend a claim and thereby avoids the insurer being under any liability, there is no entitlement to an indemnity against the costs and expenses incurred in defending successfully the liability which would otherwise have arisen under the insurance, in the absence of some express provision to that effect.

In marine insurance whether the clause is implied has not been tested. As stated above, marine policies commonly include a sue and labour clause.

The expenses incurred by the assured have to be incurred to prevent or minimise the loss which would have otherwise been covered by the policy. For instance if the policy is for total loss only and if the expenditure incurred was to prevent a partial loss of the subject matter insured, the insurer is not liable for the expenses incurred by the assured.[188] The assured's right to claim the expenses does not depend on its success in preventing the loss.[189]

Additionally, the expenses have to be reasonably incurred. In *Lee v Southern Insurance Company*[190] a cargo of palm oil was insured for the voyage from Cameroon to Liverpool. During her

---

185. For instance in *Kuwait Airways Corp & Anor v Kuwait Insurance Co SAK* [1999] CLC 934; [1999] 1 Lloyd's Rep 803 the relevant clause was in the following wording: "Sue, labour and costs and expenses and salvage charges and expenses incurred by on or on behalf of the assured in or about the defence, safety, preservation and recovery of the insured property and also [extraordinary general average sacrifice and expenditure] and costs and expenses arising out of all search and rescue operations. Provided always that these costs and expenses shall be included in computing the losses hereinbefore provided for, notwithstanding that the company may have paid for a total loss."
186. *Yorkshire Water v Sun Alliance & London Insurance* [1997] CLC 213; [1997] 2 Lloyd's Rep 21.
187. *AstraZeneca Insurance Co Ltd v XL Insurance (Bermuda) Ltd* [2013] EWHC 349 (Comm); [2013] Lloyd's Rep I.R. 290 [137]. Appeal was dismissed [2013] EWCA Civ 1660; [2014] Lloyd's Rep IR 509
188. *Great Indian Peninsula Railway Company v Saunders* (1862) 2 Best and Smith 266; *Booth v Gair* (1863) 15 CB NS 291.
189. *Kuwait Airways Corp & Anor v Kuwait Insurance Co SAK* [1999] CLC 934, Lord Hobhouse, 948.
190. (1869–70) LR 5 CP 397.

voyage the ship encountered bad weather off the coast of Ireland; and, after having sustained considerable damage, she was stranded on the Welsh Coast, near Pwllheli, and drifted on to the beach. The assured spent £212 to forward the cargo to Liverpool by rail. The ship might have been repaired and in the meantime the cargo could have been stored in a warehouse before reshipment onto the vessel once it was repaired, the total cost of which would have been about £70. The assured therefore was entitled to claim only the reasonable amount to save the insured cargo, that was £70.

(ii) Duration of the duty

The date that the claim form (formerly writ) is issued is taken into account in determining the date at which the subject matter insured became a constructive total loss.[191] In practice a notice of abandonment is served and if the insurer rejects the notice the parties agree that the writ is deemed to be issued on the date of rejection. This brings the question of when does the duty to sue and labour and therefore the right to claim the sue and labour expenses come to an end. It was held that the relevant date is the date when the claim form was actually issued[192] but not when it was deemed to be issued. On the date that a claim form is actually issued the parties' dispute has crystallised and is regulated by the rules of court. However, the writ clause or agreement provides that the insured is not prejudiced by a change of circumstances after the service of a notice of abandonment, so that the assured does not have to rush off and issue a claim form. The commercial reality is that, in many cases, at the time of the writ agreement, the vessel is still in the grip of the relevant insured peril and it is in the interests of both parties that expense continues to be incurred in mitigating the loss.[193]

(iii) Apportionment

Apportionment (or allocation) concerns the amount of sue and labour expenses that the insurer has to pay to the assured. If the steps taken by the assured prevented some uninsured risks as well as those insured the insurers would argue that they are not liable for the expenses to the extent they were spent for the uninsured risks. Technically this is true because the insurers never agreed to insure those uninsured risks that were prevented, they never collected any premium to cover that type of risk, and so why should the insurer pay for the expenses incurred to prevent or minimise them?

Apportionment may apply in marine property insurance where the subject matter insured is underinsured. Walton J in *Cunard Steamship Company Ltd v Marten*,[194] stated:

. . . the underwriters are to bear their share of any suing and labouring expenses, . . . only in the proportion of the amount underwritten to the whole value of the property or interest insured. If the assured has insured himself or goods to the extent of one-half only of the value of his property or interest in the goods insured, he, in respect of each and every item of suing and labouring expense, recovers one-half and bears one-half himself.

Thus say if the subject matter insured is insured for £5,000 whereas its actual value is £25,000, the insurer would recover 1/5 of the sue and labour expenses. More recently, the English courts

191. *Royal Boskalis Westminster NV v Mountain* [1999] QB 674; [1997] LRLR 523, at p 534, Rix J; *Polurrian Steamship Company, Limited v Young* [1915] 1 KB 922; *Ruys v Royal Exchange Assurance Corp* [1897] 2 QB 135.
192. *Suez Fortune Investments Ltd v Talbot Underwriting Ltd* [2015] EWHC 42 (Comm); [2015] 1 Lloyd's Rep 651.
193. *Atlasnavios Navegacao Lda v Navigators Insurance Co Ltd* [2014] EWHC 4133 (Comm); [2015] 1 Lloyd's Rep 117 [343], Flaux J.
194. [1902] 2 KB 624.

discussed apportionment in the context of the sue and labour expenses incurred for dual purposes. For instance, in *Atlasnavios Navegacao Lda v Navigators Insurance Co Ltd*[195] the vessel *B Atlantic* was detained in Venezuela between August 2007 and September 2009 after an underwater search of the vessel revealed three bags of cocaine weighing 132 kg strapped to her hull. The vessel and crew were arrested on 16 August 2007 and the lengthy proceedings to release the crew and *B Atlantic* were unsuccessful. In September 2009 she was abandoned to the Venezuelan court. The assured claimed for a constructive total loss as well as the expenses incurred in trying to release the vessel and her crew from the insurer. It should be noted that this case was appealed, and since the Court of Appeal[196] held that the loss was caused by an excluded peril, the sue and labour expenses were not discussed as there was no right to recovery under the insurance contract. However, it is worth noting that at first instance, Flaux J[197] rejected the insurer's argument that the assured's expenditure of US $1.4 million for legal fees were incurred for both the purpose of extricating *B Atlantic* from the insured peril and for the defence of the crew, such a dual purpose required apportionment because the latter was not an insured peril. The judge recognised that if the relevant expenditure had been incurred solely for the purpose which was not insured, that expenditure would not be recoverable as sue and labour. However, the insurer's attempt to prove that US $300,000 had been incurred in defence of the crew only was still not successful as Flaux J found that the expenditure incurred in defence of the crew was inextricably bound up with the release of the vessel. If all the crew had been released and acquitted, the vessel would have been released.[198] The judge applied an *obiter* statement in *Royal Boskalis v Mountain*[199] in which Phillips LJ stated that when the expenses were incurred to save an insured property and some human lives which were not insured by the insurance contract, apportionment would not be possible because it is not possible to assess human lives in monetary terms. As a result, whilst the sue and labour expenses may be apportioned in a marine property insurance when the subject matter insured is underinsured, in other contexts it will be a matter of proof how much exactly was spent to save an uninsured subject matter.

(iv) Failure to sue and labour

If the assured does not take necessary steps to prevent or minimise the insured risk this does not automatically deprive the assured of the policy benefits. However, the assured's inaction may be regarded as the wilful misconduct of the assured that is not covered by marine insurance policies. Therefore, if it is proved that the assured's wilful misconduct broke the chain of causation between the insured peril and the loss there may be no liability for the insurer under the insurance contract. It is worth noting that in *Netherlands v Youell*[200] Phillips LJ noted that there has not been a case since 1906 where an assured has been found guilty of failing to sue and labour. The finding was reiterated by Rix LJ in *Masefield AG v Amlin Corporate Member Ltd*.[201]

2. HULL AND MACHINERY INSURANCE

Hull and machinery insurance is a cover for the ship itself and the mechanical parts thereof. The division into "hull" and "machinery" derives from the transition from sail to steamships in the

---

195. [2014] EWHC 4133 (Comm); [2015] 1 Lloyd's Rep 117.
196. [2016] EWCA Civ 808; [2016] 2 Lloyd's Rep 351..
197. [2014] EWHC 4133 (Comm); [2015] 1 Lloyd's Rep 117 [346].
198. [2014] EWHC 4133 (Comm); [2015] 1 Lloyd's Rep 117 [346].
199. [1999] QB 674; [1997] LRLR 523 at p 647.
200. [1998] 1 Lloyd's Rep 236; [1998] CLC 44, at p 54.
201. [2011] EWCA Civ 24; [2011] 1 Lloyd's Rep 630 [76].

nineteenth century. In an important case from 1887, *The Inchmaree*,[202] it was argued that events that could happen just as well on land were not marine perils and could not be covered by a marine policy, and that problems with machinery were such land-based perils, falling outside the marine policy. The House of Lords agreed with this reasoning, but the market immediately reacted pragmatically by introducing machinery cover as an addition to the marine policy. When the old SG policy was abandoned, the two forms of cover were merged and the standard clauses now in use cover both hull and machinery perils.[203]

The main perils covered under a hull policy vary little from one set of standard terms to the next. They are perils of the seas, fire and explosion, violent theft, jettison, piracy, contact with land installations, earthquakes, volcanic eruptions and lightning, accidents in loading etc., and contact with airborne vehicles.[204] Following *The Inchmaree*, a second set of perils was also introduced and these are now grouped in what is known as the *Inchmaree* clause,[205] namely bursting of boilers and breakage of shafts, latent defects, negligence of Master or crew, negligence of repairers or charterers, or barratry. The standard hull clauses also provide partial cover for collision liability. These perils will be discussed below.

(a) Perils of the seas

The quintessential marine risk is "perils of the seas". There is no single comprehensive definition of this concept. The MIA 1906 contains a Schedule with rules for the construction of the policy, Rule 7 of which provides "The term 'perils of the seas' refers only to fortuitous accidents or casualties of the seas. It does not include the ordinary action of the wind and the waves." The rules for construction of the policy originally referred to the old SG policy (also contained in the Schedule) but can still be used for the construction of modern policies where there is no better alternative.[206] They are labelled rules for construction, not definitions, because it is emphatically not the case that they are written as exhaustive and prescriptive definitions. However, "perils of the seas" is better defined than most by its rule of construction and there is very little modern discussion of perils of the seas that does not refer to Rule 7.

In *The Cendor MOPU*[207] the Supreme Court held that in the second limb of Rule 7, the word "ordinary" refers to action and not to wind and waves, so that if the wind and waves are perfectly ordinary and such as to be expected on the particular voyage in question, but the result of such ordinary wind and waves is extraordinary, this is a loss by perils of the seas and not a loss that should be ascribed to unseaworthiness or some other cause. In other words, the question is whether the wind and waves have some extraordinary effect, rather than whether they were extraordinary in themselves.

(b) Fortuity

To recover under a marine insurance policy, it is essential that the loss was fortuitous, which means that it must not be inevitable or intentional. Absent fortuity, there is no valid loss under a marine insurance policy. The opposite of fortuity would be something predetermined, or something that is bound to happen. It is considered impermissible to insure against such certainties, simply because of the absence of fortuity. It is not a general rule of insurance that it is always

---

202. *Thames v & Mersey Marine Insurance Co v Hamilton, Fraser & Co, The Inchmaree* [1887] 12 App Cas 484.
203. Institute Hull Clauses 1983, 1995 and International Hull Clauses 2003.
204. International Hull Clauses 2003, cl 2.1.
205. International Hull Clauses 2003, cl 2.2.
206. MIA 1906, s 30(2).
207. [2010] UKSC 5; [2011] 1 Lloyd's Rep 560.

impossible to insure against certainties: for instance life insurance is essentially insurance against the unavoidable event of death. In that case, the uncertainty lies in the fact that it is unknown exactly when the death will happen, and that the policy is taken out for a long period of time. In marine insurance, where policy cover as a rule extends to only one year, an element of fortuity is needed. In *The Xantho*,[208] it was put thus: "The purpose of the policy is to secure an indemnity against accidents which may happen, not against events which must happen. " "Certainty" that a loss will happen may come in the form of intentional losses or "debility". Intentional losses can never be fortuitous because they were intended (by somebody) to happen. Losses by scuttling of the subject matter insured by the insured itself are not recoverable because of the rule against recovery in case of wilful misconduct in section 55 of the MIA 1906. This is what in *Samuel v Dumas*,[209] a case of scuttling, was referred to as "the wickedness of man" – against which a policy was not possible.

A loss by perils of the seas must be fortuitous, but the question has recently arisen what exactly it is that must be fortuitous in relation to a loss by perils of the seas? Where the peril of the seas takes the form of an ingress of seawater, is it the ingress of seawater itself or the cause of the ingress of seawater that must be fortuitous?

It had already been decided in earlier cases that it is not enough that the insured proves the fact of the ingress of seawater, but that the cause of the ingress of seawater must also be proven: see *The Popi M*[210] in which the insured was held to proof of its theory that a submarine had caused the aperture through which seawater entered the ship.

In *The DC Merwestone*[211] the judge at first instance summarised the law thus:

The fortuity may lie in what causes the hole, or what causes the seawater to reach or enter the hole, or a combination of both. If there is such a fortuity, the entry of the seawater is not the ordinary action of the wind and waves because the sea has had an extraordinary effect on the vessel.

(c) Debility and unseaworthiness

The opposite of fortuity would be something that must inevitably happen in precisely the way that it does happen. There are two main reasons why a marine insurance loss must inevitably happen, namely debility and unseaworthiness.[212] Debility essentially means that the ship is in such poor condition as almost not to be a ship anymore. It is a state much beyond unseaworthiness, although in principle both denote a ship in poor condition. The leading case on debility remains *ED Sassoon & Co v Western Assurance Co*.[213] In that case, an insurance claim for damage to a cargo of opium failed because the damage was due to the percolation of seawater through the rotten hull of a wooden hulk moored in a river and used as a store.

Unseaworthiness is dealt with by section 39 of the MIA 1906. Section 39(1) provides for an implied warranty of seaworthiness in a voyage policy. There is no such implied warranty in a time policy but section 39(5) provides that a time policy does not answer if the ship was sent to sea in an unseaworthy state and was then lost, and the shipowner was privy to the particular unseaworthiness to which the loss was attributable. Although this causation requirement is not transparent from the text of section 39(5), it is not enough that the shipowner is privy to some

208. [1887] 12 HL 503.
209. [1924] 18 Lloyd's Rep 211.
210. [1985] 1 WLR 948.
211. *Versloot Dredging BV & Anor v HDI Gerling Industrie Versicherung AG & Ors* [2013] EWHC 1666 (Comm); [2013] 2 Lloyd's Rep 131.
212. For a discussion of the related concept of inherent vice, see p 457.
213. [1912] AC 561.

other fact which also made the ship unseaworthy.[214] The concept of privity has been held to include "blind-eye knowledge",[215] meaning direct knowledge or "an actual state of mind which the law treats as equivalent to such knowledge". Privity is therefore also when the shipowner had a suspicion that the ship was not seaworthy, but did not inquire because he did not want to know the truth.[216] Although the IA 2015 did not explicitly amend section 39, it is clear that its sections 10 and 11 will modify the effect of section 39(1), and that section 11 will affect how section 39(5) is applied. The effect of the provisions of the IA on contracting out of the provisions of the Act[217] will most likely mean that if an insurer wishes to avail itself of the remedies in section 39, it must set them out explicitly in the insurance contract.

(d) The *Inchmaree* clause

At the end of the nineteenth century, steam engines and other machinery became more common at sea and a distinction between perils "of" the seas and perils "on" the seas became crucial to recovery for mechanical faults. Perils "of" the seas were wind and waves and suchlike, but the question was whether the new source of error of mechanical fault should be counted as a peril of the seas or a peril "on" the seas, like theft and other perils that, the reasoning went, could happen on land just as well as on sea and should therefore not be covered by a marine policy. A complication was when machinery was damaged due to the entry of seawater. In *Thames v & Mersey Marine Insurance Co v Hamilton, Fraser & Co (The Inchmaree)*,[218] a mechanical pump was damaged by the condensed salt from seawater. The House of Lords held that this was not a peril "of" the seas because it could just as easily have happened on land: it was not sufficient to make it a peril of the seas that it happened while preparing for a voyage or while the ship was at sea or even that it involved seawater. The common form of policy was immediately amended to say that such faults were indeed covered and the *Inchmaree* clause was born. Crew negligence was also covered by this new clause.

The clause appears as clause 2.2 in the International Hull Clauses 2003 and as clause 6.2 in the earlier forms of policy. The clause is subject to the due diligence proviso, that is, the insured can only recover: "provided that such loss or damage has not resulted from want of due diligence by the Assured, Owners or Managers". It has been held in *The Toisa Pisces*[219] that due diligence means the absence of negligence. It is the insured who must prove that it has exercised due diligence.

The perils mentioned in clause 2.2 are:

2.2.1   bursting of boilers or breakage of shafts but does not cover any of the cost of repairing or replacing the boiler which bursts or the shaft which breaks

2.2.2   any latent defect in the machinery or hull, but does not cover any of the costs of correcting the latent defect

2.2.3   negligence of Master, Officers, Crew or Pilots

2.2.4   negligence of repairers or charterers provided such repairers or charterers are not an Assured under this insurance

2.2.5   barratry of Master, Officers or Crew.

---

214. *Thomas v Tyne & Wear Insurance Association* [1917] 1 KB 938.
215. *Compania Maritima San Basilio SA v Oceanus Mutual Underwriting Association (Bermuda) Ltd (The Eurysthenes)* [1977] QB 49; [1976] 2 Lloyd's Rep 171.
216. Ibid., [25] – [26].
217. IA 2015, ss 16 and 17.
218. [1887] 12 App Cas 484.
219. *Sealion Shipping Ltd and another v Valiant Insurance Co (The Toisa Pisces)* [2012] EWHC 50 (Comm); [2012] 1 Lloyd's Rep 252. On appeal, [2012] EWCA Civ 1625; [2013] 1 Lloyd's Rep 108, this issue was not discussed.

In relation to latent defect, the pre-2003 versions of the clause refer only to latent defects, and the words "does not cover any of the costs of correcting the latent defect" are a 2003 addition. It had been held in earlier cases that the effects of a latent defect were not covered under a marine policy, because no independent physical damage had occurred. However, in *Promet Engineering (Singapore) Pte Ltd v Sturge (The Nukila)*,[220] metal fatigue cracks in the legs of an accommodation platform would, if left unrepaired, have led to the imminent collapse of the platform. The Court of Appeal held that the latent defect had not just become patent, but had caused additional damage to the subject matter insured. This interpretation of the earlier cases is reversed in the 2003 clauses.

The negligence cover under 2.2.3 derives from a clause created following the judgment in *The Inchmaree* and is a slightly inelegant phrase in that "negligence" tends to be the description of an action rather than a cause of loss. However, this has not caused a great deal of trouble in practice. It is clear that the negligence that is covered is that of the Master etc., and no other persons. The assured's own negligence is certainly not covered – this was made clear in relation to a discussion of the due diligence proviso in *The Toisa Pisces*.

For barratry, rule 11 of the Schedule to the MIA 1906 says that "The Term 'barratry' includes every wrongful act wilfully committed by the Master or crew to the prejudice of the owner, or, as the case may be, the charterer."[221] As with all named perils, it is the insured who must prove that there has been a loss by barratry. Once the facts constituting the barratry have been proven, the burden of proof shifts to the insurer to prove that the insured ordered the Master or crew member to scuttle the ship.[222]

In addition to the hull and machinery perils in clause 2 of the 2003 clauses and clause 6 of the earlier clauses, the common forms of policy also cover several other perils that are not easily understood and very peculiar to marine insurance.

(e) Three-fourths collision liability

The standard hull policies are property policies and their main function is therefore to indemnify the shipowner (or other insured) for the lost ship. The policy does also provide liability cover for collisions, but only up to three-fourths of the sums paid by the assured. This applies where the insured vessel has come into collision with another vessel and the insured has become legally liable to pay damages for loss or damage to the other ship or other property. The unwillingness of hull insurers to pay for more than three-fourths of the liabilities of shipowners for collision was a strong factor in the original creation of P&I Clubs[223] in the nineteenth century, when shipowners grouped together to share the liabilities.

(f) Salvage

Salvage exists in two forms which must be distinguished for the purposes of marine insurance. The first is common law salvage, where a volunteer salvages an object and is entitled to reward for action.[224] The second is contractual salvage, where the Master (or someone else representing

---

220. [1997] 2 Lloyd's Rep 146.
221. See fn 129.
222. *Elfie A Issaias v Marine Insurance Co Ltd (The Elias Issaias)* [1923] 15 Ll L Rep 186; this was doubted in *Piermay Shipping Co SA and Brandt's Ltd v Chester (The Michael)* [1979] 1 Lloyd's Rep 55 but confirmed in *N Michalos & Sons Maritime SA v Prudential Assurance Co Ltd (The Zinovia)* [1984] 2 Lloyd's Rep 272.
223. See further pages 482–492 in relation to P&I insurance. For further on liability for collision, see Chapter 7.
224. See further pages 240–241.

the owner) enters into a contract for salvage services.[225] Under the MIA 1906 these are covered differently. Section 65 provides that only common law salvage is covered under the policy itself. Any other expenses incurred for the preservation of the subject matter may be recoverable as sue and labour expenses.[226]

(g) General Average

General Average is also covered under the standard hull and machinery policy. General Average sacrifice is recoverable in full from the insurer, who becomes subrogated to any rights the insured may have against other participants in the maritime adventure. If the insured is liable to pay General Average contributions, a proportion of those may be recoverable from the insurer.[227]

(h) Sue and labour

As noted above,[228] the marine insurance policy, unlike other policies, usually contains an auxiliary contract permitting the recovery from the insurer of mitigation costs. This is referred to as sue and labour expenses. The sue and labour clause in a hull and machinery policy is actually best viewed not as a covered peril under the hull and machinery policy, but as a separate agreement related to the policy. The sue and labour clause provides an opportunity for the insured to incur costs in "suing and labouring" to preserve the subject matter insured. All reasonable costs necessary for the preservation of the subject matter insured can be recovered from the insurer. There are a few conditions. The subject matter insured must be in the grip of an insured peril, i.e. it must be in the process of being lost by a peril that is covered under the policy. The costs must be reasonably incurred. That assessment is made based on the skills of the average Master or other agent to sue and labour.

"Labouring" means such actions as operating the pumps or keeping the ship afloat. "Suing" means watching time bars so that they do not expire without action taken. A lawyer may therefore sometimes be an agent to sue and labour. In the case *Melinda Holdings SA v Hellenic Mutual War Risks Association*,[229] a ship had been arrested in error by the Egyptian courts and the Egyptian lawyers were considered to be agents to sue and labour.[230]

(i) Causation

Determining the cause of loss presents a few thorny issues, some of which overlap with each other. First, where there was more than one hazard operative at the time of loss, was there a single effective cause of loss? In practice, a loss event may be a messy affair with a ship in poor condition and a badly trained crew subjected to heavy weather in treacherous seas. To what degree of precision is it necessary to determine which of many operative causes was the actual cause of loss? Is it necessary to determine that one cause dominated and others should be discounted for the purposes of the insurance? Second, where there was in fact more than one cause of loss interacting to result in a loss, so that it is not correct to prefer one over another, how is this viewed technically under the insurance? If there were two equally

---

225. See further chapter/pages 241 onwards.
226. Discussed at pages 467–470 of this chapter.
227. See pages 255–260.
228. See pages 467–470.
229. Melinda Holdings SA v Hellenic Mutual War Risks Association (Bermuda) Ltd (The Silva) [2011] EWHC 181 (Comm), [2011] 2 Lloyd's Rep. 141.
230. See further pages 467–470.

effective causes and one was covered under the policy and the other was not, can the insured recover?

Sometimes multiple causes of loss operate in the form of a chain of causation where one thing leads to another. In the nineteenth century, there was great emphasis on the last operative cause of the loss. The philosophy behind this thinking was that if one began to unravel the cause of the last cause, and the cause before that, it would lead to a very complicated analysis and ultimately would become very difficult to determine the real cause of loss. In *Leyland Shipping Co Ltd v Norwich Union Fire Insurance Society Ltd*[231] the House of Lords gave permission to consider earlier causes than the very last one: in that case, a ship would not have been present in a French port where it succumbed to a storm if it had not first been torpedoed and in need of assistance. The case established the need to look for the *proximate* cause of the loss, meaning the efficient or effective cause of the loss. The events in the French port were not a *novus casus interveniens* when the ship was already in the grip of the original cause of the loss.

Especially with perils of the seas, there are often good pragmatic reasons to look to the final events before the loss for causation. In *The Miss Jay Jay*, at first instance,[232] there is an often quoted passage about chains of causation:

Nevertheless, it is clearly established that a chain of causation running – (i) initial unseaworthiness; (ii) adverse weather; (iii) loss of watertight integrity of the vessel; (iv) damage to the subject-matter insured – is treated as a loss by perils of the seas, not by unseaworthiness.[233]

Where there is genuinely more than one cause of loss in operation, and where each of the operative causes would independently have caused the subject matter to be lost, there is a rule that says that where one cause of loss is covered by the policy and the other is outside the scope of the policy, the loss is covered under the policy. However, where one cause is covered and the other is excluded (as opposed to simply not contemplated by the policy wording), such as war risks under the hull policies, the loss will not be covered.[234] This rule has lost slightly in significance following *The Cendor MOPU*,[235] wherein it was stated that the two causes must be genuinely operative and not just contributing causes. This should mean that the potential scope for taking into account more than one cause of loss should be reduced.

(j) Losses

In all forms of insurance there are total and partial losses. The MIA 1906 defines partial losses negatively: "Any loss other than a total loss, as hereinafter defined, is a partial loss."[236] The measure of indemnity for partial losses is set out in the Act: if the assured has repaired the ship, the indemnity is the reasonable cost of repairs, if the ship has been only partially repaired the assured receives the cost of repairs plus "reasonable depreciation, if any, arising from the unrepaired damage".[237] If the damage has not been repaired, the assured is entitled to reasonable depreciation or the reasonable cost of repairing, whichever is lower.[238] A partial loss that remains

---

231. [1918] AC 350.
232. [1985] 2 Lloyd's Rep 264.
233. Ibid., 271.
234. *Wayne Tank and Pump Co Ltd v Employers Liability Assurance Corporation Ltd* [1974] QB 57; [1973] 2 Lloyd's Rep 237.
235. See fn 128.
236. MIA 1906, s 56. Such losses are also referred to as "particular average" – see for instance MIA 1906, s 76.
237. Ibid., s 69(1) and (2).
238. Ibid., s 69(3).

unrepaired when the ship is totally lost is not indemnified.[239] In such a case, the insured can only recover for the subsequent total loss. Not all marine policies cover partial losses: a Total Loss Only policy will provide an indemnity only when the ship (or goods) is totally lost.

In marine insurance, total losses are subdivided into actual and constructive total losses. An actual total loss is when the ship (or cargo) is destroyed or so damaged that it can no longer be said to be a ship, or when it is not destroyed but the insured is irretrievably deprived of it for instance because it has been seized by the authorities with no prospects of recovery, or stranded with no prospects of salvage.[240] The most important example of a constructive total loss is where the costs of recovery and repair exceed the value of the ship when repaired. Another example is where an actual total loss appears unavoidable.[241]

For a ship to be a constructive total loss, it must be "reasonably abandoned" by the insured. By a notice of abandonment, the insured informs the insurer that it wishes to abandon the subject matter insured to the insurers. There is no standardised form of words, but the notice of abandonment needs to be unequivocal and clear and must inform the insurer that the insured wishes to abandon the subject matter to the insurer. Notice must be given "with reasonable diligence after the receipt of reliable information of the loss",[242] but the insured is "entitled to a reasonable time to make inquiry". The concepts of "reasonable diligence" and "reasonable time" are not given specific meaning by the Act, but there is a general provision that "what is reasonable is a question of fact",[243] meaning that these concepts must be flexible in nature and their application must depend on the circumstances. In *Connect Shipping Inc and another v Sveriges Angfartygs Assuransforening (The Swedish Club) and others (The MV Renos)*,[244] it was held that a notice of abandonment given on 1 February 2013 in respect of a loss that took place on 23 August 2012 was effective. The insured may be excused from giving a notice of abandonment where there is no possibility of benefit to the insurer.[245] The purpose of the notice of abandonment is salvage: since the insurer becomes the owner of what is left of the subject matter insured when they pay the indemnity, they should be given the opportunity to salvage as much as possible thereof even when the insured has given up hope. Recent cases on situations where no notice of abandonment was necessary include *Kastor Navigation Co Ltd v AGF Mat (The Kastor Too)*,[246] where the ship sank shortly after being consumed by a fire originating from the engine room. Fire was a covered peril but the sinking happened due to unknown causes and might therefore not be a loss by a covered peril. No notice of abandonment was given, but the court held that it was not necessary because the closeness in time of the two loss events meant that there was no possibility of benefit to the insurer. *The Kastor Too* also illustrates what may happen when there are successive losses. A partial loss followed by a total loss is not recoverable – the insured can only claim for the total loss. But an unrepaired constructive total loss is recoverable. Therefore if the insured succeeds in showing that it did not need to give notice of abandonment, it can recover for the constructive total loss, even though it could not have recovered for the partial loss.

In *Clothing Management Solutions v Beazley*[247] the insured kept sending more fabric to a sewing factory that was blighted by strikes and in the end all the fabrics disappeared and the factory

---

239. Ibid., s 77.
240. Ibid., s 57.
241. Ibid., s 60.
242. MIA 1906, s 62(3).
243. MIA 1906, s 88.
244. [2016] EWHC 1580 (Comm); [2016] Lloyd's Rep IR 601.
245. MIA 1906, s 62(7).
246. [2003] EWHC 472 (Comm); [2003] 1 Lloyd's Rep 296, affirmed [2004] EWCA Civ 277; [2004] 2 Lloyd's Rep 119.
247. [2012] EWHC 727; [2012] 1 Lloyd's Rep 571.

closed. The court held that since the insurers were at all times fully informed of the situation and could have taken action if they wished, there was no need for a notice of abandonment.

The notice of abandonment converts a partial loss into a total loss for the purpose of the measure of indemnity. Where a notice of abandonment has been successfully given, the loss is referred to as a constructive total loss. An insurer who accepts the notice of abandonment thereby also admits liability for the loss,[248] which is why insurers never accept the notice of abandonment and instead agree to put the insured in the same position as if a claim form had been issued. As remarked above in connection with sue and labour,[249] this has the effect of shielding the insured from subsequent events. The concept of constructive total loss is unique to marine insurance. Other insurances do something similar in practice, whereby a car is said to be "a write-off", but only in marine insurance has this crystallised into a rule of law.[250]

3. CARGO INSURANCE

Cargo insurance is usually concluded in the form of an open cover. Open covers are contracts negotiated in advance ensuring that an insured who regularly ships many cargoes, such as a manufacturer of goods, can declare the cargoes under the policy as and when they are shipped, instead of negotiating a separate policy for each one. The predecessor to open covers was floating policies, dealt with in section 29 of the MIA 1906 but now obsolete. Under these, each insured ship was declared to the insurer in order of dispatch, up to a cap beyond which cover ceased. Like floating policies, open covers are issued in the form of a framework contract and then individual cargoes are declared to the insurers as and when the details become known. Open covers were not in existence at the time of the MIA 1906 and there is therefore no legislation and very little case law on such policies, the effect of the declarations, or the certificates of cover issued under an open cover. Such certificates are often issued by the insured to the buyer of the cargo rather than by the insurer itself.[251]

(a) Introduction to the Institute Cargo Clauses

The Institute Cargo Clauses are a set of standard clauses used in many cargo policies. They come in three versions which are mostly identical, but the ICC (A) clauses, which are on "all risks" terms, provide a more comprehensive cover than the (B) clauses or the (C) clauses, which cover nine and seven named perils respectively.

The first predecessor of the current cargo clauses were introduced in 1912. They were revised in 1963 and again in 1982, after weighty international criticism. In 1982, the SG policy was abandoned and parts of the wording of that standard policy were transferred into the Institute Cargo Clauses. The clauses were revised again in 2009 and this latest version has been widely adopted in the cargo insurance market.

Key revisions in 2009 were a modernisation of the terminology so that where the 1982 clauses referred to "servants", the 2009 clauses use the more contemporary terminology "employees", and introduction of the language "this contract" to refer to the clauses themselves and "the contract of insurance" to refer to the open cover for the cargo policy.

---

248. Ibid., s 60(6).
249. See pages 467–470.
250. Although this is dealt with under the sub-heading hull and machinery insurance, constructive total losses are also possible in relation to cargo insurance.
251. Open covers are particularly important for cargo insurance but may also be effected for hull insurance.

(b) Scope of the policy

(i) *The voyage and the risk*

Two points are important to remember in relation to cargo insurance. First, cargo policies are voyage (and not time) policies. A voyage is between two points and therefore if the ship sails from a different point of departure than that named in the policy, the risk does not attach. This follows from section 43 of the MIA 1906 entitled, "Alteration of port of departure".

The second point is the "principle of innocent cargo" which is the reason for several of the clauses in the ICC. While a shipowner may be well aware that the ship is being sent ill equipped on a hazardous voyage, the same may not be the case for a cargo insured who may not be at all familiar with the ship and its qualities, and may not even know precisely on what ship the cargo is being transported. The sections in the MIA 1906 that exclude the insurer's liability in a few common cases of loss have therefore been modified by clauses in the Institute Cargo Clauses. Those clauses, along with any warranty implied by sections 36–48 of the MIA 1906, will now be subject to the rules in sections 10 and 11 of the IA 2015. While section 10 applies to warranties only, section 11 applies to any term.

Thus, if a ship sails for a different destination, section 44 of the MIA 1906 will mean that a hull voyage insurance policy never attaches. This applies where the voyage is changed before the ship sails, so that she sets sail for a completely different destination. The risk never attaches. Occasionally, the reason why the ship sails for a different destination may be that she has been stolen and disappears. In such a case, there is a solution for cargo, which will be unable to influence the movements of the goods, in clause 10(2) of the ICC 2009. The clause was introduced to clarify that cover remains in place if a third party disappears with the goods, following the case *Nima SARL v Deves Insurance*[252] where cargo was held unable to recover. In that case, the goods disappeared on board a so-called phantom ship.

If the voyage is changed *after* the ship has sailed, the risk will have attached, but cover then ceases from the moment the change of voyage is manifested, whether or not the ship has then left its course. This follows from section 45 of the MIA 1906. According to clause 10.1 of the Institute Cargo Clauses, the insured is held covered in such a case but may have to pay an additional premium.

Section 46 of the MIA 1906 deals with deviation, which is where the ship takes a different route from that foreseen in the policy. That section provides that the insured is discharged from liability from the moment of deviation. Unlike change of voyage, an intention to deviate is not enough, the ship must actually deviate. This is again mitigated by the Institute Cargo Clauses, clause 8.3 of which provides that the insurance remains in force during deviation.

Section 48 of the MIA 1906 on "delay", provides that the insurer is excluded from liability from the moment the delay in the voyage became unreasonable. Here, the Institute Cargo Clauses provide a variation in that clause 4.5 (see below) excludes loss caused by delay.

Section 49 explains what may be regarded as legitimate excuses for deviation and delay under sections 46 and 48. Those excuses apply also under a cargo policy, unless otherwise stated, so that it is usually permissible to deviate for example in order to save human lives[253] or where it is necessary for the safety of the ship.[254]

---

252. [2002] EWCA Civ 1132; [2003] 2 Lloyd's Rep 327.
253. MIA 1906, s 49(1)(e).
254. Ibid., s 49(1)(d).

(ii) Duration

While the MIA 1906 reflected insurance of the cargo from port to port, the modern Institute Cargo Clauses have a wider scope adapted to modern transport practices. The 1982 Clauses applied "from warehouse to warehouse", that is from the moment the goods left the warehouse until they arrived at the destination warehouse. The 2009 Clauses have been extended slightly and their cover is said to be "shelf-to-shelf", although this is just convenient shorthand for the provisions in clause 8 on "Duration".

Clause 8.1 first provides that the risk attaches, or in other words, the policy incepts, when the goods are first moved in the warehouse for the purpose of transport. This means that the land transit to the port where the ship will sail from is also covered, unlike in the MIA 1906. An insured who does not possess an insurable interest for this part of the voyage will still be covered according to clause 11.2. The cover continues "during the ordinary course of transit". What is the ordinary course of transit will be a question of what was planned or reasonable in the individual case.

Cover terminates when one of the options in clause 8.1.1 to 8.1.4 first applies. They are alternatives and therefore whichever happens first is the end point of the insurance. Clause 8.1.1 provides for termination on completion of unloading at the final warehouse; clause 8.1.2 provides for termination in case of storage in a warehouse other than "in the ordinary course of transit"; clause 8.1.3 provides for termination in case of storage in a vehicle or conveyance other than "in the ordinary course of transit"; and 8.1.4 provides that cover will cease 60 days after discharge overside from the ship. In *Bayview v Mitsui*[255] the court had to decide when cover terminated. The cargo consisted of cars in transit to the Turks & Caicos Islands but insured to Santo Domingo, where they were going to be transhipped. At Santo Domingo, they were taken into a customs compound. They disappeared from the compound at some unknown point in time and it was suspected that they had been stolen by customs officials. The court held that the customs warehouse was not a final warehouse or place of storage so that the cars were still in transit.

(iii) Perils/risks

Having ascertained that the loss can be placed within the scope and currency of the policy, the next step is to establish that the loss of the cargo was caused by a peril insured against. The cargo clauses use the word risks instead of perils, and the principal clause is clause 1. There are important differences between clause 1 as it appears in the Institute Cargo Clauses A, B and C. The ICC (A) is said to be all risks, and accordingly the only thing that needs to be proved by a claimant insured is that the loss was fortuitous, as decided by the House of Lords in *British & Foreign Marine v Gaunt*.[256]

As mentioned above, clause 1 in ICC (A) provides cover against "all risks". From the 1982 edition, the clauses are called "A" instead of "all risks". Clause 1 in ICC (B) insures against nine named risks, all in the nature of marine perils. Clause 1 in ICC (C) is limited: only seven named risks are covered. This is minimum cover and not much in use. The important risk of theft is not covered by the ICC (B) or (C) clauses, and for that reason they are only used for shipping cargoes that are subject to maritime risks, but are not likely to get stolen, such as gravel. The limited scope of risks covered naturally also means that the premium for policies on ICC (B) or (C) terms is lower.

255. [2002] EWCA Civ 1605; [2003] 1 Lloyd's Rep 131.
256. [1921] 7 Ll L Rep 62.

Clauses 2 and 3 in all three sets of cargo clauses, (A), (B) and (C), provide that the policy covers certain expenses, namely certain recovery in the case of collision liabilities, salvage awards and sue and labour expenses.

(c) Limits of cargo cover

(i) Exclusions

As with hull insurance, the burden of proof for exclusions is generally on the insurer. Most of the exclusions have their roots in the SG policy and several also correspond to provisions in the MIA 1906. Clause 4.1, wilful misconduct, mirrors section 55(2)(a) and does not contain any change compared to the Act. Clause 4.2, ordinary leakage, loss in volume and wear and tear corresponds exactly to part of section 55(2)(c). Clause 4.3, insufficient packing, was unnecessarily complex in the 1982 version and was somewhat simplified in the 2009 clauses. It excludes insurers' liability for insufficient packing and stowage where they were carried out before attachment of the risk, or where they were done after the inception of the risk by the insured itself or by its employees. Loss is covered where the packing or stowage is done after the inception of the risk by independent contractors. Clause 4.4 excludes liability for inherent vice which the Supreme Court in *The Cendor MOPU* gave a narrow interpretation so that it did not interfere with a subsequent loss by perils of the seas. Clause 4.5 excludes loss caused by delay and corresponds to section 55(2)(b) of the Marine Insurance Act. Many losses result from circumstances involving delay among other possible causes of loss and it will often be a question of which is the dominant cause. In that connection, it has been argued that delay does not obey the usual rule of causation laid down by the House of Lords in *Leyland Shipping*[257] and that delay will take over as the dominant cause of loss if it occurs after another peril. Clause 4.6 was introduced in 1982 and excludes loss caused by the insolvency of the carrying shipowner, where the insured was aware of that insolvency and still permitted the cargo to be loaded on board. There is no exception for where the insured was aware of the insolvency but was unable to stop the loading. The 2009 clauses remove assignees from the scope of the exclusion. This was introduced to protect CIF buyers who were unaware of the insolvency and did not choose the carrier. Clause 4.7 in the ICC (B) and (C) clauses excludes deliberate destruction of the subject matter insured. Clause 4.8 in the ICC (B) and (C) clauses corresponds to clause 4.7 in the ICC (A) clauses which excludes weapons employing nuclear fission.

(ii) Seaworthiness and cargo

The rules on seaworthiness of cargo are very different from those applying to ships.[258] Section 40(1) of the MIA 1906 provides that there is no requirement that cargo must be seaworthy. There is on the other hand an implied warranty in section 40(2) that the ship on which the cargo is being carried is seaworthy. This implied warranty has been modified in the cargo clauses by clause 5, by which insurers waive the implied warranty of seaworthiness but replace it with an exclusion of loss caused by unseaworthiness of the ship. The exclusion requires the insured to be privy to the unseaworthiness. As a result, cargo shipped on an unseaworthy ship is still not covered, but only if the insured was aware that the ship was not seaworthy.

---

257. *Leyland Shipping Company Ltd v Norwich Union Fire Insurance Society Ltd* [1918] AC 350.
258. For which see pages 472–473.

(d) Losses

What was said in relation to constructive total losses under hull policies[259] applies equally to cargo policies. In addition, clause 13 of the Institute Cargo Clauses limits the definition of constructive total loss compared to what follows from section 60 of the MIA 1906. Clause 13 only recognises reasonable abandonment due to a total loss being unavoidable or because costs of recovery and repair would exceed the value of cargo upon arrival as valid constructive total losses. Deprivation of possession, which is otherwise a valid constructive total loss according to section 60(2)(i), is thereby outside the scope of cargo policies. As a result, piracy events where the insured can expect to have possession of the cargo restored following negotiation and payment of a ransom cannot be considered constructive total losses.[260]

4. PROTECTION AND INDEMNITY INSURANCE

(a) Introduction

P&I Clubs provide third party liability insurance for shipowners. The modern Protection and Indemnity Associations (P&I Clubs) are the descendants of the mutual protection clubs and indemnity clubs which were founded by British shipowners in the nineteenth century in reaction to changes in the legislation affecting their third party liabilities and to the perceived failure of marine insurance companies and marine underwriters satisfactorily to respond to their needs. The distinction between protection and indemnity risks is today largely academic but originally, protection covered liabilities to personnel and for damage to property, while indemnity covered liabilities to cargo owners under a contract of carriage. Today most shipowners still obtain their third party insurance cover from P&I Clubs although it is possible to insure with other underwriters, usually for a fixed premium and with generally lower limits of cover than those offered by the clubs. Two of the features which distinguish P&I Clubs from other insurers are that they are controlled or governed by their shipowner members, which ensures their members a measure of flexibility, and that they are run on a non-profit making or mutual basis, making them economically attractive.

(b) The risks covered

The risks covered by protection and indemnity insurance are set out in detail within the rules of each club: the rules also include conditions, exceptions and limitations and other provisions, including the bye-laws relevant to the operation of the club.
    P&I risks include:

- claims for loss or damage to cargo;
- unrecoverable General Average contributions;
- liabilities to passengers, crew or others, for personal injury and death claims and including cancelled voyages;
- medical treatment and the repatriation of sick, injured or deceased crew members;

---

259. See pp 476–478 of this chapter.
260. The argument for a constructive total loss was unsuccessful at first instance and abandoned in the Court of Appeal in *Masefield AG v Amlin Corporate Member Ltd* [2011] EWCA Civ 24; [2011] 1 Lloyd's Rep 630, a case about loss by piracy where it was always expected that the ship and cargo would be returned to the owners upon the negotiation and payment of a ransom.

- crew unemployment indemnity following a casualty;
- stowaways;
- collisions – 25 per cent of damages payable to the colliding vessel;
- damage to fixed and floating objects;
- liabilities under approved towage contracts;
- wreck removal;
- expenses of marine inquiries;
- expenses incidental to the operation of ships – subject to the discretion of the club directors;
- special compensation under the 1989 Salvage Convention;
- fines, including those for pollution; and
- civil liability for pollution.

Readers who require a more detailed understanding of the cover provided are recommended to refer to the rulebook of any one of the Group clubs, most of whom make these available on their websites.

In any given period, the greatest numbers of claims experienced by a P&I Club are cargo claims and those arising from liabilities to passengers and crew; among the most expensive claims are the costs of wreck removal and repairs to fixed and floating objects. Under the London Hull form, the running-down clause covers 75 per cent of the collision liabilities: the P&I Clubs cover the remaining 25 per cent or one-fourth. In practice, this may often mean that the club is the largest underwriter sharing this risk. Under other hull forms, notably the Norwegian form and the French form, these costs are met 100 per cent by the hull underwriter. It is worth noting that if a member so chooses, clubs are able to offer 100 per cent cover for collision liabilities. This can be advantageous if security is urgently required immediately after a collision. It is interesting to note that the stated aim of the first Protection Club to be formed in 1865 was to "protect Ship-owners against their liabilities for loss of life and personal injury under the Merchant Shipping Act of 1854 *and also the risk of running down other vessels, not covered by their ordinary Marine Policies*".[261] This refers not to one-fourth of the collision liability but arises from the fact that it was then not legally possible for hull insurance to provide cover in excess of the insured value of the ship.

(c) Structure of the clubs

The clubs have a long tradition of caring for the needs of their members and have responded over the years to changes and developments in legislation affecting the liabilities of shipowners so that the scope of the cover provided has expanded considerably. The essence of the modern club nonetheless remains that it is a group of shipowners who pool or share their risks. The corporate entity which accepts the risks and which pays the claims is nowadays often located offshore, as is the management company appointed by the club to handle its affairs. Most of the English clubs originally operated within the United Kingdom using the pound sterling as their currency, but following the devaluation of the pound in the late 1960s many clubs moved offshore to such locations as Bermuda or Luxembourg, where they were able to hold their funds in US dollars and to enjoy some protection from UK exchange control. The visible presence of the club, whether in the United Kingdom or elsewhere, is likely to be the agent for the managers,

---

261. Preface to the Deed of the Shipowners' Mutual Protection Society.

who employs the underwriters and the claims handlers who are responsible for the day-to-day running of the club. Particular arrangements vary from one club to another.

Any person who has an interest in a ship may be a club member including not only shipowners but also, for example, charterers and third party ship managers. Typically, a club may include several hundred members. From their number, Directors are elected, usually holding office for three years. The Board of Directors generally meets three or four times each year. Its principal responsibilities are to determine the liabilities which are to be covered, to decide the level of calls or premium required each financial year, the ordination of club policy in general, the planning of financial strategy, particularly regarding the holding of reserve funds, the supervision of the club managers, including the handling of claims and the exercise of the Directors' discretion regarding the application of the club rules.

(d) Conditions and exceptions

It is noteworthy that in all cases, subject to the discretion of the club directors, cover is conditional on the entered vessel's classification being maintained with a Classification Society approved by the managers and upon compliance with statutory obligations including for example, SOLAS[262] (which incorporates the International Safety Management Code), the STCW (Standards of Training, Certification and Watchkeeping) Convention, 1995 and the ISPS (International Ship and Port Security) Code.[263]

Since most of the claims covered by P&I are liability claims, the club rules also require that members take the benefit of any available regime of limitation of liability. Where a member loses the right to limit, this does not deprive it necessarily of the right to claim reimbursement from the club. Under the 1976 Limitation Convention, the test for the loss of the right to limit is stricter than under the 1957 Limitation Convention: the claimant must prove that the loss resulted from the owner's personal act or omission, committed with intent to cause such loss, or recklessly and with the knowledge that such loss would probably result.[264] If this is proved, then it is likely that the owner would fall foul of sections 39(5) and 55(2) of the MIA 1906,[265] which applies to all those clubs with rules governed by English law.[266] In a Canadian case,[267] the Supreme Court held that the standard of the Convention and of "wilful misconduct" under the insurance were different. Although the conduct in question (cutting a sub-marine cable) was not "intentional or reckless" as to the resulting loss, permitting the appellants to limit liability under the Convention, it was wilful misconduct, preventing recovery from insurers.

(e) The International Group of P&I Clubs

The International Group of P&I Clubs[268] represents the collective views of its 13 member clubs and facilitates discussions between the clubs on matters of relevant interest, such as the impact on shipowners' liabilities of new international conventions or other legislation. It also provides representation for the clubs at various organisations, such as the International Maritime Organization, the International Chamber of Shipping and the European Union. Another example of the Group's

---

262. See Chapter 9 for more information on SOLAS.
263. See Chapter 9 for more information on STCW and ISPS Code.
264. 1976 Limitation Convention, art 4; see further Chapter, 7.
265. See *Compania Maritima San Basilio SA v Oceanus Mutual Underwriting Association (Bermuda) Ltd (The Eurysthenes)* [1976] 2 Lloyd's Rep 171.
266. See e.g. the UK P&I Club Rules 2013, r 42 available at www.ukpandi.com (accessed 20 January 2017).
267. *Peracomo Inc and others v Telus Communications Co and others (The "Realice")* 2014 SCC 29.
268. See www.igpandi.org (accessed 20 January 2017).

wider role is the code of practice relating to SCOPIC agreed between the International Group and the International Salvage Union.[269] In addition, the Group oversees the International Group Agreement (IGA), under which the participating clubs conduct their underwriting procedures. The Group is also responsible for the administration of the "Pooling Agreement" by which the clubs share the cost of claims in excess of US$9 million up to US$70 million. The pooling agreement also defines which types of claim can be pooled as well as the formula by which each club's contribution is calculated. Under the "Pool Reinsurance Programme", the sharing clubs negotiate the purchase of US$2 billion of reinsurance cover, bringing the total amount of funds available to US$2.1 million. The cost of any claim beyond this amount, if such a situation should arise, would be met by "overspill" funds, collected by each club from its members. It is the essence of mutual insurance that each member is the insurer of last resort. To assist with the payment of overspill claims, in 2007, the Group purchased for the first time, overspill reinsurance on behalf of each club for all categories of claim up to US$1,000 million in excess of the limit of the Group reinsurance contract.

Traditionally, for many decades, the clubs offered unlimited cover for any one claim, with two exceptions: oil pollution claims[270] which have been limited for some time and which are currently restricted to US$1,000 million and since 2007, passenger and crew claims whereby a maximum of US$3,000 million applies to each event in respect of liability to passengers and seamen with a sub-limit of US$2,000 million each event in respect of liability to passengers. In the 1990s it was decided, after a prolonged debate, to impose an overall ceiling on the cover provided, albeit at a very high level. This was in response to mounting concerns that any overspill claim in excess of the Group reinsurance limit would fall back on the clubs and thus on their members, in amounts which might not realistically be collectable. Unlimited liability for the clubs meant unlimited liability for members. There was also a fear that in some cases, some members would be unable to pay the call or might default, leaving the burden to fall on other, more prosperous members. Most members felt that while they did not object in principle to paying overspill calls, it was preferable that the amount of the call should at least be quantified. The limit of any overspill call for any ship entered in a Group club was eventually fixed at 2.5 per cent of the 1976 limitation fund for that ship. For a 10,000 gt ship, for example, the maximum overspill call would be about US$65,000. It is reckoned that this gives an effective limit for club cover for any one claim, of $4.35 billion, comprising the $2.1 billion provided by the club, the Group pool and reinsurance and approximately $2.25 billion from overspill funds.

The IGA has periodically been under the scrutiny of the relevant European Commission as being in possible restraint of free competition in insurance matters. A ten years' exemption was granted in 1986; its renewal in 1996 became the subject of intense debate and it was not until 1999 that it was conceded that the IGA was not in breach of EC principles and a further ten-year exemption was agreed. In 2010 the European Commission once again opened formal proceedings to investigate the provisions of the IGA in order to establish whether they are in breach of EU anti-trust rules. The Commission announced in 2012 that the investigation had been satisfactorily concluded and closed.

(i) Non Group P&I insurance

Most of the Group P&I Clubs were, as mentioned above, originally founded and based in the United Kingdom, with others in Scandinavia, in Japan and the United States of America. Other

---

269. See F. Rose, *Kennedy and Rose, Law of Salvage* (8th edn, Sweet & Maxwell 2013), at pp 431–440 and Chapter 7 pages 251–255 of this work.
270. See Chapter 10 on Marine Pollution from Shipping Activities.

P&I Clubs exist outside the International Group, often established to serve a particular sector of the market. The China P&I Club is an example of this, having been originally established in the 1980s in order to provide P&I cover for People's Republic of China flag ships operating within Chinese territorial waters.

(f) The managers' agents: underwriting and claims handling; calls

The role of the managers' agent or of those who deal with the everyday business of the club involves three important functions: underwriting, claims handling and the prudent investment of the club's financial reserves. The Board of Directors decide at the start of each financial year on the total amount of premium likely to be required to fund claims anticipated in that period. It is the role of the P&I underwriters to see that individual members pay the appropriate call in order to achieve that target. There is no standard tariff for P&I calls – the amount paid by each member depends entirely upon the member's loss record. Those who have a good claims record pay less: those who have a poor record pay more. Charges are levied usually in US dollars in dollars and cents per entered ton. Generally the entered tonnage nowadays is likely to be the gross tonnage. Thus it is perfectly possible for two physically identical ships to be charged different rates for P&I cover – depending upon loss record. It is worth mentioning that the P&I financial year runs from noon on 20 February each year – a relic from the days of the original hull clubs, when ships were laid up during the winter months in the northern hemisphere and were re-commissioned in mid-February.

When the financial year opens members are invoiced for the payment of an advance call, which may be settled by one payment or, more usually, paid in instalments. At some point later, generally six months or so after the end of the financial year, the directors customarily review the claims position and establish whether sufficient money has been generated by the advance call to pay claims incurred during that year. If more funds are required, they may make a supplementary call in order to balance the account. Members who elect to leave the club before the supplementary call is made are likely to be required to pay a release call in lieu or to provide an undertaking which is satisfactory to the club managers, that the eventual supplementary call will be settled.

A significant difference between market insurance and club insurance is possibly that the clubs are able to assume control of events when a situation arises on a member's ship, which is likely to lead to a claim. The shipmaster and shipowner are encouraged, when facing a potential liability, immediately to contact the club for assistance. They are also able, in overseas ports to contact the local club correspondent, who will provide further support and advice. Surveyors can be appointed and, if necessary, lawyers in order to protect the owners' interests from the outset, with the club meeting the costs. The clubs have correspondents in most ports worldwide, numbering several hundreds. Many of these are commercial correspondents and may have other shipping interests, operating as customs or ships' agents for example. Others are legal correspondents. They all however possess wide local knowledge and contacts and are able to provide valuable support to the shipmaster. They are also able to assist where required, with the provision of security if the ship is arrested or threatened with arrest.

(g) Technical advice and support

Another function filled by the managers or their agents includes the provision at all times of advice and support to members in any matters related to their business. Many clubs regularly publish materials giving topical advice on the safe and efficient operation of ships. This may include technical advice on such matters as the carriage of certain cargo products, the wording of charterparty clauses and valuable loss prevention advice. Some clubs also run a ship inspection programme, whereby the club is able to offer guidance on the management, operation or manning of members' ships, aimed at reducing their exposure to claims.

(h) "Pay to be Paid" rule: direct action

All Group club rules provide that the member in order to claim reimbursement from the club must first have been held liable for and have paid a claim. Where the member has been wound up or adjudged bankrupt before the claim is finally assessed, the member is clearly not in a position to pay the claim. The question then arises whether the claimant can sue the club directly. In 1990, two test cases were brought against two clubs in the International Group, concerning two ships, *The Fanti* and *The Padre Island*.[271] In these cases, the claimants sought to rely on the provisions of the Third Parties (Rights against Insurers) Act of 1930 whereby any rights which a defendant may have to be indemnified by insurers, are transferred, on the defendant's bankruptcy or winding up, to the claimant. The claimant may then stand in the shoes of the insured party. Section 1(3) of the Act also states that any provision in the insurance policy intended to defeat this transfer of rights, is deemed void. In the two test cases, the House of Lords held that the transfer of rights did not relieve the third party claimant of the need to fulfil the condition precedent to payment, meaning that the claimant cargo interests could not recover. Section 1(3) did not apply as "pay-to-be paid clauses were an integral part of club cover". The 1930 Act was controversial for many reasons and on 1 August 2016 was replaced when the Third Parties (Rights Against Insurers) Act 2010 entered into force. The new statute provides that rights of a third party are transferred without any conditions attached, so that clauses requiring payment to take place before an indemnity can be claimed are ineffective.[272] However, for marine insurance, this provision applies only to claims for death and personal injury,[273] where the statute now permits direct action against P&I Clubs by injured persons or surviving relatives. Such liabilities were previously honoured under Club rules, resulting in no change in practice except that there is now a legal obligation to indemnify. It is also worth mentioning that the Merchant Shipping Act 1995 fills the gap left by both Third Parties Acts in respect of pollution risks, based on the P&I Club blue card system.[274] The overall effect is that cargo interests, as before, must possess their own insurance.

Pay-to-be paid clauses apply also under the rules of those Group clubs, which are governed by a law other than English law. However, many jurisdictions have a more generous right of direct action enabling any liability claimant to proceed directly against the insurer on the basis for example of statute, resulting in jurisdiction and choice of law disputes and sometimes anti-suit injunctions.[275] It is also worth noting that in the event of an owner being bankrupt and unable to pay a claim, it is highly likely that the owner might also have failed to pay P&I calls, in which case membership of the club would have been terminated.

On occasion the clubs, entirely without prejudice to their right to invoke the "pay to be paid" rule, may be prepared to advance funds before the member has settled a claim. This procedure obviously applies where a club guarantee has been given and also where a pollution certificate

---

271. *Firma C-Trade SA v Newcastle Protection & Indemnity Association (The Fanti)* and *Socony Mobil Oil Inc and Others v West of England Shipowners Mutual Insurance Association (London) Ltd (No 2)(The Padre Island)* [1990] 2 Lloyd's Rep 191.
272. Third Parties (Rights Against Insurers) Act 2010, s 9(5).
273. Third Parties (Rights Against Insurers) Act 2010, s 9(6).
274. See Chapter 10.
275. See Chapter 1.

has been issued by the Club. Historically, in certain death or injury cases, the clubs waived their rights under the "pay to be paid" rule. Where particularly large sums of money are involved in a settlement it may make practical sense for the club to provide funds rather than requiring the member to do so. It should also be borne in mind that some recent legislation including the US Oil Pollution Act 1990 and the revised Athens Convention[276] call for direct action against insurers.

As already mentioned, English law governs the rules of most of the group clubs. From 11 May 2000 all such contracts are subject to the Contracts (Rights of Third Parties) Act 1999. Under this Act, persons who are not a party to an insurance contract may in their own right enforce a term of the contract if the contract expressly allows them to do so, or if the term in question "purports to confer a benefit on him".[277] However, the Act also allows the parties, if they wish, to make it clear in the wording of the contract that it is not their intention to confer benefits on third parties. The clubs in the International Group have accordingly amended their rules to this effect.

(i) Claims settlement: disputes

P&I Clubs in the course of a year handle many thousands of claims, most of which are cargo claims or passenger or crew liability claims. The great majority of these are settled by negotiation and without the involvement of lawyers or any legal process. Clearly, however, there are likely to be a substantial number of claims, which cannot be amicably settled and which are resolved either in the courts or by arbitration. In such cases, the club managers appoint lawyers in London or elsewhere, in the appropriate jurisdiction. Occasionally, disputes may arise between member and club over the conduct of a case or circumstances may arise where the managers may wish to reserve the club's position, possibly for example, because of a suspected breach of the club rules (such as a failure to maintain the ship in classification). In such cases, it may be appropriate for the member and the club to have separate legal representation. In the event of such a dispute not being resolved by the managers, members have the right to have their case presented to their fellow members, the directors of the club, with the request that they establish whether there has been a breach of the rules or, if they deem it suitable, that they exercise their discretion in favour of the member. Should the member not be satisfied by the directors' decision, there is an appeal procedure whereby in the first instance the case is again put before the directors as adjudicators or thereafter it may be submitted to independent arbitrators in London.

(j) Freight, demurrage and defence cover

All clubs offer freight, demurrage and defence (FD&D) or "defence" cover as an adjunct to P&I cover. The defence cover is often insured in a separate club, with a separate Board of Directors, but under the same managers. In other cases the insurance is provided by the P&I Club and is defined as a separate "class" of cover. Defence clubs provide a claims-handling service and insurance of legal costs and fees for those claims not covered by P&I. These might include disputes with shipbuilders, post-fixture disputes with charterers, disputes with suppliers including ship-chandlers or disputes with crew. The insurance provided is always discretionary and covers only the legal costs not the principal amounts in dispute.

---

276. 2002 Protocol to the Athens Convention, in force on 23 April 2014. See Chapter 6 on Carriage of Passengers.
277. Contracts (Rights of Third Parties) Act 1999, s 1(1).

(k) Mutual system

It is interesting to reflect whether shipowners in the twenty-first century, faced with the need to find insurance cover for their third party claims, would still opt for the club mutual system as did their predecessors in the nineteenth century. It may seem likely that they would, bearing in mind the success that the clubs have enjoyed over the past 150 years and the attractions of self-governing, mutual, non-profit making insurance, provided at cost.

(l) Club letters of undertaking

(i) Purpose of a letter of undertaking

The purpose of a letter of undertaking is to ensure that the vessel is not arrested in port by a creditor or to permit a ship already under arrest to sail. Whether the owner or managers are unwilling or unable to pay the underlying debt, their interest will be that the ship is enabled to continue trading and earning freight. A speedy release of the vessel is also in the interests of the creditor as it will help a shipowner or manager in financial straits to pay the debt. By the letter of undertaking, the P&I Club provides security for the debt of the shipowner or manager by undertaking to settle the debt and to accept service of *in rem* proceedings in a competent court. A letter of undertaking is also a means to allow the parties the time to discuss the precise amount of the liability and acceptable ways of paying it while avoiding litigation for as long as possible.

Most P&I Clubs make it clear in their rules that the club is under no obligation to provide bail or security on behalf of a member. However, when there has been an incident giving rise to a claim and a ship is arrested, or where there is a threat of arrest by the claimant, the P&I Club will generally agree to issue a letter of guarantee in order to avoid arrest or promptly to release the ship and allow the voyage to continue, thereby avoiding further possible delays and financial loss. The letter will state that the club undertakes to pay the addressee on demand such sum or sums, in respect of the particular claim, as may be agreed by negotiation or awarded to the addressee by final judgment of the competent court or final award of an arbitration tribunal, and no longer subject to appeal. This creates a collateral contract between the claimant and the club. It is always expressed to be in consideration of the release of the ship from arrest or the threat of arrest.

Such letters are issued on condition that: the claim is covered by the club rules and is included in the ship's terms of entry, the member's calls are paid up to date and there are no calls outstanding on that ship or any other ship in that entry, the ship is arrested or that there is an imminent threat of arrest, the ship is not in breach of club rules, for example with respect to classification, and that the wording of the letter is approved by the club managers or their agents.

The P&I Clubs, particularly those in the International Group, are scrupulous in ensuring that such letters of guarantee are always honoured according to their terms. Any default would reduce the confidence of claimants and thus the whole system of club letters of undertaking.

The alternative to a club letter for the shipowner may be the issue of a bank guarantee. In certain jurisdictions, claimants may insist on such guarantees. The disadvantage of these is first that they may take a considerable time to arrange while club letters can be issued very quickly. Also bank guarantees can be costly where club letters are provided free of charge to members. Some P&I Clubs are prepared, in some circumstances, to issue non-club bail, that is, club letters covering non-club matters, but this is usually on a short-term or interim basis, until owners are able themselves to provide suitable security.[278]

---

278. See S.J. Hazelwood and D. Semark (eds), *P&I Clubs: Law and Practice* (4th edn, Lloyd's of London Press Ltd 2010), at pp 247–262.

(ii) Construction of a letter of undertaking

General contract law is applicable to letters of undertaking, and so is the law on surety or guarantees. It has been confirmed in several cases[279] that general case law on contract interpretation applies to letters of undertaking, so that the factual matrix must be taken into account in their interpretation. As held by the Supreme Court in *Arnold v Britton*,[280] the emphasis is on the language employed by the parties with reliance on 'commercial common sense' having a limited importance. Although *Arnold v Britton* constituted a realignment in contract law more generally, its outcome aligns broadly with the cases on the construction of letters of undertaking to date. P&I Club letters of undertaking have a specific characteristic compared to other forms of surety and compared to most other forms of contract: they are not rich and precise documents negotiated over a period of time to match other documents involved in the transaction, like for instance the letters of undertaking provided as part of a credit transaction, ship construction or sale-and-leaseback of a vessel. They are one-page documents, more often than not negotiated between parties who do not do business together on a regular basis and across more than one continent. Because of the context of existing or threatened arrest of the vessel, there is usually a strong element of time pressure involved – usually letters of undertaking are negotiated in a period not much longer than a day or two.

The tendency is to interpret letters of undertaking quite literally. Although they do tend to be negotiated in emergency or urgent situations, courts tend to hold the parties to the wording of the document, unless there is cause for rectification or otherwise some obvious mistake. There are various reasons for this. The explanation provided by Gloster J in *The Rays*[281] was that the negotiations in that case had taken place over two weeks between two experienced solicitors who were each partners of their respective firms, and that the Club's solicitors had had sufficient time to review the final version of the one-page document. In *The Tutova*,[282] the judge declined to imply a term into a letter of undertaking, considering that "the LOU is a common form of document which, despite being governed by English law and subject to the jurisdiction of this court, is widely used across the world often, as here, by those whose first language is not English".[283]

As a result, the court should be "more cautious about assuming a chorus of 'yes of course'[284] than it might be in a domestic case unaffected by these considerations or the effect of different legal systems and professional assumptions".[285] The international nature and the commercial purpose of the letter of undertaking was the most important consideration in its interpretation. There are exceptions to the rule of strictly literal interpretation: in *The Rio Assu*,[286] the Court of Appeal held that a reference to the demise charterers (a corporate body) included a reference to their successors.

A narrow construction was the outcome in a case where a letter of indemnity had been provided by a P&I Club to a port in respect of the discharge of damaged containers from a ship. The

---

279. Most recently in *Canmer International Inc v UK Mutual Steamship Assurance Association (Bermuda) Ltd (The Rays)* [2005] EWHC 1694 (Comm); [2005] 2 Lloyd's Rep 479.

280. [2015] UKSC 36; [2015] AC 1619.

281. *Canmer International Inc v UK Mutual Steamship Assurance Association (Bermuda) Ltd (The Rays)* [2005] EWHC 1694 (Comm); [2005] 2 Lloyd's Rep 479.

282. *Almatrans SA v Steamship Mutual Underwriting Association (The Tutova)* [2006] EWHC 2223 (Comm); [2007] 1 Lloyd's Rep 104.

283. Ibid., [23].

284. In response to the officious bystander pointing out the need for an additional clause.

285. *The Tutova*, supra, at [23].

286. *C Itoh & Co v Companhia de Navegaçao Lloyd Brasileiro (No 2) (The Rio Assu)* [1999] 1 Lloyd's Rep 115.

liability of the Club under the letter was construed narrowly so as to encompass only fortuitous events, not the full charges of the port.[287]

A letter of undertaking may in some respects revise the contractual relationships between the parties. In *Viscous Global Investment Ltd v Palladium Navigation Corporation (The Quest)*[288] a number of bills of lading incorporated arbitration clauses from a charterparty. There were three possible charterparties to which the bills of lading might refer, each with a different arbitration clause. The competence of the constituted arbitration panel came before a judge who held that the matter was one of simple construction of the letter of undertaking, and that, on its wording, it replaced the arbitration clause in the bills of lading so that the arbitrators were competent to hear all disputes.

Case law provides few final conclusions but it is probably fair to say that the outcome will depend heavily on the wording of the letter of undertaking at issue in the individual case.

(iii) The effect of a letter of undertaking

Letters of undertaking usually also contain provisions specifying how the claim should be pursued, such as a choice of law and jurisdiction (or arbitration) clause. These are some of the most important provisions: they render the claim capable of being pursued, since the security is a private contractual matter between the parties to the letter of undertaking and only involves the court for the purpose of the arrest itself. The chosen law or jurisdiction may be different from those in the underlying claim.

Although courts are technically not involved in the letter of undertaking, they are keen to help enforce this type of security; in *The Oakwell*[289] a ship had been arrested and released upon the provision of a letter of undertaking by the shipowner's P&I Club. There followed a period of negotiations between the parties. Before the litigation started, the shipowner had sold the ship. As a result, the Club's solicitors refused to accept service of a writ *in rem*. The judge held that, in spite of the sale, the Club would be in breach of the letter of undertaking if it did not participate in the proceedings. The Club must accept service, because it would be unacceptable in the market if claimants were to find themselves in a worse position as a result of having accepted a club undertaking than if they had gone ahead and arrested. Emphasis was placed on the commercial purpose of the letter of undertaking and its role in the shipping trade.

Once security in the form of a letter of undertaking has been provided, the ship is protected from being arrested again. This presumes that sufficient security has been provided, which may not always prove the case – the provider of the security may for instance have become insolvent. In *The Ruta*,[290] the issue for decision was on what terms as to priority a claimant who had obtained security could proceed against the proceeds from a forced sale of the ship, following arrest. The claim had arisen from a collision between several ships caused by the small cargo ship, the *Ruta*. The P&I Club of the *Ruta* had provided security to the owners of the *Lutra II*, but not to the other two yachts involved in the collision, in the form of a letter of undertaking in order to secure the release of the *Ruta*. The ship was released but re-arrested and sold. The P&I Club later became insolvent, rendering the letter of undertaking worthless. Following the court-ordered sale of the *Ruta*, the creditors who had not accepted a letter of undertaking had a

---

287. *Yilport Konteyner Terminali Ve Liman Isletmeleri AS v Buxcliff KG and others (The CMA CGM Verlaine)* [2012] EWHC 3289 (Comm); [2013] 1 Lloyd's Rep 378.
288. [2014] EWHC 2654 (Comm); [2014] 2 Lloyd's Rep 600.
289. *Galaxy Energy International Ltd v Assuranceforeningen Skuld (Gjensidig) (The Oakwell)* [1999] 1 Lloyd's Rep 249.
290. [2000] 1 Lloyd's Rep 359.

priority interest in the proceeds of sale, and the question was whether the holders of the letter of undertaking, which was essentially an unsecured credit, should be granted the same priority. The judge, exercising his admiralty discretion, held that they should. The fact that the ship could technically have been re-arrested for the debt contributed to the conclusion that the priority should be the same.

There are nevertheless limits to the courts' enthusiasm for enforcing letters of undertaking. In *FSL-9 Pte Ltd v Norwegian Hull Club (The FSL New York)*,[291] the judge held that where a P&I club had issued a letter of undertaking in respect of charterers' liability to shipowners, a "liberty to apply" to have the sum of the guarantee increased could not be enforced against the Club. The right to enforce an increase in the amount lay against the charterers.

English courts now permit the use of a P&I Club letter of undertaking to replace payment of money into court for the purpose of constituting a limitation fund. In *The Atlantik Confidence*,[292] the Court of Appeal reversed the judge's ruling at first instance to hold that a guarantee, including one given by a P&I Club, can be used to constitute a limitation fund.

5. REINSURANCE

Reinsurance is defined as insurance of insurers. In order to increase their business capacity and to keep themselves solvent insurers may need reinsurance. Similar to insurance contracts, reinsurance is a subscription market whereby several reinsurers may take part in reinsuring a particular risk. Reinsurers also purchase reinsurance, which is called "retrocession".

Reinsurance policies may be proportional or non-proportional. In the proportional form the insurer and reinsurer share the risk and the premium proportionately. It should be noted that there is no double insurance here, the assured has no contract with the reinsurers, the insurer's contractual liability is to the assured and the reinsurers' liability is to the insurer (reinsured). For example, if a vessel is insured and the value of the vessel is £5 million, in the event of the actual total loss of the vessel the insurer will pay the full value to the assured and then will claim the reinsured amount from the reinsurer. If the reinsurers undertook 70 per cent of the risk reinsured, that percentage will determine the amount that the reinsurers will have to pay to the reinsured. Reinsurance can be taken out in the subscription market; therefore, it is likely that the reinsured would have other reinsurers reinsuring the rest of the 30 per cent of the risk.

In non-proportional reinsurance the reinsurers take over a sum in excess of the reinsured's retention. Non-proportional reinsurance is written in the excess of loss form, so that, for example, an insurer may insure a risk up to £20 million and then may reinsure its liability up to £20 million in excess of £5 million. This means that if the risk occurs and if the loss amounts to £20 million, the reinsured will provide the full indemnification to the assured and claim £15 million from the reinsurers. If partial loss occurs and if the loss amounts to no more than £4 million the insurer will indemnify the assured but will have no claim against the reinsurers; the reinsurance comes into play only if the reinsured's liability exceeds £5 million.

Proportional and non-proportional reinsurance may be written in the facultative form. In a facultative proportional reinsurance normally single risk is reinsured, such as insurance and then reinsurance of a vessel. Facultative non-proportional contract is a form of a treaty, another type of reinsurance. In treaties a series of direct risks are reinsured. Declarations are important in this

---

291. [2016] EWHC 1091 (Comm); [2016] 2 All ER (Comm) 576.
292. *Kairos Shipping Ltd v Enka & Co Llc (The Atlantik Confidence)* [2014] EWCA Civ 217; [2014] 1 Lloyd's Rep 586. See also Chapter 7.

type of contract because the parties set out a framework in terms of the risk reinsured. When the insurer is on risk under the original insurance it can make a declaration to the reinsurer. Whether or not the reinsurer is bound by the declaration depends on the type of the treaty. If the treaty is obligatory, any risk accepted by the reinsured which falls within the scope of the treaty is automatically ceded to the reinsurers. In such a case neither party has an option not to cede or accept. If the treaty is facultative, the reinsured is given an option to declare risks and the reinsurers are given the option to accept or reject any proposals made to them. If the treaty is in the facultative obligatory form, while the reinsured has the discretion whether or not to make a declaration, the reinsurers are bound to accept any declaration which the reinsured chooses to make. Surplus and quota share treaties are those proportional in form in which the reinsured cedes a fixed proportion of all risk accepted by it.

(a) As original

Proportional facultative reinsurance contracts normally contain a clause "subject to the same terms and conditions as original and follow the settlements of the reinsured company". By the "as original" clause the reinsurers agree that the terms of the original insurance contracts are incorporated into the reinsurance agreement.[293] In other words, the "as original" confirms that the insurance and reinsurance contracts provide "back to back" or "identical" cover so that when the insurer is liable under the original insurance contract, in principle, the reinsurers will be liable under the reinsurance contract. The presumption of "back to back" cover has been discussed in a number of cases. One of them is *Forsikringsaktieselskapet Vesta v Butcher*[294] in which a fish farm in Norway was insured and then reinsured in London. The original contract was governed by Norwegian law while the reinsurance contract was subject to English law. The original insurance contained a 24-hour watch warranty which the assured never kept. The reinsurance was "as original", therefore the same terms as the original insurance were presumed to be seen in the reinsurance contract. The insurer was liable under the original insurance because the fish farm was damaged by a severe storm and there was no chain of causation between the breach of warranty and the loss. As the law of Norway required such a chain of causation the insurers had to indemnify the assured. The reinsurer rejected the reinsured's claim for the reason that the reinsurance contract was governed by English law which requires strict compliance and no chain of causation is required for the reinsurers to seek remedy for breach of warranty. The House of Lords decided that the presumption of "back to back" cover requires interpreting the two contracts – insurance and reinsurance – in the same way which was the way that the original insurance was interpreted. Therefore, despite English law governing the reinsurance contract, the interpretation of the original insurance under Norwegian law was binding for the reinsurers and they had to indemnify the reinsured.

While this was the position regarding the "back to back" presumption, the House of Lords delivered – according to some, including the author – a controversial decision in *Wasa International Insurance Co Ltd v Lexington Insurance Co*.[295] In *Wasa* the assured and the reinsured were both based in the United States. The original insurance was for three years, from 1 July 1977 until 1 July 1980, and it insured the assured against "all loss of or damage to property". The risk was reinsured in London by a number of reinsurers on a facultative proportional contract. The reinsurance was "as original" and the cover was to be provided for 36 months from 1 July 1977.

---

293. *HIH Casualty & General Insurance Ltd v New Hampshire Insurance Co* [2001] EWCA Civ 735; [2001] 2 Lloyd's Rep 161.
294. [1989] 1 Lloyd's Rep 331.
295. [2009] UKHL 40; [2009] Lloyd's Rep IR 675.

The assured was instructed by the US Environmental Protection Agency to clean up contamination which had occurred at various of its sites. Further investigation showed that the damage had occurred as early as in the 1940s at some 35 sites within, and 23 outside, the United States. Proceedings were commenced against the insurers on risk from the 1940s until 1990, although a number could not be identified or had gone out of business. Accordingly, the assured argued that the insurers who were on risk at any time in the period of damage were jointly and severally liable for all of it. An action against the insurer was brought in the State of Washington in reliance on a Service of Suit clause in the contract which entitled the assured to "submit to the jurisdiction of any Court of Competent jurisdiction within the United States". The Washington Supreme Court decided that the law of Pennsylvania governed the contract and under the relevant law "all" within the insuring clause of "[t]his policy insures against all physical loss of, or damage to, the insured property" had its literal meaning. Therefore the word "all" prevailed over the time limitation clause "from 1977 till 1980" and the insurers were liable for the loss which occurred over a 50-year period. The insurers thus had to indemnify the assured and their claim against the reinsurers, who reinsured almost 98 per cent of the risk, was settled by those reinsurers. Two of the reinsurers contested the claim and the House of Lords decided for the reinsurers. In the view of the House of Lords, the fact that the original insurance contract contained a Service of Suit clause which entitled the assured to sue the insurer in any of the competent jurisdictions within the United States brought uncertainty into the reinsurance contract. The House of Lords distinguished *Forsikringsaktieselskapet Vesta v Butcher*[296] in which the parties, according to their lordships, had known at the time the reinsurance contract had been made that the original insurance was to be governed by the law of Norway; therefore, the reinsurers could have contemplated how the original insurance contract was going to be interpreted under the relevant local law. However, because of the Service of Suit clause in the reinsurance contract in *Wasa* it had not been possible for the reinsurers to contemplate at the time they contracted with the reinsured the possible interpretations of the original insurance cover; the assured could bring an action against the insurer in any of the competent jurisdictions in the United States and the relevant court would determine the applicable law under their conflict of laws rules. Therefore, such an uncertainty prevented the application of the presumption of "back to back" cover and the House of Lords concluded that the three-year time limitation clause was to be construed under English law, where the word "all" would not have prevailed over the time period clause but had to be read together with it. It should be noted that the House of Lords did not make any negative comments on the presumption of "back to back" cover. Their Lordships were of the view that the presumption did not apply to *Wasa*.

As stated above, "as original" incorporates original insurance terms into reinsurance, however, unusual terms as well as ancillary terms are not incorporated.[297] Arbitration, jurisdiction or choice of law clauses are examples of ancillary terms which are not concerned with the scope of the contracts but are dispute resolution clauses. If the parties intend to incorporate such terms, general words of incorporation will not suffice[298] and they are required to incorporate such clauses expressly, by using specific wording such as "arbitration clause is incorporated". Moreover, unusual terms or terms which are inapt to reinsurance contract cannot be incorporated. For instance, if the assured is required to bring a claim against the reinsured within 12 months after

---

296. [1989] 1 Lloyd's Rep 331.
297. *Home Insurance Co of New York v Victoria Montreal Fire Insurance Co* [1907] AC 59.
298. See e.g. *Gan Insurance Co Ltd v Tai Ping Insurance Co Ltd (No 1)* [1999] Lloyd's Rep IR 472 with regard to incorporation of choice of law clauses. See at pp 477–478 and the recent case law that general words of incorporation will suffice to incorporate a governing law clause (but not a jurisdiction or arbitration clause) from a charterparty into a bill of lading.

the loss, the same period clause cannot apply in the reinsurance context because before making a claim against the reinsurer the reinsured's liability needs to be established which might take longer than 12 months after the loss has occurred.[299]

The presumption of back to back cover does not operate in non-proportional reinsurance.[300] However, where the reinsurance is worded as original, in a non-proportional agreement, the tendency is to read the original insurance and reinsurance policy terms in the same manner, that is, as it was read under the original insurance. In *Tokio Marine Europe Insurance Ltd v Novae Corporate Underwriting Ltd*[301] Hamblen J held that the word "occurrence" was to be interpreted in the same way in the insurance, reinsurance and the retrocession agreements. As "occurrence" was defined in the original insurance, that determined the reinsured's liability and that was incorporated into the retrocession.[302] Against that background, the judge held that if the parties had intended a different type of occurrence to *be* covered by the retrocession they would surely have clearly spelt out i) that that was the intention and ii) what the different meaning was to be.[303]

(b) "Follow the settlements" clauses

In principle, the reinsured has to establish two matters before making a claim against the reinsurers: (1) the reinsured was liable under the original insurance; (2) the loss falls within the reinsurance cover. With regard to establishing liability under the original insurance policy, the assured might have sued the reinsured or there might have been an arbitration award against the reinsured and in favour of the assured which, in principle, will establish the reinsured's liability under the original policy.[304] The reinsured, alternatively, might have settled the claim with the assured without litigating or arbitrating it. Unlike judgments or arbitration awards, the reinsurers can object to establishing liability by such a settlement. However, to enable the reinsured to submit his claim to the reinsurers in reliance on a settlement with the assured the parties may include a "follow the settlements" clause in the reinsurance contract. The "follow the settlements" clause requires the reinsured to prove two matters in his claim against the reinsurers: (1) that the settlement was *bona fide* and businesslike and (2) that the loss falls within the reinsurance cover. The first limb, thus, is concerned with the original insurance coverage, i.e. proof of reinsured's liability under the original insurance contract. With regard to the second limb that the loss falls within the reinsurance coverage, the reference is made to the contract of reinsurance. If the reinsurance contract contains the "as original" clause, that clause will then require looking at what the original insurance terms and conditions are regarding the coverage. Since, in principle, "as original" confirms the presumption of "back to back" (or "identical") cover between the original insurance and reinsurance contracts, the reinsured's good faith settlement which establishes liability under the original insurance contract will also establish that the loss falls within the reinsurance contract.

The presumption of "back to back" cover is subject to a provision which ousts the presumption. This may occur when, for instance, the reinsurance contract contains a limitation which the

---

299. *Home Insurance Co of New York v Victoria Montreal Fire Insurance Co* [1907] AC 59.

300. *AXA Reinsurance (UK) Ltd v Field* [1996] 2 Lloyd's Rep 233; *Tokio Marine Europe Insurance Ltd v Novae Corporate Underwriting Ltd* [2013] EWHC 3362 (Comm); [2014] Lloyd's Rep IR 490 [35].

301. [2013] EWHC 3362 (Comm); [2014] Lloyd's Rep IR 490.

302. Ibid., [60].

303. Ibid., [61].

304. Although a judgment could prove the reinsured's liability there have been comments by the judges which negate the effect of a judgment in terms of proof of reinsured's liability. Discussion on those cases is beyond the scope of this chapter but the reader might refer to *Astrazeneca Insurance Co Ltd v XL Insurance (Bermuda) Ltd* [2013] EWCA Civ 1660; [2014] Lloyd's Rep IR 509.

original insurance does not. In *Youell v Bland Welch & Co Ltd (No 1)*[305] the reinsurance contract provided cover up to 48 months from the attachment of the risk, whereas the original insurance did not have such a limitation period. The loss occurred in about the 50th month after the risk attached. The reinsurers were not liable to the reinsured.

(c) Claims provisions

The reinsured's liability under the original insurance forms the reinsurers' liability. On the other hand, there is no privity of contract between the assured and the reinsurers and the litigation process or the settlement, as the case may be, all take part between the assured and the reinsured, independent of the reinsurers. Reinsurers, however, if they wish to intervene in such process, may include a "claims control" or "claims co-operation" clause in the reinsurance contract. "Claims control" clauses entitle the reinsurers to take over the relevant process, settlement or litigation or arbitration, as the case may be, and to handle it on behalf of the reinsured.[306] "Claims co-operation"[307] clauses do not give such a wide power to the reinsurers. However, they require the reinsured to co-operate with the reinsurers either by virtue of giving notification of a claim or loss, or not settling the claim without informing the reinsurers about the settlement. If the reinsured is in breach of a "claims control" or "claims co-operation" clause the remedy depends on the nature of the term in question. As stated above, insurance conditions are interpreted differently from conditions in contract law. Insurance conditions can be in the form of a mere condition or a condition precedent. As mentioned before, a breach of a mere condition has the same effect as a breach of an innominate term in general contract law, in that the remedy depends on the seriousness of the consequences of the breach. Conditions precedent are similar to warranties as their breach discharges the insurer from liability automatically. However, the difference from warranties is that while breach of a warranty terminates the risk and therefore there will be no further claim under the policy, breach of a condition precedent does not affect the future performances under the policy; the policy still stands between the parties; the assured loses the claim which is tainted by the breach but in the future, if he complies with the condition precedent, may still be able to make claims under the policy. Waiver of a breach of a condition precedent is subject to the same rules as that of warranties in that only proof of promissory estoppel might prove waiver.[308]

If a reinsurance contract contains both a "follow the settlements" clause as well as a "claims control" or "claims co-operation" clause, whether the reinsurers are still under the obligation to follow the settlements despite the breach of the latter type is a controversial matter as it will not be easy to reconcile the agreement to follow a *bona fide* settlement and at the same time ask the reinsured not to settle the claim before seeking the reinsurers' consent. If the relevant claims term is a condition precedent it is unlikely that the reinsurers have to follow the settlement. In such a case, since the reinsurers will be discharged automatically from liability with regard to

305. [1992] 2 Lloyd's Rep 127.

306. E.g. see "The underwriters hereon shall control the negotiations and settlements of any claims under this policy. In this event the underwriters hereon will not be liable to pay any claim not controlled as set out above": *Eagle Star Insurance Co Ltd v Cresswell* [2004] EWCA Civ 602; [2004] Lloyd's Rep IR 537.

307. *Insurance Co of Africa v Scor (UK) Reinsurance Co Ltd* [1985] 1 Lloyd's Rep 312:

It is a condition precedent to liability under this Insurance that all claims be notified immediately to the Underwriters subscribing to this Policy and the Reassured hereby undertake in arriving at the settlement of any claim, that they will co-operate with the Reassured Underwriters and that no settlement shall be made without the approval of the Underwriters subscribing to this Policy.

308. *Kosmar Villa Holidays Plc v Trustees of Syndicate 1243* [2008] EWCA Civ 147; [2008] Lloyd's Rep IR 489.

the relevant claim, even if the reinsured proves actual liability he will not be entitled to make a claim. However, if the clause is a mere condition the reinsurers should be obliged to follow the settlements unless the breach is so serious that it entitles the reinsurers to terminate the contract.

It should be noted that the law reform introduced by the Insurance Act 2015 as explained at the outset of this chapter (the duty of fair presentation of the risk, warranties and terms that are not relevant to the actual loss) applies also to reinsurance contracts. As noted above, section 11 of the IA 2015 applies only to risk mitigation clauses. Therefore, the interpretation of the claims provisions as set out by the common law – explained above – is left untouched by the IA 2015.

CHAPTER 12

PROCEDURES FOR ENFORCEMENT

Michael Tsimplis

1. ENFORCEMENT OF MARITIME CLAIMS

(a) Introduction

Where a ship has caused damage a claimant may face significant challenges to reparation. The ship that caused the damage will most probably belong to a foreign company and could well be the only asset of the defendant. Thus, if the ship sails away, the claimant would then have to chase the defendant shipowner in a foreign jurisdiction. Even if the claimant succeeds in bringing a claim or in having a domestic judgment recognised in the foreign jurisdiction, it could well turn out that the ship has been sold and there are no other assets against which the judgment can be enforced. Thus detaining the ship is in practice the best option for the claimant in order to bring the owner before the courts and obtain compensation for the damage suffered. However, depriving the defendant shipowner of the use of its property without due notice and without proving the claim before a court is, as a matter of legal principle, wrong.[1]

Historically the problem has been resolved by assuming that, for some special claims, the ship is the defendant. Where the defendant ship was in the port, action could be taken against it, thereby avoiding the problems of establishing jurisdiction against the foreign defendant ship-owner. As a consequence the shipowner was then put into the position of either abandoning the ship to its creditors or turning up in court and defending the claim against the ship thus submitting to the court's jurisdiction. The option to abandon the ship provided a practical way of limiting liability while the right to detain the ship for these special claims provided the origins of the action *in rem*.

Presently two international conventions, the International Convention Relating to the Arrest of Sea-Going Ships, Brussels, 1952 (1952 Arrest Convention) and the International Convention on the Arrest of Ships 1999 (1999 Arrest Convention) provide the international framework for these special maritime rules. The UK is a signatory to the 1952 Arrest Convention and has rewritten the text of this convention within the rules related to the Admiralty jurisdiction of the High Court.[2] In addition a significant part of the English rules and law related to ship arrest are contained in the Civil Procedure Rules and the Practice Direction for Admiralty claims and in case law.

This chapter describes the Admiralty jurisdiction of the High Court, the Admiralty procedure for the arrest[3] of a ship under an action *in rem* and links these procedures with those of limitation of liability.

(b) The Admiralty jurisdiction of the High Court

The Admiralty jurisdiction of the High Court is described in sections 20–24 of the Senior Courts Act 1981 (SCA 1981). However, the wording of section 20 includes in the Admiralty jurisdiction of the High Court not only the heads of jurisdiction described within the SCA 1981 but also any previous[4] and any future Admiralty jurisdiction assigned to the High Court. The Admiralty jurisdiction of the High Court applies in respect of all vessels, British or not, in relation to all claims wherever they occur[5] and to all ship mortgages.[6]

The 1952 Arrest Convention and the 1952 International Convention on Certain Rules Concerning Civil Jurisdiction in Matters of Collision, Brussels, (1952 Collision Jurisdiction Convention) are both enacted into English law as parts of the SCA 1981.

---

1. See for example the difficulties in the development of the freezing injunction in *Lister v Stubbs* [1890] 45 ChD 1; *Mareva Compania Naviera SA v International Bulkcarriers SA (The Mareva)* [1975] 2 Lloyd's Rep 509 (CA) and *Nippon Yusen v Karageorgis* [1975] 2 Lloyd's Rep 137; [1975] 1 WLR 1093 (CA).

2. See D.C. Jackson, *Enforcement of Maritime Claims* (4th edn, LLP 2005) (hereinafter "Jackson") for a detailed analysis of the Admiralty jurisdiction. See also A. Mandaraka-Sheppard, *Modern Maritime Law Volume 1: Jurisdiction and Risks* (3rd edn, Informa 2013), ch 1.

3. Art 1(2) of the Arrest Convention 1952 describes "Arrest" as "the detention of a ship by judicial process to secure a maritime claim, but does not include the seizure of a ship in execution or satisfaction of a judgment". However, no equivalent definition exists in English law. See *The Anna H* [1995] 1 Lloyd's Rep 11(CA) for the difference between the *definition* and the *purpose* of arrest under English law.

4. SCA 1981, s 20(1)(b).

5. For cargo and wreck, even if the cargo or wreck are found on land, SCA 1981, s 20(7)(b).

6. SCA 1981, s 21(7).

The Civil Procedure Rules for Admiralty[7] Part 61 (CPR 61) and the accompanying Practice Direction (PD 61) must be considered together with the SCA 1981 in order to understand the Admiralty jurisdiction and procedures.

The Admiralty jurisdiction encompasses jurisdiction for a list of claims,[8] which are the claims covered by the 1952 Arrest Convention[9] and all claims under the Merchant Shipping Act 1995 (hereinafter MSA 1995). Thus most shipping claims, like collision damage, salvage, towage, claims arising from charterparties or bills of lading,[10] provisions to a ship, wreck removal, ownership and mortgage disputes for ships etc., are subject to the Admiralty jurisdiction of the High Court.[11] In addition claims for oil pollution from ships,[12] and limitation of liability issues[13] are also subject to the Admiralty jurisdiction of the High Court. Some actions, in particular those including limitation of liability actions can only be started in the Admiralty Court.[14] However, this does not apply to other actions for which the Admiralty Court does not have exclusive jurisdiction.[15]

(c) Enforcement

Two procedures of enforcement are available under the Admiralty jurisdiction of the High Court. The first, the action *in personam*, is the ordinary action against a named defendant.[16] The action *in personam* is in general available in all cases where the High Court has jurisdiction on the merits except in cases where the jurisdiction is constrained under section 22 of the SCA 1981. This section refers to collision cases.[17] In addition where an international convention and its implementation in the MSA 1995 restricts such an action it is arguable that an action *in personam* will not be available.[18]

---

7. The civil procedure system in England and Wales has undergone major reform with the development of the Civil Procedure Rules (CPR). A reform aiming, amongst other things, to make the process of litigation more understandable to the public. For this reason many Latin terms were replaced with English terms. The CPR for Admiralty entered into force on 25 March 2002 replacing Part 49f, primarily by CPR Part 61 and Practice Direction 61 (PD 61), but also partly by CPR Part 58 and PD 58 in relation to actions against a defendant; the *in personam* action under the previous procedural rules. The term *in personam* is still retained under the SCA 1981. The ninth edition of the "Admiralty and Commercial Court Guide" (updated March 2016) in Section N covers Admiralty matters.

8. Included in SCA 1981, s 20(2).

9. Art 1. However, pre-existing Admiralty jurisdiction not expressly included in the SCA 1981 is expressly incorporated by s 20. Note that the 1999 Arrest Convention came into force on 14 September 2011 and as of 2 March 2017 has been ratified by 11 states but not the United Kingdom. Small changes are to be introduced into English law if the UK becomes a party to the 1999 Arrest Convention and this convention comes into force. See Richard Shaw and Nicholas Gaskell, "The Arrest Convention 1999" (1999) 4 LMCLQ 470–490.

10. Whether contractually or otherwise. See *Samick Lines Co Ltd v Owners of the ship "Antonis P Lemos" (The Antonis P Lemos)* [1985] AC 711; [1985] 1 Lloyd's Rep 283 (HL).

11. SCA 1981, s 20(2) and (3).

12. SCA 1981, s 20(5).

13. SCA 1981, s 20(3)(c) interpreting s 20(1)(b).

14. CPR 61.2(1)(c) includes, all actions *in rem*, all actions under the Merchant Shipping Act 1995, ship collision, pilotage and towage disputes, ownership disputes, loss of life and personal injury under SCA 1981, s 20(2)(f), master and crew member claims for wages, limitation and salvage claims.

15. CPR 61.2. Such claims include charterparty and bill of lading claims.

16. The CPR has removed the reference to the action *in personam* from the court procedure. But as the term "action *in personam*" still exists within the SCA 1981 the deletion of the definition is not very helpful.

17. In collision cases, s 22 of the SCA 1981 permits an action (or a counterclaim) *in personam* only where the defendant is resident or has a place of business in England or Wales, or where the collision took place in inland waters or in a port of England or Wales or there are already proceedings (or proceedings have already been determined) by the High Court. Otherwise there is no jurisdiction for an *in personam* action in collision cases whether such an action is started under the Admiralty jurisdiction of the High Court or otherwise (s 22(7) of the SCA 1981).

18. Where an international convention prescribes jurisdiction for another state, the SCA 1981 would not automatically restrict the initiation of an action *in personam* although the action may then be stayed or dismissed for lack of jurisdiction. In collision cases, it appears that it is not even permissible to start an action if the provisions of s 22 of the SCA 1981 are satisfied. There could be practical differences where, for example, time bars are involved.

The second, the action *in rem*, is an action against the ship or ships of named or unnamed defendants only available under the Admiralty jurisdiction of the High Court.

The nature of the action *in rem* has been argued as an action against the ship itself as if the ship is a distinct legal entity from the defendant, or as a legal device putting pressure on the shipowner to defend. In practice what matters is whether the ship and the shipowner can be considered as distinct parties in a claim *in rem* and a claim *in personam* concerning the same cause of action. This question has been answered, under European and English law, in the negative.

First, the European Court of Justice held that for the application of the provisions on multiple proceedings of the EC Jurisdiction Convention, actions *in rem* and actions *in personam* are between the same parties.[19] Thus within the EU framework of jurisdiction and enforcement there is no such distinction.

More importantly, in a case where there was a judgment in the Indian Courts, and an action *in rem* in respect of the same cause of action was later initiated before the English courts, the House of Lords held that for the purpose of section 34 of the Civil Jurisdiction and Judgments Act 1982, the action *in rem* and the action *in personam* are between the same parties. Thus because of the foreign judgment *in personam* section 34 barred an action *in rem*.[20] The decision in *The Indian Grace (No 2)* did not decide cases where a maritime lien is the basis of the action *in rem* thus the issue remains open in relation to maritime liens.[21]

The *Indian Grace (No 2)* decision is problematic in several aspects. Where an action *in rem* is initiated and the ship is arrested and sold because the owner did not enter a court appearance *The Indian Grace (No 2)* suggests that the claimant *in rem*, if the sale of the ship has not fully satisfied its claim, will not be entitled to obtain judgment *in personam* for the residual claim. Thus by utilising the particular procedure developed for ensuring the availability of some security for maritime claims the claimant may jeopardise successful recovery especially if other creditors are also to be satisfied by the judicial sale.[22]

It is very common in shipping to have claims *in personam* submitted to arbitration, following an arbitration agreement between the parties. Courts will normally support the parties' agreement and stay their proceedings.[23] However, difficulties arise when the relevant claim submitted to arbitration can also be supported by an action *in rem*. Thus where the ship is arrested and the shipowner appears to defend the court must stay all proceedings and let the arbitrators decide the case on the merits. This would normally mean *in rem* proceedings too. However, arbitrators do not have jurisdiction to decide a claim *in rem* and arrest of the ship as security for an arbitration award is not sustainable[24] without express statutory authorisation such as granted in English law under s 11 of the Arbitration Act 1996. In *The Rena K*[25] it was held that the court has discretion, when staying its proceedings for the benefit of arbitration proceedings, to decide whether a ship arrest will continue based on whether there is the possibility that the stay of the court proceedings may later be lifted. It was argued by the shipowners that because a claim in arbitration merges with the arbitration award there is no possibility of the stay being lifted even if the shipowner fails to satisfy the arbitration award and thus the ship must, at the time the *in*

19. *Owners of Cargo Lately Laden on Board the Tatry v Owners of the Maciej Rataj (The Maciej Rataj)* ECJ (C-406/92) [1995] 1 Lloyd's Rep 302; [1994] ECR I-5439.
20. *Republic of India and the Government of the Republic of India (Ministry of Defence) v India Steamship Co Ltd (The Indian Grace) (No 2)* [1998] 1 Lloyd's Rep 1; [1997] 4 All ER 380.
21. See the discussion in Jackson, *Enforcement of Maritime Claims* (fn 2), in ch 17.
22. See the discussion in *Comandate Marine Corp v Pan Australia Shipping Pty Ltd*. [2006] FCAFC 192, Federal Court of Australia.
23. See *Raukuna Moana Fisheries Ltd v The Ship Irina Zharkikh* [2001] 2 NZLR 801.
24. *The Rena K* [1979] QB 377.
25. [1979] QB 377.

personam proceedings are stayed, be unconditionally released. Brandon J rejected this, stating that it has been held that

> a cause of action *in rem*, being of a different character from a cause of action *in personam*, does not merge in a judgment *in personam*, but remains available to the person who has it so long as, and to the extent that, such judgment remains unsatisfied.[26]

This decision enabled courts to ensure security is available in appropriate arbitration cases. The *Indian Grace (No 2)* undermines this decision and its practical consequence. Thus it is not surprising that several common law courts have distinguished or rejected the general rationale behind *The Indian Grace (No 2)*.[27] Comments in a recent decision[28] suggest that *The Indian Grace (No 2)* is authority for the way section 34 of the Civil Jurisdiction and Judgments Act 1982 operates. However, it is difficult to see how this can be achieved as several parts of the judgment and the analysis are clearly broader in character. Under English law, the action *in rem* can best be described nowadays as a procedural tool with which a claimant can force the defendant shipowner to appear in front of an English court or risk losing its ship. This is because the action *in rem* carries with it, in the general case, a right to apply to the Court for the arrest of the vessel under CPR 61.5. There is however, the possibility that maritime liens do carry with them additional rights not available to claims established by the SCA 1981 and that these rights could provide for a solution different from that established under *The Indian Grace (No 2)*. This would be difficult to argue on procedural grounds because there is no differentiation in the way the *in rem* procedure operates under the SCA 1981 for maritime liens and other claims. Thus, only differentiation on pre-existing rights would be permissible.

Arrest of a ship as security for a civil claim is only available under the Admiralty jurisdiction of the High Court. However, not all claims subject to the Admiralty jurisdiction carry with them a right to arrest the ship of the defendant. From the claims listed under section 20(2) of the SCA 1981 all but section 20(2)(d) can lead to the arrest of some property of the defendant.[29]

The SCA 1981 specifies, under section 21, three groups of claims that can be enforced by an action *in rem* (Figure 12.1).

(i) Action in rem *in respect of claims to the possession or ownership of a ship*

The first category of claims[30] includes claims related to ownership and possession of the ship or the shares related to the ship, disputes between co-owners related to possession, employment or earnings of the ship, claims on mortgages or charges on a ship and claims related to the forfeiture or condemnation of the ship or its cargo and the restoration of goods or cargo.[31] We will refer to these claims as "ownership" claims. In respect of *ownership* claims the action *in rem* can be against the ship or other property involved in the ownership dispute.

---

26. *The Rena K* [1979] QB 377, at p 405.
27. *Comandate Marine Corp v Pan Australia Shipping Pty Ltd* [2006] FCAFC 192, Federal Court of Australia; *Raukuna Moana Fisheries Ltd v The Ship Irina Zharkikh* [2001] 2 NZLR 801.
28. *Stolt Kestrel Bv v Sener Petrol Denizcilik Ticaret As (The "Stolt Kestrel" and The "Niyazi S") Cde Sa v Sure Wind Marine Ltd (The "Sb Seaguard" and The "Odyssée")* [2015] EWCA Civ 1035; [2016] 1 Lloyd's Rep 125; [2015] Lloyd's Rep Plus 82.
29. See *Owners of Cargo Lately Laden on Board the MV Erkowit v Owners of the Eschersheim (The Eschersheim, the Jade and the Erkowit) (HL)* [1976] 1 WLR 430; [1976] 2 Lloyd's Rep 1.
30. SCA 1981, s 21(2).
31. SCA 1981, s 21(2) referring to ss 20(a), 20(b), 20(c) and 20(s).

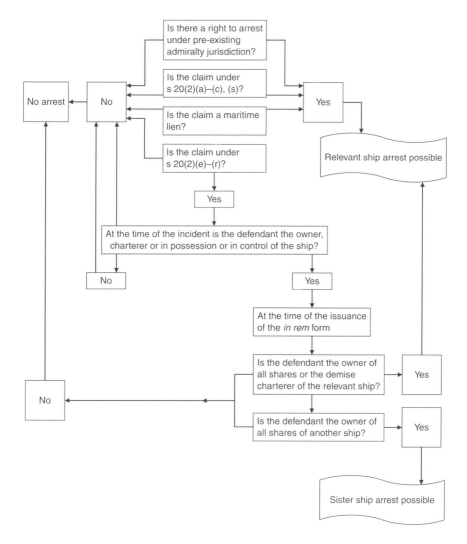

Figure 12.1 An outline of the rights *in rem* and arrest under the SCA 1981

Notes

Note that other restrictions may also apply. For example, sovereign immunity, earlier arrest or foreign or domestic judgment *in personam* or lack of personal responsibility of the shipowner may act as barriers to arrest. Note also that the claim must relate to one identifiable ship and that only one ship can be arrested per claim.

(ii) *Action* in rem *arising from maritime liens*

Section 21(3) of the SCA 1981 permits an action *in rem* against the relevant ship, cargo or freight[32] when a maritime lien is in existence. The claims that carry maritime liens are neither defined nor listed within the SCA 1981. However, it is well established that, under English law, maritime liens arise in respect of collision claims, salvage claims, crew and master's wages,

---

32. Only freight at risk is subject to the lien.

master's disbursements, bottomry and respondentia.[33] Maritime liens will be discussed further below.

(iii) Action in rem in respect of other claims

The third category of claims for which an action *in rem* is permitted involves a wide variety of shipping claims except "ownership" claims (Figure 12.1). These are listed in section 20(2) (e) – (r) of SCA 1981. Thus, claims for collision and pollution damages, claims for loss of life and personal injury on a ship, claims arising out of a charterparty or a contract of carriage of cargo, cargo damage, salvage claims under the 1989 Salvage Convention or otherwise, towage claims, pilotage claims, claims in respect of supplies to the ship, ship repair and construction claims, dock charges and dues, claims related to the crew and master's wages, claims in relation to master's, agent's and charterer's disbursements, and General Average claims are all entitled to an action *in rem* under section 21(4) of the SCA 1981.

The action *in rem* for this category of claims is different in two respects from the previously discussed ownership[34] and the maritime liens[35] categories. The first difference concerns the property that can be arrested. Claims *in rem* under section 21(4) can lead to the arrest of the ship involved in the claim but also to another ship which is under the same ownership, usually called a *sister ship*.[36]

The second difference concerns the satisfaction of specific conditions for the action *in rem* to be permissible. The fulfilment of these conditions is to be assessed for some conditions at the time the claim arises and for other conditions at the time the claim form *in rem* is issued.

Thus at the time of the action that created the claim the conditions that must be met are that (a) the claim must be linked to a ship, this we will call the *relevant ship* and (b) the person who would be personally liable (the *relevant person*)[37] under the claim is either the legal owner (if registration is required the registered owner) or the charterer[38] or in possession or in control[39] of the *relevant ship*. This condition needs to be fulfilled whether the claim *in rem* is against the relevant ship or a sister ship.

At the time the action *in rem* is initiated the condition is that the *relevant person* is either the owner in respect of all shares or the demise charterer of the *relevant ship*. For an action *in rem* against a sister ship the condition that needs to be fulfilled at the time the action *in rem* is initiated is that the *relevant person* is the owner in respect of all shares of the *sister ship*.

---

33. *The Bold Buccleugh* [1851] 7 Moo PC 267. Bottomry bonds were a form of loan signed by the master and secured on the ship. These were used to obtain supplies or services for the ship without undue delay (see, for example, *Douglas v Owners of Yacht St George (The St George)* [1926] 25 Ll L Rep 482, one of the last cases on a bottomry claim). These bonds were considered to give rights against the ship, protected by a maritime lien. Respondentia concerned similar rights in respect of loans against the value of the cargo. Both bottomry and respondentia were methods by which the difficulties of transferring information and funds were dealt with and they are both presently obsolete.
34. SCA 1981, s 21(2).
35. SCA 1981, s 21(3).
36. SCA 1981, s 21(4).
37. The terminology used by s 21(4) of the SCA1981 is "the person who would be liable on the claim in an action in personam ('the relevant person')". The "relevant person" is only used to establish the link between the property against which the action *in rem* is undertaken and the owner of that property and does not require first to show that the relevant person is in fact liable for the complaint. Of course if the relevant person is not in fact liable, the property arrested will be released.
38. The term charterer includes demise, time and voyage charterers as well as slot charterers. See *The Span Terza* [1982] 1 Lloyd's Rep 225 and *The Mediterranean Shipping Co SA v Polish Ocean Lines (The Tychy) (No 2)* [1999] 2 Lloyd's Rep 11.
39. See *Chimbusco Pan Nation Petro-Chemical Co Ltd v The owners and/or demise charterers of the ship or vessel Decurion* [2013] HKCA 180 for a discussion of the term "in control".

Although this section only mentions the arrest of the ship, the interpretation of the word "ship" has been held to include all property on board the ship including bunkers and cargo if owned by the defendant shipowner.[40] The wording of section 21(4) permits the shipowner to arrest a ship owned by a charterer for a charterparty claim. This is a significant extension of the scope of arrest and may be a significant advantage for the shipowner.

Claims supported by maritime liens which provide for the arrest of the relevant ship are also covered by section 21(4), which permits arrest of a sister ship too. For example, where there is a claim for a salvage reward the salvors can either arrest the ship they have assisted, under section 21(3), in which case they can claim the priority of the maritime lien, or they can proceed against a ship under the same ownership as provided in section 21(4). However, although more than one ship can be named in the claim form, only one can be arrested in respect of each claim.[41]

The choice made on whether to arrest the relevant ship or a sister ship will determine the priority of the claim, the time at which the rights *in rem* attach to the ship and the security available as the value of the ships may be significantly different.

It is important to note that the courts interpret the wording of section 20(2) strictly. Therefore if a claim is not covered by the relevant sub-section and there is no authority outside the SCA 1981 which permits arrest for such a claim, then only an action *in personam* is possible, even if the claim appears to be maritime in nature or it involves maritime parties.[42]

In addition, the ownership requirements described under section 21(4) have also been interpreted strictly. Thus, where a Soviet State company became a privatised Russian company, arrest of the relevant ship belonging originally to the Soviet company and then to its Russian successor was not permitted as there had been a change of legal personality under the applicable Russian law.[43] By contrast where the shipowning company goes into voluntary liquidation, beneficial ownership does not change.[44]

In another case judicial proceedings including arrest were avoided through a letter of undertaking promising to instruct solicitors to accept service of *in rem* and *in personam* proceedings. The ship was later sold. The shipowner claimed that the wording of section 21(4) of the SCA 1981 was not fulfilled because the owner at the time of issuance of the claim form *in rem* was different from the owner at the time of the incident. The High Court rejected this claim and obliged the defending shipowner who was in breach of the undertakings agreement to accept service of the *in rem* claim form.[45]

Under English law, the organisation of a fleet into a group of one-ship sister companies successfully avoids the provisions of section 21(4) (Figure 12.2). The Court of Appeal in *The Evpo*

---

40. *The Silia* [1981] 2 Lloyd's Rep 534; [1981] Com LR 256 1981 WL 186630. Difficulties arise where the charterer owns the bunkers (see *Stellar Chartering and Brokerage Inc v Efibanca-Ente Finanziario Intercambiario SpA (The Span Terza No 2)* (HL) [1984] 1 Lloyd's Rep 119, 120; see also *The Yuta Bondarovskaya* [1998] 2 Lloyd's Rep 357) or where the ship is under arrest and cargo is not (CPR 61.8(8)) and where goods and materials not directly for the use of the ship but for the passengers have been supplied to the ship (*The Edinburgh Castle* [1999] 2 Lloyd's Rep 362).

41. SCA 1981, s 21(8) and *The Tjaskemolen Now Named Visvliet (No 2)* [1997] 2 Lloyd's Rep 476.

42. See *Gatoil International Inc v Arkwright-Boston Manufacturers Mutual Insurance Co and Others (The Sandrina)* (HL) [1985] 1 Lloyd's Rep 181 relating to unpaid insurance premiums, *Petrofina SA v AOT Ltd (The Maersk Nimrod)* [1991] 1 Lloyd's Rep 269 for a demurrage provision in a c.i.f. contract, and *The River Rima* [1987] 2 Lloyd's Rep 106; [1988] 2 All ER 641 related to an agreement of container leasing to ships. In all cases there was no action *in rem* available.

43. *Centro Latino Americano de Commercio Exterior SA v Owners of the Ship "Kommunar" (The Kommunar") (No 2)* [1997] 1 Lloyd's Rep 8.

44. *International Transportation Service Inc v Owners and/or Demise Charterers of the Ship or Vessel Convenience Container* [2006] 2 Lloyd's Rep 556.

45. *Galaxy Energy International Ltd. and Corona Trading Associates SA v Assuranceforeningen Skuld (Ejensidie) (The Oakwell)* [1999] 1 Lloyd's Rep 249.

Agnic,[46] where the same shipowner held the shares of several one-ship owning companies interpreted the term "owner" in section 21(4) as referring to the registered owner alone. Thus actions *in rem* against the other companies owned by the same shipowner were not permitted and the corporate structure chosen by the shipowner was respected. Only where the corporate structure is changed for the purpose of avoiding the satisfaction of a claim, or where the corporate structure is illegal, will the English court exercise their inherent discretion to "lift the corporate veil" and identify the beneficial owner.

The Supreme Court in *Petrodel Resources Ltd v Prest*[47] re-examined the law in this area on facts which had nothing to do with shipping but instead was concerned with divorce and orders to companies, which belonged to the husband and which owned property, to transfer such property to the wife as part of the divorce settlement. The Supreme Court comprised seven Justices who based their unanimous decision on different grounds. The discussion and decision on "piercing the corporate veil" was not necessary to decide the case, so strictly speaking it is *obiter*. However, the range of the views expressed will be the basis for future similar litigation. Lord Sumption considered the earlier law and concluded that "the principle that the court may be justified in piercing the corporate veil if a company's separate legal personality is being abused for the purpose of some relevant wrongdoing is well established in the authorities."[48] In analysing the relevant wrongdoing he considered the considerations of "sham" or "facade" as unhelpful and instead analysed the case law on the "concealment" and "evasion" principles. The first concerns situations where the courts do not permit the existence of a company to hide a wrongdoer. Such situations do not, according to Lord Sumption, disregard the corporate structure and therefore are not "piercing the corporate veil". In addition, he identified cases where the evasion principle was in question which were truly disregarding the corporate veil: "It is that the court may disregard the corporate veil if there is a legal right against the person in control of it which exists independently of the company's involvement, and a company is interposed so that the separate legal personality of the company will defeat the right or frustrate its enforcement."[49] He formulated the principle as follows:

I conclude that there is a limited principle of English law which applies when a person is under an existing legal obligation or liability or subject to an existing legal restriction which he deliberately evades or whose enforcement he deliberately frustrates by interposing a company under his control. The court may then pierce the corporate veil for the purpose, and only for the purpose, of depriving the company or its controller of the advantage that they would otherwise have obtained by the company's separate legal personality. The principle is properly described as a limited one, because in almost every case where the test is satisfied, the facts will in practice disclose a legal relationship between the company and its controller which will make it unnecessary to pierce the corporate veil.

Because the companies were created well before the divorce they were neither developed to conceal nor to evade any liabilities for the divorce and the corporate veil was not pierced.[50] Lord Neuberger agreed with the distinction between concealment and evasion. He summed up the case law by saying: "whenever the doctrine is really needed, it never seems to apply"[51] and agreed with the aforementioned formulation of the principle. Lady Hale, with whom Lord

---

46. *The Evpo Agnic* [1988] 2 Lloyd's Rep 411 (CA).
47. [2013] UKSC 34; [2013] 2 AC 415.
48. Ibid., [27].
49. Ibid., [28].
50. But the wife succeeded on the basis of the Matrimonial Causes Act, 1973.
51. Ibid., [79].

Wilson agreed, expressed doubts as to whether the categorisation of concealment and evasion is one that works for all cases and continued:

They may simply be examples of the principle that the individuals who operate limited companies should not be allowed to take unconscionable advantage of the people with whom they do business. But what the cases do have in common is that the separate legal personality is being disregarded in order to obtain a remedy against someone other than the company in respect of a liability which would otherwise be that of the company alone (if it existed at all). In the converse case, where it is sought to convert the personal liability of the owner or controller into a liability of the company, it is usually more appropriate to rely upon the concepts of agency and of the "directing mind".[52]

Lord Mance, agreeing with the analysis of the case law by Lord Sumption, said:

What can be said with confidence is that the strength of the principle in Salomon's case and the number of other tools which the law has available mean that, if there are other situations in which piercing the veil may be relevant as a final fall-back, they are likely to be novel and very rare.[53]

He suggested that where there is concealment, other analysis like agency or nominee, trustee – beneficiary) may be used. Lord Clarke agreed with the existence of the doctrine, noted that its limits are unclear and that it is to be used "when all other more conventional remedies have proved to be of no assistance." He considered that Lord Sumption's conclusion that it may only be done in evasion cases "should not be definitively adopted unless and until the court has heard detailed submissions upon it."[54] Finally, Lord Walker considered that "piercing the corporate veil" is not a doctrine at all, in the sense of a coherent principle or rule of law. It is simply a label – often, as Lord Sumption observes, used indiscriminately – to describe the disparate occasions on which some rule of law produces apparent exceptions to the principle of the separate juristic personality of a body corporate... ".[55]

The multiplicity of approaches is arguably not helpful in setting a workable rule and the distinction between evasion and concealment cases.[56]

Where a bareboat charter is terminated because the vessel sinks and the owner subsequently incurs expenses for wreck removal for which it would normally be indemnified under the charter, the first requirement of section 21(4) is not satisfied and a ship of the charterer cannot be arrested.[57]

(d) Procedure for claims *in rem*

The procedure relating to actions *in rem* is governed by the Civil Procedure Rules (CPR) part 61 and its corresponding Practice Direction (PD 61). The claimant simply issues a claim on a

---

52. Ibid., [92].
53. Ibid., [100].
54. Ibid., [103].
55. Ibid., [106].
56. *The Saudi Prince* [1982] 2 Lloyd's Rep 255. In that shipping case, the sole shareholder of a company owning a ship which has incurred liability for cargo damage and owning also the *Saudi Prince*, transferred the latter to another company which he owned 80 per cent with his children owning the residual 20 per cent. He then applied for the release of the *Saudi Prince* from arrest on the ground that s 21(4) of the SCA 1981 was not satisfied because he was not the beneficial owner of all shares in the *Saudi Prince*. The court considered the transaction as a sham and permitted the arrest to stand. This case would probably fall under the evasion categorisation.
57. *Afluflet SA v Vinave Empresa de Navegaçao Maritima LDA (The Faial)* [2000] 1 Lloyd's Rep 473. Novation will also have the same effect, see *The Tychy (No 2)* [2001] 2 Lloyd's Rep 403 (CA).

(a)

(b)

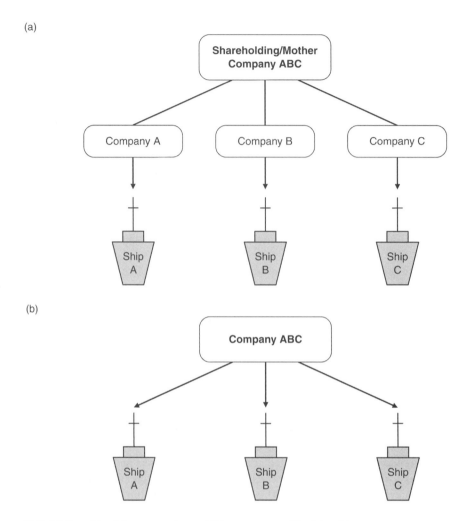

Figure 12.2 (a) One-ship sister companies and (b) a company with sister ships

Note
Arrest under s 21(4) of the SCA 1981 is only possible in (b).

special *in rem* claim form,[58] which must be served within 12 months.[59] The methods of service of an *in rem* claim form include service on the *res* itself,[60] as it was done traditionally, but it can also be effected in some other ways. For example, if the property to be served is in the custody of a person who will not permit access to it, service may be effected by leaving a copy of the *in rem* claim form with that person.[61] Where the parties agree that service may be effected upon a named person, for example a firm of solicitors, service can be effected on this named person. In addition, provided that the ship or property is within the jurisdiction, service may also be effected in any other manner directed by the court under CPR 6.15. This means that the court in

58. CPR 61.3(2) and PD, para 61.3.1.
59. See CPR, para 61.3(5). The form can then be renewed.
60. CPR, para 61 3.6.
61. CPR 61 3.6(2).

appropriate circumstances may make an order permitting service in any manner not specifically authorised by the rule,[62] for example serving the claim form on a vessel equipped with a fax machine, as the ship is sailing within territorial waters.[63]

The particulars of claim must be contained within the claim form or, otherwise, must be served on the defendant within 75 days from the day they are issued.[64] This period is longer than the relevant period for a claim *in personam*, i.e. 14 days, and ought to be sufficient time to allow a claimant to collect, and its lawyers to collate and review properly, the necessary information to particularise the claim. An acknowledgement of service must be filed in every action *in rem*.[65] After filing an acknowledgement of service the claim continues to be a claim *in rem*. However, the procedure relating to the claim becomes the same as the procedure relating to a claim *in personam*.[66] Under CPR 24.3(2)(b) it is not possible for a claimant to obtain summary judgment in an action *in rem*. The issue of default judgments in actions *in rem* is dealt with in CPR 61.9 and PD paragraph 61.9, where the different conditions applying for a judgment in default in collision cases (CPR 61.9(2))[67] and in other cases (CPR 61.9(1))[68] are spelt out.

(e) Action *in rem* in respect of collisions

A collision action is commenced by issuing a specific claim form.[69] An acknowledgement of service is compulsory whether the claim is *in rem* or *in personam*.[70] The acknowledgement of service triggers the lodging of a Collision Statement.[71] Briefly, unless the defendant contests the jurisdiction of the court, the parties are obliged to file their Collision Statements within two months as from the date when the acknowledgement of service is filed[72] and that statement must be supported by a statement of truth.[73] The requirement of lodging Collision Statements by the parties to a collision action makes the serving of Particulars of Claim unnecessary.[74]

(f) Arrest

Provided that an action *in rem* is available under section 21 of the SCA 1981 the right to arrest the defendant's ship arises.[75] Following an appropriate application the Admiralty Court will issue a warrant of arrest which will be served by the Admiralty Marshal or its nominated substitute

---

62. CPR 6.15.
63. Where the vessel is passing through the territorial waters without using or without any intention to use any coastal facilities it may not be possible to arrest it as a matter under/in accordance with art 3 of UNCLOS 1982 defining the right of innocent passage.
64. CPR 61(3)(3).
65. CPR 61(4), within 14 days after service of the claim form..
66. See PD, para 61.3.10. The only exception is that the claimant has 75 days for the service of the particulars. The wording refers to the need to "follow the procedure applicable to a claim proceeding in the Commercial list".
67. This is only available if no collision statement has been filed within the required time.
68. This is available when no acknowledgment of service has been filed within the permitted period or when a defence has not been filed within the permitted period.
69. The form is ADM3. PD, para 61.4.
70. *In personam* claims are dealt with in Part 58, subject to the provisions of CPR 61 and PD 61 relating to collision and limitation claims (see PD, para 61.12.1). This arrangement does not appear to alter the existing practice.
71. CPR 61.5. Previously called Preliminary Act.
72. See CPR 61.4(5). PD para 61.4.5 provides that the law relating to Preliminary Acts continues to apply to Collision Statements.
73. See CPR 61.4(6)(b).
74. See CPR 61.4(2).
75. See CPR 61.5 which extends the right to arrest to judgment creditors.

on the ship.[76] The application for arrest includes an undertaking to pay the Admiralty Marshal's expenses and a sworn declaration of facts.[77]

An arrest may be effected by service of the arrest warrant on the vessel itself, by fixing the warrant on the outside of the property, or by serving notice of the issue of the warrant on the vessel itself, or by just giving notice to those in charge of the property.[78] The master is usually the person in charge of the ship, thus service of the warrant of arrest on the ship's owner or managers would not be an effective service of the warrant or notice of its issuance.

Normally ships are arrested when in an English port. If the vessel is under innocent passage, a warrant of arrest arguably cannot be served.[79] If the vessel has called or is planning to call at an English port, the warrant of arrest can be validly served. However, very rarely has arrest been effected when the ship has been underway within English territorial waters and only where the Admiralty Marshal had the support of the vessel's crew.

(i) Consequences of the arrest of the ship

The arrested ship cannot be moved without the Court's permission and may also be immobilised or prevented from sailing.[80] It follows that the vessel cannot trade even if it were to trade only within English territorial waters.[81] The person that moves a ship under arrest is in contempt of court and liable for fines or imprisonment.[82] Another consequence of arrest is that English jurisdiction on the merits is established by the arrest of the ship.[83] This arises from the practical need to be able to satisfy a claimant where the security is available. Finally, unless the shipowner puts up security in order to have the ship released from arrest, the ship will be sold and the claimants will be paid out of the proceeds of sale.

Difficulties may arise where a ship is under arrest but its cargo is not or vice versa. The Admiralty Marshal has in such circumstances authority to apply to the Court for the discharge of the cargo and the release of the property not arrested.[84]

(ii) Release of the ship under arrest

The shipowner can have its ship released by providing security.[85] In England the security amount required to release the vessel is based on the claimant's best arguable case plus interest and costs,

---

76. CPR 61.5(8).

77. See PD 61.5(3). The declaration must be accompanied with a statement of truth stating the nature of the claim or counterclaim, that the claim has not been satisfied, that it arises in connection with a ship as well as the name of that ship. In addition the property and, where the property is a ship, the name of the ship, her port of registry, as well as the amount of the security sought. In addition, if the action *in rem* is brought under s 21(4) SCA 1981, all the relevant details that satisfy that the claims are under s 21(4) will need to be contained in the statement, and if it is a foreign vessel and where appropriate under intergovernmental agreements, it will be added that notice has been filed with the consul of the flag State. Also in a claim for oil pollution under s 153 of the MSA 1995, the facts relied on as establishing that the court is not prevented from considering the claim by reason of s 166(2) the MSA 1995.

78. PD, para 61.5(5).

79. UNCLOS 1982, art 28, except if the civil liability has been incurred "in the course of for the purpose of "the particular passage.

80. CPR 61.5(9).

81. *Greenmar Navigation v Owners of Ships Bazias 3 and Bazias 4 and Sally Line (The Bazias 3 and The Bazias 4)* (CA) [1993] QB 673; [1993] 1 Lloyd's Rep 101.

82. *The Merdeka* [1982] 1 Lloyd's Rep 401 and CPR 81.

83. *The Anna H* (fn 3). Under English law, service of the claim form *in rem* on the defendant even without arrest is enough to establish jurisdiction on the merits. However, under art 7 of the Arrest Convention 1952 jurisdiction on the merits is established upon the arrest of the ship. The latter is relevant when the establishment of jurisdiction under the Recast Jurisdiction Regulation is concerned, *The Deichland* [1990] QB 361; [1989] 2 Lloyd's Rep 113.

84. CPR 61.8(8). Problems related to liability for the expenses incurred may arise, see for example *The Jogoo* [1981] 1 Lloyd's Rep 513 where the cargo owners had to pay for removal and sue the shipowner for breach of contract.

85. The procedure for releasing the ship from arrest is described in CPR 61.8.

which is usually the subject of negotiation. Where there is no agreement the Court may decide on the type and amount of security.[86] The security cannot exceed the value of the ship.[87]

The ship will also be released if a limitation fund is constituted in accordance with the 1996 Limitation Convention,[88] or, if the claim is under the 1992 CLC as enacted,[89] when an appropriate fund is established.

(iii) Judicial sale

The arrested ship or property will also be released from arrest after judicial sale. Judicial sale is a crucial component in the enforcement mechanism ensuring that where the shipowner does submit to the jurisdiction of the Court or does not provide security either because it does not want to or cannot do so, the claimant will be paid out of the sale proceeds of the property arrested. Judicial sale can be effected at any stage of the proceedings even if the merits of the case have not been decided.[90] The rationale for this discretion is that there could be circumstances in which keeping the ship under arrest would mean increasing expenses which will diminish any subsequent amount recovered by the judicial sale of the ship.[91] In such a case the ship is sold and the amount obtained replaces the ship. However, payment out of the proceeds of the sale is only made to claimants who have obtained favourable judgments and subject to priorities as determined by the court.[92] In this way the claimant's position is optimised.

The court has authority to sell the ship if any party to the litigation, including the shipowner, applies for the ship's sale.[93] However, the shipowner cannot sell the ship itself as it may be in contempt of the arrest order.[94] The most important consequence of a judicial sale is that it releases the ship from all claims against it.[95]

(iv) Caution against arrest and caution against the release of the ship

The shipowner or the P&I Club can prevent ship arrest by entering a caution against arrest in the Admiralty and Commercial Registry. The person filing the caution against arrest undertakes to acknowledge service of the claim form and provide security for the claim, interest and costs or, if that person has already established a limitation fund under the 1996 LLMC, to confirm this fact and acknowledge service against the limitation fund.[96] However, the filing of a caution against arrest does not stop the claimant from arresting the ship, for example for the purpose of establishing English jurisdiction on the merits,[97] although the court may

---

86. *The Moschanthy* [1971] Lloyd's Rep 37. See also CPR 61.6 and *Global Marine Drilling v Triton Holdings (The Sovereign Explorer) (No 2)* [2001] 1 Lloyd's Rep 60.

87. CPR 61.6(3).

88. MSA 1995, Schedule 7, art 13. See Chapter 7, page 276, provided that the claim on which arrest was based is subject to limitation.

89. MSA 1995, s 159 and s 160. See Chapter 10, page 373, for claims under the CLC.

90. CPR 61.10.

91. *The Myrto* [1978] 1 Lloyd's Rep 11; 1978 WL 57210 (CA).

92. CPR 61.10(5).

93. CPR 61.10(1).

94. *The Cerro Colorado* [1993] 1 Lloyd's Rep 58. The Admiralty Marshall will normally ask for valuation of the ship and bids to ensure that the judicial sale is done in the way most beneficial to all creditors. However, in one exceptional case, *The M/V Union Gold, The M/V Union Silver, The M/V Union Emerald, The M/V Union Pluto* [2013] EWHC 1696 (Admlty); [2013] 1 Lloyd's Law Rep 68 the court exceptionally permitted a sale to a party agreed by the arresting mortgagee without valuation in order to secure a contract for the employment of the ship.

95. Ibid. See also *The Acrux (No 2)* [1962] 1 Lloyd's Rep 405.

96. CPR 61.7(2).

97. *The Anna H* (fn 3).

order the discharge of the arrest and may make the claimant pay any damages caused by the arrest.[98]

If the ship is already under arrest by one claimant other claimants may arrest the vessel too but such an action is of little use because priority of claims is not dependent on whether the right to arrest has been exercised or not.[99] Note though that if the claimant who has arrested the vessel obtains security, then the vessel will be released and the claims of other claimants may be jeopardised. To avoid such a situation an entry in the Admiralty and Commercial Registry of a caution against release is available to claimants with claims *in rem*.[100] As a result when the ship is to be released, the parties that have entered a caution against release will be notified in order to take action and arrest the ship if necessary and the ship will not be released without this party's consent.[101] However, entry of a caution against release may entitle the shipowner to damages for delay.[102]

The court has discretion to permit the re-arrest of a ship where it is fair and appropriate,[103] for example where the security provided turns out to be worthless or insufficient. Only one ship can be arrested for each claim, and multiple arrests for the same claim are not permissible.[104]

(v) Damages for wrongful arrest

Unless the arrest is done with bad faith or gross negligence there is no remedy for damages for the ship wrongfully arrested.[105] This makes arrest a very powerful weapon in the hands of a claimant because without consideration of the monetary value of the claim advanced and without examining the strength of the claim on the merits, the defendant's ship will be stopped from trading with only a remote possibility of an obligation on the claimant to pay damages.[106] Thus, in the general case it is very difficult to obtain damages from an arresting party. This has been both criticised[107] and supported.[108] It is submitted that the rule is justified in view of the general procedure of arrest, which does not distinguish between the different types of *in rem* actions available under the SCA 1981. The rule arguably arises from the protection and the rights afforded to maritime liens. *The Evangelismos* concerned an arrest following a collision. The rule is protective of the weaker claimants, for example crew members or the master. It is also protective of collision damage claimants and non-professional salvors. However, the development of statutory rights *in rem* created commercial claims where the claimants are financially stronger than the shipowner and they would clearly be capable of providing security. Nevertheless, the rule of *The Evangelismos* protects all arresting claimants irrespective of their financial strength or character of claims. For the crew and the master it is clear that an undertaking for damages or a requirement for security may be making the right of arrest practically unavailable to them because of the risks involved. In some cases this would also be true for other claimants *in rem*.

---

98. CPR 61.7(5).
99. However, arresting a ship which is under arrest by another claimant is expressly permitted under CPR 61.8(1).
100. CPR 61.8(2).
101. CPR 61.8(4).
102. CPR 61.8(4).
103. *Owners of the Carbonnade v Owners of the Ruta (The Ruta)* [2000] 1 WLR 2068; [2000] 1 Lloyd's Rep 359. See also CPR 61.6(2).
104. SCA 1981, s 21(8).
105. *Xenos v Aldersley (The Evangelismos)* 14 ER 945; [1858] 12 Moo PC 352. See also *The Kommunar No 2* (fn 43).
106. The test only applies where there is no caution against arrest or release. Where such cautions have been entered and the ship is subsequently arrested recovery of damages would be easier.
107. B. Eder, "Wrongful Arrest for Ships- A time for Change" (2013) 38 Tul. Mar LJ 115, 118. See also A Mandaraka-Sheppard, "Wrongful Arrest of Ships: A case for Reform" (2013) 19 JIML 41.
108. M. Davies, "Wrongful Arrest of Ships: A Time for Change – A Reply to Sir Bernard Eder" (2013) 38 Tul. Mar LJ 137.

It is submitted that a discretionary provision enabling the Admiralty Marshal to require counter security and the court to impose damages under a more lenient test than that presently applicable for all *in rem* claims except claims by the crew and the master would be fairer and more appropriate, albeit more complicated.

Despite the reluctance of the English courts to award damages for wrongful arrest there is one case where an English Court has awarded damages for a wrongful arrest in Nigeria.[109] While the case involved very serious violations by the arresting party it is submitted that, with respect to damages for wrongful arrest, it is plainly wrong for two reasons. First because as a matter of Article 6 of the 1952 Arrest Convention this is for the arresting court. Second, under English law, arrest is only available under an action *in rem* and in accordance with the procedural rules which require the ship to be within the jurisdiction.

(g) Priority of claims

Where the claims against the ship exceed the amount available for the compensation of the various claims, whether this amount is the security obtained or the proceeds of sale of the ship, disputes arise as to which claim will be satisfied first. Five categories of claims can be identified: the Admiralty Court's expenses related to the ship's arrest and management while the ship was under arrest, maritime liens, mortgages, other claims enforceable by an action *in rem* under section 21 of the SCA 1981 and other claims *in personam* not carrying an action *in rem*.

Maritime liens cover claims arising from the absolutely essential elements of shipping, namely the master's and crew's wages and disbursements of the master, salvage claims and damage claims caused by the ship. They also include bottomry and respondentia which were emergency funding mechanisms for the shipping adventure.[110]

Most ships are mortgaged. The financiers of the shipping adventure, the mortgagees, require their investment to be secured against the ship. In practice if the mortgage of the arrested ship were to be paid first, little would be left for other claimants. However, this would create problems in running the ship because, if crew members knew that any unpaid wages would probably not be recoverable because the banks had priority, they would be reluctant to go to sea. Similarly, salvors would hesitate to get involved with the salvage of a stricken vessel if they could lose their claim to mortgagees. Furthermore one can easily imagine the outcry after a collision, if loss of life and personal injury claims remained unpaid so that the bank which financed the negligent shipowner was to be repaid first. It is therefore not surprising that priority *in rem* is given to the claims that correspond to maritime liens and these claims will be paid before the mortgagees are paid. Of course not every claim *in rem* can be considered superior to the mortgagees' claim because then banks would probably not finance shipping. Involvement with the ship under bills of lading, charterparties, supplies, repairs, towage contracts etc., are all contractual as mortgages are and in each case there is a choice to interact with the defendant shipowner. Within this group, registered mortgages[111] have priority over later actions *in rem* which do not carry a maritime lien.[112]

---

109. *Gulf of Azov v Idisi* [2001] EWCA Civ 505; [2001] 1 Lloyd's Rep 727.

110. See fn 33.

111. See *The Shizelle* [1992] 2 Lloyd's Rep 444 for a discussion on the position of unregistered mortgages on unregistered ships.

112. See for example *The Two Ellens* [1869–72] LR 3A & E 345; *Donald Johnson and Others v John Alexander Black (The Two Ellens)* (Judicial Committee) [1871–73] LR 4 PC 161; 17 ER 361; [1872] 8 Moo PC NS 398; 1871 WL 13751. In this case the right of the mortgagee to possession and sale of the vessel under the mortgage were considered to be superior to claims of repair costs which, as it was decided in this case, did not carry the status of maritime liens. See also *The Leoborg (No 2)* [1964] 1 Lloyd's Rep 380.

Thus the distribution of the proceeds of the judicial sale or the security after judgment is as follows: the court's and harbour authorities'[113] claims are paid first, followed by maritime liens, followed by mortgages and the other *in rem* claims after them. Any other claims not enforceable by an action *in rem* would then probably have access to any remaining amount but they will need to follow normal enforcement procedures.

Priority of claims between maritime liens is subject to the court's discretion.[114] Extensive case law can be found determining the relevant priority in specific circumstances. For example, salvage generally comes first[115] on the basis that the availability of the ship as security for arrest would not exist without the salvage. Following the same argument between two salvage claims the latest has priority. However, older cases must be read subject to the court's discretion as expressed in *The Ruta*.[116] A registered mortgagee has priority over all mortgages registered after and all unregistered mortgages created before.[117]

Claims *in rem* which are not maritime liens are subordinated to maritime liens, whenever created, and to mortgages created before them. Statutory rights *in rem* between themselves rank probably *pari passu*.[118]

A possessory lien[119] ranks before all later claims, provided that possession is retained.[120]

(h) Limitation actions

Under English law there are three ways under which one may seek limitation of liability. The first way is where a party raises limitation as a defence when sued.[121] The second way in which limitation of liability can be asserted is by issuing a limitation claim form naming at least one defendant in the limitation action and describing all others. The claim form must then be served on all named defendants. The claimant can apply for a restricted limitation decree against all defendants who have admitted the right to limit liability and against any defendant who fails to file a defence challenging limitation within the required period.[122] Finally, the more general situation is where a party seeks a general limitation decree under a limitation action. This is available also where named defendants do not admit the right to limit liability.[123] These are

---

113. These are usually based on specific statutory rights. *British Transport Docks Board v Owners of the Proceeds of Sale of the Charger, Probe, Vigia, Dideki, Surveyor, Constellation, Errol and Regency (The Charger) (No 1)* [1966] 1 Lloyd's Rep 670; [1966] 3 All ER 117, *The Blitz* [1992] 2 Lloyd's Rep 441. If the claim of the authority is not in the capacity of being an authority but one equivalent to that of a civil claimant, then it is strongly arguable that the priority will be determined on the basis of the civil claim and not under the statute.

114. *The Ruta* (fn 103), where priority was linked to public policy not only in the UK but in other countries too.

115. *The Lyrma (No 2)* [1978] 2 Lloyd's Rep 30.

116. See fn 103.

117. MSA 1995, Schedule 1, ss 7–14, and 1993 Registration Regulations. Questions arise in respect of the priority of mortgages on unregistered ships as well as foreign registered and unregistered mortgages. See Jackson (fn 2), for a detailed discussion.

118. *Festival Holidays Limited v The Demise Charterers of the ship Ocean Glory 1 (The Ocean Glory 1)* [2002] 1 Lloyd's Rep 679; 2001 WL 1560842.

119. The exercise of a possessory lien is a form of self-help. The person who has possession of the property of another in respect of which it has a claim, usually of unpaid services, retains possession of the property until paid by the property's owner. This right of possession is recognised in common law. See for example *The Gaupen* [1925] 22 Ll L Rep 57; *The Ally* [1952] 2 Lloyd's Rep 427 and *The Tergeste* [1903] P 26 (CA).

120. See the discussion in the recent New Zealand Court case *Babcock Fitzroy Ltd v The Ship "M/V Southern Pasifika"* [2012] NZHC 1254; [2012] 2 Lloyd's Rep 423.

121. PD para 61.11(10.18) states that "Nothing in Rule 61.11 prevents limitation being relied on by way of defence".

122. A "restricted decree", where one or more defendants admit the right to limit, may be brought by counterclaim under CPR 61.11(22)(a). A "general decree", where limitation is not admitted, may be brought by counterclaim, but only with permission of the courts (see CPR 61.11(22)).

123. CPR 61.11(12). In that case, the claimant must within seven days of the filing of a defence or after the time to do so has expired, apply for a case management conference (PD 61.11 (10.7)). The Registrar has discretion to grant a limitation decree, or order service of a defence or disclosure by the claimant or make other case management directions (PD 61.11(10.8)).

those proceedings whereby a claimant (for example, a shipowner) may seek an order confirming that its total liability arising out of a particular incident is limited to a certain figure pursuant to the relevant legislation. A limitation fund can be established before or after a limitation claim has been started[124] either by the initiative of the claimant who may pay the limitation amount into court[125] or by order of the court following the granting of a limitation decree.[126] The establishment of the limitation fund does not transfer the rights to these amounts to those claiming against the fund and payments from the limitation fund can only be made when ordered by the court.[127] The claimant must give notice to all named defendants including the date of payment, the amount of limitation and the interest paid into court together with the value of the monetary unit used in the calculation of the limitation fund.[128]

2. MARITIME LIENS[129]

Maritime liens are rights which attach to the ship[130] at the time of the incident.[131] These rights remain attached to the ship even after the ship is sold. As a consequence, when a maritime lien is in existence the ship can be arrested after its sale even if the new owner, who would have to put up security or lose the ship, has nothing to do with the incident which gave rise to the maritime lien. The ability of maritime liens to survive the private sale of the ship is easier understood by reference to the personification theory.

By contrast, rights *in rem* under the SCA 1981 arise at the time of the issuance of the claim form *in rem*. If the ship is sold before the claim form is issued, the claimant will be deprived of the right to arrest the ship. However, an action against a sister ship may then be available, an option not available with a maritime lien.

Maritime liens are enforceable by an action *in rem* to which they are entitled under section 21(3) of the SCA 1981. Their differences and distinction from the other claims *in rem* arise directly from case law.[132] Notably this poses the question whether the modification of the categories of claims with time would also modify the claims which attract maritime liens. For example the statutory action *in rem* in relation to salvage[133] includes claims under the 1989 Salvage Convention which in turn include claims for Special Compensation under Article 14, or may well include claims under the SCOPIC Clause. Would then, a salvage claim for special compensation or under SCOPIC, be secured by a maritime lien or would the maritime lien be restricted to what was perceived as a salvage reward at the time *The Bold Buccleugh*[134] was

---

124. CPR 61.11.19.

125. CPR 61.11.18.

126. CPR 61.11.13. However, under this section the court also enjoys the right to order "other arrangements for payment against the claims subject to limitation".

127. CPR 61.11.21.

128. PD 61.11.10.13.

129. There are several international conventions dealing with maritime liens and mortgages. However, the only one in force is the International Convention on Maritime Liens and Mortgages 1993, Geneva, April 1993. This entered into force on 5 September 2004. The UK is not a party to the Convention. However, the priority structure of the Convention on Maritime Liens and Mortgages 1926, which was signed but not ratified by Great Britain, the Maritime Liens and Mortgages Convention of 1967 and Maritime Liens and Mortgages Convention of 1993 was taken into account in *The Ruta* (fn 102).

130. Also cargo or freight.

131. *The Bold Buccleugh* (fn 33). Arguably they are created at the time the right to claim is created. In a collision that would be the time of the incident but for salvage and crew claims for salaries would probably be the time payment becomes due.

132. *C & CJ Northcote v the Owners of the Henrich BJ RN (The Heinrich Bjorn)* (HL) [1886] 11 App Cas 270, at p 278; *Two Ellens* (fn 112). Although historically the view changed repeatedly until settled to the present one.

133. SCA 1981, s 20(2)(j).

134. See fn 33.

decided? Strong policy arguments suggest that the first interpretation is preferable although this would mean that maritime liens even if not created by statute are extended by statute indirectly through the expansion of the relevant definitions.

Maritime liens are probably not transferable rights. Thus, for example, where an agent pays off outstanding crew wages which arose before the arrest, he does not then become entitled to the maritime lien which the crew wages normally attract but rather is only a claimant with a statutory right *in rem*.[135] It is unclear whether a maritime lien can be assigned, with the exception of bottomry.[136] However, bottomry, respondentia and master's disbursements all share a common characteristic in that they provide funding for the continuation of the shipping adventure. Why they should be differentiated in relation to assignment is unclear.

The maritime lien for wages arises even without the personal liability of the shipowner[137] and irrespective of the contract of employment, but conversely the damage lien does require the personal liability of the owner.[138] For other liens the issue is not decided. The decisions providing for maritime liens to arise against the ship without the personal liability of the shipowner support the personification theory and may become subject to revision in the future.

Maritime liens rank above mortgages and statutory rights arising from section 21(4). Thus exercising a maritime lien would give higher priority than mortgages or other actions *in rem* created by the SCA 1981 under section 21(2) or (4).

An interesting and difficult issue is whether maritime liens recognised under foreign law are to be recognised as such in English proceedings thus taking priority over other claims. For example, where a claim was for the repairs on a ship effected in a foreign country, and the law of that country supported the enforcement of such claim by a maritime lien, the question was asked whether the claim continued to be supported by a maritime lien even where the arrest was effected in a forum in which these claims were not so supported. The answer given by the Privy Council was[139] that the maritime lien is procedural in character and therefore a matter for the law of the forum, in other words foreign maritime liens would not be recognised as such unless they also have the same character under English law.[140] Arguments in support of the law applicable to the dispute have been made by several academics. This would mean that for a contractual claim the law of the contract would determine the character of the lien. Thus where a contract for repairs or bunker provisions governed by US law is breached, the right, it is argued, should

---

135. *The Petone* [1917] P 198; *The Leoborg (No 2)* (fn 112).

136. *The Petone*, ibid. Subrogation of rights under a statute, for example, the Marine Insurance Act 1906, would arguably include rights of recovery. It is also arguable that priority and other advantages of the maritime lien may also be subrogated by statute.

137. See for a recent case *Crew Members of the Ever Success v Owners of the Ever Success (The Ever Success)* [1999] 1 Lloyd's Rep 824; 1998 WL 1045100.

138. See as examples: *The Tasmania* [1888] LR 13 PD 110. However, where the vessel is in the hands of a third party under a demise charter the maritime lien attaches: *The Father Thames* [1979] 2 Lloyd's Rep 364.

139. *Bankers Trust International Ltd v Todd Shipyards Corporation (The Halcyon Isle)* [1980] 2 Lloyd's Rep 325; [1981] AC 221. See also the decision of the Full Court of the Federal Court of Australia where a preference for the *lex fori* was expressed. For a commentary see Davies Martin (2017), Recognition of foreign maritime liens, LMCLQ, [2017], part 2, pp 206–212.

140. The situation is more complicated with the application of the Rome I and II Regulations. Regulation (EC) No 593/2008 of the European Parliament and of the Council of 17 June 2008 on the law applicable to contractual obligations (Rome I), provides for the application of the law expressly or impliedly chosen by the parties (art 3) or some law in the absence of choice (art 4) and specifies that this law will decide "the various ways of extinguishing obligations, and prescription and limitation of actions"; art 12(d). Thus it is at least arguable that the applicable law will also decide whether a claim is a maritime lien or not rather than the law of the forum. Similarly Regulation (EC) No 864/2007 of the European Parliament and of the Council of 11 July 2007 on the law applicable to non-contractual obligations (Rome II) provides for the application of the law where the damage occurred (art 4) and that this law determines amongst other things "the manner in which an obligation may be extinguished" (art 15(h)) thus pointing away from the law of the forum with respect to the type of lien supporting a non-contractual claim.

be a maritime lien because it is recognised as such, statutorily or otherwise by the US courts. Where the ship's mortgage and all other debts are also under the same law then a strong argument that this is a fair arrangement can be made. However, in the more general case this position, it is submitted, can lead to unsatisfactory consequences. A general example may be given with respect to wage claims by seafarers. A rare but not impossible scenario is that they are employed by contracts concluded under different laws. On the assumption that some laws would provide for a maritime lien and some others would not, the proposed alternative would lead to differing priorities for crew claims against the same ship, certainly an unsatisfactory position.

3. ARREST AND CROSS-BORDER INSOLVENCY

When a ship is to be arrested following an action *in rem* the rights of third parties like cargo owners, or charterers are not taken into account. Nor are the rights of the shipowner who will not be able to recover damages from a claimant unless the conduct is one of bad faith or gross negligence. The claimant is, in English law, a secured creditor. For maritime liens the claimant becomes a secured creditor at the time the maritime lien arises,[141] for statutory rights *in rem*, when the action *in rem* starts by issuing the *in rem* claim form.[142] The position of each claimant in terms of priority is determined by the Court, but, save for claims by the Admiralty Marshall and other authorities, maritime liens rank above registered mortgages which, in turn, rank above statutory rights *in rem*.

The position becomes more complicated when the shipowning company becomes subject to insolvency proceedings either voluntarily or as a result of court orders. The basic arrangement of the companies legislation is that, subject to statutory provisions concerning preferential payments,[143] unsecured creditors are to rank *pari passu*. To achieve this objective, enforcement actions against the assets of the company are restricted. The Insolvency Act 1986 has various provisions protecting an insolvent company from enforcement and permitting such actions only with permission by the court. Would then the rights *in rem* still be enforceable and give priority to the maritime claimants or are insolvency proceedings a way by which maritime priorities are undermined? The arguments could differ when the claimant *in rem* is already a secured creditor, which depends on whether the claim is a maritime lien or the *in rem* form has been issued, and when he is not. There may also be a difference depending on whether or not the *in rem* form has been served.

For maritime liens, it is established in *Re Rio Grande Do Sul Steamship Co*[144] that enforcement of the lien is permissible even if the company is in liquidation.[145] In *The Cella*[146] it was confirmed that the claimant is a secured creditor when the ship is arrested and therefore entitled to the security. In *The Zafiro*[147] the judge considered *The Cella* as good law. However, he had to consider a different situation because the ship in the former case was arrested between the time notice of the creditors' meeting was given for voluntary winding up of the company and the time the

---

141. *The Bold Buccleaugh* (fn 33).
142. *Owners of Cargo Laden on Board the Monica Smith v Owners of the Monica Smith (The Monica S)* [1967] 2 Lloyd's Rep 113.
143. *Re Redman (Builders) Ltd* [1964] 1 WLR 541.
144. (1877) 5 ChD 282.
145. This case concerned a claim by the master for wages. The position was confirmed by the Court of Appeal in *Re Aro Co Ltd* [1980] Ch 196.
146. *The Cella* (1888) 13 PD 82.
147. *John Carlbom & Co Ltd v Zafiro (Owners) (The Zafiro)* [1959] 1 Lloyd's Rep 359.

resolution to wind up the company was taken.[148] The court held that the claimants were entitled to the arrest and to the security this provided for their claim. The judge also stated: "I have no doubt that, under section 228, even a maritime lien (which, of course, is superior to a statutory lien) gives way to a Court order for compulsory winding up, if the arrest in respect of the maritime lien succeeds the order, unless the Court gives leave."[149] In *Re Aro*[150] the company was in compulsory liquidation and the providers of bunkers had entered a caveat against release of the ship, which was arrested by another creditor, and had issued a claim form *in rem* and *in personam* which had not been served. The Court of Appeal applied *The Monica S* and found that the claimants were secured creditors and that, even if they were not, the court would exercise its discretion in permitting them to enforce their claim *in rem*. It follows that if, in the case of a statutory lien, the claim form *in rem* is not issued at the time the insolvency proceedings are initiated, the claimant is not a secured creditor and it would then depend on the court's discretion whether admiralty enforcement will be permitted. In *Re Lineas Navieras Bolivianas SAM*[151] the case concerned an unregistered foreign company whose ship was arrested by one claimant while other claimants *in rem* issued claims between the presentation of the winding-up petition and the date of the winding-up order. The Court applied *Re Aro* and held that the claimant who arrested and proceeded to judicial sale did not need leave from the court because he was a secured creditor while the other *in rem* claimants did require leave to proceed, which was granted by the court. There is no decision for *in rem* claims initiated after a winding-up order has been made. Such claims will need leave to proceed. A difficulty will exist in fulfilling section 21(4) of the SCA 1981 because a winding-up order has, in English law, the effect of divesting the company of the beneficial ownership of the property[152] and therefore it is unlikely that a right for an *in rem* action will exist.[153]

The situation becomes more complicated when the insolvent debtor is in one country but has assets in other jurisdictions or indeed ships which move between jurisdictions. This is termed "cross-border insolvency" and raises significant issues of conflict of laws as well as enforcement. There is no international convention governing the rules. However, the Model Law on Cross-Border Insolvency of the United Nations Commission on International Trade Law has rules for helping States to co-operate by, in essence, assisting the proceedings of the State where the company is located.[154] This is given the force of law and incorporated by the Cross-Border Insolvency Regulations 2006.[155] The CBI Regulations contain provisions supporting foreign insolvency proceedings by staying execution and enforcement in the UK against property of

---

148. The case was decided on the basis of the Companies Act, 1948, s 325, which provided:

(1) Where a creditor has issued execution against the goods . . . of a company . . . and the company is subsequently wound up, he shall not be entitled to retain the benefit of the execution . . . against the liquidator in the winding up . . . unless he has completed the execution . . . before the commencement of the winding up:

Provided that-

(a) where any creditor has had notice of a meeting having been called at which a resolution for voluntary winding up is to be proposed, the date on which the creditor so had notice shall, for the purposes of the foregoing provision, be substituted for the date of the commencement of the winding up.

149. *John Carlbom & Co Ltd v Zafiro (Owners) (The Zafiro)* [1959] 1 Lloyd's Rep 359, 367.
150. *Re Aro Co Ltd* [1980] Ch 196.
151. [1995] BCC 666. This was decided under the 1986 Insolvency Act.
152. *Ayerst (Inspector of Taxes) v C&K (Construction) Ltd* [1976] AC 167.
153. Note that the Hong-Kong Courts have preferred the alternative solution. See *International Transportation Service Inc v The Owners and/or Demise Charterers of the Ship or Vessel "Convenience Container"* [2006] HKCFI 465; [2006] 1 Lloyd's Rep Plus 91.
154. Currently legislation based on the model law is in force in 41 States. See www.uncitral.org/uncitral/en/uncitral_texts/insolvency/1997Model_status.html (accessed 17 February 2017).
155. SI 2006/1030.

the insolvent company.[156] However, the rights of creditors including secured creditors are to be taken into account by the court when providing relief.[157] How these Regulations affect proceedings can be seen in *The Sanko Mineral*,[158]a case where Japanese insolvency proceedings were underway and the ship was arrested in England by the mortgagee with the permission of the liquidator.[159] A cargo owner who had obtained a US maritime lien attempted to arrest the ship to enforce a cargo claim. While the English court found the contractual claim time barred because the one-year time bar for initiating arbitration proceedings had expired, it nevertheless withheld from the proceeds of sale an amount corresponding to the claim by the cargo owner because the validity of the claim was to be decided by the Japanese courts.

There is also an EC Regulation on insolvency proceedings which deals with cross border insolvency in Member States.[160] It provides that jurisdiction is with the courts of the Member State where the centre of the "debtor's main interests is situated".[161] However, Article 5[162] of the Regulation provides that "insolvency proceedings shall not affect the rights *in rem* of creditors or third parties"[163] with respect to assets in other Member States. The Virgos-Schmidt report[164] makes it clear that the definition of the term "*in rem*" is intended to be defined by the national law of each Member State and is not affected by the law where the opening proceedings are commenced.[165] Thus it would be English law which will determine the fate of an admiralty claim *in rem* for a ship arrested in England even if the proceedings are undertaken in another EU Member State. Article 5.2 does, however, prescribe some "*in rem*" rights not affected by the foreign insolvency proceedings, the intention being that these are common for all Member States. These include the "exclusive right to have a claim met, in particular a right guaranteed by a lien in respect of the claim...".[166] This supports further the proposition that all maritime liens as well as statutory rights *in rem* already in existence at the time the foreign insolvency proceedings are initiated will be subject to the decisions of the English courts. Because the intention of the Regulation is to protect such creditors in accordance with the security arrangements each national law provides, it is submitted that the priority provided to *in rem* claimants under English law ought to be applicable under the EU system too.[167]

---

156. Ibid., ss 19–21.

157. Ibid., s 22.

158. [2014] EWHC 3927 (Admlty); [2015] 1 Lloyd's Law Rep 247.

159. It must be noted that sale of the ship by the Admiralty Court is arguably more effective than a sale by a liquidator or receiver because it cleanses the ship from other maritime claims.

160. Council Regulation (EC) No 1346/2000 of 29 May 2000 on insolvency proceedings, O J L160/1, resolve the issues of applicable law, jurisdiction etc. for insolvency proceedings in the EU. Regulation (EU) 2015/848 of the European Parliament and Council of 20 May 2015 on insolvency proceedings (recast), O J L141/19 will apply to insolvency proceedings opened after 26 June 2017 (art 84(1)).

161. Art 3.1

162. Regulation 2015/848, art 8.

163. Art 5.1 refers to "tangible or intangible, moveable or immoveable assets – both specific assets and collections of indefinite assets as a whole which change from time to time – belonging to the debtor which are situated within the territory of another Member State at the time of the opening of proceedings."

164. Report on the Convention on Insolvency Proceedings, Rep. 6500/96, Brussels, 3 May 1996.

165. Ibid., p. 69.

166. Regulation 1346/2000, art 5.2(b).

167. While the position under English law is clear, under other legal systems the situation may differ under very difficult commercial situations. For example, the recent bankruptcy of a big container company led to loaded containerships being kept out of port by order of the administrator of the company in order to avoid arrest of the ship on entry into the discharge port. See, for example, *Yu v STX Pan Ocean Co Ltd (South Korea) in the matter of STX Pan Ocean Co Ltd (receivers appointed in South Korea)* [2013] FCA 680, an Australian case permitting the arrest of a ship while the shipowner was under receivership proceedings in South Korea. See also *Yakushiji v Daiichi Chu Kisen Kaisha* [2015] FCA 1170, *HUR v Samsun Logix Corporation* [2015] FCA 1154 and *Kim v SW Shipping Co Limited* [2016] FCA 428 where the court permitted arrest. However, in *Tai-Soo Suk v Hanjin Shipping Co Ltd* [2016] FCA 1404 protective orders against arrest of ship, cargo and bunkers have been issued to enable the vessel to discharge. The judge differentiated maritime liens.

4. FREEZING INJUNCTIONS[168]

A freezing injunction,[169] is a court order aimed at securing funds for the satisfaction of a legal right. It is not restricted to maritime claims but it is granted in support of claims *in personam*. The purpose of the freezing injunction is "to prevent a defendant from taking action designed to frustrate subsequent orders of the court".[170] However, it has also been described as used to protect the satisfaction of a legal right.[171] A freezing injunction can be granted before or after judgment and can concern all or part of the assets of the defendant within the English jurisdiction or worldwide. It is routinely assisted by an order for disclosure of assets.[172]

Freezing injunctions are not pre-trial attachments and do not give rise to a lien or give priority to the applicant's claim.[173] To that extent they are not pre-trial security for the claim in the way the arrest of the ship is.

An action to restrict a defendant from dealing with its property before judgment was considered up to 1975 as not available to a claimant.[174] The reason was that without a judgment it is arguably unfair to restrain the defendant from dealing with his property.[175] However, in two cases[176] in 1975 the Court of Appeal had to deal with *ex parte* applications by shipowners complaining that foreign time charterers whose only assets within the jurisdiction were bank accounts in London, had not paid hire. The shipowners feared that the money would be removed from the jurisdiction thus leaving them empty handed. In both cases the Court of Appeal issued injunctions restraining the defendants from dealing with the money in the bank. The issuance of the injunction succeeded in making the time charterers pay. The absence of the defendant from the jurisdiction was the basis of distinguishing earlier case law which concerned an application for restricting a defendant within the jurisdiction from disposing of its property.[177]

(a) When can the English courts issue a freezing injunction?

Since 1975 the use and the scope of the freezing injunction has increased and, aided by significant statutory changes and judicial improvisation, it has now become a "nuclear weapon" of the law.[178] Today this type of injunction is available against any defendant whether within the jurisdiction or not and for any type of asset whether the asset is in England or not.[179]

---

168. A full account of freezing injunctions is beyond the scope of this book. Several books have treated this topic, e.g. S. Gee, *Commercial Injunctions* (formerly *Mareva Injunctions and Anton Piller Relief*) (6th edn, Sweet & Maxwell 2014); A. Briggs, *Civil Jurisdiction and Judgments* (6th edn, Informa 2015).

169. Originally called "Mareva injunction".

170. *Derby & Co Ltd and Others v Weldon and Others (Nos 3 and 4)* [1990] Ch 65 (CA).

171. *C Inc Plc v Mrs L and Mr L* [2001] 2 Lloyd's Rep 459.

172. The court has discretion under CPR Part 25.1(1)(g) to order disclosure of information related to property or assets which "are or may be the subject of an application of a freezing injunction". Nevertheless this does not create a free standing option for the court, that is, one cannot apply for disclosure and then on the basis of the information collected apply for a freezing injunction (*Andrew Frederick Parker v CS Structured Credit Fund Limited, Elegant Hotels Limited* [2003] EWHC 391; [2003] 1 WLR 1680).

173. *Cretanor Maritime Co Ltd v Irish Marine Management Ltd (The Cretan Harmony)* [1978] 1 Lloyd's Rep 425; *Gangway Ltd v Caledonian Park Investments (Jersey) Ltd* [2001] 2 Lloyd's Rep 715. See also *Kastner v Jason* [2004] EWCA Civ 1599; [2005] 1 Lloyd's Rep 397.

174. *Lister v Stubbs* [1890] 45 Ch D 1.

175. This was already happening, of course with ship arrest, but in 1890 the personification theory for the claim *in rem* was strong.

176. *Nippon Yusen Kaisha v G. and J Karageorgis* [1975] 2 Lloyd's Rep 137; [1975] 1 WLR 1093 and *Mareva Compania Naviera SA v International Bulkcarriers SA* [1975] 2 Lloyd's Rep 509 (CA).

177. *Lister v Stubbs* [1890] 45 Ch D 1.

178. *Bank Mellat v Nikpour* [1985] FSR 87 (CA) at p 92 (Donaldson LJ).

179. SCA 1981, s 37(3).

The High Court[180] has discretion to grant freezing orders in support of a wide variety of proceedings.

Thus there is jurisdiction to grant a freezing order in respect of cases where the English court has jurisdiction[181] on the merits or which relate to the enforcement of English judgments. In addition there is jurisdiction to grant a freezing injunction in support of proceedings in an EU Member State under the Recast Jurisdiction Regulation[182] or in relation to any other proceedings to be heard by any other foreign court whether in an EU Member State or not.[183] Freezing injunctions are also available for arbitration proceedings under the Arbitration Act 1996[184] and also under other statutory provisions.[185]

Within the Recast Jurisdiction Regulation[186] freezing injunctions are covered as provisional measures under Article 35.[187] In addition, in respect of enforcement of judgments from other EU Member States' courts, Article 40[188] permits the granting of a freezing injunction in respect of the defendant's property linked with the English jurisdiction but not in respect of property abroad.[189]

Procedural issues are presently dealt with in CPR Part 25. No standard forms are needed but an example is provided in Practice Direction PD 25. Applications can, in urgent cases, be made over the phone.[190]

(b) When will the English courts issue a freezing injunction?

The granting of a freezing injunction is discretionary and is normally done without notice to the defendant. Because the freezing injunction is for the purpose of assisting the substantive proceedings if there is no accrued legal right there can be no injunction.[191] For example, a freezing injunction will not be granted for a breach of contract which has not yet materialised.[192]

180. But not the county courts see: *Schmidt v Wong* [2005] EWCA Civ 1506; [2006] 1 WLR 561.

181. Note that there must be an intention to start proceedings immediately, otherwise there is no jurisdiction available to the courts see *Fourie v Le Roux* [2007] UKHL 1; [2007] 1 WLR 320.

182. s 25 of the Civil Jurisdiction and Judgments Act 1982 extends the jurisdiction to grant interim relief for proceedings that have or were to be commenced before one of the European Union courts (and if the proceedings fall within the Regulation's substantive scope of application).

183. In addition the CJJA 1982 (Interim relief) Order 1997 extends the application of s 25(1) to all proceedings commenced or to be commenced in a non-EU Member State and for all proceedings commenced or to be commenced before a court in an EU Member State for subject matters outside the Recast Jurisdiction Regulation.

184. s 44 of the Arbitration Act 1996 gives jurisdiction to grant freezing orders in support of arbitrations within or outside the jurisdiction. For the position before the Arbitration Act 1996 see *Channel Tunnel Group Ltd v Balfour Beatty Construction Ltd* (HL) [1993] 1 Lloyd's Rep 291; [1993] AC 334. Under s 49(1) of the Arbitration Act 1996 the parties may agree to give power to arbitrators to issue freezing orders (*Kastner v Jason* (fn 173)). See also *Mobil Cerro Negro v Petroleos de Venezuela SA* [2008] EWHC 532 (Comm); [2008] 1 Lloyd's Rep 684.

185. For example, under s 380(3) of the Financial Services and Markets Act 2000 ("FSMA") the Financial Services Authority can apply to the courts for a freezing injunction.

186. Regulation (EU) No 1215/2012 of the European Parliament and of the Council of 12 December 2012 on jurisdiction and the recognition and enforcement of judgments in civil and commercial matters (recast) O J L351/1 (the Recast Jurisdiction Regulation) which will apply to proceedings commenced on or after 10 January 2015 replacing Regulation 44/2001 which still applies to proceedings commenced before that date.

187. Regulation 44/2001, art 31.

188. See Regulation 44/2001, art 47.

189. *Banco Nacional de Comercio Exterior SNC v Empresa de Telecommunicaciones de Cuba SA, British Telecommunications Plc (intervening)* [2007] 2 Lloyd's Rep 484 (CA).

190. Practice Direction PD 25(4.2). See also CPR 6B.3(1) for leave to serve out of the jurisdiction.

191. The only alternative available is a *quia timet* injunction. This is different from a freezing injunction and is only available where the anticipated act is wrongful. In a freezing injunction removal of the assets from the jurisdiction is not necessarily wrongful (*Mercedes Benz AG v Herbert Heinz Horst Leiduck* [1995] 2 Lloyd's Rep 417; [1996] AC 284 (PC)).

192. *Veracruz Transportation Inc v V C Shipping Co Inc and den Norske Bank A/S (The Veracruz I)* [1992] 1 Lloyd's Rep 353 (CA) and see also *Swift-Fortune Ltd v Magnifica Marine SA (The Capaz Duckling)* [2008] 1 Lloyd's Rep 54; [2007] EWHC 1630 (Comm) (QBD (Comm)).

Provided that the court has jurisdiction under one of the various heads and there is a legal right to be protected then the court will have discretion to grant the injunction. The burden of persuading the court to grant the injunction is on the applicant, as the defendant is in most cases unaware of the application for a freezing injunction.[193] The applicant for a freezing injunction must first have a "good arguable case" that is one "which is more than barely capable of serious argument, but not necessarily one which the judge considers would have a better than fifty per cent chance of success".[194]

In addition the applicant must demonstrate that there is a real risk that the judgment will go unsatisfied without the injunction.[195] The mere existence of the defendant's assets within the jurisdiction is not enough to persuade the Court to grant an injunction.[196] In demonstrating the risk of dissipation of the defendant's assets the previous conduct and the financial standing of the defendant is relevant as well as the type of assets. For example, where the defendant is a foreign company, the country in which it is incorporated, the difficulty of enforcing judgments and the availability of financial information in that country are all factors to be considered by the court.[197] The fact that the defendant is short of funds is not enough to demonstrate a risk of dissipation of assets.[198]

A freezing injunction can also be issued against a third party holding the assets of the defendant under an agency, trust or any other legal arrangement[199] including the appointment of a receiver. In such cases the risk of dissipation has to be shown in respect of the third party.[200]

In attempting to persuade the court to issue the freezing injunction the applicant has a duty to make full and frank disclosure of all the matters relevant to the application including any possible defences and also its financial ability to make an undertaking to the court that it can pay damages to the defendant and to third parties.[201] Breach of the obligation of full and frank disclosure will generally result in the discharge of the freezing injunction. Nevertheless the court retains its jurisdiction to issue a new freezing injunction but will only do so when the breach of the obligation was not of a serious nature.[202]

In summary, the following must be demonstrated:

a) There must be a legal right to be protected;
b) The court must have jurisdiction to issue an injunction; and
c) The claimant must:
  • show it has a good arguable case;
  • show there is a risk of dissipation of assets;
  • make full and frank disclosure; and

---

193. Simply because otherwise it could remove any of its assets from the English jurisdiction.

194. *Ninemia Maritime Corporation v Trave Schiffahrtsgesellschaft M B H und Co KG (The Niedersachsen)* (CA) [1983] 2 Lloyd's Rep 600, 605.

195. *Ketchum International Plc v Group Public Relations Holdings Ltd and Others* (CA) [1997] 1 WLR 4.

196. *Third Chandris Shipping Corporation Western Sealane and Aggelikai Ptera Compania Maritima SA v Unimarine SA (The Genie, Pythia and Angelic Wings)* [1979] 2 Lloyd's Rep 184.

197. Ibid., see also *The Niedersachsen* (fn 194).

198. *Midas Merchant Bank Plc v Senator Musa Bello, Aisha Musa Bello* [2002] EWCA Civ 1496.

199. For example in the *Western Bulk Shipowning Iii A/S v Carbofer Maritime Trading Aps and others (The Western Moscow)* [2012] EWHC 1224 (Comm); [2012] 2 Lloyd's Rep 163 freezing orders have been granted on the application of shipowners against sub-charterers of the ship to protect the lien on sub-hire. See also *TSB Private Bank International SA v Chabra* [1992] 1 WLR 231.

200. *Gill & Others v Flightwise Travel Service Ltd & Another* [2003] EWHC 3082.

201. *The Genie, Pythia and Angelic Wings* (fn 195), and *Thane Investments Ltd v Tomlinson (No 1)* [2003] EWCA Civ 1272.

202. For example, see *The Arena Corporation Limited (In provisional Liquidation) v Peter Schroeder* [2003] EWHC 1089 (Ch).

- show that he would be able to pay damages to the defendant or third parties if needed. And finally

d) The court must consider it just and convenient to issue the injunction[203]

In addition to the above requirements, where the freezing injunction is in support of foreign proceedings there is a statutory requirement to examine whether it is expedient to grant the injunction.[204] In respect of a case which is or will be heard by the court of another EU Member State because Article 35 of the Recast Jurisdiction Regulation[205] permits the use of provisional remedies in all European courts to assist cases before the court of any EU Member State it is more likely that freezing injunctions would be considered expedient.[206] The granting of the freezing injunction in such a case would be subject amongst others to the existence of a real connecting link between the subject matter of the freezing injunction and the territorial jurisdiction of the English court.[207] When such a link is not present, for example in respect of a worldwide freezing order, the freezing injunction may be considered inexpedient.[208] Where the case in support of which the freezing injunction is sought is heard by the court of a non-EU Member State two factors would affect the decision: where the defendant is resident or domiciled and the reaction of the court seized of the dispute.[209] In general the English court will not normally issue orders which are unlikely to be followed.[210]

Freezing orders are judgments within the meaning of the Recast Jurisdiction Regulation and therefore directly enforceable in all EU Member States provided that they are final.[211]

(c) Consequences of the freezing injunction on the defendant

Freezing orders can be destructive for the defendant long before the case on the merits is heard. When the freezing order is granted, it is up to the applicant to inform the defendant and any third parties. From that point on, the defendant can apply to the court to modify the order. However, if the defendant does not obey the injunction it is in contempt of court and can be imprisoned.[212] If the defendant violates the freezing order then it is liable for the consequences even if the court later decides that it did not have jurisdiction to grant the injunction in the first place.[213]

Thus the defendant cannot use any assets to the extent set out in the freezing order. However, the injunction is not a way of putting undue pressure on the defendant and the court would

---

203. In relation to this, the court takes into account all other relevant circumstances. It may consider the impact the freezing injunction may have on the defendant as well as on third parties and, for worldwide injunctions, on foreign courts. However, from the moment the freezing order has been issued it must be construed strictly in accordance with what it says see *JSC BTA Bank v Ablyazov* [2015] UKSC 64; [2015] 2 Lloyd's Rep 546.

204. Civil Jurisdiction and Judgments Act 1982, s 25(3). Guidelines on how this is to be decided are set out in *Royal Bank Of Scotland Plc v Fal Oil Co Ltd And Others* [2012] EWHC 3628 (Comm); [2013] 1 Lloyd's Rep 327.

205. Regulation 44/2001, art 31.

206. *Republic of Haiti and Others v Jean-Claude Duvalier and Others* [1989] 1 Lloyd's Rep 111; [1990] 1 QB 202 (CA).

207. See *Banco Nacional de Comercio Exterior SNC v Empresa de Telecommunicaciones de Cuba SA British Telecommunications Plc (intervening)* (fn 189), applying *Van Uden Maritime BV (t/a Van Uden Africa Line) v Kommanditgesellschaft in Firma Deco-Line* (C391/95) [1999] QB 1225; [1998] ECR I-7091.

208. *Banco Nacional de Comercio Exterior SNC v Empresa de Telecommunicaciones de Cuba SA British Telecommunications Plc (intervening)* (fn 189).

209. *Credit Suisse Fides Trust v Cuoghi* [1998] QB 818 (CA).

210. *Motorola Credit Corporation v Cem Gengiz Uzan, Aysegul Akay* [2003] EWCA Civ 752; [2004] EWHC 3169 (Comm).

211. *Cyprus Popular Bank Public Co Ltd v Vgenopoulos And Others* [2016] EWHC 1442 (QB); [2016] 2 Lloyd's Rep 177.

212. *Angelo Perotti v Kenneth Corbett and Others* [2002] EWCA Civ 1993.

213. *Motorola Credit Corporation v Cem Gengiz Uzan, Aysegul Akay* (fn 210).

permit the defendant to carry on in business in the ordinary way and, for individuals, it usually allows *inter alia* reasonable living expenses, legal costs and hospital bills. Business payments scheduled before the issuance of the freezing order may also be allowed if they are genuine.[214]

The defendant may be entitled to damages if the injunction is wrongfully obtained. Thus, where a company was being driven into administrative receivership after the claimant wrongfully obtained the injunction the company was able to recover damages based on the value of the company immediately before the injunction.[215] The award of damages depends on whether the freezing injunction was wrongfully issued, not on whether the claim was successful. The question to be asked is whether the defendant was stopped, by the freezing injunction, from doing something that it was entitled to do. Thus damages may be awarded even where the claim is successful as this only proves that the claim was "a good arguable" one. The award is subject to the court's discretion which may take into account the conduct of the defendant and relying on that the court may decline to award damages. In all cases causation of damages by the injunction is needed.[216]

Where the defendant is entitled to limit its liability the freezing order will be restricted to the amount of limitation.[217] Arguably as soon as a limitation fund is established the freezing injunction should be discharged because there is no risk of dissipation of assets anymore.

(d) Consequences of the freezing injunction on third parties

Third parties who have been notified about the freezing injunction will be in contempt of court if they fail to comply with it. If they are unhappy with the order because they can suffer damage or they are unclear as to its effect they are entitled to seek clarification or modification by the issuing court. The functioning of the freezing order is heavily reliant on the behaviour of third parties who either hold assets, for example banks, or commercially interact with the defendant.

In general, pre-existing commercial transactions against the defendant's assets will be permitted. Thus banks can exercise any pre-existing rights of set-off.[218] A bank can also realise securities with only the obligation that this is done "in good faith in the ordinary course of business". The claimant does not have any interest in the assets and therefore cannot control the way the securities are realised.[219]

The effects the freezing injunction has on innocent third parties are taken very seriously into account by the courts. If the interference with the activities of the third party is not too great, the undertaking in damages by the applicant is considered sufficient.[220] However, the award of damages is not automatic but it depends on the court's discretion.[221] Where an injunction

---

214. *TDK Tape Distributor (UK) Ltd v Videochoice Ltd and Others* [1986] 1 WLR 141.

215. *Johnson Control Systems Ltd v Techni-Track Europa Ltd (In Administrative Receivership)* [2003] EWCA Civ 1126; 91 Con LR 88. The company was forced into receivership by its creditors who called for payments of debts as soon as they found out about the freezing injunction.

216. For example see *Panos Eliades, Panix Promotions limited, Panix of the US Inc v Lennox Lewis* [2005] EWHC 2966.

217. *Kairos Shipping Ltd and another v Enka & Co llc and others (The Atlantik Confidence)* [2013] EWHC 1904 (Comm) reversed on appeal but not on this point [2014] EWCA Civ 217; [2014] 1 Lloyd's Rep 586.

218. *Z Ltd. v A-Z and AA-LL* [1982] Lloyd's Rep 240; [1982] QB 558 (CA).

219. *Gangway Ltd v Caledonian Park Investments* (fn 173).

220. Note that an authority acting within its public duty will not in general be required to make an undertaking for damages (*The Financial Services Authority (Respondent) v Sinaloa Gold plc and others (Respondents) and Barclays Bank plc (Appellant)* [2013] UKSC 11; [2013] 2 AC 28).

221. *Yukong Line Limited of Korea v Rendsburg Investments Corp of Liberia* 2000 WL 1881248; [2001] Lloyd's Rep 113 (CA).

interferes unreasonably with the third party's activities, the court may refrain from granting the injunction.[222]

If notice of a freezing injunction is given to a bank but the bank negligently pays money out of these particular accounts the only remedy is contempt of court and the court order does not create a duty of care for the bank. Thus no liability in negligence for the bank in such a case can be established.[223]

(e) Worldwide freezing injunctions

A freezing injunction concerned with assets outside the English jurisdiction can only be effective in preserving the foreign assets if it is recognised by the court of the country where the assets are situated.[224] In order to assess whether the granting of such an order is appropriate the court will assess whether the claimant should be permitted to attempt the enforcement of its claim in the foreign court where the assets exist. In order to make this assessment the English courts require to be informed about the law of the foreign court in order to ensure that the freezing order will not have an excessive effect. Such orders are usually granted in the presence of the defendant and with an undertaking that the applicant will not try to enforce it in the foreign court without the permission of the English court.[225] The burden of proof is on the claimant in respect of the existence of the defendant's assets abroad although the claimant only needs to show "a real prospect that the assets are in the country where enforcement is sought".[226]

The position of third parties in cases where a worldwide freezing injunction is concerned poses additional difficulties. Banks, for example, that can be served with the freezing injunction in England but also have branches abroad can be put in a difficult position. If they ignore the freezing injunction they may well be held in contempt of court. On the other hand, if they comply with the freezing injunction both in their English branch and abroad they will be in breach of their contract with the defendant and this contract may be subject to foreign jurisdiction and/or law. In addition the courts of the State where they are situated may issue conflicting orders and then the bank will have to act in breach of the orders of one of the two courts. Damages are not considered by the English courts as an adequate remedy in such circumstances because damage to reputation and regulatory consequences as well as criminal liability may be involved.

These difficulties are resolved by the inclusion of a proviso in the freezing injunction by which the parties affected outside the jurisdiction are expressly protected. The form of the proviso has developed in case law. Thus unless the injunction is declared enforceable by the court of the country concerned, only entities subject to the jurisdiction of the English court and the defendant are subject to a worldwide freezing order.[227] Another provision available in the standard form of a freezing injunction, to the effect that the injunction does not prevent the third party from

---

222. *Galaxia Maritime SA v Mineralimportexport (The Eleftherios)* [1982] 1WLR 539; [1982] 1 Lloyd's Rep 351. A case where an injunction was granted against cargo owners to the effect that the cargo was not to be removed from the jurisdiction. The shipowners were given notice of the injunction. Consequently if they sailed they would have been in contempt of court. The shipowners applied for the injunction to be discharged and the Court of Appeal accepted their appeal in spite of the undertaking of damages given by the claimant.

223. *Commissioners of Customs & Excise v Barclays Bank Plc* [2004] EWHC 122; [2005] 1 Lloyd's Rep 165; [2006] EWCA Civ 1155; reversed by HL judgment [2006] UKHL 28; [2006] 2 Lloyd's Rep 327.

224. It is always effective if the defendant comes within the jurisdiction of the English Courts. Permission must be obtained before enforcement abroad is sought (see PD 25).

225. *Dadourian Group Int Inc & Others v Paul Francis Simms and Others* [2005] 2 All ER 651.

226. *Dadourian Group Int Inc v Paul Francis Simms* and Others [2006] EWCA Civ 399; [2006] 2 Lloyd's Rep 327. See also the guidelines developed there.

227. *Babanaft Co International SA v Bassatne* [1990] Ch 13; [1988] 2 Lloyd's Rep 435 (CA) and *Derby & Co and Others v Weldon and Others (Nos 3 and 4)* [1990] Ch 65 (CA).

complying with what it reasonably believes are its contractual or other obligations in the country where the assets exist or under the law of the contract or court decisions, should generally be included unless it is inappropriate. These provisions include criminal and civil obligations.[228]

(f) Assets subject to the freezing injunction

Any property or other asset with monetary values either owned by the defendant or held on behalf of the defendant by a third party can be used to satisfy the judgment. The property can be situated anywhere in the world.[229] Thus a ship can be subject to a freezing injunction as part of an *in personam* action against the shipowner.[230] Such an action would be a useful device if the particular claim does not fall within the Admiralty jurisdiction so as to authorise arrest.[231] However, as a matter of the court's discretion such orders would rarely be granted because they are likely to interfere with the rights of innocent third parties, such as charterers or cargo owners.[232] Freezing injunctions are not pretrial attachments, the party obtaining one is not a secured creditor and they do not give rise to a lien.[233] It follows that where there is insolvency, national or cross-border, the existence of a freezing injunction would not afford priority to the party obtaining it.

228. *Bank of China v NBM LLC and Others* [2002] 1 Lloyd's Rep 1 (first instance); [2002] 1 Lloyd's Rep 506 (CA) and now in the example of the freezing injunction in PD 25: Interim Injunction.
229. *Babanaft Co International v Bassatne* (fn 226).
230. *The Rena K* [1978] 1 Lloyd's Rep 545; [1979] QB 377, but most probably not in support of an action *in rem*: *The Stolt Filia* [1980] LMLN 15.
231. *The Irina Zharkiakh and The Ksenia Zharkikh* [2001] 2 Lloyd's Rep 319; 2001 WL 949854.
232. Cf. *The Rena K* (fn 24).
233. *Cretanor Maritime Co Ltd v Irish Marine Management Ltd. (The "Cretan Harmony")* [1978] 1 Lloyd's Rep 425; *Gangway Ltd v Caledonian Park Investments* [2001] 2 Lloyd's Rep 715. See also *Kastner v Jason* [2004] EWCA Civ 1599; [2005] 1 Lloyd's Rep 397.

CHAPTER 13

THE APPLICATION OF THE EU COMPETITION RULES TO THE MARINE SECTOR

Andrea Lista

1. THE MEANING OF COMPETITION LAW – THE GENERAL PICTURE

Competition law is a constantly developing legal field. Although it is characterised by an idiosyncratic and technical nature, competition law has a great deal of influence on every area of law and on rules of politics and economic policy.

Its principal function is to "safeguard and promote the competitive process, with the aim of ensuring an optimum allocation of resources in a market and to maximise consumer welfare.

In other words, competition law regulates market activities in order to preserve a free market system. In a market without any form of control, undertakings would be naturally inclined to collude to fix prices, those in a dominant position to abuse their market strength and mergers might inevitably lead to excessive concentrations of economic power. Such practices can hinder or inhibit the competitive process."[1]

The aim of competition law is therefore to regulate the relationships between undertakings selling goods or providing services of the same kind at the same time to an identifiable group of customers within the same geographical market.

The creation of the European Economic Community in 1957 started a process of economic integration which saw the Commission and the European Courts building a complex and extensive framework of competition law principles, which Member States are compelled to fulfil.[2] It is important to bear in mind that EU competition law is a unique legislative framework: it has been structured on the basis of the different historical and legal experiences that have shaped national competition laws of the various Member States and has been superimposed on them.

EU competition law includes four main policy areas arising from the Treaty rules:

(i)   the control of any type of cartels, or control of collusion and other anti-competitive practices which have an effect on the EU (Article 101 TFEU);[3]

(ii) the prohibition of monopolies, or of any abuse of dominant market positions (governed by Article 102);

(iii) the control of direct and indirect aid given by EU Member States to companies (State aid, covered under Article 107);

(iv) the control of proposed mergers, acquisitions and joint ventures involving companies having a defined amount of turnover in the EU/EEA (governed by Article 102 and by Council Regulation 139/2004 EC (the "Merger Regulation")).

This chapter will consider these policy areas in turn below in conjunction with their application to the maritime sector.

2. ARTICLE 101 TFEU AND THE CONTROL OF COLLUSIVE BEHAVIOURS

Article 101 TFEU prohibits all agreements between undertakings, decisions by associations of undertakings and concerted practices which may affect trade between Member States and which have as their object or effect the prevention, restriction or distortion of competition within the common market.

---

1. See A Lista, *EU Competition Law and the Financial Services Sector* (Routledge 2012), p 36.

2. EU competition law is destined to prevail in case of contrast with national law of Member States by virtue of the principle of primacy of EU Law established by the European Court of Justice (ECJ) in the case *Costa v Enel* C-6/64, EU:C:1964:66, [1964] ECR 585.

3. The chapter reflects the current nomenclature and numeration of the Treaty of Lisbon (Treaty on the Functioning of the European Union, TFEU) which entered into force on 1 December 2009. Art 101 of the TFEU was previously art 81 of the Treaty Establishing European Community, TEEC. EU legislation, which entered into force prior to the Treaty of Lisbon, will be referred to as "EC Legislation" according to the original nomenclature related to the previous European treaties. Likewise, reference to the European Courts will sometimes be made according to the past nomenclature, i.e. "European Court of Justice (ECJ)" which is now the Court of Justice of the European Union, and "Court of First Instance".

Article 101 is structured into three paragraphs. The first paragraph of Article 101 lays down a general prohibition of any collusive behaviour between undertakings having as its object or effect the restriction, prevention or distortion of competition in the market. This prohibition has a widespread area of application which involves both informal agreements (gentlemen's agreements) and concerted practices, i.e. forms of practical collusion where undertakings adopt the same behaviour raising or lowering prices at the same time in absence of a formal agreement (i.e. without having physically agreed to do so). Further, Article 101 covers both horizontal agreements (agreements between undertakings occupying the same position in the production or distribution chain, e.g. agreements between retailers) and vertical agreements (between undertakings having a different position in the production or distribution chain, e.g. agreements between retailers and suppliers), effectively outlawing the operation of cartels within the EU.

Horizontal agreements represent the most serious threat to competition, and include the so-called "hard core" restrictions, i.e. price-fixing, establishment of quotas and market sharing. Information exchange agreements are another very controversial form of horizontal agreements due to their capability of facilitating collusive conduct among competing firms, as such agreements are likely to enhance the possibility of monitoring competitors' conduct. Vertical agreements can also represent a danger to competition as they tend to lead to the so-called "market foreclosure", i.e. the effect of exclusive distribution agreements between producers and distributors of setting aside market participation of other firms.

The second paragraph of Article 101 renders any arrangement prohibited by Article 101(1) automatically void.

Finally, the third paragraph of Article 101 lays down an "exemption" mechanism allowing arrangements caught by Article 101 to remain in existence. In practice, Article 101(3) provides for an exemption of any collusive practice capable of impairing competition in so far as it creates efficiencies that outweigh the restriction of competition, consumers obtain a fair share of those benefits, there are no less restrictive means of achieving the efficiencies and competition is not eliminated altogether.[4]

Article 101(3) constitutes the basis for the so-called "Block Exemption Regulations" that have been introduced by the Commission over the years in order to grant exemption on a large scale to specific kinds of agreements.

(a) The application of Article 101 TFEU to the shipping industry

There is no reason in theory why Article 101 should not apply to maritime transport. However, for many years the competition law system created by Article 101 of the EU Treaty did not find application in the field of maritime transport. One feasible reason for this was the fact that, before the accession of the UK, Ireland and Denmark in 1973 and Greece in 1981, most transport between the Member States was landbound.

Another reason may be found in the long tradition of self-regulation characterising the international shipping industry. Its self-regulatory system was based partly on agreements among carriers, concluded in order to provide stability to the maritime transport sector (conferences), and partly on a particular form of alliance among carriers, the aim of which was to share the high costs involved in managing container fleets and to improve the quality of the service (consortia).

---

4. Price-fixing agreements cannot, nevertheless, be exempted. The only example of price-fixing agreements exempted was the block exemption for freight-rate fixing by liner conferences in the EU maritime transport sector under Regulation 4056/86 which was repealed in 2006.

The very first attempt at regulating competition in the maritime transport sector at EU level was the simultaneous promulgation in 1986 of four Regulations: Council Regulations (EEC) Nos 4055/86,[5] 4058/86,[6] 4057/86,[7] and 4056/86.[8]

Council Regulations (EEC) 4055/86 and 4058/86 ensured the application of the principle of freedom of services to the maritime transport sector. Council Regulation (EEC) No 4057/86 aimed to eliminate distortion of competition coming from third-country carriers. Finally, the cardinal piece of legislation relating to the maritime sector was the controversial Council Regulation (EEC) No 4056/86, which entered into force on 1 July 1986 and was repealed in 2006.[9] The Regulation contained both substantive and procedural rules relating to the application of competition law to international maritime transport services from or to one or more Community ports, other than tramp vessel services.[10]

Before considering the current situation and possible future scenarios, the analysis will briefly focus on Regulation 4056/86 and the past regime, as this will enable us to evaluate the evolution of the regulatory framework and to appreciate better the current status quo.

(b) The past regime: Regulation 4056/86 and the block exemption for liner conferences

Regulation 4056/86 used to lay down detailed rules for the application of Article 101 TFEU to international maritime transport services, empowering the European Commission to investigate alleged infringements.

The Regulation provided for an automatic open-ended block exemption for liner conferences (i.e. associations of shipowners operating the transport of cargo, chiefly by container on the same route, served by a secretariat) and for agreements between transport users and the latter concerning the use of the conference services. The Regulation applied only to certain types of maritime transport services. For instance, it did not apply to any activity not intended as a "transport" service; consequently, ancillary services or transport-related activity (e.g. travel agency, shipping agency, ship broking) did not fall within the scope of the Regulation. Further, the definition of liner conference only embraced the carriage of cargo and not the carriage of passengers.

The block exemption was enshrined into Article 3 of the Regulation, which provided an exemption for agreements, decisions and concerted practices of all or part of the members of one or more liner conferences of container vessels. That block exemption had some *sui generis*

---

5. Council Regulation (EEC) No 4055/86 of 22 December 1986 applying the principle of freedom to provide services to maritime transport between Member States and between Member States and third countries, OJ L 378, 31/12/1986.

6. Council Regulation (EEC) No 4058/86 of 22 December 1986 concerning co-ordinated action to safeguard free access to cargoes in ocean trades, OJ L 378, 31.12.1986.

7. Council Regulation (EEC) No 4057/86 of 22 December 1986 on unfair pricing practices in maritime transport OJ L 378, 31.12.1986.

8. Council Regulation (EEC) No 4056/86 laying down detailed rules for the application of Articles 85 and 86 [now 81 and 82] of the Treaty to maritime transport (Liner shipping conferences). OJ L 378, 31.12.1986, 31.12.1986

9. Replaced by Council Regulation (EC) No 1419/2006 of 25 September 2006 repealing Regulation (EEC) No 4056/86 laying down detailed rules for the application of Articles 85 and 86 of the Treaty to maritime transport, and amending Regulation (EC) No 1/2003 as regards the extension of its scope to include cabotage and international tramp services OJ L 269, 28.9.2006.

10. Council Regulation (EEC) No 4056/86, art 1(3)(a) defined "tramp vessel services" as the transport of goods in bulk or in break-bulk in a vessel chartered wholly or partly to one or more shippers on the basis of a voyage or time charter or any other form of contract for non-regularly scheduled or non advertised sailings where the freight rates are freely negotiated case by case in accordance with the conditions of supply and demand.

The fourth recital to Regulation 4056/86 provided that tramp vessel services were excluded because the rates for these services are negotiated on an ad hoc basis in accordance with the level of supply and demand patterns prevailing in the market. Tramp vessel services are subject to the transitional provisions of EU competition rules (i.e. TFEU, arts 104 and 105).

traits compared to the norm. Indeed, unlike other block exemptions, it was not subject to renewal but unlimited in time, and it also allowed the use of joint price-fixing and capacity regulation – practices not permitted by any other block exemption. As a result, it tolerated any type of co-operation between carriers, provided that it fulfilled the terms and conditions established in Article 4 of the Regulation (i.e. subject to the condition that the "agreement, decision or concerted practice shall not, within the common market, cause detriment to certain ports, transport users or carriers by applying for the carriage of the same goods and in the area covered by the agreement, decision or concerted practice, rates and conditions of carriage which differ according to the country of origin or destination or port of loading or discharge, unless such rates or conditions can be economically justified"[11]).

The rationale behind the introduction of the block exemption was that, at the time of the adoption of Regulation 4056/86, the Council and the Commission believed that liner conferences were necessary to enhance productivity and capacity utilisation, reduce costs, improve the quality of services and grant stability to the maritime sector. While originally seen as a useful tool, Regulation 4056/86 and the block exemption for price-fixing became increasingly controversial.

Opponents of the block exemption claimed that liner conferences were effectively able to act as a monopoly, representing a threat to competition within the meaning of Article 101.

The economics of the situation are relatively straightforward – within a market, any sort of agreement to fix prices constitutes an impediment to competition, in that it removes the possibility of offering the same service at different prices. As might be expected, the legal aspect is far more complex. The ruling of the European Court of Justice in *Pronuptia de Paris GmbH v Irmgard Schillgalis*[12] determined that restrictions on competition do not represent a distortion of competition within the meaning of Article 101, as long as they are objectively necessary in order to provide for the successful functioning of an economic system. In other words, the Court is willing to weigh up the advantages and disadvantages of an agreement related to competition.

Applying this precedent to the maritime transport sector, the argument was that liner conferences were necessary in order to provide stability in the sector.

(c) The repeal of Regulation 4056/86

The decision to undertake a review of the block exemption regulation for liner conferences was triggered by different, concurring factors. First, the block exemption for liner conferences was, as established above, in many ways exceptional.[13]

In addition to that, unlike almost all other block exemptions, the block exemption for liner conferences was not subject to time limits and had never been reviewed. Another incentive for the review process was the publication in April 2002 of a *Report on Competition Policy in Liner Shipping*[14] by the Secretariat of the OECD. The Report raised serious doubts as to the validity of the assumption that collective rate setting by members of a liner conference was an indispensable pre-requisite for efficient liner shipping services.

According to the Report, there was no evidence of a positive influence from the anti-trust exemptions for price-fixing granted by Regulation 4056/86. In particular, the Report outlined the possibility of enhancing the efficiency of the sector by other means than liner conferences,

11. See Regulation 4056/86, art 4 above.
12. *Pronuptia de Paris GmbH v Irmgard Schillgalis* C-161/84, EU:C:1986:41 [1986] ECR 353.
13. As previously mentioned, the peculiarity of Regulation 4056/86 was that it granted an exemption for a hardcore restriction of competition such as horizontal forms of price-fixing.
14. OECD *Report on Competition Policy in Liner Shipping* www.oecd.org/daf/competition/competition-issues-in-liner-shipping.htm (accessed 8 March 2017).

by adopting agreements aimed at reducing costs. The Report also emphasised the exclusion from the maritime transport market of new independent operators, willing to provide liner services but not in the position to compete with the liner conferences due to the block exemption.

In October 2004 the Commission published its *White Paper on the Review of Regulation (EEC) No 4056/86, applying the EC Competition Rules to Maritime Transport*.[15] The purpose of the White Paper was to assess whether to modify or repeal the provisions of Regulation 4056/86, based on an analysis of the current situation in the maritime transport sector.

The White Paper discussed whether, in the current market situation, there remained any justification under Article 101(3) of the Treaty for the block exemption for freight rate-fixing by liner conferences. The White Paper emphasised the extent to which the liner shipping market had changed in the two decades since the adoption of Regulation 4056/86. In particular, the role of independent carriers offering liner shipping services outside a conference framework had become considerably more important. Furthermore, the Commission recognised how forms of co-operation between carriers not involving price-fixing practices (such as consortia and alliances) had increased considerably. The White Paper also highlighted the significant growth of individual confidential contracting between carriers and shippers, by means of individual service contracts. The analysis resulted in serious doubts about the compatibility of the block exemption for liner conferences with the EU competition law system.

As a direct result of the Commission White Paper, Council Regulation 1419/2006[16] was adopted in September 2006. Regulation 1419/2006, repealed Regulation 4056/86 and its block exemption for liner conferences agreements, subject to a transitional period of two years for existing liner conferences.

The repeal of Regulation 4056/86 which used to exempt liner conferences from the application of EU competition rules represented an enormous change in the maritime industry, almost a quantum leap. The dawn of a new regulatory era began inevitably carrying a certain degree of uncertainty in relation to the application of new rules (which are actually old ones) to the maritime sector.

In order to assist maritime undertakings in the self-assessment of the compatibility of their agreements vis-à-vis Article 101, on 1 July 2008 the Commission issued its Guidelines on the Application of Article 101 to Maritime Transport Services.[17]

(d) The Commission Guidelines on the application of Article 101 TFEU to maritime transport services

The Guidelines cover the following topics: (i) definition of "liner shipping" and "tramp shipping"; (ii) effect on trade between Member States; (iii) the "relevant market" definition; (iv) horizontal agreements in the maritime transport sector (technical agreements, information exchange agreements between competitors in liner shipping, pool agreements in tramp shipping).

(i) Definition of "liner shipping" and "tramp shipping"

The Guidelines define "liner shipping" as services involving the transport of cargo, chiefly by container, on a regular basis to ports of a particular geographic route, generally known as a trade.

---

15. Commission *White Paper on the Review of Regulation (EEC) No 4056/86, applying the EC Competition Rules to Maritime Transport* (COM/2004/0675).

16. Council Regulation 1419/2006, OJ L 269/1, repealing Regulation (EEC) No 4056/86 laying down detailed rules for the application of arts 85 and 86 of the Treaty to maritime transport, and amending Regulation (EC) No 1/2003 as regards the extension of its scope to include cabotage and international tramp services.

17. OJ 2008 C245/2.

Further characteristics of liner shipping are identified with the fact that timetables and sailing dates are advertised in advance and services are available to any transport user.

In line with Regulation (EEC) No 4056/86, the Guidelines define the transport of goods in bulk or in break bulk as a form of transport where "the freight rates are freely negotiated case by case in accordance with the conditions of supply and demand".[18] It is mostly the unscheduled transport of one single commodity which fills a vessel. The Commission has identified a series of characteristics specific to specialised transport which render it distinct from liner services and tramp vessel services. They involve the provision of regular services for a particular cargo type. The service is usually provided on the basis of contracts of affreightment using specialised vessels technically adapted and/or built to transport specific cargo.[19]

The Guidelines apply also to "cabotage" services intended as the provision of maritime transport services including tramp and liner shipping, linking two or more ports in the same Member State. Although the Guidelines do not specifically address cabotage services they nevertheless apply to these services in so far as they are provided either as liner or tramp shipping services.

The range of application of the guidelines is well specified, although many would have preferred a wider definition of liner shipping so as to include also the transport of cargo not chiefly by container and specialised transport.

(ii) Effect on trade between Member States

Article 101 of the Treaty applies to all agreements which may appreciably affect trade between Member States. According to the Guidelines, in order for there to be an effect on trade, it must be possible to foresee with a sufficient degree of probability on the basis of a set of objective factors of law or fact that the agreement or conduct may have an influence, direct or indirect, actual or potential, on the pattern of trade between Member States.

Indeed, the Commission emphasised that "transport services offered by liner shipping and tramp operators are often international in nature linking Community ports with third countries and/or involving exports and imports between two or more Member States (i.e. intra Community trade)".[20] The Guidelines point out that in most cases they are likely to affect trade between Member States, *inter alia*, "on account of the impact they have on the markets for the provision of transport and intermediary services".[21]

Effect on trade between Member States is of particular relevance to maritime cabotage services since it determines the scope of application of Article 101 of the Treaty. The Guidelines emphasise that the extent to which such services may affect trade between Member States must be evaluated on a case-by-case basis.

Since the impact on trade between Member States must be appreciable, the main question is related to how "appreciability" is to be assessed in liner, tramp and cabotage services. The Guidelines do not clarify whether this assessment will be appraised by reference to the position and the importance of the relevant undertakings in relation to a specific shipping service, or be carried out in more concrete terms (i.e. by taking into account the various market conditions). Past experience seems to suggest the former; nevertheless the assessment of the impact on trade

---

18. See the Commission Guidelines on the Application of Article 101 to Maritime Transport Services, above (see also fn 10 above).

19. See Commission Decision No 94/980/EC of 19 October 1994 in Case IV/34.446 – *Trans-Atlantic Agreement*, OJ L 376, 31 December 1994, at p 1.

20. Ibid.

21. Ibid.

between Member States will definitely vary and be considered on a case-by-case basis. It is therefore very difficult to foresee any clear pattern.

(iii) The relevant market definition

In order to assess the effects on competition of an agreement for the purposes of Article 101 of the Treaty, it is necessary to define the relevant product and geographic market. The main purpose of market definition is to identify in a systematic way the competitive constraints faced by an undertaking. According to the Guidelines, the relevant product market comprises "all those products and/or services which are regarded as interchangeable or substitutable by the consumer, by reason of the products' characteristics, their prices and their intended use".[22]

The relevant geographic market comprises the area "in which the undertakings concerned are involved in the supply and demand of products or services, in which the conditions of competition are sufficiently homogeneous and which can be distinguished from neighbouring areas because the conditions of competition are appreciably different in those areas".[23]

When it comes to *liner shipping*, the Guidelines identify containerised liner shipping as the relevant product market, since usually "only a very small proportion of the goods carried can easily be switched to other modes of transport (e.g. air transport service)".[24] The Guidelines also specify that it may be appropriate under certain circumstances to define a narrower product market limited to a particular type of product transported by sea. For example, "the transport of perishable goods could be limited to reefer containers or include transport in conventional reefer vessels".[25]

According to the Commission, while it is possible in exceptional circumstances for some substitution to take place between break bulk and container transport, "there appears to be no lasting change over from container towards bulk. For the vast majority of categories of goods and users of containerised goods, break bulk does not offer a reasonable alternative to containerised liner shipping which thus remains a separate product market".[26]

As for the relevant geographic dimension of liner shipping, the geographical market in liner cases is identified by the Guidelines as a range of ports in northern Europe or in the Mediterranean. Since shipping services from the Mediterranean are only marginally substitutable for those from northern European ports, these have been identified as separate markets.

Tramp services are also the object of detailed indications in relation to the identification of the relevant market in its geographic and product dimensions. The Guidelines first indicate elements to take into account when determining the relevant product market from the demand side (demand substitution); from this perspective, the "main terms of an individual transport request are a starting point for defining relevant service markets in tramp shipping since they generally identify the essential elements of the transport requirement at issue. Depending on the transport users' specific needs, they will be made up of negotiable and non-negotiable elements. Once identified, a negotiable element of the main terms, for example the vessel type or size, may indicate, for instance, that the relevant market with respect to this specific element is wider than laid down in the initial transport requirement."[27]

22. Ibid.
23. Ibid. According to the Commission, "carrier (or carriers) cannot have a significant impact on the conditions of the market if customers are in a position to switch easily to other service providers".
24. Ibid.
25. Ibid.
26. Ibid.
27. Ibid.

The Guidelines also specify that the nature of the service in tramp shipping may differ and there is a variety of transport contracts. Consequently, it may be necessary to "ascertain whether the demand side considers the services provided under time charter contracts, voyage charter contracts and contracts of affreightment to be substitutable. Should this be the case, they may belong to the same relevant market. Vessel types are usually subdivided into a number of standard industrial sizes. Therefore, the substitutability of different vessel sizes needs to be assessed case by case so as to ascertain whether each vessel size constitutes a separate relevant market."[28]

According to the Guidelines, the relevant product market of tramp services needs to be "identified also from the supply side (supply substitution), and the physical and technical conditions of the cargo to be carried and the vessel type provide the first indications as to the relevant market from the supply side. If vessels can be adjusted to transport a particular cargo at negligible cost and in a short time frame, different tramp shipping service providers are able to compete for the transport of this cargo. In such circumstances, the relevant market from the supply side will comprise more than one type of vessel.[29] Nevertheless, the Guidelines do note that the ability of specialised service providers to compete for the transport of other cargo may be limited due to the fact that in tramp shipping, port calls are made in response to individual demand. Mobility of vessels "may however be limited by terminal and draught restrictions or environmental standards for particular vessel types in certain ports or regions".[30]

Additional factors to be taken into account are the reliability of the service provider, security, safety and regulatory requirements which may influence supply and demand-side substitutability (e.g. the double hull requirement for tankers in Community waters).

As for the geographic dimension, the Guidelines specify that when it comes to tramp services, certain geographic markets may be defined on "a directional basis or may occur only temporarily for instance when climatic conditions or harvest periods allow".[31]

(iv) Horizontal agreements in the maritime transport sector

Co-operation agreements are a common feature of maritime transport markets. Considering that these agreements may be entered into by actual or potential competitors and may adversely affect the parameters of competition, undertakings must take special care to ensure that they comply with the competition rules.

The Guidelines mainly relate to technical agreements, information exchange agreements between competitors in liner shipping, and pool agreements in tramp shipping.

Technical agreements whose sole object and effect is to implement technical improvements or to achieve technical co-operation will not fall under Article 101. Agreements relating to the implementation of environmental standards fall into this category, whereas agreements between competitors which pertain to price, capacity or other parameters of competition will, in principle, not fall into this category and are thus void.

According to the Guidelines, the exchange of commercially sensitive and individualised market data may, under certain circumstances, breach Article 101 TFEU. The Guidelines specify that the "actual or potential effects of an information exchange must be considered on a case by case basis as the results of the assessment depend on a combination of factors, each specific to an individual case".[32] The structure of the market where the exchange takes place and

28. Ibid.
29. Ibid.
30. Ibid.
31. Ibid.
32. See the Commission Guidelines on the Application of Article 101 to Maritime Transport Services, above.

the characteristics of the information exchange are two key elements that the Commission will examine when assessing an information exchange. The assessment must consider "the actual or potential effects of the information exchange compared to the competitive situation that would result in the absence of the information exchange agreement".[33] To be caught by Article 101, the exchange must have an appreciable adverse impact on the parameters of competition. In identifying the impact on competition of information exchange agreements, a key role will be played by the content and the age of the data exchanged and the frequency of the exchange.

The Guidelines emphasise, nevertheless, that an exchange of information between carriers that "restricts competition may nonetheless create efficiencies (e.g. such as better planning of investments and more efficient use of capacity). Such efficiencies will have to be substantiated and passed on to customers and weighed against the anti-competitive effects of the information exchange in the framework of Article 101(3)."[34]

The most recurrent form of horizontal co-operation in the tramp shipping sector is identified by the Guidelines in the shipping pools. A standard shipping pool brings together a number of similar vessels under different ownership and operated under a single administration. As considered in the following, without the shield of protection offered by the block exemption, shipping pools will be considered as forms of price-fixing practices having as their object and effect the co-ordination of their capacity and customer sharing, in the light of the restriction of each member's commercial freedom to operate freely in the shipping market in a competitive manner. All this is clearly against Article 101.

The Guidelines on the application of the TFEU to the maritime transport services expired in September 2013 and have not been renewed by the Commission. The decision of the Commission to let the Guidelines expire constitutes another significant step in the direction of subjecting maritime transport to the full application of EU competition law.

(e) The current scenario for liner conferences

The repeal of Regulation 4056/86 leaves the liner shipping sector fully exposed to the application of Article 101 of the TFEU directly under the European Commission's jurisdiction.[35] This means that starting from October 2008 (the end of the transitional period of Regulation 1419/2006) agreements between carriers having the object or effect of preventing, restricting or distorting competition and capable of affecting trade between Member States are prohibited, void and unenforceable in respect of their restrictions.

As from October 2008, shipping pools (either in the classic form of administration-controlled pools managed by a separate company, or member-controlled pools under the operational management of one or more members of the pool) are unlawful under EU law. In other words, agreements between carriers related to the operation of scheduled maritime transport services, whose object or effect is to fix the rates and conditions of carriage, fall within the meaning of Article 101.

On a general level, examples of agreements which are now caught by Article 101 are, *inter alia*, agreements fixing purchase/selling prices or other trading conditions, agreements limiting or controlling production, markets, technical development or investment, market sharing agreements, agreements on information sharing of sensitive information, e.g. pricing, capacity, joint purchasing/selling agreements.

---

33. Ibid.
34. Ibid.
35. The European Commission is the relevant Community institution which enforces the EU competition rules.

Consequently, any EU or non-EU carrier currently a member of liner conferences operating on trade routes to or from EU ports, which continue to fix prices and regulate capacity on those routes after October 2008, are subject to substantial fines being imposed on the parties to the agreement if discovered by the European Commission.

(f) The way forward: possibility of individual exemption under Article 101(3)

The analysis will now shift to the legal assessment of horizontal agreements in the maritime sector.

Under the current status quo, the only possibility for the survival of forms of co-operation between maritime undertakings, is through an individual exemption under Article 101(3). The repeal of the block exemption granted by Regulation 4056/86 does not preclude the possibility of an individual exemption. A block exemption is merely an exemption granted on a large scale to specific kinds of agreement. In its absence, maritime undertakings are still in a position to obtain an individual ad hoc exemption, in so far as they can prove that their agreements satisfy the four conditions listed by Article 101(3). First, such agreements will need to create efficiencies (in terms of improving the provision of the service or promoting economic or technical progress). Second, consumers must be allowed to share the benefits of those efficiencies. Third, the agreements should not contain restrictions on competition beyond strictly indispensable restraints. Finally, they must not eliminate competition altogether.

If the above conditions are satisfied, the shipping pools will be able to benefit from an individual exemption. The prerogative of granting individual exemption under Article 101(3) used to be in the power of the Commission. Since 1 May 2004 (after the entry into force of Regulation 1/2003),[36] the Commission lost this prerogative and henceforth individual exemptions are considered a legal requirement to be automatically granted by national courts and competition authorities if the conditions are met.

As a consequence, the process of evaluation of the existence of the conditions for an exemption laid down by Article 101(3) is now known as a "self-assessment" exercise to be carried out by the parties involved with the support of economists and legal advisers prior to the official evaluation of the competent national authorities. The burden of proof lies on the party involved who will need to support its claim to exemption with strong arguments.

In practice, the starting point for the assessment of the maritime pools will be their impact (actual or potential) on competition. This means that if the impact on competition is appreciable and trade between Member States is affected, in order to obtain individual exemption, shipping pools will have to prove that their agreements are necessary in order to provide their services. This can be difficult to prove, especially in the presence of the so-called hardcore restrictions of competition, i.e. price-fixing, limitation of output (hence capacity regulation) and customer or market sharing. Under such circumstances the standard of proof for the fulfilment of the conditions enshrined in Article 101(3) is particularly high.

According to the Commission Guidelines on the Application of Article 101 to maritime transport services,[37] the Commission in assessing whether to exempt or not co-operation agreements in the maritime transport market will take into account, *inter alia*, the impact of such agreements on the shipping market, prices, costs, quality, frequency and differentiation of the service provided, in conjunction with innovation, marketing and commercialisation of the service.

---

36. Council Regulation (EU) No 1/2003 of 16 December 2002 on the implementation of the rules on competition laid down in Articles 81 and 82 of the Treaty, OJ L 1, 4 January 2003, at pp 1–25.

37. Guidelines on the Application of Article 81 to maritime transport services, OJ C 245, 26 September 2008, at pp 2–14.

A good argument in support of the claim for an exemption could be therefore the provision of irrefutable evidence of the creation of remarkable efficiencies in conjunction with a considerable decrease of the costs of the services.

If, by contrast, the effects (actual or potential) of the pool on competition are not appreciable, the scenario changes radically. Agreements between small and medium-sized maritime undertakings or agreements between undertakings having very small market shares fall outside the scope of application of Article 101, as explained by the Commission in its *De Minimis Notice*.[38]

Agreements between undertakings occupying the same position in the production/distribution chain (horizontal agreements) having a joint market share below 10 per cent will be allowed without the need for an individual exemption in so far as they do not involve price-fixing, output limitation or forms of customer and market sharing, for instance, a shipping pool involving maritime undertakings with a joint share of the market below 10 per cent. Agreements between undertakings having a different position in the market (vertical agreements) will be considered lawful in so far as they do not involve more than 15 per cent of the market share (e.g. an agreement between an owner and a shipper covering no more than 15 per cent of the market).

Competition in the liner conferences market has been yet again subject to scrutiny in recent times by the OECD, which, in 2015 published a *Summary on the Roundtable on Competition Issues in Liner Shipping*.[39]

The conclusions of the Summary point out that, although liner shipping consortia can create market efficiencies, they can indeed give rise to competition concerns. This is so because "very large players are involved in the main alliances and these alliances cover very high shares of trade in the main routes".[40]

According to the OECD, a major concern lies with the fact that consortia could lead to costs alignment and could entail forms of tacit collusion due to the large share of trade of liner shipping alliances, as well as the fact that "they can promote their members' access to key strategic information regarding competing carriers which are members of the same agreement".[41]

Another concern outlined in the Summary relates to "the trend towards increasing concentration, driven by carriers' expectations to achieve additional efficiencies through mergers".[42]

According to the OECD, concentration in liner conferences is even higher if due consideration is given to the synergies between firms through alliances and consortia agreements. To this end, the suggestion here would be to scrutinise carefully the effects of possible mergers between carriers in view of the alliances and synergies of the members of the post merger

---

38. Commission Notice on agreements of minor importance which do not appreciably restrict competition under art 81(1) of the Treaty establishing the European Community (*de minimis*), OJ C 368, 22 December 2001, at pp 13–15.

39. OECD *Summary on the Roundtable on Competition Issues in Liner Shipping, DAF/COMP/WP2/M(2015)1/ANN3, 27/11/2015.*

40. Ibid.

41. Ibid. The Summary points out that, in terms of statistics, "there are currently four large strategic alliances, namely '2M', 'G6', 'Ocean 3' and 'CKYH'. These alliances have emerged as a consolidation of much smaller alliances, all of which included the most important liner shipping companies. Measuring the degree of coverage of consortia and alliances can be challenging as virtually all players are involved in some form of consortia or alliance for single or multiple trades. However, for illustrative purposes, alliances can be said to account for about 75 per cent of the transpacific trade. The Asia–North Europe trades are now only operated by global alliance players. In these trades, 2M holds 32 per cent of the total capacity, CKYHE accounts for 26 per cent, G6 for 23 per cent and Ocean Three represents 19 per cent of the total capacity allocated to these trades. "

42. Ibid. According to OECD investigations, "while the share of the top players in the industry has been increasing, the sector still shows some fragmentation. Market structures depend on the particular trade in question: for example, on the Asia-Europe trade, the five top carriers (Maersk, MSC, the CMA-CGM group, Hapag-Lloyd and Evergreen Line) control half of the market capacity, even though the total number of carriers is still large."

conglomerate with third parties, so as to avoid a move towards "excessive concentration and interdependency".[43]

(g) Article 101 and the tramp shipping and cabotage sectors

Regulation 1419/2006 assimilates the tramp shipping (the non-regular maritime transport of bulk cargo not containerised oil, agricultural and chemical products) and cabotage (unscheduled maritime transport services taking place exclusively between ports in one EU Member State) sectors to all the other sectors of the economy. This means that Article 101 TFEU now fully applies also to these two sectors of the maritime industry.

The transitional period covering liner conferences does not apply to tramp shipping and cabotage which have therefore been subject to the application of Article 101 since October 2006. As a result, the Commission has already initiated investigations related to agreements concerning the parcel tankers market.

The impact of the application of Article 101 to the tramp shipping and cabotage sectors affects, *in primis*, any form of horizontal agreements between maritime undertakings. Pools or other forms of co-operation between actual or potential competitors involving the direct or indirect determination of rates, limitations on output, market or customer sharing, information exchange and any other anti-competitive practices are subject to intense scrutiny.

Such pools *prima facie* represent a blatant price-fixing practice capable of limiting output and considerably restricting competition. More specifically, competition concerns arise because in a typical tramp shipping or cabotage pool, the pool manager is usually empowered to negotiate contracts and rates with customers on behalf of all the other members or ships belonging to the pool (the pool manager usually also takes sole responsibility for fleet scheduling, the determination of voyage and time charters, as well as for other influential management operations).

In order to obtain an individual exemption under Article 101(3), such forms of hard-core restrictions will be subject to a severe burden of proof falling on the parties to the agreement.

As for liner conferences, the application of the Commission's *De Minimis Notice* will result in the automatic exemption of horizontal agreements between undertakings whose combined market share is below 10 per cent only in so far as they do not involve price-fixing, output limitation or forms of customer and market sharing. Since pools in the tramp shipping and cabotage sectors usually involve such practices, the *De Minimis Notice* cannot in this case be considered a useful tool.

The most recurrent form of horizontal co-operation in the tramp and cabotage shipping sectors are shipping pools. There is no universal model for a pool. Some features do, however, appear to be common to all pools in the different market segments as follows. Like the liner conferences agreements, standard tramp and cabotage shipping pools

bring together a number of similar vessels under different ownership and operated under a single administration. A pool manager is normally responsible for the commercial management (for instance, joint

---

43. Ibid. Interestingly, the Summary warns vis-à-vis a recent trend of vertical integration in liner conferences. According to the OECD "the deployment of mega-vessels has given added relevance to port operations because they can potentially constitute an operational bottleneck undermining total transit times and service reliability and limiting the efficient use of vessels". As a result, "ocean carriers have begun to acquire container terminal facilities to reduce physical bottlenecks (e.g., nautical accessibility, undersized infra- and supra-structures) and thereby safeguard their maritime investments by boosting operational performance. Vertical integration also allows carriers to acquire control of stevedoring costs and provides shipping lines with the opportunity to invest in a business that is highly correlated and synergic with their core activity".

The OECD Summary advocates for a careful consideration and counter-balancing of the efficiencies which may arise from vertical integration vis-à-vis the risk that "vertically integrated port authorities could withhold access to important upstream infrastructure to their rivals, e.g., by awarding container terminals to their vertically integrated unit carriers".

marketing), negotiation of freight rates and centralisation of incomes and voyage costs and commercial operations (planning vessel movements and instructing vessels, nominating agents in ports, keeping customers updated, issuing freight invoices, ordering bunkers, collecting the vessels' earnings and distributing them under a pre-arranged weighting system etc.).[44]

The pool manager often "acts under the supervision of a general executive committee representing the vessel owners. The technical operation of vessels remains the responsibility of each owner (safety, crew, repairs, maintenance etc.). Although they market their services jointly, the pool members perform the services individually."[45]

It follows from this description that the essential characteristic of standard tramp and cabotage shipping pools lies with joint selling, alongside with elements of joint production. The guidance on both joint selling, as a variant of a joint commercialisation agreement, and joint production in the Commission Guidelines on the applicability of Article 101 of the Treaty to horizontal co-operation agreements, is therefore relevant. However, given the various elements of differentiation characterising the structure of pools, each pool must be assessed on a case-by-case basis. In so far as tramp and cabotage pools have as their object or effect the co-ordination of the competitive behaviour of their parents, the co-ordination "shall be appraised in accordance with the criteria of Article 101(1) with a view to establishing whether or not the operation is compatible with the common market and to determine whether it fulfils the four cumulative conditions of Article 101(3) of the Treaty".[46]

Pool agreements in the tramp shipping and cabotage sectors often also involve the provision of internal by-laws, such as the prohibition on operating vessels outside the pool, or long notice requirements in case of withdrawal of vessels from the pool, which are indeed capable of hindering competition. These provisions will inevitably be caught by Article 101. Yet again, the only possibility of escape is represented by an individual exemption under Article 101(3), but this will require a careful self-assessment by the parties involved in the pool. In these circumstances the situation is very delicate and the chances of obtaining an exemption reduced to the minimum, as we need to bear in mind that under Article 101(3) individual exemption can be granted only in the presence of the creation of economic efficiencies in the market and not only for the benefit of the owners pooling their vessels. Since such membership rules do not provide any benefits to consumers, the possibilities for their exemption are minimal.

Further, pools cannot reduce competition in the sector preventing the access to the market by external players or effectively reducing their possibility to compete with the pool.

By contrast, the impact of Regulation 1419/2006 on vertical agreements related to the tramp shipping and cabotage sectors is not particularly severe. Agreements between parties occupying a different position in the supply chain, e.g. requirements contracts, bareboat, management agreements, time or voyage charters, should be safe in so far as they do not contain anti-competitive clauses. Thus, agreements providing exclusivity of supply or purchase, long-term commitment obligations or long notice periods will require an individual exemption.

(h) Shipping consortia

Liner shipping carriers transport cargo on the basis of advertised timetables to ports on specifically defined geographic routes. For the purposes of the EU anti-trust rules, consortia are forms of operational co-operation between liner shipping companies with a view to rationalising costs.[47]

---

44. See the definition given by the EU Commission in the Memo "Antitrust: Draft Guidelines for maritime transport", Memo/07/355.
45. Ibid.
46. See the Guidelines on the Application of Article 81 to maritime transport services, above, at p 6.
47. Consortia are distinguished from conferences, which pursue the objective of co-ordinating tariffs.

On 29 September 2009, the Commission adopted the revised Liner Shipping Consortia Block Exemption.[48] The scope of application of the block exemption is confined to operational co-operation within a liner shipping consortium (i.e. the share of space on their respective vessels). Such co-operation is allowed only in so far as consortia do not exceed a given market share threshold in the relevant market where they operate of 30 per cent.[49]

The Consortia Regulation clarifies the definition of a consortium in two ways. First, a consortium can consist of "an agreement or a set of interrelated agreements between two or more vessel-operating carriers which provide international liner shipping services exclusively for the carriage of cargo relating to one or more trades, the object of which is to bring about co-operation in the joint operation of a maritime transport service".[50] Second, the definition of a consortium is extended to all international liner shipping services of cargo, whether or not such services are provided "chiefly by container",[51] designed to improve the service that would be offered individually by each of its members in the absence of the consortium, in order to rationalise their operations by means of technical, operational and/or commercial arrangements. "Liner shipping" is defined as the "transport of goods on a regular basis on a particular route or routes between ports and in accordance with timetables and sailing dates advertised in advance and available, even on an occasional basis, to any transport user against payment."[52]

In order to benefit from the block exemption, an agreement between a consortium member and a third party is required to fulfil all conditions of the Consortia Regulation with emphasis on the market share threshold. Indeed, the Regulation provides for a list of exempted activities generally considered indispensable for the provision of a joint liner shipping service, such as co-ordination and joint fixing of timetables, determination of the ports of call, pooling of vessels or exchange of space.[53]

---

48. Regulation (EC) No 906/2009 on the application of art 81(3) of the Treaty to certain categories of agreements, decisions and concerted practices between liner shipping companies (consortia) (the "Consortia Regulation") OJ L 256, 29 September 2009, at pp 31–34.

49. Art 5(1) of the Consortia Regulation clarifies that the market share of a consortium is "the sum of the individual market shares of the consortium members. The individual market share of a consortium member includes all volumes carried by that member, whether within the consortium in question or outside that consortium, be it on the member's own vessels or on its behalf on third party vessels on the basis of a slot charter agreement or any other co-operation agreement" (Consortia Regulation, art 5(2)). When assessing the market share condition, liner carriers must determine the relevant product and geographic market or markets where the consortium operates. In doing so, carriers are assisted by the Guidelines on the Application of Article 101 to maritime transport services analysed above.

50. See the definition provided by Regulation (EC) No 906/2009 on the application of art 81(3) of the Treaty to certain categories of agreements, decisions and concerted practices between liner shipping companies (consortia), above.

51. Including consortia operating ro-ro and semi-container vessels.

52. See the definition provided by Regulation (EC) No 906/2009 on the application of art 81(3) of the Treaty to certain categories of agreements, decisions and concerted practices between liner shipping companies (consortia), above.

53. More specifically, the Regulation exempts:

1. the joint operation of liner shipping services including any of the following activities:
    (a) the co-ordination and/or joint fixing of sailing timetables and the determination of ports of call;
    (b) the exchange, sale or cross-chartering of space or slots on vessels;
    (c) the pooling of vessels and/or port installations;
    (d) the use of one or more joint operations offices;
    (e) the provision of containers, chassis and other equipment and/or the rental, leasing or purchase contracts for such equipment;
2. capacity adjustments in response to fluctuations in supply and demand;
3. the joint operation or use of port terminals and related services (such as lighterage or stevedoring services);
4. any other activity ancillary to those referred to in points 1, 2 and 3 which is necessary for their implementation, such as:
    (a) the use of a computerised data exchange system;
    (b) an obligation on members of a consortium to use in the relevant market or markets vessels allocated to the consortium and to refrain from chartering space on vessels belonging to third parties;
    (c) an obligation on members of a consortium not to assign or charter space to other vessel-operating carriers in the relevant market or markets except with the prior consent of the other members of the consortium.

Another prerequisite for the exemption is the obligation of the consortium to give members the right to withdraw without financial or other penalty such as, in particular, an obligation to cease all transport activity in the relevant market or markets in question, whether or not coupled with the condition that such activity may be resumed after a certain period has elapsed.

Lastly, the block exemption does not apply to a consortium which, "directly or indirectly, in isolation or in combination with other factors under the control of the parties, has as its object the fixing of prices when selling liner shipping services to third parties, the limitation of capacity or sales and the allocation of markets or customers".[54]

After the repeal of the maritime transport guidelines, the only surviving set of specific anti-trust rules applicable to the maritime industry will be the Consortia Regulation[55] which expired in April 2015, and was renewed for other five years until 2020.[56]

Traditionally, consortia are viewed as an essential means to allow the market survival of small vessel operating carriers. On the downside, consortia allow information exchange capable of facilitating tacit collusion. A growing trend in consolidation of the maritime industry coupled with the desire of the European Commission to avoid the use of specific industry regulation appeared in the past to indicate a possible repeal of the Consortia Regulation, which in the end has been renewed.

(i) General consequences in case of non-compliance with Article 101

The consequences for non-compliance can be extremely severe. The competition authorities (the Commission together with the relevant national anti-trust authorities, e.g. the Competition and Markets Authority in the UK) have a wide range of powers in order to ensure the compliance of agreements and pools with Article 101. First, they are endowed with large investigative powers which allow them to require information on agreements, and carry out dawn raids on private and business premises in order to collect evidence related to potential anti-competitive behaviours.

Furthermore, in case of violation of Article 101 they are allowed to impose fines of up to 10 per cent of the worldwide group annual turnover of any party involved in the infringement, issue cease and desist orders and other interim relief measures.

3. ARTICLE 102 TFEU: ABUSES OF DOMINANT POSITION BY ONE OR MORE UNDERTAKINGS: MEANING AND ISSUES

Article 102 TFEU prohibits the abuse of dominant position by one or more undertakings within the common market or in a substantial part as incompatible with the common market in so far as it may affect trade between Member States.

Such abuse may, in particular, consist of: directly or indirectly imposing unfair purchase or selling prices or other unfair trading conditions; limiting production, markets or technical development to the prejudice of consumers; applying dissimilar conditions to equivalent transactions with other trading parties, thereby placing them at a competitive disadvantage; or making the conclusion of contracts subject to acceptance by the other parties of supplementary obligations which, by their nature or according to commercial usage, have no connection with the subject of such contracts.

54. Except for the capacity adjustments referred to in art 3(2).
55. See fn 48.
56. See Commission Press Release of 24/06/2014.

The essence of Article 102 is to control market power. The prohibition on abuses of dominant position provided by Article 102 incorporates three cumulative elements.[57]

First, one or more undertakings need to acquire a dominant position within the Common Market or in a substantial part thereof. The concept of dominance does not exist in the abstract, but only in relation to a particular market,[58] intended as a clearly defined geographical area where a product is marketed and where the conditions of competition are sufficiently homogeneous for the effect of the economic power of the undertaking to be evaluated.[59] The relevant market needs thus to be identified in its geographical and product dimensions prior to the assessment of dominance which is mainly based on the analysis of the share of the market occupied by a specific undertaking in conjunction with the assessment of the market share of its nearest competitor.

Nevertheless, it needs to be emphasised that a dominant position within a market is not illicit in itself; it is the abuse of that position which is illegitimate. Accordingly, in order to trigger the application of Article 102 the undertaking or undertakings concerned must have abused that position of dominance.[60]

Lastly, the abuse of that position must affect trade between Member States. If the abuse of a dominant position does not affect the trade between the Member States, Article 102 will not be relevant.

These requirements all need to be satisfied and are considered below in the context of the shipping trade.

Contrary to Article 101 (which, as established above, did not fully apply to shipping undertakings until October 2008), Article 102 has always applied to the maritime industry. Article 8(1) of Regulation 4056/86 provided that an abuse of dominance within the meaning of Article 102 was prohibited without the need for a prior decision to that effect, whereas Article 8(2) provided that the Commission may withdraw the block exemption for liner conferences where the conduct of the conference had effects which were incompatible with Article 102.

The entry into force of Regulation 1419/2006 did not change the previous scenario: Article 102 currently fully applies to the maritime sector, and, as it will be readily appreciated, the application of Article 102 has been particularly relevant in the context of ports.

(a) The identification of the relevant geographic market in the maritime sector

As previously established, the definition of the relevant market is a core element for the application of Article 102. The reason for this is obvious: the abuse of dominant position needs to be identified in relation to a particular market. For example, two dominant stevedores in the port of Southampton (UK) refusing to supply their services would not have any material impact on stevedoring services in Genoa (Italy) because they operate in two separate markets.

We have seen that the geographical market may be defined as "the space comprising the geographical area in which the conditions of competition are sufficiently homogeneous and which can on this basis be distinguished from neighbouring areas in which the conditions of competition are appreciably different".[61]

---

57. This explanation of art 102 is based on A Lista, *EU Competition Law and the Financial Services Sector* (Routledge 2012), p. 236.

58. See *Europeanballage Corporation and Continental Can Co Inc v Commission* C-6/72, EU: C:1973:22 [1973] ECR 215.

59. See *United Brands v Commission* C-27/76, EU:C:1978:22 [1978] ECR 207, and the Commission Notice on the definition of relevant market for the purposes of Community competition law, OJ C 372/5, 9 December 1997, at pp 5–13.

60. Abusive practices undertaken by non-dominant companies do not fall within the aim of the article here being considered.

61. See, *inter alia*, Commission Decision of 30.01.2008 declaring a concentration to be compatible with the common market and the functioning of the EEA Agreement (Case No COMP/M.4734 – *INEOS/ Kerling*), [72].

In the maritime sector, the geographical market may involve, for instance, a single port or a cluster of ports, or a service between two ports or two countries. For example, in a case relating to ferry services across the Baltic Sea, the geographical market may involve a single port (e.g. Stockholm) at one end of the journey. By contrast, in relation to liner traffic between the UK and Italy, the relevant geographical market may involve a range of ports (e.g. Southampton, Marseille, Genoa).

The importance of the relevant geographical market definition derives from the fact that under one market definition, a port could be dominant in a substantial part of the common market and, therefore, subject to Article 102 but the same port might not be in a dominant position under a different geographical market definition. An interesting example is *Irish Continental Group plc v Chambre de Commerce et Industries de Morlaix*.[62] In this case the object of dispute was the access to the port of Roscoff, a ferryport in Brittany in France. Brittany Ferries was the only company to operate a ferry service from Roscoff to Ireland, carrying around 100,000 passengers annually.

In November 1994, an Irish ferry company, Irish Ferries, sought access to the port of Roscoff by application to CCI de Morlaix. The parties negotiated, but CCI de Morlaix denied that there was an agreement for the access of Irish Ferries to the port of Roscoff.

The scenario of this case could have changed radically in relation to the outcome of the identification of the relevant geographic market. If the geographical market were Ireland–Brittany, then Roscoff was in a dominant position in a substantial part of the common market and subject to Article 102. By contrast, if the relevant geographical market was considered to be Ireland and the range of northern French ports generally considered (including Brittany and Normandy) then Roscoff did not occupy a dominant position.

The *raison d'etre* here was that Roscoff had a very high share of the market Ireland–Brittany, but a considerably lower percentage of the geographical market identified in Ireland and the range of northern French ports generally considered.

The geographical market can indeed be a limited market in practice especially in case of passenger car ferry services (where normally passengers choose short sea journeys. For instance, in the *Holyhead* cases,[63] Stena Sealink Ports and Stena Sealink Line which owned the port of Holyhead were accused of abuse of dominant position for their refusal to allow Sea Containers Limited to operate a fast ferry service through the central corridor between Holyhead (located in Anglesey, North Wales) and Dun Laoghaire (in Ireland). Sea Containers argued that Stena Sealink Line had a dominant position in the market for the provision of passenger and car-ferry services on the "central corridor" route between Britain and Ireland.

In order to identify the relevant geographical market, the Commission had defined three corridors: the northern, central and southern corridors. The Commission maintained that the substitutability/interchangeability of the three corridors across the Irish Sea for any traveller depended on the traveller's point of origin and his or her intended destination for the journey in question, and that the relevant geographical market in this case was represented by the central corridor.

The northern and southern corridors, with service routes between Scotland and Northern Ireland and South Wales and Ireland respectively, were in fact not considered "viable alternatives to the central corridor for the majority of leisure users, with or without cars".[64] The reason for

---

62. *Irish Continental Group plc v Chambre de Commerce et Industries de Morlaix* [1995] 5 CMLR 177 (not published in the Official Journal).

63. 94/19/EC: Commission Decision of 21 December 1993 relating to a proceeding pursuant to Article 86 of the EC Treaty (now TFEU, art 106) (IV/34.689 – *Sea Containers v Stena Sealink* – interim measures) OJ L 15, 18 January 1994, at pp 8–19.

64. Ibid., p. 12.

this was that almost one-third of Ireland's population resides in the Greater Dublin area and Holyhead is easily reached by inhabitants of Birmingham, Manchester and Liverpool.

(b) The identification of the relevant product market in the maritime sector

The identification of the relevant product market is essential in order to assess the dominance of a maritime undertaking. The definition of the relevant product market offered by the Commission and the European Courts has been to focus upon the notion of *interchangeability*, i.e. the extent to which the goods or services under scrutiny are interchangeable with other products. The notion of *interchangeability* entails the analysis of "cross-elasticities" of one specific product. The existence of high cross-elasticity indicates that the products are interchangeable; the more products tend to be interchangeable, the greater are the probabilities that, in practice, they belong to the same relevant market.

In the maritime sector, on a general level there is a difference in terms of product market definition in cases relating to *passenger* traffic rather than *commercial/cargo* traffic. The reason for this is mainly due to the fact that passengers generally are inclined to prefer short sea journeys and equally do not want to travel too far by road from either their home or destination. Conversely, the logistic allocation of the resources and ships in case of commercial/cargo traffic is usually accommodated in a different way so as to reserve the shortest and most convenient routing to *passenger* traffic.

Nevertheless, we need to bear in mind that the identification of the relevant product market is focused on the concept of interchangeability or substitutability of services. The more services are interchangeable, the more is it likely that they belong to the same relevant product market. The identification of the relevant product market can be a rather easy exercise where a port provides its services in several different product markets (e.g. the passenger liner trade, the oil tanker trade and the passenger car ferry trade). In this case, each of the services above will clearly represent the relevant product market; for instance, the oil tanker trade is not interchangeable with the passenger car ferry trade.

This identification can become far more complex in case of shipping companies operating through car and passenger carriers due to the high level of interchangeability characterising car and passenger vessels. It is essential to emphasise that the correct identification of the relevant product market is crucial in order to assess the dominance of a specific undertakings. Dominance is very much a market-specific concept, and, for instance, a port may be in a dominant position for one specific service market (e.g. the oil tanker trade) but not in the case of another product market (e.g. for passenger car ferry trade).

(c) The assessment of dominance in the maritime sector

Having identified the relevant market considered both under its product and geographical dimensions, the next step forward is represented by the assessment of the dominance of a specific undertaking. The concept of "dominant position" is not defined in Article 102 but it is generally considered in case law as a position of economic strength enjoyed by a specific undertaking which enables it to undermine, restrain and hinder competition within the relevant market. Dominance may be either individual or collective.

In order to assess whether a particular undertaking has a dominant position we need to refer in the first place to its market share. If we are dealing with a firm having a market share of around 40 per cent or more, it is highly likely that we are dealing with a dominant undertaking. Nevertheless, even lower thresholds could hide a position of dominance, especially within very fragmented markets. The relevant element is the market share of the nearest competitor. If, for instance, we are dealing with an undertaking having 25 per cent of the market and its nearest competitor has a share of 7 per cent of the same market, the former will be considered to be in a dominant position.

Other elements to be taken into account in conjunction with the market share are the financial or technical resources of the undertaking concerned, or the possibility that it eventually has to control both production and distribution within the relevant market.

All these factors will have to be taken into account in order to assess the dominance of a shipping undertaking.

In liner shipping, volume and/or capacity data have been identified as the basis for calculating market shares in several Commission decisions and Court judgments. In *Cewal I*,[65] the Court of First Instance held that, in the absence of exceptional circumstances extremely large market shares (market share of between 70 and 80 per cent) are in themselves evidence of the existence of a dominant position. Lower market shares (market share of 60 per cent on the trade in question) are capable of giving rise to a strong presumption of a dominant position.[66]

In tramp shipping markets, service providers compete for the award of transport contracts, that is to say, they sell voyages. Depending on the specific services in question, various data may be used in order to calculate the annual market shares, for instance: (a) the number of voyages; (b) the parties' volume or value share in the overall transport of a specific cargo (between port pairs or port ranges); (c) the parties' share in the market for time charter contracts; (d) the parties' capacity shares in the relevant fleet (by vessel type and size).[67]

(d) Examples of abuse of dominant position in the maritime industry

As previously mentioned, the abuse of dominant position can assume different forms, e.g. charging excessive prices, refusal to supply existing customers as well as any other type of behaviour of a dominant undertaking capable of exploiting the position of weaker market players.

In the *Cewal I* case, members of a liner conference were found to infringe Article 102 for abusing a collective dominant position by taking collective action designed to eliminate their principal competitor. Specifically, their abuse consisted of predatory prices by offering lower freight rates than their competitors and through the offer of loyalty rebates.

Another example of abuse arose from *Corsica Ferries Italia Srl v Corpo dei Piloti del Porto di Genova*,[68] where Corsica Ferries Italia SRL (hereinafter "Corsica Ferries") considered that it was the victim of an abuse of dominant position contrary to Article 102 by the Corpo dei Piloti del Porto di Genova (Corporation of Pilots of the Port of Genoa).

In Italy, piloting services were made compulsory in almost all ports, including Genoa, by decrees of the President of the Republic (failure by the captain of a vessel to use the piloting service is a criminal offence). At the time when the alleged abuse of dominant position took place, piloting services in the port of Genoa were offered at a discount to vessels permitted to carry on maritime cabotage, in other words traffic between two Italian ports. Only vessels flying the Italian flag could obtain permission to engage in maritime cabotage.

---

65. Joined Cases T-24/93 to T-26/93 and T-28/93 *Compagnie maritime belge transports and Others v Commission* [1996] ECR II-1201 (*Cewal I*).
66. See the Court of First Instance judgment in Joined Cases T-191/98, T-212/98 to 214/98, *Atlantic Container Line AB and others v Commission* [2003] ECR II-3275 (TACA), [908].
67. See Guidelines on the Application of Article 81 to maritime transport services, OJ C 245, 26 September 2008, at pp 2–14, [34].
68. *Corsica Ferries Italia Srl v Corpo dei Piloti del Porto di Genova* C-18/93, EU:T:1994:255 [1994] ECR I-1783.

Such discounts were denied to Corsica Ferries, a company established under Italian law, which operated a liner service between the port of Genoa and various Corsican ports, using two ferries registered in Panama and flying the Panamanian flag.

The European Court found that Corpo dei Piloti del Porto di Genova occupied indeed a dominant position, and considered the refusal to offer the above discounts to Corsica ferries as a discriminatory practice (i.e. an abuse of dominant position within the meaning of Article 102). Furthermore, the European Court took the view that EU law prevents a Member State from applying different tariffs for identical piloting services, depending on whether or not an undertaking operates a vessel entitled to operate cabotage services.

Another case quite illustrative of abuses of dominance in the maritime sector is the *B&I Line plc v Sealink Harbours Ltd and Sealink Stena Ltd*.[69] Stena Sealink Ltd owned, through a subsidiary company, the port of Holyhead. Stena Sealink was also providing a ferry service from Holyhead to Dun Laoghaire (located in Dublin Bay).

In order to curtail competition, Sealink Stena scheduled its ferry timetable in such a way as to be prejudicial to the operations of B&I (a competitor operating services within the same routes). B&I complained to the Commission for an alleged abuse of dominant position by Sealink Stena.

This case brought to light the application of the so-called "essential facilities" doctrine to the maritime industry. The concept of "essential facilities"[70] entails the existence of two markets, i.e. an "upstream market" and a "downstream market", together with a dominant undertaking operating in both the upstream and the downstream market. If the dominant undertaking owns an input (the essential facility), and uses that input to compete in the downstream market, it is, as a consequence, extremely difficult for a competitor to seek access to the downstream market. Two elements are therefore necessary: the ownership or control over a "facility" by a dominant undertaking and the "essentiality" of a facility.

Under EU competition law, the "essential facilities doctrine" is dealt with in conjunction with Article 102 TFEU. It is generally applied to exclusionary practices (e.g. such as refusals to supply), having the effect of abuse of a dominant position in the relevant market.[71] Whenever an essential facility is identified, the refusal of access to that facility automatically constitutes anti-competitive behaviour by the dominant undertaking.

In *B&I Line plc v Sealink Harbours Ltd and Sealink Stena Ltd*, the Commission laid down the principles that a dominant undertaking which both owns or controls and itself uses an essential facility, i.e. a facility or infrastructure without access to which competitors cannot provide services to their customers, and which refuses its competitors access to that facility or grants access to competitors only on terms less favourable than those which it gives its own services, thereby placing the competitors at a competitive disadvantage, infringes Article 102, if the other conditions of that article are met.

First, the European Commission emphasised that a port, even if it is not itself a substantial part of the common market, may be considered as such in so far as "reasonable access to the facility is indispensable for the exploitation of a transport route which is substantial for the purposes of the application of Article 102".[72]

---

69. *B&I Line plc v Sealink Harbours Ltd and Sealink Stena Ltd* Case IV/34.174.

70. This explanation of art 102 is based on the one elaborated in A Lista, *EU Competition Law and the Financial Services Sector* (Routledge 2012), p 192.

71. The first EU law case relating to the concepts of essential facilities and refusal to deal is *ICI v Commission*, C-48/69, EU:C:1972:70 [1972] ECR 619. In this case the ECJ defined the concept of "essential facility" as a "facility or infrastructure without access to which competitors cannot provide services to their customers".

72. See *B&I Line plc v Sealink Harbours Ltd and Sealink Stena Ltd*, above, [21].

Second, the European Commission considered that a company which both owns and uses an essential facility – in this case a port – should "not grant its competitors access on terms less favourable than those which it gives its own services".[73]

Therefore, the owner of an essential facility which uses its power in one market "in order to strengthen its position in another related market, in particular, by granting its competitor access to that related market on less favourable terms than those of its own services, infringes Article 102 where a competitive disadvantage is imposed upon its competitor without objective justification".[74]

Furthermore, the Commission emphasised also that the owner of the essential facility, which also uses the essential facility, may "not impose a competitive disadvantage on its competitor, also a user of the essential facility, by altering its own schedule to the detriment of the competitor's service, whereas in this case, the construction or the features of the facility are such that it is not possible to alter one competitor's service in the way chosen without harming those of others".[75] Specifically, where, as in this case, the competitor is already subject to a certain level of disruption from the dominant undertaking's activities, according to the Commission there is "a duty on the dominant undertaking not to take any action which will result in further disruption; that is so even if the latter's actions make, or are primarily intended to make, its operations more efficient. Subject to any objective elements outside its control, such an undertaking is under a duty not to impose a competitive disadvantage upon its competitor in the use of the shared facility without objective justification".[76]

(e) Impact on trade between Member States

Lastly, in order to claim the application of Article 102 it is necessary to prove that the abuse of dominant position taking place in the relevant market is capable of affecting trade between Member States. According to Article 102, once the relevant product market and the relevant geographic market are identified, it is necessary to prohibit the abuse of a dominant position of one or more undertakings that may affect the Common Market or a substantial part of it.

It is important to emphasise that it is not necessary for the abuse of dominant position to extend over the territory of two or more Member States in order to affect Community trade within the meaning of Article 102. Even an abuse of dominant position which remains confined within the territory of a single Member State will be caught by Article 102 in so far as it is capable, actually or potentially, of directly or indirectly affecting trade between Member States.[77]

In *Merci Convenzionali Porto di Genova SpA v Siderurgica Gabrielli SpA*[78] a number of dock companies in Italy had enjoyed a monopoly in the provision of stevedoring services. Under the Italian rules, Siderurgica Gabrielli was obliged to apply to Merci Convenzionali Porto di Genova SpA (an undertaking with the exclusive right to organise dock work in the Port of Genoa for ordinary goods), for the unloading of a cargo of steel.

As often happens in Italy, the employees of Merci Convenzionali Porto di Genova SpA went on strike and consequently the cargo was unloaded three months late. Siderurgica Gabrielli

---

73. Ibid.
74. Ibid.
75. Ibid.
76. Ibid.
77. See *British Airways v Commission* C-T-219/99, EU:T:2003:343 [2003] ECR II-5917.
78. *Merci Convenzionali Porto di Genova SpA v Siderurgica Gabrielli SpA* OJ 1997 L301/27, [1998] 4 CMLR 91 (on appeal, *Merci Convenzionali Porto di Genova SpA v Siderurgica Gabrielli SpA* C-179/90, EU:C:1991:464 [1991] ECR I-5889, [1994] 4 CMLR 422).

instituted proceedings vis-à-vis Merci Convenzionali Porto di Genova SpA in an Italian court claiming, *inter alia*, an abuse of dominant position under Article 102 TFEU.

The question was referred to the European Court,[79] which found that Merci Convenzionali Porto di Genova SpA had abused its dominant position. Interestingly, although the abuse was confined within one port (the port of Genoa), the situation, according to the Court, was indeed capable of affecting trade between Member States and having an impact on the internal market.

More specifically, the ECJ emphasised that the port of Genoa is a substantial part of the common market and the abuse of dominant position was indeed capable of affecting trade between Member States because of: (i) the extent of the activity at the port of Genoa; (ii) the fact that Genoa is one of the most important ports within the Community; (iii) the fact that Genoa is the most important port in Italy; (iv) users frequently do not have a choice about using the port of Genoa because of that port's infrastructure.[80]

In light of *Merci Convenzionali Porto di Genova SpA v Siderurgica Gabrielli SpA*, it appears clear that the element of the impact of the abuse of dominant position on the internal market or a substantial part thereof and its possibility of affecting trade between Member States will easily be fulfilled whenever the abuse takes place in an important port, or a port equipped with specific infrastructures not easily available elsewhere.

4. STATE AID

State aid is a *sui generis* element of the EU competition policy regime. As the EU comprises independent Member States, "competition policy could be rendered in practice ineffective if Member States were allowed to provide financial support to national companies indiscriminately".[81]

Article 107(1) TFEU provides that any aid granted by a Member State or through State resources in any form whatsoever which distorts or threatens to distort competition by favouring certain undertakings or the production of certain goods shall, in so far as it affects trade between Member States, be incompatible with the Common Market.

The objective of State aid control, as laid down in the Treaty, is "to ensure that government interventions do not distort competition and intra-community trade. The EU Treaty does not define the concept of 'aid'. The absence of a definition has assisted the Commission and the Courts by allowing them a considerable degree of discretion. The aid may take the form of any financial support, whether in the form of capital lending, reduction in the tax levied or a shareholding or stake by a Member State in a company so as artificially to assist that company."[82] In essence, any "aid granted by a Member State or through State resources in any form whatsoever capable of distorting competition by favouring certain undertakings or the production of certain goods is, in so far as it affects trade between Member States, deemed to be incompatible with the Common Market".[83]

---

79. National courts are compelled to enforce Community law; nevertheless they cannot decide its validity and are not allowed to interpret it. In case of doubts related to the interpretation, validity or application of EU law, under TFEU, art 267, national courts can initiate preliminary ruling proceedings and refer a question to the CJEU.

80. *See Merci Convenzionali Porto di Genova SpA v Siderurgica Gabrielli SpA* [1991] ECR I-5889, [1994] 4 CMLR 422, at p. 436.

81. A Lista, *EU Competition Law and the Financial Services Sector* (Routledge 2012).

82. Ibid.

83. Ibid.

Nevertheless, Article 107(3) provides a mechanism whereby aid may be authorised under specific circumstances.[84]

In the maritime industry, State aid has been particularly controversial in the ports sector. The reason for this is that ports often receive State aid and therefore need to ensure that the support which they receive is compatible with Article 106 TFEU.

The situation is particularly delicate if considered within the context of the internal market. For instance, the port of Genoa in Italy may be in competition with the port of Southampton; if the port of Genoa were to receive some form of financial support from the Italian authorities, this competition would inevitably become unbalanced and unfair.

The problem here is that, in reality, State aid is very common in the case of ports; this is mainly due to the nature of *quasi* "public service" characterising port activities, and to the enormous financial effort necessary in order to render ports operative.

The situation is also quite complex due to the very low level of disclosure of State financial support to ports which very often deny being in receipt of any form of State aid. Overall, Article 107(3)(a) appears to be of vast application when it comes to ports located in financially depressed areas. As previously mentioned, Article 107(3)(a) provides that forms of aid aiming to promote the economic development of areas where the standard of living is abnormally low or where there is serious underemployment may be compatible with the Common Market. This provision is very important for ports located in areas of economic deprivation.

In 1999, the Commission adopted a Decision related to *the 1999 French Port Sector Scheme aiming at supporting* the French port sector.[85] The French port sector benefited from substantial public financial support particularly in relation to heavy port facilities (cranes, etc.).

The Commission considered the aim of the proposed aid scheme as to render the provision of cargo handling services more efficient and productive. A scheme notified to the Commission provided for a proposed reduction of the tax base for the French "taxe professionnelle" for the private cargo handling with a view to modernisation and more rational organisation of these services.

The Commission considered such aid compatible with EU law, provided that the aid remained confined to the fiscal year(s) when the investments in such equipment were made (and during the subsequent amortisation of the equipment until the expiry of the scheme).

The aid was also subject to the condition that the French authorities supplied the Commission with appropriate annual reports about the implementation of the aid scheme.

If the Commission was prepared to consider the State aid granted by the French Government to ports compatible with the Treaty (subject to the aforementioned conditions), the same did not

---

84. According to TFEU, art 107(3), the following may be considered to be compatible with the Common Market:

    (a) aid to promote the economic development of areas where the standard of living is abnormally low or where there is serious underemployment;

    (b) aid to promote the execution of an important project of common European interest or to remedy a serious disturbance in the economy of a Member State;

    (c) aid to facilitate the development of certain economic activities or of certain economic areas, where such aid does not adversely affect trading conditions to an extent contrary to the common interest. However, the aids granted to shipbuilding as of 1 January 1957 shall, in so far as they serve only to compensate for the absence of customs protection, be progressively reduced under the same conditions as apply to the elimination of customs duties, subject to the provisions of this Treaty concerning common commercial policy towards third countries;

    (d) aid to promote culture and heritage conservation where such aid does not affect trading conditions and competition in the Community to an extent that is contrary to the common interest;

    (e) such other categories of aid as may be specified by decision of the Council acting by a qualified majority on a proposal from the Commission.

85. Commission Decision of 30 March 1999 on State aid which France is planning to grant as development aid in the sale of two cruise vessels to be built by Chantiers de l'Atlantique and operated by Renaissance Financial in French Polynesia, OJ L 292, 13 November 1999, at pp 23–26.

happen in *Bretagne Angleterre Irlande*.[86] Here, the State aid at issue related to the package purchase of travel vouchers by the Basque authorities on the Bilbao–Portsmouth route.

The intervener, Ferries Golfo de Vizcaya, contended that the Basque authorities' undertaking
to purchase in advance certain quantities of travel vouchers to be used within a certain period was
to be considered as a commercial transaction germane to the business of shipping companies.

Even though, according to the Spanish Government, the payment to Ferries Golfo de Vizcaya
represented the *quid pro quo* for the travel vouchers purchased by the regional authorities, the
Commission took the view that the 1992 agreement incorporated elements of State aid, as the
agreed conditions of the transaction were in contrast with Article 107.

Another important decision related to State aid in the maritime sector (which this time did not
affect ports) is the one adopted by the Commission in *CalMac and NorthLink*.[87] The case concerned
the provision of regular ferry shipping services between the Scottish mainland and the islands off
the west and north coasts of Scotland. These services were mainly provided under public service
contracts with CalMac and NorthLink benefiting from compensation for their performance.

Having established that the financial support received by the aforementioned ferry operators
fell within the concept of State aid within the meaning of Article 107 TFEU, the analysis of the
Commission shifted to the assessment of whether the aid was capable of affecting trade between
Member States following the guidelines provided by the Courts of Justice in the case *Altmark*.[88]

Ultimately, the Commission found the State aid granted to CalMac and NorthLink compatible
with Article 106(2) of the Treaty, since, in its opinion, the maritime undertakings concerned by the
decision have not been "overcompensated for the provision of the public service tasks they were
entrusted with, and there was no sufficient evidence of anti-competitive behaviour that would have
artificially raised the public service costs, thereby causing an undue distortion of competition".[89]

---

86. *Bretagne Angleterre Irlande* C-T-14/96, EU:T:1999:12 [1999] ECR II-139.

87. Commission Decision of 28 October 2009 on the State aid C 16/08 (ex NN 105/05 and NN 35/07) implemented
by the United Kingdom of Great Britain and Northern Ireland – Subsidies to CalMac and NorthLink for maritime transport services in Scotland, OJ L 45/33, 18 February 2011, at pp 33–71.

88. *Altmark Trans GmbH and Regierungspräsidium Magdeburg v Nahverkehrsgesellschaft Altmark GmbH*,
C-280/00, EU:C:2003:415 [2003] ECR I-7747. In this case, the Court of Justice specified that the condition for the
application of art 92(1) of the EU Treaty (now, after amendment, TFEU, art 107(1)) that the aid must be such as to affect
trade between Member States does not depend on the local or regional character of the transport services supplied or on
the scale of the field of activity concerned. However,

> public subsidies intended to enable the operation of urban, suburban or regional scheduled transport services are not
> caught by that provision where such subsidies are to be regarded as compensation for the services provided by the
> recipient undertakings in order to discharge public service obligations. For the purpose of applying that criterion, it
> is for the national court to ascertain that the following conditions are satisfied:
>
> • first, the recipient undertaking is actually required to discharge public service obligations and those obligations
>   have been clearly defined;
> • second, the parameters on the basis of which the compensation is calculated have been established beforehand in
>   an objective and transparent manner;
> • third, the compensation does not exceed what is necessary to cover all or part of the costs incurred in discharging
>   the public service obligations, taking into account the relevant receipts and a reasonable profit for discharging
>   those obligations;
> • fourth, where the undertaking which is to discharge public service obligations is not chosen in a public procure-
>   ment procedure, the level of compensation needed has been determined on the basis of an analysis of the costs
>   which a typical undertaking, well run and adequately provided with means of transport so as to be able to meet
>   the necessary public service requirements, would have incurred in discharging those obligations, taking into
>   account the relevant receipts and a reasonable profit for discharging the obligations.

89. Commission Decision of 28 October 2009 on the State aid C 16/08 (ex NN 105/05 and NN 35/07) implemented
by the United Kingdom of Great Britain and Northern Ireland – Subsidies to CalMac and NorthLink for maritime transport services in Scotland, above, at p 42.

ANDREA LISTA

On a general level, it is crucial that ports or other maritime undertakings determine whether or not any assistance which they expect to receive, represents State aid within the meaning of Article 107. Any form of aid should in fact be notified to, and approved by, the European Commission before the aid is effectively provided.

Where a specific form of assistance qualified as State aid, then the relevant Member State is under the obligation to notify the European Commission of the proposed form of financial support. In case of public service, the scrutiny of the Commission will rotate around the proportionality and cost effectiveness of public compensation.

5. THE EU MERGER REGULATION FRAMEWORK

Council Regulation (EC) No 139/2004 (the "Merger Regulation") represents the EU mergers regulatory framework[90] whose foremost aim is to monitor and regulate mergers and concentrations having "Community dimensions"[91] capable of hindering competition in the internal market.

The two foremost concepts enshrined in the Merger Regulation are the concept of concentration and the notion of "Community dimension".

A concentration is defined as a change of control on a lasting basis resulting from: "(i) the merger of two or more previously independent undertakings, or (ii) the acquisition of one or more persons already controlling at least one undertaking, or by one or more undertakings, whether by purchase of securities or assets, by contract or by any other means, of direct or indirect control of the whole or parts of one or more other undertakings".[92]

The creation of a joint venture performing on a lasting basis all the functions of an autonomous economic entity also constitutes a concentration.[93]

The concept of "Community dimension" is delineated by worldwide and EU-wide turnover[94] of the undertakings concerned.[95]

Concentrations having Community dimensions must be notified to the Commission without delay,[96] and the Commission has the power to approve or deny a concentration. Under the

90. Council Regulation (EC) No 139/2004 of 20 January 2004 on the control of concentrations between undertakings, OJ L 24, 29 January 2004, at pp 1–22, which repealed Council Regulation (EEC) No 4064/89, the previous EU regulative framework of mergers and acquisitions.
91. See Merger Regulation, art 1.
92. Ibid., art 2.
93. Ibid., art 3.
94. Ibid., art 1. Turnover is defined by the Regulation as (art 5):

the amounts derived by the undertakings concerned in the preceding financial year from the sale of products and the provision of services falling within the undertakings' ordinary activities after deduction of sales rebates and of value added tax and other taxes directly related to turnover.

Where parts only of an undertaking are to be acquired, then only the turnover attributable to the parts being acquired will be taken into account in order to determine whether the thresholds are met. (art 5(2))
95. Concentrations are of a "Community dimension" where the merging parties' (the "undertakings concerned"):
  (i) combined world-wide turnover is superior to €5 billion and each of at least two of the merging parties realised superior to €250 million turnover in the EU, unless each of the merging parties obtains more than 2/3 of its EU turnover in one and the same Member State, or;
  (ii) combined world-wide turnover is superior to €2.5 billion; in each of at least three Member States, the combined turnover of the merging parties is superior to €100 million; in each of those three Member States, the turnover of each of at least two of the merging parties is superior to €25 million; the Community-wide turnover of each of at least two of the merging parties is superior to €100 million; unless each of the merging parties obtains more than 2/3 of its EU turnover.
96. Merger Regulation, art 7(2a).

552

Merger Regulation, the main task of the Commission is in fact to assess the eventual creation or enhancement of a dominant position within the internal market.[97]

The criteria by virtue of which the Commission approves or prohibits a concentration are laid down by Article 2 of the Merger Regulation, and are basically structured on the basis of Article 102. Adopting the phraseology of Article 102, the Regulation prohibits a concentration in case it "would significantly impede effective competition, in the common market or in a substantial part of it, in particular as a result of the creation or strengthening of a dominant position".[98]

In assessing the impact of the concentration on the market, the Commission may also consider the market position of the undertakings concerned and their economic and financial power, the alternatives available to suppliers and users, their access to supplies or markets, any legal or other barriers to entry, supply and demand trends for the relevant goods and services, the interests of the intermediate and ultimate consumers, and the development of technical and economic progress provided that it is to consumers' advantage and does not form an obstacle to competition.[99]

The assessment of the creation or extension of a dominant position in the shipping trade is the result of a complex economic analysis which takes into consideration three elements as outlined in the following.

The first element to be considered is the geographical dimension of the market (relevant geographical market); secondly, the product dimension of the market (relevant product market) is taken into consideration; finally, the market shares of the undertakings concerned is the last factor analysed. When it comes to the shipping industry, these elements have been characterised by the Commission through a series of decisions analysed below.

The first important merger in the shipping sector was the creation of the P&O/Nedlloyd Container Line Ltd.[100] Through this merger, the UK Peninsular and Oriental Steam Navigation Co. ("P&O") and the Dutch Royal Nedlloyd NV ("Nedlloyd") acquired joint control of P&O Nedlloyd Container Line Ltd ("P&O Nedlloyd").

P&O engaged in a wide range of maritime activities (including passenger and cargo shipping, and integrated transportation and warehousing), whereas Nedlloyd was an international logistics services company specialised in container logistics. The activities of both P&O and Nedlloyd included ocean container shipping and related landside activities.

The Commission defined the relevant geographic market as a service supplied between a range of ports on either the northern European or the Mediterranean coast and a range of ports in another continent or region.

Interestingly, the Commission emphasised that, on a general level, transport to and from northern Europe constitutes a relevant service market for liner shipping services. However, P&O and Nedlloyd contended that in certain trades the geographical scope of the liner shipping service was indistinguishable between northern Europe and the Mediterranean, due to improved land transport links with the rest of the continent. The Commission rejected this claim, indicating that "the possibility of inland transport or maritime transhipment between northern Europe and the

---

97. The assessment of concentrations having a Community dimension is the exclusive competence of the Commission. Nevertheless, the Commission may by means of a decision refer a notified concentration to the competent authorities of the Member State concerned in case

    (a) a concentration threatens to affect significantly competition in a market within that Member State, which presents all the characteristics of a distinct market; or

    (b) a concentration affects competition in a market within that Member State, which presents all the characteristics of a distinct market and which does not constitute a substantial part of the common market. See Merger Regulation, art 9(2).

98. See Merger Regulation, art 2(3).

99. Ibid., art 2(1).

100. Case No IV/M.831, *P&O/Nedlloyd*, 19 December 1996.

Mediterranean did not lead to facility of substitution to any considerable extent".[101] According to the Commission, this distinction is reinforced by, for example, northern European ports, such as Antwerp, being cheaper to use than their Mediterranean counterparts, for example, La Spezia. Furthermore, the Commission specified that there is "only limited substitution between ports in these regions and it can therefore be concluded that northern Europe and the Mediterranean do not belong to the same relevant market".[102]

This definition of the relevant geographical market for liner shipping services was reiterated by the Commission in *Maersk/Safmarine*,[103] *Taca*[104] and, in the largest ever merger in the liner shipping sector, *Maersk/Sea-Land*,[105] where the Commission found that container shipping to and from northern Europe constitutes a distinct market from transport to and from the Mediterranean.

As for the relevant product market, the Commission in *P&O/Nedlloyd* emphasised that "non-liner shipping services, either in the form of chartering the whole or part of vessels by individual customers, 'tramp' operations, being unscheduled sea transport, and specialised transport, i.e. ships developed for transporting specific goods, do not compete with liner shipping services".[106]

Liner shipping services, according to the Commission, may be distinguished from these other modes of transport in three ways:

first, customers demand scheduled transport in order to meet production runs and delivery deadlines. Second, the vast majority of customers require flexibility in available space – something unavailable when whole or parts of ships are to be chartered. Finally, specialised transport constitutes a reasonable alternative only for a few shippers who have large quantities of only a few categories of goods to transport for which such ships have to be available.[107]

Nevertheless, in its decision in *Maersk/Ponl*,[108] the Commission has considered transport for refrigerated goods a possibly narrower product market in the market for containerised liner shipping services. This consideration is based on the fact that the transport of refrigerated goods could be limited to reefer (refrigerated) containers only or could include transport in conventional reefer (refrigerated) vessels. Moreover, according to the Commission, "from a demand-side perspective, certain goods such as fruit, meat and dairy products must be shipped under refrigerated conditions. For this reason, non-reefer containers are not considered as a substitute for reefer containers".[109]

Finally, in relation to the concrete evaluation of the impact of mergers on the shipping market, the assessment of the Commission in this final stage aims at identifying possible concentrations having Community dimensions, and leading to the eventual creation or enhancement of a dominant position within the internal market. In order to perform this delicate test, the Commission has carefully evaluated the possible co-ordinated effects and synergies in shipping markets where the merging shipping undertakings were parties to co-operative arrangements such as liner conferences, consortia or pools.

Under such circumstances, the analysis of the Commission focuses on the possible synergies between competitors arising as a consequence of a possible merger, which may increase the risk of co-ordinated or parallel behaviours.

In relation to past case law, in *Maersk/Safmarine*[110] the Commission has considered, for instance, whether the parties' increased vertical integration in the liner shipping services,

101. Ibid., [7].
102. Ibid.
103. Case No IV/M.1474, *Maersk/Safmarine*.
104. Case No IV/35.134, *Taca*.
105. Case No IV/M.165, *Maersk/Sea-Land*.
106. Case No IV/M.831, *P&O/Nedlloyd*, above [7].
107. Ibid.
108. Case No Comp/M.3829 – *Maersk/Ponl*, decision of 29 July 2005.
109. Ibid., [9].
110. See fn 103.

resulting from the combination of their respective terminal operations, could strengthen their position in the container shipping market. Similarly, in *Maersk/Ponl*[111] the Commission analysed the effects that the merger between Maersk and Ponl might have on conferences and consortia depending on the parties' membership.

The Commission identified two general scenarios that may give rise to concern: the first scenario arose in cases where the merging parties were currently in the same conference or consortium and remained members after the merger. Depending on the structure of the conference or consortium (see below), however, this could lead to a strengthening of the internal cohesion and eventually lead to the merged entity controlling the conference.

The second scenario arose since in some instances, Maersk was in a conference or consortium, but Ponl was not, even though it was active in the same trade. This link would enable Maersk to take part in the exchange of information within the conference and/or the consortium.[112]

Based on the above considerations, the Commission carried out its analysis of co-ordinated effects in as many as 22 different trades.

The decision in *Maersk/Ponl* clearly shows that the assessment of mergers and acquisitions in the shipping sector is subject to intense and very strict scrutiny by the Commission.[113]

(a) Recent mergers decisions in the EU maritime sector

In recent years, a series of mergers in the EU maritime sector have been allowed by the Commission.

On 22 May 2015, the European Commission received notification of a proposed concentration by which the undertaking CMA CGM SA ("CMA CGM", France controlled by Merit Corporation (Lebanon), Yildirim holding (Turkey) and Caisse des Dépôts et Consignations (France)) intended to acquire control of the whole of the undertaking Oldenburg-Portugiesische Dampfschiffs-Rhederei ("OPDR", Germany, controlled by Bernhard Schulte GmbH & Co KG (Germany) by way of purchase of shares).[114]

The transaction was referred to the Commission under Article 4(5) of the Merger Regulation and was therefore deemed to have an EU dimension. The transaction originally exceeded the filing thresholds in Germany, Austria, Portugal, Spain and Cyprus.[115]

In terms of market identification, the claim of the parties involved in the merger was that their activities mainly overlapped on the markets for intra-European door-to-door transport, although they also provided stand-alone short-sea container shipping. Further, vertical relationships were also in place between their shipping and transport activity and CMA CGM's activity as a provider of freight forwarding services and a terminal services operator.[116]

Although the parties were very active in the Ro-Ro shipping market, their submission pointed out no areas of overlap.

---

111. See fn 108.

112. The Commission pointed out that "Maersk could use the commercially sensitive information exchanged therein to adapt over time its conduct in the market, thus increasing the risk of market sharing or lessening of competition between itself and the other members of the conference or the consortium. Even without integrating itself into the conference or the consortium, Maersk would no longer be an independent competitor because it controlled a member of the conference or the consortium" (see Case No Comp/M.3829 – *Maersk/Ponl*, above, [36].)

113. A similar level of analysis aiming at identifying possible concentrations having Community dimensions and leading to the eventual creation or enhancement of a dominant position within the internal market, does not emerge in Commission decisions related to different sectors, e.g. the insurance market.

114. Case M.7523 – CMA CGM/ OPDR, Commission decision pursuant to Article 6(1)(b) of Council Regulation No 139/20041 and Article 57 of the Agreement on the European Economic Area.

115. Ibid., [8].

116. Ibid., [20].

In considering the relevant market, the Commission defined the door-to-door transport as "services consisting in taking up cargo at an agreed point and delivering it to another agreed point. Customers decide where the point of loading and point of delivery are situated and transport services providers adapt to this".[117] Since the cargo is containerised, it can travel on vessels, trucks, trains and barges. The claim of CMA CGM was that customers take three factors into account when selecting a supplier for their transport needs:

frequency of departures, transit time and price. While short sea shipping is usually the cheapest mode, trucks are faster and often offer a higher frequency of departures, which often makes it a preferable choice for perishable goods. Transport by train and barges usually needs to be complemented by trucking in order to offer a door-to-door transport service, and barges play a role only in certain areas of Europe.[118]

Despite the aforementioned differentiating elements, CMA CGM's submission was that, from a customer's perspective, in-land and sea transport are substitutable or interchangeable with one another, and that, as a consequence, the relevant product market was the market for door-to-door multi-modal transport services.[119]

Up until the decision in CMA CGM/ OPDR, the Commission has never defined the door-to-door transport market and left open whether short-sea container shipping services compete with other forms of transport.[120] The Commission has, however, accepted a market for unitised transport in which maritime services compete with other modes used for door-to-door services in antitrust cases.[121]

Considering that containerised cargo can easily be transported on trucks, the Commission noted that there seems to be a high degree of substitutability between sea transport and truck transport. In its words, within the intra-European market, "customers who would consider maritime transportation can often also opt for transport by truck. Likewise, sea transport may often be an option for customers of truck transportation services (depending on their needs in terms of frequency and flexibility)".[122]

117. Ibid., [24].
118. Ibid.
119. Ibid. As we established in the above, the concept of 'interchangeability' lies at the core of the identification of the relevant product market, a key factor in the ascertainment of a possible position of dominance.
120. See M.1651 – Maersk/Sea-Land, recital 9;, and M.5756 – DFDS/Norfolk, recital 12.
121. See Case M.7523 – *CMA CGM/ OPDR*, [26]. See also Case IV/36.253 – *P&O Stena Line* of 26 January 1999 – recitals 20 (b) and 38.
122. See Case M.7523 – *CMA CGM/ OPDR*, [26]. Nevertheless, the analysis of the Commission did find some differentiating elements within the context of door-to-door transport services (see Case M.7523 – *CMA CGM/ OPDR*, [29]–[30], where it is stated that:

> As concerns the different modes of transport, some differences exist. While trucks can reach any given point accessible by road (or potentially by means of ferry), i.e. virtually any loading and delivery point chosen by the customer, rail or ship carriers need to arrange for the first/last mile to be performed by trucks if the point of origin or destination is not accessible by ship or train. Ship and train operators do this either by subcontracting the first/last mile of the journey to a truck company or by internalising these operations (i.e. by operating their own trucks). Similarly, truck operators may need to subcontract with vessel operators in order to reach areas in the UK, Morocco, etc. Moreover, trucks may offer greater flexibility than ships or trains because they are independent of fixed schedules and can reach any point connected by road. The market investigation also showed, however, that transport by truck can be substantially more expensive than transport by ship or rail. Price as well as frequency and travel duration may therefore be the main differentiating criteria from a customer's perspective between door-to-door services by a truck operator or door-to-door service by a train/ship operator (if both are available for a given route).

From a demand-side perspective, it might therefore not matter so much how exactly the transport of the freight is being carried out, as long as the customers' needs in terms of price, frequency, capacity and transport duration are met. Not all customers are completely indifferent as to the mode of transport used, because they may be price sensitive, want to reduce their carbon footprint or need a high degree of flexibility. However, there appears to still be a large number of customers, for which all operators, irrespective of the mode of transport employed, are an alternative option.

All that considered, the conclusion reached by the Commission in terms of relevant market of door-to-door services was that there is a market for door-to-door transport services, including all modes of transportation, "as transport operators often need to combine different modes of transport in order to provide a full door-to-door service, it appears that sea vessel operators, truck, rail and barge companies offering door-to-door transport ultimately compete on the provision of multimodal transport services".[123]

Alongside the door-to-door transport sector, the merger in CMA CGM/ OPDR also involved the market for short-sea container shipping.

Here, despite the claim of the parties involved in the merger that the short-sea container shipping was only marginally touched upon by the prospective merger, the Commission claimed that the short-sea container shipping represented a separate market to be separately considered for the purpose of the identification of a possible conglomerate.

Indeed, the Commission pointed out that, in its decisional practice, cases involving short-sea container shipping, can potentially be distinguished, for the purpose of the identification of the relevant market: (a) from deep sea container shipping (i.e. deep sea shipping); (b) from bulk shipping (i.e. non-containerised shipping); and (c) from Ro-Ro shipping.[124]

Further possible differentiations can be made between liner (scheduled services) and charter, tramp or specialised transport services (ad hoc services), as well as reefer and non-reefer services (i.e. refrigerated or not). According to the Commission's case practice, in trades with a share of reefer containers in relation to all containerised cargo below 10 per cent in both directions, transport in reefer containers is not assessed separately, but as part of the overall market for container liner shipping services.[125]

The conclusions of the Commission were that there may still be a "separate short-sea container shipping services market independent from an all-encompassing door-to-door transport services market".[126] Indeed, some customers may wish to utilise short-shipping services due to their cheaper nature and lower carbon footprint.

In terms of geographic market for container shipping services, in the past the Commission distinguished single trades, and defined them by the range of ports served at both ends of the service.[127] In case M.7268 – *CSAV/Hapag Lloyd*,[128] a case related to deep sea container shipping, the Commission further differentiated between the "legs of each trade", defined as "one of the two directions of a trade (e.g. on the trade connecting Northern Europe to North America and back, Northern Europe–North America is the first leg and North America–Northern Europe is the second leg)".[129] Given that the market conditions on the two directions of a trade can be significantly different, in particular in the case of "trade imbalances or different characteristics of the products shipped",[130] the Commission reached the conclusion that each leg represents a separate market.

---

123. See Case M.7523 – *CMA CGM/ OPDR*, above, [31].
124. Ibid., [40]. See, e.g., cases M.3829 – *Maersk/ PONL*, recital 7; M.3973 – *CMA CGM/Delmas*, recital 6; M.5398 – Hutchison/Evergreen, recital 12; M.5756 – DFDS/NORFOLK, recital 11 and following; M.6305 – DFDS/ C.RO Ports/Älvsborg, recital 19; M.7268 – *CSAV/ HGV/ Kühne Maritime/ Hapag-Llyod AG*, recitals 15 and following.
125. See Case M.7523 – *CMA CGM/ OPDR*, [40]. The Commission points out that in trades with a share of reefer containers below 10 per cent of total capacity, vessels have in general more reefer facilities than actually used. Shipping companies will therefore be able to shift volume from transport of warm containers to transport of reefer containers in the short term and without significant additional costs; M.3829 – Maersk/PONL, recital 10; M.3863 – *TUI/CP Ships*, recital 8; M.3973 – *CMA CGM/Delmas*, recital 7.
126. See Case M.7523 – *CMA CGM/ OPDR*, [47].
127. Ibid., [53]. See M.3973 – *CMA CGM/Delmas*, recital 8; M.6278 – *Kühne/HGV/TUI/Hapag-Lloyd*, recital 22.
128. See M.7268 – *CSAV / HGV / Kühne Maritime / Hapag-Lloyd AG*.
129. See Case M.7523 – *CMA CGM/ OPDR*, [54].
130. Ibid.

After analysing the various market components involved in the prospective merger, the Commission reached the conclusion that the transaction did not raise competition concerns within the context of intra-European door-to-door multimodal transport services, despite the high combined market shares of the parties involved (60 per cent), due to the varied nature of this kind of transport services.

The same conclusions were reached in relation to the market for short sea container shipping. Furthermore, despite the presence of high combined market shares (60/70 per cent), the Commission did not find any actual or potential danger in terms of competition within the internal market, due to the presence of low barriers to entry, the imminent entrance of new players into the market, and the existence of road services as valid alternative means of transportation.

The decision in *CMA CGM/ OPDR* is of great interest. In the first place, it epitomises the difficulties in assessing competition within a complex, differentiated and segmented market, such as the multimodal transport sector, and its container shipping branches.

Secondly, it is important to emphasise that the approach of the Commission in terms of assessment of combined market shares within these sectors has proven to be quite lenient; indeed, combined market shares of 60/70 per cent (such as the ones identified by the Commission), are normally likely to give rise to serious competition concerns.

The discerning elements which here ultimately lead to leniency appear to be represented by the low barriers to market entry, in conjunction with alternatives such as road transport.

Another significant merger decision is the one issued in the case *DFDS/ C.RO Ports/ Älvsborg*.[131] Here, the proposed merger regarded DFDS (a Danish undertaking involved in roll-on/roll-off and container shipping, terminal services in Norway, Denmark, the United Kingdom, France and the Netherlands) and, C.RO Ports and Alvsborg (two providers of Ro-Ro terminal services).[132]

The transaction was found to have a Community dimension, as the parties' combined aggregate turnover was more than EUR 100 million.[133] The Commission identified the market for Ro-Ro services as the relevant market for the purpose of the competition assessment. Indeed, the decision observes that "Ro-Ro vessels require different terminal infrastructure from other types of vessels such as Lift-on/Lift-off ("Lo-Lo") vessels or vessels carrying bulk freight."[134]

The competitive assessment of the merger in this case raised doubts in terms of the vertical links between Älvsborg and DFDS and CLdN. More specifically, concerns arose in respect of DFDS' and C.RO Ports' ability and incentive, through Älvsborg, to "foreclose rival short-sea Ro-Ro shipping companies from providing shipping services to customers on the Sweden–UK and Sweden–Belgium/Northern France corridors by foreclosing access to Älvsborg".[135]

The Commission concluded that even on the basis of the narrowest possible market definitions, i.e. "the markets for (i) short-sea Ro-Ro terminal services to pure Ro-Ro vessels in Gothenburg; (ii) Ro-Ro freight shipping services from Sweden to the UK; and (iii) Ro-Ro freight

---

131. Case No COMP/M.6305 – *DFDS/ C.RO Ports/ Älvsborg,* Commission decision pursuant to art 6(1)(b) of Council Regulation No 139/2004.

132. C.RO Ports provides Ro-Ro terminal services in the United Kingdom, Belgium and the Netherlands, whereas Älvsborg provides Ro-Ro terminal services at the Port of Gothenburg in Sweden.

133. Pursuant to art 1(3) of the Merger Regulation, Council Regulation (EC) No 139/2004 of 20 January 2004 on the control of concentrations between undertakings (the EC Merger Regulation) (Text with EEA relevance) OJ L 24, 29.1.2004.

134. Case No COMP/M.6305 – *DFDS/ C.RO Ports/ Älvsborg,* [12]. Any further attempt to narrow down the Ro-Ro services market was considered futile by the Commission since "the conclusion on whether or not a distinction should be made between terminal services depending on the vessel type or between deep-sea and short-sea services can however be left open for the purposes of this decision as no competition concerns arise even under the narrowest market definition of short-sea terminal services to pure Ro-Ro vessels" ([14]).

135. Ibid., [34].

shipping services from Sweden to Belgium/Northern France",[136] the transaction did not give rise to serious competition concerns.

According to the Commission, even if it were the case that DFDS and C.RO Ports could prevent competitors from having access to Älvborg, or render the terms and conditions on which access would be granted less attractive to competitors, DFDS and C.RO Ports "would not have the ability to foreclose competitors from the relevant downstream markets since the recent entry by North Sea Ro-Ro on the Gothenburg – UK route from the neighbouring Logent Car Terminal shows that Älvsborg is not an essential facility and alternative terminals exist even within the Gothenburg harbour".[137]

In essence, due to the alternatives present, the transaction did not amount to a concentration of market power within the context of an "essential facility". As established in the above, the concept of "essential facility' entails the existence of an essential infrastructure with which undertakings operating in a specific sector need to engage in order to provide their services.[138]

In the presence of an essential facility, mergers and concentrations of market powers are very carefully scrutinised, so as to ensure that the merger does not have adverse effects vis-à-vis third parties wishing to have access to the market.

Within the context of the maritime industry, it is therefore extremely important to assess whether there is the infrastructure in place in terms of ports, cargo transportation etc. which could amount to essential facilities; under those circumstances, mergers and potential anticompetitive behaviours are much more likely to be held incompatible with the internal market.

Another important recent merger in the field of container shipping services is represented by the case *CSAV/ HGV/ KÜHNE MARITIME/ HAPAG-LLOYD AG*.[139] Here, four major container shipping services operators were allowed by the Commission to merge their services subject to specific conditions enshrined in the decision.

The relevant market was identified as the market for container liner shipping, which was distinguished from non-liner shipping (tramp, specialised transport) because of "regularity and frequency of the service".[140] In addition, the use of container transportation was considered to be differentiated from other non-containerised transport (bulk, vessel).[141]

The consideration of the *ex post* transaction market lead the Commission to the conclusion that effective competition in the sector could be retained due to the presence of Maersk, the market leader independent of the parties and the parties' consortia, as well as two other consortia (i.e. CKYH, now CKYHE and MSC SCI120).

Nevertheless, differently from the cases considered above, the merger in this case was not a "no-strings attached' affair.

Indeed, the Commission subjected the clearance of the merger under scrutiny to two main conditions, namely that: a) the parties involved will not, within five years from the Effective Date, "become a member of any consortia to which MSC Mediterranean Shipping Company SA (MSC) is a member on a Relevant Trade",[142] and: b) that the Parties will not become a member of "any consortia to which AP Moller-Maersk Group (Maersk) is a member on a Relevant Trade

---

136. Ibid.
137. Case No *COMP/M.6305 – DFDS/ C.RO Ports/ Älvsborg*, [42]. Indeed, the Commission found that a free Ro-Ro berth was actually available at one of the terminals in Gothenburg.
138. For an analysis of the concept of 'essential facility' under EU law, please see S.J. Evrard, "Essential Facility in the Eurooean Union: Bronner and Beyond" (2014) 10 Colum. J Eur. L. 491.
139. Case M.7268 – *CSAV/ HGV/ KÜHNE MARITIME/ HAPAG-LLOYD AG* Commission decision pursuant to art 6(1)(b) in conjunction with art 6(2) of Council Regulation No 139/2004, OJ L 24, 29.1.2004, p. 1.
140. Ibid., [16].
141. A possible narrower product market is, according to the Commission, "that for the transport of refrigerated goods, which could be limited to reefer containers only or could also include transport in conventional reefer vessels" (ibid., [17]).
142. Ibid., at Section C of the Commitments Addendum.

before the earlier of 1 January 2017 or the date on which the widening of the Panama Canal is completed".[143]

A similar fate occurred in the merger between *CMA CGM/NOL*,[144] which was also conditional on specific commitments superimposed vis-à-vis the parties involved in the transaction.

The merger concerned the market for deep-sea container liner shipping services, which involved consortia in terms of joint co-operation between the undertakings involved.

The counter-factual analysis undertaken by the Commission lead to the conclusion that in the post-transaction reality, the combined entity would therefore

(i) have the ability to influence decisions regarding the level and the allocation of capacity, (ii) participate in the setting of ports of call and schedules, and (iii) have access to information on capacity for a broader range of consortia and competitors than CMA, CGM, and NOL had individually before the mergers took place, with specific reference to the G6 consortium agreement which included APL (a NOL affiliated undertaking), Hapag-Lloyd Aktiengesellschaft ("HL"), Hyundai Merchant Marine Co Ltd ("HMM"), Mitsui OSK Lines, Ltd ("MOL"); Nippon Yusen Kaisha ("NYK"); and Orient Overseas Container Line Limited ("OOCL").[145]

As a result, the proposed merger raised serious concerns about its compatibility with the internal market, and was subject to specific commitments to be undertaken by the parties involved. The foremost commitments were APL's withdrawal from the G6 consortium, alongside the undertaking by the parties that they will not, "within [confidential business secret] years from the date on which APL's withdrawal from G6 takes effect, re-join any substantially similar form of the [confidential business secret] G6 Alliance on the relevant trades with the G6 Signatories as a group".[146]

The most recent clearance of a merger in the maritime industry is the container shipping merger between Hapag-Lloyd and United Arab Shipping Company ("UASC").[147]

The European Commission has decided to clear, under the EU Merger Regulation, the proposed acquisition of UASC by Hapag-Lloyd of Germany, both undertakings operating within the container liner shipping industry.

As with the decision in *CMA CGM/NOL*, competition concerns arose in relation to the fact that both UASC and Hapag-Lloyd were party to already existing liner shipping consortia with other maritime undertakings.

The clearance was therefore made conditional upon "the withdrawal of UASC from a consortium on the trade routes between Northern Europe and North America, where the merged entity would have faced insufficient competitive constraint".[148]

This recent trend of mergers in the maritime sector has generated a certain level of consolidation at EU level. It is worth noticing that, compared to the past, the Commission was prepared to allow mergers even in the presence of high market shares. This is linked, in legal teleological terms, with the fragmentation of the relevant market allowed by the Commission in light of the cross-elasticities between different types of transport with specific reference to the multimodal transport market.

---

143. Ibid.
144. Case M.7908 – CMA CGM/NOL,Commission decision pursuant to art 6(1)(b) in conjunction with art 6(2) of Council Regulation No 139/20041 and art 57 of the Agreement on the European Economic Area, 29.04.2016.
145. Ibid., [65].
146. Ibid., [4] of the Commitments Addendum.
147. Hapag-Lloyd and UASC, n.y.r., as per EU Commission Press Release, Brussels, 23 November 2016 IP/16/3942.
148. Ibid.

The international dimension of the maritime sector, alongside the high level of interchangeability with roadside transport within the internal market can indeed lead to a very narrow interpretation of the relevant product market in maritime transport.

The situation can become even more complex if one considers that maritime undertakings involved in mergers may carry out different types of services, leading to further ramifications in terms of relevant product market.

In order to counter-balance the narrow dimension of the relevant product market, as established above, the Commission has carefully scrutinised the post-merger implications of possible conglomerates in terms of synergies with third parties, and possible further alliances, subjecting mergers to specific conditions.

Will that suffice in order to avoid consolidation and mitigate possible adverse effects vis-à-vis competition in the maritime industry? *Posteritas iudicet.*

6. CONCLUDING REMARKS

This chapter has emphasised the need for the shipping industry to comply with EU competition law. As we have seen, the four areas of the EU anti-trust regulatory framework (i.e. Articles 101–102, Article 107, and the Merger Regulation) currently find full application to the maritime industry.

(a) Compliance with Article 101

Article 101 prohibits any collusive behaviour between shipping companies whose aim or effect is the restriction, prevention or distortion of the competition in the maritime industry.

Since October 2008 (the end of the transitional period of Regulation 1419/2006), liner conferences and shipping pools (either in the classic form of administration-controlled pools managed by a separate company, or member-controlled pools under the operational management of one or more members of the pool) capable of affecting trade between Member States are prohibited, void and unenforceable in respect of their restrictions.

This means that liner conference agreements between carriers related to the operation of scheduled maritime transport services, whose object or effect is to fix the rates and conditions of carriage, will fall within the meaning of Article 101.

In the tramp shipping and cabotage sectors, the impact of the application of Article 101 affects pools or other forms of co-operation between actual or potential competitors involving the direct or indirect determination of rates, limitations on output, the sharing of markets or customers, information exchange and any other anti-competitive practices.

In the light of their characteristics, liner conferences (subject to the transitional period), tramp shipping or cabotage pools *prima facie* represent a blatant price-fixing practice capable of limiting output and considerably restricting competition. In practice, the starting point for the assessment of their legality is represented by their impact (actual or potential) on competition. If the impact on competition is minimal and remains confined within the limits as per the Commission's *De Minimis* notice (10 per cent of the market share in the case of horizontal agreements, 15 per cent for vertical agreements), pools will be automatically allowed in so far as they do not involve price-fixing, output limitation or forms of sharing of markets or customers.

While the theory is clear, it is often uncertain where the line must be drawn in practice as liner conferences, tramp shipping or cabotage pools always involve elements capable of limiting output and hindering competition.

The best option is therefore an individual exemption under Article 101(3). First, we have seen that under this article, maritime pools might obtain an individual ad hoc exemption, in so far as their agreements satisfy the four conditions listed by Article 101(3). Such agreements will need therefore first to create efficiencies (in terms of improving the provision of the service or promoting economic or technical progress). Second, consumers must be allowed to share the benefits of those efficiencies. Third, the agreements should not contain restrictions on competition beyond the strictly indispensable restraints. Finally, they must not eliminate competition altogether. If the above conditions are fulfilled, shipping pools may benefit from an individual exemption to be automatically granted by national courts and competition authorities.

It has been emphasised that the burden of proof in support of the exemption claim for shipping pools lies on the party involved, who will need to support its claim with strong evidence in order to overcome the incompatibility with Article 101. For instance, proving that shipping pools increase the efficiencies of the service is not enough to obtain an exemption, if consumers will not share some of the benefits, or the conditions of the pools go beyond what can be considered as strictly indispensable restrictions.

Scrutiny is very strict and will take into account *inter alia*, the impact of such agreements on the shipping market, prices, costs, quality, frequency and differentiation of the service provided, in conjunction with innovation, marketing and commercialisation of the service.

A good starting argument in support of the claim for an exemption could be the provision of unquestionable evidence of the creation of remarkable efficiencies in conjunction with a considerable decrease of the costs of the services.

Consequently, pool membership rules such as the prohibition on operating vessels outside the pool, or long notice requirements in case of withdrawal of vessels from the pool, will be very difficult to justify as they do not seem to give rise to any evident benefit for consumers.

(b) Compliance with Article 102

The application of Article 102 has been particularly relevant in the context of ports.

Article 102 is triggered only in the presence of an abuse of dominant position capable of affecting trade between Member States. This abuse of dominance needs to be identified within the context of a market considered in its geographical and product dimensions.

In the maritime sector the geographical market may involve, for instance, a single port or a cluster of ports, or a service between two ports or two countries. Most importantly, the geographical market can indeed be a limited market, especially in case of passenger car ferry services where passengers are usually inclined to choose short sea journeys. This element can, in practice, be of crucial importance as the narrower the geographical market, the higher the possibilities that a maritime undertaking occupies a dominant position.

The identification of the relevant product market is another essential element in order to assess the dominance of a maritime undertaking. The relevant product market is focused on the concept of interchangeability or substitutability of services. The more services are interchangeable, the more likely it is that they belong to the same relevant product market.

On a general level, there is a difference in terms of product market definition in cases relating to *passenger* traffic as opposed to *commercial/cargo* traffic. In case a port provides its services in several different product markets (e.g. the passenger liner trade, the oil tanker trade and the passenger car ferry trade), each service will represent a different product market, as for instance the oil tanker trade is not interchangeable with the passenger car ferry trade.

This identification of the relevant product market can be more complicated in the case of shipping companies operating car and passenger carriers, due to the high level of interchangeability characterising car and passenger vessels.

As for the assessment of dominance, in the absence of exceptional circumstances extremely large market shares (between 70 and 80 per cent) are in themselves evidence of the existence of a dominant position. Lower market shares (60 per cent on the trade in question) are capable of giving rise to a strong presumption of a dominant position.

The maritime undertaking in a dominant position may not discriminate in favour of its own activities in a related market. In particular, the owner of an essential facility (e.g. a port without access to which competitors cannot provide services to their customers), which uses its power in one market in order to strengthen its position in another related market, in particular, by granting its competitor access to that related market on less favourable terms than those of its own services, infringes Article 102 where a competitive disadvantage is imposed upon its competitor without objective justification.

Finally, although an abuse remains confined within one port, the situation is still capable of affecting trade between Member States and having an impact on the internal market if the port in question operates on a large scale and it is equipped with specific infrastructures not readily available elsewhere.

(c) State aid

In the maritime industry, State aid prevents ports from receiving financial support by Member States. As previously mentioned, Article 107(3)(a) provides that forms of aid aiming to promote the economic development of areas where the standard of living is abnormally low or where there is serious underemployment may be compatible with the Common Market. This provision is very important for ports located in areas of economic deprivation.

On a general level, it is crucial that ports determine whether or not any assistance which they expect to receive, represents State aid within the meaning of Article 107 TFEU (with the exemption as per Article 107(3)(a) above, any form of direct or indirect financial subsidy qualifies as State aid).

Where a specific form of assistance qualifies as State aid, then the relevant Member State is under the obligation to notify the European Commission of the proposed form of financial support.

(d) Merger regulation of the shipping industry

As previously mentioned, the EU mergers regulatory framework fully applies to the maritime industry, and aims at avoiding the creation or extension of a dominant position capable of affecting competition within the shipping sector in the internal market.

The assessment of the creation or extension of a dominant position in the shipping industry is the result of an economic analysis considering three elements: the geographical dimension of the market (relevant geographic market), the product dimension of the market and, finally, the market shares of the undertakings concerned.

The geographical dimension of shipping mergers has been considered by the Commission with a rather narrow approach. For instance, in the liner shipping services due to the limited substitution between ports in northern Europe and the Mediterranean, transport to and from northern Europe is deemed to represent the relevant geographical market. Yet again, this is a crucial aspect to be taken into account by shipping undertakings planning a merger, as the narrower the geographic dimension of the merger, the higher the possibilities that the merger will be considered capable of hindering competition.

As for the relevant product market, non-liner shipping services, either in the form of chartering the whole or part of vessels by individual customers, "tramp" operations, being unscheduled sea transport, and specialised transport do not compete with liner shipping services. Non-liner shipping services and liner shipping services therefore represents two separate product markets (within the market for containerised liner shipping services, transport for refrigerated goods can represent a possible narrower product market).

Finally, in relation to the concrete evaluation of the impact of mergers in the shipping market, the assessment of the merger aims at identifying possible concentrations having Community dimensions and leading to the eventual creation or enhancement of a dominant position within the internal market. In order to evaluate shipping mergers, the Commission will consider not only the merger itself, but also the possible synergies between competitors arising as a consequence of a merger, which may increase the risk of co-ordinated or parallel behaviours.

The analysis of co-ordinated effects is subject to intense and very strict scrutiny by the Commission especially in shipping markets where the merging shipping undertakings are parties to co-operative arrangements such as liner conferences, consortia or pools. In such cases, the concentration would not change the total market share of the conference or consortium. Nevertheless, in conjunction with the structure of the conference or consortium, this could lead to a strengthening of the internal cohesion and eventually lead to the merged entity controlling the conference.

Shipping companies operating in consortia or pools need therefore to evaluate any possible side effects post-merger carefully if they intend to avoid the censure of the Commission. Maritime undertakings operating individually may also be subject to an intense scrutiny in relation to the creation of possible synergies, co-ordinated or parallel behaviours arising as a result of a merger.

However, for many years Regulation 4056/86 EU used to lay down an automatic open-ended block exemption for liner conferences (i.e. associations of shipowners operating the transport of cargo, chiefly by container on the same route, served by a secretariat) and for agreements between transport users and the latter concerning the use of the conference services. As from 18 October 2008, this scenario radically changed leaving the liner shipping sector exposed to the application of Article 101 TFEU directly under the European Commission's jurisdiction. This means that since October 2008 (the end of the transitional period of Regulation 1419/2006), agreements between carriers having the object or effect of preventing, restricting or distorting the competition and capable of affecting trade between Member States are prohibited, void and unenforceable in respect of their restrictions.

Shipping pools (either in the classic form of administration-controlled pools managed by a separate company, or member-controlled pools under the operational management of one or more members of the pool) are from then on unlawful, and agreements between carriers related to the operation of scheduled maritime transport services whose object or effect is to fix the rates and conditions of carriage, fall within the meaning of Article 101.

On a general level, examples of agreements which are caught by Article 101 are, *inter alia*, agreements fixing purchase/selling prices or other trading conditions, agreements limiting or controlling production, markets, technical development or investment, market sharing agreements, agreements on information sharing of sensitive information, e.g. pricing, capacity, joint purchasing/selling agreements.

Consequently, any EU or non-EU carrier currently a member of liner conferences operating on trade routes to or from EU ports, which continue to fix prices and regulate capacity on those routes are, since October 2008, subject to substantial fines being imposed on the parties to the agreement if discovered by the European Commission.

Without the shield of protection offered by the block exemption, shipping pools will be considered as forms of price-fixing practices having as their object and effect the co-ordination of their capacity and customers sharing, in light of the restriction of each member's commercial freedom to freely operate in the shipping market in a competitive manner. All this is clearly against Article 101.

Where does this new scenario leave shipping pools then? It has been established that the only possibility for their survival would be through an individual exemption under Article 101(3). The repeal of the block exemption granted by Regulation 4056/86, in fact, does not preclude the possibility of an individual exemption. A block exemption is merely an exemption granted on a large scale to specific kinds of agreement. In its absence, maritime undertakings are still in the position to obtain an individual ad hoc exemption, in so far as they are in the position to prove that their agreements satisfy the four conditions listed by Article 101(3). Such agreements need therefore in the first place to create efficiencies (in terms of improving the provision of the service or promoting economic or technical progress). Second, consumers must be allowed to share the benefits of those efficiencies. Third, the agreements should not contain restrictions on competition beyond the strictly indispensable restraints. Finally, they must not eliminate competition altogether.

If the above conditions are satisfied, the shipping pools are in the position to benefit from an individual exemption. The prerogative of granting individual exemption under Article 101(3) used to be in the power of the Commission. Since 1 May 2004 (after the entry into force of Regulation 1/2003),[149] the Commission has lost this prerogative and henceforth individual exemptions are considered a legal requirement to be automatically granted by national courts and competition authorities if the conditions are met.

As a consequence, the process of evaluation of the existence of the conditions for an exemption laid down by Article 101(3) is now known as a "self-assessment" exercise to be carried out by the parties involved with the support of economists and legal advisers prior to the official evaluation of the competent national authorities. The burden of proof lies on the parties involved who need to support their claim to exemption with strong arguments.

---

149. Council Regulation (EC) No 1/2003 of 16 December 2002 on the implementation of the rules on competition laid down in Articles 81 and 82 of the Treaty, OJ L 1, 4 January 2003, at pp 1–25.

BIBLIOGRAPHY

Aikens, R., Bools, M. and Lord, R., *Bills of Lading*, 2nd edn (2015, Informa Law from Routledge).

Anderson, D., "Freedoms of the High Seas in the Modern Law of the Sea" in Freestone, D., Barnes, R. and Ong, D. (eds), *The Law of the Sea: Progress and Prospects* (2006, Oxford University Press).

Baatz, Y., Debattista, C., Lorenzon, F., Serdy, A., Staniland, H. and Tsimplis, M., *The Rotterdam Rules: A Practical Annotation* (2009, Informa Law from Routledge).

Baughen, S., *Shipping Law*, 6th edn (2015, Routledge-Cavendish).

Beale, H. (ed.), *Chitty on Contracts*, 32nd edn (2016, Sweet & Maxwell).

Bennett, H., *Law of Marine Insurance*, 2nd edn (2006, Oxford University Press).

Bridge, M. (ed.), *Benjamin's Sale of Goods*, 9th edn (2014, Sweet & Maxwell).

Briggs, A. and Rees, P., *Civil Jurisdiction and Judgments*, 6th edn (2015, Informa Law from Routledge).

Brown, E.D., *The International Law of the Sea* (1994, Ashgate Publishing).

Churchill, R.R. and Lowe, A.V., *The Law of the Sea*, 3rd edn (1999, Manchester University Press).

Clarke, M., (ed.), *Maritime Law Evolving: Thirty Years at Southampton* (2013, Hart Publishing Ltd).

Coghlin, T., Baker, A.W., Kenny, J., Kimball, J.D. and Belknap, T., *Time Charters*, 7th edn (2014, Informa Law from Routledge).

Coles, R. and Lorenzon, F., *Law of Yachts and Yachting* (2012, Informa Law from Routledge).

Coles, R. and Watt, E., *Ship Registration: Law and Practice*, 2nd edn (2009, Informa Law from Routledge).

Collins, L.A., Morse, C.G.J., McClean, D., Briggs, A., Harris, J., McLachlan, C. and Hill J., *Dicey, Morris & Collins: The Conflict of Laws*, 15th edn (2012, Sweet & Maxwell).

Cooke, J., Taylor, A., Kimball, J.D., Martowski, D. and Lambert, L., *Voyage Charters*, 4th edn (2014, Informa Law from Routledge).

Crawford, J., *Brownlie's Principles of Public International Law*, 8th edn (2012, Oxford University Press).

Curtis, S., *The Law of Shipbuilding Contracts*, 4th edn (2012, Informa Law from Routledge).

Davies, D., *Commencement of Laytime*, 4th edn (2006, Informa Law from Routledge).

Davies, M. (gen. ed.), *Jurisdiction and Forum Selection in International Maritime Law: Essays in Honor of Robert Force* (2005, Kluwer Law International).

De la Rue, C., Anderson, C.B. and Marion, M., *Shipping and the Environment*, 2nd edn (2009, Informa Law from Routledge).

Debattista, C., *Bills of Lading in Export Trade*, 3rd edn (2008, Bloomsbury Professional).

Debattista, C. and Lorenzon, F., *Sale of Ships under the Singapore Form* (2013, LexisNexis).

Dickinson, A., *The Rome II Regulation: The Law Applicable to Non-Contractual Obligations* (2008, Oxford University Press).

Dromgoole, S. and Gaskell, N.J.J., "Interests in Wrecks" in Palmer, N. and McKendrick, E. (eds), *Interests in Goods*, 2nd edn (1998, Informa Law from Routledge).

Dunt, J., *Marine Cargo Insurance*, 2nd edn (2015, Informa Law from Routledge).

Eder, B., Bennett, H., Berry, S., Foxton, D. and Smith, C., *Scrutton on Charterparties*, 23rd edn (2015, Sweet & Maxwell).

Falkanger, T., Bull, H.J. and Brautaset, L., *Scandinavian Maritime Law: The Norwegian Perspective*, 3rd edn (2011, Universitetsforlaget AS).

Fogarty, A.R.M., *Merchant Shipping Legislation*, 2nd edn (2004, Informa Law from Routledge).

Gaskell, N., Asariotis, R. and Baatz, Y., *Bills of Lading: Law and Contracts* (2000, Informa Law from Routledge).

Gaskell, N.J.J., *Current Law Statutes, Merchant Shipping Act* 1995, Chapter 21 (1995, Sweet & Maxwell).

Gaskell, N.J.J., *Merchant Shipping Act and Maritime Security Act 1997: Current Law Statutes* (1997, Sweet & Maxwell).

Gaskell, N.J.J., "Decision Making and the Legal Committee of the IMO" (2003) 18 *International Journal of Marine and Coastal Law* 155.

Gaskell, N.J.J., Debattista, C. and Swatton, R.J., *Chorley and Giles' Shipping Law*, 8th edn (1987, Pearson Education Ltd).

Gault, S., Hazelwood, S., Tettenborn, A. and Girvin, S., et al (eds), *Marsden and Gault on Collisions at Sea*, 14th edn (2016, Sweet & Maxwell).

Gilman, J., Merkin, R., Blanchard, C. and Templeman, M., (eds), *Arnould's Law on Marine Insurance*, 18th edn (2013, Sweet & Maxwell).

Girvin, S., *Carriage of Goods by Sea*, 2nd edn (2011, Oxford University Press).

Goldrein, I., Hannaford, M. and Turner, P., *Ship Sale and Purchase*, 6th edn (2012, Informa Law from Routledge).

Gürses, Ö., *The Insurance of Commercial Risks: Law and Practice*, 5th edn (2016, Sweet & Maxwell Ltd)

Gürses, Ö., *Marine Insurance Law*, 2nd edn (2016, Routledge)

Gürses, Ö., *Reinsuring Clauses* (2010, Informa Law)

Halsbury's Laws of England, Volume 91, Sale of Goods and Supply of Services, 5th edn (2012, LexisNexis Butterworths).

Harris, D.J. and Sivakumaran, S., *Cases and Materials on International Law*, 8th edn (2015, Sweet & Maxwell).

Hazelwood, S.J. and Semark, D., *P&I Clubs: Law and Practice*, 4th edn (2010, Informa Law from Routledge).

Hill, C., *Maritime Law*, 6th edn (2003, Informa Law from Routledge).

Hill, J. and Chong, A., *International Commercial Disputes: Commercial Conflict of Laws in English Courts*, 4th edn (2010, Hart Publishing).

Hill, J. and Ni Shuillebhain, M., *Clarkson & Hill's Conflict of Laws*, 5th edn (2016, Oxford University Press).

ICC, *ICC Uniform Customs and Practice for Documentary Credits*, 2007 Revision, ICC Publication No 600 (2007, ICC).

ICC, *Incoterms 2010: ICC Rules for the Use of Domestic and International Trade Terms*, ICC Publication No 715 (2010, ICC).

ICS, *The STCW Convention*, 3rd edn (2010, Marisec).

IMO, *Maritime Security: Guidance for Ship Operators on the IMO International Ship and Port Facility Security (ISPS) Code* (2003, Marisec).

IMO, *SOLAS: International Convention for the Safety of Life at Sea* (2014, IMO).

ICS, *Guidelines on the Application of the ISM Code*, 4th edn (2010, Marisec).

Jackson, D.C., *Enforcement of Maritime Claims*, 4th edn (2005, Informa Law from Routledge).

Lavelle, J., (ed.), *The Maritime Labour Convention 2006: International Labour Law Redefined* (2013, Informa Law from Routledge).

Lorenzon, F. and Baatz, Y., *Sassoon: CIF and FOB Contracts*, 6th edn (2016, Sweet & Maxwell).

Lowe, A.V., "The Right of Entry into Maritime Ports in International Law" (1977) 14 *San Diego Law Review* 597.

Lowe, V., *International Law* (2007, Oxford University Press).

McClean, D. and Ruiz Abou-Nigm, V., *Morris: the Conflict of Laws*, 9th edn (2016, Sweet & Maxwell).

Macdonald, C. and Karia, C. (gen. eds), *Butterworths Commercial Court and Arbitration Pleadings* (2005, Bloomsbury Professional).

McKendrick, E., (ed.), *Goode on Commercial Law*, 5th edn (2017, Penguin Books).

Mandaraka-Sheppard, A., *Modern Maritime Law*, 2 vols, 3rd edn (2013, Informa Law from Routledge).

Merkin, R., Hjalmarsson, J., Bugra, A. and Lavelle, J., *Marine Insurance Legislation*, 5th edn (2014, Informa Law from Routledge).

Nordquist, M.H. and Norton Moore, J. (eds), *Current Maritime Issues and the International Maritime Organization* (1999, Martinus Nijhoff).

Osborne, D. Bowtle, G., and Buss, C., *The Law of Ship Mortgages*, 2nd edn (2016, Informa Law from Routledge).

Palmer, N. and McKendrick, E., *Interests in Goods*, 2nd edn (1998, Informa Law from Routledge).

Plender, R. and Wilderspin, M., *The European Contracts Convention: The Rome Convention on the Choice of Law for Contracts*, 2nd edn (2001, Sweet & Maxwell).

Rainey, S., *The Law of Tug and Tow and Offshore Contracts*, 3rd edn (2011, Informa Law from Routledge).

Reeder, J., *Brice on Maritime Law of Salvage*, 5th edn (2012, Sweet & Maxwell).

Reynolds, B. and Tsimplis, M., *Shipowners' Limitation of Liability* (2013, Kluwer Law International).

Rose, F.D., *Marine Insurance Law and Practice*, 2nd edn (2012, Informa Law from Routledge).

Rose, F.D., *Kennedy's Law of Salvage*, 8th edn (2013, Sweet & Maxwell).

Schofield, J., *Laytime and Demurrage*, 7th edn (2016, Informa Law from Routledge).

Serdy, A. and Bliss, M., "Prompt Release of Fishing Vessels: State Practice in the Light of the Cases before the International Tribunal for the Law of the Sea" in Oude Elferink, A.G. and Rothwell, D.R. (eds), *Oceans Management in the 21st Century: Institutional Frameworks and Responses* (2004, Martinus Nijhoff).

Strong, M. and Herring, P., *The Sale of Ships: The Norwegian Saleform*, 3rd edn (2016, LexisNexis).

Sturley, M., Fujita, T. and van der Ziel, G., *The Rotterdam Rules* (2010, Sweet & Maxwell).

Tetley, W., *Marine Cargo Claims*, 4th edn (2008, Editions Yvon Blais).

Thomas, D.R. (gen. ed.), *Liability Regimes in Contemporary Maritime Law* (2007, Informa Law from Routledge).

Thomas, D.R., *Modern Law of Marine Insurance*, Vol. 1 (1996, LLP).

Thomas, D.R., *Modern Law of Marine Insurance*, Vol. 2 (2002, Informa Law from Routledge).

Thomas, D.R., *Modern Law of Marine Insurance*, Vol. 3 (2009, Informa Law from Routledge).

Thomas, D.R., *Modern Law of Marine Insurance*, Vol. 4 (2015, Informa Law from Routledge).

Thomas, D.R. (ed.), *A New Convention for the Carriage of Goods by Sea: The Rotterdam Rules* (2009, Lawtext Publishing Limited).

Thomas, D.R. (ed.), *The Carriage of Goods by Sea under the Rotterdam Rules* (2010, Lloyd's List).

Todd, P., *Principles of the Carriage of Goods by Sea* (Routledge, 2016),

Treitel, G. and Reynolds, F. (eds), *Carver on Bills of Lading*, 3rd edn (2012, Sweet & Maxwell).

Von Ziegler, A., Zunarelli, S. and Schelin, J., *The Rotterdam Rules 2008* (2010, Wolters Kluwer).

Wilson, J., *Carriage of Goods by Sea*, 7th edn (2010, Pearson Education Ltd).

Wolfrum, R., Rosenne, S. and Blanco-Bazan, A., "IMO Interface with the Law of the Sea Convention" in Nordquist, M.H. and Norton Moore, J (eds) *Current Maritime Issues and the International Maritime Organization* (1999, Martinus Nijhoff).

INDEX